Child Custody Help SourceBook

Win Your Child Custody War

by Charlotte Hardwick

ISBN: 1-58747-024-1

The publisher may be contacted about this book and other titles at:

SAN 299-9358

Pale Horse Publishing

T (936) 327-1104 F (936) 967-8962

E-Mail divorce@livingston.net

World Wide Web http://www.custodywar.com

P.O.Box 1447, Livingston, Texas 77360-1447 U.S.A.

Dedication

I consider this book to be one of the most important works of my life and dedicate it to the most important people in my life: David, my husband; Adelle and Ben Dichter, my parents; to Goldie and Ruben Kirsch, Rae and Alex Dichter, my grandparents; and to Kelly, Joshua and Bethany, our much-loved children.

"Making the decision to have a child is momentous.

It is to decide forever to have your heart go walking around outside your body."

Elizabeth Stone

Acknowledgments

I appreciate the help of the many people who shared information and ideas with me. Most expressed a heartfelt desire to save other souls the pain and expense this experience cost them. I am especially grateful to those who took the time to read all or part of the manuscript and make valuable suggestions:

Attorney Janice Palmer, and her associates and staff in Mesa, Arizona also provided exceptionally competent and professional services, meeting our needs with sensitivity and attention to detail during our child custody battle.

I owe special thanks to the members of my family for their support and love.

To my spouse, you are without a doubt "Still the Best."

I have stood with parents who have suffered the death of a child. I could not distance myself from the pain they felt and I cried with them. They pleaded to God or to me or anyone who would listen, "I would do *Anything* to see my child just one more time."

This is the Anything

You will travel any distance.
You will tap all resources.
You will hold your tongue when hurt and angry.
You will abandon persons who do not share your devotion.
You will do without comforts, even necessities.
You will adjust your entire life.

You will learn to get along with the devil if necessary.
You will do whatever it takes.

This is the Anything.

Seeing your child may be short in time and uncomfortable in location.
It is all you have, but it will allow you to see your child one more time.

This is the Anything.

The repeated pain of separation is the pain of grief and death with each leaving. Repetition does not make it any easier to endure the pain.

This is the Anything.

In exchange for getting to see your child one more time, it is your responsibility to make sure your child does not feel or see the pain you endure, only the joy of this coming together and the expectation of the next meeting at this parting.

This is the Anything

by Charlotte Hardwick

Reviews and praise for WIN YOUR CHILD CUSTODY WAR

"**Win Your Child Custody War**, has given me the most amount of knowledge in the least amount of time. I have purchased everything available. The hype the others offered quickly became as obnoxious as a faulty septic tank. All too soon the lack of information did surface and became embarrassing. Embarrassing for the authors for their poor product and embarrassing for me to get so little for my money. A parents attitude toward a book ought to be similar to a gold miner's attitude toward gold: get every last bit of value out of it. Custody of your child is to important for inferior books. This book is a true collaboration between the author and the reader." **Dan (Stonewall) Jackson Austin, TX**

"I knew half of my efforts to win custody of my children were wasted. **Win Your Child Custody War**, helped me figure out which half. I had all the ingredients for being the custodial parent. This book gave me the recipe.

"I am really impressed and proud to have your books in my "custody". I love your books and what you do! **Jody Seidler, Santa Monica, CA 1999 Makinglemonade.com**

"**Win Your Child Custody War**, is a must read for anyone who is dealing with, or may in the future deal with, a child custody battle; in fact I would even recommend it for someone who has already been there, and is still trying to figure out what hit them, and why. The chapter on how to select and work with an attorney by itself makes this book worth its weight in gold (no small feat, as this is a hefty volume). This chapter should be required reading for all parents headed towards a contested custody matter, and for attorneys as well. Anne P. Mitchell, Esq., Founder/Director, **Fathers Rights & Equality Exchange (F.R.E.E.)**, Mother.

"I can't decide whether to characterize **Win Your Child Custody War** as the 20th Century response to Sun-Tzu's **The Art of War**, or as an indispensable **Bible** for the modern divorcing parent. I am astonished at the breadth and detail afforded here. This book contains more information than any other ten books on divorce put together!" Jim Anderson, Noncustodial Dad of Sari, Editor, **Infocus Newsletter, FOCUS: Children And The Other Parent**, Parents Organization, Salt Lake City, UT.

"Within these pages the various scenarios play themselves out, from the negotiated settlement to the full nuclear exchange. **Win Your Child Custody War** is not only an entertaining allegory of war and peace, however. It bulges with strategic techniques on the handling of the players (including you) in your ordeal of battle. Examples of professional reports from the various troops under your command, and explanations on interpreting their real meaning. Checklists and blank forms help you, the prospective commander, formulate and stick to the best tactical strategy for your own custodial conflagration. There are many more helpful books on making peace and recovering from defeats than this one, but if you are thrust into war, make no mistake about it; you need this book." Brent Wellman, This review was written for **FREE Thoughts** of **Fathers' Rights and Equality Exchange (F.R.E.E.)** San Diego, CA. reprinted (with permission) in the **Family Guardian Journal**

"**Win Your Child Custody War** really helped us out with our evaluation and everything else. It taught us a lot. Thanks!" Kelly Rea, Noncustodial Mom, San Jose, CA

"**Win Your Child Custody War** goes a long way down the right road for parents and children. Innovative methods for problem solving and maintaining the vital links that must exist between parents and children." Ed Winter, Cofounder, Custody Exchange Centers, Inc. Los Angeles, CA

"Win Your Child Custody War was presented to our group as a seminar. I am not exaggerating when I tell you the effect on our membership was dynamite." Lyle Fullmer, Custodial Dad, and Program coordinator of **Dads Helping Dads**, Temple, TX.

"Thank you, Thank you, Thank you. **Win Your Child Custody War**, is a very worth while publication." **Coy Slaton**, Boca Raton, FL January 2000

More reviews of WIN YOUR CHILD CUSTODY WAR

"We received your manual on Friday. It has so much information in it and is already helping me mentally. I am better equipped to help my husband gain custody of his little girl. We are glad to see so much of what we have let go wrong is fixable. **Win Your Child Custody War** is a GREAT book!" Gevette King mom and step-mom, Fremont, CA.

"The information is instantaneously usable. I still lost sleep last night. Not because I faced another night of despair, but because I didn't want to take time out to rest. There is so much I am now doing to make my case work. It's the first time in 25 years anything gave me as much assurance as my Teddy Bear. The bear was the illusion of help **Win Your Child Custody War** is the tool I needed." George Reme, Crisis Counselor New York, NY

"I was immobilized by what was happening to me. This manual made me aware of the hidden agendas of the people around me and improved my progress. This manual guided me out of the pit and gave me an aerial view of the terrain. Routing me around the inconspicuous pitfalls. The best money I spent was on **Win Your Child Custody War.** It Works!" Steve Scheffe, Custodial Parent of my three sons, Phx., AZ.

"Thank you so very much, on behalf of our entire Board. We are absolutely thrilled at the vast amount of valuable information in **Win Your Child Custody War**. Many major points are what we have been telling our members for years. Your manual is outstanding." Vesuvio Mann Charles, for The Board of **Fathers For Equal Rights**. Miami, FL.

"Thank you for the opportunity to review **Win Your Child Custody War**. I will be using parts of this text in training our new domestic relations judges." Kenneth Fields, Superior Court, Presiding Judge, Domestic Relations, Phx., AZ.

"**Win Your Child Custody War** is the 'Text Book" on proper parental conduct during a custody battle, a workbook in the best sense, containing exercises to enhance self awareness, to stimulate positive responses and induce new levels of communication." Steve Chiton, Father 50/50 custody, Miami, FL.

"**Win Your Child Custody War** is a book for all parents dealing with any child custody issue. The depth and breath of the information will make the reader aware of the complexity of custody issues, and what must be done to win in our legal system." Boyer Cole, N.M.D. Author and father, Flagstaff, AZ.

"**Win Your Child Custody War** should definitely be in the hands of those about to face one of the most unnerving challenges of their lives. It's amazing what people don't know. The manual is extremely easy to reference, to understand, no legal mumbo jumbo, with the various prospects involved beautifully outlined." Ralph & Marietta Marchese, grandparents, Phoenix, AZ.

"The manual **Win Your Child Custody War** might be the difference between winning and losing your case." Lynella Grant, mother, Attorney, Author Denver, CO.

"**Win Your Child Custody War** has leveled the playing field for my son and ensured my ongoing contact with my grandchildren." Bea Davi, Grandmother, Warren, PA.

"Indispensable. **Win Your Child Custody War** gives you an insiders grasp of the entire custody process without the years of pain. Having been on both sides of this issue, I find this book sets the standards for information and results. It is an important contribution to the welfare of families during and after a child custody war." Marsha Temple, President of **Family and Friends in Support of Children of Divorce**, Phx., AZ.

More reviews of WIN YOUR CHILD CUSTODY WAR

"**Win Your Child Custody War** is highly praised by parents, attorneys, psychologists and parenting groups. The manual explains in detail what to expect during custody proceedings and how to maximize efforts to gain custody. It defines legal constricts, suggests how to present oneself to various legal agencies, and identifies factors to consider prior to appearing in court. The personal history shared brings an immediacy to the material which stresses the serious results of custody proceedings. Perhaps the best praise for this book can be summed up as follows: **Win Your Child Custody War** keeps the focus of custody proceedings where it belongs - on the welfare of the child." Penny Kariznowi, Arizona Authors' Association, Phoenix, AZ

"**Win Your Child Custody War** is Incredible!" Marie Witkin Kargman, A.M. Harvard, J.D. DePaul, clinical family sociologist and specialist in Family Law for 30 years. Former associate editor of "The Family Coordinator" Editorial Board of the Journal of Divorce, the Governor's Advisory Council on Home & Family in Boston, MA.

"After reading **Win Your Child Custody War**, I realized I wanted sole custody for all the wrong reasons. My attitude adjustment allowed her attitude adjustment and we worked out the best plan for all of us." Balor Rui, father, Peoria, IL.

"This is a drop dead great piece of work. My mother bought a copy of **Win Your Child Custody War** and sent it to me. I bought a copy and gave it to my soon to be X. We all won. My little girl has two happy homes instead of one broken home. Thank you" Frank Smith, father and Teacher, Turlock, CA.

"I just received '**Win Your Child Custody War'** and I'm impressed by the extensive research demonstrated here. You've certainly done your homework on this subject, and I rate it an "A" in content. I also understand why you ask the price you do for this tome: it's worth it!" Joseph McLaughlin father, Author of **The Zen of Golf**, Associate Professor of English, Stark Technical College, Canton, OH.

"It arrived this afternoon - looks like it is all you cracked it up to be. But you know we almost did not buy it, here is why: When I read your ad online, I called all the bookstores, the University Book Store, Tower and Barnes & Nobel and even asked about it on the alt.child-support news group. I was informed it was an old book printed in 1994, and it would take 3 to 5 weeks to get a copy. What we did do was go to each of the book stores with the index printed out and tried to match the data to other books - no luck - we spent the whole day going through those three book stores. We are in the middle of a custody case and finding REAL information is like finding hen's teeth. We re-read the index and decided to get it anyways. When I did get my copy I read upon opening the book that it is updated every year. I figure after 3 readings we should be ready to outline a complete battle plan - one is already forming and we are glad we sent for the **Win Your Child Custody War** manual." James McFarland, Seattle, WA

"I can't tell you how long I looked or how much I needed this book. This clean clear note of sanity is a real blessing. I didn't understand how people who stood so close to the foot of the cross could have to go through so much hell at the hands of criminal ignorant people. The Win Your Child Custody War manual confirmed what were doing right and gave many excellent options. Get it before you need it. Get it after you blew it. It can help no matter where you are when you find it." Nelson Cambridge, Richmond, MN

"**Win Your Child Custody War** covered many details of which I would never have thought. I bought it. I used it. It made the difference. I recommend it to other parents every day of the week. God Bless You." Mark E. Whitt, joint custody father, Phx., AZ.

"Wow! What a book! I'm still jumping all over **Win Your Child Custody War**! So many interesting and fascinating things to read and utilize!" David W. Funk, Dad and Noncustodial Dad, Tomball, TX.

More reviews of WIN YOUR CHILD CUSTODY WAR

"**Win Your Child Custody War** helped me deal with a psychotic personality on the other side without becoming one myself. My child and I were spared a lot of grief because of this manual. God Bless You." Don Edmonds, Sole Custody father, Houston, TX.

"My attorney told me to buy this book! First, I trusted the system to protect me and my child. Seeing there was no interest in our welfare, I dropped my case and a lot of money in an attorneys lap. In less than six months he stopped answering my calls and did nothing. I hired a new attorney. At our first appointment she told me to buy **Win Your Child Custody War**. I thought she was telling me to buy the manual so she wouldn't have to help. Since then I can see that my attorney has given me a lot of good advice. Telling me to buy this book was the best. Before I got this book I thought the court and even my own attorney just weren't listening to my concerns. With my understanding of the real issues, I have stopped wasting my time on what the court considers, emotion driven non-issues. Now I understand the process and can be a real part of the team. Helping things along and getting better results is gratifying. I wish I had this book five months ago". Kelly Duvall, kellykatt@hotbot.com from Houston, TX, February 18, 1999

"I thought I had it tough until **Win Your Child Custody War** made me aware of some of the problems other people face. I am sure that just knowing what could happen helped me guard against many of the pitfalls." Dawn Winchester, Mother, Nurse KC., MO

"All the info you need to get organized. This is a great book if you need to build a winning child custody case or rework a losing one. Anything over 600 pages, may seem far too long, but the book contains little repetition and has a huge index. The author warns against over reacting to False Allegations of Abuse, Parental Alienation Syndrome and Lies while giving you ideas on how to document the truth. Taking the issue from the 'he said - she said' category to hard evidence really makes a difference. The author says, you are not judged by what is done to you, but by how you respond to what is done to you. This is some powerful stuff. Lots of information, lots of examples, a fantastic reference guide. Hardwick has a relaxed, interesting style of writing. I do hope she keeps on producing more valuable information!" Liza Whitehorse, Deadwood, SD

"My book arrived three working days after I ordered it! Great book - easy to use and very informative. I have read enough of **Win Your Child Custody War** to know this is just what I needed. I should have had it ten months ago. I could have avoided a lot of problems. Information about cases that set precedent as recently as 1989 were very helpful. The first thing it did for me was put my case in prospective by showing me what others faced and overcame. I found the book to be surprisingly interesting. It's very unusual to find a topic that appears to be so horrible, such as a child custody case, brought to life in such a masterful way. It looks like this book was originally written for men. I am a Mother's Rights advocate and will use any good weapon to fight my battle. I recommend the book to anyone involved in this life altering challenge. Carol Lee from Effingham, Il

"I saw **Win Your Child Custody War** at my x-girlfriends house and decided if she had it I needed it. It was the smartest thing I ever did. I had noticed huge changes in the way Jody was dealing with me and now I know why. This is the first time in this fight I feel the playing field is level. Things are easier, sometimes happier now. Jacob Kildare, Never been married Father, Turtle Creek, PA

"I never wanted or needed help from anyone in my life. I thought if you couldn't handle your own problems privately and efficiently there was something wrong with you. I was wrong. When it comes to something as important as your child and you need it you must ask for help. **Win Your Child Custody War** is the help I needed. I still have my dignity and my little girl". J.D. Haute, Los Angeles, CA.

Disclaimer

The materials provided within are for your personal information, education, and communication, but should not be construed as legal advice between an attorney and client; mere reading, review or other use of this information does not create an attorney-client relationship with the author or any other person who assisted in creating this manual. Furthermore, neither the author nor those who helped create this web site are liable for any damages you may suffer if you use it; that includes direct, incidental, consequential, indirect, or punitive damages arising out of your access to, or use of, the manual. Some jurisdictions may not permit the exclusion of implied warranties, so some of the above exclusions may not apply to you, depending upon where you reside. No reader should act on the basis of any information contained in this manual or provided through listings from this manual without seeking appropriate legal advice from an attorney. No prediction of results should be inferred from the information provided within.

Like any manual, this one is no substitute for legal advice. Although the author and publisher have exhaustively researched all sources to ensure the accuracy and completeness of the information contained in this manual, we assume no responsibility for errors, inaccuracies, omissions, or any inconsistency herein. Any slights to people or organizations are unintentional. Readers should use their own judgment or consult an attorney for specific applications to their individual problems.

This manual does not contain legal advice. We do not warrant the fitness of form or process in this manual for use in a court of law, and we express no legal opinions in providing the educational resources in this manual. You are encouraged to collect relevant cases and give them to your attorney so he has better tools to work with in your case.

Items are not to be considered legal advice or to create any lawyer-client relationship. Articles may include some obsolete information. In addition, taking any legal information out of context, i.e., using it in a different court or a subtly different kind of case, or without the training to understand all of what it means or doing research to verify it, usually has disastrous consequences.

We encourage those involved in custody issues to consider utilizing the tremendous collection of information and case cites available in your location in researching your case, to give to your attorney. Those who go to court with the facts are likely to do better than those who do not. Laws on child custody and divorce change daily and vary from state to state. Laws that govern information gathering and presentation vary from state to state. It may be legal to gather data using a device in one jurisdiction, and against the law to present, in court, data gathered using that device in the jurisdiction in which your case is being adjudicated.

Various products discussed, services described, techniques explained and devices identified in the manual may be illegal to possess or employ in your state. It is your responsibility to confirm the legality of any process or service you consider employing.

Any connection you might have with the violation of such laws will impose a mandatory prison sentence. It is your responsibility to find out what is legal where you live and what is not, before using any device or service that would put your future at risk. You cannot care for your child from jail. The findings and forms in this manual are for reference and informational purposes only. No guarantees, warranties or representations, expressed or implied are made as to their correctness or legal effect in specific situations. Neither the author nor the publisher, or others who have contributed information, assume any liability or responsibility for the use or misuse of the information contained in this manual.

The names used in this manual are not the actual names of real persons. These names are fictitious. The incidents in this manual are true but may be a composite of several situations experienced by the author and/or people interviewed. The message of this manual is to be prepared and to know there is an element of chance in the Child Custody War. Having said this, this manual will greatly increase your chance of winning.

The Small Print: This response is for information and discussion purposes only. It isn't meant to be legal advice and you shouldn't treat it as such. If you want legal advice, speak with a local lawyer familiar with your state's laws who can review "all" of the facts and the law applicable to your situation.

Credentials Vs Credibility

My credentials and research. I am not an attorney, psychologist, judge or mediator. I am an expert on winning child custody because I have done it. The professionals in the field of custody only know the experience from the perspective of their individual expertise. Those who have experienced the war on a personal level are ethically rejoined from allowing their personal experiences to color their performance. I countered false accusations of rape, child abuse, neglect, nonsupport, and harassment. I faced bad advice, lies, kidnapping, misinformation, parental interference, intimidation, character assassination, implied threats, overt acts of violence, financial drain, emotional turmoil, self doubt, fear for our child's safety, problems I was causing myself, and a horrible strain on my marriage. The opposing attorney aggravated every situation, and a gender biased judge who prolonged the process by almost a year increasing our costs by an additional $10,000.00 to the total of $82,000.00 we spent by the end of 1993.

The information was available to the court through the defendant's depositions, certified copies of documents, the court appointed mediator's report and a separate psychological evaluation ordered by the court. It was obvious to everyone but the judge, that the defendant in this case did not give honest testimony and did not offer the best home for our child. In the end, the court-appointed psychologist made the custody decision. Unable or unwilling to see and deal with the real issues, the defendant blamed everyone else for her loss of custody: her free attorney, our competent (but not free) attorney, the judge, mediator, conciliation court officer, psychologist and us.

My spouse and I have enjoyed a good marriage since 1984 in what is a second marriage for us both. We have solid employment and a stable home life with no history of alcohol, drugs, family problems or difficulties with the law.

The Other Parent, single again, has been divorced three times. In February of 2000 she had another child increasing the total to five children from three fathers. She, two of her older male children and her assorted spouses and companions have committed felonies and have long, well-documented histories of antisocial behavior and instability. Having moved eight times and changed jobs four times in the last six years indicates the poor soul may never have a stable life. All efforts to work with her in the past were met with were met with passive or outright aggression.

Happily, today we have custody of our healthy, lovely, wonderful child. Our marriage is stronger and happier than ever. We have an opportunity to be kind with the other parent and take a great deal of pride in our efforts.

This compendium of information and options I developed has worked well for me and so many others that I want you to know about it. It will work for you and your child, too. Initially, we did not understand that we were at war. For months we allowed the other side to manipulate us.

During this period we lost precious time and spent a great deal of money unnecessarily. When we realized what we were up against, we tried to find help. The legal advice we found was solid as it pertained to the law, but the law never seemed to apply when we needed it. No one could give us any idea of where to start improving our position or even explain what was really happening. We only knew that these frightening events and expensive legal procedures were sapping our energy and rapidly draining our resources. Our past and present lives had never been under such scrutiny as they were now. We had never been deposed, did not know what an interrogatory was, and had never been psychologically evaluated.

Not only did we have to go through these procedures, we had to pay for them. In addition, the judge ordered us to pay part of the opposition's expenses. As we spent time, money and effort on products, books and services, we became expert consumers. The spy shops made many exotic, high-tech items available. Had we used them as instructed, I would have written this manual from my very own cell in a federal prison. Some professionals and services we hired "took us to the cleaners." Others gave us not only our money's worth, but a world of emotional support and will remain our friends forever. We learned to arrive at each new challenge as prepared as possible.

Table of Contents

If You Don't Know Where You're Going,

You Can't Get There From Here.

This manual will help you see where you really are,

identify exactly where you can go,

and give you options that will get you there.

Chapter 1: War or Peace 11
Questions Asked and Answered 11
Pray for Peace - Prepare for War 15
Intended Audience 15
Where Do You Fit? 15
Married - Unmarried Parents 15
Whose Custody Case is this Anyway? 17
Best Interest? 17
Who Should Not Fight for Custody 18
Reasons People Say They Have Custody 18
Worst Reasons to Fight for Custody 18
Abuse Excuse 19
Dead Hand 19
Children as Pawns 19
Factors Influencing Court Decisions 19
Common Custody Arrangements 19
Interim or Temporary Custody 20
Sole Custody 20
Joint Custody 20
Physical and Legal 20
Joint Physical 20
Joint Legal 20
Split Custody 20
Alternating or Divided 21
Bird's Nest Custody 21
Visitation 21
Suddenly Super Parent 21
Grandparent Visitation 22
Exercising Visitation 22
Successful Visitation 22
Your Interference with Your Visitation 22
Parental Interference with Visitation 23
Visitation Bond 23
Police 24
Police and Restraining Orders 24
Life's Time-line 24
If You're on a Short Time Line 25
Non-Custodial Parent's Emotions 25
Issues - Non-Issues 25
Their Problem or Yours 25
Child Endangerment 26
Opposition is a Control Freak 26
Control Freak and No Responsibility 26
Blended Family 26
Mental Illness 26
Lengthy Child Care 26
Verbal or Mental Abuse 26
False Accusations 26
Frequent Moving 26
Physical Abuse 26
Alcohol Use or Abuse 27
Drug Use or Abuse 27
Other Parent Only Wants to Hurt Me 27

Visitation Denial or Interference 27
Lying to Child, You and the Court 27
Kidnapping 27
Kidnapping Threat 27
Domestic Violence 28
New Significant Other or Step-parent 28
Alternative Lifestyle 28
Best Interest of the Child 28
Neglect 28
Poor Living Conditions 28
Responsibility for Problems 28
Your Expectations 28

Chapter 2: You Are the Package 30
State of Mind or Mindlessness 30
Safety Nets 31
Group I Need Doesn't Exist 31
Not Comfortable In Self Help Groups 31
Why Are You Here? 31
New Relationships 32
Invest in Yourself 32
On the Hot Seat, So What? 32
Unsolicited Help 32
"Thanks, but No Thanks" 33
The Rescuer 33
Rest and Relaxation 33
Aid to the Enemy 33
Right Thinking 34
It's Your Battle Because 34
Delegation 34
Personal Security 34
Bunker (Your Home) 34
Demilitarized Zone 35
Maneuvers, Planned Action 35
Retraining 36
From Now On 36
No Sniveling or Whining 37
The Most Important Witness 37
Dress for Custody Success 38
What Do I Tell People on My Side? 38
Confidentiality - My Witnesses 38
I Think I Need a Shrink 38
Confidentiality - Shrink 38
When the Police are Called 39
Things You Can Get Arrested For 39
If You Are Arrested 40
Inventories 41
Confidentiality - Inventories 41
Relationship Inventory Example #1 44
Relationship Inventory Example #2 45
Opposition's Inventory Example 45
Child's Inventory Example 45
Parent as a Soldier 46
Ask Yourself the Real Question 46
Desiderata 46
Duck Muck 47
The One I Feed 48
Proper Responses 48
Victim or Victor 49
Security, Privacy on the Internet 50
Your Computer Their Attorney 50

Chapter 3: Strategies 51
Reality Check 51
Well, Get Over It 52
Desire vs Reality 52
Looking Past 2001 53
Changes in the Wind 54
Strategic Interaction 55
Strategy = Planning 55
Deliberate, Insightful, Rational Enemy 56
Specific Techniques 56
Live and Let Live 57
Tit For Tat 57
Look Ahead 57
Tester 57
Tranquilizer 57
Exploitative or Permanent Retaliation 57
Attrition 57
Deterrence 57
Reciprocity 58
Random 58
Agendas 58
Changing Strategies 58
Defensive Behaviors 58
Remedies To Defensive Behaviors 59
Delay 59
Strategic Case Boosters 59
Activities to Cultivate 64

Chapter 4: Conflict Resolution 65
Problems the Other Parent Causes 65
Why They Do What they Do 67
Pre-Contact Planning 69
Negotiation 70
Why Cooperate? 70
Why Will the Opposition Cooperate? 71
Reduce Differences 71
Aim to Negotiate, Not to Win 71
Overcoming Obstacles 72
Discover Hidden Agendas 72
Children's Agenda 72
Concerns that Affect Children's Agendas 73

Conflict 73
Methods of Thinking 73
Individual's Moral Obligation 74
Changing Strategies 74
Not Really the Same 74
Using a Professional to Negotiate 75
Mediators 75
Attorneys 75
Three Reasons to Negotiate 75
Right Place and Time to Negotiate 75
Preparation 76
Assumptions 76
Guidelines for Discussion 76
How to Negotiate 77
Is the Negotiation Going Well? 77

Chapter 5: Friend or Enemy? 80
Make Words Work for You 80
It's Your Army; Impose Censorship 81
Loose Lips Sink Ships 81
Security Breach 81
If You Disregard This Advice 82
Fear and Communication 82
Assertive Communication Evaluation 83
Dealing with Fear 84
News Flash Junkies 84
Safe Answers 84
Friendly Fire 85
People Who Cause Damage 85
Important Questions to Ponder 86
Family In-laws and Outlaws 86
Your Parents 86
Opposition's Parents 86
The Agendas of Your Friends 87
Friendly Strangers 87
Know Your Enemy 88
Data Sheet 88
Noncombatants 88
Data Sheet Form 88
Information and Mis-information 89
Source of Information 90
Case Killers 91
Quick List of Activities to Avoid 95
Hurt You Worse Than Them 95
Anger and Joy 95
You've Been In Court Too Long When 95

Chapter 6: Logs as Documentation 97
Reasons for Documentation 97
Detective 99
Attorney 99
Evaluator 99
Guardian ad Litem 99
Telephone Log 99
Methods of Documentation 99
Websites as Evidence 101
Chain of Evidence 103
Spoliation of Evidence 103
Crucial Data to Record 104
Simplicity and Speed 104
Confidentiality - Documentation 105
Codes for Log Book 105
Contact Log Example 1991-2001 106
Take Photos of Everything 127
Where they Will Do the Most Good 127
The Dark Side 128

Chapter 7: Equipment & Services 129
Equipment 129
Invasion of Privacy 132
Services 132
Day Care Workers 133
Legal Transcribers 133
Parent Locator Service 134
Testing Services 135
Drug Tests 135
Urine Analysis 135
Passive Inhalation 135
Hair Analysis 135
Will You Take a Drug Test 136
Lie Detector Test 136
Maternity & Paternity Testing 137
DNA - Genetic Testing 137
Court Ordered 137
DNA Samples From Many Sources 137
Challenges to DNA Testing 138
Computer Data Retrieval 139
I Have Evidence - No One Cares 139
Confidentiality - Services 140

Chapter 8: Attorney 141
Right to Free Counsel 141
Legal Aid 142
Representing Yourself 142
No ProSe Recovery of Attorney Fees 142
Getting Started ProSe 143
Precedent 143
My Humble Opinion 143
Shared Attorney 143
You are the Commander 143
How to Find an Attorney 144
Initial Consultation 145

Reasons They Won't Take Your Case 145
Good Old Attorney System 146
More Bang for the Buck 146
Not So Secret "Secret Weapon" 147
Don't Hire Attorneys Who 147
Sorting Out the Bad Apples 148
Before 10:00 A.M. After 5:00 P.M. 148
The Bad Rap Attorneys Get 148
Confidentiality - Attorney 149
Cannot Do 149
Can Do 149
Keep a Good Attorney Happy 150
Military Attorney 150
Case Analysis 151
Communicate with Your Attorney 151
Advised to Violate Court Order 152
Restraining Order 152
Communicating with the Enemy 152
Sex and Your Attorney 153
Before You Talk, Assign or Request 153
Win Opposition Attorney to Your Side? 154
Get Rid of Their Attorney 155
Attorney Invoice 155
Attorney and the Liar 155
Accessory to Your Crime 156
Reasons Attorney Will Fire You 156
My Way or the Highway 157
Please Release Me, Let Me Go 157
Reasons to Fire Your Attorney 157
Handling a Bad Attorney 158
New Attorney = Delay 158
Lawsuits Against Attorneys 158
Suing Your Attorney 158

Chapter 9: Detectives 165
Covert Intelligence Division 165
Can Do 165
Right One for You 166
Interview the Detective 168
Understanding the Costs 168
Avoid Hot Shots 169
A Snake Is A Snake Is ... 169
Keep A Good Detective Happy 169
Help Your Detective 169
Stay Alert 169
Opposition's Detective 171
Are You Being Watched? 171
Getting the Evidence 171
Detective Assignment Form #1 172
Assignment Example #2 174
Assignment Example #3 176
Discovery Bonus In Detective Report 177
Assignment Example #4 177
Assignment Example #5 178
Assignment Example #6 179
Confidentiality - Detective 179
Sex and Your Detective 180
Detective Turns Into An Outlaw 180
Filing A Formal Complaint 180

Chapter 10: Evaluations 181
Purpose for an Evaluation 181
Types of Evaluations 181
Who and Why are Evaluators Used? 182
Best Attitude with the Evaluator 182
Facing the Other Parent 183
When There are Two of You 185
How Much Weight Do They Carry? 186
Parental Alienation Syndrome (PAS) 186
Other Parent is a Chameleon 188
False Accusations of PAS 189
Change Where the Children Live? 189
What are Evaluators Observing 189
Confidentiality - Evaluator 190
If You Gotta Go 190
Make This Easier for Your Children 190
Evaluator's Report #1 191
Evaluator's Report #2 194
Evaluator's Report #3 197
Evaluator's Report #4 198
Evaluator's Report #5 199
Home Study 200
What Costs are Involved? 200
Get Ready for the Home Study 201
The Book of Your Life 201
Examples of Letters of Support 202
Letters of Love 205
Letter to Document Order Violation 205
Help from Hell 205
What are they Looking for? 208
Evaluating the Evaluation 208
Child's Hospital Visit List 209
Data Submitted to Identify Concerns 210
Frequent Moving 210
Home Study Example, Report #1 210
Comparing Apples to Oranges 210
Condition of Child Report Form #1 211
Condition of Child Report Form #2 212
Home Study Example, Report #2 212
Eliminate the Trash 216
Flaws in the Process 216
The Second Home Study 216
Evaluating the Home Study 216
Filing a Formal Complaint 217

Chapter 11: Experts 218
Qualifications to be an Expert 219
Costs Involved in Using Experts 219
What Can Experts Do? 220
Some Experts are Prostitutes 221
Hiring Your Expert 222
Confidentiality - Expert 223
Your Expert In Court 224
Attacking an Expert's Qualifications 225
Opposition's Expert 225
Loose Cannon 225
Deposing Your Opponent's Expert 225
Opponent's Expert in Court 228
New Stricter Standards for Experts 229

Chapter 12: Psychologists & Tests 230
War of the Minds 230
Who Can Perform Psychological Tests 230
Check Out the Psychologist 230
Psychologist Contact Log 231
Best Attitude with the Psychologist 231
Before You See the Psychologist 232
Facing the Other Parent 232
Recommendation = Decision 232
When There are Two of You 233
What are they Looking for? 233
Specific Positive Character Traits 233
Send Up Warning Flags Early 233
The Process of Evaluation 233
Concerns that can be Documented 234
Will You Take a Drug Test? 235
Drug Tests 236
Random Testing 236
Court Room Samples 236
Hair Analysis 236
Urine Analysis 237
False Positives 237
Passive Inhalation 237
Prescription Drug Abuse 237
Psychological Tests for Adults 238
Before You See the Psychologist 239
Confidentiality and the Psychologist 239
Sex and the Psychologist 239
Filing a Formal Complaint 239
Change Where the Children Live? 240
Tests for Children and Adolescents 240
Psychological Evaluation #1 241
Psychological Evaluation #2 246
What to Do about a Bad Evaluation 248
Filing a Formal Complaint 249
Evaluating the Psychologist Example #1 250
Evaluating the Psychologist Example #2 251
Evaluating the Psychologist Example #3 252

Chapter 13: Children's Perspective 253
Child and Parent Match 253
But I Want to Stay with You 253
Children Who Want to Choose 254
Children Who Cannot Choose 255
Hearing the Child's Voice 256
Go Where they are Heard 256
Child's Realities 256
Dealing with Your Child's Fears 257
Loss 257
Monsters 257
Failure 257
Trying 257
The Future 257
Not Doing the Right Thing 258
Abandonment 258
Time 258
Fear 258
Not Being Important 258
What You Can Do To Help 259
Discipline 259
That's Not What I Meant to Say 259
Styles of Parental Discipline 260
Television 260
Activities 260
You Are Always On My Mind 261
Places to Find Activities 262
Religion 263
Division of Church and State 263
Intra-Faith Custody Challenges 263
Visitation 264
International Travel 264
Fear of Flying 265
My Child Hates Visitation 266
Custodial Responsibilities 266
Non-Custodial Responsibilities 266
I Don't Want to Visit You Anymore 267
Whim or Survival 267
A Phone Call Away 267
Document Now For Later 267
Parental Alienation Syndrome 268
Alienation Messages 268
Unconscious Messages 268
Conscious Messages 268
Combating PAS 269
Children's Responsibilities 269
Information Children Should Know 270
Walk the Talk 270
Help Your Children Be Responsible 270
Seeing Abuse is Abuse 271

Move Away 271
No Move Away Provision 271
Best Interest Move Away 271
Limited Presumption for Move Away 272
Presumption for Move Away 272
Buying the Pain Away 272
Too Much Hurt... Accidentally 272
Such Behavior is Bad Parenting 273
Guidelines for Interviewing Children 273
Confidentiality - Your Children 273
Revenge 274
Second-Hand Smoke and Children 274
Court's Reaction 275

Chapter 14: Lies and Perjury 276
Types of Lies 276
Types of Liars 277
Some of the Best Reasons not to Lie 277
Conflicting Truths 277
Memory's Imperfections 278
Exaggerations and Fabrications 278
Portrait of the Liar 278
When is Someone Lying 279
Lies by Strangers 279
Lies by Familiars 279
Seeing the Pattern of the Liar 280
Why Liars Get Caught 280
Liars even Lie to Themselves 280
Recruiting Troops 280
Defense Against Lies 281
The Grand Lie 282
Handling the Liar 282
Lie Suppression 282
Sue the Liar 283
Using Their Lies against Them 283
Proof or Poof 284
Impeachment of a Witness 284
Children and the Liar 284
When Children Lie 285
Where Do You Fit? 285
Non-Fatal Flaw 285
Your Lies 286
Cold Turkey Truth 286
How to Start Repairing the Damage 286
Correcting Old Lies 287
Identifying the Liar to Others 290
Telling the Awful Truth 290
Perjury in Family Court! 291
Attorneys and Lies 291
The Court Will Call a Liar a Liar 291
No Lie Double Talk 291

Chapter 15: Panic Situations 293
Pro Active Steps 293
Learning from the Pain of Others 294
Panic Situations, Examples 294
01 Legal Papers 294
02 Misappropriation of Money 295
03 Other Parent Has Moved Child 295
04 Phone Harassment at Work 295
05 Bruises on Your Child 296
06 Implied Threats 296
07 Accusation of Abuse 296
08 Abandonment 296
09 Restriction of Child's Calls 297
10 Child Not Available for Pick up 297
11 Public Display of Affection 297
12 Interference with Child's Mail 298
13 Dangerous Living Conditions 298
14 Denial of Holiday Visitation 298
15 Phone Calls That Upset the Child 299
16 Child In Danger 299
17 Change in Exchange Location 299
18 Moving Child without Consent 299
19 Restriction of Time with Child 300
20 Other Parent Bad-mouthing You 300
21 Working Things Out, Need Room 300
22 Denial of Contact 301
23 Other Parent Costing You Fees 301
24 Parental Alienation Syndrome 301
25 Demand for Information 302
26 Disneyland Parent 302
27 Denial of Grandparent Visitation 302
28 Secret Filing of Court Documents 302
29 Differences in Parenting Style 303
30 Conflict during Exchange 303
31 Misuse of Psych Evaluation 303
32 Ex Parte Hearing - Order 304
33 Children Pressuring Parent 304
34 No Money, No Attorney 304
35 Other Attorney Costing Money 305
36 Grandparents' Custody Interrupted 305
37 Child's Affidavit of Preference 305
38 Teenager Won't Go to Visitation 306
39 Attorney Wants to Quit 306
40 We Comply, They Don't 306
41 Accusation of Sexual Abuse 307
42 Visitation Home Is Dangerous 307
43 Opposition Won't Pay 307
44 Lied, Forged and Ignored the Court 308
45 Parent Threatens Suicide 308
46 Religion as Grounds for Custody 308
47 My Lawyer Really Screwed Me 308
48 Won't Supply Insurance Card 309

49 Volunteer Spy 309
50 Relationship With the Judge 309
51 Internet Lurking 310
52 Prosecution for Perjury 310
53 Constant Public Harassment 310
54 Change of Circumstances 311
55 Lesbian Mom 311
56 Ex-Husband Excluded as Guardian 311
57 Credit Report Without Permission 311
58 Bio- Dad v Adoptive Parents 311
59 Step-Mom Wants Custody 312
60 Computer Evidence 312
61 EX Won't Complete Move 312
62 Military Non-Support 313
63 Unfit Parent 313
64 Interfering With Grandparent 314
65 They Searched My House 314
66 Confidentiality of Case File 315
67 Fined for Attorney Advice 315
68 Opposition Grinding Me Down 315
69 Leaving Country Owes Support 315
70 Former Spouse Tips Police 316
71 Bipolar Disorder 316
72 Child's Right to Choose 316
73 Forcing Me Back to Court 317
74 Child's Medial Problem Ignored 317
Evaluating Your Panic Situation 317
Your Panic Situation List 318
Anger 320
Dealing With Your Anger 320
The Anger of Others 321
Anger in Our Children 321

Chapter 16: Abuse, Allegations, Kidnapping 324
Abuse 324
Categories of Neglect and Abuse 324
Exposure to Abuse and Violence 326
Indications of Negligence or Abuse 327
Children's Reactions to Abuse 327
Penalty for Reporting Suspected Abuse 328
Child Protective Services 328
When CPS Gets A Call 328
Grounds to Continue the Investigation 330
Court Ordered Cooperation 332
When CPS Knocks at Your Door 332
Removal of the Children 332
Abuser's Reaction to Investigation 333
Arrest for Abuse 333
Getting Your Child Back from CPS 333
Has Your Child Been Abused? 334
Munchausen Syndrome by Proxy 334
Allegations 335
Allegation of Abuse 335
Preventing False Allegations 336
Dealing with False Allegations 336
False Allegations Examined 337
Profile Precursors for False Accuser 338
Post Accusation Accuser Behavior 338
Children Supporting False Accusations 338
Requesting Supervised Visitation 338
Complying with Supervised Visitation 339
Supervised Visitation Options 339
Abduction-Resistant Children 339
Disproving False Accusations 339
Sue for False Accusations 339
Types of Supervised Visitation 340
Reason for Referral 340
Reporting to the Court 340
Requesting Supervised Visitation 341
For the other Parent 341
Supervised Visitation for Yourself 341
Complying with Supervised Visitation 341
Child in Danger 342
Violence Lethality Assessment 342
Police 343
Violent Patterns Won't Change 343
If You are Forced to Leave 343
Kidnapping 343
Prevention 343
Profile of the Abductor 344
Kidnapping Warning Signals 344
Has Your Child Been Kidnapped? 345
Emotions When Kidnapping Occurs 346
Abduction Retrieval Questionnaire 346
Legal Steps to Get Your Child Back 347
People Trail or the Family Tree 348
The Paper Trail 349
Places to Look 349
Money 350

Chapter 17: Discovery / Deposition 351
Feast or Famine 351
Surprise and Ambush 351
I Have to Tell Them What? 352
Fruit of the Poisonous Tree 352
Interrogatory 352
Objecting in Interrogatory 352
Production and Inspection 353
Documents and Records 353
Tape-recorded Conversations 354
Confidentiality - Documentation 354
Photographs and Video Tapes 354
Medical Records 354

First Strike 355
Deposition 355
Explanation of a Deposition 355
Four Reasons to Depose Someone 355
Costs for Deposition 356
Best Time to Depose 356
Second Deposition 356
Prepare for a Deposition 356
Your Deposition 356
Psychological and Emotional Preparation 356
Attorney Preparation 357
Information is not Protected 358
Deposition Instructions 358
During Your Deposition 359
Facing the Mad Dog Attorney 360
Check Your Deposition 361
Ending the Deposition 361
Correcting Mistakes on Deposition 361
False Documentation 362
Who Would You Depose? 362
Opposition's Deposition 363
During the Oppositions's Deposition 363
Check the Opposition's Deposition 363
Check the Expert's Deposition 364
Your Witnesses' Deposition 364
Example of Deposition Indexing 364
Evidence to Disprove Statements 364
Failure to Comply with Discovery 364

Chapter 18: Judges 368
Perception of Hierarchy in Law 368
Two Levels of Law 368
Welcome to the Hotel California 369
Jurisdiction Shopping 369
Getting a Good Judge 369
Like No Other Law 370
Research Your Judge 370
Those Who Render Opinions 370
Which Judge is Mine? 371
Who Do You Think You Are Talking To? 371
A Judge Should Be Removed When 371
Judges Can Step Down 374
Get Rid of a Bad Judge 375
Whose Custody Case is this Anyway? 376
How Judges Decide 376
What Judges Cannot Do 376
What You Cannot Do with the Judge 376
Your Expectations 377
Examples of Judges' Rulings 379
A Matter of Perception 379
Judicial Immunity 380
Abuse of Discretion 380
Filing a Formal Complaint 380
Confidentiality - Judge 380
Judge's Ruling on Motion 380
Judge or Jury 380

Chapter 19: Court 382
Time Line 382
The Ultimate Battlefield 383
Types of Courts 383
Types of Cases 392
Are All Court Appearances Equal? 392
Pre-trial Conference 392
How Subpoenas Work 392
Court Before Court 392
Your Case Strategy 393
Court Presentation Outline Form 393
Non-Issue 394
Your Assignment 394
Refreshed Memory 394
Last Review 395
What Is a Witness? 395
Confidentiality - Witnesses 395
Your Children Testifying in Court 395
Competence of Child to Testify 395
Knowing Truth from Lie 395
Helping Your Child Testify 396
Challenging a Child's Testimony 396
Suppress Child's Testimony 397
Fear, Bias, Prejudice or Interest 397
Content of Child's Testimony 397
Anger Against You 398
Contempt of Court 398
Filing a Contempt Motion 398
Speak to Inequity 403
Visual Impact on the Court 404
Clothes Make the Witness 404
Major Problem Areas 404
In the Eye of the Beholder 405
In Court 405
Witnesses' Demeanor 405
Attitude 406
What a Witness Cannot Do 406
Witness Guide for Questions 406
Dodging Enemy Fire 407
Their Bullet Your Target 408
Types of Questions 408
Types of Questioning 409
Direct Examination 409
Cross Examination 409
Re-Direct 409
Not Sure! Not Sure? 410
Frontal Assault 410

Hey, Were All on the Same Side Here 410
People Who will be Attending the Trial 410
What Will Happen In Court? 411
It Ain't Over When It's Over 412
Appeal the Threat 412
The Appeal Process 413
Should You Worry? 414
Confidentiality - Court 414
Inexperienced Not Vexatious Litigator 414
Civil Appeal Example 416
Modification 419

Chapter 20: Costs 421
I Don't Understand Why No One Cares 421
When Your War Chest Is Spent 421
Two Ways To Significantly Cut Costs 423
Costs Go on Forever 423
Bankruptcy 425
Acknowledgement of Paternity 426
2001 DHHS Poverty Guidelines 426
Dependent According to the Court 426
Are You Poor Enough? 427
Dependent According to the IRS 427
Dependent Credits 428
Hidden Assets 428
Tax Gifts and Insurance Ownership 428
Earned Income Credit 428
Use a Good Tax Advisor 428
Adoption of Child and Termination of Rights 428
Voluntary Relinquishment of Parental Rights 429
Petition for Termination/Adoption of Stepchild 432
Social Study Report of Investigator 434
Decree Terminating Parental Rights 435

Chapter 21: Child Support 437
Income 437
Self Employment 438
Lottery Winnings 439
Hidden Sources of Income 440
Financial Child Support Theory 443
Child Support Decision Modeling 444
Ability to Pay 445
Ability to Earn 445
Daily Expenses 445
Costs to Rear A Child 445
Child Support Expense Survey 446
Child Support Obligation Starts When 446
Child Support Ends When 446
How Much Support is Appropriate? 449
Too Much or Too Little? 449
Support Below the Guidelines 450
Departures from the Guidelines 450
Temporary Modification 450
No See - No Pay 451
Can't See No-pay 451
Can't Pay 451
Advised Not to Pay 451
Who, When, How, Where to Pay 451
No Place to Send Payment 452
No Court Order in Place 452
Appeal Doesn't Stop Support 452
Best Attitude for Paying Child Support 452
Remove the Sting of Paying 452
Child Support as a Expense/Debit 453
Security for Support Awards 453
Insurance 453
Out-Of-Pocket Medical Expenses 454
Child Support and Bankruptcy 454
Child Support as Income 454
Best Attitude for Receiving Support 454
Is Child Support on the Children? 454
Best/Worst States for Collection 455
Child Support Doesn't Come 455
Where Child Support is Spent 455
Collection Methods 456
International Support Enforcement 457
Statute of Limitations 458
Criminal Non-support 458
Under the Table Employment 459
Assistance with Back Child Support 460
Waiting Too Long to Collect 460
Military Service and Child Support 460
Child Support Court Cases 461
Religious Objection to Paying Support 461
Support Reduced for Time with Child 463
Reduced by Child's Disability Benefits 463
Father's Debt Service 463
Forced to Provide College Education 464
Hardship Income Deduction Reversed 464
Child Support for Kidnapped Child 464
Case Behind License Revocation 464
Federal Government Force States to Comply 464
Canadian Child Support 466

Chapter 22: End or Beginning 467
Forgiveness 467
When You Win Custody 467
Is This the Win I Wanted? 468
Mental House Cleaning 468
The Hard Part 468
To Build a Healthy Child 468
And the Beat Goes On 469
When You Lose Custody 469

Emotions and Feelings 469
Many Emotions - Most Hurt 470
Now is not Forever 471
Making the Not-so-good Better 471
Let Go 472
Normal Feelings 472
Usual Challenges 472
Helpful Applications 473
Safe Answers 473
Concentrate on the Children 474
New Traditions 475
Holidays 475
Major Holidays 477
After You're Gone 478
Seek Support 478
Start a Support Group 479
ANYWAY 479

Chapter 23: Cases / Decisions 481
DNA 482
Paternity Suits May Never be Settled 482
Can't Sue Wife for Lying About Paternity 482
Documents Produced by Mistake 486
Tender Years Doctrine 487
Override of Right to Travel 487
Pro Se 487
Pro Se Not Held Same As Licensed Attorney 487
Recording Telephone Conversations 487
Real Advantage Test 489
Shared Parenting 489
Doubtfire Clause or First Right of Refusal 490
Custodial Mother Allowed to Move 491
Tort - Interference/Relationship 492
Custodial Interference Damages 492
Parents Who Smoke 492
Parental Alienation Syndrome 495
Malicious Mother Syndrome 496
Kidnapping 497
Kidnapping Damages Awarded 507
Emergency Jurisdiction Ends 508
Termination of Parental Rights 509
Psychological Parent 509
Passport Restrictions for Child Support 514
Lottery Payments Frozen 516
Parenting Constitutional Right 516
Fair Law - Unfair Enforcement 519
Fifth Amendment 519
Protective Laws May Not Hide Child 519
Judges are not Immune 520
Grandparent 520
Grandparents Custody Despite Father 522
Religion 522
Parents Can't Choose Modification 524
Change of Circumstance 525
Does a Police Liability Case Exist? 526
Expunged Records 527
Lesbian and Gay Parents 527
Disallowing a Child to Testify 551

Glossary of Terms 564

Index 607

Chapter 1: War or Peace

Questions Asked and Answered

Q. "The bad parent in the examples in this manual are almost always women. Is this manual anti-women?"

- *A.* No. The opposition in your case may be male or female. It just happens the opposition in our case was a woman. Most of the documents used as examples are from our case with the names changed. We think the best parent for the child is both parents, and we work hard to make sure the child gets just that.

Q. "If I use all this information and do everything legally, will I gain custody of my child, guaranteed?"

- *A.* There are no guarantees in this life. This information will help you avoid the most common mistakes people make, resulting in loss of the custody of their children.

Q. The other parent has custody and there is no way I can say there is any reason the court should change the decision. The problem I do have is that there are many times I could take care of the children when the other parent can't, but they go to a baby-sitter or other relative instead of me. What can I do about it?

- *A.* Most state guidelines clearly state that parental care is preferred over surrogate care. Therefore, unless there is a history of child abuse, the courts will enforce a non-custodial parents request to provide care for the children. Some parents' rights groups refer to this as the Doubtfire Clause in honor of the movie "Mrs. Doubtfire" staring Robin Williams.

Q. "A lot of what has gone on in my past personal life is now embarrassing. Will this manual tell me how to hide that stuff?"

- *A.* Most legal proceedings are a matter of public record. In some instances the judge may seal the case. This is usually to protect the child, not to make adult participants more comfortable. Incidents that happened before the birth of the child or have happened out of knowledge of the child and have precipitated no legal recourse other than this trial are usually not allowed to be presented. Your attorney can assess whether or not much of what you are concerned about will be relevant to this case. Keeping irrelevant information from the permanent records is one of the valuable services a competent attorney can perform.

Q. "I am tired of all of this. I want to give up my rights. How do I do that?"

A. You can give up your rights very easily. Don't take the time to visit your children and offer your parenting skills to help improve their lives. You effectively exit the lives of your children. Thereby, giving up your rights. If you do give up your rights now, you may find it very difficult or impossible to gain a legal right to re-enter their lives in the future. It is also important to note that even if you choose to give up your "rights" as they pertain to the children, the court will not allow you to give up your parental responsibilities for their economic and legal welfare.

A. The only way the court will lift the legal and economic responsibility for your children from you is if another similar parent is willing and able to take on those responsibilities. Precisely, if the other parent establishes a proper legal union (marriage) and the new mate is willing to adopt your children, there is a process for you to wave you rights and responsibilities and let the new parent step into the parenting role.

Q. "A great deal of what you cover in this manual seems to involve extreme circumstances and unstable people. We are both decent, reasonable and responsible adults. I don't foresee any of that in my case. Can this manual still help?"

A. Reasonable people do unreasonable things when faced with having someone tell them when and how they may see their children. Advice from family, friends and professionals will also affect how the other side reacts to this stressful process. The more information you have about what can happen, the more problems you can avoid and the more efficiently you will handle your case.

Q. "Does this manual tell me what I can do to get even with the other side for all the pain they have caused me?"

A. Revenge is not covered in this manual because revenge will not help you do what is best for you or your child. The judicial system and mediators consider vengeful acts to be indications of instability; therefore, they would not see you as an acceptable guardian for your child should you choose to be vengeful. Nothing else yields such unreliable results as trying to get even.

Q. "Does everything I need to do to win custody cost huge amounts of money?"

A. This is an expensive process. However, you can do many things to reduce the costs. Understanding what is possible as well as having your information in order and listening to the professionals you hire will cut your expenses. Preparation is ninety percent of the fight. You can do fifty percent of the preparation.

Q. "Why have custody battles become so ugly?"

A. In the past, custody of children was usually handled as part of a "fault" divorce, and custody awards were dictated by the issues raised as grounds for the divorce. Now, a divorce in two-thirds of the states of the United States requires only that one of the parties feels that the union is "irretrievably broken," allowing for a "no-fault" divorce. Therefore, the process does not allow for painful issues such as adultery, fraud, alcoholism, drug addiction, insanity, mental or physical cruelty or desertion causing the break in the marriage to be aired. These issues may be pertinent regarding custody only where the character of the parent becomes relevant.

Q. "I won custody of my children two years ago, but my former spouse keeps dragging me into court. Why isn't this over yet?"

A. Because you and/or your former spouse haven't come to the realization that you will have to get along better now than you ever did before. Old grievances will have to be put aside, and your new lives as not-living-together parents must start. Unless something horrific happens to you, your children will remain in your custody. As the winner, attempt to help the other parent learn to live with the situation. It won't be easy. It always takes the parent who loses custody longer to heal from the ordeal.

Q. "What if the wrong person uses this system?"

A. This data may enable the person to see there is no way to change his or her life enough to gain or retain custody of the child. Acceptance of this fact may expedite matters. On the other hand, if someone is attempting to follow the form of how to do things right while avoiding the identification of the problems they are causing, are in denial of personal shortcomings, and will not or can not change, this manual will not accomplish masking the inadequacies the professionals we'll see.

Finally if a parent with a great number of shortcomings, but who is primarily concerned about the welfare of the child, has long term contact with that child and practices the behaviors in this manual long enough to gain custody or visitation, he or she will be a better parent. Either way, your child wins.

Q. "Initially the other parent looks more socially acceptable and conservative, but any professional evaluation will indicate that the other parent is unstable and that I am the right parent to raise my child. I feel the system is unjust, and the only way to change it is to fight it. Why can't I fight things through my own way, instead of buckling under this stupid legal system?"

A. The only opportunity you had to fight it through in your own way was before the courts became involved. Now, you are on the legal battlefield where the rules have been in place for hundreds of years. The rules are set up to favor the prepared and equipped. It doesn't matter if you are fighting in the snow, the forest, or the court. If you are not dressed in the right kind of camouflage you *will* be the first casualty. Additionally, you can't fight two battles at once. Choose the one that is the most important to you now. Many fight their own custody battles and then go back to change the system.

Q. "What if both sides use this manual?"

A. If they follow the advice of this manual, they will fight a cleaner battle and cause less harm to the child they both love. They will become better parents and may be able to better deal with each other. You may find, in fact, that you are all on the same side. Your child's.

Q. "I think the other parent is systematically buying off the evaluators, my attorney and the judge. How can I stop this from happening?

A. It would take several hundred million dollars. No one has enough money to bribe all these people.

Q. "I would be interested in locating law books that pertain to the final judgement, violations of the court order so I can reverse custody. "

A. It does not work that way. The Law is a growing animal. Each day decisions are rendered according to how a case is presented and how a judge rules on his or her interpretation of the law and previous cases. Each ruling has an affect on the rulings that come after it. Each person must document (that is make proven, demonstrable evidence) of violations of court orders. They must be presented in the correct form at the proper time in the jurisdiction of the case at the time. At the time of this printing there is no compendium of case decisions, violations of those decisions or precipitation in the reversal of custody cases in existence.

Q. "I am the residential parent. The other parent is irresponsible in all respects. She spends money on things she wants before paying for utilities or insurance. She can't keep a job and is always moving back with her parents. Her personal relationships are chaotic and short lived. Her life is one excuse and crisis after another. When she is in love, she forgets about the children except to show them off. She offers no financial and very little emotional support. Will this manual help me remove this negative influence from my children's lives?"

A. The courts don't want to permanently remove parents from the lives of their children. She may be a less than perfect wife, daughter and mother, but she is all you, her parents and your children have. This manual will help you document the stable life you offer your children and the challenged existence she lives. This could be critical data if she decides to attempt to modify custody.

Q. "The other parent has custody of my child and won't take care of simple things like his teeth. I only get him every other weekend and drive four hours to pick him up. By the time we get back to our town on Saturday afternoon all the dentists are closed This is only one of the problems, but one that really bothers me. Can I get the court to see this neglect and give me custody?"

A. The court won't reverse custody over lack of dental care. This book will help you find the solutions to this problem which is to get a dental appointment in the town in which the child lives and drive the four hours back after his teeth are fixed. The court will view your inaction as harshly as the custodial parents. Fix what you can and document the rest.

Q. "My child hates going with the other parent. She suffers so, as soon as she knows the day is getting close.
When it gets down to hours before a visit she begins to shake and often becomes physically ill. How can I get the court to understand how hard this is on her and that she should not be subjected to such suffering?

A. It is critical to make sure there are no medical, psychological or abuse issues that professionals should address.

A. What you see and what the other parent and the court see are all different perceptions. Your perception is clearly stated in your question. The other parent sees the stressed child that was waiting for the visitation exchange. Then the other parent sees the child relax and enjoy the parenting time that is available. Often the other parent sees the same stressors exhibited by the child in the same or to lessor degrees as time to return to you approaches. The court sees parents subconsciously merging their own needs with those of the child. Often projecting the parents angry feelings to the child making the child fearful of each time the parents must interact.

A. It is the legal responsibility of each parent to follow the intent of any access or visitation order. It is the moral responsibility of each parent to make all contact with the other parent as easy on the child as possible. Research has shown that in the adult lives of children of divorce, the children know who was causing the problems at exchange. Regardless of what they were told at the time

Q. "I have posted information on some law news groups on the internet and sent a synopsis of my case to several attorneys' sites. Ultimately they have all said I have a very good case. All of these professionals are in other states. When I take the same information to attorneys in my state, they tell me to forget it. Can I handle this case using this manual without an attorney?"

A. The out of state out of jurisdiction might be venturing opinions on a point of law which might be true in ninety-five percent of the US, but not in the particular jurisdiction in which you are involved. Licensed lawyers are subject to getting blasted for practicing law outside their jurisdiction when they give free and correct advice on the net. We don't advise going after your case with only this manual to help you. You do need a good attorney.

Q. We are still married but don't live together. I would like to get legal custody of our children since they live with me.

A. Both parents in a marriage have equal custody of the children. If the parents were married when the children were born, custody is only assigned to one parent as a result of a divorce. If you decide to divorce an attorney will help you protect your rights. Things get started when the plaintiff (the person originating the suit) creates a legal pleading called "complaint for divorce" which is filed with the Clerk of Courts, along with instructions for service and payment of the filing fee. This document will include the request for custody. The plaintiff must attend all of the hearings required by the court, and prepared all the necessary papers. Usually the person asking for the divorce will have to appear at a hearing and give testimony under oath and bring a witness who will also testify, and prepare and bring all the necessary paperwork to complete the case. These may include complaint for divorce, dissolution, service, filing fee, parenting affidavit, parent education seminar (each curt has its own).

Q. The Court has ordered that my soon to be ex-spouse and I go to Family Conciliation. Do I have to go? Is this for marriage counseling?

A. You must attend Conciliation to complete the divorce in most states. Family Conciliation Services seldom deals with reconciliation of a marriage. This department's primary role is to evaluate the future decision making and living arrangements for the minor children in contested divorces. When the parties are able to agree about the parenting issues, only one visit may be needed. If there isn't a complete agreement more appointments may be needed to see each parent with the children and the parents separately. In rare instances there is a spontaneous reconciliation.

Pray for Peace - Prepare for War

Our goal is not to make you paranoid. It is to offer you an awareness of some of the dangerous and difficult positions in which you may be placed. Then, to place at your disposal some successful methods to deal with these situations.
Having read this manual, you will be ready to formulate clear, logical thought and action patterns adaptable to your individual challenges.

Child custody conflicts typically produce situations resulting in intense emotions that often lead to unacceptable behavior. Inappropriate behavior can permanently damage your chance to retain or obtain custody of your children. This manual identifies these situations and will help you deal with those situations in the most appropriate manner.

One half of knowing what you want is knowing what you must give up to get it. You will have more than enough challenges thrust upon you from the outside to test your character; do not entertain exaggerated fearful images. Don't let the fears you face on a daily basis immobilize you. Most of what could happen never does.

Intended Audience

The primary audience for this how-to system is the parent who is serious about winning and maintaining custody of a child. It does not matter whether the parent is male, female, a grandparent, disabled, a step-parent, married, single, wealthy, financially restricted, a mother or father. A child custody war rarely involves only the children and the parents of the children. The short-term emotional and financial impact of this kind of litigation also affects family and friends. Long-term emotional scars and financial indebtedness may never be completely erased.

Painfully aware of the economics of this process, I have tried to choose the products, services and procedures that produce the maximum amount of information in the shortest time for the least cost. However, my ultimate concern is for the quality of information. Quality should not be sacrificed solely because of cost.

This system will not make an expert out of you. It will help you identify situations in which you will need the expertise of professionals and give you an idea of where to find them and what to expect from them. You must tailor this information to fit your unique situation and the laws of the state in which you and your children live.

Although many suggestions in this manual can improve your interpersonal and parenting skills, it will not enable you to mask dangerous or illegal behaviors. Use this system in dealing with your children, the opposition, attorneys, judges, mediators, police, detectives, your friends, relatives, threats (real and perceived), and your own feelings.

Where Do You Fit?

"If there are no guarantees that I can win, why should I put my children or myself through this process?" Because there are no guarantees that you will lose.

Review your health and life insurance policies, retirement and survivor benefits on profit sharing, company retirement and your Last Will and Testament. Interstate succession laws may conflict with your wishes as they affect your children.

Make sure that if something happens to you during this process, your enemies don't get control of your assets. The people and positions we will address are mothers, fathers, grandparents, psychological parents, step-parents, step-grandparents and significant others. Identify your position in this equation. It will allow you to establish realistic long-term goals, install safety nets, and begin doing what is necessary to win.

Married - Unmarried Parents

Parents: people who bring another into existence.

Children are no longer bastardized by the circumstances of their birth. Parents are no longer ostracized if they have children out of wedlock.

The 2000 Census figures showed that 5 percent of all households were unmarried-couple, non-traditional arrangement homes. The numbers released so far do not disclose how many unmarried-partner homes were made up of same-sex couples.

The best circumstances possible for children is to be raised in a home with two loving parents who love each other.

The second best circumstances possible for children is to be co-parented by two cooperative loving adults that put the welfare of the children before their own desires.

The third best circumstance possible for children is to live with a residential parent that supports and encourages children to have a loving relationship with all the people the children care about.

Mother

The bulk of conservative public sentiment is on your side. Mature judges are convinced that the natural mothers of children are automatically best suited and equipped to care for their children. As a mother fighting for her children, you have a leg up on anyone who wishes to oppose you. Historical and biological weight are on your side. Many judges have presided over criminal court before they sit on a domestic relations bench and see more "bad" men than women. All things resist change, especially judges and the legal system. Other mothers fighting for custody and parenting groups are important in times of stress for friendship and support. Join one.

Father

You are on the crest of a new wave of thinking. Recently, public opinion has shifted to the premise that parenting skills are a matter of individual nurturing ability rather than gender. Psychologists and mediators in domestic relations tend to be younger than the judges are. Their training is more in line with popular current trends. In their eyes, the care-giver need not automatically be the children's mother. In addition, there is a mountain of legislation pending and passing that offer all parents' equal rights and responsibilities with regard to children. When fathers fight for custody all the way through court, they win more than 60% of the time. This is, in part, because if a father knows he has a good case, he will go as far as it takes and he will do whatever is necessary to win. Generally, men have years of resource evaluation and goal-oriented game plan practice. They have worked hard for years to have access to, and fit into, the "good old boy system." Fathers produce and control the bulk of family income.

Therefore, before a court makes a decision that controls how this money will be distributed, fathers have a financial advantage. They can afford to hire better attorneys and fight longer in court. Fathers' rights groups are more militant than the parents' rights groups. Find a group with which you can talk.

Grandparent

You raised your children and now, if necessary or given the opportunity, you are raising their children. Five percent of children live with people other than their parents, and you are the largest and most established group of people rescuing children. Economic depressions and social epidemics like drugs and AIDS have sent more and more children home to grandparents. Often a grandparent must fight one's own child for custody of grandchildren in order to protect their lives. Children are being given access to their grandparents through court ordered visitation in several states. If you have been the primary caregiver for your grandchildren for over six months in a state or county other than the one in which the parents of your grandchildren live you may have the right and responsibility to petition the court for Managing Conservatorship of your grandchildren.

Your abilities and desires to raise your grandchildren are winning battles all over the country, most notably in states where "Best Interest" and "What Is, Shall Remain" or "Status Quo" are the criteria for placement. There are Grandparent support groups and parenting groups all over America.

Psychological Parent

You are the parent in practice, but you have no biological or legal relationship to the child. The courts acknowledge the relationship when you and the children have a close relationship and consider you parent and child or when the biological parent encouraged this relationship.

You may be granted the responsibility of children's support and the privilege of visitation. Michigan 1987, Atkinson v. Atkinson: "A spouse who is not a biological or adoptive parent may be granted custody or visitation under the notion of Equitable Parent." Arizona District 1. 1993 Finck v. Finck: "If a child knows you 'only as a parent' then the court recognizes that relationship for visitation."

You are in much the same position as grandparents. "Best interest of the child" States offer you the best opportunity to care for and protect the children you love. Many parents' rights groups are providing a place for you to get support and information.

Possessory Conservatorship is being granted in many states to a person who is not a blood relative and may be granted custody by the court if the person can demonstrate substantial past contact with the child.

Step-parents and Step-grandparents

You are in the worst position. You will give your love, time and money to your child or grandchild, but have the fewest rights or considerations in public opinion or in the courts. That does not mean you should surrender.
The children need the love you feel for them and you matter to them. If, in fact, you are the best parent that life has to offer these children, staying in contact with these children will improve their existence on this earth. Keep fighting.

Significant Other

Because your significant other cares about his or her children and you care about this person, you may be completely immersed in a custody case. You may be the driving force that keeps things moving, the only element that keeps any sanity in all of this craziness, and be providing the financial ability to stay in the battle for the long run. Make sure the parent of these children is more interested in custody of these children than you are, and that it's not simply a vendetta.

If this case looks driven or controlled by you rather than the parents, you could be causing problems. If you finish the parents' sentences, do more talking to the attorney, and are apt to make copious notes to the attorney during court, you may actually cause problems. An attorney will have a husband, wife, father, mother or significant other stay out of court as much as possible if they give the appearance of power or passion.

Whose Custody Case is this Anyway?

In this war of endurance and attrition, you need to and should accept, appropriate support and assistance from the people who care about you and your children. Appropriate support includes a calm, reassuring listener, finder of knowledge, and information to full financial support. Inappropriate help includes fanatics anxious to make personal sacrifice or doing questionable activities to meet your goals.

Make sure your case does not look driven or controlled by someone else. It is advisable to help your husband, wife, father, mother or significant other be, and appear as a support person, rather than a leader. If this person finishes your sentences for you, does more talking than you do, and makes promises or decisions for you, you have this problem. If you are in this battle because it is your opportunity for external validation from your parents or others, you are in this fight for the wrong reason. If you lose the battle you will be blamed by the very people you need approval from and if you win they will feel it was because of their efforts.

Mediators, Psychologists and Judges are very sensitive to a case that looks driven or controlled by someone other than the parents of the children. Questions come to mind, including: Is this parent interested in custody, or is their significant other interested in custody? Is this custody case a vendetta of rivals for a parent's attention rather than the welfare of the children? Why does this person seem more assaulted by the process than the other parent of the children does? Often an attorney will have your husband, wife, father, mother or significant other stay out of the limelight as much as possible if they give the appearance of power or passion. Accept the healthy help offered by the people who care about you. But do not hand over control of your case to anyone.

Best Interest?

The earliest case we could identify was U.S. v. Green, 1824, a case citing best interest standard. With all preceding cases in mind, the courts will decide for a less-than-perfect situation in order to provide continuity for the children. Don't be surprised if the court decides against changes intended to improve things for the children.

Once an agreement to set a schedule is reached, it is important to the court that the schedule not be altered. **Your children love both parents.** Your opinion of the other parent is no indication of the kind of parent he or she is for your children. It is not unusual for a person to be a good parent, yet be only adequate as a spouse or employee.

Your children have the right to have access to, and the love of, each parent without interference. **Your children need to feel and be safe, secure and protected from physical, emotional and sexual abuse.** Your children's needs at different ages must be considered carefully. Children will accept or be unaware of the distinction between a combative or cooperative relationship their parents have with each other. Your children will do better if both parents are willing to work together.

Forcing children to choose one parent or the other will cause much more damage to the children than to the other parent. Best interest of the child is subjective. Each person viewing the case may have a different perception of what is in the best interest of the child. The courts have consistently ruled that, "Parents cannot always be deemed to be acting on the child's behalf."
An obvious example is when a parent has been convicted of physically abusing a child.

One parent may feel the child should reside with that parent because the parent has and is raising siblings of the child. The other parent may feel that social and school problems exhibited by those very same children are evidence that the child should not live in that house. At the same time, a mediator may feel the child would be appropriately cared for in either home.

A parent's personal needs and agenda will often influenced that parent's notion of the best interest of the child.

Who Should Not Fight for Custody

Some people need to build a life for themselves before they attempt to build a life for their children. It may be the first opportunity circumstance has ever offered. Letting the other parent raise the children free of negative interference will provide a better future for the children and for them.

Providing a safe place for your children to be cared for, while you build a viable and happy future for yourself, is one of the greatest things you can do for yourself and your children.

People give as many reasons for fighting for the custody of their children, as there are children. Very few of the reasons given are valid. Many are based on the adult's need to retain control of the children that the adult treats as another piece of property or as a tool to cause the other parent pain.

Every decision you make in this regard should be tested by the question; "Will the results of this decision be in the best interests of my children?"

There are several excellent books written by adult survivors of custody battles, retelling how they suffered as children. Some of these survivors have successfully coped with the scars inflicted on them as children, and some will never heal.

Reasons People Say They Have Custody

As I interviewed people who had custody of their children, these were the responses I received:
Did they all have legal custody? No.
Is the best interest of the child in each example served? No.

As you can see, some of these reasons are less than perfect:

- The children asked to stay with me.
- I won the child custody lawsuit.
- The other parent did not want to go to court.
- I kidnapped the children.
- We agreed that I would have the children.
- Other parent needed fewer obligations.
- I am the better parent of the two.
- The other parent just disappeared.
- The other parent's new partner did not get along with the children.

Worst Reasons to Fight for Custody

- The other parent wants the children so I want them.
- I have been paying the kid's bills all these years.
- I need someone to love me.
- Having the children will give me the ability to punish the other parent.
- I am the parent, so I deserve to have custody.
- I need the tax deduction or child support.
- People will think badly of me if I don't have my children.
- Keeping the children gives me control over the other parent.

Abuse Excuse

Because life is not fair or easy, many things happen to us. One may be a victim of child abuse, neglect or a horrible accident. But if you survive the terrible thing that happened to you, you must make the decision to go on with your life and make it the best it can be for you and your children.

Dead Hand

Only a few people make the journey from birth to death in one complete piece. Some face challenges from birth. Others are the victims of circumstance because of where or when they were born. Still others are harmed by the misdeeds of others. A surprising number of people are damaged by their own actions.

If you have faced any of these challenges and survived you have won. The size of the challenge or why you had to face it is less important than the fact that you have survived. Children born with a physical challenge or subjected to brutality or sexual abuse are blameless for the trials they have endured. As the children become adults it is vital that they accept that they have survived to inhibit their ability to face new challenges or rewards.

If you lose the use of your right hand, it is terrible. But the quality of your life is up to you, not your hand.

Don't let your dead hand rule your life.

Children as Pawns

Nothing is more terrifying than the possibility of losing contact with your children. The opposition knows this and may capitalize on this by requesting custody when that person would be unable or unwilling to give your children a good home. The other parent may want to cause you pain, get revenge, get money or control other people's lives. Understanding that this might be the opposition's motive may prepare you for the fight.

Factors Influencing Court Decisions

Judges are supposed to weigh carefully all significant factors relevant to a child's welfare and best interest. Incorrectly, we would like to think that custody issues, more than most litigated matters, are determined primarily by their unique patterns. In reality the number and variety of cases assigned to each judge prevents careful determinations of custody. The judges must establish broad guidelines to determine what generally constitutes a child's "best interest".

In determining what constitutes a child's best interest, judges are theoretically supposed to consider the following:

- Best interest of the child
- Relationship between each parent and the child.
- Any instance of child or spousal abuse.
- Results of any testing.
- Ages and sexes of the children.
- Adjustment and length of time of the children to their environment.
- Child's need for special, emotional or physical care.
- Child's wishes, if of sufficient age.
- Parent's desires and agreements between the parents.
- Educational needs of the child.
- Separation of siblings.
- Length of time child has been in the custodial home.
- Permanence of any proposed home.
- Mental and physical health of the parents.
- Prior custody determinations.
- Hostility levels between parents.
- Flexibility of each parent to work with the other parent.
- General parenting skills.
- Substance abuse by either parent.
- Religious concerns.
- Morality of the parents.
- Care-taking arrangements prior to and after separation.
- Likelihood that custodial parent will remove child from jurisdiction.
- A parent will alienate the affections of the child from the other parent.

Common Custody Arrangements

Custody contemplates the primary question of, which parent the children will live and how much time each parent will spend with the children. There are as many formulas for custody as there are imaginations. It appears that no country in the world has the answer to the problem of where children should be placed when the biological parents are not living together. Legal terminology or definitions may vary from state to state. The information you get about the custody laws in your state today may be out of date by next month.

Make no mistake; the laws of this country are written by adults to protect their interests, not to protect the interests of the children. There have been many studies in the last fifteen years that compare the welfare of children in intact families, sole paternal, sole maternal and joint custody situations. If you are interested in protecting your children, honestly attempt to decide where the best future home for them would be, and make sure that is where the children end up. If you are not equipped to make this evaluation, get professional assistance. Search your heart and make the right decision for the children.

This section is included to indicate the variation from state to state and to give you an idea of what is going on where you live. You are advised to get a current update from your attorney.

Interim or Temporary Custody

Once the court becomes part of the formula one of the parents will be designated as the temporary or interim custodian and establish fixed-schedule visitation arrangements for the other parent. The court most often accepts these motions. Most often the Interim or Temporary arrangements become the permanent custody order. However, a non-custodial parent can win custody of the children by demonstrating to the court that the family structure at the time of the temporary order did not reflect the long-term family arrangements before the temporary order. Other factors that could encourage the court to award the non-custodial parent would be degeneration in the children's health, school grades and mental attitude. Documentation is essential to any presentation.

Sole Custody

Provides one caretaker with the custodial position, including total control and legal responsibility for the children. Choice of where the children live within the state in which custody was decided, and who has access (other than those set forth in the visitation guidelines) to them is entirely up to this person, with some instruction from the court. Each state has minimum fixed-schedule visitation guidelines established for non-custodial parents and grandparents.

Joint Custody

Joint Physical Custody. The children live with one parent during the school year and the other parent has "visitation" during that school year. Then the children spend the entire school vacation, a period of three or more months, with the non-custodial parent.

Physical and Legal

Both parents are responsible for the children's behavior and needs. Time with the children and expenses for them are divided. The children customarily reside with one parent. This does not necessarily mean that the child is with each parent fifty percent of the time or that one of the parents does not have the obligation of child support.

Joint Physical

Both parents are responsible for the children's needs. Time with the children and expenses for them are divided, not necessarily on a 50/50 basis. The children customarily reside with one parent. That parent has the legal control. Joint custody does not necessarily mean equal parenting time.

Joint Legal

One parent is designated as the custodial parent. Both parents have legal responsibility, but the children may live with one parent. Decisions are made jointly. This does not necessarily mean that the child is with each parent fifty percent of the time or that one of the parents does not have the obligation of child support.

Split Custody

Some children from the family live with one parent, and some children live with the other parent. Visitation is on a schedule. This is seldom ordered unless it is an established system the family has been successfully functioning with for a reasonable length of time and all affected parties agree.

Alternating or Divided

The children are moved from one parent to the other on a schedule. The parent with custody at the time makes the legal decisions. This takes a great deal of cooperation from everyone involved.

Therefore, alternating or divided custody is seldom ordered unless it is an established system within which the family has been successfully functioning for a reasonable length of time and all affected parties agree.

Bird's Nest Custody

The children stay in the family home and the parents move in and out. The parents may maintain other residences or stay with friends or relatives. This arrangement is wonderful for the children and can work if the parents want it to. This is seldom ordered unless it is an established system within which the family has been successfully functioning for a reasonable length of time and all affected parties agree.

Visitation

As you prepare for war, visitation becomes a key issue. There are many types of visitation including: fixed-schedule visitation, reasonable visitation, overnight visitation, weekend visitation, summer visitation, long distance visitation, telephone visitation, e-mail visitation, computer visitation and mail visitation. A non-custodial parent who does not use the visitation given is seen as not interested in spending time with the children. A custodial parent interfering with the children visiting the other parent is seen by the court as a person who will disconnect the children from the people they love for their own purposes.

Visitation is a Right of the Children.

Visitation is not the right of either parent. It is not a tool for the residential caretaker of the children to control or hurt the nonresidential parent. The companionship and care that visitation encourages is a very important part of child support. This concept is one of the most misunderstood in the custody arena.

The parent fortunate enough to be the residential caregiver has the responsibility to assist the children, not hamper the efforts of the non-custodial parent. Statistically, non-custodial parents do not follow the visitation schedule, even when it is exactly what they requested. In most cases, the non-custodial parent will ask for more visitation or parenting time than that parent can reasonably exercise or on occasion really want. Children whose non-custodial parent exercises all of the parenting time offered are very lucky.

Suddenly Super Parent

If a parent has been a devoted parent in the past, there is every reason to believe the children can depend on that level of care and attention in the future. Parents and children who are used to continual exposure to one another and are suddenly forced to compress all their feelings into a relatively short time span, will feel awkward and the situation may be painful. How often children come in contact with a non-custodial parent following a separation is a key factor in the time they will require to recover from the trauma.

If this person has become "devoted" only since the custody battle began, it may be because the conflict has opened the person's eyes to the importance of their relationship with their children. If the feelings are not deeply rooted, the other parent may revert to old ways when the custody case drags on or is over.

Children will be seduced by an increase in affection and time from a parent who has always been distant. All you can do is help the children enjoy this bounty while it is there, and understand if and when it disappears. Don't steal any of the happiness the children are experiencing now with dire predictions of abandonment later. You will end up the "bad guy."

Make a notation in your contact log as soon as you notice the increase in attention. If there is a danger of the children being disappointed by a non-custodial parent missing visitation for any reason, have some backup plans made to salve their wounded feelings.

If you know the children are being stood-up intentionally, or the non-custodial parent frequently fails to show up, document the infractions to submit later for a reduction in visitation allowed. This is a good time to remind you that there is a value in keeping a log, even after you have won your custody war. If you lost the war, keep trying to improve yourself and your life. Nothing is forever. Your children may <u>want</u> to live with you when they are older. If your life is stable and sane, a judge is likely to listen to the children. Children of divorce who heal well are children who have two responsible, healthy parents even though they live in two different households.

Grandparent Visitation

Citing the importance of the extended family in the development of children, the courts had put legislation into place that gave visitation to grandparents. To determine visitation privileges for grandparents, the court examined the involvement the individuals had with the children in the past, age and general health of the adults and desire of the children.

Grandparents with this kind of interest often subsidize the needs of the children. If the grandparents were infrequent visitors in the past and the grandparent's interest is to harass the custodial parent rather than to spend time with the children, the court would deny visitation.

As the year 2000 began the Supreme Court of the United States is considering the question of parent's rights verses grandparent rights. During 2001 several states have ruled for parents seeking to raise their children without interference and others have ruled in favor of the grandparents. Grandparents are presenting the value the extended family has to the short and long-term emotional health of the children. Parents are concerned that their right to raise their children without interference from others is under siege. Additionally, many of these parents say their efforts are essential to protect the children from emotional, psychological, physical or sexual abuse that they themselves suffered as children at the hands of these same parents/grandparents. The questions of grandparent visitation and grandparent custody of children are entirely different issues.

Exercising Visitation

If your children live with the other parent and you have been given visitation through some instrument of the court, it is your responsibility to exercise that visitation. Follow the visitation order to the letter. If the custodial parent allows you additional time with your children, be polite and appreciative and note the additional time in your log. If your children live with you and the non-custodial parent does not attempt to exercise the visitation, do everything to lessen the negative impact on your children's emotions and make a notation for each missed visitation in your log. It would be difficult in the future for a parent to ask for additional visitation time if the past visitation was not exercised to the fullest.

Successful Visitation

- Residential parents should have the child(ren)'s schedule ready for the nonresidential parent.
- Nonresidential parents should have telephone numbers ready for normal contact and emergency contact by the residential parent.
- If there is more than one child, and the opportunity arises, make separate plans for each child according to their developmental needs and abilities. A teenager will want more time with their friends or independent activity while a ten-year-old will want to do more things with you.
- Reserve time to be alone with your children. You don't need to go any place special, but give them an opportunity to talk to you without any interruptions. Do something special with your children without anyone else around.
- Allow life to go on as usual. Have your children accompany you as you fulfill your responsibilities and commitments. Encourage your children to become a part of that lifestyle.
- Never have your children carry messages for you, especially ones that will upset the other parent. Talk with the other parent in private or on the telephone.
- Never speak negatively about the opposition or their activities to the children.
- Don't question the children about the other parent's activities or relationships.
- Give your children chores or responsibilities while visiting with you at your home.
- Establish and maintain boundaries for the children's behavior. Discipline your children with love.

Your Interference with Your Visitation

If your personal discomfort or strain at the thought of facing the other parent or inability to fit your children into your business or personal schedule keeps you from calling or spending time with your children, you are the person responsible for interfering with the visitation.

No excuses or explanations will satisfy your children or the courts, now or when dealing with your conscience later.

Parental Interference with Visitation

If someone is preventing you from exercising your visitation, there are some very effective options for you to try. It is illegal to interfere with court ordered visitation, but it is not a high priority for law enforcement. Therefore, it is best for you to attempt to correct the situation yourself.

In most cases taking someone with you can solve the problem. The best option is a neutral, unimpeachable, third party. A cool, calm friend or a support person from a parent's rights group are two very good options.

Your attorney can pursue several legal "remedies" that yield varying degrees of success. Save some money by doing the foundation work yourself. Lay out your plan and get your attorney's opinion as to legality of form and purpose and opportunity for success. If your attorney has never faced this problem before, you will both find the following lists helpful. Non-attorneys are very intimidated when they receive copies of filed documents (even if they carry no real weight with the court) and may feel compelled to comply because they feel "the court" is watching them again. Once you have built evidence of a pattern the court can see, then have your attorney go after the opposition in court.

Handling Interference with Visitation

One example of how to deal with and document parental interference with visitation is one non-custodial parent's routine:

1. In advance of the date of visitation, you or your attorney should construct a "Notice of Exercise of Parenting Time" that states exactly what the court order says about the visitation. Identify the date, time, place for pick up and the items to accompany the children.

2. The non-custodial parent would file with the court and send by courier or registered mail a court stamped copy to the custodial parent or parent's attorney two weeks before scheduled visitation.

3. The non-custodial parent would arrive with police "Civil Standby" to keep the peace during an attempted pick up of the children to exercise parental rights, with copies of court order and Notice of Exercise of Parenting Time in hand.

4. Anytime visitation is denied, the non-custodial parent should file a "Notice to Court of Denial of Parental Access."

5. When you go to court submit highly specified fixed-schedule visitation schedules that include, transfer sites, monitors, and reasonable timely penalties for noncompliance. The schedule must include the precise dates and times when visitation is to begin and end. There must be no room for an outside observer to interpret to be any different than those outlined by the court.

6. Visitation will need to be renewed on a periodic basis, as defined by the court. The exchange site should be the lobby of a police station, a church leader's office, day care center office, school principal's office or the main entrance to a shopping center.

7. The court must direct all the parties around the custodial parent to comply and specify the penalties that will be imposed if the court order is violated, and it must carry out those penalties as necessary.

8. The court order should include a precisely worded authorization to all law enforcement officers to execute the transfer of children as specified in the court order. Additionally, it should direct the police to assist the victimized parent in locating his or her child. If this is an ongoing problem, the police may be directed by the court order to arrest the violating parent.

Visitation Bond

Where there is a history of custodial interference or a likelihood of future interference, you may ask the court to order the potential abductor to post a bond, payable to you, to ensure that the children are returned or released in compliance with the order. Along with a fixed-schedule visitation the visitation bond works like a bail bond and may be available through the same sources. The forfeit of the bond in case of noncompliance with the visitation order does not remove other penalties the law may hold for the noncompliant parent.

If you are the parent requesting visitation, but are falsely accused of looking for an opportunity to kidnap your child, you could ease the mind of the other parent by offering to post a visitation bond. It isn't fair, but if you post the bond and return the child in accordance with the visitation guidelines you have shown yourself to be a problem solver in this situation.

Police

There is not a great deal in this manual about the police. Because there is very little they can really do to help you. The officer on the front line has little or no training in domestic relations. The officer's superior wants the family disturbance handled quickly so the officer can go on to "real police work". And the city, state, and federal government agencies have no funding or inducement to take any new or innovative approach that may or may not work. Therefore, it is in your best interest not to *need* an officer.

If getting upset so you can yell and make a scene is what you want, then at least be aware that you are in fact going to pick a fight. You may feel some short-lived satisfaction in stirring things up, or you may induce the other parent to do something you are unable to predict or defend against. A confrontational attitude will cause you and your children more harm than good.

If you are going to pick up or drop off your children or some other necessary task that requires interaction with the other parent, make it your responsibility to accomplish your goal without participating in anything negative. Do not take part in any action or exchange of words that will upset your children.

If the other parent always picks a fight with you during each encounter, do not fight back. Review the last several exchanges of angry words and prepare alternative responses that will not incite the other parent. Have any information or items ready if the other parent has reason to expect them from you. Arrive on time. Mind your own business. It will take more thinking and planning to win, but it is worth it. Take the steps necessary to defuse dangerous situations and enable the other parent to do what you want easily and without cost or embarrassment. Of course it sounds like you are "giving in," but it may be the difference between getting what you want or not. If you cannot control your own emotions, get a neutral person to accompany you or ignore the assaults of the opposition, then you may have to call the police.

When you go to the police, you will need to have a cool head and the court documents designating the fixed-schedule visitation to support the charges you are making and a list of witnesses and statements. Avoid angry statements and foul language no matter how upset you feel. Law enforcement personnel can execute warrants for entry and arrest and communicate with other police departments. If the abuse continues, the non-custodial parent can petition the court for a modification of visitation or custody.

Check to see if case law in your state has designated interfering with visitation as child abuse. If it has then it may help to have a copy of the decision with you since all child abuse is a criminal offense.

If a police officer is under subpoena, he/she cannot absent him or herself from the trial without accounting to the court later. There could be severe repercussions.

Police and Restraining Orders

Keep in mind that the police officer is an officer of the court and must enforce orders or the court.

A rising trend is people filing suit against police officers who fail to enforce restraining orders.

Life's Time-line

You have probably seen a chart that shows a history of the world using thousands of years in small increments. It diagrams the time line from earth's formation through the first plant and animal fossil skeletal remains found to our exploration of space. This permits the viewer to put events in proper perspective. Chart your life using single years. The challenges of the custody battle can limit your ability to see beyond the emotional and financial restrictions that engulf you.

The chart with your childhood, upper level schooling, employment, marriage(s) and projected future will let you put things into perspective. The important things in your life always take a considerable amount of time. Your custody battle is one of those important things. This chart will enable you to deal with the short-term pain better by allowing you to visualize the long-term, more acceptable future. This exercise can empower you to reach an understanding and reasoning that will enable you to formulate responses and facilitate your children's return to your life when they are ready, without additional delay caused by any guilt that the children might feel.

If You're on a Short Time Line

If custody of your children is in question as part of a divorce in a state that has "no-fault" divorce, or if the relationship or situation with the opposition has deteriorated, you are on a very short time line. A very short time line usually means hours, not days or weeks. Don't feel discouraged if they have beaten you to the punch on some of these moves; accomplish what you can.

1. Don't move out of your home if it means moving away from your children. If forced to move out, find a place within blocks of the old residence. If your children are of school age, make sure your new home is in the same school district. This will help if your attorney requests 50/50 shared time or, if you cannot get a temporary order for full custody. If the opposition moves out with or without the children, change the locks and install a burglar alarm system.

2. Hire an attorney and file as the plaintiff requesting custody of your children. If it is possible in your state, have your attorney get an ex-parte order granting you temporary custody effective right away, and then proceed to make the temporary order permanent. If a request for temporary custody is not probable, request an order that limits the other parent from moving the children out of the school district.

3. Do not sign anything without having your attorney look at it first. If you can't afford to retain an attorney full-time, hire one to examine and advise on this document only.

4. Close all joint checking, savings and credit card accounts. Make a cashier check for 50% of the monies in the accounts and send it to the opposition. If you take any more than half, you will start a pattern of behavior the courts will look critically upon. Open your own checking, savings and credit card accounts.

5. Stay in touch with your family and friends. Do not disconnect from your work and personal support systems.

6. Start keeping a daily or incident log. If you can do it accurately, go back to the beginning of the problem.

7. Take care of yourself and do not do anything you would be ashamed for your children, parents or minister to know about.

Non-Custodial Parent's Emotions

The emotions that accompany visitation are difficult. Initially you are elated that you will have time with your children. Then, the unhappy realization that you will have to face the custodial parent descends on you. Anxiety about the exchange begins to build in the pit of your stomach.

Once you accomplish the pick up of your children you must put aside any apprehension you feel and any unhappiness that you were unable to prevent. Endeavor to make the time with your children as calm and rewarding for you both as possible.

Have something planned for you to do after you take your children back after visitation. The activity will shorten the sadness and grieving you will feel.

Issues - Non-Issues

Sometimes the problems we face are not considered issues by the court. Focusing on the wrong issues can waste your time. Knowing the difference between an Issue and a Non-Issue is critical. A quick discussion of the most common complaints will help you fine-tune your efforts. These categories are not presented in any specific order.

Their Problem or Yours

Issues should be documented and presented to the court. An issue is the opposition's problem. Non-issues are your problem. You should correct them to the best of your ability. The opposition doesn't care, and won't help. You must find a way to handle and defuse any non-issues. Any non-issue you cannot correct you must learn to accept.

Child Endangerment

Issue. Only if it can be documented that the children are in obvious, imminent and not correctable danger. Usually, there must be a documented history of injury to the child. Often third party professional sworn testimony is necessary.

Opposition is a Control Freak

Non-issue. Living in a controlled environment is not a threat to the lives of the children. Additionally, if you feel the other parent is a 'control freak', in most cases the court hears from the other parent that, 'You have no sense of responsibility'. The court considers it a wash.

Control Freak and No Responsibility

This is a very complex combination of choices. Normally we see a person as controlling or irresponsible.

In most cases this is a non-issue because the court will only see it as a personality clash. On the other hand, the combination could make it an issue if you can document the behaviors that would impact the child.

Blended Family

Non-issue. The courts run both ways on this issue. Often they will give the blended family a great deal of time to adjust to the stresses. Evaluators will consider the impact on a child more seriously. Blended families could consist of (a) siblings from several family groups now comprising one family (b) a racially blended family (c) a religiously blended family (d) a same sex blended family.

Mental Illness

Issue. Proven mental illness in the initial custody battle is a valid reason for the court not to award custody to one parent. A newly developed mental illness that can be documented with observation of unstable behavior by impartial third parties is grounds for reversal of custody.

Lengthy Child Care

Issue. If a custodial parent must have others take care of the child for extended lengths of time (10 hours + a day M-F) and the non-custodial parent is available and willing to care for the child; the court will often modify an order to read that the non-custodial parent has first right of refusal over outside day care. This also applies to older children in the family watching, but not necessarily giving proper care and loving attention to the child. The older siblings should be allowed to be children, not stand-in parents. The court sometimes refers to this as 'the Doubtfire clause' from the movie by Robin Williams.

Verbal or Mental Abuse

Non-issue. If the abuse is against you, the court does not care.

Issue: If the abuse is against the child, make or get a fill-in 'Incident Report' form that can be used by you and your child as well as third party non-related witnesses, to document the problems. Tape-recorded statements may be critical to substantiate the abuse.

False Accusations

Non-issue/issue. As accusations are made and proven false, a pattern emerges against the accuser. Evaluators and psychologists place more weight on this than the court does. Keep your cool and get it documented. Once you are found innocent by child protective services or whoever must investigate the incident, the accusing parent looks bad. Future claims are not taken as seriously.

Frequent Moving

Issue. Almost anything a person does before the birth of the child is a non-issue. Chart all the places the other parent has lived since the birth of the child. If you know how many other people lived there and how many bathrooms and bedrooms the places had, list that also. Stability in a child's life is critical.

Physical Abuse

Issue. Make or get a fill-in 'Incident Report' form that can be used by you and third party non-related witnesses, to document the problems. Photos and tape-recorded statements are critical. If the abuse is against you, call the police. If the abuse is against the child, get the school and the police involved.

Alcohol Use or Abuse

Issue. The children in the care of a parent whose judgement or ability to care for the children because he or she is too drunk to care for them shows negligence and abuse. Driving while drunk with the children in the car is abuse. A good example of 'bullet proof' documentation would be an 'Incident Report" form filled out and signed by the baby-sitter or day care that the parent was intoxicated when they picked up the children.

Drug Use or Abuse

Issue. The use or abuse of prescription or street drugs is a problem that can be tested for. Make sure you can also pass any screening you may wish the other parent to undergo. Many kinds of testing are available. Most test for drugs currently in a persons system. Testing of hair for drugs can show evidence of drug use for weeks, months and years in the past depending on the length of the hair available for testing

Other Parent Only Wants to Hurt Me

Non-Issue. Actually they are so busy screwing things up and then attempting to fix them they don't have many evenings to spend wondering what they can do tomorrow to make you miserable. Often the things that hurt you most were done unintentionally. Your only option is to get a thicker skin. You don't believe them when they tell you something good why should you always believe them when they tell you something bad.

Visitation Denial or Interference

Issue. Custody is being reversed on these grounds. You must have, consistent documentation. It would be important to ask the court to change an order from reasonable visitation to fixed-schedule visitation to see it that will solve the problem.

If it does not, each time you go to get your child and are denied access, you need to fill out an Incident Report Form. It would make a great deal of difference if you take an impartial, non-related person with you. A fill-in form would help them make a hard evidence statement rather than it being your word against the other parent's word. If you are denied your visitation during telephone conversations, have an impartial, non-related person listen in on the call and fill out the Incident Report Form. You may want to talk to your attorney about filling a Contempt of Court complaint for denial of visitation each time you have this problem.

Lying to Child, You and the Court

Non-issue. You are right. It is wrong for the other parent to lie and it is wrong that you can do nothing about it. When your child says, "Janice says you lie to me all the time," the proper response is, "I am sorry Janice feels that way. Do you think I lie to you?"

Issue. To make their lies an issue there is a great deal of documentation required. You will have to determine what issues are important to the court and only document them. The original lie. The proof of the lie. Organization of the information. Charting, graphing, or photos if necessary. Avoid turning this into a one person's word against the other shouting match. The court will not allow this to happen. Proving a person lied to the court, in court, is one way to get the court to act. Make sure it is an important issue, not something the court will see as a non-issue.

Kidnapping

Issue. Once a parent has kidnapped it is fairly easy to convince an evaluator or the court that it may happen again. I am fairly sure this is not the only incident you have dealt with. You must keep a contact log.

Kidnapping Threat

When people threaten to kidnap or express fear that you will kidnap, there is a real problem. Make data sheets on all the people around the other parent. This will enable you to find your child if necessary. Teach your child to call you at work, at home, your best friend's house. Let your child practice calling you and other family and friends collect. Show the child where they live on a map of the United States.

Make sure your child knows your entire name and how to tell the police to get in touch with you. Tell your child that if he is taken he can dial 911 when no one is around and hide the telephone when it is off the hook. The police will come to help the child.

Domestic Violence

Non-Issue. Seeing domestic violence is abuse, but the courts usually don't do anything about it unless the child is the target of the violence.

New Significant Other or Step-parent

Non-Issue. Often a new person in the life of your ex gives you someone you can give information to and get information from without all the old hurt and arguments starting again. Issue: On the other hand, if you are concerned, have a background check run on this person. Learn everything you can about who they are and where they came from. Fill out a 'Data Sheet' on new significant others, especially if there is a quick turnover in them. Charting the rapid change of the guard may be something an evaluator might look at seriously. Other than that, the only time a new adult in the life of your ex concerns the court is, if they are on drugs, drive drunk with your children in the vehicle or have been convicted of a sexual offense against a child.

Alternative Lifestyle

Non-Issue/Issue. It really depends upon the political and social climate where you live if being gay or lesbian is going to be an issue or not. There is a checker board of decisions for and against the homosexual parent.

Best Interest of the Child

Almost a Non-Issue. Best interest of the child is almost a non-issue because both parents feel they offer a life that is in the best interest of the child. Most custody statutes are modeled after the Uniform Marriage and Divorce Act. Section 402 lists the criteria that a decision maker should consider in determining the best interest of a child.

Any allegation would have to be proven to have a negative effect on the child involved.

Neglect

Issue. Neglect is only a step away from abuse. Make or get a 'Condition of Child' form (example in this manual) that can be used by you and third party non-related witnesses, to document the problems. The parenting style of one raised with only one or two other siblings will be very different from one raised in a household of six children.

Non-Issue. Neglect that can be identified and corrected by the complaining parent is not an issue. The professionals and the courts feel that if you become aware of something your child needs, you should fill the need. A common problem is dental care. The complaining parent feels that Dental Neglect is an outward manifestation of the inferior overall care the child receives. The judge will not reverse custody or award custody on this issue.

Poor Living Conditions

This is a “quicksand” area. There is no crime in being poor, although it can make for less than perfect living conditions.

If you are the poor one, show that you are doing the best you can. Keep your home clean and safe. Demonstrate how you are able to compensate with more one on one time with your child. If you are the one who can offer the child better living conditions, make it clear without putting the other parent down. A comparison of the neighborhoods, security, support systems and opportunities each home has to offer may be your best shot. Your Best Tool Will Always Be Documentation.

Responsibility for Problems

Take full responsibility for the particular circumstance in which you find yourself. The reality of your life is the result of what you've done thus far. You never harvest in the same season that you've planted in. It takes time for your effort to take root and become real. If you cannot (or will not) take responsibility for what is, you cannot change it and make it better. Take responsibility for where you are now.

Your Expectations

A great deal of what we go through is pre-set by our expectations about the world, the laws, the court and other people. The way it really is:

- The world is not, and never was safe or fare.
- The laws and the constitution give you a few specific rights.
- The laws define what you can do to stop someone from violating your rights.
- There is no agency or person who will go after someone who has violated your rights.

- Your rights and another's rights may be in direct conflict.
- Just laws give you justice, not the Justice System.
- The court is in place to render a decision in accordance with the law as it exists at the time of the violation.
- The other parent is responsible of taking the best care of him or herself, as he or she sees it, and the children that he or she can. If that's all you ever expect of him or her you will never be disappointed.
- It is your responsibility to take the best care of yourself and your children, as you see it, as you can. That is all the other parent has the right to expect of you.

Common Custody Myths

People with good intentions, especially people who have never been through the challenge, make winning child custody seem simple. It is not.

What is not true for most people is thinking if they would just change one of the following statements their dream of being with their children unchallenged would magically happen. Each individual statement, alone and by itself is for most people not true in and of itself.

If God were #1 in your life you wouldn't be having this problem.	Not True!
If you had been a better person you wouldn't have to worry about fighting for child custody.	Not True!
There must some hidden abuse, or emotional reason behind why you are in court.	Not True!
There is nothing you can do to influence the court in your favor.	Not True!
If only you had more self-control you wouldn't be involved in family dynamic problem.	Not True!
There is nothing you can do to correct the mistakes you have made in the past.	Not True!
If you really loved your children you could make the relationship work with the other parent.	Not True!
The courts have swung so far the other way, you have no chance of winning.	Not True!
You will have to change everything about your life to be with your children.	Not True!
If you had unlimited money you would win custody with no problem.	Not True!
The other parent has completely destroyed any chance you had of winning.	Not True!
You can get through this litigation quickly, easily, and inexpensively.	Not True!
You can count on the justice system to protect your rights.	Not True!
This pain will be going on for the rest of your life.	Not True!
If you don't fight for custody of you children you are a bad parent.	Not True!
If you don't win custody of your children, people will think you are a bad person and parent.	Not True!

Yes, some of the statements above do apply to some people. They can make some simple changes to correct one bad behavior or attitude.

However, for the most part it is much more complicated than just one issue per person. For most people a custody battle is complex and multifaceted. A combination of the comments stated, and many outside issues.

To get closure you will need time, support and a great deal of effort on your part. We are here to help you along the way. Through painful ignorance to thoughtful understanding.

Chapter 2: You Are the Package

Attempting to control everything around you will cause frustration and exhaustion. Focus on yourself and what you can realistically accomplish. You are the most important single element in this war. You are the financier, organizer, backbone, and the living proof of the life you offer your children. You are the person in control and the most important witness, even if you do not testify.

The kind of person you are speaks so loudly to others that they cannot hear what you say. How you deport yourself can solidify a win or insure a loss. Friend and foe will observe your appearance, behavior and parenting skills with greater intensity from the moment you respond to or initiate any action.

Enemies will disclose and recite your weakness, take delight in your troubles and attempt to prove to the world why you do not deserve the custody of your children. Attempting to sway these people to your side is like trying to teach a pig to sing. It wastes your time and it annoys the pig.

Friends will re-evaluate their relationship with you and their opinions of your parenting abilities then demonstrate their support or lack thereof in word and/or action.

State of Mind or Mindlessness

Don't let this challenge engulf you entirely. Eat right; see your friends and family and exercise. Do something for yourself on a regular basis. Your world will often feel chaotic. Sometimes you will feel unable to deal with problems constructively. At times you may even find yourself spinning out of control in unproductive circles. The impact of events can make you feel disconnected, lost, confused and out of focus. All of this would make your enemy very happy. Prepare for these difficult times with positive activities that require your total attention.

Commit yourself to a project for a specific length of time. Physical or artistic activity that gives you a sense of achievement and success will benefit you greatly in this time of stress and offer a beneficial pattern for the future. How you conduct your day-to-day life during this time may be under observation and will have an impact on the ultimate decision-makers. Control any desire to snivel, whine or express doubt about your ability or right to win this war. Decide to remain strong, morally upright, healthy and purposeful. Your troops need a strong leader.

Just making the decision to be strong will not only help you keep up a good front with your troops, but will actually give you strength. List your strengths and weaknesses on paper or in your computer. Trust your strengths and maintain the behaviors that encourage them. Set up safety nets to limit the damage your weaknesses cause.

Safety Nets

Prepare safety nets now. Because of this child custody battle you are not like regular people anymore. You are in danger of having someone else decide if and when you can spend time with your child. From this moment on you are from another planet. You don't speak the same language as other parents. Even in a support group, you seem to speak different dialects. Everybody hangs out his or her pain like some special license to suffer. Some have fought battles you are going to face in the future and have information about what caused them problems or helped them prevail. It's not like it takes all your pain away, but it least it makes it part of something. Set up your safety nets now. Then there will be in place for times of weakness when you falter. There are support groups for everything including:

- Victims of Child Abuse
- Assertiveness Training
- Children's Rights
- Prosecute Child Abuse
- Co-dependent Behavior
- Anger
- Crisis Counseling
- Victims
- Step-family
- Death and Grief
- Debtors
- Parents in Prison
- Divorce
- Single Parents
- Alcoholics Anonymous
- Eating
- Emotions
- False Accusations
- Victims of Laws
- Fathers' Rights
- Divorce Discrimination
- Fathers Behind Bars
- Internet Talk Groups
- Grandparents' Rights
- Kidnapping
- Missing Children
- Mothers' Rights
- Single Parents

Group I Need Doesn't Exist

If the support group you need doesn't exist you may want to consider starting one. It takes a great deal of time and effort to start any kind of club or group. While it is important not to be distracted form the most important goal; you may need to start a group to get the support you need. Having the time to start a group is often more of an option for the non-custodial parent than the custodial parent. More information about starting a face to face or online support group is available in Chapter 22: The End or The Beginning in the paragraph, Start a Support Group.

Not Comfortable In Self Help Groups

If you are not interested in joining groups consider: night school, a small investment in the stock market, attending seminars, learning a new skill, volunteering at your children's school or at a senior center, redecorating, writing for sanity or profit, start a support group. Most metropolitan communities have professional counseling services with private full fee or fee schedules set according to your ability to pay, and no fee.

Why Are You Here?

We love our children for many reasons. Our children's existence validates us to society as adults. Our children link us to a future that extends past our individual life-span. Our children open new avenues of association in the community through their school, religious training, social and sport activities. Our children demonstrate to all who observe them, that we can be trusted with our country's most valuable resource. Our children give us a new mirror in which to see ourselves. Our children give our lives a positive focus.

If you get angry when you are asked, "Why do you want custody," it is probably because you are so involved in the fight that you have not had an opportunity to think it through. It is not important to be able to explain to others why you are fighting for custody. It is important that you know why you want custody of your children.

Take the time to ask yourself some questions.

- What kind of life, in general, do you want to lead on earth?
- How do you want to be remembered by your family, grandchildren?
- What effect will a custody battle have on your children?
- What ramifications will a custody battle have on your present interpersonal relationship?
- If you win custody, are the children young enough so that you can have a positive imprint before the children are making their own decisions? Twelve years old in most states.
- Where do you want to be in your life financially, physically, emotionally and professionally in five years?
- How will custody influence these plans?
- How will winning custody affect your life?
- What mark would losing custody make on your life?

There will be specific things you must do now to achieve the goals you have for the next five years. Make a list that is clear cut and achievable. Use these examples to spark your imagination.

- Get a home large enough for my children and me.
- Move to the state and school district in which my children live.
- Take parenting, relationship, and conflict resolution classes.
- Take classes to make a better living in a more fulfilling career.

New Relationships

Make sure your attorney is aware of how you spend your social time. Some states give a great deal of consideration to the moral behavior of the parents. Your associations with other adults after the breakup of your association with the other parent could be as important to the case as before the break up. Never start seeing, dating, or living with other people without your attorney's advice.

A serious side-effect of your new relationship is that there will be an intense negative response from the opposition. Increased hostility and additional activity against you will evidenced this.

Invest in Yourself

Normally there is a measurable depletion of your personal energy, resources and self-esteem during a protracted custody case. Some of the balance you must gain and maintain included:

- A feeling of focus in your daily life.
- Economic use of mental and physical energy.
- Reasonable self-discipline.
- A positive manner about life in general
- A positive feeling about yourself in particular.
- Greater respect for yourself and others.
- Harmony of your mind and your body.
- Increased courtesy to your children, family, friends, co-workers and adversaries.
- Physical agility, endurance and speed.
- Coordination, muscle tone, flexibility and strength.

On the Hot Seat, So What?

Be aware that your problem, no matter how it consumes you, is not likely to be of paramount importance to your family, friends and co-workers. Nor should it be.

Anyone consumed with the problems of another is not exhibiting a normal, healthy attitude and behavior pattern. Make an effort to pull away from yourself and maintain some contact with what is going on in their lives. For example; how their son is doing in college, their mother's arthritis situation and enjoying the job promotion of a friend. This will help you keep your problems in perspective. We underestimate our power to change ourselves. We overestimate our power to change others.

Unsolicited Help

The advice offered by your family, friends and co-workers can be of great comfort and assistance or great irritation.

People who want to help, who are truly able to help and from whom you want help should be given a copy of 'Guidelines For Helpers During A Crisis' in Chapter 21: The End - Beginning.

"Thanks, but No Thanks"

Often when others hear about your challenges, they will want to help. After a short period of time you will become tired of repeating all the horrible things you are going through. It will also become apparent that very few people can do anything to really help. Therefore, it is important to know how to say, "Thanks, but no thanks."

When dealing with people from whom you do not want help or people who are not truly able to help you should:

- Listen carefully to their advice. It may be the only assistance they can offer. It does no good to try to explain to them why a suggestion will not work.
- Answer their inquiries with appreciation and careful well-thought-out answers.
- The simplest thing you can do to keep people from feeling as if you don't appreciate their concern or that you are arguing is to listen. Listen patiently and then say, "I appreciate your help. I think you have given me some things to consider. Thank you."
- Become immediately suspicious of anyone who suggests or encourages you to take any dangerous, illegal or negative ideas or activities.

The Rescuer

When you are overwhelmed with the pressures a custody battle add to your already hectic life, you are vulnerable to the desire to hand all your problems over to someone who seems willing to handle them. There are people who are drawn to others in trouble. Their need to take over is just as compelling as your need to surrender your huge challenges. There are several dangerous problems with rescuers, even if the rescuer is a person with good intentions. First, any person willing to take on all of your problems is not dealing with their own. Second, the rescuer's personal agenda may cause you additional problems. Third, if the rescuer is unable to meet your needs and expectations you will be disappointed. Fourth, if the rescuers learns everything he or she needs to know to help you and then stops helping you will feel abandon and betrayed. Fifth, Assuming control of you case may be complicated or impossible.

Rest and Relaxation

It is important to demonstrate a practical grasp of logistics, exercise devastating aggressive tactics on the battlefield, and hold an insurgent army together through indescribable adversity. This is not all that is required to win this war. In order to stay strong, you must take some time off from the war. You must make time to see a movie, catch some sunshine or read a book. Dress up sometimes. This is especially important for you and your children if you are dealing with unstable behavior in the opposition. If you don't, you run the risk of becoming a "nut." Avoid people who make you feel bad, even if you are not sure why you feel that way when you are around them.

Some of the problems you face are the result of the pressures the system places on you. Some are the result of your enemy's efforts to hurt you. Most of the challenges you face are self-imposed. Any negative feelings you experience are real and disabling. The pressures are intensified by fatigue, hunger and the feeling that you have lost control of your life and are being victimized. There are several ways to shorten the duration of the distress you feel or alleviate it entirely.

1. When you feel sad, cry. When you feel angry, get mad. Don't hold it in.
2. Get involved in short-term: result oriented therapy.
3. Take a class in self-defense.
4. Gain and retain control over small areas of your life, one at a time.
5. Get some exercise. It improves almost everyone's appearance.
6. Don't dump responsibility for your feelings on anyone else, even if they are to blame.

Aid to the Enemy

Sometimes it will seem as if you are working harder to please your enemy than your friends. Usually, you will have to push your troops along, rather than lead them. You will have to watch the troops that get paid just as carefully as the volunteers to make sure each assignment is completed.

This is not a beauty pageant, spitting contest, endurance test, or popularity poll, although, on occasion, elements of all of these will surface. Take extra vitamins and be ready for the swimsuit competition.

Right Thinking

Always try again. Try one more time. Then yet again. Know you can.

There are always alternatives.Anything is possible.

Learn from each experience, the losses and the wins.Really listen.

It's not an insurmountable problem; it is a challenge.Reevaluate your priorities.

Find new ways to look at situations or to do things.The investment is worth it.

You are the right person for this fight.

It's Your Battle Because

The outcome of this war will affect you and your children more than it will anyone who helps you fight the battles. You will have to guide as much of the process as humanly possible. Keep after everyone, take control, and be willing to be the one who assaults the enemy bunker alone. If you want to win this war, start your attack now. This manual will provide you with experience, insight, strategies and guts. Keep tabs on everyone from the messenger boy to your attorney.

Delegation

Work is accomplished in one of two ways: first, by changing the position of matter at or near the earth's surface relative to the other matter; second, by getting other people to do so.

Decide what you can and must do yourself, then delegate the other things to your troops. It is your responsibility to give the tasks to people who are willing and capable of doing the job. Make sure they understand the time restrictions affecting this specific job. You must check back to see if the job was accomplished correctly. By assigning some tasks to others, you will be free to lead the battle and make decisions.

Make sure assignments you have delegated are done on time in order to produce the results you need. If someone in your army fails, it is you and your children who will suffer.

Personal Security

Although you may not feel paranoid, you should be more careful. If you have not been concerned about personal security in the past, this would be the right time to establish some family guidelines or re-evaluate the ones you do have in place. Simple things like screening your telephone calls and locking the doors and windows of your home before you leave for the day can go a long way toward a better over-all level of safety.

If a member of your family has moved, and you wish to restrict access to your home and office you will have to;

- Change the locks and hide the keys in a new place.
- Check the message on your answering machine to make sure it is still valid.
- Submit change of address cards to the Post Office to route mail correctly.
- Get a post office box in your name if you don't want your mail accessible to others.
- Install burglar alarm systems and use them.
- Lock the doors to your vehicle when you are in it.
- Lock the doors to your vehicle when you leave it unattended.
- Install locking gas caps on your vehicle(s).
- Ask your neighbors to inform you if anyone asks questions about you.
- Ask your employer to inform you if anyone asks questions about you.
- Be aware of people and vehicles in your vicinity.
- Attempt to vary your weekly schedule.
- Copy important documents and put the originals in a bank safe deposit box.

Bunker (Your Home)

Because of the static nature of the battle, your home is your bunker. It should be a secure place to rest, nurture your family, and carry on the business of family life. It is also your headquarters for the planning and operation of the war.

Your bunker is more comfortable than the tents, huts, foxholes, trenches and dugouts it replaces --- but sometimes it is more vulnerable.

Make an assessment of your bunker for the safety of its occupants with regard to the supplies and furnishings in the interior and the exterior. Pay particular attention to dangerous areas such as swimming pools and busy streets. Small children will gain confidence by seeing you act confidently. Older children will appreciate gaining control of their primary environment. This can eliminate a great deal of normal fear or panic in an emergency. Make bunker safety a game and practice it several times a year. Since you want your children to see your confidence, make a practice run of each exercise before you work with your children.

- **Stranger on the Telephone.** Show children how you would handle an unknown person and give them statements they might say or questions they might ask. Do several rehearsal calls to improve the children's skills.
- **Stranger at the Door.** Role play with children to show them how an unknown person may attempt entrance and how to deal with the situation.
- **Fire Drill.** Have a daytime and nighttime safety drill with your children. Do the daytime drill first. Exit the house, and have everyone meet at a specific place outside to count heads. Do the same drill on hands and knees to teach the children to avoid the danger of smoke.

  Do this from several places in the home to give the children more than one option in case of any kind of danger. Once your children have the daytime drill under control, do the same procedure at night in a darkened house. Stress the importance of following your instructions exactly and quickly.
- **Exterior Survey.** In daylight, examine the outside of your home to determine how difficult it would be to break into your bunker. Fix any problems you discover.
- **Night Inspection.** It's important to see what can be observed going on inside your bunker from the outside at night. Know what things are supposed to look like around your home in the dark. Learn how to get around the interior and exterior of your home at night without the assistance of light.
- **Peeping Tom Law.** There is another valid reason to gain and maintain control of what can be seen, photographed or video taped inside your home at night from the outside. Most people think the Peeping Tom Law allows them to call the police and press charges if someone is spying on them. In most jurisdictions the peeping Tom must be on your property to be in violation of the law. In other words, any place the eye can go a camera or video recorder can go. This means a person could suspend a camera outside a window of your apartment, house, condo, mobile home, and legally observe and record anything happening in your home without your permission. Additionally, this kind of activity could constitute a real threat to your children.

Demilitarized Zone

In order to protect your children's sense of well-being, make it very clear to your opposition that your bunker will not be a battleground. Communicate that you will not attack the other parent's home, and you will not permit hostile behavior at your home. If confronted by an aggressive enemy at your bunker, take all legal measures to defuse, contain and prevent the situation from occurring again. If this does not work, move away from the problem. Legally, geographically or whatever it takes.

Maneuvers, Planned Action

If you keep doing what you've always done, you'll continue getting what you've always gotten. Therefore, a plan of action is necessary to facilitate the changes you want.

A maneuver by definition is an action planned or taken toward the accomplishment of a purpose with efficiency. The way a specific situation is handled can destroy years of positive groundwork when there are no planned maneuvers. There is no way to make a plan of action for every incident that may happen. Establishing an attitude by which most situations are handled will give you direction and guidance for unforeseen challenges.

- **At Work:** How will you be notified of emergencies at home? Can you leave your job without endangering your permanent position? Who will cover your obligations if you must leave the job? How will the company handle any assault on you, or it, by the other parent? Is your vehicle (personal or company) safe while you are at work?

Does the company offer counseling or human resource assistance for this situation?

- **At Home:** If you have to be late getting home from work, who will pick up the children? Who will take care of the children if you are sick?

Retraining

Good or bad, we train people how to treat us. With each new encounter, we reinforce patterns established in the past. Respect must be earned and expected. If you allow people to deal with you without regard for your feelings or needs, if you deal with others without consideration for their feelings or needs, no respect will grow. It is possible to respect a person without loving or even liking that person.

The first step is to establish and maintain an appreciation of your own worth.

Second, when dealing with others, be aware of their needs without sacrificing yours. Be courteous and considerate even if it is not reciprocated. Be assertive while avoiding aggressive behaviors.

The third step is to reward the behavior you want. People will continue behaviors for which they are compensated or rewarded. The reward they want could be to anger you to attain a specific goal.

If what they are doing does not get the reaction or reward they want, they will eventually stop and attempt an alternative course of action. A pattern of strategies or tactics may become apparent. Awareness of these patterns will help you deal with the process. As you are firm, but reasonable in your dealings with others, you will be training them as to how you expect to be treated. The re-training will be difficult for everyone. You may momentarily slip back into nonproductive behaviors. As soon as you are aware of the backsliding, stop and regain your new pattern.

Others will consider your new attitude as fleeting, and they will attempt to force you back into the familiar roles of the past. Change occurs slowly in any relationship. Even a small change will be tested many times to see if you really mean it." Don't get discouraged if you fall on your face several times as you try to put theory into practice. You may find that you start out fine, but then blow it when things heat up. Getting derailed is just part of the process, so be patient with yourself. You will have many opportunities to get back on track...and try again.

If you can't be a good example of how you want to be treated, then you'll have to be a horrible warning for others.

From Now On

Everyone knows that you feel a great deal of pressure whenever you have contact with the other parent, with or without others observing:

1. Always act and speak as if you are being audio and video taped. *You probably are.*

2. Review why you are about to have contact; picking up or returning the child(ren); calling with information the other parent needs; or other necessary contact.

3. Rehearse what you have to say or do. This will give you confidence and control.

4. If there is a history of, or threat of, violence or accusations, do not have contact with the other parent without a third, unimpeachable witness.

5. Listen to the opposition. Do not interrupt what is being said to defend yourself or to make your point. You know how the other parent feels about you and what that person will say. If an answer is required, have reasonable non-aggressive responses ready or do not answer at all.

6. Be clear about why you are there or what you want to say.

7. If the other parent interrupts your activity or statement, wait patiently until that person is finished. Do not get angry or respond to any indictment. If you answer the accusations you are giving the other parent control of the situation. Retain awareness of and control your body language.

8. Once you have been given back the "floor," resume your statement. Each time the other parent interrupts, wait patiently again.

9. Always sincerely thank the other parent for any kindness or time.

No Sniveling or Whining

Adult behavior dictates that when we are not treated fairly we must let it go and go on with our lives. Voicing dissatisfaction, resentment, disappointment, or regret in an adult manner is acceptable if done correctly. Whining displays a lack of control over oneself and fear of being overwhelmed by an unfair world.

While you may not feel responsible for the problem or have the ability or opportunity to resolve the problem, it is unacceptable to complain about the problem in public or to someone who is unable to correct the situation. The world is not going to operate under your standard of perfection or fairness.

For hundreds of years it was not polite to discuss personal problems or family challenges in public. In the nineteen sixties people were encouraged to free their private demons and "tell it like it is." The nineteen seventies became the "I want to share my pain" and group therapy era. The eighties were remarkable for the assistance and programs that were organized. The nineties were infamous for the gross exploitation and commercialization of the embarrassing secrets people were willing to share in print and on television. As we enter the new millennium we are hardened to the pain of others and expect them to show responsibility for themselves and a willingness to take control of their lives, focusing on the main points and working to positive solutions.

It is normal and acceptable to feel defensive and angry. It is not acceptable to inflict these feelings on others by exhibiting these feelings by whining, sniveling, complaining, pouting, having tantrums or any other defeatist behaviors. Eliminate these and any other negative activities you are demonstrating including:

- Calling people late at night to talk or ask them to come over because you are upset. Regardless of the pain you are in, your troops have lives of their own. Be cautious about how intrusive your behavior may be upon their relationships or employment. Don't drain them emotionally or financially. Late at night, there is nothing they can do to help the situation.
- Your friends probably have to work tomorrow or take care of their own family responsibilities, and you have disturbed their rest. Contact a crisis hotline for someone with whom you can talk.
- Behavior requiring rescue include excessive use of alcohol, incorrect use of prescription drugs, manic-depressive behaviors, use of illegal drugs or threats of suicide. These demonstrate your inability to cope with the pressures associated with a custody battle. This behavior is impossible to hide from the opposition and is deadly to your case. Even your troops may question your stability.
- Expecting others to immerse themselves in your problems and pain is dependent and codependent behavior. This action is smothering for normal, healthy people and will cause them to avoid you.
- Requiring an opinion from everyone about each incident that occurs, commonly include behaviors the opposition exhibits to incite you or offensive letters from the opposition's attorney. Aside from your troop's real desire to assist you through this time, it will be difficult for them to see the great harm done to you by the petty offenses the opposition commits. You will begin to look easily distracted from the important goals, bewildered by the complexity of the situation and out of control. You may even be saying too much to a spy or within earshot of enemy troops. In any case, it's all part of the opposition's game. Harden yourself to these tactics.
- Calling friends and your attorney many times through the day and verbalizing your reoccurring insecurity can have the effect of instilling doubt about you in your troops. Demonstrating your lack of meaningful direction will ruin the morale of your troops. Constant whining will harden your friends to your pain and eliminate some of your safe havens when you really need them.

A Strong Confident Leader attracts good people and power to the cause. This encourages positive, healthy activity, offering the best possibility for a win. It is just as important to do right as to be right.

A Weak Leader that requires constant reassurance of his or her right to win and ability to do so, quickly exhausts, discourages and alienates good troops, stalling a win.

The Most Important Witness

Witnesses are the people who support the validity of evidence by swearing where it came from or how they came to know of its existence.

You are the most important witness before, during and after any appearance with a mediator, psychologist, the court or anyone who may testify or judge you. You may testify to what you have seen, heard or done. Any other information would be "hearsay" and therefore not allowed.

Dress for Custody Success

I have met the Enemy and it is I. This could be the most important realization for a parent during a custody case. Most parents feel the enemy is the other parent or the legal system. Once the parent is able to recognize self-caused problems and works to correct those problems, things begin to improve.

Some of the issues one must face are enormous and not immediately fixable. How one dresses is one of the easier and least expensive parts. Getting dressed to go some place or do something, is part of the preparation for the event. Clothing helps us maintain the proper demeanor for the environment we are in and indicates to others how we expect to be treated. You should dress appropriately for the task at hand. Casual old clothes are for yard work and nice dress-up clothes for parent/teacher meetings. Not dressing neatly at all times is a mistake. It is best to avoid black T-shirts, especially with motorcycle logos, acid or hard rock band imprints.

Expressing your individuality could detract from the value of your testimony and cost you the custody of your children. It's not fair and it's not right, but that's the way it is. If your appearance is exotic or unusual, you need to make some changes. If the opposition presents photos of you in your exotic attire, your attorney can argue that your new image reflects your new conformity to a conservative life-style. Have someone professional assist you with an appearance evaluation. Do your best to downplay or avoid the negative impact some visual messages send the court.

What Do I Tell People on My Side?

You have more control of, and you know more about your case than the average person in a custody battle. Part of that control is how you disperse information.

The more information you disperse, the less control you have. Discuss your case as little as possible. Do not explain your decisions or tactics to anyone. Your best witness could become your worst nightmare.

The welfare of your children is your goal, but your witnesses may have their own agenda. It is best to concentrate on what those witnesses have to offer and how to help them through the court experience. Supply anyone who must testify in deposition or court with the "Witnesses Guide to Testifying at Deposition or in Court" offered in the back of this book.

Confidentiality - My Witnesses

There is no such thing as confidentiality. Every word spoken to a witness for your side can become ammunition for the opposition and/or public record. It is best not to give any witness any information the person does not already have.

If practiced in the appropriate circumstances, rightly placed silence can be interpreted as confidence. Confidence is born of strength.

I Think I Need a Shrink

In daily life and in court, you must appear normal in behavior, in control of your emotions and purposeful in your actions. How do you do this when your mind and heart are an emotional quagmire? Talk to someone, someone safe. If you think you need a shrink, you do. Find a professional to help you through these trying times. There are full-pay, private, pay-according-to-income and free public mental health programs available in most communities. A professional can help keep you on track.

As with most professions you must be a licensed professional in that vocation to be governed by the rules. Psychologists, counselors, therapists and mediators are some of the designations used by these professionals. Each has it's own educational and professional standards. You must understand the differences in order to make the best choice.

Confidentiality - Shrink

Confidentiality laws that govern these professionals in most states are clear cut. The laws only govern doctors and licensed mental health caregivers. Carefully check the laws in your state.

Doctor-patient privilege relationships rest on the premise that "The keeper of the records has a primary obligation to the client." Normally the confidence between a therapist and a patient can only be broken under specific circumstances.

Secret Help From Psychologist

One parent we interviewed explained how to get psychological assistance during a custody battle without the opposition finding out:

"I contacted a highly recommended psychologist and explained that I was experiencing a great deal of stress and anger during my custody battle. I wanted to be able to have the guidance of a professional without the other parent finding out, because I felt this would be used against me in court. The psychologist accepted the fact and that I was not willing to give my real name, any telephone number or address. Arrangements were made for cash payments and I was assigned an assumed name under, which my file could be kept. I didn't tell anyone about the doctor and I received the help I needed."

Some of the situations could include:

- Patient indicates to the therapist that he may kill himself or another person.
- Therapist strongly suspects that child abuse or neglect may be taking place.
- A court order from a judge demands a breech of confidence.
- The patient gives the therapist permission to release the records.
- The patient threatens the life of the therapist.
- Client tells or gives the information to another person.
- The custodial parent who impedes the ongoing visitation of the non-custodial parent loses custody of children.

When the Police are Called

The police can be called by anyone witnessing the situation. Your children, a neighbor, you, the other parent, anyone. Domestic disturbance calls are the most hazardous calls for the police officer. From experience the officer knows he or she may be exposed to a greater level of personal threat. The officer arrives at your situation in that frame of mind. It is important that you do not transfer any of the hostility you feel towards the other people in your confrontation to the officer. Don't make any statements or movements that the officer could interpret as threatening.

- When the police are called to a domestic disturbance their primary task is to defuse the situation. They can't solve the problems you have been having for months or years.
- The officer is more inclined to believe the person that is calm rather than the person that is hysterical. On an intellectual level the officer knows that just because a person appears rational it does not mean they are telling the truth. But, it is very difficult for an officer to get the facts from a person who is out of control.
- The officer will inquire as to the nature of the problem. Describe the current incident only, in the simplest terms possible. You must avoid vulgar language. You must avoid any statement that includes a possible admission of a crime, example, "I grabbed her arm," can be charged as an assault and battery. This statement can be used against you even though you have not been advised of your rights.
- If two officers responded to the call they attempt to separate the parties to defuse the situation and get less adulterated information about how each person viewed the incident. One officer responding to a call will attempt to separate the parties. A person refusing to be separated from the incident may be arrested.
- If both parties insist on pressing charges, both may be arrested and any children will be put in the care of the child protective services. Children are held in protective custody for twenty-four to forty-eight hours minimum. This gives the court time to assign a caseworker. The number of files and severity of the cases being handled by that individual determines how long your children will be in the custody of child protective services. The children may not be released to either parent if the caseworker feels they may be in danger in the future.
- You can be arrested even if you were the one assaulted or the one who made the call.

Things You Can Get Arrested For

If an officer thinks you need to be arrested you will be. Listed below are some of the charges an officer could use to take you to jail.

- failure to identify to a police officer
- violation of protective order

- false report to an officer
- injury to a child
- assault
- harassment
- family violence
- assault with deadly weapon
- burn ban violation
- criminal trespass
- criminal mischief
- disorderly conduct
- public intoxication
- criminal nonsupport
- burglary of a habitation (even your own)
- disturbing the peace
- harboring a runaway child
- possession of a controlled substance
- terroristic threat
- interfere with public duties
- thwarting child's mandatory attendance at school

Removing your own clothes from you house after a court has issued a Order Of Protection that instructs you stay away from the property can result in several charges including violation of a court order and burglary of a habitation.

Allowing your child to stay with you when the other parent has custody and the child has left that parent's home without permission you can be charged with interference with parenting and harboring a runaway child.

Therefore, any situation that has the potential for confrontation must be avoided. If you are confronted with a situation that has gone bad, walk away. Don't make yourself more of a victim.

If You Are Arrested

Getting arrested is usually an unexpected piece of misery. Once your bail's been posted, if your car's been impounded, you find yourself stuck out in the boonies, just one more element of distress after a night of humiliations. If you may be accused of domestic violence or child abuse, you can expect to be arrested. It may not happen, but it would be wise to set up some safety nets, just in case. Keep the name of your attorney in your wallet, get to know a bail bond person and make arrangements for bail, in case it ever becomes necessary. Read through this list.

1. Do not resist arrest. In addition to getting arrested, which is going to happen no matter what you do, you may also get beat up. Any resistance will be considered aggressive, so you may also be charged with resisting arrest and assaulting an officer. Even if you are found innocent of the original charges you may still end up getting convicted of resisting arrest and assaulting the officer. These are *misdemeanors*, which are a fairly serious offense. If the officers say you used a weapon (a gun, baseball bat, briefcase, your car) to try to resist, it is a *felony*. If an officer approaches you and you have <u>anything</u> (car key, pen, cell phone or wallet) in your hand, drop it, and step away from it. Once either of these charges goes on your record, any law enforcement person will be informed that you are dangerous and may be armed.

2. If you are arrested as a result of a domestic violence call, you may attest to your innocence. Once you are being seriously questioned, the investigation begins to focus on you, or you are informed that you are being arrested, you should be advised of your Miranda Rights. Invoke your right to remain silent. Shut up. Do not give any statements.

3. Do not sign anything. If they insist that you sign something before you can be released, *you must read the entire thing*. If you have any questions or concerns about the document refuse to sign it until an attorney can look at it. You have a constitutional right not to make a statement to the police. Even if they tell you that you are not a suspect, do not talk to them. There is always a chance that you may become a suspect. Always assume that they are investigating you personally. Often a "Nice Person Cop" will come in saying something like, "You can probably clear this up in just a few minutes if you will give a statement." Do not accept the statement that helping the police will help you in your case. It will not.

4. Demand to speak to your lawyer, immediately. You have a constitutional right to speak to your lawyer before being questioned by the police, but only if you request one. However, this does

not mean that the police cannot put you in a lineup or do what the law considers non-invasive procedures such as photographing and finger printing before your lawyer gets there.

Once you have demanded to speak to your attorney, do not speak to the police until your lawyer speaks to you. You will go through a lot less hell if you have made arrangements to be able to contact your attorney in this emergency, in advance.

5. Do not talk to your cell-mates. They may inform on you to get leniency in their cases. You may have to talk to them in order to survive in the jail, but you do not have to discuss the specifics of your case.

6. Call and have a relative go to a bail bondsman. Hopefully, you have made arrangements in advance in case you needed bail. Advance arrangements can speed your release by hours or days. Generally bail bonds are sold for about ten percent of the amount of bail. This amount is not refundable.

7. Don't miss any court dates. If you skip your court date, the bail is forfeited, the property you put up for security will be forfeited and you will still have the legal charges against you. If one of your dearest relatives or friends posted the bail and you don't show, the bail bondsman will collect the entire amount of your bail from that person. Failing to appear at trial will result in forfeiture of the bond and an all points bulletin for your arrest.

8. If you are arrested and have had anything at all to drink, you should refuse to admit anything at all including if you drank or how much you have had to drink. You will be required to take a field sobriety test. If you have been drinking nothing is going to stop this arrest. Giving a breath test that shows a blood alcohol over .01 (or whatever is considered drunk in your state) is going to be admissible as evidence and will likely result in a complication of the original charges. Behave and don't do anything that will aggravate the situation

9. If your children are with you and you are arrested (depending on your state procedures) they will be handed over to the other parent or child protective services.

10. If you cannot afford to hire an attorney you can have one appointed for you. When you do this, you will be getting potluck. You may get a good lawyer or you may get a really poor one. In order to get one appointed for you, you will have to sign a document stating that you are indigent or cannot afford an attorney.

- There are several cases in Chapter 23: Cases, Studies, Decisions, Rulings, in the heading "Arrested" that may directly affect you and your case.

Inventories

Inventories become a biography of your personal life and relationship with the opposition and your children. The process is therapeutic and requires that you take an unbiased look at your life. The inventories will help your attorney understand where you have been and help you identify where you may go.

The savings in money for you and the time saved for your attorney are secondary, but vital. The process of thinking about the relationship and writing it down will allow you to have a clearer picture of your association with the other parent. Mediators and psychologists will be asking many of these questions. Attorneys often use this form to get a thorough understanding of everything you know about your case. It is not unusual for the inventories to run thirty pages long.

Confidentiality - Inventories

There is no confidentiality if you do not work at it. Every word spoken to anyone, or document you create, or document created about your personal or business life can become ammunition for the opposition and/or public record.

Do not discuss your inventories with anyone. When you make a decision to give the information to a professional, be aware if this person is bound legally to keep the information private. Then, understand what private means in your state.

Inventory for Randall Long

I actually have _4_ children, this case concerns one of them. The child(ren)'s age(s) in this matter *ten months*.

[x] I live in the same state as my child(ren) [ ] I live in another state.

[ ] My child(ren) have lived with me for _ *10 months*__ (weeks, months, years.)
Or if the child(ren) live with the other parent. *We share the custody.*
[x] My child(ren) spends _*1/2 time* ___hours a (week, month, year) with me.
[x] I have given up or lost custody of other children. First wife Gina has custody of our three sons ages 25, 22 and 18.
[ ] I have not given up or lost custody of other children.
I am _*39*__ years old. Last year of formal education completed _*4*_ years of College_
I have taken parenting classes [x] yes [ ] no If no, I am willing to take parenting classes [ ] yes [] no
I have an attorney or ability to hire one [x] yes [] no
I qualify for legal aid [ ] yes [x] no
I have the support of my family [x] yes [ ] no
My family lives in my town [x] yes [x] no *My parents don't/ wife does*
I am: [ ] single [x] married [ ] separated [ ] divorced *1* time(s)
I live in a:
[x] separate house [ ] duplex [ ] apartment [ ] high security building [ ] trailer [] good neighborhood
[ ] bad neighborhood
I live:
[ ] alone [ ] alone with children [ ] with my spouse [x] with my spouse and children[ ] with my parents [ ] with my parents and children [ ] with several people [ ] with my platonic friend[ ] living with someone, I am engaged to be married
At home we have:
[x] washing machine [x] clothes dryer [x] dishwasher [x] pets [ ] open yard[x] fenced yard[ ] siblings of the child(ren)
I have lived here:
[ ] ___ days [ ] ___ weeks [ ] ___ months [*x*] _*4*_ years
In the last four years, I have lived in __*1*____ places.
I work:[ ] self-employed [ ] unemployed [x] disabled
[ ] full-time from_______ to_______, _______days a week.
[ ] part time from_______ to_______, _______days a week.
At work, I have: My wife owns her own company so we have benefits.
[x] insurance [ ] profit sharing [x] paid holidays [ ] credit union [ ] other benefits
My job supports ______ people
I meet my monthly expenses: [ ] with difficulty [x] easily

I have a problem with: [ ] drugs [ ] alcohol [ ] the law [ ] my family [x] my health [ ] _________
My general appearance is:
[ ] unusual [x] up scale [ ] blue collar [ ] OK [ ] modern [ ] not so good [ ] I have to be me
As it concerns the general appearance of my living environment, my home is:
[x] very clean [ ] clean [ ] lived in [ ] always a mess
My personal associations and friendships are:
[ ] not close [x] very close [ ] work only [ ] family only[x] for many years[ ] never family
What can you offer your child that the other parent cannot? I can stay home with Bobby, giving him a great deal of attention, and take him places. Provide a safe clean environment with unlimited opportunities to learn and grow.
Is there anything in your past or present that would cause a court to deny you custody? Nothing.

Inventory for Amber Jones

The other parent actually has _*4*_ children, this case concerns _*1*_ of them.
The child(ren)s ages in this matter *8 months old*
[x] The other parent lives in the same state as my child(ren). Temporary.
[x] The other parent lives in another state. *Amber & kids live in Washington State.*
My children live with me and the other parent spends _*1/2 time*_ hours a (week, month, year) with the child(ren)
[ ] The other parent has given up or lost custody of other children.
[x] The other parent has not given up or lost custody of other children.
She is _34_ years old. Last year of formal education 12th Grade
The other parent has taken parenting classes [ ] yes [x] no
If no, the other parent would be willing to take parenting classes [ ] yes [x] no
Amber feels she is a good parent and has three other children to prove it.
The other parent has an attorney or has the ability to hire one [x] yes [ ] no
She said her current husband makes $60,000 a year, but is using legal aid
The other parent qualifies for legal aid [ ] yes [x] no not legally.
The other parent has the support of his or her family [x] yes [x] no
The other parent's family lives in the same town [x] yes [ ] no

The other parent is: [ ] single [ ] married [ ] separated [x] divorced _*3*_ times
[x] living with someone [ ] engaged to be married
The other parent lives in a:
[ ] separate house [ ] duplex [ ] trailer [ ] apartment [] high security building [ ] good neighborhood
[] bad neighborhood
At home, the other parent has:
[ ] washer [ ] dryer [ ] pets [x] open yard [ ] dishwasher [x] siblings of the child [ ] fenced yard
The other parent lives: [ ] alone [ ] alone with children [x] spouse and children[ ] parents [ ] several people [ ] platonic friend
The other parent has lived there: Amber left other children behind in Washington State with her new in-laws. It must have been hard for them all because the children had only met the people 4 days before their mother left them to return to Arizona; she was gone eight months.
[x] _*4*_ days [ ] ___ weeks [ ] ___ months [ ] ___ years
In the last four years, the other parent has lived in: _*8*__ places
The other parent's job supports __*5*____ people
The other parent meets monthly expenses: [x] with difficulty [ ] easily
The other parent works: [ ] self-employed[ ] unemployed [ ] disabled
[ ] full-time from ___*10:00am*___ to____*6:00pm*_, __*6*__days a week
[ ] part time from________ to________, _______days a week
At work, the other parent has: no benefits, works at Ice Cream Queen
[ ] insurance [ ] profit sharing [ ] paid holidays [ ] other benefits
The other parent has a problem with: [x] drugs [x] alcohol [x] the law [x] family [x] health
The other parent's general appearance is: [ ] unusual [ ] up scale [ ] modern [x] blue collar [ ] OK [x] not so good
As it concerns the general appearance of the other parent's living environment the home is:
[ ] very clean [ ] clean [ ] lived in [ ] a little messy[x] always a mess
The other parent's personal associations and friendships are:
[ ] not close [x] very close [x] work only [ ] family only[ ] for many years [ ] never family
What the other parent can offer your child that you cannot? *Close association with his step-siblings.*

Is there anything in your opposition's past or present that can cause the court to deny the other parent custody? *A great deal of documented questionable decision-making.*

Inventory for Bobby Long

Child's name: *Bobby Long* My child's age _*4 Years*_
What was the custody arrangement before the separation or divorce and what is it now? *We shared child care for 2 years and I have had primary custody for 2 years. Bobby's mother moved to another state and has seven weeks a year visitation.*
How has the child adapted to the change? *He seems happy and lighthearted*
What grade does the child attend school? _*Pre K*_ *at Children's House*
What is the child's temperament? *Happy, willing to please*
How is the child reacting to the separation or divorce? *With confusion. It is hard for him to understand why everyone he loves cannot be near him all of the time.*
How does the child interact with other children? *Bobby plays well and enjoys competition with children his own age and loves babies*
What method of discipline works best with the child? *1-2-3 Time Out*
The method discipline that produces the worst result is? *Taking away privileges or toys.*
How has the child's standard of living changed? *It stayed the same.*
The feelings my child has expressed about the current parenting arrangement are: *He loves both his mom and dad, but wants to remain living with his dad. Bobby expresses a great deal of trepidation about leaving his home to go for visitation and a great deal of relief when he returns. To lessen the stress, he is told about visitation only hours before he is to leave*
How does the child expresses anger and fear? *Bobby is verbal and asks what will happen to me when frightened and is willing to stand up for what he wants and argue his side when angry*
What is the child's normal bedtime? *8:30 - 9:00 P.M. very easily*
What time does the child wake up each day? *About 7:00 A.M.*
In what mood does the child usually wake up? *Happy*

Have there been any changes in the child's sleep and wake up schedule in the last year? *Only during visitation*
What is the child's favorite breakfast food? *Anything he can fix himself like cereal or toaster waffles*
What is the child's favorite lunch meal? *Grilled Cheese sandwiches*
What is the child's favorite dinner meal? *Spaghetti or pizza*
Can the child cook? *He prepares cold cereal and makes muffins and cookies with me.*
Have there been any changes in the child's diet and eating habits in the last year? *Nothing major. Bobby does decide what he wants to eat at restaurants*
Child's favorite color? *Red*
Child's favorite book? *All of them. Any book someone is willing to read with him. Bobby looks forward to the Sunday Comics.*
Child's favorite toy? *Hot Wheels*
Child's favorite clothes? *Baseball Uniform*
Child's favorite pastime? *Outdoor activities that involve team effort*
Child's feelings about church are? *His friends do not attend, has no interest in church.*
Changes in my child's church attendance in the last year? *None*
Child's least favorite pastime? *Taking a bath*
Child's favorite sport? *Baseball, fishing*
Child's least favorite sport? *He loves them all*
Child's feelings about school? *Bobby loves school*
Child has regular lessons in? *Karate, swimming*
Child would like regular lessons in?
Child has and uses a library card [x] T [ ] F
Child enjoys books about? *Animals and Children*
The child, compared to other children of the same age, is developing? The doctor and his teachers say "at a normal rate:" I think that he is a genius.
In the past year my child has reacted to change? *Bobby does not like change. He will ignore events or people that move too fast.*
I help my child with change by? *Talking about where something is now, how it can change, how the change will be to his benefit and help him to be part of the event.*
The child reacts to fear by? *Coming to me for comfort or refusing to move.*
I help my child cope with fear by? *Talking to him, Reminding him of other things he has mastered that he once feared, doing the feared thing first, doing the feared thing with him, reducing the feared thing in smaller more manageable parts.*
My child sees the future as __ *Exciting*
When grown, my child wants to be__ *A Doctor*
When grown I would like to see my child happy, some kind of professional
The one place my child would love to go with me? *Bobby loves to go everywhere with me and because of my schedule, is able to accompany me much of the time.*
One thing I would like people to know about my child is? *Bobby is a really good natured, happy, loving and smart kid.*
The best arrangement as far as custody for my child would be? *If Bobby's mother could live in the same city we live in so he could have contact with both of his parents. If that is not possible, I think Bobby should stay with me.*

Relationship Inventory Example #1

In The Beginning

- How we met: *Katie is my daughter and Joe was her husband.*
- Length of our relationship before the child's conception: I k*new Katie 22 years and Joe 2 years.*
- Our relationship before the child's conception: *Very close*
- Circumstances of conception: *During the normal marital experience.*
- Relationship during pregnancy: *Good.*
- Medical problems during pregnancy or birth: *Katie and Joe drank a little and smoked marijuana a little.*
- The birth: *I was there and it was a normal delivery.*
- Relationship immediately before the birth: *Good.*
- Relationship immediately after the birth: *The were having financial and relationship difficulties so they moved in with my husband and me.*
- How long did the relationship last after the birth: *They both went back to work and began to have relationship problems because they wanted an open marriage. Because I was there to take care of the baby one or both would be absent from the home for days at a time.*
- How things stand now: *Joe moved out of state to get a better job and Katie has moved in with her third new relationship. She leaves the baby with*

us most of the time, but picks him up for a few days every couple of months.

Where Things Are Going

- How I want things to be: *I would like to have legal custody and have Katie visit the baby whenever she wants to, Joe also.*
- The way the other parent wants things to be: *Katie wants to have legal custody so she can still get food stamps and a welfare check.*
- What I am afraid of: *Katie will pick the baby up and never come back. I don't think she is drug free or can take proper care of the baby.*
- What the other parent is afraid of: *Me running her life.*
- Best possible outcome: *Katie to stop using drugs and learn to take care of herself and her baby.*
- Worst possible outcome: *Court lets Katie take the baby away.*
- Probable outcome: *The baby has lived with us for 18 months. They will probably give us temporary custody.*
- Best interests of my child: *Katie and Joe find themselves and become good parents.*

Relationship Inventory Example #2

In The Beginning

- How we met: *Worked with my wife, became a friend.*
- Length of our relationship before my child's conception: *1 1/2 years*
- Our relationship before my child's conception: *Comfortable*
- Circumstances of conception: *Consensual sex.*
- Relationship during pregnancy: *Comfortable, civil.*
- Medical problems during pregnancy or birth: *Pregnancy fine.*
- The birth: *Amber almost hemorrhaged to death after delivery.*
- Relationship immediately before the birth: *Fine, saw Amber daily.*
- Relationship immediately after the birth: *Cooperative*
- How long did the relationship last after the birth: *8 months.*
- How things stand now: *Very strained, she is unpredictable.*

Where Things Are Going

- How I want things to be: *Cooperative.*
- The way the other parent wants things to be: *Me out of the picture.*
- What I am afraid of: *Amber will disappear with Bobby again.*
- What the other parent is afraid of: *I will get custody of Bobby.*
- Best possible outcome: *Amber to move back to Arizona.*
- Worst possible outcome: *Court lets Amber take Bobby away.*
- Probable outcome: Shared custody, *I hope.*
- Best interests of my child: *Bobby has access to both parents.*

Your Inventory Example

Complete this form as honestly as you can to get a look at how you appear to others and check as many boxes as apply. Do this exercise in pencil so you can make changes as they occur in your life. Mediators and psychologists will ask many of these questions. The savings in money and time for you and your attorney are secondary, but vital.

The inventories will help your attorney understand where you have been and help you identify where you may go.

Opposition's Inventory Example

Complete this form with as much information as you honestly know. This will allow you to get a look at how the opposition appears to others. Complete and mark as many boxes as you can. Leave blank the spaces requesting information you do not have at this time. Later fill in the spaces as the data becomes available. Do it in pencil so you can make changes as they occur in the other parent's life.

Child's Inventory Example

How well do you know your child? It is possible to love your child very much and not really be aware of the child as a separate person? If you are able to answer all of these questions, then you are headed in the right direction.

If there are a lot of unanswered questions on this page, it is probably time to really get to know your child. Copy this form. Fill one out for each child.

Parent as a Soldier

- I am a loving parent soldier.
- I am a volunteer, knowing well the hazards of my calling.
- I pledge to uphold honor and integrity in all I am and in all I do.
- I will strive always to excel in every art of parenting.
- I will always do as I ought rather than what I would like.
- I will not fail those with whom I serve.
- I will not bring shame upon myself or my child(ren).
- My goal is to survive in any mission and live to succeed again.
- I serve with the welfare of my child(ren) always on my mind and in my heart.
- I will never surrender the well-being of my child(ren) though I am the first and last to fight for their well-being.
- I will keep my mind and body clean, alert and strong, for this is my responsibility to those who depend upon me.
- I know that I will be called upon to perform tasks in isolation from my child(ren) far from family and friends. With the help and guidance of my Higher Power, I will conquer my fears and survive.

I am a parent soldier, a member of my child(ren)'s infantry. May my Higher Power grant that I may not be found wanting. I will not fail this sacred trust.

Ask Yourself the Real Question

Which would you rather have: to get what you want OR for your children to have what they need? As a baby, your cries brought someone to comfort you. As you grew, your cries became less effective. As a baby, you were unhappy for a short while if your desires were not met. Some adults remain unhappy for years if they don't get what they want. Don't let the disappointments of the past ruin your future. Let them go; move on to a more positive, fulfilling life.

Your state of mind must be a matter of your own decision, such as how you plan to take care of your children, handle this case, pay the bills, and live through the difficult times to come. Decide to enjoy the things that are good and work to correct the things that are bad. Look at each event as it happens and find something in it from, which you can profit. If you have someone to love and someone who loves and supports your efforts, you are very lucky. It helps to have someone remind you to keep a contact log when everything seems quiet or to use as a sounding board when you are confused or perplexed. Remember, this person is on your team. Don't use anyone in your army as a punching bag when you are angry or upset. The enemy would enjoy the thought of your fighting because of them. Be the first to say, "I'm sorry." Don't lose the joy you have between you during this ordeal.

If you do not have a helper, use the contact log to express yourself. It is a very good way to blow off steam without hurting anyone's feelings or saying things that could cause you problems later. When you have had time to cool off, edit any inflammatory verbiage out of the text.

This document may become part of the public court record someday. How you say the things you say tells the reader a great deal about the kind of person you really are. Make an effort to see happy movies. Subscribe to health and self-improvement magazines. Read uplifting books to establish safety nets for times when you are fatigued and your normal defenses are low.

Desiderata

Go placidly amid the noise and the haste, and remember what peace there may be in silence. As far as possible, without surrender, be on good terms with all persons.

Speak your truth quietly and clearly; and listen to others, even to the dull and ignorant; they too have their story.

Avoid loud and aggressive persons; they are vexatious to the spirit. If you compare yourself with others, you may become vain or bitter, for always there will be greater and lesser persons than yourself.

Enjoy your achievements as well as your plans. Keep interested in your own career, however humble, it is a real possession in the changing fortunes of time.

Exercise caution in your business affairs, for the world is full of trickery. But let this not blind you to what virtue there is; many persons strive for high ideals, and everywhere life is full of heroism.

Be yourself. Especially do not feign affection. Neither be cynical about love; for in the face of all aridity and disenchantment, it is as perennial as the grass.

Take kindly the counsel of the years, gracefully surrendering the things of youth. Nurture strength of spirit to shield you in sudden misfortune. But do not distress yourself with dark imaginings. Many fears are born of fatigue and loneliness.

Beyond a wholesome discipline, be gentle with yourself. You are a child of the universe no less than the trees and the stars; you have a right to be here. And whether or not it is clear to you, no doubt the universe is unfolding as it should.

Therefore, be at peace with God, whatever you conceive him to be. And whatever your labours and aspirations, in the noisy confusion of life, keep peace in your soul. With all its sham, drudgery and broken dreams, it is still a beautiful world.

Be cheerful. Strive to be happy.
Max Ehrmann, 1927

Read and listen to healing healthy words for support and strength.

If you are in too much pain to be able to make the Desiderata part of your life, try a dose of *Duck Muck.*

Duck Muck

Definition: Duck muck is that slimy stuff around a lake. It contains, among other things, water, mud, duck poop, slime, dead bugs, moss, worms, algae, feathers, grass, mosquito larvae, microbes, tadpoles and urine. It looks offensive, smells nauseating, sounds horrible and feels disgusting. The very idea of it is repugnant.

Therapeutic usage: The subjective responses we have to situations we encounter are referred to as emotions. Some that have varying degrees of status in our society include: love, pain, fear, stress, hate, affection, attachment, devotion, fondness, adoration, worship, fidelity, loyalty and passion. The emotion that has no status at all is self-pity.

Our society has very little patience with us feeling sorry for ourselves. Often, we do feel horribly bad and need sympathy. The people that care about us may never have been sympathetic or have tired of being compassionate and supportive. Some of us don't have anyone to support our emotions during difficult times. To stay psychologically healthy, all strong emotion should be released. Occasionally the proper thing to feel is self-pity.

Indications: Severe and overwhelming feelings of rejection, distress, melancholy, sadness, defeat, sorrow, grief and regret are indicators. Ongoing symptoms include lack of sleep, loss of appetite, overeating for comfort, over-indulgence in any activity - including work - smoking, drinking, crying, calling friends in the middle of the night, emotional outbursts, and lack of all feeling.

Dosage: Find a private place where you will not be disturbed. Make a list of all the hurtful things said and done to you, all the times you feel you failed, the times in your life others have failed you, all the hopes and dreams you will never realize, and anything else that causes you distress and pain.

Visualize the things on your list as all the components in the duck muck around the lake. Put away any pretence of happiness or good spirits you have for others and get down in the duck muck. Just feel sorry for yourself. Really get down in it. Shove it in your ears, poke it up your nose and rub it into your hair. Wallow in it. Cry. Scream. Feel the hurt. Enjoy the strong emotion. As you feel the pain and hurt without reservation, the things that inhabit your duck muck will shrink in size, eventually disappearing entirely. Flounder, tumble, roll, in the misery of such strong horrible stuff.

Concluding Treatment: When you are finally, really done, pull your emotions out of the muck and stagger to a cleansing mental shower. Wash all the duck muck off, watch it go down the drain, and leave it behind.

Make a new list of positive things you will do to improve your life. Resolve to avoid people who destroy the goodness and happiness in your life. Decide what is important to you. List small steps you can make to begin to accomplish those goals.

You will feel better and look better. The people that care about you will see a new positive strength they didn't see before.

Caution: Properly used, duck muck has a true curative healing affect, but it should only be used after all good efforts and prayers have been exhausted. Duck muck may be habit forming, addictive, and of course, it will always be repugnant.

This prescription is for persons suffering huge disappointment and pain.

The concept for Duck Muck was condensed from an idea explained to C. Hardwick by Kate Pich.

The One I Feed

The grandfather's little grandson often came in the evenings to sit at his knee and ask the many questions that children ask. One day the grandson came to his grandfather with a look of anger on his face.

Grandfather said, "Come, sit, tell me what has happened today."

The child sat and leaned his chin on his grandfather's knee. Looking up into the wrinkled, nut brown face and the kind dark eyes; the child's anger turned to quiet tears.

The boy said, "I went to the town today with my father to trade the furs he has collected over the past several months. I was happy to go because father said that since I had helped him with the trapping, I could get something for me.

Something that I wanted. I was excited to be in the trading post. I have not been there before. I looked at many things and finally found a metal knife. It was small, but a good size for me, so father got it for me."

Here the boy laid his head against his grandfather's knee and became silent. The grandfather, softly placed his hand on the boy's raven hair and said, "and then what happened?"

Without lifting his head, the boy said, "I went outside to wait for father and to admire my new knife in the sunlight. Some town boys came by and saw me. They got all around me and started saying bad things. They called me dirty and stupid and said that I should not have such a fine knife. The largest of these boys pushed me back, and I fell over one of the other boys.

I dropped my knife. One of them snatched it up, and they all ran away, laughing." Here the boy's anger returned, "I hate them. I hate them all!"

The grandfather, with eyes that had seen too much, lifted his grandson's face so his eyes looked into the boy's. Grandfather said, "Let me tell you a story. I too, at times, have felt a great hate for those that have taken so much, with no sorrow for what they do. But hate wears you down, and does not hurt your enemy. It is like taking poison and wishing your enemy would die. I have struggled with these feelings many times.

It is as if there are two wolves inside me. One is white and one is black. The White Wolf is good and does no harm. He lives in harmony with all around him and does not take offense when no offense was intended. He will only fight when it is right to do so, and in the right way.

But the Black Wolf is full of anger. The littlest thing will set him into a fit of temper. He fights everyone, all the time, for no reason. He cannot think because his anger and hate are so great. It is helpless anger, for his anger will change nothing. Sometimes it is hard to live with these two wolves inside me, for both of them try to dominate my spirit."

The boy looked intently into his grandfather's eyes, and asked, "Which one wins Grandfather?"

The grandfather smiled and said, "The one I feed." Written by Vicki Smith

Proper Responses

Everyone needs emotional support during a crisis. Sometimes all you can do is listen: It is difficult to assist someone who needs compassion. Use these examples:

- **Your Friend Says**

I feel guilty and angry with the children. They expect me to match everything the other parent does.

Good Answer

I can see this is painful for you.

Poor Answer

You started this, "I can do everything better than them" competition.

- **Your Friend Says**

I felt so helpless when my former spouse was so critical of me.

Good Answer

That's an awful feeling.

Poor Answer

That's generally how you deal with people.

- **Your Friend Says**

I don't think you are really trying to help me.

Good Answer

That hurt my feelings. What made you say that?.

Poor Answer

How could you say that to me?

- **Your Friend Says**

I don't have time for anyone with problems bigger than mine.

Good Answer

Each of deals with what we can.

Poor Answer

That's very self-centered of you.

- **Your Friend Says**

I had to watch the teacher introduce my former spouse's new mate as my child's parent. I was embarrassed and hurt.

Good Answer

Your feelings were understandable.

Poor Answer

You don't live here anyway, why should you care.

Guidelines for Helpers During a Crisis

- Listen without comment.
- Offer advice only when specifically asked.
- Do not be offended if your recommended action is not implemented.
- Show respect don't baby or debilitate.
- Do not probe for information.
- Maintain boundaries between your life and the person you are helping.
- Do not encourage dangerous or illegal thinking or action.
- Follow through with any task you have accepted quickly and carefully.
- Assume responsibility for minor necessary daily chores.
- Do not take over, assume back-up position.
- Challenge any dangerous, illegal or negative behavior.
- Encourage positive healing, dealing and growth.
- Stay involved by communicating and participating.
- Don't discuss your friend's problems with anyone.
- Take care of yourself.

Victim or Victor

You should take some time to consider these statements and what they have to do with your life and situation.

- No decision or choice you make is going to be made in a vacuum.
- Every decision or choice has a result or reaction.
- Problems aren't going to change until you do.
- It is up to you to do the hard thing. If you don't you will have to do something worse.
- You will be affected by the poor choices of others, but it is not an excuse for you to make poor choices.
- You have thrown enough fits in your life to know they don't fix anything.

Security, Privacy on the Internet

Anonymity, security and privacy on the Internet are a real concern. During this difficult time we wish for a place to feel safe expressing ourselves. The Internet seemed like a perfect answer. We could communicate with people who won't be defending the otherside or bringing up information we wish to forget. We could log-in with an anonymous name Talk to others that would share our anger and pain. Sometimes they even offered suggestions. Some interesting ideas and some obviously foolish.

The problem is that there is no perfect security or anonymity. Even if you use an anonymous browser, all anonymous browsing sites log users. They log the exact time you were on the system and can correlate your user name with your true identity in spite of statements to the contrary and will do so under order of the courts. Anonymous browser sites leave certain protocols. Any one can determine your user agent and your referred with PHP or SSI routines, and they can from the logs determine what pseudonym you used for that connection. Because most of us pay by check or credit card, this can be correlated with your real name and address.

All e-mail, remail and Usenet news posting are logged. There is pending federal legislation to require providers to maintain and make logs available for longer than the six months some do voluntarily now. Even the best anonomyzer services will give you up to a summons when ordered to by the court. It comes down to a matter of money. They simply can't afford the cost of defending litigation that would allow them to protect your name.

Anonymous browsers and remailers do not hide your computer from the network and that information is recorded. That has the effect of negating any effort at anonymity. Your computer contains everything you wanted to keep private unless you use PGP wipe or some such, but who can remember to do that or does?

In addition to the information the browsers collect the programs you install have Trojan programs and back door gateways for government agencies to keep track of your information. We can't tell because their code is not open source. You probably would be surprised at how many programs are gateways for some agency to get into your computer.

Some surf in stealth without using an anonymous browser by surfing piggyback on top of another link. That is safer browsing in stealth than using an anonymous service. If you want privacy, security, safety, then turn off your computer.

Your Computer Their Attorney

Information on your computer is just a vulnerable as any other evidence. The information about anonymity or security or privacy was offered to let you know that your computer is not the only place where your computer on-line or off-line activities can be tracked. Therefore, any information you decline to produce may be produced from other sources.

The only saving grace is that many attorneys are still unfamiliar with discovery as it affects computers.

Chapter 3: Strategies

Looking forward to victory is exciting. You expect a win to be rewarding, vindicating, cleansing and gratifying. To do this you must establish your strategies and techniques. First of all, there is no guarantee of a win in any war. Second, there is rarely a real win in any war. Consider how Dwight D. Eisenhower, a winning general in World War II, felt about war:

"Every gun that is made, every warship launched, every rocket fired signifies, in the final sense, a theft from those who hunger and are not fed, those who are cold and are not clothed.

This world in arms is not spending money alone. It is spending the sweat of its laborers, the genius of its scientists, the hopes of its children... This is not a way of life at all in any true sense."

The thefts mentioned, the hungry not fed, clothed and sheltered whose hopes are shattered, are the children you love because your resources and energies are spent on the battle. The sweat and genius wasted are yours. This war will be your way of life for two to five years. The wounds on all sides will take lifetimes to heal. Therefore, your primary goal must be whatever constitutes the best interest of your children.

Custody decisions are made every day. Many custody battles are waged publicly in court. Other custody battles are negotiated privately, decided privately, and approved by the court. Every custody situation is unique because each involves different circumstances and individuals.

Reality Check

It is time for you to think about what you consider "a win." Then you can decide if negotiated peace --- or all out war --- will accomplish your goal. Are you operating from your self interest or for your child?

It is common to negotiate a "better" settlement with the opposition than you can be "awarded" by the court. Begin to construct a powerful cohesive position from, which to negotiate or wage war.

This chapter will help you understand how the current attitudes in domestic relations will affect you and your opposition.

You will need to consider your resources, abilities, and willingness to cooperate with the other parent. You will also need to take into account how your behavior affects your children, and whatever particular needs and desires they might have.

Such an assessment will help you identify your deficiencies. Do not be offended by the word "deficiencies." After all, no one is perfect, and you are taking responsibility for your good and bad traits. Attend parenting classes. Some of your established patterns of behavior may not be in the best interest of your children. Do not rely on your instincts.

When you fail to admit and accept your responsibility for all of your experiences and blame others, you are giving away your freedom to change yourself and control your life.

This chapter also helps you identify deficiencies in the opposition's war machine, allowing you to negotiate a fair custody arrangement. If that fails, being aware of the opposition's deficiencies may require that you capitalize on the opposition's mistakes to win custody. Then you can be as generous as you care to be.

If there is no opportunity to negotiate a healthy, workable custody settlement for your children, you must consider war. Some of the most important things to think about before you jump into battle include your children's ability to survive a custody battle and your emotional and financial ability to wage a war. Also consider the enemy's ability and desire to fight.

While you're taking a look at the situation, establish a positive mindset. To begin, increase your knowledge of child custody matters and start doing some things that will improve or secure your position.

You are hurt and angry. You want to rip the living heart out of the person who has caused you so much pain and worry and eat it in front of the jerk, daring him or her to say a word. You want to take your children far away and live happily forever after and never hear from that idiot again.

Well, Get Over It

That is not how the real world works. Probably it would not be in the best interest of your children.

Eventually children want and seek contact with both their parents and extended family, including biological parents, adoptive parents, step-parents, grandparents, psychological parents, foster parents and siblings. The trend has fostered a growing number of support groups to help people contact lost relatives. This knowledge should help diminish or alleviate feelings of rejection or disappointment when your children begin this quest. You can help your children in this search and earn a great deal of love and respect from them.

At this time you must decide what you will consider "a win." If you use your resources and energy for an unrealistic goal, you will achieve your own defeat. Determine the real possibilities and set your goal. Look at the possibilities and the chances of them happening.

Desire vs Reality

"We spelled out a shared parenting agreement on paper that we have actually been doing for seven months and presented it to the court for approval. The judge decided it was not workable and imposed a plan neither of us can live with. We want to make the judge approve our original plan."

- It is difficult to make a judge do anything the judge does not want to do. Find a psychologist who is considered a "friend of the court" and request an evaluation of the two parenting plans. If the evaluator agrees with you, there may be an opportunity to present the professional's recommendation to the court.

"I want to be awarded sole custody, giving the opposition very limited visitation."

- Visitation of less than two weekends a month is rare unless the non-custodial parent resides out-of-state. Visitation of less than seven weeks a year is rare for out-of-state visitation.

"I know the opposition is as capable and caring as I am, and I want to work out a 50/50 joint custody and shared responsibility agreement."

- If you are able to work this out with the opposition, you will have to prepare your homework carefully before you take the plan to the judge. If a judge feels that the proposed plan will not work because of personal bias or previous experience in court, that judge may not approve your agreement. If you have outlined the plan and can demonstrate that the system has been in effect for a reasonable period of time with no problems, you may increase the chances that the judge will accept your plan.

The judge may, in fact, impose one with which the court is more familiar. Find instances in existing decisions that support what you have agreed to. This will limit the ability of the judge to circumvent your wishes.

"The opposition is not interested in visiting the children and would leave me alone and stop harassing me if I didn't accept the child support the court ordered."

- You could get counseling, legal assistance or return the money the court sends you each month from the other parent.

"I want to be awarded sole custody and for my children to never have contact with the opposition again."

- A parent is rarely permanently denied access to his or her children, even with a history and conviction of child abuse. To protect the children, the contact may be restricted to "supervised visitation." In other cases, visitation guidelines or visitation guidelines for long distance visitation are considered and adjusted to meet the needs of the children and abilities of the parents.

"Two years ago we worked out a shared parenting agreement, without involving attorneys or the courts, that allowed the children to live with the opposition most of the time. The other parent has a much larger income and provides everything except the children's clothes, which I provide.

My life-style has changed, and I could spend more time with the children, but the opposition ignores my requests. I want to go to court to get more time with my children."

- Start by checking the visitation and child support guidelines for your state. Approaching the court on any question opens the entire case to review any existing agreement. If you, as the non-custodial parent, are not paying child support according to the current guidelines, you could end up seeing your children on a more restricted basis and paying a larger percentage of your income for support. It may be to your advantage to stay out of the legal system and work things out with the custodial parent.

"Two years ago I was awarded sole custody of my child who is now five. The other parent has standard long distance visitation and telephone contact. Telephone contact is rarely exercised, and visitation is consistent, but on very short notice. The other parent's home life is unstable. The other children (twelve and fifteen) are in constant difficulties with the law for serious assault and drug-related infractions. I do not want my child in the care of the older children when away at visitation. Additionally, I am tired of dealing with such a hostile person."

- A parent is responsible for the welfare of the children. It is your responsibility to find a way for this child to spend time with the other parent and still protect the child from abuse from the step-siblings. Enlist assistance from the court in your area and child protection services where the child must go for visitation. The other parent may never be any easier to deal with. You must find ways and means to meet your child's needs, follow the court orders and protect your child.

"We live in the same neighborhood and our children come and go from our homes at will. I have started a serious relationship with another person and expect to marry in the next year. Every time my ex gets mad at me, the children are signed up for a new activity that requires money and/or transport that I am better equipped to provide. If I express any objection my ex and the children question my interest in their welfare. At this point we have karate, scouts, school events, attendance at birthday parties for friends, little league, choir, ballet, soccer, 4-H and little theater. At this point I don't have an evening or weekend to myself."

- You feel like you're being manipulated because you are. Children need all of the life lessons these activities provide, but you should not be the only parent required to facilitate the children's attendance. Chart the activities on a calendar. With the help of your children and ex attempt to work out a more equitable plan that might include the children's car-pooling with other families for some events.

Looking Past 2001

At the present time a single parent on welfare may be granted custody in preference to a two-parent, upper middle class, working household. The ability to lavish attention and time on a child is winning over money, status, and "quality time."

Fathers in greater numbers are winning custody of multiple children from mothers with similar incomes and abilities, where fathers are shown to demonstrate superior parenting skills and better decision-making abilities as they pertain to the children. Dads are not only winning custody, but are being awarded child support.

Some parties enter a shared-custody agreement that requires the children to change residences every six months. This is one of the more difficult, out-of-court settlements that parents and their attorneys work out, but it avoids the risk of letting a judge make the decision.

There are no guarantees. Although finding a solution that is best for the child has always been the court's aim, the idea of what is best for the child has changed dramatically through the years. In the last five years, the emphasis of the court has changed.

You cannot change the system while you are managing your own custody battle. Some parent's rights and support groups have legislative branches in their organizations. Joining a group with that ability would give you the emotional and informational support you need while giving you the opportunity to offer your input into future legislative changes.

You can get the best professional help affordable and counter any attitudes or behaviors that could cause you trouble. You can understand the process, learn the correct "language" to express yourself, and improve your chances within the legal structure.

Even if you cannot win custody, you can still have a positive, ongoing impact on the life of your children. History provides many examples of a country winning the war against an invader and collapsing from within because it was so damaged from the conflict. In medicine, it occurs when the operation is a success, but the patient dies.

The saddest result of a custody war is children so devastated by the battles fought by the people who love them, that they can never grow into loving, complete human beings.

Changes in the Wind

If you have not noticed the winds of change where you live, these are some of the things you can expect in the not-so-distant future:

- A court, in determining custody, shall not prefer a parent as custodian because of that parent's sex.
- Casino as well as Lotto and tax refunds will be garnished to meet back child support obligations.
- Joint custody will become either the authorized or mandated starting point for deciding custody of children.
- A custodial parent will be prohibited from removing children from the jurisdiction, when both parents live in one jurisdiction, or when it substantially interferes with the non-moving parent's joint custody or visitation to the detriment of the children.
- It is in the best interests of children to have frequent, meaningful and continuing access to the non-custodial parent (or both parents).
- States will set up "Do It Yourself" court services that help and educate the consumer to file court papers correctly to speed up the process when parents are unable to afford good legal assistance and to unplug the bottleneck in the family law arena. In Arizona, the Maricopa County system has initiated an outstanding and highly successful pilot program called the Family Support Center (602) 506-3762
- The custodial parent who impedes the ongoing visitation of the non-custodial parent loses custody of children.
- The states will strive to assist unwed fathers who want to acknowledge and establish a legal link to their children at birth by signing documents like the "Recognition of Parentage." This strengthens the father's connection to his children and their sense of identity and self-esteem.
- There is no *prima facie* right to sole custody for either parent.
- States are requiring that parents who are parties to dissolution of marriage proceedings participate in an educational consultative program designed to prepare parents to assist their children in coping with the divorce. Remember, The children are always watching.

Strategy in a child custody war is primarily concerned with the formulation of solid policy and clarification of goals. This may involve the selection of new healthy alliances, maintenance of solid associations.

It may also mean evaluating or dropping of alliances that are harmful to your objective. Tactics of war are the methods designed to shore up your defensive position, employ positive systems for offense, and maintain the emotional, financial and physical ability to wage war. You must make a plan.

Strategic Interaction

Understanding Strategic Interaction between you and the other individuals in your case will strengthen your position because you will make better decisions. If you assume that the opposition will always make the move you fear most, it will lead you to expect that the other will never cooperate.

This will encourage you to be absent from the real battle while fighting an imagined war in your mind, and ultimately caring more for short-term wins, discounting the consequences for the future. It is never safe to assume that the only priority of the opposition is that they are "out to get you." The opposition has many pressures and priorities of which you are unaware. The continuing opportunity of interaction is necessary for the development of cooperation, but is not sufficient if the opposition is never encouraged to participate. Your efforts will be judged by their results.

Strategy = Planning

1. Strategy = short and long-range planning. As Commander-in-Chief, devise your strategy! Establish the needs of your children and your desire and right to engage your opposition.

2. Enlist your troops and mobilize their skills to mount your campaign! Survey the terrain and your financial ability to gain ground while still protecting your children from stray enemy bullets or friendly fire.

3. Gather your data ammunition, load your guns and prepare to deploy your professional armaments, such as attorneys and detectives. Present a solid front to the enemy, observers, and mediators.

4. Once fully supplied and supported, execute your battle plan offensive. Shore up any weakened defensive positions and maintain damage control while your attorney directs the legal maneuvers.

5. Contain any battle damage while building a well-constructed case to win the war being waged before the psychologist or judge.

6. Establish a lasting plan to maintain peace.

7. Your strategy should not be etched in stone. Just almost.

8. Any strategy you form to ensure peace or to make war must be strong enough to hold up under the strain of constant testing.

9. Your strategy must be flexible enough to bend rather than break .

10. Your strategy must be solid enough in its entirety that it will not collapse over the long-term.

11. Your strategy must include a plan A, plan B and plan C.

12. You cannot consider making changes or actually implementing changes in your strategy when you are tired, hungry or frightened.

13. Your strategy must include how you will handle defeats as well as how you will celebrate the victories.

14. Your strategy will strengthen if you determine why each plan worked or failed.

Winning Battles or Games = Strategy

In 1994 two Americans and a German won the Nobel Prize in economics for work identifying that companies do business, governments make decisions and armies fight battles much the way people play poker and chess. Understanding the systems of competition and cooperation are tremendously important to the custody battle.

You can handle yourself and your opposition with less work and more success if you understand how each of you thinks.

Discussion of strategy here is conducted with the assumption that you are dealing with a person from a social group you understand. Americans negotiate and cooperate best with other Americans. This would be true of any individuals from the same country because there are many situations and attitudes that are already understood by both. Whereas, discussion with a person from another country may be complicated by lack of foundation or information about the customs, laws and accepted attitudes by one or both participants.

The fact is you may be dealing with a person that is incompetent. Most don't know they are incompetent. To make matters more complicated, they are usually supremely confident of their abilities. This happens because the skills required for competence are the same skills necessary to recognize competence.

This deficiency in self-monitoring skills causes incompetent people to suffer not only from the erroneous conclusions they make that lead to poor choices, but then they are incapable of recognizing their inadequacy. A few of the reasons people overestimate their own abilities includes lack of solid guidelines, clear feedback and training in logical thinking. Additionally, incompetent individuals are not able or willing to recognize competence in others.

Deliberate, Insightful, Rational Enemy

In order to understand why the opposition does what they do, you should not assume that the enemy is deliberate, insightful or rational. The opposition may be operating without making conscious choices, using instead their own standard operation procedures, instincts, habits, imitations or poor advice from others rather than attempting to maximize their rewards. This person does the same thing over and over again, getting less than favorable results, but expecting a better outcome. What does influence the opposition?

- Past experiences the opposition has had with you or others.
- How information is communicated to the opposition.
- The direct influence of third parties on the opposition.
- The problems of implementing a choice.
- What the opposition thinks they'd be giving up.
- What the opposition thinks they will gain.
- What the opposition thinks you have done in the past.
- What the opposition thinks the family, neighbors, church, community or society will think of them.

It is necessary to know how much the opposition is willing to cooperate in order to decide on a strategy. It is not necessary to be friends to develop cooperation.

A Tactic is a Technique is a Strategy

Strategy is making a plan. The plan you devise to deal with a specific incident is a tactic. The standard manner with which you deal with a person or circumstance is a technique. Determining, which tactic and technique will best help you attain your ultimate goal is strategy.

One cooperates with the opposition because one must. It does not matter how this custody decision is made, you will have to deal with this other parent until the youngest child is eighteen years old. The strategy you use and the results of each engagement will affect future contact with the opposition. At first, all of the techniques work. It quickly becomes evident that the poorest, more exploitative techniques produce less and less results. The more positive techniques produce better results for everyone.

Specific Techniques

Whether you are aware of it or not, you are negotiating and cooperating throughout your day: Choosing the correct clothes to make the desired impression. You negotiate and cooperate to get the children dressed, fed and out the door for school. You move in and out of traffic with other vehicles, get along with coworkers, employees, vendors, customers and bosses. You wait for a turn on equipment at the gym, merge into line at the grocery store, keeping your enemies at bay and your loved ones happy.

The techniques you used were probably learned by trial and error. Sometimes you learn from your mistakes, sometimes you don't understand what made things go wrong. Often becoming aware of specific techniques makes you more successful. Listen, watch, and think to become aware of the techniques you and the people around you use and which ones produce the best results.

There are specific techniques of negotiation/ cooperation. Identify the techniques you used in the past and make any adjustments necessary. Make your attorney aware of the techniques the opposition uses and identify your strategy for the future. The primary indicator of which strategic type your opponent is using would be your observations of the past actions. The strategy and techniques the other parent uses will be influenced by the people around at the time, but you will be able to identify the techniques that person will depend upon.

Let's examine what they are and how they work.

Live and Let Live

This is the maintenance of restraint as long as the opposition reciprocates it. Although willing to retaliate for unintentional problems caused by the opposition, this strategy will attempt to determine if the problem was intentional or not.

- Live and Let Live can give satisfactory results for the long-term.

Tit For Tat

After the first move, each successive move then does whatever the other person did on the previous move. A move in a negative direction can therefore set off a long string of recriminations and counter recriminations. Both sides suffer.

Kind and forgiving moves can make life easier for everyone. This strategy may or may not retaliate for unintentional problems caused by the opposition.

- Tit for Tat can give satisfactory results for the long-term.

Look Ahead

This is a deliberate attempt to understand the opposition and then to make a choice that will yield the best long-term results based upon this understanding.

After each move, this technique updates the assumptions and again selects the choice that will then maximize the long-term. Unwilling to retaliate for unintentional problems caused by the opposition, this strategy will attempt to determine if the problem was intentional or not.

- Look Ahead can offer the best results for the long-term.

Tester

This strategy is willing to exploit softies or unsuspecting opponents, but is prepared to back off if the opposition shows it won't be exploited. This person will usually fall back on Tit for Tat and is apt to retaliate for unintentional problems caused by the opposition.

- Tester offers poor results for the long-term.

Tranquilizer

This type will first seek to establish a mutual rewarding relationship with the opposition. Only then does the tranquilizer cautiously try to see if he/ she will be allowed to get away with something. The tranquilizer is apt to retaliate for unintentional problems caused by the opposition.

- Tranquilizer can offer a little less than satisfactory results for the long-term.

Exploitative or Permanent Retaliation

This strategy exploits the weakness or kindness of the opposition as well as any rules. Although this strategy looks promising at first, it can destroy the very environment it needs for its own success. This strategy will retaliate for unintentional problems caused by the opposition.

- Exploitative or Permanent Retaliation provides poor results for the long-term.

Attrition

This is a strategy whereby equal losses (in money or manpower) from both sides mean a net gain for the side with the most resources. In this case a lose-lose situation is a win-for-one-side. This strategy may or may not retaliate for unintentional problems caused by the opposition.

- Attrition can offer a little less than satisfactory results for the long-term.

Deterrence

Such a strategy establishes a reputation as a bully for squeezing the most out of the opposition, while at the same time not tolerating any request or demand the bully sees as unreasonable. Any attempt by the opposition to not cooperate will provoke swift retaliation and the understanding that the bully will never cooperate again even after only one mistake.

One purpose of having a reputation as a bully is to achieve deterrence by means of a credible threat.

Two Bullies will drive the process into a downward spiral with a long series of mutual punishment. This strategy will always retaliate for unintentional problems caused by the opposition.

- Deterrence offers poor results for the long-term.

Reciprocity

This is a strategy of give and receive mutually. It is a more positive strategy than Tit for tat, because it is the process of giving value as a reward for being given value. Retaliation would reflect the negative process of reciprocity.

This strategy would avoid retaliating for unintentional problems caused by the opposition.

- Reciprocity can give better than satisfactory results for the long-term.

Random

Less a strategy or technique and more of an uncooperative or unorganized participant without a clear goal, this strategy may use all of the strategies without waiting for results from one before initiating another. This strategy may or may not retaliate for unintentional problems caused by the opposition.

- Random can yield poor results for the long-term.

Agendas

Agenda is a conscious or unconscious plan that may or may not be formally contrived to ensure the results desired by an individual. The more people involved in the visitation exchange, rule setting, negotiation, decision-making and evaluation on each side the more personal agendas there are with which you have to deal.

At the onset of the custody dispute, you may have been only dealing with the other parent. Now you have the grandparents, significant other, and people and pressures of which you are totally unaware, exerting influence on the other parent. As new people and their personal agendas enter either side of the contest, new opportunities will present themselves. The significant other may be interested in getting things settled down so the other parent will be ready to start a new and lasting relationship, whereas the grandparents want to assure contact with your children.

The people you count on for support may have hidden agendas as to which you are not aware. As you work with anyone, listen to what they are really saying and constantly revise your evaluation of why they are involved in this conflict and if their actions support their words. Someone else's agenda, though not identical to yours, may, in fact, assist you greatly. Others may have malicious agendas that you are unable or unwilling to see.

Changing Strategies

Get a solid understanding of your ultimate goal and the strategies you have used in the past. Once you become aware of the strategy the opposition is using, choose the most positive technique available. You may find that the opposition is more willing to cooperate than you expected. If you feel it is necessary to change strategies, do so after a great deal of consideration. Feeling a constant need to change your strategy indicates you are not committed to your goal and will yield no positive results. Strategy is a long-term plan, not a whim.

It is counter-productive to choose the strategy that looks most damaging to the opposition, rather than the most helpful for the long-term. Professional observers can put a name on what is going on, but the untrained, while unable to label what is happening, can easily identify the techniques used and the motivation of each person.

Defensive Behaviors

Defensive behaviors are a protective guard against an anticipated attack or a fixed position from which an individual would rather not move. If a person arrives at the negotiation in a defensive stance, your ability to put that person at ease will dictate the mood of the entire project.

Unaware of what the opposition is truly communicating, a solution might be reached that will be destructive to the overall goals of everyone in attendance. Learn to recognize the early signs of disagreement, suspicion, uncertainty, rejection, doubt, discomfort, or discontent, which will complicate the situation and inhibit agreement. Use them as guide posts without becoming defensive yourself.

Specific Defensive Behaviors

1. Arms crossed on chest (men).
2. Arms crossed below breasts (women).
3. Hand covering mouth or chest or hand holding throat.

4. Any item used as a shield such as a notebook, clipboard, or purse.

5. A person straddling backwards in a chair may look relaxed, but the back of the chair may actually offer the protection of a shield to the person.

Remedies To Defensive Behaviors

Do something that allows the person to open up. Hand the person something they would want to accept, or consider. If we can supply assurance where needed, our opposition can be encouraged to be cooperative.

Specific Defensive Behaviors

- Tilting head and face down.
- Person not willing to look at you at all.
- Person is leaning back in chair.
- Glances at the ceiling, watches the exit door.
- Body twisted away from opposing person.
- Sitting with body is pointing toward the exit.
- Crossed legs pointed toward exit.
- Legs crossed with the ankle resting on other knee in a figure four position.

Remedies

Change the subject to a point in which the person has special interest or control.

If all efforts fail, allow the person to leave. It does you no good in the long run to keep talking to someone who is telling you that he or she is anxious to leave.

Specific Defensive Behaviors

- Chip on the shoulder or outright aggression.
- Placing obstructions in the way of all ideas and suggestions.
- Suspicion of each part or package under discussion.
- Agreement without commitment, just to finish the process.

Remedies

Ask if there is a specific way the person would like this session to be handled. Offer to let the other person make the initial presentations.

Delay

Delay or pausing to think is usually either the way someone has always dealt with you or a person exercising extreme caution. If you have seen this tactic before, accept that this is how things are going to proceed. If you are unaccustomed to this tactic, relax and adjust your pace. A person who uses delay as a normal tactic or as a new-found method may delay after each proposal made to them. Delays may be for no apparent reason, sometimes as many as five times an hour. To delay or stall for time to think over a situation before raising more opposition, asking for clarification, or posing a question, is more of a positive gesture than negative as it shows a willingness to stay and work things out rather than flee.

The three most common delaying tactics are:

- Pinching the nose while squinting. This means the person is having difficulty seeing the answer they need.
- Pacing ritual is a very positive gesture. One should not speak to the pacer. It will interfere with what they are trying to decide. Wait until the pacer interrupts the silence to comment or ask a question.
- Putting tools (eyeglasses, pens, and pencils) in mouth. This signals that I am thinking because there is something in my mouth and I can't talk. Delay can also communicate resistance, impose a halt or time out, express anger, and relieve or build emotional tension.

Strategic Case Boosters

You can do many things big and small to improve or secure your position. Encourage good habits. Some you already have, and some you may wish to establish. All constructive behaviors and actions will affect your children's lives and your case in a positive manner.

Negative behaviors and actions will impact your children's life and your case in a detrimental manner. Work toward using constructive behavior in your life and in this case.

Be careful that you do not let your own negative thinking or other people's negative thinking undermine the good you are attempting to do. Negative thinking can make you appear to act in an erratic manner. Concentrate on building a solid, visible bond with your children.

Follow the suggestions that you can at this time. When you review this information later, you will be surprised at how many more positive activities you have begun.

1. Establish yourself as the parent seen by the children's doctor, teachers, scout leader, neighbors and minister.

2. Don't worry about the clothes and toys that go to the children's other home and don't return. Your children still have the use of the things you have purchased. After all, that is why you bought the items.

3. Keep a detailed log or diary for an extended length of time, even if things are going well. A year or two from now you may need to refer to what was happening yesterday,

4. If you become aware that your children are experiencing emotional difficulties because of this custody case, get professional help right away.

5. Accept the "help" your children give. Not everything needs to be done "right." If you can, simply say, "You made the bed. Good for you," and leave the bed as the child made it even though it is not perfect.

6. Help your children enjoy the things the other parent does and buys for them. Remove any guilt they have about these feelings of happiness. Let the children know, "We all love you and want you to have nice things and nice experiences in both families."

7. Be aware of behavioral changes in your children.

8. Be proactive not reactive.

9. Your children's feelings are more important to you than you being right or proving the other parent wrong.

10. Have your children accompany you to buy a flowering bush or tree (as your yard or patio space allows). As a team you can plant and fertilize it. Each time the children are with you, the ritual of caring for the project will be something you do together. It will anchor the children to your home and to you while they are away from you. The children will think of you when ever they see the same plant.

11. Identify and use reliable, unbiased witnesses.

12. Make sure that if you have control of the children's report cards, school notes, special awards and results of medical exams, you send copies to the other parent as quickly as possible.

13. If you become aware that there are shortages of supplies for the children in the other household, offer to fill some of these needs for the other parent. Do this in a manner that will allow the opposition to accept. A gesture of help, offered in a negative manner, indicates that you intend to discredit the other parent, rather than help the children.

14. Experience is what you get when you didn't get what you wanted.

15. Consider your children's emotional health and well-being. Think of how they feel when things are said or done. Learn what is important to your children and make an effort to understand things from their point of view. Speak on your child's level and listen to what the child is trying to express, rather than just the words.

16. Take some time to think about anything negative that has happened. Try to analyze the entire matter and identify any actions you made that affected the situation adversely. Prepare an alternative and more constructive course of action in the event you are placed in a similar spot again.

17. Be open and free with your affirmation of the achievements and positive actions of your children. Do not criticize. There are lots of right ways to do things.

18. Follow court orders and mutual agreements regarding visitation and support to the letter.

19. Assure your children that the problems you and the other parent are having are the result of adult behavior and not the children's behavior.

20. If something of the children's is broken when they are with you, fix it and send it home in good order. It reduces the aggravation with the other parent and shows your children that you care about what is important to them.

21. Let the child know that you are very happy he or she can be with you. Do it often.

22. Instead of no, try to say yes, automatically, first.

23. Attend every occasion that the children or you feel is important. Such events would be graduations, religious occasions, family events, awards, recitals, tournaments, weekly sporting events or ceremonies. These are once in a lifetime events, even if you would rather avoid the other parent or their family. Most of these events are once in a lifetime for a child and important memories. Be there and make it happy for the child and as easy for the other parent as possible. If your obvious attendance will cause a big commotion, make a point of not being obvious. Take photos of your child if necessary, so you can demonstrate to the child and others that you were there.

24. Be as kind as you can as soon as you can. You never know how soon it will be too late.

25. Be the parent and allow your children to be children.

26. The right way may be the hardest, but when you get to rest, you get to rest easy.

27. Make plans. If time with your children is limited, make the most of it with several activity options that can be adjusted according to how they feel, your financial limitations, and weather conditions. Visit family and friends, indoor physical fitness centers, or plan a day of activities around your home. Have a plan A, plan B and plan C. If everything falls apart, be prepared to handle the disappointment with grace.

28. Take photos of everything. Including child-oriented projects you and your "significant other" do with your children. Happy events are important to you now, to your case soon, and to your children forever. It is also necessary to document dirty, unsafe or worrisome conditions to which your children are exposed. If you are ever accused of something, or fear that you may be, taking a photo with a camera that prints the date on the photo is a very good defense.

29. If it does not affect the welfare of your children, let unkind words or deeds go unanswered.

30. Your children's names on special cups or T-shirts from you to have at their other home gives you a constant presence. Personalized school notebooks and pencils will also remind the children that you were thinking of them.

31. Handle discussions or disagreements with the other parent over the telephone or privately, out of sight and hearing of the child. This will decrease the amount of stress felt by the child at times of pick up or return or when both parents are able to attend an event with the child.

32. Let your children know that they belong with both parents in both homes and that you want them to feel good about being happy in each environment. Include each child as a member of the family with the chance to give and receive affection, express anger, and learn how to manage these feelings in themselves and from other members of the family.

33. Make an effort to fill your life with people who love you and treat you well. This will give you the strength to fight when necessary.

34. The freedom I want is not to do what I like, but to do what I ought.

35. When you send letters and notes to your children, keep them up-beat and include a piece of chewing gum, some jokes or a dollar bill.

36. Seek professional guidance to correct any antisocial or dysfunctional attitudes or behaviors your children may exhibit. Mediators and judges are favorably impressed with parents who are able to put their own embarrassment aside to make sure their children receive positive help to heal emotional problems. This assures that the children will function more efficiently as adults.

37. Children are never detached spectators when their parents fight. Learn to restrain yourself to protect your children.

38. Take good care of the pets, gardens and things that are important and must be left behind by your children when they have to be away from your home. Your children are suffering many losses of which you are not aware. Each one compounds the great sadness your children feel. Do your best to safeguard those things your children need not lose.

39. Information will give you confidence. Confidence will give you control. Control will give you perspective. Perspective will give you strength. Strength will give you power. Power will give you the WIN.

40. If you have a church home and have been thinking about attending church on a regular basis, this is a good time to renew those bonds. If you have not established religious ties, consider doing so now. Most mediators and judges attend church.

41. Watch for unusual behavior your child may exhibit when dealing with a specific person, place or circumstance. Aggressive or drastically subdued behavior may indicate unspoken fears your child may have or a need for specific attention.

42. Be open and free with your affirmation of the achievements and positive actions of your child. Do not criticize. There are many right ways to do things.

43. It is easier to get forgiveness than it is to get permission.

44. Try to spend as much time with your child as you can. If court orders or distance limit the time you can spend with the child, stay in touch in other ways. Send letters, post cards and call (at reasonable hours) if you cannot make a physical appearance. Keep promises to your child.

45. It is common for parents to have hundreds of photos of their children with the other parent, playing with neighbor children or pets and not have any of themselves with their children. Have other people take photos of you and your children.

46. When your small child is tugging at your clothes and whining, kneel down, look your child in the eye and ask what is wrong.

47. Often it is easier to get teenagers to talk with you when you aren't looking directly at them. Turn off the radio in the car and encourage your teen to participate in a conversation. This takes practice.

48. Do something new and constructive for yourself. Start walking a mile in the morning before you get ready for work. Learn to make stained glass at the community center. Take an evening class for automotive repair at the junior college or learn some other new skill.

49. Assure your children of both parents' love.

50. Affection should be expressed in many ways, verbally, physically, and emotionally. Express your feelings for your children in loving words like, "I love you," "I like the kind of person you are," and "I think you are a very special child." Be physically affectionate. Lavish your children with hugs and kisses, cuddle your children while reading a story or watching television. Sit together while playing, hold hands while walking, or work closely together on a project.

51. Carefully let the child know that even though the child does not live with you, he or she remains in your heart.

52. Keep all receipts. Mark purchases made specifically for the child and total separately on the receipt. Try to pay for products and services for the child with a separate check, listing the check number on the receipt. Do not attribute all general purchases to the child. Keep receipts of purchases for the child in a separate box or file.

53. Get the children a subscription to a magazine that would be of interest to them. Then every month, when it arrives, the children will be reminded that you thought of them.

54. As you mourn the things you wanted and did not get, remember to celebrate all the things you did not want and did not get.

55. Plan for your next meeting with a difficult person. Write down the sequence of events the

way they usually happen. Now change the way you would have dealt with the situation. List other options you have tried that have had some success and several new options. Review your lists just before you have to see this person.

You will feel a new control. Do not be drawn into the old pattern.

56. Learn to accept your child as a person separate from yourself and the other parent. Find ways to demonstrate your acceptance. Share your child's hobby, school successes, and sports achievements.

57. Make sure all child support or spousal maintenance is current in this or any other matter before you enter this custody battle. Any back money owed will give you "dirty hands" in the eyes of the court. Children are very hurt that a parent does not care enough about them to send money for their food and clothing.

58. Separate your child from unacceptable actions. You love your child, but may not like what that child is doing at a given moment. Help your child understand the difference.

59. Be honest with your child. It is easier for your child to understand that you have made mistakes and are embarrassed about something, than it is to know that his parent is a liar.

60. The public library has newspapers you may read at no cost. The paper lists activities and events for you and your child to attend.

61. Follow court orders and mutual agreements regarding visitation and support to the letter.

62. When you are very angry or upset, walk around the block, counting each step as you take it, concentrating on your place and the length of stride. This will rest your emotions and give the dangerous part of your feelings a chance to cool off.

63. At the end of each day make a plan for the next day. Example: 7:30A.M. go to work, 11:30A.M. lunch with Shawn, 5:00P.M. exchange books at library, 7:00P.M. call children, 8:00P.M. watch movie Forrest Gump.

64. Be patient and kind to your child and to yourself.

65. Do try to make peace with the other parent. Try again and again. Start new each time. It is worth it for the child.

66. Talk to your children about what is important in their lives - soccer games, piano recitals, report cards and their best friends.

67. The work will wait while you show the child the rainbow. The rainbow won't wait while you do the work.

68. Keep the lines of communication open between you and the other parent.

69. Subscribe to the newspaper in your city. If you cannot afford daily delivery, get a subscription for Sunday only, or make it a point to pick up the Sunday edition.

70. Engage your child in conversation. Listen to what your child says.

71. Be aware that children learn chiefly by the example of their early caregivers. They learn quickly by what they see, not by what they are told.

72. Help older children remember the things that are important to the other parent and grandparents, such as birthdays, mother, father and grandparent days. The child will appreciate your assistance in pleasing someone the child cares about. It also shows the child that he or she can be somewhat neutral in this custody battle and is free to give and receive love from both sides. Your child will appreciate your unselfish and reasonable behavior.

73. Keep a calendar in a convenient place for the children. Help them mark important dates, such as events at school, as well as ones you have planned with the children, family and friends like birthdays and anniversaries.

74. Work with the future. Time is on your side.

75. Keep yourself and your child in a safe, non-threatening environment.

76. Follow your plan and your dream will become your goal.

* There are more than 1,500 of these helpful listings in "Killers and Boosters for Custody Litigants" available in the back of this manual.

Activities to Cultivate

- Maintain child's appearance and health with regular medical and dental visits. No matter who the court says is supposed to pay for it.
- Read to stay current on childcare ideas.
- Be seen with your child.
- Keep your appearance conservative and clean.
- Establish and/or maintain regular schedules.
- Make plans for spending positive time with your child.
- Enjoy scheduled and impromptu family outings, such as picnics, zoo day or the park.
- Attend religious services regularly.
- Express your emotions in an adult manner.
- Engage in regular exercise.
- Keep a safe and clean vehicle.
- Seek activities that you and your child can both enjoy.
- Spend time with other parents and their children.
- Help your child enjoy the good things in life.
- Keep a camera with film close at hand.
- Ask people to take photos of you with your children with your camera.

It is possible to make some small times of peace even in a heated battle. During the Second World War it was common on several battle fronts that exchange of fire, including bombs, were lighter at meal times to allow both sides to eat. An essential element of strategy should be to incorporate more cooperation and peace into the battle until there is more peace and less war. Hopefully peace will eventually break out on all fronts.

Chapter 4: Conflict Resolution

Q. Can you win without ever firing a shot? A. YES
Q. How? A. NEGOTIATE

Problems the Other Parent Causes

Problems are not created or dealt with in a vacuum. Many factors influence them. Some you can control. Some you must only be aware of to change the negative impact on you and your case. Any positive changes you can make in your attitude about what is going on or your response to the problems will help you now and your case in the short and long run.

In life you are judged not by what was done to you, but by how you responded to what was done to you. If something terrible is done to you and you react in a bad way, you lose twice. You lose once because you were hurt by what happened; the second time because your reaction escalated the problem or demonstrated your bad side. You may have reacted because of concern for your children's welfare, from habit, concern for yourself, emotion, situation, anger, or revenge.

By examining any unpleasant occurrence you gain a degree of control. Once a situation happens we tend to put it behind us as if it is never going to happen again. Often we are surprised.

It is helpful to identify what is happening and why you react the way you do. If you are not happy with the same situations repeating themselves, you can devise and practice new methods to handle the old problems. You can't fix everything by yourself, but you can identify the incidents that keep happening, and change their outcome. This exercise is important if any of these statements are true.

- We argue about everything.
- Every time I have to talk to them I get upset. The stress often starts days or weeks before the actual meeting.
- I argue with the people I love over these people I can't stand.
- I feel everything I do is examined and viewed in a negative light and used against me.
- They want too much control over what I do.
- I never know what they are going to do to me next and I feel threatened all the time.

Common Problem Situations	
1.	They will not give me the children's things they need for visitation.
2.	They don't return the children's things after visitation.
3.	They tell lies about me to my children.
4.	They tell lies about me to other people.
5.	They always pick up/deliver the children at the wrong time.
6.	They make a scene or argument at every pick up or drop off of the children.
7.	They won't let me talk to the children.
8.	When I go to pick up the children for visitation, they aren't there.
9.	They tell my children I don't love them.
10.	They don't spend the child support money on things my children need.
11.	They tell the children they can't have things because I don't send enough money.
12.	They accuse me of everything including child abuse.
13.	The other parents accuse me of improper behavior when dealing with them.
14.	They criticize everything I do.
15.	They threaten me when I pick up/deliver my children.
16.	They call me at all hours of the day and night.

- Don't worry about listing them in any specific order, just get them all down. Your problems may be more basic than the ones listed here, but that doesn't make them less important than the challenges other parent's face. Learning to deal with the small problems will keep them from growing into insurmountable obstacles. Your problems may be much more complicated than the ones listed here, but that doesn't mean that you can't find new solutions for dealing with them. Common Challenges.

If you don't feel you have any problems, but the other parent does, you may want to list the things that seem to bother them and find solutions for those. The reduction of problems you and the other parent feel will reduce the stress your children must endure. Any reduction in stress and animosity will make future negotiations proceed more quickly.

Once the incidents are listed, think about the last time each incident happened. Often our reaction has less to do with what actually happened, but a great deal to do with other factors. Explore some of these:

- **Habit.** A reaction and mode of behaving by constant repetition that may no longer be serving you well.
- **Children's Welfare.** If what is being said or done is really going to hurt your children.
- **My Welfare**. If what is being said or done is really going to hurt you.
- **Emotional.** Memory and pain from the past may be making this situation more hurtful than necessary.
- **Situational.** If your reaction had more to do with who said or did something or who else was there.
- **Knee-Jerk.** Lack of preparation allows more actions or words to feel like assaults and cause defensive, less than perfect, responses.
- **Anger.** Fear/feeling of loss will cause emotional excitement inducing intense displeasure.

- **Revenge.** Is the act of inflicting or the intent to inflict injury in return for injury. Revenge will cause you more trouble.
- **3rd Party.** Others are influencing how you respond to this situation

If you are able to identify a pattern in your responses to the incidents, you may be able to adjust your attitude, limiting the amount of control the opposition has over your life.

Incident List	
List the arguments and situations that cause you problems with the other parent.	
1.	Amber won't return Bobby's things after visitation.
2.	Amber won't communicate with me about anything, even Bobby.
3.	Bobby won't ask to call me because he says it makes Amber mad.
4.	Amber won't let Bobby call Rebecca Mom when he is at her house.
5.	Bobby visits Amber in Washington five times a year. As soon as he gets home, she starts telling him about when he will be going back to visit. These conversations make him cry.

Opposition's Motivation
What motivates the other parent to do the things he or she does when dealing with you.
Motivation
Habit. It is how this person has always behaved.
Children's Welfare. The other parent is really worried about the welfare of the children.
His or Her own Welfare. The other parent says he or she is frightened of me.
Emotional. It was an emotionally motivated action.
Situational. It was a situationally motivated action.
Knee-Jerk. The other parent was reacting to something he or she thinks I did.
Anger. He or she was angry.
Revenge. Everything the other parent does is based on revenge.
3rd Party. Someone else is controlling the other parent.

Why They Do What they Do

The opposition may be motivated by any and all of the reasons listed. They may even be motivated by factors of which you are totally unaware.

You may be aggravating the situation either inadvertently or by design. Aggravation of the situation is not going to serve you or the best interests of your children. It is important for you to attempt to understand why the opposition does what they do. It is more important to know that you will be judged by what you do not what the opposition does.

In most cases you have known this person for a long time. You may have been warned by one of the opposition's former significant others and just didn't believe what you were hearing.

You may even have watched the opposition react in this manner when dealing with others.

In the past this attitude and behavior may have served your purpose. Whether this did or did not serve your purposes, you should not be surprised when these old behaviors show up to cause you problems. You are also aware of what feeds the flame of these behaviors and what it takes to calm this person down.

Reaction Chart

Using the corresponding numbered situations you listed on the INCIDENT LIST fill in your current reactions to the situation on this chart using an "X" Use an "O" for the problems you will need professional help with in the future.

Situation number	1.	2.	3.	4.	5.	6.	7.	8.	9.	10.	11.	12.
Fear born of experience												
Fear born of rumor												
Fear born of unknown												
Habit	x											
Children's Welfare		0	0	x	0							
My Welfare												
Emotional	x		x	x								
Situational		x										
Knee-Jerk												
Anger	x	x	x	x								
Revenge												
3rd Party		x										
Let it go												

The new responses for situations #1

You will practice for old arguments and situations.

I will duplicate the things Bobby wants to take with him to his mother's and keep a list so I know what he has at his other home. I will not make this a duplication an issue with Amber or be upset if Bobby needs me to replace something that broke while it was at his mother's home.

The things I send are Bobby's and he will get to use them at Amber's house.

I assure Bobby that the things he has here at home will be safe while he is at his mothers home.

I will let Bobby know the things we send for visitation can stay in Washington. He should not worry about what comes back and what doesn't.

I will convince Bobby that we love him, no matter where he may be and that we really want him to have a great time with his other family.

The new responses for situations #2 You will practice for old arguments and situations.
I will keep trying to communicate with Amber. I will focus on issues she will be happy to address, rather than upset about.
I will strive to keep my communications with Amber free of emotion and professional. I will send copies of my communication with Amber to my attorney.
I will keep out of Amber's personal business. I will avoid making unkind comments.

The new responses for situations #3 You will practice for old arguments and situations.
I have given Bobby an 800 number so he can call home if he wishes to and when he gets an opportunity.
Bobby is usually gone for only eight days at a time for most holidays and six weeks in the summer. I am going to get used to these black-out periods of not getting to talk to him until he is older and can work it out from that end.
I will remember that bobby is a separate person and may not fee the same suffering I feel. If necessary I will get professional help for Bobby and for myself to help us deal with our feelings.

The new responses for situations #4 You will practice for old arguments and situations.
I have decided to not be concerned with what Amber needs to tell Bobby to make her feel better. I will not make an issue of the things Bobby tells me about things his mother said or did when he was with her.
I will tell Bobby to do what his mother says when he is in Washington with Amber. That nothing he says or does there will keep me from loving him.
We will tell Bobby he can call Rebecca Mom when he is with Rebecca and us when he is with his mother. That is OK with us. Bobby must be assured that he is not betraying us by loving his mother.
I know it must be very hard for Amber to not have Bobby living with her most of the time. If she has to express her pain as anger with us and this is something she has to do to survive, it's OK with me.
I will be prepared to be polite, kind, patient and calm when I must interact with Amber. I will never again behave in a manner that will upset Bobby or set a bad example for him. I will keep in mind why we are interacting with each other and move to that goal.

Pre-Contact Planning

Many situations that cause problems can be avoided by thinking through the meeting or contact you are to have with the other parent before you have to face them.

There are no new arguments. You can describe what will happen before you even go.

Don't fall into that trap again. Know why you are meeting with this person and what you want to accomplish. Then, within reason, don't be diverted from your plan.

Contact Goal Form
Reason for contact: *Taking Bobby to the police station so Amber can pick him up for his spring break in Washington.*
People who will be there: *Amber, Bobby and I.*
Situations I must avoid: *Don't get mad if she won't respond to anything I say.*
People or things that will help make this contact easier: *Being at the police department keeps her from making accusations later. Have Bobby carry his backpack so Amber can't refuse to take it from me.*
Positive affect this will have on my child(ren): *If no one gets upset during the exchange, the children will feel less stress.*

Negotiation

You know this person better than the attorney or mediator. Think about what is really important to this person. Examples would include staying involved in the children's activities and money. Often one parent will maintain an issue as the "one non-negotiable" point. The issue may only be important to the obstinate parent as a weapon.

It will become the "deal breaker" whenever the other parent steps out of line. It is important to defuse this issue as early in the process as possible. Be careful not to give up too much for this non-negotiable point.

When it is obvious that there will be a separation or divorce, it usually takes some time before professionals are involved. You can eliminate many problems by designing some methods of handling what were everyday events. Now responsibilities for the children must be divided between two families rather than one. Address the children's best interests first. It is important to address the needs of each child separately. Then address the parental convenience issues. Offer in writing through a neutral party (a trained counselor, if possible) some methods of:

Time-sharing, including holiday provisions
Emergency notification
Responsibility for religious, educational, medical
Exchange of information
Money arrangements

Be sure to include a travel restriction, which requires both parents' written permission for the children to vacation or move out of state. Considering the size of some states such as Alaska, California, and Texas, the restriction might be the county. If you are able to negotiate this document, it will go a long way in protecting both parents' interests and the children's peace of mind.

Why Cooperate?

You have to decide if you love your children more than you hate the opposition. If you love your children more, then you must cooperate. Your children will suffer much less if you and the opposition cooperate and communicate. If you have an open line of communication, ask the opposition to make a list of what that parent wants regarding the children, and what that parent is willing to let you have.

Say or spell out, "Bearing in mind our children's best interest, what do you want and what are you willing to let me have?"

Offer a list of what you want, as it pertains to the children, and what you are willing to let the other parent have.

Because points of agreement won't be issues, there may be less to negotiate than you think, especially if both parents negotiate each issue with the children's best interest in mind. Experience also teaches us that people and nations behave wisely when they have exhausted all other alternatives.

Why Will the Opposition Cooperate?

Eliminate the negative behaviors of the past, show through word and deed that you are willing to be fair, and you prove that you have the welfare of your children as your goal. Then, it will be easier for the other parent to see there is a better opportunity to get what he or she wants from you than from the courts.

By demonstrating that you are prepared and well armed, the opposition will see that in fact they have exhausted all other alternatives.

Reduce Differences

To make negotiation successful it is important to reduce the obvious differences, because nobody cooperates with anybody who seems to be against them. Some of the easier differences are sensory such as visual and audio, making them very powerful. Powerful because you are synchronizing your behavior to theirs and sending comforting messages without vocalizing. Style of dress, body posture, energy level and volume of voice. If the opposition comes from work in a uniform, it would be better not to show up in three-piece suit type attire. If their speech patterns are quiet and deliberate, adopt that level of volume and slow down when you speak.

State your positive intent. Message could be: "We are all here to make the weekend and holiday exchange easier on Molly and Matthew."

Aim to Negotiate, Not to Win

You will be disappointed if you expect to "win" on every issue. Repress the desire to get this negotiation completed. The person anxious to settle things so they can go on with a new life negotiates with a severe disadvantage. That person is likely to make many concessions they would not ordinarily make. Rarely is either side happy about every negotiated point. Even the fairest negotiation leaves both sides somewhat dissatisfied.

- Start new.
- Aim to be giving, honest, generous, forgiving, committed, polite, clear, respectful, sincere, accepting.
- Discuss one subject at a time. Example: Bedtime on school nights.
- Accept that what the opposition says it will do, it will do. Example: The other parent has never dropped your children off on time. Accept the statement, "I will have the children home by 7:00 p.m. every Sunday night."
- Express how you feel; do not make accusations. Example of poor communication: "You never let the kids call me when they are with you." Example of good communication: "Please remind the kids to call me collect every two or three days. I really miss them."
- Do not bring up old problems or incidents that will start an argument. Example of poor communication". "You never reminded the kids to call me when you took them to Florida for vacation." Point: Stay focused on the topic at hand. Example of good communication: "I will really try to remind them to call."
- Be willing to go the distance in patience and understanding for the peace of mind and sense of order this will help your children establish.
- Offer only positive constructive ideas.
- Do not indulge in name-calling. Example of poor communication: "You are always such a jerk about his friends coming over to play." Example of good communication: "Is there a time when his friends can come over that will not make problems for you?"
- It doesn't matter how you see the truth or what the truth is. The other person's perception is what is real to that person.
- When you are negotiating, give the other parent something <u>that</u> <u>parent</u> values. Do not decide what the other parent needs and offer that. Find out what the opposition <u>wants</u> and make it available.
- Be aware of the problems the other parent feels you cause.
- Attempt to accomplish the things you need to without causing the other parent anxiety and ask the other parent to do the same.

- If you meet with a great deal of hostility at first, stay calm. Emotions the other parent is experiencing will cycle up and down. You may also be receiving the anger from situations unrelated to you or this custody matter.
- If you meet with a great deal of hostility, stay calm. Everyone's emotions will cycle up and down. Both sides may also feel stress or anger from situations unrelated to this custody matter.
- Pay attention to any changes in the thinking or cooperation techniques of the opposition.
- If necessary be willing (but not overly eager) to change your strategy and methods to get the results you desire.

Overcoming Obstacles

K.I.S.S. means "Keep It Simple Stupid."

1. You are aware of the situations that cause the opposition concern. Don't cause those situations. It will only slow the process.

2. There are no new arguments in this relationship. Don't start any of the old arguments. They are not important.

3. You are aware of the "standard" statements that provoke arguments and the automatic answers the opposition will give that usually bring any discussion to an end. If necessary, make a list of the statements and incidents that cause problems. Design some new answers and solutions that the opposition will be able to accept.

4. Avoid topics that cause problems until you find answers the other parent will be able to accept. You are doing this for your children.

5. If a topic stops the discussion dead, change the focus to a more workable topic.

Discover Hidden Agendas

Agenda: A conscious or unconscious plan that may or may not be formally contrived to ensure the results desired by an individual.

The more people involved in the negotiation the more personal agendas there are with, which you have to deal. Even the people you count on for support may have hidden agendas.

The agendas of others will also affect what is happening with the other parent, although there may be no recognition of agendas hidden or otherwise.

- Your significant other may want you to win custody, feeling it will help you be ready to settle down and remarry.
- A co-worker of yours is devoted to your effort because, if you become a full-time parent, your job position will become available.
- Your best friend and you are both romantically interested in someone who has no interest in children, and your winning custody would eliminate you from the competition.
- Your parents may want to maintain contact with the children and/or the other parent.
- One of your troops has an old axe to grind with the other parent and is helping you to cause that person some heartache.
- You may just be the "Cause Of The Month" for a person with nothing better to do.

If their agenda is not identical to yours, but accomplishes what you want, their hidden agenda should be fine with you. As you work with others listen to what they are really saying. Constantly revise your evaluation of why they are involved in this conflict, if their actions support their words, and if your goals still serve their needs. When what you want no longer serves their needs, your usefulness to them is greatly diminished and so may be the support that they give you or you may expect from them be diminished.

Children's Agenda

When children under ten years of age are involved, you must consider the situation and be responsive to their needs. Older children may have endured a great deal of pain that you are not aware of. They may feel if they don't take care of their own needs no one will. Children who are articulate and aware of the situation can and will tell you how they feel and what they need. It is important to listen to their concerns without expressing or imposing your desires on them. The child's needs cannot be sacrificed to protect your feelings. Make an effort to see your desires and the child's need as the separate issues they are. If your desires and needs are in direct opposition to your child's, it will be necessary to reevaluate the situation with an uninvolved neutral professional.

Concerns that Affect Children's Agendas

1. Make sure the parent I am with now does not get angry with me.
2. Do not cause either parent any pain.
3. Maintain contact with both parents.
4. Have assurance that they may give love and get love from both parents.
5. Know who will take care of child if something happens to the parents.
6. Maintain contact with extended family.
7. Know they will have a safe secure place to live.
8. Know what will be happening in their lives in the future.
9. Know their possessions will be safe in the children's absence.
10. Maintain contact with neighborhood and school friends.
11. Have consistency in education and religious training.
12. Be assured they are not responsible for the conflict of their parents.

Children also have hidden agendas. Agendas will change as the custody case drags on and the children tend to become alternately victims and manipulators of their parents. When adults use children as pawns in a custody battle, the children parrot an adult's agenda. Psychologists, mediators and guardian ad litems watch for indications of parental propaganda and specifically alienation messages when they speak with children and explore the children's agendas.

Conflict

A relationship should not be destroyed by a difference in opinion. Conflict should not be seen as an insurmountable obstacle, but as an opportunity. See the positive aspects of conflict as both parents express concern for the children's welfare. Pick your battles. Some issues affect your children's welfare more than others do. Let them win on the points that cause you no uneasiness. Concentrate on the important points. If you demonstrate a willingness to work things out, eventually the opposition may become more reasonable.

Methods of Thinking

Analytical

Is a method whereby each situation is dissected, dividing a complex whole into its constituent parts in order to view each part more clearly. This kind of thinker is likely to consider all facts presented. This type of thinker would say, "What does it mean, bottom line?" This person wants to be seen as serious, focused and self-controlled. They see things as right or wrong. In conflict the analytical thinker will become unbearably unemotional.

Emotional

Is a method governed by the emotional state of the person at the time. These thinkers are not likely to consider facts that do not support their position. This type of thinker would say, "What does it mean to me?" This person wants to be seen as fair, sensitive, sympathetic, and considerate. This person sees things as fair or unfair. In conflict the emotional thinker will become fearful and overly emotional.

Linear

Is a method whereby the person follows a predetermined line of reasoning. These people may not let facts sway them from the direction, which they have chosen to follow. This type of thinker would say, "Where is this leading?" This person wants to be seen as sensible, methodical and exacting. This person sees things as right or wrong. In conflict the linear thinker will become obsessed with attempting to back-track to see where the breakdown in the process occurred.

Abstract

Abstract thinking uses conceptual rather than concrete existence for decision making. This kind of thinker may or may not consider all facts presented. This type of thinker would say, "What is the result?"

This person wants to be seen as innovative and impressive.

This person sees things as right or wrong. In conflict the abstract thinker may blame others for the problem.

Mediative

Avoids making decisions without a great deal of thought. This kind of thinker is likely to consider all facts presented. This type of thinker would say, "What are the other options?" This person wants to be seen as insightful and involved. This person sees things as fair or unfair. In conflict the medative thinker will become disconnected and unemotional.

Calculative

Reasoning will determine the value, cost, time and effect of any decision. This kind of thinker is likely to consider all facts presented. This type of thinker would say, "What do I have to do to get it?" This person sees things as right or wrong. This type of person wants to be seen as decisive and nonconforming. In conflict the calculative thinker will become controlling.

Rational

Employs reasoning to approach decisions or problems. This kind of thinker is likely to consider all facts presented. This type of thinker would say, "What does it do?" This person wants to be seen as stable and direct. This person sees things as appropriate or inappropriate. In conflict the rational thinker will become angry when dealing with emotional people.

Secular Humanism

If you decide where your support should be placed based on secular humanism ethics, each issue may be viewed in many shades of gray. This is because the right or wrong of any particular act is consequence oriented. Moral reference points are floating, not fixed.

Individual's Moral Obligation

The individual's moral obligation is limited to taking the best course of action "for him or her" while taking into account all of the circumstances. The obligation to obey any law becomes an empty concept unless it directly adds to the consequences. Diversity abounds with each individual. These individuals feel the laws should fit their personal needs. Sometimes these people find similarly minded persons. The group citing its uniqueness may agitate for special privileges. These individuals or groups feel that laws, rules, and regulations are to be obeyed only if the results will benefit them.

The laws are unable to foresee all of the consequences of any action and therefore may seem unbending to some. Judges and juries are sometimes able to see why an individual acted as he did, but are uncomfortable with this kind of evaluation of situations. Testimony with this bias is not easily understood and accepted. It often makes the person who justifies their actions with secular humanism ethics look self-serving. There may be only a difference in how each of you processes the information given rather than a conscious effort to be uncooperative. The best tool for resolving conflict is for each parent to pose this question to any proposal that they are not pleased with: "Is that what is best for (put in the children's names here)?"

Changing Strategies

Get a solid understanding of your ultimate goal and tactics you have used in the past. Once you become aware of the approach the opposition is using, choose the most positive technique available. You may find that the opposition is more willing to cooperate than you expected. If you feel it is necessary to change plan, do so after a great deal of thought. Feeling a constant need to change your strategy indicates you are not committed to your goal and will yield no positive results. Strategy is a long-term plan, not a whim. It is counterproductive to choose what looks like the most damaging tactics to the opposition, rather than the most helpful for the long-term.

Observers, professional or not, will easily identify negative strategies even if they are sugar coated.

1. Do not start with your best offer.
2. Start the negotiation where the opposition thinks you will. It is easier on their nerves, and you will not lose as much.
3. Work toward your best offer.

Not Really the Same

During negotiation it is important to know these terms and understand that they usually involve a third party and are not interchangeable:

Arbitrate: to decide something in dispute on merit and evidence without the mutual agreement of the disputing parties

Conciliate: to pacify anger or agitation, may make a recommendation without the mutual agreement of the disputing parties

Mediate: to come between disagreeing elements, with the mutual agreement of the disputing parties

Negotiate: to bring about mutual agreement of the disputing parties

Using a Professional to Negotiate

There is no solid rule of procedure. Professionals have several formats they adapt to the person's problems and place for the negotiation. Sometimes the parties (the parents or the parents alone and their attorneys) all meet in one room with the professional. Other times the professional shuttles between the angry participants. Still, other professionals meet with the parents separately for private appointments.

Mediators

Many problems can be defused by using a professional mediator. You should choose a mediator that is a mental health professional with formal training and experience in conflict resolution and family court matters. The mediator guides the participants through the decision-making process, but does not make any decisions for the participants. The outcome of the mediation remains completely in the hands of the participants.

Parties who wish to come to a settlement, may select a mediator or the court may appoint one. Private mediators seem to be less intrusive than those appointed by the court. Professionals working for the state seem to be overburdened and burned out. The Professionals investigate in detail the environments and people influencing the welfare of your children. A court appointed professional may be asked by the court to offer an opinion as to the placement of the children and visitation.

Attorneys

Attorneys experienced in the process of four-way mediation can give you the flexibility of the mediator and the information about your responsibilities as well as the protection of your rights. An attorney's expertise in conflict resolution and mediation can pave the way.

You and your attorney should understand what you want and what you are willing to give up before you meet with the opposition. Since you are paying your attorney to be present, let the professional do the talking. At the proper moment let your attorney "give away" the points you and your attorney have decided to concede.

The outcome of the mediation can be the final document presented to the court.

Do not use your attorney for negotiation if this person is combative or inexperienced in conflict resolution. Proof of conflict resolution training may properly be requested.

One parent reported that a $1,000.00 bonus per attorney helped encourage a speedy win-win settlement.

Three Reasons to Negotiate

There are only three reasons for negotiation - **communicating** the results of actions taken; **creating** planned action to eliminate future strife; or **deciding** among alternative actions. If you're at a meeting with some other purpose, you're wasting time. No negotiation should go beyond the scheduled time. If you get bogged down on a point, postpone it for a future meeting.

Praise should be earnest and public. The person running the negotiation should squelch any criticism.

Right Place and Time to Negotiate

Choose a quiet, neutral place for the meeting that may be adapted for either a one-or-two room format. Check out the room to be used for the negotiation in advance. It is important to eliminate any animosity that jockeying for position could cause when the parties enter.

It is crucial to note that a person who feels at a disadvantage or in a subordinate position will be less inclined to negotiate in good faith. The assurance of a level playing field will encourage a feeling of cooperativeness. Make sure all chairs are the same (with or without arms), use a round table or eliminate chairs at the head and foot of an oblong or rectangular table. To make negotiating work, you have to watch the other person as well as listen to the words. Nonverbal communication of what we really feel about the situation is as automatic as is the response of others to that communication. Ignoring what the other person is telling you will not improve the situation. Watching for defensive, as well as accepting, behaviors can speed the process.

Preparation

Once the other parent has agreed to negotiate, and in advance of the meeting, read and give a copy of the Outline for Discussion Form, Assumptions, Parent to Parent Guidelines, Child's Bill of Rights and The Parent's Bill of Rights to the other parent. Indicate your willingness to abide by any statements listed by initialing them. Understand your opposition and know what is important to that person.

Assumptions

These assumptions are based on the premise that:

1. Both parents are emotionally and morally fit.
2. Both parents desire to have an ongoing relationship with the children.
3. Both parents are willing and able to carry out the childcare plan.
4. Both parents prefer a negotiated solution to a court-imposed solution.
5. Both parents feel it is in the children's best interest for each parent to have frequent, meaningful, and continuing access to them.
6. Both parents feel that frequent, meaningful, and continuing access to the children offers them a sense of significance. "I am a person. I am important and I count."
7. Both parents feel that the children need reliability, predictability and consistency from both parents.
8. Both parents feel the children need to be shielded from parental arguments, recriminations, accusations and blame.
9. Nobody should be deprived of financial security.
10. Nobody should profit at the other's expense.
11. If the other parent will not agree to the assumptions, the negotiation will still proceed more quickly and successfully if you start from this frame of mind.
12. The important things are always simple.
13. The simple things are always hard.

Guidelines for Discussion

If, through unforeseeable circumstances, either parent is unable to follow through with the time-sharing arrangements involving the children, that parent will notify the other parent as soon as possible.

The parents agree that the children may accompany either parent for any other occasion as may be mutually agreeable, convenient and in the children's best interests.

Both parents agree that each shall promptly inform the other of any emergency or other significant event, which involves the children.

Both parents agree that when childcare is needed, the other parent will be considered as the care provider of choice for the children for periods exceeding six hours.

Neither parent shall change the children's residence from the state, or travel with the children outside the state, for longer than seven days without prior written consent of the other parent or order of the court.

Each parent agrees to respect the other's parenting style, privacy and authority in order to provide a reasonable degree of consistency in the children's upbringing.

If major changes arise, which make the present childcare plan no longer feasible, the parents shall agree to renegotiate their plan with a conciliation services counselor or private mediator prior to any changes taking place, or any court actions being initiated.

Each parent agrees to encourage love and respect between the children and the other parent, and neither shall do anything, which may knowingly hamper the other's parent-child relationship. Agree to solve the problem, to tell the truth, accept the other parent's version of an event as another view, not a lie, not to interrupt, and not to call names.

How to Negotiate

If you don't have the benefit of a professional to guide the process, work it through, one step at a time. Be sure to make and bring copies of all the forms in case the other parent did not get the originals or forgot them.

After you complete your Outline for Discussion Form, request an appointment time to meet with the other parent to compare the forms. You may find there is more you agree on than you disagree on.

- A very carefully defined residency and visitation agreement can solve many problems before they arise.
- Handle the needs of each child separately.
- There is no one plan that will work for every situation. These are good guidelines to start with. If you and the opposition cannot work things out in a reasonable manner, the court will.
- Choose a time of day when you will both feel rested.
- Pick a place where the two of you can talk without help from outside influences that one or both of you may feel are hostile.
- Do the easy parts first. Any point that slows things down should be put aside for later in the day or another time.
- Once a point is agreed upon, do not rehash it.
- Write every point on which you agree in detail.
- Be specific about what you are saying; avoid generalities.
- When there is disagreement, offer a compromise.
- If necessary, meet again to finish. It may take several appointments. If you come to an impasse, have the final meeting with a professional mediator.

Is the Negotiation Going Well?

When things are going well, you will see some readiness, compromise, reassurance, acceptance and cooperation. These are identified by obvious orientation toward action gestures, such as hands on hips, leaning forward with forearms on thighs, sitting on edge of chair, or other positions.

- Head cocked or tilted slightly to one side while listening.
- Jackets and sweaters being unbuttoned or coming off
- Both sides uncross arms and legs
- Both sides are leaning forward in a non-confrontational manner
- They begin to make statements like: "Will our holiday start on the first or the thirty-first?" "Which weekend will be mine?" "I need this date changed because of my job."
- One or both hands are on side or under face or head while leaning forward.
- Opposition moves closer to the table.
- One of the people on the opposition begins to support some of the points you have offered.

Outline for Discussion Form

I, _ *Randall Long* _____, would like to propose these guidelines for the care and responsibility of Bobby Long to Establish Physical Residence Of Child

Weekday Schedule *I will pick up Bobby from Amber at 6:00 a.m. Amber will pick Bobby up from me when she gets off work.*

Weekend Schedule *We will alternate weekends*

Summer Months *Same as winter*

Summer Vacation *Either parent may take Bobby for their vacation*

Travel Arrangements __ *The parent who is to have Bobby will be responsible for picking him up if it is for visitation. For vacation the person taking Bobby on vacation will be responsible for travel arrangements. The vacationing parent will let the other parent know how to contact them in the case of emergency.*

Professional Day Care or Parent Care

During the normal schedule when a parent must rely on someone else to take care of the child(ren) for more than three hours less than twice in a 30-day period, a relative or professional day-care or caregiver may be used.

During the normal schedule when a parent must rely on someone else to take care of the child(ren) for more than three hours more than twice in a 30-day period, the non-scheduled parent may have the opportunity to care for the child(ren). *I agree with the statement above. RL*

Holiday Schedule

Holiday Schedule takes priority over regular schedule.

"Day" means from 8 a.m. To 8 p.m. "Night" means 8 p.m. To 8 a.m.

"Shared Day" means 8 a.m. To 1 p.m. And 1 p.m. To 8 p.m.

"Even" means even-numbered years, like 1998. "Odd" means odd-numbered years, like 1999.

"Airline flights" are to be as close to noon departure as possible. Parent who is to have time with the child is responsible for pick up and transportation of child. Odd years: Morning with Dad, afternoons with Mom

Child's Birthday Even years: *Morning with Mom, afternoons with Dad*

Easter *Same as Birthday*

Mother's Day *All day with Mom, Amber Jones*

Mother's Birthday *All day with Mom, Amber Jones*

Father's Day *All day with Dad, Randall Long*

Father's Birthday *All day with Dad, Randall Long*

July 4th *Same as Birthday*Thanksgiving *Same as Birthday*

Christmas Eve *Same as Birthday*Christmas Day *Same as Birthday*

Some of these categories may require that one person make a decision at the time a situation arises. Choose the best solution for most of the time. Put your initial next to that option, or both parents sign if it is a joint effort.

Educational Arrangements

Parents will make major educational decisions together. [*X*] Yes [ ] No or ____________________ will make all educational decisions.

Social Activities

During School

After School

Evening

Weekend

Medical and Dental Arrangements

Both parents will authorize emergency treatment by the parent who has the child at the time. Parents will make major medical decisions together. Parents will keep each other informed as to names, addresses and telephone numbers of all health care providers.

Each parent will be notified of emergency medical care for child by the other parent within _2_ hours of any event that requires more than $250.00 of medical treatment.

Insurance will be covered by *Randall Long*

Medical costs will be covered by *Randall Long's insurance*

Dental costs will be covered by *Randall Long's insurance*

Any Medical or Dental costs not covered by insurance will be paid by *50% by each parent within 120 days of the billing*

Monetary Arrangements

School clothes will be provided by *Randall Long, Amber Jones when willing or able*

Play clothes will be provided by *Randall Long, Amber Jones when able*

Special uniforms or outfits will be provided by *Randall Long, Amber Jones*

Food will be provided for, or food expenses will be paid by *Randall Long, Amber Jones when willing or able*

School supplies, books, photos, yearbooks and expenses will be provided by *Randall Long, Amber Jones when willing or able*

Spending money *Randall Long, Amber Jones when willing or able*

Money for extra activities will be supplied by *Randall Long, Amber Jones when willing or able*

Additional Considerations

Neither parent may take Bobby out of Arizona without written permission of the other parent as long as both parents reside there.

Bobby's medical care, when he is in Arizona, will be taken care of by his pediatrician only, not by the county medical center.

We enter these negotiations without prejudice and for settlement purposes only. This form may not be introduced into any court or administrative proceeding without the written permission of both parties.

We will make every effort for initial negotiations to take place within _5_ days.

Chapter 5: Friend or Enemy?

A negotiated peace or all-out war --- it's not a decision to make in a hurry. Sometimes the decision is made for you. In any case, it is important that you stop causing yourself problems. Here is the best way to start. Contested custody decisions are rarely settled in less than one year. Your past and present life will be under closer scrutiny than a presidential candidate's. Your attorney will tell you that most people do not lose custody because they are bad people or parents. Most lose custody because they have caused themselves to look callous, flaky, vindictive, uncooperative, and/or easily driven to hysterics.

This chapter will prepare you for the calm control you need to feel, as well as exhibit. In any war, it is important to begin to think and behave like a winner. Decide to be in charge. Be *proactive* by making short-term (today and this week) and long-term (six, twelve, or eighteen month) plans. Because the opposition does not have this manual, the opposition will be at a great disadvantage by responding in a *reactive* posture to situations on a moment by moment basis. Make words work for you rather than against you. Be aware of what you say and whom you say it to. Know who can hurt you by trying to help. See everyone as someone's soldier. Learn to differentiate worthwhile information from information calculated to cause you harm. Let the winds of war blow around you in all their fury while you stand firm and keep your eye on the prize.

Make Words Work for You

More often than not, it's not what you say, but how you say it that conveys the message. The way you express yourself is very important. You will be communicating with mediators, judges, attorneys, and other people with control over decisions affecting the rest of your life.

Using proper English is not the most important consideration in communication. Sometimes you will find it necessary to express anger, concern, pain, fear, disappointment and other emotions. Be aware of your tone. It is important to say what you feel without appearing bitter, vindictive, condemnatory, dangerous, or out of control.

If you use socially accepted wording, there will be less chance for you to slip when you are upset or caught off guard. You will find that using less acidic wording helps you cool heated and potentially dangerous situations, giving you the upper hand. The person in control can speak quietly and powerfully. Hostile attitudes will work against you, instead of against your target. Also, consider the impact of the language to which your children are exposed.

It is worth your time to learn to avoid offensive, aggressive wording. The importance of your children's future intensifies everything you feel -- most notably, the pain, panic and fear. Learn to express these emotions in an acceptable manner. It is impossible not to feel the emotions with all the raw edges and damage they cause, but the satisfaction or momentary relief you gain from using abusive language will cost you too much.

Learn to make words work for you. For example, if you want to offer to pay for the installation and monthly charges for telephone service, so that you may have contact with your children, carefully choose words that will not demean or embarrass the other parent.

If the opposition says "no" to a reasonably worded request, the opposition has demonstrated an attitude that is unreasonable and uncooperative. If the opposition says "yes," you all win.

It's Your Army; Impose Censorship

Even in wars fought by countries, much of the ammunition fired at the enemy is words. Once real bullets are fired and hit or miss their mark, they are finished. In this war your words and deeds are ammunition. Unlike bullets, they can be fired back at you, not once, but many times. Do not arm your enemy with ammunition that can kill your case.

Controlling how you voice your feelings and needs is only one part of your responsibility. You are responsible for how your army communicates with the opposition. Insist on reviewing all correspondence that is created by your troops, including your attorney's, before it is sent.

Communication between attorneys should be monitored, but with a minimum of interference. You are not qualified to dictate the legal verbiage, but you can and should influence the tone of the correspondence.

Some attorneys resist this close observation. Important as it is to not offend the general of your army, you are still the Commander-in-Chief. You are also paying the costs and living with the results of these exercises.

Your long-term relationship with the other side gives you insight into the person most influenced by the communication. Attempt to put yourself in the opposition's place when he or she receives the information or material you are sending. Prepare the correspondence in a manner that will allow this person to respond the way you want.

Loose Lips Sink Ships

"Loose Lips Sink Ships" was a World War II warning to our people on the home front, as well as to our soldiers, to avoid leaking information on troop strength, artillery and ship location, supply availability and future plans.

1. Do not talk just to hear your own voice.

2. Do not talk to a kind stranger who shows an interest in your problems and has a few minutes.

3. Do not talk to old friends to bring them up-to-date on what has been going on in your life.

Vital information will eventually fall into the hands of the Enemy, the Enemy is anyone who does not share your goal. Also, be careful of what you say in front of the children --- they will repeat what they hear.

4. Steer clear of horror stories. Listening politely to awful things other parents have endured can be upsetting. The person speaking may feel they are warning you. In fact rather than helping you be prepared the stories may cause you additional stress. A nice way to stop the talker may be to just say, "I have heard all the horror stories. Please spare me from the negative information."

Security Breach

There are other potential leaks, such as employees of the professionals you have hired and your e-mail. I'm mentioning them, because most people who use a service or a computer think of the outside people or the machine to be the most likely hole. Check all possible leaks, including the possibility of you talking in your sleep. Never forget anything when researching security-breaches.

If You Disregard This Advice

If you disregard this advice, you have just shot yourself in the foot. If you have never had this experience...

It hurts like Hell. You feel stupid. And, you have positively identified yourself to the world as an idiot.

"Loose Lips Sink Ships." Its meaning is as relevant in a child custody war today as it was in World War II. **Do not do your thinking out loud.** Learn to keep your own counsel.

For example: Do not discuss your decision to use a private detective or discuss information that has developed as the investigation progresses. Such decisions are not appropriate topics for casual conversation. This is your private life. Always be aware to whom you are speaking and of what you are talking. Decide the worst possible thing this person could do with this information. If you are not prepared for the worst to happen, do not relate information that could damage your case.

Communication Skills Include Knowing When Not to Talk.

Fear and Communication

The way in which you communicate is often influenced by whom you are attempting to communicate with and your history with that person. The difference is so apparent that someone listening to you speak on the telephone can tell with whom you are talking, without being able to hear the other person on the line. As an example, you may sound excited talking to your best friend, patient when listening to your grandmother and defensive when listening to someone attempting to collect money you don't feel they deserve.

While it is easy to see why we can be happily excited or patient, it is much harder to understand why fear and anger come on so quickly. To our astonishment, even situations we thought we were prepared for can inflict huge amounts of stress that we display as fear and anger. Our history with the person is the key. Relationships between people who feel equal may not last longer than relationships between partners that feel unequal, but do tend to end with less hostility. The level of hostility between people who feel victimized and/or used can eliminate any dialogue, even if it would benefit both parties.

Unequal relationships form for many reasons. Often it serves both parties to allow a person who is accustomed to, or likes, confrontation to be in control, and a person willing to follow, to stand back and still have his or her needs met. As the association evolves, the growth of one or both of the parties may cause discontent with the established pattern. A generalization that could apply would be that the town bully is feared. The people the town bully protects have some power because of that fear.

An assertive personality might be tired of fighting battles created by others. Sometimes there is only an outward appearance of one member being the tough one and the other being the nice one. The publicly tough one, may be tired of outwardly fighting the battles for two in the public eye, when in fact that person feels manipulated by a needy, or passively aggressive personality. On the other hand, a strong personality may desire even more control.

The non-assertive personality may feel subjected to the same tactics used on everyone else. With time, the non-assertive personality becomes unwilling to accept the control that once felt like safety. The bully in our example manipulates outsiders and the people the bully is protecting because that is what a bully does. Conversely, a non-assertive personality may have learned from watching the assertive personality and is now comfortable fighting his or her own battles.

The problems arise when one party wants to change things and the other party is unwilling to let go. This can happen when both parties are unhappy with the relationship, but one would rather be unhappy and have things remain the same rather than face the prospect of change. Growth that causes you to change your position as a leader or follower can cause hostility in the other person. Hostility from the other person can affect your attitude and cause you to react in non-productive ways.

An aggressive, sarcastic or fearful attitude can damage your attempts to get the opposition to work with you to accomplish something for your children. Learning to be assertive rather than aggressive is important. If you feel intimidated you may come off in a defensive manner that will look aggressive.

Awareness of how you communicate and why is the first step. If the manner in which you communicate is contributing to negative results, it is in your best interest to change your behavior.

Successfully changing the way you communicate takes effort.

Becoming verbally fit is no different than becoming physically fit. It takes recognition of where you are now, commitment to change and practice. Improving your ability to communicate assertively will become easier with practice.

Assertive Communication Evaluation

1. The opposition finds it easy to take advantage of me. True False
2. I avoid expressing my dissatisfaction to avoid confrontation. True False
3. The opposition makes jokes at my expense and pretend they are kidding. True False
4. The opposition is always putting me down. True False
5. I don't say what I really feel just to keep the peace. True False
6. I don't trust anything the opposition says, even if it's nice. True False
7. The opposition answers statements I make as if I'm asking permission or a question. True False
8. I fold my arms across my chest and look down at the floor when I speak to the opposition. True False
9. To avoid confrontation, I apologize for, or disclaim my own statements. True False
10. I feel threatened or guilty when I say no to the opposition's requests. True False
11. I tell the opposition too much and give too many details when I explain something. True False
12. The opposition pressures me into making snap decisions. True False
13. I often lose my courage at the last moment and don't say what I planned to say. True False
14. I respond defensively to everything. True False
15. I am nervous about dealing with the opposition because I am rarely successful. True False
16. I feel I must give excuses when I say no. True False
17. I usually say yes when I want to say no. True False
18. I respond defensively because I don't have time to choose my words. True False
19. I feel uncomfortable when taking credit for my accomplishments. True False
20. I accept what I'm offered even when it's not what I wanted or expected. True False
21. I am more reluctant to speak up in this custody situation. True False
22. I buffer my words with, "My lawyer (boyfriend, girlfriend, father, wife, husband, the judge) says..." to give my words more credibility. True False
23. I let them inconvenience me to avoid conflict. True False
24. I am forced to follow through with decisions I've made even when I don't feel good about them. True False
25. I feel ganged-up-on even if there is only one of the opposition present. True False
26. The opposition scrutinizes every decision I make. True False

Now you're ready to take a look at your responses.

If you did not answer true to any of the statements, you may want to see if you aren't pushing the other parent too hard. If you are walking all over the other parent and happen to be getting away with it, you may be sorry later. Insisting on a total win in every situation for your side, can become a habit. Evaluators and psychologists will look upon your relentless need for victory negatively.

If you answered true to a few of the statements, you are probably attempting to work with the opposition and are very uncomfortable. Giving in is uncomfortable, but it demonstrates your willingness to work things out and exercises your desire to have your children be the real winners.

If you answered true to most or all of the statements, you need to take some assertiveness training and work on your self-esteem. Your children learn primarily by watching how you deal with others. If your children see you bullied and taken advantage of, they will either think that is the proper way for them to behave or adopt your behaviors for handling difficult situations. If your behavior is not serving you well, it will not serve your children well either. For yourself and for your children, learn to deal with others fairly while taking good care of yourself.

Dealing with Fear

Dealing with fear is an important part of gaining and maintaining control. As you look back on your life, you will see that most of the trouble you worried about, never happened. Do this exercise when you think everything is hopeless. List the cause of your pessimism on a sheet of paper; next to each cause, document the evidence that it is real and not imagined. For each real cause, write down at least one way to counteract it.

News Flash Junkies

If you have been free with information and updates on your case up to this point, it will be difficult to wean your fan club from the news-flash syndrome. As you have learned, not everyone has your best interests at heart. As you become more selective about what information goes out, and where, you will notice a change of attitude in questionable friends. Beware of people pumping for information instead of understanding your restraint. The easiest way to divert attention from your private matters is to ask about matters important in their lives. Most people are not nearly as interested in what you have to say as they are in what they want to say. Ask them a question about their lives.

Safe Answers

Because you can't prepare for every conversation or discern why a question is being asked, instantaneously having a catalogue of safe answers ready is a powerful tool. Listed below are some common questions you will face on a daily basis and suggestions for safe answers. Having safe answers ready also gives you a feeling of control.

Q. How are things going with the custody case?

- *A.* Well, you know how it is when the attorneys get started on it. You are never sure where things stand.
- *A.* I don't really know. We are just waiting for the court to make the decisions.
- *A.* Same as always. Hurry up and wait.
- *A.* Let's talk about something less stressful. How are things going for you?

Q. I heard you gave your children away. Why?

- *A.* What do you mean by that?
- *A.* Why do you want to know?
- *A.* My children have two parents and we are the best qualified to decide what is best for our children.

Q. Why don't your children live with you?

- *A.* Why do you want to know?
- *A.* We all decided the children are where they need to be.
- *A.* I am not the one who gets to decide where the children live and I do not wish to discuss it any further.

Q. Why don't you let me get rid of the other side for you?

- *A.* No, the other side would just come back to haunt me for the rest of my life.
- *A.* Don't even kid like that. This is too important.
- *A.* I pray that nothing happens to them. I would get the blame if an airplane fell on them.
- *A.* Don't be so angry. It doesn't do any of us any good.
- *A.* What have you been doing with your time?

Q. Are you going to fight for custody of your children?

- *A.* I will do what's best for my children. Thank you for your concern. I will call you if I wish to discuss it further.
- *A.* That, as well as other questions about my children, are not welcome at this time.

Q. Are they still giving you problems with the baby?

- *A.* Things have been pretty quiet for a long time now.
- *A.* I am sure things will work out the way they are supposed to.

A. We are all working to make this time as easy as possible.

A. Please don't ask about the case every time you see me. I appreciate your concern, but it wears me out.

Q. What is going on now?

A. Nothing new.

A. I'll let you know if anything interesting happens.

A. Not much. Do you have any plans for the summer?

Q. How can I help you?

A. Pray.

A. Knowing you are there helps.

A. There is nothing anyone can do for now.

A. You are the person I get to talk to about other things. That would help me the most.

Friendly Fire

Friendly fire is just as deadly as enemy fire. Being shot or bombed by one's own troops or allies has cost many lives as well as battles. The enemy is easier to watch than someone you consider a friend trying to help.

Now is the time to identify family and well-wishers who could cause problems. This emotional time requires you to use your head. If someone could not be trusted to keep a confidence in the past, don't trust that person to keep a confidence now. Remember, anyone may be envious or hold an old grudge against you. Don't set that knowledge aside now.

This does not mean you should isolate yourself and become suspicious of everyone. Be aware. Limiting the number of confidants you have will eliminate the need for damage control later.

People Who Cause Damage

Anyone with information about your case or power to control your case can cause damage. It may or may not be intentional, this is who and why they can cause problems. By maintaining who has what information you can control where it goes. If you gain and maintain firm and reasonable control of your case you can limit short-term problems and long-term damage.

A person trying to stay friends with both parties may decide to share information in the interest of fairness.

A family member or witness with too much information may discuss the case with a longtime friend or a friend who is tied to the other family.

Some people will talk to anyone. Do not let your custody case become the weekly soap opera at the hair styling salon or health club.

Some people talk to feel important. You might be able to identify these people by their eagerness to tell you everything they know about what the other people are doing, while pumping you for details about your case. You may be tempted to use this type of person to spread mis-information. Avoid this temptation. This practice will backfire.

Your attorney may be hesitant to offend or anger the judge because the attorney may have to face that judge in another case. Question your attorney's reluctance to respectfully challenge any valid point of law or procedure. The attorney's actions must reflect your best interest, not the attorney's.

A professional investigator, psychologist or expert you have hired who will not be able to give credible testimony or can be discredited by the other side can damage your case. Investigate the background of all witnesses and credentials of the professionals.

Some people enjoy stirring up trouble, to see what will happen. They do not care, or may not be aware of, how much damage their actions can cause.

Any person advising you to, or offering to, act in socially unacceptable, vindictive or illegal ways against the opposition can cause you damage.

A friend or acquaintance who has agreed to testify on your behalf, who has been made aware of confidential information you intend to use, can decide not to testify or may even change sides.

Any acquaintance who has damaging data, or is willing to fabricate or embellish negative information about you, may be willing to testify against you. Make sure you fill out a data sheet on anyone who might become important.

A friend who will do <u>anything</u> to help you may do more damage than good. Discourage your friends from acting on their own.

People who decide to do something they think will help your case or avenge some wrong they believe has been done to you can damage your case. Make it very clear to the people who care about you and your children that anything they do may affect your case negatively. Instruct them to talk to you in advance about any action they are considering.

Some persons manifest extreme and often dangerous ardor, fervor or attachment to a person or a cause. (Sometimes referred to as fiends, freaks, maniacs, nuts, extremists or zealots.) A large number of these wild warriors are looking for a cause. These people are fanatics and will do you much more harm than good.

Your children are so young they do not understand that they are being used as a spy by the opposition. Sometimes an older child attempts to "fix" the broken relationship or manage the situation him or herself.

You may be your own worst enemy. You will be amazed at how often you are responsible for pulling friendly fire down on yourself. The incidence of massive fatalities from friendly fire in a conventional war and in a child custody war are well documented. Anticipation of this problem prevents you from causing yourself irreparable damage. The members of your army should be given information on a need-to-know basis only.

Important Questions to Ponder

Is the enemy of my enemy not my friend?

No

Is the friend of my enemy not my enemy?

Yes

Family In-laws and Outlaws

If you have always been able to count on your family for positive support, then cling to the love, strength and power your family can provide. However, not all the members of your family may be loyal, so remain cautious with the information you share. If you have never tested the strength of your family, or historically have only been offered negative criticism, or if some family members have never been on your side, stay away from them. Family can also be friends. Cousins, siblings, uncles, aunts and grandparents who know you and your faults, and still love you, can provide some of the deepest, long-lasting friendships. You will need this kind of support during the times to come.

Your Parents

Your parents find themselves facing the very real threat of losing contact with your children. Because your parents dearly love your children, they may deeply fear losing them. They may also feel great sorrow because of their feelings of helplessness. If they wish, they can be of great help.

Your parents may be able to assist you monetarily by sharing a multi-generational home with you, or with childcare while you're at work. Your parents' emotional stake in their grandchild is great, and their exposure to loss is enormous. However, the laws are for the protection of the child and the parent only --- not the other relatives.

Discourage your parents from discussing what is going on with the opposition's parents. If these people have been good friends for many years, they may attempt to help "you kids" work things out. Impress on them how important it is that you be the one in charge. In most instances, only you have status in a custody battle. Discourage your parents from acting unilaterally. Be patient and listen to their suggestions and worries. Tell your parents you will consider what they have said and always thank them for their thoughts.

Opposition's Parents

The opposition's parents have the same feelings your parents have. If you have had a good association with them and they are close to your children, do what you can reasonably do to maintain the relationship. Children need the extended family. To be on the safe side, do not discuss what is going on in the custody case with them.

Talk about the weather, the children's progress or how their aches and pains are doing.

Above all, do not discuss problems you are having with the opposition. Do not make snide remarks, or voice an opinion about the opposition's life-style, treatment of the children, new relationships, or other subjects that may hurt or alienate your opposition's parents.

Your Children

Sometimes our children become our friends and confidants. Unless a proper perspective is kept on the parent-child relationship, this can be a dangerous pattern for the child's development. This is especially true when the parent is under a great deal of emotional pressure. It takes a great deal of self-control and some practice, but you should avoid confiding or complaining about adult problems to your children.

Children are survivors. They are compelled to tell each parent exactly what that parent needs to hear. Your children may not feel free to express their true emotions to you or the other parent.

Friends, Your Extended Family

Friendships tend to be compartmentalized relationships. It is especially important now. Think of these compartments as an opportunity to leave one emotional environment and enter another. Being able to change emotional environments for a rest is as important as being able to change physical environments.

Far Away Friends

Distant friends are usually from back home or from college days. They only hear your side and wouldn't believe anything else anyway. Even though you don't see them for years at a time, knowing they are there makes everything easier.

Closest Friends

Your best and closest friends will usually be more helpful and less demanding than family. Although they share your pain, they do not feel the fear of losing a part of their family, as your relatives do. Because they have less to lose, they can be more objective and more supportive. Use discretion even when talking to your best friends.

Old Friends

Don't fill in all the details of your life to an old friend that suddenly shows up after a long absence. Former friends are the most dangerous. They don't love you anymore, and they know everything about your past.

On-the-Job Friends

Work friends are the people who can help you concentrate on work challenges and business goals. They can give you a solid diversion from your personal problems. Do not burden them with your trials and tribulations. The information you give them could be used against you in a job evaluation. Keep your job separate from your personal life. This does not work at all if you happen to be employed at the same place where the opposition works.

Buddies and Pals

Buddies are the people you're happy to see and who are happy to see you. These casual friendships tend to be numerous and require the least amount of involvement. In many cases you don't tell them your personal problems, so you have some people to spend time with that won't be asking “heavy” questions. Shooting pool, golfing or shopping with one of these buddies can give you a much-needed emotional break.

Online Friends

Chat rooms and usergroups on the Internet can be good sources of companionship, ideas and information. The problem is that you don’t know with whom you are really communicating.

New Friends

This can be a very lonely time in your life. If you are not “connected” in your community or have never made strong alliances, you may easily be drawn into new associations. New friends are as dangerous as former friends are.

Don't stop making friends, but take more time than usual. Don't talk about any of your personal problems, especially your child custody case. An attentive new friend could be a detective hired by your opposition.

The Agendas of Your Friends

Become aware of other people’s agendas. Consider how the agenda may change and the impact it may have on your efforts.

Friendly Strangers

In the past, families and individuals generally lived and died in the town in which they were born. They kept their problems and private business to themselves.

You did not talk about your problems to your friends or acquaintances. Among many changes in the 1960’s the message was to tell it like it is. The message of the 70’s and 80’s was share your pain, that you will find others and heal together. None of this will help your custody case. Read “No Sniveling or Whining” in Chapter 2.

You can't share your problems with friendly strangers. They may be detectives or unfriendlies sent to cause you real harm.

Know Your Enemy

You have to know your enemy. The more information you are able to gather about the opposition and the people around your children and the opposition the better prepared you are.

Data Sheet

The least powerful soldier in a war is the foot soldier, the private. The private has the ability to wound or kill the most powerful soldier, the general. The opposition's privates are just as important to watch as the opposition's general.

Build a data sheet on all of the enemy troops involved in your case. As you begin to fill out each data sheet, you will be surprised at how little you know about the people you considered lovers and friends. The data sheet provided in this manual is designed so that you will be able to insert new information as it becomes available. As new enemy troops come into play, begin data sheets on them.

New players may include the opposition's family members, not in the picture until now, and any new personal relationships they form. Be alert to where information can be found. Listen to any stories the other side may tell about things that have happened at work or at a party. The opportunities that new relationships offer are sometimes bragged about. Listen carefully with your brain, not your ego.

Your investigator and attorney need more information about the other parent than you would normally have. Filling in as much information as you can on the data sheet enables the professionals to be more productive as they work for you.

The data sheet is a very powerful tool in locating your children in the event of a parental kidnapping. People do not just run away with children. They usually run to a specific place, aided by friends and relatives. The data sheets can give you important leads as to where they might have gone.

Your attorney will want a data sheet on anyone called to testify in order to gauge the strength or necessity of possible testimony.

As you fill in a data sheet, you become aware of how well you know your enemy and just how well your enemy may know you.

Noncombatants

Noncoms rarely exist in a war zone. Family, friends, neighbors, young children, adult children, coworkers, and others, are pressed to, or voluntarily choose sides. The information on these people may be more accessible than information on the other parent. Primarily, this is because the noncoms are not making a concerted attempt to hide information. Therefore, a data sheet on a noncom may help you find vital data.

Data Sheet Form

Data Sheet Form Example

Date: January 5, 1993

Name(s): *James William Jones; Jim Jones; JJ; Gear Jammer Jim. He was born James William Turner, but his mother married Mr. Jones who then adopted James.*

Social Security Number: *111-44-0000*

Address: *902 E. Whitten, Eloy, AZ --- Currently, 1167 N. Madison, Eloy, AZ. 1990 and 2202 Palm Court, Long Beach, CA. 1990*

Date Of Birth: *01/17/62 or 63*

Place Of Birth: *Anderson, IN.*

Driver's License Number: *Unknown*

State Of Issue: *One from Arizona and one from Colorado*

Race: *Caucasian*

Height: *6'1" (usually wears boots) WEIGHT: 180 to 250 lbs.*

Hair Color And Length: *Lt. brown, balding on top, shoulder length*

Eye Color And Vision Correction: *Hazel, no correction. Wears sunglasses*

Build: *Heavy-set and sturdy looking*

Complexion: *Fair*

Facial Hair: *beard and mustache*

Scars, Marks, Tattoos, Moles, Distinguishing Features: *Sacred heart, Harley Davidson, and assorted other tattoos on arms; scar on forehead above right eyebrow.*

Deformities, Handicaps, Limp: *None.*

Religion: *Catholic. Church attendance unknown.*

Military, Branch, When, Where, Rank: *Army, 1980. Dishonorable discharge, served in the Philippines.*

Favorite Foods: *Likes to go out often for pizza or Italian food.*

Unique Clothing: *Always wears black leather jacket, jeans, T-shirt and boots.*
Hobbies: *Collects guns, especially handguns.*
Sports: *Fishing. Likes motorcycle and auto racing on television. Sometimes attends drag races.*
Sports Licenses: *hunting, drawn for elk in 1985. Uses his dad's boat; takes it to the lake several times each summer.*
Business Licenses: *Auto mechanic certificate from American Auto Mechanic Institute.*
Habits: *Smokes, drinks moderately, drug use includes smoking, sniffing, injection and pills.*
Places Frequented: *Mike's Lounge, 4 X 4 Bar, Hog Haven.*
High School Attended, Graduated: *Westown High, AZ. GED in 1980.*
College Attended, Graduated: *No college.*
Arrests Or Convictions: *All in Arizona, Weapons. 1981; Drugs 1982 and 83; Driving without a license 1985; Drugs 1992.*
Vehicles: *Honda Motorcycle in parts; uses parents' truck, #EER-767, AZ.*
Organizations: *Motorcycle Mechanics Institute.*
Politics, Party Registration: *Democrat, unknown if registered.*
Property Owned, Leased, Rented: *Did own a house on West Melvin in Phoenix in 1982.*
Business: *None.*
Employer: *Previously --- AP Fuel, 4001 W. Indian School Rd. Now Granger's Exxon, 5102 W. Glendale Avenue.*
Siblings: *Bob Jones in Tulsa, OK.*
Credit Or Airline Cards: *none.*
Regular Subscriptions To Publications: *Easy Rider, Popular Mechanics.*
Names Of Others Involved In This Case That This Person Knows Or Is Associated With: *Amber, Les Cable, Mike Miller, Don Denison*
Family Or Friends Living In Other States: *Motorcycle club member Colorado. Uncle in Houston, TX. Brother somewhere in Southern California.*
Other States In Which Subject Has Mentioned Wanting To Live: *Served some military time in the Philippines and has talked about Southern California. Mention of letters from guy in Denver, CO.*
Former Spouses' Names, Addresses, and Employers: *He was married to Jenny, who worked at Lenney's. They lived with her parents on Pinchot in Avondale, AZ.*
Former Lovers' Names, Addresses, and Employers: *He lived with Kathy Jenret, who worked at Big Shot Truck Stop. They lived with her girlfriend, Patty, in Tempe, AZ.*
Special Information: *He thinks he can act and was talking about taking acting lessons or getting an agent. When in jail he learned how to "cook" crystal meth.*
Special Knowledge About The Case Or Other People In The Case: *Spends a great deal of time where the principals in this case work and has lived with almost everyone involved in this case at some time or another.*

It is more advantageous to fill out a data sheet on someone and never need it, than to be caught without it if you do need it. Your detective or attorney may see connections between some of the minor players that you haven't noticed and could save you a great deal of grief.

Information and Mis-information

During World War I, there was Matahari. World War II had Tokyo Rose. Viet Nam had its Hanoi Hanna. These people were experts at dispersing a great deal of misinformation -- with a little valid information mixed in to confuse and undermine their enemies' war efforts. These people were very effective.

The names listed all happen to be women because most of the troops were men. The feminine voices that broadcast via radio were very appealing and, therefore, very effective. Watch for the most effective weapon against you in your own war.

On the whole, our society has safeguards set in place to assure that information we get has some validity to it. Misinformation is designed to look true and to deceive.

So, unless you've had experience in the armed services, or are employed in law enforcement, you are not trained to dissect data before accepting it as truthful and reliable.

Now is the time to use all of your resources to gather information for your case. Then, with information you have validated, make definite tactical decisions. Some of the information may shock, anger or frighten you. In most cases it is best not to react openly.

You need more than a "poker face;" you need to control your entire body. Teach your body to show that you are confident. Learn to stand with your arms held easily at your sides. Avoid crossing your arms across your chest. It gives the appearance of a frightened person attempting to protect himself. Look cool, calm, in control, and unconcerned about anything the opposition may say or do. Standing and moving this way will even convince you.

Too much is going on for you to remember everything. Make note of any information that comes your way. Its value may only become apparent weeks or months later. The situations and conditions surrounding you and the opposition will not remain the same.

Every event offers opportunities to discover more data. Weigh it with objectivity.

To consider what is really happening, how you feel about it, and if there is something you can or should do about it, examine the information using the following diagnostic questions:

- Is this new information?
- Who and where did the information come from?
- Whose side has this source chosen to be on?
- Is there any question about this person's loyalty?
- What is the personal agenda of this person?
- What does the information reveal?
- What does the information really say?
- Could this be misinformation?
- Will this information really have any ramification on the situation?
- Is there any actual urgency to dispersing this data?
- The opposition may have intended for me to get this data. Even so, is it good for me to have or use it?
- What would the opposition want me to do with this information if the opposition knew I had it?
- What is the most damage I could cause myself with this data?
- Does it confirm or support other information, or contradict and discredit other information?
- Is there any way to corroborate the truth of this information?
- Is the information or situation in the proper hands?

Once you have analyzed the data and made a determination, it is time to take action, and make out an incident report to fax to your detective and/or attorney, if appropriate. Enter it in your contact log. Only after completing the above steps should you consider taking action. Make sure it is legal, prudent, and carefully thought out.

Do not discuss the information with anyone else to see what he or see may think about the content, validity or what you should do. The wrong people will become aware of what you are doing. Any free advice you get will be worth just what you pay for it now and cost you a great deal later. In most cases, the value of a particular piece of information depends on its source.

Source of Information

Your Attorney

Communicate with your attorney. Keep your foot on solid legal ground by explaining what you want to do and listen to the advice you are paying to receive. Listen to all the attorney's advice even if the instructions are something you don't want to hear.

Opposition's Attorney

This communication should properly come to you through your attorney. Your counsel will advise you as to your options and the best course of action. The opposition's attorney should never communicate directly with you if you have an attorney of your own. This includes any personnel form from the attorney's office.

Your Private Investigator

Make sure your attorney is aware of any important information discovered. If your detective gives you hard copy reports, fax these to your attorney with your comments. Hard copy reports are subject to subpoena; verbal reports are difficult to verify later.

From the Opposition

If the information has upset you, enter it into the contact log. If necessary, fill out an incident report and fax it to your detective and/or attorney. You probably don't believe the opposition when it tells you something good, so why do you believe it when they tell you something to upset you?

Outside or Questionable Source

Note it in your contact log and send your attorney and/or detective an incident report.

Documents

Learn how to search public records for information on the enemy. Detectives and paralegals, can also do this, but you will pay for their time and expertise.

Certified copies cost a little more, but are usually accepted as evidence in court. Attorneys can subpoena copies of the opposition's credit card statements, telephone bills, banking records, tax returns, detective reports they have paid for, and medical records.

Your own records are just as vulnerable as the opposition's records. Documents are usually produced in duplicate or triplicate. School, medical and credit records are routinely dispersed to many agencies without your knowledge or permission. A third rate detective can identify your eating, bill paying and drinking habits, marital status, membership affiliation, and much more from a week's collection of garbage from the cans behind your home.

Your Child

Your child may be an unintentional spy. Do not fall into the easy trap of asking your child what is going on at the other house, or grilling the child about the other parent's activities or associates. A younger child does not understand the consequences of his or her words, and older children may attempt to prove their love or loyalty to you by attempting to spy. The opposition may be aware of what the child is doing and use the child to give you misinformation. Even if it is the child's idea now, the child will resent you later for taking advantage of his or her vulnerability.

You

You should be the best source of new information. Learn to see and hear everything. Do not be so involved with protecting your ego, or scoring points by making insults when you drop off the children, that you miss the suspicious automobile's license plate number, fail to smell the alcohol or marijuana, or forget to grab the camera and get an important photo.

You could be your worst enemy by exposing your strategy or putting yourself in a bad light. Plug any information leaks. Make a thoughtful decision about the kinds of information you make public. Anything you say to anyone will become common knowledge.

Case Killers

Identify and stop activities, behaviors, and bad habits that will destroy your case. Some you are already working on, some you don't see and some overwhelm you. Many individualists feel that appearance is especially superficial. They are unable or unwilling to conform to other peoples' ideas about what they should be and how they should act. "I should be judged for what I am and what I do, not what others think I should be or do." That's right. But that is not the way it works in the custody warfare arena. If you are not interested in taking professional advice regarding questionable activities, learn to eat with a spoon. The guards do not give you knives and forks in jail. More importantly, you cannot take care of your children from a prison cell. If you choose to ignore any chapter in this manual, don't let it be this one. Often you can win a child custody case by being the best of the bad options.

1. You cannot live in fear or hatred for extended periods of time. These strong emotions will make you and your children physically and psychologically ill.

2. You cannot cause the opposition additional distress. It will backfire on you.

3. You cannot do anything illegal. You cannot engage in questionable activities. Usually, it is best to even avoid the appearance of questionable activities. In order to win, there are some things that you <u>cannot</u> do. If you are considering doing something questionable, but are not sure you should, don't. Consider how you would feel, or what you would do, if such action was taken against you. If what you're considering doing will make the situation worse, it will affect your case negatively. If you are not sure about doing something, ask your attorney, police department, or your private detective. Use common sense.

4. Last year there were things you considered doing to make things better, but you did not do them. A year from now you may still wish you had started them.

5. If you protest long enough that you are right without any consideration of how the facts appear to others, you will be wrong

6. Sometimes being pushed to the wall gives you the momentum you need to change something.

7. You cannot spend time daydreaming about the happy times you had with the opposition in the past.

8. You cannot do everything in an attempt to please and win back the opposition to the kind of relationship you desire.

9. The costs of a custody case may force you to work more hours. However, you should not work overtime when your children are staying with you. Your children should spend most of their designated time with you, not in childcare or with others.

10. You cannot stop keeping a detailed log because things seem to be going well. You have dealt with these people and know that the opposition has not changed. Let the appearance of normal behavior, after years of unreasonable behavior, serve as a warning.

11. You cannot violate <u>any</u> court order for <u>any</u> reason.

12. You cannot falsify receipts or attribute purchases not specifically for the children to the expense records you are keeping for them. You cannot attribute general household purchases to the cost of caring for your children.

13. Nothing produces such odd results as trying to get even.

14. You cannot use your children as pawns to ransom things or favors from the opposition.

15. You cannot let your children do without basic necessities. If you are unable to supply seasonal clothing, vitamins, age-appropriate food (with ongoing input from the baby's doctor), it is your responsibility to petition the other parent and/or social service organizations to get what your child needs. Your attorney may assist you in this.

16. You cannot harass, bribe, threaten, or coerce anyone in person or on the telephone. You cannot have another person do these things on your behalf.

17. You cannot refuse proper supplies for the children's needs from the other parent. Make the other parent aware of shortages in a manner that will permit him or her to offer assistance.

18. You cannot discuss with the children any problems you may be having with the other parent. There is nothing they can do to improve the situation, and it will cause a great deal of additional stress on them.

19. You cannot have anything to do with drugs. You cannot hold drugs for a friend. You cannot package or transport drugs. You cannot buy, sell or trade drugs. You cannot have anything to do with people involved with drugs.

20. You cannot worry about winning. It's really about getting what you want. Sometimes you lose now to get what you want later.

21. Beware of friends applauding inappropriate behavior. They do not understand the risks you are really taking.

22. You cannot spend the short time you have with your children lamenting about how limited the visit is. Do not wait until the children arrive to decide what to do. Do not agonize over the activities you are unable to provide because of time, money, or personal inability. If you have made plans, but the children arrive with alternate activities that seem important to them, make every attempt to be flexible and fulfill their needs.

23. Too fast old. Too slow smart.

24. Fun is a good thing, but only when it doesn't spoil something better.

25. You cannot use your children to remind the other parent about money or other obligations.

26. It is never "OK" to hit or spank a child or commit other acts of violence.

27. False accusations are easily disproved and make the accuser appear to be a vindictive pathological liar.

28. If you can't say something nice about the other parent, don't say anything.

29. You may not cause the other side to lose his or her employment or interfere with his or her ability to earn a living.

30. You cannot tap or bug the opposition's telephone, even if you supplied the telephone and are paying for the service.

31. You cannot yell at, cuss out, or berate attorneys, police, judges, court mediators or the opposition, no matter how upset you are.

32. Parents' priorities change during a custody case. Children's priorities do not. They still need to love and be loved by both their parents.

33. You cannot criticize the other parent in the presence of the children or let others criticize the other parent in the presence of the children.

34. You cannot blame the opposition for all the problems that caused the failure of your relationship.

35. You cannot make your children inaccessible to the other parent when the children are in your care. The other parent must have reasonable telephone contact with the children during their normal waking hours. Guidelines for checking on an infant would be 8:00 a.m. to 8:00 p.m. Calls to and from children old enough to talk may reasonably be limited to ten minutes per child, and would be adjusted according to the age and maturity of the child. If you cannot afford a telephone, ask if the other parent would be willing to bear the cost of a telephone to have easier access to the children.

36. You cannot spread gossip about the other parent.

37. You cannot attach tracking devices to vehicles in most states.

38. If a phone is too costly for you or the other parent to provide, inquire about a digital pager. It would be reasonable for you to call back within an hour of the pager's signal. The court considers a willingness to cooperate with the other parent a key issue in deciding custody.

39. Never get advice from someone if you have ever had doubts about their sanity or honorable intentions.

40. You cannot pump your children for information about the other parent's life-style, friends or anything else.

41. If you are in a chemical dependency program, you cannot drop out. If you have dropped out, go back and complete the program.

42. You cannot attempt to sneak information to the court or psychologist.

43. You cannot use aggressive or negative language to refer to or describe the opposition. You should not do it in public or in private because it will reinforce a bad habit. It also exposes your children to antisocial terminology that they will invariably repeat at the most inopportune time.

44. You cannot make a scene in front of coworkers, family, friends or your children.

45. You cannot lie to your attorney. Lying is stupid and will prevent the attorney from doing a good job for you.

46. You cannot call the other parent at their job.

47. You cannot get arrested for anything. Any arrest will impact negatively on your suitability as a good parent.

48. You cannot fight with the opposition in the presence of your children.

49. You cannot refuse to give prompt, responsible information about the children's health, location, or welfare to the other parent.

50. When things are really bad and they are after your butt, answer the phone.

51. Do not bring up the opposition's problems with sex or drugs if they are not current.

52. You cannot violate international, federal, state, county, city, or the moral laws of the community in which you live. You are the one responsible for finding out if any activities you are considering doing yourself, asking someone else to do, or hiring someone else to do, are against the law. It is your business to know what is legal and what is not.

53. There is no absolute failure. Sometimes we just don't get all the results we expected.

54. Totally and completely forgive yourself for the mistakes of the past.

55. Do everything necessary to not make the same mistakes again.

56. Do not build your entire case on the testimony of one person. The judge may disqualify or refuse to hear the testimony or the person may not show up for court.

57. You cannot make your children choose between you and the opposition.

58. Remain vigilant and keep listening for any deficiencies or trial balloons you see the opposition send up. If something the opposition does or says today would have caused you concern when things were at their worst, do not pass it over now. Really examine what has happened. Make the proper people aware, using an incident report, and then proceed carefully.

59. You cannot invade the privacy of the other side's home with electronic video or listening devices.

60. You cannot disconnect the children from established patterns. If your children live in the other parent's home fifty percent of the time or more, attempt to maintain the same sleeping, eating, and homework routines established there.

61. Don't attempt to handle everything at once. Break problems or projects into bite-size chunks.

62. Do not disappoint your children by not showing up when you have made plans or promises.

63. Don't approach every problem with an open mouth.

64. You cannot expect your children to make up for all of the love you may have missed.

65. You cannot be emotionally dependent on your children to fulfill your psychological or physical needs, or to take away the hurt others have caused you.

66. You cannot become confused about what you want. Concentrate on what is important. Motivate yourself and your army. Separate what is not really important from what is.

67. You cannot let your attorney aggravate this already sensitive situation with inflammatory words when communicating with the opposition. If you have hired a "Mad Dog" attorney, this will be a major problem for you all through the case.

68. You're no loser. They quit long ago.

69. You cannot leave angry messages on their answering machine.

70. You cannot have your children carry messages to the other parent in order to spare yourself a confrontation. The stress this causes your children is very harmful.

71. The test of a first-rate intelligence is the ability to hold two opposing ideas in mind at the same time and still retain the ability to function.

72. Be able to see that things are hopeless and yet be determined to make them otherwise.

73. You cannot disappoint your children. Do not make plans or promises beyond your abilities to deliver. If you must change plans, communicate at the children's level of understanding as to why this has happened and when the promise or plan can be carried out. If you encounter this problem more than once, examine your abilities and adjust your commitments. Children do not rebound from repeated disappointments. You must build trust.

74. You cannot change the system by fighting it during your case. Work within the current standards and procedures.

75. You cannot ignore the possibility that you may not get what you want in this war.

76. Ignorance of the law is no defense. If you do not know the law, ask a professional.

77. You must not appear vindictive.

78. You cannot give the opposition more power than they really have.

79. If you can't bend, you will break.

80. Don't be an immovable object. Be an irresistible force.

There are more than 1,500 of these helpful listings in 'Custody Case Killers and Boosters' available in the back of this manual.

Quick List of Activities to Avoid

- Frequenting bars and keeping late hours
- Abusing illegal or prescription drugs
- Smoking or drinking alcohol in the presence of the children
- Leaving the children with inappropriate caretakers
- Displaying erratic behavior and outbursts of temper
- Sporting unusual attire, strange hair styles, new tattoos
- Getting arrested or associating with friends who get into trouble
- Engaging in dangerous sports or fast and reckless driving
- Using foul language or repeating dirty jokes
- Working excessive overtime or bringing work home regularly
- Changing jobs or residences frequently
- Overspending on custody support services
- Eating to dull the pain you feel during stressful times

Hurt You Worse Than Them

Fostering feelings of vindictiveness and hatefulness will poison you with the venom of your anger. It will cause you to look and feel older, make you physically ill, encourage you to do stupid things, and give anyone watching a very dark view of your personality. Make an effort to forgive the people who attempt to hurt you (it gets easier with practice) for three reasons:

1. It will drive the opposition crazy. This should give you some comfort.

2. It will make your position look stronger to opposition and the courts.

3. It is much healthier for you and your children.

What if... The other parent is doing <u>all</u> of these things wrong?"

"It doesn't matter.

It is none of your business.

But you may ask me again when

You aren't doing <u>any</u> of these things wrong."

Anger and Joy

You will be dealing with many emotions, often in rapid secession or at the same time. Anger with the other parent will often encourage you to be pleased when bad things happen to them. Even if the problems they are having will not necessarily help you with your case. This is especially true if these problems are of their own making.

One of the more healthy reasons you are happy when your enemy is in trouble is the affirmation of your negative opinion of that person. Frequently the next emotion you will feel is shame. Shame that you found joy in someone else's pain. We are taught that it is wrong to be happy when bad things are happening to others. It really isn't healthy for your character or for your child to see you delight in the sorrows of others. Avoid gossiping about the information. Dwelling on their problems will make you look petty and mean spirited. Decide if the information will advance your case in a positive manner. Document and log the incident, if appropriate.

You've Been In Court Too Long When

1. You are starting to question if the battle of defending yourself from a crazed ex-spouse is worth the time, money, and frustration.

2. Your kids mention that they always know when their parents are going to court because

grandma comes to visit "mysteriously" the day before the hearing.

3. You dream about courtroom battles instead of beautiful beaches.

4. You know more divorced people than married people.

5. Your attorney has started referring people to you for advice on the child custody battle process.

6. You have almost run through all of the child psychologists in an area either in evaluation or you know them socially.

7. Your attorney has more of your money than you do.

8. You've outlasted all of the original staff at your attorney's office, other than the attorney and the court, including the judge.

9. The opposing attorney actually shows off articles you've written on custody to non-involved attorneys.

10. The judge calls you by your first name.

11. You start to understand why the court does some of the things it does, and you agree.

Source: Dean Hughson, Dad/Husband/Thinker/Friend, and editor of 'View From the Net' column for Self-Help Magazine.

Chapter 6: Logs as Documentation

This chapter will show you how to keep one of the most important kinds of documentation, contact logs. Attorneys will sometimes discourage clients from keeping contact logs. Because in most cases a log is kept by an interested party and therefore, discounted by the court as hearsay evidence. Even if contact logs aren't accepted as evidence they may create time lines, which support other documentation and evidence.

The real value of the logs becomes apparent when dealing with professionals, not bound by the court's rules of evidence. These professionals include: child protective service counselors, home study evaluators, police, psychologists, guardian ad litem and other friends of the court.

Reasons for Documentation

Documentation is the best defense against false accusations and the best way to prove your concerns are valid. The Importance Of A Contact Log Cannot Be Overstated. The contact log is a critical weapon in your child custody war. Many products and pieces of equipment can make this work easier and more efficient. Numerous professionals offer services that will help you in your record keeping and documentation. Using these goods and services will help put your mind at ease.

If you are unable to do anything else for yourself, keep a log. Other than having a client behave, attorneys say it is the most valuable tool they can get. The contact log can be the most lethal, offensive weapon and the most effective defensive weapon.

The legal process to obtain custody of your children may only last six months, or it may go on for seventeen years. If you do not need your daily log now, you may need it in the years ahead. The log will allow you to refer to a specific event with an accuracy that could not be matched by the most perfect memory. Take time to examine the full-page Contact Log Examples in this chapter. These documents may hold a tremendous amount of weight with the courts. Scanning your log will assist you in identifying critical behavior patterns in the opposition that your attorney, mediators, and judges will want to be aware of.

Keep your log on a daily basis and it will have more authority, hold greater validity, and create a more complete picture.

Sporadic records of horrific incidents will appear too slanted. You must demonstrate that you know when things are good as will as when they are bad. A daily log also carries greater legal weight and gets around "hearsay" restrictions on evidence. The opposition should not be doing these things either.

Watch for these behaviors and log any problems you see on your side or that of the other party. Entries reflecting months of calm and routine observations will discredit unsubstantiated claims of upheaval.

Contact Log for Visitation Pick-Up and Drop-Off

Date	Time	Pick-Up	Date	Time	Drop-Off
01/07	6:00pm	Mike and Kate picked up the children. I asked them to make sure the kids buckled up. Mike was in my face saying I should mind my own business his breath smelled of beer and pot.	01/09	8:30pm	Mike and Kate smelled of beer when they dropped the children back home.
01/12	6:00pm	When Mike and Kate picked up the children, I asked that someone help her finish the homework that we didn't have time to finish.	01/14	4:30pm	When Tammie got home from school she said she got an S- on her report because no one would help her finish her homework.
01/14	6:00pm	Mike picked up the children and then called me fifteen minutes later. He had an accident and his car was disabled. When I got there, the police were waiting for me to take the children home. They had arrested Mike for DUI. see Guardian Log			
01/19	6:00pm	Kate picked up the children. I asked where Mike was, but she wouldn't answer.	01/20		When Tammie and Lee got home from school they said Mike was still in jail and they didn't get to see him.
01/21	6:00pm	Kate picked up the children for the weekend. She would not speak to me.	01/23	8:30pm	Kate & Mike dropped-off the children. Lee and Tammie are forbidden to talk about what is going on at Mike's.

Conversely, if the log documents the child's bruises, doctor's visits, and sleep problems, all doubt is removed.

This log must become part of your daily routine, just like brushing your teeth. A simple contact log should be kept with any person or company important to your case including the professionals whether ordered by the court, forced on you or someone you hired.

Accurate record keeping and documentation can provide proof of appropriate behavior, inappropriate behavior, harmful behavior, disprove false allegations against you, and document your concerns. Often it is important to show that you did respond quickly to information or an incident, regardless of the ultimate outcome. A contact log will accomplish this by indicating when you got information, where you got the information, what you did and when you took that action. Knowing that you will have to log information requires that you establish reasonable patterns of information gathering, processing and response.

You have no control over the actions of others and there is very little you can do to fix or prevent any problem they cause. If you have attempted take action in the past and met with no success or penalty, you may have given up further attempts to meddle in the same or similar problems when they reoccurred. Ultimately, you may actually be penalized or punished for not attempting to intervene. The court may feel that it was your responsibility to do something more. Your logs can be used to show the action or inaction of those you notified or went to for help, offering explanation or defense of your position. As an example: The court order requires that you release you children to the other parent and his spouse for visitation. You have made the court aware (by letter to the guardian ad litem) of the fact that the children are allowed to ride in their vehicle without seat belts and the other parent drives after drinking too much alcohol. You have made notation in your log that the other parent seems to act drunk and smells of beer and marijuana. Your contact log with the other parent can reflect your concern.

Your log with the guardian can show that you have on several occasions called and/or written about the smell of dope and beer. Your contact log with your attorney can show that you requested substance testing for the other parent. If you don't get any response from these professionals, you should log a second and third attempt and the response or lack thereof.

Detective

Keep track of each contact with your detective. If you are recording the detective's verbal reports to you, indicate the tape number, date and short synopses of the information. An example of the Detective Communication Notes, which is an easy method of documentation is in Chapter 9: Detective.

Attorney

Documentation of each contact with your attorney keeps your case moving, helps you check the billing and saves you money. An example of the Attorney Communication Notes, which is an easy method of documentation is in Chapter 8: Attorney.

Evaluator

Documentation of each contact with your attorney keeps your case moving and saves you money. An example of the Evaluator Contact Log, which is an easy method of documentation is in Chapter 10: Evaluations.

Guardian ad Litem

Documentation of each contact with the child's GAL is important if the professional is doing a good job and more important if you are concerned.

Telephone Log

Telephone logs are important for non-custodial parents to demonstrate to the court now and your children later, how hard you work to stay in touch.

Logs are important for custodial parents when children are away for visitation.

Methods of Documentation

The decision to keep a contact log is less important than which method you use. You can start with one technique and change to others until you have the system that works best. Some are easier to catch up in than others. But don't let the fact that you haven't entered anything in your log for a period of time keep you from starting again. Often you are able to fill in the blank days weeks or months later.

Appointment Book

If you, like many business people, are already in the habit of working with an appointment book to better organize your time, designate a place each day in your existing system for updating the important notes about your children. Many business people use time systems or appointment books for their work and personal activities.

Long-haul truck drivers can use their truckers log the same way. Draw a line down just as you would for tire inspection or coffee break. Just list your location and what the stop was for. If you are using this kind of system with success, adding your "contact log" information to it is an excellent idea.

Telephone Contact Log		
02/27/00	2:00 pm	Gloria had a good day at church and lunch at grams. She is excited about her new teacher.
02/28/00	4:45 pm	I spoke with Tina, Katrina and Lynn. Gloria was having her friends over for dinner.
02/29/00	4:45 pm	No answer.
03/01/00	4:45 pm	No answer.
03/02/00	4:45 pm	Gloria said she and her aunt went shopping Tuesday after school. Has a lot of homework tonight.
03/03/00	4:45 pm	Gloria got the package I sent. Loves the coat and scarf.
03/04/00	4:45 pm	No answer.
03/05/00	4:45 pm	Gloria went to church with Tina and her family. Says she misses and loves me.
03/06/00	4:45 pm	Gloria's dad said he got the tickets for spring break visitation. She said she is excited to come.
03/07/00	4:45 pm	Ronald said Gloria is spending the night with Lynn so they can be at school early for band.

Calendar Contact Log						
Sun.	Mon.	Tue.	Wed.	Thu.	Fri.	Sat.
1 Pick up Cathy at 3:00 for dance lesson	2 Joe to pick up kids for two weeks Tue	3 Pick up went OK. Joe was 1 hour late.	4 Kids called to say hi.	5	6	7 Joe called, kids getting on Lynn's nerves.
8	9 School called kids late Thu, Fri & Mon.	10 Got Child Support ck.	11 Lynn called to have me watch kids Fri. night	12	13 Kids stayed over night with me.	14 Lynn & Joe picked up kids at 10:00am
15	16 Kids called, having fun.	17 Joe brought kids home with new clothes	18	19	20	21
22 Kids will be	23 gone with	24 Lynn & Joe	25 all week. I	26 get them	27 all next wee	28 week!!!

Calendar

A calendar with room to make simple notes on a daily basis may be adequate if there isn't a great deal of strife.

Computer

Because many of the entries in your contact log will be repetitive, you may find that a computer is the ideal method of record keeping. You can design your own format, or use our example. The program should allow easy reference by name, date, or event. Whether you set up your own system or use an established program, there are several types of information important enough for you to record.

Fill-In Form

Design a fill-in form that will fit in a standard, three-ring binder or can be reduced, using a copy machine, to fit in your appointment book. Use a form that allows you to insert data quickly and easily. It will be necessary to photocopy entries on a regular basis and put these copies in a safe place. An outstanding example of a fill-in form is the 'Condition of Child Report Form'.

Index Cards

Index cards work especially well if you are only given parts of each story or conflicting information from several people. Start with a fresh pack of index cards. Keep some with you at all times. Make note of the date, time and persons involved in any incident, call or contact that happens. Ideas and options are also good to list. The index cards permit a variety of approaches: timetables, relationships, the known and the unknown, motives and speculations. Using index cards of different colors to keep information relating to specific persons or events may assist you in seeing patterns. It may help to pin the cards to a bulletin board in a private, but accessible place. In idle moments you can arrange and rearrange the data according to time line or connection to specific persons or incidents. Follow the column of information and watch the sequence of events unfold. It is valuable to realize how different a detail can look when it's seen out of context. Like the pieces in a puzzle, the shape of reality seems to shift according to circumstance. What seems strange or unusual can make perfect sense when it's placed in the proper setting. Conversely, what seems unremarkable can suddenly yield precious secrets when placed against a different backdrop.

This is an excellent way of keeping track of each new "crisis" the opposition brings to a head. After a period of time you will be able to chart the approach of the next assault. Giving you an opportunity to prepare for the "emergency".

Notebook

Small notebooks are easy to carry around and handy to make notes in. However, because of their size, they are also easy to lose and forget. The notebook method is great if you have clean penmanship and good follow-up skills. Photocopy your pages regularly and put these copies in a safe place.

Tape Recorder

If your penmanship is poor, make cassette tapes of information you wish to record. Be sure to label and safeguard your recorded tapes. Eventually, you will need to have the tapes transcribed. Duplicate these regularly and put them in a safe place.

Admissible Evidence

One of the important reasons to document is to produce evidence. No one will have the time or interest to look at all the evidence you produce. Therefore, it is important to gather everything you can; sort out what is of real value to your case; and assemble it in the most compact and easy to understand format available. The important question is, "What is Admissible Evidence?" The real answer is, "Any evidence the judge wishes to see." The judge may properly receive only admissible evidence, but need not permit a party to introduce all admissible evidence. Using his or her discretion, the judge may exclude otherwise admissible evidence when the court determines that its possible value is outweighed by negative factors such as undue consumption of time.

Websites as Evidence

Because it is very difficult to tamper with the information on a website they are usually accepted as evidence. A wide range of website evidence is admitted by the courts Generally, a printout of information from a website can be admitted just like ordinary paper evidence.

The best way to admit website evidence is to persuade the other party to agree to its authenticity. Alternately, it would be reasonable to assume that the website can be admitted in a manner similar to the basis for authenticating photographs. A witness can testify that it is what they saw and what they printed out after typing in a particular Internet address or using specific key words in a search.

It is important to use the Internet since a lot of information only exists in electronic format and is not available anywhere else. Although lots of evidence can be obtained elsewhere, its not as easy, cheap, or quick to get as it is on the Internet. Situations where "you have two weeks to respond to a motion and are scrambling to get whatever information is possible make the Internet a valuable source.

To overcome the reluctance of some judges to admit website evidence, because of the risks that the website was "hacked" or that the download or printout of the website data was manipulated, you might arrange to have the evidence downloaded from the website by an independent third party, such as an paralegal or investigator, or get the testimony of the site's "webmaster." Alternatively, once you are aware of it's existence, if the evidence can also be obtained from another source, get it that way. It may be more expensive or slower to obtain, but may carry more weight with the court.

Available Information

In addition to personal and company websites an extensive range of evidence can be found on Internet websites including:

Corporate financial information:
http://www.tenk wizard.com
http://www. internetprospector.org/secstate.html.

Liens and UCC Filings
http://www.informations4business.com
http://www.choicepointonline.com
Medical Information:
http://www.fda.gov

The Merck Manual of Diagnosis and Therapy:
http://www.merck.com
http://www.mdconsult.com
Has a doctor has ever been sanctioned:
http://www.searchpointe.com.

Product and Drug Information:
http://www.nhtsa.dot.gov;
http://www.cpsc.gov
http://www.osha.gov

Prescription drugs and medical devices:
http://www.fda.gov
http://www.rxlist.com

Used Car Values
http://www.kbb.com
http://www.nadaguides.com.

Stock Prices
http://chart.yahoo.com
http://www.wallstreetcity.com.

Housing Prices:
http://www.reale state.yahoo.com/realestate
http://www.realtor.com.
Weather Information
http://www.noaa.gov.

Birth Dates
http:www.anybirthday.com.

Federal government's 27 million web pages:
http://www.firstgov.gov

Government Statistics:
http://www.fedstats.gov
Highway Safety:
http://www.hwysafety.org.

Federal Aviation:
http://www.faa.gov.
http://www.ntsb.gov

For individual state by state information:
http://www.custodysource.com

E-mail Evidence

It is more difficult to get the court to accept e-mail as evidence unless person listed as the sender of an e-mail message produces it in litigation and/or admits to being the sender. If the person listed as the sender denies that he or she sent the e-mail it is difficult to prove. An e-mail message can actually sent by someone who pretended to be that person by "spoofing" the message's "header". Unless the spoofer has a sophisticated program the sender can be tracked. Short of inspection the "senders" computer e-mail logs that's all you can do.

Factors that support authenticity of e-mail include:

- The e-mail message contained information that only the claimed sender would know
- The claimed sender later made statements showing knowledge of the message's contents
- The message was received from the claimed sender in response to a message that was previously sent to him or her

Chain of Evidence

Chain of evidence is a written chronological list of persons that have accessed the evidence. This is important to maintain the "purity" of the evidence to insure it hasn't been tampered with.

Evidence comes from many sources. Public records and items produced in daily life are the easiest to obtain. Often you become aware of information not as easily obtained. As an example, attempting to prove someone spends much more money than they claim to earn is difficult. You may be aware of a way to get a copy of an income tax return or a credit report on the person that would prove the statement false. Although the tax form or the credit report may prove your point, it could cause you more trouble than good. This is because you may have to account for how the document came into your possession. If he document was not available through proper sources you could have civil or criminal charges filed against you. Federal statutes may apply that could disqualify the evidence or allow suit against you.

Some of the precedent for this includes instances where an insurance company obtained an insured's credit report because it suspected a fraudulent claim. In Yang v. Government Employees Insurance Company, No. 97-8432 July 22, 1998, the Eleventh Circuit court said it was possible for them to be sued under the Fair Credit Reporting Act. The court ruled that a report could be covered by the Act even if it wasn't used for one of the listed purposes in the act. If you become aware of information from a source you cannot or should not use, you will have to obtain it from a more "acceptable" source and document that source. Make sure your trail or chain of evidence is as good as the evidence.

Don't build your entire case on any one piece of evidence.

Spoliation of Evidence

If a person or entity destroys key records or other evidence they can be sued in tort for punitive damages for "intentional spoliation of evidence." It is critical to identify the spoliation of evidence before the underlying case is resolved.

Example #1. Supreme Court. Goff v. Harold Ives Trucking Co., Inc., No. 99-1420. September 28, 2000 Ruled that the plaintiff can't sue for spoliation of evidence .

A truck company destroyed the driving logs for a driver who seriously injured the plaintiff in an accident, the company can't be sued for "intentional spoliation of evidence."

The plaintiff requested discovery of the driving logs to determine how long the driver had been on the road on the day of the accident, but the company claimed it had either lost or destroyed the records.

The plaintiff won her personal injury suit. Notwithstanding, she argued that the lack of availability of the logbooks limited her damages.

The court refused to recognize a claim for spoliation. The court stated "There are sufficient other avenues, short of creating a new cause of action, that serve to remedy the situation for a plaintiff. Most significantly, an aggrieved party can request that a jury be instructed to draw a negative inference against the spoliator. Additionally…the plaintiff can ask for discovery sanctions or seek to have a criminal prosecution initiated against the party who destroyed relevant evidence. In short, we do not find it necessary to create a new tort out of whole cloth in order to provide a party with a remedy. We are especially averse to creating a tort that would only lead to duplicative litigation, encouraging inefficient relitigation of issues better handled within the context of the core cause of action."

There are contrary decisions from the D.C. Circuit and state courts in Alaska, Florida, New Jersey, New Mexico and Ohio.

Example #2. U.S. Court of Appeals, 9th Circuit. DeLew v. Wagner, No. 97-15778. May 11, 1998

Where police covered up evidence that an officer's wife who killed someone in a car accident had been drinking, the wrongful death plaintiff can sue them under 42 U.S.C. Sect. 1983.

The plaintiffs' lawyers should consider filing a Sect. 1983 claim anytime evidence of a conspiracy by state actors to cover up evidence comes to light. This is particularly true in states that don't acknowledge a tort claim for "spoliation of evidence."

The plaintiff (husband) sued for wrongful death in state court. During discovery, the plaintiff found evidence that the driver was drunk, but the police never conducted any sobriety tests, allowed her to leave the scene and didn't preserve any physical evidence, including skid marks.

The plaintiff moved to amend the complaint to add a claim under Sect. 1983. When the trial judge denied the motion, the plaintiff filed a separate Sect. 1983 case, and moved the case to federal court.

Denying the defendants argument that the plaintiff couldn't show a constitutional violation giving rise to a claim under Sect. 1983, the Ninth Circuit said, "The plaintiff has indeed alleged a constitutional violation, namely, that the defendants violated the plaintiff's right of meaningful access to the courts by covering up the true facts surrounding the death."

It cited a Sixth Circuit case, which held that a cover-up of evidence can give rise to a Sect. 1983 suit. (Swekel v. City of River Rouge, 119 F.3d 1259 (1997).

There's "an independent cause of action" if you can show that your access to state court has been defeated. Even if you don't win this kind of case, this decision is meaningful because it puts state actors on notice. The plaintiff could still have a viable Sect. 1983 claim even if he won in state court, because the success of a right of access claim depends on whether the case could be "fully litigated," not on what the verdict turns out to be.

Probably, the plaintiff could sue if the defendants' cover-up prevented him from collecting from additional parties, or prevented him from collecting punitive damages.

In 2001 the California Supreme Court rejected a tort case for "spoliation of evidence."

Crucial Data to Record

- Accurate pickup and return dates, times and address of children for you and the opposition.
- Children's health and immunization record.
- Living conditions with other parent.
- Incidents and statements involving potential witnesses.
- Incidents that affect the children's well-being including negligence, incompetence of the other caregiver, or abuse.
- Money spent for children, attorney, private investigator, child support payments, or money sent to assist the other parent, with amount and check number.
- Time specially allotted to child-centered activities you feel are important.
- School grade fluctuation and absenteeism.
- Anything else you think is important.
- Children's weight gain and loss associated with visitation.

Simplicity and Speed

You can devise a code for your log, which will facilitate the making of entries and expedite compilation of data. The following codes are an indication of the kinds of codes you can devise. The age of your children or the kinds of information important to your case will determine the information and coding necessary. This type of diary or log may be subject to the process of discovery by the opposition. It is best not to mention its existence to anyone except your attorney. When the time comes, this system of coding will help you and others (mediators, psychologists, judges, home study specialists, and others) find key information quickly and easily.

To facilitate the process of identifying what is really important to the professional who may see the log, check with your attorney to make sure that the timing on any information you give the professional is OK for the opposition to see now. Copy the entire log to substantiate the information.

- Highlight the important sentences with a light blue marker.
- Don't over do the highlighting or too much won't be read either. If the professional finds your highlighted sentence important, the professional can read more.

One of the many not-so-obvious messages your log can convey to the reader is your stability and the normalcy with, which you live your life. Some of the other messages you might make sure the log sends are:

- Contact, communication and support of your family.
- Your healthy interest in family sports.
- Frequent contact with the children's teachers and minister.
- Regular health and dental visits for the children.

Confidentiality - Documentation

All record keeping documentation may be subject to the process of DISCOVERY. Therefore, it is important to decide how and what you will document, who is aware of what you are doing and what documentation exists.

In the event that documentation must be presented for inspection to the opposition, you may not feel too concerned if it is not easy to hear, read or sort. Once information is entered into the case and is filed with the court, it becomes public record. Public records may be viewed by anyone who knows where to find them and wishes to inspect or copy them.

Some documents may be protected by attorney work product. If your attorney shows you this documentation, do not discuss it with anyone. Do not mention their existence in your contact logs. If your attorney gives you copies of these documents, do not show them to anyone.

Codes for Log Book

Explanation Of Codes For Example Log Entries:

L Lies: Indicate when you are told lies.

P Photo: Photographs or videos taken.

A Abuse: Back up notation with photos, paperwork from doctor, emergency room, child protective services, and check numbers and amounts for treatment.

D Dirt: Filth or insect bites observed anywhere pertaining to the children. Take photos and statements from others about worrisome conditions.

DR. Call or Visit to Doctor, Dentist or Hospital: Note if child was sick or if it was a regular check up. Record check number and amount paid.

HRS Hours Spent with Children: How much time you spent with your child may become a key issue.

HRS+Hours Spent with Children, Plus Overnight: This entry can indicate the children may be legally in the custody of the other parent, but in fact really lives with you.

N/INegligence, Incompetence: Photos and statements from witnesses are important to validate your concerns.

$ Dollar Sign: Designates the money you spent for your children.

XXX Inflicted distress: Incidents that cause you or your children unnecessary concern.

The more XXX's the more distress.

The following entries demonstrate the value of keeping a log in the custody case of Randall Long versus Amber Jones.

Note the use of codes at the beginning of each entry. These are specifically selected log sheets extracted from four years of entries. If you are attempting to follow the story, pay close attention to the dates as you read these examples. It will demonstrate how important dates and good record keeping can be as you enter data in your logs.

Customize Your Log

Each parent faces different challenges. Customize your log to help you document the real issues in your case.

If you have had an opportunity to get to know what is important to your judge keep those things in mind. As an example if he or she is tired of hearing about father's rights or is suspicious of claims of Parental Alienation Syndrome, don't push those issues.

Some judges never approve home studies and others depend on them to actually make their decisions. A home study professional is more sensitive to quality of life issues, where the judge is more interested in issues that are addressed by the laws.

Contact Log Example 1991-2001

1991

TUE. OCT. 15, 91 N/I

Amber came to my wife's office with her carload of kids. It looked like an invasion. Amber said she was out of prenatal vitamins and needed some money. Amber's former husband, James, had been calling and harassing her all night, and she said she was as tired as she looked. I followed them outside as they left. It's cold and her children aren't dressed right. I don't know how she can concentrate enough to drive safely. It looks like a hockey game going on inside the car as it goes down the street.

Value of the Following Entries
In July, after nine months of shared parenting, Amber took Bobby to Washington without Randall's knowledge. When a judge forced her to return to Arizona, Amber leveled several serious accusations:
a) Bobby was conceived because Randall raped Amber.
b) Randall never attempted to spend, or spent, any time with Bobby.
c) Randall never financially supported or cared about Bobby.
Information in the following entries indicated that Amber's behavior was not consistent with the allegation of rape. These dated entries accompanied by photos, checks and receipts indicated the parents of the child were amenable and jointly cared for the child. This went a long way toward disproving false allegations. In deposition twelve months later, Amber unintentionally validated information listed in these entries.

WED. OCT. 16, 91 D

I put a new door in the jam between the living room and a bedroom at Amber's house. I told Rebecca my wife, I was worried about the unsanitary conditions there. I didn't feel there was much I could do about it. When Amber came over, Rebecca asked if we could send Mac, our cleaning guy, to her house to shine things up for her before the baby came. Amber became very mad and stormed out.

THU. OCT. 17, 91 HP P

Amber called at 1:00pm saying she was in labor at the hospital and wanted to know when I was coming. It took me an hour to get things rounded up to get there. Amber's girlfriend, Doris, and her sister, Eunice, were in the room when I arrived. The nurse came in and said we would have to leave. Amber said, "I was told the father of the baby could stay." The nurse said I could stay, causing Eunice to get angry. Eunice and Doris left the room. Doris came back in saying, "Eunice told the nurses that they better watch Randall, because he is going to steal the baby as soon as it is born." Amber was in labor for forty minutes. Bobby was born today at 6:45pm I cut the umbilical cord and the nurse put Bobby in a heated bed. The nurse told the doctor Bobby was not breathing correctly. So the doctor and the nurse took him to the newborn nursery and put him in a respirator.

I was alone in the room with Amber while we waited for word about how Bobby was doing. Amber was doing the post-delivery abdomen massage the doctor told her to do. We talked and she said her ex-husband James had never been at the birth of any of his children, and that's why it was important to her to have me here. Amber stopped talking, and I could see her breathing was not right. Her face was turning gray. I moved to the end of the table. There was blood coming out of her very fast. I ran into the hall and called for a nurse. They told me I must leave the room and they got busy taking care of her.

An hour later the doctor came out into the hall and said Amber would be fine. They sent me down to the nursery, and I fed my son his first bottle. The nurse took a picture of us. I left the hospital at 10:00pm

MON. OCT. 28, 91 8 HRS HP P $51.15

7:00am I went to the hospital to see how Bobby and Amber were doing. I took photos of Bobby and Amber in her room and visited for several hours. I took Bobby and Amber home with me at 6:00pm Amber could not get Bobby to nurse or take

formula, and he cried from 7:00pm to 2:00am Actually she was never able to nurse him at all. I called the doctor and he had me take Bobby and Amber to the emergency room ($51.15 CK#4836). They worked with the baby and told us he would be fine, and we could go home.
Amber said, "I had trouble with my last kid and my mother took care of him for the first three weeks."

TUE. OCT. 29, 91 5 HRS+ $85.96

Amber and I spent last night at my home. She is ill-at-ease taking care of a newborn. With so many younger brothers and sisters I thought she would be more confident. Amber can't get Bobby to nurse at all. She gets frustrated quickly and hands the baby to me and I gave him water from the bottle the hospital sent home with us. At 8:00am, I took Amber and Bobby to her mother's house. I don't feel good about leaving Bobby there. It feels like a cold, stark cold institution with bare floors, walls, and beds everywhere. Amber has told us on several occasions that her mother is a manic-depressive and an alcoholic and is sometimes so depressed she is suicidal.
5:30pm I picked up Bobby and Amber and took them back to my home. When Amber said they were settled in I went to Wal-Mart to buy some things Amber needed to take care of Bobby. $85.96, CK# 4837. 10:30pm My wife Rebecca, called from the airport in New York and would be home tomorrow morning. She was worried when I told her about the baby's trip to the hospital.

Value of this Entry
The one bad incident in the following entry does not indicate incompetence or neglect, but a log documenting a history of poor child care choices and life-style decisions can. Condition of Child Report Form (example in Chapter 21) filled out by other responsible people will make hearsay into evidence. Later entries were documented over a dozen different incidents similar to this one.

WED. OCT. 30, 91 3 HRS+ N/I P

Bobby hates to be unwrapped. I can see he likes to feel the blankets snug around him, and he yells when he is naked. I took photos of Amber giving the baby a bath in my kitchen sink; he hated it. 8:00am I took Bobby and Amber to her mother's. 5:30pm I went to Amber's mother's house to pick Bobby and Amber up to take them home. Amber was walking across the dirt yard of the house from the neighbor on the west. She was wearing a blouse that covered her shoulders and sweat pants, with Bobby draped over her arm, wearing only a diaper and a Onesie T-shirt. I had a jacket on because it was quite cool. I asked, "Why do you have the baby outside without a blanket on him?" Amber was annoyed and said, "I was only out here visiting with the neighbor for a few minutes." I brought them home. Amber had her Polaroid camera and took photos of Bobby and me.

Value of this Entry
Lack of family communication and support surface in logs and detective reports. Willingness to deal in a less - than - honest manner became evident.

THU. NOV. 2, 91 14 HRS D

6:00am I picked up Bobby at Amber's work. His clothes were dirty. 4:00pm, Amber picked up Bobby and supplies in the front office. Amber was more abrupt than usual and rushed out the door.

Value of this Entry
The following July 2, 1992, notation about Amber's attitude did not seem important at the time, but the difference in mood was unusual enough to be noticed and noted. In deposition on October 10, Amber testified that on July 2, 1992, she was in court for her arrest for attempting to smuggle drugs into a prison on June 23, 1991, when she was four months pregnant. Documentation of the reasons Amber gave for wanting to move are established, in incidents like June 10th, then testified to on October 10, then changed constantly through the case.

WED. DEC. 10, 91 9.5 HRS XXX D

6:00am I picked up Bobby at Amber's work. He was wearing the clothes I had put on him yesterday morning. 4:30pm, Amber came for Bobby. She said, "Mike, my new husband is afraid of James and wants to move to Washington. I have to do something to get my kids away from James's violent influence. We had already moved out of one house and into another to hide from him. James is especially hard on my oldest son, Jerome, and I am tired of him victimizing all of us. James's bothers my parents, and I don't get along with my family anyway, and I can't stand to listen to my crazy mother any longer."

I said I love my son. You can move, but Bobby will have to stay. Amber said, "He is my kid and no one tells me what I can do with my kids." I told her I would fight her on it. As Amber left, she said, "I'll tell Mike to forget about moving."

1992

THU. JAN. 11, 92 14 HRS+

I picked up Bobby at 6:00am at Amber's work. When I called my attorney about Amber's desire to move, she told me not to worry about it because of the agreement. Mac cleaned the house today. Amber picked up Bobby at 4:00pm Amber said her sister Eunice still didn't have her children back from Child Protective Services and could only have supervised visitation. So Eunice spends her time upsetting Amber. Amber was excited because Eunice had qualified for a welfare apartment and would be moving out soon. It has been hard with two adults and five children in that three-bedroom house. Amber returned baby Bobby, and he stayed with me overnight.

Value of this Entry
Psychologists and mediators could see what was happening on a daily basis throughout the log sheets. In addition, the log sheets documented Randall's response to incidents.
In the following entries, it is clear that Randall did not know of Amber's ultimate decision to move. When Amber later claimed that Randall had agreed to Bobby's relocation, this entry helped to indicate that was not true.

SAT. JUN. 13, 92 12 HRS+ D

8:00am I picked up Bobby for the weekend. Amber invited me into the house. I followed her back to her bedroom where Bobby's bed was. The room was a mess. Amber has lived here over a year and the waterbed wasn't even assembled. It's just a bubble on the floor. She pulled some baby clothes from a pile, cleared a surface and changed the baby. I hate to have him in that house. We stopped at Village Inn Restaurant for breakfast. I pulled the Babywipes out of the diaper bag. There was a cockroach clinging to the box. The waitress watched Bobby so I could take the box out to kill the roach.

THU. JUL. 2, 92 14 HRS+ L

6:00am I picked up Bobby at Amber's work. We ate breakfast at P&A, and I gave Bobby his bath. Ann and Joanne were with us all day, and I had to compete for the baby's time. Amber picked up Bobby at the office at 4:00pm She came back with the baby at 4:45pm. She spent a long time with me, and we talked about the weekend. It was Thursday night, so the baby was going to stay with me overnight. Amber wanted to pick Bobby up at 10:00am on Friday at my home. She said she and Doris were taking all the kids to visit some friends in Pine for the July 4th weekend. We agreed that she would bring Bobby back Sunday between 1:00 and 2:00pm for the night. We talked about Christmas. Amber said Mike's parents would be in town and that was supposed to be my weekend. I told her I was willing to trade time now, since I wanted to take Bobby to spend Thanksgiving with my parents in California.

FRI. JUL. 3, 92 5.5 HRS L

At 11:30am Amber and her friend Doris came to pick up Bobby for the weekend. They left Amber's other children and Doris' children outside in the pickup truck. Mike's boat was hooked up. They sat in our family room and told us all about the big 4th of July barbecue and camp-out in Pine. Amber said she would see me around 2:00pm Sunday.

Value of this Entry
In her deposition Oct. 10th, Amber stated first that she had discussed with Randall about moving Bobby to Washington State, and he said if the court said it was OK she could. Later in the same deposition, she said she knew he strongly objected to any suggestion that Bobby might be relocated.

SAT. JUL. 4, 92

Had a yard sale. The people started showing up at 6:00am and did not stop coming until after 5:00pm We do not ever want to do this again; it is too much work. Rebecca's mom came to help out all day.

SUN. JUL. 5, 92 XXXX $44.66

I went to Fry's ($44.66 cash for baby food) while Rebecca held down the fort at our yard sale. The yard sale is winding down. Bobby is due at 2:00 --- no show. At 4:00pm --- no show. Called Amber's home --- no answer. Called again at 5:00pm --- No answer. Amber called me to say she moved with Bobby to Washington and was not coming back. Amber said we would have to work it out later about the baby. I asked her about the mediated agreement we had in court. She said she checked, and it wasn't on file. I asked for a phone number, and she hung up. We drove to the house Amber had been living with Mike and the children.

It was empty, except for a big pile of garbage in front for the trash man. I didn't want to believe that she would do this. I can't think straight, eat, stand still, or sleep.

MON. JUL. 6, 92 XXXX DR.C

Rebecca has stopped running her company in order to help me. Our families are devastated and say they feel helpless. I called the baby doctor to see if Amber had taken Bobby's medical records with her, in case he got sick. She did not. He expressed concern and offered any assistance he could. I don't know where my son is or if he is OK or not. I called everyone I could think of for help. Bobby's toys are all over the house and office. Every time I turn around, he is there --- but he isn't. I cannot imagine what kind of sick mind would put another person through this agony. No call from Amber about Bobby.

TUE. JUL. 7, 92 XXXX

Rebecca and I spent our day trying to find my son. My attorney found an address for Amber in Washington on papers filed with the court 5/18/92. My attorney was working on papers to notify Amber that my son must be returned to Arizona. Amber called at 5:20pm to say that Bobby was OK.

I pleaded for a telephone number, but she said, "Mike said he did not want me to give it to you." She also said no when I asked to come to Washington to see my son. We talked about five minutes, and she said she might call in a week. There is not a television show or commercial without a baby in it. I just want to scream all the time. My heart is aching badly. You can't go out of the house and you can't stay inside. It is criminal to put people through this.

WED. JUL. 8, 92 XXXX

Rebecca spends the day with me. We try not to go crazy or make ourselves sick. This has affected everyone connected with our lives as well as Rebecca's business. I can't believe anyone would do this to someone on purpose. I do not think I have ever felt so much pain. My attorney sent the documents to Amber, Federal Express, and she should have them tomorrow. Amber called at 10:00pm to give me the phone number and address in Washington. Amber said she did so because Mike was on the road and his parents said she should. She said, "I will be going to Seattle to look for work because I need to find a place of my own and I can't make ends meet without working." I asked who would take care of Bobby while she was at work, and she said she would get a baby-sitter.

THU. JUL. 9, 92 XXXX $746.00

Rebecca and I feel better knowing where the baby is. Thank God Mike has responsible parents. We can't go anywhere. Everyone asks about Bobby and we both start crying. I still don't know what to do. My attorney said we are morally and legally right when I called her with more information on Amber then went to her office to work out the papers to bring my son home.

My attorney said I have a right to see Bobby this weekend, so I called the travel agent and bought a ticket to go to Washington ($746. ck# 4172). Mac cleaned the house today. No call from Amber in Washington about Bobby.

Value of this Entry
As repetitious as it seems, keeping a log will help prove important points later. In the following entry, July 2nd, Amber claims she had to move because she was unable to find work. Randall's log indicates he picked up Bobby at her job on July 2. A call to Amber's former employer indicated she gave 2 weeks notice before moving and quitting her job.

FRI. JUL. 10, 92 XXXX

I arrived at my attorney's office. She said that Amber had called in response to the papers and is mad, saying, "I am not going to let Randall have the kid for the weekend. I left Phoenix because I can't find work or get along with my family." Amber called back about 40 minutes later, saying, "I will be back in Phoenix tomorrow just long enough to get legal papers to take my kid back." When I called the travel agency to cancel my ticket to Washington, they said it was nonrefundable and non-changeable.

SAT. JUL. 11, 92 12 HRS+ D $40.52

Amber called at 7:00am Gave me the address, 7702 E. 44TH Lane, Apt. 11. It is her sister Eunice's two-bedroom apartment, provided by the Department of Welfare. 8:00am Rebecca and I arrived to pick up Bobby. Amber was standing outside with Bobby. I told her I would have him back to her at 8:00pm, Sunday. Eunice glared at us, and we were interrupted by her saying to her own baby crawling on the sidewalk dressed only in a soiled diaper, "Get into the house before they rape you."

From the open doorway of the apartment, you could see the place looked like Amber's house always did, a mess with garbage and clothes laying around.

Amber handed me the diaper bag containing some diapers and medication. Bobby was very quiet, uncommunicative, or crying a lot. He had dirty ears and fingernails, a bruise, and a mark on his head. Bobby was not saying daddy or the other cooing, clicking, and baby sounds he was making before Amber took him away just one week ago. The baby just makes a sound like a growling grunt to express himself. It made me very worried. Bobby wanted to be held all day. After a bath, breakfast and nap, we took him to Buster Brown for new shoes ($40.52, ck# 4174).

SUN. JUL. 12, 92 14 HRS XXX

Bobby could not settle down in his bed last night, so I put him between Rebecca and me. He slept quietly. I stayed awake most of the night listening to him breath. I knew I loved my son before this happened, but now my feelings are magnified. Even though Bobby was withdrawn, he seemed, after a few minutes, to recognize everyone who came to say "hi." We had visitors all day, including our family, some friends, and three employees.

It was as if they did not believe he was back in Phoenix until they saw him. Bobby had become accustomed to many visitors all his life in Rebecca's office, but Bobby was very quiet and subdued. Mom was a primary teacher, and said he will pull out of it in a few days. Dropped Bobby off at 7:45 pm. I gave Amber the diaper bag, now containing 2 cans of formula, 8 jars of baby food, Babywipes and diapers. Told Amber I would pick up Bobby at 6:00am She said, "No, it's not in the agreement. I'm not working, so you can't have Bobby except for Thursday nights and every other weekend." I told her to read the agreement. Amber called back at 9:30pm saying, "Don't go to my sister's. I will be staying at a friend's and will bring Bobby by on Thursday night." I explained the agreement she signed again and told her I was going to have the attorney do the paperwork., I needed to have my parental rights protected. Amber called back at 10:15pm and said, "You can pick up Bobby at my sister's at 6:00am tomorrow. I am going to an attorney. If you aren't there on time I am taking him with me and you won't get him until next weekend."

Value of this Entry
At a later date, it may be necessary for people who witness events to testify. Have them read through your entry when you make it and have them put their signature next to the incident. This will help you find the information when it is needed for review during sessions with the mediator, the psychologist and your attorney or in court.

MON. JUL. 13, 92 9 HRS D $37.00

6:00am Amber had him dressed, but without shoes. From the open doorway, the apartment was filthy and smelled bad. Amber said she would pick him up at 4:00pm. Bobby's shoes were not in the diaper bag, and there were no bottles of milk or juice in the bag to hold him over until I could get him something. None of the supplies were used. I called the attorney to ask about the weekend. Amber called the office about picking up Bobby at 2:00pm instead of 4:00pm, since her sister Eunice had an appointment at 4:24. I said, "OK." At 1:00pm. I took Bobby to the baby doctor ($37, ck# 4178). His nose was plugged, and he needed his nine-months' shots. The doctor was glad Bobby was back and happy he was well. Amber did not show up at 2:00. She came at 4:45pm. Amber arrived and picked up Bobby. I asked for a telephone number. Amber said, "I told you my sister can't afford a telephone. If you want me to have one, you will just have to pay for it." I gave Amber the diaper bag containing supplies.

TUE. JUL. 14, 92 9 HRS D $2,550.00

6:00am Picked Bobby up at Amber's. Bobby is dirty and had on the same clothes I put on him after his bath yesterday. There was food and dirt on his arms and on his feet under the socks.

From the look of his feet, she must have had him barefoot. None of the baby care or food supplies were used out of the diaper bag. After breakfast at Village Inn, I was bathing Bobby and noticed insect bites on his chest and stomach. I called the doctor's office and applied the cream they suggested. He took a long nap after our walk. Sent my attorney $2,550, ck# 4117. 3:00pm Amber came for Bobby and the diaper bag. Her sister was in the car.

WED. JUL. 15, 92 9HRS D

Same as yesterday.

Value of this Entry
Notations in these entries indicate that Amber is not complying with the court's order, allowing parents telephone contact with or about the child. Each time an incident of noncompliance occurred, Randall reported it to his attorney using an Incident Report Form. Randall's attorney then notified Amber's attorney in writing, creating yet another traceable record.

THU. JUL. 16, 92 12HRS+

6:00am Picked Bobby up at Amber's sister's apt. It took Amber 15 minutes to come to the door this morning. Bobby looks like he has been bitten by something new on his chest and stomach, and under his clothes his little body is very dirty. None of the supplies were used out of the diaper bag to take care of Bobby. Bobby and I ate breakfast at Village Inn, and after his bath and nap, we took the truck to Bill's Radiator. Amber picked Bobby up at 2:30pm and brought him back at 5:10pm. We took Bobby to the Pier. Everyone was happy that he was safe and back home.

FRI. JUL. 17, 92 9HRS

Bobby slept quietly last night and ate French toast and Hawaiian Delight for breakfast. 3:20pm. When Amber picked up Bobby, I asked if I could have a contact telephone number as ordered by the court. She said, "I don't have one of my own. I have to walk all the way to the laundry room in the complex." I asked her if she would call since the laundry room is only 200 yards from her door. She said, "I'll try," as she picked up the diaper bag.

SAT. JUL. 18, 92 and SUN. JUL. 19, 92

No call from Amber about Bobby.

MON. JUL. 20, 92 9HRS D

8:00am Picked Bobby up at Amber's sister's apt. Bobby was wide-awake and smiled and reached for me as soon as Amber opened the door. The house is filthy and disgusting. I asked how the baby was this weekend. Amber gave me a "go-to-hell" look and slammed the door in my face. No supplies were used out of the diaper bag. The poor baby had dirt in the creases under each arm and in the inside of his elbows. He must crawl around in just a diaper like baby Elmer. He was wearing the same blue knit outfit I put on him Friday morning after his bath, and it had not been washed. Breakfast was more play than eat.

Just as we finished Bobby's bath, Don and Sue came by with baby Adam, Don wanted us to baby-sit Sue and Adam for him while he did some jobs. Amber called and said she would come for Bobby at 4:30pm after her doctor's appointment. I handed Amber the diaper bag containing supplies.

TUE. JUL. 21, 92 9 HRS

At 6:00am I arrived to pick up Bobby at Amber's sister's apartment. Amber was mad and said she spoke to an attorney yesterday. The baby does not like the "tang stuff" Amber puts in his bottle. If her old house was any indication, the front room of this apartment is a mess. But it is probably much cleaner than the rooms I can't see. None of the supplies were used out of the diaper bag to take care of Bobby. 2:00 Rebecca, Bobby and I were at my attorney's office before court to determine if Bobby was to stay here or go to Washington. The judge listened to our attorney's reasons that Bobby should stay and Amber's reasons for leaving. The judge said he did not feel Amber was being honest with the court and said, "Bobby may not leave the state with either parent, and the agreement signed with the conciliation court is to be honored." Amber was really mad. She thought the judge would just let her take the baby back. When we got out of court at 4:45pm, Amber grabbed Bobby and the diaper bag and stormed out. When we got back to the office, Amber called and said, "You just better tell Rebecca's family the truth about us." I faxed my attorney an Incident Report Form to advise her of the call.

Value of this Entry
The following notations in the log indicate that Amber is negligent and not complying with nutritional requirements ordered by Bobby's pediatrician. Randall will have to supplement Bobby's diet with vitamins and additional attention to good nutrition.

WED. JUL. 22, 92 9HRS N/I DR.C

6:00am Picked Bobby up at Amber's sister's apt. His bottle was dirty and had powdered milk caked inside the bottom.

After his bath and breakfast, I called the baby doctor and asked about vitamins because, apparently, Amber had taken Bobby off formula. The doctor told me Bobby should stay on formula for the first year and to get some vitamins. When Amber picked Bobby up at 4:15pm, I told her the doctor wanted Bobby on formula for at least a year and if she needed some, I could give it to her. She said, "I can get him what I think he needs" and left. I handed Amber the diaper bag containing supplies.

THU. JUL. 23, 92 14HRS+ D

6:00am Picked up Bobby. No supplies were used out of the diaper bag to take care of Bobby. I took Bobby into the bathroom at Paul's Cafe to clean his face, hands, arms, and legs before breakfast. Amber picked Bobby up at 2:30pm. Brought him back at 4:45pm saying, "I'll call later to see how my son is." Ate dinner at the Pier. Mac cleaned the house today. No call from Amber.

FRI. JUL. 24, 92 9HRS

Bobby and I stayed home and played in the pool and he napped. Amber arrived at 4:00pm.

SAT. JUL. 25, 92 12HRS+ $10.84

8:00am Rebecca and I picked up Bobby. On arrival at her apartment, Eunice made a crack to me that I could not really hear and Amber told her to shut up. None of the supplies were used. Picked up some baby food and cookies at Smart & Final ($10.84, ck# 4189) and some feed at The Stock Shop. The guy let Bobby pet the baby bunnies.

Value of this Entry
Notations of the following entries indicate a pattern that neither Amber nor Mike attempt to use proper legal safety measures for the baby in the car. This pattern is confirmed in a detective's report. It is arguable as to whether this constitutes negligence, incompetence or abuse and may indicate a lack of concern in other areas.

TUE. JUL. 28, 92 9HRS I/N $27.94

6:00am Picked up Bobby. The baby and I went to Smitty's ($27.94, ck# 4193) after lunch and a nap. Amber, Mike and Eunice came to pick up Bobby at 4:00pm. I handed Amber the diaper bag. Eunice was standing there muttering obscenities. Amber asked, "Will you pick up Bobby at "Food for Less" (grocery store) at 24 East Bell Road tomorrow at 6:00am?" I told her I would. Amber carried Bobby out to the car and got in on the driver's side and handed Bobby to Mike. They pulled out of the parking lot with the baby on Mike's lap, not in the baby's car seat. I called my attorney's office and voiced my concern about the car seat.

WED. JUL. 29, 92 9HRS I/N

5:45am we were at "Food For Less" waiting for Amber to bring Bobby. At 6:00am Amber drove her car up to the front of our truck. Bobby was not in the baby car seat; he was on Mike's lap. I asked Amber, "How come Bobby is not in the baby car seat?" She did not answer, turned, and went back to her car. None of the supplies were used. Bobby ate oatmeal at Village Inn and made a mess with the orange juice. Amber picked up Bobby at 4:00. Gave Amber the diaper bag. Amber carried Bobby out to the car and got in on the driver's side and handed Bobby to Mike. She looked back at me, standing at the window, daring me to say something again. They pulled out of the parking lot with the baby standing on Mike's lap, not in the baby car seat.

THU. JUL. 30, 92 12HRS+ D

6:00am Picked Bobby up at Amber's. These people live like pigs and treat the children like furniture. None of the supplies were used out of the diaper bag to take care of Bobby. Bobby ate scrambled eggs at Village Inn.

After his bath and nap at the office we went to

Discovery Zone. The baby cried when we left the building, but was sleeping before we got to Bethany Home Road. Amber picked up Bobby at 4:00pm and brought him back at 5:00.

Value of this Entry
In the deposition October 10, 1991, Amber testified she was forced to move to Washington to get her children away from James Miller because he was a violent drug dealer and she had no idea where he was now.
Her deposition seemed to indicate a positive shift in life-style. However, the following entry clearly indicates that James Miller is still a part of her life, and that there has been no significant change in lifestyle.

THU. NOV. 12, 92 12HRS+ D

Picked up Bobby at 6:00am at Amber's sister's apt. I asked how he was doing. She said, "Fine." We had a nice day with lunch at Encanto Park. 3:45pm Amber came to pick up Bobby in James Miller's vehicle. Amber picked up the clean clothes I put out for Bobby and his coat. Because Amber used James's vehicle, on the way home we passed the shop where he was working. Amber was carrying Bobby and getting into James's vehicle with him so we turned around. They pulled into a trailer park and a little while later, we followed them in. Amber and James were visiting with some other people. James saw us and jumped into the vehicle and took off after us. He tailgated us then swung around to get in front and slammed on his brakes. I did not hit him and made a right turn down the street. I called the police and made a report of the incident. When we got home, James had called and in a very low voice said "Don't just drive through next time. Stop by and visit. We might have a lot to talk about." I called Mr. Solomon and told him that Amber was exposing Bobby to James. Mr. Solomon thought it was important that Amber no longer see James.

TUE. DEC. 1, 92 10HRS

Picked up Bobby at 6:00 at Amber's sister's apt. I asked how he was doing. She said, "OK"... The apartment was a mess. Amber's current husband [Mike Jones] is on the road as a truck driver and James Miller's truck was in the west side parking lot. Bobby ate strawberries and oatmeal before his vitamins and nap. Linda and Ron brought their baby Christine to the office for the day. Christine is only nine months old, but she weighs 28 lbs., being so fat that she only crawls a little. Bobby is so taken with her. He brings her toys and cookies and pats her on the head. After we went to lunch at Garcia's, Linda and I took the babies shopping. Got back at 4:10pm, Amber arrived 4:14.

WED. DEC. 2, 92 9HRS N/I

Picked up Bobby at 6:00am at Amber's sister's apt. Amber's car and James Miller's Chevrolet truck were in the west parking lot. 3:10pm Amber came to pick up Bobby as I came into the lobby of the office. Amber picked up the clean clothes I put out for Bobby and his coat. I handed Bobby's coat to Amber and she started to leave. Rebecca was sitting in the lobby visiting with her mother and another lady and said to Amber, "You have your coat on; you should put the baby's coat on him before you take him outside in the cold." Amber did not hesitate to take him out the door without his coat, saying, "I will take care of it."

SAT. DEC. 5, 92

6:00pm Amber called to tell me Bobby had been running in the house this morning and hit his head very hard. She took him to the emergency room free clinic at the hospital and they did x-rays. There was no fracture. I asked to talk to him. She said, "No his cousins had him outside."

MON. DEC. 8, 92 10HRS

Picked up Bobby at 6:00am. Both Amber's and James's vehicles are in the parking lot. Bobby's head has a huge lump, abrasion and bruising even after 3 days.

Amber arrived to pick up Bobby at 4:00pm. I handed Amber the diaper bag containing supplies. Amber called to say she just wanted me to know she was going to keep Bobby for the week of Christmas. I told her we would have to see Mr. Solomon tomorrow.

MON. DEC. 14, 92 9HRS

Picked up Bobby at 6:00am at Amber's sister's apt. Amber's car and James Miller's Chevy truck were in the west parking lot. Amber arrived to pick up Bobby at 3:50pm. I handed Amber the diaper bag. I told Amber to call Mr. Solomon because he said the normal daily schedule will be in place for the week and she gets him in the morning Christmas day and

I get Bobby for New Year's evening.

FRI. DEC. 25, 92 9HRS

6:00pm Amber brought Bobby to my home in James Miller's vehicle. Her sister Eunice and her two children were also in the El Camino.

1993

FRI. FEB. 5, 93

Picked up Bobby at 6:00am at Amber's apt. Ok, it looks like this is almost over. We have court at 1:30pm today. Mom will be here to watch Bobby, and all our witnesses called to let us know everything is ready. I can't believe it. The Judge would not hear anything. He would not let either of the attorneys talk or any of the witnesses testify. He ordered that Bobby is to go to Washington with Amber this afternoon for the next three weeks and then back to me. This is to continue until a home study can be done in Washington. We are devastated. Amber picked up Bobby at 5:00pm
She didn't say anything. She just smirked.

FRI. FEB. 26, 93

Amber brought Bobby back this morning at 9:00am. She said they drove straight through.

MON. MAR. 1, 93 $30.00

It is wonderful having Bobby back. With Amber in Washington trying to put together an acceptable home for the evaluator, we don't have to give him back each night. He seems very quiet, but very happy to be home. Took him to the pediatrician for a check up. He has a cold.

THU. MAR. 18, 93 $30.00

Took Bobby to the pediatrician for a well baby check up before we have to take him back to Washington.

FRI. MAR. 19, 93 $1,594.00

We took Bobby back to Amber today. God, this is hard. He does really well on the airplane. Between the airline tickets, rental car, food and hotel, it costs about $1,600.00 to take him to Washington. Amber had moved from the duplex in Nola to an apartment complex in Star without letting me know.

FRI. APR. 9, 93

Amber brought Bobby back this morning at 9:35am. She brought all of the children with her in the car this time.

MON. APR. 12, 93 $30.00

Bobby is back. It is great. During his well baby check up, the pediatrician said Bobby lost weight just like last time.

THU. MAR. 18, 93 $30.00

Took Bobby to the pediatrician for a well baby check up before we have to take him back to Washington.

FRI. APR. 30, 93 $1,594.00

We took Bobby back to Amber today. I hate this. He slept most of the plane ride this time.

FRI. MAY. 21, 93

Amber brought Bobby back this morning at 10:00am. She looked exhausted from the drive.
I know it's a lot cheaper than flying, but I think a 3-day car drive is too hard on both of them.

MON. MAY. 24, 93 $30.00

Bobby is home. During his well baby check up, the pediatrician said Bobby lost weight again.

THU. JUN. 10, 93

We have court today and on the 22nd, so we don't have to take Bobby to Washington. That's wonderful.

THU. JUN. 22, 93

4:00pm We went to court again. With all the witnesses and documentation, the judge stopped the proceedings. He was not willing to make a decision. We must agree to have the decision by a psychologist as binding. We all finally agreed. The Judge changed the alternating visitation from every three weeks to every five. Sometimes I think this will go on forever. I made our appointment with the psychologist. Amber left for Washington with Bobby at 6:00pm

SUN. JUL. 18, 93

Amber brought Bobby back this morning at 9:45am.

MON. JUL. 19, 93 $30.00

Bobby is home. During his well baby check up, the pediatrician said Bobby lost weight again.

WED. AUG. 11, 93 $500.00

First appointment with the psychologist. No idea how we did.

MON. AUG. 23, 93 $500.00

We had our second appointment with the psychologist.

TUE. AUG. 24, 93 $30.00

Took Bobby to the pediatrician for a well baby check up before we have to take him back to Washington.

WED. AUG. 25, 93 $1,594.00

Took Bobby back to Washington today. It doesn't get any easier.

THU. AUG. 26, 93 $30.00

We had our third appointment with the psychologist and he got to meet Bobby.

MON. AUG. 30, 93 $500.00

I went to the psychologist alone. He is professional and distant. I think I answered about a hundred questions. God, I wish I knew how I was doing.

TUE. SEP. 07, 93 $30.00

Took Bobby to the pediatrician for a well baby check up before we have to take him back to Washington.

WED. SEP. 08, 93 $1,594.00

We took Bobby back to Amber today. We had the same stewardess we had on other trips and she played with Bobby. Amber acted the way she usually does, but I had proof this time, and the psychologist read the sworn statement the witness made.

SUN. SEP. 26, 93

Amber was supposed to return Bobby this morning, but she didn't. I called her and she said she could not afford to bring him and then would not answer the telephone the rest of the day.

MON. SEP. 27, 93 $1,850.00

Our attorney is filing contempt of court charges if Amber does not return Bobby to Arizona by noon on Wednesday. Court and Attorney $1,850.00

WED. SEP. 29, 93

Our judge is on vacation and the substitute judge did not find Amber in contempt, but did say she must comply. Amber said if we want him back we will have to pay for the airline ticket. We said we would and that she should call us back with the flight information. She said she already had it and told us when to be at the airport tomorrow with a check for $331.00

THU. SEP. 30, 93 $331.00

I had the check ready and when Bobby saw us he ran to me and jumped into my arms burying his face in my shoulder.
Amber didn't have her glasses on and was squinting into the crowd looking for us. I called her name and waved. She came over to us snatched the check and turned without saying good-bye to Bobby. He didn't notice.

FRI. OCT. 1, 93 $30.00

During his well baby check up, the pediatrician said Bobby lost weight again.

TUE. OCT. 26, 93

Our attorney Catharine called to tell us I have been awarded sole custody of Bobby, and the psychologist's report was accepted as the custody order. Amber will have Bobby for seven weeks out of the year for visitation.
Bobby has been well and happy. Amber hasn't called to see how Bobby is in weeks.

Value of this Entry
Once custody is decided the emphasis of the information in the contact log may change. Randall no longer felt it was necessary to list the money spent for Bobby's care.

MON. DEC. 27, 1993

8:00am Amber arrived at the office with James's brother Paul to pick Bobby up for Christmas week visitation. It was the first time we had seen or heard from Amber since custody was awarded. 11:00am. We met our attorney at court for final ruling on visitation and child support. I was really shocked when I saw Amber. She had always dressed in a business like manner for court, but today she was in faded Levis and grubby shoes, shirt and jacket with her hair a mess and no makeup. She did not look this bedraggled when she picked up Bobby this morning. In the judge's chambers, Amber said she no longer made $800.00 a month because she had a cut in pay and was the sole support of her other three children with no other income. The judge asked if there were any other changes in her financial statement. Amber said no. Our attorney produced proof that she had regular substantial income from three other sources, that she lived with James the father of her other children, and he makes over $2,000.00 per month. The judge seemed irritated by Amber's antics and awarded me child support using the guidelines.

WED. DEC. 29, 1993

10:00am I called Amber to see how Bobby was doing. Amber's oldest son answered the telephone and told me Bobby was doing fine and let me talk to him.

1994

SAT. JAN. 1, 1994

10:00am I called Amber to see how Bobby was doing. She said he was OK and let me talk to him.

MON. JAN. 3, 1994

I flew out of Phoenix last night to Seattle, spent the night and picked up a detective to accompany me to Amber's to pick up Bobby. Her oldest son saw us pull into the apartment complex.

We arrived at Amber's door at 8:00am and knocked on the door. The door opened, Bobby walked out, and Amber closed the door. As we were getting in the car, Amber appeared at the door and called to Bobby, "Don't worry baby,

Mommie will get you back as soon as she wins her Appeal."

MON. FEB. 20, 94

Amber called to see how Bobby is doing, then spoke to him for approximately 2 minutes. First call since I picked up Bobby Jan. 3rd.

FRI. MAR. 18, 94

8:00am Amber arrived at the office with a man we didn't know. We said good bye to Bobby and followed them out to a Bronco. Amber jumped in the back seat with Bobby. There was no child car seat in the vehicle so I told him they could not take the baby. We stood in the door of the vehicle preventing the man from driving away. The man called me a rapist and cussed at me. Bobby was crying and became so upset he threw up. Amber decided to have us clean up the baby and they would return with a car seat. They came back with the seat in about an hour. The baby was calm, and they left.

MON. MAR. 21, 94

10:00am I called to see how Bobby was doing. Amber answered the telephone, so I said "Hi Amber, how's Bobby?" She said she was not Amber, but her daughter. I said "Right, how's Bobby?" She said he was fine and let me talk to him.

THU. MAR. 24, 94

6:00pm I called Amber to see how Bobby was doing. Amber's youngest son answered the telephone and told me Bobby was doing good and let me talk to him.

FRI. MAR. 25, 94

12:00pm We arrived at the Police Station in Amber's town. The officer asked, which address we were going to. I told him the address and told him Amber and James lived there. He said, "Yeah, I have arrested James a couple of times". The officer accompanied us to the house, and the officer and I went up to the door. Amber had a short plump biker-looking guy there guarding the door. Amber opened the door and her oldest son Jerome yanked Bobby from a nap directly into the sunlight. The baby started to cry. Jerome handed me Bobby, and as we started to leave the door, Amber said "You could have told me he was sick when I picked him up." I said "He had a well baby check up the day before you picked him up." Amber said "Sure you did, well here is his medicine." As I was getting into the car she called to the still crying child that she made no attempt to comfort and said, "Mama loves you baby, and I will get you back soon." The neighbors looked as if I was tearing a child from its mother's breast. Amber was in her glory. She likes lots of audience for her performance. I thanked the officer and called the doctor listed on the medicine. He said Amber brought Bobby in late yesterday afternoon and what he had, can happen overnight.

SUN. MAR. 27, 94

When we got home, there were several messages from Amber. I called her and told her he was fine. She did not ask for him.

WED. MAY. 18, 94

Received court papers. Amber had withdrawn her Appeal.

THU. JUN. 18, 94

Amber called to change the summer visitation schedule. I told her the court prohibited any changes after April 15 of each year. I quoted the sentence to her, "To avoid conflict and misunderstanding, the visitation schedule is suggested to be fixed, and should not be extended or adjusted if either parent is unable to exercise their visitation as outlined." Amber talked to Bobby for several minutes.

FRI. JUL. 1, 94

My attorney called Amber's attorney to find out what time Amber would be picking up Bobby.
Amber's attorney called our attorney. He said Amber would not be coming to pick up Bobby for this visitation, but that she would pick him up in six weeks.

THU. JUL. 28, 94

Bobby had his well baby physical check up before his trip.

FRI. JUL. 29, 94

8:00am I took Bobby to the police department so Amber could take him for the three week visit at her house in Washington. Amber refused the knapsack Bobby had packed for his trip saying, "He has his things at my house, I don't need that stuff." Bobby made a fuss when she tried to give me back his Aladdin book so she let him take that.

MON. AUG. 1, 94

10:00am I called to talk to Bobby. Lucy said he was gone with Amber, and she did not know when they would be home. 5:00pm Lucy said he was gone with Amber, and she did not know when they would be home. 7:00pm I got the answering machine.

TUE. AUG. 2, 94

10:30am I called to talk to Bobby. I got the answering machine, left a message. 8:00pm Left a message again.

WED. AUG. 3, 94 Same as previous

THU. AUG. 4, 94

9:45am I called to talk to Bobby. I got the answering machine, left a message. 7:00pm I got the answering machine, left a message saying my attorney would file charges. Amber called right back within 3 minutes, saying, "I am not going to wait around my house all day waiting for your call." She said Bobby was fine. I got to talk to him for 2 minutes. It was wonderful to hear his voice. I could hear the other children calling him to go outside.

MON. AUG. 8 & 9, 94 Same as previous

WED. AUG. 10, 94

I can't believe what is going on now.
Ms. March of Texas Child Protective Services called to investigate an anonymous charge of sexual child abuse and neglect from Washington state against Rebecca. I spoke to Ms. March for almost an hour. We made an appointment for the next day.

THU. AUG. 11, 94

9:00am I dropped the custody papers off at Ms. March's office. 10:30am I called to talk to Bobby. I got the answering machine, left a message. 8:00pm I got the answering machine, left a message.

FRI. AUG. 12, 94

9:00am I called to talk to Bobby. I got the answering machine, left a message. 4:45pm Jerome answered the telephone. I got to talk to Bobby. Amber got on the telephone and asked why the rest of the work had not been done on Bobby's teeth. I told her it was scheduled. She said we didn't care about Bobby's teeth and they could just fall out. I told her that was bull. Amber hung up on me.

MON. AUG. 15, 94

9:45am I called to talk to Bobby. I got the answering machine, left a message. 8:00pm I got the answering machine, left a message.

TUE. AUG. 16, 17 & 18, 94 Same as previous

I called my attorney and asked her to call Amber's attorney to confirm that Amber got the notice I sent saying,
I would be there to pick up Bobby tomorrow. My attorney advised me that Amber had filed papers in Arizona. Since my wife was under investigation for sexual child abuse, Bobby should not be returned to me, and requested a change of custody because of the sexual abuse and neglect. I faxed my attorney the report from Child Protective Services, saying there

was no evidence that the child had ever been abused. So my attorney said go pick up Bobby and don't worry.

FRI. AUG. 19, 94

7:45am Two blocks from the police station in Washington, Jerome threw a rock at our car. Bobby was happy to see me and buried his face in my neck. Amber said his Aladdin book was at the baby-sitters 60 miles away and she was late for work. We headed for 3-days at Disney Land.

MON. AUG. 22, 94

Bobby had his well baby physical check up after his trip. Amber called and talked to Bobby for 15 minutes.

THU. AUG. 25, 94

Amber called and talked to Bobby for 10 minutes.

MON. AUG. 29, 94

Amber called and talked to Bobby for 5 minutes.

TUE. SEP. 6, 94

Amber called and talked to Bobby for 10 minutes.

SAT. OCT. 1, 94

Jerome called at 1:00pm asking to talk to Bobby. I told him he was down for a nap. Jerome asked if I would wake him up. I said no, that he would be up in one hour. Amber called at 6:00pm and talked to Bobby. She had Bobby talk to several neighbor kids, her three children, and then accused me of taking the telephone away. Bobby did not want the phone after he had been talking to people for an hour.

SAT. OCT. 15, 94

Lucy called and asked to speak to Bobby. I told her that her Mom would have to make the call, then she could talk to him. Amber called at 6:00pm and talked to Bobby.

TUE. OCT. 21, 94

Bobby got three letters from Amber today, a Birthday card, an I-love-you-son card, and a Halloween card. I helped him put them up on the corkboard in his room.

TUE. NOV. 1, 94

Amber did not show up in court for the hearing on the papers she had filed that Bobby should not be returned to me, and requesting a change of custody because of the sexual abuse and neglect charges. The Judge looked at the final report from Ms. March, whose opinion was that the charges were false, and he dismissed the case with prejudice.

MON. NOV. 28, 94

Amber called at 1:15pm. I told her Bobby was napping and he would be up in one hour. She said she would call back. She didn't.

MON. DEC. 5, 94

Got a letter from Amber's attorney she would be picking up Bobby at 10:00am for Christmas.

THU. DEC. 15, 94

Bobby had his well baby physical check up before his trip. He also had a meeting with Dr. Savant for a well baby psychological check up.

FRI. DEC. 16, 94

Amber called me at 9:00am "Well, are you going to bring him to me or not?" I told her the attorney set it up for 10:00, but I would get there as soon as I could. I arrived at the police department at 9:30. Amber refused Bobby's backpack saying "I have everything he needs. I don't need that stuff." Even the dispatcher at the police department was astonished and commented about the venom in Amber's voice.

MON. DEC. 19, 94

10:30am I called to talk to Bobby. I got the answering machine, left a message. 8:00pm I got the answering machine, left a message.

MON. DEC. 19, 94

Same as previous

TUE. DEC. 20, 94

I got to speak to Bobby for 5 minutes.

THU. DEC. 22, 94

Same as previous
11:00am I called to talk to Bobby. I got the answering machine, left a message. 8:00pm I got the answering machine, left a message.

FRI. DEC. 23, 94

Jerome accompanied Amber to the police station in Star to bring Bobby to me. They were 15 minutes late. Jerome was very hostile to Rebecca and me and called us filthy names. Amber glowed with pride that Jerome was attacking us on her behalf. We left for the airport and spent a week at my parent's home in California.

1995

TUE. FEB. 9, 95

Bobby had his well baby physical check up after his trip.
He also had a meeting with Dr. Savant for a well baby psychological after visitation check up. The psychologist is concerned about the things Bobby tells her, but she won't go into detail with us.

TUE. MAR. 8, 95

1:25pm Amber called to talk to Bobby. I told her he was at Wal-Mart with Rebecca and they would be back in one hour. She said, "I thought he was always with you" and hung up.

TUE. MAR. 21, 95

I filed papers for Amber to have supervised visitation until Bobby is 7 years old. Ms. March of Texas Child Protective Services and Mrs. Savant the psychologist, have both suggested it would be best for Bobby.

TUE. JUL. 4, 95

Haven't heard anything from Amber in four months. She hasn't even a called to see how Bobby is doing. Her attorney is to have her interrogatories back to our attorney tomorrow for court August 24th.

MON. JUL. 24, 95

Our attorney has not heard from Amber or her attorney. The phone number we had for her is disconnected.

TUE. AUG. 1, 95

Our attorney got a packet from Amber's attorney containing copies of the complaints Amber filed against the original judge and the psychologist and a litany of new and old accusations against Rebecca and me, but, none of the financial documentation requested in the interrogatories.

TUE. AUG. 23, 95

Bobby had his well child check up at the doctor and psychologist this morning. Amber's attorney said she will be in town this afternoon. She has not called to set up a visit for before or after court, but if Amber wants to see Bobby, I wanted him to be able to spend some time with her without delay or me feeling the threat of new accusations.

WED. AUG. 24, 95

Amber didn't call last evening, but she did come to court. After hearing the testimony, the judge expressed little confidence in Amber's ability to tell the truth. My attorney presented evidence that Amber's two sons had been in a lot of serious trouble with the police. The psychologist testified that from what Bobby was saying the time he spends in Washington state is spent in the care of these two boys and is very scary. The judge felt there was not enough evidence that Bobby is in danger when in her care. There would not be supervised visitation in Texas, but he would make Bobby's visits with Amber more structured in Washington as to who would take care take of him when she is working. The judge asked Amber if she made any attempt to see Bobby before or after court. She said no and asked if she could take Bobby to Washington for the next nine weeks. He said he would not do that to Bobby since she had not maintained contact and she was virtually a stranger to him. The judge asked Amber to stay in town for a few days to let Bobby have some time with her. Amber said, "No, I have to be to work in the morning." The judge ordered Amber to spend from 3:30pm till 7:00pm before she left town with Bobby and to call him every Wednesday. Her next scheduled visitations are 5-days at Thanksgiving and a week that includes Christmas. We delivered Bobby to Amber on time and picked him up at seven. Bobby was happy to see Amber and he was happy to see us come back for him. He is very confused. We answer his questions and just let him talk about it. He is calming down.

WED. AUG. 31, 95

Amber called at 5:00pm, and Bobby spoke to her for about ten minutes and was happy to get the call. Bobby has been talking about Amber a great deal. He calls her his Nother Mommie and wants to know why she doesn't come again. I said, "She will come as soon as she can." Bobby woke with nightmares at 11:00pm, and I spent the night in his room.

WED. SEP. 6, 95

Amber called at 7:00pm, and Bobby spoke for about twenty minutes. Bobby got to speak to a brother and his sister. Bobby says he would like his nother Mommie to visit, but he does not want to go there. Bobby made fewer comments about Amber this week.

WED. SEP. 13, 95

Amber called at 4:30pm, and Bobby spoke to her for about fifteen minutes and was happy to get the call. We are all doing better. Bobby made no references to Amber this week.

WED. SEP. 20, 95

Amber called at 5:00pm, and Bobby spoke to her for about ten minutes and was happy to get the call. We are all doing better.

WED. NOV. 22, 95

No calls from Amber Sept.20 to date.
Amber picked up Bobby at Police department for Thanksgiving visit. I told her I would be calling Bobby on the 24th.

THU. NOV. 24, 95

James answered the phone and said Amber was not home. I called back in one hour and spoke to Bobby. Bobby said he had to live there from now on because he came from Amber's tummy not Rebecca's. I told him he could visit any time he wanted, but he lived here. He said OK.

SAT. NOV. 26, 95

At the Star Police Department, Bobby came running up to me, anxious to go home.

SAT. NOV. 29, 95

Amber called to say she would be picking Bobby up December 24th for Christmas. She did not ask to speak to Bobby. Amber's attorney still has not filed the papers from the August 24th court hearing and its costing me attorney fees every time my attorney asks for them.

SUN. DEC. 24, 95

Amber picked Bobby up at the police department. He was very hesitant to go with her. She did not kiss or hug him hello she just put him in the car.

WED. DEC. 27, 95

I called Bobby and we spoke for 15 minutes. God I miss him.

SUN. DEC. 31, 95

I picked Bobby up at the police department in Washington. He ran to me and wrapped his arms around my neck and wouldn't let go. Amber said the big sore on his mouth is only a cold sore and there was a tube of ointment in his bag to take care of it. We had to spend 6 hours in the airport. He was sitting or laying on me all the time. Nice. He said the girl (looked about 12 years old) with Amber was his baby-sitter and he was with her all the time. Bobby said he did not want to go back there.

1996

TUE. JAN. 2, 96

Doctor said the sore on Bobby's mouth is impetigo and very contagious and could cause other problems and that the salve that was sent with Bobby would have spread the problem not cure it. Bobby can't go to school until his sore is gone that will be about 2 weeks.
We don't mind having him home. Dr. Savant talked to Bobby and said if we go back to court for anything she wants to be there.

WED. FEB. 21, 96

My attorney called. We have court March 8, 1996, because Amber's attorney never filed the papers from court last August. No calls from Amber.

THU. MAR. 7, 96

My attorney called Amber's attorney and got a continuance until August 8, 1996. He also notified me that she would be picking Bobby up for spring break March 9th.

SAT. MAR. 9, 96

Amber picked Bobby up at 10:30am at the police department. She didn't want to take the backpack he put his things in. I told her those things were important to him and she took it saying "I'll just leave it in the rent a car." Bobby looked very distressed.

WED. MAR. 13, 96

I got to talk to Bobby for about fifteen minutes. I miss him so much.

SUN. MAR. 17, 96

Picked up Bobby at the police department in Washington.

WED. JUN. 19, 96

Amber called our home and Rebecca's daughter told her we would be home in one hour. Amber did not call back.

Value of this Entry
It often felt as if there was no longer any reason to keep a contact log. But when it became necessary to demonstrate how little contact Bobby had with Amber the contact log was crucial.

THU. AUG. 8, 96

We went to court. Because Amber's attorney did not file the papers from last year the judge reconsidered all the documentation about the legal problems Amber's son Jerome was having. We presented at that time and documentation of how seldom Amber attempted to contact Bobby and the problems he had with each visit. The psychologist, Bobby's teacher, Rebecca's daughter and Amber and I all testified. The judge said Amber could have only 10-days of summer vacation rather than 7 weeks and she was to keep Jerome and Bobby from having contact in any form. He also said if Amber does not call every Wednesday night at 7:30 there would be no more visitation and no more court. Bobby flew away for the 10-day summer visit with Amber at 3:00pm

WED. AUG. 13, 96

I called Bobby and visited for 15 minutes.

WED. AUG. 17, 96

I called Bobby and visited for 15 minutes. I told him I loved him and I would see him tomorrow.

WED. AUG. 20, 96

I picked up Bobby at the police department. His obvious joy at seeing me makes me feel like a million dollars.

THU, AUG. 21, 96

Bobby saw Dr. Savant today.
Amber called Bobby at 7:30pm. Every Wednesday from Aug. 21 through Wed. Dec. 11, 96

WED. DEC. 18, 96

Amber called Bobby at 7:30pm. Bobby said they have a bunch of presents there for him and a new bicycle. He is excited about the trip. I talked to her and she said she would be picking Bobby up at 10:00 Saturday morning. I told her I did not get the court ordered visitation notification from her attorney 31-days advance of the pick up date. I had not purchased a ticket to pick him up after the visit so she should call her attorney to see what they could do about getting me an airline ticket.

THU. DEC. 19, 96

My attorney called. Amber's attorney had not followed Amber's instructions and did not send out the proper notification so Amber's attorney would arrange for my ticket.

SAT. DEC. 21, 96

Bobby opened five Christmas gifts before he dressed to go to Washington for his Christmas visit. He picked two of the small transformer toys to take with him. Amber picked Bobby up at the police station. This is the first time he said he wanted to go so letting him go is much easier.

WED. DEC. 25, 96

I called Bobby and wished him a Merry Christmas. He said they didn't get him the things they promised, but he was having a good time. He was happy to hear I would be picking him up Sunday.

FRI. DEC. 28, 96

I called Bobby and talked for about ten minutes. He was ready to come home and looked forward to seeing me Sunday.

SUN. DEC. 29, 96

I have my Bobby back and we had a good trip home. I think he grew three inches in 8-days.

1997

WED. JAN. 1, 1997

Amber called Bobby at 7:30pm. Amber only missed 5 calls to Bobby from January through June 4th

SUN. JUN. 8, 1997

Amber picked Bobby up for three weeks of his seven week summer visit. He was nervous, but we worked hard to make sure he knew he would be fine and have a good time once he got there. Amber shoved Bobby into the car and drove off without a word

WED. JUN. 11, 1997

I called Bobby. His conversation was guarded, but he said he was fine and having a good time. He wanted to know when I was coming to get him.

WED. JUN. 18, 1997

I called Bobby. He wanted to know if I would come and get him tomorrow. I asked if he was ok and he said yes I just want you to come and get me tomorrow. He was very insistent. I told him I could come in one more week.

WED. JUN. 25, 1997

I called Bobby. He started off with telling me I needed to come and get him tomorrow. I told him it would be only four more days. He was not happy about that.

SUN. JUN. 29, 1997

I picked Bobby up at 8:30am at the police station. He wrapped his arms around my neck and didn't want to let go. We flew home and spent the night in a hotel near the airport and the next day at Astro World. At four we headed home to Rebecca. Amber called Bobby twice in the four weeks between the first and second part of his visitation.

THU. JUL. 25, 1997

Amber and her attorney and my attorney and I went to courthouse this morning. She wears baggy clothes, but she looks pregnant. Her live in James got himself fixed over ten years ago. I have no idea whose baby this one might be. The judge didn't want to hear any of the arguments and ordered the attorneys to work it through and bring him the results or neither of them was going to like what he did. My attorney showed her attorney the documented evidence of 11 major violations of the court order since we were last in court in August 8, 1996. They agreed to change the visitation to standard for this state. Amber was angry because under the old order she would eventually have had Bobby for the entire summer. With this order the visitation will remain at 42-days only.

SUN. JUL. 27, 1997

Amber was waiting for us when I arrived at the police station to drop Bobby for the second half of his visitation. He hugged and kissed me goodbye and turned to his mother. She grabbed his hand and said to me, "You just love making my life miserable."

WED. JUL. 30, 1997

I called Bobby he is doing fine. I sure miss him.

WED. AUG. 6, 1997

I called Bobby. He said they are going to visit Grandma in Arizona next week so he will call me from there. He is doing fine.

WED. AUG. 13, 1997

Bobby called me from Phoenix. He said his mom, big sister, her baby, and one brother drove to grandmas. He was having a good time.

WED. AUG. 20, 1997

I called Bobby. He asked if I would come and get him. I told him I would be there in 4-days. He said he had a nice visit in Arizona and that it was a long drive.

SUN. AUG. 24, 1997

Amber brought Bobby to the police station with her younger son. She is definitely going to have a baby. Bobby was glad to see me and hugged my neck as I carried him out to the car.

WED. SEP. 3, 1997

No call from Amber. Bobby was upset that she did not call, but did not want to call her.

WED. SEP. 10, 1997

Amber called Bobby and said she didn't call last week because she was in the hospital for two days. Bobby told us that and then put the telephone up to his ear again. The conversation was short and when he got off the telephone he was very upset. When I asked what was the matter he said his Mommie said he could not talk about it to me. He woke up crying twice and I put him in bed with us. He keeps asking Rebecca's daughter, whose baby is due this month, if her baby is alive or not.

SAT. SEP. 12, 1997

Bobby's best friend Jason spent the night last night. They played outside on the trampoline and rode KoKo around the back yard. They came in smelling very much like the pony. Jason took his shower first. While Bobby was in the shower, Jason said he was sorry Bobby's other mom's baby died and that he and Bobby decided to pray for the baby in church tomorrow. I told him I thought that would be very good.

SUN. SEP. 13, 1997

At church the boys prayed for Amber's dead baby. They had their entire Sunday school class praying with them. Bobby will stand right next to Rebecca and I and talk to the other children about the baby, but he does not mention it directly to us.

WED. SEP. 17, 24, OCT. 1, 8, 15, 22, 1997

Amber called and talked to Bobby.

WED. OCT. 29, 1997

Amber called and talked to Bobby. She wanted to know if he got the birthday card she sent. He read it to her.

WED. NOV. 5, 12, 19, 21, 1997

Amber picked up Bobby for Thanksgiving.

FRI. NOV. 28, 1997

I picked up Bobby from Amber in Washington. He said he had a nice visit and got to see his brothers, sister, niece and nephew.

WED. DEC. 3, 10, 1997

Amber called and talked to Bobby.

WED. DEC. 7, 1997

Amber called and talked to Bobby. He told her we were flying to Phoenix for Christmas. She wanted to know, which day and on what flight we would be returning. I told Bobby to tell her we didn't have the tickets from Rebecca's brother yet. Because the trip was a gift from them to us, I did not have the information yet. That was true, but I was also concerned about any trouble she could have her family cause for me in Arizona.

FRI. DEC. 14, 1997

All five of us flew into Phoenix tonight. Rebecca's brother rented a car for us, then decided it wasn't good enough and gave us his new car to use. They gave us the entire up stairs of their big home and made sure we had everything. Bobby slept in his cousin's room. The boys are the same age and get along great.

WED. DEC. 17, 1997

We forwarded the phone from home to Phoenix. Amber called and talked to Bobby. She asked, which day and flight we would be going back to Texas on. Saying "I'll see you there." Bobby was concerned about Amber's comment.

THU. DEC. 25, 1997

We had a wonderful visit with our family in Phoenix. All five of us loaded on to the plane to fly home. Bobby and Rebecca were playing a Game Boy, in the seats behind me on the plane. They talked happily and were kidding each other over the game. The last person to load the plane was Amber, she said, "Hi, Randall. Hi, Rebecca. I told you I would be here." She didn't say another word as she proceeded to the back of the plane. I turned in my seat. Bobby had a look of panic on his face and was frozen in place. He looked at me and said, "Are you going to let her take me now?" I told him, "No, you are going home with us tonight. She will pick you up tomorrow at 11:00 in the morning. OK?" Bobby seemed to relax a little. He wiggled to get under Rebecca's arm and cuddled against her side and went directly to sleep. When the flight landed, our family waited to let the crowd off the plane. Amber went by without a look or a word. I carried Bobby off the plane.

FRI. DEC. 26, 1997

Bobby slept through the ride home from the airport and quietly through the night. He woke early and in a very good mood. I fixed breakfast for the family and we read some stories. Around ten he finally mentioned his trip with his mom. We got his bag ready and he seemed fine. Amber was at the police department when I got there with Bobby. She didn't say a word. Just put him into the car after I kissed him good bye and told him to be a good boy and have a good time.

WED. DEC. 31, 1997

I called Bobby. He said he was having a nice time and wanted to know when I would be picking him up. I told him I would call next Wednesday and pick him up the next Saturday.

1998

WED. JAN. 7, 1998

I called Bobby. He said he loved me and wanted to know when I would be there. I told him I would be there to pick him up in three days.

SAT JAN. 10, 14, 21, 28, FEB. 4, 11, 18, 25, MAR. 4, 11, 1998

Amber called and talked to Bobby.

FRI. MAR. 13, 1998

Amber picked Bobby up for Spring Break.

WED. MAR. 14, 1998

I called Washington and talked to Bobby.

SAT. MAR. 21, 1998

I picked Bobby up from Amber.

WED. MAR. 18, 25, APR. 1, 8, 15, 22, 29, MAY. 6, 13, 20, 27, 1998

Amber called and talked to Bobby.

WED. JUN. 3, 1998

Amber called and talked to Bobby. He woke at 3:00am with a rash and temperature. The doctor had me give him Dimetap and put Calamine lotion on the rash.

WED. JUN. 10, 1998

Amber called and talked to Bobby. He is expressing a lot of anxiety about the summer visit.

WED. JUN. 13, 1998

Amber called and talked to Bobby.

WED. JUN. 17, 1998

Amber picked Bobby up for the 6 week summer vacation.

WED. JUN. 24, 1998

I called and talked to Bobby. He said he is having a good time.

WED. JUL. 1, 1998

I called and talked to Bobby. His mom is taking him to Phoenix.

WED. JUL. 8, 1998

Bobby called. He said they had a good drive from Washington to Phoenix, but he is glad to be out of the van.

WED. JUL. 15, 1998

I called and talked to Bobby. He asked when I was coming to get him. I told him to look at the calendar I put in his suitcase. He said his mom keeps the suitcase in her closet and he isn't allowed to go in there. When I told him, two more weeks he said that was too long. How bout I come tomorrow.

WED. JUL. 22, 1998

I called and talked to Bobby. He said I need to come to get him. When I told him five more days he said how about four?

WED. JUL. 27, 1998

I picked Bobby up in Washington this morning. He is glued to me. Feels great. Bobby said Amber records his calls with me and he doesn't like it.

WED. AUG. 5, 1998

Amber called and talked to Bobby. She mentioned his Christmas visitation and he said, "I am not ready to think about that yet."

WED. AUG. 12, 1998

Amber called and talked to Bobby.

WED. AUG. 19, 26, SEP. 2, 9, 16, 23, 30, OCT. 7, 14, 21, 28, NOV. 4, 11, 18, 25, 1998

Amber called and talked to Bobby.

WED. DEC. 2, 1998

Amber called and talked to Bobby. He counted the days until Amber is to pick him up and he became upset. Bobby woke up several times during the night crying and asking why he had to go. We told him his mother loves and misses him and that he will have a good time. Bobby has broken out in a rash all over his body and a cold sore has formed on his bottom lip. The doctor gave him something for the itching and said it's just nerves.

WED. DEC. 9, 1998

Amber called and talked to Bobby.

WED. DEC. 16, 1998

Amber called and talked to Bobby.

WED. DEC. 18, 1998

Amber picked Bobby up for Christmas visitation.

WED. DEC. 22, 1998

I called and talked to Bobby. He said he was having a good time.

SAT. DEC. 26, 1998

My daughter and granddaughter came with me to Washington to pick up Bobby. Then we flew on to California to spend a week with my family. Bobby said that he went to court two times when he was visiting his mother. One because his brother was in trouble and once because his step sister and her boyfriend were hitting her two year old boy. The baby sitter had taken pictures of bruises on the child and reported it to family services. Bobby was upset because he heard the family lie in court and was worried about the two year old boy. He didn't think it was right that the step sister said as they were leaving court, "We really fooled them big time" and laughed. Rebecca called the Washington children's services. They called us in California and talked to Bobby.

WED. DEC. 30, 1998

I had Bobby call Amber since she didn't have my mother's telephone number.

1999

WED. JAN. 6, 1999

Amber called and talked to Bobby.

Value of this Entry
The log gives witness to the fact that with time things do cool down. This log also shows no extra effort made on Ambers part to be anything, but minimally in contact in order to comply with court orders. Only a birthday card and no additional calls packages or reminders of her motherhood. We would never have believed things would ever get this calm.

WED. JAN. 13, 20, 27, FEB. 3, 10, 17, 24, MAR 3, 10, 1999

Amber called and talked to Bobby.

WED. MAR 17, 1999

Amber called and talked to Bobby. Bobby insisted on sleeping with us and has been counting down the days until Amber is to pick him up. Bobby woke up crying with a temperature and a rash all over his body and two cold sores have formed on his bottom lip. The doctor said it is just nerves again and gave him something for the itching and the cold sores.

WED. MAR 24, 31, APR 7, 14, 21, 28, MAY 5, 12, 19, 26, 1999

WED. JUNE 2, 1999

Amber called and talked to Bobby. Rebecca spoke to Amber and let her know that if she wanted to spend the day with Bobby at Astroworld rather than at the mall we would send the family season pass.

Amber said the court order would only let her pick him up at 6:00pm and her flight would leave at 10:50pm Therefore, she wouldn't have time to take him anywhere. We told her we would make him available at noon if she wished. Amber said that would be fine. Rebecca said she would print a map off the Internet with the driving directions. Amber said fine and resumed her conversation with Bobby.

SAT. JUN 5, 1999

Bobby went to Camp Pine Trails. Since his little league team hasn't lost any games they are allowing us to pick him up each evening for two hours for the play-offs. He was really excited about baseball and camp. Bobby packed for camp a week ahead of time.

FRI. JUNE 11, 1999

Picked Bobby up from camp and registered him for next year. His team won the championship. His Mother picks him up for six weeks of summer visitation in four days.

TUE. JUNE 14, 1999

I met Amber at noon for the exchange. I handed her Bobby's rolling suitcase and the envelope with Bobby's Astroworld season pass and the map. She said, "Uh, OK." She still doesn't hug and kiss him hello. I don't know why that bothers me, but it does.

TUE. JUNE 15, 1999

I called Bobby this evening. He said they had a good trip back, but did not go to Astroworld. Bobby said Amber was not going to do anything Rebecca was trying to make her do. Bobby said they saw a funny movie and played video games at the mall. I told Bobby we could go to Astroworld anytime and I was glad he had a good time. Rebecca and I were amazed at Amber's reaction to the effort we had made to accommodate her. But we think it will take some time. We have made a conscious decision to make things easier for Amber and it will take a while before she will get used to it.

WED. JUNE 16, 23, 30, JULY 7, 14, 21, 1999

I called Bobby this evening. He's doing fine.

MON. JULY 26, 1999

I picked Bobby up in Washington. My step-daughter and her two-year old came with me. We are going to play in the snow in the mountains and visit grandma in California. Then return home in a week.

WED. AUG. 4, 11, 18, 25, SEP. 1, 8, 15, 22, 29, OCT. 6, 13, 20, 27, NOV. 3, 10, 17, 1999

Amber called to talk to Bobby.

SAT. NOV. 20, 1999

This is Bobby's first flight alone. He was upset about it for weeks. I put him on the non-stop, direct flight, but it wasn't easy for any of us. A pilot was on his way home and made friends with Bobby before they boarded the flight. I called Amber's house at 8:00pm Washington state time. Bobby said he did fine, but he didn't like it. I told him I was proud of him and I loved him.

WED. NOV. 24, 1999

I called and talked to Bobby. He said he is having a good time and doesn't want to fly home alone. I can't get off work but we are trying to work something out.

SAT. NOV. 27, 1999

Rebecca flew up to Washington to escort Bobby back. She said the exchange went well with Amber.

WED. DEC. 1, 8, 15, 22, 1999

Amber called Bobby.

SUN. DEC. 22, 1999

I put Bobby on the plane to visit Amber for Christmas.

WED. DEC. 29, 1999

I called and talked to Bobby.

2000

SUN. JAN. 2, 2000

I picked Bobby up at the airport. He said he did much better flying this time.

WED. JAN 5, 12, 19, 26, FEB. 2, 9, 2000

Amber called to tell Bobby he had a new baby brother. Bobby is thrilled.

WED. FEB. 16, 23, MAR. 1, 8, 15, 22, 29, APR. 5, 12, 2000

Amber called to talk to Bobby.

SAT. APR 14, 2000

We took Bobby to the airport for Spring Break visit.

FRI. APR 21, 2000

I picked Bobby up at the airport.

WED. APR. 26, MAY. 3, 10, 17, 24, 2000

Amber called to talk to Bobby. The call in April Bobby told his Amber he broke his arm at his friends home and the cast was really cool.

WED. AUG. 16, 23, MAR. 1, 8, 15, 22, 29, APR. 5, 12, 19, 26, MAY 2, 9, 16, 23, 2000

Amber called to talk to Bobby.

MON. MAY 29, 2000

We took Bobby to the airport for Summer Vacation visit.

WED. MAY 31, JUN. 7, 14, 21, 28, JUL. 5, 2000

I called to talk to Bobby. He hates being at the baby-sitter all day. When he said there was nothing to do but watch TV. I asked Amber if I could send Bobby a box of activities. I sent puzzles, models, art supplies, games and trick cards.

SUN. JUL 9, 2000

I picked Bobby up at the airport. He was glad to be home and looked great.

WED. JUL. 19, 26, AUG 2, 9, 16, 23, 30, SEP. 6, 20, 27, OCT. 4, 11, 25, NOV. 1, 22, 29, DEC. 6, 13, 2000

Amber called to talk to Bobby.

TUE. DEC 19, 2000

We took Bobby to the airport for Christmas visit. He bought and wrapped all his gifts himself.

TUE. DEC. 26, 2000

I picked Bobby up at the airport. He said that he and his mom and the baby spend a quiet Christmas.

2001

WED. JAN. 6, 13, 20, 27, FEB 3, 31, 2001

Amber called to talk to Bobby. On February 3rd she

said that Bobby was so unhappy during the summer visits that rather than have him stay for six weeks she would have him come one. Maybe later in the year she and the baby would fly out to see Bobby here. I told her that would be fine. When she called back on the 31st Amber said she was working on her schedule to see when would be the best time for him to come.

WED. MAR20, 27, APR 4, 18, 25, 2001

Amber called to talk to Bobby. Amber told Bobby she was not going to have him visit for a week in the summer, she was going to come here instead. I told her we would pay for her hotel when she came.

WED. MAY 2, 16, 2001

Amber called to talk to Bobby.

SUN. MAY 17, 2001

6:30am Bobby woke me up with a cup of coffee. Then invited me out to the kitchen for my Father's Day Breakfast. Bobby with a little help had made cinnamon rolls for breakfast. Bobby, Rebecca and my Mother-In-Law made a nice little celebration for me. Bobby and I got to Canoe Central at 8:30am and were on the river all day. We had lunch at Dutton's Point and swam at Sandy Bottom. On the way home we ate at Los Mesa Grande and took dinner home to Rebecca and Grandma. This was the first Father's Day Bobby has been home in seven years. It was wonderful.

WED. MAY 23, 2001

Amber called to talk to Bobby. She said that she decided to have him come after all. Amber didn't know just when but she would let him know.

WED. MAY 30, 2001

Amber called to talk to Bobby. Still doesn't know when she wants him to come but knows he will have a great time when he does. They have moved on to the top of a mountain. Since they are snowed in from the middle of November until February she told them she wouldn't be able to see him for Thanksgiving or Christmas. He didn't seem to be upset by the call.

WED. JUN 13, 2001

Amber called to talk to Bobby. They had a good talk. He said she still doesn't know when she will send for him. Then he ran back outside to play with the other boys.

End of Log Entries

Photos

Taking photographs of your children can be one of the most rewarding parts of this process. The pictures will give you comfort when you cannot be with your children and remind you of why all of this is worth the trouble. It is important for you to have photos of you with your children. One of the primary problems of compiling these photos is that usually there is not a third person to take the photos. This problem can be overcome by using a camera with an automatic setting or scheduling a photo day once a month with a friend or relative.

Take Photos of Everything

Take photos of all the things that you are proud of and want to share --- happy times like birthday parties, bath time, playing with pets, cuddling with grandma, and other family members, as well as your children's rooms and toys.

Before you take the photos of your children, take a moment to look around to see what else will appear in the snapshot. Change your angle to eliminate unwanted objects or pick up anything scattered around that will make the area look messy. Take photos of all the things that cause you concern for your children. Some of the worrisome things would be bruises, bug bites, scratches, severe diaper rash, grubby clothing, dirty or cluttered environment. Take photos to disprove allegations made against you.

Supply older children with cameras and film. This allows them to capture in a photo what is important to them and gives you another avenue of insight as to their feelings.

Give your children photos of things important to them. At an age as young as fifteen months, they can identify themselves, you, and their pets. The photos you give small children will not survive sticky fingers and tooth marks on corners, so only give them duplicates.

Where they Will Do the Most Good

Photos in your children's possession helps them to maintain a feeling of being connected to you by having something to actually hold.

Give your children photos of themselves, their pets, and yourself taken together during happy times in your home. These can provide a constant, positive link between you and your children when they are away from you.

Photos help your children see they are really a part of your life. Put the children's photos, artwork and awards on display in your home. This shows your children they have a presence even when they are not in residence. Assist your children by displaying photos from the children's other parent or family, and home in the children's room. This simple action demonstrates you want the children to feel happy in all of the situations in which the children live.

The Dark Side

The weapons of this war are identical to the weapons of any war. A weapon can be used for defense or offense. Any weapon can be used against the warrior who brought it to the battle. Because of this problem, not everyone agrees with the wisdom of keeping a log or diary.

Generally speaking, it is good to keep a detailed record of what goes on. Be careful how zealously you represent the wrongs the opposition has inflicted on you. Exercise caution when deciding to whom you will present either knowledge that the log exists or the log itself. There are evaluators, mediators, judges, and attorneys for the opposition who feel that meticulous record keeping is "evidence "that a person is compulsive, controlling or obsessed.

When we asked evaluators, mediators, judges, and attorneys for the opposition who felt uncomfortable with meticulous record keeping; "What should a person do who is dealing with inconsistencies, false accusations, and behaviors that threaten the well being of one's children?"

The room gets very quiet and no reasonable answer is forthcoming.

Often you will hear it stated that the log won't be accepted as evidence at court, so it's a waste of time to do all that work. Even if the court will not accept your log as evidence, it is amazing how often a guardian ad litem or psychologist will take time to look them over. Indexing will improve the chances of a professional examining your work.

The psychologist may be more interested in how you view the problems than in what was happening at any specific time. For this reason it may be a good idea to have someone you trust read intermittent entries in your log. This person would be able to tell you if you sound accusatory or vengeful in your entries.

Chapter 7: Equipment & Services

The principals' acceptance or rejection of systems they view as too expensive or overly complicated may determine the pace of progress in a child custody war. When you wage war, you need adequate armaments. In our day-to-day life, some of us use computers to earn a living, and some of us operate heavy equipment. This chapter is about the armaments necessary in your arsenal for the child custody war.

Your intelligence and ability to reason things out will always be your best weapon. As you decide what you can and cannot afford, remember, "Stone knives and bear skins in the hands of the right person can win against all the high-tech equipment in the world." It makes the battle much more difficult for the under-equipped, but I have witnessed low-tech passion win against hi-tech snobbery.

Equipment

All methods of producing, reproducing or transmitting information by any means, electronic or mechanical, including photocopying, recording or by any information storage or retrieval system is open to the process of discovery.

Calendar

It is important to keep track of court dates and appointments with mediators, attorneys, and anything else that has to do with your children. If your calendar notes are brief, you can also use them as a daily log for pickup and return times for your children.

Caller ID

This is a service offered by the telephone companies in some areas that allows you to see the name and telephone number of anyone calling your telephone. There is a blocking service for people who do not want their number to show on Caller ID. You probably should subscribe to both services.

Camera, 35 MM

Use a 35mm camera that records the date, or date and time, of the photo. The advantage of 24-exposure film over 36-exposure is that it is faster to complete the roll for processing. Usually, 400 speed film is adequate for indoors and 200 for outdoors. If your skills are limited, check out a library book and read about the basics of taking good photographs.

Camera, Video

A video camera can be the second most valuable piece of equipment. It is small and very efficient with a price under $300.00. It can be your best shot at showing an evaluator your home, recording that papers were properly served to the opposition and offer evidence of how exchange for visitation was handled. A little known, but very powerful use of the video is its use during the process of discovery. The attorney can include a video inspection of the opposition's home in a motion for production and inspection. The attorney informs the opposition of the time and date as well as who will be coming. Video can be a lethal custody weapon and has been around for years. Parent's rights groups have successfully used them in "parent stand by situations" recent improvements and miniaturization in the technology have made them much smaller and easier to operate.

As a result, they are turning up in more child custody cases all the time. Video cameras can be used to document who is taking care of a child, behavior of the adults during visitation exchange or living conditions among many other things. Serious pitfalls can be avoided if you have your attorney review the video before court. The attorney may even have you shoot the scenario again to include or exclude information. This will help the attorney to prepare to overcome the objections of the opposition attorney. Scripting when and were you will shoot may also help. A two-minute video can make a stronger impression on the court than the world's best expert. The opposition's attorney's lack of familiarity with video evidence often causes them to forget to isolate objectionable portions. Because they are surprised or intimidated they may forget traditional objections that might be applicable portions of the video, which could be cumulative or inflammatory and make specific arguments to judge.

If you discover that the opposition will be presenting a video, make sure your attorney has reviewed it in order to prepare the proper objections to protect you.

Cellular Telephone

Cell phones are small and convenient. They are also not as private as conventional telephones. It may be possible for others to hear your calls on a cell phone. It is possible for others to get copies of your cell telephone bill and call record. The call record will not tell you to whom the call was made or who made the call, but it will tell you from what number to what number, what time the call was made and the length of time the connection remained open.

Computer

If you are familiar with computers, keeping a contact log will be much easier for you. The easier it is to keep the log complete and current, the more valid the document will be when you need it. Hand-held computers are making the task much easier.

Those final documents you send to clients and opponents may inadvertently include your entire thought process on the issue, including information you decided the recipient should not see.

If you are using Microsoft Word, you will have to take some extra precautions before submitting the information to your attorney or the court. Your final documents will contain imbedded versions of earlier drafts, complete with corrections and deletions. It only takes is a few quick clicks of the mouse for others to gain access to the old document. To view the old documents, pull down the "Tools" menu in Microsoft Word, click "Track Changes," select "Highlight Changes," click all three boxes and the changes will appear. To avoid this problem, pull down the "Tools" menu, highlight "Track Changes," and then click on "Accept or Reject Changes." You will then get a dialogue box that allows you to accept or reject each change, or click "Accept All Changes."

Contact Log

A Contact Log should be kept whenever you interact with the other parent, people or events important to the custody action. The entries may occur several times each day or remain inactive for months at a time. The log can be kept in a notebook, on a calendar, on a recorded tape, or on a computer.

Fax Machine

Fax machines allow you to send a copy of a photo or document over the telephone lines in seconds. Most business offices, including doctor's, attorneys, and detectives, have "fax ability." If you are unable to purchase a fax machine and you find it necessary to get data to someone who has a fax, most copy centers offer fax service at a reasonable price.

Many computers have modems and software that allow you to fax directly from your home or business computer.

Home Testing Kits

For years people had to rely on doctor's offices for all testing procedures. The first home test kits were blood glucose monitors. They became available in the late 1960's. Now there are home tests for the detection of illicit drugs, tobacco, colorectal and bladder cancers, blood cholesterol, urinary tract infection, HIV and Hepatitis C, DNA, alcohol use, female fertility, pregnancy, ovulation, testing your home for lead, radon, and pesticides. The drugs for which there are tests include; THC (marijuana, hashish, cannabis), cocaine (coke, crack), opiates (heroin, codeine based prescriptions), amphetamines (speed, uppers), methamphetamines (ecstacy), pcp-phencyclidine (angel dust), barbiturates (barbs, downers, reds), benzodiazepines (valium, librium, xanax), hair drug test and drug residue identification wipes.

Some tests claim to be FDA approved and are available through the Mayo Foundation for Medical Education and Research. Many are not FDA approved and may not be safe or effective. It is also important to be aware that there are states that prohibit the sale of home testing kits for people. Many home tests are available on the Internet and at retail drugstore chains such as CVS Corp., Eckerd Co. and Walgreen Co.

It is doubtful that the results of any home test kit would be admissible in court. Here are some guidelines for using any kind of home test kit:

- When purchasing and then when using the kit, check the expiration date. Don't use any kit with an expired date.
- Avoid keeping the test kit in places where it may be exposed to extreme temperatures, like the trunk of your car.
- Read the instructions carefully. Don't begin until you understand each step.
- If a test requires exact timing, be precise. Use a stopwatch or a watch that counts seconds.
- Before you open the test kit think ahead to what you will do once you get the results. What steps will you take if the results are positive, negative, or unclear? It may make you think twice about using that test.

Internet

"Internet visitation" with web cameras, e-mail, and online chat can enhance long distance contact. School papers an artwork can be scanned and placed on a web site that parent or child can load or access. E-mail and real time chat are additional visitation options. The internet certainly can't replace physical contact with the child or presence at their school events but it is much better than a phone call once a week.

Be aware that when information is sent over the Internet, it's difficult to keep it secure and private. If you tell your child negative things about the other parent it can be accessed by the other parent and could affect further contact with your child as well as pending and future custody and support agreements.

Pager

Pagers offer many of the advantages of the mobile telephone with much less expense. Business people, homemakers, students, and children use them with great success.

Paper Shredder

Paper shredders are an effective method of keeping a great deal of information out of unauthorized hands. All paper including envelopes, applications, documents generated on your computer or correspondence that you have decided is trash should be shredded. Often detectives use a persons trash as the primary source of personal information.

Tape Recorder

Pocket recorders are useful during face-to-face verbal communication with the other parent, your attorney, detective, or for making notes to yourself. NOTE #1: The speed of the recorder determines the quality of the recording. Record on the highest speed possible on the machine you are using. Duplication or transcription require clear clean originals.

Telephone Answering Machine

Connecting an answering machine to your telephone can accomplish several things: allow you to include:

- a message telling the operator that you are willing to accept collect calls from your children

- you are late but on the way to meet/pick them up
- offer an alternative number to your pager or another telephone on which you can be reached in case of an emergency.

In some states it is prohibited to record conversations on the telephone without the express permission of all parties.

The exception to this rule may be messages left on answering machines. These may be admissible in court since the person did know they were leaving their words on the machine. Keep important tapes in a safe place.

NOTE #2: Double-check the laws in your state as to how, where, and when you may record conversations with other people.

Telephone, Cellular, Mobile

A mobile telephone gives the other parent access to you. It does not restrict you to specific addresses or locations. When you are at a specific address for an extended length of time, either call-forward the calls from your mobile number to that phone, or leave the mobile phone on its charger.

Some of the mobile communications systems have a "Follow Me" service. All inbound and outbound telephone numbers are listed on the bill. It isn't possible to prove to whom someone spoke at a specific number, but it is possible to see how many times a number was called, when the calls were made and how long they lasted.

Telephone, Recorder on Phone

There are special suction cups and plug-in phone devices to make the process of recording easier and of a higher quality. Check with a dependable authority as to the legality in your state. In addition, because of the differing state laws governing electronic recording of conversations between private parties, parents are advised to err on the side of caution when recording or disclosing an interstate telephone call. The safest strategy is to assume that the stricter state law will apply. For example, a parent located in Texas who records a telephone conversation without the consent of a party located in Oregon would not violate Texas law, but could be liable under Oregon law. A court located in Texas may apply Oregon law, depending on its "conflict of laws" rules. Therefore, an aggrieved party may choose to file suit in either jurisdiction, depending on which law is more favorable to the party's claim.

Invasion of Privacy

Suits for invasion of privacy or violation of a wiretapping statute aren't new, but the methods are new The most common are downloading e-mail files, retrieving records of Internet "chat room" activity, or intercepting cell-phone conversations or beeper messages.

The federal statute, 18 U.S.C. Sect. 2510, excludes certain actors and types of communications. But some state wiretapping statutes are more expansive. For example, New Jersey's statute includes "electronic storage of wire communications" in its definition of prohibited interceptions, which could include e-mail messages, Statutes can provide for civil and criminal penalties

As for privacy claims, a person's expectation of privacy in computer files may depend on who owns the computer and if the person has a private e-mail account.

Confidentiality-Equipment

Any equipment or documentation proving you purchased or rented equipment may be subject to the process of DISCOVERY. Therefore, it is important to decide how you will attain equipment, what you will do with it, and who is aware of what you are doing. In the event that the court is made aware that you purchased equipment that is illegal in your jurisdiction, it would be difficult to prove that once you had the equipment you did not use it.

Services

There are many professional service companies that can keep the processes you require completely legal, safe, and cost-efficient. These explanations are by no means all inclusive, but will give you an understanding of some of the help available. The list that follows is alphabetical, not in order of importance.

Accident Investigation Services

This service is more commonly used for vehicle and industrial mishaps than in domestic cases. If a situation arises where you feel there is a problem, and the damage is not explained satisfactorily, you may consider this option.

Arbitration

Arbitration is a procedure in which a designated arbiter decides a dispute on its merits and evidence. Arbitration is nonbinding or binding. This is not the same as "going to court" and does not include the same court rules, issues, or enforcement. Be cautious with arbitration because you may be required to waive your right to appeal, or waive your right to a jury trial. Don't depend on companies for referrals since it is only reasonable that if they alienate the companies, the referrals stop. Investigate former cases in which the arbitration professional has been involved.

Attorney

Attorneys are bound by the rules of confidentiality and cannot be compelled to reveal to others anything that you have told them. An attorney is authorized to practice law in the courts or to serve clients in the capacity of legal agent or advisor.

Conciliation Court

Conciliation or mediation have essentially inter-changeable meanings in some states. Most states have special departments in their family law courts to assist in mediation and determination of child custody matters. Call the information telephone number in your state or county.

Day Care Workers

A working parent can gain a great deal of information about his or her children from day-care providers. The validity of this statement has a great deal to do with the competency and accountability of the facility chosen. Because your children may spend as much as ten hours a day in the care of others, it is vital that you establish and maintain open communication about your children's problems and achievements. These professionals are very aware of the strain custody matters exert on children and will usually help you identify and deal with behavior problems observed after non-custodial visitation. Make a record of day-care workers' comments in your daily log. Make sure that parental access to your children is strictly monitored in disputed custody matters. If you want this person's observations to be part of the court's records, the day care worker will have to testify in court in person.

Detective

If you have reason to believe that the daily routine described by the opposition is not accurate, a professional investigator can document one day, or a week of real-time activity. The documented activities of a day or week would indicate the behavior as a pattern. This procedure is expensive, but valuable. A mediator or judge could see the report of a reliable third party. If you want this person's observations to be part of the court's records the detective will have to testify in court in person. There are several examples of a detective's reports in this manual. They are included to demonstrate the instructions that will produce the best results. Additionally, the examples will as inform you as to what could be found out about you.

Doctors

If possible, your children should see the same physician for immunizations, well child checkups, and sick child appointments. This is important for them, because a doctor familiar with the children can detect small, but significant changes in them. The doctor can also be called on to testify in the instance of real or imagined child abuse.

Medical records may be entered into evidence without the doctor being present. If you want this person's observations to be part of the court's records, the doctor will have to testify in court in person. Since the emotional and psychological, as well as physical well-being of your children is important, maintain the same solid guidelines for psychologists and counselors.

Legal Transcribers

tape-recorded data can be easily lost, damaged or erased. Working with a hard copy of your tapes is more efficient and effective than winding and rewinding tapes to find specific data. If your tapes are clear and easy to hear, use a professional service. You should budget approximately $5.00 per transcribed double spaced page. If tapes are hard to understand, because of outside noise, it can cost $45.00 per tape to clean up the interference. Transcribed pages copied to a CD can be easily reproduced, searched and printed as many times as necessary.

Parent Locator Service

The Federal Parent Locator Service is a computerized national location network operated by the Office of Child Support Enforcement (OCSE). *Authorized persons (any agent or attorney of any state having an agreement with OCSE)* can access the system to locate people suspected of parental kidnapping and for the limited purpose of criminal enforcement actions in civil court proceedings. In addition to obtaining information from the Department of Health and Human Services, it can also access the Social Security Administration, the Internal Revenue Service, State Employment Security Agencies, the National Personnel Records Center, the Department of Defense, the Veterans Administration, and the Selective Service System to find a person. Contact the prosecuting attorney, the local police, or a judge to find the procedures necessary to use the service in your state. See the Chapter 21: Child Support, for more information.

Parenting Classes

Classes voluntarily taken to gain or improve your parenting skills can go a long way to impress an evaluator. Parenting classes are indicated if you haven't taken care of babies or children by yourself. If CPS or the court indicates that they think there may be some areas in which you need instruction. If you have been taking care of children all your life, but are now being criticized for the way you discipline or care for them. New ideas and methods are evolving all the time and your interest in being the best parent you can be is noteworthy. Always ask for a certificate of completion.

Paralegal Service & Legal Technicians

A paralegal is a person, other than a licensed attorney, who is employed to perform a variety of tasks associated with law practice, which can be done by one not authorized to practice law. These people are wonderful to employ as witness stand-by when you must pick up or return your children in a hostile environment. Paralegal services can be a one person office who is a specialist or may have several people who can scour public legal records and prior cases that might be pertinent to your case. They write briefs and produce documents. Good ones will work their hearts out for you. Their experience can prevent you from wasting your time learning where to find the information you need. They may even have some suggestions about additional pertinent information. Often paralegals are available through your attorney's office or can be contacted through a parent's right's group.

Patrol Service

A patrol service offers regular, routed service past one or several addresses at set or varying times to check the location of vehicles. A weekly or monthly rate is easily established. A report from a licensed service will hold more weight than a report from a family member or a friend. The court feels that a third impartial party especially a professional service will be impartial. In most cases the client that hires the service never meets the employee of the company that actually performs the service.

Spy Shops

An amazing selection of gadgets, paraphernalia and information exists in spy shops. Use your head and find out from your attorney or the police what is legal to use where you live. Many devices are illegal, but the devices to detect illegal devices are legal. You can use detection devices to protect yourself and document the use of illegal equipment being used against you. These shops also attract some very unusual people. Be careful of whom you talk or listen to in these places.

Teachers

All through children's school years, the working parent must rely a great deal on the children's teachers for information about the children. Children who exhibit normal behavior patterns are often considered untroubled by the custody battle. Children sometimes want things to be back to the way they were or appear to be normal, and they are in denial about the situation in which they find themselves. Occasionally children are playing the system and their parents to their own advantage. You will need the cooperation of your children's teachers to watch for any of these behaviors. Because your support at home is pivotal to your children's progress in school, most teachers welcome an actively involved parent. Establish and maintain open communication about your children's problems, goals, and achievements. Keep a record of teachers' pertinent comments in your daily log. Attend parent teacher conferences. Stop in to see the teachers often.

Make sure your children's teachers know how much you care about the progress your children are making in school. Do not be critical of the other parent to the teacher. Volunteer in the classroom.

Travel Agent

It does not cost more to use a travel agent than to buy directly from an airline. Travel agents will compare routes and rates to save you time and money. Your travel agent will be aware of special rates and promotions offered by the airlines, as well as new routing that becomes available. Because the terminology can be confusing, it helps to have a professional working with you. For example, "nonstop" sounds the same as "direct routing." However, "nonstop" means getting on the plane, flying, and getting off at your destination with no stops. With "direct routing" you do not change planes, but may have one or two stops en route to your destination. Therefore, "nonstop" is usually easier on a child than "direct routing."

Do not accept electronic ticketing without a receipt or a written record. Electronic tickets cannot be regenerated and no record will exist if the computers at the airport are down. Whenever possible fly mid week. Avoid traveling on Saturdays in December and January 2nd. They are the highest traffic days of the year. If you must travel on high volume days book your flight for the first flight of the day. Check for traffic, weather and flight delays before you leave the house to drive to the airport. Make sure you get to the airport two hours before departure time for domestic flights and three hours for international.

It is important to enroll in the frequent flyer programs offered by most airlines. They have many benefits. Buying Frequent Flyer Coupons to reduce the expense of visitation is a new option. One company that sells frequent flyer coupons and is experienced with the problems of children's visitation transportation is World Wide Travel (800) 424-5312.

Testing Services

Laboratories perform many types of testing including: microbiology, chemistry, water, food, cosmetics, medical device testing, alliteration, explosive atmosphere, flow, function, modal analysis, pressure stress screening, pesticides, paternity forensics, genetics and drugs. Make sure you have the right kind of company or laboratory for the testing or service you require.

Drug Tests

Clinical and analytical services are done for individuals, consultants, attorneys and the regulated community. Some laboratories offer full instrumentation and mobile refractories. It is important that you find an accredited laboratory that has experience producing court admissible results.

Urine Analysis

The Center for Disease Control and the National Institute on Drug Abuse ran a nine-year study on the accuracy of private sector laboratories. Private sector labs are not licensed, and there has been no legislation requiring employee training of even minimum wage employees. Sixty-six out of a hundred samples showed false positives. On the other hand, accuracy for screening known abusers under "blind test" conditions was one hundred percent inaccurate. The urine sample itself may be too acidic or alkaline, subject's use of medication, passive inhalation, use of prescription medication or ingestion of legal food substances can trigger a positive test result. See Drug Tests in Chapter 12: Psychologists.

What can make your test results come out wrong?

- Mishandling by tester.
- Urine specimens that have gone stale.
- Specimen's reaction to temperature extremes. Urine that is too acidic or alkaline.
- Subject's use of medication.
- Subject's eating spicy foods.

Passive Inhalation

Is defined as inadvertent exposure to marijuana when others are smoking it. Judges are not interested in hearing Passive inhalation as an excuse or defense. See Drug Tests in Chapter 12: Psychologists.

Hair Analysis

The court likes hair analysis because drugs remain in the hair giving a record of the pattern of drug use. See Drug Tests in Chapter 12: Psychologists.

Will You Take a Drug Test

With all of this in mind, what do you say if asked, "Will you take a drug test?" Say yes. Being asked if you would take a drug test is not the same as being asked when will you take a drug test. If the opposition, judge, psychologist, your attorney or you decide that you should take a drug test, you should:

1. List all medications you have taken in the last six months. List the brand names and the form in which they were taken. Example: pill, syrup, powder, inhalant. All tests cross-react with something.
2. Request a list of all over-the-counter and prescription drugs and other ingestible substances known to cross-react with the test that will be used.
3. Schedule your test for afternoon.
4. Drink lots of water to clean out your system. Also, coffee, tea, and fruit juices are excellent.
5. Avoid alcohol.
6. Sweat any impurities out of your system with exercise, saunas, and steam baths.
7. Take B-complex vitamins; they are good for your general health.

   If you feel it will help your case, have a drug test taken without notifying anyone, and if you get the results you want, offer the results to your attorney. If the test shows a positive result, request another type of test.

Lie Detector Test

The lie detector/polygraph machine is an electromechanical instrument that simultaneously measures and records certain physiological changes in the human body, which are believed to be involuntarily and caused by the subject's conscious attempts to deceive the questioner.

The operator connects the subject to the machine and asks some obviously true and false questions to establish a response pattern for the subject. The operator then asks the real questions. Once the machine has recorded the subject's responses to the questions propounded by the operator, the operator interprets the results.

The courts almost uniformly reject the results of a "polygraph," when offered in evidence for the purpose of establishing guilt or innocence, because of its lack of reliability. Military Rule of Evidence 707, prohibits polygraph results from being introduced at trial although the U.S. Government through its Department of Defense conducted more than 400,000 lie-detector tests between 1981 and 1997 to ferret out spies and criminals.

On March 31, 1998, the Supreme Court ruled that criminal defendants have no constitutional right to introduce at trial, lie-detector test results that support their claims of innocence. The ruling does not violate his Sixth Amendment right to present a vigorous defense. There is no constitutional right to present polygraph evidence. It is commonly assumed that since lie detector tests are not accepted as evidence in court in most cases, they carry no weight.

This assumption is not entirely correct.

Most people, including professionals, are more suspicious of someone who refuses to take a lie detector test and less suspicious of someone who volunteers for the test. The paradox is that we are not entirely sure if someone is found to be telling the truth when using the test.

Psychologists will tell you that it is virtually impossible to tell if someone is lying, but that it is possible to tell if someone believes what they are saying. Therefore, it is necessary for a person to grasp the reality of a situation before that person can consciously decide to be truthful or lie. If one's perception of reality is not solid, the truth becomes whatever that person needs it to be at that moment.

If you have been falsely accused of an act, and there is no way for you to prove yourself innocent, you may wish to pay for a test. The idea of taking a polygraph scares most reasonable people.

There are things you can do to make taking a polygraph more tolerable and increase the chances of the results you want. More than half of the people who take lie detector tests fail it or comes out inconclusive. Proper preparation and a thorough understanding of the process make a great deal of difference. It is important to use a company the court will recognize to make sure the operator will ask questions that satisfy the investigators or the court. Because there is such a controversy about the validity of these tests, do not tell anyone you have taken a lie detector test unless you have received favorable results. Tests can cost anywhere from $150 to $1,000.

If you pass the test with flying colors, make it available to mediators and judges; it can't hurt.

Maternity & Paternity Testing

Any parent may initiate a paternity action. If the guardian (mother, father, grandparent, for example) applies for Aid to Families with Dependent Children (AFDC), the agency will require the guardian to identify the names of both parents of the children. The agency will then initiate action to get reimbursed from the parents of the children.

In a case of abandonment or denial of maternity, a woman could be tested for maternity in order to establish responsibility for the reimbursement of AFDC payments. If the parents were not married, but by admission or agreement are acknowledged mother and acknowledged father, they are required to pay support for the children. It is always easier to establish the mother of children. If the mother is the guardian of the children, the agency will require the mother to name the father in order to qualify for assistance. If the father denies paternity, the agency will initiate a paternity suit in an effort to get reimbursed by the father for money paid to the mother for support of the children. Children born "out of wedlock" are no longer considered "illegitimate" children. They have all the rights of "legitimate" children born into a marriage.

If there is any question in your mind of your children's parentage, get tested.

If you have been the "parent in fact," having loved, cared for and supported these children, you may not care what a test says. On the other hand, if you have been the "parent in fact" for an appreciable period of time, you may be financially responsible for the children regardless of what the paternity test says.

Many states assign the responsibility for the children to the presumed father. Some of the criteria used are:

1. If the children were conceived or born within the structure of the marriage.
2. If a formal marriage was established after the birth and he agreed to have his name on the birth certificate.
3. If he presented the children to others as his and said that he was the father.

DNA - Genetic Testing

DNA (Deoxyribonucleic acid) is the genetic material in the cells of your body. Every nucleated cell has forty-six chromosomes, except the sperm cells from the man and the egg of the woman, which only contain twenty-three chromosomes each. At the moment of conception, there are forty-six chromosomes necessary to create a person. A person receives half of his/her genetic material or DNA from the biological mother, and the other half from the biological father. If a child is carried in the womb of another woman because of invitro fertilization and implantation, the biological mother, not the host mother, is the DNA contributor.

Court Ordered

The court may order DNA testing as a matter of procedure or at the request of one parent or guardian over the objections of the other parent or guardian. If you want testing under the observation of the court and there is no case pending the parent may file a Paternity Action by delivering relatively simple paperwork to the local district court. Then ask the court to order the testing.

If you just want to know and have access to the child you can set up an appointment with Planned Parenthood. They can provide all sorts of information and guidance to single parents including DNA in a professional, confidential environment.

DNA Samples From Many Sources

DNA testing is much more than a blood test. It can be performed on a much wider variety of samples, including blood cells, cheek cells, tissue samples from living or deceased people, and semen. Since blood types, such as A, B, O, and the Rh factor, are more common within the population, the power to differentiate individuals is not as high as with DNA testing. Every person's DNA is unique except for identical twins. Since it is so specific, just like a fingerprint, DNA testing is the most powerful form of testing. Our results are often 10 to 100 times more accurate than what the courts require. The Human Leucocyte Antigen (HLA) test, used to match blood type, tissue, race and other genetic factors, is ninety-eight percent accurate to confirm paternity, and one hundred percent to rule out paternity and the most often used.

DNA Testing includes two major components.

- The first involves the molecular biological techniques that allow analysts to directly examine a DNA sample.
- The second has to do with population genetics. To interpret the DNA test to calculate the degree to which different samples are associated.

Since small communities don't have laboratories with DNA testing equipment, some national laboratories have made arrangements with local hospitals.

You pay a small fee to the hospital for the blood or swab sample to be taken. In order to maintain the proper chain of custody over the samples, the hospital sends the specimens directly to the laboratory. The results are available in about fifteen days. Most laboratories will not give the results of the testing over the telephone. The results are sent to the address you chose when you contracted for the service. Paternity tests using drawn blood or mouth swab cost $145.00 per person for the mother, father, and child. The court usually will determine who will pay these costs unless one side volunteers to pay the expenses.

Participant Samples Needed for DNA Testing

Test	Samples Necessary
To Identify Mother	Child and Mother or Both Mothers' Parents
To Identify Father of a Child	Child and Mother and Father or Both Sets of Grandparents
To Identify Father of a Fetus	Fetus and Mother and Father or Both Sets of Grandparents
To Identify Siblings	All Children to be Identified
To Identify a Person	Sample from the Person to be Identified

Necessary for DNA Testing

For accurate results, make sure:

1. the child is over six months of age.
2. the lab checks proper photo identification of each person.
3. the lab has adults initial the seal placed over each sample.
4. all of you are in good health and have not received a blood transfusion in the past six months.

Challenges to DNA Testing

Short tandem repeats (STRs) is a method of testing that uses very small sample of DNA and a machine called a 310 Genetic Analyzer. The test comes in a kit/package, including the software and the machine.

STRs are areas of DNA where certain sequences of genetic code repeat themselves. Scientists have not figured out what function STRs serve, but they are useful for modification purposes because although different people may have the same sequence, they will have different lengths. For example, one person may have CATGCATG, while another person has CATGCATGCATG. STR testing exploits these differences in length. More than one location on the chromosome is targeted to reduce the chance of coincidental matches.

STRs are not generally accepted in the scientific community because such small samples are more sensitive to contamination or picking up extraneous DNA. In addition, the results may be invalid if the DNA sample has mixed contributors or is of a low quality.

California, Colorado and Vermont have excluded DNA evidence because some to the testing methods haven't been proven valid and reliable.

In order to challenge the DNA findings it would be necessary to get the whole DNA file. This would include the raw data and copies of the raw material before it is massaged by the examiners and to have somebody screen it for you. Parts of a test not reported could be very useful.

Computer Data Retrieval

Landmark years for Cyber Evidence were 1998 and 1999. Attorneys have been able to present evidence that convicted a guilty party and/or provided alibis for innocent clients.

Companies that do computer data retrieval don't work on a contingency basis since sometimes the evidence never was there or can't be found.

Some of the tasks that can be accomplished are:

- dating when files were last accessed
- determine if the date has been altered
- pinpointing attempts to conceal
- identifying attempts to destroy information
- recognizing attempts to fabricate data
- retrieving e-mail from months or years
- reconstructing financial records
- when and what web sites have been visited
- identifying files that have been downloaded
- retrieving an electronic copy of a document containing text that was removed from the final version
- spotting fax machines that can contain exact duplicates of several hundred of the last pages received
- computer faxed documents sent or received can remain on the computer indefinitely
- e-mail business communications including intra company memorandum or letters

I Have Evidence - No One Cares

If you have any concerns about the opposition's behaviors or attitudes that "you think evaluators" or the court need to be aware of, you are told you must have proof. Proof is necessary in order to avoid the he said, she said stalemates.

This can be very frustrating since so much of what you have done, in an attempt to get along, ends up validating the opposition's bad behavior. The court may even feel that your passive or positive behavior negates the harmful effects the opposition's negative behavior has on your children.

In order to set the record straight you work very hard to get the evidence to prove that your concerns are valid. Once you have proof something has been or is happening it is difficult know when to reveal the evidence or to get the right people to look at it. In family court, proof or evidence isn't required to meet the strict guidelines necessary in criminal court. However, the closer you can get to those standards the more weight your evidence will have.

Evidence comes in many forms. Physical evidence is one of the most difficult because you must know exactly how to go about recognizing, documenting, preserving, marking, collecting and packaging physical evidence You may be looking for very large evidence such as a hole punched in a door or something small like a fingerprint on a page.

Each category of evidence has to be properly handled, documented, marked, packaged, tagged and preserved for later examination by a scientific expert. Basics would include setting the scene perimeter and preparing a sketch. This gives you the foundation to demonstrate beyond any shadow of a doubt that direct physical contact did in fact occur between the scene, and a person

Even if you do manage to observe a problem, and even if you do manage to conduct an immediate, proper and though scene investigation - including preserving the scene, taking dozens of overall and close-up photographs, making a detailed sketch, casting, collecting, vacuuming, scraping, marking and preserving, it won't do you the least bit of good.

Why? Because you are an advocate. An advocate has an interest in the outcome of what the evidence has to prove. In order for evidence to be validated it must be analyzed and interpreted by unbiased scientific experts in a laboratory. The problem is, no lab director is going to accept, much less examine, physical evidence collected by an unsuppressed advocate. This is because the lab will be required to issue a report based upon the physical evidence. Therefore, they will not expend their time or risk their hard-earned reputation examining evidence that lacks a reliable chain-of-custody.

A proper chain-of-custody would involve: discovery, preservation, documentation and collection of the evidence by a professional. A professional is someone who will seek out and evaluate the evidence in an unbiased manner before coming to a conclusion and present that evidence with professional indifference as to the outcome, not caring if it helps or hurts a specific party in a case. See Chapter 9: Detectives, Finding the Evidence.

Confidentiality - Services

Any company or service you employ will create documentation, including phone logs, messages you have left, billing, employee observation of the person contracting the services, internal reports, memos, and test results that are subject to the process of discovery.

Decide how you will attain the services you need, what you will do with the information, and who inside and outside of that service is aware of who you are and what you are doing. Some documentation may be protected by attorney work product. Any documentation your attorney shows you should not be discussed with anyone. Do not mention its existence in your contact logs. If your attorney gives you copies of these documents, do not leave them laying around or show them to anyone.

Equipment & Service Options

Equipment and Service Options	Using	Considering	Notes
Camera, 35 mm/ Camera, Video	X		
Computer	X		at work
Contact Log	X		
Fax Machine		X	
Phone, Cellular, Mobile, Pager, Caller ID		X	
Telephone, Answering Machine, Recorder	X		
Telephone Answering Machine	X		
Attorney	X		
Conciliation Court	X		court ordered
Day Care Workers			
Detective	X		
Doctors	X		
Legal Transcribers			
Paralegal Service		X	
Travel Agent	X		
Drug Tests/ Urine or Hair Analysis			
Lie Detector Test		X	
DNA/ Paternity Testing			
Citizen Stand By			

Chapter 8: Attorney

You are the Commander-in-Chief of this army and you need a General for your army. Having made the decision to fight the custody war, you must find the professional soldier who will listen to what you want from this action and provide tactical and strategic support. Although lawyers go through the same basic courses in the first year of law school, their interests diverge in the second and third year. Rare is the practicing lawyer who can field every question in every sphere of law. You must find a lawyer who specializes in family law.

Right to Free Counsel

The U.S. Congress passed the law that is the root of 28 USC 1915 in 1892. The intent of the law is clear from the following quote taken from the congressional record of 1892, page 5199. The following is the explanation of Mr. Culberson, of Texas regarding the intent of the law concerning appointment of counsel for middle class and poor citizens.

"Mr. Speaker, the effect of this bill, if it should become law, will be to open the courts of the United States to a class of persons who are now denied the right of bringing suits in the courts of the United States, that have no money or property by which to comply with the rules of the courts in respect to costs. This bill provides that any individual in this class who files an affidavit that he is not able to pay the money that is required to be deposited, or to give security for the costs, he may proceed, in forma pauperis, and at the end of the lawsuit a judgement of costs is issued as in other cases."

Nowhere in this explanation is there a limit placed upon the right whereby the benefits of the law are limited to persons that may face time in jail. Yet in 1981, the U.S. Supreme Court stated in Lassiter: "There is a presumption that an indigent litigant has a right to appointed counsel only when, if he loses, he may be deprived of his physical liberty.......". For many hundreds of years before the passing of this law, another law protected the citizen known as 11 Henry 7, and that law did not limit the right to counsel to those who may be imprisoned. Nevertheless, our Supreme Court in the Lassiter ruling declared that "we the people" were not entitled to the protection of counsel passed by our Congress unless we were to be threatened with jail time.

The resulting effect of the ruling of the court.

First, citizens can be forced into court and lose everything they own to attorneys, all the while being denied the protection of counsel. This means that in child custody battles you are not entitled to free counsel.

Legal Aid

In 1974 Congress established the Legal Services Corporation to provide free legal assistance in civil matters for eligible individuals and families. A staff attorney will handle your case, or it can be referred to a local private attorney. Most cases are resolved by mediation. Only about 15 percent of the cases handled by this group of attorneys end in court.

Eligibility is determined after you fill out a simple form listing size of family and income. High child care expenses and provable inability to hire private legal assistance are factors that are considered. Call the Federal Information Center for a list of the offices near your home. If the first person you talk to in the local office questions your income before sending out preliminary information, they are looking for a number like $6,000.00 a year. Since there are many other factors that influence the amount of income you can earn and still be eligible, do not let this person stop you.

Legal Clinics

Legal clinics that advertise on television, billboards, or the back of the telephone book survive on volume. "Uncontested Divorce $250.00" may lure you into the first call or office visit, but watch for the add-ons. The additional charges may include $50.00 per child, $20.00 per vehicle, $35.00 per bank account.

Many charge a small down payment and weekly or monthly payment as the case progresses. If the fee is dependent on a monthly payment, the attorney may not feel induced to speed the process along or negotiate an early settlement. Therefore, the bottom line is this: a legal clinic may not in fact cost less than a sole practitioner. Legal clinics rely heavily on the work of associates called paralegals. This cuts down the personal contact the attorney has with your case and the contact you may have with your attorney.

Representing Yourself

Laws are made to offer justice and equity to the people. It is the responsibility of the court to process the cases and make judgments that are in accordance with the laws. It is not the responsibility of the court to teach you how to conduct a proper case. It is the responsibility of the court to render a decision. Law school teaches the difficult and exacting mix of research, the art of interpretation and skill of presentation for the price of more than ten thousand dollars a year for four years for a full-time student.

Representing yourself is called ProSe, and The Constitution of the United States gives you the right to represent yourself in custody court. You must decide if it is advisable for you to be your own Attorney in such an important case. It takes a stalwart soul who has the ability, initiative, guts, time, and fortitude to fight the battle alone and win. Usually, the drive is borne out of the necessity to save money rather than an inner voice that says it is the best route. The person that can do this successfully is the exception, not the rule. A course of action may be to follow the precedent set by a similar case.

While you may feel you have more control over your costs you are giving up some important advantages. Since it is not the responsibility of the court to teach you law, judges quickly become impatient with attorneys or laypeople who don't know what they are doing. Protecting information that would have been considered Work-Product Privilege may now be vulnerable to discovery.

No ProSe Recovery of Attorney Fees

(Parker v. Rodwell, Philadelphia Court of Common Pleas case #001828), A pro se litigant asked for attorney's fees for two full days in a law library learning libel and torturous interference law and about $20.00 for copies, an additional day drafting the complaint. He was encouraged when he collected an attorney fee of $20.00 plus costs in a small claims case. Generally even an attorney cannot collect a fee even when representing himself, not even for costs such as copying, filing fees, mailing costs, and service costs. Since pro se are not licensed, attorneys were paid for their services, they cannot be reimbursed for those fees. A pro se litigant did collect funds paid to an attorney acting as a coach/advisor, but only for the time he actually spent working for the litigant.

With the billings, he was able to show that all invoices had been paid.

Getting Started *ProSe*

You will have to acquire a reasonable understanding of form and procedure and of how to protect your rights and not offend the court by stepping on the rights of the opposition in court.

As complicated as the "Pleading And Practice Forms" are for any state, tracking the twisted maze of precedents is much more difficult. The process of locating the legal decisions pertinent to your case is not only difficult, but also time consuming.

Understanding the legalese they are written in, with the myriad of citations and references, and using them to your best advantage is much harder. You can find the law in the college law library and in the public county law library near the court house.

Law students receive exhaustive instruction on how to properly use the law library, and it takes them three or four months before they are effective.

If you have no other option other than ProSe, you can use the opposition's previous cases as a blueprint from which to model your case. Public records of the attorney's previous cases are filed and available to anyone who wishes to read them. You can study their pleadings, briefs, motions, letters to the court, written discovery such as interrogatories, and responses to the same documents you received from the opposition and modify the forms and documents to suit your needs. Your advantage over the opposition's attorney is that you are only working on one case. If you were inclined to do so, you could bury them in paperwork.

Precedent

Attempting to break new legal ground during your custody battle is much more difficult than utilizing the concept of "precedent" or doing things the way they have been done before. Precedent is used in deciding many kinds of legal issues. For example, if one parent moves out, leaving the child with the other parent, it would be difficult for the leaving parent to get custody. Another example is if you request a reduction in support payments because you lost or quit a high income job. It may be hard to convince a court that you are unable to find employment at that level now. Precedent in life and in court is an important legal principle and can give you a template to follow in filing your documents and making your arguments.

My Humble Opinion

You cannot win a contested custody battle without a good attorney. It is crucial to get good legal help as early in the process as possible.

You can cause your case irreparable damage in the initial stages without wise counsel. It is entirely your responsibility to hire the best attorney you can afford. Choose an attorney who will negotiate fairly and aggressively for your rights. Your attorney should be a good strategist who knows you cannot sacrifice the war to win a skirmish. Your attorney should be more concerned about your case than about achieving star status. Above all, your attorney should have firm control of the processes necessary to speed a slow system and do what is best for your children and your case. You will want an experienced, well-seasoned veteran to be your general. Consider your attorney's experience, reputation, education, personal sense of pride, fair play, and ego. Your attorney must fight very personally for your victory and be determined not to lose. You must be of clear mind and have a determined goal at every meeting and court appearance.

Shared Attorney

If you and the other parent have used the same attorney as "the family" or "the business" attorney in the past, neither of you should use that attorney now. Many conflicts of interest and confidentiality issues that will cloud the issue at hand.

You are the Commander

Because you are the Commander-in-Chief of this army, use your team members and supplies to their best ability and to your best advantage. Every minute you spend now picking the best attorney you can find will save you hours of time, hundreds of dollars, and years of pain.

Handle your case the way you want it done, with reasonable diligence and solid advice from the professionals you hire. Your attorney will assist you in identifying the real enemy and choosing a battle plan to accomplish your goal.

The attorney has been battle-tested and can evaluate the strength of each strategy.

Your attorney will initiate action in your case and respond under your direction to action taken against you.

Attorney Evaluation Form

Good or reasonable answer mark the box with a "+".

Flaky or wrong answer mark the box with a "-".

No answer or not sure mark the box with a "?".

Has this attorney been to court at least four times in the last year?	X		
Does his attorney have experience before a judge? A jury?	X		
Does this attorney express an interest in and a willingness to use mediation, if it is in your best interest?	X		
Do you feel comfortable dealing with this person?	X		
Does this attorney behave in a professional manner?	X		
This is not a matter of equal rights hiring. This must be a person who can win your case. Will the sex, age, or any other factor regarding this attorney assist your case?	X		X
Do you understand what this attorney is saying, and do you have faith in the information given to you?	X		
Has this person identified the merits in your case and explained how you can win?	X		
Did this person identify problems in your case and explain how to overcome them?	X		
Did this person take the time to talk to you without office or telephone interruptions?	X		
Hire the very best attorney you can. Can you afford to hire this person?	X		
Does this person have associates or paralegals?	X		
Is this person able to demonstrate a level of competence in custody matters to your satisfaction?	X		
Do you understand how this person gets paid and when?	X		
Can this person provide you with a written resume?		X	
How often will this person be out of the office in court, at conventions, on vacation during the next 2 years? Who will handle you when this person is not available?	X		
Under what circumstances would you refund all or part of the retainer fee?	X		
This is the hardest question to ask, but do it. Really listen to the answer, especially if you get an answer you don't like from more than one attorney. "Do I have solid grounds for this litigation, or is my case without merit?"	X		

How to Find an Attorney

1. Talk to attorneys you have contact with and ask them to refer you to family practice specialists.
2. If you are working with a private investigator you trust, ask for some suggestions.
3. Ask other parents who have been in custody battles. They are easy to find at the local

parents' right's group meeting.

4. Sit in the domestic relations courtroom during custody hearings and watch some attorneys work.

5. The State Bar Association and attorneys' Referral Service are two other adequate starting places.

6. Call the offices of well-known and respected publications in the judicial community of the state in which you live for several recommendations.

7. As a last resort consult the Martindale-Hubbell Law Directory at the library.

8. Talk to more than one attorney. Get a second opinion. Make sure you like and respect your choice. You are going to have to depend on each other.

Initial Consultation

Make sure you talk and listen during the initial consultation. Take the list of impressions you want to gather, as well as a list of specific questions about your case, and remember to ask them. Do not attempt to put down the answers, just grade the response.

Review the "Attorney Evaluation Form" before your appointment. Have a list of questions about your case ready. Don't be rushed into a decision. At the conclusion of your appointment, tell the attorney you will call tomorrow and advise as to what you have decided to do.

Take These Things to the Consultation

- Take only copies of your paperwork. Keep the originals in a safe place.
- A full chronology (time line of everything that has happened) of your relationship and the problem.
- Relationship, Personal and Opposition Inventory
- Child's Daily Routine Inventory
- Any mediated or negotiated agreements
- List of what the opposition wants
- Police or prison records of you and opposition
- Photos of all parents and children
- A list of what you want
- Check for the initial retainer

Reasons They Won't Take Your Case

1. The other parent has already contacted the attorney.

2. Attorney has a conflict of interest.

3. Attorney feels you are not being entirely honest.

4. Attorney feels you will not follow his or her advice.

5. Attorney feels you are not communicating (listening as well as talking).

6. Attorney feels you are behaving in an inappropriate manner.

7. Attorney feels your expectations are not reasonable or flexible.

8. Attorney feels your case is without merit.

9. Attorney does not have enough experience in domestic relations law.

10. Attorney hates working in domestic relations law.

11. Attorney has not been successful in cases similar to yours.

12. Attorney feels you perceive everything as an emergency.

13. Attorney feels you cannot afford the legal fees.

14. Attorney feels your style and the attorney's style are not compatible.

15. Attorney just has too much work already.

16. Attorney does not wish to take a case that was *pro se* because that type of client is too strong willed to work with comfortably.

17. Attorney does not wish to take a case that has already begun the process, a case from which you have already fired other attorneys, or a case from which other attorneys have already withdrawn.

Good Old Attorney System

Attorneys who specialize in domestic law will probably try several cases against each other over the years. They attend many of the same professional events and may even work on committees together.

Camaraderie develops naturally over the years. Just because your attorney and the opposition's attorney lunch together, does not mean that they are being disloyal to their clients. Your attorney is professionally committed to the best result for you, given the facts of your case and the law.

If your attorney is known for carefully accepting clients with meritorious cases, you can benefit from your attorney's good reputation. Since the cases your attorney represented in the past were solid, your case will appear solid by association.

If the other attorney has faced your attorney on previous cases and lost, the other attorney may be anxious to settle rather than face another defeat. The opposition may be part of a large firm that accepts a client's case and then assigns it to the first available associate. Another common opponent for your attorney is a "divorce mill" that will accept anyone that answers the advertisement and has some cash down and will sign a contract for monthly payments.

Free legal aid attorneys have very little choice about whom they represent if the client seems to meet the guidelines for that organization. Pleasant greetings and small talk in the hall does not indicate that your attorney likes or respects the other attorney. On the other hand, it would not be professional behavior for your attorney to be hostile, rude, or mean to the opposition's attorney. Such behavior often harms rather than helps your case.

Attorney Comparison Form Choose a letter to represent each attorney and rate him or her in each category. A. Best choice B. Would be satisfactory C. Last choice	A	B	C
Willing to go to court if necessary, but would work to avoid it.	X	X	X
Expresses a willingness to use and had success with mediation.	X		X
Level of comfort while dealing with this person.	X		
Professional manner of attorney and staff.			
This person could win your case.	X	X	
Understanding the attorney and faith in the information given.	X		
Evaluation of the case merits agree with yours.	X	X	X
Ability to identify and overcome problems in your case.	X		
Reasonable time and attention was devoted to your meeting.	X	X	X
Retainer and costs within reason.			X
Sufficient support staff including office, associates or paralegals.	X	X	
Demonstrated competence in custody matters.	X		X
Can this person provide you with a written resume?			
Availability during the next 2 years.	X	X	X
Feels you have solid grounds to pursue or defend for this litigation.	X	X	X

More Bang for the Buck

It is hard to tell if you get a better attorney if you spend more money, but this is what the numbers look like. The cost of hiring an attorney can vary greatly.

A single practitioner in a small farming

community may charge less than two hundred dollars an hour. A partner in a sixty person law firm charges five hundred an hour. Many attorneys use a formula that breaks up the hour into six parts.

This simplifies the billing process for them as they round up to the next ten minute point. The formula would look like this:

Work charged to time in *Unit Time (hours) .6 = number of hours* X *hourly rate* = Total.

Attorney Fee Comparison for 3.12 hours Billed							
Hourly Rate	Total	Hourly Rate	Total	Hourly Rate	Total	Hourly Rate	Total
$125.00	$390.00	$225.00	$720.00	$325.00	$1,014.00	$425.00	$1,326.00
$150.00	$468.00	$250.00	$780.00	$350.00	$1,092.00	$450.00	$1,404.00
$175.00	$546.00	$275.00	$858.00	$375.00	$1,170.00	$475.00	$1,482.00
$200.00	$624.00	$300.00	$936.00	$400.00	$1,248.00	$500.00	$1,560.00

Promissory Note

You are under no legal obligation to sign a Confession of Judgment or a Promissory Note or agree to a lien or mortgage on your home or other property to cover legal fees. You should not waive your rights to dispute a bill for legal services.

Not So Secret "Secret Weapon"

Not all attorneys charge for the initial consultation. As you interview for representation, you may become aware that there are very few really good custody attorneys in your area. Once you have talked about your case with any attorney, they are legally and ethically barred from representing the opposition by attorney-client privilege. This could prevent the opposition from having representation you cannot afford, or fear. When the only purpose of talking to an attorney is to eliminate that attorney as an option for the opposition, d**o not** take any documents with you. Document your visit to each attorney. You may be required to prove you consulted with this person a year from now.

1. Document the time and day you made your appointment and the day and time of your interview with this attorney. Take a list of some questions to ask and an Attorney Form.

2. Give the attorney your name, name of the opposition, why there is a dispute, and what you want the outcome to be. If there has been contact with the opposition the attorney will tell you.

3. Make notes about what the attorney said, ask for one of the attorney's business cards while you are in the office and write down the name of the receptionist. If this consultation is only to eliminate this attorney from the opposition's options, do not take any documents with you.

Don't Hire Attorneys Who

- Forget simple things over and over again.
- Do not return your calls in a reasonable period of time.
- Say, "We can get the whole thing done for $595.00."
- Say, "Agree to it now and we will change it later."
- Refuse to negotiate. Particular points on your behalf in the way you wish them done. This is not the same as when your attorney advises you that your chances would be better if you follow another path. If you decide, after listening to your attorney's professional advice, that you prefer to proceed in the direction being advised against, the attorney should either vigorously pursue that direction or tell you to find someone else to represent your case.
- Say, "I can get everything you want; the opposition will get nothing."
- Say, "You have a 'sure win' case."
- Automatically reject any suggestion or request

from the opposition. Attorneys with reputations as "litigators" refuse to cooperate with opposing counsel and prolong the process at your expense. Doing it the hard way increases your emotional duress, court costs and attorney fees.

- Say, "I have the judges in my pocket."
- Say, "We can always appeal."

Sorting Out the Bad Apples

Avoid "Show Boat," "High Profile," "Mad Dog" attorneys. You want an attorney interested in your welfare, not their talk show opportunity or personal revenge. Attorneys with a frivolous or vicious reputation will only cause you problems. They are wounded warriors from their own battles and want each win to cause as much damage as possible. The "high" they anticipate from the blood and gore during the battle keeps them from negotiating in good faith. Such attorneys are notorious for lack of follow through. An attorney willing to use illegal or nasty tricks on the opposition will use them on you if you ever have a falling out.

Dirty tricks intended to hurt the opposition will cause additional stress and hardship for you and your children. This is very damaging to the children involved. Once an attorney has information about a case from one side, that attorney cannot represent the opposition in the same law suit. Therefore, you can use a "Secret Weapon" explained earlier in this chapter, to eliminate the possibility of your opposition hiring an attorney you cannot afford or to eliminate the "Mad Dog." This is an innovative way to eliminate the "Mad Dog" from the opposition's options. No matter how desperate you feel, once in the "Mad Dog's" office, don't be fooled into thinking it is worth it to you to take a chance on this person. This is a dangerous person for you and your children to have contact with. Do not be seduced by the promise of a "Sure Win" and hire this person. They are combative, contentious, belligerent, abrasive, and aggressive, causing more problems for their clients than they solve.

If you find out you have picked a bad apple after you have hired him or her, don't multiply your misfortune, but fire that attorney right away.

Positive Attributes

The positive attributes to look for in an attorney are: honesty, strong sense of justice, free from improper influence, desire to win, fair, candid, equal, equitable, objective, just, nondiscriminatory, nonpartisan, square, unbiased, uncolored, unprejudiced, and solidly on your team.

Before 10:00 A.M. After 5:00 P.M.

Because attorneys are handling several cases at any given time, it is unreasonable to call them at home. They are usually not accessible on weekends, holidays, and after business hours. Check with your attorney about leaving messages on the answering machine or answering service when the office is not open.

Problem	**Call**
Legal Emergency	Attorney
Spiritual	Religious Counselor
Medical Emergency	Doctor, Hospital
Talk or Yell	Hot Line, Friend
Emotional Emergency	Psychologist
Civil Emergency	Police

Make sure your attorney has rapid, hard-copy access to information developed by the detective, or an incident report from you in case something happens. Your attorney will tell you which situations require which specific action, investigation, or patience and calmness on your part.

The Bad Rap Attorneys Get

You will hear about how useless and crooked attorneys are, that they always take advantage and make problems bigger so they can charge larger fees, and that you should avoid them at all costs. Avoiding an attorney in this matter could cost you your children.

In my experience, the people who have had bad experiences with their own attorneys, were not handling their cases with the assistance of a good attorney.

Others did not cooperate with their attorney, lied, withheld information, or were totally in the wrong and unwilling to admit it, so they blamed their lost case on the attorney. Such persons had, in fact, dropped their problems into the lap of an attorney and waited for the results they felt they deserved.

Find good legal representation to assist you in handling your case. Then you will both need to work hard together as a team. It is also helpful to remember that your attorney did not create the system and cannot change it.

Confidentiality - Attorney

The relationship between an attorney and a client is highly confidential. Often called the Attorney Client Privilege it is defined as: The indefinite protection of oral, written, actions or gestures of communication between an attorney and client in the course of the professional relationship and cannot be disclosed without the consent of the client. The privilege protects discussion of past crimes, but does not extend to the client's proposed commission of future crimes. The confidentiality does include law clerks, stenographers, or interpreters employed by the attorney.

There is even a higher degree of confidentiality than you have with your doctor or priest. The law imposes many restrictions on these professionals about information or documents shown or given to them. Attorney client privilege relationship rests on the premises that, "The keeper of the records has a primary obligation to the client." The services of other professionals such as detectives or psychiatrists, may be protected by the Attorney-client privilege if the attorney hires the professional in the course of the attorney work product function.

Normally the confidence between an attorney and client can only be broken under the following circumstances:

- A court order from a judge demands a breech of confidence.
- The client gives the attorney permission to release the records.
- The client threatens the life of the attorney.

Your relationship with your lawyer is privileged; however, if you choose to talk about what is going on in your case to family, friends or others, then you waive this privilege. Most often the privilege is waived inadvertently. You talk to your significant other and they talk to a best friend or parent. Soon your privileged information is public knowledge. That means that no conversation or evidence is protected and you may give away the strategies of your case.

If relatives, friends or associates of yours accompany you to the appointment, the confidentiality may be destroyed. Telling others what you have discussed with your attorney, or allowing others to read the correspondence between you and your lawyer, destroys confidentiality.

The attorney client privilege is in place to protect the client, not the attorney. In rare cases the privilege is compromised by attorney error as in a case concerning Documents Produced by Mistake, in Chapter 17: Discovery and Deposition.

Cannot Do

Your lawyer cannot

- guarantee results.
- punish the opposition for all that has happened to you.
- handle matters that are beyond the scope of your agreement.
- act against the best interests of your children.
- protect you from the truth.
- win custody for you if you are not a good parent.
- change the attitude of the court or the laws.
- get you everything you want.
- begin or pursue the legal battle without an initial retainer and prompt payment.
- feed your unrealistic expectations.
- accept your information or evidence without skepticism.

Can Do

Most of what is listed here is not only what the attorney can do, but what the attorney must do by the ethical and legal requirements of the law in order to demonstrate that the attorney has given you proper representation. One of the primary tasks the attorney performs is to interpret and translate child custody law from "Legalese" to layperson's language.

If you listen to the advice, it will keep you from inadvertently breaking the law. Some of the other services are:

- Prepare a strategy with the best chance of success.
- Help you maintain contact with your children.
- Identify any real threats made by the opposition and the opposition's attorney.
- Identify which of your concerns are valid and which can be dismissed.
- Educate you about the realities of the child custody world.

- Provide the comfort of having someone powerful on your side.
- Subpoena and depose friendly and hostile witnesses.
- Advance claims in your best interest.
- Argue motions for temporary and permanent custody.
- Answer communications from the opposing counsel.
- Answer communications from the court in a proper manner.
- Obtain an Order for Evaluations by custody experts.
- Exercise all legal options on your behalf.
- Communicate with you on a regular basis.
- Make intelligent assessment of challenges and responses.
- Advise you of your changing options.
- Prepare and present your case for trial.
- Negotiate the best possible settlement.
- Request the court appoint an attorney for the children.
- Advise you of alternative strategies.
- Help you identify problems you are causing yourself.
- Advise you to stop if you tell him/her you are going to do something stupid.
- Apply his or her experience regarding the judge, other attorney, and experts.
- Hold down your losses.

Keep a Good Attorney Happy

Attorneys require clients to pay an initial retainer to insure that the clients have a material stake in this lawsuit equal to the effort the client wants the attorney to make on the client's behalf. Clients who resist paying an initial retainer are indicating that they don't wish to make the financial commitment necessary or don't have the resources to pay for the work they want done. If you have found the right attorney, make sure you show the same effort in getting the attorney paid as you want exhibited in your case.

Once you have established a relationship, always tell the truth. Communicate honestly and completely. Prepare for your physical or telephonic meetings with your attorney by reviewing all of the recent materials received from the attorney since the last meeting and relate them back to previous documents. Follow your attorney's advice regardless of what your friends, family or hairdresser has to say. If your attorney gives you information you don't like and then the judge makes a decision or comment that confirms it, accept the information and proceed. Do not bring your children to meetings with your attorney. You and your attorney need to concentrate on your case. Demonstrate that you are willing and able to assist in your case. You will face many crushing disappointments. Avoid remaining intensely bitter or upset, even after a reasonable "cooling off" period. It will only delay your progress on the case. Review the monthly statement from your attorney as soon as it arrives. If you have questions about your statement, call your attorney within 10 days of receiving your bill. Even though you may be seeking reimbursement of legal fees from the opposition by court order, you are responsible for your attorney's fees.

Pay your attorney on time, so he or she can do the work you are requesting. If you have a problem paying, talk to your attorney right away to set up suitable payment arrangements. During an interview I asked an attorney, "Doesn't all this heartache get to you?" The answer came quickly, "I can't let it get to me, I have to keep my wits about me to be able to do a good job for them. But the fact is, I never can forget any of them."

Military Attorney

A military child custody divorce attorney is necessary when representing the needs of the military and the nonmilitary spouse in a child custody battle because specialized knowledge is required. Federal law and regulations frequently govern or limit the capabilities of the individual state courts. Jurisdiction, insurance, and health benefits all involve the complicated rules. If you are an active duty member, retired from active duty, or the spouse of an active duty or retired member, it is very important that you select an experienced attorney. Even if proper benefits are awarded the children when the retired member dies, these benefits stop. Therefore, insuring the military benefits is very important. Your attorney should have been a military attorney and handled military related divorces with military personnel as regular clients.

Very few attorneys have a working knowledge of this area, so if you are not able to hire an attorney with the correct credentials it is advisable to bring in a qualified consultant.

Case Analysis

If you are handling your own case or have lost confidence in the attorney you are working with, have another attorney do a check-up on your case. The analysis can be done at an hourly rate with a written summary. An estimate of time and cost will allow you to budget, and the summary may either give you confidence in the course you have chosen, or new paths to follow.

Once Over Lightly

Keep all communications from your lawyer in a private place. Since child custody generally involves continued contact with the other parent, and since circumstances change, be prepared to face such issues as remarriage, relocation, changed income, illness, and bankruptcy.

- Behave yourself.
- Panic and emotions have no place in the decision-making process.
- At all times act in a manner that would make your children proud.
- Be kind and firm.
- Don't let important decisions be influenced more by emotions than economic common sense.
- Separate your emotions from the economics and practical issues
- Avoid advice from nonprofessionals.
- Understand your options
- Channel your energies, and then make informed decisions.

Attorney Communication Notes Date 2 Nov. 92 Time Start 10:50a.m. Time Finished 11:10P.M.
Information the attorney has asked for and I have ready. Certified copy of Bobby's Birth Certificate Copies of the pediatrician's records
Information the attorney has asked for and I don't have ready. Interrogatories are not complete, but they will be on Thursday the 5th
The things the attorney said would be ready.
The things the attorney said would be ready, but I still need. Stacy still has not sent us a current billing.
Topics I need to discuss. The patrol service says that Amber takes Bobby to James' trailer park to spend the nights when Amber's husband, Mike, is out of town. I think Bobby is in a drug and gun environment there. Is there anything I can do about it?

Keeping detailed communication notes will make the job of helping a good attorney easier and suing a bad attorney possible. Make copies of your notes and staple them to the invoices you receive from the attorney's office.

Communicate with Your Attorney

Make a list of what you want to talk about before you call or go to see your attorney. Leave space on your list for answers and dates. Place a notation in your log or appointment book for a few days before the deadline to call your attorney's secretary for a progress report. Understand what overall time lines are critical to your case.

Make sure you keep a file and get copies of all documents the opposition has filed or communications from the court as soon as your attorney receives them (a fax machine is critical for this process).

Ask what action each document requires of "our side" and what deadlines apply. Place a notation in your log or appointment book for a few

days before the due date to see if the "answer" will be completed on time.
Require that a copy be sent to you before it is formally submitted. Read and understand what the document says and why. Call again on the due date to confirm that the deadline was met.

Keep all legal papers by order of date in a three ring binder. Most documents filed require an answer or are an answer.

Save your log and appointment book notes so you do not ask for work to be done twice. If you are calling your attorney more than once a day and your children are safe and no one is bleeding, you are calling too often. Establish an agenda of what you want to discuss with your attorney before you call. It will make your attorney happy and you more productive.

Advised to Violate Court Order

If you have been issued an order by the court, to do or not do something, you must comply.

Any grounds to remove or change the court order must be submitted to the court by filing proper motions for the court to consider. This gets a little hazy in some instances.

Family court is the only place that people tend to look at a court order as a 'suggestion' rather than a demand for action or inaction. Failure to comply with a court order can result in fine, imprisonment and/or loss of your case without the chance for appeal.

This is true even if you hold what you think is new law or a letter from your attorney telling you that you need not to obey the court order. You are obligated to comply with the court's instructions. The attorney may be fined or sanctioned for advising you to disregard a court order, but you will still be the one violating the order.

Restraining Order

A restraining order is a good illustration because it limits the access of a person to another person or persons, place or thing. It also limits a person protected by the restraining order from the same access to the person being restrained. If the protected person violates the restraining order, it does not invalidate the court order. It is the obligation of the restrained person to present that information to the court. Then the court will either compel the protected person to abide by the restraining order or the court may remove the order.

As an example: Juan Garcia, requested from the court and was granted, a six month restraining order that kept Gloria Garcia, his wife, from any contact with Juan and their children Jesus and Maria. The order stated that the Gloria's violent temper put Juan and the children in danger. Juan delivered copies of the document to his employer, the manager of his apartment building and the children's school. Five weeks into the time period Juan had to go to another city for five days of training that his job required. He called Gloria and asked her to take care of the children at his apartment until his return. Gloria contacted her attorney, and asked him to file a motion for the court to vacate the restraining order. Gloria's attorney said he was swamped and could not get to it, telling Gloria that since Juan had called her violating the court order and not the reverse, he felt she would be safe proceeding without approaching the court. When Gloria attempted to pick the children up at school the police were called. The principal and police waited while Gloria contacted Juan. Juan faxed permission to release the children to Gloria and she was permitted to leave with the children. Before she left, Gloria asked the principal of the school for a written statement of the incident and the police officer for a copy of the police report.

The next day her attorney filed an emergency motion to vacate the restraining order. Gloria was able to show the court that Juan did not really see her as a threat to their children. The attorney gave poor counsel and Gloria was more cautious in her dealings with him in the future.

Communicating with the Enemy

Letters your attorney writes may accomplish more than the obvious task. Sometimes the other parent hires an incompetent and/or disreputable attorney. This can cause you many problems including delays, additional paperwork and filings by your attorney just to keep things moving. A disreputable attorney may press irrelevant points, non-issues, or issues already settled by the court in order to pump up the billable hours. An incompetent attorney may not file papers in a timely manner, miss court dates, and a myriad of other things wasting their client's money as well as your attorney's time (which costs you money). A letter from your attorney to the other attorney, specifically pointing out each misdeed or legal blunder, what should have properly been done and that the costly maneuvers are squandering their client's money. The letter may be ignored by the attorney but the client will probably find it of interest. The other parent may not know they have hired a dud. This is costing you both money and pain and is not doing your children any good.

You are legally entitled to copies of all communications your attorney receives about your case and any communications your attorney sends out pertaining to your case. It is illegal for your attorney to communicate with the other parent directly. It is not illegal for you to give the other parent a copy of the letter your attorney wrote to their attorney. While an attorney represents you, it is unethical for the opposition attorney, or anyone from that attorneys office, to communicate directly with you. Even if you call the opposition's attorney, the opposition's attorney should refer you back to your attorney.

Sex and Your Attorney

You are very vulnerable at this time, and it is a severe breach of trust for your attorney to make romantic or sexual advances during this association. Your attorney is aware of the emotional turmoil you have been in and of the phenomenon of transference of affection that some clients experience.

Your need for assurance and approval at this time gives others a disproportional amount of influence over you. It is just as unethical for the attorney to succumb to your advances. It is the attorney's responsibility to realign the relationship if you step out of line.

Don't take the chance of offending or alienating a fine attorney by acting in a sexually provocative manner. Once a breach of conduct on either side has occurred, the trust and effectiveness of the team is diminished. One incident can permanently damage the future association because one person or the other may feel pursued or rejected.

This kind of distraction from the important goal can be fatal to your case.

Taking the chance of offending the professional by communicating or behaving in a sexually provocative manner is stupid. Once a breach of conduct on either side has occurred, the value and validity of the evaluation or therapy is destroyed. There is no way to measure the damage that can be caused to your case now, and you permanently, if there is any sexual misconduct with the psychologist.

Record and Report

Usually, you are calling your attorney because of something that has happened. You are excited and upset. You want something done or explained right now. Fill out an incident report to help you think the matter through and get your thoughts in order. You should fill in an incident report form even when you know your attorney is not immediately available. Fax or mail it to the law office. An experienced staff person will probably advise you to calm down and wait for instructions from the attorney.

Later, if necessary, there will be a written report somewhere besides in your head. The completeness and clarity of your reports will lend an additional measure of validity to your explanation of any problem. Modify or design incident report forms to fit your parameters. Everyone has different issues to deal with and a generic form may not suit your needs.

Before You Talk, Assign or Request

Stay on top of anything that is happening with your case. Communicate with your attorney in writing when ever possible. A fax machine will facilitate this. It is important that you retain a copy of everything you send to your attorney and of everything sent to you. If you ask your attorney to send a letter to opposing counsel, to depose a specific witness, or to make a motion, you should submit this request in writing.

Whenever you talk to your attorney, it costs you money. You are paying for your attorney's education and experience. Everything you ask an attorney to do costs time and money.

Think things over before you call your attorney. Make notes and write down your questions before you call, and then take notes from the answers they give you. Make sure your attorney understands what you want from the legal process before you spend their time and your money. Your attorney will tell you what they can and cannot do, as well as what you can and cannot ask other professionals to do. Read more about the expenses in Chapter 20: Costs.

Incident Report for Visitation

Date: __ *October 10, 1997* ___ Time: __ *8:30pm* ___

I was asked to accompany ___*Levi Peck*___ as a ___*private person* ___

Our purpose was to *Pick up child from the mother to facilitate visitation* _ *at* _*627 Regent Place*____________________

[ ] Could not gain access to the property
[X] No one answered the door
[ ] Someone answered the door, but said child was not available for pick up
[ ] The child was there, but was not allowed to go with us.

Synopsis if necessary? *At 6:00pm on Oct. 6, 1997, Levi called Nancy to let her know he would be at her house Friday 9:00am to pick the child up for the weekend visitation. He had to leave a message on the answering machine. He called back at 8:00pm and spoke to Nancy. She said she had things to do and it would not be convenient for the visit. Levi said he would be there on time to pick up his child. The phone was on the speaker, and I could hear both sides of the conversation. When we arrived to pick up the child it did not appear that anyone was home. We waited 30 minutes and then left.*

My Name:___ *Jerry Norderling*____ Phone: __ *555-1212* ___

Incident Report Form

Day and Date __*Sat. 10/29/93*________ Time ___ *4:45 PM*_________

What happened? *I was taking Bobby to Amber's house so she could have him for Saturday and Sunday. The house was abandoned when I got there. There were no drapes so I looked in the front window. The house appeared to be empty.*

Who was there? *Amber's live-in boyfriend James drove up and told me to take Bobby to Amber's work and that they had moved. I took the baby to her.*

Our next move? *I don't know*

What I want you to do? *Nothing, I just think they should have notified me before I attempted to return the baby.*

sent by: *Randall Long copy* sent to: *Catherine Law*

Win Opposition Attorney to Your Side?

When dealing with the attorney(s) or staff for the other parent, make an effort to act in a professional manner. Venting your anger and frustration on them will waste your energy and delay your progress towards your goals. In other circumstances you and this attorney could have been working together on a case.

It is also unwise to attempt to make friends with their attorney(s). Friendliness on the part of the other attorney is a professional's demeanor, even in an adversarial relationship. They know where their paycheck is coming from and there is no doubt to whom their loyalty is owed. You will never be able to convince them you are a good person and that they should turn their backs on their client and take your side. This is just one more case in a long career, in which you barely exist, for only a moment of time.

If an attorney represents you it is unethical for the other parent's attorney to communicate directly with you even if you initiate the communication.

Get Rid of Their Attorney

If you feel the other attorney is a liar, a cheat, and does everything possible to aggravate each situation there is still nothing you can do about getting that person removed as the attorney for the opposition.
It is impossible for you to get rid of the other parent's attorney if the other parent is happy with that person. If you are attempting to disqualify the other attorney because of things the attorney has done or is doing to you, it will not work. We have watched people spend thousands of dollars and months of effort and get no satisfaction for their effort. It really is a non-issue and you should devote your time and energy to the real issues.

The attorney is to do the best for his or her client that is possible with the time and resources (money) given as tools. Not for the children, not for you, not even for the law, just for his or her client. He does not need to be fair to you or the children. Put the jerk out of your mind. It does not matter. Really. In fact the attorneys love it when you waste your time and energy on this. They just laugh it off if they give it any thought at all. It is one of the signs that your emotions are running your case instead of your brain. It will be easier for you to function if you remember that the other parent and the attorney are not one and that their motivations are not identical. You should deal with them separately. The attorney is only using experience and brain on this case. The other parent is experiencing the same emotional ups and downs that you are. The advantage to all the attorneys in this case is that their families will be as they were when you showed up and the outcome of your case will have no impact on their future.

Date	**Attorney Invoice for Service**	Time	Charge
6/09/93	telephone call to Randall/ telephone call to Solomon/ telephone call to Randall	1.00	150.00
6/10/93	preparation and court appearance	2.00	300.00
6/18/93	review the home study from Solomon	0.30	45.00
6/21/93	telephone call to Randall/ telephone call to Solomon	0.60	90.00
6/22/93	review file, telephone call to Randall, telephone call to Solomon	1.30	195.00
6/23/93	court appearance on behalf of client, telephone call to Randall, prepare for court appearance	3.30	495.00
6/24/93	telephone call to Randall, telephone call to Macini/ telephone call to Eli/ research re: 52 (f) for cause	3.00	300.00
6/25/93	telephone call to Randall re: sending files to Solomon	0.30	45.00
	Total Due		$1,620.

Attorney Invoice

Have a list in front of you itemizing what you want to speak to your attorney about, with a place at the top of your page to put down the time you start to speak.

Make a note of anything your attorney says will be done and when or what you have requested and ask when those things will be accomplished.

Put the time you finish speaking with your attorney under the start time. This will give you the ability to check the billing you get from your attorney. Keep in mind there is a great deal of time spent doing the things you have requested as well as the usual tasks required for preparation and review of documents and information.

Attorney and the Liar

Because attorneys are trained to be other people's champions, and to take only one side of a dispute, they are often dangerously ready to take up the cause of the wounded client and run off blindly in a crusade of zealous advocacy. It is obvious that some attorneys never even think to question what the client says. This is a mistake. These clients cause others a lot of grief and pain. They turn our legal system into an instrument of terrorism, and as they make fools of themselves, they make attorneys and judges look like villains.

If you identify this in your attorney you will either have to replace or keep a tight reign on the attorney.

If you identify this flaw in the opposition's attorney you will want to keep an eye on the information on which that attorney seems to be basing the case. In some instances the attorney has been seduced by the halo effect and is unable to disbelieve anything their client says or believe anything from the opposition. An attorney is compelled to press for more information from his own clients in order to investigate contrary evidence made available by the opposition's attorney. The attorney may not continue to accept in good faith information supplied by the client until opposition counsel produces compelling evidence. The attorney may be liable for sanction under Rule 11 of the Federal Rules of Civil Procedure where opposing counsel provided him with evidence that the client was lying, but the attorney failed to investigate.

Case law would include, U.S. District Court District of Mass. Schiebel Elektronische Geraete GMBH v. Polestar Technologies No. 97-10231-REK. August 3, 1998. Sometimes a client will claim that the attorney encouraged the client to lie.

Accessory to Your Crime

Not reporting a crime to which one had prior knowledge makes one an accessory before the fact, if the crime is committed. Having knowledge of a crime after a crime has been committed makes one an accessory after the fact. To avoid these ramifications, one must refuse to listen to anyone talking about doing something illegal.

If one is unable to avoid obtaining the knowledge of the actions of another, one must report the wrongdoing to the proper authorities as soon as he/she knows the crime has been committed. During the course of a custody war, your self-control and sanity will be tested. Do not blow off steam in your attorney's office by listing the horrible things you would like to do to the opposition. Attorney confidentiality does not include listening to you plan illegal activities such as destroying the personal property of others, inflicting bodily harm on another or even destroying your own property in the care of others. If you slip, the attorney will probably respond to your pronouncements with something like, "I do not want to hear about, or know about, anything you are planning that is illegal. I am an officer of the court."

Reasons Attorney Will Fire You

Often when an attorney fires you it will sound like, "There are some new very complicated issues in your case and you should get someone more knowledgeable in the field," or "Clearly you're not happy with me. Probably the best thing you can do is get another lawyer." There are many reasons an attorney will fire you. Some of the most common forms of client misconduct are, that the attorney feels you are:

- Lying
- Not following the attorney's advice
- High-maintenance client
- Ungrateful and unappreciative
- Acting as if everything is an emergency
- Not communicating
- Abusive to attorney's support staff
- A miserable person to deal with
- Behaving in an inappropriate manner
- Not paying the bill

Attorneys have an ethical obligation to provide you with zealous representation. They can't bail out of your case seven days before trial. If you want rid of the attorney as badly as the attorney wants rid of you there is no problem. But if it will hurt your case for the attorney to drop out, and depending on how far along the case is, the attorney may need permission from the court to drop your case. It is the judge's prerogative and many judges will never, ever allow an attorney to get rid of a client who wants to keep the attorney. When an attorney does fire you, you should receive a disengagement letter via certified mail stating that the attorney is closing your file and it should contain:

- An explanation of why the attorney has withdrawn.
- Reasons that the withdrawal doesn't reflect negatively on the merits of your case.
- A recommendation as to whether you should seek other counsel.

- An account of outstanding fees with the dollar amount.
- Arrangements to transfer the case file from the attorney to you.
- A list of all pending deadlines in your case.

My Way or the Highway

"My Way or the Highway" is one of the things an attorney will say to a client that is getting too hard to handle. If you have a good attorney, and have been given this ultimatum, you'd better think about cleaning up your act. It is very difficult to hire another attorney as it gets late in the game. You have explained your situation so many times by now that you will leave out important facts. The new attorney will have a new set of ideas and style that may be crippled by the efforts of the first attorney. You will have to pay the new attorney to read through every piece of paper produced by everyone up to this point. Attorneys have a saying for it: stepping into someone else's underwear.

Please Release Me, Let Me Go

If you don't want to release your attorney from your case, you can put up a fight. Once your attorney has sent you a letter or notified the court of the attorney's withdraw from your case, you would send a letter to the judge explaining why attempting to find new counsel would harm your case.

Some of the reasons would include the time restrictions and monetary considerations of bringing another attorney up to speed on your case. Pointing out (if true) that the other parent has contacted all of the other attorneys within a reasonable distance. A list of the attorneys may be helpful.

Inclusion of your attorney is communication notes and the attorney's billing could substantiate any claims you may have of unfinished business.

Judges don't like attorneys to walk away from a case that has gone to court. Often they will keep the attorney on the case.

Although keeping an attorney that does not want to represent you may not offer you the best representation, it may be better than nothing. Keep in mind that this person will be watching how they deal with you because the judge will be watching the attorney.

Reasons to Fire Your Attorney

Plea to Judge to Keep Attorney Example

Mrs. Judith Sormer
23 Blue Lane, Phoenix, AZ 85003

April 30, 2001

Judge Harold Grange,

As of May 5, 2001 my attorney for the past two years has notified me he will not act in my behalf on any legal matters. We are to appear before you on May 30, 2001 and I have contacted all 18 attorneys in the county. Non will take my case at this late date. If attorney Sackson is allow to abandon my case it will cause irreparable damage to my case. Please don't allow this to happen. I have enclosed copies of the billing from my payment record to the attorneys office.

Thank you for your time in this matter.
Mrs. Judith Sormer
cc: Mr. Sackson attorney
Mr. Jack Lenden attorney for Mr. Sormer

Because we need our attorney so badly it is common for a parent to be experiencing several problems with the attorney before we have finally had it. Some of the common reasons we fire an attorney are because the attorney is:

- Not behaving in a professional manner with you
- Forcing you to surrender your rights
- Giving you dangerous advice
- Giving you incorrect or illegal advice
- Failing to follow through
- Incorrectly billing you
- Failing to communicate
- Not filing papers in a timely manner
- Failing to show up in court
- Overly co-operative with other attorney
- Lying

Once you have made the decision to fire an attorney you may want to review your attorney communication log to see if there's something the attorney should have done or something the attorney did wrong that needs to be fixed before you sever the relationship. The attorney may want to stick with you to protect himself against further risks and to undo any mistakes and perform functions that the attorney should have taken care of earlier in the case.

Handling a Bad Attorney

If you feel your attorney is not doing a good job for you, find another attorney. Then send your old attorney a letter with instructions to file a motion to withdraw from the case.
Send a copy to the judge.

It is illegal for your attorney to record your conversations with him/her without your specific knowledge and agreement.

In most states attorneys cannot force you to pay your bill first, but the attorney may delay returning your files to you or may withhold your files from the new attorney causing you additional legal problems.

Attorney Discharge Letter Example

Ms. Judith Sormer
2332 Blue Lane, Phoenix, AZ 85003
April 30, 2001
Mr. Inadequate Lawyer,

As of May 5, 2001 please do not act in my behalf on any legal matters. Please forward my files to the office of Mr. New Lawyer at 333 E. Virginia, Phoenix, Arizona 85003.

Thank you for your time in this matter.
Ms. Judith Sormer
cc: Judge Harold Grange
Mr. Jackson Leaderman attorney for Mr. Jack Former Spouse
Mr. New Lawyer

If you have communicated in writing and paid your bills in good faith, but your attorney has not performed adequately on your behalf, you may have a case for legal malpractice (which is a civil suit for money damages). Your other option is to file a grievance with the State Bar Association, which could deprive him of his license to practice law.

You can avoid many of the problems by doing a proper evaluation of prospective attorneys before you hire one. Use the **Attorney Evaluation Form** in this chapter. Once you have evaluated several candidates then compare them to each other using the **Attorney Comparison Form** in this chapter, to give you the best attorney available.

New Attorney = Delay

If you must hire a new attorney the court will usually grant a delay. The length of the delay will depend on how complicated your case is, the pressure of cases on the docket and the judge's whim. Use this time to fix anything you have been doing wrong and document anything the opposition may be doing wrong.

Lawsuits Against Attorneys

Jordache Enterprises v. Brobeck, Phlenger & Harrison CA Supreme Court. Jordach was sued for selling knockoffs of Guess jeans. Jordache sued Brobeck, Phlenger & Harrison for malpractice because they didn't inform Jordache that the cases might have been covered by its insurance.

Suing Your Attorney

Just because you feel you received a bad result in court, that does not mean that the lawyer has committed malpractice. You may have received the best results possible under the circumstances. If your attorney's incompetence or unethical or illegal behavior causes you to lose contact with your children or custody of them then you should choose one of three courses of action.

1. Do nothing at all.

2. File a grievance with the State Bar Association. If valid, the Bar may subject the attorney to disciplinary action. Loss suffered as a result of an attorney's action is not recoverable through the lawyer grievance system. You will have to file a civil case to get damages (money).

3. Contact another attorney (there are attorneys with this specialty) and file a malpractice suit against the first attorney. Most attorneys do not accept legal malpractice cases on a contingency basis unless the hard, solid, provable, collectable damages exceed $100,000, because malpractice cases are usually highly contested and strongly defended cases.

4. File a statement of claim with the Small Claims Court for as long as the amount that you are owed is less than $5K (this will vary from state to state). You file and serve a complaint. You won't go though the process of Discovery. You will just tell

your story to the judge. Go over it repeatedly until you can tell it in a straightforward manner (Keep It Simple Stupid). This is a very cheap option as you don't need a lawyer and your chances are good since no real law is applied there. This should be your advantage when suing a professional lawyer. Because, no matter how important the lawyer thinks he is, it will still be up to the Judge's discretion, the law that he applies is not a precedent law.

If he likes you and feels that your claim is just, you'll be the winner.

The burden of proof for malpractice is on a "more likely than not" basis of all four elements necessary to prove negligence.

1. Breach of Attorney-Client Relationship. A lawyer commits malpractice when a client (with or without retainer or payment) asks for legal advice and the lawyer gives advice with the lawyer knowing that the client will rely on that advice. In some states you may sue another party's litigation attorney for legal malpractice. This is most common in domestic relations disputes.

2. Attorney Fails on the part of the attorney to the client to show a Duty of Care

3. A lawyer commits malpractice when he or she does not demonstrate reasonably or competently of a person having a legal duty, created by his or her undertaking, to act primarily for the benefit of another in matters connected with determining and implementing a strategy to be followed to achieve the client's legal goals.

4. Breach of Duty

5. A lawyer breaches his or her professional duty of care if he or she fails to provide reasonably competent representation. You may be required to prove that an alternative course of action would have provided a different result.

6. As a Direct and Proximate Result A lawyer commits malpractice when a client can prove damage was incurred as a result of the lawyer's action and could not and would not have happened if the attorney had chosen a different course of action.

A lawyer commits malpractice when he or she fails to provide quality legal services to a client through an error or omission and/or fails to provide the services that meet the minimum standard of care of a licensed attorney. Proven incompetence may offer you solid grounds for Appeal in your custody case. Attorneys must be able to demonstrate that they used sufficient care and diligence in representing and advising their clients. If your attorney settled your case without your permission, did not file papers on time, used your money for other than your case, or forged your signature, you probably have grounds for suit. An attorney may have an opportunity to reveal confidential information about you in order to defend against the malpractice suit you file.

Help from the Bar Association

Filing against the attorney with the bar association serves to punish rather than a tort lawsuit for money. The stated purpose and nature of lawyer discipline proceedings and sanctions proceedings is to protect the public and the administration of justice from lawyers who have not discharged, will not discharge, or are unlikely to discharge their professional duties to clients, the public, the legal system, and the legal profession properly.

As a point of information, in many states including California, there is no statute of limitations on state bar complaints. An attorney has a duty under Business and Professions Code section 6068, subdivision (o)(7) to report to the bar, the reversal of a case based on the attorney's misconduct, gross incompetence, or willful misrepresentation. The courts feel a need to protect the integrity of the legal system, and to insure the administration of justice.

As with the penal system the courts feel they should, when and where appropriate, rehabilitate the lawyer. Sanctions for misconduct apply to all licensed lawyers. Lawyers who are not actively practicing law, but who are serving in such roles as corporate officers, public officials, or law professors, do not lose their association with the legal profession because of their primary occupation.

The public expects that anyone who is admitted to the practice of law, regardless of daily occupational activities, will conform to the minimum ethical standards of the legal profession. If the lawyer fails to meet these standards, appropriate sanctions should be imposed.

All of that sounds wonderful because you have a place to go for help with a bad attorney. But once you have removed the emotional questions and delineate the real issues to construct a presentable convincing case you must submit the information to the State Bar Association.

If they determine there is clear and convincing evidence that a member of the legal profession has violated a provision of the Rules of Professional Conduct (or applicable standard under the laws of the jurisdiction where the proceeding is brought), they decide how to deal with the attorney. Some of the criteria used to do this is: minor misconduct, when they perceive that there is little or no injury to a client, the public, the legal system, or the profession, and when there is little likelihood of repetition by the lawyer, private discipline may be imposed. If they feel that grievous injury to a client, the public, the legal system, or the profession has occurred they reprimand, suspend or disbar the attorney. Sanctions are imposed on a lawyer upon a finding or acknowledgment that the lawyer has engaged in professional misconduct. Disbarment terminates the individual's status as a lawyer.

Although the legal profession in general and lawyers strongly oppose it, public proceedings, after probable cause is found, and public sanctions is the approach favored by the general public.

Individual lawyers may prefer to avoid the embarrassment and stigma associated with a public sanction, but the profession and the public as a whole will benefit. The more you know about how effectively the disciplinary system works, the more confidence you will have in that system. If there is approval of the system, it is hoped that public confidence in the profession's ability to discipline itself will be assured. Primarily the Bar Associations are concerned with:

Violations: Duties to Clients

Failure to:
Preserve the Client's Property: Cases involving the failure to preserve client property:
Preserve the Client's Confidences: Cases involving improper revelation of information relating to representation of a client.
Avoid Conflicts Of Interest: Cases involving conflicts of interest.
Lack of:
Competence: Cases involving failure of the attorney to provide competent representation to a client.
Candor: Cases where the lawyer engages in fraud, deceit, or misrepresentation directed toward a client.
Diligence: Cases involving a failure to act with reasonable diligence and promptness in representing a client.

Violations: Duties to the Public

Failure To Maintain Personal Integrity: Cases involving commission of a criminal act that reflects adversely on the lawyer's honesty, trustworthiness, or fitness as a lawyer in other respects, or in cases with conduct involving dishonesty, fraud, deceit, or misrepresentation.

Failure To Maintain The Public Trust: Cases involving public officials who engage in conduct that is prejudicial to the administration of justice, or who state or imply an ability to influence improperly, a government agency or official.

Violations: Duties to the Legal System

False Statements, Fraud, and Misrepresentation: Cases involving conduct that is prejudicial to the administration of justice or that involves dishonesty, fraud, deceit, or misrepresentation to a court.

Abuse of the Legal Process: Cases involving failure to expedite litigation or bring a meritorious claim, or failure to obey any obligation under the rules of a tribunal except for an open refusal based on an assertion that no valid obligation exists.

Violations: Duties as a Professional

False Advertising: Cases involving false or misleading communication about the lawyer or the lawyer's services, improper communication of fields of practice, improper solicitation of professional employment from a prospective client, unreasonable or improper fees, unauthorized practice of law, improper withdrawal from representation, or failure to report professional misconduct.

Cases involving prior discipline and prior Discipline Orders

Admonishment

Admonishment is the lowest form of discipline, which declares the conduct of the lawyer improper, but does not limit the lawyer's right to practice. Admonishment is appropriate when a lawyer:

(a) is negligent in dealing with client property and causes little or no actual or potential injury to a client, or where there is a technical violation of trust account rules, or where there is an unintentional mishandling of client property.

(b) negligently reveals information relating to: representation of a client not otherwise lawfully permitted to be disclosed and this disclosure causes little or no actual or potential injury to a client.

(c) is negligent in determining whether the lawyer may materially affect the representation of a client may be materially affected by the lawyer's own interests, or whether the representation will adversely affect another client, and causes little or no injury or potential injury to a client.

(d) is negligent and does not act with reasonable diligence in representing a client, and causes little or no actual or potential injury to a client.

(e) engages in an isolated instance of negligence in determining whether he or she is competent to handle a legal matter, and causes little or no injury to a client.

(f) negligently fails to provide a client with accurate or complete information, and causes little or no actual or potential injury to the client.

(g) engages in any other conduct that reflects adversely on the lawyer's fitness to practice law.

(h) in an official or governmental position, negligently fails to follow proper procedures or rules, and causes little or no actual or potential injury to a party or to the integrity of the legal process.

(i) is negligent in determining whether submitted statements or documents are false, or in failing to disclose material information upon learning of its falsity, and causes little or no actual or potential injury to a party, or causes little or no adverse or potentially adverse effect on the legal proceeding.

(j) negligently fails to comply with a court order or rule, and causes little or no injury to a party, or causes little or no actual or potential interference with a legal proceeding

(k) negligently engages in an improper communication with an individual in the legal system, and causes little or no actual or potential injury to a party, or causes little or no actual or potential interference with the outcome of the legal proceeding.

(l) is negligent in determining whether the lawyer's conduct violates a duty owed as a professional, and causes little or no actual or potential injury to a client, the public, or the legal system.

(note) Admonishment is not an appropriate sanction when a lawyer violates the terms of a prior disciplinary order, or when a lawyer has engaged in the same or similar misconduct in the past.

Suspension

Suspension is the removal of a lawyer from the practice of law for a specified minimum period of time. A suspension of a specific amount of time (example: ninety (90) days or less shall not require proof of rehabilitation or passage of the bar examination. A suspension of more than ninety (90) days) should require proof of rehabilitation and may require passage of all or part of the local Bar Association examination. Often no suspension shall be ordered for a specific period of time in excess of three years.

Suspension is appropriate when a lawyer:

(a) knows or should know that he is dealing improperly with client property and causes injury or potential injury to a client.

(b) knows of a conflict of interest and does not fully disclose to a client the possible effect of that conflict, and causes injury or potential injury to a client.

(c) knowingly reveals information relating to the representation of a client not otherwise lawfully permitted to be disclosed, and this disclosure causes injury or potential injury to a client.

(d) knowingly fails to perform services for a client and causes injury or potential injury to a client

(e) a lawyer engages in a pattern of neglect and causes injury or potential injury to a client.

(f) engages in an area of practice in which the lawyer knows he or she is not competent, and causes injury or potential injury to a client.

(g) knowingly deceives a client, and causes injury or potential injury to the client.

(h) knowingly engages in criminal conduct that seriously and adversely reflects on the lawyer's fitness to practice.

(i) in an official or governmental position

knowingly fails to follow proper procedures or rules, and causes injury or potential injury to a party or to the integrity of the legal process.

(j) knows that false statements or documents are being submitted to the court, or that material information is improperly being withheld, and takes no remedial action.

(k) knows that he or she is violating a court order or rule, and causes injury or potential injury to a client or a party, or causes interference or potential interference with a legal proceeding.

(l) engages in communication with an individual in the legal system when the lawyer knows that such communication is improper, and causes injury or potential injury to a party or causes interference or potential interference with the outcome of the legal proceeding.

(m) knowingly engages in conduct that is a violation of a duty owed as a professional and causes injury or potential injury to a client, the public, or the legal system.

(n) has been publicly reprimanded for the same or similar conduct and engages in further similar acts of misconduct that cause injury or potential injury to a client, the public, the legal system, or the profession.

Interim suspension is the temporary suspension of a lawyer from the practice of law pending imposition of final discipline. Interim suspension includes: (a) suspension upon conviction of a "serious crime", or

(b) suspension when the lawyer's continuing conduct is, or is likely to, cause immediate and serious injury to a client or the public.

Probation is a sanction that allows a lawyer to practice law under specified conditions. Probation can be imposed alone or in conjunction with any other disciplinary measure; probation can also be imposed as a condition of readmission or reinstatement.

Other sanctions and remedies, which may be imposed include: (a) restitution, (b) assessment of costs, (c) limitation upon practice, (d) appointment of a receiver, (e) requirement that the lawyer take the bar examination or professional responsibility examination, (f) requirement that the lawyer attend continuing education courses, (g) other requirements that the state's highest court or disciplinary board deems consistent with the purposes of lawyer sanctions.

Reciprocal discipline is the imposition of a disciplinary sanction on a lawyer who has been disciplined in another jurisdiction.

Public Reprimand

Public Reprimand, also known as censure or public censure, is a form of public discipline, which declares the conduct of the lawyer improper, but does not limit the lawyer's right to practice. Public Reprimand is appropriate when a lawyer:

(a) is negligent in dealing with client property and causes injury or potential injury to a client.

(b) negligently reveals information relating to representation of a client not otherwise lawfully permitted to be disclosed and this disclosure causes injury or potential injury to a client.

(c) is negligent in determining whether the representation of a client may be materially affected by the lawyer's own interests, or whether the representation will adversely affect another client, and causes injury or potential injury to a client.

(d) demonstrates failure to understand relevant legal doctrines or procedures and causes injury or potential injury to a client

(e) is negligent in determining whether he or she is competent to handle a legal matter and causes injury or potential injury to a client.

(f) is negligent and does not act with reasonable diligence in representing a client, and causes injury or potential injury to a client. Public Reprimand is appropriate when a lawyer negligently fails to provide a client with accurate or complete information, and causes injury or potential injury to the client.

(g) knowingly engages in any other conduct that involves dishonesty, fraud, deceit, or misrepresentation and that adversely reflects on the lawyer's fitness to practice law.

(h) in an official or governmental position negligently fails to follow proper procedures or rules, and causes injury or potential injury to a party or to the integrity of the legal process.

(i) is negligent either in determining whether statements or documents are false, or in taking remedial action when material information is withheld.

(j) negligently fails to comply with a court

order or rule, and causes injury or potential injury to a client or other party, or causes interference or potential interference with a legal proceeding.

(k) is negligent in determining whether it is proper to engage in communication with an individual in the legal system, and causes injury or potential injury to a party, or interference or potential interference with the outcome of the legal proceeding.

(l) negligently engages in conduct that is a violation of a duty owed as a professional and causes injury or potential injury to a client, the public, or the legal system.

(m) negligently violates the terms of a prior disciplinary order and such violation causes injury or potential injury to a client, the public, the legal system, or the profession.

(n) has received a private reprimand for the same or similar misconduct and engages in further similar acts of misconduct.

Disbarment

Disbarment is the act of expelling a lawyer from the practice of law. To expel from the bar, or the legal profession; to deprive (an attorney, barrister, or counselor) of his or her status and privileges as such. Disbarment is the most serious sanction the Bar Associations can impose. Appropriate when a lawyer:

(a) intentionally or knowingly converts client property regardless of injury or potential injury.

(b) with the intent to benefit the lawyer or another, intentionally reveals information relating to representation of a client not otherwise lawfully permitted to be disclosed and this disclosure causes injury or potential injury to a client.

(c) without the informed consent of the client engages in representation of a client knowing that the lawyer's interests are adverse to the client's with the intent to benefit the lawyer or another, causes serious or potentially serious injury to the client

(d) simultaneously represents clients that the lawyer knows have adverse interests with the intent to benefit the lawyer or another, and causes serious or potentially serious injury to a client.

(e) represents a client in a matter substantially related to a matter in which the interests of a present or former client are materially adverse, and knowingly uses information relating to the representation of a client with the intent to benefit the lawyer or another, and causes serious or potentially serious injury to a client.

(f) abandons the practice and causes serious or potentially serious injury to a client

(g) knowingly fails to perform services for a client and causes serious or potentially serious injury to a client

(h) engages in a pattern of neglect with respect to client matters and causes serious or potentially serious injury to a client.

(i) course of conduct demonstrates that the lawyer does not understand the most fundamental legal doctrines or procedures, and the lawyer's conduct causes injury or potential injury to a client.

(j) knowingly or intentionally deceives a client with the intent to benefit the lawyer or another regardless of injury or potential injury.

(k) is convicted of a felony under applicable law; or

(l) engages in serious criminal conduct, a necessary element of which includes, intentional interference with the administration of justice, false swearing, misrepresentation, fraud, extortion, misappropriation, or theft.

(g) engages in the sale, distribution or importation of controlled substances.

(h) engages in the intentional killing of another; or

(i) attempts or conspires or solicits another to commit a crime

(j) engages in any other intentional conduct involving dishonesty, fraud, deceit.

(k) misrepresentation that seriously adversely reflects on the lawyer's fitness to practice.

(l) in an official or governmental position knowingly misuses the position with the intent to obtain a significant benefit or advantage for himself or another, or with the intent to cause serious or potentially serious injury to a party or to the integrity of the legal process.

(m) with the intent to deceive the court, knowingly makes a false statement or submits a false document

(n) improperly withholds material information, and causes serious or potentially serious injury to a party, or causes a significant or potentially significant adverse effect on the legal proceeding.

(o) knowingly violates a court order or rule with the intent to obtain a benefit for the lawyer or another, and causes serious injury or potentially serious injury to a party or causes serious or potentially serious interference with a legal proceeding.

(p) intentionally directly or indirectly tampers with a witness

(q) makes an unauthorized ex parte communication with a judge or juror with intent to affect the outcome of the proceeding.

(r) intentionally engages in conduct that is a violation of a duty owed as a professional with the intent to obtain a benefit for the lawyer or another, and causes serious or potentially serious injury to a client, the public, or the legal system.

(s) intentionally violates the terms of a prior disciplinary order and such violation causes injury to a client, the public, the legal system, or the profession

(t) has been suspended for the same or similar misconduct, and intentionally engages in further similar acts of misconduct.

If you are attempting to prove misconduct you would be wise to identify any aggravating and mitigating circumstances that the court may consider in deciding what sanction to impose include:

(a) prior disciplinary offenses; (b) dishonest or selfish motive;

(c) a pattern of misconduct; (d) multiple offenses;

(e) bad faith obstruction of the disciplinary proceeding by intentionally failing to comply with rules or orders of the disciplinary agency;

(f) submission of false evidence, false statements, or other deceptive practices during the disciplinary process;

(g) refusal to acknowledge wrongful nature of conduct; (h) vulnerability of victim;

(i) substantial experience in the practice of law;

(j) indifference to making restitution.

Chapter 9: Detectives

Covert Intelligence Division

In the child custody wars, this is the "Covert Intelligence Division." Don't waste your time having a detective follow good people around waiting for them to do something bad. It will not matter to a judge that the opposition is developing new interpersonal relationships. This part of your army should spend its time documenting bad people doing bad things. That's all.

One of the very best reasons for using a detective is that most of the procedures required to gather information about the opposition such as following, taking photos, asking questions and watching them, are now considered "stalking". In some cases stalking someone is a federal crime punishable by up to five years in prison. A professional is also less likely to be observed or involved in an altercation with the opposition than you or a friend of yours might be.

I found very few detectives who looked or behaved like television private investigators. Don't be disappointed. The subject (the person you are checking on) would notice the tall, good-looking hunk or remember the beautiful bombshell. To accomplish your objectives, it is critical for the investigator to blend, without notice, into an office setting, be easily lost in a swap meet crowd or grocery store, and be quickly and entirely forgotten after personal contact with your subject.

Make sure your detective is licensed and, above all, very street smart. This may be a difficult call if the detective is smooth and you are not street smart. Many agencies are made up of only one or two regular employees, who have many associates they call on, as needed. One experienced investigator told me, "My work is best described as hours of research, weeks of boredom, relieved by twenty minutes of panic, and a wonderful high when I complete an assignment successfully."

Can Do

Detectives are usually more accessible on weekends, holidays, and after regular business hours than are attorneys. As an important part of your team, the private investigator may be able to defuse your emotions and help you find positive actions to take when an incident causes panic, pain or stress. The private detective will keep you informed of the progress on your case and require your assistance in analyzing facts.

The investigation may change directions several times as one avenue of information proves useless and another opportunity is identified. A change of direction may involve a change in the service being used. Always ask how the cost to you is affected. A detective can be your eyes and ears in situations that may otherwise remain inaccessible to you. There is a peace of mind that comes with knowing that someone is able to document problems that only you have seen until now. Sometimes your investigator can calm you by letting you know that a bad situation you felt existed was, in fact, harmless, or that the false front the opposition has established will not hold up in court. The calming effect of knowing that you have help and something is being done to bring matters to a close in your favor cannot be underrated. This feeling relieves you and lets you act in a more positive manner. You have an army; you are not alone.

Finding One

Your first reaction will be to reach out in a panic to anyone who seems willing to help you. Calm down and make the best choice for your challenge. These are your children, your money, your problem. It is not possible to hire the "grunt work" and put it out of your mind. Be sure to hire someone you can work with for the long haul.

Your attorney probably has a number of private investigators he had used in the past. Because of your relationship with your attorney, this is usually the most reliable and workable option. After your attorney has recommended several, interview them and choose the one you can work with the best. Pay the investigator directly, as some attorneys add a mark-up to defray the cost of paying the detective while still waiting for payment from you. Also, tell the investigator that you intend to maintain control over the costs and information developed.

Contact the state government agency that licenses private investigators in the state in which you intend to hire a detective. When you call that agency you will find that standard department policy prohibits recommending one detective agency over another. Rules aside, often an individual will give you several telephone numbers of agents with whom he or she is familiar.

The public library has a reference book of associations that is updated each year and will give you the telephone number of several detective and private investigator groups you could call for a recommendation.

The worst option, equal to using only the telephone book, is asking people you know for the name of a detective. Moreover, asking friends for a recommendation may alert the opposition of your intentions. Individual private detectives and agencies belong to professional groups. Contacting these groups, as well as any the agency itself may have given you, may assist you in verifying the length of time in business and stability of the individual or company. Check any references given to you by the agency you are considering hiring. Hiring the right private investigator could be crucial to your case. Make sure, by investigation, that this is an ethical and trustworthy person. It is best to choose one who is a member of a recognized organization, such as the California Licensed Investigators, World Association of Detectives or Council of International Investigators.

Right One for You

When hiring a detective, you may be required to reveal a great deal of sensitive information about your life. Some of this is necessary so that you can prove that you have the right to look for the information you seek. One great advantage of finding an investigator through your attorney is that this step is skipped entirely.

Your relationship with a detective or agency may go on for a long time, and it will cost you a great deal of money. Make sure these people can do what they say they can do and that you trust them. Also, be sure that you can communicate directly with the agent assigned to your case.

When you call for an initial appointment, give a short statement about your case, such as, "I am involved in a contested child custody matter that may require surveillance, investigation, and contact with the opposition. Are you experienced in this area, and are you interested in talking to me about it?"

Once you identify a company's interest, set a time and place to meet, in the detective's office, if possible. Let the detective know you will want to see an example of a finished report. The detective should be able to cross out names on a closed file to show you what to expect.

Detective Evaluation Form Good or reasonable answer, mark the box with a "+". Flaky or wrong answer, mark the box with a "-". No answer or you are not sure, mark the box with a"?".	+	-	?
Does this person have prior experience with your attorney?	X		
If not, is the detective willing to give you names and telephone numbers of attorneys they have worked with?	X		
Are you comfortable with how & where the appointment was set?	X		
Did he/she demonstrate sufficient experience in custody matters?	X		
How many times has the detective testified in child custody cases? _ *MANY*__. Ask for names and telephone numbers.	X		
Has this investigator demonstrated, "credibility"?	X		
When you listened to the detective describe normal practice and procedures, did you feel the detective's judgment was trustworthy?	X		
Will the detective be creative enough to accomplish your goals and knowledgeable enough to give you advice to keep you legal?	X		
Did the methods and processes described sound professional?	X		
Is the detective willing to show you the method used for keeping proper records?	X		
Has your agent been employed as a detective long enough to have the required expertise?	X		
Did you hear any warning bells in your head? *NO*			
Do you understand how much the detective gets paid and when?	X		
Did the detective seem to think your goals were reasonable?	X		
Did the detective seem interested in taking your case?	X		
Notes:			

When you meet with the detective, restate the short explanation of your problem and ask for similar examples of assignments handled in the past. Inquire as to the method the detective will use to communicate, with you during the investigation. Written reports can be subpoenaed from your investigator by the opposition. Verbal reports are harder to keep straight, refer back to, or present in court. Your investigator may be required to testify by either attorney.

Ask about the specific techniques and equipment used, what kind of results you might look for, and the estimated length of time usually required. Then shut-up and listen. It is important to really hear what is said, not what you want to hear. You may want to take notes or record the conversation.

It is best to evaluate what you have seen and heard without the pressure of the detective waiting for a decision. You do not have to hire any of them on the spot or hire the first individual or company you talk to.

Interview the Detective

Review any evaluation form before your appointment. Have a list of questions about your case ready. Don't be rushed into a decision. At the conclusion of your appointment, tell the detective you will call tomorrow and advise him as to what you have decided to do,

Understanding the Costs

Private investigators have several ways to charge for their services. When using the services of a detective agency for a specific job, do not assume that a new avenue of investigation suggested is included in what you are already paying.

For example: you have hired a detective to do surveillance at an hourly rate. During the surveillance the detective informs you that a driver's license and motor vehicle search might speed up the process.

Ask what information that may produce, when you might expect to have it, and how much more that will cost. Always fill out the private investigator assignment form. Everything you ask a private investigator to do costs him (or her) time, money, favors saved from contacts and associates, hours of research, and draws on years of experience.

Understand what you want from your detective agency before you spend their time and your money. Explain what you are trying to accomplish or what you think you need to know or document. Initially, the detective will assist you in asking the correct questions to get the information you need.

As you become accustomed to working with this person, you will learn a little of the technical language of the industry.

Your ability to communicate with the detective more efficiently will ease the process along. Just as importantly, the professional private investigator will tell you what you may and may not hire a detective to do, and why.

In most countries of the world, as well as in the USA, **if you hire someone to do something that breaks the law, you are just as criminally liable for prosecution as the person committing the crime.** In some well publicized cases the perpetrator of the crime has plea bargained a lighter sentence for him/herself by turning State's Evidence against the person that asked them to, or paid them to, commit the crime.

The cost for professional investigative services can be as little as $25 for a simple computer report to $75 per hour per operative, with a four-hour minimum in a medium-sized metropolitan community. To start an investigation, a retainer of $200 to $1,000 is usually required. Read more about the expense of investigation in Chapter 20: Costs.

Contract or Agreement

Your initial contract is the detective's promise to do specific work for a set dollar amount. You promise to pay for that work in a prescribed manner. The original contract should only be changed or added to in writing by the person proposing the change, signed, dated, and returned by the person accepting the amendment. Copies of each specific job and rate you are quoted, accompanied with check paid, can help you avoid billing problems later.

Detective Retainer Agreement

I, ___Randall Long _ (your name), hereafter called "the Client," hereby retain ____L. Hammer___ (detective's name), hereafter called "the Detective." The Detective is to investigate and perform legal functions to prepare and present evidence in a contested, child custody dispute. Detective will take all reasonable steps necessary in a timely manner to collect information and present the best possible case for an award of custody to the client. Hourly rate of $ ___75.00__ per hour for investigative services and $ __125.00__ per hour for court preparation and testimony. A retainer against fees of $_500.00__ has been submitted by the Client and accepted by the Detective.

Hourly rate _____$55.00___________Date __July 3, 1992__

Client _Randall Long_______________ Detective ___L. Hammer________________

Fee Schedule

Ask for a fee schedule. The experienced investigator will be able to give you a bottom line as to what this type of work usually costs. The statement I have heard most often is, "There are a few variables, but it should not cost any more than ________." (You will be quoted an amount.)

Use the Detective Retainer Form in this manual. It gives you the ability to give instructions as to the type of work you want done and what dollar amount the agency may not exceed.

Ask for the agreement in writing. Many investigators have a contract or retainer agreement incorporated into their fee schedule. Accept it if you are comfortable with what they present.

Avoid Hot Shots

Anyone you have seen on the afternoon or late evening talk show circuit, or read about in your newspaper is making a big name for him or herself by exploiting the cases the investigator was hired to work on. Your case could be the next one the hot shot sits up laughing about. People like this are more interested in the foreign sports car they drive and in seeing their names in print, than in making sure a proper job is done for the client. It is amazing how poorly they are thought of in their own professional community. Avoid high visibility investigators.

A Snake Is A Snake Is ...

In your enthusiasm to "get" the opposition, do not hire a detective or any professional who is willing to employ "dirty tricks" or break the law. If detectives seem unconscionable, unprincipled, deceitful, scheming, improper, unseemly, corrupt, crooked, dishonest, questionable, shady, sinister, underhanded, unethical, bribable and unprincipled, they are. It is not because they think you are such a wonderful person with a worthwhile mission that they will do these things only this time to help you; it is because they are this way all of the time.

Such a detective will be willing to do these same "dirty tricks" and worse to you if circumstances change. A snake is a snake. Snake handlers get snake bite more often than people who avoid the reptiles altogether.

Proper Record Keeping

Without meticulous documentation, your case can fall apart in court. You can end up looking like a liar and your attorney a fool. The opposition's attorney loves nothing better than discovering that a detective hasn't kept proper records because this often indicates that person may also be lax in other areas such as keeping the investigation within lawful limits.

Keep A Good Detective Happy

Pay your investigator's fees on time. This will allow the investigator to do the work you are requesting. If you feel your investigator is not doing a good job for you, find another investigator and send your old investigator a fax or letter instructing him or her to deliver your file, or make an appointment to pick up your file and pay the final bill.

Always save your copy of the fax and the transmission log proving delivery.

Help Your Detective

Copy and fill out the Assignment Form in this manual and give this to your detective for each assignment. It will help you to organize your thoughts and lead to a better understanding of what your expenditures will be.

If you need the report in a specific format, make a form for the detective to fill in.

Supply a Data Sheet on all people the report or investigation concerns. Photos that you provide of persons, vehicles, and buildings will save time.

Keeping yourself available by telephone is adequate.

If something happens that you think your detective should know about, copy the Incident Form in this manual, fill in the data, and fax, if time is of the essence.

Stay Alert

You have hired a detective, but you are not relieved of your responsibility to contribute new information. Initially, you are the best source of information your detective will have. Once the detective begins the investigation, the "subject" will be the best source of data. Keep your eyes open. Watch out for "smoke screens" and other diversionary tactics. The opposition may attempt to keep you too busy to notice something important.

A common tactic is to make a smart remark that encourages you to respond angrily. For example: you have become so involved with answering the obvious attack leveled at you that you do not notice that there is no child safety seat in the car. You and your children just lost a battle.

Be aware of the make and license plates on the vehicles in which the opposition interacts with your children and the children's verbal and nonverbal responses. It is much better if you are on speaking terms with the opposition. Listen to stories about the opposition's past, hobbies, vacations and jobs.

Encourage detail without asking threatening questions, while getting additional information for your data sheet. Make notes as soon as possible. This is crucial data if the opposition attempts to disappear. People do not just run away with children. They usually run to a logical or predetermined place.

Detective Communication Notes

Date *Wed. 6 Oct. 99* Time Start *2:00P.M.* Time Finished *2:10P.M.*

I called for an appointment. Spoke to John Boxer who was recommended to me by Betty Darcy. After a short explanation of my needs we set a meeting time for Friday at 9:00am in his office at 2025 North LePant #17.

Date *Fri. 8 Oct. 99* Time Start *9:00A.M.* Time Finished *10:30A.M.*

John Boxer asked me many questions about my case, what I wanted from him and what I was going to do with the information. I asked about his background, experience in this type of case, how he did his work, basis for billing and what I could expect. He typed up an agreement and we signed it. We settled on telephone updates that I was free to record and a written report each week. I gave him a check for two thousand dollars.

Date *Fri. 22 Oct. 99* Time Start *3:55P.M.* Time Finished *4:15P.M.*

John Boxer called with the first weekly report. He said the children spent each evening after school entirely with their step-mother. Dad didn't get home until after ten on each evening. Dad left the house to go to work by six in the morning and the children were taken to school by their step-mom at eight in the morning. Step-mother attended Lon's soft ball practice and Karen's Girl Scout meeting. John Boxer said he would mail a copy of the activity schedule for both children so I would be able to attend their events. A written more detailed copy of the report was already in the mail to me. I got the report in Monday's mail.

Date *Fri. 15 Oct. 99* Time Start *4:00P.M.* Time Finished *4:25P.M.*

John Boxer called with the weekly report. The children spent each evening after school with their step-mother. Dad didn't get home until after ten on each evening and left the house to go to work every day by six in the morning. Step-mom took the children to school and attended Lon's soft ball practice and took Karen to her gymnastics class. John Boxer suggested that I volunteer time at the children's school to get to see them during the day. A written copy of the report was in the mail to me. I got the report in Tuesday's mail.

Date *Fri. 29 Oct. 99* Time Start *4:15P.M.* Time Finished *4:35P.M.*

John Boxer called with the weekly report. The children didn't see their dad at all this week because of a business trip. Step-mother took them to school, picked them up and made sure Lon got to his guitar lesson and soft ball practice. Karen had no special activities this week, but did spend last Friday night at Jennifer's house. John Boxer said he'd mail the report to me. I got the report in Monday's mail.

Opposition's Detective

Do not assume that if you are being followed, or you are aware that questions are being asked about you, that the opposition has hired a professional. The fact that you are aware of a presence indicates that it may not be a professional.

Are You Being Watched?

If there is nothing negative to report, a detective will be hard pressed to manufacture data. See report #6. The opposition may be forced to submit a report full of good information about you in order to present the negative point they did identify. The most damaging information a detective can give in court is usually negative data received directly from the subject (person being investigated) of the investigation. Don't supply anyone with information to use against you.

Behave as if you are being watched twenty-four hours a day. If you think your normal routine would not meet with the approval of the courts, now is as good a time as any to eliminate people, places, and practices that can cost you your children. Do things the right way. You may enjoy the lack of tension in your life.

Once your attorney decides the time is appropriate to exercise the process of "Discovery," these reports can be requested. This will require the opposition to give you copies of any written detective reports --- before going to court.

Your attorney can subpoena the agency's records as they pertain to this case. Once you identify the detective agency being employed by the opposition, contact the licensing board in your state. Make an effort to ascertain the agency's credibility or lack thereof. Ask your detective for information about XYZ Agency. If you can afford the expense, have your investigator spend an hour interviewing XYZ Agency, as if looking to hire XYZ for a case. XYZ Agency may give your investigator some information about your case without using names to impress the potential client.

The testimony of a sloppy or inexperienced detective can severely damage the opposition's case or yours. It is always a mistake to rely on any one factor to win your case. It is as much of a mistake to count on one mistake on their side to lose the case for them.

Research Opposition's Detective

Make an effort to identify the detective or agency being used to collect data about you. If the information being given to the opposition is in the form of reports, this is information your attorney can request during the process of discovery. As a matter of personal safety, be aware of the vehicles and people around you. Really look at the people around you and take down vehicle descriptions and license plate numbers.

If the opposition has the money, a full background check on you and anyone with whom you are associating can be expected. The cost of these reports, if only one state is involved, is $250 per person or more. The next best report would be a "week in the life of" on you. Depending on your hours and the amount of travel you do each day, this could cost $500 a day or more. An example of such a report included in this chapter will show you how the document may read. Unless you have no conflicting information, a judge or mediator may assume that one week is a good indication of how you spend every week.

If you are conducting your life in a proper manner, the opposition's investigator could be your best witness. The report will only contain what the professional found in public records and sees or hears first hand.

The professional detective will not jeopardize a life's work by telling lies for someone who has hired him or her. The professional has learned not to put his or her neck on the line for a two-week assignment, no matter how persuasive, physically or monetarily, a client tries to be.

Getting the Evidence

Read Chapter 7: Equipment and Services, I Have Evidence - No One Cares. Once you have gained an understanding of the complexities of recognizing, documenting, preserving, marking, collecting, packaging physical evidence as well as maintaining a clean chain of custody, it becomes very clear how a good detective can help your case.

As an advocate it would be a good idea to gather any information you can from a distance. Send the detective in the right direction without too much help from you and let the detective find the evidence. This is done so that if the need arises for your detective to testify in court he or she can tell the truth about how the evidence came to light.

If you have chosen a professional with a law enforcement background the detective may have a lab that will produce results the court will accept.

Detective Assignment Form #1

To: Fingerprint Investigations
Attn.: Lars Nelson
Phone: 555-2100 **Fax**: 555-2200
From: Randall Long
Phone: 444-3100 **Fax**: 444-3101
Start Assignment: any time after January 3, 1993 for 5 days 4 hours per day from 7:00 p.m.
End Assignment: before January 15, 1993
Rate Quoted: $25.00 per hour, plus expenses
Purpose: Identify present environment surrounding Bobby when in the care of his mother, Amber.
Location:: Happy Time Mobile Home Park 6522 West Holt Ave., Space 77, Glendale, AZ
Specific Inquiries:

- General welfare of Bobby Long.
- Does Amber give proper maternal supervision, play time and cuddling?
- Is the environment healthy for a 14-month old?
- What is the supply of baby food, vitamins, whole milk, diapers, winter clothing and toys in the trailer?
- Does Amber insist on Bobby's being in a child seat during transport?
- Relationship with parents, sisters, and brothers? Do they help her?
- What are her plans if she is not awarded custody?

Detective Report Example #1

Fingerprint Detective Agency
File: # 0182239 Final Report

Date: January 13, 1993
Re: Bobby Long when in the care of Amber Calle Jones
Happy Time Mobile Home Park
7522 West Holt Ave, Space 77, Glendale, AZ

Initial Assignment: Develop a record in accordance with attached Private Investigator's Assignment Form.

Friday, January 8, 1993. Undercover Agent set up light housekeeping at the trailer she rented two spaces south of James Miller's trailer. Agent was in possession of a Motor Vehicle Department photograph of James and a photo of Amber and baby Bobby.

Assignment Report: During the afternoon, Agent sat outside her trailer for a period of time and did observe the area, the occupants of the other trailers, the manager, and the occupants of the trailer between that of the subject Amber and the Agent. The occupants of the trailer between that of the Agent and the subject talked to the Agent in an effort to be neighborly.

Agent accepted their invitation to sit with them and drink a beer at the entry to their trailer, placing our Agent next to the subject's trailer and in an excellent position to observe the same and its occupant's activities without arousing suspicion. The Agent's neighbors introduced themselves as Jerry and Ted. Jerry readily admits that he is a manic-depressive. Ted is excessively withdrawn to the point of mental hospitalization, and both men were there for treatment of the mental illness they both had.

Jerry described James and Amber and stated that they lived next door with her baby. The Agent questioned the men further concerning Amber until Jerry admitted that except for hearing them arguing, they knew very little about their neighbors.

The subject's trailer was darkened except for a single interior light. It was padlocked. There was every indication that the trailer was not occupied.

Agent spent time establishing that she was unemployed and hiding out from her husband in the midst of a divorce action and was available as a baby-sitter. Agent felt other tenants of near by trailers and the manager accepted her as an ordinary resident.

Agent left the trailer park Friday Jan., 8, 1993, 8:00 p.m. Agent arrived at the trailer park Saturday, Jan. 9, 1993. 7:00 a.m.

Agent arrived back at the rented trailer in an effort to preserve her position as resident. At approximately 7:30 a.m., Agent was walking in the area near her trailer. The trailer park manager called her over and they talked across from Amber's trailer.

8:00 a.m. As Agent and the manager talked, they observed the client (Randall) and his wife as they went to Amber's trailer to pick up Bobby. It was during this conversation that the manager told Agent that police officers arrested James Miller in front of Amber's trailer some time during the night of January 5. The police got him out of the trailer by pretending that their automobile had malfunctioned. They called upon James Miller for assistance, and when he bent over to look at the car, he was handcuffed and removed to the downtown jail.

According to the manager, Amber said James is presently incarcerated at Cochise Prison and will be there for the next thirty days unless he provides $3,000 for back child support. He further indicated that James' parents came to the trailer after he was arrested, and took back their automobile because James' parents did not want Amber to drive it.

At this point, Agent observed the subject Amber who had exited her own trailer and was unlocking a bicycle that was chained to the trailer. In an effort to get closer, Agent asked the manager to help her work the hatchback release on her car.

As the manager and Agent grew closer, Amber told the manager that she was going to ride her bike to Cochise Jail. Agent then introduced herself to Amber and offered her a ride in her car to Cochise since Agent had nothing else to do. The subject readily accepted.

During the drive, Amber told Agent that her baby's father had raped her, and she had three older children living in Washington. Agent mentioned to Amber that she had no electricity in her trailer and would not have until Monday or Tuesday, and that it was very cold in there.

Amber thereupon invited Agent to stay with her in the subject's trailer, because she was alone and sometimes felt uncomfortable, because her trailer door did not lock from the inside. Amber said she was trying to get someone to go with her to a local bar to shoot pool and visit with the bouncer.

Subject Amber states she has sixteen brothers and sisters and describes her mother as being crazy.

Amber went on to state that her baby is a year old, and she is in a legal battle for his custody. She states that she is allowed to have the baby every night and every other weekend.

Thereafter she began to describe her marital situation. The subject, Amber, states that she is now living with her ex-husband. Her present husband is an old, fat, gross, truck driver and she had been married to him and divorced from him on a prior occasion. After her first divorce from him, she married Mr. Miller and then divorced him. She then remarried her present truck driver husband to get this custody thing settled.

Agent drove Amber to the Cochise Tower Prison, and Amber went inside. Support Agent proceeded to secure documentation concerning the true reason for Mr. Miller's incarceration.

James Miller Current Criminal Charges

1. Possession of dangerous drugs
2. Possession of marijuana
3. Possession of drug paraphernalia

Being held in lieu of bail in the amount of $1,000.00

On the ride back to the trailer, Amber told Agent that James was arrested because "the baby's father told the cops a bunch of lies." Amber said, "A couple of months ago, I found out my present husband is currently married to a lady in Florida." Amber told Agent, "That is fine with me because now I don't have to file for divorce since I'm not really married." Amber told Agent that her other children were with her husband's parents in Washington, and she had not seen them since the second week of July the previous year.

Amber stated she did not have a telephone, but did have James Miller's pager. Subject stated that she is "very much in love with James Miller" and that they have great sex together. However, she wants the house with the white picket fence, and Miller does not want any sort of normal life. Amber states that James Miller left her every time he got her pregnant, ever since the first time when she was fifteen years old and unmarried. Amber told Agent she was going back to Washington February 18, 1993, and never coming back.

Agent and Amber ate and prepared to go out for the evening. There were several leather jackets in the closet, and Agent remarked about it. Amber told Agent that James stole those jackets and that he will steal whatever is available. Agent and Amber left for the bar, Sometimes Crazy, 4205 West Holt Avenue.

During her conversations, the subject Amber mentioned that she does not get along with her family and believes that her mother is crazed. She does not feel she would get any help from any family member and has never asked them. Subject states that James Miller and Mike Jones hate each other. They met several days before Miller was arrested.

The subject and the Agent went to the bar Sometimes Crazy where they played pool until after 1:00 am. Subject consumed five Bloody Mary drinks during the evening, but never appeared intoxicated. It was at this time that Agent learned from Amber that James Miller supplied narcotics to

the bouncer. Subject also mentioned that James presently smokes crystal-methamphetamines.
It appears that the subject Amber has a garnishment order for Miller's wages while they are living together in his parent's trailer.

Subject Amber showed to Agent a mark on her arm where her sister bit her. She had been living with her sister, whom Amber described as mentally unbalanced, until the previous week and was thrown out after the fight. That's why she is living at Miller's trailer.

Subject Amber states that she and Miller fight and argue all the time, primarily because he is a narcotics abuser, lies constantly about everything, and is a thief.

Subject Amber states that Miller says that he loves his kids, but that he doesn't want to have anything to do with taking care of them and refuses to financially support them. Amber states that she and Miller have great sex. Amber does consider herself married to Jones.

She adds, incidentally, that Jones was imprisoned on a narcotics charge. She states that Jones was convicted because someone informed upon him to the police. The police informant was later killed in a mysterious car accident.

After the bar closed, subject Amber and Agent went to a restaurant for breakfast. Subject Amber stated that Miller acted as a police informant when he gave information about the "Unclean Twelve Motorcycle Club." On another occasion, Miller tried to blow up the Unclean Twelve Clubhouse.

Amber's trailer is a twenty feet long by ten feet wide, fifth wheel unit set up for one adult. There are no facilities for a healthy, active, year-old boy. Agent observes that the subject Amber has covered the platform section over the fifth wheel with several blankets and a pillow.

This results in a large flat sleeping area, which has no springs or soft surface. The baby, Bobby, is said to sleep with the subject Amber in that area. There is no baby car seat on the premises and no baby food. There are no baby toys except for a plastic phone in the sleeping area. One dirty baby bottle was seen. No vitamins or supplemental winter clothing were observed.

Monday, January 11, 1993. Subject Amber exited an automobile carrying Bobby and a bag of groceries and invited Agent into trailer. Subject Amber had a letter from Miller in jail she proceeded to read aloud.

In the letter Miller states that he loves Amber and Bobby and wishes to be with them. He states that he had decided to "quit using drugs." Agent drove subject Amber and Bobby to Bank of America and Wards.

During the ride to and from, the baby Bobby sat on Amber's lap. It must be stated here that the subject Amber does not request or insist that Bobby be restrained in a baby car seat during transport and refuses to have the baby ride in the rear to have his own seat belt.

Agent mentioned to Amber that the plastic bottle carried by the baby Bobby seemed to be dirty or contained a brownish liquid. Subject replied that the liquid was milk and the bottle may look that way because she doesn't have a bottle brush.

Agent asked why the baby's father didn't get some things for the baby. Amber stated she could take care of Bobby and didn't want anything from him. When they got back to the trailer, subject Amber mentioned that the client always remarked about how dirty the baby is when he is returned to them and that Randall sends clean clothes with Bobby in which Amber would dress the boy and returns the dirty ones in a bag. The baby was asleep at 8:30 p.m. and Amber was asleep at 11:00 p.m.

The alarm clock went off at 5:30 a.m. At some time later there was a knock at the door, subject Amber passed the Agent's sleeping area, carrying Bobby. The door was opened, the baby was passed through the door, and the door was closed. No voices were heard. The subject went back to bed. Agent left.

It is noted that her plans to be Mrs. Jones in Washington conflict with her re-union with the "changed" Miller, but that is what she said (at different times). This report concludes our assignment in this matter.

Assignment Example #2

Investigator Assignment Form

To: ACME Investigations Attn.: Sonja
Phone: 555-2100 Fax: 555-2200
From: Loraine Newton
Phone.: 444-3100 Fax: 444-3101
Communicate with [X] Me only Via [X] Telephone
[ ]Fax [ ]Report [ ] Wait for call

Start Assignment: January 22, 1998
End Assignment: When my $2,000.00 is spent
Rate Quoted: $40.00 per hour, plus expenses
Purpose: To identify living conditions for Beth and Lynn Newton when at their father's home in their father's custody?

Location: Justin Newton's house #3 Woodsy Road, Modesto, CA
Specific Inquiries:
How many hours each day does their father care for the girls?
Are the children well supervised?
Is the home clean?

Detective Report Example #2
Final Report

ACME Investigations File: 1998 Newton
Date: February 2, 1998

Operative: Mike Reed

Initial Assignment: Develop a record in accordance with attached Assignment Form.

Friday, January 23, 1998. I pulled my pick-up truck with boat and trailer into the huge parking area in front of a house with a mail box identifying it as the "Newton's".

There were two little girls playing with some puppies next to a refuse pile on the opposite side of the parking area. A woman about twenty-eight years old dressed in a halter top and shorts came out of the small house within a minute of my arrival. I showed her a poorly drawn map and asked for directions to Don Pedro Lake. She said I would never find it with this map and added some lines to it with my pen. I noticed an old boat and trailer next to the house and asked about it. She said they were for sale, but didn't know how much.

I asked for and got permission to take some pictures of it for my friend who may want to buy it. I asked if her husband would be home soon so I could ask some questions about the boat. She said he works real late. I took the opportunity to photograph the house and the children playing. She said her husband worked at one of the resorts on the lake. I asked his name and she said just ask for Justin, everyone knew him. As I got in my truck she smiled and said to come back if the map didn't work. I asked if she wanted to come along and she said she would love to, but as usual she had to watch her husband's kids, maybe another time.

I found Justin in the bar at the Lakeside Resort. I showed him my map and explained how I saw the boat and trailer he had for sale. I asked him if since tomorrow was Saturday would he have the day off so I could take a closer look at the boat?

He said this was his day off, but he didn't tell his wife that because he didn't want to hang around the house. I told him I was up for a long weekend, and he said to come by his place the next morning around eight.

I dropped my boat and trailer at a campground and waited until sundown to head back out to the Newton's house. I parked about a quarter of a mile past the Newton house and walked back. There was very little moonlight. A security light attached to the house shone out into the parking area. The surrounding woods allowed me to walk right up to the hog wire fence at the back of the house. Most of the inside lights were on, and I was able to photograph the inside of each room of the small house (two bedrooms, living room, bathroom and kitchen) from the back side. The children were asleep on a bare mattress with what appeared to be old urine stains. The children were apparently still wearing the panties they were playing outside in earlier that afternoon. Their little bodies looked un-bathed.

I visited with Justin and his wife from eight (8:00 am) in the morning until nine thirty (9:30 am) when Justin had to get ready to be at work at ten. I was invited in the house, but declined coffee when I observed the unsanitary condition of the kitchen. They explained that she watched the kids and sold Avon cosmetics to the neighbors.

He worked until after ten most nights to make enough money to get to live up here in such a nice area. The children were ignored unless they were crying or demanding attention. There were a few toys scattered around. Both children had numerous insect bites on their legs, arms chests and backs. The younger child had evidence of a recent severe sun burn.

Enclosed you will find twenty-two photographs. Any taken during the day were with permission. The photographs at night of the inside of the house were taken from a vantage point off their property taking advantage of the Peeping Tom Law.

End of this report

Assignment Example #3

Investigator Assignment Form

To: Mellon & Barnes

Attn.: JR Jackson

Phone: 555-2100 Fax: 555-2200

From: Rob Haddon
Phone.: 444-3100 Fax: 444-3101
Start Assignment: 01/01/2000 for 15 days 10 hours per day from 7:00 p.m.
End Assignment: before January 15, 2000
Rate Quoted: $175.00 per hour/ 4 hour minimum

Purpose: Since the divorce was filed my wife said she has permanently quit her job and has no residual resources. Therefore the judge is considering giving her an enormous amount of temporary child support and alimony. She has been a highly paid professional making over $200,000.00 per year on her job. I want to know if; in fact, she has permanently quit her job, does she has any other source of income. Avoid direct contact with Rita or my children. Any evidence must be collected in a manner that will allow it to be submitted as evidence in court. The detective will be required to testify as to manner and methods used to gather information. Exercise all good practice and procedure in accordance with state law.

Location: 220110 Moon Valley Trail, Scottsdale, Arizona

Detective Report Example #3

Final Report

Mellon & Barnes Operative: Trish Ong Financial Investigative Officer

In the assignment time I was unable to identify a solid employment link, but several other indications show a healthy flow of funds.

Although the subject claims to have exhausted her financial resources evidence of stockpiling and overpayment of accounts was started in November of 1999. I picked up the garbage from the alley of the subjects home each morning at 2:30am.

Information from account statements.

1. Children's Village Montessori School. Tuition for Lydia Haddon is paid through the remainder of this Pre-K year ($6,755.00) kindergarten ($13,000.00) and first grade ($14,300.00) including a special field trip fund ($3,500.00).
2. Judson School. Tuition for Robbie Haddon is paid through to the completion of this year ($24,000.00) and his seventh and eighth grade years ($83,200.00).
3. Valley Travel has a deposit for vacation's not yet designated totaling ($62,220.00)
4. Sprint Communication account number 7731725333001 has a positive balance of ($5,205.00)
5. Moon Valley Electric account number 220110 has a positive balance of ($4,400.00)
6. Arizona Republic account number had 4151006 has a positive balance of ($626.00)
7. Salt River Project Water for the home address has a positive balance of ($9,200.00)
8. Chevron Credit Card number has a positive balance of ($3,228.00)
9. Master Card Account number 6033928 has a positive balance of ($11,600.00)
10. American Express Card number 0114067288 has a positive balance of ($15,500.00)
11. Scottsdale Country Club Membership has been paid through December 31, 2005 ($50,000.00)
12. Charter Home Services has paid up extended warranty policy on all home appliances through 01/2006 ($2,800.00)
13. AOL on line service for account number 8275854207 has a positive balance of ($2,160.00)
14. Moon Valley Veterinary Clinic has a positive balance of ($2,145.00)

Information from receipts.

1. Toshiba 400MHz Pentium II, L2 Cache 512K, HDD 14GB, Display 14.1"XGA TFT, 56K Modem, DVD ($3,799.00)
2. Tektronix Phaser 840 Printer Extended 128MB ($4,195.00)

3. ScanJet 6390Cse ($899.00)
4. Xerox Fax Telecopier 7024 ($1,800.00)
5. Xerox Copier ($2,455.00)
6. Palmpilot ($2,800)
7. Olympus D-620L Digital Camera ($995.00)
8. Fire Proof Safe 1,200 pound ($2,600.00)
9. U.S.West Equipment installation four telephone lines ($120.00)
10. Office Max desk, chair, two bookcases, file cabinet ($3,800.00)

Daily observation of the subject.

Rita Haddon does not leave her home until eleven thirty each weekday. She meets various people from her former office at the Biltmore Hotel Restaurant. Rita always eats a salad and drinks mineral water. There is always an exchange of folders. After lunch Rita often shops at the Galleria on Scottsdale Road. I photographed the folders left on the passenger seat through the car window on six occasions. Photos attached to this report. The files appeared to be client files from her former employer.

The children are with Rita all day both days of the weekend on the second, and fourth weekend of each month.
Respectfully submitted, *Trish Ong* End of Report

Discovery Bonus In Detective Report

Detectives are hired to catch someone doing something wrong. If you are a good person and parent, in proper control of your life, the detective report the opposition has on you can be some of your strongest evidence.

This happens in at least two ways. The first, would be if the assignment form is requesting information about you that has no bearing on the well being of your children. The second would be if the report shows that you have been behaving exactly as you said you have been.

Generally, all evidence, including photos, notes, tapes, and interviews the detective produced are open to discovery. Anyone with a copy of the requested evidence may be required to produce them. In some instances, if the attorney hired the detective, the information gathered may be protected as attorney work-product privilege. There are severe legal complications that can be imposed if they refuse to comply.

In most instances this case is more important to you and the other parent and very few others would be willing to pay fines or go to jail to help one side win over the other.

Anyone volunteering to make such a sacrifice for your case should be viewed with suspicion. This type of action, even with the best intentions, is against the law. If you are responsible for or implicated in any way, you could lose much more than this lawsuit.

The next example is something you would never want to be responsible for producing, but would be great to have your attorney find when you exercise your right of discovery. Failure to disclose the information requested can result in sanctions, jail or forfeit of the case in question.

Assignment Example #4

Investigator Assignment Form

To: Stonewall Investigations
Attn.: Lindy
Phone 555-2100 Fax: 555-555-2200
From: Cindy Lesto
Phone: 333-3100 Fax: 333-3101
Communicate with [X] Me only
Via: [ ] Telephone [ ] Fax [ ] Report [X] Wait for call

Start Assignment: April 27, 2001
End Assignment: When asset search is completed.
Rate Quoted: $2,500.00 Flat Rate
Purpose: To document where income from former family business goes.

Location: Next Century Real Estate
Specific Inquiries:
My ex-husband claims that business has dropped off so much that he can only make minimal child support payments.
Who actually owns the business?
Does he own his house and car?
What are Jack Lesto's assets?
What happened to the assets I listed on page 2 of this assignment?

Detective Report Example #4

Stonewall Investigations File: Jack White
Date: June 30, 2001
Assignment Agent: Richard Lemon

Final Report

I made contact with Joe Lesto and his current wife Katrina Lesto when I entered Next Century Real Estate office. I gave them a ninety day exclusive listing on three small properties for sale with their company. I was in the office for approximately two hours. During the conversation I told them my wife was fooling around on me and I wanted to dump some properties before I considered any legal action. They said they understood because Joe had gone through the same thing with his first wife. We made an appointment for the next evening to have dinner and discuss the possible listing of some other properties and the possibility of my purchasing a new place to live.

At our dinner appointment Joe and Katrina were sympathetic to my personal problems. I told them I was concerned that since I had a successful business, my wife would get a lot of child support. They offered many helpful suggestions on how to shelter my income and assets. They explained that even though their business was doing very well they were able to show the court they had very little profit. Their very creative bookkeeping showed they could not even afford a family car. Of course the two new company cars complete with insurance and gas cards, were driven exclusively by Joe and Katrina. While said they were able to show the court they could not even afford inexpensive vacations. They said they got around this because they travel for their company to lovely vacation spots in the summer and ski resorts in the winter. Joe was issued a very small paycheck while Katrina make the salary of a top manager. Finally since Katrina had to work full time the company paid for the cleaning lady, lawn service at their home.

During my two subsequent meetings I was unable to garner any additional useful information.

End of Report

Assignment Example #5

Investigator Assignment Form

To: International Investigations
Attn.: Solon
Phone: 555-1212 Fax: 555-2200
From: Loraine Newton
Phone: 444-3100 Fax: 444-6767
Communicate with [X] Me [X] My Attorney Via [X] Telephone [X] Fax [X] Report [ ] Wait for call

Start Assignment: May 1, 1999
End Assignment:: When you get written instruction to stop.
Rate Quoted: $95.00 per hour, plus expenses.
Purpose: To document how and with whom Jack spends his time.

Work Product: Mrs. Ramirez, your attorney has requested availability of supervising team member and full report for pre-trial conference and possible court appearance. She has authorized our fee schedule and will remit payment when full report is submitted to her. Mrs. Ramirez has requested that a Summery Report only be sent to you.
Location: Jack White, 36 Bryn Mawr Road, Carlsile, Pa 17013
Specific Inquiries:
Is Jack still doing drugs?
Who is living with him?
Where is he taking the kids when he kidnaps them?
Is Jack really working?

Detective Report Example #5

Final Report

International Investigations
File: Jack White Date: May 31, 1999

Team #4 Supervisor: Jens Riner
Team Member: Jim Colter
Team Member: Ryan Jacobs
Team Member: Ray Gardino
Team Member: Abby Lister

Investigation Summery

The various members of Team #4 kept Jack White under observation for thirty continuous days. Three of the team members have had conversations with Jack himself. Team #4 has interviewed his neighbors, co-workers, supervisor and more than twenty of his acquaintances/friends and his children while they were in his custody. All of which are included in the court ready version of the report. Except for the children, when they are in residence, there are no other people living in Jacks house.
Jack has advanced to a supervisory position at the company at which he works. He has been there nineteen months. He signed up for the 401K

retirement plan and the Christmas Club when he became eligible (one year minimum employment). He is on the company bowling league and participates in the company outreach program for disadvantaged youth. Jack is making mortgage payments on a three-bedroom house four blocks from the school his children attend. We do not see any indications of a man preparing to kidnap his children and move to another place.

We have determined that Jack White is clean and sober of all alcohol and drugs. Our team has found no evidence of past juvenile or adult use of any drugs and minimum use of alcohol as an adult. End of Summery

Assignment Example #6

Sandra Walker Investigations
Background investigation on Janita Jeffery.
Flat rate fee of $450.00

Detective Report Example #6

Janita Jeffery is currently a News Anchor Person at TV 3 in Austin Texas. She is a 34 year old black woman who is presently engaged to Arthur Trinity also of Austin. Mr. Trinity has custody of his five year old son and is a 35 year old white male who owns a small accounting firm. The neighbor reports that Ms. Jeffery has been living with Mr. Trinity and his son, as a family, for a period four months as the time of this report.

Ms. Jeffery was born in Austin in 1967. She attended Crocket Elementary, Central High School and the University of Austin. Her grades were always in the upper 5% of the class and she has no record of truancy or poor behavior. Ms. Jeffery lived in her parents home all through her school years.

After graduation from the University of Austin in 1988 Ms. Jeffery took a job with KIKK Radio as a secretary. Occasionally she would fill-in if the news person was not available. In 1990 she was given the on-air responsibility of the morning drive time traffic and news.

TV 3 offered Ms. Jeffery the position of News Anchor Person in 1992. She has been in that position with growing responsibilities ever since. Ms. Jeffery moved into an apartment when she took the position with TV 3. Moving again when she moved in with Mr. Trinity and his son.

Under the guise of doing an article about Ms. Jefferys:

I called Ms. Jeffery's work number and they were happy to answer all my questions about her. There are no indications of problems on the job or with any of her work associates.

I interviewed her parents and the neighbors around her parents home.

I interviewed teachers and administration at the schools she attended.

I researched her name at the superior court clerk's office. There were no felony convictions or dockets with Ms. Jeffery's name on them.

I got the same results form the municipal court records and the sheriff's department.

Ms. Jeffery does not hold a U.S. Passport.

Ms. Jeffery was registered to vote and had been since old enough to do so.

I ran all four major investigatory software programs using her name, social security number, date and place of birth, and drivers license number. There were no files on Ms. Jeffery.

I briefly interviewed Ms. Jeffery and found her to be open and ungraded. She seems to be exactally the person she appears to be on TV 3.

End of Report

Confidentiality - Detective

The relationship between a detective and a client is confidential between you and a reputable detective, but there is no confidentiality protected by the law. The law imposes no special restrictions on these professionals about information or documents shown or given to them.

A detective-client privilege relationship rests on the premises that "The keeper of the records has a primary obligation to the law of the land and then to the client."

Once documents protected by doctor-patient or attorney-client confidentiality are shown or given to a detective, the protections are no longer in place. Be careful what you decide to show this professional.

The exposure of information produced by a detective through the process of discovery can be slowed.
Instruct the detective to send everything directly to you and not maintain an in house file on your case.

The confidence between a detective and client can be broken under many circumstances including:

A court order from a judge demands a breech of confidence.

The client gives the detective permission to release the records.

The records are requested by subpoena.

Sex and Your Detective

You are as vulnerable as you will ever be. This is a new situation for you, but this is an old one for the detective. The detective has seen hundreds of people in your state of mind and knows how the relationship with you and your case will go the first time you meet. It is not only a breach of trust for your detective to make romantic or sexual advances during this association, it's predatory. It is just as unethical for the detective to succumb to your advances. It is the responsibility of the detective to realign the relationship immediately if you step out of line. A detective that will take advantage of you will also be willing to use your actions, information you have supplied or information you have paid him to gather, against you. This kind of distraction from the important goal can be fatal to your case.

Detective Turns Into An Outlaw

Example:

January 2. Client hired Fingerprint Detective Agency, paying a $1,000 retainer. The assignment was to watch and attempt to make contact with the other parent. Written assignment designated four hours a day, starting any day after January 3, at 7:00 p.m. and be completed before Friday the 15th. The rate quoted was $25 per hour, plus expenses.

August 7 11:00 a.m. Saturday morning the **Owner** of Fingerprint Detective Agency called the **Client** from a telephone booth at Lenney's Restaurant down the street from the Subject's trailer, reporting that the undercover person had made contact with the subject and everything was going well.

12:00 Noon. The **Owner** of Fingerprint called back to report that the undercover and the subject had become fast friends and were going out drinking that evening.

2:00 p.m. The **Owner** of Fingerprint called back and said, "We have everything you need. The place is full of drugs and undercover has completed all the specific inquiries you wanted made. We will need another $2,500 to finish everything up."

Client: "You have not worked enough hours to use up my deposit."

Owner Fingerprint: "That's what we will need to finish everything up. Is your child important to you or not?"

Client: "I don't know where I can get that much more money."

Owner Fingerprint: "We would accept a post-dated check. Take care of it Monday."

If this person is dishonest enough to extort money from you in such a manner, what kind of a witness will he or she prove to be when it is time to go to court? Is the report to be trusted?

Filing A Formal Complaint

If you feel that you have been unfairly treated, consider filing a complaint with the court, the licensing authority for detectives in your state, and professional organizations to which the detective is a member.

Chapter 10: Evaluations

Roll up your sleeves. This is where you dig in with the help of the army you have assembled. You can make things happen by presenting all the positive factors in your life and show how they stabilize and improve the quality of your children's lives. Carefully submit any documented information that you feel will identify problems on the opposition.

Purpose for an Evaluation

The purpose of an evaluation is to 1) identify the motivations and behaviors that are causing an impasse in the settling of the case; 2) to assess the parenting abilities of the individuals; 3) determine compliance with existing court orders; 4) determine what custody location would be most beneficial to the child; 5) determine if a fixed-schedule visitation would be beneficial to the child.

Less obvious observations will be made of parent focus, boundaries, child issues verses parent issues and reciprocal parent behaviors.

Types of Evaluations

It may be more advantageous to request a court-ordered evaluation rather than a privately obtained assessment. All parties are compelled by the court to participate with its ordered evaluation whereas, opposing parties may not cooperate with a private evaluator. Evaluations are accomplished by a combination of these methods:

- Two or three interviews
- Scoring and interpretation of several standardized personality and parenting tests
- Reading background information
- Telephone consultation with attorneys, social workers, collateral information sources
- Observation of interaction between parent and child
- Report preparation
- Court testimony may or may not be required.

Interview: By physical meeting with or telephone contact and may include the adult principals in the custody dispute, the children that are the focus of the dispute, children related or who do or will have contact with these children, adults that do have or will have contact with the parents or the children themselves.

Documents may be accepted and considered during the interview. Interview as a method is used extensively by conciliation and home study evaluations.

Observation: In the evaluator's facility or principal's home and may include the adult principals in the custody dispute, the children that are the focus of the dispute, children related or who do or will have contact with these children, adults who do have or will have contact with the parents of the children themselves. Documents may be accepted and considered during the interview. Observation is used extensively in physical examination, psychological evaluation, chemical testing and home study.

Testing: In the evaluator's facility and may include physical, chemical and/or psychological testing of the adult principals in the custody dispute, the children that are the focus of the dispute, children related or who do or will have contact with these children, adults who do have or will have close contact with the parents or the children themselves in the home. Testing is used extensively in physical examination, psychological evaluation and chemical testing.

Who and Why are Evaluators Used?

Evaluators are usually mental health professionals with formal training and experienced in family court matters. Some evaluators are trained to do custody evaluations and only perform this service for the court. When the court wants more information than the attorneys may wish to present in court, evaluators are appointed. They gather specific facts that might be compared to make a better determination for the long-term welfare of the children. The evaluator may wish to see the environments and speak to the people influencing the welfare of your children. The product of the evaluation will be a written report that will contain recommendations as to placement of the children and visitation schedule.

A good judge will appoint an evaluator to take a closer look at the circumstances in the case. The judge's aim is to make the best possible decision for the children within the limits of the law. A judge may hoist the entire decision of custody and visitation on the evaluator.

Avoid the *sua sponte* appointment by your judge. The evaluator must have knowledge challenges such as:
PAS, (Parental Alienation Syndrome)
MMS (Malicious Mother Syndrome)
FFS (Fulsome Father Syndrome)
BPD (Bi Polar Disorder) An inability or impaired ability to regulate emotions.
OCD (Obsessive Compulsive Disorder)
DID (Dissociative Identity Disorder)
RAD (Repressed Memory Disorder)
ODD (Oppositional Defiant Disorder)

The evaluator will attempt to determine how they impact a child custody battle. You can protect yourself by making sure the evaluator is a Ph.D. who will adhere to guidelines set forth by the APA. Evaluators with the designations L.C.S.W., or M.S.W. should be avoided if possible since they are not bound by the professional ethics of the Ph.D. Prepare a list of qualified evaluators from which the opposition may choose a name.

Best Attitude with the Evaluator

Be the first one to see the evaluator. Be on time for your appointment. Make sure your appearance is neat, clean and conservative. Be open and honest with the evaluator. The evaluator is trained to hear what you say, understand what you mean, and read your body language. He or she is trained to identify a hundred different signals you give that you do not even know you are sending. Do show a confident attitude. Listen attentively and maintain eye contact when you are speaking to the evaluator.

Do not become frustrated if your children behave in an unacceptable manner during the observation period. The evaluator is more concerned with how you respond to your children than with how good their manners are.

Have a very clear image of what kind of parent you are. The evaluator is less interested in a parent that works long hours to keep a child in brand name clothes and state-of-the-art toys. They want to see a parent who knows how the children are doing in school, who their friends are, what stories they have this parent read at bedtime and if the parent participates in the children's activities on a regular basis.

Identify your relationship with the children. The evaluator knows that working parents often work harder at the relationship with their children to compensate for the large blocks of time the parent must be away from them.

Demonstrate how you capitalize on the time you do have with your children.

Avoid overacting, interrupting, speaking too fast, getting angry, and arguing with the evaluator. Your motives will be looked at in great detail. Any indication that a parent is seeking custody to avoid paying child support will be branded a "Financial Child Abuser." Don't mix the separate issues of the time you want to spend with your children with money. If questioned, make it clear that you see the issues separately and will make sure your children have as much emotional and financial support as necessary.

Mediators and Evaluators

Often you will be ordered to mediation. The court hopes things can be worked out to avoid open court. The mediator may or may not be required to report to the court. Often they are only there to help work out a solution. Ask your mediator what his role is. Read "From Now On" in Chapter 2, in this manual.

Reviewing this list before each appointment will give you control and the evaluator a consistent picture of you.

Facing the Other Parent

Many evaluators schedule at least one joint meeting with both sides of a conflict to personally observe the dynamics of the relationship. It is critical that you leave this professional with the knowledge that you are a responsible, well mannered adult whose main concern is the well being of your children.

You know how the opposition will react to you and what they will say. If you have someone to practice with, do so. If you don't have someone to help you prepare for this meeting, you can still be properly prepared. Make a list of the things you know they will say. Add things you are afraid they will bring up. List your answers and their answers to your answers. List the things you want to mention and what you think they will have to say about those topics. Read what you have written out loud and attempt to reword your responses so they will get your point across without sounding hostile or defensive.

To Facilitate this Impression

1. In advance of the meeting, make a list of points you think the opposition will raise.
   (a) Make note of the points with which you agree. (b) Decide which of the opposition's points are real issues. (c) Be prepared to address these concerns with positive responses.

2. Make a list of no more than 4 or 5 concerns you want to verbalize. Don't nit pick.

3. (a) Only address issues that affect the children. By making a list you can avoid repetition and control the desire to accumulate a list of irritants and transgressions that will stand in the way of the conflict resolution. (b) Identify the situations that trigger conflict in your association with the other parent.

4. Make a list of what the opposition usually says or does to make you upset.

5. (a) Decide not to respond by getting upset. (b) Prepare at least two ways to respond in a non-aggressive and non-accusatory way to any indictment made by the other parent, BUT only if the evaluator requests that you do answer the charge.

6. Make a list of negative behaviors and attitudes you do not want to exhibit. Avoid loud sighing, exaggerated expressions, outbursts, remarks, noises like drumming of fingers and any other provocations.

7. Prepare yourself emotionally to face this person by Role Playing with someone you trust. Explain to your partner what you are trying to do. Have your partner be you and you be the other parent. Create some of the situations you think you might face.

8. (a) Rehearse your major points out loud in front of a mirror or a friend several times to gain clarity of thought, confidence and control. (b) When the professional asks what you want to say, state your concerns from the child's advantage. Poor example: "I think the other parent should make decisions from a more responsible point of view rather than from hormones." Good example:

"I feel the other parent has used some questionable decision making abilities when it comes to the children." Be polite, but clear about what you want to say. (c) The other parent will interrupt your statements and answers. Expect it and do not respond unless the professional instructs you to do so.

9. Dress as if you are going to an important business meeting. Keep you manner professional.

10. Do not attempt to run the meeting.

11. Listen and obey the ground rules.

12. Address your answers and comments to the evaluator. Even if you are answering a challenge from the other parent. This will keep you from getting angry. Inside an angry person is a hurt person. It is easier to keep yourself under control than it is to regain your self-control once you lose it.

13. When asked, focus on the problem that is giving you the most problem now. Only tell your view of the situation. Opinions of your parents, friends or current spouses are not relevant.

14. State your side using neutral language. Example: don't say, "She does everything she can to keep me from seeing the children." do say, "I feel my time with the children is curtailed even more than the court order says it should be." The evaluator will then ask for specifics including who, what, when, where, who in what way and under what condition.

15. This may be your first opportunity to hear the other side's story. It is critical for your case that you hear and understand what they think is important. Don't interrupt the other parent during any statement. The evaluator will give you an opportunity to tell your side.

16. If asked you may say, "I hear what you say and understand your feelings. What did I say that made you feel that way?"

17. Deal with the issue the professional addresses. Everything will be discussed before this process is completed. Dealing with one problem at a time eliminates resistance.

18. The professional's job is not to decide who is right or wrong. It is the professional's job to gather information. It is your job to make sure the professional understands your story as you see it. If you feel the professional does not understand your point, ask the professional a direct question. Example: "Mr. Hall, do you understand that I feel my ex-wife will agree to comply at this meeting and then either instruct or allow her baby-sitter and parents to keep the children from calling me or accepting my calls?" Don't get angry. Gain an understanding of what the professional does understand.

19. If the professional asks, "Do you mean...[+your conclusion]?" Don't begin to speak until you have listened to the entire statement. Attempt to answer with a "yes" or "no." Allow the professional to ask clarifying questions. If you are using words that sound like you want to work things out, but use an aggressive tone in your voice or body language, the professional may re-state the question.

20. Don't attempt to make the professional agree or sympathize with you. This will cause the professional to get side-tracked keeping him from understanding the nature and scope of the problem.

21. The professional is to find out how each of you sees the problem. Don't become distressed it the professional seems to accept the other side of the story. In most cases, there is no right or wrong. There is only a difference in perception. The difference in perceptions you and the other parent have are, in fact, part of the problem.

22. The professional may summarize the points in each disputant's story. "As you see it [problem1] + [problem2] + [problem3] + [problem4] then ask, "Do I understand you correctly?"

23. Ask about the next step in this process.

24. Make notes of anything the professional wants you to bring if there is to be another meeting.

25. At the end of the meeting, thank the professional and the other parent for his or her time.

When There are Two of You

In addition to presenting yourself for evaluation the professional will want to meet anyone else the children will be interacting with on a regular basis in a home setting. The positive support you can demonstrate from your *significant other* (husband, wife, betrothed, person you are living with on an intimate basis) is important.

Home Study Evaluator Contact Log
Date *Mon. 2 Feb. 99* Time Start *1:00P.M.* Time Finished 1*:25P.M.* We appeared in the court of the Honorable Stonewall Jackson. Preliminary statements and facts were presented. Judge Jackson ordered home study of each home and offered our attorneys a list of evaluators from which to choose. The attorneys agreed on Perry Maston. Judge Jackson instructed us each to contact Mr. Perry and set a schedule for evaluation and that each parent would have to pay for their own.
Date *Mon. 2 Feb. 99* Time Start *3:15P.M.* Time Finished 3*:20P.M.* I called Mr. Perry's office as soon as I got home from court. Mr. Perry's secretary set the in home evaluation for the first available date which is April 6, 1999. I asked for the payment information and she said she would mail out the procedure and billing.
Date *Tue. 30 March 99* Time Start *9:30A.M.* Time Finished 9:40.*M.* I called Mr. Perry's secretary to let her know my appointment was in a week and I still did not have the procedure information or billing. Ms. Porelon said she would get it into the mail today. I asked when the other parent in our case had his appointment set for and she said he hadn't even called to schedule his evaluation.
Date *Tue. 6 April 99* Time Start *2:15P.M.* Time Finished 4:50P.*M.* Mr. Perry arrived forty-five minutes later than the procedure letter I received yesterday said he would. Mr. Perry toured the house and yard. He asked what advantages I thought I could offer the children over what the other parent had to offer. Mr. Perry made notes, took the names, addresses and telephone numbers of people I thought he should contact, and accepted the 'Book of Our Life' I make for him. When he asked me about my concerns as far as the other parent, I showed him the section in the back of the book that identified my worries. He visited with the children and their friends as they arrived when school let out at just after three thirty. As Mr. Perry was getting ready to leave I asked when the other parent in our case had his appointment. After checking his notes he said that evaluation was not set until June third because they only called the office last week. I asked Mr. Perry when I would have the results of my evaluation. He said they issue both evaluations at the same time.
Date *Fri. 25 June 99* Time Start *9:30A.M.* Time Finished 9:35A*M.* I called Mr. Perry's office to see when the evaluation reports would be ready. Ms. Porelon said it would be anytime from forty-five to sixty days before the evaluations would be finished and that they could not be sent out until the other parent paid the balance on his bill.
Date *Fri. 3 Sept. 99* Time Start *9:05A.M.* Time Finished 9:10A*M.* I called Mr. Perry's office to see if the evaluations were finished. Ms. Porelon said they would be mailed out to the attorneys on the fifteenth. I was so frustrated and upset because of all the delays that I started to cry. Ms. Porelon attempted to calm me down and said that I shouldn't worry because the evaluation results were very telling and everything was going to be all right for my children and I. I called my attorney with the information.
Date *Fri. 17 Sept. 99* Time Start *10:00A.M.* Time Finished 10:15A*M.* My attorney called. After reading the evaluations, she and the other attorney consulted and the other side has decided that the settlement offer for custody, visitation and support are acceptable.

Evaluators are very sensitive to a case driven or controlled by someone other than the parents of the children. It becomes worrisome because many questions come to mind, including: Is this parent interested in custody or is their significant other interested in custody? Is this custody case a vendetta of rivals for a parent's attention rather than the welfare of the children?

One's ability to identify this flaw in the opposition's character while showing stability in their own interpersonal relationships has a superior position.

Read through the chapter, "You Are The Package" with your significant other. This experience, although less formal, is a type of testimony and may be the deciding factor.

The manner in which you and your significant other relate to each other on a verbal and non-verbal level will be observed, studied and noted by the professional.

Touching in the presence of the professional should be gestures of assurance and reassurance rather than touching that shows rights of possession or intimate feelings.

How Much Weight Do They Carry?

Recommendation = Decision

The evaluator's recommendation is adopted by the court 90% of the time. Therefore, the professional's recommendation carries a great deal of weight with the judge. It is out of the ordinary for the court not to follow the evaluator's recommendation.

Evaluators are not governed by "rules of evidence" and are usually willing to consider any data you present. The information and manner in which you present it says as much about you as the data itself. Negative information about the opposition should be in the form of certified copies of court records or third party reports from reliable companies. Avoid accusations. Recriminations, with or without proof, reflect badly on you. Let the evidence say the "ugly" things. Statements made about keeping the children from the other parent or protecting them will weigh heavily against you.

Positive information about you, such as accomplishments, letters, photos, and your children's achievements while in your care, is important. You will probably be asked what you would offer the opposition. Understand what the court considers proper visitation for your children. If you offer less visitation than the court's guidelines, your offer will look too restrictive to the evaluator.

Parental Alienation Syndrome (PAS)

Practically all custody disputes generate some hostility between the parents. When both parents are concerned for the long-term welfare of their children they work to resolve the conflicts quickly. In other cases many hostile charges are leveled.

It is common for the Evaluator to make a determination as to the truth of the accusations. Often initial hostility diminishes with time and workable systems take over. Sometimes one or both parents are unable to put aside the emotional trials and they feel compelled to maintain a level of animosity. In some instances one parent is compelled to eliminate the other parent from the life of the child at any cost. Any false information given to a child or an adult meant to eventually get to the child, any visitation withheld, any conscious or unconscious messages that demean a parent in a child's eyes is brainwashing.

Parental Alienation Syndrome (PAS). PAS is the process of one parent willfully making the child develop an obsessive, irrational hatred of the other parent. The child will see the hated parent as the one causing all the problems the child and loved parent experience. The bond with the primary parent is psychologically strong, but sick. Mothers are most often identified as the parent guilty of PAS. Although as fathers are being awarded custody with greater frequency they are being accused of PAS more often.

Many evaluators, judges and courts have not yet accepted that PAS even exists. If a parent insists on attempting to prove they are under siege while at the same time attempting to educate an unwilling student the parent loses both battles. Therefore, we think it is important to approach the subject of PAS very carefully. If you identify that the professional or court you are dealing with is aware of and understands that PAS does in fact exist and knows the truly hidden damage it does to children, you can work in a straightforward manner.

But, if you detect any concern about the "theory of PAS" you must back off and proceed in a more careful manner. With these professionals you must demonstrate the negative results caused by specific words used and behavior that causes adverse and harmful attitudes to be expressed by the children. Then the professional can identify the "PAS" behavior under any label they wish. It is said that a rose by any other name smells as sweet. So don't be troubled if the professional is able to see the problem, but calls it something else.

The evaluator may talk with you about the interviews with the children before they occur, to tell you how to prepare them. Most evaluators make a great effort not to distress the children by placing them in a position of having to state a preference or tell anything about either parent, which might be negative.

The children will be interviewed about general issues such as school, friends, activities and interests, and about family activities and interaction. When the issue of separation arises, the children will tell a great deal about how the separation is affecting them and how the situation might be improved. Children coached, over-prepared, or placing blame are obvious. This is not considered a positive action on the part of the parent and may indicate PAS. Do not instruct the child to say certain things or to not say certain things. Do not indicate that the evaluator is your friend, nor that the evaluator might take the child away from you. Remain matter-of-fact, neutral, and brief in what you do say. Something like, "This woman/man is going to help us make the best arrangement for how you will spend time with both your [other parent] and me." Generally it is good to tell the children very little about what to say--urge them to be open and honest. Do not promise them that their talk with the evaluator will be kept confidential, as it likely will not.

What's Not PAS

First it is important to know what does not constitute PAS. If only the parent is participating in the process of making the target parent the bad person, it is not PAS.

These examples are bad parenting and may or may not be part of PAS. They could include: the other parent: tells the children lies about you; tells the children things about you that are true, but only serve to hurt you in the children's eyes; tells the children that all the bad things that happen to them, are happening because of something you did or did not do; schedules the children's lives in order to eliminate your time with them; or making the children give up something to spend time with you.

This messages indicates to the children that you are unimportant even harmful in their lives. The other parent attempts to replace you as a parental figure with another person; acts angry or hurt when the children seem happy to be with you; threatens to harm him or herself if the children want to be with you; blames any shortage in the children's lives on your lack of love or financial support.

What is Parental Alienation Syndrome? Although all of these may be elements of PAS they are not in and of themselves PAS.

The problem becomes Parental Alienation Syndrome when the parent brainwashes the children long enough for the children to actively participate in negative verbalization and actions toward the target parent.

To further aggravate the problem many professionals, rather than learn about the problem, encourage the courts to exclude PAS testimony. They see PAS as a theoretical disorder in children that arises almost exclusively in child custody disputes. In most PAS cases it is claimed that one parent (usually the one with custody) encourages the children to hate the target parent - often leading to false allegations of physical and sexual abuse.

Psychologists and courts feel it is extremely difficult to prove where the child's negative feelings originated.

The professionals feel there is no observational, factual data or direct sense experience as evidence supporting the PAS theory. Because PAS has not been subjected to long-term extensive meaningful peer review or publication the professionals are reticent to offer you help. In fact, some experts in the field have discredited the theory. They argue that PAS is dangerous because its rapid wide dissemination and misuse in the family law community, is lending a questionable aura to the theory. Feeling that any disorder identified in some other profession has little validity.

It is as if we the people on the front line of the battle are too stupid to correctly identify what is happening to our children. What is the best weapon against PAS? The best weapon against PAS and other lies is documentation.

If you feel you are the target of PAS it is important not to start doing it yourself. Professionals who acknowledge PAS say it is often a reciprocal behavior.

What is Parent Alienation Syndrome

PAS is a type of brain washing that involves the children in vindictive thought and behavior aimed at alienating the target parent. The loved parent and the children work together to get the parent that is the target of scorn out of their lives. Children display specific symptoms that the theory of Parent Alienation Syndrome behaviors identifies can range from mild, moderate, overt and severe. They are as follows:

The child

- feels justified in treating the target parent badly.
- sees any family or friends of the target parent as the child's enemies.
- exhibits relentless hatred for the target parent without being able to say why.
- parrots the loved parent and their cause against the target parent.
- does not want to speak on the phone to, visit with or spend any time with the target parent.
- believes many negative sometimes irrational things about the target parent.
- is unable to differentiate between personal experience and related information and hates the target parent for faulty reasons.
- can't remember anything good about the target parent.
- is unable to see anything the target parent does as good.
- relives any past perceived wrongdoing.
- champions the alienating parent's grievances against the target parent.
- becomes ill or angry when having to deal with or talk about the target parent.
- step-parent, grandparent or others join forces with the alienating parent to convince the children to hate the target parent because they too believe the unconfirmed and bad stories. The alienating parent often quickly replaces the role of the targeted parent with a new relationship.

The alienating parent refuses to communicate in any way with the target parent even under the most serious of circumstances concerning the child. What does this do to the child?

Other Parent is a Chameleon

"The other parent can charm anyone." Since a competent assessment includes skilled clinical interview and history-taking, objective measures of personality and parenting characteristics, and some outside interviews known as "collateral checking."

The evaluator will likely review information you supply including previous treatment records, talk with some people you have supplied telephone numbers for in the community who know of the issues first hand and who can comment on the other parents and your parenting skills, and finally, observe each of you in interaction with the child(ren). By interviewing each member of the family several times, the evaluator can attempt to clarify apparent contradictions in the data, and by exercising good clinical judgment, it is generally possible for the evaluator to arrive at a fairly clear impression of the family dynamics, the needs and wishes of the children, and the strengths and weaknesses of each parent in meeting the needs of the children.

Some of the personalities the evaluators watch for are:

- Nay-Sayer: They are deadly to morale since they are able to defeat a good plan with a barrage of reasons as to why it won't work. Distressed at the idea of trying anything, they drive others to despair.
- Commander: They are often confrontational, directed and angry displaying the ultimate in pushy and aggressive behavior. They see any compromise as a weakness and are willing to threaten.
- Agreer: They will agree with the point of one person and agree with the opposing point just as readily. Their overwhelming desire to please everyone causes them to agree to everything causing them to break promises and commitments.
- Know-It-All: They have no tolerance for any method or opinion, but their own. They never doubt their opinion and will not accept contradiction, correction or blame.
- Procrastinator: Puts off even small decisions until its too late. To avoid conflict or blame, all decisions must make themselves.
- Sniper: They are expert at identifying your weaknesses and using them against you. They do

it behind your back to your face and in public to humiliate you.

- The Bomb: They take control by exploding suddenly and exaggerating and ranting about things that have nothing to do with the circumstances.

With the exception of child abuse, children will and should desire contact with both parents. The extended length of the conflict combined with its permanence seriously endangers the mental health and psychological development of the children.

It does this by disallowing the children to experience the full range of feelings for both parents that are normal and necessary for an emotionally well adjusted individual.

The negative impact of parental alienation syndrome on the children is equally harmful if the alienating parent's intentions are to protect the child or hurt the target parent. Unless the children are in imminent danger, it is the responsibility of the guardian of the children to make sure contact is established and maintained with the other parent.

False Accusations of PAS

False accusations of PAS (Parental Alienation Syndrome) can be made by either side in a custody dispute. Primarily it is the non-custodial parent making the accusations against the custodial parent. Although PAS does occur it is not as prevalent as one might think.

If you are dealing with another parent that is difficult and/or finds it difficult to deal with you, one side or the other may feel there are sinister intentions at work to influence the children. Influence on the children is dependent on the age, emotional make-up, auxiliary contacts, and agenda of the child. The pain and panic of being accused of negatively influencing your children can distort your perceptions of your position and the other parent's power.

First, if you feel you are dealing with a liar you have to stop selectively believing that person. If you don't believe them when they say something about helping you or the children, you must not believe them when they say something that will hurt.

Second, the accuser's view of the situation belongs only to that person. The professionals will make a determination as to the presence of PAS or its absence. Third, you have a lot to do with making yourself a victim. You have to stop giving the other parent more power than they actually have. You have to document what you have done because that will also show what you have not done. If you are not involved in PAS, settle down. Your children won't be displaying the indications of PAS. Cruel, stupid behavior is seen on both sides. Avoid being part of the problem. That will make you part of the solution.

Change Where the Children Live?

False accusations of PAS could change where the children live. **What Is, Shall Remain,** also known as Status Quo, means the children will remain where they have been residing, unless a problem (obvious and imminent danger to the children) can be proven to exist. This situation rarely exists and is very difficult to prove even when it does.

More often than not a parent living away from the children will have to relocate to have more frequent contact with the children. It would be best to find a home on the same block or within walking distance for the children. A parent fighting for custody of children that reside in a state other than that in which the children live and not in the state with jurisdiction for the case has little or no chance of winning custody. Relocating to the state in which the children live and filing a request for a court-order that the other parent not be allowed to leave the state with the children would be the only valid remedy.

What are Evaluators Observing

The following Positive and Negative behaviors are taken into account whenever parents and children are observed together. A parent attempting to force positive behaviors is not able to perform consistently.

Guidelines for Evaluators

The primary purpose of a child custody evaluation should be to assess the short and long-term needs of the children, with focus on the parenting capacity of the adults and social, psychological and developmental needs of the children. In many cases it is difficult to distinguish between the job of the evaluator and the psychologist.

It is the Responsibility of the Psychologist to:

- Attain and gain specialized training, experience and on-going training.
- Avoid multiple relationships.
- Maintain an objective, impartial stance.
- Be aware of social and personal biases, but engage in non-discriminatory practice.
- Make certain the scope of the evaluation will be determined by the nature of the referral question.
- Obtain informed consent from all adults and, as appropriate, inform the children.
- Inform all participants about limits of your confidentiality and legal disclosure of information.
- Use multiple methods of data gathering.
- Render opinions regarding only individuals and their psychological functioning you have personally evaluated.
- Neither over interpret or inappropriately interpret clinical or assessment data.
- Maintain written records.
- Make recommendations that are based upon what is in the psychological interest of the children.
- Clarify financial, visitation and other necessary arrangements.

Confidentiality - Evaluator

There is no confidentiality. Every word spoken to the evaluator and any test results may go into the final evaluation and becomes part of the court record, which becomes public record.

The only exception is if the judge seals the records to protect the children. If you tell the evaluator information that you and your psychologist or attorney has determined is confidential you have waived the right of confidentiality for this information. You may have even opened the door to other areas you did not want exposed.

If You Gotta Go

Once aware that it will be necessary to be evaluated, make an appointment, the first available on the evaluator's schedule. It is important to be the first one to which the evaluator speaks. Evaluators are trained to be neutral, but they are human. If you have made a positive impression, something called the "Positive Halo Effect" kicks in. It will be difficult for the opposition to change the good impression you have established.

If the information human beings are hearing does not correspond with the information they are seeing, they will believe what they see.

Listed under Positive and Negative on the next pages are some things evaluators and psychologists are trained to watch for when you are dealing with your children.

It would be a good exercise to have someone rate your behavior. If they identify a number of negative traits, you may have some problems of which you are not aware. An awareness of these behaviors may help you and a professional identify problem areas and eventually improve the quality of life that you and your children share.

Make This Easier for Your Children

You can make this ordeal easier for the children. Your nervousness will be felt by your children. Calm the children with loving touches, cuddles and hugs. Explain to older children why you are on edge.

Dress your children in comfortable clothing. Children who are comfortable will behave better and act more natural. If your children are old enough to pick out their own clothing, let them. Do not be concerned by what they choose.

If you are uncomfortable with your children's choice of attire, tell the psychologist who was in charge of wardrobe that day. Example; "Becka chose to ware all her pretty things to see you today." or "Mike wanted you to see that he can make his own wardrobe choices".

If your child has a blanket, Teddy bear, or pacifier that is always within reach, let this object of comfort come along.

The evaluator or psychologist has observed thousands of children, and there is nothing your children can do to upset or surprise this professional.

Listen to the psychologist carefully when he gives you instructions or asks you questions. He is probably following a set of guidelines. It is your responsibility to hide your insecurities and worry from your children.

Becoming Aware of My Actions with My Children	
The Way I Will Learn To Be With My Child	**Things I Will Stop**
Set reasonable limits for child	Controlling
State consequences for undesirable actions	Threatening my child
Be willing to follow up with corrective measures	Slapping or hurting my child
Be tolerant of dissent behavior	Demanding compliance
Use a pleasant voice quality	Use baby talk or talk over child's head
Allow expression of feelings	Withhold attention and/or affection
Use appropriate language level to child	Not look at child when speaking to child
Be physically affectionate with child	Using blank expression toward child
Have eye contact with child	Stiffness in handling child
Use facial expressions to show approval	Disregard child's concerns
Be flexible in my communication with my child	Stiffness in handling my child
Lean toward and get close to child	Keeping physical distance from child
Be aware of child	Being self-absorbed
Encourage child	Criticizing child

Evaluator's Report #1

Conciliation Services of The Superior Court of The State of Arizona

January 14, 1993

Family Assessment Re: Randall Long/ Amber Jones (aka Miller)

DR#: 92-42487 **S#:** S-5174 GD **Referred by:** Honorable. L.L. Baplon

Attorney for Mother: Faith Beli **Attorney for Father:** Catharine Law

Mediation Conducted: February 12, 1992

Introduction:

Randall Long and Amber Jones, who were never married to each other, have a 14 month old son named Bobby. Bobby was born on October 27, 1991. During the first weeks of Bobby's life, he lived primarily with his mother. Since that time, however, both parents have been very actively involved in his care. Each parent currently has Bobby for some portion of every weekday and weekends have been alternated. In a February 1992 meeting at Conciliation Services, both parents agreed to make the informal parenting plan they instituted upon Bobby's birth permanent.

The present controversy began in July 1992 when Mrs. Jones moved to Washington with Bobby and her other three children from a prior marriage. Mr. Long immediately brought this issue to the court's attention. Soon after relocating, Mrs. Jones returned to Arizona with Bobby. She left her three other children in Washington, where they lived with her present husband's parents.

The court referred the case to Conciliation Services for a family assessment.

Objective and Background Information:

Amber Jones, age 32, has four children: Lucy, age 14, Byron age 11, Jerome, age 10, and Bobby, age 14 months. The father of her three oldest children is her ex-husband, James Miller, a man described by Mrs. Jones as a violent drug dealer. In fact, she cited wanting to isolate the children from his harmful influence. Nevertheless, Mrs. Jones is temporarily living with Bobby in a trailer owned by Mr. Miller. She has also been using Mr. Miller's vehicle. Prior to living at Mr. Miller's trailer, Mrs. Jones lived at her sister's apartment in HUD housing, but she was forced to move because she said Mr. Long complained to HUD.

Mrs. Jones' present husband, Mike Jones, age 41, is a long-distance truck driver. Their present marriage is actually the second time. Mr. and Mrs. Jones have been married to each other. Their brief first marriage was in the late 1970's. For many years after their first marriage ended, Mr. and Mrs. Jones only had telephonic contact with each other.

They re-met in March 1992, and got remarried one month later.

Randall Long, age 40, a former truck driver, suffered a degree of permanent disability because of injuries sustained in an accident. He helps his present wife Rebecca, age 44, run her warehouse business. Mr. and Mrs. Long live in a leased five bedroom house, where Bobby has his own room.

Mr. Long was married once previously, but his ex-wife and their two sons moved to Washington in 1979. He has no contact with his teenage sons, a fact he attributes to his ex-wife's insistence. A document produced by Mrs. Jones indicated that Mr. Long, in 1985, owed his ex-wife more than seven thousand dollars in delinquent child support.

Mr. Long produced documents to show resolution of delinquent support due to the trucking accident that resulted in his disability. Support is no longer delinquent.

Synopsis:

The parties involved in this family assessment have known each other for several years. Bobby is the unplanned result of casual sex between the parties. In fact Mr. Long impregnated Mrs. Jones one time before Bobby was conceived.

It was reported by Mrs. Jones that the fetus was aborted when Mrs. Jones' then husband, James Miller, punched her in the stomach.

Many years ago Rebecca Long dated James Miller while he was married to Amber Jones. For several years in the late 1980's and early 1990's, Amber Jones worked at Rebecca Long's company. All of this business and personal familiarity seems to have heightened the animosity between the parties. Mrs. Jones wants to move to Washington with Bobby and start a life with her second husband and other children. Randall and Rebecca Long are convinced that Bobby would be better off living with them. Accusations and counter-accusations are volleyed between both camps.

First of all, Mrs. Jones claims that Bobby was conceived as a result of Mr. Long raping her. She levels this serious charge despite the fact that, by her own admission, she was too "plowed" (drunk) to remember having sex with Mr. Long that night. She reports that she didn't realize they had intercourse until she turned up pregnant. Her lack of memory about this incident casts doubt on her claim that she was raped. Mr. and Mrs. Long categorically deny that sex was forced upon Mrs. Jones.

Mr. Long questions the decision-making ability of Mrs. Jones with regard to the people to whom she has exposed the children. For example, in 1989 and 1990, Mrs. Jones acknowledges co-habituating with a man she describes as a "biker."

She terminated this relationship because of this man's excessive drinking. Mr. Long also wonders about the stability of Mrs. Jones' present marriage, implying that it is only a marriage of convenience to allow Mrs. Jones to get custody of this child, get off welfare and be supported by a man. (Mrs. Jones replies, saying that her current husband loves all of her children and he has a positive relationship with each of them).

Mrs. Jones and her husband Mike reported to Conciliation Services that they had not experienced any arrests or legal difficulties. However, Mr. Long supplied information about Mrs. Jones' arrest and a report indicating that Mr. Jones was charged with grand theft in 1971 and ended up serving over 5 years in prison. Mrs. Jones's arrest was a very serious lapse of judgment, according to Mr. Long. It occurred in June 1991 when Mrs. Jones was arrested for attempting to deliver nine balloons filled with marijuana to a male friend serving time at the prison. The police report indicates that her three older children were with her and that she handed some of the drugs to the then five year old son of the convict she went to visit. Although Mrs. Jones blames a female companion who accompanied her to the prison as the real culprit, she later reached a plea agreement in which she received probation to a charge of solicitation to promote prison contraband.

Mrs. Jones describes her fine and two year probation as a "slap on the wrist" and down plays the importance or seriousness of this incident.

What also bothers Mr. Long is the fact that recently Mrs. Jones has been in association with her ex-husband, James Miller.

Mr. Long does not understand why Mrs. Jones is associating with a man Mrs. Jones said caused her so much grief in the past. Mrs. Jones states that Mr. Miller is only helping her and denies rekindling a romantic relationship.

Mrs. Jones reports that she once found staple holes in the bottom of Bobby's feet and she has observed black eyes and bruises on the child. She is quick to point out that she does not suspect Mr. or Mrs. Long have abused Bobby. However, she said she reported these incidents to Child Protective Services, because she did not want the Longs to blame her for these injuries to Bobby. CPS has no record.

Mr. Long furnished a report from Bobby's doctor, which indicated that the pediatrician had not seen any abuse or neglect of the child. The Doctor noted that both parents participated in Bobby's care, but Bobby was brought in primarily by his father.

Mr. Long alleges that Mrs. Jones doesn't always use a child car seat while driving and generally is nonchalant about Bobby's hygiene. As an example of his claim, he recalls the time Mrs. Jones returned Bobby's diaper bag with a cockroach inside. Mrs. Jones produced a photo of the child car seat she uses for Bobby and dismisses Mr. Long's complaints about dirty clothing.

Profoundly upset when Mrs. Jones took Bobby to Washington, Mr. Long has kept a detailed diary, including photographs of his daily contacts with Bobby.

Since her return from Washington, he even hired a detective to perform surveillance of Bobby when with Mrs. Jones. Until Mrs. Jones moved to Washington, Mr. and Mrs. Long state, their intention was always to co-parent with her.

Due to their belief that Mrs. Jones does not have sufficient financial resources or parenting skills to properly care for Bobby full-time, the Longs are requesting custody.

Mrs. Jones wishes to move back to Washington with Bobby. She reports that her husband's income ($35,000 per year) will allow her to stay home full-time with Bobby. She says that Bobby really has four parents: herself and her husband, and Mr. and Mrs. Long. She wants Bobby to see his father, she claims, but it will be difficult to share the child if the child's primary residence is in the state of Washington.

She reports that since her original parenting agreement with Mr. Long was never converted into an official court order, she is legally free to relocate Bobby.

Evaluation:

Both of Bobby's parents provided many witness letters testifying to their respective parenting skills. There is no question about the fact that Bobby is a much-loved child.

Mrs. Jones and Mr. Long started out by being very cooperative regarding Bobby, but regrettably the situation has deteriorated into a lot of sniping and mudslinging after Mrs. Jones took Bobby.

Mr. Long and his wife want their home in Arizona to be Bobby's primary residence. Mrs. Jones and her husband intend to move Bobby to Washington. In order to determine the best possible living arrangements for Bobby, one must examine the appropriateness of decisions each parent has made.

Mr. Long has been a very active father. Since he helps in his wife's office, he is able to provide a lot of attention and care to Bobby on a daily basis. The fact that he does not have to maintain full-time competitive employment allows him to spend much time with Bobby. His wife is very encouraging and supportive of his effort to attain custody. It is very likely that his campaign for custody, which consisted of keeping copious notes about parenting issues and the hiring of a detective, is fueled by the loss he feels due to the fact that he has no relationship with his older children.

However, if Mr. Long is going to criticize the way Mrs. Jones parents her older children, then he must be willing to accept some criticism for not maintaining a relationship with his older sons.

Despite his suspiciousness of and resentment toward Mrs. Jones, Mr. Long is an appropriate parent. He has the resources to meet Bobby's needs.

Mrs. Jones must accept the fact that, for the most part, the present misunderstanding stemmed from her decision to relocate Bobby to another state. Although she had some convincing reasons to move, she seemed unconcerned with the developing relationship between Bobby and his father. While she said she wanted Bobby to see his father, the practical effect of moving a pre-verbal child to another state is to sever his relationship with the other parent. Moving to Washington fulfilled Mrs. Jones' wishes quite well, but did not fully take into account Bobby's needs. Mrs. Jones' remarriage to Mike Jones, a man who can financially support her, is designed to allow her to be a full-time mother. The move to Washington was a consequence of her decision to get remarried.

Mrs. Jones' claim that she was raped strains her credibility. It is also noteworthy that Mrs. and Mr. Jones, when asked about any arrests or legal difficulties, failed to mention his theft conviction or prison term or her drug arrest.

These incidents lead one to suspect that Mr. or Mrs. Jones may distort or deny events to their advantage.

Although Mrs. Jones' three older children could not be interviewed for this evaluation, one wonders how the children reacted to the alcoholic behavior exhibited by the boyfriend with whom Mrs. Jones co-habited in 1989 and 1990.

Mrs. Jones' move to Washington last summer has also left them living in another state without either parent for the last six months.

The marijuana smuggling conviction, as well as the cockroach-in-the-diaper-bag episode, call into question Mrs. Jones' judgment and cleanliness, respectively. Mrs. Jones is a loving parent, but her decisions and life-style have exposed her older children, and may expose Bobby in the future, to an unacceptable degree of uncertainty and turmoil.

Recommendations:

It is recommended that custody of Bobby be granted to Mr. Long.

If Mrs. Jones remains in Arizona, a fixed-schedule visitation arrangement like the present court order would appear to be in Bobby's best interest. It would have to be modified when Bobby reaches school age. At that time, the parties should participate in mediation and devise a new visitation schedule.

If Mrs. Jones decides to move back to Washington (and this would be the decidedly less advisable course of action, because it would disrupt her relationship with Bobby), she should be able to see Bobby whenever she travels back to Arizona. Also, she should be allowed to have Bobby come to her home in Washington for two 2- week periods per year, with this time to expand as Bobby gets older.

Respectfully submitted this 14th day of January, 1993.

Paul Solomon, Family Counselor End of Evaluation.

Evaluator's Report #2

Destiny Cheyene Ph.,D.
Family Directions
34 Sand Dollar, Malibu, CA

I have been assigned evaluations for the parents involved in a divorce/child custody dispute. Scheduling:
Ms. Strong 04/16, 04/23, 04/30/2001
Mr. Strong 05/07, 05/14, 05/21/2001
Ms. & Mr. Strong 05/28/2001
Brittany, Justin and Samantha Strong 05/28/2001

The information in this report is produced singularly from three one-hour interview sessions with Ms. Strong. Ms. Strong did not show up for the joint session with Mr. Strong.

Although I request the names of family or friends that could support her efforts and information, she submitted no collateral contacts.

Ms. Strong

Session 1

Ms. Strong arrived at our first session on time in office-job-appropriate dress. Her attitude was upbeat, animated and enthusiastic.

Ms. Strong initiated conversation which evolved into a monologue, while opening a briefcase to show me a three-inch stack of boilerplate pretrial motions, marginally coherent, largely well intended, reasonably well-researched, and totally predictable legal documents she had produced. I listened carefully as she explained that she was fighting for custody of her three children pro se. Ms. Strong said she was up against a controlling, vengeful soon-to-be-ex-husband and his money.

The money was buying a team of three attorneys, twenty-two para-legals, two private investigators, a huge private law library and high-security office with valet parking.

Ms. Strong responded to all questions about parenting, her personal relationship with her husband and the children with antidotal information about Mr. Strong and his single-minded pursuit to destroy her.

Ms. Strong

Session 2

Ms. Strong arrived at our second on time but a day early. She returned on the correct day, but twenty minutes late. Her clothes were exotic and best suited to an evening of dancing. She was tired, distracted and non-responsive.

I asked about her post-marriage inter-personal relationships. Admittedly, the man she left her husband for was a poor choice, but she claims he had her fooled completely. She explained that her move to California for six months was a cooling-off time in order to give the children some time with their father.

Ms. Strong feels that her desire to have her own life is what propelled Mr. Strong into his scorched earth policy against her She feels his only reason for pursuing custody of the children is to hurt her. Ms. Strong gave several examples of how Mr. Strong and the legal system are victimizing her.

Ms. Strong relishes in the pleasure of bad judgment and is no longer capable of reflective analysis. When she describes a bad situation she has experienced she does not see where she may have contributed to the problem. If Ms. Strong avoids dire consequences, she is unable to reproduce the positive decisions or behaviors that may have produced the end result.

Ms. Strong is interested in hardship demonstrated by her attraction to the "bad-boy with a rescue mentality." When confronted with misdeed or poor judgment, Ms. Strong is unable to admit fault or apologize. She feels any apology would be tantamount to an admission of failure.

When asked, Ms. Strong said she would give up her boy friend if she had to, to keep her children.

Ms. Strong

Session 3

Ms. Strong arrived at our third session an hour early. She was wearing a service station uniform. Her demeanor was that of a woman attempting to sit in a burning building.

Ms. Strong initiated conversation about her children for the first time. She said she had been the primary caretaker, stay at home mom for all three until Samantha the youngest started first grade eight months ago. With the children gone most of the time and her husband's lack of interest in their marriage she was board.

Ms. Strong said she had been watching the house across the street that had been rented to a young couple. When the wife left, several men moved in and there seemed to be a party going on all the time. Ms. Strong accepted an invitation one afternoon and became a regular.

The arguments started when Mr. Strong questioned the way she was caring for the children and the house. He objected to her new friends and asked her about money and electronics that were disappearing from their home.

Ms. Strong feels that Mr. Strong is only interested in punishing her for trying to be her own person.

The information in this report is produced from three one-hour interview sessions with Mr. Strong. Mrs. Strong did show up for the joint session, Ms. Strong did not show.

Collateral contacts included Mr. Strong's parents, Mike Wilest, Mr. Strong's best friend of thirty years. Julie and Tim Able, next door neighbors to the Strong family for ten years, and letters from co-workers, family and friends.

Mr. Strong

Session 1

Mr. Strong arrived at our first session on time in office-job-appropriate dress. His attitude was concerned and cautious.

I asked him why he seemed so pensive. Mr. Strong explained, "My attorney said that your recommendation would determine where our children would live and I don't know what you want to hear from me." I told Mr. Strong I wanted to hear whatever he wanted to tell me.

Mr. Strong said his children were bright and loving with strong individual personalities. He was

very concerned about the long-term effects this custody battle could have on them. He said Ms. Strong had been very involved and loving wife and mother since the birth of Brittany who was now twelve. When Justin was born four years later she seemed at her happiest.
Just as Justin started first grade Samantha was born and their home was the hub of all the good things in the world.

Mr. Strong felt Ms. Strong had become distant and began to demonstrate mood-swings in the last two years. He had encouraged her to have a physical to see if she was suffering anemia. When Samantha started school, Ms. Strong began to dress and act in a manner that was inconsistent with her role as a wife and mother. Mr. Strong said she stopped keeping the house picked up. He said, the cleaning people reported that on several occasions they found plastic bags of dope and white powder. When he asked Ms. Strong about the dope she said the cleaning people were lying. Several evenings when Mr. Strong came home late from work the children were eating junk food and up past their bedtime. They said mom was across the street if they needed her.

Mr. Strong said it all came to a head when Mr. Strong went across the street at six one Wednesday evening and found Ms. Strong asleep and naked in bed with one of her new friends.

Mr. Strong asked her to leave the family house. She returned to the family home some time the next day to get some of her things. Ms. Strong did not communicate with anyone.

After six months the police called Mr. Strong at two in the morning and notified him that they had his wife in custody and to please come to get her. Ms. Strong was thirty pounds lighter with a tattoo of a butterfly on her hip. Mr. Strong took her home and the children were happy to see her and frightened by her appearance.

(Mr. Strong handed me two legal documents. Restraining order (quashed) and Petition for Divorce and Temporary order for Custody)

The day after her return home, Ms. Strong filed a restraining order against Mr. Strong. He was ordered to stay away from his wife, the children and the house. Mr. Strong moved in to a hotel. Ten days later Mr. Strong, his attorney, the children and their attorney appeared on the restraining order.

Ms. Strong testified that Mr. Strong beat her and held her prisoner.

Mr. Strong and the children testified that there was no hostility or even harsh words.

The judge quashed the restraining order and granted Mr. Strong's attorney's request that Ms. Strong be removed from the family home until the divorce case was settled.

Mr. Strong

Session 2

Mr. Strong arrived at our second session on time in office-job-appropriate dress. His attitude was appropriate.

Mr. Strong brought a proposed parenting plan that would keep the children involved with their mother but in his care. It included a letter from his employer that notified me of the time schedule he had been working for the last seven months. His workweek scheduled him in the office (20 minutes from his home) from 9:00 a.m. to 4:00 p.m. Monday, Tuesday, Wednesday and Thursday. Additionally, he was scheduled on line from 9:00 p.m. to 11:00 p.m. the same days. The letter notified me that this flex-schedule had also been working out for a single mother with the same company.

We discussed his role as full-time-dad and his back-up and support plans for childcare.

Mr. Strong has no romantic interests at this time but says he does get a great deal of attention at the soccer games and PTA meetings.

Mr. Strong

Session 3

Mr. Strong arrived at our third session on time in office-job-appropriate dress. His attitude was appropriate.

Mr. Strong was concerned that the children were not seeing enough of their mother. Her contact with them was erratic and accusatory. He felt they were feeling abandoned and guilty. Mr. Strong was looking for ways to deal with the questions they were beginning to ask.

We identified some places in times that the children could visit with their mother that would be more comfortable for her.

Conclusion:

At this time I feel that Mr. Strong is the more appropriate parent to act as guardian. His desire and ability to parent as well as his support team are key to this decision.

Ms. Strong is encouraged to maintain contact with her children and petition the court for more visitations, as she is able to exercise them.

These evaluations have been assigned the parents involved in a child custody dispute.

Evaluator's Report #3

Destiny Cheyene Ph.,D.
Family Directions
34 Sand Dollar, Malibu, CA

Scheduling:
Ms. Bell 04/16 Interview, 04/23/2001 Testing
Mr. Hale 05/07 Interview, 05/14, Testing05/21/2001
James Hale 05/28/2001 Interview

The information in this report is produced from scheduled appointments, tests, documentation and collateral contacts.

Ms. Bell

Session 1

Ms. Bell arrived for our session on time and dressed appropriately.

Ms. Bell reported that she and Mr. Hale were married for a year and on half. Mr. Hale left when James was six-months-old. The Hales were divorced shortly after that. There was virtually no contact with Mr. Hale or his family for eight years. Child support has not been forthcoming because Mr. Hale works in family businesses and shows no hard income.

Ms. Bell married Brian Bell when James was three-years-old. Mr. Bell has been a father to James in all the meaningful ways.

Ms. Bell explains that Mr. Hale's mother has recently expressed an interest in her grandson and has encouraged and financed Mr. Hale's desire and court case. Ms. Bell is concerned because the senior Mr. Hale was a judge and even though retired has a great deal of influence in the community.

Ms. Bell, because of Mr. Bell has the finances and support to resist this custody suit. She does feel the two and a half years it has been going on is emotionally and psychologically taxing on James and her marriage.

Ms. Bell gave me certified copies of nine motions filed by Mr. Hale against her in the past twenty-nine months.

3 for change of custodial parent

4 (one each for) notification of tutoring, doctors appointments, club activities and church affiliation

2 extended out of country visitation

The judge denied all these motions.

Ms. Bell

Session 2

Ms. Bell arrived on time for testing and dressed appropriately.

She completed her test and left the office.

Mr. Hale

Session 3

Ms. Hale arrived for our session on time and dressed appropriately.

Mr. Hale reported that he left the marriage because Ms. Bell became frigid when James was born. He left the baby with his mother but feels that James needs his real father now.

Mr. Hale says his family has a lot more to offer James than the Bells do. He feels that James lives too structured a life and will rebel if he doesn't get to try some things when he is young.

When questioned, he admits that there has been no interference with his attempts to see James and that he has not been financially responsible.

Mr. Hale married last year and feels that the new wife will be an excellent mother to James.

Session 2

Mr. Hale

Mr. Hale arrived on time for testing and dressed appropriately.

He completed his test and left the office.

James Hale arrived for our session on time and dressed appropriately.

James introduced me to his stepfather Mr. Bell in the lobby. We moved to my office for our session.

James is an integument good-looking apparently well-adjusted boy of ten. He expressed love for his mother and step-father as well as a mind interest in his biological father. James was a little mystified in Mr. Hales interest in him. "My dad makes a big deal about coming to pick me up and then doesn't know what to do with me after that. I like grandmother and Grandfather Hale but I don't know them too good. They like my dad a lot better when I am with him." He explained.

When asked where he wants to live, James is very clear that he is happy where he is now.

When asked about the problem between his parents he just shrugs.

Conclusion:

Primary custody should remain with Ms. Bell. I find nothing to indicate that James would be better cared for with his father Mr. Hale.

Evaluator's Report #4

Destiny Cheyene Ph.,D.
Family Directions
34 Sand Dollar, Malibu, CA
An evaluation has been ordered for
Patrick White and Venus White

First Session:

There is a history of parent to parent violence that has gone on for seven years. There has been no parent to child violence, but the children have witnessed their parents discord.

At present the parents still reside in the same home but are involved in a divorce and child custody dispute.

Neither parent presented as the better or worse parent.

I am concerned that the children live in a situation that can become volatile at any time. Even when the parents live apart there may still be a danger of violence if appropriate action is not taken.

After an initial session with each parent I recommended that they each:
Keep a journal
Choose a sport or hobby that will require total concentration
Maintain your Anger Diary
Attend a parent class.
Attend an anger management class
Participate in conflict resolution
Return in sixty days.

Second Session:
Patrick White and Venus White
Returned with mixed results on their assignments

Patrick
Did not keep a journal
Joined an adult baseball league
Did not maintain your Anger Diary
Did complete the parenting classes
Did not complete the anger management classes
Did not participate in conflict resolution classes

Venus
Kept an extensive journal
Did not get involved in a hobby sport
Maintained her Anger Diary
Did complete the parenting classes
Did complete the anger management classes
Did not participate in conflict resolution classes

Patrick and Venus reported that they are experiencing fewer arguments and have endeavored to stop all confrontations in front of the children. They have jointly asked their attorneys to avoid aggravating the divorce process.

I asked them to work on their previous assignments and report back in thirty days.

Patrick White and Venus White

Patrick and Venus returned with a joint parenting agreement.

After review of the parenting agreement, I sent a request for the attorneys to draft a temporary order that followed the parenting agreement.

The order designates that I review the situation and interview the parents and children in six months.

Patrick White and Venus White and Chenille, Jamal and Accria their children participated in a roundtable session in my office. Because of a personal emergency this evaluation was delayed for two months.

The children expressed their satisfaction with the joint parenting agreement.

The children have remained in the family home and the parents have moved out.

Patrick lives with the children the even numbered months of the year.

Venus lives with the children the odd numbered months of the year.

All school events, holidays and celebrations are held family style with both parents in attendance.

Household costs are split 60/40 with Venus taking the larger responsibility because her income is larger.

The adults live with their own parents when they are not living with the children.

Conclusion:

I have extended the temporary status of this joint parenting agreement for an additional six months. If there are no incidences of violence in that time I will recommend that the court make this temporary order permanent.

Evaluator's Report #5

Douglas Boxlightner Ph.,D.
327 Ridge Road Suite #D, ABQ, NM
A parent-parent and a parent-child evaluation has been ordered for Wolfgang Blake (8 years old) and his parents Serendipity and Ronald Blake.
The purpose of the evaluation is to determine who will have the responsibility of residential parent.

Wolfgang is a healthy, well adjusted, engaging child who loves and enjoys both of his parents. His desire is to have his parents together again. Wolfgang has accepted the situation as it is with a sturdy resolve.

Mr. Ronald Blake

I was able to fit into Ronald Blake's calendar first so I scheduled an office and home visit with him.

Mr. Blake greeted me in the lobby of his five person, CPA firm which is located in a downtown hi-rise. He was dressed in a conservative but expensive looking dark gray suit and showed me his office which included a play-area homework room set up for Wolfgang. The carpeted room has a desk, couch and entertainment set-up with books, toys and videos which appear to be age appropriate. Wolfgang seemed to be at home and familiar with the surroundings and interacted well with the office personal. When he is with his father on weekends and evenings and Mr. Blake's schedule dictates Wolfgang goes to the office with his father.

Mr. Blake's home is up-scale and clean. His attire was somewhat casual but his demeanor was still very formal. Although he seemed extremely reserved to me, there was definitely a strong warm physical and emotional bond between father and son. Father and son went into a great deal of explanation of Wolfgang's interest in team sports and his position and abilities at baseball, soccer, basketball and swim team. They also shared some stories about their once a month golf game.

Wolfgang's room at home was almost a reproduction of the room at the office with the addition of clothing and more personal items on the walls. Once Wolfgang was off doing his homework, Mr. Blake expressed his concerns about Mrs. Blake's friends and disinterest in wearing clothing. He feels Wolfgang does not get enough supervision when with his mother.

Mrs. Serendipity Blake

Mrs. Blake lives on the second level of a huge barn converted into a home/studio. The home is an experience of visual and acoustic wonder which is inviting and disorganized. The entire ground level is a studio/showroom. Primarily Mrs. Blake works in clay and she makes and sells remarkably innovative and beautiful impressionistic pieces. Mrs. Blake greeted me in a flowing floor-length caftan and felt it was very important to explain the origin of her first name. She proceeded to explain; "Although both of my parents were there, my parents did not meet at the original Woodstock. But, did spend some hours together, dancing naked in the field at the reunion twenty years later. They parted with phone numbers and no real intention of ever seeing each other again. Five months later my mother called my father to tell him that I had been conceived. My father said "it must be serendipity that we met and conceived a child." He drove from Nags Head North Carolina to Albuquerque New Mexico, non-stop, to marry my mother. They named me, Serendipity and lived happily ever after."

Wolfgang seemed to have the run of the studio and played with clay and interacted comfortably with an odd assortment of people who came and went as we conducted our interview.

Mrs. Blake said she was originally taken with Mr. Blake when they met their last year in college. He was such a sharp contrast to the bohemian people that surrounded her during her childhood and young adult life. What appealed to her ten years ago now looked restricted. Mrs. Blake felt that Mr. Blake was too controlling and wouldn't let Wolfgang find himself. Mrs. Blake did not seem concerned that Wolfgang was present during her somewhat negative description of his father. Mrs. Blake and Wolfgang were physically and emotionally affectionate.

Once Wolfgang was across the room, I asked her to address the concerns Mr. Blake had expressed. Mrs. Blake was astonished that I had given an ear to such nonsense. She felt that freedom of movement and contact with as many people as possible were what would give Wolfgang the

experiences to cope with later life. She felt that Mr. Blake was so dull because his parents had never allowed him an opportunity to taste life until he met her. "And then" she said "it was already too late." When I asked her about Mr. Blake's statement about Mrs. Blake's reluctance to wear clothes she responded, "I take antibiotics to deal with my adult acne and that causes yeast infections.
So often I only wear huge loose fitting t-shirts without panties. In fact I'm not wearing any panties now." Mrs. Blake chatted on non-stop about her work and interesting friends. I asked about Wolfgang's interest in sports. Mrs. Blake said she resented Mr. Blake forcing Wolfgang into such highly competitive testosterone charged war games. Mrs. Blake said she never attended the competitions because they were usually when she had to be at a gallery showing. As a matter of fact she informed me that Jon her live-in boyfriend was exhibiting his work at a large gallery in the colony and she was going to have to hurry off to help. Mrs. Blake said her schedule would be hectic until the end of the season. When I asked to see her son's room she summoned Wolfgang to take me upstairs.

Wolfgang's room was a riot of color which included a bed, bookcase, TV, Nintento, boom-box, toys and clothes everywhere. He seemed to be as comfortable in this home as he was with his father.

Conclusion.

Wolfgang has access to both of his parents and they have access to him. Mr. Blake appears to have the greater interest in a hands-on parent-child relationship. I think that each parent has a great deal to teach their son and that assigning Mr. Blake as residential parent will insure a stable home and ongoing access to the love and support of both parents.

End of Report

Home Study

Home study is one of the evaluation tools the court system uses to measure your ability to provide a proper physical and emotional environment for your child. The home visit also gives the evaluator a more relaxed and natural setting in which to observe the family structure and the child's interaction with parents and siblings.

It is common for the court to order a home study on the "questionable" parent and not for the "stable" parent. If the court orders home study for one parent, have your attorney request that the court order a home study at each parent's house. A judicial delay of months could result if later the judge decides a home study is necessary for the second parent.

When the home study is done under ideal conditions, the same person inspects both homes. This study can make a great deal of difference in the outcome of the case. As uncomfortable as this examination may make you feel, it can be the deciding factor in your favor. Take this opportunity to demonstrate the safe, clean, stable, loving, and happy surroundings your child enjoys while with you.

If one professional is going to do both home studies, make sure you schedule your appointment first. If you have made a good impression, the "Positive Halo Effect," again kicks in. It will be difficult for the opposition to change the good impression you have established. If the information human beings are hearing does not correspond with the information they are seeing, they will believe what they see. The home study person will not be impressed with material wealth if the emotional needs of the child are not being met. Conversely, there is no crime in being poor. The only crime is to let your child do without basic material necessities if supplies are available through any source.

Therefore, a welfare parent may be rich in time, ability, and nurturing skills and a better option for custodial control of a child than two working, wealthy parents with a full-time nanny. The professionals assigned by the state to make the home study are interested in the welfare of the child. Evaluators are experienced and not easily fooled by surface appearance and a few new toys.

The evaluator will ask about toys, pets, and established routines allegedly in the home if they are not apparent during the tour and visit. Home study may involve more than one visit to the family. It may also include separate interviews with the parents and siblings. Present your home in its best light. Have family and friends speak about your strengths. Indicate problems in the child's other environment without hysterics.

What Costs are Involved?

The cost of home study will vary from $475 to $1,500 per home and may involve an appointment in the evaluator's office, one or two visits to your home, other places the child regularly spends time, and a written evaluation. If you are self-employed or work in a non-traditional environment, the evaluation may include your place of work. There will be an additional charge for this extended evaluation.

Get Ready for the Home Study

Schedule your home study as soon as you become aware one is required. This will indicate that you are ready, willing and able to comply with whatever is required. It may be several weeks before the professional can fit you into the schedule. If the same person is doing the evaluation on both homes, your positive presentation will make anything negative the opposition says sound hollow. Home study professionals are not constricted, as is your judge, by the "laws of evidence." This is your opportunity to have someone with influence look at everything you feel is important. Evidence you cannot submit to the court, you can offer to the home study person. This is a chance to show someone, "The Book of Your Life".

The Book of Your Life

The book should contain positive information about you. This book can point out your strengths without you looking like you are bragging and any negative information about the opposition (without making you look vindictive).

This suggestion requires advance planning and a great deal of effort. It may be necessary to assemble everything in a three-ring binder with index and subject dividers. To maintain some organization of the information. Make a copy of the book and submit it to the home study person. It will convey your concern and dedication to your child. Many times the home study person will include your binder as part of their report. Include:

1. Photos of your children's rooms or areas.
2. Candid photos of you and your children, extended family and pets.
3. Letters from friends, employers, children's teachers, ministers and family.
4. List of the back-up people and resources you have to take care of your child if the child becomes ill at school or you are delayed by an emergency and are unable to pick your child up.
5. Certificates for parenting classes completed.
6. Completion documents for any rehabilitative classes or programs.
7. Comparative evaluations showing your strengths and stability against the opposition's shortcomings.
8. Chart documented information such as weight loss and gain or school grades or absenteeism. This will insure that facts that seem apparent to you are not inadvertently or purposely misread. People retain 15% of what they hear, 50% of what they see and 85% of what they see and hear. So people are more apt to believe what is seen, not what is heard.
9. Important parts of Depositions or other sworn statements in which the opposition spoke well of you or contradicted itself.
10. Arrest or negative records on the opposition.
11. Written agreements (with their signature, or in their handwriting if possible) that are being used or that the opposition has violated.
12. The last page should be an upbeat, forward looking synopsis of what you want for your child.

Letters from Family and Friends

Ask people who know you and have seen you with your child to write a letter about the relationship they see between you and your child, with comments as to how long they have known you and their opinion of your ability and willingness to care for your child. Included are several examples you may use as guidelines to help your friends and neighbors. It is important to remind the family to highlight your positive points rather than dwell on the other parent's lack of ability. You can speed up this process by weeks if you give people an envelope with your name, address and stamp, ready to send the letter back to you.

This is an evaluation of you and the environment you offer your child. Have copies of any articles, recommendations or certificates of completion that you have received regarding your work with children or classes that would positively impact your child. A letter from your employer as to your reliability, length of employment, and future with the company is very good. Include a letter from your landlord or mortgage company about the length of time you have lived in one place, made payments, been prompt in paying, and as to your stability.

If your supporters need help to draft a letter that lets them say what they feel, offer the following examples to them.

Examples of Letters of Support

from a Friend #1

To Whom It May Concern:

On or about December 15, 1985, after an introduction by a mutual friend and Rebecca's becoming aware that we had no home, Rebecca Long and her daughter Goldie, who was seven years old, offered me and my two small children, ages six and three, a place to stay in the big house on Geneva Way. In the three months that we lived with them, I found the home environment to be filled with warmth and love. Rebecca kept the home in a clean and well-supervised manner.

After moving out of Rebecca's home, I maintained a close relationship with her and had the opportunity to watch Goldie grow into a happy and well-adjusted young lady. Not once during the following years did I ever visit Rebecca's home and find Goldie to be deprived of food, clothing, love or supervision. My children have remained very fond of Rebecca because of the closeness developed during the time they lived with her.

Rebecca's marriage to Randall Long completed the picture and provided Goldie with the father she never had and Rebecca a gentle, loving husband.

My observation of the relationships are that Rebecca and Randall have a stable, loving and sharing marriage. Goldie, although married in April, is truly the "daddy's girl," and I have noticed that she trusts him enough to confide in him concerning her problems, plus comes to him for comforting when she is upset.

I have been able to observe Randall's and Rebecca's interaction with Bobby. I have recently finished school, and Rebecca offered to allow me to use the equipment at Long's warehouse to make a current resume in order to find a job. Sometimes I am in the office five days in any one week, using Long's office as a home base.

I have been able to get acquainted with Bobby. Rebecca's treatment of Bobby reflects the same love and tenderness that she used with Goldie. Rebecca and Bobby exhibit bonding as that of a mother and child.

Randall's love for Bobby is very obvious and shows through in everything he does for the child. Randall is always playing with his son, in addition to feeding, bathing, and changing diapers. Rebecca has made her company a welcome place for Bobby, with a nursery for him next to Randall's office, and a fenced, grassy playground outside with swings and toys. During the course of the day, everyone in the office helps with Bobby. Also, Bobby has the added plus of being played with by the employees and visitors to Long's warehouse.

Sincerely, Susan Peterson

From Son-in-Law #2

September 8, 1992

To Whom it May Concern:

As the son-in-law of Randall and Rebecca Long, and working in Rebecca's company, I see Bobby every day during the week and family gatherings.

My dealings with Amber have been very limited except for about once a week, carrying supplies she has had Randall purchase from our office to her car.

I don't know Amber, and I try not to judge people, but what sticks in my mind about her the most is when one day Amber came to pick up Bobby, and Randall asked if Amber had gotten a telephone as required by the agreement, and she replied sharply, "I cannot afford one, but if you pay for it, I'll have it put in." Amber stormed out of the office with Bobby.

Randall is my wife's stepfather, but you would not know it by watching how they get along as a family. When my wife told me about her parents, she warned me at first of how protective they were of her and her little brother.

At first I was intimidated by the size of this bear of a man. But once I saw how kind and gentle he was with Bobby, I was not intimidated anymore. I have watched Randall bathe and change Bobby's clothes every morning. This is obviously necessary when he is picked up from Amber's house. Bobby is always fully dressed in the office, except during his bath time. Randall feeds and plays with his son all day and is the kind of father I will strive to be.

Rebecca has changed the emphasis of her company to limit her travel to twice a year and removed all responsibility Randall had assumed in past years so he may devote his time to his son. Rebecca could not treat her own child any better and loves Bobby as if he were her own.

They both love Bobby very much, and being an adopted child, I am very aware of how parents and children interact.

I feel that any child that has so much love all around him is truly a lucky one. Sincerely, Ward Cotter

from Mother-in-Law #3

To Whom it May Concern:

I was a primary school teacher for 26 years, and a first grade teacher the last 16 years. Now retired, I continued to substitute until three years ago. I wish to present my own observation of the care given to Bobby by his father, Randall, and Randall's wife, Rebecca, my daughter. I am keenly aware of the influence parents can have on a child's future development and adjustment, especially if it is done with patience, love and positive guidance.

This father maintains a routine of feeding, cleaning and interpersonal activities that could be a standard for all caregivers. After all, this is what helps develop communication skills and emotional stability. Rebecca is very devoted to Bobby and is supportive of Randall. She also expresses her love for Randall's son in word and deed.

They have been playing games with Bobby that parallel his maturation, all of which tend to increase awareness, strength and manual dexterity. Regular contact with family and friends, visits to parks and the zoo, and frequent home get-togethers have all been part of Bobby's environment. Bobby is already being introduced to the joy of reading as Rebecca and Randall read books with him and tell him stories.

Our family supports the efforts of Rebecca and Randall in their effort to care for Bobby and assist him in maintaining contact with everyone who loves him. He may not be a child of our blood, but he is certainly the child of our hearts.

In closing I would like to say that almost everyone comments on how Bobby's face lights up when he looks at and reaches up for his father to pick him up. As a member of the older generation, I find it so heartwarming to see this gentle man being so involved with his son.

Sincerely, Ann Butler (Rebecca's Mother)

from Opposition's Co-worker #4

To Whom It May Concern:

On numerous occasions, winter and summer, I observed Amber leave her four children unsupervised in her car at Rebecca Long's business for a period of 20 minutes or more. The children often spent their time outside the car, playing in an area where semi-trucks were pulling out and backing into the loading docks.

On February 25, 1991, I observed Amber and another co-worker, Chuck, smoking marijuana on the way back from a pick-up the three of us did for Long's office.

Amber talked to me about the arrangement with her boyfriend in jail, saying she was watching his kid till he got out so they could get married and have another kid.

She took his kid and her other three kids to the prison frequently. There was a photo of him in his jail clothes on her desk.

In sharp contrast, I have observed Randall on many occasions that he was unaware of, taking care of Bobby. Randall shows a lot of love and gives top priority to the needs of his son.

Regards, Allen Richards

from Friend #5

To Whom it May Concern:

I have been employed at Pier Restaurant for sixteen years, and I have had the privilege of becoming a requested waitress and friend for Rebecca and Randall Long for ten years.

I have seen the tender, loving care that Randall gives to Bobby. It is so apparent even in a child as young as Bobby.

I also feel that Rebecca and Randall can give Bobby financial stability in his future. But even more important, there is this genuine love between a father and son.

I have also been to Rebecca and Randall's home on several occasions, and the atmosphere is so comfortable. Bobby is a very contented little boy. I have taken my grandchildren with me, and I myself feel very comfortable in their home. No mother could possibly give better care and more affection than what I have seen Rebecca give to Bobby.

Having been in their home, they seem to me like a perfect family unit.
And I, as a mother of two now-grown daughters and grandmother of three, couldn't possibly have given more love and affection than I have seen displayed by this loving couple. I feel that if you knew Randall and Rebecca as I do, you could see that Bobby should be with his father.

Thank you for the opportunity to write on their behalf.

Sincerely, Andrea Johns September 23, 1992

from Employee #6

To Whom It May Concern: Oct. 8, 1992

I was an employee at Rebecca Long's business from March 3, 1991, through September 8, 1992. During that time I got to know Randall and Rebecca quite well --- and Bobby too! I watched the baby and daddy grow together and bond together. When Bobby looks at his daddy, his whole face lights up, and he gets the biggest, happiest grin on his face! You cannot possibly miss the love there is between them. I have never seen a happier, more contented baby than Bobby when he's with his daddy. And bless Rebecca, she loves little Bobby with all her heart. They are so good to him, and they deserve to be his parents. I don't know Amber very well, but what I do know, I don't like her. When she would come to pick up Bobby, she would leave her kids out in the hot car. I think that's awful! She was always much less than polite toward me.

Respectfully yours, Patty Leland

from Employer #7

To Whom It May Concern: Oct. 5, 1992

I was Randall Long's team leader for three years with All American Trucking. He was one of the best drivers I supervised. His dependability and conscientious attention to policy and service were a credit to our company.

Randall and Rebecca drove the lower forty-eight States as a Double Operator Team for our New Products Division and earned Safe Driver Team Award for no accidents, incidents or loss of cargo for seven consecutive months.

We were sorry to lose him to the disability caused in the truck accident he had while working with our company. Given the opportunity, we as a company and I as a supervisor would welcome him back. He holds our highest regard.

Sincerely, Albert Trelli, All American Trucking

from Caregiver #8

To Whom It May Concern,

Before Julie Hall started taking care of the children, Kyle Hall would drop the children off and pick them up without letting me know what kind of night or weekend the children had or asking how they had done during the day. Kyle didn't seem to have any plan for alternate care for the children if they were too sick to come to or stay at day care. On several occasions it became evident that Kyle had given the children large doses of children's medication so they would appear well enough to come to day care. The children would appear sleepy until the medication wore off and then fever, coughing and runny noses would reappear. When called to pick the children up because of illness he would take as much as three hours to arrive. Kyle would always have excuses for not paying the bill on time and often was late arriving to pick the children up at the end of the day.

Julie is conscientious about letting us know anything about the children that may affect their attitude or behavior for the day. She always asks how each one did each day and addresses any information that requires attention. Julie has a back-up day care and arrives within twenty minutes if the children require non-scheduled pick up for any reason. Her bill is paid on time and the children seem well adjusted to the change in residence and parental custodianship.

Kindest regards, Lucinda Moran Director

from Teacher #9

To whom it may concern,

I have been asked by the father of Geralyn Goode to comment on her progress during the last two semesters of this school year. I believe I was asked to offer my opinion because I had Jerry Goode in my class last year and Geralyn this year. The comments I am about to make are not the opinion of the Salines Elementary School or any other persons, they are my opinion and responsibility alone.

In the last two semesters of this year Geralyn's attitude, behavior, demeanor, attendance and grades have improved greatly. She seems happy and rested when she arrives at school. Her homework is completed and her clothes are clean and pressed. She has not been tardy and has not missed any school days. Geralyn has always been a dear child who was eager to please and easy to learn. I have visited with Jerry twice in the last thirty days when he stopped by my classroom. His appearance was markedly improved since he spent last year in my class.

His attitude was very positive as he spoke about all the activities he and his dad were doing together. Jerry is very bright and needs the intense attention he is getting from his father. Both children have all the basic qualities and abilities to achieve good things in their lives, but they both need the solid support and encouragement they appear to be getting since moving to their father's home.

You may feel free to contact me through the school if you have any questions.

Sincerely, Maria Woods

Letters of Love

One of the great benefits of this exercise is reading the wonderful things your family, friends and supporters have written about you. Keep copies of the ones that mean the most to you with you at all times. When you are experiencing a bad day, read your fan mail.

Letter to Document Order Violation

September 20, 1996
In The Interest of Bobby Long
Judge Phillip Dewarte,

As a friend of the court I am compelled to relay some information to the court.

When Bobby returned from the ten day visitation with his mother in August he requested a visit with me and his father made an appointment.

During play therapy Bobby stated, "Some people call me butt-head."

I asked him how he felt about being called that name and he responded, "its not nice."

I asked him who called him the name and he said "My brother Mike."

I inquired as to whether it happened a long time ago and Bobby responded, "No, he said that to me when I saw him on my visit to my Nother Mommie. We went to the Boy's Ranch to pick him up an he started calling me that in the back seat."

In court I had expressed dire concerns about the general supervision of Bobby and specifically exposure to his older brother Jerome Smith. I was greatly relieved when you specifically enjoined Amber Smith from allowing any contact including Jerome's weekends and the eight-hour home visit times.

I am alarmed that within days of your clear directive to Amber Smith that she violated the court's instructions with apparent disregard for Bobby's well-being.
I am at your service if you have any questions.
Relinda Stewart
CC
Attorney John Green for Amber Smith
Attorney Gary Country for Randall Long

Help from Hell

There are many advantages of dealing fairly with people once an altercation has been resolved. Win, lose or draw, you may have to interact with this person again. An example you will see often is when a politician graciously concedes an election to the opposition, pledging to assist the winner and urging supporters to do the same. It is common to fear demons from our past.

In this example, Randall would not have considered contacting Gina after a hard divorce twenty years ago. Randall did not, Amber did, and these were the results. Transcript Of Telephone Deposition
Questions by Catharine Law Answers by Gina Douglas (former wife of Randall Long)

CL: Catharine Law (Randall's Attorney): (Dialing)

GD: Gina Douglas (Randall's First Wife): Hello.

CL: This is Catharine Law, may I speak to Gina Douglas?

GD: This is Gina.

CL: I called to arrange the telephone

deposition we discussed yesterday. It is all right with you if I tape this and have it transcribed?

GD: Yes, that would be fine, I would like a copy of it when your secretary gets it done.

CL: Thank you, I would appreciate that. Okay, we spoke briefly yesterday afternoon.

GD: Yes, we did.

CL: The reason that we spoke was that you called me. Why did you call?

GD: When I arrived home at two yesterday afternoon there was a dirty van blocking my driveway so I parked on the street. A man and a woman who looked like they were going door to door asking for newspapers and tin cans were standing at my front door talking to my husband. As I got to the door I handed my baby daughter and a package to my husband.

The woman said her name was Amber and that she was having problems with my ex-husband Randall. Amber never introduced the rough looking man with her. She began to ask very personal questions about my life and relationship with Randall while straining to see over my shoulder to look into my home. Amber said she had been raped by Randall two years ago. She wanted to know if my boys knew they had a baby brother as a result of their father's assault. I told her they did not know about the child even if the accusation was true. She became hysterical and irate with me because my boys didn't know and she insisted they had a right to see the child and know what their father had done to her.

I tried to explain to her that I have a very private, sheltered life and don't want my children to meet the child. It was fortunate they weren't home.

She stated that she was entitled to a large cash settlement and that my boys were entitled to some also. Amber said her father-in-law Elmer Jones used to be in law enforcement as a prison guard, and he was trying to have Randall arrested today when he landed in Seattle to bring the child to Amber for visitation.

She and Elmer arranged to have him arrested for my back child support. I told her that had been cleared up years ago.

I said "Look I can't help you. I have nothing to do with this. I haven't seen Randall in 15 years. I really don't want to get involved. I have nothing to say to you. Will you please go away." Amber then began a story about Randall, saying that she loved Randall and thought they could have had a good life together if it weren't for Rebecca. Then she added a story about a molestation then back to a rape. I told her I could not help her and kept asking her to go away. Amber refused to leave my door.

I was very upset that she was accusing my ex-husband of things I was not involved in and didn't want to hear. I wanted to know how she came to my residence when she had no right to invade my privacy. So I asked, "How did you get my address?" Amber did not answer my question, but started to rehash the entire diatribe. I fear this woman is going to continually pursue me now because she knows where to find me.

CL: You were divorced from Randall Long, sixteen years ago. Before you were divorced, did he have anything to do with your kids?

GD: There were irreconcilable differences, but it had nothing to do with the children. He was a very good father to them. Very supportive, in fact, I did not work. Unfortunately, Randall worked long hours, but when he did come home we always did family activities with the boys.

We went fishing, camping and we played ball with them. He brought them lots of toys and put a big pool in the backyard. He was a very caring, giving father even cooking dinner for us once in a while. Randall changed diapers and did a lot of things that at that time, sixteen years ago, I think that other men we knew would not even consider doing.

CL: After the divorce, was there any dispute about his contact with the boys?

GD: The boys were so torn because of the divorce, they didn't understand. I moved to Washington. Randall wanted to see the boys, but it wasn't possible for either of us to transport three children.

Then I remarried, and the boys got busy with summertime activities. Randall was always there for the boys. In fact in the last sixteen years if I needed something he has always been there. If they needed clothes, he sent money or gift certificates. When my second husband passed away, I called Randall, and he and his present wife Rebecca were there for me. We live our own separate lives, but if there is an emergency we know how to contact each other.

CL: When Amber showed up on your doorstep, did you have prior indication that someone was going to come visit with you?

GD: No. And, I felt very violated, let alone saying all these awful things.

My current husband felt assaulted and fears that Amber will come back and contact my children with this whole spew. We think she will continue to hound us.

CL: Was she talking like a calm person? Tell me how she was delivering the message.

GD: She was irate, bitter, and vile as far as the denouncement about Randall. Never once did she mention this child's welfare, that she was looking out for the child, or that she wanted to nurture or protect him. She wanted some dirt on Randall so she could pin him against the wall. She wanted me to say he was a bad man, a horrible father and wouldn't support his children.

CL: Have you had any other incidents that brought Randall into your present life?

GD: I had a strange call from the Washington State District Attorney's office because some ludicrous accusations were made on my behalf against Randall. Until now I didn't know why I got the call. Evidently, Amber or this father-in-law of hers called the D. A.'s office and tried to raise a stink.

CL: Had you been contacted by Amber's attorney?

GD: Yes. I have a letter dated December 7th. It reads, "Dear Mrs. Douglas, I represent Mrs. Amber Jones in a custody procedure filed by Randall Long for the custody of their child. I understand from Amber that you are Mr. Long's former wife. It would be very helpful to us if you would telephone collect to discuss Mr. Long's relationship with your children.

We will not be revealing your whereabouts to him. Thank you for your cooperation. Ms. Faith Beli, Esq."

The bottom of the letter indicates a copy was sent to Amber, so I guess that's how she got my address. I didn't respond because I didn't have anything that would help her case. But I have had phone conversations with Randall and Rebecca. His wife is very nice very caring and giving person also. Rebecca has always been sympathetic to me and understanding.

Rebecca has gone out of her way when she wasn't obligated to make sure they've helped me out whenever I've called.

CL: Did Randall know at that point where you were living?

GD: Yes, he's always known. In case of emergency, we could contact each other.

CL: Did Amber say anything else about the child?

GD: No. She said the company Rebecca owns makes millions and I was entitled to this money.

I explained that Rebecca's company didn't have anything to do with me. I am a typical middle class person, and I feel sorry for people who have hard times. Amber looked as if she only has hard times, but she didn't look or sound like a kind, caring mother. I was wondering where the other three children were, since she and this man were standing at my front door screeching at me.

CL: In your experience with Randall, what kind of man was he?

GD: In my opinion I don't think Randall has done anything to this woman. I find this pretty far fetched as I've know him for twenty-one years. When I met Randall, I had a small child, and Randall accepted him as his own flesh and blood. When the other two children were born, Randall never showed any partialities to the others. Randall always made sure we had a very nice home. We had a well-rounded, very nurturing home and the boys just didn't run rampant in the neighborhood. He always looked out for the welfare of the children as well as myself. For the five years we were married, I felt that he was a very gracious, giving man.

CL: Ok, why did you call me?

GD: I contacted you to make it clear I do not want Amber or that man coming to my home again. She is living in Star, Washington, which is close to my home. I don't want her trying to badger me into anything. I do not want her accosting my children. I need to put a stop to this, because my current husband and I are afraid that Amber is going to come back, and one of my children is going to answer the door, and she is going to go into this rage again about their father, and it is going to do traumatic harm to them. If this woman does come again I will call the police and get a restraining order.

I would advise the Court of Arizona to pay attention to Amber's whereabouts because she indicated to me that she will do whatever it takes to

keep that child from Randall and Canada is very close to here. I think she will continue to make up more ludicrous statements, which I will not back up, and I don't want to be involved in saying vile things about a man that was never vile towards me or his children. As you are Randall's attorney, I felt you were the right person to contact. I feel after meeting Amber, that if anyone deserves that baby or can provide an adequate home with compassion and love, I feel that the child is a lot better off with Randall and Rebecca than Amber.
I would like you to contact the other attorney and let her know what I have said.

CL: Thank you very much for your call. Do you have any objection to me using the tape we're making at the present to give to Conciliation Services or the Court?

GD: I have no objection to that. And he can contact me, if he wishes to do so.

What are they Looking for?

The evaluator will be looking at the total environment surrounding the children including support from the extended family. The family's connection to community as well as the micro environment of the home will be noted.

Some of the specific observations and questions will be:

Does the child have a room of his or her own or share a room with other children of the same or the opposite sex? Is there enough room for privacy and a designated place to put the child's own things, allowing for a sense of space? What methods are used when handling the children in situations, happy or stressful, while the evaluator is in the home? Have age appropriate safety measures been taken? Such as safety latches on drawers and cabinets. Locks on gates leading to swimming pools, lakes, rivers, streams, roads and large or dangerous animals.

Have cleaning supplies, automotive liquids, tools, prescription drugs and medicines been moved out of reach? Are sports, fishing and hunting equipment, including guns and ammunition, locked away? Are swimming pools, spas and hot tubs fenced and locked? Are the children an incorporated part of the family and home?

- Do family members deal with each other in a comfortable manner?
- Do the children, if maturity permits, have the freedom to use the telephone to make calls to or receive calls from the other parent?
- Are there adequate supplies of diapers, formula, milk, food, toys, books, weather-appropriate clothing, vitamins, and basic medications appropriate for the children's age and personal development on hand?
- Is there an atmosphere of respect and affection in the home?
- Is the children's presence represented in the home with photos on display or pictures and art work made by them?
- Is there access to a safe, supervised, outside, play area with developmental opportunities?
- Are the children handled in a consistent manner in regard to attention, affection and discipline?
- Are there arrangements for alternative inside play areas?
- Is family behavior consistent? Do the members fit together and function like a family?
- Is there opportunity for the parent to take a "Time Out" from the children, while leaving them with a responsible, caring adult?
- Interviews with neighbors and people who have visited the home describing the normal living conditions in your home would be helpful. This will allow you to contradict any unfavorable statements in the social worker's report.

Evaluating the Evaluation

Evaluate every interview you have. Look for your strong and weak points. When you and your attorney have an opportunity to review the recommendation, rate it. Use the example in this chapter. If you are happy with the recommendation, enjoy the win. Keep up the good work.

If you are dissatisfied with statements or conclusions, you have an opportunity to disprove or change things to which you object. Make a bad report work for you by identifying the things or actions that require change. This gives you an opportunity to change your appearance, behavior and attitude. Submit documentation to challenge incorrect information. Institute and document systems to change those things the report identified as negative activities and behaviors.

Because everything with the courts takes time,

any and all efforts to change will defuse the negative impact of the "old" report. As an example, start parenting classes, establish new positive acquaintances, or request regular substance testing.

Child's Hospital Visit List

Tyler Allen Tree's Hospital List for Six Months of 1999			
Date	**Admitted**	**Hospital**	**Complaint**
1/1/99	no	County General ER	Burn on hand from fireworks
1/5/99	no	County General ER	Fell off trike, black eye, skinned forehead, nose and chin
1/23/99	no	Saint Joseph's ER	Frostbite on ears and fingers.
2/11/99	no	Saint Joseph's ER	Drank dish soap from under kitchen sink
2/23/99	no	Glendale Baptist ER	Fell off second floor outside steps. Bruises and broken arm.
2/25/99	yes	Samaritan Health ER	Ate entire bottle of baby aspirin.
3/9/99	yes	Saint Joseph's ER	Throwing up, cause unknown.
3/28/99	no	County General ER	Burned hand on stove.
4/2/99	yes	Children's HR	Ate cigarette butts from ash tray.
4/25/99	yes	Baptist Hospital ER	Trouble breathing, keeping down food.
5/5/99	yes	Mid-Town ER Clinic	Ate ant killer granules.

Amber's Homes Since Bobby's Birth				
Date	Owner	Addresses	Rooms	Occupants
10/17/91	Amber	105 Alder Phoenix., AZ	3Br 1Ba	2-A 2-B 4-C (8)
05/03/92	Amber & Mike	9507 Weldon, Phoenix., AZ	3Br 1Ba	2-A 1-B 3-C (6)
07/04/92	Mike's Mom	42 Tee Ln., Nola, WA	3Br 1Ba Trailer	4-A 1-B 3-C (8)
07/10/92	Sister's HUD	1207 21st. St. Phoenix., AZ	3Br 1Ba Apt	3-A 2-B 1-C (6)
01/01/93	James' Mom	4448 Glenn Drive, Glndl., AZ	1 Room 1Ba	3-A 1-B (4)
01/15/93	Amber & Mike	5110 N. 27th Ave, Phx., AZ	3Br 1Ba Apt.	2-A 1-B (3)
02/05/93	Mike's Mom	42 Tee Ln., Nola, WA	3Br 1Ba Trailer	4-A 1-B 3-C (8)
03/19/93	Amber & Mike	168 Tame Street, Star, WA	3Br 1Ba Apt.	2-A 1-B 3-C (6)
08/07/93	Amber & James	863 Normal Star, WA	3Br 1Ba Apt.	2-A 1-B 3-C (6)

A- Adults C-Children B-Babies ( )-Total People

My wife and I have lived in the same beautiful, five-bedroom home on two acres in which Bobby has his own room. I have paid my lease of $1,325.00 a month for four years. Attached to this document is a letter of recommendation from Carol Beck the woman who owns my home.

In Chapter 12: Psychologists, there is a list of over 30 things that can be documented and charted. There will be others you can think of since behavior or activity creates a pattern that can be charted. One unexpected benefit of charting is that an activity or behavior that seemed bizarre may make more sense once you see the diagram assembled, defusing any anguish you felt.

Data Submitted to Identify Concerns

During the investigation the home study person may ask if you have any concerns as to the welfare of your children when with the other parent. Verbalization is very important at this point. State your points simply in writing.
Offer documentation in the form of photos, arrest records, or court papers to validate your worries of abuse, problems with the law, or anything else you feel is important. You should have the capacity to present all documentation in two forms. One for The Book of Your Life, and the other as a poster size exhibit for court. Spread sheets offer the most difficult exhibit with which to deliver your message. Photos, maps, graphs and charts offer a clearer and faster vehicle to get your point across.

Frequent Moving

An example of what you might say, "I am concerned about the instability of my son Bobby's environment when he is with his mother, Amber. As an example, this is a list of Amber's addresses since Bobby was born (October 17, 1991 - August 17, 1993) two years ago.

These addresses are listed on legal documents filed with the court. Photos of each house are attached to this letter."

Home Study Example, Report #1

Shawn Jameson Counselor/Mediator
3433 East Squaw Peak, Phoenix, AZ
Mr. Solomon, Conciliation Court June 2, 1993

On 4/29/93 I made a home visit to Randall and Rebecca Long's home, and on 5/17/93 I made a visit to their place of business.

Home Evaluation. Their home is located one block north of Camelview Road and 82nd Street. The development is Indian Trail Farms, and each lot contains two acres.

The home was very clean, nicely furnished, and very obviously a child lived there. The house had five bedrooms, three of which are used to house visiting family members and clients of the business who need overnight accommodations periodically. They have two dogs, several chickens and ducks, seven sheep, a cow and two horses. The house has been child-proofed and presents a safe environment for Bobby. Bobby's room is appropriately decorated, and he has many toys, most of them educational.

Randall and Bobby were present at the time of the visit, and I was impressed by the way Randall handled Bobby. Bobby was testing Randall by repeating some unacceptable behaviors and Randall quietly and firmly told him no, and the behavior stopped. There was an affectionate give and take between them.

Business Evaluation. The family business does mostly warehousing and is one block east of Center Street and four blocks south of Main Street. The entire area is filled with business and warehouses because of the railroad access.

The baby's playroom/bedroom is next to Randall's office and can be seen from Randall's desk. The business office is very large, and Bobby has a lot of space to play in.

The area of the warehouse with storage is off base to Bobby unless accompanied by an adult. It is not easily accessible, and Bobby could not possibly gain entry without help.

Behind the warehouse is a 20' X 40' fenced-in grassy play yard with a jungle gym, slides and toys. A picnic table and chairs are available for adults and children to sit and relax or eat. The office is safe for Bobby and has a sleeping, play, and eating area for him. Both the house and place of business have been professionally child-proofed and cater to Bobby's care, well-being, and comfort. I saw nothing that would indicate that Bobby is not being well taken care of. Sincerely yours,

Shawn Jamison, M.A. **End of Report.**

Comparing Apples to Oranges

The validity of home studies can vary because of the professional standards of the community, training of the evaluator, personal bias of the evaluator and influence the subject of the evaluation has on the evaluator.

Two professionals who were acquainted and were comfortable with competency of the other preformed home studies #1 and #2 in this chapter within 30 days and 1395 miles of each other. Both studies meet the professional guidelines. The problem of comparing the evaluations becomes very difficult due in part to the form and style used by each evaluator. One evaluator was extremely compassionate and the other professionally clinical.

To eliminate some the problem it is important to make sure one professional performs the home study on both residences. This may entail additional costs that could be substantial.

Condition of Child Report Form #1

Date: _*August 2, 1997*___ Time: *4:00pm* ___

I was asked to accompany ___*Linda Carter*___ as:

[ ] a Sheriff/Police Officer [x] a private person as an observer *Linda's Sister*

[ ] a medical or psychological observer [ ] we held documentation to allow our action

Our purpose was to *see the appearance of her child and the house where the child lives with her father* .

Location: __*1680 N. Highland*____ Child's name __*Debbie*__________________ The child was:

[ ] Alone [X] Dirty [ ] Ill [ ] Hurt [ ] Not there [ ] Other

Synopsis if necessary? *We arrived at 3:30 and the baby-sitter let us in saying she was living there now to take care of the baby.*

Debbie was sitting on the living room floor her sleepers, which had stains of food on the front and the knees and tops of the feet were very dirty from crawling on the floor in the house. Debbie had green mucus coming out of her nose and crusted on her cheeks and chin. Her diaper was soiled and soaked. Linda asked for a diaper and clothes for Debbie.

There were old french fries, cigarettes and an ashtray with cigarette butts in it on a coffee table Debbie can pull herself up to. Baby bottles with orange juice, milk and some empty were scattered around the house. Some looked several days old.

I took a photo of Debbie on the floor and put the camera away while the baby-sitter was out of the room. The baby-sitter dug through a pile of clothes in the bedroom on the floor and found a jumper, but no blouse, sox or shoes.

Debbie has a severe diaper rash she did not have when I was there five days ago and her father picked her up.

My Name:__ *Donna Nelson-Carter*_ Contact Information: _*Home 555-1212*__*Work 555-1313*_

Collateral Contact List

Please contact the people I have on this list for information that is important to your study of the parenting issues that will determine custody of my children. You may contact me at 555-6666 Gene Pepper.

Person Contact Information Knowledge
Mark Bookman Emerson School Guidance counselor for both boys. Has seen marks where she hit them
Jill Robinson Faith Methodist Church Woman who calls me when my ex-wife forgets to pick the boys up
Trudy & Sal Sackowitz 555-2222 Neighbors for 15 years. Where the boys go when they can't find mom
Kit Green 555-5555 Sitter who has had the boys for three nights at a time without word from their mother.

Condition of Child Report Form #2

Date: __*April 11, 1997*___ Time: __*2:30pm*___

I was asked to accompany ___*Elizabeth Summer*___ as:

[ ] a Sheriff/Police Officer [ ] a private person as an observer

[x] a medical or psychological observer [ ] we held documentation to allow our action

Our purpose was to *Wait for Elizabeth's x-husband to pick the children up for this weekend visitation* _ *at*

Location: _ *902 East Wiletta Street* ________________________

Child(ren)'s name(s) __*Eddie and Patty's*__________________ The child(ren) were:

[ ] Alone [ ] Dirty [ ] Ill [ ] Hurt [ ] Not there [ ] Other

Synopsis if necessary? *Elizabeth has been accused of sending the children dirty, un-fed and with ragged clothes. I have been here for every pick up and drop off of the children for six months. The children are always rested, fed and well clothed for the weather. Elizabeth makes an effort to include in their overnight bags things purchased for them by their father. Mike has never asked who I am or why I am always there for the exchange, but he has seen me each time. The children come and go in approximately the same condition from each of the parents.*

My Name:___*Carol Dodlite R.N.*___ Contact Information: __*H 555-1212*__ *W 555-3131*______

Home Study Example, Report #2

Helen Hodge, MS Counselor/Mediator
9562 24th Place, New Fair, Washington

Referred by: Mr. Solomon, MSW, Conciliation Court

A home evaluation was conducted on 5/10/93 at Amber Jones' residence.

Present were Amber Jones, her children Lucy, age 14, Byron, age 12, Jerome, age 10, and Bobby, age 18 months. Also present were Mike Jones's Parents, Cathy Jones, age 65 and Local Jones, age 66. Due to Mike Smith's work schedule, he was interviewed prior to the home visit. Amber Jones and Byron were interviewed again at Amber's request on May 19, 1993. James Miller, Amber's first husband, was interviewed on May 26, 1993.

Home Visit:

Amber and the children reside in a three-bedroom, one bath duplex on a cul-de-sac in a newer neighborhood in Star, Washington. Star is a small farming community 12 miles from Seattle.

There appeared to be numerous children in the neighborhood. Both Lucy and Byron had friends come to visit while the interview was being conducted. The home was clean and adequately furnished. Lucy had a room of her own, and the three boys shared another bedroom. Bobby had his own bed tucked between the older boys' beds.

Amber recounted the following information to supplement the Arizona evaluation report of January 14, 1993. According to Amber, the present conflict came about because a secretary in the Arizona court told her that nothing had been filed in the court records that prevented her from moving with Bobby from Arizona to Washington.

With that understanding, Amber said she made arrangements to move on May 18, 1992. She took a letter to the court stating she married Mike Jones April 2, 1992, and planned to move to Washington in June 1992.

Amber stated that on April 4, 1992, she had signed under duress a mediated order agreeing to the previous parenting agreement. Amber stated at the time of the signing, Randall had his wife, Rebecca, take Bobby to a secret place and told Amber that Bobby would not be returned until she signed the agreement.

Amber said she signed under those conditions because she planned to remain in Arizona anyway. It was only later that she and Mike decided to move to Washington to get the children away from the high crime area and to provide a better environment for them.

Amber admits having little recollection of Bobby's conception. She stated that Rebecca took her out drinking and that since she was not sober enough to drive, slept on a bed at Randall and Rebecca's home. Amber said Rebecca told her later that Amber had tried to fend off Randall's sexual advances. But Amber is unclear about what happened that night.

In regard to the questions posed by Randall about Amber's decision-making and choice of male companions, Amber states;

A. She has had three primary relationships, Mike Jones, James Miller, and Thomas "TomTom" Ester. Amber states TomTom, who rides a motorcycle, didn't start drinking excessively until his mother died. When he did, Amber said, she ended the relationship within a 3-4 week period of time.

B. Initially Amber denied any problems in the relationship with Mike. However, Amber requested a second interview.

C. At the second interview, Amber stated she was leaving John because of his continuing physical abuse of Byron and his demeaning and demanding manner with her. She said she originally was afraid to say she was leaving him as he had her convinced that if the court knew, she would lose Bobby.

D. After talking to the Children's Services worker, she realized she needed to be honest and report fully on what had happened.

E. Amber admits making a "stupid mistake" in being involved with attempted transportation of marijuana balloons to Wayne Brier in the prison. She states that it was her female companion's idea and that it was the companion's balloons that were found. Amber was fined $358 and placed on three years of summary probation.

F. Amber said that she did live in the trailer occupied by James Miller, but that while she was there, James was in jail for non-payment of child support.

G. She said that when he got out she moved into an apartment. James has reactivated his relationship with their children. Amber states, "James is no longer using drugs."

H. Regarding the allegation that she returned Bobby in "dirty or grubby clothes," Amber said those were the clothes Randall had given her for Bobby to wear when she returned him to Randall's home.

I. Amber denied ever leaving her older children without a caregiver when she was away from home with the Longs. She said her mother and a female friend supervised the children when she wasn't available.

J. She believes the report of a cockroach in the diaper bag was blown out of proportion. She said the roach was more likely to have gotten in the bag at the warehouse where she stated there are mice and roaches. She contends her sister's apartment did not have roaches.

K. Amber states that she was the primary parent for Bobby for the first three months of his life as she was breast feeding him. She said Randall tried to take Bobby and get her to tell people she was the surrogate mother. She states Randall offered her a car and $100 per month during the pregnancy.

L. According to Amber, she returned to work when Bobby was four months old. She worked from 6 am to 2:30 p.m. and attended school 2 nights a week, 4 hours a night. She was attending school to improve her ability to provide for the children. She said Randall made it look like he had custody when he was really just watching Bobby while she worked and went to school.

Concerns:

Amber voiced the following concerns about Randall and Rebecca:

1. Randall has refused Amber access to Bobby. He denied her the scheduled Christmas visitation, hid Bobby and threatened to not return him unless Amber signed the mediated agreement.

2. Randall is working for Rebecca while receiving Social Security disability benefits, which she believes is illegal. Amber states, "Randall is under investigation presently by Social Security Administration."

3. Randall takes Bobby to the warehouse when he is there, thus exposing Bobby to hazardous

materials and situations. Amber contends Randall was to stay home when he had Bobby in his care.

4. Randall has refused to give Amber Bobby's medication. More recently Randall repeated Bobby's shots after Amber had shown him paperwork from the county health department stating she had provided the shots.

5. Randall's residence doesn't have a fence around the pool, making it a potential hazard.

6. Randall makes harassing telephone calls to Amber on a daily basis, making accusations about her parenting.

7. Rebecca harasses Amber when she returns Bobby.

Additional Information:

Amber and Mike Jones initially did not reveal the physical abuse allegations pending against Mike Jones. When I asked Amber about those allegations at the home visit, she was surprised I knew about them and stated there had been "a little scuffle" between Mike and Byron when Byron back talked her. She said Mike slapped Byron across the mouth and Byron fell, bruising his back. Later, at her request, she met with me to describe Mike hitting Byron across the mouth and encouraging Byron to hit him so Mike could "throw him through the wall." Byron had a cut lip and bruises when he went to school three days later. The school counselor reported the incident to the Children's Services Division.

Mike was told to remain out of the home, and a hearing will be scheduled for May 19, 1993. According to Amber, Mike will be proceeding to trial on the matter.

Amber said she finalized her decision to leave Mike that night because Mike wanted to send Byron to live with James in Arizona. She said she did not want to send Byron away and resented Mike's demanding and abusive ways.

Interviews:

Mike Jones

Mike stated to this interviewer that Amber would have lost custody if he had not talked to the judge. He said it was after he talked to the judge that the home study was ordered. Mike Jones is no longer in the family home, and Amber believes her marriage to him may be invalid as she believes he is still married to a previous wife.

Amber Jones

Amber is presently working at an ice cream store. She hopes to be able to quit work and remain home with Bobby and the children. She is presently living with James Miller, her first husband and the father of the three oldest children. Amber stated that James moved to Washington after Byron called him and told him about the incident with Mike. They have been together since that time and plan to remarry if the relationship continues as it is now.

If Amber is awarded custody, she proposes that Randall have Bobby for six weeks in the summer, alternate Thanksgiving and Christmas vacations, with additional times arranged when Randall is in Washington. She was unable to think about Randall having custody and what visitation she would want.

Later she contacted me and said, "If Randall got custody I will move back to Arizona." Amber hoped she wouldn't have to do so since she was sure Washington state was a better environment for the older children and would provide a better environment for Bobby in the future.

James Miller

James Miller was interviewed after this evaluator became aware of the above information. James confirmed he moved to Washington after Byron told him about Mike hitting him. He had been telephoning the children since Amber and he began talking in Arizona.

James responded to questions about his being in jail. He said he has been picked up three times and held briefly for non-payment of child support, but that when the state checks his record they find he has paid and let him out. The only other legal difficulty he had was when his car was repossessed for non-payment. James said he was stopped for a faulty taillight.

The officer found the owner's drugs in the car. James said he was cited for that, but that the drugs weren't his. He is willing to be tested for drugs at any time.

James is presently working as a mechanic at a car dealership. He learned that trade during his rehabilitation from a motorcycle wreck. He would like to remain in Washington and buy a house. He wants to remarry Amber. He believes Bobby should be with his brothers and sister.

He thinks Randall should have a relationship with Bobby but was not certain how that should be structured.

The Children

The children were interviewed separately at the residence. At the time they spoke positively about Mike Jones.

When I re-interviewed Byron, he gave me a more detailed accounting that matched the information I had from the Children Services Division of the physical abuse incident by Mike.

All of the children were very affectionate and caring with Bobby. Bobby went to each of the children while I was in the home. Lucy took Bobby out to play. Byron sat with Bobby while he drank a bottle.

Jerome let him play with a game and appropriately took away the small pieces. Each of the children told me they would like to have their brother live with them. Lucy expressed concern that Bobby seemed confused the first few days when he returned from Arizona.

Children's Services Division

Children's Services Division became involved when the school counselor reported the alleged abuse. CSD interviewed Mike, Amber and Byron. Mike was ordered out of the home and not to have contact until after the hearing.

When Amber originally spoke to the CSD worker, Amber told the caseworker she was leaving Mike because of the physical abuse of Byron. Amber, James and the children have started family counseling through CSD. The family therapist has had two sessions with them. The therapy is to be ongoing. Amber has also been referred for parenting classes. She is actively following through on making those arrangements according to the CSD caseworker.

Conclusion

There is no question that Amber and the children have had a difficult lifestyle. Amber believes that she will be able to start fresh in Washington. She states the children are doing better in school, have nicer friends, and the support of the school staff. Byron is receiving individual counseling, Jerome is receiving specialized help, and Lucy is doing well. Amber believes Bobby will also benefit in this atmosphere.

Amber states she and James will continue spending time together and if the relationship continues positively, they will remarry. She states that given what happened with Mike, she wants to wait a while before she remarries.

Having interviewed only Amber and her family, I can only make observations rather than recommendations as to the custody of Bobby. Those observations are:

Amber remarried Mike after being together for approximately one month. Amber is planning on eventually remarrying James. They reportedly began their relationship after Mike hit Byron at the beginning of April. According to Amber, they began talking when James helped her in Arizona.

Amber did not initially tell me about the physical abuse charge against Mike, her plans to leave him, or that James had moved to Washington. However, Amber did voluntarily contact me later to set the record straight. The rental house Amber resides in provides adequate housing for the family. While Bobby would be sharing a bedroom with his brothers, there is sufficient room and he does have his own bed.

Bobby relates well to each of his brothers and sister. They appear to be very affectionate and appropriate with him.

With the ongoing friction between the parents, there appears to be some question if Bobby would become further enmeshed in his parents' battle if his parents have more frequent contact with each other. I believe it is possible that with the support of the schools and CSD, Amber may be able to make the fresh start she envisions. If she is able to maintain the present residence and not have to move the children, it appears to be the beginning of a stable environment. Whether the relationship with James will continue or be healthy is unknown. Certainly both James and Amber seem convinced it will. But a few months ago Amber was saying the same about the relationship with Mike. James is working as a mechanic and would be able to provide for the family. The state of Washington has a solid mental health network that Amber has already accessed and that can provide a safety net for this family.

Helen Hodge, MS End of Report

Eliminate the Trash

You will feel many emotions when you review the home study of the other parent. While observations of the opposition's habitat and conclusions of the professional may be helpful to your case you, may feel embarrassed and incensed by accusations and statements made by other people interviewed.

Often the evaluator will include in the final document comments made by persons interviewed in the Home Study.

Home Study and Social Studies are subject to rules of evidence in most states. Therefore, hearsay facts "need not be admissible in evidence". Request the removal of all hearsay from the Home Study before it is read into or accepted as evidence.

Flaws in the Process

Even with the additional information the home study may offer the court, there are some major problems with the Home Study process. As you recognize these shortcomings, you may be able to lessen their negative impact on your case. The professionals who do home studies see so many really bad environments, that they may not note shortcomings in the opposition's house. Evaluators that are desensitized to conditions you may find very upsetting at the children's other home.

Also, because an appointment for home study is made in advance, the environment can be altered for a short period of time to make a more favorable impression. Don't make yourself crazy worrying about the opposition taking this opportunity to create an "ideal home picture" for the evaluator. The opposition, in all probability, will not know how. Although it is ideal for one professional to do the study on both homes, the court often assigns a different evaluator to each home because of distance or time restraints. The use of more than one evaluator effectively reduce the court's ability to compare the two environments. It also limits your ability to derive maximum benefits from the evaluations. Since the evaluations come from two professionals (who may have any number of biases), using dissimilar methods for information gathering and reporting, you could end up with finished products that defy comparison on any level. One way to circumvent this obstacle is to request from the court the names of several outside professionals that might be hired to complete evaluations on both residences. Another option is to scan previous cases adjudicated by this judge and find a professional whom the judge previously appointed and apparently trusted. This strategy is indicated if the judge states (or is able to research) that any previous decisions that were based in any part on this professional's assessment. Some judges order parental evaluations and home studies by court-appointed professionals and then ignore the recommendations once submitted. Your attorney can respectfully request a reason for this type of decision on the part of the judge. Unless evidence has been submitted that indicates the evaluations are not valid, a judge ignoring the data may be exposing the decision to the process of Appeal.

The Second Home Study

Initially you may be angry at what the report says about you. It may be very difficult for you to accept the statements and conclusions. The report and its conclusions carry a great deal of weight with the court so you must decide how to handle it.

Your options really only include loud protestations and insistence on how you have been misrepresented and defamed or giving up or fixing what the professional feels is dysfunctional.

Read the evaluation to identify the stated shortcomings and determine what action you can take to change the conclusions. Once you have made the changes and attended the classes the home study recommended, request a second home study. Attempt to get the professional who did the original evaluation to reevaluate your home. The additional expense of the second home study can go a long way to demonstrate to the court your desire to be the best possible parent you can be and provide a positive healthy home for your children.

Evaluating the Home Study

When you and your attorney have an opportunity to review the home study, rate it. If you are happy with the home study evaluation, keep up the good work. Compare your home study to the home study for the opposition and see if you can use the comparison in your case. If you are dissatisfied with statements or conclusions, make this an opportunity to disprove or change things. Make a bad report work for you. Immediately fix any problems the study identified. Submit documentation to challenge incorrect information or

improvements.
Change those things in your life that the report identified as negative or inadequate. Then get a new or updated home study. Because everything with the courts takes time, any and all efforts to change the negative impact of the "old" report will help. Since the merit of the evaluation can be greatly compromised by a poor evaluator you must do something to fix the problem. A rushed, uninterested or distracted evaluator isn't doing a good job and may cost you contact with your children. Contact your attorney immediately with a written evaluation that points out the problems. Your attorney can request a new evaluator or a reevaluation even before the first one is complete. Specific complaints would be: The evaluator kept talking about his personal life. The evaluator was telling me things about the other parent that was none of my business. The evaluator seemed confused and inexperienced. List examples and quote statements made by the evaluator to demonstrate each of these problems you have identified.

Filing a Formal Complaint

If you feel that you have been unfairly treated, consider filing a complaint with the court and professional organizations of which the evaluator is a member. The complaint must list incidents in which the evaluator did not follow the code of ethics or the evaluator did not use proven techniques for their recommendations. The complaint must deal with facts not emotions. An evaluator who spends 20 minutes at your home, talks about the evaluator's personal problems, seems uninterested in what you have to demonstrate, complains about the excessive number of cases assigned, or seems preoccupied with fitting you into a specific mold are valid concerns.

Chapter 11: Experts

Experts can make or break a case. The expert's mere presence on the case enlarges the importance of the case. Complex matters and little-known procedures are custom-tailored for the expert witness. The case actually determines the necessity for an expert. Your attorney will advise you as to how much value an expert can be to your case or the damage the opposition's expert can cause. You can't stop a tank with a squirt gun, and you can't waste your time firing mortar shells at a flea.

Many people want to use an expert to "lay blame' on the opposition. Blame is not a healthy dynamic and the court does not want to hear it.

What is an Expert

An expert witness is a person who possesses special knowledge or skill on a subject beyond common experience. That does not mean that others who are knowledgeable on that subject or in that profession consider the witness to be an expert. As an example: A person with eleven years of experience working at three different summer camps for children may be accepted as an expert on how children cope with short-term separation anxiety.

If there is a dispute as to whether a witness is qualified, the attorneys will each argue the point and then the Judge must make a decision on the adequacy of the witness's qualifications before permitting testimony. The proponent of the expert witness has the burden of proving by a preponderance of evidence that the expert witness is appropriately qualified.

Expert witnesses acquire qualification through experience, training, or education. Ideally your expert has all three, but it is not necessary. Any one of these elements is sufficient. For example, a day care worker, through experience alone, may qualify as an expert witness to testify as to an opinion of the effectiveness of a certain method for correcting a child's behavior. A child psychologist may have an impressive academic education on this subject, but lack the years of hands on daily experience of the day care worker.

The difference in cost between these two expert witnesses could affect your ability to have an expert testify on your behalf or not.

The child psychologist may cost two thousand dollars for preparation, deposition and court, while the day care worker less than five hundred dollars.

Kinds of Experts

Practical experts are experts whose opinions are based on practical information, which they acquired from within their particular field of expertise. The opposition may depose practical experts, and their notes and reports are open to discovery.

Academic experts have significant academic qualifications and have developed the basis for their expert testimony while involved in education. The opposition may depose academic experts, and their notes, reports, previous testimony in other cases and published works are open to discovery.

Employee experts can testify to the custom and practice regarding the responsibility of various employees and the various standards and practices of the employer. The opposition may depose employee experts, and their notes, reports and work history are open to discovery. The employees work-related employee evaluations may also be requested to indicate the employee's opinion of the employee, in order to reflect positively or negatively on the expert's testimony.

Consulting experts are hired for the purpose of working directly in consultation with the attorneys but who are not expected to testify. The advantage with this type of expert is that discussions, evaluations, notes, and reports between the consulting expert and attorney falls within the work-product privilege, which is not open to discovery. The expert remains a consultant until the expert's name is disclosed as a witness. As long as the expert is a consultant only, the expert's work is privileged. The opposition may not depose the consulting experts, and their notes and reports are not open to discovery.

Testifying experts are retained for the purpose of appearing in court. The opposition may depose testifying experts, and all sources of information from which their opinion was formed are open to discovery.

Qualifications to be an Expert

There are experts in every field. A witness's testimony is limited by their qualifications and the witness may not testify beyond his or her competency. For example, an examining physician may be quite qualified to state that a child had bruises on a leg. This does not mean, however, that the physician should be permitted to testify that, in his or her opinion, the defendant inflicted the bruises. At issue is whether or not your case needs information to go before the judge that cannot be obtained in any other way.

Q. Do I need an expert?

A. This is a judgment call you must make with the assistance of your attorney.

Q. Can I afford the expense?

A. Most experts charge from $100 to $300 per hour, with a 4-hour minimum for their work, and a flat rate for court appearance starting at $600 for a half day.

Q. Does the opinion of an expert make a big difference in a case?

A. Some judges won't even listen to an expert they did not call in to the case. To avoid this problem, research other cases in which the judge used a specific expert as a "friend of the court" and hire that person.

Q. If the opposition is using an expert, do I need to have an expert to challenge his or her testimony?

A. You can check out the danger posed by the opposition's expert before trial. The opposition must include the names of experts on its witness list. After checking the opposition's witness list, you must decide whether to use an expert. Often cases hinge on the "battle of the experts." Sometimes, experts cancel each other out.

Q. How can my attorney question an expert?

A. Have your expert give your attorney a crash course on the information to be discussed. Your attorney can usually gain enough information about any subject to properly question the expert.

The stronger the expert witness's qualifications, the greater the weight the jury may give the expert's testimony. It is the responsibility of the judge to determine whether the expert is qualified to testify on the particular subject matter on the basis of the qualifications presented. The jury weighs the expert's testimony, and in doing so, the jury is to consider the qualifications of the expert.

Costs Involved in Using Experts

Experts charge a premium for their work. They

should be able to give you an estimate of hours necessary to complete a specific type of investigation. Ask for a fee schedule and get a retainer signed. Under the Civil Rights Act of 1964, when a winning party is awarded attorney's fees, reimbursement of expert witness fees can now be recovered as part of attorney's fees.

As with the other professionals you hire, you can effectively reduce the amount of the expert's fee by actively participating in the gathering information available through public records. It is important to tell your experts what you wish to gain from the work you want done. Experts should fight to win the case for you, as far as the information and documentation allows.

Attorneys are no longer allowed to seek income tax records and similar financial documents to prove the amounts that the experts earned to show that those experts might be biased or interested in the results of the litigation. The Supreme Court opined that the disclosure of personal financial information by expert witnesses was unnecessarily burdensome, intrusive and could discourage qualified witnesses from serving as expert witnesses in litigation. Instead, experts need only generally estimate the number of clients seen, consultations held, and evaluations performed for litigation purposes.

What Can Experts Do?

Unlike other witnesses, experts can offer an opinion based on their experience and credentials in addition to what they have personally seen and heard. Individuals or companies can offer expert opinions about:

- Present value calculations for personal property, real estate
- Accident reconstruction
- Wage and benefit projection
- Wage and benefit loss
- Employability
- Earning potential
- Rehabilitation
- Medical health
- Dental health
- Mental health
- Child care and nurturing
- Any field of vocation or avocation

What Experts Cannot Do

An expert may not testify to legal conclusions in the guise of expert opinion. An expert may not attempt to define a statutory term when its definition is a matter of law.

An expert cannot stretch beyond the truth. All conclusions and testimony may rely only upon the facts, which can be demonstrated or proven. An expert may not overstate his or her opinion.

How to Find an Expert

Your attorney is the best source, since he or she may have used this kind of expert in other cases.

Many experts have their own websites on the Internet that include articles they have written, level of experience, discussion groups they host.

Identify a city, state, or federal agency that regulates or does the kind of occupation or work in which you need an expert. Some examples would be:

Arson --- contact the fire department for the name of an investigator.

Child abuse --- call child protective services for a referral.

Accident investigation --- call the police department. Look up court cases like yours in which an expert may have been used.

Most states have a publication that reports the results of court cases to attorneys. Such a publication may publish a compendium of experts. Other sources of information about experts are:

Commercial referral services provide attorneys with large pools of expert witnesses and consultants. They advertise in the telephone book, on the Internet, association magazines and journals published by bar associations.

Personal recommendations are the most common method for locating expert witnesses and eliminate much of the unknown from the process of selecting an expert.

Professional organizations and publications that list members of professional groups in a particular field of expertise provide an excellent source of potential experts. Check your public library for these helpful resources:

- Encyclopedia of Associations (Gale Research Co., Detroit)
- National Trade And Professional Associations Directory (Columbia Books, Washington, D.C.)
- Lawyer's Desk Reference (Bancroft-Whitney Co., San Francisco).

What to look for in Experts

Stay away from detectives, family counselors -- or anyone -- who claims to be an expert about everything. Make sure your experts have records and credentials in the field and in court. Some experts produce outstanding investigations with documentation, but cannot hold their own in court. This is counterproductive and may work against you. Make sure your expert is willing to call in other experts if the investigation enters an unfamiliar area.

There is much confusion about who may be qualified as an expert. It is important that you do not enlist the services of a person that can be discredited. As an example, there are three kinds of professionals who can provide the best kind of expert evaluations and expert testimony in cases of the alleged sexual abuse of children: psychiatrists, psychologists, and social workers. All three professions are subject to licensing in all fifty states. Confusion regarding professionals in mental health arise when they use designations such as "psychotherapist", "therapist", "family therapist", "psychoanalyst", "counselor", "family counselor" and "caseworker", which generally, (dependent upon state law) are not protected titles.

Most evaluations performed in child sexual abuse allegations are performed by caseworkers that are individuals with limited or no education, mental health practice, procedure, evaluation and treatment. Caseworkers are employed (some are actually volunteers) by agencies because of budgetary restraints. Some caseworkers have some education and training in social work, and various aspects of social service. These people will not be found testifying in criminal and civil cases of alleged sexual abuse. Because of the increase in child custody cases, evaluation is a growth industry.

As you understand how limited the number of people available are to take on the monumental task of properly processing all these cases, you will see how important it is to have the right expert and to check out the opposition's expert. Many people take courses in which they are trained by others of questionable qualifications and given a certificate that has no merit. You must be intimately familiar with the qualifications of caseworkers in your jurisdiction. Are they required to hold college degrees? Are they required to participate in ongoing education? What exactly is the "in-service" training that these workers receive?

You must perform the appropriate homework with regard to the qualifications of agency personnel involved in your case. Often you will be surprised to find out the background of the opposition's "star" expert -- but not as surprised as the court! Request and verify any certifications the expert claims to have by asking what certifications are available in that area of expertise and by obtaining copies of these certificates. Check all the references your expert presents. Use a list or chart to keep track.

Over or Under-Exposed

Inquire as to how many cases of this kind the expert has testified in; how many were for the prosecution and how many for the defense, and the outcome of these proceedings. Four to six cases a year are good numbers. Your expert should not be hired merely to repeat your side of the case. The expert should be supportive of your position, but careful not to overstate his or her opinion in such a way that the testimony lacks credibility. To avoid the potential for impeachment, you need to know whether your expert has ever expressed opinions, which are inconsistent with his present opinion on your case. Your attorney should ask the expert for a list of all publications and copies of any articles or speeches relating to the issues on which the expert's opinion testimony would be given. Additionally, your attorney should obtain and review copies of prior testimony of the expert, particularly in any case involving similar issues.

Some Experts are Prostitutes

Some experts are prostitutes by reputation and practice. This is critical because an expert without the respect and confidence of the court is less than worthless. He or she is dangerous. A bad expert can make a solid case look flaky. Spend a lot of time checking out anyone that you expect to put on the stand as an expert witness. It is also important to avoid the "professional court expert," because too much time in court is as bad as too little.

This professional has probably testified on

both sides of the issue in prior cases. The opposition's attorney may find that out and use it to discredit your expert.

The judge rules on whether an expert will be permitted to testify. The opposing attorney can object, so the expert needs strong qualifications.

Verification of Expert Witness	Date Requested	Date Received
Name and Title Scott Harrison PHD		
Education Baylor College of Medicine & University of Texas Medical School	03/01/2000	03/22/2000
Diplomas and Certificates	03/01/2000	03/22/2000
In-the-field Hands-on Experience	03/01/2000	03/27/2000
Reports	03/01/2000	03/24/2000
Courtroom Experience	03/01/2000	03/31/2000
Other cases and what the outcomes have been.	03/01/2000	03/31/2000
Articles and Opinions Published in Professional Journals.	03/01/2000	03/22/2000
List of Standard Industry Tests the Expert Uses.	03/01/2000	03/27/2000
Certification of/or qualification required to give these tests.	03/01/2000	03/29/2000
Professional Groups in, which Membership is Maintained.	03/01/2000	03/29/2000
Write to the agency of certification, asking for the agency's list of requirements and an application packet.	03/01/2000	04/05/2000
You will want to know if experience and ongoing education are required, or if only a payment of money gets this certification.	03/01/2000	
Ask the expert if there is anything in their personal or professional background that could cause you problems.	03/01/2000	03/27/2000

Request an example of the expert's work by asking for "a John Doe case" for the defendant and then the same case presented for the plaintiff. (A John Doe case is usually one in which the names have been blacked out to maintain the confidentiality of the persons.)

You do not want to see the same evidence manipulated to present the different sides. You want to see that the expert would pull different information from the case to confirm the results rather than just manipulate one bit of data or statistics.

For example, you do not want to see on one side of this case that the expert used data to indicate, "There is no hope for full recovery." And on the opposition, the expert used the same data manipulated to indicate, "There is every reason to believe there will be a full recovery." You must see different information and examples supporting the opposing side. An expert's testimony in your case can be challenged by contradictory testimony given by this expert in a previous trial. It may also be challenged by a more distinguished expert's testimony.

Hiring Your Expert

It is best to hire the expert first as a consultant if possible and then decide whether to use him or her at the trial.

Explain the exact issue or issues the expert is to address. Any limitations on the information coming from the expert should be determined since all information communicated to the testifying expert is discoverable.

The expert should be well informed on any issue in the case, which might relate to the basics or the ultimate opinion expressed. But the focus of the expert should be narrow to be credible.

Inform the expert of what he or she is expected to do and on what terms. By defining the scope and objectives, the expert will be able to set resource and time commitments. Make sure the expert understands the scope of your adversary's discovery rights. All contents in the expert's file on your case should be those that counsel and the expert do not object to producing to opposing counsel. Putting preliminary opinions, impressions or other thoughts in writing makes those preliminary opinions, impressions or other thoughts discoverable and may also create a waiver with respect to any prior preliminary opinions, impressions or other thoughts.

Have the expert request information or items the expert wants to review by telephone and without notes in the file until the matter has been discussed with your attorney. Everything, which is shown to your expert becomes discoverable. As a result, much of counsel's case could easily be subject to discovery by virtue of an overly aggressive expert attempting to review any and all items related to the case.

Tests for Expert Opinion

An expert's opinion must meet three separate, but related tests:

1) The information must be known or seen during or before the hearing at which the opinion is expressed. This assures that the expert knows the facts of the case.

2) The information must be of a type that reasonably may be relied upon by experts in forming an opinion upon the subject to which the expert's testimony relates, whether or not such information is admissible or not.

3) The opinion of an expert must not only be on the subject, but must be founded on relevant reliable information.

An expert may rely on logs, photos, incident report forms, detective reports, charts, statements and other information that might not be admissible evidence. Experts are not absolutely prohibited from relying on information provided by lay persons when reaching their conclusions. Although the court should consider the propriety of relying on such information, the judge will often rely on the expert's discretion.

In some fields such as medicine, an expert may rely on hearsay, statements made by, and information received from other doctors, nurses and patients, which are considered truthful. In other fields requiring expert testimony, an expert may not rely on the statements of witnesses to events.

An expert may use hearsay (information from a third source) to support an opinion, if the elements of necessity and reliability are established. Even so, the expert may not testify to the out-of-court statements of another as independent proof of that fact.

Confidentiality - Expert

Your attorney must know what the expert has reviewed or consulted in order to make sure that the expert has examined enough material to provide a credible basis for an opinion and to prevent unintended disclosure of case materials.

The relationship between an expert and a client is confidential to you, but it is not protected by the law. The law imposes no special restrictions on these professionals about information or documents shown or given to them or produced by them. An expert for the opposition is not concerned with your concerns about confidentiality. In fact, the opposition may use an expert to make specific information admissible.

Once documents or information protected by doctor-patient or attorney-client confidentiality are shown or given to an expert, the protections are no longer in place. Therefore, be careful what you decide to show this professional. Expert-client privilege relationship rests on the premise that "The keeper of the records has a primary obligation to the law of the land and then to the client." The confidence between an expert and client can be broken under many circumstances including: A court order from a judge demanding a breech of confidence. The client giving the expert permission to release the records. The records being requested by subpoena.

Preparing Your Expert for Court

Your expert will have all the passion and conviction you feel when you get your report or commitment from him or her. There can be several reasons for this enthusiasm, including: what is right, concern for the child's welfare, expert's ego, need of the job, or other reasons.

Time and other factors can dilute the potency of the expert's message. It is heartbreaking to watch your key witness turn to mush before your eyes. You can avoid this tragedy by deposing your expert while the passion is at its height. This will make a record of the important aspects of the testimony. Make sure your expert gets a copy of the deposition and reads it prior to the court date. This will increase your expenses and may increase your chances of getting your message across.

If your expert has deposition and court experience, you may not need to prepare the expert. Some experts offer a video of a previous testimony to show you their courtroom style. In any case it would not hurt to remind your expert that opposing counsel will attempt to illicit inconsistent testimony, which will undermine your expert's credibility. Even an expert should be told not to stretch beyond the truth. The demeanor of the expert may significantly affect opposing counsel's estimate of the persuasiveness of the expert, as well as the relative potential for success in the case. The expert should not argue with the opposing counsel.

Remind the expert to correct any mistake in his or her testimony, before the end of the deposition, after conferring with your attorney. The expert should, accordingly, request a recess and should advise counsel of the mistake. Together, counsel and the expert should agree upon the best way to correct the record.

Your Expert In Court

The expert will be required to give his or her educational background, including all formal and informal training that bears in any way on the work done in the present case, and employment history in chronological order. The expert will have to describe his or her qualifications in such a way as to illustrate that the expert is qualified to testify. The expert will also be required to provide a list of the professional societies and organizations to which he or she belongs, any lectures in a relevant area, any articles, books or papers in the area, participation in the drafting of any relevant legislation or anything else of relevance to the matter at hand.

The expert should also be prepared to describe prior experience as a litigation expert including:

- How long the expert has been testifying as an expert in these types of cases.
- The number of cases in which the expert has been retained as a consultant, for deposition, and/or testified at trial.
- Percentage the expert has worked for plaintiff as opposed to defendant.
- How many of the expert's prior cases have involved the same issue as the one in which the expert is about to testify.
- How many times the expert has previously testified on behalf of the same law firm.

The expert will be asked to state the date on which he or she was first contacted and set forth the circumstances of the original contact. The expert will be asked to describe the nature of the assignment and rates and methods of billing. The expert will be asked how many total hours were spent on the case beginning with the date the expert was retained (time sheets may be required) and why. They may be asked the number of hours devoted to each category:

a. Hours spent discussing the case with the lawyer presenting the expert, with the party or parties, with other experts, and with other independent individuals, as well as the subject matter of each of the discussions.

b. Hours spent reading and the subject matter that has been read, including, but not limited to, depositions, interrogatories, answers, pleadings, documents in the file, and secondary sources such as key documents to the case, periodicals, reports, articles, studies, treatises and other related materials.

c. How the remainder of the time has been spent. Any interviews or on site inspections.

The expert should be ready to identify the categories included within the file, which may include photographs, calculations, legal records, notes, deposition transcripts, statements of witnesses, charts and graphs. The attorney presenting the expert should have already produced the expert's report. The expert should be prepared to provide additional copies of the report. If the expert has not prepared a report, he or she will be asked whether there are plans to prepare such a report in the future, and if so, the expert should be aware that opposing counsel will ask the expert to deliver a copy when it is provided. To the extent that the expert was assisted by an assistant, the expert should be prepared to describe the nature of the work performed by the assistant.

The expert will be asked to state his or her opinion with respect to certain key issues in the case and the basis for each of the opinions reached. The basis for the opinion should include:

> Any admissible evidence, such as photographs, records or testimony, upon, which the expert relies in reaching his or her opinion; similar situations on which the expert relies; assumptions, conjectures, reasoning that forms the basis for the opinion, the corroboration, any other reason the expert may have for reaching the particular opinion, including any books, articles, or treatises upon, which the expert has relied.

Attacking an Expert's Qualifications

The expert will be attacked on the basis of the opinion. This can be avoided if the expert is fully aware of all of the facts upon, which the opinion is based; he should know, which facts are significant such that a change in the facts would necessitate a change in the opinion; and he should be fully prepared to describe all of the considerations for reaching the opinion.

Another line of attack is based upon hypothetical or changed facts. This is an area where the expert should focus with counsel prior to the deposition. Counsel and the expert should go over each of the key facts to determine what changes in the opinion would have to be made given certain factual changes. What facts cannot be changed without destroying the opinion?

Finally the opposition's attorney will try to get the expert to agree with some or all of the premises of the opponent's case or of testimony by the opponent's expert. The expert should be made fully aware prior to cross-examination of the key premises in the opposition's case. The extent to wish the expert is forced to agree to such a key premise, may very well damage the viability of his or her own opinion and the overall success of the case. Where possible, the expert should be thoroughly prepared to avoid admitting any key premise of the opposition's case or of the opposition's expert testimony.

Rehabilitating After Cross

Counsel must make a determination of whether his or her expert needs to be rehabilitated on re-direct examination. When counsel is proceeding before the court, particularly a jury, counsel can demonstrate significant confidence in the testimony of his or her expert by choosing not to attempt to rehabilitate the expert. Also, attempting to rehabilitate your expert on a point, which is not important, or on which his testimony is truly and unavoidably weak, may backfire by simply reinforcing the jury's perception of the weakness. Where the expert must be rehabilitated, counsel should confine re-direct examination to specific critical areas. The rehabilitation should be precise and efficient. Examining one's own expert on re-direct can afford your opponent an opportunity to revisit and reinforce your expert's weakest areas on re-cross if the re-direct examination is not carefully circumscribed.

Opposition's Expert

If the opposition is using an expert, you can usually find out who it is and what their written reports say during the process of discovery. Your attorney can ask for the names of witnesses the opposition expects to call to the stand.

It is useful to exercise "discovery" as soon as the litigation is initiated and again just before the court date. In some states the opposition has up to sixty days to answer the interrogatories, so adjust your timetable to what "just before" means in your state.

Since there is no generally recognized training for experts in sex abuse, the expert presented by the opposition may be easier to discount.

Loose Cannon

It is common for an attorney to list an expert witness without formally notifying the witness.

Take this opportunity to have your attorney speak to any experts listed by the opposition. If the expert has not been contracted with the opposition, and your attorney thinks it would be helpful, you can pay a retainer and bind that expert to your side. You may wish to "tie up" this expert, forfeit your retainer, and not use the expert at all.

Deposing Your Opponent's Expert

Check all references, especially those listed in the expert's promotional material, including education, in-the-field hands-on experience, courtroom experience, and professional groups in which the expert claims to maintain membership.

Verify the value of any certifications claimed by writing to the agency of certification, asking for a list of requirements. The organization will send you a packet, looking for a new customer. You want to know if experience and ongoing education are required, or if only a payment of money got this certification.

Deposing the opposition's expert can be one of the most important parts of your case preparation.

Ask for and examine the declaration of expert witness. It must be signed by the other attorney and must contain a statement of the witness's qualifications, the general substance of the expected testimony, and a representation that the expert has agreed to testify at trial. The expert must be sufficiently familiar with the action to provide a meaningful deposition concerning his expected testimony and its basis, and a statement of the expert's hourly and daily fee for providing deposition testimony.

You may depose any or all of the experts listed by the other party. The party requesting the deposition must pay the expert's reasonable and customary fee for time actually spent in the deposition.

At the same time demand all discoverable reports and writings of experts that are subject to the requirement of an expert witness declaration. If the expert fails to comply, the trial court must exclude the testimony of the expert, upon the objection of a party who has complied in a timely and complete manner.

A list may include:

- All documents reflecting or relating to any communication between the expert and opposing counsel, including such things as engagement letters.
- All documents reflecting any communication relating to the engagement, including any communications with witnesses.
- All documents reflecting or relating to any preliminary opinions or conclusions.
- All documents consulted or relied upon by the expert in connection with the engagement including those he consulted or relied upon in forming his opinions.
- All documents relating to his educational, employment, and professional history and any other documents reflecting or relating to his qualifications to testify.
- All documents reflecting other cases in which he has testified as an expert, including any documents, including transcripts, that reflect the substance of his testimony, the terms of his engagement, the court in which the action was pending, or the outcome of the case.
- Copies of all professional publications that he has written or been a contributor.
- All other documents relating to the engagement, the opinions he expects to give, or the opinions he was asked to consider giving. Before the deposition, you should learn as much as you can about your opponent's expert, his area of expertise, and the potential weak spots in his opinions. Your own expert is one source of such information, but you should not limit yourself to any one source. There are two schools of thought about whether it is better to try to take the deposition of your opponent's expert before or after that of your expert. If your expert goes last, your opponent will have had the benefit of seeing what a really good deposition of an expert looks like. He will also have a pretty good idea of your theories to help him prepare for his deposition of your expert. On the other hand, your expert will have the benefit of knowing what the opposition's expert said and can avoid pitfalls and help you to develop lines of inquiry.

In the deposition, your attorney's goal will be to exhaust the witness's qualifications, preparations to reach the opinion, and the opinions. Your attorney will explore with the expert all the areas the attorney expects to cover with your witnesses, get any admissions, and explore any possible sources of bias. Your attorney will exhaust the witness's qualifications by first getting a narrative description of all of the qualifications and experiences that the expert believes qualify him to give an opinion in your case. Look for differences between the facts of this case and situations with which the witness has had experience. This will produce a list of facts in this case with which the witness is unfamiliar or inexperienced. Your attorney may attack the credibility of the witness at trial with questions like, "Isn't it a fact that you've never treated even a single child abused by a parent with indications of Munchausen Syndrome by proxy?"

Your attorney will look for differences between the kind of opinion that the witness seeks to give at trial and the kind of opinion that the witness is required to form in his own work. For example, the district manager of a chain of day care centers who is being called to give an opinion about the suitability of a religious school preferred by the defendant to the public school insisted upon by the plaintiff may never be called upon to make educational recommendations in his daily work of supervising personal and office operations.

The goal with this kind of questioning is to limit the areas of the witness's expertise to exclude some or all of the areas material to the case. As with all similar types of questioning, it is important to ask the closeout questions. For example, you should not leave the area of the witness's qualifications until you get an unequivocal "no" to a question like, "Do you have any other qualifications or experiences that fit you to express an opinion in this case?"

After your attorney has exhausted the witness's qualifications, the same thing will be done with respect to the witness's preparation to render an opinion. Your attorney will want to know everything the witness did and should not leave this area until you get a satisfactory answer to the closeout questions. Then, your attorney will get specific about what was not done. Following up with questions like: Would it have been helpful to have done specific additional items of preparation? Would the results of the additional procedures have changed your opinions in any respect? Why or why not? The attorney will then ask open ended questions about what additional preparation or procedures might have been helpful and the reasons why or why not. Why were any admittedly valuable procedures not done? For each opinion your attorney will:

Find out all the facts upon, which it is based. Find out the basis, if any, for those facts. Ask whether relevant alternative facts might result in a different conclusion. Find out why or why not. Ask the closeout questions.

Determine the witness's degree of confidence in each of his opinions in an attempt to distinguish between firmly held conclusions and mere guesswork or speculation. This works two ways: (a.) If the witness admits that some of his opinions, conclusions, or assumptions are less than secure, the opinions will carry less weight. (b.) If the witness claims an improbable degree of confidence in the opinions, it may hurt the witness's credibility.

Ask the witness all the questions that might be asked your own expert. Opinions on many matters may support your theories and will be far more convincing on these points than those of your own witness. For each answer that contradicts your own expert or theory:

Find out the precise nature of the disagreement.

Find out whether the contradictory opinions are based on different assumptions. If so, ask whether the expert's opinion would change if he accepted the same facts as your expert. Ask him what other changes in the facts might change his opinions. If there are no facts that could change his opinion, or he says that obviously material facts wouldn't affect his opinions, he won't be very credible. If he admits that certain facts would change his opinion, maybe you can prove those facts at trial and turn him, in effect, into your witness.

Find out whether there is more than one school of thought in the community of experts. If so, see if you can get the hostile expert to admit that there is a substantial body of thought that supports your position.

During the course of completing the above lines of questioning, you should have gotten most of the useful admissions that could be obtained concerning the expert's expertise, preparation, opinions, and assumptions. In addition, try to get admissions concerning the expertise of your own experts and the reliability of any treatises, tests, or other sources of information upon which you intend to rely.

Ask the witness about the documents. Start by asking how the documents he brought with him or provided through counsel were gathered or selected. Ask about each category of document requested and ask whether the witness knows of any documents in the category that were not produced. Also ask pointed questions about more specific kinds of documents that fall into the categories and that were not produced, but that you believe or suspect exist. Ask whether the witness reviewed any documents when he was preparing to testify, including personal notes, and make sure that you have copies of them.

Finally, explore any possible sources of bias or interest. In particular, you should ask about the witness's relationship with the parties, with your opponent's counsel, with the plaintiffs' or defendants' bar and terms of the witness's compensation.

Opponent's Expert in Court

- Stipulate to the qualifications of their expert witness unless clearly shaky.
- Ask for the full amount the expert will get paid for the work-up and testifying in court.
- Does the witness consider him or herself free from bias or prejudice?
- Who actually did interviews, administered tests, interpreted the test results?
- What was the witness's prior testimony in cases for this attorney?
- How much time was spent on each part of the process? Time with subject, time analyzing reports and tests, or their procedures.
- Has this witness ever made a mistake? Name and date of case? Was it significant?

The only thing more challenging and dangerous for an attorney than cross examining an expert witness is asking a question to which the attorney does not know the answer. Careful preparation is the only safeguard since the expert usually controls the testimony by being very knowledgeable in the area of testimony. Prompting by the attorney's own expert and reading prior testimony of the expert will enable the attorney to successfully cross examine and zero in on the weaknesses of the expert or the expert's testimony.

Your attorney's summarization of the deposition taken of the expert witness for your case and comparison with prior depositions that your attorney summarized, given in other cases will often produce many helpful statements that will assist in your case. Any articles, books, editorials or previous cases may contradict the expert's opinion offered in your case. Next, determine if this expert relies heavily on any other expert. Has that expert published or testified with an opinion that disagrees with an opinion offered in your case. Your attorney will never be able to win on a toe-to-toe match with the expert. Your attorney must be knowledgeable in the area so that if the expert goes too far the attorney can expose the expert as a hired gun.

Your attorney should always cross examine an expert witness. It is better to help the court question whether the expert has seen all the evidence or was handing out the opposing attorney's pre-printed opinion. Allowing an expert witness to give opinions without challenge may indicate to the court that the expert is fair, correct and the opinion is so strong it cannot be challenged.

Even the best expert witness can be challenged using some of these starting points:

Bias in the expert witness can always be proven because of friendship, money or a relationship with the attorney or the attorney's client.

A disproportionate amount of time in court in comparison to the amount of time spent in the expert's given field of expertise should be identified. The number of times an expert witness has testified on behalf of the particular lawyer or law firm evidences bias.

Keep in mind that no matter how qualified an expert witness may be in a given field, there are probably levels that the expert has not reached. For example, if the expert witness only has a master's degree, your attorney may point out that the expert lacks a Ph.D. Make sure that a Ph.D. is offered in that field.

If the expert is not published, or has not held any teaching positions in colleges or universities, this may be an indication that others don't agree with the expert. You need to check out this information before your attorney has to face the expert in court. The attorney's staff can do this research, but it is much more expensive than if you do it yourself. Often your attorney can get the opposing expert to testify in general principles that are consistent with your case. Your attorney will ask basic, helpful, leading questions that cannot be denied, so the expert will have to admit the facts suggested in the question or appear foolish.

Your attorney will always point out that the expert received the facts and materials from the opposing attorney. Your attorney will then offer pertinent evidence of which the expert is unaware. Then attempt to elicit agreement that this evidence would have altered the final conclusion. Your attorney will use hypothetical questions in order to change the facts so that they are consistent with your side of the case; then, ask the expert controlled questions within the restricted scenarios that the attorney has presented.
This will allow your version of the case to be heard through the opposing expert. Your attorney won't allow the expert too much room when testifying. The question will be in a long detailed factual

pattern followed by a direct leading question relating to the facts presented hypothetically. Even if the expert refuses to provide a favorable response, your attorney has told the court your side of the story by using the hypothetical question.

You can impeach the expert witness with an article, journal or chapter of a book from the expert's field. You will almost always be able to find research, positions and opinions that are contrary to the expert witness's opinion. Your own expert witness can usually identify exactly what you need quickly. With what you have found, your attorney can attempt to have the expert witness agree that the author of the article in the journal, or the chapter in the book, or treatise is authoritative or at least a well recognized expert in the field.

Next, your attorney will identify the article or chapter, read the relevant portions that contradict the opinion of the expert, and then ask the expert if he or she agrees with the statement that you just read. It does not matter whether the expert agrees or disagrees. You and your attorney have effectively demonstrated to the court that other published experts do not agree with the opposing witness's position.

Your expert may be able to identify an error in the opposing expert's investigation or calculations.

Your attorney will choose only two or three areas of attack at trial. If your attorney attempted to use all of them, the cross examination becomes too lengthy or confusing and the longer an opposing expert witness is on the stand, the greater the likelihood that the expert will hurt your case.

Therefore, your attorney will hit two or three areas of attack, expose the expert's weak points, then politely thank the expert and sit down.

New Stricter Standards for Experts

The U.S. Supreme Court is expected to clarify the screening test established for "scientific" testimony applying it to all expert testimony. Getting doctors, accountants, attorneys, real estate appraisers, sociologists, handwriting experts, economists, engineers and other experts admitted at trial is becoming much harder both in state and federal courts.

Chapter 12: Psychologists & Tests

In 98% of the cases both parents are fit parents. If they have gotten as far as psychological testing it is because they have not been able to separate ex-spousal issues from parental issues.

War of the Minds

If the judge cannot or will not make a decision, or the options for the children are not clear to the judge, a battery of tests may be ordered. The following explanations should take a lot of the fear out of the process, making your results more stable. Some kinds of testing, including drug and paternity, are becoming more common.

Who Can Perform Psychological Tests

Psychological testing must be performed or supervised by mental health professionals who have been appropriately educated and trained in the administration and interpretation of psychological tests. A trained technician can, under supervision, administer and score a psychological test, but the interpretation and reporting of findings of such tests must only be done by individuals with appropriate assessment training.

A licensed psychologist should be familiar with the standards for educational and psychological testing (APA, 1985). All mental health professionals who use the tests should be familiar with both their state's testing guidelines and the ethical guidelines relating to their specific subjects or topics.

Check Out the Psychologist

If the court-ordered decision of this professional is binding, you have in fact a new "judge." As with any professional assigned to your case, research the work the psychologist has done. Your attorney or someone known to your attorney has examples of the work.

Read the reports to decide if this person can be fair. The psychologist's primary concern should be the children's welfare. Have your attorney reject any professional with whom you are not comfortable or whose work is unknown. In one case the attorney for one side rejected seven psychologists. There is no way to be sure if that maneuver made the difference, but that attorney's client did win custody.

Psychologist Contact Log

Contact Log with Dr. Stewart
Date *Tue. 7 Dec. 99* Time Start Time Finished Letter arrived today from my attorney saying the court agreed to the psychological evaluations we had requested for both parents. I called the Dr. Stewart designated in the letter and was given an appointment at ten in the morning on December 22 for my wife and I to take a MMPI-III. I am to come back at two in the afternoon for a meeting with just me and Dr. Stewart. Then he wants to see my wife and I on the 27th. January 10, he wants to see my wife, the children and I for one hour.
Date *Wed. 22 Dec. 99* Time Start *10:00A.M.* Time Finished 12*:40P.M.* My wife and I finished the MMPI-III and turned them into the receptionist in Dr. Stewart's office. We had lunch and I hung around until my appointment at two. We talked from two until three forty-five. I asked if he ever found for the fathers. He said in about forty percent of the cases the decision was for shared joint custody, 30 percent for the parent who currently had custody and twenty-five percent for the parent that had been the non-custodial parent at the time of the psychological testing. Dr. Stewart said a larger number of fathers had temporary custody at the time of the testing in the last eighteen months than in previous years. The doctor said since the children are spending an almost equal amount of time with each parent, there was no way to predict the outcome in our case.
Date *Thus. 27 Jan. 00* Time Start *9:00:30A.M.* Time Finished *11:05A.M.* I have a much better feeling about our meeting with Dr. Stewart than my wife does. She felt he was too concerned with her life before she married me. I told her not to worry about it. I think the doctor asked my wife many of the questions he asked me last week to see if her answers were comparable with mine. He seemed concerned about the issues that worried us.
Date *Mon. 10 Jan. 00* Time Start *9:00A.M.* Time Finished 10.30A*.M.* Our family meeting with Dr. Stewart was much easier than I thought it would be. The kids liked him right away. Little Brenda alternated between Dr. Stewart's lap and mine the entire session. Maggie and Adam sat on each side of my wife and seemed less interested in our conversation with the doctor than I would have liked. We ran over time because near the end of the session Adam began to describe our weekends at the cabin and Maggie and he got so excited answering the doctor's questions that Dr. Stewart became distracted.
Date *Fri. 25 June 99* Time Start *9:30A.M.* Time Finished 9:35A*M.* My attorney called with the results of Dr. Stewart's testing. It has given me residential parent status with generous visitation for their mother.

Best Attitude with the Psychologist

Be open and honest. These professionals are trained differently from the mediator. If you have been evaluated by a mediator and now face a psychologist, you have an indication of how you will respond and how the professional will see you. If you were happy with the mediator's evaluation and have been maintaining and reinforcing positive behaviors, you are doing fine. If the mediator's report was negative, you have had an opportunity to change any negative behaviors identified at that time. If you have not been through the mediation process, it will help if you read the section on mediators.

If one psychologist is going to do the testing on both parents, make sure you schedule your appointment first. If you have made a positive impression, something called the "Halo Effect" kicks in. The Halo Effect is a filter that the subconscious mind uses to confirm the initial impression formed about a person. All subsequent information and events will be viewed through this filter to validate the first judgment. Even though they are aware of the Positive and Negative Halo

Effect, it still works almost as well with professionals as it does with the general public. It will be difficult for the opposition to change the positive impression you established.

The psychologist makes observations during the process of evaluation, looking for behavior patterns. He or she notes what you wear, how punctual you are, whether your statements are consistent with how you behave, how you react to occurrences in the facility related and unrelated to your interview and your desire or resistance to communicate openly.

Make your appointment for the first available opening in the psychologist's schedule. If your children are to be seen by the psychologist, but the opposition appears to have difficulty with the schedule, let the other parent and the professional know that you can adjust your schedule to have the children there when necessary.

You should register any objections or complaints about the psychologist or evaluation process, through your attorney to the court, before the report is submitted. Once the evaluation has been submitted to the court, you have little recourse. A valid, well documented complaint can encourage the court to appoint a new psychologist.

Before You See the Psychologist

Before you see the evaluator, read "From Now On" in Chapter 2: You Are The Package, in this manual. Reviewing this list before each appointment will give you a feeling of control and give the evaluator a consistent picture of you.

Facing the Other Parent

Many psychologists schedule at least one joint meeting with both sides in conflict to personally observe the dynamics of the relationship. It is critical that you leave this professional with the knowledge that you are a responsible, well mannered adult whose main concern is the well-being of your children. To facilitate this impression: (1) Make a list of what you think the opposition will bring up. (2) Decide, which of the opposition's points are real issues. (3) Make a list of four or five concerns you want to verbalize addressing the real issues. (4) Make a list of what the opposition usually says to upset you. (5) Decide not to respond by getting upset. (6) Respond in a non-aggressive and non-accusatory way to the indictment if the evaluator requests that you do answer the charge. (7) Make a list of negative behaviors and attitudes you do not want to exhibit.

Listen to the opposition and do not interrupt to defend yourself from what is being said or to make your point.

- You know how the other parent feels about you and what will be said. Prepare yourself emotionally to face this person.
- It is also obvious that you feel a great deal of pressure and so does the other parent. Rehearsal of your major points and concerns will allow you clarity of thought, confidence and control.
- The psychologists will ask for your side. Be clear about what you want to say.
- If the other parent interrupts your statement, wait patiently while they say what they wish. Do not get angry or respond to the new indictment. If you answer the accusations, you are giving the other parent control of the agenda. Remain aware of your body language keeping it open and confident without seeming cold and aloof.
- The psychologist will bring the question back to you. Once you have been given back the "floor," resume your statement. Each time the other parent interrupts, wait patiently again.
- The psychologist will appreciate having one sane controlled person at this meeting.
- Always thank the psychologist for his time and patience.

Recommendation = Decision

Usually, the recommendation is accepted by the courts and signed by the judge without change of content, but with some additions to satisfy legal aspects.

Psychological studies are not governed by "rules of evidence." A psychologist is usually willing to consider any data you present. The information and manner in which you present it says as much about you as does the data itself.

The psychologist may charge an additional fee to read home studies, detective reports, mediation evaluations and other information. Pay it! Pay it! Pay it! It could be the most important investment you make.

When There are Two of You

In addition to presenting yourself for evaluation, the professional will want to test anyone else the children will be interacting with on a regular basis in the children's home setting.
The positive support you can demonstrate from your significant other (husband, wife, betrothed, person you are living with on an intimate basis) is important. Read through the chapter "You Are The Package" with your significant other. This experience, although less formal, is a critical type of testimony and may be the deciding factor.

The manner in which you and your significant other relate to each other on a verbal and nonverbal level will be observed and noted by the professional. Any touching in the presence of the professional should be gestures of assurance and reassurance, such as patting an arm or holding a hand, rather than touching that indicates possession, such as a hand on a thigh.

What are they Looking for?

As soon as you are aware an evaluation is required, make an appointment for the first time available on the professional's schedule. Make an honest presentation of yourself and offer the psychologist documented information that will raise issues the opposition may be unwilling to deal with in an honest manner.

Discuss with your attorney any pertinent negative information about you or your situation and be ready to talk about it in an honest, open manner. Be ready to answer any questions raised, whether you feel it is relevant or not, even if presented by the opposition.

Specific Positive Character Traits

The psychologist is interested in your ability and willingness to do the things listed below. The professional is even more significantly interested in your children's perception of your willingness, and the children's dependence and reliance on you for these things. The results are important to the evaluation and very important to the children's welfare.

- Requires family chores done by the child(ren).
- Participates in child's activities.
- Listens when child speaks.
- Remains calm during frightening situations or arguments.
- Maintains a generally happy frame of mind.
- Keeps promises to the child and others.
- Makes new things more comfortable for the child.
- Enjoys time with others.
- Will be there for the child in an emergency.
- Makes sure homework gets done.
- Settles arguments fairly.
- Answers sexual and religious questions.
- Assists in caring for pets and precious possessions.
- Participates in family, neighborhood, school and community projects.
- Exercises patience with child and others.
- Speaks up over unfairness.
- Accepts criticism.
- Remains firm about bedtime.
- Manages money.
- Helps face fear.

Send Up Warning Flags Early

If you have agreed or the court has ordered that the decision of the psychologist be binding, you must insure that you are treated fairly. Any hint of gender bias against you, unprofessional behavior, indications of incompetence or misconduct, must be reported at the time you see it. Telephone your attorney and follow up in writing. The only limit to the number of times you can change a psychologist is the patience of the court. Once the evaluation is made, cries of injustice will fall on deaf ears.

The Process of Evaluation

The family evaluation will involve several phases. Arrive at each appointment on time, rested and properly nourished. Each member of the family may have a private session. Those old enough will have a written test. Then there will be a family group session with the psychologist. Normally there is a standard set of questions that the psychologist asks. These questions provide a broad range of information that may not be evident to you on the surface. It is vitally important that you answer the verbal and written questions stating how you really feel, not with the answers you think the psychologist wants, or what you think is "normal." Such manufactured answers will work against you.

It is unlikely that you will ever see the actual results of the tests on either you or the opposition. Generally, you will see a copy of the Custody Evaluation after it is sent to your attorney.

Data Submitted: Identify Abilities

The data you submit should contain positive information about you. Read how to assemble The Book of Your Life in Chapter 10: Evaluations. This book can point out your strengths without you looking like a braggart and any negative information about the opposition, without making you look vindictive.

Data Submitted: Identify Concerns

During the investigation, the psychologist may ask if you have any concerns as to the welfare of your children when with the other parent. Verbiage and charting are very important at this point. State your points by offering documentation of photos, school health, or arrest records, or court papers to validate your worries of abuse, problems with the law, or anything else you feel is important. Many things that can be documented and charted.

Concerns that can be Documented

Information That Can Be Documented	
Absenteeism From School	Injuries, Adult's
Arrest Record Of Adult	Injuries, Child's
Arrest Record Of Child	Interference With Your Visitation
Bed Wetting	Medication, Adult's
Change Of Address	Medication, Child's
Change Of Schools	Missing Needed Medical Appointments, Child's
Child Support Payments	Money For Support (Extra)
Child's Activities	Running Away From Home
Child's Activities Designed To Interfere With Your Visitation	Special Medical Emergencies, Adult's
Child's Grades	Special Medical Emergencies, Child's
Church Attendance	Telephone Contact With Child
Drug Use and History Of Drug Use	Time Child Spends With Parent and Others
Hours Worked pre/post Custody Battle Started , Parent A	TV Hours, Child's
Hours Worked pre/post Custody Battle Started, Parent B	Visitation Adjustment
How Support Money Is Spent	Weight Gain, Child's
Illness, Adult's	Weight Loss, Child's
Illness, Child's	Welfare Payments Into Home

School Year September 1992-1993 Laurie Lemony First & Second Quarter							
Week	**Days Absent**	**Days Tardy**	**Grade Average**	**Week**	**Days Absent**	**Days Tardy**	**Grade Average**
1 (A)	15	8	C-	1 (B)	0	0	C+
2 (A)	12	6	C	2 (B)	0	0	C+
3 (A)	22	3	C-	3 (B)	0	0	B
4 (A)	9	10	C-	4 (B)	0	0	B
5 (B)	3 *	0	C	5 (A)	25	5	C-
6 (B)	1	0	C	6 (A)	12	8	C

School Year September 1992-1993 Laurie Lemony Third & Fourth Quarter							
Week	**Days Absent**	**Days Tardy**	**Grade Average**	**Week**	**Days Absent**	**Days Tardy**	**Grade Average**
1 (A)	6	9	C-	1 (B)	0	0	C+
2 (A)	9	11	C	2 (B)	0	0	B
3 (A)	26	8	D	3 (B)	0	0	B
4 (A)	15	10	C-	4 (B)			
5 (B)	1	0	C	5 (A)			
6 (B)	0	0	C+	6 (A)			

(A) Signifies the semesters that Laurie was living with parent A
(B) Signifies the semesters that Laurie was living with parent B
* Laurie was returned to parent B by parent A one week into the semester and only missed school during that week.

Example Data

I am submitting this school attendance and grade chart for my daughter Laurie Lemony to show a direct correlation between school attendance and where Laurie lives at the time. Laurie enjoys school and welcomes help with her homework. Copies of the report cards used to compile this chart are available. The card reports six, six week reporting periods.

Will You Take a Drug Test?

What do you say if asked, "Will you take a drug test?" Say yes. Being asked <u>if</u> you would take a drug test is not the same as being asked <u>when</u> you will take a drug test. If the opposition, judge, psychologist, your attorney or you decide that you should take a drug test, you should:

1. Make a list of all medications you have taken in the last six months. List the brand names and the form in which they were taken. Example --- pill, syrup, powder, inhalant. All tests cross-react with something.

2. Request a list of all over-the-counter and prescription drugs and other ingestible substances known to cross-react with the test that will be used.

3. Schedule your test for afternoon.

4. Drink lots of water to clean out your system. Also, caffeine free coffee, tea, and fruit juices are excellent.

5. Avoid alcohol.

6. Sweat any impurities out of your system with exercise, saunas, and steam baths.

7. Take B-complex vitamins; they are good for your general health.

If it will help your case, have a drug test taken without notifying anyone, and if you get the results you want, offer the results to your attorney.
If the test shows a positive result, request another type of test.

Drug Tests

The Supreme Court has upheld drug testing for federal employees and people employed in the private sector with jobs that impact the public safety. While there is no direct link between these policies and custody litigation, the rulings have to be interpreted as reflecting our society's general acceptance of drug testing. By the year 2002 one out of five custody battles will require that one or both parties be tested for drugs.

Random Testing

Patterns of abuse or addiction can be detected by regular testing. Testing can also disprove false accusations. You may feel that because you do not take drugs, this is an area with which you will have no problems. Random (unannounced or spot testing) testing offers the best opportunity to demonstrate a drug free life-style or to ensnare the drug user or abuser. Advocates of drug testing believe that an optimum level of deterrence can be achieved by a combining frequent and unannounced testing. Example: a parent assigned to this test schedule requests contact with his or her children several times a week.

In addition to a urine test every Monday morning the parent may be required to test with-out prior notice one to three additional times during the month when he or she arrives to visit with the children. This technique has proven to be an effective deterrent when used consistently.

Court Room Samples

During court an attorney can request that the judge order the bailiff to take a sample of hair from both parents. Your attorney could expresses concern that the opposition will not go for the test or will try some trick to thwart the results if another time and place are set for removal of the samples. The attorney should be prepared to offer a kit with:

- sterilized scissors
- evidence bags and tables
- express postage paid envelope to mail the evidence bags
- payment ability such as a credit card number with expiration date
- a list of several laboratories for the judge or bailiff to choose from
- instruction sheet to the lab with areas to list fax numbers of the judge and both attorneys to send the results

Once the samples are collected and sealed the bailiff can send them to the lab. The judge may not care for this courtroom antic or may see it as a way to resolve an important issue. This tactic can be very powerful if you have been falsely accused of drug use or you are sure the other parent is involved with drugs. This drastic maneuver indicates that you want the problem addressed immediately and are not afraid to face the results. Often the opposition will just admit to past drug use rather than submit to testing.

Hair Analysis

The basis for hair analysis is that drugs circulating in the bloodstream are transferred to and embedded in the cortex of growing hair fibers. These drugs remain in the hair and move away from the head as the hair grows recording the pattern of drug use. Hair from a persons head five inches long gives you a drug history of nine to twelve months. Slower growing body hair can extend the history to several years.

The method used for analysis starts with taking strands of hair from the scalp and then cutting the strands into sections that correspond to the periods of interest. As an example: hair from within one inch of the scalp would give evidence of drug use from the last two months. The hair samples are then chemically destroyed and then examining the resulting extract using essentially the same techniques used in urinalysis.

Urine Analysis

Because urinalysis reveals the types of drugs taken and provides some indication as to quantities taken, it can be used as a diagnostic aid in evaluating the nature of the involvement with drugs. It can be used to monitor treatment progress and provide credible and timely information on a person's continued use or abstinence from drugs. Drug testing can be used in a therapeutic sense as well. For example, a positive test during rehabilitation can be used to confront denial of continued drug use. Even occasional use can be spotted by drug testing so steps can be taken by treatment professionals to keep the person from reverting to a pattern of regular use. When handled skillfully, drug testing can help parents in rehabilitation to resist peer pressure and attain the drug-free status necessary to maintain contact with their children.

Retention Times of Drugs in Urine	
Amphetamine	48 hours
Barbiturate (short-acting)	24 hours
Barbiturate (long-acting)	2-3 weeks
Benzodiazepines	72 hours
Cannabinoids	5-11 days/ more
Cocaine	2-4 days
Methadone	72 hours
Methaqualone	14 days
Opiates	24 hours
Phencyclidine	8 days

False Positives

There is a problem called "false positives," which could cause your reputation and/or ability to earn a living to be at risk. "Positive" means that there is an indication of a controlled substance in the subject specimen tested. Many everyday foods, liquids, over-the-counter drugs, pain relievers with ibuprofen, as well as legal prescription drugs may give incorrect "evidence" that you use illicit drugs when, in fact, you do not. Poppy seeds and codeine may show up as morphine. Valium has been known to appear as angel dust. Ninety percent of all these chemicals may produce positive findings in the body for three months.

The Center for Disease Control and the National Institute on Drug Abuse ran a nine-year study on the accuracy of private sector laboratories. Private sector labs are not licensed, and there has been no legislation requiring employee training of even minimum wage employees. Sixty-six out of a hundred samples showed false positives.

On the other hand, accuracy for screening known abusers under "blind test" conditions was one hundred percent inaccurate.

What can make your test results come out wrong?

- Mishandling by tester.
- Urine specimens that have gone stale.
- Specimen's reaction to extremes of heat and cold.
- Urine that is too acid or alkaline.
- Subject's use of medication.

Passive Inhalation

Inadvertent exposure to marijuana is frequently cited, but clinical studies show that it is unlikely that a non-smoking individual can passively inhale sufficient marijuana smoke to result in a high enough concentration for marijuana to be detected in standard urinalysis.

Prescription Drug Abuse

Prescription drugs are the fastest-growing component of personal health expenditures and will exceed $80 billion in 2001. More than 4 million people are abusing prescription drugs in America.

Even proper use of prescription drugs can be the deciding factor in a child custody case. In cases where parents are equally appropriate, willing and able to be primary resident parent, even proper legal prescription drug use can penalize one of the parents.

Bob a father of two was taking Xanax for severe panic attacks. The attacks began when the computer software company Bob worked for was purchased by a much larger company and his quota was dramatically increased. A company insurance HMO psychiatrist prescribed the sedative. Bob was amazed when the pills solved everything replacing panic with a feeling of calm, control and self confidence. During his divorce when a decision had to be made about the custody of his two sons, Bob's prescription use was the only negative factor that the evaluator designated as the deciding one.

Kim and her husband were already having problems when she hurt her back working for a local grocery store as a checker. The workmans compensation doctor put her on Percocet for pain. When Kim's husband was able to show the psychologist doing the family evaluation that Kim was getting her prescription filled through three different pharmicies. Copies of the pharmacy receipts gave credence to his concern that Kim was taking many times the proper dosage.

The husband explained that the children had to be driven to school, church and special events and that Kim should not drive under the influence of Percocet even with proper dosage. Additionally, he felt that alone in the home Kim may not be able to take proper care of the children. The evaluation was well balanced in all aspects except for the focus on Kim's prescription drug use and possible abuse. Kim's husband was awarded custody of the children.

Abuse of prescription drugs is more often the cause of the loss of custody that merely the legal use.

Frequently several drugs in one category or multiple categories of drugs are abused at the same time. This happens over a period of time because the body builds up a tolerance and needs more to feel the beneficial effects of the drug. The four categories that are abused most often are pain relievers, tranquilizers, sedatives and stimulants. They can be administered; by injection, pill, liquid, patch, powder, inhaler, suppository and cream.

The problem of prescription drug abuse has become so critical that in May of 2001 state attorneys general said they will study and make recommendations to their legislatures.

Many states are looking at the innovative controlled substances programs in Nevada and Nebraska. All prescriptions are entered into a database. The computer scans more than 2 million controlled-substance prescriptions each year. It can flag the identify of persons given specific drugs either by several doctors or in unusually large quantities. The names are given doctors and pharmacies that decide if the patients need help. Some people find help at Pills Anonymous meetings.

Psychological Tests for Adults

You may feel nervous when you find out you must take a psychological test. The good news is, that is normal. The bad news is that most of us try too hard. The test can even indicate that we are attempting to please the tester rather than give a true reading of our feelings. That can produce the opposite outcome of the results you wanted. Just answer the questions as truthfully as you can. Don't attempt to second guess the test.

Minnesota Multiphasic Personality Inventory (MMPI)

Composed of 567 statements to which a subject must reply uses a "true" or "false" reply. This test can correctly identify persons with particular psychiatric problems. At this time, this is the most commonly used test. In 1989 the test was entirely revamped and renamed on a sample based upon the typical nature of the United States population (based upon U.S. Census data) and included 2600 subjects from across every region in the United States. Based upon this, its validity for help in diagnosing and understanding people with psychological problems is invaluable.

On the MMPI, some of the questions don't have an appropriate answer. The idea is to select the best possible one. Once the test is completed the results are evaluated by a computer in the professionals office and sometimes sent off to a larger database.

The results give a great deal of information and by comparing the information the professional may draw many conclusions.

Rorschach

Ten standardized inkblots. Subject is asked to verbally elaborate on what is seen in the inkblots and where the image begins, under the directive that there is no right answer. Inkblots are the classical miscellaneous projective drawings and have been used by psychologists for many years as a way of tapping the unconscious of patients. In oversimplified form, the theory holds that the unconscious will strongly contribute to responses made under ambiguous conditions.

Thematic Apperception Test (TAT)

The cards contain a black and white picture of people in circumstances that invite responses having psychological overtones. The person being tested is asked what he or she thinks is going on in each picture and how the people feel. The idea is for the person being tested to project his or her fantasies, feelings, patterns of relationships, needs and conflicts.

Weschler Adult Intelligence Scale

The WAIS was specifically designed to test (verbal and nonverbal) intelligence, with the ability to identify strengths and weaknesses in each.
The test includes six verbal and five performance subtests.

Adult Sentence Completions

Basically unfinished sentences are posed that the person is asked to finish. For example: "I wish _____" the idea being that unconscious material gets reported.

Sixteen Personality Factor Questionnaire

List of sixteen interrelated traits that describe an individual personality. This is a standardized test, not unlike the MMPI. Lots of questions, which when factor analyzed break down into sixteen dimensions. Also known as the 16PF. The particular dimensions are in pairs, high scores meaning one thing, low another. It's not either or, but somewhere between each of these sixteen pairs--the score tells you where on each of the sixteen continua.

Kinetic Family Drawings

Parent-Child Interaction Test

Before You See the Psychologist

Read "Whose Custody Case Is This Anyway?!" Chapter 1: War or Peace.

Confidentiality and the Psychologist

There is no confidentiality. Every word spoken to the psychologist and any test results may go into the final evaluation and becomes part of the court record, which becomes public record. The only exception is if the judge seals the records to protect the children.

Sex and the Psychologist

Even if you are normally a logical person, this period of your life will cause you to operate more often from an emotional level. Finding people you feel believe in you (friends, attorneys, detectives, psychologists) and want to help, encourages you to shift strong emotions to the "helper." This shifting is called transference. Helpers may or may not be aware of this phenomena. Transference is usually desperate and intense.

Transference is temporary with no resemblance to the real emotional bonds that grow from time and trust rather than an emotional rebounding. Your need for assurance and encouragement at this time gives others a disproportional amount of influence over you.

When you consult a professional for counseling, it is the emotional trust and bonding that occurs that allows the psychologist to help you during therapy. The professional is trained to observe, analyze, understand, assist and guide. Psychological techniques exploited by unscrupulous persons can be used to manipulate.

It is a gross breach of trust, conduct and ethics for the psychologist to make romantic or sexual advances during this association. It is just as unethical for psychologists to succumb to your advances. A responsible psychologist will immediately realign the relationship if you behave inappropriately. Offending the professional by communicating or behaving in a provocative manner is stupid. Once a breach of conduct on either side has occurred, the value and validity of the evaluation or therapy is destroyed. There is no way to measure the damage that can be caused to your case and you permanently, if there is any sexual misconduct with the psychologist. It is unethical for a psychologist to have a personal relationship with a patient within five years of the last time they met professionally.

Filing a Formal Complaint

If you feel that you have been unfairly treated, consider filing a complaint with the professional organizations to which the psychologist belongs. The complaint must list incidents in which the psychologist did not follow the code of ethics or did not use proven techniques for their recommendations. In the event of sexual contact, consider legal action.

Change Where the Children Live?

It could. This person's opinion is very important. A recommendation in your favor could go a long way in overcoming or maintaining status quo meaning, What Is, Shall Remain. In status quo, the children will remain where the children have been residing, unless a problem (obvious danger to the children) can be proven to exist.

Tests for Children and Adolescents

The children's tests are similar in results to the tests for adults, but are adapted to suit the child's needs and abilities. In psychology, the general mental ability involved in processes such as calculating, reasoning, classifying, learning, the use of language, and adjusting to new situations. It is widely accepted that although potential intelligence is related to heredity, the environment is a critical factor in determining the extent of its expression. Since the concept of intelligence is elusive, it has generally been defined by psychologists as that which is measured by intelligence tests.

Bricklin Perceptual Scales

A research-based custody test which measures a child's perceptions of each parent in four critical areas: competency, supportiveness, consistency, and admirable traits. It is aimed at children who are age six and older.

WISC

Currently the Wechsler Intelligence Scale for Children is the most widely used intelligence test. It has been revised recently because there were some problems with it and the most commonly used version at this time is the third version.

WAIS-III

Wechsler Adult Intelligence Scales-III is the most accepted intelligence test for adults. Often used in forensic or custody evaluation.

Stanford-Binet Intelligence Testing

This is another intelligence test. It is the first American intelligence test to use the term, "I.Q." and one of the most widely utilized tests of its kind. This test measures intelligence in adolescents and adults.

Thematic or Children's Apperception

In this test, more commonly referred to as the "TAT", an adolescent is asked to tell a story about black and white pictures that are presented. It's used to examine social-emotional components of the personality of adolescents.

Miscellaneous Projective Drawings

Projective tests have been used for many years as a way of tapping the unconscious of patients. In oversimplified form, the theory holds that the unconscious will strongly contribute to responses made under ambiguous conditions.

Bender Gestalt

There are more than one. For example, in the Bender Gestalt Visual/Motor, the child copies geometric designs from nine cards. This test is a frequently used assessment tool that evaluates visual-motor abilities of children aged five to eleven.

Wide Range Achievement Test

The test is a far-reaching scale for overall evaluation and age-appropriate comparisons.

Family Eruptions Test

Simply put, all seven of these tests are used as tools to interpret a child's perception of his own world and familial environment. An art therapist, for example, may ask a child to draw a picture of his family and compare the relationships between family members (Is one apart from the others? Is one abnormally large? Small?) to help determine how the child views himself or herself in the world.

Tasks of Emotional Development Test

These are a series of tests used to determine where a child or adult stands in terms of a pre-established norm for emotional development. Different tests are administered for adults than for children.

Miscellaneous Anxiety Inventories

Helps identify anxieties and their causes and is used as an aid to help the person who is taking the test to overcome these anxieties, especially if they have debilitating effects, which prevent the subject from experiencing a fulfilling life.

Strange Situation Test

A measure of attachment developed and tested primarily with children not in child care. In it, researchers expose infants to a mild stress by separating them from their mothers for a few minutes.

Secure infants reestablish positive contact with their mothers following the separation. They hug their mothers, stay close to them or seem reassured by her return. Insecure infants either ignore and avoid their mothers or are not reassured by her return.

Psychological Evaluation #1

W. Bowersock, Ph.D., P.C.
Clinical Psychologist
902 East Wiletta Street, Mesa, Arizona 95255
October 25, 1993
The Honorable L.L. BAPLON
Superior Court of Arizona, Maricopa County
Domestic Relations Division Re: Long Vs. Jones
201 W. Jefferson, Phoenix, AZ 95003 Custody Evaluation

Referral:

The undersigned psychologist was appointed through the court order to conduct a family evaluation in the above referenced case. The following report summarizes assessment findings and offers recommendations concerning the custody and visitation schedule of Bobby Long (DOB - 10/17/91)

Procedures

Individual Interviews:

Randall Long, father. Rebecca Long, stepmother. Amber Jones, mother James Miller, Mrs. Jones' former spouse.

Joint interviews:

Father, stepmother and child.
Mother, stepfather, and step-siblings.
Observational assessment of parent-child and sibling interactions.
Administration of personality assessment to all adults.

Additional interviews with the mother's three other children.

Documents & Materials Reviewed:

Letters from each parent. Re: visitation issues
Booklet of information supplied by Mr. Long including:

Photographs.
Temporary visitation orders.
Mediated agreement, April 1992
Deposition transcript, Mrs. Jones - Oct.1992
Transcript of trial proceedings - July 19,1993
Conciliation Services evaluation report 1/3/93.
Criminal plea, re: Mrs. Jones and Mr. Miller.
Transcript of telephone conversation with Mr. Long's first wife.

Collateral Contacts: none

Family/Marital History:

The family history is characterized by a complex intertwining of entangled personal and work relationships. The biological parents, Mr. Long and Mrs. Jones, were never married. Rebecca Long owns a warehouse business.

Both Mr. Miller and Mrs. Jones previously worked for her. Mrs. Long and Mr. Miller acknowledge that they had a prior relationship in approximately 1981. This was before Mrs. Long married Mr. Long. Mrs. Jones and Mr. Miller were still married, but had been experiencing serious marital problems for some time.

Mr. and Mrs. Long were married in 1984. Mr. Long was aware of the past relationships between Mrs. Long, Mrs. Jones and Mr. Miller.

Mrs. Jones divorced Mr. Miller in 1987, reporting he had a serious substance abuse problem primarily involving crystal methamphetamine. She also describes him as being physically abusive toward her and being emotionally and verbally abusive to her and their three children.

Mrs. Jones has been pregnant twice by Mr. Long. The first pregnancy ended in a miscarriage. Mrs. Jones stated the miscarriage occurred after her ex-husband, Mr. Miller. discovered that pregnancy, became enraged, and punched her in the stomach.

The relationship existed for several years and had temporarily abated in 1990. However, it resumed in late 1990. This resulted in a second pregnancy, the one, which led to the birth of Bobby.

Despite whatever other complaints are being aired now about the relationship, that relationship actually represented an unusual extended family, one, which served to satisfy the unmeet dependency needs of the adults.

Subsequent to Bobby's birth, a struggle over custody ensued. Initially, Mr. Long and Mrs. Jones reached a court mediated agreement in April 1992. This really was an extension of a schedule they had been following after Mrs. Jones returned to work after Bobby's birth.

Their mediated agreement assigned daytime child care responsibilities to Mr. Long. Mrs. Jones assumed nighttime overnight care. In addition, Mr. Long kept Bobby overnight once per week, and until 9:00 p.m. on a second evening as Mrs. Jones was attending school. The parents also alternated weekend care. This schedule remained in effect until July 1992, when Mrs. Jones moved to Washington State and did not return Bobby. At the time she had married Mr. Jones.

Mr. Long instituted suit that required Mrs. Jones to immediately return to Arizona. Temporary court orders were issued. Bobby Long was ordered to remain in Arizona pending the outcome of a custody hearing. Mrs. Jones then left her three older children in Washington for eight months with her new in-laws, so she could remain in Arizona to maintain contact with Bobby.

Subsequent court orders in February 1993 permitted the mother to relocate to Washington and established an alternating three week visitation schedule between parents for Bobby. This subsequently amended to an alternating five week schedule in August 1993.

There is no history of physical abuse between Mr. Long and Mrs. Jones. There are no indications that Bobby has been physically mistreated either. However, concerns have been expressed by Mr. Long regarding Mrs. Jones's emotional stability, criminal background, relationship problems and quality of care she provides to Bobby.

Mrs. Jones has contended that she has always raised her other three children without the interference of their father. She feels that it would be to Bobby's advantage to be raised within her family setting. She expressed dissatisfaction with Mr. Long being so controlling of the parent-child relationship.

Both parents were distrustful that the other would fail to return their son consistent with the current court order.

Mr. Long does not use day care, nor rely upon family members or private sitters to assist him with child care. He does help in his wife's business.

He has converted a separate office into a child's room so he can care for Bobby while he is there. Mr. Long has resided in the same home since 1988.

Upon the last date of interview, Mrs. Jones was again living with Mr. Miller, who apparently moved to Oregon in April 1993, after learning about one of his sons being physically abused by Mrs. Jones' then husband, Mr. Jones. The family is attending family counseling. Mrs. Jones works as a shift supervisor at a fast food restaurant. Her work hours run from approximately 4:00 to 10:00 p.m. five days a week.

However, her work schedule varies. Mr. Miller reported being steadily employed as an auto mechanic.

He works 9:00 a.m. to 5:00 p.m. Monday through Friday.

Mrs. Jones has three older children: Lucy(15), Byron(12), Jerome(11). When Bobby visits, she relies upon either her daughter or teenage baby-sitter to provide afternoon child care until Mr. Miller returns home from work.

Each parent was desirous of being awarded sole custody.

They are not cooperative in resolving issues affecting Bobby. They are unlikely to reestablish residency within the same state.

Parental Adjustment:

Randall Long appears to be a quiet, passive and nurturing individual. He does not present with any history of violence or aggression. He is currently disabled due to a 1983 trucking accident. Mr. Long has been married before. He has not maintained contact with his older children. However, he apparently has provided financial support.

Mr. Long does not present a prior history of mental health treatment or substance abuse problems. He has never been arrested. Although the relationship between the adults in this case is atypical, there is nothing to suggest that Mr. Long suffers from a serious maladjustment. Personality test findings indicate Mr. Long tends to be shy and withdrawn. He may not readily form relationships and may feel more comfortable with a rural life-style. He also appears to be bothered by ongoing problems of pain and discomfort. These are residual injuries sustained in the former trucking accident. He is most concerned about health-related matters. There are no indications he suffers behavioral problems, which would limit his ability to parent.

Rebecca Long is an entrepreneur. She is the one who basically provides for the financial support of the family, while Mr. Long provides the bulk of the child care. Mrs. Long represents herself as being rebellious, impulsive, and challenging of authority. She readily acknowledges having a liberal attitude about acceptable sexual relationships. However, she described her relationship with Mr. Long as satisfying and loving.

Mrs. Long does not fit the typical female role. She was married once before. She has one daughter, now in her early twenties. Following her divorce, she was awarded sole custody of her daughter.

She has never been arrested, treated for substance abuse problems, or been involved in prior mental health treatment. Mrs. Long's test findings were valid and within normal limits. She also appears to be a hard-driving individual, one who may become excited by or interested in the exploits of antisocial characters. However, there is no history of antisocial behavior.

Amber Jones presents an unstable background of interpersonal relationships. She quickly jumps from one marriage or intimate relationship into another. Mrs. Jones has been involved in three major relationships: Randall Long, Mike Jones and James Miller. The later two individuals she has been married to a total of three times. She has three children by Mr. Miller. She is now currently residing with him, while pursuing divorce for the second time from Mr. Jones. Mrs. Jones has evidenced poor judgment and borderline criminal activity. She had been found guilty of attempting to smuggle drugs into a prison system. She is very dependent on others and has yet to learn how to rely upon herself to survive. Mrs. Jones has frequently moved. Her older children have attended many different schools. She was hoping she could reconstruct her relationship with Mr. Miller.

Mrs. Jones denied being treated for a substance abuse problem. However, she did acknowledge that when she was involved with the Longs she often drank to excess. She is now involved, for the first time, in family counseling.

Test results indicated that Mrs. Jones most likely suffers from a personality disorder. She is unlikely to deal with anger and confrontation constructively. She is prone to express her hostility in indirect ways including: lack of cooperation, purposeful obstruction, and defiance. She also is likely to be very dependant and insecure. She may have developed a view of the world in which she feels mistreated and given a raw deal. These characteristics are probably long-standing in nature and unrelated to the current stresses associated with the custody battle.

James Miller also presents a history of instability. He has suffered from serious substance abuse problems. It was unclear to this examiner when he last used alcohol or drugs. Record review indicated he accepted a plea bargain in early 1993 regarding drug possession.

Mr. Miller denied ever being abusive. However, this directly contradicts statements made by Mrs. Jones about being punched by him when she was formerly pregnant. He has been married only once, to Mrs. Jones. He describes her as being his high school sweetheart. He acknowledged having formally abused marijuana, speed and crystal. He was motivated to attempt to resurrect his family and marriage. Despite his substance abuse problem, he has not been involved in any kind of treatment program. His current relationship with Mrs. Jones is in flux.

Personality test findings were invalid, due to an excessive tendency to present himself in a socially desirable and acceptable fashion. It is best to avoid offering an interpretation of this profile in light of the distorted response tendency.

Child's Adjustment:

Bobby is almost two years old. He is not yet toilet trained. He has a limited vocabulary. In fact, Mrs. Long was aware that this child may be exhibiting some delayed speech.

When observed, he was noted to grunt and point and frequently say "huh". Bobby was not observed to display discernible speech. This may be an area that should be more closely monitored for possible future speech intervention. Health-wise, Bobby is essentially fine.

However, there is some documented evidence to indicate that whenever he has returned from placement with the mother, he has lost approximately one or two pounds. The family doctor responsible for his pediatric care has commented that this is a rather unusual finding.

Bobby also was having a problem with rotting teeth. Mr. Long had taken his son to both the family doctor and a pediatric dentist. His teeth have been capped and bonded to prevent further decay. He was informed this condition was due to permitting his son to go to sleep with a bottle of milk in his bed. Mrs. Jones stated she had never given her child milk at night anyway, so she was not responsible for this problem.

When observed, Bobby appeared to be happy and pleasant. If anything, he was provided with too much attention by Mrs. Jones' family.

This reached the point where everyone was giving Bobby instructions, a situation, which appeared to over-stimulate him.

As mentioned, Mrs. Jones' children were also included for interview.

They confirmed having moved several times. They did not know Mr. Long. They deny that they have ever been physically mistreated by their father, James Miller. However, one child, Byron (twelve), appears to have a serious behavioral problem involving anger management. He was once struck and injured by his stepfather, Mike Jones. This incident occurred in his mother's presence.

<u>Parent-child Interactions:</u>

Bobby was responsive to everyone with whom he was observed. He evidenced no discomfort with and seemed to relate well to James Miller. Likewise, he was very comfortable with Rebecca Long and was often noted to request and receive attention and affection from her.

Both parents indicate when Bobby returns from visiting the other parent, he exhibits increased aggression typified by hitting, biting and pinching, behaviors, which may last one to two weeks. As this is occurring in both homes, this appears to reflect adjustment difficulties following visitation exchanges.

Bobby was observed to readily interact with his father and stepmother. Both adults were willing to get on the floor and play with him. Bobby was very relaxed and comfortable with them.

When observed with only Mrs. Jones and Mr. Miller, Bobby also appeared relaxed and calm. Mrs. Jones assumed more direct parental involvement when the other children were absent. She was responsive to Bobby and provided him with affection.

None of the adults involved appear to be at risk of improperly disciplining Bobby. All four adults interviewed appear to adopt a non-abusive punitive style of discipline.

<u>Conclusions:</u>

1. There is a distinct difference in the personal and interpersonal stability of the parents. Mr. Long is the one who is more stable.

2. Mrs. Jones's life is in flux. She has frequently jumped from one relationship to another, and in light of the past history of marital problems, it is too early to determine whether the family situation is stable.

3. Mr. Long is the one who can offer Bobby the most stability.

4. The current visitation exchange schedule appears to have an adverse behavior effect on Bobby. Modification in this arrangement is needed.

<u>Recommendations:</u>

1. In light of the family and personal backgrounds, and the child's adjustment, it is recommended that Mr. Long be awarded sole custodial control and care of his son.

2. Visitation with the mother is advised to be scheduled consistent with long distance visitation guidelines. Given Bobby's young age, it is recommended that contact over the summertime be divided into two segments until he reaches kindergarten age.

3. Given the conflicts and existing lack of cooperation between the parties, this visitation schedule must be scheduled in advance. Holidays should be shared and alternated. To avoid conflict and misunderstanding, the visitation schedule is suggested to be fixed and should not be extended or adjusted if either parent is unable to exercise their visitation as outlined.

4. It is advised that Mrs. Jones not only attend family therapy, but also involve herself in individual treatment. She should focus on issues of assertiveness, and overcoming her excessive dependency and insecurity, which have led her to jump from one relationship into another.

5. Telephonic contact between homes should also be designated. It is recommended that this be limited to twice per week. However, as Bobby grows older, and develops language skills, it would be anticipated that this would be expanded. A balance must be developed between intrusiveness and a desire to remain in touch with a child residing out of state.

6. Although Bobby may not be sleeping with his parents, it is advisable that he be moved into his own room to promote his developing a sense of independence and competency.

End Of Report

Evaluation #1/ Addendum

W. Bowersock, Ph.D., P.C. October 25, 1993
902 East Wiletta Street, Mesa, Arizona 95255
The Honorable L.L. BAPLON
Superior Court of Arizona, Maricopa County, Domestic Relations Division
Re: Long vs. Jones

Report Addendum

Dear Judge Baplon;

In response to concerns expressed about my report not being specific regarding summer access, I offer the following suggestions, which are consistent with Maricopa County long distance visitation guidelines. These recommendations take into consideration Bobby's age (2) and are based upon the assumption that visitation will be increased as he grows older.

<u>The following guidelines are suggested:</u>

Age ... Summer Access

2 years old ... Five weeks total visitation divided into two segments of Three weeks and Two weeks each.

3 and 4 years old ... Six weeks visitation, divided into two three week segments.

5 years old ... Six weeks visitation, divided into two sessions; the first four weeks and the second two week's in length.

6 years old ... Six consecutive week's visitation

7 and older years old ... Eight consecutive week's visitation.

The parents are advised to provide the undersigned evaluator or any other designated mental health professional, by April 15th of each year, with a copy of their summer vacation plan. This is to include any special events they would like to attend as a family. These will then be considered when developing each summer's vacation schedule.

Regarding holiday access, for ease of scheduling and to avoid misinterpretation, Christmas, Thanksgiving, and Spring holiday will run coincidental to the school calendar.

During <u>odd number</u> years, Mr. Long will have the following visitation: Spring Break and the first week of Christmas Holiday. Mrs. Jones will have Thanksgiving and the second week of Christmas Holiday.

During <u>even numbered</u> years, Mr. Long will have Thanksgiving, and the second week of Christmas Holiday. During <u>odd number</u> years, Mrs. Jones will have the following visitation: Spring Break and the first week of Christmas Holiday.

Thanksgiving holiday will run from Wednesday evening through Sunday evening. The first week of Christmas holiday will run from the Friday afternoon of the last day of school through the following Saturday (eight days later).

Bobby will be exchanged on the Saturday of the middle weekend. He will be returned to the primary residential parent on Sunday evening, the night before school resumes.

As the need for interstate transportation is likely to continue, when air travel is chosen:

Bobby is to be placed on the flight closest to noontime as possible.

I hope that this addendum provides a more detailed understanding of the summer and holiday access.

Very truly yours.
W. Bowersock, Ph.D., P.C. End of Addendum

Psychological Evaluation #2

W. Bowersock, Ph.D., P.C.
Clinical Psychologist
902 E. Wiletta Street, Mesa, AZ 95255
December 27, 1993

The Honorable P.J. Lassater
Superior Court of Arizona, Maricopa County, Domestic Relations Division
201 W. Jefferson, Phoenix, AZ 95003
Re: Jesus Hernandez
Custody Evaluation Referral

The undersigned psychologist was appointed by the Honorable P.J. Lassater as the mental health professional to conduct a family evaluation in the above-referenced case. The following report summarizes my findings and recommendations regarding the custody of Jesus (Jesse) Hernandez (age five).

Procedures:

Interviews and Testing:
Individual interview with each parent and joint interview of each parent and child.
Observational assessment of parent-child interactions.
Administration of personality assessment to each parent.
Documents Reviewed: Petition affidavit of Permanent Custody.

Family/marital History:

1. Rosie Moro and Joe Hernandez were never married. They met in 1986 and dated off and on until Ms. Moro became pregnant. Their child Jesse was born in 1988. He is now five (5) years old.

2. Only ten (10) days after the child's birth, Mr. Hernandez moved to San Diego, California, to finish a ten-month tour with the Navy.

3. The couple apparently separated in the beginning of Ms. Moro's pregnancy. They did attempt to co-residence in the early stages of her pregnancy. They lived together until Mr. Hernandez moved to San Diego for his military service.

4. From the time Jesse was born, the maternal grandparents have been the primary and most consistent child care provider. Although the exact amount of time they devoted to child care is disputed, they provided between four (4) to five (5) days care until Jesse's father completed his military service. Independent of the disputed amount of care provided, the maternal grandparents have been a steady parental influence for their grandson.

5. The couple did live in San Diego, California, for five (5) months after Mr. Hernandez completed his military service. They subsequently returned to Arizona and moved in with the maternal grandparents. They briefly obtained an apartment for three (3) months, but then moved in with the paternal grandmother for approximately six (6) months. They again moved into their own place, but separated for the final time in August 1992, only one (1) month later.

6. During the time the couple resided in Arizona, the maternal grandparents still continued to play an active role in care-taking. The maternal grandparents reported after discovering their grandson was placed in daily day care for two (2) weeks, ten (10) hours a day, and they again insisted on providing in-home care for Jesse.

7. Ms. Moro moved in with her parents October 1992. Mr. Hernandez is now living with a girlfriend, whom he regards as his fiance.

8. The relationship between Mr. Hernandez and Ms. Moro was both physically and emotionally abusive. Each apparently denigrated the other, while Mr. Hernandez acknowledges being responsible for most of the physical violence.

9. After the final separation, the couple reached an apparent oral agreement about Jesse living primarily with Ms. Moro. However, the couple disputed the intent of how long this placement was to last. Mr. Hernandez indicated that the placement was to last only until he could complete his training. Ms. Moro indicated this agreement had no time limit.

10. Mr. Hernandez is employed as an automotive mechanic five (5) days a week, and has received a promotion to shop foreman after two (2) years.

11. Ms. Moro apparently works as a stock clerk at a grocery store four (4) days a week for minimum wage. She is hoping to eventually take her State Boards to certify herself as a nail care specialist.

12. Temporary custody was awarded to the mother in November 1992. In consideration of his work schedule, the court awarded Mr. Hernandez visitation every other Saturday from 9:00 a.m. through Monday at 7:00 a.m.

13. Mr. Hernandez has been consistent with visitation since it was ordered. However, parental reports vary regarding the amount of time he spent providing child care before the court order was issued.

14. Ms. Moro reported that Mr. Hernandez had been sporadic in his contact and would frequently keep Jesse less than anticipated. Some of these contacts were not overnight, and at other times, he apparently failed to appear for visitation without providing notice of postponement. Mr. Hernandez indicated he always visited his son on weekends and during the week while Jesse resided at the maternal grandparents' home.

15. Problems between the maternal grandmother and father, and mother and father's fiance have been reported during visitation exchange.

16. Mr. Hernandez was willing to enter into a shared custody agreement, while Ms. Moro believes sole custody was indicated. Mr. Hernandez wished to keep the mother's visitation liberal, but unspecified. Ms. Moro stated the father should receive basic guideline, alternate weekend contact.

<u>Parental Adjustment:</u>

1. Rosie Moro dropped out of school after completing the ninth grade. She has unsuccessfully attempted to pass the GED examination twice. She apparently must have the GED before she can take the Board Certification as a Nail Technician.

2. Ms. Moro appears to present with learning difficulties. Although she stated she was disinterested in school and unmotivated to perform, she appeared to suffer from educational weaknesses.

3. Mr. Hernandez is a high school graduate. He does not present with a history of learning disability. He did complete a year of college.

4. Of the two adults, Mr. Hernandez presents a significant history of family dysfunction. This included a family history marked by divorce, molestation of himself and other children by his natural father, physically abusive discipline, and witnessing domestic violence within his family. He does not present a current problem or past history of alcohol or drug abuse.

5. Both parents have apparently been fairly steadily employed.

6. Ms. Moro comes from an intact family. Her parents have been married thirty-five years. She maintains close ties to her family and does receive their support with child care.

7. Results of personality testing indicated defensive test taking attitudes. Although such is typically found in custody evaluations, Mr. Hernandez exhibited this to such an extent as to invalidate his test results. Test findings concerning Ms. Moro were valid and within normal limits. Mr. Hernandez was so guarded during personality assessment that he is unlikely to self-disclose any personal weaknesses.

8. Due to their central role in Jesse's life, the maternal grandparents were interviewed. They appear to have a well-balanced and intact marriage. They are committed to providing whatever assistance is needed for their grandson. Neither one presents a history of alcohol or drug abuse, past mental health treatment, or antisocial behavior. Although Mr. Hernandez accused the maternal grandfather of being motivated to replace him as a father, assessment revealed his intentions to be based solely on what was best for his grandson.

<u>Child's Adjustment:</u>

1. Jesse is a verbal 5-year-old child who appeared to display age-appropriate behavior. Jesse does not present with any significant medical or developmental problems. However, he has been

prone to frequent ear infections.

2. Jesse has a fleeting notion of what is occurring within the family. He was aware that his mom and dad do not live together and that his father now has a girlfriend.

3. Jesse attends a preschool program five (5) days per week. Reportedly, he is well adjusted socially. The grandparents reported the preschool has noticed that Jesse is more fatigued on the days his father returns him to school.

4. Although Mr. Hernandez complained about the mother or her family failing to adequately provide for Jesse's medical care, this was not confirmed.

Parent - Child Relationships:

1. Observations of parent/child interactions supported the conclusion that Jesse is attached to each.

2. Mr. Hernandez exhibited considerable caring, patience, comfort, and affection toward his son. He could set limits and provide his son with needed direction. Jesse responded quite well to his father.

3. Jesse was observed to be very comfortable in his mother's presence. Ms. Moro related to her son appropriately. She also was able to set limits and was observed to encourage and praise her son.

4. Unfortunately, while in his son's presence, Mr. Hernandez complained about what he believed was the inadequate care and treatment his son was receiving from the mother and grandparents. While Mr. Hernandez did criticize the mother in front of his son, Ms. Moro did not do likewise.

Conclusions:

1. The role of the maternal grandparents appears to be the most important and steady parental influence Jesse has known to date. To remove him from the grandparents' care would appear ill-advised at this time.

2. Of the two parents, Ms. Moro displays more positive signs of emotional adjustment than was assessed with the father.

Recommendations:

1. Sole custody to the mother appears indicated.

2. It is recommended that the maternal grandparents continue to provide supportive child care. They are an important source of security, consistency, and caring for the child.

3. Visitation with the father is suggested to be alternate weekends from Friday, 6:00 p.m. until Monday at 9:00 am. In addition, one day midweek overnight contact, with the same time frame, is also suggested. Mr. Hernandez would be responsible for transportation. Should Mr. Hernandez's work schedule change, a new visitation schedule would then be arranged.

4. Holidays are to be shared and alternated. Each parent is entitled to spend up to fourteen consecutive days for out-of-town vacation travel with their son. Phone contact between parent and child may be daily, but should be limited to approximately ten minutes per call.

5. All major decisions impacting this child's life should be made by the mother. This will prevent open conflict from erupting between the parents over child care issues.

6. It is recommended both parents submit documentation of completion of a parent training program.

7. If arguments are occurring during visitation exchange, the court may wish to consider either designation of a third party to assist in the exchange or identifying a neutral site for Jesse's transfer.

W. Bowersock, Ph. D. End of Report.

What to Do about a Bad Evaluation

If the recommendation is not fair or you are not happy with it, you may attempt to submit additional testing or documentation to amend incorrect information. It is worth your time to correct any problems identified in the report and document your efforts.

Many psychologists jump into a custody case eager to become an advocate and clearly disregard the very strict new rules of the American Psychological Association Guidelines for Custody Evaluations. The limitations that APA Guidelines place on the work of psychologists in custody evaluation cases should be emphasized. Therefore, every one of the guidelines provides good cross-examination material if a negative evaluation is a factor at trial.

One should ask what special education this particular expert has in the special aspects of this custody case. Is the supposed expert highly qualified in questions of sexual abuse, over-parenting, alcoholism, homosexuality? Also, psychologists are required to avoid "multiple relationships" with a patient. Thus a treating psychologist should not be the evaluator.

Filing a Formal Complaint

It is a waste of your time to file a complaint if you are not happy with the results and the professional did the evaluation correctly. You may want to have a second opinion of the evaluation report. If you do submit it for opinion, don't do a bunch of explaining about the results. Just submit the report for an honest evaluation. If this professional comes to the same conclusion the original evaluator did, you must rethink your situation. You may ask the evaluator what you can do to improve your status.

If you feel that you have been unfairly treated, consider filing a complaint with the court and professional organizations of which the psychologist is a member. See, Chapter 10: Evaluations, Filing A Formal Complaint.

Evaluating the Psychologist

Your demeanor during the interviews should be serious about the process and open with your attitude. Fill out a copy of this form after each appointment with the psychologist.

Review it and fax it to your attorney. Have your significant other fill out a form each time. If you are having problems with the psychologist, now is the time to let your attorney know about it, not after the evaluation and recommendation have been made.

Evaluating the Psychologist Example #1
Did the psychologist keep the appointment and arrive on schedule? Yes. I arrived early and he didn't make me wait.
Did the psychologist explain the process and answer your questions? Yes. I was very worried and he calmed me down. I told him my specific fears and he explained why I should not worry.
Did the psychologist maintain an objective, impartial attitude? He was hard to read, but I did feel I got a fair hearing. He asked me to address several charges made by the other parent and I felt he was willing to hear my side.
Did the psychologist exhibit any personal biases? I asked if he felt that one parent may be a better parent than the other because of sex and he said his determinations were on a case by case basis with about a 50/50 split.
Did the psychologist answer your questions? For the most part. I will have some more for the next meeting.
Did the psychologist lead or ram rod your answers? *No.*
Did the psychologist inform participants about the limits of confidentiality and disclosure of information? *Yes*
Did the psychologist use multiple methods of data gathering? Yes. Tests, interviews and review of documents.
Did the evaluator indicate interest in the physical, emotional and psychological interest of the children? Yes. A lot of the discussion we had was about the children and the affect this ordeal was having on them.
Did the psychologist encourage you to submit additional information and give you a phone number or some other ability to do so? Yes. He said to call if I had questions or additional data.
Did the psychologist say anything specific that encouraged you? Just that a decision was only weeks away rather than months.
Did the psychologist say anything specific that discouraged you? *No* **Did the psychologist make any statements that caused you concern?** *No*
What was your overall feeling about how you and you partner presented for the evaluation? I think I was able to show him that I want my children to be OK when this is over and am willing to do whatever it takes.

Evaluating the Psychologist Example #2
Did the psychologist keep the appointment and arrive on schedule? I guess. There were a bunch of people in the waiting room when I got there, and I felt like everyone knew why I was there.
Did the psychologist explain the process and answer your questions? He said I had to come back two more times. Once with my children and next time for a Minnesota test.
Did the psychologist maintain an objective, impartial attitude? I think most of the questions he asked don't have anything to do with custody and are none of his business.
Did the psychologist exhibit any personal biases? I didn't like him and I don't think he liked me. He wanted to know about all the stuff the other parent has made up about me.
Did the psychologist answer your questions? *I didn't ask any. I just wanted out of there. I don't have any faith in psychology.*
Did the psychologist lead or ram rod your answers? *No.*
Did the psychologist inform participants about the limits of confidentiality and disclosure of information? He said everything I say to him goes in the report.
Did the psychologist use multiple methods of data gathering? *I don't know.*
Did the evaluator indicate interest in the physical, emotional and psychological interest of the children? He asked how my kids were doing. I asked him how they were supposed to be doing with all this crap the other parent was pulling. He didn't have a real answer for me.
Did the psychologist encourage you to submit additional information and give you a phone number or some other ability to do so? Yea., but I don't think it will really help .
Did the psychologist say anything specific that encouraged you? *No.*
Did the psychologist say anything specific that discouraged you? *No* **Did the psychologist make any statements that caused you concern?** *No*
What was your overall feeling about how you and your partner presented for the evaluation? "I asked him if the judge always did what he suggested and he said not always so I think this was a waste of time."

Evaluating the Psychologist Example #3
Did the psychologist keep the appointment and arrive on schedule? It took four months to schedule the evaluations, but once it started she was fine.
Did the psychologist explain the process and answer your questions? She answered my questions about what she was going to do, but not exactally what would be done with the results. She said no when I asked if I could see the results of the individual evaluation sheets.
Did the psychologist maintain an objective, impartial attitude? I didn't like having to explain copies of documents that my soon to be former spouse gave to her. I thought there wasn't supposed to be any mud slinging.
Did the psychologist exhibit any personal biases? Not particularly.
Did the psychologist answer your questions? She said the questions I was asking about what and when the court would decide were not in her area.
Did the psychologist lead or ram rod your answers? *No.*
Did the psychologist inform participants about the limits of confidentiality and disclosure of information? She said there weren't any.
Did the psychologist use multiple methods of data gathering? Interview, tests and documentation.
Did the evaluator indicate interest in the physical, emotional and psychological interest of the children? Yes. She offered some suggestions for making things easier for them.
Did the psychologist encourage you to submit additional information and give you a phone number or some other ability to do so? Yes. I attempted to put the same things about my life before her that I could see my soon to be former spouse was presenting. I just wasn't as well prepared as he was.
Did the psychologist say anything specific that encouraged you? *No.*
Did the psychologist say anything specific that discouraged you? *She just said things would eventually get better.* **Did the psychologist make any statements that caused you concern?** *No*
What was your overall feeling about how you and your partner presented for the evaluation? I don't have anyone at this time, but I think I did Ok. I feel better now that is over. My soon to be former spouse is a salesman and normally everyone just loves him. I don't think she was fooled by "Mr. Wonderful" and "Miss Gee I Am Just So Cute."

Chapter 13: Children's Perspective

Every year more than one million children begin to face the challenges of the child custody battle. Until each state creates special family courts that use specially trained psychiatrists, social workers, attorneys and judges, the process will remain a process that often takes eighteen months.

One of the common problems children face during a custody battle is that they become less a child and more a prize that must be won. Even under normal circumstances, time for children is often shuffled around the need to earn a living and daily adult responsibilities to keep things running. The purpose of this chapter is to sensitize us to the pain and pressure our children feel and give us some ways to ease that burden.

Child and Parent Match

You may not be the appropriate parent to care for your child during every stage through, which the child passes. A person terrorized by infants may be at ease with toddlers. One may feel that primary school children consume a person's entire life, but feel comfortable with teenagers.

When both parents are available to the children in one home, children often gravitate to one parent for a period of time and then to the other. The excited greeting and homecoming of the working parent by the child will sometimes astonish a homemaker parent who has cared for and entertained a child all day. Children generally greet lesser contact parents and loved ones with a great deal of joy. The greater contact parent should learn to enjoy this event with and for the child. Children need to share the events that make them happy.

But I Want to Stay with You

Partings generally cause a great amount of pressure and distress for children. It is normal and expected for children to tell people they love, "We want to stay with you. Don't leave us here. We don't want to visit our other house."

Children are very good at reading non-verbal communication. Since it reassures you of the children's love and warms your heart when they say they don't want to leave, you respond affectionately. When the children say these words, you hug and kiss them and tell them you also love them. Since their words are rewarded with affection and approval, the words will be repeated another time.

But in fact, the other parent probably hears the same thing at the other end. As the children become aware of the power they hold to control your emotions or manipulate situations to their benefit, they will do just that.

You may feel your children are innocents and subject to the manipulation of the other parent. This is usually true only in part. As children watch one side or both manipulate the people or situations around them, the children learn the process and use it just as they would learn any other behaviors. This indicates the children are intelligent and able to adapt to the emotional and psychological environment in which they live. It is entirely a matter of survival.

Once you are aware that what you hear is affected by the agenda of the children as well as yours and the other parents, you will be better able to deal with how your children give you information and the content of the communication.

10, 9, 8, 7, 6, 5, 4, 3, 2, 1, Lift Off

Prepare yourself emotionally for the children to leave. Put your feelings aside and make the process as easy on the children as possible.

If you know that once they get to the other parent's house they do in fact have a good time, say "You are going to have a wonderful time with Grandma (or Dad or Mom). Remember how you like to play with Spot and Fluffy."

If you know the children really do not enjoy the visit, but must go, say "You know this is the weekend you go to Grandma (or Dad or Mom). Remember you always come home after and I will see you then."

One way to ease the stress of departure is to help the children make something like cookies to take to the other home. Then the event becomes a "taking something to" excitement rather than a "leaving behind" sad time.

By preparing for difficult situations and communicating without high emotion, your control skills will grow. You will be able to teach your children how to accept and enjoy the present circumstances (even if they are not perfect) and adapt to new situations. The ability to adapt to new situations is essential to your children's survival.

Children Who Want to Choose

The desires of the children are important to the court. To assist in making their decisions, mediators and judges use many methods to determine where the children have the best options. At a certain age (which varies from jurisdiction to jurisdiction), the court gives greater weight to the children's opinion.

Often children will sign an 'Affidavit of Preference' or 'Choice of Managing Conservator By Child Twelve Years Or Older' under pressure for one parent and then sign one under pressure for the other parent when the document's existence comes to light.

Because a second affidavit of preference for one parent usually follows the first submitted by the other parent, attorneys often advise against this tactic. This indicates to the court the children are attempting to please the people they love.

The court may even override the document if the judge feels the child's choice does not represent the child's best interest. Judges respond with varying degrees of acceptance when a form called a Choice Of Managing Conservator By Child is submitted on behalf of a child since the desires of a young person are subject to change with the high emotion of the custody case and the intense drama of puberty.

Some judges let a family divide itself, with the children splitting up to go to separated parents. Is this good? In some cases it is the best solution available. Help make your children's choices easier.

Even after the decision is made regarding residency, additional decisions must be made. It is your responsibility to resolve conflicts, so that your children do not have to choose between you.

It is important to deal daily with the problems your children face in a manner that helps you bond with them. Positive reinforcement of good behavior, as well as redirection away from negative behavior, can lead to a stronger bond between you and your children. Seeing things from a child's view is not something we are trained to do. We don't even know how to help children gain the right vocabulary to express themselves. Put yourself in your children's shoes. See through their eyes, and hear through their ears.

Exploring the ways children see things will help you understand that the child's perception of an event is the reality in which the children must function. Rejecting the child's perception of an event and explaining the adult reality will often cause distress and confusion in the child. This happens because the adult explanation of the reality is too abstract for the child.

Children Who Cannot Choose

Most children should not be put in the position of having to choose one parent over the other. Being forced to choose can cause short-term behavioral problems and long-term emotional problems.

The children's feelings can include: confusion, anger, guilt,
distrust and can be exhibited by: illness, regression in social and developmental behaviors, hostility, submersion in school, sports, or imaginary friends, manipulation, acting out or withdrawal.

Professionals watch for signs that a parent is exerting undue pressure on children to chose them over the other parent. Understanding the negative effects of this activity, the professional can be prejudiced against the offending parent.Affidavit of Preference, Example:

NO. 95-003858

In The Interest Of	*In The District Court
Jennie Ann Rose	*224th District Court, Peoria County, Ohio
Donald Lee Rose	*
and,	*
Linda Marie Rose	*

Choice Of Managing Conservator

By Child Twelve Years Or Older

BEFORE ME, the undersigned authority, on this day personally appeared Linda Marie Rose, who by me duly sworn, made the following statements and swore that they were true:

"I, Linda Marie Rose, am a child whose conservatorship in being sought. I am 12 years of age or older."

"Subject to the approval of the Court, I choose my grandmother Lillian Rose to serve as my managing conservator."

"I understand that the managing conservator is the person with whom I will live and the person who will have the duty to provide for my care, control, and protection."

SIGNED on ___April 5th____, 19 _96_. ______*Linda Marie Rose*________ Linda Marie Rose

SIGNED under oath before me by Linda Marie Rose on April 5th, 1996.

___Mark Jackson__ Notary Public State Of Ohio Mark Jackson Commission Expires 05/05/2008

Hearing the Child's Voice

Make the effort to gain an understanding of the child's perception of an event.
Deal with your child's concerns from the child's level and ability to cope.

1. Talk to your child about any incident that may arise. Ask your child what the child has seen and how the child feels about it.

2. Explain that it is normal to have strong positive and negative feelings.

3. Find out what conclusions the child has come to about each incident. Set the child straight if the observations are not correct.

4. Assure your child you will keep the child safe, even if you are not sure you can.

5. Make an effort to be sensitive to situations that are happy, sad or violent. Let your child see that an adult feels and copes in a responsible manner with adult feelings.

Go Where they are Heard

Your communication skills with your children will grow, and you will be able to better teach them how to understand new situations. Because new situations case the most fear, children will gravitate toward the parent that has the time and the willingness to be with them when the children will have to face the unknown.

Another factor you should consider is that there are times when your children have a better chance of being heard by the court than you. This can be very shaky ground. It is common for children to tell the parent posing the question, what that parent wants to hear. Your children, in total honesty, may be telling each parent," I want to live with you."

Choosing the other parent is not an indictment of you by your child. Even when a child is given a choice, the child often feels there is no real choice. The child faces a no-win situation.

Your children are reaching for what they need now. These needs change and your children can request a change of residence later. We will explore a few common situations that cause stress in children and some ways parents can deal with the stress from the children's perspective.

Child's Realities

- I did not get to decide if the family stayed together or broke apart.
- One day everything was real good, and the next day our whole life was ruined.
- All the family rules keep changing.
- Sometimes they take away our telephone, car or electricity.
- I am not sure my parent can keep a place for us to live.
- My parents always said they loved each other and now they hate each other. If I do something wrong, they might start to hate me too.
- When I go for visitation, they say bad things about the parent I live with. I know the things aren't true, but it still hurts my feelings.
- My parent does not care enough about me to send child support money for food or clothes.
- If I like the "new" friend or parent, my real parent will be upset.
- At my desk it is hard to study; I keep thinking about the bad fights and yelling at home.
- I didn't get to choose the new family that will join with ours.
- If I had been a better kid, this would not have happened to my family.
- I am scared all the time.
- I think I am stuck here and nothing will ever be happy again.
- If the little kids get hurt, I will get into a lot of trouble.
- I don't like some new adult acting like my new parent.
- I was the big kid in the family; then I had the responsibilities of my parent who left; now I have to take orders from the two new bigger kids in the family.
- its hard to sleep cause I wake up from nightmares.
- I have to take care of the younger kids and don't get any time to do any school activities or play.
- The other kids know I am responsible for everything so they do things wrong just to get me in trouble.
- The big kids pick on me and make me do things and my parents don't care.

- I do not like the new kids in the family.
- If I am really good, everything will go back to the way it was.
- I don't have a room of my own or a private place for my things.
- I feel like something bad is going to happen all the time.
- My parents talk to me about grown up private things about their lives that scare and embarrass me.
- I want to just stay away at my friend's house and be in that family.
- When I go for visitation, they are mad that I don't want to stay there.
- I would like things to go back to the way they were before my parent left.
- I like where I live now, but the parent I don't live with talks to me all the time about moving to live there.

Dealing with Your Child's Fears

Growing with your children is much more rewarding than attempting to pull confused, frightened children into adult reality. Children often feel the failure of the marriage was caused because they were not a good enough child. Self-doubts, criticism and fears are intensified. Be less fearful yourself, and teach your children to live with a positive frame of mind. Do not disregard the fears your children express or gloss over their importance. Listen to what your child has to say. Help your children express their thoughts completely and attempt to eliminate the causes of their distress.

Loss

Children have a huge fear of loss. Loss of your love an companionship. Loss of contact with the other people they love. Loss of their toys and clothes. Loss of their friends when they go away to visitation. Loss of the new friends made while they were on visitation. It takes an enormous amount of love and patience to help children feel secure.

Monsters

There are real and dangerous monsters in the thick darkness that surrounds a child in the night. Leave a light on in the hall or put a night-light in the child's room. Do whatever it takes to get rid of the monsters. Placing a "Police Teddy" in a chair, in the closet, or under the bed sometimes solves this problem. Talk to the librarian in the children's section at your public library for titles of children's books that will help children overcome their fear of monsters.

Failure

It is essential to teach your children to love themselves as a precursor to accepting themselves as valuable persons. Once children accept their value as persons, they will be able to accept affection and approval from others and believe it is deserved. Children seek the company of adults who nurture them and who demonstrate delight in their presence. Tell your children how wonderful they are and do it often.

Small accomplishments give children the confidence to tackle bigger challenges. Playing games and sports with your children can start them on a winning path. You will always win in any competition against your children. It is better to offer a partnership in activities, so that your children can feel the supportive power of your strength or ability. Then you all win and share the success. Show your children how to enjoy the success of others when others win. It will remove the sting of defeat and make your children sought after by friends and peers throughout life.

Trying

It doesn't take very many failures to make children afraid to try new things. Teach children that, although they cannot be good at everything, new things can be wonderful and sometimes a lot of fun to try. Tell them when you are going to try something new and how you feel about it. Let them see your concern and willingness to try anyway. It doesn't matter if you fail or succeed, share what happens with your children. Your example will give them the courage to try.

The Future

Make plans with your children and carry those plans through to completion. It is important to start with a small project of short duration. A small goal with a short interval that produces success is important. Small projects like a Christmas Savings Fund, planting and harvesting or building something to make things easier are good places to start.

Assist the children in making plans that will accomplish something that is important to them. Making a gift of cookies for grandparents or the other parent. Teach them to make an alternative plan in case the original plan gets "rained out." Your interest in your children's plans shows them how important they are to you.

Not Doing the Right Thing

You are the primary person your children depend on for information. Children seek approval and you are your children's primary judge. Repeatedly, your children look to you for approval and verification of information from other sources. Therefore, in a moment of frustration or anger, if you thoughtlessly tell your children they are stupid, ugly, clumsy, bad or other hurtful things, the children will believe you. If given this negative information often enough or with enough volume, your children will believe you and be damaged for the rest of their lives.

If you hear yourself saying things like, "You spilled the milk again. Why are you so clumsy?" The "again" should let you know that this child is being set up to fail. Practice safe, pressure-releasing statements. An example would be, "Oh oh! Let's clean it up. Next time we'll pour only half a glass."

Be sure to catch your children doing something right as often as possible. Acknowledge your children's positive behavior even after something negative happens (like the spilled milk) with words like, "Thank you for grabbing the towel so fast to clean this up," or, "That was smart of you to grab those papers out of the way before the milk got on the papers.

Thank you." Your children watch you for indications of the right way to feel about things in general, as well as how to respond to specific situations that happen. Moods are contagious. Be sure your children are picking up the signals you want them to receive and are learning from your positive responses.

Abandonment

Hugs are as important to your teenager as they are to your newborn. No one can be spoiled by being snuggled, touched, and held by people who love them. Touch is the wonder drug of the ages. It improves your children's self-image, speeds healing, encourages weight gain in premature babies, instills a feeling of security, reduces crying and fussiness in infants, and improves learning ability. Your child needs to feel as safe and secure as a baby kangaroo in its mother's pouch.

Time

Time is a very difficult concept for children to understand. The time away from you can seem like an eternity for the younger children who have no concept of how long they will be separated from you. When they are away, your children feel an enormous loss of security, and the focus of their young lives is gone. So, as your children mature, give them markers to watch for to indicate when your time together is approaching.

Give them projects to work on while you are separated to ease the parting and give excitement to the reunion as their work is presented.

Give your children something to deliver to someone in the other home and put the emphasis on delivering the item, rather than on leaving you. A special blanket or Teddy bear can provide comfort in a lonely, confusing and frustrating world. It can also demonstrate to your children the rewards of taking care of the things that are important. Your children will appreciate the concern you demonstrate for the things they value. There are children who feel responsible for the welfare of their parents. Children panic at the thought of what will happen to that parent, if the child is not there to care for and protect the parent. This problem requires professional assistance.

Fear

Encourage self-confidence, spontaneity, enthusiasm, hope, and responsibility in your children. Let your children see the effects of these attitudes in your successes. Children who seek success and happiness with an optimistic attitude will find life easier than a child prepared for disappointment and failure.

Not Being Important

Children are instructed, told, re-directed, ordered, talked at and talked over by people bigger than they are. Children will want to spend more time with you, if you actually listen to them. Sometimes children will stammer and hesitate because they are accustomed to being interrupted or corrected while talking.

As the children realize that you will listen to them for as long as it takes to communicate, they will relax and gain confidence in speaking to you.

As consummate observers, children will watch your reactions to what is done to you and what you think is valuable and important. If crisis, illness or achievement get your attention, that is what the children may exhibit to gain attention.

What You Can Do To Help

- Be less fearful yourself. Do what you can, where you are, with what you have.
- Get your hands on some good reading material designed to help children undergoing stress.
- Establish and maintain good rapport with teachers and coaches that work with your children at school. Communicate with teachers and school administrators on a regular basis.
- Your children will have a difficult time remembering the good things and happy times.

Talk to your children about the happy things that happened each day, including the days your children were with the other parent. It is easier to ask the right kind of questions if you stay involved with their lives.

- Don't be too hard on yourself or your children.
- Help your children keep a journal or diary. This is the child's journal; don't be controlling or judgmental about what goes into it. If the child wishes, let it be private. As your contact log helps you work things through, this journal can help your child.
- Discipline should be predictable and flexible enough to address the growing needs and added stress that your child is experiencing. There are many books on discipline, read several.

Discipline

The goal of discipline or setting limits and rules is to help the child to gain self-control, learn self-help skills, and to feel good about himself or herself while relating in an enjoyable way with others.

Maintaining discipline during a custody battle is more difficult than under normal circumstances. The additional stress of the situation may cause children to test each situation with more enthusiasm than usual.

It is important to discipline children for their transgressions only. Some important points to remember are:

- Do not discipline all your children for the misbehavior of one.
- Do not vent your anger about the situation on your children.
- Do not withdraw your love or affection for misbehavior.
- Do not discipline for mistakes, only for misbehavior.
- Do not ridicule, belittle, insult, embarrass, shame or humiliate or use as discipline.
- Do not scream and yell.
- Do not specifically say or imply your children are a burden.
- Do not let your emotional state determine the kind or severity of the discipline.
- Make limits clear and short.
- Think of the example you set for the children when dealing with problems.
- Ignore inappropriate behavior whenever possible.
- Redirect misbehavior whenever possible.
- Offer children choices. Then respect the choice made.
- Help children see the cause and effect of their behavior whenever possible.
- Teach manners in private.
- Help children understand the reasons why certain behavior is expected.
- Stay out of children's conflicts as much as possible.
- Make sure your tone of voice matches the situation.
- Tell children what they can do rather than what they cannot do.

That's Not What I Meant to Say

Its easy to say you shouldn't be critical, hostile or ridicule your children. In fact, the stress of the custody battle may cause you to speak unkindly to your children. This is more likely to occur when they need you most. The times when you are exhausted from your job and the challenges the other person is causing. If you hear yourself saying anything like the fowling statements, you need to rethink how you speak to your children. Here are some examples of Bad Speak and Good Speak.

- **Bad Speak:** Won't you ever learn?

  Good Speak: That's hard. Let me show you.

- **Bad Speak:** Why do you always drop things?

  Good Speak: Its just an accident. Here is a towel, let's clean it up

- **Bad Speak:** You are being a brat.

  Good Speak: I know you are disappointed. I know how bad that feels

- **Bad Speak:** Can't you do anything right?

  Good Speak: Good try. Hold it with both hands next time.

Styles of Parental Discipline

The parent who must have perfect children:

These parents are controlling and demanding. There is no joy in or love and acceptance of a child's normal behavior. There is no forgiveness if any of the many rules are broken. Discipline takes the form of physical or emotional punishment. Punishment does not teach children how to do things right, but only shows them what will get them punished. The children of these parents will feel unloved and unlovable and have broken spirits that will make them withdrawn or aggressive.

The parent-pal:

These parents have no problem showing love and affection for their children and may be more emotionally dependant upon the children than is good for the relationship. Although discipline is threatened, it is never actually administered because these parents are afraid the children will withdraw their love. The children of these parents will have problems accepting limits and may exhibit an attitude of entitlement into adulthood.

The busy parent:

These parents are not necessarily living outside of the home. Parents emerged in their jobs or personal lives or problems may become distant and uninvolved. These parents don't set limits or discipline their children. With children there is no such thing as benign neglect. These children will be too insecure to develop healthy relationships. These children will rebel against authority and social skills.

Effective parent:

This parent shows love and affection, sets reasonable limits and uses guidance rather than discipline to reinforce and teach proper self-control and decision making. These children will develop other good relationships because they are secure in their ability to love and be loved. These parents learn from the mistakes they make and grow with their children.

Television

Under normal circumstances children are drawn to television. During a child custody battle children may withdraw into the fantasy world of happy families, free spirited unfettered teenagers and super-heroes who can fix anything with special powers. Rather than offering real relief from the unhappiness in their lives, children who watch a lot of television seem more aggressive.

The toy commercials encourage children to desire toys that may not be appropriate for the children or too expensive for the family to afford. The message that some commercials give is that you won't be happy until you have this toy and parents who love their children want them to be happy. The foods shown in commercials are often high in fat, sugar, salt and show children eating with their friends rather than with family members.

- Schedule chores, television, reading, game playing and quiet time together.
- Television programs you want to watch together should guide the scheduling of TV.
- Watch television with your children so you can discuss the program and answer their questions.

Activities

Deciding how to spend the time you have with your children can be difficult. These guidelines will give you a place to start. Infants enjoy being held, talked to, and cuddled. A toddler's short attention span and abundance of energy require more space and a great deal of physical activity. As the children gain maturity, they enjoys simple, quick-to-complete, hands-on projects that produce results that can be manipulated, floated, flown --- or eaten.

If the children associate you with early, stress-free successes, it will give the children the confidence to tackle larger projects and come to you for loving support. Gauge plans to the level of ability and interest of your children. The secret to having a successful outing or project with your children is the preparation you do before the children are involved.

Gather materials, pack a lunch, read the instructions, arrange transportation, or make reservations. Have several well thought out backup plans to put in operation should circumstances (such as the weather) foil your original plans.

As your children become more individual, it will be important to identify activities in which you have a shared interest. A few examples of things to do together would be cooking, golfing, reading, rock collecting, automotive repair, gardening, stock car racing, sewing, making stained glass, camping, or art classes.

Any positive activity will work that involves making plans and working together and will produce results in which the children feel a personal sense of accomplishment and a bonding with you.

Avoid overloading your child with activities. Help them expand their horizons by enrolling them in classes in which you may participate with them or watch them in:

- Gymnastics and Exercise Classes - Gymboree, Aerobikids, Kids in Action, YMCA and Weebodies
- Music Classes - Kindermusik Beginnings, School Band, School or Church Choir
- Art Classes - Arts a La Carte, Icky Sticky-Ooey Gooey, School of Art
- Swimming Classes - YMCA, Private Lessons, Public Park Lessons
- Ice Skating Classes - Ice Rinks (some located in large shopping malls) usually offer beginner classes
- Sports - Neighborhood sporting good stores have information about local teams
- Computer Classes - Futurekids, Computer Kids, Computer PlayGround, Kid Bytes

You are not expected to entertain your children twenty-four hours a day if they live with you most of the time. Having a shared interest to pursue and look forward to will enrich your relationship. This will also dispel the idea for the children that all the fun stuff happens with the "Disneyland Parent" whom the children see only twice a month.

If your children have limited time with you, and you are able to devote part of this time to a shared interest, your visit will be more rewarding for both of you. Adults who spent their formative years being shuttled between parents recall fishing activities with much more fondness than the amusement park days.

You Are Always On My Mind

Stay in touch if you are the custodial parent with the children away on visitation or a non-custodial parent when the children are away with the custodial parent. It is not important if the children are seven blocks away or across the globe. Reading is important to the current development of your children and critical to their success later in life. That makes sending magazines to your children thoughtful and valuable. Plan ahead so letters and phone calls will come when the children are available. Send magazine subscriptions to the address where the child spends a great deal of time, either the permanent residence or the summer visitation home. These publications are listed by the appropriate age of the child.

The options you are offered for your children are diverse in subjects covered and price.

Age of Child **Magazine**
6 - 24 Months.**Babybug** (800) 827-0227
P.O. Box 592, Mt. Morris, IL 61054-0592 [12]
2-6 Yrs.**Sesame Street Magazine**
P.O. Box 52000, Bolder, CO 80321-2000 [10]
2-6 Yrs.**Mickey Mouse Magazine** (515) 243-4543
P.O. Box 10598, Des Moines, IA 50340 [4]
2-7 Yrs.**Ladybug, Young Children** (800) 284-7257
Cricket Country, POB 50284, Bldr. CO 80323 [12]
2-5 Yrs.**Turtle Magazine** (317) 636-8881 $16.95
P.O. Box 7133, Red Oak, LA 51591-0133 [8]
3-5 Yrs.**Your Big Backyard** (800) 432-6564
1400 16th St., N.W., WA, D.C. 20036-2266 [12]
4-9 Yrs.**Chickadee** (800) 387-4379
255 Great Arrow., Buffalo, NY 14207-3082 [10]
4-12 Yrs.**Highlights for Children** (800) 848-8922
P.O. Box 182167, Columbus, OH 43218

There are several magazines for each age group and as the children get older their interests may become very specialized and there are many magazines to cover those interests. Some other magazine options are:

Air & Space $19.97
Alfred Hitchcock's Mysteries $34.97
American Astronomy $21.99
Archaeology $19.97
Auto Racing Digest $23.94
Backpacker $16.21
Baseball Digest $23.94
Basketball Digest $23.94
Bicycling $13.00
Bird Talk $34.99
Bowling Digest $21.97
Boy's Life $15.95
Car Craft $19.95
Car & Driver $22.99
Cat Fancy $34.99
Champion Crossword Puzzles $16.50
Child Life $16.95
Children's Digest $16.95
Children's Playmate $16.95
Crafts $21.98
Custom Classic Trucks $19.95
Dell Word Search Puzzles $11.97
Discover $35.40
Dog Fancy $34.99
Football Digest $23.94
Golf $21.94
Golf World $69.00
Four Wheel & Off Road $24.00
Four-Wheeler $24.00
Game Pro $24.95
Horse & Horseman $34.99
Horse Illustrated $27.99
Hot Rod $24.00
Humpty Dumpty $16.95
I Love Cats $24.00
Inside Karate $19.97
Inside Kungfu $19.97
Inside Sports $29.99
International Boxing Digest $29.50
Isaac Asimov's Science Fiction $27.97
Jack & Jill $16.95
Kit Planes $29.97
Motor Trend $24.00
Mountain Biker $30.00
Mustangs & Fords $21.96
NBA Inside Stuff $19.95
Outdoor Life $22.00
Outside $19.97
PC Gamer $29.50PC Games $22.97
Plane & Pilot $19.99
Popular Electronics $19.95
Popular Hot Rodding $22.00
Popular Science $19.95
Road And Track $22.00
Rodale's Scuba Diving $19.97
Seventeen $24.95
Skateboarding $19.95
SKI $13.99
SKIING $13.99
Skin Diver $22.97
Snow Boarding $22.95
Soccer Digest $22.00
Sporting News $88.20
Sports Illustrated $88.56
Sport Truck $19.94
Stock Car Racing $29.99
Surfing $19.95 Tennis $23.94
Teen $24.95
U.S. Kids $19.95
Young Miss $20.00

Places to Find Activities

- The public library has books and scheduled activities.
- The public library has a magazine section with a large number of publications expressly for parents seeking ideas on family activities.
- The newspaper has a children's section and a

leisure section listing activities.

- Try your community center, YMCA and YWCA.
- The book stores have guide books for your city.
- Book stores also have craft books.
- The hobby or craft shop has age-appropriate projects. Your house of worship has holiday and evening events.4-H Clubs of America has projects for urban children as well as rural.
- Check out the Boys and Girls Clubs Of America.
- Museums have many childrens' programs.
- Call the city parks and recreation for additional suggestions.

Religion

Substantiation that religion is important to all the peoples of the world is that each of the seven days of the week is designated as the Sabbath by various nationalities and religions.

Monday is the Greek Sabbath, Tuesday the Persian, Wednesday the Assyrian, Thursday the Egyptian, Friday the Turkish, Saturday the Jewish and Sunday the Christian. Religion can have a stabilizing influence for you in the child custody wars. Attempting to hide a negative life-style by claiming to be a devout follower of the faith will most assuredly backfire. If you have not attended religious services and are not comfortable doing so, don't go.

If you have a religious "home" and the support that comes with a religious family, you are fortunate. Most denominations devote a great deal of their time and effort to offering social activities, family service support, extended family programs, as well as religious training. Many find this to be a wonderful place to establish long-term friendships in a refreshing and uplifting atmosphere. Because religious organizations are interested in you as an individual and have a great deal of experience in dealing with family matters, they may provide special counseling that applies specifically to your needs.

Children enjoy the happy hubbub and seasonal ritual of the social activities in Bible and Hebrew School. Religious involvement gives your children another source of positive attention, activity and friendships. In many families, religious services and events, holidays, or birthday parties are the only opportunities children have to get dressed up.

There are no entirely safe places in the world. (There never were.) Do not drop your children off and trust that everyone who comes in contact with them have their best interest at heart. Take part in your children's extra-circular activities and organizations, religious or otherwise.

If you feel a need for religious ties, there are many options to consider. You can find a religious "home," by visiting house of worship in your community.

Division of Church and State

Child custody and divorce courts can't interfere with parents' religious training of their children. The division of church and state means that the way a parent raises a child is a constitutionally protected right of privacy. The only time the state can interfere with a parent's right to teach kids his religion is if he has harmed the children by exposing them to his religion. The next reality is that regardless of who's right or wrong, the kids will suffer from a protracted battle between the parents. No religion wants a parent to sacrifice the well-being of the children in order to comply church dogma.

Intra-Faith Custody Challenges

The court can make a relatively easy call if there is clear risk of physical harm to the children. But in most cases, courts are reluctant to settle religious disputes between parents. In the majority of these cases there is no clear right or wrong - just an intense disagreement, based on religious doctrine, about how children should be raised. Judges do not want to interfere with the parent's constitutional right to freedom of religion. Competing religious beliefs are bound to be a factor in litigation around custody, visitation and even schooling. We think of interfaith unions when a Christian and a Jew have children.

Many of the same issues can arise in same-faith custody battles when the parents have different beliefs within a religion. As an example, one parent is an Orthodox Jew and insists that Sabbath and kosher laws be observed and the other parent is a reform Jew that is not interested in observing those laws. Therefore, it's common for parents who practice the same faith in different degrees of strictness to fight over the same kinds of issues as parents of completely different religions. Many of these disputes arise when one parent wants:

- The children not trick-or-treating or say the Pledge of Allegiance, even when the children are with the non-Jehava's Witness parents.
- To use where the child goes to church as a form of keeping score.
- The children to attend parochial school, and the other parent doesn't want the children to have that type of intensive exposure to that religion.
- To have visitation during religious holidays, even if the parent normally wouldn't have the children during those periods.
- To have the children attend church or temple of their own religion when the other parent has custody.

Visitation

Visitation Is a Right of the Child. A Happy Safe Visitation Is the Responsibility of the Adults.

The companionship and care that visitation encourages is a very important part of child support. This concept is one of the most misunderstood in the custody arena. The parent fortunate enough to be the residential caregiver has the responsibility to assist the children in having a strong relationship with the non-custodial parent. Non-custodial parents must make every effort to fit into the children's schedule. Statistically, non-custodial parents don't follow the visitation schedule, even when it is exactly what they requested. In most cases the non-custodial parent will ask for more visitation than that parent can reasonably exercise or on occasion really want. Children whose non-custodial parent exercises all of the visitation offered are very lucky.

If a parent has been a devoted parent in the past, there is every reason to believe the children can depend on that level of care and attention in the future.

A parent and children who are used to continual exposure to one another and then are suddenly forced to compress all their feelings into a relatively short time span, will feel awkward and the situation may be painful. How often children come in contact with a non-custodial parent following a separation is a key factor in the time they require to recover from the trauma.

Children will be seduced by an increase in affection and time from a parent who has always been distant. All you can do is help the children enjoy this bounty while it is there, and understand if, and when, it disappears. Don't steal any of the happiness the children are experiencing now with dire predictions of abandonment later. You will end up being the "bad guy." Make a notation in your contact log as soon as you notice the increase in attention.

If there is danger of the children being disappointed by a non-custodial parent missing visitation, for any reason, have some backup plans made to salve their wounded feelings. If you know the children are being stood-up intentionally, or the non-custodial parent frequently fails to show up, document the infractions to submit later for a reduction in visitation allowed. Children of divorce who heal well are children who have two responsible, healthy parents even though they live in two different households.

International Travel

If visitation involves long distance travel, you can remove many of the problems by having the proper court documentation, identification, visas, passports, and notarized permission papers prepared in advance. Many travel destinations such as Australia, Brazil, the Caribbean and Mexico require special authorization when only one parent or guardian is traveling with a child. Since 1986, Canada is asking many arriving parents, whether traveling separately or with a spouse, to provide some form of identification for any accompanying children under the age of eighteen. The purpose of these requirements is to thwart kidnapping attempts, including parental abductions. Canada's International Project Return is an arm of Canada Customs. Many countries are observing and instituting programs that mirror Canada's clean, effective project.

Before You Buy the Tickets:

1. Get proper IDs for both of you. The Motor Vehicle Division or Police department can make photo ID for parents and children. Call them to find out what documentation you will need to present to get the photo IDs.

2. If you are not the custodial parent, and the custodial parent will help you, create a letter from the custodial parent giving you permission

to cross international borders with your children. Include as much travel information as possible including departure date, airlines, countries, hotels, tours and return dates. Make certain the custodial parent's name, address and phone number (home and work). Have this letter notarized

3. If you are not the custodial parent, and the custodial parent will not help you, get a certified (stamps and official signatures are very important in other countries) copy of your divorce/custody decree. Create a letter identifying where the decree gives you permission to cross international borders with your children. Include as much travel information as possible including departure date, airlines, countries, hotels, tours and return dates. It will help if you have the name, address and phone number of your attorney or the presiding judge (if you are on good terms with the judge). It would be advisable to get a trip specific decree for this trip. Have all letters notarized or certified.

4. If you are the custodial parent, have a complete original (if possible) of relevant papers with you. All single parents are suspect. Get a certified (stamps and official signatures are very important in other countries) copy of your divorce/custody decree. Create a letter identifying where the decree gives you permission to cross international borders with your children.

Include as much travel information as possible including departure date, airlines, countries, hotels, tours and return dates. Have the name, address and phone number of your attorney or the presiding judge (if you are on good terms with the judge). If possible, get a trip specific decree for this trip. Have all letters notarized or certified.

5. Contact the tourist offices or embassies of the countries you will pass through or visit to get all the rules and regulations in writing that apply. It would serve you well to attempt to establish a personal relationship with a key person. Get the contact home and work phone numbers to help shorten delays or eliminate problems during your trip.

6. Often the person checking your documents in the foreign country has never seen or heard the requirements explained to you. Therefore, any instructions you have in printed form or by letter from their tourist office or embassy will help a great deal if there is a question thousands of miles away from home. A week before you leave, contact the tourist offices of the countries where you will travel. Make certain no policies have changed before you travel to that country with your children. Check with the Department of State to see if there are any tourist or travel advisors for the countries through or to which you will travel.

Once you get to your destination:

1. Check in with the American Embassy

2. Keep a complete set of ID and documents for you and your children with you at all times. Many foreign hotels demand your passport or will not allow you to check in. Often they will accept a copy of the cover and photo page.

3. Have your child carry a copy of his/her ID, itinerary, and emergency contact information with him or her at all times. Make a point of meeting the day and night managers of the hotels in which you stay, getting emergency contact numbers from them.

4. Keep your children within arm's reach during all sight-seeing or tours.

Airlines are subject to fines if they fail to observe the foreign entry requirements set by the countries where they land. Foreign entry requirements can change overnight, and circumstances vary depending on whether the parents are divorced or separated, whether one parent has sole custody or custody is shared, whether a parent is deceased or if a child is in the care of one or more guardians. Foreign entry requirements by country can be obtained by calling the State Department's Citizens Emergency Center, (202) 647-5225, and requesting the appropriate Consular Information Sheet.

Fear of Flying

Long distance visitation requires children to fly. Sometimes alone. The airlines offer a chaperon service. The thirty to sixty dollar fee is paid at check-in. Buttons identifying the children as special travelers are put on their chests and the airline assumes responsibility for getting the children to the destination airport and make them available to an adult with identification that matches information given by a parent at the beginning of the flight.

The first flight may be very difficult for the children. It is easier on them if two or more are traveling. Providing the children with a backpack containing activities and snacks will make the time pass faster and diminish their anxiety. Once the children have completed their first long distance visitation they will feel more confident about future trips.

Since judges know thousands of children travel every year for visitation without any problems, they will not excuse your children because they are showing a great deal of fear and anxiety. Therefore, it is your responsibility to make this as easy on your children as possible.

If you don't get your children on the plane to meet the long distance visitation ordered by the court you may go to jail or lose custody of your children.

My Child Hates Visitation

"My child hates to go to visitation. As soon as my seven year old child finds out he will be picked up for visitation, he becomes upset. He cries and becomes moody. We have tried to prepare him several weeks in advance, but this just extends the period of time he is miserable. He clings to us and wakes in the night with bad dreams.

For the last three visits we have only told him a day or two before the other parent arrives. This shortens the time he frets about going.

Every time we pick him up at the end of his visit he says he never wants to go back."

As miserable as your children seem, this is something they have to do. In most states if you do not make your child go to visitation you can be put in jail.

Help make the preparation for the trip as easy as possible. Remind the child of any of the good things the children have at the other house: pets, siblings, special activities and the other parent that they do love and who loves them. List the things, people and events that will be here when they come home. Be firm about the fact that they must go.

Custodial Responsibilities

As the custodial parent you have the responsibility to satisfy the court order and make your child as comfortable with the process as possible. One of the primary reasons our children react so negatively to visitation is that we have not given them permission to go to visitation. We may have said the words, but even the words we used or the way we said them or our tone of voice gives a much different message. Supervised visitation has the same parent responsibilities.

The messages you should give your children are:

1. I love you.
2. It's ok to go.
3. It's ok to love your other parent.
4. It's ok to have a good time on your visit.
5. I will be fine while you are gone.
6. I will be here when you get back.
7. I will love you when you get back.

If your children don't know and believe these things, then you have not fulfilled your responsibilities. As bad as that is for your children now it can also permanently damage your long-term relationship with your children. Additionally, a psychologist or family relationship professional will be able to identify the problems you are causing.

Ultimately your children's unwillingness to go to visitation could indicate to the court that you are attempting to subvert the court order by causing your child additional distress. Lapses in the other parent's ability to behave responsibly, requires additional responsibility in your behavior.

Non-Custodial Responsibilities

As the non-custodial parent you have the responsibility to assist the custodial parent satisfy the court order. You can do this by following the court order to the letter. Send your notice of visitation in the manner the court dictated. Maintain all the contact the court and the other parent will allow you to. Make plans for the time with your child. Don't make extravagant promises you may not be able to keep or that make the custodial parent look bad. It is normal for your children to have

separation anxiety about leaving the custodial home. Don't let it hurt your feelings. Supervised visitation has the same parental responsibilities.
Proper messages to give your children are:

1. I love you all the time.
2. It's ok to want to go back to all your things and friends.
3. It's ok to love your other parent.
4. This is going to be a nice time and you will have a good time during our family time together.
5. I will be fine while you are gone.
6. I will be here when you get back.
7. I will love you no matter where you live.
8. I will always be here when you need me.

Just as with the custodial parent- if your children don't know and believe these things, then you have not fulfilled your responsibilities. As bad as that is for your children now it can also permanently damage your long-term relationship with your children. As the "odd-man-out" you may always be expected to be the one causing problems by psychologist or family relationship professionals. Therefore, you must be on your most child aware good behavior.

Eventually your children's willingness or unwillingness to go to visitation will be determined by the level of stress exerted on them at both ends of each visitation event. Lapses in the other parent's ability to behave responsibly, requires additional responsibility in your behavior.

I Don't Want to Visit You Anymore

Children can be influenced into telling a parent, "I don't want to go with you anymore." Or children, exhausted, confused, angry or attempting to prove loyalty to one parent, may decide to sever his or her ties with the other parent. In either case, the court may either listen to the children or the parent who wishes to alienate the other parent or force the child to visitation under threat of parental arrest and/or juvenile detention for the child.

Whim or Survival

Once you determine this is not a whim, but something the children seem committed to, let it go for now. You can fight, but if the children are clear and persistent in the demand, or old enough for the court to listen to, you will lose. The children do not understand what this is doing to you and are dealing with a difficult set of circumstances as best they can. Your prolonged battle will only solidify the children's resolve.

A Phone Call Away

Regardless of where the idea came from, this is one of those times in life when you have to back off and comply with the children's request. Make sure the children know how to contact you if they change their minds. There is usually a change of heart during puberty. If the alienation was the product of a vindictive parent the children lived with, they may never forgive the person that compelled them to expel a parent and for the years lost with that parent.

Document Now For Later

If all contact has been denied to you, first deal with your anger and pain. My Kids Don't Live With Me Anymore by Doreen Virtue, is a book that can help you deal with much of the emotional trauma. It explains what you feel and why, from the onslaught of emotions to waking up angry and the social stigma of being a parent without custody.

Whether you live far away, or in the same town as your children, send Birthday, Easter, Christmas, Halloween and have-been-thinking-about-you cards. Even if you are sure the children are getting the mail, send a duplicate card to the children, addressed to them, to your address and save them for the children when contact is reestablished.

Use this system if you are not allowed to send mail directly to the children. Buying, penning your personal message and sending the card will help you deal with the loss now. Later you can show that the children were never out of your thoughts.

"Later" is very important because sometimes grown children don't know why you did stop seeing them. The feeling of abandonment can be erased from a young person's emotions when a parent can prove the parent's intent was to stay in touch with the children.

Parents who have saved letters, savings bonds and gifts for as much as eight years, tell us the impact on the children, when the cache is finally delivered, is life changing for the children and effectively dispels any messages of abandonment or lack of love the children may have heard from a vindictive, controlling parent.

Parental Alienation Syndrome

Parent Alienation Syndrome is a parent trying with success at a conscious level to alienate children from the other parent with the assistance of the children. The children's actual interactions would be far more positive without the negative influence of the alienating parent.

While it was common at one point in time to immediately assume that a parent that alienated children from the other parent was automatically the wrong parent to choose as the primary custodial parent, that is no longer the case. It is now considered proper behavior when the intent is to protect children from a dangerous parent. It is psychologically harmful to children to be deprived of a healthy relationship with one parent. This is why it is essential that visitation agreements to insure the emotional bond of the children with both parents be protected. There is substantial research indicating children need contact with adults of both sexes for balanced development.

Alienation Messages

Unconscious Messages

Some alienating parents are unaware of their emotions or motivation to alienate, or the effects of their unconscious behavior on the children. These parents tend to deny their motivation and actions, and will insist that the opposite is true. These parents may be intolerant of the other parent at events important to the children.

They openly express little value in the children's communication with or relationship with the target parent. On occasion the alienating parent will understand the theoretical importance of the other parent, but will identify character deficiencies the target parent exhibits that would be harmful to the children. Since the alienating parent's words and actions don't coincide with their statements, it is obvious that their view of the other parent is affected.

1. "You can go for a visit if you want. But, I won't force you to go."
2. "I'm glad you had a nice visitation, but let's talk about something else."
3. "It doesn't matter if you missed your weekly call, you can talk to her next week."
4. "Yes, he is your dad, but you have two dads now."
5. "I wish it didn't cause them so much trouble to have you there."

Conscious Messages

Alienating parents are anxious to voice their feelings and motivations. Informing you that the target parent was never any value to the children and is only pursuing the children to hurt the alienating parent, they explain that the target parent is controlling and so deceptive that even they were fooled for a long time. Now that they are aware of the danger the target parent presents, they feel compelled to make every effort to protect the children. They want and need your pity and support to protect their children, stating as fact that the target parent is intentionally causing harm to the children. Alienating parents are willing, even anxious, to involve the children in the litigation.

1. "I can tell who you love more by where you want to live."
2. "They have each other. I only have you."
3. "If you leave me, I will lose the money they send. I can't afford our house and there won't be enough money for food."
4. "We were both left behind, so why do you think they want you now?"
5. "That parent used to love me. When will the love you get stop?"
6. "What will happen to me when you leave me too?"
7. Children witness, or see evidence of, or are told about domestic violence.
8. "Are they doing bad things to you?"

9. “You don’t like being there. It upsets your stomach every time.”

Combating PAS

Children say different things to different people. Children say to each parent what that parent lets the children know they need and expect to hear from them. Therefore, the child says different things to each parent by saying what they think the adults want to hear. The child’s instinct feels this is necessary to survive. Children fit their responses to the expectations of adults, especially those adults who are in a position of current control.

Each parent will take what the child has said at face value and not believe the other parent’s claim that they have been told the opposite.

Professionals that deal with the successful adjustment of children after the separation of their parents feel that continued contact with both parents is critical. Adult egos, needs and desires must be put aside. Children can’t appreciate the short or long-term effects of not having meaningful contact with one parent. There can be long-term damage to the child’s development caused by losing contact with either parent. Often the parent on the outside must accomplish this alone. The following will give you some guidelines to follow:

1. Find out what the child is actually saying to the other parent. The child may feel the other parent’s fear and is afraid of hurting the person that takes care of the child. Determine if the child is having these emotions or is the child expressing feelings or concerns of the other parent. Calm the fears of both the child and the parent.

2. The absence of one parent, for whatever reason, may have been so frightening that the child does not want to do anything, which might cause the loss of the other parent.

After all, the child doesn’t know who would take care of the child if that parent left. Assure the child and the other parent you are there to enrich the child’s life not put it at risk.

3. If you are attempting to reestablish contact and the child was very young at the time of the separation, the child may in fact view you as a stranger. The idea of going away with a stranger may be frightening. Present a plan to handle the visitation differently. Use a controlled environment such as a contact center or day-care center, and ask that it be reviewed by both parties and an observer from the visitation facility in three months.

4. The child is afraid to choose because it is aware of the animosity between the parents; and may therefore think that going will cause horrific changes in the normalcy of life. A child should not be expected to make this kind of decision. A decision needs to be imposed by a mediator or the court. This removes the burden of making the decision and eliminates most feelings of betrayal when they go to visitation.

Children’s Responsibilities

- Keep a list of friends’ names and addresses next to the telephone.
- Tell parents about any new people hanging around, especially if they make you feel weird.
- Post your schedule on the calendar with times and addresses so you can be found in an emergency.
- Use a buddy system. Never walk or ride bikes alone, day or night.
- If someone grabs your buddy:

  1. Pay attention to what the grabber looked like:

     A. Male, female, white, black, Asian, Indian, Hispanic, glasses, hair color, hair long or short, fat or thin, tattoos, scars, mustache, beard, color of clothes, uniform?

     B. Color and type of vehicle, license number on vehicle and state where vehicle is from, window tint, dents.

  2. Run for help. You aren’t big enough to save your friend, but adults and the police can. Time is the most important thing.

- Set up a code word with your brothers and sisters and friends. Have some word you or your friend will say to let the other one know something is wrong when you can’t talk. A word you would never use any other time like “my head hurts like an artichoke or you are a real artichoke.” The use of the WORD will let your friend know you need help and to get away and get help now.
- Let your family and friends know where you are. Be aware of where they are if needed in an

emergency.

- Be aware of where you are all the time and where the closest "safe" place is. These are places where people are twenty-four hours a day like the fire department, police department, funeral home, hospital, all night markets, gas station, McDonald's Restaurant or open twenty-four hour a day Wal-Mart.
- Get to know the business people and neighbors you can help and can help you. Keep your parents informed about who these people are.

Information Children Should Know

- The child's own first, middle, last name
- Home telephone number
- Emergency telephone number (relative or close friend)
- How to dial 911 and ask for help and give location
- Physical address of child's primary residence
- City and state of primary residence
- Full name of primary caretaker
- Name of foods or medicines to which the child is allergic
- Name and dosage medicines the child must have
- Name of teacher and school child attends
- Secret Word known only to family
- Learn the number for Child Find, which is "1 800 I AM LOST" to get help.
- Learn S.K.Y. (SCREAM - KICK- YELL) This can save a child's life if someone attempts to force the child into a vehicle or building.
- Tell your children they do not have to do what bad grown-ups tell them to do.
- Tell your children that if anything unusual happens or if anyone tells them that you are dead or do not love them anymore, they should be immediately suspicious. Make sure that your children understand that you will always love them no matter what they think they have done, and that you want to share your life with them.

Special Note:

As a safety precaution, exercise or trial run, have an adult or teen the child does not know, attempt to trick the secret word out of the child. If the child is easily fooled, more instruction is necessary.

Walk the Talk

Children are more likely to be open about their activities if you are open about yours. Make it a family "tradition" to keep each other informed and therefore involved with each other's lives. This will also give you something to talk to each other about.

Help Your Children Be Responsible

- Put an address book and pen next to the telephone. Help your children establish and maintain a list of their friends' names, addresses and birthdays. Help children pick out cards and send out holiday cards such as Christmas, Thanksgiving, Birthday, Valentine's Day, Easter and Halloween to their friends as a non-intrusive way of updating the list.
- Ask your children about any new people hanging around, especially if they make your child feel weird or apprehensive. Check this person out right away.
- Post your schedule of activities on the calendar with times and addresses of where you can be found in an emergency in one color like green and have each of your children add their information in other colors.
- Ask them to list, which buddy they will be with for each event. Never tolerate walking or riding bikes alone, day or night or lack of information from the children.
- Do some practice observations. Tell your children to pay attention to everything going on for the next few minutes. Then ask questions about some specific person they should have seen like: What nationality did the person appear to be? Did the person wear glasses, wear mustache or beard? What color and how long or short was the hair? What about the other factors: fat or thin, tattoos, scars, color of clothes, uniform and vehicles. They should also get to ask you questions.
- Set up a code word with your children.
- Let your family and friends know where you will be and be aware of where they will be if needed in an emergency.
- Get a passport for each of your children and put them in a safety deposit box at the bank.
- Notify the United States Passport office of any

threat to take your children out of country.

Seeing Abuse is Abuse

Verbal, Physical, Emotional or Sexual Abuse against the children, against the people the children care about or in the children's presence or within the children's knowledge is a crime of violence against them that will leave permanent scars.

Abuse, kidnapping and allegations are discussed in depth in Chapter 16.

Move Away

Twenty years ago the custodial parent, usually the mother, could move her children whenever and wherever she wanted. In the past ten years the courts were reticent to let a parent move children if the move would substantially interfere with the contact of the children with the non-custodial parent. Since1997, the courts are making it easier for parents to move a child out-of-state, parents should make sure there is a "relocation clause" in their divorce or child custody agreement.

A "require notice" clause in the custody agreement could go a long way toward protecting your contact with your child. Example: The custodial parent can't move without giving sixty days notice or getting judicial permission. This can give the non-custodial parent a chance to go to court and persuade a judge not to allow the move.

If the custodial parent moves without permission he/she is in violation of a court order. Additional provisions could provide for the immediate transfer of temporary custody and the suspension of support payments if the custodial parent violates the notice requirement. Even if it is not enforceable, it provides a disincentive to move in the middle of the night.

No Move Away Provision

With a "no move" clause, the custodial parent knows he or she has to go into court and say everything agreed to is now not true. Depending upon the time-line, the judge may feel the first agreement was not made in good faith. The language in the decree may make a judge think twice before rubber-stamping a relocation order. In addition, the moving parent opens the case for other considerations that person does not want set forth.

This could take the emphasis off the best interest of the child and present someone to the court who is in violation of a provision that binds the parent rather than protects the child. The move away agreement might also provide for a generous alternative visitation schedule in the event of a move, and spell out who will pay for travel expenses. That could make relocation more acceptable to the parent left behind and, if there's a conflict later, reassure the court that the non-custodial parent will still be able to see the children. An agreement between the parties permitting relocation and it's incorporation into a court order, has a good chance of being enforced.

Illinois puts the burden on the custodial parent to show that a move should be allowed.
In re Marriage of Smith, No. 79036 (1996);
In re Marriage of Eckert, 518 N.E.2d 1041 (1988).

Best Interest Move Away

A relocation clause won't prevent all relocation if the move looks to the best interests of the children, but it may help. To fight a relocation, include specific statement of the children's 'best interests.' An example would be:

1. It is presently in the best interest of the children to reside in Nebraska. It is anticipated that residence within Nebraska will continue to be in the best interest and provide the most stability within the children's minority.

2. The children see their non-custodial parent on a regular basis. The non-custodial parent is with the children fifty-five percent of 'quality' (time when the children are not sleeping or at school) parenting time.

3. The children enjoy weekly contact with grandparents, aunts, uncles, cousins, and step-siblings in the area.

4. The children have been in the same school district and church community for the last ten years.

5. The children participate in baseball, basketball, ballet lessons, soccer, Sunday school, Boy Scouts, karate lessons, swim team and 4H.

Additionally, include a 'burden of proof' clause for the custodial parent in justifying a move, or that a move will be considered a "substantial change in circumstances" that will reopen the custody issue.

These states don't have a presumption and say that a move should be allowed if it is in the best interests of the child.

North Dakota Supreme Court. Keller v. Keller, No.980068. September 29, 1998
Alaska. McQuade v. McQuade, 901 P.2d 421 (1995).
California. In re Marriage of Burgess, 913 P.2d 473 (1996).
Connecticut. Blake v. Blake, 541 A.2d 1201 (1988).
Idaho. Osteraas v. Osteraas, 859 P.2d 948 (1993).
IN. Lamb v. Wenning, 600 N.E.2d 96 (1992).
ME. Rowland v. Kingman, 629 A.2d 613 (1993).
MD. Domingues v. Johnson, 593 A.2d 1133 (1991).
NY. Tropea v. Tropea, 665 N.E.2d 145 (1996).

Limited Presumption for Move Away

State Supreme Court decisions have limited presumption in favor of moving. The custodial parent has established a "good faith" reason for the move. Then the burden of proof becomes the challenge for the non-custodial parent.

- CO. In re Marriage of Francis, 919 P.2d 776 (1996) (reason must be "sensible").
- NY Sara P. v. Richard T., NY FamCt Monroe City, NYIJ (3/13/98)
- MA. Yannas v. Frondistou-Yannas, 481 N.E.2d 1153 (1985).
- NV. Trent v. Trent, 890 P.2d 1309 (1995).
- NJ. Holder v. Polanski, 544 A.2d 852 (1988); Cooper v. Cooper, 491 A.2d 606 (1984).
- PA Baldwin v. Baldwin, PaSupCt., No. 1662 Pitts. (1997, 4/8/98

Presumption for Move Away

The Presumption in Favor of Move Away has caused so much litigation about it that some family lawyers specialize in 'move away' cases. The move away laws in every state are experiencing daily change. It is vital to include a move away clause in any child custody agreement or decision. If there is nothing agreed to or ordered and in writing it will become much harder to prevent a move. The agreement can simply provide that the custodial parent can't move the children out of state.

These State Supreme Court decisions that have Presumption in Favor of Moving that presumes that a parent should be able to move the children. The burden is on the other parent to show that this shouldn't be allowed.

The high courts in California, Colorado and New York have made it easier for parents to move. The Tennessee Supreme court held that a parent should always be allowed to move unless she is doing so just to be vindictive or unless the child would be in physical danger.

Alabama. Ex parte Murphy, 670 So.2d 51 (1995).
FL Russenberger v. Russenberger, 669 So.2d 1044 (1996).
MN. Silbaugh v. Silbaugh, 543 N.W.2d 639 (1996); Auge v. Auge, 334 N.W.2d 393 (1983).
MS Bell v. Bell, 572 So.2d 841 (1990).
MT. Lorenz v. Lorenz, 788 P.2d 328 (1990); In re Marriage of Hogstad, 914 P.2d 584 (1996).
NE. Harder v. Harder, 524 N.W.2d 325 (1994).
ND. McDonough v. Murphy, 539 N.W.2d 313 (N.D. 1995).
SD. Fortin v. Fortin, 500 N.W.2d 229 (1993); Fossum v. Fossum, 545 N.W.2d 828 (1996).
TN. Aaby v. Strange, 924 S.W.2d 623 (1996).
VT Lane v. Schenck, 614 A.2d 786 (1992).
WI. Bohms v. Bohms, 424 N.W.2d 408 (1988).
WY. Love v. Love, 851 P.2d 1283 (1993).

Buying the Pain Away

Toys * Books * Games * Trips. There may be a tendency to buy more things for your children during this process. You may notice the other parent spending more than ever before. Don't panic. It will not ruin the children's values, spoil them forever, or win their love away from you if you are unwilling or unable to get into the "toy wars." It is normal for a non-custodial parent to think of the children when absent for extended periods of time and buy things to patch the empty feeling in his or her heart.

As the gifts come home, help your children enjoy the gifts and properly care for them. This practice usually fades with time. If the non-custodial parent has more money than time and can take the children to Disneyland, remember to help make this a happy time. The attitude with, which you handle the news and the things you pack to facilitate the trip will show your children that you want them to fully enjoy the opportunity.

Too Much Hurt... Accidentally

Some of the things that cause children the

greatest pain now and the most damage later are:

- Using the children to carry angry messages back and forth.
- Children experiencing constant or big changes in their lives without warning.
- A parent attempting to prove how bad the other parent is.
- One parent denying the children time with the other parent.
- Parents burdening children with financial and legal worries.
- Children witnessing violence or evidence of violence.

Such Behavior is Bad Parenting

If you are exhibiting some of the listed behaviors, seek help to correct these behaviors as soon as possible. A combination of poor choices and behaviors can cost you the custody of your children. The court will not accept a history of poor choices and behaviors as mistakes you have made that are really someone elses fault.

If the opposition is exhibiting some of the listed behaviors, seek professional help for you and your children in dealing with the problems they cause. People who may be able to help or make recommendations are:

Family counselor

A Psychologist

Your attorney

Your Family Physician

Guidelines for Interviewing Children

1. All interviews of the child should be videotaped. Videotaping is seen as providing an incentive for interviewers to use proper techniques. Procedures and information obtained during the interview must be accurately documented to avoid criticism of the interviewer's techniques.

2. An attempt to tap into a child's accurate free recall by encouraging the child to tell in his or her own words what has happened. Questions should be open-ended to encouraging the child to provide a free narrative. Responses such as "and then what happened" should be used to encourage details.

3. Age-appropriate instructions such as, "I don't want you to say something that didn't happen, but if something did happen, I want you to tell me about it" can be given. The child should be discouraged from trying to answer questions when the answer is not known.

4. The Criterion Based Content Analysis/ Statement Validity Analysis technique is proper. Assuming an account based on memory for an actual event will differ in content and quality from accounts that are based on fabricated, learned, or suggestion. A relatively complete statement obtained as soon as possible after the child has disclosed an incident and the interview designed to obtain as much free narrative as possible. The interview is tape-recorded and transcribed for analysis.

5. Avoid pressure, coercion, leading questions and selective reinforcement of responses. Repeated questions should be avoided since this tells the child the previous answers were not acceptable.

6. Assess previous formal and informal interviews with the child witness. An expert can provide helpful information about the investigation and the resulting statements from the child even if not allowed to interview the child before the trial. The progress of the case, along with the procedures followed by the previous evaluators, must be carefully examined in order to assess possible contamination of the child's testimony.

Confidentiality - Your Children

There is no Parent-Child Privilege in the law. Nothing is confidential when you are dealing with children. Once they are aware of something, decide it is common knowledge. Tell your children the truth.

Do not tell your children information they do not *need to know*. Do not instruct them to hide information or circumstances from anyone. They cannot accomplish this successfully. Your children observing your inability to understand the truth or attempting to hide the truth will diminish you in their eyes. Once they see you being less than truthful with anyone, they will be suspect of your ability to be truthful with them. Do not attempt to change information or have a child lie for you. The professional evaluators can spot children under pressure to lie. This will count very heavily against the offending parent. It also subjects the children to a great deal of stress.

Revenge

The desire for revenge is a very normal, but negative motivation. Bogging you down in obsessive fantasies about striking back to get satisfaction creates additional frustration and unhappiness working against your emotional well-being. Despite how sweet the idea of the perfect revenge may be or the moment of satisfaction it could offer, it keeps stirring up the emotional chaos. It is not necessary to forgive others for the things they have done to you in order to stop wanting revenge. Letting go of your need for revenge is difficult, but it is clearly a healthy step. Because early childhood experiences play a pivotal role in character development, what your children see you do is critical.

If your children see you behave in a forgiving and understanding manner when you are angry or hurt, that is what the children will learn.

If your children see you strike back or act in a retaliatory and vengeful way, that is how they will learn to react to pain in their lives.

When you feel vengeful, find some positive methods for analyzing the reason someone hurt you.

- They didn't even know I would be affected by their reaction.
- I am not really involved and should not let this bother me.
- It was their only course of action.
- This is how they respond to everything.
- They are bad people.

Then find some reasonable ways to deal with your feelings.

- I will dismiss harm done to me unintentionally.
- I will avoid sticking my nose where it does not belong.
- I will attempt to project what their reaction will be to upcoming situations.
- I will avoid causing negative reactions to my actions.
- I will protect myself from unreasonable reactions from others.
- I will work through my initial reaction and decide how I really want to deal with each situation.
- I will help my child understand what happened and how and why I decided to handle the situation the way I did.

Second-Hand Smoke and Children

The 1994 U.S. Surgeon General's report states that second-hand smoke harms children. Children who breathe second-hand smoke have more ear infections, more severe asthma attacks and more breathing problems than children who live in smoke-free homes. Where tobacco use is allowed, children often have no way of protecting themselves from exposure to second-hand smoke. The report also discusses the increased neonatal and infant mortality rates for children whose parents smoke.

The pathological arterial change, which causes atherosclerosis has also been observed in the umbilical arteries of infants born not only to mothers who smoke, but also to mothers who have been exposed to second-hand smoke. Paternal as well as maternal smoking is associated with low infant birth weight. Parental smoking is also a significant risk factor for postnatal deaths, especially due to respiratory disease and sudden infant death syndrome (SIDS). There is sound evidence that exposure to second-hand smoke in childhood is associated with an increased probability of developing asthma among certain at-risk children, and suggestive evidence that children who are not at risk and are exposed to second-hand smoke may have a higher-than-average risk of developing asthma. For asthmatic children, second-hand smoke has a causal role in asthmatic-related morbidity.

Exposure to second-hand smoke represents a serious pediatric problem, which has been estimated to double the risk of infection and death in children.

They must be protected from the adverse health hazards of involuntary exposure to second-hand smoke. Parents who don't believe that second-hand smoke makes children sick or who don't believe that parents' smoking will encourage children to start are twice as likely to allow their children to be exposed. Studies show that most smokers fail to protect the young children who live with them.

All smoke contains cancer-causing chemicals. Second-hand smoke comes from all tobacco products, including pipe tobacco and cigars. There are about 2,000 chemicals in tobacco smoke. In smokers themselves, smoke reduces the capacity of the blood to carry oxygen to the tissues and increases the stickiness of the blood. This happens because second-hand smoke is a Class A carcinogen. That puts it in a class with 15 other substances, including asbestos, radon and benzene, that are known to cause cancer in human beings. Doctors are saying that virtually everything that they know active smoking does to the circulatory system is probably the same thing is happening to the bodies of people who inhale second-hand smoke. It directly damages the lining of the arteries. The surgeon general has estimated that approximately three thousand Americans die each year from passive smoking, which causes lung cancer.

The mainstream smoke the smoker inhales contains only fifteen percent of the smoke from a cigarette. The other eighty-five percent is accounted for in side-stream and inhaled smoke. Side-stream smoke is the smoke coming from the cigarette between puffs. Side-stream smoke has more tar, nicotine, carbon monoxide and other chemicals than the smoke inhaled through the cigarette itself. Second-hand smoke is a combination of: mainstream, side-stream and exhaled smoke, inhaled and then breathed out by the smoker. Passive smoking is the breathing in of second-hand smoke. These facts were confirmed and strengthened by the 1992 U.S. Environmental Protection Agency (EPA) assessment of the health effects of second-hand smoke.

Second-Hand Marijuana Smoke

Second hand smoke of any type is never good for children. Studies indicate that marijuana components do get stored in mom's body fat and release over time. The major side effect seen in babies and children exposed to marijuana is sleepiness, which can slow their physical development and overall development.

Additionally, there is no way to know what is added to street drugs to stretch the product so the dealer can make more money. Without knowing what is in the marijuana, there is no way to protect your children from these extra ingredients. The other concern is that the people who sell marijuana have even stronger drugs that they offer and are in general, people you don't want around your children. If the dealer knows how to find you they know how to find your children. If children see the parents they love use drugs, it is easier for them to accept drug use; just as children with parents who smoke cigarettes are more likely to smoke cigarettes themselves.

Court's Reaction

The courts are now dealing with parents who smoke and willfully and knowingly exposing their children to second-hand smoke. Rulings include:

- Ordered custodial and non-custodial parents to restrict smoking when the children are present or before exercising a period of custody.
- Consider that the smoking habits of significant others, older siblings, grandparents and any other person who has frequent contact with the child may be a factor in a child custody decision.
- Made an initial determination of custody or transferred custody from the parent who smokes to the nonsmoker parent.
- Awarded custody to a nonsmoking relative or other third party if both parents smoke.
- Determined that second-hand smoke from parental smoking is one factor that should be used when determining the custody arrangement of a child.
- Retained jurisdiction for a period of months after entering a custody order to check on parental compliance with orders.
- Ordered a parent who is trying to quit smoking to test for non-smoking compliance.

Chapter 14: Lies and Perjury

Lie: Intentional false statement.

Perjury: The traditional definition is the criminal offense of lying under oath, a willful and corrupt sworn statement made without sincere belief in its truth and made in a judicial proceeding regarding a material matter. Today, the statutes have been broadened so that in some jurisdictions any false swearing in a legal instrument or legal setting is perjury. It is chargeable even if it is not material and even though it is not presented in a judicial proceeding. Some statutes group perjury, false swearing, and making false written statements together as different degrees of the same crime, often loosely called perjury. Perjury can be punishable by imprisonment. See Subornation of Perjury in the glossary. Lies can throw a wrench into the cogs of the best war machine.

> If there is a Murphy's Law about telling lies, it reads:
>
> Your lie will surface at the worst possible time for you,
>
> cause the most damage to your case,
>
> and afford you the least amount of opportunity to make amends.

As a child, you were directed to always tell the truth. At the same time, you observed Mom instructing everyone in the house to tell Aunt Kim that Mom is out shopping for the day, because Mom does not want to talk to Kim. Dad calls in sick to work, so he can take you fishing. As an adult, honesty is identified as the primary indication of character while you observe people you respect inflating the value of their business to get a better selling price. Friends give you confidential information about their clients and brag about cheating on income taxes, insurance claims or getting back too much change at the store.

Types of Lies

White lies, bragging, song and dance, fibs, canards, bending the truth, telling tales, falsehoods, cock-and-bull, distortion, inaccuracy, adopting other people's stories as one's own, untruths, little lies, misrepresentations, falsities, stretching the facts, fish stories, exaggeration, libel, perjury, flim-flam, omissions, misstatements, half truths, embellishments, forgotten old lies --- They get to be part of how we all function.

The lies you normally fear are lies the opposition tells about you that the decision makers may believe. These are in fact the easiest to handle, with one exception, *The Grand Lie*. The Grand Lie is a falsehood that is so enormous and outrageous that all other issues are trivialized. The most common at this time is, the false accusation of sexual abuse against a minor child. Even if all accusations are proven untrue, there is always residual damage to the accused.

The real problem is any lie you have told because your character may be questioned.

Types of Liars

It isn't that the liar can't see the solution. It is that they can't see the problem.

Psychologists will tell you it is virtually impossible to tell if someone is lying, but that it is possible to tell if someone believes what they are saying. Therefore, it is necessary for a person to grasp the reality of a situation in order to consciously decide to be truthful or lie. If one's perception of reality is not solid, the truth becomes whatever that person needs it to be at that moment.

If you are unaccustomed to dealing with other than occasional, socially acceptable lies, you may need more explanation of what is going on in the liar's mind. Initially, we tend to feel that we did not understand or that we missed something rather than see we have been lied to. Being lied to can undermine your sense of trust in everyone and everything. A white lie can seem outrageous to the person to whom the lie is told. There are varying degrees of personality disorder that exhibit an extensive pattern of lying.

These range from a normal desire to avoid conflict, being aware that they have manipulated the truth, to rearranging reality to suit one's needs and not being aware that what they are saying is not the truth. The frequency of the lies, as well as the scope of the lies, indicates the degree of dysfunction.

The most extreme liar is the pathological liar. There is no way to identify the pathological liar except by the trail of victims they leave behind. These liars are especially insidious because they seek out and feed on specific types of victims, and the carnage is so complete. These liars are able to undermine the self-worth of the victim to the point that the victim is unaware of how much they were damaged. If they do recognize the damage done to them, they think they are the only one and are somehow responsible. The most common extreme we usually deal with is the psychological liar. The psychological liar is living the reality of what he or she is talking about at the moment the lie is being told. There is no set length of time that any one lie must exist. The lie may live for many years or a new lie/reality may form with the next person to whom the liar speaks. For the liar, what they are saying is the truth. The liar feels all the emotions that reality would "normally" invoke.

Because the lie is their reality, they are initially able to convince others by their passion and sincerity. The liar expects others to see the situation as it is seen by the liar. The feeling the liar gets of bringing someone along adds momentum and power to his message.

Some of the Best Reasons not to Lie

The truth always has a way of coming out.

Once a mediator, judge or jury has classified a person as a liar, very little of what that person says afterwards will change that opinion.

Depositions, statements, letters, notes, recordings, cancelled checks bank statements, pay stubs, IRS returns, personal diaries, receipts, and witnesses can all be used to prove that a lie has been told.
It is impossible to keep lies straight.
Lies tend to multiply.
Lying makes a victim of the liar, waiting for exploitation.
Lies count heavily against the liar.
Lies under oath are very hard to explain away.

Anyone who knows a person is a liar will identify the liar to anyone who asks.

Conflicting Truths

It is possible for two truths to appear to be opposite information. This can be caused by a combination of things including: perspective, the halo effect and previous history with any of the other players. An incident can be related to convey contradictory messages. Example:

1. The parent's negligence was apparent when the child was able to gain access to the pool area.

2. The parent provided all possible protection available to protect the child.

Many of the truths we cling to depend on our point of view. When the self-interest of the parents takes precedence over what would serve the child, there will always be an opportunity for conflict.

Memory's Imperfections

In addition to conflicting truths there is also the problem of memory's imperfections. Memory malfunctions can cause a great deal of the problem with telling or finding the truth in a matter.

The most common is the weakening or loss of memory over time. It's normal because of all the new information we add daily and is the culprit in many memory problems. Many of us even call ourselves absent-minded because we didn't pay close attention to the forgotten thing to begin with.

Compounding the problem is when a specific piece of information was known to us but it is now blocked. It is common for the blocked information to return when we are no longer thinking about the original question days later.

In court memories may be implanted by suggestion as a result of leading questions or comments when a person is trying to recall an experience.

Incorrectly remembering that a friend told you something you heard on television, or that a story originally told to you and retold by you has become a memory of something you have done rather than something you merely heard. This common phenomena is called misattribution.

If we unknowingly and unconsciously rewrite a previous experience we will have a skewed rendering of a specific incident, or even of

an extended period in our lives, which says more about how we feel now than about what happened then. This forms a bias for relating experiences we have had or witness.

Exaggerations and Fabrications

Suspicions encourage one to believe and fear exaggeration and fabrication. You know if the other side will try to bolster their story or not. Even having one's adversary doesn't present at the telling of a story doesn't always keep exaggeration and fabrication in check. There are several reasons for this. They feel telling the tale their way will sway the listener, there are other parties present that have already heard the exaggeration or fabrication and they need to stick with the story or they actually have begun to believe the bloated story themselves.

If you feel you must protest, do it in a controlled, polite way.

Portrait of the Liar

Liars do not see themselves or what they do the same way others see them. Liars are victims who think they can insulate themselves with misrepresentations. Victims are people who have been subjected to oppression, loss or suffering inflicted by the actions of others or as a result of their own actions. Lying is one of the many techniques for survival used by the emotionally abused. Once a person has been emotionally abused and feels powerless, he comes to understand the process of victimization and the power gained by the victimizer. It is common for the victim to become a victimizer. The liar sees *truth* as something to use, rather than be controlled by it. The only value of truth is what he can do with it, not that it is a yardstick, which he can measure information and behavior against. It is easier to deal with liars if you understand how the world looks to them. They are:

- judging the value of any person or event exclusively from their own self-interests
- convinced they are smarter than everyone else
- inclined to believe what they are saying
- able to project their feelings as if these originated with another person
- obsessive in their need to control situations and people
- prone to generalize and exaggerate
- only interested in the short-term benefits
- determined to destroy anything that does not serve their purposes
- convinced they have a right to do what they do
- not subject to remorse for the damage their lies cause
- never to blame
- labeling everyone as an ally or an enemy
- compelled to win at any price
- devoid of real weapons and use lies to assault

- self-righteous
- are unable to learn
- unaware of the burdens their lies place on others
- impatient
- able to disassociate themselves from their lies
- inclined to believe everyone else would do or is doing what they themselves are doing

When is Someone Lying

We have all experienced the discomfort of realizing that information we have accepted as fact is not true. By watching for some standard body language, you may be able to see the silent signals most people exhibit when they begin to lie. One of the ways you may identify if a remembrance is concocted or accurately recited is to watch where a person's eyes go when they are speaking. People tend to look up and to the side to pull information from memory, and down if constructing new circumstances.

Another indication of a liar is when he or she recites an event, and the syntax of this sentence moves from the past to the present. Trust your instincts. If you feel something is not true, you are probably right. Liars are aware that lying is not socially acceptable. The liar will probably be watching your body language to see if what they say is being accepted or rejected. If you do not seem convinced, the liar may press more information into the lie to give it more power.

If confronted with their lie, liars will prove not only that the situation justifies any action they took, but that they were forced to lie or blame you for making them lie. Your reaction to the occasional liar or the pathological liar should be the same.
Listen carefully (record if legal in your area), document and have your information substantiated by a witness in writing, or by other documents that prove conflicting information.

Lying is a mistake. Remember, don't interrupt your enemies when they are making a mistake.

Lies by Strangers

An opportunity to watch a person's behavior before you speak with them would be valuable. This would give you an opportunity to compare and assess their mannerisms, helping you to identify a change in demeanor. The person's face, then their words, then their body language should send each message.

There are a wide number of mannerisms that people normally do not exhibit unless they are under stress. Lying is, for most people, stressful. Exhibiting any of the listed specific behaviors does not prove that someone is lying, but may indicate stress. Some behaviors worth attention are:

- blushing or blanching
- keeping hands buried in pockets or behind their backs
- avoidance of eye contact
- use of hesitation between words, non-words and statements
- attributing statements to sources you cannot verify
- covering mouth while talking, or mumbling, wetting their lips
- pupil dilation, blinking rapidly, looking down at the floor
- scratching their head while talking
- putting their hand to their throat, rubbing the back of their neck, increase in volume or decrease in volume, expressions and emotions out of synchronization with words
- facial expressions that lag behind what the words convey
- strained or stressed tone of voice
- the story changes when asked to repeat for clarification or detail, making the attack very personal against you
- constantly clearing their throat, swallowing repeatedly
- anxious to finish present business and get away from you

Lies by Familiars

Lover, friend, acquaintance, confidant, intimate, mate, alter ego, best friend, bosom friend, ally, colleague, partner, or anyone you are on good and usually familiar terms with, are all familiars. Finding out you have been associated with a liar and/or that you have believed someone's lies for years, can be a terrible shock. The blindfolds of love, need, fear and desire are smoke screens that can be removed by distance from persons or events, allowing patterns to become evident.

You have observed this person's behavior so often you may have become blind to the things you would notice in a stranger. Pay attention to and compare the mannerisms with which you are familiar, noticing any change in demeanor.

Seeing the Pattern of the Liar

Once you get past the feelings of pain and betrayal, you will have a new way to protect yourself. The liar will be unaware of your 'enhanced vision' unless you announce it. Don't. Now that you know with whom you deal, make a study of which mannerisms accompany their lies. Make your observations and double-check your conclusions. Make note of any sequence that could be followed by an observer. Recruit someone you trust to test your results to see if, when observing the liar, they see the same sequential behavior pattern you identified. If your associate does not see what you saw, make every attempt to identify where the discrepancy is. If necessary, start over. Once your observations prove correct, you can identify this pattern to your attorney and/or an evaluator. Identifying the pattern of the liar to *truth tellers* is difficult because truth tellers expect the truth from others.

Evaluators rarely have the interest or are afforded the proper amount of time to sort out all the accusations in any case. Often the information presented by one side to identify problems with the opposition is stilted or incomplete. Alerting the evaluator to an identifiable pattern should assist the professional.

Example: "There is always a protective crossing of arms over the chest before Shawn begins a lie."

Why Liars Get Caught

The most common reason liars get caught is that they can't keep track of all the lies they have told and to whom they were told.

If two people with conflicting information from the liar confront the liar, the liar will sacrifice the feelings or reputation of one of the others to save his or her own face rather than admit to the lie.

Liars may not always anticipate when they will need to lie and therefore may not have the lie rehearsed. It is also impossible to anticipate all the situations that could arise or the questions that could be asked. Even the most skillful liar occasionally slips and blurts out the truth.

As an example: The attorney asked, "Three months ago the court ordered you to cease all contact with and to keep your child away from Mr. Morrel. When was the last time you took your child to Mr. Morrel's house?"

Miss Hall: "I have not seen or talked to him since."

Attorney: "Isn't it a fact, that you had a date with Morrel on the night your child overdosed on the pain pills?"

Miss Hall: "I cancelled the date earlier that day."

The instant the words left her lips, Miss Hall knew she had misspoke.

Liars even Lie to Themselves

NEWS FLASH: Of all the people liars lie to, they lie most often to themselves. Their self-deception will cause more damage to their case than your strongest weapon. Simply let their own statements and sworn testimony contradict each other.

Self-deception allows a person to find more acceptable reasons for the rejections felt or the problems encountered, rather than deal with unpleasant truths of one's own shortcomings. Any information that conflicts with the fabricated persona is subconsciously filtered out. The compounding of information and proof against the liar does not convince the liar of the truth, but causes extreme anxiety, triggering a flight or fight reaction. Dealing with the truth means the liar would have to do something to fix the real problems.

Recruiting Troops

Even when your day-to-day life is uneventful, you need to know that people approve of you as a person and that they approve of your life goals. During an armed conflict, it becomes vital to have the support and comfort of allies. Longtime friends, loving family, and hired professionals are the best people to fill these needs. These kinds of relationships are built on mutual trust and honesty.

If the liar does not have the support of honestly won soldiers, the liar will enlist help in any way possible. The most powerful method of capturing helpers for someone that sees themselves as a victim is Save Me. This method is accomplished by first, giving new recruits "facts" that will invoke pity and sympathy and identification of the liar as a victim. Second, by fostering a desire on the part of the listener to offer support and protection. Third, making obvious what small thing the recruit can do that will help the victim. Fourth, bathing the victim in a Positive Halo Effect. The facts must be detailed, painful, and horrendous enough to guarantee that the recruit will blindly mistrust --- even hate --- anyone who appears to be in opposition to the person they have decided to help. Therefore, a Negative Halo Effect automatically is attached to the victim's enemies. All information is subconsciously filtered through the Halo Effect, insuring that conclusions reached support the recruit's established opinion of the victim.

Once committed to the liar's cause, the soldier's own pride is at stake. The soldier must help the liar win against the evil enemy. The soldier's own sense of self-worth will usually prevent him or her from seeing the truth. This investment will be compounded when the soldier recruits friends and family into the liar's army.

The troops actually see the problems with what the liar is saying, but their commitment is so strong that they "suspend their belief" for this person and manage to keep it in place for all other functions in their lives. Even documented evidence of the liar's misdeeds will be dismissed by the loyal soldiers as elaborate attempts by the enemy to discredit their worthy friend. As time goes on, the liar will be required to manufacture more "facts" to ensure the loyalty of the troops. Soldiers enraged by the "facts" sometimes engage in fanatical behavior.

Such behavior is often encouraged by the liar, who feels this is an exhibition of true loyalty.
It seems that nothing is as strong in human beings as the craving to believe in something that is obviously wrong.

Initially, you will feel angry that someone is telling lies about you. You will be mortified that people are willing to believe such horrible things. You will realize that what they think is unimportant. You will understand that their blind support of the liar will actually hurt the liar and help you later.

The troops, having accepted the "facts," inadvertently move the liar into a manufactured reality in which the liar begins to feel secure and self-righteous. The liar is trapped, which adds more pressure to an already difficult situation.

The liar, caught up in the manufactured reality, uses lots of resources to support these lies. The liar has less time to identify the real problems in life, delaying or preventing the liar from taking the positive steps necessary to build a solid custody case.

It is a mistake to let yourself be deceived by anyone. It is a more lethal mistake to deceive yourself. Let the liar enjoy the "fortress" of self-deception. It offers the liar no real protection; the fortress will collapse, leaving the liar's troops forever angry and alienated.

Understanding what is going on will give you the patience that is the key to dealing with this person. It will cost you fewer resources to let the liar self-destruct than to engage the liar in a full-blown battle. If you allow him or her to self-destruct, you will be blameless for the liar's destruction.

Once you have identified a soldier as being in the opposition's army, fill out a data sheet on the new recruit. When you are close to the situation, it can be difficult to know who are the cavalry and who are the decoys.

One of the hardest lessons to learn is that it is useless to attempt to win your opposition's soldier over to your army. Information you reveal in an attempt to convert recruits will not be believed and will be relayed to the enemy.

Defense Against Lies

Don't waste time defending yourself against frivolous lies. Once you are aware that this tactic will be used against you, decide not to let each barrage upset you. Your energetic effort would give the lies more credence than if you ignore them. Conducting your life in a proper manner and keeping a contact log will allow you to easily disprove untruths.

Often the liar will find some bit of negative information about you and embellish it in order to make the offense appear more dastardly. The exaggeration may actually make the original information look so ridiculous that no one will accept it at all.

The Grand Lie

Defending yourself against The Grand Lie can involve psychologists, lie detectors, experts, employers, former spouses, contact log and enormous amounts of money. VOCAL (Victims of Child Abuse Laws), a national organization working to protect the civil rights of those falsely accused of child abuse or neglect and to protect children from their abusers.

Even once you have proven your innocence, things will still never return to the way they were before the accusation. Some people will always doubt you, and you will find yourself monitoring every interaction with all children.

Handling the Liar

You have three options when you know a person has lied to you: let the liar off the hook, don't acknowledge the lie, or confront the liar. Don't handle this situation in a manner that will let you win this small war now and make you feel good now. Lying is a mistake. It will become apparent to the liar that it was a mistake. Handle this in a manner that will do you the most good in the long run, to help you win the big war.

1. Let the liar off the hook. In order to deal with this person in the future, you may allow them a way out. (a) "I see there has been a misunderstanding and we have the opportunity to set things straight." (b) "It looks as if things have gotten scrambled. Why don't you take some time to reassess the situation and get back to me with your answer, tomorrow?" (c) "Let me give you the information I have. It may change your response."

2. You can challenge the statement made by the liar without calling the person a liar. This is accomplished by starting your answer to their statement with "but." As an example: the liar says, "You aren't home when I come to pick up the children."

Your answer can be, "But, you are supposed to call the evening before you come and we are always home by 8:00 p.m. because the children have to be in bed by 8:30." Once you have given your statement, stop talking. One strong rebuttal is much more powerful than multiple arguments.

3. If you do not wish to confront the liar, act as you normally would have in the past. You wish to let the liar off the hook. You say, "That's not the way I see it. Take a look at it from this side and let me know what you think." Or "Here is some information you may not be aware of." Or "That's not the way I heard it happened. Why don't you check your sources and get back to me?" Or "It may have looked that way to you, but the documentation submitted is solid enough that you should consider your facts again."

4. Some additional options:

- If you wish to confront the liar, stare at the person unflinchingly.
- Ask the person to repeat the statement. If the statement has changed, remind the person of what was said previously.
- If the lie is outrageous, laugh out loud.
- Make a show of writing down the "facts" as stated.
- Ask for the date and spelling of a name of a person or place mentioned.
- Raise your eyebrows.
- Repeat the lie as stated with a question in your voice.
- If there is a way to verify the statement while the person is there, do it .
- If you can't tolerate it any longer, stop talking.
- Inform the person you are finished.
- Don't let the person reengage you in conversation or debate.
- Gather your things and leave.
- Avoid contact with this person in the future.
- If you must communicate again, record the conversation or take a reliable witness with you.

Lie Suppression

Somewhere in their brains, lairs know lying is wrong. If they are so disconnected that they don't know it is wrong they still know they don't want to get caught. In order to keep going they use some common techniques to suppress the discovery of their lies. They don't seem to understand that these techniques don't always work.

Enthusiastic, credible sounding allegations of poor judgment, neglect and abuse can bring an incorrect judgment for custody or the reversal of a custody decision. When the accused lacks an understanding of what is happening and an effective, fact-based defense, other techniques must be employed. The success of the liar using these techniques depends heavily upon the ignorance, lack of understanding of the accused and an understanding that very few outside parties have much at stake in this process.

- If only you are aware that they lied they dummy up. If no one important knows about it, it didn't happen.
- Explaining that they were only the receivers of the information, not the originators and therefore not responsible for if the information is correct or not.
- When the lies come to light they become indignant saying "How dare you accuse me of such a thing?"
- Often they will identify the proof as "rumors" or, "lies on your part" regardless of eyewitness or documented evidence.
- They will say you are "paranoid" or "hysterical." since no one is "out to get you."
- Attacking the weakest aspects of your defense. Even creating new charges.
- Calling you names like "control-freak," "redneck," "biker," "dead-beat," "workaholic," and, of course, "child abuser." Using counter accusations heavily loaded verbs and adjectives when describing their defense and listing your new crimes.
- They will keep things hostile in order to avoid a fair and open discovery of the facts.
- Refusing to accept as true any of your motives and suggest that you are not really interested in the welfare of the children, but are simply pursuing your own selfish agendas
- Involving the authorities who must investigate any accusation offering them a new unwitting ally.
- Dismissing your information as "old news."
- Confession and avoidance by coming half-clean may create the impression of candor and honesty. While admitting only to relatively harmless, less-than-vindictive "mistakes" the rest of what they have said may be accepted as the truth.
- Another track is to fall-back position quite different from the one originally taken. "Well, it may not have been actual child abuse, but it was obviously child neglect."
- Explain that the situation is impossibly complex and the truth as ultimately unknowable.
- Changing the subject to past unsolvable problems.
- Reporting new incriminating facts, and then make nothing of them rather than proving existing information.

Sue the Liar

You may only sue for defamation in a tort case. If you are considering a lawsuit against the Liar, read ""Sue For False Accusations" in Chapter 16: Abuse, Kidnapping and Allegations.

Only the District Attorney (D.A.) for the State can prosecute for perjury, It is not as simple as you might think. The primary problem with trying to get a D.A. to prosecute perjury is the matter of prosecutorial resources. The D.A. has a limited budget, which precludes prosecuting every crime, particularly to the fullest. Budget restrictions are the primary reason for plea bargains. Therefore, by only prosecuting the good cases, the D.A. produces a nearly 100% conviction rate.

The second consideration is that it generally requires that the person being prosecuted (a) actually make two statements of fact, under oath, (b) both of which cannot be true, and (c) both of which are material to the matter at hand. Testimony at conflict with that of another witness doesn't qualify. The evidence is not likely to get past the three primary hurdles since they're so difficult to prove. The D.A. won't mess with bad cases. Most perjury cases fall into this category.

Finally, your custody case is only important to you and the other people involved in the suit. The D.A. would be hard pressed to explain to the other taxpayers why this type of case could be considered as important as prosecuting capital crimes.

Using Their Lies against Them

Remember that whistle-blowing invites censure. The way to avoid these recriminations is to use the proper timing and messengers. Using your "evidence" too soon is like firing your best weapons when the enemy is well out of striking range. Your attorney will counsel you as to the best time and method for firing your weapons. When you are "in the right," it is especially important to avoid any appearance of being vindictive.

Proof or Poof

You need to determine the differences between:
What you feel.
What you think.
What you know.
What you can prove.

These are all very different things. Photos, signed documents, reliable third-party testimony constitute acceptable evidence. The opposition is as wrong as wrong can be, and you can prove it. What do you do with the evidence? Talk to your attorney. The three most important factors to consider regarding potentially damaging information about the opposition are:

1. Timing. 2. Timing. 3. Timing.

Use the information when it will do your case the most good. If the liar is accustomed to telling lies, you may be able to find a pattern of lies. Don't worry that this person will change overnight. The liar won't change.

The liar can't change. The liar doesn't think there is anything to change. The liar doesn't want to change. If you keep looking and listening, you will amass an amazing amount of information.

Locate any document, especially sworn statements, in which false information was given. You may be able to locate other sworn statements with contradictory information. Letters in the liar's handwriting or statements signed by the liar are very good. The data may not look important now, but its value may become evident when you really need it.

If you find evidence of criminal records, obtain a complete set of certified documents for each and every incident. Some of the documents you are looking for are: arresting officer's report, booking, detective's follow-up report, arraignment, trial record and sentencing.
If the person was incarcerated, attempt to obtain a record of behavior while he or she was under the control of the penal system. When you submit evidence of the liar's wrongdoing, you will be accused of harassment. You will be threatened with legal action. You will be accused of putting his or her ability to earn a living in jeopardy.

Impeachment of a Witness

Lies of the opposition should, in some cases, not be challenged. If the person becomes comfortable lying, you may be able to use it to your advantage later. One of the most effective ways of catching the liar is impeaching a witness at trial through the use of depositions and inconsistent statements. Unfortunately, you will have to do a great deal of the work for your attorney. The attorney needs your help to know what questions to ask at deposition and to know what authenticated documentation or proof there is that there were inconsistent statements. In court your attorney should allow the witness to bring to life the lie by asking the witness the following questions:
Do you remember having given a statement to (person's name) regarding how the accident occurred?
Did you give that statement freely?
Who was present when you gave your statement?
When was the statement given?

The witness should then be shown the proof and asked the following question: "I show you what has been marked as Plaintiff's Exhibit 'A' for identification. Is this a copy of your sworn statement?" Finally, read the relevant portion of the statement that directly contradicts the trial testimony of the witness. Impeachment through the use of depositions or documented inconsistent statements should be accomplished in an organized fashion and should be performed smoothly and directly. The relevant pages and sections of the deposition should be marked and highlighted beforehand so the questioner will not fumble through pages or lose control of the witness.

It is rewarding and impressive to see your attorney properly impeach a liar through the use of inconsistent statements in documents or in a deposition. It is a very simple procedure to learn and, once mastered, will prove to be an effective means of cross-examining even the most "dangerous" witness at trial.

Children and the Liar

Children believe their parents are good. They should. Children will eventually know when a parent is telling lies and will see the lies are self-serving for the liar. This information will not affect the love the children have for the parent. It should not. A liar is not necessarily a bad parent.

Seeing someone they love lie, children may decide that lying is not so bad. It may even entice them to use lies in their lives. If children have an opportunity to see that the lies backfire on the adult producing negative consequences and more problems, the children may make a decision to avoid lying themselves.

When the adult is caught in a lie by another adult because the children have told the truth, it is common for the adult to accuse the children of lying and then admonish the children for lying. This telephone conversation is an example;

Randall: Bobby, you have been gone five days. Why haven't you called?
Bobby: I wanted to, but Mom won't let me.
Randall: You know the judge said you could call anytime you want to, don't you?
Bobby: I wanted to call you even at the airport, but she said, "No."
Randall: Do you want me to talk to your mom?
Bobby: Yes. Please tell her I could call. "Mom, Dad wants to talk to you."
Amber: Yeah
Randall: Amber, please let Bobby call when he wants. It's in the court order.
Amber: He has never asked to call.
Randall: He uses the phone here all the time. He calls his grandmother, his friends and me from his friends' homes when he is away for the afternoon. It isn't reasonable for him to act differently at your house. Please let him call.
Amber: Sure. Here's Bobby. Bobby, don't you lie to your father.
Bobby: Dad, I did ask to call, but she gets mad.
Randall: You could call from the baby-sitter's house.
Bobby: The baby-sitter said my special number doesn't work from her house.
Randall: That 800 number works from anywhere. I will call the lawyer tomorrow.
Bobby: Tell him to tell the judge to tell my Mom I can call.

When Children Lie

Children pressured or enticed to be part of the lie will suffer more damage longer than children allowed to remain outside of the conspiracy. When children are encouraged or forced to lie for a parent they love and then have to witness the pain it causes someone else they love, they may experience permanent psychological dysfunction.

Since the long-term goal is to help your children incorporate a conscience into their lives, don't over-react to the lie. You know that your children mean well. Try to understand how the child saw what was happening. Attempt to understand the circumstances that led to the episode. If the child's perception of the event was not correct, explain the difference between what did happen and how the child understood it. Explain the difference between wishful thinking or fantasies and reality.

Don't overwhelm children by cornering them to make them face the truth. A violent reaction will make the children associate disapproval with anger which they fear. Even mild disapproval will make the children feel guilty. If your children are involved in adult intrigue and conspiracy, you and the children may require counseling to learn to deal with the lies now and circumvent any long-term consequences.

Where Do You Fit?

[] I tell the truth in all matters. Whatever transpires after that, happens. It's not my responsibility.
[] I tell the truth, but will lie to be polite or avoid hurting someone's feelings.
[] I normally tell the truth, but occasionally lie.
[] I like to tell the truth, but will lie to protect myself.
[] I do whatever I have to do to get by.
[] I say what I think people want me to say.
[] My life is private so I tell them lies so they won't know anything about me.

Some people feel their only defense is lying. Lying can also be a symptom of delusions, schizophrenia and paranoia.

Non-Fatal Flaw

A non-fatal flaw is something that is wrong and could affect this case. If it is wrong, but does not affect this case, it is a non-issue and should be protected by your attorney.

If you identify a flaw, you should face *it*, deal with *it*, fix *it* if you can, prepare to deal with it if the opposition brings it up, or point *it* out before the opposition finds out about *it*. In this way, the non-fatal flaw will increase your credibility and improve your case. Old lies are one example of a non-fatal flaw you can and should attack.

Your Lies

Lies of any kind can destroy your custody case. This chapter is designed to help you deal with lies whether in the past or present, so that you can minimize the damage you could inadvertently cause to your case. Telling the truth, like any other good behavior, is learned behavior and takes practice.

Your lies negatively affect how others feel about you.

Most people will not knowingly become liars to protect you or your lies. If you are able to force a truthful person to lie for you, you have probably destroyed any friendship, loyalty, or respect that person had for you.

It is a common belief that if someone is a liar, that person is also a thief.

Your lies negatively affect how you feel about the people who know you have lied.

It is very easy to forgive others their mistakes; it takes more grit and gumption to forgive them for having witnessed yours.

If you know you lied, they know you lied, and you know they know you lied.

It is hard to face someone who knows you have lied in the past and who thinks you will probably do it again. Such a person will never be sure if you have been truthful. In any case, such a person knows that if you decide to, you will lie again.

Cold Turkey Truth

If you catch yourself telling a lie, stop what you are saying and say, "That was a lie." Then tell the truth. If it is something you do not wish to talk about, don't. It is better to tell someone, "I really do not want to talk about this," than to make up something.

How to Start Repairing the Damage

Every expert and professional will tell you: Above all, do not lie. Correct old lies as soon as possible. Do not create new lies to explain old lies.

If you have lied in the past, make a list of any lies you have told, the date you lied, if the lie is currently maintained, what the truth is, the reason you lied, and who knows about each lie. Go over the list with your attorney and ask about how to handle these matters.

There is a vast gulf between crimes and employee misconduct. It is a span an otherwise good employee may successfully cross. Our lies are primarily minor indiscretions that in their worst form would not get us prosecuted, but might get us fired.

Telling the truth about old situations that were handled with lies may be easier than you think. The most fearsome thing about lies is worrying about the truth coming out. Once the truth is out, whatever will happen will happen. You will probably feel a great sense of relief. The consequences are usually not nearly as bad as you imagine. Ask any person who has lied and then told the truth. Getting things out in the open has a healing effect.

April 14, 1912, the steamship Titanic of the White Star Line, sailing on her maiden voyage from Southampton England to New York, was sunk at sea by a collision with a submerged iceberg. The Chairman of the Board of White Star Line pressured the captain to shorten the projected arrival time, badgering him to ignore warnings from the crew about the worsening conditions at sea. After the collision with the iceberg, the Chairman abandoned the captain, sinking ship, passengers and crew, scrambling to safety. The lives of fifteen hundred people were lost. He was cowardly, irresponsible and despicable. Very few people even know or cared that he sailed with the vessel.

Your misdeeds are most assuredly smaller and will also be lost in time. Tell the truth as simply and cleanly as you can. Don't become the voice of truth for anyone else. Coming clean for others will buy you more problems than you can afford, especially at this time.

Lies, especially old ones, can very often be reasonably explained in several ways; for example, one's age when telling the lie. Many lies have outlived their perceived usefulness.

The length of time one has let lies remain unresolved adds to one's fears of their discovery. Moral values may have been different at the time a lie was told, or the feared impact on an economic situation might have prompted a lie. Never attempt to justify an old lie with a new lie.

We don't lie because the truth is difficult to see. Usually, it is visible at a glance. We lie because it is more comfortable.

This kind of comfort doesn't last very long. Witnesses hate finding out, under questioning, in court, that they believed a lie. It is easier for your witnesses to be "in the know" about what is really going on. Telling the truth about your lies before the opposition does, can deflect the main assault against your case.

Judges, mediators, psychologists, and reasonable people will think more of you for confronting the skeletons in your closet than if you stubbornly stick to your lie when the truth can be determined.

Correcting Old Lies

Correcting old lies doesn't have to be a major production. Several times in this manual we tell you to be kind to yourself. Once you have dispensed with your own old lies, you will see this is one of the kindest things anyone can do for him or herself. Don't beat yourself up with it. Just do it.

In a non-court environment, one of the easiest methods is to work a conversation around so that an old lie comes up. You could laugh and say, "I can't believe anyone really thought that was true" or "That old lie did me a lot more good twenty years ago than it does now."

In court, avoid any attempt at humor and state the truth simply. As an example "I was eighteen years old at the time. Why would anyone have believed I had already served three years in Viet Nam?"

Done correctly, this makes perfectly clear that the old lie was obviously nonsensical. This allows them to see the joke rather than making people feel they were taken in, and therefore, much easier for them to dismiss. Be straightforward or be creative, but clean up the old lies as soon as possible. Use these examples to examine your alternatives:

Old Lie:
Twelve years ago, I was divorced when my child was an infant.
Truth:
The other parent of my child and I were never married.
Reason I lied:
I have generally lived in places where a birth out-of-wedlock was unacceptable. That was twelve years ago, and the attitudes about this seem better now, but it would be hard for my child to deal with this information even now.

Old Lie:
I told my ex-in-law that the divorce and custody case were all my fault.
Truth:
I did not cheat or lie, but my ex-spouse did.
Reason I lied:
I did not feel like hurting my ex-in-law's feelings. I cared about these people for too long, and they need to be able to support their child.

Old Lie:
I have never been in the military.
Truth:
I was dishonorably discharged from the Navy.
Reason I lied:
First, I was embarrassed then it was the post-Viet Nam era, and military service was unpopular. It was twenty-eight years ago; I was just a kid.

Old Lie:
I agreed to all their verbal requests and demands.
Truth:
I did not have any intention of giving up the rights the court had given me.
Reason I lied:
It was easier to agree at the time than get into a big fight.

Old Lie:
When moving to this new company, I inflated my seniority and remaining ties with my old company, implying that I could still place junior associates with my old firm.
Truth:
I barely got out of there without going to jail.
Reason I lied:
I needed a job, and would have told them I was a transvestite if it was necessary to end the months of unemployment.

Old Lie:
I missed court because I was very ill.
Truth:
I overslept because I had been out drinking the night before.
Reason I lied:
I really am concerned about my children. I had so much pressure for so long, I went out with some friends to blow off steam and overdid it.
I felt the judge would not listen or understand, so I lied.

Old Lie:
I just open my mouth and start lying. Everything I said was a lie. Even when I try to fix the lie, I end up telling another lie.
Truth:
It happens every time I start to talk.
Reason I lied:
It happens when I'm standing in the line at the grocery store for two minutes, or stuck on an airplane for six hours. I have no idea why I do it. I see myself doing it and I just can't stop. My friends treat me like I have a drinking problem, except it is a lying problem.

Old Lie:
I never knew my parents; they died when I was a baby.
Truth:
I never got along with my family and left home at sixteen.
Reason I lied:
My family was abusive and dysfunctional. I had all the pain and humiliation I was willing to take.

Old Lie:
When I applied for my job, I submitted information on my resume about undergraduate work and on-the-job work experience that was required for the position.
Truth:
I have not done most of the things I listed.
Reason I lied:
A great opportunity opened up at a very good company. Knowing it was critical to fill the position quickly, I schmoozed the interviewer enough so that my credentials were not verified.
I needed a better job and knew I was under qualified.

Old Lie:
When I moved into this new community, they assumed some very nice things about me.
Truth:
I have never been anyone important. When people gave nice, but incorrect information about me, I did not correct them. As time went on, misinformation built on misinformation, and I made no attempt to correct it.
Reason I lied:
I was flattered that people were so impressed with me and by what they thought of me, I let them think what they wanted.

Old Lie:
I told my friends at work that I had slept with another employee who works at our company. I gave them lurid details about the relationship several times a week for several months.
Truth:
I have never had anything, but a business-related conversation at the office, with this person.
Reason I lied:
The first time I mentioned this person, I had drunk half a dozen drinks with some of my co-workers. They were so impressed that I had scored, I was unwilling to rectify or stop enlarging the lie. I wanted to impress them and it raised my level of confidence.

Old Lie:
I stood there while my friend lied, telling someone that we had worked out an important very lucrative deal.
Truth:
This friend and I were always trying get-rich-quick schemes. We did not do the deal he said we did. Everything we touched turned into manure.
I didn't actually tell a lie. I just agreed with my friend's statements.
Reason I lied:
The people listening to our story were really impressed; they spread the story as they introduced us to others. It gave us credibility, and people gave us respect.

Old Lie:
I was raped by the father of my child.

Truth:

After being involved with this person for a long time, I didn't get everything out of the deal I wanted.

Reason I lied:

I knew that people would feel sorry and offer me help more easily. I was able to get free legal assistance by charging abuse. The authorities did not have any way to verify or disprove my statements.

Old Lie:

I have never been arrested.

Truth:

I was caught red-handed and pleaded guilty to a class four felony.

Reason I lied:

I have spent a good deal of my life around the kinds of people who get into a lot of trouble. When other people keep getting away with things, it does not seem so wrong after a while. This was my first and only offense, and I received probation. The sentence was light, and I learned my lesson.

Old Lie:

I told the other parent I was thinking of leaving my spouse.

Truth:

Nothing is happening in my marriage.

Reason I lied:

I wanted them to think something was going on so they would waste their time with misinformation.

Old Lie:

I just kept making the same indictments over and over again.

Truth:

None of the things I was saying were true.

Reason I lied:

There was no way for the opposition to defend themselves. I could see the Judge did not like the opposition and wanted to win, so this was my best shot at winning.

Old Lie:

I always attempt to tell the truth.

Truth:

I have lied about so many things that I cannot remember all of my lies.

Reason I lied:

I wanted acceptance. I never felt that I was good enough, had enough, or could be enough. So, I told people what I thought they wanted to hear.

Old Lie:

I said I only made $200.00 a week after taxes.

Truth:

My income is twice what I stated, but much less than I need to pay my bills.

Reason I lied:

They really don't need my money; there is a lot more money in the other home than in mine. I heard they would take a big percentage of my income, and I didn't know how I would live on what was left.

Old Lie:

I have never been involved with drugs or alcohol.

Truth:

I required rehabilitation for chemical abuse in 1981.

Reason I lied:

I have been able to rebuild my life around good people. I did not think they could accept my past.

Old Lie:

I told everyone that a mutual acquaintance had AIDS.

Truth:

This person is not sick, just slender.

Reason I lied:

I hate this person and wanted to cause all the trouble and pain I could.

Old Lie:

I took on additional responsibility that my entry level job did not allow and was accepted as a professional because of the completeness of my work. Later, when asked, I told them I did in fact have the certification necessary for the procedure.

Truth:

I had only seen the advanced procedure done.

Reason I lied:

I lied about my training to avoid getting in trouble.

Old Lie:

I was just telling a bunch of outrageous and funny stories.

Truth:

The stories were exaggerations of several experiences of my own and stories I had heard from others through the years and adopted as my own. I was having a great time making everyone laugh. I did not consider if anyone was taking me seriously.

Reason I lied:

I love being the center of attention. I did not really feel I was lying.

Old Lie:

I was not at my parents' house when everyone got involved in that scheme. I heard about it later, but I did not approve or take part in it.

Truth:

I was there and even participated in the planning and execution. It was exciting, and we thought we were too smart to get caught.

Reason I lied:

I thought that if I told a lie, I would stay out of trouble.

Old Lie:

When I go someplace where I am not known, I become a new person. Anyone I want to be.

Truth:

I have never felt important.

Reason I lied:

I am happiest when I can be someone new, exciting and smart to other people.

Old Lie:

I have known that person for a long time and I know marriage vows don't mean anything in her life.

Truth:

I don't have any information about her private life.

Reason I lied:

That woman has always been my enemy. She has lied to me and about me, so I did not feel it was wrong to lie about her.

Identifying the Liar to Others

Sometimes when we are attempting to show a listener that the other parent is a liar, the information we are forced to give makes us look worse than the liar.

Statements like: "They lie about everything." "You can't trust anything they say." "They will say anything to get what they want." Reflect as badly on the speaker as they do on the target of the statement. Re-stating the information in a less accusatory or hostile manner will accomplish the message more efficiently.

Examples would include; "I am not comfortable relying on the information I get from them." "Their prospective is often slanted by their wants rather than the children's needs." "They tend to live in a flexible reality."

When attempting to inform professionals that they are dealing with a liar it is best to do so with documented evidence rather than anecdotal stories. The stories tend to put things in a "he said - she said" context where solid evidence can't be discarded as readily.

It is unnerving to have to identify the liar to each professional, evaluator or decision maker along the way; unnerving, but necessary. It is helpful if the professional on one level happens to make a statement as to the lack of truth in statements mad by the other parent in any reports or decisions they make. Examples would be; "Ms. Smith, I don't feel you are being honest with this court." "Amber changed the information initially given when faced with her previous statements." These statements by other professionals become a powerful element of documented evidence to present to the next professional.

One interesting observation is that sometimes the liar becomes aware of his past mistakes. Although, rather than learning from past mistakes, usually the liar doesn't learn not to lie. They tend to change the lies to something they think will be more acceptable. Often the liar will blame the condemning professional for not understanding what was really said or fabricating the statement. Because you have documented the event or evidence, the new lies only work in your favor.

Telling the Awful Truth

Even truthful assertions of fact may be actionable. As an example, the public disclosure of private facts can be grounds for a successful lawsuit, even if it involves completely truthful assertions. Companies that make their living as tattletales have to be careful what they print and who they report stories about. Not everyone doing something in public is considered a public figure legally. Nor is the fact that an official complaint has been made a guarantee of "accuracy."

Perjury in Family Court!

Perjury is not prosecuted in Family Court!
Perjury is not prosecuted in Family Court!
Perjury is not prosecuted in Family Court!

It is not fair or right. It just is. You must hire a new lawyer and file suit in civil court.

Attorneys and Lies

Advising a parent to gain a tactical advantage by using false information violates the law and the Attorney's Code of Professional Conduct even if the attorney is not involved in the presentation of the case to the court.

An attorney shall not knowingly mislead the court. If an attorney does act upon false information the attorney is required to notify the court and the opposition. If the attorney persists in presenting the information even after the attorney is notified about the problem, the attorney may be subject to fines or sanctions.

Even if an attorney filed a groundless suit because he was misled by his client, he can still be liable under Rule 11 of the Federal Rules of Civil Procedure where opposing counsel provided him with evidence that the client was lying, but he failed to investigate, says a U.S. District Court in Massachusetts.

The client had sued another company for breach of contract, claiming that the parties had entered into a joint venture. The company moved for Rule 11 sanctions on the grounds that the lawyer had failed to investigate whether his client had a valid claim against the company. The lawyer argued that he wasn't responsible for any Rule 11 violations because he had relied in good faith on information from the client that turned out to be false. But the court said that Rule 11 did not permit the attorney to rely on "the deliberately false assurances of high-level officials of the company that he represents [just] because he had earlier dealings with them, and had come to the belief that their representations were always reliable... "Here, the very nature of the assurances he was receiving, in the face of evidence to the contrary made available to him by defendants and their counsel, created a compelling need for him to press for more information from his own clients rather than taking the position that he could continue to rely until defense counsel produced compelling evidence." U.S. District Court for Massachusetts. Schiebel Elektronische Geraete GMBH v. Polestar Technologies, Inc., No. 97-10231-REK. August 3, 1998.

The Court Will Call a Liar a Liar

Often the court is clear without being rude about its opinion of a witness. As an example, a judge may say, "The witness seems to have considerable indifference toward the truth." Or "I don't feel you are being entirely honest with the court Mr. Hart.

This Won't Change Where the Children Live

Although the court does not like being lied to, it feels that the jails are full of real criminals and that the court must expeditiously move past as many minor obstructions as possible. The court may not feel that the past or present ability to recognize the truth or tell the truth indicates what kind of parent one may be. The court may not make the final decision.

What Is, Shall Remain: Also known as Status Quo, this means the children will remain where they have been residing, unless a problem (obvious and imminent danger to the children) can be proven to exist. There does not seem to be any drive in the courts to remove children from an environment where the truth is absent or rarely used.

No Lie Double Talk

We feel that if persons are caught lying in court, they are perjuring themselves and should suffer dire consequences. Because finding the "Truth" in many instances is impractical or impossible, the effort is rarely made by the court.

On one hand, we tell you "absolutely do not lie." On the other hand, we tell you that the lies told by the opposition sometimes won't hurt them, and it may not affect the case in the end. It CAN and MAY make a difference. If a person believes he is telling the truth, but is factually incorrect, he's neither a liar nor perjurer. If he knowingly and intentionally makes factually incorrect statements under oath, he is both a liar and perjurer. If the statement is not made under oath, he is merely a liar.

Parents often comment that the opposing attorney is a "liar" or "perjurer." If opposing counsel makes a factually incorrect statement, it doesn't necessarily mean he is lying. Who knows what he believes, or what his client told him? Try to stay calm when this happens. Perjury may run rampant in child custody trials. Criminal prosecution for perjury in civil cases is virtually non-existent.

No one likes being lied to, especially judges. The "jerk" factor often decides cases. Which party is the bigger jerk? Judges are human. They often like one side more than the other. Point out your oppositions' perjury at trial, and the opposition will assume "jerk" status.

Chapter 15: Panic Situations

Custody battles often result in potentially explosive situations. You may feel an enormous amount of panic of anger or even rage. These feelings, even if justified, are not your allies. They may cause you to act in illegal or socially unacceptable ways. Control your fear and anger and act in a responsible manner.

Anger is an internal response to external stimuli. To control your anger in a responsible manner will also limit the pain and trouble it causes you as well as diminish the power others have over your life. There is nothing you can do about what other people do, but you can avoid distortion, magnification, essential thinking and mind reading that will make things seem much worse than they really are. An example of distortion in your thinking would be destructive labeling such as, "Pat has always been lazy." An example of magnification in your thinking would be, "Everything is ruined now." An example of essential thinking is, "If I can't do it this the way I have always done it, it just can't be done." An example of mind reading is, "They didn't include me, so they must not think I know what I am doing."

You can prevent or reverse the negative effects of anger with a Power Step. Planning ahead for the situations that you know will cause anger and preparing to take some Pro Active Steps.

Pro Active Steps

I can't do anything to change that now.
I will do better at the next meeting.
They are doing the best they can.
I will ask if I can be involved in the process.
I will count to ten very slowly before I respond.

How you handle the things that happen to you is more important than what is actually happening.

Said another way, you are responsible for what you do and say, not for what is done or said to or against you. Learn to utilize intelligence, threat analysis, security measures and crisis management.

The opposition will be held blameless if you "misunderstand" something they have said or done and do something stupid or illegal. It is easier to respond in an appropriate manner if you have all the information available or are aware of how others have handled similar matters.

Not knowing the entire story or being under the threat of losing contact with your children, causes fear. Fear of the unknown causes panic. For instance, if someone threatens to tell everyone you are an ax murderer, and you know that the worst thing you have done is drive fifteen miles per hour over the speed limit, you laugh.

On the other hand, if the amount of time you have with your children is limited, and you are aware that steps are being taken to reduce or eliminate your time together, the panic you feel may cause you to seriously consider becoming an ax murderer.

Learning from the Pain of Others

When exposed to real or manufactured crises, it is best to seek a safe place to express your panic-induced anger. There is nothing wrong with blowing off steam. In fact, it is generally considered healthy. Since anger may impair your judgment, be aware of anyone near enough to hear anything you may say. Do not express your anxiety or anger within hearing distance of possible enemy troops. The enemy could testify in court later that you were volatile, exhibited hostile behavior, and appeared out of control. Delay any action for at least one hour to help you avoid a spontaneous and possibly regrettable reaction. Take a swift walk around the block. Do not get in your car when you are upset. Your children need you in one piece, not fighting another lawsuit because you were not able to concentrate on traffic.

If you have any doubts about the wisdom of your contemplated plans, abandon them. Ask yourself if there is any way a specific action could damage your case. Consider what action you would take against the opposition if they did to you what you are considering doing to them. Fill out an incident report to get a firm understanding of what has happened and make an entry in your contact log. Call the appropriate person, your attorney, detective or minister. If you have the support of someone who is very levelheaded and whom you can trust, bounce your reactions off that person. Make sure this person understands his or her role. That person's role is to calm you down, help you see as many sides as possible to the incident, stay as unemotional as possible, and offer constructive ways for you to respond. Most often the best response is to do nothing.

Your susceptibility to pain and your elevated sensitivity to the words and actions of others during this challenge in your life may prompt you to react inappropriately, especially if you feel bullied. This chapter is designed to make you aware of some common problems, help you analyze the situation, make some reasonable decisions, and avoid some pitfalls. Even though the specific problem you are facing may not be discussed here, these examples of the more common challenges will give you some solid guidelines. A great deal of panic is situational. An incident that would normally not cause you any concern may take on terrific importance or pressure during a custody battle. If you don't face any of the problems listed in the following pages, you may benefit from using these examples to put your situation in perspective.

Panic Situations, Examples

01 Legal Papers

You arrive home after a hard week of working and find filed documents in the mail box. The documents state that you are violent when dealing with your children. You must appear at a hearing to defend against charges because the other parent is asking the court to issue an Order of Protection for the children against you. It is 6:15 p.m. Friday, and there is no way for you to talk to your attorney until Monday at 10:00am.

What This Means

It is possible the attorney believes false information that has been presented by the other parent. Unless the other attorney has seen evidence to indicate you are dangerous, this action is unwarranted. Tactics like this may be used to unnerve and/or build a track record to discredit you. This strategy can be very destructive to the entire process and is generally used by an inept or unscrupulous attorney.

Reasonable Reaction

If you have done nothing wrong, settle down. When interacting with the opposition this weekend, act as if nothing has happened. The opposition knows you are supposed to get the notice, but may not be sure when you will receive it. You are expected to explode. They want you to explode. If you go "ballistic," it will strengthen the opposition's case and damage yours.

If you think there may be a problem, take an unimpeachable third party with you.

Remember why you are having contact with these people and practice some non-reactive responses to the static they usually give you.

Your cool, calm, normal demeanor will unnerve the opposition. Do not allow the opposition to pull you into a verbal or physical confrontation.

If you are concerned about the opposition's behavior or your own behavior, take a calm responsible person with you. Fill out an Incident Report form and send it to your attorney so it will be there first thing Monday morning. Begin to assemble the proof you will need to have the charges legally dismissed. If accusations are raised against you and dismissed repeatedly, the judge will see a pattern of harassment.

02 Misappropriation of Money

You are in the military and are separated from your spouse and child. Your child was having emotional problems, so the other parent took your child for psychiatric services. CHAMPUS (military medical insurance) said they sent payment directly to the other parent who was to pay the counseling service.

The other parent now says the temporary court order says you are to pay medical bills and is unwilling to discuss the matter any further with you. Actually the current court order orders you to pay for any expenses not covered by CHAMPUS. You requested a paper trail from CHAMPUS, but they refuse because information can only be released to the custodial parent.

What This Means

The other parent is being dishonest. The insurance company is probably worried about violating the Privacy Act.

Reasonable Action

It is reasonable to have a proper accounting and complete information on any bill you are expected to pay. Record the name of each person you talk to at the insurance company, and give the insurance company a copy of the court orders you have now. Consult your attorney. If the insurance company becomes unreasonable, call the insurance commission and file a complaint.

03 Other Parent Has Moved Child

You arrive on time at the opposition's house to pick up your child at the end of the other parent's regularly scheduled weekend. The house is empty. It looks like the opposition has moved, taking your child without informing you.

What This Means

The other parent may have been unable to reach you to tell you about the move and perhaps has left information on your answering machine or with one of your relatives. The opposition may have mixed up the pickup time.

On the other hand, the other parent may have decided to run with the child.

Reasonable Action

If you have not been home, check your answering machine to see if any message was left. If this is not the case, call all relatives and friends the opposition keeps in touch with for information. Contact the landlord for a forwarding address. Look through any trash left at the house for an indication of where the opposition may have gone. If you feel sure the opposition has left the area, and you have a document restricting the transportation of the child without your permission, read the information in this chapter on kidnapping.

Call your attorney. If this person has not had successful experience with parental kidnapping problems, copy the section in Chapter 16: Abuse and Kidnapping, Legal Steps To Getting Your Child Back, and give it to the attorney.

04 Phone Harassment at Work

The non-custodial parent calls at various times during the day and evening on the home and business numbers to yell at you or the child. This person is very angry. The calls are always upsetting and unsettle you for many hours after the call.

What This Means

The non-custodial parent is probably very upset and doing the best he or she can with circumstances. Or, you are still dealing with a jerk. Since you don't know, which telephone line or when the assault is coming, you get uptight every time the telephone rings.

Reasonable Action

Get a copy of your employer's personal call policy. Have your attorney send a letter notifying the opposition it is illegal for them to interfere with your ability to earn a living along with the company's telephone policy. The company may have to file criminal charges if the problem persists. If you have your own company or are self-employed and can afford Caller ID or an additional telephone line to which only the other parent will have the number, you can trace the place from which the hostile calls will come. When that line rings you have a moment to get mentally prepared to deal with the other parent. This has the calming affect of removing the "threat" from your business life. In the letter to the other parent, have your attorney outline generous, but specific times the other parent may call to talk to you about the child or to speak with the child. Reasonably, this will be during the child's normal waking hours and when the child is home from school. Fill out an Incident Report Form.

05 Bruises on Your Child

You pick up the child for the weekend. Hours later, when you're bathing the child, you notice marks on the arms and bruises on the back and buttocks.

What This Means

Probable child abuse. This does not necessarily mean the other parent or someone living in the home did it.

Reasonable Action

Call the child's doctor right away and ask what he/she wants you to do. If the doctor is not responsive or is unavailable, take the child to the emergency room. Call your attorney. It may be necessary to call Child Protective Services.

06 Implied Threats

There have only been words and posturing so far, but you feel bullied and threatened by the other parent's "friends" each time you arrive to pick up or return your child. Whenever the other parent comes to your home or work, the friends come along and there is a scene that is upsetting and frightening.

What This Means

This tactic is probably designed to intimidate you so that you will stop coming to pick up the child.

Reasonable Action

Most cities have established exchange points for parents because this is a common problem. This must be requested by you and ordered by the court.

The process is sometimes called Expedited Visitation. If that option is not available, request "Civil Standby" from the police for each exchange. Or have the most calm responsible person you know available to accompany you for pick up and return.

Other options are to take a third unimpeachable witness with you and/or a person with a video camera to tape the exchange.

07 Accusation of Abuse

The other parent picked up the child an hour ago. Now that parent calls asking where the child got the black eye. You know the child had no black eye when the other parent collected the child.

What This Means

There really is a problem. Either the other parent has injured the child, or the other parent is trying to set you up on a child abuse charge.

Reasonable Action

Tell the other parent to meet you at the child's doctor's office, emergency room, or the police department right away. If the opposition agrees to do this, go. Take someone with you who saw that the child was okay when you handed him to the other parent. If the other parent refuses, make a note in your log. Ask anyone with you at the time to make a written statement, including time, date, and condition of the child when last seen. Advise your attorney and the child's doctor via fax, and mail in an incident report form.

08 Abandonment

You come home from work and find a note telling you the person you are married to or have been living with has left you and that your child is at the neighbor's house.

What This Means

You and your child have been abandoned.

Reasonable Action

If you don't have an attorney, get one now. File for divorce and custody of your child. Change the locks on the house, install a burglar alarm, and have the car re-keyed.

Close your bank accounts and open new ones in your name only. Get a safety deposit box for all important family documents you should remove from the home. Close your charge accounts. Do all of this immediately. You may have only a matter of hours, not days.

09 Restriction of Child's Calls

The court has granted you twice weekly telephone visitation with your children. Your children are not allowed to call you because of the long distance charges.

What This Means

There may be a financial problem in the home, and additional telephone bills cannot be paid.

Or the other parent wishes to keep your children from communicating with you.

Reasonable Action

Tell your child how to call you collect. Give the child a telephone "Call Me Card." This is a nice idea because you may allow the child to call grandparents also. Or you may install a 1 800 or 888 number at your home for your child to use to call you. Give your toll free number to the child's doctor and principal and teacher at your child's school.

Send a letter to the other parent advising of the telephone arrangements you have made for the child and request their cooperation. If the problem persists, ask the court to order the other parent to allow the child to call. Eventually the child will find opportunities to call.

10 Child Not Available for Pick up

You arrive at a previously arranged date, time, and place to pick up the child and are told by a person answering the door that neither the child nor the other parent is there. You inquire as to where your child is and are told to go away.

What This Means

The parent did not let anyone at that address know where he or she would be. The parent is late. Or the person you were speaking to was giving you a bad time.

Reasonable Action

Leave the premises, if that is what you were instructed to do. Call the police and request a Citizen's Backup so you can return to the door and make further inquiries as to the location of your child. Wait for the officer. Explain your problem. Follow the officer's advice. Ask the officer to give you some kind of report or incident number. Keep on your person, at all times, a copy of any court order and documents that prove your relationship to the child and your right to pick up the child at that time and day. Officers in some jurisdictions may not assist you without these documents. Fill out an Incident Report Form. Some states have laws, which allow for prosecution of those who interfere with visitation or reversal of custody for very bad cases. Petition the court for a supervised visitation exchange location. The police department is a good location.

11 Public Display of Affection

You and the other parent are separated and you arrive at your former residence to pick up your child for visitation. Your not-yet-X and his or her "new live-in love" are all over each other in front of the child. You feel insulted, angry and jealous.

It is in violation of your marriage vows, and not the kind of behavior to which you want your child exposed.

What This Means

The opposition is establishing a new romantic relationship. This is normal, if not socially acceptable, behavior. The court has no interest in the opposition's infidelity and feels it has nothing to do with determining who is the better parent. The courts are aware of, but are uninterested, in the outrage felt by one parent when the other parent is "finding" him or herself. If the opposition can convince the court the "new relationship" is stable, you can end up looking like a One-Parent household against a Two-Parent household.

Reasonable Action

Avoid making comments either to the opposition or the child about the new relationship.

Put new people on a Data Sheet form and pay attention to what is said and any vehicles that appear. Keep track of the number of relationships in which the other parent is involved.

The court will be sensitive to your child's being exposed to six new live-in partners in a year. Avoid doing anything that could be considered stalking. Keep your own transient romantic relationships on a back burner. If you have a good, dependable, reliable partner, introduce this person into your family life in a smooth, matter-of-fact manner.

12 Interference with Child's Mail

Because you live out of state, you have been sending your child a letter each week. During your regular summer visitation, your child says that no letters were given to him by the other parent.

What This Means

Someone at that home does not wish the child to have any more contact with you than necessary.

Reasonable Action

If the child is old enough and the Post Office (companies like Mail Boxes, Etc. are in most cities) is close enough, rent a post office box for your child. The small boxes are less than $100.00 a year. You can put your name and the child's on the box. Anyone else entering the box without permission or through threats or coercion is violating federal law.

13 Dangerous Living Conditions

Your child lives with you half of the time and with the other parent the rest of the time. When the child was brought to you today, you were given a piece of paper with an address on it and told to drop the child off at the opposition's new address. You know this to be the residence of someone the opposition once lived with and has described in sworn statements as "a dangerous, violent drug dealer."

You have even seen evidence that this person has abused the other parent on previous occasions, causing the other parent to go into hiding.

What This Means

The statements made by the opposition about this person were not true. Or the drug dealer is supplying something the opposition wants. You are frightened for your child and not very comfortable about having to deal with this person during pick up and return of the child.

Reasonable Action

There is nothing you can do about where the other parent lives.

If you can afford to, hire a detective to make observations about how your child is cared for while in this environment. If the danger can be documented with photos and reports, the court may do something about a temporary custody order to have the child live with you on a full-time basis.

14 Denial of Holiday Visitation

You have arrived at an agreement to share holidays, and this holiday, it is your turn. You have purchased tickets and made reservations. Now the other parent has changed his or her mind about the child's going with you.

What This Means

There may be a problem that the other parent is unable or unwilling to discuss, which caused a change of mind. Or, the other parent is just being difficult.

Reasonable Action

Make every effort to control your disappointment and anger. This is not the first disappointment in your life, and you have survived the others. Ask if there is something you can do to facilitate the child's going with you, or if there is some specific objection that can be resolved. Because there may not be anything you can do about the other parent's change of mind, short of going to court, it is important to try to work this out. If all else fails, call your attorney. In any event, record the event in your contact log and fill out an Incident Report form and send it to your attorney. Have agreements filed and make court orders to strengthen your position if your visitation access is in danger of being violated. In the future, always buy tickets that can be changed.

15 Phone Calls That Upset the Child

You have custody of your child, and the other parent has what the court decided is reasonable visitation for an out-of-state parent. The other parent does not normally exercise all of the visitation awarded by the court. Each week the other parent calls, making extravagant claims to your child about wonderful presents and all the people who love the child who are waiting at the other house. The other parent tells the child he or she loves the child and asks the child why you won't let the child come to visit. Each time this happens, the child is upset, exhibiting painful "ulcer" symptoms for hours, and cannot understand why you will not find the money to send the child to the other parent.

What This Means

The other parent really misses the child, and does not understand the stress these actions create in the child.

Or the other parent feels that if the child exerts enough pressure, you will do what they want.

Reasonable Action

Record the calls, if it is legal in the state in which you live. If recording is not an option, have another responsible adult listen to subsequent calls. Send a letter to the other parent, telling that parent how upset the child becomes. Make an attempt to identify the problem without placing blame. Describe the incident in your contact log. If the character of the calls does not change, enlist the assistance of a child psychologist to have the request come from a professional. If the problem persists, appeal to the court for relief.

16 Child In Danger

Your child has been treated for swallowing a toxic liquid while in the care of the custodial parent. This is the third time this has happened this year. When you contact the Poison Center, they will not give you any information because you are not the custodial parent.

What This Means

There is a very real threat to the life of your child. It is your responsibility to remove the child from the danger.

Reasonable Action

As a parent of this child, you have the right to any documents that emergency or medical facilities have about these incidents. Present proof of parental status. If the emergency or medical facility still refuses to release information about your child to you, your attorney may be able to subpoena or formally request the information for you.

With documented proof of this neglect, you may be able to remove the child from the home where this keeps occurring, by obtaining an emergency hearing for Temporary Custody from the court. Testing within days of the incident may give evidence the child was exposed to dangerous chemicals. Make an entry in your contact log any time you suspect this kind of neglect. Send your attorney an Incident Report form.

17 Change in Exchange Location

You receive a letter from the opposition's attorney, stating that at the end of the visitation period you are to return your child to a public place at 1:00 p.m., rather than at the other parent's house at 5:00 p.m., as you usually do. The attorney has threatened to petition to have you held in contempt of court if you fail to comply.

What This Means

This is just tough attorney talk designed to rough you up. When your attorney reads the same document, that part of the rhetoric will be ignored.

Reasonable Action

If you don't mind taking the child back to the designated place at 1:00, do it. If you object to the time or place or cannot comply, have your attorney offer a compromise. If you have always returned your child to the other house at a specific time, the other attorney probably cannot force you to change the routine without an order of the court.

18 Moving Child without Consent

You live in a different state than your child and the custodial parent. For the past two years it has costs you about $300.00 each time to pick up your child for twice a month visitation.

Thirty days before you are to pick up your child for summer vacation, the custodial parent's attorney notifies your attorney of the custodial parent's new address in a state much farther away. It will now cost you double the money, the inconvenience of using a rental vehicle and usually an additional day in travel time.

What This Means

If you do not live in the same state in which your child and the custodial parent live, there is little you can do to prevent the residence of the child from being moved. If you have notice that the other family intends to move, but has not yet done so, you may be able to move your residence to the state in which they live, and through your attorney request that the court issue a temporary restraining order to keep them from moving your child out of the state in which you now reside. This probably will not work even if you can submit proof that you have moved there permanently.

Reasonable Action

This is one of those times when there is probably nothing you can do.

19 Restriction of Time with Child

You have been taking care of your child the larger part of every day since the separation five months ago. The opposition filed papers for a Hearing To Show Cause to restrict your time.

The court issued Temporary Orders that change your time with your child to four hours every other Tuesday evening. Your attorney said there are fifteen days to file an objection. You are destroyed and feel the world is caving in on you.

What This Means

Feel the hurt, wallow in the pain, cry.

The opposition has won round one. Ask your attorney if the order has been signed, if not you may not have to comply with it until it is.

Reasonable Action

It is time to give in or dig in. As soon as you are able to function, make a plan. Request supervised visitation until this is settled. This will allow you ongoing contact and demonstrate that although the circumstances are difficult, you intend to spend time with your child. Talk to your attorney. Talk to people in your parenting groups. In some states like California, you can request a "timely Statement of Decision". This requires that a judge explain his reasoning. Find out why the court feels this is good for your child. If they are wrong, prove why it is bad. Fight on.

20 Other Parent Bad-mouthing You

Your children, eight and twelve years old, are telling you the other parent is telling them outrageous things about you and how you feel about them.

What This Means

The other parent is unaware, negligent or so intent on causing you pain, the other parent doesn't care that this negative activity is extremely harmful to the children.

Reasonable Action

As the children tell you or ask you about what has been said, you can defuse the potential harm by asking questions: "Do you think I don't love you because I can't send more money? Do I treat you like you are too much trouble for me to pick up on weekends?" Avoid making disparaging comments about the other parent. A safe response is, "I am sorry your Mom/Dad feels that way." Consult a child psychologist for other responses or counseling for your child.

21 Working Things Out, Need Room

The only system the two of you have worked out well is taking care of the children. Everything else is dangerously strained. The big problem arises because you and the other parent are having a great deal of trouble being civil to each other even in front of the children. There is no outside social life causing problems here. You both just want to work and take care of your children.

Neither of you wants to move out because the children need you both and would suffer emotionally and economically, and neither of you can afford a place of your own.

What This Means

Two reasonable people are attempting to cooperate to raise their children, but the living area is too small. You both need some space and/or counseling.

Reasonable Action

If it is possible where you live, put a motor home next to the house. One parent can use it to live in as an apartment. This maintains the close proximity for the children, but gives the parents some room. You may be able to borrow one from a family member, friend, your church, or rent one. Counseling may give you methods for conflict reduction and resolution. Most communities have professional assistance offered on a sliding fee schedule.

22 Denial of Contact

Your child was picked up by the non-custodial parent seven days ago for a three-week visit in another state. At that time, the other parent refused the clothes and personal items the child packed for the visit. The child had to make a fuss in order to be allowed to take a book. The other parent also refused to state a time and day that you could call to talk to your child. When you do call, the older children tell you the other parent and your child are not at home and they do not know when they will return. Sometimes you can hear your child playing in the room. Usually, you get an answering machine. Your messages have been polite and you have offered to accept collect calls to get a call back. None of your calls are returned.

What This Means

The other parent has no regard for the right of the child to maintain contact with you and no interest in your concern for your child.

Reasonable Action

Notify your attorney using an Incident Report Form. Document (witness and photos) the other parent's refusal of the child's personal items.

This behavior reflects parent's lack of understanding that a child needs to be able to keep the things that are important to the child. Have a third unimpeachable witness listen on a speaker telephone and record the call each time you attempt to contact your child. If necessary, leave a carefully worded message on their answering machine offering to accept collect calls from the child and inquiring about the child's well-being.

You can arrange to make your call to your child from the office of a professional who will document your time of arrival, the telephone number you called, your conversation with others if a speaker phone is used, or message you left on an answering machine.

Documenting parental interference with court-ordered contact eliminates your identification of this problem as being your word against the other parent's word. This behavior indicates to the court that this person is not a good candidate in the future for the responsibilities of custodial parent, facilitating and guarding the right of the child to maintain contact with the non-custodial parent.

23 Other Parent Costing You Fees

The other parent does not have an attorney and the unhappy calls to your attorney cost you $423.00 last month.

What This Means

You need to take control of the situation. Your attorney is your employee.

Reasonable Action

Notify your attorney to limit the calls to five minutes per call, per day or written correspondence or not to accept calls until the other parent gets an attorney.

24 Parental Alienation Syndrome

The other parent has brainwashed your nine year old, and now the child has told you and the court that visiting you makes the child very unhappy. You are very hurt and angry because the child has shut you out entirely and refuses to talk to you about what is really happening. You know the other parent is responsible for this erosion of your relationship with your child.

What This Means

You have probably been effectively removed from your child's life for the time being.

Reasonable Action

Notify your attorney. Back off. The court will not make a child visit someone the child does not want to see. It is impossible to prove what the other parent has done. Read "I don't want to visit you anymore" in, Chapter 13: Children's Perspective.

A prolonged fight over this matter pits you against the child, not the other parent.

25 Demand for Information

You just received a huge envelope from the opposition's attorney containing an interrogatory with over fifty very personal questions and demands for business, tax and banking records for the last five years. You were only married for two years and your child is less than a year old. Your attorney won't be back from vacation until four days after the interrogatories are due back to the other attorney.

What This Means

This is normal procedure for a custody suit. Your attorney will want to review the requested information and response data before it is submitted to the opposition.

Reasonable Action

Since you will probably have to produce most of what has been requested, begin to answer the questions and assemble the data. Before the deadline date for submission of the documents contact your attorney's office and ask the secretary to send correspondence notifying the opposition attorney there will be a delay in the return of the interrogatories and why. Have the secretary send you a copy for your file.

26 Disneyland Parent

The other parent picks up the children the first and third weekend of each month. They always go to exciting events and come home with new clothes and expensive toys. The children are promised that if the judge decides they live at that house, they can have these things every day and never do homework or household chores again. The letdown after each visit makes the children behave badly, and they resent your more structured real life existence. Any request you make for help in the house is countered with how things would be if they lived with the other parent. They no longer take care of the new things because they know more are coming.

What This Means

The other parent is behaving in an irresponsible manner by buying the children a fantasy.

Reasonable Action

Talk to the other parent about the permanent damage the children's unrealistic views could have. If you do not get assurances that the misinformation will stop and see evidence that it has.

Call your attorney and/or contact a child psychologist for a report on this activity and help for the children.

27 Denial of Grandparent Visitation

You have been denied visitation with your grandchildren since their parents separated. In addition to missing the children, the financial assistance you have always supplied the grandchildren by buying their clothes is no longer accepted.

This adds greatly to the sorrow you feel from the loss of contact.

What This Means

The parent who is the primary custodian of the children is behaving in an irresponsible manner by denying the children the emotional and financial support of their extended family.

Reasonable Action

Contact your attorney about Grandparents' Rights and visitation in your state. In the interim, identify a family member the custodial parent trusts and has sympathy for you. Buy the things you feel the children need and give them to this person to give to the custodial parent without mentioning you. If you are more concerned with the child having the clothing than you are with getting credit for buying the clothing, you have accomplished your objective.

28 Secret Filing of Court Documents

You called your children yesterday and everything seemed normal. You called today to make arrangements for the weekend and the telephone was disconnected. The other parent's employer said two weeks notice had been given, and yesterday was the last day worked. You had negotiated and signed a separation agreement that said neither of you could move the children without proper notification and consent by the other parent. Your attorney found that the other parent filed notice with the court two months ago that they would be moving out of the country at this time. The notice said copies had been mailed to you and your attorney, and if you did not respond in thirty days it would be assumed that you agreed to the move. Neither your attorney or you got any notice from the other parent or the court.

What This Means

The opposition has been filing papers with the court without your knowledge.

Reasonable Action

Your attorney will have to file an Emergency Order to Show Cause to keep the children from leaving the country. Once this has been accomplished, you must notify the U.S. State Department, the airlines, and the airports. Once a month (more often if necessary) check your file at the court and make sure that you are aware of everything that has or is being filed.

29 Differences in Parenting Style

When visiting the other parent on weekends, your teenage son says he is allowed to drive the car with his seven and eight year-old step-brothers on short errands. Being seventeen, and having his license less than two months, you fear he is more interested in speed and girls than in safety or child care. Along with concern for all three children, you are also concerned about your liability as the custodial parent.

What This Means

The child and the other parent are experimenting with responsibility and privilege.

The other parent is responsible probably for any legal liability when your son is visiting, but it is best to check with an attorney. Many states have a rule called The Family Purpose Doctrine, which makes the owner of the car liable for injuries caused by a spouse or child while driving the car on a family errand.

Reasonable Action

You cannot control what happens when your child is at the other home. Trust in your son's good judgment and hold your tongue. Any reservations you express will be interpreted as a lack of faith in your son. At his age, your support of his efforts at positive growth are important.

30 Conflict during Exchange

Your stomach is upset every time you prepare to pick up or return the children. Your ex-spouse makes insulting remarks or starts an argument that always results in a yelling match with the children in tears. Therefore, each exchange is an emotional disaster for everyone. It casts a shadow over any plans you have made for a nice visit. Your oldest child has even suggested that to avoid the conflict you should not pick them up for visitation anymore.

What This Means

The children are willing to sacrifice anything to eliminate the horrible confrontations. Your ex-spouse is not dealing with visitation as something that is good for the children and something each parent should help the children enjoy. You are contributing to the problem either on a conscious or subconscious level.

Reasonable Action

Since the primary reason you are there is to pick up your children for a wonderful visit, decide before you go that no matter what your ex-spouse says or does you will not participate in making matters worse.

There are really only four or five set arguments you keep having with this person. Script them out on paper.

1. What they usually say. 2. What you always answer. 3. What they always say back.

Now prepare some new answers that will defuse the problem.

Keep your answers polite and short. Let the other parent know you will make contact for an appointment to discuss any problems.

31 Misuse of Psych Evaluation

The other parent hired a psychologist to destroy you during your custody case. You have always been very involved in the lives of your children. The psychologist never tested you and only spoke to you over the telephone for a short interview. The evaluation labeled you unbalanced and dangerous for your children. The judge attributed the final decision in large part to the results of the psychologist's report and made you pay for the work.

What This Means

The other parent is behaving in an irresponsible manner for the long-range health of your children.

Reasonable Action

Hire an expert to examine your complaints. Problem areas would be improper behavior, use of the word "proven" if no proof existed, illegal or unethical behavior, opinions of things if there is no hard proof of testing or direct observation and inappropriate billing practices on the evaluator's behalf. If impropriety is proven, consider making a complaint with the proper professional governing body, Better Business Bureau, and professional organizations.

32 Ex Parte Hearing - Order

At work today you were served with a Restraining Order preventing you from returning to your home, backed up with the threat of jail if you attempt to do so. There has never been any violence in your relationship before now.

What This Means

The opposition has approached the court and requested an emergency Exparte Hearing and made claims of violence in order to get you out of the house.

Reasonable Action

1. Notify your attorney and follow the advice given. Request permission to follow steps 2 through 5.

2. Call the police for a civil backup to escort you to your home so you can get your clothing, toiletries, and personal belongings.

3. On the back of the Restraining Order is a notice informing you that you have a right to a full evidentiary hearing on the charges against you and that this hearing must be granted within five days of your request. Request a court reporter at the hearing.

4. Get a statement from the police department about the lack of domestic disturbance calls to your home. Bring reliable witnesses to prove you are not violent and request the judge reverse the decision.

5. Show up for court dressed correctly, state your side calmly and honestly.

6. To avoid having another Exparte order against you, talk to the clerks at both the Superior and District Court about your concern. Give them your telephone numbers to facilitate notification so you can appear in court on short notice in the future.

7. Request supervised visitation until this is settled to maintain contact with your child.

33 Children Pressuring Parent

The other parent tells the children that you are responsible for the breakup of your home and that you can put it back together if you decide to move home. Your children plead with you to make things the way they used to be.

What This Means

The other parent is in denial and feels the children can influence you to change the situation. Short-term denial helps one cope with things that are hard to accept.

Reasonable Action

Let your children know you love them and that you are sorry the other parent feels that way, but the old family situation will never return. You may wish to get counseling for you and your children to deal with feelings and make the future more acceptable for you all.

34 No Money, No Attorney

The other parent dragged you into court sixty-five days ago and you did OK. You are entitled to pick up your child in another state in two weeks for a week visitation for Thanksgiving and a week at Christmas. The judge has to hand down the final decision or you are only permitted to visit your child in the state where the other parent lives. You can't afford to miss a week of work, fly round trip, rent a car, stay in a hotel and feed yourself for a week. You are very short of money and have only paid $100.00 of the $1,500.00 your attorney billed. Your attorney will not return your calls.

What This Means

Your attorney won't submit the necessary papers to the court until the bill is paid, and the judge won't hand down the decision until the proper papers are submitted.

The courts do not require attorneys to do work for which they have not been paid. Once the attorney is paid, it can take several weeks before you can get the papers required from the judge. Unless you are able to get your attorney paid in the next day or so, you will probably not be able to pick up your child for Thanksgiving. Even your visitation for Christmas is in danger.

Reasonable Action

Get some payment to your attorney. Every time you get money for anything, paycheck, yard sale, or giving plasma, send something against the bill and your attorney will start returning your calls.

35 Other Attorney Costing Money

The other attorney won't file any of the papers the judge ordered. Your attorney is doing the other attorney's work and charging you for it. You want to take advantage of this problem the other parent is having and just let it go, waiting for the other attorney to default or the court to take action.

What This Means

The other parent has hired another bad attorney. It is unclear as to whether the attorney is unresponsive because of non-payment or ineptitude. Procedural obligations by the opposition remain unfulfilled.

You are not excused from your obligations because of the other attorney's inaction. Your attorney advises that the court may look disapprovingly at any action that looks as if you are taking unfair advantage.

Your attorney is forced to send each communication to the opposition numerous times and to write and file documents to keep the case from shutting down. You are billed for all of this additional work.

Reasonable Action

Ask your attorney to request sanctions against the other attorney. Advise your attorney to let the other attorney know you intend to file a grievance. Domestic relations is the one practice of law in which more grievances are filed by the person on the opposition than by the attorney's own client.

If the other attorney chooses to ignore the warning, you must be prepared to follow through. You will not get any immediate relief from the problem, but there should be some satisfaction in knowing this will cause the attorney a great deal of trouble for a long time. File a grievance for each major infraction. Investigate the feasibility of a civil suit for money. If you are able to give evidence to the court of all the communication your attorney has sent to the opposing attorney without response (you can do this with the bill from your attorney, because you are billed for communication sent out and communication received, reviewed and answered) the judge can advise, reprimand or sanction the errant attorney.

36 Grandparents' Custody Interrupted

Our daughter and her husband shipped our three grandchildren (seven, nine, and twelve-year-olds) to us a year ago saying they needed time to work out problems in their marriage.

The children adjusted well and showed marked improvement in their health and school grades. Eight months later they wanted the children back, but the children wanted to stay. We filed a legal action to continue caring for the children because jurisdiction had changed once the children had been in our county six months. The court has given us temporary custody. The parents have filed a divorce petition in their county, and we have been ordered to return the children.

What This Means

A divorce proceeding takes precedence over a custody proceeding. The children must be returned according to the court order. The parents may really be involved in a divorce, or they are using this action to derail your efforts.

Reasonable Action

Your attorney may file an intervention in the divorce case as it concerns custody of the children. Much depends on the attitude of the judge and the documentation you are able to submit to prove the best interest of the children is for them to live with you.

37 Child's Affidavit of Preference

Your thirteen-year-old has lived primarily with you for the year since the marriage separation, and has signed an Affidavit of Preference stating a desire to live with the other parent while spending the weekend there. The other parent is acting like the decision is now a "done deal". You are sad and feel betrayed. Your child offered to sign a new affidavit in your favor or cancel the one that is signed when you became upset.

What This Means

The child wants to be with both parents. The child wants everyone to be happy. In addition the child wants to be where the child can get his or her way most often. As a matter of survival, some children become adept at manipulating the situation. A new affidavit will indicate to the court that the child is under a great deal of pressure and that the child doesn't really know what the child wants. The affidavit does not seal a judge's decision in any case.

The judge may feel that there has been undue influence exerted by the parent the child has chosen or that what the child wants is not in the child's best interest. Under the best circumstances, a judge will only add an affidavit as evidence to the equation of the decision.

Reasonable Action

Talk to your attorney. Your child may need time with a professional counselor to work out his or her feelings. Listen to what your child is really saying. This may be a cry for attention or an indication of real problems.

38 Teenager Won't Go to Visitation

After years of not seeing our child, the other parent requested and received visitation. The child refuses to go, citing many problems, including: interference with long established scheduled activities, strong dislike of parent's new significant other, negative comments about our family and home and a less than clean environment. The other parent thinks I am causing this problem.

What This Means

The child is really not happy and wishes to adjust the situation.

Reasonable Action

Talk to the youngster. If the court has ordered visitation, the court can insist that you and your child comply. The court is intolerant of anyone not obeying its orders.

Judges have ordered the parent who cannot or will not make a child go to visitation to pay a fine and serve jail time. In extreme cases the teenagers have been ordered to spend time in juvenile detention centers.

39 Attorney Wants to Quit

When I filed for divorce and custody, the other parent expressed no interest, telling me to do whatever I wanted. Three months ago, I hired an attorney and paid $1,500.00. Now, one week before the scheduled court appearance, we received interrogatories from an attorney hired by the other parent, and it looks like there will be a fight for everything from the children to the used furniture in the attic. My attorney said I need to come up with $3,000.00 more or the attorney will resign from my case.

What This Means

The case has gone from uncontested to contested and has become a great deal more work for your attorney.

Reasonable Action

Talk to your attorney about a payment plan. This isn't your fault or your attorney's fault, it is just a matter of business. The judge may not allow your attorney to resign, but a legal action is difficult enough when the team is happy and working together and almost impossible when it's not. An attorney forced to remain on a case who does not demonstrate due diligence may be subject to complaint, grievance or a malpractice suit.

40 We Comply, They Don't

My attorney and I have obeyed every order of the court. The other parent and attorney ignore every instruction or court order that is not in their favor, forcing us to file additional requests for documentation or compliance. Now the judge thinks we are causing the problems. Since the opposition is not punished for noncompliance, I do not want to do the things the court orders me to do.

What This Means

This is life. You and your attorney comply because you do not want to be the ones in noncompliance on a day the judge decides to get tough.

Reasonable Action

Remain in compliance and don't dwell on that which you cannot change.

41 Accusation of Sexual Abuse

The other parent picked up your three-and-a-half-year-old child Friday morning at eight for long distance summer visitation to last three weeks. At ten Saturday morning Child Protective Services (CPS) in your city is on the telephone. An anonymous sexual child abuse charge has been filed against you. The accusation says that on the airplane on Saturday your child pulled down his pants and attempted to put his penis in the other parent's mouth, saying that's what you do with him at home. The CPS Investigator makes an appointment to interview you, your child and inspect the child's environment. A week later you are served papers by the other parent's attorney that request the court grant an emergency change of custody since you are under investigation for child abuse.

Your child is interviewed in the state where the other parent lives, and the report says there is no indication of abuse. The investigator in your state reports there is no indication that there is any truth to the charges. You fly to the state where custody was granted to defend against the change of conservatorship and the case is thrown out.

What This Means

There really is a problem with the other parent that you can do nothing about. The CPS in your area is now aware that you are under fire and can be your best ally if the other parent files false charges again. Document the problem.

Reasonable Action

Don't react when you deal with the other parent. Just keep taking good care of your child and yourself.

42 Visitation Home Is Dangerous

Both parents and step-brothers where your child goes for visitation have a fifteen year documented history of problems with the police and drugs in each city they have lived. Your child is to live in that home with little supervision other than fourteen and sixteen-year-old males who have arrest records including, drive-by shooting, drug treatment, drugs for sale, assaulting other children and running away from home. You have presented police records to document these dangers in court, and the judge still rules that the child will go for visitation because it has not been proven that being exposed to these factors during the four to seven weeks in the summer and four assorted weeks the rest of the year will cause the child permanent harm.

What This Means

It is amazing that the judge even looked at or considered the police records of the other children. You probably got more out of that information than you could have hoped for. There are problems, but the judge cannot protect the child against all of the things that might happen. If something does happen to the child, the judge can keep the child from an environment that did in fact harm the child.

Reasonable Action

Don't drive yourself crazy with worry. Your child will go and come home OK. Make the going as comfortable for the child as possible and the readjustment upon return as smooth as possible.

Be very patient if the child brings home unacceptable language or behavior. Don't over react. Just tell the child, "We don't talk or act that way here".

43 Opposition Won't Pay

The other parent was ordered to pay fifty percent of some medical bills that amount to $800.00 owed for our child and court costs for an appeal filed then dropped, that my attorney did some work to defend. The attorney I have now in a different state says the judge here will probably make the other parent pay the medical order. On the other hand, the attorney advises not asking for the $700.00 in attorney's fees because the judge will feel it puts an undue burden on the other parent. The other parent was assessed this order to stop the filing of frivolous claims against me, and I did have to pay the money to the other attorney already.

What This Means

Your attorney may know something about the judge that you don't.

Reasonable Action

Do something to keep the order for attorney's fees alive (like sending a letter requesting payment to the other parent or filing it where you live) and then proceed in small claims court after the court has given you the medical money. In most jurisdictions, you can get the court to limit the amount of time, they have to pay a judgment. If they have not started paying within the allotted time they can be found in contempt and fines can be added to the judgment or they can be jailed.

44 Lied, Forged and Ignored the Court

I have documented evidence the other parent violated the court's direct orders, forged documents they presented in court and lied on the stand, but my attorney doesn't want to hear about it.

What This Means

After an extended time in the process, your attorney and the judge just stop hearing what you have to say. If you are the non-custodial parent, unless the children are in imminent physical danger in the situation they are in, the custody of the children will not be changed. If you are the custodial parent, and attempt to make the non-custodial parent comply with the court orders, the court will generally feel you are just picking on the other parent.

Reasonable Action

This is one of those times when if you don't have a lot of money to throw at the problem you are going to have to live with it.

45 Parent Threatens Suicide

For the last five months, and until custody is decided by the court, our ten-year-old's time is divided almost equally between the other parent's home and mine. At dinner tonight, he said the thing that worries him most is that if the judge gives me custody his other parent will commit suicide. I was so stunned I didn't know what to say. I knew something was bothering him, but when I would ask directly, he would always say, "It's nothing."

What This Means

The other parent has decided to pull out all the stops and will do anything to manipulate the child. Or the other parent is having a breakdown because of the stress of this ordeal.

Reasonable Action

Get some psychological help for your child. Suicide kills more than the person that kills him or herself. It devastates entire families and spreads like a plague. Even if no other people actually kill themselves, the guilt felt by the survivors often ruins many lives. Fill out an incident report and fax it to your attorney advising what your child said, what you have done and asking what to do next.

46 Religion as Grounds for Custody

We met, became friends, dated, courted and married in a church that does not believe in blood transfusions or organ transplants as well as some other generally accepted medical treatment and procedures.

We have three children and attended church and religious functions as a family until he was required to travel extensively for the company that employs him. He is in love with the woman coworker he has been traveling with and is suing for divorce and custody of our children on the grounds that I don't allow proper medical care for our children. I know his religious feelings have not changed because he refused one trip because it required an inoculation.

What This Means

He wants his freedom from you and custody of the children and is unable to find any other grounds for his action.

Reasonable Action

All you can do is request marriage counseling and/or get an attorney. Your marriage is probably over, but the chance of custody being given to a traveling parent when there is a good parent who need not travel is very slim.

47 My Lawyer Really Screwed Me

Our child and the other parent live clear across the country from me. When I exercise visitation I must drive an hour to the airport, fly for six hours, rent a car and drive for another hour to pick up my child. They schedule the court appearances so I don't have to make extra trips.
I appreciate that, but it makes each visit more difficult because I have to go to court about half of the time. Last month we went to court and my attorney left me out in the hall and went into another room with the other attorney and parent. When they came out he told me that since they could prove a long list of things I have done wrong he made the best deal for me he could by changing everything over to the standard visitation and child support for

the state in which the child lives. I got the papers today and the document gives me less time with my child and increases the benefits I have to provide. This is not what my attorney told me before or after court.

What This Means

You have very poor communication with your attorney, you only hear what you want to hear, or you have a bad attorney. If you are doing things wrong, you must find out why you are doing things that will be used against you in regards to your child. Then you must stop these activities. Get professional help if necessary.

Reasonable Action

If the papers have been signed by the judge they are now a court order. It is reasonable for the court to want all of the custody cases in their jurisdiction to be standardized. It reduces the number of court appearances required to settle disputes. You can hire a new attorney and start from square one, but your chances of changing things are slim. If you intend to fire your attorney, anyway, you can file a grievance against him with the state bar association.

48 Won't Supply Insurance Card

We have had temporary custody of the children for almost two years while awaiting the final judgment The other parent was ordered to supply insurance cards for the children, but ignores our requests. Each time something else comes up, we have our attorney ask their attorney about the cards. Nothing is happening.

What This Means

Waiting for others is not working. If it is important to you, then you have to act. It may appear that you haven't made enough effort.

Reasonable Action

Call the company for which the other parent works and ask to speak to the Human Resources person. That person will be able to give you the name of the Insurance Company and its telephone number. You should be able to get a plan benefit summary and coverage information. You may still need the help of your attorney to get an insurance card from the other parent. There may be an ability for you to buy insurance and have it automatically added to the amount of child support the other parent is paying. Additionally, there may be penalties for the other parent such as having to reimburse you for the expenses you have had to pay out of pocket. If none of that works, contact the insurance commissioner in your state. They can get action very quickly and may be able to get reimbursements directly to you.

49 Volunteer Spy

I have custody of my son. He visits his mother on the other coast five times a year. It is a very strained relationship. For over a year I have been getting calls from a woman with whom she works. I have never seen this woman and don't even know her name or how she got my home phone number. The information she gives me is very damning to my son's mother and very helpful to me on several occasions because it eliminates many surprises and lets me know what is really going on there. I am pretty good at telling when my son's mother is blowing off steam or is really plotting. This is the second time someone in her life has gone out of their way to help me by giving me extensive information. At this time the information is that my son's mother is planning to move back to the state in which I won custody of our son. We don't live there and the court in our state has jurisdiction so I don't feel threatened.

What This Means

Your son's mother may have some psychological problems that others identify and want to guard your son against or she just talks too much for her own good. If you are not soliciting the assistance and strangers to you are attempting to safeguard your son you can only be grateful.

Reasonable Action

It sounds like you are being cautious with the information. Keep it up.

50 Relationship With the Judge

My brother-in-law went to a father's rights meeting. It turned out my ex-husband was there and is a member. He was sitting and talking with a man for about a half hour before the meeting started. When the meeting was called to order my ex-husband introduced the man he had been talking with as the speaker for the evening, a judge. When my brother-in-law told me the judge's name, I realized he is the judge in our case and I think my ex-husband has an unfair opportunity to influence him.

What This Means

Judges and attorneys are making an effort to speak at parent's rights groups all over the country. This gives people an opportunity to ask questions in order to better understand the system.

Reasonable Action

Fill out an incident report form and fax or mail it to your attorney. The attorney can decide the best course of action if one is indicated.

51 Internet Lurking

For the last two years I have been communicating with other parents involved in custody battles on the Internet by posting messages on several discussion groups. I described several of the problems that my ex-wife caused and asked for advice. I blew off a lot of steam and got and gave some good and bad advice. I found out today that my ex-wife has been lurking on the groups to which I have been posting. She has read and printed out every one of my posts. I don't have any of them, but I know sometimes I got pretty hot. I am afraid she will be using these against me in court.

What This Means

You have had your electronic foot in your mouth. You have some major damage control to do.

Reasonable Action

Keep posting and start being more careful about what you ask and advise others about. Print out or save your communications. If your X-wife wishes to use your Internet communications, you will have your more current communications to show how you are healing and dealing with the stresses of the custody case.

52 Prosecution for Perjury

The other parent has been caught lying in court several times. My attorney and the courts seem uninterested in charging the other parent with perjury.

What This Means

A lie under oath may not be perjury if the lies were not material to the case.

Reasonable Action

Put it out of your head. It is not going to do your case any good and you are wasting your time and money attempting to get anything done about it.

53 Constant Public Harassment

Each time I pick up or drop off my daughter, I am subjected to being recorded on audio and/or video tape by the "paramour" of my ex-wife. Today, when we walked out of the courtroom, he placed his little micro cassette recorder in MY FACE and tried to record a conversation between my ex and I. I don't think this is legal. I want to knock him down if he does it again. Can I get this harassment to cease, legally? From what I understand, this guy is in the eyes of the Court - a legal STRANGER to my daughter. Do I have to keep putting up with this?

What This Means

This reaction very likely is what they are trying to provoke. If you lose your temper and strike -- or push, shove, even threaten -- him, you strengthen their position and weaken yours. Smile pretty and wave for the camera. When the microphone arrives, speak about what a wonderful child you have or ignore your wife's friend. They are probably recording every telephone conversation you have with that side, even the telephone conversations you are having with your child.

Reasonable Action

If you are in a public place, such as a courthouse, you have no expectation of privacy. Your ex-wife may be recording you with a hidden recorder at other times. Knocking this guy on his rear if he does this again would have legal repercussions.

In most states your action would constitute battery, which is a misdemeanor.

The momentary satisfaction can cost you a criminal record, and the possibility of a year in the county jail and $2500 fine. Additionally, he could file a civil suit against you. Keep a record of each incident in your log. If possible, have a friend take photographs or videotape the guy as he tapes you. Document, document, document. You will probably have to keep putting up with this if you want to see your daughter. You have little recourse at this point.

So keep putting up with it -- until he takes his little campaign one step too far.

54 Change of Circumstances

Three years ago, I won custody of my three children, primarily because my ex was having problems with stability, drinking and drugs at the time. She has been clean and sober for a year. She keeps telling the children her lawyer is working to help her get them back. The children are happy and healthy here and want things to stay as they are. We are in a new cycle of promises to the children and threats to me.

What This Means

She is telling her lawyer there are substantive problems in your home and he is attempting to build a case on the points she has raised. Or, being unable to face the reality of her situation and the future as only a part-time parent, her ego forces her to struggle valiantly against what she sees as an unfair system.

Reasonable Action

By awarding you the primary caregiver responsibility, the Court has said: "It is a finding of FACT that the best interest of the children is served by having them in your custody. The mother would have to prove that a material change in your circumstances has taken place in order to get that order changed." Merely a change in her circumstances was not enough to justify a change in custody. Courts like stability.

55 Lesbian Mom

I was a partner to another woman for six years. Two years ago we decided to have a child. She was artificially inseminated and had our son. I have been the stay at home mom while she built her career. Now she wants to separate and take our son with her. She says I have no rights.

What This Means

She is attempting to claim custody as the birth parent. You do have rights because you "stood in the shoes of a parent to the child and should be accorded the status of parent in parity with the other parent."

Reasonable Action

Document your activities with your child and get a good lawyer to pursue your rights as a Parent in Fact.

56 Ex-Husband Excluded as Guardian

My wife and I are expecting a baby, but our marriage has been in trouble for some time. Her parents have always hated me and say they will make sure I not only lose custody, but won't even get it if my wife dies at some time in the future. They have a great deal of money and power. I am just a working stiff, but an honest, working stiff.

What This Means

They are just blowing hot air unless your conduct is notoriously bad, you are incapacitated or are incapable of taking care of the child or the judge finds you otherwise unsuitable, which would be a hard case to prove.

Reasonable Action

Stay out of trouble. Try to work things out with your wife. Pay your child support if you are ordered to do so. Use the visitation and parenting time the court gives you. Don't interact with your in-laws without a witness.

57 Credit Report Without Permission

My ex-husband's attorney got a copy of my credit report to imply that I was an irresponsible person and could not take care of my child. I told him it was illegal to do that without my permission. The lawyer said that credit reports could be obtained where there is a legitimate business need for the information.

What This Means

Probably that the lawyer acted in an unprofessional manner. Act, 15 U.S.C1681 *et seq.* Allows credit reports to be obtained where there is a legitimate business need for the information in connection with a business transaction involving the consumer. This allows obtaining credit reports to prepare for litigation.

Litigation only in limited instances, as in a case to collect a debt owed by the consumer.

Reasonable Action

Sue the attorney.

58 Bio- Dad v Adoptive Parents

It turns out my ex-girlfriend was pregnant

when we broke up. I found out she bore our child when she filed to have my father's rights terminated so she could put the baby up for adoption. She says it's none of my business since I don't have the ability to take care of my baby as well as the prospective adoptive parents.

What This Means

Since the mother's conduct kept you from your child, you shouldn't have to compete with the prospective adoptive parents. To require a comparison between you and the prospective adoptive parents would be unfair and unreasonable.

Reasonable Action

If you are a fit parent and you want to raise your child, you will have to build a case and file for custody.

Dawson v. Emerson. Michigan gives you precedent.

59 Step-Mom Wants Custody

I have cared for my husband's child for our entire marriage of more than six years. I was the person that took her to the doctor and provided all the parenting a small child needs including registering her for school and participating in her after school activities. My husband left me and took the child to his parents who can't or won't take proper care of her.

What This Means

You have been the parent in fact and have a good case for winning custody.

Reasonable Action

Document what you have done to raise your child and file for custody.

Ellison v. Ramos. North Carolina gives you precedent.

60 Computer Evidence

Our son Devon lives with me. Bill my ex-husband gave our son his old computer from his office. Bill said he cleaned out the data files and loaded games, an encyclopedia and a web account for Devon. Bill said if I would e-mail him an accounting of how I spent the child support on Devon he would stop causing me problems in court. I bought a home and small business accounting system and loaded it into the computer in order to make compliance with his request possible. While loading the program, he asked if I wanted it to update the existing data and I said, yes. Bill's books for the last five years were then loaded on the program. It indicated he has been paying a third of the child support he should have been because he has been lying about his personal income from his business. I have had to work two jobs because of this skin-flint.

What This Means

Your ex-husband has handed you hard evidence. It's a good bet you can get the child support changed. You may even have a case for criminal charges. The possibility of additional stress to your son must be considered. Even if your ex-husband had not handed the evidence to you, these records were available through the process of discovery. Your attorney could have asked for a court order forcing your ex-husband to produce an external storage device known as a "Bernoulli disk," which can be sent to a professional for analysis. It has been legal to get computer-based evidence for over twenty-seven years, but there wasn't much produced that would affect family court until personal computers became prevalent about seven years ago.

Reasonable Action

Stay calm and call your attorney. The attorney should start with a carefully-crafted interrogatory or deposition.

61 EX Won't Complete Move

I have complied with a move and she has been dragging her feet. I have joint legal and physical custody every other month, but I had my attorney put in the papers that the last parent remaining in Nevada would maintain custody. That was because she had made a motion to move to Wyoming one month before the divorce was final. I did make the move, within one month after the divorce. Now, I have driven twenty-eight times to Nevada to see my children.

I have had two attorneys. They are the only two attorneys in our area. The first is the DA now, so I lost him, then I got his partner. Now, he is the public attorney, and is very busy.

I have filed everything you can think of, and the ex-wife has had every delay you can think of, including her attorney's maternity leave. The story goes on and I have it well-documented. I have even had to file bankruptcy. I will be in Nevada on my next visitation. I even went to the expense of maintaining two residents (one in Wyo. and one in Nev.), so that I could be involved in the children's school on my month.

What This Means

You feel the other parent should be legally compelled to move because of the motion she filed. You want the court to see the huge effort you have made to be where you thought your children would be living. You want the court to see the financial sacrifice you have made to be with your children.

You want the court to make her complete the move. The court will see you as a controlling person willing to respond erratically and back up poor decisions to the detriment of your financial future and bring into question your judgment as it may impact the lives of your children. In the end, the court will not make her move and you may have helped her establish grounds with which to challenge the joint custody. At best, the court will see it as a non-issue. At worst, the court will feel you are harassing your ex.

Reasonable Action

Stop all legal action. Talk to the attorney about the proper way to stop this suit. Live where your children live. Don't only be involved with your children during the month you have custody, be involved every month. Concentrate on making their lives better no matter where you all live.

62 Military Non-Support

My ex is in the military and because he enjoys the challenge, manages to keep himself stationed in the world's hot spots. He loves the duty, but it makes getting child support on a regular basis very difficult. He gets far enough behind to require me to hire a lawyer to get anything. It is still necessary to personally serve him with a summons and petition for any legal action. This process is almost impossible since he is always overseas and it is not possible to compel military authority to serve the summons. I have requested that military authority serve him, but service only is allowed with my ex's consent. A friend of mine in the same position wrote a letter to her ex's commanding officer.

She stated that she understood that failure to support dependents constitutes "service-discrediting" misconduct. Under military regulations, the service member must then be counseled regarding his obligations. She was informed that administrative discharge proceedings were initiated because his service-discrediting conduct continued. In this scale down of the military climate, I am afraid to make problems for my ex, but I need the help.

What This Means

Even though a letter to your ex's commanding officer could be very effective, you should exercise restraint in taking action that could jeopardize your ex's employment. Obtaining an involuntary allotment may be a better solution. With your state court support order and an arrearage equal to or exceeding the support required for a two-month period, an involuntary allotment is available and preferable to garnishment because the definition of "disposable earnings" includes basic pay, basic allowance for quarters, basic allowance for subsistence, sea pay, special pay, and other allowances.

Reasonable Action

Address your request for a "mandatory allotment" to the military finance center. Make sure that the arrearages are stated and documented. The finance center notifies the member that an involuntary allotment is started. Arrearage may be collected in a similar fashion. The maximum amount of the allotment is generally sixty percent of disposable earnings or fifty percent if the member is supporting other family members, inclusive of allowances.

63 Unfit Parent

Besides such obvious factors as substance abuse and domestic violence, how does the court determine whether a parent is "UNFIT"? Do education and income levels matter in such decisions?

Is a psychologist called in for his "expert" evaluation? Where is the borderline between "acceptable" and "unfit". Are general guidelines published for judges? Does education and income levels matter in such decisions?

What This Means

Suspected substance abuse and domestic violence are indications that a parent may be unfit. Even though you may know the other parent is an abuser (in any sense) you must have documented proof. Documentation is much more involved than you just noting incidents in your contact log. An evaluation or home study can be requested by someone, including the judge (because the case is too involved to hear in court. Or the judge doesn't have the guts to make an unpopular decision). As a point of information, the court never pays for these evaluations. One or both parents pay. Parents may request evaluation because they know they are a better option for the child and feel a psychologist will be more sensitive to the human issues rather than points of law. Usually, a lower income is not used against a parent. In fact, a higher income may indicate that a parent must spend more time at work and therefore is less accessible than that of the lower income parent.

Reasonable Action

You must document everything. Even if the abuses are documented, the court may disregard them if they do not put the child's life in imminent danger. There is not a published guideline for unfitness that judges must abide. It is a matter of personal experience and bias with each judge. A new judge may be more sensitive than one who just rotated off a criminal bench. It is important to gather the right information. Eliminate the non-issues (as the court sees them) and present the documentation to the person that has the ability to do the most for your child with that information. Often a psychologist will look at issues the court just doesn't care about.

64 Interfering With Grandparent

Our daughter has married a man who won't let us visit our grandson from her previous union. She insisted that her dad (my husband) intervened and the results were much less than perfect. We have filed for visitation rights and now our daughter has stopped all contact with us or our grandson. She says her husband won't allow it. Her therapist says she is being pulled apart by all of us. From what she has told us, he physically abuses her and the boy and we think her current husband is controlling every aspect of her life. He says that's what we are doing. Every time our daughter pleads with us to, or insists that we rescue her, we end up in a worse position.

What This Means

Your daughter is taking no responsibility for her life and is in fact pitting everyone against each other in order to be a victim. Or, she really can't help herself.

Reasonable Action

Follow through with your case and attempt to avoid criticizing the husband and conflict when possible. You probably have to stop attempting to rescue her before you and your husband drown in all this dependent and codependent behavior. Get some professional assistance.

65 They Searched My House

I have temporary custody of my child and live in a small town. Like most people here I don't lock my doors. Most people don't even take the keys out of their vehicles in town or at their homes. One day last month the closet light was on in my bedroom when I got home from work. I lay my clothes out the night before, so I never turn on the light to use my closet in the morning. I didn't think much of it at the time. Now the opposition has presented photographs taken inside my home to an evaluator. They did not have a search warrant or my permission.

What This Means

You need to lock your doors, windows and animal entrances. If there is no apparent forced entry they may have picked the lock or had a superintendent (if you live in an apartment) let them in. Breaking and entering another's home or business is a crime in every state.

Reasonable Action

Your attorney can request through discovery, copies of the photos and information under oath. How the witness obtained or became aware of the evidence can be questioned. Only the police have to concern themselves with legal searches and probable cause. You may have some trespass or theft issues the attorney should examine. The evaluator may disregard the photos because of how they were obtained. The method may destroy any value the opposition may have hoped to obtain from their production. This action could prejudice the court against the opposition, and the court could order the evaluator to disregard the photos.

66 Confidentiality of Case File

I was going over my case with my attorney in her office. I asked about a note in the margin on the psychological evaluation that had been completed on me. At first she was confused and did not recognize the handwriting. After telling me that no one did or was supposed to have access to my file she left the office with the file. Returning she advised that a senior partner had reviewed the file and made some notes in it. She said things to ease my concern, but I don't think she was very happy about the intrusion. Now, I don't know just how confidential my communications are with her or why someone else is looking into my case.

What This Means

Someone is tampering with her sensitive client information.

Reasonable Action

You should be concerned. Speak to your attorney. This situation must be corrected. She needs to add or change her password in her computer and lock the files she's worried about. The senior partner must have her permission to review her files.

67 Fined for Attorney Advice

I was having a problem with how my child's father was taking care of him. I called my attorney and he told me to not allow my child to go to the court ordered visitation with his father until the situation was corrected. I asked the attorney to send me a letter stating the advice, but it never came. I did not let my child go for three visitations. In court the judge admonished the father for the problem and me for violating the court order. The judge did not say a word to my attorney for telling me to violate the order. I had to pay both attorneys.

What This Means

Your attorney gave you poor advice.

Reasonable Action

Every attorney and judge we spoke to agreed that you got very bad advice. If your attorney agreed the child was in danger, an emergency order for protection should be filed. Only the judge can give you permission to withhold court ordered visitation.

68 Opposition Grinding Me Down

When the other parent picks the children up he is always early. He brings them back late, very dirty and ill fed. The children are usually cranky and exhausted. It's never so bad that their lives are in danger or a reasonable issue to raise with the court. when I remind him that he is late bringing them back, he says, "It was only half an hour and it was the traffic.

Isn't that right kids?" I find this exhausting and it makes me short tempered. His attitude is cavalier when I question any of these problems.

What This Means

He's doing a great job of wearing you down. He's attempting to make you angry enough to act vindictive. Most people would say that mothers are just more adept at parenting than fathers and allowances must be made.

Reasonable Action

Rather than confront him about the situation again, work at solving the problem. Ask, "What can we do to make drop-offs and pick-ups work better for all of us?" It may take some time to get a response you can work with. Or, decide he can't tell time, and is doing the best he can. You can't change him and you are compounding the impact his harassment has on you. Adjust your thinking to find his lack of organization and parenting skills silly rather than aggravating. Much of the behavior will stop if he isn't getting the response he wants. If he accelerates his activities to a level that others will find harmful to the children, consider taking it back to court. In the interim, be as patient as you would be with any other dim-witted person.

69 Leaving Country Owes Support

I have custody of our children and the mother has never met her child support obligation. It now amounts to over fifteen thousand dollars. I have been unable to collect because she works as a private subcontractor for large companies. The contract is usually finished and paid before I know she has been working again. She has been offered a huge contract overseas and it looks like she will be completely out of my reach.

What This Means

You have a great opportunity to collect your support. You must act quickly.

Reasonable Action

The Secretary of State must deny a passport to a person who is in arrears of child support of more than $5,000 upon certification to that effect by the Secretary of Health and Human Services Sections 370, 652(k) and 654(31) of the Personal Responsibility and Work Opportunity Reconciliation Act of 1996 (PRWORA) (Pub. L. 104-193), which amends 42 U.S.C. 452,. Get your documentation in order and get going.

70 Former Spouse Tips Police

My ex-wife has remarried and lives in a very large upscale neighborhood. I am black (she is not) and my car is not the best. On several occasions when I left her house after dropping off the children I have been stopped by the police. The officers have said they are responding to anonymous calls. Some of the calls include: a 'suspicious person' cruising the neighborhood, a black drug dealer and drunken driving. They have usually been polite, and they have always let me go. Sometimes they only keep me there ten minutes other times as long as an hour.

What This Means

Your ex-wife is probably responsible for the problem.

Reasonable Action

You or your attorney should contact the police department and ask for suggestions. Additionally, in 1999 the Maryland Court of Appeals, in Cartnail v. State, where police stopped a driver based on a tip that three black men had committed an armed robbery and fled in a gold or tan Mazda in "no known direction," this violated the Fourth Amendment, reversing an appellate court.

71 Bipolar Disorder

Besides taking care of my two children my greatest challenge is dealing with rapid cycling Bipolar Disorder (manic-depression). This illness has increased the amount of stress I experience every day, in my relationships with family and friends, and especially my ex-husband. This is happens because of my unpredictable energy level and my oscillating outlook on life. I have had custody of our children since our divorce five years ago. I have requested an increase in child support and my ex-husband and his new wife are attempting to get custody of our children. I am on medication and am not dangerous to my children or myself. They are using my disorder as the only challenge to my retaining custody.

What This Means

Your ex-husband thinks he can do a better job than you can and/or doesn't want to pay the additional child support.

Reasonable Action

You must document the kind of mother you are and have been. If it will help your case talk to your medical and mental health professionals for positive documentation and deposition on you wellbeing. Be prepared. Don't panic. You can be your best or worst witness.

72 Child's Right to Choose

My sixteen year old daughter wants to go live with her father. She says, "I won't stay living here anymore. If you won't let me live with my father, I'll just run away. And if you bring me back, I'll run away again. I don't care if you put me in jury or jail. You can ground me forever or take away all my privileges, I will leave as soon as you aren't watching. I told her there is no law that gives her the right to choose, but that a judge weighs in a large number of factors. She said, "A girl at school just did this so she knows she can do it to.

What This Means

Your daughter will eventually win this one, and she knows it. Your ex-husband may or may not have anything to do with the situation coming to a head at this time.

Reasonable Action

Legally the child doesn't have a right to choose. Judges would really like to carefully evaluate the custody factors and make a decision on that information. Years of experience has proven that you can't really keep a teenager where they don't want to be. This teenage extortion will work so you may as well make it as easy on yourself as possible. You could request a six month temporary change in custody. With a review for permanent status at end of that time. Your child and the other parent may find it isn't what they thought it would be. If the child's request is based in maturity the judge will find it easier to grant the change. Documentation such as school grades and attendance as well as proper juvenile behavior will make the decision easier for everyone.

73 Forcing Me Back to Court

I have had custody of our children for three years. The other parent keeps taking me back to court every six months. The filings alternate from accusations of denial of access to modification of support and visitation. I don't do anything to interfere with visitation or access and my attorney and court costs are killing me. He goes pro se and is getting very proficient and well known at the courthouse.

What This Means

This parent feels abused and is learning about and using the legal system to get his needs met. On the other hand, as custodial parent, it is your responsibility to actively encourage a positive relationship between the other parent and the children. He may be able to build the case that you are in fact doing nothing either way. In this case that would reflect negatively on you at court.

Reasonable Action

The court doesn't want you two showing up in court any more than you do. You have a little more power if the court has found the majority of his cases groundless or found against him. Compile an easy to read chart showing the dates and title of each filing, and the outcome. This visual aid may encourage the judge to reprimand him if he files further suits. Your attorney could ask the judge to rule that the other side would have to pay all court costs and attorney fees for future suits. You may consider a civil case for Vexatious Litigation.

74 Child's Medial Problem Ignored

Even at three our son exhibited symptoms of hyperactivity, and never outgrew it. By the time he was 5 we couldn't take him anywhere because he made so much noise and was in constant movement. He couldn't keep his hands off other children and was fidgeting, squirming when trying to sit. He couldn't wait his turn in line, talked excessively, and moved from one activity to another at lightning speed. He spoke and did things without considering the impact on others or himself. At 7 he was diagnosed with Attention Deficit Disorder (ADD). He is responding well to medication, school intervention, behavior modification, training I went through as a parent, changed his diet and supplement with vitamins and minerals. Two years ago after our divorce his father decided that there was nothing wrong with his son and disregards all instructions from the doctor for medication and diet. By the time I get him back from summer visitation he is wild and it takes weeks to get back to normal.

What This Means

This parent can't or won't deal with fact that his child is not without challenge. Some of what you see in your child's behavior upon return from visitation may be the normal readjustment period that many children experience.

Reasonable Action

You can't change the other parent. The summer interruption in your child's medication and diet won't cause permanent damage. Work on your feelings of fear and anger and strive to accept what you cannot change. Unless the child is on medication for a life-threatening disorder the court won't help.

Evaluating Your Panic Situation

Keep a Panic Situations Log separate and in addition to the contact log you should be keeping. List, number and date of any panic situations you must deal with as they come up. Examples of situations in this chapter will show you how to describe what is happening. You will begin to see patterns in the other parent's behavior and take steps to do effective damage control or eliminate the problem before it arises. The patterns of behavior exhibited by what the other parent does and how you evaluate and respond will give any professional to whom you show the log a very clear picture of the past and present. Usually, a professional evaluator, ad litem or psychologist will be willing to look at a Panic Situation Log when he or she would have been unwilling to listen to a verbal litany of offenses by the other parent. Start with #1 and proceed as far as necessary.

Your Panic Situation List

Although if you never show this list to anyone, it will serve several very important functions. The first, is that taking the time to diagnose the situation to put it on paper will keep you from responding with a knee-jerk reaction that will compound your problems. Second, it will help you decide on a reasonable course of action.

Third, you not only will begin to see patterns of behavior, but you will be able to accurately predict the opposition's next step.

Additionally, the positive therapeutic value to you is immeasurable.

___ Title of Situation

Date and description of the situation as clearly as it was presented to you.

What This Means

Evaluation of what the problem really was.

Reasonable Action

How you dealt with the situation. Does it relate to any other situation you have dealt with?

Randall's Panic Situation List

Most of Randall's situations are listed above with the forty-five other situations experienced by others. They have been listed in the order they happened to Randall.

Your list should be included in the Book Of Your Life that you submit to evaluators and decision makers through the years as necessary.

01 Interference with Parenting Time

Amber called and said she wanted her mother to watch Bobby two days a week so Bobby and her mother could bond. I said I was not willing to give up two days a week of watching my son while Amber worked. Amber said if you don't agree, I won't let you have him at all.

What This Means

Amber does not feel anyone should interfere with what she has decided to do when it concerns her son.

Reasonable Action

For now you will have to do what Amber wants you to do. Try to talk to her about it. If that fails, you may have to appeal to the courts for some relief.

02 Forced Mediation

Amber dropped a note on my kitchen counter saying she had made an appointment at mediation and I better be there. I feel like this is her show and they are going to impose a bunch of new rules and obligations on me. I pay all of Bobby's bills and deliver food and supplies to her home once a week and on demand. Amber wants child support, but I don't know what for since I do the child care unless she takes the child to her mother.

What This Means

This parent feels she can use the system to force you to do what she wants you to do.

Reasonable Action

This may be your opportunity to improve your situation. Make a list of everything you are doing for your son now. Take your receipts and the parenting plan you want. Let the mediator know you want the child care days Amber has given to her mother back.

The courts favor a parent's care over any other care. The mediation is not binding. Go and mediate in good faith.

03 Parental Kidnapping

Amber moved Bobby to Washington without telling me she that she was doing so. In the mediation she forced me into and whose results we finally agreed upon, neither of us could move Bobby out of state.

What This Means

This parent does not feel anyone should interfere with the way she has decided to raise her child. She feels any agreement that no longer suits her is no longer binding.

Reasonable Action

Find out where she has taken your child. Have your attorney serve her with papers ordering her to bring the child and appear at a hearing to return the child to your state. If you have not done so, file a suit for custody

05 Failure to Return Child

Amber refused to bring Bobby back at the end of her visitation

What This Means

This parent cannot or will not comply with the court order.

Reasonable Action

File a complaint with the court. If the other parent will bring the child back if you pay for the fare, arrange to have the money ready in exchange for your child.

The court can do it without costing you the "fare", but it will take more time and cost you attorney fees. It is not right or fair, but it will get your child back. After all, that is what you really want.

06 False Accusations of Abuse

Amber filed anonymous sexual abuse charges against Rebecca. The complaint said the child stood on his mother's lap on a crowded airplane and said, "Becky, Pee Pee Mouth" and attempted to put his penis in his mother's mouth.

What This Means

This parent has pulled out all the stops and is attempting to use any means available to reverse custody. If there were no witnesses on the airplane, there is probably no case.

Reasonable Action

Cooperate with the investigation of Child Protective Services. Amber had exhausted all the other avenues of assault so she tried this one. The normalcy of Rebecca's relationship with Bobby, as well as the fact that no sexual abuse was mentioned or indicated for the four previous years of the child's life he had lived in a secure happy home with his father and step-mother.

Have your attorney get copies of the original complaint and any statements of witnesses and professionals who interviewed the child.

07 Attorney Wanted to Quit

I received a letter from my attorney stating, "I would suggest that you obtain new counsel to represent you. I am having a difficult time finding the enthusiasm to continue pressing for further hearings after all the hearings I have already been in on your behalf.

When I initially agreed to represent you, I did not envision a situation where I would have to request a court hearing arguing over the same thing every time the mother chooses to exercise her limited visitation. I do not believe the judge will be enthusiastic at hearing more about what may be perceived to objective outsiders as nothing more than a continued grudge match.

There is very limited time that Bobby is with the mother, assuming your home life is as stable as it seems (and I have no reason to believe otherwise). Bobby is going through less than what a lot of other children have to deal with in situations where their parents are not together."

What This Means

The case has gone on for so long my attorney has lost sight of what is really happening.

Reasonable Action

First, I made notes, then I called my attorney and asked to give a quick review of how things looked from my side. My attorney said he would listen, so I proceeded.

"First of all, I am looking for another attorney. Now I would like to review this case from our first meeting. When I first came to your office I already had custody of Bobby for eight months. I told you Amber was vindictive and everything would be a fight. With that information you charged me an initial retainer of three thousand dollars."

Dear Mr. Country,

(1) I told you Bobby's visitation with his mother required over two thousand miles of travel each way and it appeared her home was an active criminally violent atmosphere. I wanted Amber to be restricted to supervised visitation in this state rather than in her home state until Bobby was eight years old. You strongly recommended that we go for Termination of her Parental Rights. (2) In 1994, we had extensive dental work done for Bobby and requested her court-ordered portion of the money. You also requested payment via her attorney several times in 1994,1995 and 1996. (3) Most of the court appearances have arisen because the original court order from Arizona was very specific, and Amber pressed to subvert the order at each visitation.

This is not an over caring mother as evidenced by the judge's having to order her to call

Bobby once a week rather than once every six months. (4) In November 1996, we submitted documentation to you that encouraged the court to admonish Amber from allowing any contact between Bobby and his oldest brother. We submitted documentation that proved Amber took Bobby to a juvenile detention facility to visit the older brother therefore violating that court order within three days of the order. (5) You said "Since Amber was just here in November, the court would not make her appear on this violation." We submitted documentation that proved for the entire Christmas visitation the older brother was not only home, but was in charge of the care of Bobby. (6) You said we could not do anything until she was going to be in town. Now in May you wish to resign from our case because you have lost enthusiasm to continue. You stated in your letter that we seem to harass Amber by serving her with subpoenas each time she attempts to exercise her limited visitation. We do not make any decisions without your valuable and costly advice. We always follow your advice. I feel Amber's attorney has ignored communications, delayed filing required court orders and ignored court orders entirely in some cases causing delay, subversion costing me more than two thousand above and beyond the original three thousand."

Epilog

My attorney said he would appear on the pending court date for me. He was much tougher and more effective than he had been in a long time. He demonstrated to the court that Amber and her attorney were not responding in good faith to correspondence or court orders. After court he said I didn't need to find another attorney.

Anger

Anger usually indicates that our focus has shifted from what is essential for the welfare of our children to exerting the effort necessary to fulfill our desires or needs. Anger can erupt at any moment, and it's not always directed at a person. Sometimes we get angry at circumstances. We're frustrated because we believe we're about to lose something we thought was secure. We feel anger when we realize we may not gain something we expected or our personal goals are frustrated.

What usually makes us angry is our lack of control over people and circumstances. Anger without true danger may expose our self-centered agenda. To deal with anger we must come to grips with the fact that we are not all-powerful. We need to determine why we're angry. Blocked goals are the most common causes of anger, and anger over blocked goals reveals our selfish nature. Anger can imprison us. Fear reveals our attitude toward personal loss. The greater the loss, the greater the fear. Worry, a form of fear, is preoccupation with the possibility that we can lose something valuable. Most of us express fear as anger.

Dealing With Your Anger

1. Different perspectives and ways of reacting do not necessarily mean that one person is "right" and the other "wrong." Even in an intensely focused dispute we recognize that there are as many ways of seeing the problem. You're missing the point if you are fighting about who has the "truth".

2. Always be prepared for whom you will be dealing and how they react in situations that involve you. Take time to think about the problems that may arise. Decide, which issues require you to establish or maintain a position. Understand, which issues are not important. Be willing to back off on any challenge to those unimportant issues.

3. Recognize that each adult is responsible for his or her own behavior. Don't blame the new significant-other because your former spouses says that person is responsible for the breakdown in communication. If you are angry about a problem, it is your responsibility to find a new way to approach the situation. Direct your attention to the correct person.

4. Take a stand and speak up when an issue is important to you. It is a mistake to stay silent if it will make you feel bitter, resentful or unhappy. Don't address every injustice and irritation. Often letting something go can be the best answer and an act of maturity.

5. If your goal is to change an entrenched negative pattern, the worst time to speak up may be when

you are feeling angry. Insist on some temporary distance. You can always say, "I need a little time to sort out my thoughts. I will send you an e-mail or call so we can talk about this."

6. Don't confront, blame, interpret, shame, name call, threatening, assume, diagnose, label, analyze, preach, moralize, order, warn, interrogate, ridicule, lecture, project or bring up old arguments.

- Commands

  You should.... You shouldn't...

  You'd better... You ought to....

  You're suppose to.... You can't...

  You will.... You must...

- Comparisons

  You're just like... That's like...

  ______wouldn't...

  That's not the way ____would

- Ignoring

  That's Irrelevant Don't bother. Whatever...

- Exaggerations

  Always... Never... Constantly...

  Forever... Everybody... Nobody...

7. The other side will stop listening and start defending themselves if you start criticizing, blaming or holding them responsible for your feelings or reactions. Learn to express yourself without using "you" in any of the sentences. Say, "I think..." "I feel.". "I want..." or "Help me understand". Have your statement say exactly what you feel.

8. Don't participate arguments that reoccur and go nowhere. Don't spin your wheels trying to convince the other side of the "rightness" of your position. If the other person can't or won't hear you, simply say, "I understand that you disagree, but I guess we see the problem differently."

9. Avoid speaking through a the children or untrained persons. If you are angry try "I was upset when you didn't come. You're important to the children and I know you wanted to be there."

10. If you think of the other parent as the otherside or the enemy you will destroy every opportunity for communication. You will turn every conversations into an argument. This will escalate emotions to unmanageable levels. This can cause your targets to lose their tempers and make them defensive or worse offensive. Many times we do not even notice we are using these types of words or phrases. You can improve your ability to communicate and benefit your children by avoiding using these words and phrases.

The Anger of Others

1. Minimize risks to yourself and others when confronted by an angry person. It may be necessary to remove yourself and your children from the area.

2. Evaluate your response options quickly and then select one of your prearranged action plans.

3. Present a calm, serious appearance.

4. Speak softly.

5. Talk in a non-judgmental manner (don't "shame, blame" or patronize).

6. Put physical space between you and the other person. You may want to have a piece of furniture, such as a desk, between the two of you.

7. Try to have someone else with you for help and support.

8. Encourage the person to talk to you and explain the situation from her perspective.

9. Try to not let the person stand between you and an exit.

10. Don't make promises you can't keep.

11. After you've experienced a problem like this, made an incident report form and send it to your attorney.

Anger in Our Children

Children may express anger and aggression

more freely when their parents are embroiled in child custody disputes. Often they feel like everyone is using them to gain control over the opposition rather than really caring about what the children are experiencing.

Our actions should be motivated by the need to protect and to reach our children on the level at which they need attention. Not by a desire to punish the children so we can get back to what is important to us. Parents should show children that they accept the children's feelings, while suggesting alternative ways to express the feelings.

It is not enough to tell children their behaviors are unacceptable. We must teach them acceptable ways of expressing themselves and coping with new and difficult situations. We must communicate exotically what we expect of them.

1. Catch your children doing something right. Tell the children when they have done something that pleases you. Respond to positive efforts to reinforce good behavior. You will find countless opportunities during the day to make such comments as "I like the way you helped set the table for dinner without being reminded"; "I appreciate your hanging up your clothes before school this morning."; "You were really quiet while I was on the phone"; "I'm glad you shared your crayons with your sister"; "I like the way you try to think of others"; and "Thank you for telling the truth about what really happened."

2. Ignore inappropriate behavior that can be tolerated. This doesn't mean that you should ignore the children, just the behavior. The "ignoring" has to be planned and consistent. Even though this behavior may be tolerated, the children must recognize that it is inappropriate.

3. Provide physical outlets and other alternatives. It is important for children to have opportunities for physical exercise, both at home and at school.

4. Positively manipulate the child's surroundings. Aggressive behavior is encouraged by allowing children to play violent video games, view wrestling on television or placing children in tough, tempting situations. We should try to plan the surroundings so that certain things are less apt to happen. Stop a "problem" activity and substitute, a more desirable one. Rules and regulations, as well as physical space, may be too confining.

5. Closeness and touching are important to children. Move physically closer to the children to curb their angry impulses. Young children are often calmed by having an adult come close by and express interest in their activities. Children naturally try to involve adults in what they are doing, and the adult is often annoyed at being bothered. Very young children (and children who are emotionally deprived) seem to need much more adult involvement in their interests. Children about to use toys or tools in a destructive way are sometimes easily stopped by an adult who expresses interest in having the object shown to him. An outburst from older children struggling with a difficult reading selection can be assisted by a caring adult who moves near the children to say, "Show me, which words are giving you trouble."

6. Be ready to show affection. Sometimes all that is needed for angry children to regain control is a sudden hug or other impulsive show of affection. Children with serious emotional problems, however, may have trouble accepting affection.

7. Ease tension through humor. Kidding the children out of temper tantrums or outbursts offers the children opportunities to "save face." However, it is important to distinguish between face-saving humor and sarcasm, teasing, or ridicule.

8. Appeal directly to the child. Tell him or her how you feel and ask for consideration. For example, a parent may gain a child's cooperation by saying, "I know that noise you're making doesn't usually bother me, but today I've got a headache, so could you find something else you'd enjoy doing?"

9. Explain situations. Help the children understand the cause of a stressed situation. We often fail to realize how easily young children can begin to react properly once they understand the cause of their frustration.

10. Use physical restraint. Occasionally a children may lose control so completely that he has to be physically restrained or removed from the scene

to prevent him from hurting himself or others. This may also "save face" for the child. Physical restraint or removal from the scene should not be viewed by the children as punishment, but as a means of saying, "You can't do that." In such situations, an adult cannot afford to lose his or her temper and taunting remarks by other children should not be tolerated.

11. Children feel powerless. Encourage children to see their strengths as well as their weaknesses. Help them to see that they can reach their goals.

12. Promises of future pleasure can be used both to start and to stop behavior. This is not bribery. We must know what the children like--what brings them pleasure--and we must deliver on our promises. Use promises and rewards.

13. Limits should be clearly explained and enforced. Children should be free to function within those limits. When appropriate say "NO!"

14. Tell the children that you accept their angry feelings, but offer other suggestions for expressing them. Teach children to put their angry feelings into words, rather than fists or fits.

15. Build a child's positive self-image. Encourage them to see themselves as valued and valuable people. Help them see the value in all the people they love.

16. There is a fine line between punishment that is hostile toward a children and punishment that is educational. Use punishment cautiously.

17. Parents should be aware of the powerful influence of their actions on a child's behavior. Model appropriate behavior.

18. Allow the children individually to express themselves verbally. Talking helps children have control and thus reduces acting out behavior. Encourage the children to say, "I don't like bedtime here. At my other house I get to stay up late."

Chapter 16: Abuse, Allegations, Kidnapping

Abuse

Child Abuse: Any psychological, emotional, physical or sexual assault on a child. Verbal, physical, emotional or sexual abuse against the child, against the people the child cares about or in the child's presence or within the child's knowledge is a crime against the child that will leave permanent scars.

The specter of child abuse looms heavily over our society. It is so pervasive that parents are more watchful and aware than ever before. The definition of child abuse includes many things, including willfully and knowingly exposing their children to second-hand smoke. The language and definitions used in the child abuse and neglect laws of some states may be interpreted so that parental smoking around children is considered a form of child abuse. It is possible that professionals, like psychologists, pediatricians or certain care-givers, may be required to report a child suffering from symptoms caused by exposure to secondhand smoke to the appropriate child protection agencies. There are many books and articles that explain how abuse effects not only the abused child, but the children of that child many years later. It is your job to protect your child from this crime, and it is also your job to protect yourself from the crime of false accusations.

Parents should be watchful of any unusual condition in the children, such as intoxication, stress, fatigue, anger, fear or any evidence of abuse.

Categories of Neglect and Abuse

The following are an example of the statutory definitions of abuse under, which CPS in some jurisdictions operate in fulfilling their mandate to receive and investigate allegations of physical abuse and intervene with rehabilitative services.

Abuse means the infliction or allowing of injury, impairment of function or disfigurement or the infliction of or allowing another person to cause serious emotional damage as evidenced by severe anxiety, depression, withdrawal or untoward aggressive behavior and which emotional damage is diagnosed by a medical doctor or psychologist and which is caused by the acts or omissions of an individual having care, custody and control of a child. Abuse is inflicting or allowing sexual abuse, sexual conduct, sexual assault, molestation, commercial sexual exploitation, sexual exploitation,

incest or prostitution.
Physical injury is further defined by some criminal statutes as the impairment of physical condition that includes, but shall not be limited to any skin bruising, pressure sores, bleeding, failure to thrive, malnutrition, dehydration, burns, fracture of any bone, sub-dural hematoma, soft tissue swelling, injury to any internal organ or any physical condition, which imperils health or welfare.

Physical Abuse implies that the child victim is physically injured by the actions, whether or not intentional, of the caretaker. There are many definitions of abuse within the culture and value system of the community in which it occurs.

Serious Physical Injury means physical injury, which creates a reasonable risk of death, or which causes serious or permanent disfigurement, or serious impairment of health or loss or protracted impairment of the function of any bodily organ or limb.

Neglect means the inability or unwillingness of a parent, guardian or custodian of a child to provide that child with supervision, food, clothing, shelter or medical care if that inability or unwillingness causes substantial risk of harm to the child's health or welfare, except if the inability of a parent, guardian or custodian to provide services to meet the needs of a child with a disability or chronic illness is solely the result of the unavailability of reasonable services. Sexual Abuse

Sexual Abuse is defined as the involvement of dependent, developmentally immature children and adolescents in sexual activities that they do not fully comprehend, to which they are unable to give informed consent, or that violate the social taboos of family roles. Sexual Abuse is any act designed to stimulate a child sexually, or to use a child for the sexual stimulation either of the perpetrator or of another person.

Sexual Misuse is defined as exposure of a child to sexual stimulation inappropriate for the child's age and role in the family.Sexual offenses Against Children include sexual abuse and misuse. A person commits sexual abuse by intentionally or knowingly engaging in sexual contact with any person fifteen or more years of age without consent of that person or with any person who is under fifteen years of age if the sexual contact involves only the female breast.

Sexual Conduct with a Minor is when a person commits sexual conduct with a minor by intentionally or knowingly engaging in sexual intercourse or oral sexual contact with any person who is under eighteen years of age.

Sexual Assault is when a person commits sexual assault by intentionally or knowingly engaging in sexual intercourse or oral sexual contact with any person without consent of such person.

Molestation of a Child when a person commits molestation of a child by intentionally or knowingly engaging in or causing a person to engage in sexual contact, except sexual contact with the female breast, with a child under fifteen years of age.

Commercial Sexual Exploitation of a Minor when a person knowingly:

(1) Using, employing, persuading, enticing, inducing or coercing a minor to engage in or assist others to engage in exploitive exhibition or other sexual conduct for the purpose of producing any visual or print medium or live act depicting such conduct;

(2) Using, employing, persuading, enticing inducing or coercing a minor to expose the genitals or anus or the areola or nipple of the female breast for financial or commercial gain;

(3) Permitting a minor under such person's custody or control to engage in or assist others to engage in exploitive exhibition or other sexual conduct for the purpose of producing any visual or print media or live act depicting such conduct;

(4) Transporting or financing the transportation of any minor through or across the state with the intent that such minor engage in prostitution, exploitive exhibition or other sexual conduct for the purpose of producing a visual or print medium or live act depicting such conduct. Sexual Exploitation of a Minor A person commits sexual exploitation of a minor by knowingly:

(1) Recording, filming, photographing, developing or duplicating any visual or print medium in which minors are engaged in exploitive exhibition or other sexual conduct;

(2) Distributing, transporting, exhibiting, receiving, selling, purchasing, possessing or exchanging any visual or print medium in which minors are engaged in exploitive exhibition or other sexual conduct. Incest Persons who are fifteen or more years of age and are within the degrees of

consanguinity within, which marriages are declared by law to be incestuous and void.
Those who knowingly intermarry with each other, or who knowingly commit fornication or adultery with each other.

Child Prostitution is when a person commits child prostitution by knowingly:

(1) Causing any minor to engage in prostitution;

(2) Using any minor for purposes of prostitution;

(3) Permitting a minor under such persons custody or control to engage in prostitution;

(4) Receiving any benefit for or on account of procuring or placing a minor in any place or in the charge or custody of any person for the purpose of prostitution;

(5) Receiving any benefit pursuant to an agreement to participate in the proceeds of prostitution of a minor;

(6) Financing, managing, supervising, controlling or owning, either alone or in association with others, prostitution activity involving a minor;

(7) Transporting or financing the transportation of any minor through or across this state with the intent that such minor engage in prostitution." Emotional Abuse

Emotional Abuse is evidenced by severe anxiety, depression, withdrawal, or improper aggressive behavior as diagnosed by a medical doctor or psychologist and caused by the acts or omissions of the parent or caretaker.

Emotional Maltreatment includes blaming, belittling or rejecting a child, constantly treating siblings unequally, and persistent lack of concern by the caretaker for the child's welfare. Emotional maltreatment is rarely manifest in physical signs, particularly in the normal school setting; speech disorders, lags in physical development, and failure to thrive syndrome are physical indicators of emotional maltreatment. More often it is observed through behavioral indicators, and even these indicators may not be immediately apparent. While emotional maltreatment does occur alone, it often accompanies physical abuse and sometimes sexual abuse. Emotionally maltreated children are not always physically abused. But physically abused children are almost always emotionally maltreated as well.

Abandoned Is defined as "the failure of the parent to provide reasonable support and to maintain regular contact with the child, including the providing of normal supervision, when such failure is accompanied by an intention on the part of the parent to permit such condition to continue for an indefinite period in the future. Abandoned includes a judicial finding that a parent has made only minimal efforts to support and communicate with the child. Failure to maintain a normal parental relationship with the child without just cause for a period of six months shall constitute prima facie evidence of abandonment.

Non–Sexual Exploitation There is not a legal definition for exploitation; however, it is defined for CPS purposes to mean the use of a child by a parent, guardian or custodian for material gain, which may include forcing the child to panhandle, steal or perform other illegal activities.

Failure to Protect It is not only the responsibility of a parent to not abuse a child but also to protect a child form abuse.

In New Hampshire In the case of Samantha L., Tina Langlais' 9-year-old daughter had to be hospitalized for two months. Langlais claimed her daughter's injuries weren't the result of abuse, but the state division for children, youth and families claimed that they were. A state district court found that Langlais hadn't abused her daughter, but that she failed to protect her from abuse. It awarded Langlais custody, but gave legal supervision to the state.

Langlais appealed, but a superior court affirmed the lower court's ruling that the child had been abused. It gave custody to the state because Langlais refused to acknowledge the abuse. The supreme court affirmed. "When a parent shirks the responsibility to assist a child in coping with abuse or fails to realize that the abuse occurred, that child falls within the definition of an abused and neglected child... and can be removed from parental custody," it said.

The state may assume custody of a child if her parents won't acknowledge that she is being abused, the state supreme court has ruled.

Exposure to Abuse and Violence

Recognizing exposure to abuse and/or violence is a complicated process. There are behaviors that are characteristic of children who experience family violence or abusive behavior. Repetition of abuse toward children or adults when these children become adults is a serious consideration.

- **Aggressive behavior.** Some of these children may act aggressively at home, in school, and toward others. This may also include destroying property or theft.
- **Role reversal.** Often an older child is forced to accept responsibility for caring for younger siblings and/or household duties due to the parents' own dysfunctions.
- **Self-destructive behavior.** Abused children may be sexually promiscuous or exhibit self-mutilating behaviors as they vent their anger or seek attention from others.
- **Running away.** This may be seen as the only alternative for escaping.
- **Shy, withdrawn behavior.** These children may not interact with others. They may go undetected as being troubled because of this lack of attention to self.
- **Substance abuse.** This behavior is often modeled after parents' behavior and is used as a means of psychological escape.
- **Truancy.** Sometimes abused children fail to attend school because they either feel they have to stay home to control things or else they fear detection of the home problems by their peers.
- **Violence toward parents.** Children may turn on parents during adolescence or adulthood.

This information originated from: Barnett, Pittman, Ragan, and Salus, "Family Violence: Intervention Strategies", W.A., D.C. U.S. Department of Health and Human Services, U.S. Government Printing Office, May 1980.

Indications of Negligence or Abuse

- Insect or parasite bites
- Soiled clothing
- Soiled bed
- Poor skin hygiene
- Pallor, sunken eyes, cheeks
- Dehydration, mal-nourishment with illness
- Dehydration without illness
- Weight loss
- Evidence of inadequate or inappropriate administration of medication
- Burns possibly caused by cigarette, acid or friction
- Lack of bandages on injuries or stitches when indicated
- Injury that has not been cared for properly
- Implausible explanation for injury
- Bruises, welts, discoloration, cuts, lacerations, puncture wounds.
- New bruises, welts, discoloration, cuts, lacerations or puncture wounds, which are structurally similar to an object, or where an old and new wound can be observed at the same time
- Signs of confinement (rooms locked from outside, bars on windows or nailed closed)
- Imposition of isolation of the child from family and family situations
- Restriction of the activity of the child within normal age appropriate social situations
- Lack of amenities for the child such as toys, books, games, personal grooming items and appropriate clothing

Children's Reactions to Abuse

Agitation, anxiety

Ambivalence

A poor self-image

Inability to trust

Aggressive behavior

Passive and withdrawn behavior

Hyperactivity

Attachment Disorder

Refusal to go to school

Clinging behaviors

Persistent fears

Sleep disturbances

Loss of concentration

Behavior problems

Physical complaints

Withdrawal from family/friends

Preoccupation School failure

Drug and alcohol abuse

Anger

Contradictory statements

Denial

DepressionFearHelplessness

Hesitation to talk openly

Implausible stories

Non-responsiveness

Resignation

Failure to Thrive

Penalty for Reporting Suspected Abuse

In most states the laws for reporting child abuse prohibit retaliation against a person who reports suspected abuse in good faith. But if the person reporting has no substantiated evidence, the state authorities are reluctant to disrupt the family. Physicians and school teachers are required to report any evidence of abuse.

Although some anonymous referrals may have less validity, they should be handled in the same manner as other reports. Caseworkers must gather the same information from the anonymous reporter as they would from any other reporter. Caseworkers should also explore the reason for his/her anonymity. It is important to explain to the reporter the reasons why the agency needs the reporter's name and telephone number. In addition, caseworkers should assure the reporter that unless court action is required, his/her confidentiality will be maintained. In addition, reports from an estranged spouse regarding the other parent's care of the children often create suspicion among CPS caseworkers. Such reports should be handled in the same manner as other reports.

Child Protective Services

CPS may play during a child custody dispute. The name of the agency may be different in your community, but the goal the organization will be the same. Your understanding of their goals will limit the damage false claims against you could have or give more weight to any report necessary to protect your children.

The type of abuse reported and the level of risk to the child determines how CPS responds to a report. Reports of neglect and abuse are categorized as high risk, low risk, moderate risk and potential risk.

It starts when an individual or professional reports that a person presently under the age of eighteen (18) is the subject of physical, sexual or emotional abuse, neglect, abandonment or exploitation. Most often the complaint is against a parent or guardian.

The primary goal of the agency is to assure the safety and well-being of children.

The secondary goal is to focuses on the family as a whole and will enable children to remain safely in their own homes unless it is not in their best interest.

When CPS Gets A Call

This may be your first contact with CPS, but they have been through this entire process thousands of times. They don't just run out the door as soon as a call comes in. Agencies must accept any report that meets the statutory and agency guidelines.

These guidelines include:

1. Determine if the report meets the agency guidelines Some agencies provide caseworkers with guidelines for screening particular types of reports.

2. Determining the credibility of the report by examining the consistency of information being reported. If the information being reported is considered a valid complaint it will be accepted for an initial assessment/investigation. These as well as other questions will be asked to help the caseworkers evaluate the report:

- Is the reporter willing to give his/her name, address, and telephone number?
- What is the reporter's relationship to the victim and family?
- How well does the reporter know the family?
- If the reporter knew of previous abuse or neglect, why is he/she reporting now?
- How does the reporter know about the case?
- Does the reporter stand to gain anything for reporting or from the report being validated?
- Has the reporter made previous unfounded reports on this family?
- Is the reporter willing to meet with a caseworker

in person if needed?

- Does the reporter appear to be intoxicated, extremely bitter, angry, or exhibiting behavior that which would make the caseworker question his/her competency?
- Can or will the reporter refer CPS to others who know about the situation?
- What does the reporter hope will happen as a result of the report?

The answers to these questions will determine the urgency of the response. Risk assessment models have been established to guide the caseworkers' decision regarding the response time. Models may include checklists, matrices, and scales.

Factors Necessitating An Immediate Response:

Type of Maltreatment

- Life-threatening living conditions exist.
- Cruel, bizarre, or sadistic punishment or treatment.
- Indications that abusive acts are premeditated.
- The child is currently being physically abused.
- There are previous reports of abuse or neglect.
- Multiple injuries are alleged.
- Previous suspicious injuries are reported.
- Injuries are located on the head, neck
- Injuries are located on the genitals or internally.
- Medical attention is needed.
- Uncertainty exists regarding the severity of the abuse or neglect.
- Instruments are used in the abuse.
- The child is alone or has been abandoned and is not competent to provide his/her own care.
- Incidents have increased in intensity and frequency.

The Child

- The child is under 6 years of age and/or cannot protect him/herself.
- The child is fearful of the parent/caretaker or of going home.
- The child has a disabling condition that makes him/her completely dependent on the parent/caretaker for care.
- The child is immediately accessible to the perpetrator.
- The child is suicidal.

The Parent(s)/Caretaker(s)

- The parent/caretaker exhibits bizarre behavior and is not taking prescribed medication.
- The abuse or neglect is related to alcohol or drug abuse, and the parent/caretaker is currently intoxicated or high on drugs.
- The parent/caretaker is described as volatile or dangerous.
- Parents'/caretakers' view of the child is bizarre (such as, the parent/caretaker believes the child is possessed by the devil).

The Family

- The family is transient or new to the community.
- The parent/caretaker is hiding the child.
- The family is physically and socially isolated.
- Family members are threatening or out of control.
- There are indications of domestic violence.

Once those factors have been considered the caseworker must establish the Intake Process in order to gather sufficient information from the reporter and agency records to be able to:

- **Gathering Information From the Reporter** The more comprehensive the information provided by the reporter, the better able caseworkers are to determine the appropriateness of the report for CPS intervention, the level of risk to the child, and the urgency of the response needed. Information gathering should focus on demographic information about the child and family; information about the alleged maltreatment; and information about the child, the parents/caretakers, and the family as a whole.
- **Information Regarding the Alleged Maltreatment** Information about the nature, severity, and chronicity of the alleged maltreatment and where it occurred. The nature of the maltreatment regarding the specific characteristics of the maltreatment and the parental acts or omissions.

  Physical abuse: burning, beating, kicking, biting, and other physical abuse.

  Neglect: abandonment, withholding of needed medical care, lack of supervision, lack of adequate food or shelter, emotional deprivation, failure to register or send to school, and failure to thrive.

Sexual abuse and/or exploitation: fondling, masturbation, oral or anal sex, sexual intercourse, pornography, and forced prostitution.

Emotional abuse: constant berating and rejecting treatment, scape-goating a particular child, and bizarre/cruel/ritualistic forms of punishment (such as, locking a child in a dark closet, tying a child to a bedpost, and demeaning a child).

Parental/caretaker acts/omissions: (such as, accidental vs. intentional or premeditated, disregard for the child's age or condition, and instruments used).

Severity and Location of the Maltreatment

Extent of the physical or emotional injury to the child (such as, second and third degree burns on half of the child's body, withdrawal, suicidal behavior, and excessive fear).

Place of the injury on the child's body.

Reoccurrence of the maltreatment.

Information gathering should focus on:

- whether there have been prior incidents of abuse or neglect
- how long the abuse or neglect has been occurring
- whether abuse or neglect has increased in frequency or remained relatively constant

Location of the incident. It is important to ascertain the setting where the actual abuse or neglect occurred (such as, home, school, or supermarket).

Grounds to Continue the Investigation

Most States require reports to include three components:

1. a child under 18 years of age
2. a parent or caretaker responsible for the care of the child; and incidences
3. circumstances, conditions, or omissions contributing to abuse or neglect that indicate that the child's health or welfare has been harmed or threatened.

If it is determined that the report is inappropriate for CPS, no initial assessment/ investigation will occur; however, information and referral services may be provided. Almost every State requires that a report alleging maltreatment by a non-caretaker must be referred immediately to law enforcement personnel. If it is determined that the allegations constitute abuse or neglect or the risk of maltreatment, then an initial assessment/ investigation will be conducted.

Child and Family Assessment Outline

Once a permanent caseworker has been assigned a detailed assessment of the family will take place. The inquire will probably include:

Parents' History

1. Childhood experiences: level of nurturing, relationships with parents and siblings, income and housing situation, urban versus rural environment
2. Type of discipline as a child
3. Meaning of culture to their current views
4. Educational background
5. Sexual development
6. Relationships with others (historically); are there meaningful long-term connections to others?
7. Employment record
8. Criminal background
9. Emotional stability over time
10. Physical health history

Parents' Health, Mental Health, and Behavior

1. Feelings about self in relation to the world at large
2. Emotional stability: any previous diagnoses of mental illness, observations of behavior and emotions, level of adaptation, reactions to others such as: impulsivity, hostility
3. Life style, such as, chaotic, crisis style, stable

4. Use of drugs or alcohol
5. Methods of coping with stress
6. Physical health status
7. Level of intelligence
8. Attitudes toward violence

Parenting Attitudes and Behaviors

1. Viewpoint and expectations of children
2. Knowledge of child development
3. Attitudes about parenting including discipline
4. Daily parenting approach
5. Comfort in parenting role
6. Primary caretaker
7. Use of outside child care
8. Nurturing behaviors, such as: listening and talking to child, display of affection, attachment and bonding
9. Knowledge of nutrition, appropriate medical care

Child's Health, Mental Health, and Behavior

1. Age appropriateness of behavior
2. General personality and behaviors such as: hyperactivity, acting out, withdrawn behavior, and other unusual behaviors.
3. School functioning
4. Physical health including any disabilities
5. Developmental level, such as, language, and motor skills.
6. Recent changes in behavior or functioning
7. Substance or alcohol use
8. Relationships with peers
9. Intelligence level
10. Attitudes toward parents, such as, fearful, or protective.

Family Functioning

1. Roles and relationships among family members including marital and sexual relationships
2. Methods and level of communication
3. Level of affection
4. Methods for dealing with conflict, problem solving, responding to stress
5. Open versus closed family system
6. Power and control, family decision making
7. Nature of family, such as, blended family, single parent family, or birth of new child.
8. Family activities, such as, outings, or vacations.
9. Who actually performs family tasks, such as, housekeeping, management of family finances, grocery shopping, and cooking.

Environment

1. Income
2. Housing: health and hygiene, safety
3. Neighborhood: safety, crime, violence
4. Rural versus urban
5. Affiliation with community church, clubs, or other groups
6. Accessibility to resources and social support

Relationships With Others

1. Extended family
2. Friends, neighbors, and others who may support the family
3. Nature of relationships (if any), example: close, superficial
4. Boyfriends/girlfriends of single parents and the role they have in the family

Response to Agency and Other Community Professionals

1. Previous use of outside agencies

2. Level of trust in professionals in general
3. Awareness of community resources

The response time is determined by combinations of risk factors that reflect the level of risk to a child.

A psychotic parent who is having delusions about killing an infant. Children alleged to have been maltreated who are under the age of 6 or otherwise unable to care for themselves and are left alone.
A suicidal 11-year-old, an alcoholic parent, and an apathetic and indifferent parent. A 3-year-old with bruises and lacerations on several surface areas of the body and a previous fracture, and a single parent addicted to crack. A 9-year-old girl who discloses to her teacher that a male relative has been forcing her to have sexual intercourse and that she is fearful of going home. Caseworkers determine how quickly the agency must respond to a particular case by considering the factors in the case that individually present a risk to the child and also the risk factors that in combination present an even greater risk to the child. The presence of several factors and one or more combinations of factors requires an immediate response by CPS.

Every State and local CPS agency has established required response times. The requirements vary from community to community. In some States, CPS must initiate an investigation of all cases within 24 hours. In other States, cases determined to present a high concern for the child would require a CPS caseworker to respond immediately or at least within 24 hours. And, for cases where there is a risk of harm, but not imminent danger, the initial assessment/investigation may begin within 24, 48, or 72 hours or up to 5 days, depending on State law.

Court Ordered Cooperation

You are obligated to cooperate with the CPS professional if there is a court order. You have no other obligation to cooperate.

When CPS Knocks at Your Door

The initial confrontation with CPS (Child Protective Services) is frightening. Usually, you have no warning that CPS is coming. A visit from CPS can happen to a custodial or non-custodial parent. It helps if you know and understand what CPS can and cannot do.

Because all CPS agencies are understaffed, underpaid they can make mistakes. The valid complaints they investigate are truly horrible. Therefore, they don't start off in a friendly state of mind. In any case this person is not your enemy. This person is doing a very difficult job. They meet allot of very bad people and it is their job to protect children.

CPS professionals is at your door responding to a complaint that identifies that children are in danger. It is their job to use the law or intimidation tactics to get their job done. This professional is not your friend.

These legal and standard precautions should be followed when any officer of the court or peace officer knocks on your door. Be prepared for the professionals to say, "You should really let us in unless you have something to hide". If you have decided not to comply with the request, don't be encouraged or intimidated to change your mind. It won't make things easier in court later if it comes to that.

- If you are not shown a warrant, ask if they have one.
- If they have a warrant, let them in and while they are there, read the document to see what it allows them to do.

If you have one, call your attorney.

Children may not be removed from your home unless the CPS professional has a court order (California and New York may be the only exceptions).

Most reports to CPS are anonymous. The professional is mandated by law to check out the complaint. They know that only an allegation has been made. You may wish to let them know that you are involved in a divorce or child custody dispute. They know that many of these reports are generated during these legal disputes.

Removal of the Children

If CPS is removing the children from your home make a record of exactally what is happening. Record everything that happens using a tape recorder, video, still camera, third party witness, documentation and contact log. Pay close attention to the procedure used by CPS and the police.

Document how your children are reacting to the process.

Dealing with False Reports

If you say nothing at all, they will be inclined to think that you are hiding something, and will continue to pester you. If you choose to answer the questions, answer in as minimal a way as possible. Do not volunteer any information that they do not ask for. Offer to (insist if you can) meet with them in their office or at a another place rather than your home. If they don't have a warrant, don't allow them access to your kids without a lawyer present. If they threaten to interview your kids against your will (at school, say), then have your lawyer send a letter to the school stating that they are under no circumstances to allow anyone from the government to speak or touch your child.

Make sure that the caseworker knows you have a right to privacy, that you are a very private person, and are not sure what is happening is ethical. Make sure they have just cause before they barge into your life. Insist on your innocence; that you have done nothing wrong, and that what they are doing could possible constitute harassment and abuse in and of itself.

Let them know that you are willing to answer any question they may have, but you must protect your children. There have been many cases where CPS has destroyed families without cause.

The approach one parent took when CPS was on the doorstep was to say, "I am closing the door. I will not lock it. I am not inviting you in, but, I am not stopping you either. If you enter my home it will be against my wishes and I will take legal action."

Make all legal efforts to find out as many details as you can about where the false allegation originated. You won't be able to get the person's name from CPS. You should be able to put enough details together to figure out who made the complaint.

It is normal to attempt to distance yourself from the origiator of the complaint. If it came from school, talk with the principal about who made the false allegation and why. Let the principal know that you want to understand and help solve the problem. If they are not interested in helping let the principal know you will sue if it ever happens again. You may consider pulling your children from that school and enroll them in another. In every and all encounters with the social workers and anyone connected with CPS record everything either by videotape or audio. At the very least, have a note pad in hand and jot down everything said, and have a bound copy of your notes notarized immediately. This will increase your credibility and makes it possible for your notes to serve as evidence against the child snatchers in a court of law. Take preemptive action If you find yourself in a situation where false allegations are made against you regularly. You should consider legal action to prevent and stop the onslaught of false allegations. Eventually a "pattern", emerges. You must make sure that the pattern shows a clean parenting record on your side and a history of false accusations on the other.

Abuser's Reaction to Investigation

Suspected probable abuser will:

- not allow child to answer questions for him or her self
- not allow child to be interviewed outside his or her presence
- not assist the child in this process
- show an attitude of indifference or anger toward the child
- blame the child
- have a previous history of abuse of the child or others
- give conflicting accounts of incidents
- object to any observation or change in his or her contact with the child

Arrest for Abuse

All forms of child abuse are crimes. If the investigation concludes that abuse has occurred, and there is probable cause that further abuse will occur the police may arrest the person they think is responsible.

Getting Your Child Back from CPS

If you have a lawyer, listen to the lawyer. Make sure he or she has copies of your documentation of the removal of the children.

The responsibility of CPS is to protect your children not make you comfortable. If you were having someone investigated for abusing your children you would want CPS to exercise all due care before they let that person have access to your children again. Your attitude with CPS will have a great deal to do with how long it takes you to get your children back.

Your cooperation with this difficult process is essential. Become familiar with the practice and procedures that the agency must follow. Ask your attorney for advice. Get and give information in writing when ever possible. If it is legal in your state record phone calls with everyone at CPS with whom you speak.

Ask what you have to do to get your children back. Keep a contact log. Date, time, who you talked to, what you said, what the CPS professional said.

Complete any tests, and classes they suggest. Do what ever they ask you to do with a positive attitude. Remain involved and active in your case. Build a Book of Your Life for CPS. Maintain constant and polite communication with your caseworker.

If you can't get your case worker to respond contact that persons superior. Be firm and proper in all your dealings with CPS.

Has Your Child Been Abused?

1. Stay calm. It will make things much harder for the child if you become hysterical. Report any suspicion of child abuse. If the abuse is within the family, report it to the local Child Protection Agency. If the abuse is outside of the family, report it to the police or district attorney's office. Individuals reporting in good faith are immune from prosecution. The agency will evaluate and take action to protect the child.

2. When your child tells you about sexual abuse, give a supportive, caring response. This will be the first step towards getting help for the child and reestablishing his or her trust in adults.

3. Record an audio or video statement from the child with as little prompting from an adult as possible. If you think there has been physical contact, the child should have a physical evaluation from the doctor. Consult your pediatrician or family physician, who may refer you to a physician who specializes in evaluating and treating sexual abuse.

4. The examining doctor will evaluate the child's condition and treat any physical problem related to the abuse, gather evidence to help protect the child, and reassure the child that he or she is all right.

5. The child should also have a psychiatric evaluation to find out how the sexual abuse has affected him or her. It will be important to determine whether ongoing professional help is necessary for the child to deal with the trauma of the abuse.

6. Other members of the family may need to speak with the psychiatrist so they can provide support to the child and other family members who may be upset by the abuse.

7. When a child is asked to testify, special considerations--such as video taping, frequent breaks, exclusion of spectators, and the option not to face the accused--make the experience less stressful.

8. Adults, because of their maturity and knowledge, are always the ones to blame when they abuse children. The abused children should never be blamed.

Munchausen Syndrome by Proxy

A problem that parents that work long hours or non-custodial parents have is determining if they have a very sickly child or if the custodial parent is keeping the child sick to maintain control of the child and/or get attention or sympathy for themselves. Munchausen Syndrome by Proxy (MSBP) is a disorder in which a parent informs health care professionals of symptoms of fabricated disorders or exaggerates or actually induce in their children. This makes them a concerned parent in need of attention, sympathy, and support that they feel unable to obtain in any other way. These parents gain external gratification and acceptance as the child's champion, savior or co-victim with the child. MSBP is a severe form of child abuse. It tends to be a serial crime and a parent afflicted with this disorder may torture and kill one child after another attempting to meet their own needs. It is unusual for a parent to abuse more than one child at a time. Some of the behaviors exhibited by parents with MSBP are:

- Deliberately mislead others into thinking their children have serious medical or psychological problems.

- Change doctors or facilities to find a more sympathetic environment or one that can be manipulated more easily.
- Learn from each contact with health care professionals of symptoms to claim on the visit with the next professional.
- Exaggerating symptoms often resulting in extraordinary numbers of medication trials, diagnostic tests, hospitalizations, and even surgery.
- Induce seizure in infants and children.
- Withhold medication or over medicate.
- Falsify or adulterate lab results.
- Aggravate an existing medical problem by manipulating a wound so it doesn't heal.
- Induce an actual illness by injecting their child with bacteria to cause infection.

Allegations

Allegation: To bring forward for consideration a claim of one party against the other. A statement of issue, which the contributing party is prepared to prove.

Making false allegations against the other parent can cause you, at the very least, to look like a liar and at the most to lose custody of your children. When an allegation is made, even in the context of high conflict litigation, it must be taken very seriously and fully investigated to determine its validity.

The safety of the children is paramount. By their very nature, the allegations shift the emphasis of the case away from all other issues and onto the accused.

Allegations of abuse of children need to be dealt with immediately by a competent professional: 1) one who fully understands sexual, physical and emotional abuse of children; 2) one who understands family systems; 3) one who understands divorce and custody litigation; 4) one who understands the impact of an abuse accusation on the custody process; 5) one who can assess the truth and relevance of the allegations; 6) one who understands motivation for the allegations; 7) one who can assess the safety and welfare of the children; 8) one who can make recommendations as to the best placement and visitation arrangements for the children.

Allegation of Abuse

Any allegation of abuse must be taken seriously. When a child tells you that he or she has been physically or sexually abused, you may feel uncomfortable. Do not alarm the child, discount what the child is saying or make judgmental comments. If you cannot deal with the problem call a professional for assistance.

- Most children will first hint of an abuse problem and see what will happen. If they feel someone is listening and the child himself won't get in trouble, the child will begin to tell what is going on.
- Encourage the child to speak freely. Make it clear to the child that you understand and believe what he or she is saying.
- Most children want to understand why this happened to them.
- Let the child know that sometimes bad things happen to good people and that the child is not a bad person because this happened to him or her.
- Most children will feel responsible for the abuse and will believe that somehow they caused it to happen.
- Tell the child that he or she is not to blame for the abuse no matter what the abuser said.
- Most children will think the abuse is a form of punishment for real or imagined wrongdoings.
- Let the child know that there is nothing the child could have done bad enough to make this happen.
- The child may feel frightened if the abuser has threatened to harm the child or other family members as punishment for telling the secret.
- Assure the child that he or she did the right thing in telling. Finally, offer the child protection, and promise that you will promptly take steps to see that the abuse stops.
- The child may fear losing his or her family, home, food or support from the abuser.
- The basic survival needs of the child may be jeopardized by the report of abuse compounding the problem for the child and anyone wishing to help the child.
- Children who are close to the abuser may feel fear or guilt about revealing the secret.

- Assure the child that he or she has done the right thing and that you will help resolve the problem.

Preventing False Allegations

If you think the other parent may be capable of falsely accusing you of child abuse or sexual child abuse, you should take steps to prevent the accusation. If you follow these precautions you will find it much easier to answer the allegations and to disprove them.

No one is safe from false accusation concerning opposite sex child, same sex child, biological child, adopted child, step child, grand child, great-grandchild, brother, sister, niece, nephew, cousin and/or any person with whom the child may have contact.

- Have your children meet with a qualified child psychologist several times while things are going well so the professional can get to know your child. Then if there is an accusation of abuse, the professional will have a base-line of behavior from which to question and test the children.
- Only take your child to one qualified doctor for all complaints. The doctor will call in consulting professionals, if necessary.
- Avoid doing all your child's medical visits in the emergency room.
- Always have someone with you when you are in the child's hospital room.
- Don't sleep in the same bed or even same room as your children. Often children will ask to do so if it was the norm during the time they lived with both parents or because the custody situation has caused additional stress or fear in the children. Just don't do it.
- On camping trips have the children sleep in their own sleeping bags.
- Never be naked around your children.
- Avoid having your children naked around you.
- Always sleep in pajamas when your children are staying at your home at night.
- Always have your children sleep in pajamas.
- Once a child can safely go the toilette and bathe alone, don't accompany them into the bathroom.
- Do not bathe or shower with your children.
- If your child needs assistance in the bathroom and is the opposite sex from yours, whenever possible have someone who is the same sex as your child assist them.
- If the children complain of a genital soreness or problem have the assistance of another adult that will remain above suspicion to help you examine the children.
- If you think there has been sexual contact with anyone, don't examine the children yourself. Take the children to the doctor or emergency room.
- If the other parent ever threatens that they will accuse you of child abuse, document the threat.
- If there has been history of abuse or false accusations of abuse, document the information.
- If you are under extreme threat of false allegations of abuse always have a witness around when you are with your children.

If You Are Arrested. Read 'If You Are Arrested' in Chapter 2: You Are The Package.

Dealing with False Allegations

1. If you are accused of abuse, realize just how much trouble you are in.
2. Get an attorney immediately. You can't afford not to have one.
3. Connect with your support system including contacting a non-custodial parents' rights organization, for meetings, resources, support, and understanding
4. Figure just what kind of monetary resources you have. You will need them.
5. Make a list of witnesses and get their written, signed statements.
6. Find the experts in false allegations and start reading the reference material you can find.
7. Look into lie detector and DNA testing.
8. Make reasonable efforts to maintain contact with your children. If you have previously been accused of abuse and found innocent, present that information to the investigator and court immediately. Get copies of medical records, any abuse examination and psychological examinations. If they indicate no abuse, take

them to the judge and ask that contact not be severed. As an alternative, use these documents to request supervised visitation during the investigation.

9. Don't wait for the investigating agency to contact you. Make sure you have the name of the agency and investigator assigned to your case. Set up a meeting so the person will get to know the kind of person you are.

10. Read the chapter "You Are the Package" before you go to the first meeting. Give the investigator a list of names and phone numbers of people you think will vouch for you including your minister or rabbi, employers, friends, relatives, the children's teachers, doctors and people who have observed you with your children and have trusted you with their children.

11. If the findings of the investigation are against you, the attorney can advise you as to the next step you must take. If the findings of the investigation indicate that the accusations were false, your attorney may assist you in exploring the option of filing suit against the other parent. Your judge needs to know if you have been able to prove that you were falsely accused.

12. In some cases the judge will see that the other parent was attempting to alienate your children and move the decision of custody in your favor.

False Allegations Examined

Each state has its own child protective law, which mandates a prompt investigation of each allegation of child abuse, whether physical or sexual.

The agency, without making any findings, usually recommends to the court that all contact between the accused and the children be cut off pending the results of the investigation.

The intention is to protect the children since ongoing contact with a real abuser could intimidate the child's testimony.

Under normal situations allegations of sexual abuse made by children are accepted as true. But it has become common for false accusations to arise in custody disputes.

Occasionally, the court will ask a child psychiatrist to help determine whether the child is telling the truth, or whether it will hurt the child to speak in court about the abuse.

Even when an allegation is made in the context of high conflict litigation, it must be taken very seriously and fully investigated to determine its validity. Each allegation accusing a parent of behavior harmful to the children and their safety is paramount.

By their very nature, the allegations shift the emphasis of the investigation onto the accused. The allegations tend to trivialize all other matters and leave a harmful residue on the accused. Allegations of abuse of a child need to be dealt with immediately by a competent professional who fully understands:

1) emotional, sexual and/or physical abuse of children

2) family systems

3) divorce and custody litigation and the impact of accusations on the system

4) methods for assessing validity of statements

5) scientific knowledge concerning memory, recall, and suggestibility

6) sources of influence on statement contents and allegation

7) psychological approaches and techniques for interviewing witnesses

8) statement validity assessment in criminal and civil proceedings

An expert must assess the truth and relevance of the allegations, the motivation for the allegations, assess the safety and welfare of the children and make recommendations as to the best placement and visitation arrangements for the children.

Special notice should be taken of the time frame of the allegations. If there was no mention of problems or history of abuse for this family or individual prior to the custody dispute, the person making the allegation should be as suspect as the person being scrutinized.

It is psychologically damaging to children to be brainwashed with lies and made to be an active party to false allegations. Children may be willing conspirators if they feel involvement in the conspiracy is the only way to be assured of some security.

Profile Precursors for False Accuser

Although false allegations could be made by almost anyone, there are several indicators or precursors that are often present. Because you did or do care about the other parent, you will probably have more information about them than your attorney or an evaluator. If several of these indicators are present you should make your attorney aware of the facts.

1. If there is a history of abuse in the family. Either to the other parent directly or a sibling of the other parent.
2. If there is a history of rape or accusations of rape.
3. If there is a history of another family member alleging abuse during a custody battle.
4. If there is a history of children being removed from the family due to allegations of, or actual abuse.
5. If the other parent has exhibited unethical behavior in the past.
6. If the other parent is attempting to exercise complete control over their relationship or your relationship with your child.
7. If the other parent's effort to control becomes more pronounced the more you resist.
8. If the other parent feels the court doesn't see things their way.
9. If the other parent is in therapy for being a "survivor of abuse".
10. If the other parent has a history of vilifying anyone that disagrees with them or they dislike.
11. If the other parent filed allegations against any other spouse or ex-spouse.

Post Accusation Accuser Behavior

Parents of children who have been abused are as traumatized by the experience as their children. It is usually difficult to get them to talk about what has happened and it doesn't get any easier for them as time passes. These parents often experience anger, grief, guilt, shame, and a great deal of pain. Conversely, the reactions of a false accuser is more often accusatory and baneful to others. Some of the behaviors exhibited may be:

- Compelled to tell everyone they talk to about the sexual ordeal their children were exposed to.
- Refuse to accept any alternative explanation for the claim of abuse.
- Demand the investigation proceed rapidly and with the results they dictate.
- Willing to add horrific detail and new accusations to encourage action.
- Subject the child to many physical and psychological examinations.
- Takes no responsibility for what they allege happened to the child.

Children Supporting False Accusations

Testimony about sexual child abuse often comes directly from the child. There may be many indications that the accusation is false. Some examples would be:

- The child lacks the demeanor or appearance of a traumatized individual.
- The child changes the identity of the persons involved, the number of incidents and how frightened or hurt the child claims to have been.
- Child's responses sound coached or rehearsed.
- Child's description describes preposterous scenarios.
- Child is comfortable around the accused abuser unless accusing parent is present.
- The child is offering information about the incident to any adult present.
- The child uses language or descriptions inappropriate to the age of the child.

Requesting Supervised Visitation

If you have reason to believe your children are in danger of being abducted or are being abused, it is your responsibility to insist on Supervised Visitation. This process can mean the children are not to leave their primary residence with the other person or that visitation will be at a neutral facility with appointed or hired observers when the children will be in contact with the adult or siblings in question. If children are being abused, they want the abuse to stop, but the children don't necessarily want to lose that parent.

Complying with Supervised Visitation

If an allegation of abuse has been made against you, Supervised Visitation will allow your children to continue to have contact with you while you disprove the charges.

Children already live a supervised life and will not be as sensitive to the supervised contact as you are. Your reaction to the process will indicate to the children what their reaction should be.

1. Don't feel like a criminal. These professionals see more than eighty-five percent of the abuse charges dropped or disproved.

2. Adjust your attitude to turn this into a positive experience. This will allow you to make the best impression on everyone connected with the supervised visitation experience.

3. As soon as you know where the visitation is to take place, visit the facility. Meet the director and ask about rules and solicit suggestions about how to make this easier for your children.

4. On the days you are scheduled for visitation, arrive early and visit with your observer. The positive reports from the visitation liaison person can be a major plus to your case. Never speak negatively about the other parent. Keep notes about when you arrived, who your observer was, when the children arrived, how they looked and acted, what time they were picked up by the other parent and anything the observer said to you.

5. Take messages from and reports about other members of the family your children may not be able to visit with at this time. Make sure the messages are up beat and not offensive to the other parent.

6. Bring activities to do with your children during the visit. Make things you want the children to take home with them. This gives your children a way to stay connected with you when away from you.

Supervised Visitation Options

Whether you have requested supervised visitation or it is being imposed on you, there are several options. Among the poorest is when the subject requiring supervision has control over the place and/or person assigned for the supervision, primarily because additional charges could be made against the subject. Therefore, it is not a good idea if the subject's fiance is supposed to supervise the visitation in the subject's home. A good option would be at the child's day-care or school during regular hours. The best option would be to have the supervised visitations take place at an established contact and exchange facility. You may be able to locate one in your area by contacting the Supervised Visitation Network (218) 327-6735, http://www.SVNetwork.org

Abduction-Resistant Children

Children want to be responsible for themselves from a very early age. Nothing makes children abduction proof. In the event of an abduction, there may be opportunities for the children to assist the rescue.

You can help your children learn basic information, the foundation of survival. Make knowing this information a game for younger (three to seven years old) children and a requirement for older children.

Disproving False Accusations

Many steps are necessary to prove you are innocent of abusing your children. Don't delay in getting started. Facts, such as: there were never any concerns or reports of abuse before the custody action and that the other parent allowed you to take the children after the abuse was reported are important. Get the best professional and legal assistance you can find.

Sue for False Accusations

Most people don't want and can't afford a second law suit. If you have exhausted all other avenues of action to stop the false accusations you may wish to consider filing a lawsuit to stop this abuse. In most cases the attorney you have hired for the custody case will not file the new suit.

There are several legal tests that must be met and several personal questions you must ponder before you consider a tort suit for defamation:

1. Has the accuser diminished your reputation with accusations? There is very little you can do about someone using the truth against you. However, if the accusation can be proven to be false and vicious enough, you may have a case for slander, libel, invasion of privacy, or infliction of emotional distress.

2. If the false accusation was made verbally, was it heard by someone other than yourself? It is not necessary that the other person(s) believe the accusation, only that they heard it and that they knew the accusation referred to you.

3. If the false accusation is made in writing, was it seen by someone other than yourself? It is not necessary that the other person(s) believe the accusation, only that they heard it and that they knew the accusation referred to you.

4. Can you and your children and your family afford (the money, time, emotional trauma) of additional litigation at this time?

5. Is there another less taxing way to make the offending party stop this behavior?

6. If you do win, is there anything you want (such as money) and can get in addition to the cessation of the behavior? Is there really any opportunity to collect the judgment if you win?

7. Will you have to hire an additional attorney or will your custody attorney pursue this as a separate action on your behalf?

Types of Supervised Visitation

Supervised visitation is an international intervention strategy that enables children to continue, establish and/or re-establish a relationship with a parent.

This contact may be advantageous for the child with the understanding that the parent it is thought or known to be, or has been accused of being, a physical or emotional risk to a child and from whom the child is separated. Parents who utilize the methodology of supervised visitation to visit their children are either court ordered to do so or cooperate with this interactive process as recommended by counsel. There are a number of options available to meet the age of the children, distance between parent and child, the amount of risk the child faces in visiting with the parent and the amount of hostility between the parents. The options include:

Telephonic monitoring

Neutrally supportive supervision

Internet monitoring

Actively supportive or facilitated

Monitored exchange/changeover

Therapeutic supervision

Monitored visitation

Protective supervision

Observed visitation

Educative supervision

On-site supervision

Off-site supervision

Supervised Visitation Staff

Supervised visitation is done by clinically trained professionals, child care professionals, volunteers, law enforcement professionals, clergy, private service providers. These people work in agency-based, court-based or private practice organizations.

Reason for Referral

There are many reasons for a referral for supervised visitation including:

- Allegations of access denial.
- Unresolved conflict between parents.
- Lengthy separation of child and parent.
- No previous relationship between and child.
- History of domestic violence.
- Abduction concerns.
- History of mental health problems.
- History of substance abuse.
- Concerns about parenting skills.
- Concerns about emotional or physical abuse of the children.

Reporting to the Court

Each court will have it's own expectations or standard reporting procedures. Reporting procedures should specifically address:

- Frequency of reports: either immediately upon incident, upon request from the court or other agency, by subpoena or periodically.
- Reporting method: written, video or verbal.
- Report format may be one or a combination of the following:

1. DETAILED OBSERVATION: Offers a comprehensive account of events that took place between the parents and between the parent and children. Providers may use a checklist during the visit, which records the level of adherence to visitation arrangements by the parents. For example: compliance with scheduling and program rules. Providers may also wish to include an objective account of all behaviors and actions observed between the parent and child as they occur.

2. SUMMARY: These reports provide an overview of the interaction that took place between the parents and the parent and child during a supervised visit. The report must be factual, objective and absent of any professional recommendation. Unlike the detailed observation report, the summary report does not contain a comprehensive list of all behaviors observed between the parent and children. Instead this report is meant to provide the court with a brief synopsis of the visitation.

3. INCIDENT: Incident reports provide a detailed account of potentially harmful behavior exhibited by a parent, either towards the children, other parent, or program staff, during the supervised visit. Typically the provider observes a behavior or action from the parent that she/he perceives as an indication for alarm and will immediately submit a detailed account of the parent's behavior, how the incident occurred, and the reaction of the children. Once again, this is strictly a factual account and does not offer an opinion as to what course of action should be sought regarding this incident.

4. EVALUATIVE: Evaluative reports provide an assessment that offers professional opinions and recommendations as the observed contact between the parent and children. It is generally inappropriate for the provider to offer reports that express professional opinions based upon observations. In cases of reunification, programs may be requested by the court to make future visitation recommendations. However, without prior approval from the judge, a program should not offer a report that provides advice or expresses opinions, specifically, an opinion about the appropriate future course of access between a parent and a child who have been supervised by a program.

Requesting Supervised Visitation

For the other Parent

If you have reason to believe that your children are in danger of being abducted or are being abused, it is your responsibility to insist on supervised visitation. This process can mean the children are not to leave the primary residence with any person.

In extremely hostile situations, visitation will be at a neutral facility with appointed or hired observers when the children will be in contact with the adult or siblings in question.

Supervised visitation will allow your children to continue to have contact with a person the children care about while the charges are developed or disproved.

Your children already live a supervised life and will not be as sensitive to the supervised contact as the adult may be. Your reaction to the process will indicate to the children what their reaction should be.

Supervised Visitation for Yourself

Complying with Supervised Visitation

If an allegation of abuse has been made against you, supervised visitation will allow your children to continue to have contact with you while you disprove the charges. If you have requested visitation for yourself, it will be easier to comply than if it has been imposed upon you. Supervised visitation is much better for the children than no visitation.

1. Don't feel like a criminal. These professionals see more than 85% of the abuse charges dropped or disproved.

2. Adjust your attitude to turn this into a positive experience. This will allow you to make the

best impression on everyone connected with the supervised visitation experience.

3. As soon as you know where the visitation is to take place, visit the facility. Meet the director and ask about rules and solicit suggestions about how to make this easier for your children.

4. On the days you are scheduled for visitation, arrive early and visit with your observer. The positive reports from the visitation liaison person can be a major plus to your case. Never speak negatively about the other parent. Keep notes about when you arrived, who your observer was, when the children arrived, how they looked and acted, what time they were picked up by the other parent and anything the observer said to you.

5. Take messages from and reports about other members of the family that your children may not be able to visit with at this time. Make sure the messages are upbeat and not offensive to the other parent.

6. Bring activities to do with your children during the visit. Make things you want the children to take home with them. This gives your children a way to stay connected with you when away from you.

In some jurisdictions you will not be allowed any contact with your child if there is any indication that the child may be in danger in your company.

Child in Danger

If the lives of your children are in serious danger, start with the legal steps available to you. Make the problem your children and you are having with abuse a very public one. Don't be embarrassed. You are not responsible for the actions of another person who is abusive. You are responsible for how you respond to that abuse. If you see any indication of abuse, seek medical treatment and get copies of all documents.

- File a complaint by making out a police report; get copies of all documents.
- Take photos of bruises, abrasions or broken bones with time and date.
- Document each incident in your contact log.
- Send your attorney an incident report followed by a telephone call.

If the injuries are the result of normal childhood activities, the hospital or doctor will tell you so. It is better to know for sure, and perhaps feel foolish about your fears, than to take the chance you might be letting your children live in an abusive situation.

Your children depend on you to provide for their physical and emotional safety, as well as their peace of mind. Make sure their doctor, the local police, Child Protective Services, neighbors, teachers, principals, relatives, your church, friends and media (if you can work it out) know what is happening.

It may be difficult for others to believe that your child is facing serious danger or abuse if you have done a good job of covering for the abuser for many years. With proof, you can get a judge to issue a restraining order or order for protection. Getting the child out of the abusive environment through shelters and foster homes is less desirable. If this is the only choice available, take it, but be aware that you may not have much control over how things are handled.

Violence Lethality Assessment

Research has found that there are certain factors that are important in assessing the lethality potential in a particular situation. However, predicting lethality is difficult, as all serious battering relationships can be unpredictable and have the potential to flare up quickly. Nonetheless, the reported presence of some of these factors can be used to assist you in making judgments about the level of protection necessary at any particular moment:

Increased violent episodes
Severity of violence is escalating
Intoxication and drug abuse
Threats to harm the children
Forced or threatened sex acts
Suicide threats or attempts
Access to weapons
Psychiatric impairment of the victim or abuser
Proximity of victim and abuser
Abuser's need for control of contact around children
Current life stress
Previous criminal history
Presence of new relationship
Defiance of court orders or judicial system

Police

The information you have heard that a person must be missing for seventy-two hours before you can get the police to take a report and start looking for them does not apply to missing minors. So if your children are missing, call the police right away. The police will ask if you have called the other parent to see if your children are there or if you have called the police, friends, former neighbors, people with the church or school where the other parent lives. In any other instance of requiring assistance, before you call the police read Chapter 3: Prepare For Both, as it pertains to the police. If you have been involved in an incident and the police were called, a police report should have been filled out. In most states, you just go to the agency in the city you want to get the police report from and pay the fee. You will need the name of one of the persons involved and the date of the incident.

If the child is found it is important to notify the police immediately.

If you file a missing or kidnapped child report and it is discovered that you did know where the child was, you can be charged with filing a false report. The District Attorney can ask for the maximum penalty, which can be substantial fine and jail time if you are found guilty.

Violent Patterns Won't Change

As you have seen in the past, you will not get any lasting relief from the threats and abuse against you, your child, your family or friends, even if you do what the abusive person says to do. Abusers abuse. You cannot stop the abuser from following through on threats against others by complying with demands. If there is a chance that your child will be hurt or killed, you must leave immediately. Inform anyone else the abuser has told you he or she will harm. Inform your attorney and the police.

Whatever is going to happen, is going to happen. So take action immediately. If there is a chance that your child will be hurt or killed, it is your responsibility to remove your child from that danger immediately.

If You are Forced to Leave

If there is no custody order limiting transport of your children, then you must take them away for their welfare:

1. Talk to your attorney about your intentions. If you feel you must relocate your children, make sure your reasons are valid. If you can prove the children were in imminent danger and/or there is a record of abuse, you will have a better chance of resisting law enforcement intervention. See if your attorney can get some legal documents in place to protect you and your position.

2. Have your attorney notify the other parent as quickly as possible that the child is with you and is well.

3. Your attorney's office may be used as the place for the other parent to call when the other parent needs you to call or if the other parent wants to speak to the children. Ask your attorney to send a next-day letter by certified mail, notifying the other parent of a contact address and telephone number to put his or her mind at ease about the children's well-being.

4. Have your attorney advise the FBI that your children have not been kidnapped.

5. Have your attorney start the legal process that will keep you and your children safe.

Kidnapping

Abduction, whether committed by a stranger or a parent, is one of the most vicious of all crimes. If your child is taken by strangers, there are county, state, federal and international agencies that may assist you. Kidnapping by a parent is an entirely different matter.

In some states, the initial divorce filing produces a mandatory preliminary injunction, which orders that neither parent remove the children from the jurisdiction, pending the final decree of divorce.

In most states, kidnapping a child in violation of a custody order is a felony.

If you are considering kidnapping, do not do it. It can damage your chances for custody and visitation forever.

Prevention

1. Obtain legal custody of your children **or** establish your legal right to ongoing, regularly scheduled access to them. Specify in the

custody order the exact times and locations for visitation.

2. Ask for special prevention provisions in the custody decree. Restrict movement of the children out of state without your written permission. Request specific penalties for interference with access or return of the children, such as permanent loss of contact with the children or posting a bond payable to the injured parent.

3. File the custody decree in the other parent's home county. Use counseling or mediation to resolve problems.

4. Notify schools, day care centers, and baby-sitters of custody orders by giving them certified copies. Give them specific information, in writing, about who and when and how other people may have access to or pick up your children.

5. Get a passport issued for your children and keep it in a safe place.

6. Notify the U.S. Department of State and the U.S. Passport Office that your children are not to leave the country without your written consent.

7. Teach your children to use pay phones, call collect, call 911, e-mail and cellular telephone.

8. Keep current data sheets on the other parent and anyone with whom the other parent associates.

9. Teach them to be able to identify in which state they live.

10. Help them learn your phone numbers and those of other family members they may need to contact.

Profile of the Abductor

The following information is provided by the Royal Canadian Mounted Police and may be used to construct an overall profile of a parental abduction:

- The mother, father or a caregiver that has bonded to the child, is likely to abduct the child.
- Mothers tend to abduct their children after a court order is made. Fathers tend to abduct their child before a court order.
- Mothers who abduct their children tend to keep them for a longer time than fathers who abduct.
- The age range for abducting parents is 28 to 40 years.
- Fathers are usually employed while the mothers are more likely to be unemployed.
- Socio-economic factors vary from case to case.
- Few studies have identified a psychological or sociological profile of the abducting parent.
- The majority of children are between three and seven years of age.
- Children taken out of the country tend to be older (i.e., over the age of eight years).
- Both male and female children are equally likely to be abducted.
- Children tend to be taken from the home. They are less likely to be taken from another residence or from a school yard.
- Most searching parents report the abduction of the child to the police on the day it occurred.
- There is, however, a large proportion of searching parents who delay in reporting the incident.
- Communication usually occurs between the searching parent and the abductor.
- The majority of parental abductions are short-term and resolved within seven days.
- Various modes of transportation are used to move the child.
- Children tend to be taken during weekends or summer or winter holidays.
- The parent abducting the child tends not to use physical force.

** Accomplices are used in less than half the cases. They are usually family members or current partners.

Sexual and physical abuse occurs in a small percentage of the cases. Studies on this issue must be interpreted with extreme caution.

Kidnapping Warning Signals

Other than fear for the children's well-being, the most common emotions that precipitate parental kidnapping are hopelessness and anger. A parent who is convinced there is no hope of staying involved in the lives of the children may feel there is nothing to lose by disappearing with the children.

Many parents who experience the trauma of kidnapping by the other parent tell us they should have seen the warning signs. In retrospect there were many, but they didn't seem important because the abandoned parent wasn't paying attention. It is difficult to build a trusting relationship with the other parent as it concerns the child and still remain vigilant against kidnapping.

There may be anger with the decision the court has made or is certain to make or anger with the other parent for attempting to build a new life without including the angry parent. In these cases, the kidnapping is done to hurt the other parent rather than for a desire to care for the children.

Any direct threat or suggestion of kidnapping should be taken seriously. Parents should always be alert to stranger and acquaintance as well as parental abduction. Many of the warning signals will be present in any custody case, but if more signals are active than inactive, there is definitely a problem.

Be especially alert if the other parent has always been or has become:

[] irresponsible
[] easily angered
[] delusional
[] depressed
[] impulsive
[] erratic or disorganized
[] hostile or abusive
[] disruptive or accusatory
[] vengeful
[] paranoid
[] apathetic or withdrawn
[] subject to hearing voices
[] exhibits self-destructive behavior
[] dependent on alcohol
[] seems beaten and without hope
[] neglectful of others in their care
[] dependent on prescription or illegal drugs
[] new or increased problems of the law
[] unable to behave properly in social settings
[] contact with family or friends in another country
[] poor or deteriorating record of employment
[] employed in a job that encourages or facilitates relocation

The insidious part of this problem is that you must be aware of any drastic or sudden change in the attitude or behavior of the other parent. If you have been dealing with a reasonable person and can see that he or she is becoming erratic and unreasonable, you must become more alert to the threat of kidnapping. Conversely, if you have been dealing with an erratic and unreasonable person and his or her behavior has suddenly become reasonable and agreeable, you must also watch for the threat of kidnapping.

Has Your Child Been Kidnapped?

1. Make a careful search of your home and property and check with child's friends and favorite play areas.

2. Call all neighbors, friends and relatives.

3. Prepare a full description of your child including birthmarks, scars or other identifying marks, a recent photo, description of child's clothing worn that day, medical problems if any, any recent problems at home or school, with an announcement about a possible abduction by spouse.

4. Possible runaway; are clothes or prized possessions missing?

First, you must decide if your child has been kidnapped. If the other parent has not returned the child at the conclusion of a regular visit or has informed you that he or she has no intention of returning the child, the other parent may feel the action taken is to protect the child from some real or imagined danger. If this is the case, the opposition will probably tell you or someone why he or she feels the child cannot be returned.

Normally, when the perpetrator is informed of the repercussions, legal remedies being taken, others that are available, and the possible consequences if the child is not promptly returned, the opposition returns the child immediately. This may be interpreted by the court as parental interference. **If you determine that the child has been kidnapped, do not let your emotional state of mind or panic allow you to do anything that later could be considered stupid or illegal.**

So far, you have not broken the law; the opposition has. Settle down and catch your breath. Regardless of how much pain you are in right now, this may be the best thing that has happened for your case. If you have done nothing to put your child in danger, and there is no record of abuse, there is no excuse for this kidnapping.

It will put the kidnapper in a very bad light. How you respond will determine how this terrible situation will be examined.

Emotions When Kidnapping Occurs

If your child has been kidnapped, there are several emotions you may experience. Anticipate fear, panic, anxiety and periods of morbid depression. Expect the people you love and count on to say all the wrong things. Without meaning to, they will increase your fear and anticipation of horrible consequences. It is normal to want to isolate yourself in your pain and fear, but it is not healthy. Make an effort to not abandon remaining children or family members.

Eliminate discussions about whose fault the abduction was. The only culprit is the kidnapper. Contact support groups for guidance and counseling. Members of these organizations can help you cope with the roller coaster of emotions.

Abduction Retrieval Questionnaire

Complete this questionnaire. It is designed to provide details as easily as possible.

1. Details of the Applicant(s)

Mother [X] Father [ ] Grandmother [ ] Grandfather [ ] Other ____________________ [ ]

If two people with legal status (such as mother and father or father and grandmother) are filling out this questionnaire, include information for both.

First, Middle and Last name *Susan Irene Jeferies*

Date and Place of Birth *Watertown, NY April 5, 1972*

County, City, State and Country of Residence *Holland County, City of Chester, IN, USA*

Nationality (ies) *American of Dutch decent*

Occupation *Secretary in a law office*

Address at which the applicant can be contacted *102 West Weld, Chester, IN*

Home Telephone: *(555)442-1212*

Work Telephone: *(555) 422-1212*

Name of Attorney (if any) *Jackson DeMichaels*

Name of Firm *Bieter and DeMichaels*

Address of Attorney *22 Tree Line Court, Chester, IN*

Telephone: *(555) 422-1212*Fax: *(555) 466-1212*e-mail: *demichaels?@aol.com*

Details of the Remedy Required by the Applicant

Please check appropriate situation

Enforcement of rights of Custody and return of child(ren) *[X]*

Enforcement of rights of access [ ]

2. Details of Child(ren)

Continue on separate page if necessary

First, Middle, Last, Age, Date, and Place of Birth

1. *Lisa Ann Jeferies 8 years old, December 11, 1992*

2. *Justin David Jeferies 6 years old, November 16, 1994*

3. Country of residence (immediately before removal)

   USA

4. Passport or identity Card if child holds a separate passport (if not indicate whether child is included on parent's passport)

   1. Lisa, *None that I knew of.*

   2. Justin, *None that I knew of.*

5. Nationality (ies)

   1. Lisa, *American of Dutch decent on mother's side and German decent on father's side.*

   2. Justin, *American of Dutch decent on mother's side and German decent on father's side.*

6. Description(s) (attach a recent photograph)

   1. *Lisa, 51" tall, 70lbs, blue eyes, straight blond hair to her waist,*

   2. *Justin, 46" tall, 58lbs, blue eyes with glasses, curly blond hair.*

7. Details of Missing Parent or Person you believe has the child (ren)

Mother [ ] Father [X] Grandmother [ ] Grandfather [ ] Other ____________________ [ ]

First, Middle and Last Name *David Justin Jeffrey*

Date and place of birth *Upper Sanduskey January 23, 1970*

Nationality *American of German decent*

Occupation *Computer programmer*

Residence *Unknown*

Passport or Identity Card No. *None that I knew of.*

Relationship to child(ren) *Father*

Description (attach photo if available) *6'2" tall, 180lbs, blond hair cut business length, blue eyes*

Last known address(es) (in the country in which this person now resides) *74 Towne, Troy, IL USA*

8. Place Where The Child(ren) Is (Are) Thought To Be

   Unknown

9. Details of other persons where the child(ren) may have been taken who might be able to supply additional information on the whereabouts of the child(ren) or taker of the child(ren).

David's mother, Cindy Jeferies 333 Desert Park Trail, Tucson, AZ (602) 555-1212 Says she hasn't heard from him since the children disappeared. But she assures me that he loves them and is taking proper care of them.

David's older sister, Judy Davidson 11237 Sky Line Drive, Park City UT (I don't have her phone number) Hates me and wouldn't talk to me if I did have her number.

David's younger sister, Dawn Jeferies 12 North Hoyden Road apt 18, Tempe AZ (602) 555-2121 She hasn't seen David, but thinks he is with family.

10. Brief Details of the Time, Date, Place and Circumstances of the Removal of the Child(ren).

December 26, 1999 David picked the children up for their New Years visit. The children called me New Years Eve to wish me a happy new year and we all said bye until we would see each other again January 6, 2000. David did not bring them home at dinner time as he usually did and the cell phone number I had for him was disconnected. I haven't seen or heard from any of them since.

11. Details of Court Proceedings that have Taken Place or are Taking Place (such as Divorce, Child Custody, Contact). Attach copies of the final decision in each matter.

We were divorced June 10, 1998. David asked for joint custody. That's what the court awarded, but assigned me as the custodial parent and he had visitation each Wednesday night overnight and the first, third and fifth weekend of each month. David was angry because he thought joint custody meant he would have the children fifty percent of the time. He asked me to change the arrangement to half time with me and half time with him. We tried alternating a week at each home for four months. The children were exhausted and they were missing school. I insisted we go back to the court-ordered visitation. He instituted suit to make the fifty-fifty custody. After a year of legal wrangling, the court found against him and he had to pay his attorney and mine. He was still mad about that when he disappeared with the children.

12. Other Relevant Matters

    None

13. Arrangements for the Return of the Child(ren)

Please indicate whether the applicant is prepared to travel to the state or country to which the children have been taken, both to attend the court hearing if necessary, and to collect the child(ren) should the application be successful or indicate any other person who could do so on their behalf.

I will fly or drive to pick up the children, or forward funds to whomever or wherever necessary. I will do whatever is necessary.

...*Susan Irene Jeferies*.....*January 11, 2000*....
Signature of applicant or their attorney and Date

Legal Steps to Get Your Child Back

It is time to find your child and make the right moves to have your child returned to you ---- maybe forever.

The parent who defies a court order and leaves the state with a child may never be trusted by the legal system again. As the victimized parent, you will bear the responsibility for gathering information, pursuing leads and establishing the location of an absconding parent. This includes making contact with friends and family of the perpetrator. You will be in a better position than anyone else to understand the information as you collect it.

Everything must be done in order as you and your attorney enlist the assistance of law enforcement agencies. Your attorney can help keep you legal as you prepare the package for the authorities. Normally, you should have your attorney start civil proceedings to enforce the custody order to secure return of your child.

At the same time, you should encourage criminal proceedings by the state prosecutor to be started. You are pushing to get your child back. The state's interest is to protect the integrity of its judicial determinations. The state does not care how you feel about their case. Therefore, you cannot rely on the criminal process to protect your custody rights. The state's case against the other parent will not necessarily result in the automatic return of your child to you. The state the child was taken to now may become involved, if the offending parent resists your efforts. Contact the "National Center for Missing and Exploited Children" and request their book titled, "Family Abduction," How to Prevent Abduction and What to Do If Your Child Is Abducted.

Assemble all documentation of court decrees and custody orders to determine jurisdiction. The non-custodial parent uses the uniform Child Custody Jurisdiction Act to determine jurisdiction to petition for custody in the local family court.

1. Ask the local police what documentation they require to issue a warrant for the arrest of the kidnapping parent. Present that documentation and get a copy of the warrant. Get copies of any prior warrants against the abducting parent.

2. Ask the police officials to submit information about the missing child and abducting parent to the National Crime Information Center computer.

3. Contact the state prosecutor or district attorney to request the U.S. attorneys to issue a federal Unauthorized Flight to Avoid Prosecution (UFAP) arrest warrant.

4. Take the UFAP to the FBI and ask them to assist in the investigation and to use the services of the Federal Parent Locator Service.

5. Ask the FBI to request the U.S. Attorney's Office to revoke the passport of the kidnapper.

6. Call the National Center for Missing and Exploited Children (800) 843-5678 and register your child.

7. Contact Medical Network for Missing Children, telephone (914) 967-6854 Fax (914) 337-4006

8. File a request with your State Parent Locator System, requesting the location of the abducting parent.

9. Have your attorney investigate the possibility of civil remedies of a tort suit against the kidnapper and those who assisted in the abduction. This will often exert enough pressure so that to avoid prosecution, the kidnapper's friends or family members will assist you in getting the safe return of your child.

10. Give your attorney copies of Data Sheets on the abducting parent, family members and friends who may know of the other parent's whereabouts.

11. Contact your local newspaper, television and radio stations to bring your story public attention and gain community support.

12. Full Faith and Credit means that judges must recognize and enforce valid decrees and judgments issued by courts in other states. This is not automatic. The person seeking the enforcement must take the legal steps required by the state the person is seeking assistance from. "Comity" is a term meaning other countries recognize United States custody orders and the United States recognizing theirs.

Even if the other parent is found guilty, he or she does not automatically lose visitation rights. Only a judge's decision can change the original court order.

People Trail or the Family Tree

Often it is easier to locate family members of the other parent than it is to locate the other parent. This is primarily because the family members are not attempting to hide from you. A visit to the courthouse in the city in which these people live may produce a great deal of information about them that is in common with the person for which you are looking.

If you think the person is hiding your children with relatives, but you have no idea of who or where the relatives are, you might consider climbing their family tree. The family tree offers much more than history. It can identify family members you were not aware existed. Halbert's Family Heritage Publishing publishes informative, useful family heritage reference books for some family names. Data is researched in America and eleven different countries, and names and addresses are printed in alphabetical order by state, province or county. If the family name you are researching is available, the cost per family name is under $50.00.

Experts in this field are located at the Family History Library of The Church of Jesus Christ of Latter-Day Saints. People there can tell you how to get a chart to start the process.

Once you have filled in as much of a chart as possible and presented it along with copies of pertinent documents, such as birth certificates and marriage licenses, the experts can give you an estimate of the time and cost involved to add information to the chart. On the Internet and World Wide Web, there are huge groups of amateur and professional genealogists willing and able to assist in putting together a family tree.

The Paper Trail

We can change where we are, but we cannot change what we are. When it becomes evident that you must find someone, there are several valid trails to follow. Whether you do the work yourself or hire a private investigator, there is still a great deal of information you must assemble. Start by filling out a Data Sheet and consider the avenues of information the following list may bring to mind. Does the opposition have or do any of these traceable things?

VA benefits

Subscription to magazines

License vehicles

Children's school records transferred

Fly an airplane

Parent's school records transferred

Voter Registration

Uses A Prescription Medicine

Pet licensing

Get Loans for Vehicles or Property

Has a Web Page

Shows or Breeds Animals

Uses the Internet

Life-long member of anything

Files income taxes

Appears in criminal or civil court

Uses credit cards

Membership in book or other clubs

Works union

Has Been a Litigant In Lawsuits

Has a telephone

Owns or owned a business

E-mail address

Uses cellular phones

Hunting or fishing license

Attends worship services

Buys from catalogues

Works in a specific trade

Buys products online

Change of address to postal service

Purchases and uses travelers checks

Western Union transfer of money

Participates in sports bowling, golf

Mailing list of favorite charities

Uses the Public Library

Roadside auto or travel club

Medication

Awaiting an inheritance

Corporate papers

Has been listed in telephone books

Filed business ownership

Cable television subscriber

Professional license

Professional registration

Frequent flyer club

Involved in an ongoing lawsuit

Lottery winnings

News or chat groups on the Internet

Church membership roster

Prescription eye glasses/ contact lenses

Sports, hobbies

Competitive events

Compile yearly or lifetime scores

Places to Look

Local telephone book

Criss-cross directory

National telephone book

Court house

Civil and criminal records

Corporation commission filings

Motor vehicle registration

Computer data bases

Websites

Class Reunions

Money

One of the most common mistakes made by people attempting to disappear is that they are not willing to give up everything. They think they can give up the inconvenient things (like you) in their lives and keep the parts that help make them comfortable and that are convenient. Money in the form of income is one of the easiest ways to track someone who does not wish to be located.

Rents or payments on property owned
Allowances
Monies from trust accounts
Student loans
Social security
Disability payments
Military payments or death benefits
Stock, bonds, dividends
Retirement Payouts
Oil, water and gas leases
Government benefits for children
AFDC and food stamps
Payments from an inheritance
Lottery winning in payments

Chapter 17: Discovery / Deposition

Goal of Discovery

Discovery should be undertaken with the following goals in mind: marshalling the facts necessary to prepare for trial; confirming the initial good faith judgment that suit is warranted; narrowing and clarifying the issues; refining the theory and presentation of the case; preview the trial demeanor of witnesses and counsel; avoiding surprise at trial; and the preservation of evidence.

The only general limitation imposed on the admissibility of evidence is that it be relevant; that is, the evidence must be rationally related to the issues in the case in that it tends to prove or disprove the issues which have to be decided.

Relevance is thus the fundamental limitation on discovery. Further, evidence can be relevant and inadmissible if it is prejudicial, misleading, or confusing.L. Hampton, L. Moskowitz, S. Moskowitz, & F. Silberberg, "Discovery," Family Law Litigation Guide with Forms (Matthew Bender 1993) (discussion of general purposes of discovery).

Feast or Famine

Answering discovery seems to be handled in a variety of ways. A few attorneys produce what is requested in the proper time. Some attorneys give you as little information as possible and only after many requests. Others hide the trees in the forest. Each request is met with boxes and boxes of information that the receiving attorney must spend hundreds of hours and thousands of the client's dollars to sift through. Often the documents for one case will be stacked half way up the wall in the attorney's office.

Requesting discovery is managed just as differently. Some attorneys make little or no effort at discovery, while others are masters of plundering private papers using the legal process.

Surprise and Ambush

This is how Perry Mason got all the bad guys to confess: Good Ol' Perry would drop some heavy information on them and catch them by surprise. In shock, the bad guys would spill the beans right there on the witness stand in front of everybody.

In 1937, the Federal Rules of Civil Procedure required "Pretrial Discovery."

This process uses documents as tools to make demands for information. Most states have accepted this practice in custody cases. Discovery allows both sides to see what the other is bringing to court. Keep in mind that, the standard for introduction into evidence is stricter than that for discoverable material. You may have to prove the information is valid even if you obtained it in discovery, depending on your state's laws on procedure or evidence.

I Have to Tell Them What?

Being aware of the process and its tools will help you understand that during discovery, if requested, you must deliver a great deal of information you consider private. Nothing makes delivering information to the opposition easy.

Knowing you must comply does eliminate the shock and may affect how you compile and store information that may be requested. Failure to produce properly requested data may prejudice the court against your case and cause sanctions to be requested, and possibly levied, against you. It is dangerous to destroy records that may be requested by the court. Most financial, criminal and medical records can be reconstructed in several ways. Your attorney will advise you as to how to respond when a request for documents and evidence arrives.

Properly used, these legal tools eliminate the chance of your being victimized by "Surprise and Ambush."

Conversely, your attorney will inform you of which of the following processes will serve you best in gathering information from the opposition.
Some of the processes used to extract information are:

Interrogatories

Request for Production and Inspection

Deposition

Request for Admission

Fruit of the Poisonous Tree

Fruit of the Poisonous Tree is a term used in criminal law that says, since the evidence was unlawfully obtained, it bears the "taint" of that illegality. Even though your case is in Family Court, most of the attorneys and judges have worked in Criminal Court and tainted evidence is not something they want to see. Evidence you want to present in court could be discounted or disqualified if the judge doesn't like the way it was gathered. Ultimately, the court will decide if you knowingly received or should have known something was illegally obtained. If you or your attorney are concerned with how some information was obtained, you may wish to obtain it from a more "acceptable" source and document that source. Any and all information obtained as a result of the tainted evidence is inadmissible.

Interrogatory

This act of seeking truth or knowledge about something, a formal request on paper submitted from one side to the opposition to request specific, listed information is an Interrogatory. Second and Third Interrogatories are commonly requested. Failure to comply can cause you to be cited by the court or could even cost you your case. They may ask anything remotely connected with the children. As an example you can ask for the names and social security numbers of anyone taking care of or living in the house with the children.

Objecting in Interrogatory

Request for information is not necessarily an assurance that it is proper for them to ask for or that you tare required to produce the information. Rather than immediately produce the requested information you can object to the request with a statement.

Examples:

#1. Respondent objects to this Request since it seeks to obtain information, which is protected from discovery by the attorney/client, attorney work-product, investigative and consulting expert privileges. Subject to the foregoing objections, respondent will make responsive documents available for inspection and copying to Movant's attorney or someone acting on his/her behalf at a mutually agreeable time and place.

#2. Respondent objects to this Request since it is overbroad, harassing and practically impossible to fully and completely answer as phrased. Subject to the foregoing objections, respondent will make responsive documents available for inspection and copying to Movant's attorney or someone acting on his/her behalf at a mutually agreeable time and place.

#3. Respondent objects since the information

required is beyond the scope of discovery in a Request pursuant to Rule 168 and other applicable rules of the Texas Rules of Civil Procedure.
Subject to the foregoing objections, respondent will make responsive documents available for inspection and copying to Movant's attorney or someone acting on his/her behalf at a mutually agreeable time and place.

#4. Respondent objects that this is repetitious and unduly burdensome and harassing. Subject to the foregoing objections, respondent will make responsive documents available for inspection and copying to Movant's attorney or someone acting on his/her behalf at a mutually agreeable time and place.

#5. Respondent objects to this Request on the grounds that it requests information that is irrelevant and immaterial and not calculated to lead to the discovery of admissible evidence. Respondent further objects since this Request is intended to merely harass and annoy this respondent, and constitutes an invasion of his/her personal, constitutional and property rights. Subject to the foregoing objections, respondent will make responsive documents available for inspection and copying to Movant's attorney or someone acting on his/her behalf at a mutually agreeable time and place.

The last line in each objection is letting the court know that, if the court rules that the information must be made available, you are willing to comply.

Production and Inspection

The production of documents may be required at any stage of the custody process. The documents listed here may surprise and show you that one of the things court can do is make your private life public. Although some of these documents can be protected, you will be and can be required to produce them. Specific documents either side may request are:

Address books & appointment books
Answering machine tapes
Banking records
Calendars, personal, kitchen, business
Checking, savings & credit card accounts
Computer print-outs
Computer Hard Drives
Criminal records
Court orders
Credit card applications
Credit card statements and receipts
Detective reports
Diaries or journals, business or personal
Drug prescriptions
Employment records
Expense account records
Financial statements
Home videos & photos
Income statements
Life insurance applications and policies
Loan applications and payment records
Medical records, including therapists
Orders for protection
Photo Graphs
Previous civil and criminal cases
Restraining orders
Receipts for products and services
School records, children's and adult's
tape-recorded conversations
Tax records
Telephone records

Documents and Records

It is important to distinguish between documents and records. A document is a physical item that is usually a written, typed or printed documents such as letters, memos, reports, receipts, invoices, faxes, pictures, and maps. These items can be uniquely identified by placing identifying stamps, labels, or bar codes in obvious locations on the items.

A record is usually an item in a database with a unique number identifier and date that can be indexed. By categorizing the item important characteristics and contents of the document are easily identified. If you assign each item an index number and description important information can be found easily; and yours won't need to repeatedly examine each document individually. They need only search the indexed records.

Records can reflect individual people, specific events, or whatever else is determined to be meaningful to a case. Records can be small parts of documents, individual documents or collections of documents For example, an individual document may be made up of parts of several documents such as a deposition.

Documents

You must be able to answer the following questions in order to establish the foundation for a document to be admitted into evidence:

- Where did you get this document?
- Are you familiar with the signature of Miss Jacobs (the person who signed letter)?
- How are you familiar with Mr. Smith's signature?
- When shown this document, do you recognize the signature at the bottom of this letter?
- Whose signature is it?

Tape-recorded Conversations

If you are submitting legally recorded conversations as evidence, you should be able to answer the following questions in order to establish the foundation for tape recordings to the event they need to be admitted into evidence:

- Who recorded this tape?
- Where was it recorded?
- Have you heard this recording before this time?
- What was the purpose of the recording?
- Are you familiar with the people whose voices are on the recording?
- Have you had the opportunity to hear the voice of Mr. X before?
- How many times have you heard his voice?
- Have you had the opportunity to hear the voice of Mr. Y before?
- How many times have you heard his voice?
- Tell us how you are familiar with Mr. X's voice?
- Do you recognize the first voice to speak?
- To whom does the voice belong?
- Do you recognize the second voice to speak?
- To whom does the voice belong?

Confidentiality - Documentation

Once any of this information is entered into the case and is filed with the court, it becomes public record. Public records may be viewed by anyone who knows where to find them and wishes to inspect or copy them. Therefore, old court cases can be a bountiful source of information.

Photographs and Video Tapes

If you are submitting recorded conversations as evidence you should be able to answer the following questions in order to establish the foundation for tape recordings to the event they need to be admitted into evidence:

- Do you recognize what is shown in this photograph (tape)?
- Do you know who took this photograph (tape)?
- Do you know why this photograph (tape) was taken?
- Are you familiar with the scene (person, product, place) portrayed in this photograph (tape)?
- How are you familiar with the scene portrayed in the photograph (tape)?
- Does the scene portrayed in the photograph (tape) fairly and accurately represent the scene as you remember it ?
- Who took this photograph (recorded this tape)?

Medical Records

Medical records may be maintained by many persons, including a physician, surgeon, dentist, registered nurse, dispensing optician, registered physical therapist, podiatrist, licensed psychologist, osteopathic physician, chiropractor, clinical laboratory bioanalyst, clinical laboratory technologist, pharmacist or the companies or departments for which they work.

When medical records are required, the professionals may want the attorney to formerly request them with a written authorization, This may be a letter or form signed by an adult patient, by the guardian or conservator of his or her person or estate, or in the case of a minor, by a parent or guardian of the minor, or by the personal representative or an heir of a deceased patient.

In some cases a subpoena may be required. All reasonable costs incurred by any person or entity making records available may be charged against the person whose written authorization required the availability of the records. Current documentation will be less expensive than archived information.

The confidentiality of the documents is maintained to protect the patient not the hospital, physician or other staff.

In Veronica L. Baker v. Oakwood Hospital Corporation in Michigan, Veronica L. Baker filed a motion to compel disclosure of certain medical records she claimed were essential to her wrongful discharge case against Oakwood Hospital Corporation. A lower court said that the material requested was sufficiently relevant. But the court of appeals said that the physician-patient privilege applies even when the patient's names aren't disclosed. "The physician-patient privilege prohibits the unauthorized disclosure of patient medical records, including when the patients are not parties to the action," the court said.

First Strike

It is said in the legal profession that eighty percent of the real work is done before a case goes to court. Many feel that if the job is well done, the case will never get to court because the outcome will have become apparent to all involved. At this time, a settlement may be the best course of action for everyone involved, once your attorney has identified where you stand and what your choices are and suggests the best course of action.

All of this has a great deal to do with how experienced your attorney is in this kind of litigation; how complete the documentation is that you produce; how honest you have been with your attorney; and if you listened to and carried out your counselor's instructions. The taking of a deposition can be the turning point in your case. You can lose a solid case if you do not handle the deposition process well. What follows is a layperson's guide to the deposition.

Deposition

Discovery or Examination Before Trial (EBT), is a formal request for oral information; an act of seeking truth or knowledge by presenting questions to the individual being deposed and recording, by one of several means, the answers given. Depositions were usually taken in an attorneys office, which allowed for the time, space personal and equipment necessary to complete the process.

Now depositions can be taken anywhere, anytime including from a home, school, the office, hospital, jail or hotel room via the Internet. It is even possible to send comments and suggestions to the deposing attorneys. To further enhance the process it is possible to use a transcript repository that will make the deposition immediately available in multiple transcript formats.

Explanation of a Deposition

A deposition is a fact-finding expedition for the party requesting and paying for the deposition. The attorney can question and cross-examine a friendly or unfriendly witness under oath, outside the hearing of the judge, in advance of the trial.

Unless you can accomplish one of these purposes or some other specific goal with a deposition, don't waste your money.

Four Reasons to Depose Someone

1. A deposition gives you the opportunity to confirm information and verify documents you intend to use as exhibits.

2. A deposition can be used to clear away lies, past and present, and to get to the truth. On occasion, a person being deposed will lie. If you have proof of lies, or can get proof, this will effectively reduce the opposition's progress.

3. Questions can be posed to probe for unknown data. It is common for a person who is nervous and inexperienced in legal procedure to say much more than is necessary or prudent.

4. Sometimes the attorney will use a deposition to transmit information to the opposition.

Deposition could be used to harass a person, but it is a foolish way to spend money and time. It would be possible to lose the patience or sympathy of a judge or jury if they feel you went out of your way to harass the other parent. In rare cases an attorney may use a deposition to convince his or her own client that there is no case.

Rules of Deposition

Some states have no rules of deposition. In the states that do, they define from whom, how, where, when and why a deposition will be taken. Exceptions to these rules are also listed. Rules of deposition vary from state to state and according to the type of litigation. Some states have a rule that limits the length of time a deposition can go on in some kinds of cases. This rule may be waived if requested by your attorney.

Ask your attorney if this rule applies to your case and discuss whether taking this course would be to your advantage. To eliminate the practice of some attorneys who would depose everyone even remotely connected with the case, some states have limited deposition to the principals in the case only, with very strict exceptions.

Costs for Deposition

The costs of a deposition include your attorney's fees, the court reporter's fee, and any expert's fees. Budget a minimum of $250 per hour during the deposition. The cost may look prohibitive, but the finished document can be worth its weight in gold.

Best Time to Depose

In most cases, it is best to depose the opposition's side, as well as primary witnesses, as soon as possible. Memories of actual events are fresher and are unadulterated with additional data from other sources. In domestic relations cases, there are usually fewer bad feelings in the early stages of the process.

The opposition will feel kinder toward you, less angry at things the opposition thinks you have done, and less critical of your requests than it will be as the case drags on.

Second Deposition

Regardless of the expense, a second or third deposition may be very important to your case. Your best defense may be to use the opposition's own words transcribed in a previous deposition. Changes in circumstances such as marital status, earning ability, passing from noncriminal to criminal status, and health may dictate the necessity of a new deposition. If a great deal of time elapses from the deposition date to the court date, another deposition may be to your advantage.

This deposition will let you update information. The attorney may ask a question posed in a previous deposition and get a response that contradicts answers given the first time. Your attorney will advise you as to what is best for the kind of litigation in which you are involved. If you are to be deposed for a second or third time or after one of your witnesses has been deposed, be sure to reread and be familiar with any information previously given.

Prepare for a Deposition

Several days before the deposition make necessary arrangements for child care, transportation, leave of absence from work, and any other obligation, you may have.

The Night Before a Deposition

For court tomorrow choose conservative, comfortable clothes. You may be in the deposition three or more hours. Put antacids, cough drops, tissues, and the last-minute notes for your attorney in your pocket or purse. Make sure your car has gas or that you have the money for the bus or taxi.

If you have never been to the place where the deposition will take place, get a map and good instructions on how to get there. Check your alarm clock again.

If you are driving and the place you are going is downtown, take at least $20 and park in an all-day parking lot or garage. This reduces the stress and is more reasonable than driving around looking for an empty parking space and worrying about the parking meter.

Deposition First Thing in the Morning

Have your clothes laid out the night before, ready to put on. Have your morning cup of coffee to wake up, if necessary. After that, avoid coffee, tea or soda pop that contain caffeine until the deposition is over. Stick to cold water. Studies show that caffeine is a deterrent to concentration and memory recall when under stress.

Deposition Later in the Day

If you will be going to the deposition from a place other than home, assemble your clothes and a small clean-up kit to take with you. You will feel more in control if you are clean and fresh.

If you are aware that your attorney is allergic to your after-shave or perfume, don't use it. It is important that nothing you do affect your attorney negatively. If you do use perfume, remember that a little scent goes a long way in a closed room.

Your Deposition

Psychological and Emotional

Preparation

- Do not go to be deposed without a good attorney at your side. Decide to listen to what your attorney tells you to do --- and do it. Make an appointment to meet with your attorney a day or two before the deposition is scheduled. If it is not possible to meet in person, a telephone conference is better than nothing. Listen carefully to the instructions your attorney gives you before and during the deposition.
- Your deposition will be taken in the opposition attorney's office. Don't visit with any of the personnel in the enemy camp before your deposition, during breaks or after the deposition. If you need to speak with your attorney, and cannot find a private or "bug free" room, go outside. Discuss these tactics and your feelings with your attorney. Your attorney may be able to give you some advice about handling any fear or animosity you feel.
- The other parent and possibly their significant other will probably be there when you are being deposed. It is the other party's right. Get accustomed to the idea, so you can appear calm and unconcerned when the opposition arrives. This is probably not comfortable for the opposition either, and it will unnerve the opposition if this situation does not cause you noticeable distress.
- The old fashioned technique was for the questioning attorney to be aggressive. The more modern tactic most commonly used is to be very cordial, friendly and caring during all or part of your deposition. Be prepared for both. Ask your attorney about the opposing attorney and what suggestions can be offered to handle this person.
- The kinder tactic encourages you to lower your protective guard and puts you off balance. If someone is nice to you, there is a desire to try to give that person the answers he or she wants. Don't do it. Never forget --- it is the opposition against you. The answers the opposition's attorney wants to hear are not necessarily the answers you want to give. There are only two sides in this skirmish --- yours and theirs.

Do not forget, which side the other attorney is on.

Approaching your deposition with the right mindset is important to the mood for the entire case.

No New News Is Good News

During the deposition is not a good time for your attorney to learn anything new about you or your case. If you have not done so yet, come clean. Tell your attorney anything you have withheld.

Tell your attorney about any lies you may have told in the past and decide together how to handle the lies. A deposition is a sworn statement. It looks like the court reporter is putting it on paper, but it is being cast in stone forever. Do not lie. Subjects that do not apply to this matter and that you are not required to talk about should be clear in your mind. This will help you avoid talking about these topics accidentally. Decide, which areas will be painful, embarrassing, or uncomfortable. Discuss attitudes that will help you face these challenges as you map out a strategy to answer difficult questions. You will be better prepared and less likely to say something that will damage your case if you do this. If your attorney has the time and thinks it will help, ask to practice some questions and answers that may come up during deposition. Discuss the subjects and documents that are sure to be questioned and try to anticipate any surprise questions. Do some role-playing until you feel comfortable and confident with your answers.

Attorney Preparation

This is the least expensive part of the deposition process, because you are only paying for your attorney's time. It is also the most important part, because this is where the foundation of your case is built. The costs are directly affected by the volume of data requested and the type of case in which you are involved.

Your attorney will organize and review all of the information you have supplied and any information gathered from other sources. If your attorney thinks it is important to meet for an hour or two a few days before the deposition, make every effort to fit this appointment time into your schedule and this expense into your budget. With your attorney's help, you may be able to settle this case out of court in a short period of time. You can reduce the amount of your attorney's time and charges if you:

- Supply certified documents, or certified copies of documents, when possible.
- Make sure all documents are dated. If the document was not dated, but did arrive via postal

service or regulated carrier, copy the waybill or envelope in which it arrived.

- If there are handwritten or foreign language documents, attach typed translated versions.
- Keep a copy of each document you submit in the event any additional copies are required.
- Type a note on a contrasting color of paper and attach to the front of the document explaining the importance of this document to the attorney.
- Index long documents or groups of photos, documents or other evidence.

Information is not Protected

If you become involved in a lawsuit, you must be ready to suffer the scrutiny it brings. It is not unusual for an attorney whose client has deep enough pockets, to depose everyone who may testify. For the most part, the testimony invoked is not for the sake of information, but rather to annoy the witness and put him or her on notice that skeletons could be summoned from the closet. When it comes to deposing the principals in the lawsuit, anything may be asked. Examples could include: How much money do you have in the bank? Where did that money come from? Who can write checks on your account? Do you ever use your money to pay the bills that come to your spouse? What kind of cars do you have? When did you get them? How much did you pay for them? Are you under the influence of any drugs or alcohol?

Instructions from the Opposition

Deposition instructions are given by the opposing attorney to the deponent (person to be deposed) at the deposition before the deposition begins. If the deponent is accompanied by an attorney, the instructions are given orally. Supposedly, this is to reinforce the instructions already given by the attorney accompanying the Deponent. It is important for you to find out what is law and what the attorney wants. The instructions from the opposing attorney are a mixture of what the attorney wants and the law. Not everything the attorney instructs you to do is required by law.

You can easily identify the differences between what the attorney for your side has told you and what the opposition attorney is telling you. The following is an example of deposition instructions from the opposition's attorney.

Deposition Instructions

This proceeding is know as a deposition. The person transcribing the proceeding is a certified court reporter and also a notary public who has placed you under oath. During the course of this proceeding, I, and perhaps other of the counsel present here today, will be asking you questions pertaining to this lawsuit.

Although this proceeding is being held in an informal atmosphere, you have been placed under oath, your testimony here today has the same force and effect and is subject to the same penalties as if you were testifying in a courtroom before a judge. Specifically, you are subject to the penalty of perjury.

Perjury is defined as willful, and contrary to an oath administered, stating as true any material fact, which one knows to be false. The penalty for perjury may be imprisonment for not less than one (1) year, nor more than fourteen (14) years. You are advised that an unqualified statement of that which you do not know to be true is equivalent to a statement of that which you know to be false.

If, at any time during the deposition, you feel that any question is ambiguous or unintelligible, or that you are unable to understand it, or you fail to hear the question for any reason whatsoever, please tell the person asking you the question. If you do not so indicate, it will be presumed that you have heard and have understood each question and that your answer to each question is based upon your complete and full understanding thereof.

If, after a question has been posed to you, you have any question yourself relating to what has been inquired about, please ask the person who posed the question before you answer the question.

The reporter is only able to transcribe audible responses, so please do not nod your head, shake your head, or say "ahha" or "haah". Further, the reporter can usually record the words of only one person speaking at a time, so please allow time for the question to be completed before you respond. You will normally be allowed to finish each and every answer before a new question is posed.

At the conclusion of this deposition, the reporter will transcribe these proceedings into a booklet form.

You will have an opportunity to read that booklet and make any changes in your testimony, as it is given here today.

I will be entitled to ask you why you made such changes and comment upon those changes before a judge or jury trial of this action. Because of this fact, it is important that all of your answers be full, complete, and correct.

If I ask you about any conversation you have had in the past, and you are unable to recall the exact words used in the conversation, you may state that you are unable to recall those exact words, and then you may give me the gist or substance of any such conversations that you recall.

If I ask you whether you have any information upon a particular subject and you have overheard other persons conversing with each other regarding it, or have seen correspondence or documentation regarding it, please tell me that you do have such information, and indicate the source as either a conversation or documentation, or otherwise from which it was derived. In answering, please do not be concerned with whether or not your answer is hearsay or concern yourself with any technical rules of evidence you think may preclude answering.

Our purpose here today is not to trap you, or to trick you in any manner, but simply to ascertain and discover that information about the facts that you have within your knowledge concerning this lawsuit.

At the conclusion of this deposition, the attorneys present may, by agreement, stipulate that you sign the booklet containing your testimony in the presence of any notary public, rather than the reporter who is here today, taking and transcribing this deposition. If we do so, it will upon the expressed understanding and your promise, that you will, upon receipt of the deposition, promptly and as expeditiously as possible, read it, correct it, if you feel it is necessary, and sign it in the presence of a notary public, and return it to the office from which it was sent to you.

Do you understand everything that you have just read? (Please circle) YES NO

Do you have any questions pertaining to either the procedure, or what is about to transpire, insofar as this deposition is concerned? If so, please ask them of me now.

Please indicate that you have read and understood all of the foregoing, by signing this document where indicated below.

Signature of Deponent ________________________

Exhibit # ______ to the Deposition of __________

taken on ____________, 20 ___

During Your Deposition

The following list of tactics will help you respond effectively to questions:

- This is an important time to be assertive and truthful and to avoid being aggressive and less than truthful.
- Don't attempt to make a point, embarrass the enemy, tell your side, debate with the other attorney, or get revenge for all the injustices you have suffered. It will backfire. The other attorney will encourage any attempt you make to do these things.
- Remain consistent with whom you say you are. If you cannot sit for extended lengths of time, if you must eat, take medication, or go to the bathroom frequently, do not feel uncomfortable about letting your attorney know. Have your attorney schedule these breaks in the deposition. This will not hurt your case and may, in fact, help it along.
- Listen carefully to the entire question before you begin to think of your answer.
- Pause for a moment to allow your attorney to object to the question, if necessary. This gives you a few moments to put your thoughts in order.
- If your attorney does object, it is probably for the record, and you may, in fact, be instructed by your attorney to answer the question. This may also be a warning from your attorney that you are skating on thin ice. So, be careful but honest with your answer.
- If you can't answer the question after your attorney instructs you to do so, don't. The opposition attorney will have to go to the judge to get a ruling to force you to. The other attorney may or may not go that far to get an answer.
- Answer only the question. Do not go into any detail. The more you say now, the more you will be required to remember later. Do not supply the opposition with ammunition that can be used against you later.
- Do not answer general questions. The opposition's attorney is fishing for information to

use against you. Example: "Tell me about your childhood."

Your proper answer to this could be, "That is an inappropriate question." or "Please be more specific."

- Do not make up details based on a spotty or forgotten memory because the attorney pressures you. Example: "Was it between January and March, or April and June?" Insist, "I do not remember, and I will not guess."
- Do not attempt to give an answer if the attorney bases a question on an untrue statement. Example: "You were late arriving as usual, and the other parent had to call your job looking for you that Thursday, isn't that so?" A reasonable response may be, "What you said is not true; I am never late. I was not aware a call was placed."
- Do not chew gum or use smokeless tobacco during the deposition.
- Speak clearly, audibly, and keep your answers simple and free of slang and bad language.
- Do not try to make a point; just answer the question.
- This attorney thinks he or she already knows the answers to the questions being asked. The attorney is giving you every chance to do as much damage to your case as possible. Do not do it. Stay cool and think.
- If you are asked to supply a list, finish with, "That is all I can think of now."
- Answer only, "Yes" or "No" as often as possible or "I do not remember" if that is the case.
- In the event that the other attorney does not ask, request an opportunity to inspect the document and ask the court reporter when your attorney can expect the copy they are obligated to submit. If you are told you must pay for a copy, do it.
- At the end of your deposition, the opposition's attorney should ask, "Do you want to read and sign this deposition?" Always say, "Yes." It will give you an opportunity to make sure your answers were recorded correctly, make corrections to the record, and have the document copied without having to pay extra.

Facing the Mad Dog Attorney

It is proper to ask your attorney if he or she is familiar with the opposition's attorney and what kind of treatment you can expect from this person. You can always research the opposition's attorney just as you would the judge or psychologist.

Some attorneys are vicious and ruthless. Such attorneys are willing to destroy anyone, including their own client, to win a case. These people are well known, if only by reputation, to the other attorneys and judges. With this kind of adversary, it is essential that you read and understand how to answer the questions asked and understand how to respond.

It is your attorney's responsibility to safeguard you from vicious behavior. Your attorney must be fearless in protecting you during questioning from this kind of attorney. It is your responsibility to listen to the instructions given to you by your attorney.

Make sure you and your attorney understand what you will and will not be required to tolerate. Gain assurance from your attorney that objection will be made to unseemly behavior. Keep in mind that your attorney can't object to a question just because it makes you uncomfortable. A deposition is supposed to be a non-hostile environment.

Therefore, if during the deposition, the opposition's attorney acts in a threatening, insulting, loud or abusive manner, do the following:

1. Inform the affronting attorney that you are offended and request a change in demeanor.

2. If the attack persists, ask your attorney if the opposition attorney may address you in that manner. If your attorney says "yes," you may wish to attempt to proceed. If you do not wish to proceed, go to step #4. If your attorney says "no," it is on the record. If the incident is repeated, state for the record that you feel this is hostile and degrading, and if this does not cease, you will be forced to leave.

3. Ask the court reporter if the offending statement is on the record. If the answer is affirmative, proceed to #4.

4. If the incident is repeated, state for the court reporter's record what the opposition's attorney is doing: "I have asked Attorney Toel to not yell at me. I feel threatened and forced to leave." Then leave immediately. Throw up if necessary.

There are monsters that are so bad that other attorneys may throw in the towel when the mad dog's name is listed as the opposing council.

If permitted, make arrangements to have the deposition recorded. Use a professional audio recording company. They will have the equipment to capture the offending attorney's assault.

Check Your Deposition

You should be prepared to read through your deposition a minimum of two times. You can be sure the opposition will read it twice as many times.

Most people find it difficult to read their own deposition. It will be easier if you were well-prepared and listened carefully to the instructions your attorney gave you before and during the deposition.

You will find it easier to read through your deposition if you have been truthful. Seeing your own lies transformed from words you could forget into documented evidence is awful. Knowing you gave the opposition valuable ammunition is devastating. Waiting for the lie to blow up in your face is psychologically exhausting.

Have two additionai copies made. Keep one copy unmarked and set aside to make notes to carry to court with you. Use the original copy of the deposition to give back to the court reporter with any corrections you find necessary. Put the last copy in a three-ring binder to work with now.

The first time you read through the working copy of your deposition, tab the important events or dates using stick-on notes or scraps of paper. This will give you a chance to become familiar with the document.

The second time you read through your deposition, make sure the person transcribed your words correctly. Example: You say, "I was living in Hollywood, Florida." The court reporter transcribed, "I was living in Hollywood, California."

- Spelling errors are not important unless the mistake affects the validity of the statement.
- Punctuation errors are not important unless they change the meaning of the responses you made.

Ending the Deposition

Arrange in advance with your attorney to take a short break when the attorney is ready to finish the deposition. This gives both you and your attorney a chance to collect your thoughts. It also intimidates the opposition. In private, quickly review your notes with your attorney to see if you have any questions the attorney should ask. As difficult as this advice is to follow, it will enable you to gain greater benefits from the opposition's deposition.

Tip: Go home and rest. You are not the one on the hot seat.

Correcting Mistakes on Deposition

It is not necessary to list why you think you made an incorrect response to a question. It is only necessary to make the correction. If you wish to state a reason, try to make it brief. Example:

Corrigena

The witness, Amber Jones, wishes to make the following changes or corrections in his/her testimony as originally given:

Page	Line	Correction	Reason
96	14	Accused of attempting to take narcotics into a prison	Just said it wrong
201	3	My mother was watching the children	

I declare under penalty of perjury that the foregoing is true and correct.

__Amber Jones____ Amber Jones

State of Arizona

County of Maricopa

SUBSCRIBED AND SWORN TO BEFORE ME by the said witness, Amber Jones, on this the 4th day of April 1996

_Trudy Lane____ Commission Expires:08/11/99

Trudy Jones Notary Public in and for the State of Arizona

False Documentation

Documentation is the key to most child custody cases. Good documentation can make your case. Bad documentation can kill your case. Once discovered, false documentation can put someone in jail. The severity of the punishment, if any, depends on the intent with which the documentation was created or amended. Examples of falsified documentation and possible repercussions could be:

A person may not be free of liability for wrongful acts committed indifferently because that person relied on false documentation. It is the responsibility of each person to make reasonable efforts to validate documentation.

Who Would You Depose?

List the people you would like to depose and what information they may have that you want.

Proposed List of People to Depose

Name Information

1. Amber Jones - accusation of rape, move to Washington, her arrest, how she feels about having her children witness her preparing the drugs for transport and having them see her get arrested, residential and employment moves, the arrest record of her thirteen year-old son
2. Mike Jones - prison record, abuse charge, other wife
3. James Miller - arrest in Phoenix when Amber and Bobby lived with him in trailer, physical abuse causing miscarriage, relationship with Amber
4. Mr. Solomon - evaluation and recommendations on report
5. Shawn Jameson - home study
6. Dr. Johns - about Bobby's weight loss and health, Amber's care of the baby
7. Janet Wood - Amber's co-worker about Amber's relationship with man in prison, plans to marry him, taking her other children and Bobby to visit him in jail.

Deposition Outline Form

Form filled in by: **Randall Long**

Plaintiff: defendant: **Long v Jones**

Name of person to be deposed: **Dr. Johns**

1. Relationship to this case (such as employee, co-worker, relative, former friend, neighbor): **Bobby's baby doctor**
2. Does this person have any concerns about giving testimony in this case? **No**
3. Information this witness may have that may damage the opposition's case: **He was the doctor for Amber's other children when she did not take them to the county free clinic.**
4. Information this witness may have that may damage the case: **None**
5. Information this witness has which is relevant to this matter: **Bobby's weight loss, observations of both parents with child**
6. What information does this witness have which is not relevant to this matter? **None.**
7. Special information this witness can offer about the opposition: **Knows Amber's entire family as physician for them and Bobby**
8. Relationship to individual or event in litigation: **Randall for two years, Amber for fourteen years**
9. What factors would impact his or her testimony? **He has expressed fear for the welfare of his family and himself from Amber and James**
10. Other people in this litigation with whom this person is associated: **None**
11. What does this person know that he or she does not want to talk about? **Nothing.**
12. What does this person know that you do not want him or her to talk about? **Nothing.**

Complete one of these forms for each person to be deposed.

Opposition's Deposition

Your attorney will prepare questions to ask the opposition designed to confirm information the attorney already has. The attorney will also prepare questions to elicit new information. Sometimes your attorney may even go fishing for information.

You should give your attorney a Data Sheet and a Deposition Outline Form on each person being deposed. You should make a list of all of the questions you would like your attorney to ask.

The opposing attorney will advise the opposition not to answer some questions. Some people are not smart enough to listen to their attorneys and may insist on answering a question to make a point.

If the person being deposed opens a closed area, your attorney will be able to use more of the questions you assembled for this process.

When you begin to prepare questions for your attorney to ask at the opposition's deposition, list everything. Understand, however, that you may not get to ask all these questions or receive answers to all of your questions. There will be questions you have listed that your attorney may not be able to ask initially.

Print or type your questions on white address labels. Put the questions down as you think of them. Do not worry about putting the questions in the proper order of importance. The labels allow your attorney to integrate them into already existing notes or place them in the order required.

The person being deposed may not be aware that you will be present at the deposition. It is your right to be there, and your attorney may feel it is necessary. Your attendance may cause the person being deposed to act emotionally rather than rationally. The opposition may even believe your presence has even created an opportunity to strike out at you. Understand that the other party is damaging its case by shooting at you with words, which they think will win the battle. That information should help you get through this ordeal. Actually, the opposition is giving you ammunition to win the war. Discuss any apprehension you feel with your attorney.

Absence of hostility will do more for you than your enemy because it will clear your thinking, allowing you to do your job more efficiently.

During the Oppositions's Deposition

It is difficult to listen to a question by your attorney, a person's answer to the question and take notes without missing the next question and response. Therefore, do not attempt to take long notes. Make one word notations to review with your attorney during a break.

A "poker face" refers to the ability to control your expressions so that others have no idea what you are thinking. This is the time to have a poker face and a "poker body."

Use this list as a guideline of things to avoid doing during the enemy's deposition:

- Do not laugh, snicker, roll your eyes back, or shake your head. Be prepared to hear some amazing answers. This person may know you well and would love to get to you now. Don't let it happen.
- Do not try to intimidate or make friends with the opposition, opposition's witnesses, or opposition's attorney. They are the enemy. The opposition's witness may assault you or ask you questions. You are not legally allowed to respond. Do not attempt to respond.
- Do not show any change in facial expressions.
- Do not make noises either with pencils on the table or tapping with fingers or toes.
- Do not do anything that might limit the opposition's answers. Once the opposition understands that you cannot respond or give your side, more often than not, he or she will say much more than the opposition's attorney would like.
- Listen carefully to the answers the opposition gives. Jot down additional questions for your attorney to ask. The opposition may have opened an important area for questioning that your attorney may now explore.

Check the Opposition's Deposition

You should be prepared to read the opposition's deposition several times. Don't get upset or mad every time you look at the document. Avoid discussing the contents of the document with anyone except your attorney. Most people find this difficult.

Don't let your legal challenge become neighborhood or talk show entertainment. It is best to have an additional copy made.

One copy is to give to your attorney when you are finished making notes, and one is to put in a three-ring binder to work with now. The first time you read through the working copy of the opposition's deposition, tab the important events or dates using stick-on note pads. This will give you a chance to become familiar with the document. The second time you read through the deposition, highlight in light blue any data that requires verification. Underline the statements that you can prove are false. Send the amended deposition and the documents that disprove any statements made to your attorney as soon as possible.

Check the Expert's Deposition

Take the time to read any depositions that are taken by anyone connected with your litigation. Obtain copies of all depositions, even if you have to pay for them. Once you have studied the documents, make short, clean notes of anything you think your attorney needs to be made aware. Make a list of incorrect statements. Explain how each statement is untrue and how you can disprove it. It is important that you understand the testimony of your expert as it pertains to your case. These professionals are usually willing to give you a working knowledge of the methods they used to reach their conclusions in your matter. If you or your attorney have any question about the validity of information contained in a deposition given by the opposition's expert, it is a good idea to hire another professional in that field to critique the document for you. Ask your expert to make a set of questions that will challenge any dubious statements or conclusions the opposition's expert made. Your expert should also provide the right answers and a secondary set of questions for your attorney in case they are needed in trial.

Your Witnesses' Deposition

It is in your best interest to spend the money to have your attorney present when any witness for your side is being deposed by the opposition. Your attorney may want you to be there also. It reminds the witness whose side the testimony is for and gives you a "read" as to how that witness may do in court.

You would be amazed at some of the "stupid" things your friends will say when being deposed by the opposition. Your presence will limit the natural inclination people have to try to say what the person asking questions wants to hear.

Preparation is just as important for your witness as it is for you and will prevent many disasters. Even the deposition of your expert will be better for you if you are there. Very few people have given a deposition. Most people are intimidated by what they think will happen. Fill out a deposition outline with your witness and discuss concerns thoroughly. It will help to ask your witness some questions that the other attorney is sure to pose. This preparation will help your friend do a better job for you.

Example of Deposition Indexing

It isn't reasonable to expect an evaluator, judge or psychologist to read through a deposition. Even if it is short. If there is testimony that you want to make sure the professional will read then index the document.

Indexing will keep important statements that are make from getting lost in the sea of paper. When you list the pertinent information the professional can choose to access the page with the statement. This gives the professional the opportunity to read preceding information and subsequent text at will. The professional will appreciate your conservation of his or her time and are much more responsive to a short list than a long document.

Evidence to Disprove Statements

As you find statements in the deposition that you know are false, list them. Then state why the information is not true and how you can document your facts. Make a preliminary list and submit it to your attorney. Your attorney will be able to sort out what is important to the court and eliminate the non-issues. Some things to remember are:

- Documents or reliable testimony are the only proof.
- If you know a statement is false, but are unable to prove it, put it aside for now.
- If there are a great number of lies in the deposition, it is not necessary to prove each one.
- Do your research quickly and quietly.

Failure to Comply with Discovery

The Federal Rules of Civil Procedure concerning Depositions and Discovery state in part in Rule 37. That failure to make or cooperate in discovery may allow sanctions.

A party, upon reasonable notice to other parties and all persons affected thereby, may apply for an order compelling disclosure or discovery using a motion for order compelling disclosure or discovery as follows:

(1) Appropriate Court. An application for an order to a party shall be made to the court in which the action is pending. An application for an order to a person who is not a party shall be made to the court in the district where the discovery is being, or is to be, taken.

(2) Motion. (A) If a party fails to make a disclosure required by Rule 26(a), any other party may move to compel disclosure and for appropriate sanctions.

Topic	Page	Amber Jones Deposition Index of Statements
Randall Long	46	not physically mean, mentally mean
	83	I knew it would harm Randall
Mike Jones	27	Mike was first husband, six month marriage
	29	left him for mental and physical abuse of me and my kids
	30	married James after divorced Mike
	30	after no contact for ten years, there was a thirty day relationship before second marriage to Mike
	31	physical abuse to children, mental abuse to me
Amber Jones Children	29	left children with people in Washington for eight months
	86	James would tell Byron he was no good
	145	James never supported his three children
Amber's Drug Felony	96	arrested for attempting to take narcotics into a prison
	97	used marijuana in 1981, James; gave me acid in 1982

The motion must include a certification that the movant has in good faith conferred or attempted to confer with the party not making the disclosure in an effort to secure the disclosure without court action.

(B) If a deponent fails to answer a question propounded or submitted under Rules 30 or 31, or a corporation or other entity fails to make a designation under Rule 30(b)(6) or 31(a), or a party fails to answer an interrogatory submitted under Rule 33, or if a party, in response to a request for inspection submitted under Rule 34 fails to respond, that inspection will be permitted as requested or fails to permit inspection as requested, the discovering party may move for an order compelling answer, or a designation, or an order compelling inspection in accordance with the request. The motion must include a certification that the movant has in good faith conferred or attempted to confer with the person or party failing to make the discovery in an effort to secure the information or material without court action. When taking a deposition on oral examination, the proponent of the question may complete or adjourn the examination before applying for an order.

(3) Evasive or Incomplete Disclosure, Answer, or Response. For purposes of this subdivision an evasive or incomplete disclosure, answer, or response is to be treated as a failure to disclose, answer, or respond.

(4) Expenses and Sanctions. (A) If the motion is granted or if the disclosure or requested discovery is provided after the motion was filed.
The court shall, after affording an opportunity to be heard, require the party or deponent whose conduct necessitated the motion or the party or attorney advising such conduct or both of them to pay to the moving party the reasonable expenses incurred in

making the motion, including attorney's fees, unless the court finds that the motion was filed without the Movant's first making a good faith effort to obtain the disclosure or discovery without court action, or that the opposing party's nondisclosure, response, or objection was substantially justified, or that other circumstances make an award of expenses unjust.

(B) If the motion is denied, the court may enter any protective order authorized under Rule 26(c) and shall, after affording an opportunity to be heard, require the moving party or the attorney filing the motion or both of them to pay to the party or deponent who opposed the motion, the reasonable expenses incurred in opposing the motion, including attorney's fees, unless the court finds that the making of the motion was substantially justified or that other circumstances make an award of expenses unjust.

(C) If the motion is granted in part and denied in part, the court may enter any protective order authorized under Rule 26(c) and may, after affording an opportunity to be heard, apportion the reasonable expenses incurred in relation to the motion among the parties and persons in a just manner.

(1) Sanctions by court in district where deposition is taken. If a deponent fails to be sworn or to answer a question after being directed to do so by the court in the district in which the deposition is being taken, the failure may be considered a contempt of that court.

(2) Sanctions by court in which action is pending. If a party or an officer, director, or managing agent of a party or a person designated under Rule 30(b)(6) or 31(a) to testify on behalf of a party fails to obey an order to provide or permit discovery, including an order made under subdivision (a) of this rule or Rule 35, or if a party fails to obey an order entered under Rule 26(f), the court in which the action is pending may make such orders in regard to the failure as are just, and among others the following:

(A) An order that the matters regarding, which the order was made or any other designated facts shall be taken to be established for the purposes of the action in accordance with the claim of the party obtaining the order;

(B) An order refusing to allow the disobedient party to support or oppose designated claims or defenses, or prohibiting that party from introducing designated matters in evidence;

(C) An order striking out pleadings or parts thereof, or staying further proceedings until the order is obeyed, or dismissing the action or proceeding or any part thereof, or rendering a judgment by default against the disobedient party;

(D) In lieu of any of the foregoing orders or in addition thereto, an order treating as a contempt of court the failure to obey any orders except an order to submit to a physical or mental examination;

(E) Where a party has failed to comply with an order under Rule 35(a) requiring that party to produce another for examination, such orders as are listed in paragraphs (A), (B), and (C) of this subdivision, unless the party failing to comply shows that party is unable to produce such person for examination.

In lieu of any of the foregoing orders or in addition thereto, the court shall require the party failing to obey the order or the attorney advising that party or both to pay the reasonable expenses, including attorney's fees, caused by the failure, unless the court finds that the failure was substantially justified or that other circumstances make an award of expenses unjust.

(c) Failure to disclose; False or misleading disclosure; Refusal to admit.

(1) A party that without substantial justification fails to disclose information required by Rule 26(a) or 26(e)(1) shall not, unless such failure is harmless, be permitted to use as evidence at a trial, at a hearing, or on a motion, any witness or information not so disclosed. In addition to or in lieu of this sanction, the court, on motion and after affording an opportunity to be heard, may impose other appropriate sanctions.

In addition to requiring payment of reasonable expenses, including attorney's fees, caused by the failure, these sanctions may include any of the sanctions authorized under subparagraphs (A), (B), and (C) of subdivision (b)(2) of this rule and may include informing the jury of the failure to make the disclosure.

(2) If a party fails to admit the genuineness of any document or the truth of any matter as requested under Rule 36.
If the party requesting the admissions thereafter proves the genuineness of the document or the truth of the matter, the requesting party may apply to the court for an order requiring the other party to pay the reasonable expenses incurred in making that proof, including reasonable attorney's fees. The court shall

make the order unless it finds that (A) the request was held objectionable pursuant to Rule 36(a), or (B) the admission sought was of no substantial importance, or (C) the party failing to admit had reasonable ground to believe that the party might prevail on the matter, or (D) there was other good reason for the failure to admit. (d) Failure of Party to Attend at Own Deposition or Serve Answers to Interrogatories or Respond to Request for Inspection. If a party or an officer, director, or managing agent of a party or a person designated under Rule 30(b)(6) or 31(a) to testify on behalf of a party fails (1) to appear before the officer who is to take the deposition, after being served with a proper notice, or (2) to serve answers or objections to interrogatories submitted under Rule 33, after proper service of the interrogatories, or

(3) to serve a written response to a request for inspection submitted under Rule 34, after proper service of the request, the court in which the action is pending on motion may make such orders in regard to the failure as are just, and among others it may take any action authorized under subparagraphs (A), (B), and (C) of subdivision (b)(2) of this rule.

Any motion specifying a failure under clause (2) or (3) of this subdivision shall include a certification that the movant has in good faith conferred or attempted to confer with the party failing to answer or respond in an effort to obtain such answer or response without court action. In lieu of any order or in addition thereto, the court shall require the party failing to act or the attorney advising that party or both to pay the reasonable expenses, including attorney's fees, caused by the failure unless the court finds that the failure was substantially justified or that other circumstances make an award of expenses unjust.

The failure to act described in this subdivision may not be excused on the ground that the discovery sought is objectionable unless the party failing to act has a pending motion for a protective order as provided by Rule 26(c).

(e) [Abrogated]

(f) [Repealed]

(g) Failure to participate in the framing of a discovery plan.

If a party or a party's attorney fails to participate in the development and submission of a proposed discovery plan as required by Rule 26(f), the court may, after opportunity for hearing, require such party or attorney to pay to any other party the reasonable expenses, including attorney's fees, caused by the failure.

Chapter 18: Judges

Most domestic relations or family court determinations are made by judges, not juries. Judges are appointed or voted into office, but they are not necessarily attorneys. This chapter is intended to demystify the judges and explain why they can do what they do in court. Customarily, judges in family court were themselves formerly practicing attorneys. In many jurisdictions, judges are rotated through the courts and have presided over criminal court before they sit on a domestic relations bench. In criminal court, judges see more "bad men" than "bad women." Therefore, these judges may be unaware that they feel protective of women and bias against men. This will make it necessary for a male parent to prove to the judge that he is a "good man." A tour of duty in criminal court will also make them more sensitive to the rules of evidence, procedure and more hardened to the bad things that happen in our society. Even when not filled by election, judgeships are very political and reflect the attitudes of the mainstream, forty-five-year-old to seventy-year-old voting community. All systems resist change, especially the legal system.

Perception of Hierarchy in Law

Within the legal system there appears to be a designation unrelated to the laws themselves in which status and/or authority rank the practice of one kind of law above another. Therefore, the persons working at each level are relegated to their place in the hierarchy. This is reflected in the demeanor of the law clerks who work under attorneys and judges. The more exalted the position of the boss, the more exalted the position of the assistant. Other than at the Supreme Court level, the more prestigious kind of law (by economic standards) "in rem" because it is more palatable, important, and is compensation better than "in personam."

Two Levels of Law

The lower (by legal standards) and easier kind of law is "in rem," which deals with things like real estate and money. There may be some emotion to the cases, but you are still only dealing with things. The higher kind of law is "in personam" and deals with people.

"In personam" law has a much higher time and

emotional drain on the judges and attorneys then "in rem." "In rem," may be the lower law in the land, but it is better thought of and makes more money for the attorneys than "in personam". So the prevailing consensus is that the brighter, better attorneys and judges practice at the more exalted levels of "in rem" law. Consequently, it is felt you are not getting the cream of the crop for your custody case. This is not necessarily true. Family law requires and has dedicated, caring and astute professionals.

Welcome to the Hotel California

In the 1970's, a rock group called the Eagles recorded a song titled, "Hotel California." One line states, "You can check out, but you can't leave." This may be the most accurate description of the custody process.

As citizens, we feel we have enlisted the assistance of the legal system to solve a private dispute and when this custody battle is finished, we are all restored to being private people taking care of our children. This is not so. After this case has been decided, we will be people taking care of children who are wards of the state until each child reaches the age of maturity, therefore, we are forever after answerable to the state. We can be yanked back into court at any time whether we win or lose custody. "In personam" law is more complicated when children are involved because the court in the person of the judge becomes the parent to the children. This happens because lawmakers feel that parents may not be able to act in the best interest of their children if the parents' interests are at risk or at odds with those of the children.

Jurisdiction Shopping

Judges are bound by the laws and jurisdiction in their state and work in a specific court. A case can only be heard in a court that has jurisdiction. Prior rulings may affect jurisdiction. If the parents and the children have all live in the same county for the proceeding six months and no other proceeding active anywhere else, there is no question about jurisdiction. In many places you may file in counties adjoining the county in which you live.

Many states have adopted uniform laws to eliminate some inconsistencies that occur from state to state. Those laws may include:

- Uniform Child Custody Act. Which states that the jurisdiction is with the state in which the child has resided for the proceeding six months if there were no proceedings pending in any other state.
- Family Support Act. Standardizes how payments will be made and many other issues.
- Uniform Interstate Family Support Act. Sets standards for establishing, enforcing and modifying child support.
- Parental Kidnapping Prevention Act. Authorizes the use of the Parental Locator Service so that states can find parents who have kidnapped.

Parents who understand this vital point have been known to go jurisdiction shopping for a state that would be more friendly to their case. This is an unusual option, but one that should be considered if you have the opportunity. Once you are involved in the system, there is nothing short of dying that you can do to get out of it. If the jurisdiction is out of your hands, concentrate on the judge.

Getting a Good Judge

The judicial system is huge, well organized, and feels the impact of political and budgetary pressure imposed by social and political influences. Consider the diverse variety of questions in the form of cases addressed, the numbers of new cases filed, the number of cases active at the time, and the number of cases refilled. These are all decided by people. Usually, these people are called judges. Considering the millions of laws, some over a hundred years old and impacted by the new laws and decisions that are enacted each day, it is amazing. As thousands of cases are settled, hundreds of thousands of people are released from the system and allowed to carry on with their lives. Some people will fall through the cracks.

Judges are forced to decide more cases by default than by fair hearing. It is the responsibility of the litigants to build their cases with the help of attorneys, witnesses and evidence.

It is the responsibility of the attorney to assemble the case in a proper manner and reduce the time and volume of the action to the smallest size. It is the responsibility of the judge to hear properly presented information and render an opinion as quickly as possible.

There are many good judges in our system, and they are being given more latitude with the new social attitudes about the parenting abilities and limitations of men and women and the needs of children. The good judges do not present a problem so we will spend this chapter addressing the other kinds.

Forum Shopping

Even the best judge is influenced by their own personal bias. Your attorney should work aggressively to get your case before a judge who is more likely to decide in your favor. In order to do this your attorney must be aware of the personal bias of each judge.

Like No Other Law

Custody cases are like no other law. In all other cases a question is brought before the court and a decision is reached. If there is another question about the matter a new case if filed. Custody may involve adults that are not able for one reason or another to assume the responsibility for their own wellbeing or children until they are adults. The adult or child whose custody the court overseas is a ward of the court. Once the court becomes involved with custody they remain involved until the adult is competent to care for himself or dies or the child becomes an adult. The parents of the children are allowed to care for the child at the behest of the court and in the manner the court deems fit. Since the court is your judge it is vital you get the best judge you can.

Research Your Judge

Because judges run the gambit of human behavior, type and style, it is vital that you research your judge in order to get a fair judge. It is impossible to legally get rid of a bad judge after a certain point in the custody proceedings. As soon as a judge is assigned to your case, begin to research the judge's background. Ask about your attorney's previous experience with this judge. Your attorney can solicit opinions from other attorneys. Contact local parents' rights groups. Attend meetings. Speak to other parents who may have had a case before your judge. Listen to the people you meet. Be sure to ask for the name of their attorneys, so your attorney can speak on a professional level with that attorney. Get a list of domestic relations cases in which your judge has ruled. Take this list to the records department and pull out as many of the cases as you have time to read. This will give you an indication of how the judge responds to the participants. Your attorney can tell you how to find these records. Attempt to see your judge in action. The cases are posted daily at the courthouse. The judge is in the same hearing room.

- **Ultraconservative:** Used to describe a judge that strongly resists change and often favors a prior condition.
- **Ultra Liberal:** Used to describe a judge who is not bound by traditional forms, tends to depart sharply from the usual. Is tolerant, indulgent and unorthodox, often favoring new approaches to old problems.
- **Peremptory Challenge:** Many states allow dismissal of the judge without having to prove an actual bias.

Those Who Render Opinions

It may appear on the surface that the judge has the easiest job in the courtroom. It isn't true. Judges lives are regulated by a docket calendar, a trial calendar, a motion calendar and probably a personal calendar. They must maintain control of their court room and the respect of the attorneys and other judges. Once an attorney requests a ruling everything stops. Often an attorney will ask for a decision on a case offering a specific cite case. The judge has the responsibility of determining if in fact the cite is valid and if it applies to this case. Then the judge has to make a ruling and it becomes part of a permanent record.

If you have never been involved with the judicial system, you may see judges in a Godlike light. It is important to show a person in that office proper respect, but to understand that the person is holding an office not positioned by divine province. The following statements are a mixture of facts and opinions from participants in child custody cases, including: Attorneys, fathers, non-custodial parents, children, mediators, psychologists, judges, mothers and custodial parents. Some of the statements concern specific judges and some concern the entire bench. The statements grew from anger, gratitude, envy, sadness, love, disappointment and many other emotions. Judges may:

- Be human.
- Accept or reject any testimony.
- Hate whispering in court.
- Feel no parent's rights supersede the children's rights.

- Be influenced by what you wear to court.
- Impose some alternative solutions of which you were unaware.
- Suffer from burn-out.
- Be liberal or conservative.
- Resent being forced to read the law.
- Become afraid to make any decision.
- Feel they are doing the best possible job.
- Be pro one side or the other in every case.
- See through play acting.
- Find very little joy or personal satisfaction in domestic relations court.
- Have personal prejudices.
- Really know what is better for your child in the long run than you do.
- Think they are God.
- Like or dislike your attorney.
- Try to overcome dislike for an attorney.
- Be influenced by how well your attorney is prepared.
- Drink too much at lunch.
- Be always organized/ never organized.
- Be an embarrassment to the legal community.
- Have incredible power over how an attorney conducts a case.
- Not have rested well last night.
- Expect you to behave in a civilized manner while under strain.
- Hate being lied to.
- Be very difficult to get rid of once your case is started.
- Feel that if you are clean, you will keep your children clean.
- Be protected and defended by their peers, even if not respected by them.
- Harbor resentment at having to work at a court level below their personal goal.
- Be the best judge available in this jurisdiction.
- Aren't any better at defending themselves in court than we are.

Which Judge is Mine?

In some jurisdictions you are assigned a judge that will be with you until your children are no longer wards of the court or until the judge dies. In other jurisdictions you get the luck of the draw each time you enter the court house. If there is no way to tell, which one you will get you may have to research all of them. If you can't do a through job because there are so many you may just need to sit in on a case or two for each one you can identify. Even if you don't get the right one you will have a much broader understanding of what can be done. You may even learn some important tips for running your case. Just being in the court rooms you will be able to identify some good psychologists and mediators. You may even be able to get a feel for the politics of the legal system in your city.

Who Do You Think You Are Talking To?

One of the major obstacles you may be required to deal with is the, "I-am-the-law" attitude. Humans assigned the task of interpreting, administering and/or enforcing laws seem to feel omnipotent. This begins with the entry level bureaucrat who makes you wait to file papers and becomes worse as individuals gain additional power. As the administrator of the law, which "must be right," they make you feel they are always "right." Any testing, questioning or opposing that law must make you "wrong." Therefore, you are less than worthy of their attention or concern. Anything you do that requires them to do additional work will compound their perceived assault on what is "right." The best attitude to adapt when dealing with these people is expressed when you say, "What do you need me to do. This is what I want to accomplish" or, "Tell me what you need me to do and I will try to do it." This trick does not always work, but it is your best chance.

A Judge Should Be Removed When

A judge should be removed when there is or has been:

- Any conflict of interest.
- Personal acquaintance of the judge with a principal in the case.
- Previous knowledge of the case.
- Personal interest in the case.

- Impaired judgment due to substance abuse (alcohol or drugs).
- Bias that appears with great frequency.
- Off-the-wall statements made during the proceedings.
- Published writings that voice politically incorrect viewpoints.
- Statements made about pending cases in inappropriate settings.
- Inability to listen to presented facts.
- Unwillingness to put aside personal feelings.

If you are a member of a minority and your judge does not understand the problems you face, this judge could be a problem.

Do not assume that because a judge is a member of a minority or even the same minority as you, that you do not need to investigate this judge carefully. Some members of minorities are prejudiced against their own people.

Evaluation Form for Judge #1

____ *Harmon J. Kirsch* ________

Mark the question at the end of the row for a quick reference later, but include a comment for more depth.
Very Good impression mark the box with a "+".
Fair impression mark the box with a "0".
Bad impression mark the box with a "-".

Did the judge follow proper procedure? *Seemed to*	-
Did the judge admit evidence? *Yes*	-
Did the judge allot time fairly? *Yes*	-
Did the judge remain attentive? *Yes*	-
Did the judge seem free of bias or prejudice? *No He was protecting the woman from herself*	-
Did the judge seem to lean to one side of the case or the other? *No*	-
Did the judge use the law fairly? *I think so*	-
Did the judge take notes? *Yes*	-
Did the judge ask questions? *Only one*	-
What the judge intolerant of? *Any back talk to him.*	-
What was the judge tolerant of? *Efforts of a person attempting to improve*	-
Did this judge seem tolerant of ProSe litigants? *No. He told one woman he didn't have time to teach her the law.*	-
Did you see this judge work with your attorney? *No*	-
Did the judge seem more helpful to one side than the other? *No*	-
Did the judge listen to the entire case or cut it short? *Usually, listened. I would have stopped the same ones he did.*	-
Information about this judge from any groups you belong to? *Two have been assigned to him, but not in court yet.*	-
Does your attorney have any information about this judge? *No He's new*	
Do you have any personal information about this judge? *No*	

Evaluation Form for Judge ____ *Clement Tsang* ________ #2 Mark the question at the end of the row for a quick reference later, but include a comment for more depth. Very Good impression mark the box with a "+". Fair impression mark the box with a "0". Bad impression mark the box with a "-".	
Did the judge follow proper procedure? *No*	+
Did the judge admit evidence? *Not ours*	+
Did the judge allot time fairly? *No*	+
Did the judge remain attentive? *No*	+
Did the judge seem free of bias or prejudice? *No*	-
Did the judge seem to lean to one side of the case or the other? *Yes*	+
Did the judge use the law fairly? *No*	+
Did the judge take notes? *No*	+
Did the judge ask questions? *No*	+
What the judge intolerant of? *Yes. He didn't like anything one attorney said.*	+
What was the judge tolerant of? *Everything one side wanted*	+
Did this judge seem tolerant of ProSe litigants? *I don't know thy both had attorneys*	+
Did you see this judge work with your attorney? *No*	+
Did the judge seem more helpful to one side than the other? *Yes*	+
Did the judge listen to the entire case or cut it short? *He never did let one side present their case*	+
Information about this judge from any groups you belong to? *none*	+
Does your attorney have any information about this judge? *No*	
Do you have any personal information about this judge? *No*	
After court I found out that one attorney had his office across the street from the court house. The other attorney was from a county near by. I think the judge was comfortable working with the local attorney and gave the other one the shaft. Like motions were accepted and rejected by the judge not on the merit of the motion, but on which attorney made the motion. I think we should attempt to find local representation in case we get this judge.	

Judge Comparison Form		
Donald Russell	Good	Will force parents to mediate the situation. Parent unwilling to cooperate will lose custody. Doesn't have any sympathy for pro se. Seemed even-handed. Watched this judge for a week.
James Duncan	No good	Runs hot and cold. Everything seemed to be continued, didn't seem to settle any cases. Watched this judge two days a week for four weeks.
Deadra McCall	Ok	New to the bench. Wants to really understand the case and really listens. Encourages pro se. Watched this judge three days each for two weeks.
Carl Eioler	Ok	Wants the problems solved before you get to his court. Seems willing to listen to reasonable parenting plans. Won't listen to anything about PAS or other "fads" as he called it. Watched this judge two days for two weeks.
Maxwell Franklin	Very bad	This judge is tired and hates the job. Does not want to listen and cut everyone short. No pro se tolerated at all. Watched this judge one day each for four weeks.
Gene Bolloinger	Ok	Assigns parenting class, mediation, home study and evaluation for all parents. Attorneys have to be on their toes and on time or he berates them in court. The results of the studies and evaluations are what he uses to make decisions. Very little in court testimony is permitted. This judge settled or made progress on every case he addressed. Watched this judge for three days for four weeks.
Robert Pettus	No idea	This judge never made it to court. I attempted to be in his court ten times.
Frank Stangate	Very good	Started court on time, knew the cases he was to hear, ran the trial well, listened to both sides, cut off mud slinging, issued decisions within days of the end of the hearing. Watched this judge for two weeks.
Parker Ness	Not good	Good judge one day, bad the next. I think he has a problem with blood sugar or something. No way to tell how he is going to be until the trial starts. One day he slept through one trial. Another day he seemed drunk. Watched this judge three days one week and four days the next.
Angelo Demarco	Good	Asked a lot of questions and made many comments that kept the witnesses and attorneys in line. Listened to friends of the court and experts, but did question their procedures and results. Issued more than fifty percent of his decisions at the end of the trial. Watched this judge for five days one week.

Judges Can Step Down

In small towns and communities it may be difficult to find a judge that does not know everyone in town. Or has strong ties to the well connected families. If you are a member one of these families you may feel the judge can be fair regardless of the social ties. If you are not a member of a well connected family, but face opposition that is, you will probably feel like the underdog. Judges may voluntarily remove themselves from hearing a case for any reason. This process is called recusal and causes no problem for the judge or the case if the judge does it voluntarily. Involuntary recusal or the disqualification of a judge because of judicial prejudice or bias is tricky business. If you believe that a judge cannot give your case a fair hearing, counsel can file a motion asking the judge to "recuse" him or herself. Unless the judge has a personal or business relationship that can be

documented with the opposition.
Your motion will probably fail, and may even backfire.

Judges do not want to be told that they cannot act fairly. There are cases in which a judge is on trial and all of the judges, municipal and superior, have recused themselves, making it necessary to bring in a judge from another county.

If you are unable to get away from a judge whose fairness you doubt, there are steps you can take to protect your case:

1. Do not do anything off the record. Make sure your attorney always has a court reporter when the judge is in attendance, especially in chambers. If the judge does not allow a court reporter in attendance, have your attorney object to this matter for the record.

2. Before the case goes to trial have your attorney request "a finding of facts." This requires the judge to list each point of law at which the case failed pursuant to existing statutes. Judicial error may be your best chance for appeal if the case goes against you.

3. Document any inappropriate behavior of the judge.

   Example:

   Two or more drinks at lunch while hearing your case.

   Statements made in public about your case.

   Statements made that indicate the judge holds the judicial position or the responsibility for decisions in disdain. Example "Any ape could do this job."

- "Ex Parte" (private) conversation with one of the principals and the judge in the case.

  If there is proof (photo or reliable witness) that the judge had a conversation with one of the people in the case without the other party in the case present, it is considered "ex parte."

Dear Judge, take a hike

Judges don't like releasing cases to other judges. They are aware of the number of cases assigned to them, how many are in process, how many have been completed and how many they have for one reason or another sent to another judge. As a matter of personal pride they don't want to appear to be slacking or inept at their job. Reasons judges find it acceptable are when their case load is just too large or they have a conflict of interest. Unacceptable reasons would include that their ability to be fair is in question or that they are incapable of doing the job for which they were elected or appointed. If you find it necessary to attempt to remove a judge you must be very polite and follow accepted procedures.

Steve Smith

DISTRICT JUDGE
361ST JUDICIAL DISTRICT
May 31, 2001
Mr. T.R. TynerFax (713) 888-8888
Mr. J.D. BuckhouseFax (713) 999-9999
RE: No. 32,44B- 361 In the matter of Red Jones
Dear Counsel:

I have received your Agreed Motion for Appointment of Special Judge. While I will agree to sign your order, I am somewhat perplexed as to why you did not have the courtesy to personally inform me (as opposed to informing my court coordinator) that a request would be made or the reasons for the request. Millie Cinder did call this morning with the stated reasons for the request (even though I deem it YOUR responsibility as primary counsel to contact me).

I serve as the elected judge of this court, and take that responsibility very seriously. Before requesting me to assign that responsibility to another judge (for whatever reason) I would expect counsel to contact me and give me reasons why I should decline to exercise my jurisdiction in favor of a judge who is not a resident of this county, even though he is a very qualified and capable jurist.

I would encourage you to contact the judge directly if this situation arises again. I wonder how this matter would have been handled had the elected judge been a Harris County family law judge.

Sincerely yours,

Steve Smith

Get Rid of a Bad Judge

If you feel you must get away from a bad judge, request a change of venue. Venue is changed to a different courthouse, city, county or district for the convenience of the parties or the witnesses. Sometimes this is called venue shopping. It is most easily accomplished if both attorneys are unhappy with the judge.

Whose Custody Case is this Anyway?

Judges are very sensitive to a case that looks driven or controlled by someone other than the parents of the children. It becomes worrisome because many questions come to mind including: Is this parent interested in custody or is their significant other interested in custody?

Is this custody case a vendetta of rivals for a parent's attention rather than the welfare of the children? Often an attorney will have your husband, wife, father, mother or significant other stay out of court as much as possible if they give the appearance of power or passion. If this person finishes your sentences for you, does more talking to your attorney than you do, and would be apt to make copious notes to your attorney during court, you may have this problem.

How Judges Decide

WHAT IS, SHALL REMAIN is also known as Status Quo (unless there is an obvious danger to the children). This statement reflects how most judges, psychologists and mediators feel about the custody of the child. The reasoning is that it is better for children to stay in a less than perfect situation than to inflict radical change on children if the court has no way of knowing if it will improve the situation for them.

Domestic law is vast and complex because each state makes laws to govern its people.

> There are federal laws passed by legislature. Judges in other domestic relations courts make decisions that your judge may consider as a precedent. The superior court in your state or other states make decisions that can affect the outcome of your case. The supreme court issues opinions and decisions, and there is an ever changing body of common law that impacts domestic law.

The judge's first obligation is to see that the rules of practice and procedure are followed in the case in the state in which the judge presides. Judges decide what admissible evidence in any case may be. In fact, admissible evidence is anything a judge allows to be seen or heard in court, regardless of the evidence's ability to meet legal standards of reliability or fairness.

The judge then considers "case law" which may have set a precedent that would affect this proceeding. In addition there are judicial rules that govern the judge's behavior. The judge then considers the evidence presented in the form of testimony and documentation. The decision is then strongly influenced by what the judge sees as the "best interest of the child."

If there is a law for the judge to follow, the judge will interrupt the statute to the best of his or her ability suing a process called Interpreted Statute.

If there is no case law to follow but another court has ruled with a decision that was so clearly written and well-reasoned, the judge will site Persuasive Authority and follow that ruling.

Often the attorneys will present previous case that closely resembles the case in question and the judge is able to rule using Precedent.

What Judges Cannot Do

1. Give you justice. Only a decision based on the law.

2. Give you custody because you have worked twelve hours a day for many years at a job you don't like so your family could live a good life.

3. Keep the other parent from starting new relationships.

4. Keep the other parent's new relationships away from your children.

5. Give you custody because you promise to change your lifestyle and devote more time to your children.

6. Make decisions on anything, but the information presented in court.

7. Give you custody or visitation because you are a good person.

8. Punish the other parent. Domestic relations court does not have the power or interest in meter out punishment.

What You Cannot Do with the Judge

- You cannot write letters or telephone the judge

directly. The judge is not permitted to read such letters or speak with you, your friends or relatives. If there is something you want the judge to know, your attorney should communicate if by scheduling a hearing.

- You cannot ignore a judge's instructions as to your behavior in court, how you deal with the opposition or information the judge wants you to bring to court.
- You cannot tell the judge what the judge will or will not do.
- The judge will not put up with temper tantrums either by you or your attorney.
- The judge is not there to right all the wrongs done to you by the opposition and will not be used as your tool of revenge.
- The judge will not tolerate hysterics from anyone in court.
- You cannot make a judge regret a decision to trust you, or give you a second chance.
- You cannot expect the judge to deny the opposition a fair hearing because you are convinced they are wrong or bad.
- You cannot decide the judge is in the pocket of the other lawyer, because you know they socialize together.

Your Expectations

Examples of situations listed in this chapter will give you an indication of some of the unexpected results that facing a judge could produce:

Situation # 1

You, your attorney, and your witnesses arrive at court, properly prepared to present your case. It appears the opposition is ready to proceed. The judge, without allowing either attorney to present the case, states, "I do not have enough information on which to make a decision, and I am ordering a home study done at the respondent's home. Court is dismissed until the report is submitted to me." Your attorney informs the judge there is no permanent residence in that state. The opposition lives with their in-laws. The judge, unmoved, orders the sixteen-month old child to be transported every three weeks from one parent's home to the other until the home study can be completed. Each parent is to pay the expense of returning the child to the other parent at the end of the time period.

Repercussions

Witnesses who have traveled a great distance or have taken time away from employment to appear in court may not be able to return for subsequent court dates. Expert witnesses responding to subpoena must still be paid. If witnesses are unable to testify when the date is reset, their evidence, including reports, will probably be inadmissible. The preparation time your attorney has spent, which you have paid for, is wasted.

Recourse

There is nothing you can do about the judge or the order except to accomplish the task as soon as possible. This judge may be giving the opposition enough rope to hang itself.

The judge may be putting off the decision because of a crowded court calendar. A disgusted judge may delay and extend the process to escalate the expenses for the offending litigants.

Situation # 2

As the opposition's attorney and your attorney are leaving the judge's chambers after concluding some normal pleadings, the judge states to no one in particular, "I am leaning to the respondent parent in this one." There was no court reporter to record the judge's statement.

You and your attorney are very concerned because only a little information about your case has been presented.

Repercussions

The judge's bias may produce a decision in favor of the opposition.

Recourse

Until a final decision is made, you have no recourse. Have your attorney formally insist that a court reporter be present at all future hearings in your case. Request a finding of fact requiring the judge to keep copious notes, citing each point of law on which the final decision is made.

Situation # 3

Your attorney has introduced, as witnesses on

your behalf, your child's doctor, the person who conducted your home study and examined the opposition's home study, and the court-appointed mediator. Their unanimous opinion was that you offer a superior environment for your child, and that, without reservation, the child should be placed with you. The judge interrupts the proceedings, saying, "I am not comfortable making a decision in this case. I would rather have a psychologist make the custody decision." Your attorney insists the judge hear more of the case before exploring that option. Your attorney questions the other parent, exposing several lies to the court.

Three people who worked with the respondent testify to the opposition's poor parenting skills and propensity to tell lies.

The judge stops the proceeding saying, "My position has not changed. I am unwilling to make a decision in this case." A psychologist will make the custody decision.

Plaintiff will pay seventy-five percent of the costs, and respondent will pay twenty-five percent. The child will be transported between the parents every five weeks until the psychologist has rendered a binding decision."

Repercussions

This may be the best thing that could happen. The judge has, in fact, removed him or herself from the equation.

The psychologist will be more sensitive to the best interests of the child and less interested in the rules of evidence than a judge. Testimony of witnesses already on the record and reports that the judge was not willing to consider will gain new validity.

Recourse

If you are not happy with the final decision, you can show that you did not get your day in court, and with the judge's finding of fact, you may have grounds for appeal.

Situation # 4

The opposition's attorney has filed a motion to delay the return of minor child five days before the child is to be returned from a five-week stay with the other parent. The opposition states that, because of unexpected expenses, he or she cannot afford the transportation back for the child.

The opposition claims that your actions have delayed a decision by the court-appointed psychologist, and the child should stay with the opposition until the decision is reached.

If the judge allows the delay, you may not be able to see your child for an undetermined period of time. Your attorney responds by requesting an oral argument and stating that the opposition has said on numerous occasions that he or she could afford to transport the child. Your attorney adds that the delay was requested by the psychologist and agreed to by both parents and the attorneys. Nothing happens because the judge is on vacation. Your attorney notifies the court that the opposition is in contempt of court for failing to return the child as ordered.

A judge sitting in for your judge does not find the opposition in contempt, but instructs the opposition to return the child. The opposition calls you, saying that if you want your child back, you must pay the air fare. If the other parent does not hear from you in the next two hours the entire deal is off and you will be out of luck.

Repercussions

You call your attorney and let him or her know about the call and that it will be very difficult for you to afford the new expense. Your attorney says he or she knows it is not right, but you can all go back to court. If you want the child back right now, you will just have to pay transportation expenses.

Recourse

It is just one of those things. Petition the court to change the exchange orders to indicate that the parent who is to have the child next is responsible for pick up transportation arrangements and expenses.

Situation # 5

You travel to another city in another state to pick up your child as ordered by the court. Your return flight is scheduled for later that day. When you arrive at the other parent's house, the child is not there. The child still is not there later that day or later that night.

Repercussions

You missed your flight and must now find a hotel room. Your ticket was non-changeable and non-refundable.

Recourse

With your court papers in hand, you go to the police department. They will usually tell you that the court orders from another state are not valid in their state. Therefore, you must find an attorney in the state you are in and have the papers "domesticated."

You may want to take care of this process when the final court papers are issued initially.

Situation # 6

You and your attorney were satisfied with the way the case went. The judge caught the opposition in several lies and seemed to hear and understand why your child should remain with you. The judge made several remarks that indicated you would get the results you wanted.

When everything was finished and the judge let the court know that the ruling would be made within the next thirty days, you were sure the judgment would be in your favor. The decision arrived and was not in your favor. You and your attorney were stunned.

Repercussions

You must turn your child over to the other parent. You and your child and your attorney are devastated.

Recourse

Unless you can get the judge to explain why the final decision was so different from statements the judge made in court there is probably nothing you can do about it. Appeal is very expensive and not usually successful. This happens and judges are not usually willing to reverse themselves.

Situation # 7

You become aware that there are some dangerous things happening at the other parent's home. You have a detective check things out. The report has documented ongoing and new frightening criminal activity that puts your child in danger during visitation. The information includes sixty-seven contacts with the police in the last two years by your child's fifteen-year-old step-brother, including drug and assault convictions, and ten contacts for the twelve-year-old for drugs and assault.

Your attorney filed the proper documentation listing compound negligence by the opposing attorney and the heretofore unknown hazards for your child. You are requesting supervised visitation to protect your child. The judge said he made his own investigation and requested that child protective services and the local police department make spot checks on the child. In addition, the judge said he has "sensitized" the other parent to the fact that this small child requires more adult supervision and that you must turn the child over for the visit.

Repercussions

You must turn your child over to the other parent.

Recourse

Have your attorney file papers to request a change of judge. The judge may have a bias, and it may not be appropriate for him to have acted as he did.

Examples of Judges' Rulings

"I do not feel comfortable making a ruling in this case with the evidence that has been presented. I will appoint a psychologist that the court has worked with on previous occasions, and I will find in accordance with the final report from that professional. Counsel will stop at the bailiff's desk for name and telephone number of the psychologist so your clients can make their appointments as soon as possible."

"I find that the best interest of the child will be served by approving the shared parenting plan worked out by the parties and their counsel. If the parties are not back in court for one year, this plan becomes permanent."

"Because of the animosity between these litigants, I feel there is no opportunity for reasonable exchange even when it comes to the child.

"I find for the petitioner and assign visitation in accordance with long distance guidelines to the respondent. In addition the respondent is ordered to pay child support in the amount of $295.00 per month, starting in thirty days, and is obligated to pay half of any medical and dental expenses not covered by the petitioner's insurance."

A Matter of Perception

Judges are human and fallible. A librarian does

not know all the information in the books at the library. A bank president cannot do anything he or she wants to do with all of the money on deposit. In a civilized society, the law governs the behavior of the people, and a judge is one of many people who interprets the law. The judge is not above you or the law.

Judicial Immunity

This is freedom from charge or obligation, which others are subject to, from civil liability for any acts performed in the judge's official capacity. The immunity is absolute, provided only that the judge is acting within his or her jurisdiction. The scope of the judge's jurisdiction must be constructed broadly to protect the court's independence; therefore, the judge will not be deprived of immunity because the action taken was in error, was done maliciously, or was in excess of the judge's authority; rather, the judge will be subject to liability only when the action taken was in clear absence of all jurisdiction.

Abuse of Discretion

After saying there is nothing you can do about a judge, it is important to be aware that there is some recourse. If you can find help and if you can afford the help, it may be possible to do something about the judge if you can prove abuse of discretion. abuse of discretion is: any unreasonable, unconscionable or arbitrary action taken without proper consideration of the facts and law pertaining to the matter; a standard of review applied by appellate courts in reviewing the exercise of flexible, but sensible course of action taken by trial courts and administrative agencies and persons; used by reviewing courts to upset determinations made when such determinations are wholly inconsistent with the facts and circumstances before the court, and the deductions that can reasonably be made from the facts and circumstances.

Filing a Formal Complaint

If you feel that you have been unfairly treated, consider filing a complaint with the court and the professional organizations to which the judge belongs. The complaint must list incidents in which the judge did not follow proper procedure or did not use proven techniques for their recommendations. It will probably not help your case, but it will indicate a real problem exists if many complaints are received about the same judge.

Confidentiality - Judge

There is no confidentiality. Every word spoken to a judge and taken down by the court reporter becomes public record. The only exception is if the judge seals the records to protect the children.

Judge's Ruling on Motion

NOTE: One can spend a great deal of time and expense creating long documents to have the Judge answer the motion with a one line acceptance or denial.

SUPERIOR COURT OF ARIZONA
MARICOPA COUNTY
November 24, 1993 HON. L.L. BAPLON R. Arable Deputy
No DR 92-02129
In re the Custody of BOBBY LONG
RANDALL LONG
Catharine Law
and
AMBER JONES
Faith Beli
This matter having been under advisement, Defendant/Respondent's Motion to Objection to Order submitted by Plaintiff/Petitioner's counsel is denied.
The Court has on November 22, 1993 signed the Order submitted by Plaintiff/Petitioner's counsel.
Docket Number 022

Judge or Jury

In some states you may request a jury trial for divorce or child custody. If you feel you have a strong case on an emotional level you may do better with a jury. A judge would be inclined to rule with the law where the jury may give circumstance more weight. It is common for attorneys to ask a question knowing that the opposing attorney will object and the judge will sustain the objection.

They do this because they know the bell can't be un-rung. Even when a jury is instructed to disregard a question or an answer there is no guarantee that will happen. As an example: The judge may say, "Strike the question from the record, and ladies and gentlemen, please strike the question from your mind. Mr. Match has no right to ask such a question without proof or evidence. Please remember that a question by an attorney is not testimony from a witness stand, and you may not consider it as such." Therefore, an attorney may raise a point in order to get the jury thinking along lines they may not have considered otherwise.

Trial judges have carte blanche on evidentiary rulings, and appellate courts don't throw out jury verdicts unless the evidentiary errors make a difference in the trial's outcome. Otherwise, they are legally considered "harmless error," although if it is your case that was harmed you will find it hard to believe any errors are harmless.

Chapter 19: Court

The Judicial System or Court: The branch of government, which is responsible for the resolution of disputes arising under the laws of the government. Family court is not an institution equipped to meet justice to the righteous and punishment to the corrupt. It is just another method of conflict resolution. It may be the poorest of all the available methods.

Time Line

Exactly how long your custody case will take varies with the complexity of your case and how each state handles the matter. This outline will give you an idea of what it takes to get through the process. Many elements can be added and some may be eliminated. Each process starts or stops the clock ticking.

1. **Complaint or Petition.** Is filed to notify the court and the other parent of intentions and what is wanted, such as primary custody, child support, and visitation.

2. **Response.** Must be filed within a time limit by the other parent if the complaint or petition filed does not meet their wants, needs and desires as they apply to the children. The initial complaint may be amended by the complainant until a response is filed.

3. **Temporary Orders.** Are set by the court assigning interim custody of the children and may or may not establish a new status quo. Either parent may request interim custody.

4. **Motions:** May include: Attack of jurisdiction, emergency, ex parte, for mediation, for home study, for psychological evaluation, for recusal, acceleration, continuance, to set trial, reconsideration, compel to disclosure and for sanctions to mention the most common.

5. **Discovery or Disclosure.** The process of getting information from the other parent.

6. **Negotiated, Mediated, Arbitrated Settlement.** Any method of settlement that avoids a formal court proceeding is superior to full in-court litigation.

7. **Directed or Summary Judgment.** A party may request form the court.

8. **Court.** The viewpoints of the litigants will be presented to the court under the rules of evidence and at the judge's discretion. The court may or may not make a final ruling. For any number of reasons, a judge may send the litigants to an alternate decision maker or decision making process.

9. Appeal

The Ultimate Battlefield

Because of the emotional and economic expense, court should be vigorously avoided. Strategically, it is a very poor move as too many factors over, which you have no control come into play.

A great deal of information you have about the judicial system is from television courtroom dramas. Most of it is grossly inaccurate. You probably think of your appearance in court as a one-time event, which will offer you an opportunity to tell your side of the case, listen to the opposition's declarations and have a decision reached within the hour.

Be prepared to find that a judge may hear your case and not render a decision on the evidence for a few days or many weeks. While there may be other outcomes, you must be prepared for at least these eventualities:

1. You may get the results you wanted and for which you worked.

2. You may get the results you have dreaded and worked to prevent.

3. The judge will not reach a decision at this time, keeping everyone involved in limbo for years.

4: The judge will make a decision neither side asked for or wanted.

This chapter will give you an overview of the terminology used, how the battlefield will be laid out, what basic maneuvers will look and sound like, and some of the possibilities making the process less stressful.

Types of Courts

Supreme Court of the United States

Clerk: William K. Suter, **(202) 479-3000** U.S. Supreme Court Bldg., W.A.,, DC 20543

The U.S. Supreme Court consists of nine justices, appointed for life by the President, with the advice and consent of the U.S. Senate. The Court holds one term annually, commencing on the first Monday in October. Jurisdiction: The U.S. Constitution provides that the Supreme Court is to exercise original jurisdiction in such matters as those involving foreign ambassadors and those in which a State is a party, and that appellate jurisdiction is subject to regulation by Congress. Congress has authorized the Court to, among other things, review decisions of the lower Federal courts and the highest courts of the States.

U.S. Court of Federal Claims

Clerk: David A. Lampen, **(202) 219-9657** 717 Madison Place, W.A.,, DC 20005

The U.S. Court of Federal Claims, formerly known as the U.S. Claims Court, mainly hears breach of contract claims filed by individuals and companies against the U.S. Government in those areas where such suits are allowed by Congressional waiver of sovereign immunity. Tort actions against the Government may not be filed in this court; rather, they are heard in U.S. district courts. Judges in the U.S. Court of Federal Claims are appointed by the President for fifteen year terms, subject to Senate confirmation. Appeals from Claims court decisions are to the U.S. Court of Appeals for the Federal Circuit.

U.S. Court of International Trade

Clerk: Joseph E. Lombardi, **(212) 264-2800** One Federal Plaza, New York, NY 10007

This court hears product classification and valuation determinations by the Customs Service plus appeals of unfair trade practice cases, involving antidumping and countervailing duty issues, from the Department of Commerce and the International Trade Commission. The judges are appointed for life by the President, subject to Senate confirmation.

U.S. Armed Forces Court of Appeals

Clerk of Court: Thomas F. Granahan, **(202) 761-1448** Fax: **(202) 761-4672**

450 E St. N.W., W.A.,, DC 20442-0001

Formerly known as the Court of Military Appeals, this court consists of five civilian judges.

They are appointed by the President for 15 year terms, subject to Senate confirmation. The court exercises appellate review of court-martial convictions. Its decisions prior to 1984 were final, but now are subject to Supreme Court review.

Court of Veterans' Appeals

Clerk: Robert F. Comeau, **(202) 501-5970** 625 Indiana Ave. # 900, W.A.,, DC 20004

This court was created by act of Congress in 1988 to review decisions of the Board of Veterans' Appeals whose decisions, prior to the establishment of the Court of Veterans' Appeals, were final. Appeals from the Court of Veterans' Appeals are to the U.S. Court of Appeals for the Federal Circuit. Judges are appointed for fifteen-year terms and subject to Senate confirmation.

United States Tax Court

Clerk of the Court: Charles S. Casazza, **(202) 606-8754** 400 Second St. N.W., WA., DC 20217

The Tax Court adjudicates controversies involving deficiencies or overpayments of income, estate and gift taxes. Tax Court judges are appointed by the President for fifteen year terms, subject to Senate confirmation.

U.S. Courts of Appeals

There are eleven circuit courts of appeals plus the District of Columbia Circuit and the Federal Circuit. The Federal Circuit is a specialized appellate court, its docket consisting mainly of patent appeals from the U.S. district courts and appeals.

The cases come from the U.S. Court of Federal Claims, the U.S. Court of International Trade, the Court of Veterans Appeals, and the Merit Systems Protection Board. The other circuits have appellate jurisdiction over the U.S. district courts (excluding patents) and selected federal agencies. The judges of the courts of appeals are appointed for life by the President, subject to Senate confirmation.

Federal Circuit Court

Clerk: Francis X. Gindhart **(202) 633-6550** 717 Madison Pl., N.W., # 209, W.A.,, DC 20439

Cases not referred to in the U.S. Constitution or granted to the federal court system by the laws of Congress fall under the jurisdiction of the 50 separate state court systems. Custody cases occasionally fall within the jurisdiction of or are affected by the rulings of Military, Rabbinical and Tribal courts.

Many of the state court systems are divided into three types of courts based on jurisdiction.

Appellate Court

The courts of Appellate jurisdiction include Supreme Court and the Court of Appeals. These courts hear appeals to review decisions made in a lower court.

Superior Court

The Superior Court, a court of general jurisdiction, is considered one court, but has locations in each of the counties of the state. The population of the county determines the number of authorized judgeships. The Superior Court has: (a) criminal jurisdiction over felony and high misdemeanor crimes; (b) civil jurisdiction involving amounts from $500 to $2500; (c) juvenile jurisdiction over all matters relating to persons under 18 years of age; (d) probate jurisdiction; (e) mental competency jurisdiction; and (f) appellate jurisdiction, which gives the Superior Court the authority to review decision of Justice, Police and Magistrate Courts.

Courts of Limited Special Jurisdiction

Courts of limited and special jurisdiction include Justice Courts and the Police or Magistrate Courts.

Justice of the Peace Courts have jurisdiction over: (a) low misdemeanor crimes; (b) preliminary hearings for felonies; (c) civil jurisdiction involving amounts less than $2500; (d) traffic cases; and (e) small claims cases involving less than $500.

Police or Magistrate Courts have jurisdiction over: (a) traffic cases; (b) misdemeanors; and (c) violations of city ordinances.

Military Court

Persons in the armed services are governed by The Uniform Code of Military Justice. Congress and the Courts have always recognized that the military is a unique community that needs unique rules. The UCMJ is the progeny of the Articles of War. They are simply different rules to fit unique circumstances. In many instances some consider that there is less constitutional protection, but in others there is more. As an example: 1) Miranda rights came into being in the civilian community in 1961. The military has had this since 1951, and it is an even greater protection since you must also be advised of the nature of what you are suspected of or nature of the actual charge against you. 2) Grand Jury - The Military has no grand jury system. It has Article 31 hearing, which is a hybrid grand jury / preliminary hearing system. In federal court civilians are indicted without input to the grand jury and have no right to attorney if called before it. In military at Article 31 you can have counsel and cross examine witnesses, simply you do not get to go as far as you can in a civilian preliminary hearing. State courts are not required to indict by grand jury and use preliminary hearings. Federal courts must indict by grand jury only. Article 31 falls in between. 3) Jury trial and a civilian federal trial:" twelve jurors required with a unanimous vote to convict; state felony can have six jurors, but must be unanimous to convict. Most states use twelve. Military requires two-thirds to convict and three-fourths to impose serious punishment. Military imposes punishment in a bifurcated proceeding for an all-guilt phase and punishment phase. Only death penalty cases are handled this way in civilian courts. In many civilian courts the judge imposes punishment. 4) Jury members -- Military uses blue ribbon juries, officers and senior non-commissioned officers. States and feds use anyone qualified from the voter list and some use a drivers license list. Feds used to use blue ribbon juries fifty years ago. 5) The review process in the military, after conviction, starts with the Commander who can overturn the conviction.

You then get your appeal to the court of review. The Court of Appeals in DC and Supreme Court. States and feds are about the same. 6) Jurisdiction -- The Warren Court took jurisdiction away from the military for off post offenses because Warren said military courts were to justice like military music is to music. Now that has come full circle, and the military has been given jurisdiction over all offenses committed by soldiers wherever they might occur. This implies trust by the Supreme Court in the system. In balance, the military system of justice is considered extremely fair and competent by most judges and well experienced and trained attorneys. F. Lee Baily (former Navy defense counsel) was once quoted as saying if he were guilty of a crime he would rather be tried in civilian courts. If he were innocent he would rather put his hands in the fate of a military jury.

Military Divorce

Even though your divorce involves one of you being in the military or formerly being in the military, the divorce is not handled by a military court. There are many important issues that must be addressed with which a competent family practice attorney might be unfamiliar. Therefore, selecting an attorney to handle a military divorce is critical. If your attorney doesn't have any experience with a military divorce, it may be necessary for the attorney to have a co-counsel with the experience to advise. Some of the vital issues include: How does the federal statute that covers the division of military retired pay affect your case? What are the applicable highlights of the amendments to the Act that were passed in 1990? What is the Code of Federal Regulations? What parts of it deal with military divorces? What is the Soldiers' and Sailors' Civil Relief Act and how does it relate to my situation? What are the limitations on obtaining direct payment from the pay center? How long does a spouse have to be married to a member in order for there to be an award of part of retired pay as property? How are maintenance and child support treated differently under the Act from an award of retired pay as property? What does the term "disposable retired pay" mean? Does the Act contain special jurisdictional limitation on the power of a state court to divide retirement? If there is a VA disability, how will the division of retired pay will be affected? How would the division of retired pay be affected if the member goes to work for civil service? What happens to the payments to the former spouse if she/ he dies before the member? What is the Survivor Benefit Plan? Can a court order a member to provide SBP protection for the former spouse and pay the premiums after the divorce? What are the income tax consequences of a division of retired pay as property and payments of maintenance out of retired pay? How does this state divide the retirement when the member is still on active duty?

It would also be important to know: How many cases has the attorney handled in the past year that involved military personal? How many of these cases went to trial? How many were settled?
In how many did the attorney represent the non-military or the military spouse? In how many did you represent each? What articles or publications has the attorney read on the subject in the past year? How many hours of Continuing Legal Education does the attorney have on this subject? When was the attorney's last military case? How familiar is the attorney with the Soldier's and Sailor's Civil Relief Act?

Tribal Court

The Indian Nations, located within the boundaries and protectorates of the United States of America, have all the rights and responsibilities of any other separate and sovereign nation, such as England, Australia or Japan. The custody of Native American Children is under the jurisdiction of the Tribal Court where the children are enrolled or the Tribal Court on the reservation on which the children live.

The laws that govern each reservation vary. If your children have been taken to a reservation, the decisions of the U.S. Courts will be dealt with as if you petitioned the court of any other sovereign nation.

You may be able to secure some help and guidance from: the Bureau of Indian Affairs, the Tribal Relations Branch, the Association of American Indian Affairs, the National Congress of American Indians the Bureau of Indian Affairs at the Department of the Interior, or the Division of Social Services.

Indian Child Welfare

The document that sets forth the laws concerning indian children is United States Code Title 25 - Indians Chapter 21 - Indian Child Welfare. The specific areas of interest are:

Chapter 21 - Indian Child Welfare

- 1901. Congressional findings.

Recognizing the special relationship between the United States and the Indian tribes and their members and the Federal responsibility to Indian people, the Congress finds -

(1) that clause 3, section 8, article I of the United States Constitution provides that "The Congress shall have Power * * * To regulate Commerce * * * with Indian tribes (FOOTNOTE 1) " and, through this and other constitutional authority, Congress has plenary power over Indian affairs; (FOOTNOTE 1) So in original. Probably should be capitalized.

(2) that Congress, through statutes, treaties, and the general course of dealing with Indian tribes, has assumed the responsibility for the protection and preservation of Indian tribes and their resources; (3) that there is no resource that is more vital to the continued existence and integrity of Indian tribes than their children and that the United States has a direct interest, as trustee, in protecting Indian children who are members of or are eligible for membership in an Indian tribe; (4) that an alarmingly high percentage of Indian families are broken up by the removal, often unwarranted, of their children from them by non-tribal public and private agencies and that an alarmingly high percentage of such children are placed in non-Indian foster and adoptive homes and institutions; and (5) that the States, exercising their recognized jurisdiction over Indian child custody proceedings through administrative and judicial bodies, have often failed to recognize the essential tribal relations of Indian people and the cultural and social standards prevailing in Indian communities and families.

- 1902. Congressional declaration of policy.

The Congress hereby declares that it is the policy of this Nation to protect the best interests of Indian children and to promote the stability and security of Indian tribes and families by the establishment of minimum Federal standards for the removal of Indian children from their families and the placement of such children in foster or adoptive homes, which will reflect the unique values of Indian culture, and by providing for assistance to Indian tribes in the operation of child and family service programs.

- 1903. Definitions. For the purposes of this chapter, except as may be specifically provided otherwise, the term:

(1) "child custody proceeding" shall mean and include -
(i) "foster care placement" which shall mean any action removing an Indian child from its parent or Indian custodian for temporary placement in a foster

home or institution or the home of a guardian or conservator where the parent or Indian custodian cannot have the child returned upon demand, but where parental rights have not been terminated.
(ii) "termination of parental rights" which shall mean any action resulting in the termination of the parent-child relationship;
(iii) "pre-adoptive placement" which shall mean the temporary placement of an Indian child in a foster home or institution after the termination of parental rights, but prior to or in lieu of adoptive placement; and
(iv) "adoptive placement" which shall mean the permanent placement of an Indian child for adoption, including any action resulting in a final decree of adoption. Such term or terms shall not include a placement based upon an act, which, if committed by an adult, would be deemed a crime or upon an award, in a divorce proceeding, of custody to one of the parents.
(2) "extended family member" shall be as defined by the law or custom of the Indian child's tribe or, in the absence of such law or custom, shall be a person who has reached the age of eighteen and who is the Indian child's grandparent, aunt or uncle, brother or sister, brother-in-law or sister-in-law, niece or nephew, first or second cousin, or stepparent;
(3) "Indian" means any person who is a member of an Indian tribe, or who is an Alaska Native and a member of a Regional Corporation.
A regional corporation is defined in 1606 of title 43;
(4) "Indian child" means any unmarried person who is under age eighteen and is either
(a) a member of an Indian tribe or
(b) is eligible for membership in an Indian tribe and is the biological child of a member of an Indian tribe;
(5) "Indian child's tribe" means
(a) the Indian tribe in which an Indian child is a member or eligible for membership or
(b), in the case of an Indian child who is a member of or eligible for membership in more than one tribe, the Indian tribe with which the Indian child has the more significant contacts
(6) "Indian custodian" means any Indian person who has legal custody of an Indian child under tribal law or custom or under State law or to whom temporary physical care, custody, and control has been transferred by the parent of such child;
(7) "Indian organization" means any group, association, partnership, corporation, or other legal entity owned or controlled by Indians, or a majority of whose members are Indians;
(8) "Indian tribe" means any Indian tribe, band, nation, or other organized group or community of Indians recognized as eligible for the services provided to Indians by the Secretary because of their status as Indians, including any Alaska Native village as defined in section 1602(c) of title 43;
(9) "parent" means any biological parent or parents of an Indian child or any Indian person who has lawfully adopted an Indian child, including adoptions under tribal law or custom. It does not include the unwed father where paternity has not been acknowledged or established
(10) "reservation" means Indian country as defined in section 1151 of title 18 and any lands, not covered under such section, title to which is either held by the United States in trust for the benefit of any Indian tribe or individual or held by any Indian tribe or individual subject to a restriction by the United States against alienation
(11) "Secretary" means the Secretary of the Interior
(12) "tribal court" means a court with jurisdiction over child custody proceedings and which is either a Court of Indian Offenses, a court established and operated under the code or custom of an Indian tribe, or any other administrative body of a tribe, which is vested with authority over child custody proceedings.

Subchapter I - Child Custody Proceedings

- 1911. Indian tribe jurisdiction over Indian child custody proceedings.

(a) Exclusive Jurisdiction

An Indian tribe shall have jurisdiction exclusive as to any State over any child custody proceeding involving an Indian child who resides or is domiciled within the reservation of such tribe, except where such jurisdiction is otherwise vested in the State by existing Federal law. Where an Indian child is a ward of a tribal court, the Indian tribe shall retain exclusive jurisdiction, notwithstanding the residence or domicile of the child.

(b) Transfer of proceedings; declination by tribal court

In any State court proceeding for the foster care placement of, or termination of parental rights to, an Indian child not domiciled or residing within the reservation of the Indian child's tribe, the court, in the absence of good cause to the contrary, shall transfer such proceeding to the jurisdiction of the tribe.

Absent objection by either parent, upon the petition of either parent or the Indian custodian or the Indian child's tribe: Provided, That such transfer shall be subject to declination by the tribal court of such tribe.

(c) State court proceedings; intervention

In any State court proceeding for the foster care placement of, or termination of parental rights to, an Indian child, the Indian custodian of the child and the Indian child's tribe shall have a right to intervene at any point in the proceeding.

(d) Full faith and credit to public acts, records, and judicial proceedings of Indian tribes

The United States, every State, every territory or possession of the United States, and every Indian tribe shall give full faith and credit to the public acts, records, and judicial proceedings of any Indian tribe applicable to Indian child custody proceedings to the same extent that such entities give full faith and credit to the public acts, records, and judicial proceedings of any other entity

- 1912. Pending court proceedings.

(a) Notice; time for commencement of proceedings; additional time for preparation

In any involuntary proceeding in a State court, where the court knows or has reason to know that an Indian child is involved, the party seeking the foster care placement of, or termination of parental rights to, an Indian child shall notify the parent or Indian custodian and the Indian child's tribe, by registered mail with return receipt requested, of the pending proceedings and of their right of intervention. If the identity or location of the parent or Indian custodian and the tribe cannot be determined, such notice shall be given to the Secretary in like manner, who shall have fifteen days after receipt to provide the requisite notice to the parent or Indian custodian and the tribe. No foster care placement or termination of parental rights proceeding shall be held until at least ten days after receipt of notice by the parent or Indian custodian and the tribe or the Secretary:

Provided, That the parent or Indian custodian or the tribe shall, upon request, be granted up to twenty additional days to prepare for such proceeding.

(b) Appointment of counsel

In any case in which the court determines indigency, the parent or Indian custodian shall have the right to court-appointed counsel in any removal, placement, or termination proceeding. The court may, in its discretion, appoint counsel for the child upon a finding that such appointment is in the best interest of the child. Where State law makes no provision for appointment of counsel in such proceedings, the court shall promptly notify the Secretary upon appointment of counsel, and the Secretary, upon certification of the presiding judge, shall pay reasonable fees and expenses out of funds, which may be appropriated pursuant to section 13 of this title.

(c) Examination of reports or other documents

Each party to a foster care placement or termination of parental rights proceeding under State law involving an Indian child shall have the right to examine all reports or other documents filed with the court upon, which any decision with respect to such action may be based.

(d) Remedial services and rehabilitative programs; preventive measures

Any party seeking to effect a foster care placement of, or termination of parental rights to, an Indian child under State law shall satisfy the court that active efforts have been made to provide remedial services and rehabilitative programs designed to prevent the breakup of the Indian family and that these efforts have proved unsuccessful.

(e) Foster care placement orders; evidence; determination of damage to child

No foster care placement may be ordered in such proceeding in the absence of a determination, supported by clear and convincing evidence, including testimony of qualified expert witnesses, that the continued custody of the child by the parent or Indian custodian is likely to result in serious emotional or physical damage to the child.

(f) Parental rights termination orders; evidence; determination of damage to child

No termination of parental rights may be ordered in such proceeding in the absence of a determination, supported by evidence beyond a reasonable doubt, including testimony of qualified expert witnesses, that the continued custody of the child by the parent or Indian custodian is likely to result in serious emotional or physical damage to the child.

- 1913. Parental Rights; Voluntary Termination.

(a) Consent; record; certification matters;

invalid consents

Where any parent or Indian custodian voluntarily consents to a foster care placement or to termination of parental rights, such consent shall not be valid unless executed in writing and recorded before a judge of a court of competent jurisdiction and accompanied by the presiding judge's certificate that the terms and consequences of the consent were fully explained in detail and were fully understood by the parent or Indian custodian. The court shall also certify that either the parent or Indian custodian fully understood the explanation in English or that it was interpreted into a language that the parent or Indian custodian understood. Any consent given prior to, or within ten days after, birth of the Indian child shall not be valid.

(b) Foster care placement; withdrawal of consent

Any parent or Indian custodian may withdraw consent to a foster care placement under State law at any time and, upon such withdrawal, the child shall be returned to the parent or Indian custodian.

(c) Voluntary termination of parental rights or adoptive placement; withdrawal of consent; return of custody

In any voluntary proceeding for termination of parental rights to, or adoptive placement of, an Indian child, the consent of the parent may be withdrawn for any reason at any time prior to the entry of a final decree of termination or adoption, as the case may be, and the child shall be returned to the parent.

(d) Collateral attack; vacation of decree and return of custody; limitations

After the entry of a final decree of adoption of an Indian child in any State court, the parent may withdraw consent thereto upon the grounds that consent was obtained through fraud or duress and may petition the court to vacate such decree. Upon a finding that such consent was obtained through fraud or duress, the court shall vacate such decree and return the child to the parent. No adoption, which has been effective for at least two years may be invalidated under the provisions of this subsection unless otherwise permitted under State law.

- 1914. Petition to court of competent jurisdiction to invalidate action upon showing of certain violations.

Any Indian child who is the subject of any action for foster care placement or termination of parental rights under State law, any parent or Indian custodian from whose custody such child was removed, and the Indian child's tribe may petition any court of competent jurisdiction to invalidate such action upon a showing that such action violated any provision of sections 1911, 1912, and 1913 of this title.

- 1915. Placement of Indian children.

(a) Adoptive placements; preferences

In any adoptive placement of an Indian child under State law, a preference shall be given, in the absence of good cause to the contrary, to a placement with (1) a member of the child's extended family; (2) other members of the Indian child's tribe; or (3) other Indian families.

(b) Foster care or pre-adoptive placements; criteria; preferences

Any child accepted for foster care or pre-adoptive placement shall be placed in the least restrictive setting, which most approximates a family and in which his special needs, if any, may be met. The child shall also be placed within reasonable proximity to his or her home, taking into account any special needs of the child. In any foster care or pre-adoptive placement, a preference shall be given, in the absence of good cause to the contrary, to a placement with -

(i) a member of the Indian child's extended family; (ii) a foster home licensed, approved, or specified by the Indian child's tribe; (iii) an Indian foster home licensed or approved by an authorized non-Indian licensing authority; or (iv) an institution for children approved by an Indian tribe or operated by an Indian organization, which has a program suitable to meet the Indian child's needs. (c) Tribal resolution for different order of preference; personal preference considered; anonymity in application of preferences.

In the case of a placement under subsection (a) or (b) of this section, if the Indian child's tribe shall establish a different order of preference by resolution, the agency or court effecting the placement shall follow such order so long as the placement is the least restrictive setting appropriate to the particular needs of the child, as provided in subsection (b) of this section. Where appropriate, the preference of the Indian child or parent shall be considered: Provided, That where a consenting parent evidences a desire for anonymity, the court or agency shall give weight to such desire in applying the preferences.

(d) Social and cultural standards applicable

The standards to be applied in meeting the preference requirements of this section shall be the prevailing social and cultural standards of the Indian community in which the parent or extended family resides or with which the parent or extended family members maintain social and cultural ties.

(e) Record of placement; availability

A record of each such placement, under State law, of an Indian child shall be maintained by the State in which the placement was made, evidencing the efforts to comply with the order of preference specified in this section. Such record shall be made available at any time upon the request of the Secretary or the Indian child's tribe.

- 1916. Return of custody.

(a) Petition; Best Interests Of Child

Notwithstanding State law to the contrary, whenever a final decree of adoption of an Indian child has been vacated or set aside or the adoptive parents voluntarily consent to the termination of their parental rights to the child, a biological parent or prior Indian custodian may petition for return of custody and the court shall grant such petition unless there is a showing, in a proceeding subject to the provisions of section 1912 of this title, that such return of custody is not in the best interests of the child.

(b) Removal from foster care home; placement procedure

Whenever an Indian child is removed from a foster care home or institution for the purpose of further foster care, pre-adoptive, or adoptive placement, such placement shall be in accordance with the provisions of this chapter, except in the case where an Indian child is being returned to the parent or Indian custodian from whose custody the child was originally removed.

- 1917. Tribal affiliation information and other information for protection of rights from tribal relationship; application of subject of adoptive placement; disclosure by court.

Upon application by an Indian individual who has reached the age of eighteen and who was the subject of an adoptive placement, the court, which entered the final decree shall inform such individual of the tribal affiliation, if any, of the individual's biological parents and provide such other information as may be necessary to protect any rights flowing from the individual's tribal relationship.

- 1918. Reassumption of jurisdiction over child custody proceedings.

(a) Petition; suitable plan; approval by Secretary

Any Indian tribe, which became subject to State jurisdiction pursuant to the provisions of the Act of August 15, 1953 (67 Stat. 588), as amended by title IV of the Act of April 11, 1968 (82 Stat. 73, 78), or pursuant to any other Federal law, may reassume jurisdiction over child custody proceedings. Before any Indian tribe may reassume jurisdiction over Indian child custody proceedings, such tribe shall present to the Secretary for approval a petition to reassume such jurisdiction, which includes a suitable plan to exercise such jurisdiction.

(b) Criteria applicable to consideration by Secretary; partial retrocession (1) In considering the petition and feasibility of the plan of a tribe under subsection (a) of this section, the Secretary may consider, among other things: (i) whether or not the tribe maintains a membership roll or alternative provision for clearly identifying the persons who will be affected by the reassumption of jurisdiction by the tribe; (ii) the size of the reservation or former reservation area, which will be affected by retrocession and reassumption of jurisdiction by the tribe; (iii) the population base of the tribe, or distribution of the population in homogeneous communities or geographic areas; and (iv) the feasibility of the plan in cases of mul-titribal occupation of a single reservation or geographic area. (2) In those cases where the Secretary determines that the jurisdictional provisions of section 1911(a) of this title are not feasible, he is authorized to accept partial retrocession, which will enable tribes to exercise referral jurisdiction as provided in section 1911(b) of this title, or, where appropriate, will allow them to exercise exclusive jurisdiction as provided in section 1911(a) of this title over limited community or geographic areas without regard for the reservation status of the area affected. (c) Approval of petition; publication in Federal Register; notice; reassumption period; correction of causes for disapproval

If the Secretary approves any petition under subsection (a) of this section, the Secretary shall publish notice of such approval in the Federal Register and shall notify the affected State or States of such approval.

The Indian tribe concerned shall reassume jurisdiction sixty days after publication in the Federal Register of notice of approval. If the Secretary disapproves any petition under subsection (a) of this section, the Secretary shall provide such technical assistance as may be necessary to enable the tribe to correct any deficiency, which the Secretary identified as a cause for disapproval.

(d) Pending actions or proceedings unaffected

Assumption of jurisdiction under this section shall not affect any action or proceeding over, which a court has already assumed jurisdiction, except as may be provided pursuant to any agreement under section 1919 of this title.

- 1919. Agreements between States and Indian tribes.

(a) Subject coverage

States and Indian tribes are authorized to enter into agreements with each other respecting care and custody of Indian children and jurisdiction over child custody proceedings, including agreements, which may provide for orderly transfer of jurisdiction on a case-by-case basis and agreements, which provide for concurrent jurisdiction between States and Indian tribes.

(b) Revocation; notice; actions or proceedings unaffected

Such agreements may be revoked by either party upon one hundred and eighty days' written notice to the other party.

Such revocation shall not affect any action or proceeding over, which a court has already assumed jurisdiction, unless the agreement provides otherwise.

- 1920. Improper removal of child from custody; declination of jurisdiction; forthwith return of child: danger exception.

Where any petitioner in an Indian child custody proceeding before a State court has improperly removed the child from custody of the parent or Indian custodian or has improperly retained custody after a visit or other temporary relinquishment of custody.

The court shall decline jurisdiction over such petition and shall forthwith return the child to his parent or Indian custodian unless returning the child to his parent or custodian would subject the child to a substantial and immediate danger or threat of such danger.

- 1921. Higher State or Federal standard applicable to protect rights of parent or Indian custodian of Indian child.

In any case where State or Federal law applicable to a child custody proceeding under State or Federal law provides a higher standard of protection to the rights of the parent or Indian custodian of an Indian child than the rights provided under this subchapter, the State or Federal court shall apply the State or Federal standard.

- 1922. Emergency removal or placement of child; termination; appropriate action.

Nothing in this subchapter shall be construed to prevent the emergency removal of an Indian child who is a resident of or is domiciled on a reservation, but temporarily located off the reservation, from his parent or Indian custodian or the emergency placement of such child in a foster home or institution, under applicable State law, in order to prevent imminent physical damage or harm to the child.

The State authority, official, or agency involved shall insure that the emergency removal or placement terminates immediately when such removal or placement is no longer necessary to prevent imminent physical damage or harm to the child and shall expeditiously initiate a child custody proceeding subject to the provisions of this subchapter, transfer the child to the jurisdiction of the appropriate Indian tribe, or restore the child to the parent or Indian custodian, as may be appropriate.

- 1923. Effective date.

None of the provisions of this subchapter, except sections 1911(a), 1918, and 1919 of this title, shall affect a proceeding under State law for foster care placement, termination of parental rights, pre-adoptive placement, or adoptive placement, which was initiated or completed prior to one hundred and eighty days after November 8, 1978, but shall apply to any subsequent proceeding in the same matter or subsequent proceedings affecting the custody or placement of the same child.

Types of Cases

Civil Cases

Civil Cases are one person or entity suing another person or entity for money or property.

Criminal Cases

Criminal Cases are an entity of the State suing a person or entity for breaking a law and may involve fines and prison sentencing.

Administrative Cases

Administrative Cases are a matter of due process and called for by circumstances or accepted legal standards.

Are All Court Appearances Equal?

Yes and No. To the court, they are. To you they should be. Any person who fails to appear for any ordered court date may be charged with contempt and, subject to a Bench Warrant for Arrest to be issued.

Pre-trial Conference

Make an appointment to meet and talk with your attorney for a reasonable length of time, before your court date is scheduled. This conference may take several hours or an entire day. This is not an opportunity to be social or complain about what the opposition has been doing You are paying for this time, so make it productive. You and your attorney will devise a battle plan. The plaintiff usually presents its case first, stating why this action has been brought and what it wants the court to do.

The defense has the opportunity to state the case from its perspective and answer statements of the plaintiff and make a request for action. Your attorney should be prepared to present your case in any order the judge decides to proceed. Your attorney's approach to the case will depend on who is heard first.

How Subpoenas Work

A subpoena is an order of the court to produce documents (specified in the subpoena) and/or to attend at court to give oral evidence, at the date, time and place specified. Although a subpoena is an order of a court, subpoenas are issued at an administrative level by the court at the provocative of one of the parties to the proceedings. The judge generally knows nothing about the subpoena until the date for production of the documents or the date the person attends at court to give evidence. While the documents must be produced to the court (not to the party who requested and had the subpoena served), and a person subpoenaed to give evidence must attend at court. At the proceeding the court will decide whether to permit the documents to be seen by the parties and whether questioning of the person subpoenaed will be permitted and, if so, to what extent. Don't make the mistake of delivering important documentation directly to the opposition.

Court Before Court

Long before you have your big day in court, you may have preparation, initial filings, exparte orders, response, preliminary hearings, temporary order hearings, discovery, enforcement hearings and contempt of court hearings. Actually, even after custody has been decided you may be back in court for most of these procedures. Custody cases are different from any other because it involves children (or adults requiring that others have custody of them). In other types of cases a decision is reached and the matter is concluded. A new law suit would have to be filed to address or change the decision. With child custody, the children actually become wards of the state and the state maintains continuing jurisdiction. Even if you win custody of your children, you actually have fewer rights than you did before the action began.

An initial filing is done to notify the court of ones intent to use the legal system to gain a decision in a matter. Once the other party is served, you notify the court with proof of service, that it has jurisdiction and the clock starts ticking. Then there is a waiting period, which gives the parties time to get the required procedures completed and documents filed.

This may be as short as ninety days or as long as a year; however, it actually takes as long it takes. As long as progress is being made, you will have to continue to be patient. If there is no action for a long period of time (established by rule or whim, I can't actually tell), the court may dismiss the action. If this happens the case would have to start over again, if the parties were still interested.

Preliminary hearings are different for each jurisdiction and may involve; how much time the case will need on the docket, if everything is ready such as answers to complaints, counter claims, evaluations, mediation and parenting classes. Not all cases require a preliminary hearing. The preliminary hearing may be built into the system of that court or take place because it has been requested.

Often temporary orders are issued at preliminary hearing. If court orders, temporary or permanent are not obeyed, a party may make a motion for an enforcement hearing. Eventually if all the procedural matters are handled properly, the court date can be set so the content of the case can be addressed and a decision reached.

Your Case Strategy

Your strategy will be decided by the order in which the case is presented. The petitioner has the option of deciding whether or not they want to go first. Most often it is to your advantage to be the first to present your side of the case. If you go first you can control the order in which the evidence and witnesses are presented. It keeps the opposition off balance and you get the last word before the case is determined.

Some of the elements of this planning will be to decide:

- What the main focus of your case will be.
- Which and when witnesses will be called giving you the opportunity to call your witnesses in a logical order that tells your story in the best light. It also allows you to make sure your best witnesses are heard before the judge tires and calls a halt to the proceeding.
- Your best witness will be low key and professional. Every word they utter should be a plain statement of fact, with little embellishment, simple yes and no whenever possible. The witness should offer no spin since he or she will come across as credible.
- If you have the opportunity to present your case first you may consider calling the opposition first. Even though you know you aren't going to like the things they say. There are several advantages you can gain. Primarily, you know the opposition has been prepared to testify and how to best tell their story. The opposition expected to have heard your case before they had to answer questions. Now they have no idea what will be asked. Additionally, they haven't had time to get comfortable with the surroundings or the judge and will probably give more information than their attorney would have liked. Because they have spent hours or days with their attorney focusing on the key points of their case you will hear those now rather than in the order the attorney would have liked them presented.
- If your case is presented very well and the judge feels he has heard enough from the opposition, you may be able to ask for and get a preempted verdict.
- If you are the second to present your case and you feel the opposition has left key elements out of their case (such as proving you are an unfit parent) you may ask for and get a summary judgment.
- As you know now, what you think the main focus of the opposition's case will be is important since you have to be ready for anything including being the opposition's first witness. Plan and practice with your attorney in case this happens.
- Your power will lie in all of the things you did right that the opposition did not even think of to do.

Ask your attorney to fill out a court presentation outline form for each way your attorney may handle the case. This form will help you see the battle plan your attorney intends to follow. Being informed of the plan will keep you from executing a "Charge of the Light Brigade" prematurely. It will also keep you from trying to get information into the proceeding that you think your attorney has forgotten.

Make sure your attorney has a witness outline form, a data sheet, and a subject profile for deposition Form on each person either side may call as a witness. This will give your attorney a solid basis for questioning.

Would your case present better before a judge or a jury? See, Judge or Jury in Chapter 18: Judges.

Court Presentation Outline Form

Witnesses We Will Call:

Amber Jones (if we present our case first)

Randall Long

Dr. WoodBobby's baby doctor

Mr. Solomonconciliator court evaluator

Shawn Jamesonhome study evaluator

Gary Mitchell co-worker of Amber

Patty Lead employee of Rebecca Long

Major Points We Will Cover:

Observations of parental involvement with Bobby

Amber's poor decision making abilities and unstable life

Amber's continued association with dangerous people

Amber's willingness to lie to the court

Witness the opposition will call: Amber

Major points we want to cover:

Why she left Phoenix, how many places she has lived, drug arrest

Non-Issue

It is not enough to know the law. It is important to understand how it is applied in a case like yours. The court will only deal with what the court regards as the real issues of the case. Your attorney will be able to tell you if the court has already dealt with you in regard to an issue that concerns you or why it is a non-issue.

Making a "fuss" over a non-issue will hurt your case. Wasting the court's time with non-issues is a principal mistake made by ProSe litigants.

Your Assignment

As you map out a strategy to answer difficult questions, you will become better prepared and less likely to say something damaging to your case. Discuss the subjects that will be covered. Explore areas that may arise. Try to anticipate "surprise" questions designed to catch you off guard.

- Ask your attorney, which subjects to avoid. Subjects, which do not apply to this matter and that you should not raise must be clear in your mind. The opposition may not be able to delve into your character or past acts that are not related to the question before the court. This is taboo unless you open the issue yourself by placing evidence of your good character or prior acts before the court.
- Accusations or subjects that you fear the opposition will broach should be discussed with your attorney. Many of the "skeletons" you fear would make spicy reading in the local newspaper will not pertain directly to this case and will be disallowed by the judge.
- If your attorney has the time, ask to practice some questions that you might be asked. Practicing will fix the right response in your memory and eliminate hazy answers. For example, the opposition's attorney may ask, "Did your attorney tell you what to say?" You should say, "My attorney told me not to lie. My attorney did not tell me what to say." It is illegal for an attorney to tell you what to say.
- Make charts of important documented information such as weight loss and gain or school absenteeism. This will insure facts that seem apparent to you are not inadvertently or purposely misread. People retain fifteen percent of what they hear, fifty percent of what they see and eighty-five percent of what they see and hear simultaneously.
- Ask your attorney how the opposition's attorney might handle the case. Understanding the opposition's point of view will make it easier for you.
- Practice listening to entire statements or questions people ask before you begin to think about your answer. You have the mental ability to hear and understand over six hundred words per minute and the average person speaks at less than two hundred words per minute. You have a great deal of time. Take the time you need.
- Make sure you have listened well enough to understand what the person speaking is saying. Ask for clarification if you do not understand. This important exercise will make you a better witness for your side. Practice answering only the question asked. Answer it without elaboration. Do not give a date or time or place unless you are sure. If you are not sure, say, "I do not remember." You may be pressured to guess. Don't do it.

Refreshed Memory

Review any documents you prepared to refresh your memory. Even though during court you may be presented with documents to refresh your memory that were not prepared by you (or prepared by the person who is giving the testimony) they can be used for that purpose.

The original ruling disallowing the document was reversed 10/2000 in Horton v. Switzer, et al. Michigan Court of Appeals.

Last Review

Read any documents containing your statements, such as depositions. Review what you have said in the past about subjects that will be raised. During the last few weeks and days before court, the stress becomes so great that normal people sometimes crack. It is especially important to avoid doing anything that may effect your case adversely. The advantage can shift from one side to the other in the weeks, days and hours before the trial starts. The tension and costs will become more difficult to handle. Keep your eye on the goal. Avoid people and situations that discourage and wear you down.

What Is a Witness?

Witnesses are the people who give evidence in court. A witness may testify to what he has seen, heard or done. A witness may not testify as to what someone else told him he saw or did. This or any other information would be "hearsay" and, therefore, not allowed. Witnesses have information about the case that can impact the decision of the court. Do not assume that the witness agrees with your version of the facts, even if the witness saw the same event you did at the same time. Each person's perception of an event can differ greatly. Ask your potential witnesses to give a synopsis of the events in question. This will clarify your understanding of their point of view. Do not build your entire case on the testimony of one person.

Don't panic when you see the list of witnesses presented by the opposition. They may be listing names to cause you concern when all the while they are not sure that he or she can get these people into court or what these people may testify to.

The opposition may have a powerful witness for his or her side. Nonetheless, your attorney may find part or all of the testimony more in your favor than the opposition's. The opposition is just as vulnerable to "friendly fire" as you are and may not be as aware of the possibility or be as prepared to employ effective damage control. A witness cannot be forced to testify. To avoid any legal ramifications, a witness may answer all questions, "I do not remember." It is against the law to threaten or coerce a witness.

Fill out a background outline for each witness you or the opposition may present so your attorney has a solid base on which to build or attack. Provide your witnesses with a copy of "Witnesses' Guide for Testifying for Deposition or in Court," available in the back of this manual.

Confidentiality - Witnesses

There is no confidentiality. Every word spoken to a witness for your side may become ammunition for the opposition and/or public record. It is best not to give any witness any information the person does not already have.

Your Children Testifying in Court

Testifying in court is a traumatic experience for children. Repeated questioning, lengthy delays, testifying in front of the two most important people in the children's life without hurting either one of them may increase their anxiety and sense of helplessness.

Domestic relations court generally involves only a judge rather than a jury. The judge may allow the children's testimony be presented in the judge's chambers. This limits the number of people in the office during the children's testimony.

Competence of Child to Testify

The ability of a child to perceive, recall, and communicate relevant events is a question of competence. Initially, this is a question of law for the judge, but if the witness satisfies this test, the problem becomes one of credibility, whose testimony may determine the case. To be competent, the witness must have the ability to understand the nature and significance of the oath and be able to conform his or her conduct to it. In custody cases, this issue often arises with "child" witnesses. In this case, it must be shown that the child understands the difference between right and wrong in order to be competent to testify. If the witness passes muster with the judge, it is left to the lawyer to show that the witness cannot possibly perceive, recall and communicate the relevant event effectively.

Knowing Truth from Lie

To have a child qualify to testify he or she must satisfy the two parts of the Oath-taking Competency test.

The first is, does the child know the truth from a lie. Most children are competent to testify in court as witnesses if their lawyers questioned them the right way. Determining if children five and older know what a lies is, can be established. They are able to consistently identify who is telling the truth in a stated situation. This is accomplished by telling the child a short story with a series of characters. The characters and a situation are described then the children are asked to select the characters who are telling the truth. Demonstrating a child's ability to see the lie is much more accurate than requiring a definition of a lie from a child. This is because even by age seven about half of the children can't provide a minimally sufficient definition of truth or lies. Nor could they explain the difference between the terms. Once it can be demonstrated that the child understands what the truth is, the first part of the oath-taking competency test is satisfied.

The second part of the oath-taking competency test determines if the child knows that it is wrong to lie. Using the original story the child is told that one story-character told a lie and the other story-character told the truth. Then the child is asked, which story character is going to get in trouble or did something bad. If both parts of the oath-taking competency test are satisfied the child can testify.

Helping Your Child Testify

Listed below are some steps you can take to help make this ordeal easier for the children. Testimony about an event may be easier than having to directly call an person a liar. This is true because children are afraid to tell any adult they have done something wrong, let alone call any adult a liar.

1. Formally request that the court appoint a special attorney or advocate. This person is called a Guardian Ad Litem (GAL) and ensures proper protection of the children. Usually, the GAL comes from a list of names kept by the judge, or each district court has at least one full-time GAL that is appointed by statute in every case involving allegations of child abuse. The whole point of the GAL is to be an independent advocate for the child irrespective of the parent's wishes or position on the issues.

2. Give the attorneys the children's schedule listing naps, meals, school schedule, vacation and birthday to help them pick a reasonable time and day for the children to testify. If your children have any special ways of showing fear or distress, add this to the list. Identify any special measures that may be taken to alleviate your children's anxiety during questioning.

3. Have the children wear tidy, comfortable clothes that they like.

4. Do not go over the children's testimony before the courtroom appearance. The other attorney may ask the children, "Did someone tell you to say that?" If it looks as if you have coached the children, your case could be badly damaged. Instruct your children to tell the truth. Then if the other attorney asks, what you told the children to say, they will say, "I was told to tell the truth."

5. Explain the court process to the children at a level each can understand. This will greatly reduce the stress they will feel. Take your children on a tour of the courthouse building and courtroom several days before they are scheduled to appear.

6. Notify the parties that the child is never to be asked, "What would happen to you if you told a lie?" or "If you don't tell the truth, do you know what will happen to you?' This causes the child to imagine that he or she is telling a lie, which is frightening for the child because they're afraid of the consequences. This is especially true if the child has been accused of lying and threatened by an adult when the child knew he or she was telling the truth.

7. Tell your children that if a question is confusing or not understood, they should say so.

8. Tell your children that you love them, and that everything will work out just fine.

9. There may be long delays and periods of waiting, so bring some quiet toys or books to amuse the children.

10. After the children's testimony, assure them you love them and are proud of them.

Challenging a Child's Testimony

An attorney wishing to challenge a child's testimony in court has to be careful to avoid upsetting the child and offending the court.

One way to do this is on direct examination, embark on a complex line of questions to the child, then ask no questions at all on re-direct. This will show the court that children have no place in the courtroom, and that the examiner is not going to risk emotional injury to innocent children in order to win a case.

Another way attorneys challenge a child witness' credibility is to show the child can't distinguish between what they have experienced and what they have been told. To demonstrate this, an attorney will get the child to relay information about events that are outside their personal knowledge. This can be accomplished by having the child witness testify to an event the attorney knows the child did not witness. Then question the child to establish the attorney's point. They will ask a questions to establish the mental state of the witness at the time the event was witnessed. Were they at a party? Who else was there?

Was the witness inside or outside? Was it day or night? The parts the witness doesn't remember, did someone tell them about it? It is not uncommon for a child witness to mistakenly believe they have personal knowledge of an event because they simply do not know what that term means. Therefore, the attorney must take a very simplistic approach to the inquiry and determine that their information did not come from someone they love who has never told a lie!

Suppress Child's Testimony

A hearing may be held to determine whether a child's testimony is tainted and should be suppressed. In New Jersey v. Margaret Kelly Michaels found nine factors sufficient to justify a pretrial taint hearing. They are:

1. absence of spontaneous recall;
2. interviewer bias against defendant, for what the child should be disclosing;
3. repeated leading questions;
4. multiple interviews;
5. incessant questioning;
6. vilification of defendant;
7. ongoing contact with peers and references to their statements;
8. use of threats, bribes and cajoling; and
9. failure to videotape or otherwise document the initial interview sessions.

See Michaels, at 1377. Com. v. Callahan, 1998 WL 808850 *5 (Mass.Super. 1998).

Custody appeal case contending the trial court's error in disallowing a child to testify. IN THE INDIANA COURT OF APPEALS, Sandy L. White v. Daniel G. White

Fear, Bias, Prejudice or Interest

A child witness's credibility can also be brought into question by identifying a witness's fear, bias, prejudice, partisanship, or outright corruption. Fear can be instilled through direct or implied threat.

Bias is an improper predisposition in favor of one side of a controversy, while prejudice has been defined as an improper predisposition against another. Partisanship amounts to favoritism toward one side for whatever reason. Corruption is more heinous, involving such things as bribery or false testimony.

Content of Child's Testimony

Even the testimony of a child witness must satisfy the personal knowledge requirement. That means the child must have personally seen, felt, heard or experienced the event in question. Any information to be offered by a child should be investigated by your lawyer during the discovery phase. At trial, the child can be prevented from testifying about those matters of which the child has no personal knowledge.

If it is critical to cross-examine, it is important to be as delicate and brief as possible such as asking if the child knew she would testify in court, how she knew, and who prepared her for the big day. Often, you will find that the child was in opposing counsel's office the day before. This will severely injure the credibility of the opposing party, and opposing counsel because it increases the pressure on the child witness.

Anger Against You

It is normal to experience a great deal of anger from the other parent and their supporters. This will happen even when things are going relatively well with the other parent.
The parent knows the truth, but the other parent's allies are still bearing the insult of the horrific things they believe you have done.

Your child, their child will attempt to support both of you. This is very hard on the child. The other parent's pain and anger may be reflected in the child's testimony. It is not the child's fault and you should not hold what the child says in court against the child. The child may be expressing anger against the system as well as the parents.

Contempt of Court

If there is a court order in place and a person willfully and deliberately violates a court order without a legally sufficient excuse, the person is said to be in contempt of court. If there is no court order in place, there's no contempt of court.

Conduct in court, which interferes or stops a court in the administration of its duties, is contempt of court. The willful and intentional failure to comply with a court order, judgment, or decree by a party to the action is also contempt of court which, may be punishable in a variety of ways.

The first kind of contempt is civil. Civil contempt is often addressed by incarceration of the offending person until that person complies with the court order. As an example: A man is ordered to produce family financial information for the last three years. He refuses to do so. The judge says you can sit in jail until you are willing to produce the documents we have requested. The father has "the keys to the jail house in his hands." He gets out as soon as he obeys the orders of the court.

Criminal contempt is as punishment for disobedience of a court directive, including, but not limited to, failure to pay child support and acting in a disorderly manner in open court. Criminal contempt can be detected by its consequence, which could include punishment, by incarceration for a definite time period and/or a fine. As an example: The man mentioned above has cooled his heals in jail for two weeks. He sends word to the court that he now wishes to comply with the court order. His current wife has informed the court that she has been instructed to get the documents out of the safe deposit box at the bank and deliver them to the court by 2:00pm Tuesday. By Thursday the documents have still not been delivered to the court. When contacted by the court the wife said she burned the documents because they were none of the courts business. The judge could put the wife in jail for a couple of years and fine her.

Filing a Contempt Motion

If the other parent is in violation of an order, you can file a complaint for contempt of court. In most states it is just like filing a motion relating to a pending case, except you must have it personally served on the other parent. Pay a filing fee. Then it will usually take several weeks before the court notifies you of the date your case will be heard.

In court you will have to present and prove your allegations using good records and testifying about the accuracy of your record keeping. Unless the other parent has a great excuse for not complying, the judge will probably order the other parent to comply immediately or face imprisonment. Example of Motion filed in a contempt of hearing case:

Case No. 42,843A-136

In The Case Of Kim Lee Ong, A Child

IN THE DISTRICT COURT OF CLARK COUNTY, TEXAS 136TH JUSICIAL DISTRICT

First Amended Motion For Enforcement And Order To Appear

This First Amended Motion for Enforcement is brought by Ron Lee Ong, Movant. In supp[ort, Movant shows:

1. Discovery Level

Discovery in this case is intended to be conducted under level 2 of rule 190 of the Texas Rules of Civil Procedure.

2. Movant

Movant is a resident of Beaumont, Texas. Movant is the possessory conservator of the child subject of this suit.

3. Child

Name: KIM LEE ONG

Sex: Female

Birth Place: Plano Texas

Birth Date: January 2, 1990

Present Address: 343 Waltan, Plano, TX

Social Security No: 629-16-2765

4. Jurisdiction

This Court has continuing, exclusive jurisdiction of this case as a result of prior proceedings.

5. Parties Entitled to Citation the parties entitled to notice are as follows:

a. Pam Ong, Respondent, whose address is 343 Waltan, Plano, TX,. Respondent is a joint managing conservator of the child.

Process should be served at that address.

6. Order to be Enforced

On September 21, 2000, in this cause of action, this court signed an order entitled "Agreed Temporary Orders Regarding Education and Evaluation" that appears in the minutes of this Court and attached hereto for all purposes. Such Order states in relevant part as follows:

"IT IS ORDERED, ADJUDGED AND DECREED, that:

1. The child's education and academic needs shall be directed by Harold Beeman (or his designated representative) at the Exhilarated Learning Center of Texas, 101 Central, Plano, Texas. Further, Harold Beeman shall direct the Academic Special Education Therapy for the child. The child shall be seen at all appointments at the time and place as directed by Harold Beeman. Nothing therein shall prevent the parties from agreeing to another professional educator to provide such services.

2. The parties acknowledge that the child is presently in need of medication for Attention Deficit Disorder. Both parties shall cause the child to take any medications as prescribes by Dr. Bloom, or his successor. Further, Pam Ong shall cause any prescription for the child to be filled within 24 hours of her receipt of such prescriptions and to provide such medication to the school with instructions to administer same to the child as prescribed on such medication, with the exception that Pam Ong shall retain the pills necessary for Kim Ong to take on the days she is not in school, such as weekends and holiday. Pat Ong is further to cause all re-fills and new prescriptions to be filled within 24 hours of her receipt of same;

3. The parties shall select a mutually agreed upon tutor to provide tutoring at least twice a week for a period of at least 45 minutes each for the minor child, as more fully set out herein. Prior to the selection of such tutor, or in the event the parties cannot agree, Harold Beeman shall provide the tutoring for the child at the address listed in 1. above;

4. Within 10 days of the entry of this Order, Pam Ong shall schedule any appointments with the public school district for the district in which the child is a resident for a Special Education Committee meeting for the purpose of an Admission Review and Dismissal and to timely do all acts required to qualify and enroll the minor child for services under the Rehabilitation Act, Section 504 of the I.D.E.A. Act;

5. Further, Ron Lee Ong, shall be notified by Pam Ong within four hours of her knowledge of any appointment the child has with any doctor, counselor, tutor, teacher or school administrator or any appointment she has with such person or any committee appointment she may have with any school system by faxing such notice to him at 555-555-5555.

6. Pam Ong shall, within 7 days of entry of this Order, cause Ron Lee Ong's name, address and business and home telephone listed with any school or counselor or tutor seen by this child, as the person to contact for any matters pertaining to this child, including emergencies;

7. The party in possession of the minor child shall, at the time of any appointments for the minor child as contemplated in this order, shall deliver the child to the place and at the time scheduled for such appointments, on time, and shall have the child at school on time at the beginning of each school day."

Movant was the Petitioner, Ron Lee Ong, and Respondent was the Respondent, Pan Ong, in the prior proceedings.

Said Agreed Temporary Orders Regarding

Education and Evaluation are still operative and in full force and effect. Although it was within Respondent's ability to comply, Respondent has disobeyed the Order of this court by her failure and refusal to carry out the terms of the Agreed Temporary Orders Regarding Education and Evaluation.

8. Contempt Violations

Respondent has willfully failed to comply with the order described above as follows:

Violation 1:

On or about October 5, 2000, Respondent failed and refused to deliver the child's medication to the child's school within 24 hours of her receipt of same. The medication should have been procured by Respondent on september 15, 2000 and was not delivered to the school until October 5, 2000.

Violation 2:

On or before October 5, 2000, Respondent failed and refused to give instructions to the child's school personnel regarding administering the child's medication within 24 hours of her receipt of same. The school received the child's medication on October 5, 2000 without any instructions from Respondent. Due to her violation, the school was unable to administer such medication until October 12, 2000.

Violation 3 and 4:

On or before October 5, 2000, Respondent failed and refused to send the child's medication for Movant's possession of the child from October 20, 2000 through October 22, 2000 thereby causing the child to go without her medication for three days.
On November 3, 2000, Respondent failed and refused to send the child's medication for Movant's possession of the child from November 3, 2000 through November 5, 2000 thereby causing the child to go without her medication for three days.

Violation 5:

Subsequent to the entry of the Order to be enforced, Respondent employed Caramel Rose as tutor for the child without consulting with or even contacting Movant.

Violation 6:

Subsequent to the entry of the Order to be enforced, after Respondent failed to employ a mutual agreed upon tutor for the child as set out in Violation 6 above,. Respondent further violated the Order by failing to seek Harold Beeman's assistance in tutoring the child.

Violation 7:

Subsequent to the entry of the Order to be enforced, Respondent failed and refused to schedule appointments with the school district in which the child resides for the purpose of an Admission Review and Dismissal within 10 days from the date of the Order.

Violation 8:

Subsequent to the entry of the Order to be enforced, Respondent failed and refused to do all the acts required to qualify and enroll the minor child for services under the Rehabilitation Act, Section 504 or the I.D.E.A. Act within 10 days from the date of the Order.

Violation 9:

Subsequent to the entry of the Order to be enforced, Respondent failed and refused to notify Movant within four hours of the scheduling of a meeting with the child's school personnel that took place on October 6, 2000.

Violation 10:

Subsequent to the entry of the Order to be enforced, Respondent failed and refused to notify Movant within four hours of the scheduling with the child's tutor as follows: On October 6, 2000, October 6, 2000, October 6, 2000, October 6, 2000, October 9, 2000, October 10, 2000, October 11, 2000, October 17, 2000, October 18, 2000, October 25, 2000, October 26, 2000, October 30, 2000, November 1, 2000, November 2, 2000, November 6, 2000, November 7, 2000, November 8, 2000, November 10, 2000, November 13, 2000, November 16, 2000, November 20, 2000, November 21, 2000, the child was seen by her tutor Caramel Rose.

Violation 11:

Subsequent to the entry of the Order to be enforced, Respondent failed and refused to notify Movant within four hours of the scheduling of any appointment with the Special Education committee of the school district in which the child resides.

Violation 12:

Subsequent to the entry of the Order to be enforced, Respondent failed and refused to notify Movant within four hours of the scheduling of appointments with Harold Beeman on October 6, 2000.

Violation 13:

Subsequent to the entry of the Order to be enforced, Respondent failed and refused to notify Movant within four hours of the scheduling of an appointment with Dr. Bloom which took place on October 16, 2000.

Violation 14:

Subsequent to the entry of the Order to be enforced, Respondent failed and refused to inform the child's school of Movant's name , address and telephone numbers within seven days of the entry of the Order.

Violation 15:

On or about October 3, 2000, Respondent failed and refused to timely take the child to school as ordered by this Court.

Violation 16:

On or about October 4, 2000, Respondent failed and refused to timely take the child to school as ordered by this Court.

Violation 17:

On or about October 6, 2000, Respondent failed and refused to timely take the child to school as ordered by this Court.

Violation 18:

On or about October 27, 2000, Respondent failed and refused to timely take the child to school as ordered by this Court.

Violation 19:

On or about January 19, 2000, Respondent failed and refused to timely take the child to school as ordered by this Court.

Violation 20:

On or about January 20, 2000, Respondent failed and refused to timely take the child to school as ordered by this Court.

Violation 21:

On or about January 29, 2000, Respondent failed and refused to timely take the child to school as ordered by this Court.

Violation 22:

On or about January 30, 2000, Respondent failed and refused to timely take the child to school as ordered by this Court.

Violation 23:

On or about January 31, 2000, Respondent failed and refused to timely take the child to school as ordered by this Court.

Violation 24:

On or about February 1, 2000, Respondent failed and refused to timely take the child to school as ordered by this Court.

Violation 25:

On or about February 2, 2000, Respondent failed and refused to timely take the child to school as ordered by this Court.

9. Punishment Requested

Movant requests that Respondent be held in contempt, jailed, (not to exceed six months) and fined for each violation alleged above.

Movant believes, based on the conduct of Respondent, that Respondent will continue to fail to comply with the order. Movant requests that Respondent be held in contempt, jailed and fined for each failure to comply with the order of the Court from the date of this filing to the date of the hearing on this motion.

Movant requests that Respondent be confined in the county jail (not to exceed six months) until Respondent complies with the order of the Court.

Movant request that Respondent be placed on community subversion for five years on release from jail or suspension of commitment.

10. Request for Clarification Order

Movant requests that, if the Court finds that any part of the order sought to be enforced is not specific enough to be enforced by contempt, the Court enter a clarifying order more clearly specifying the duties imposed on Respondent and giving Respondent a reasonable time within which to comply.

11. Attorney's Fees

It was necessary to secure the services of Theo L. Hays, a licensed attorney, to enforce and protect the rights of Ron Lee Ong and the child the subject of this suit. Respondent should be ordered to pay a reasonable attorney's fee, and a judgment should be rendered in favor of the attorney against Respondent; or, in the alternative, reasonable attorney's fees should be taxed as cost, and should be ordered paid directly to the undersigned attorney. Respondent should be further ordered to pay all other costs of this proceeding.

12. Alternative Dispute Resolution Statement

Movant has signed a statement on alternative resolution, which was previously filed in this matter.

13. Prayer

Movant prays that Respondent be held in contempt and punished as requested, that the Court order community supervision, that the Court Clarify any part of its prior order found not be specific enough to be enforced by contempt, for attorney's fees and costs, and for all further relief authorized by law.

Movant prays for general relief.

Respectfully submitted,

Theo L. Hays, P.C.

State Bar No. 40965100

1552 Jolie Road, Plano, TX

Defending Contempt Charges

Gather documentation and witnesses to disprove each of the charges. Example:

From Pam Ong.

Violation 1:

I have a letter from the school director attesting to the fact that I delivered the medication to the school within the proper time limit.

Violation 2:

In the above mentioned letter the school director attests to the fact that she read and understood the dosage information on the pill container. Additionally she understands that the dosage is minimal and should be administered on an as needed basis as per Dr. Bloom's instruction.

Violation 3 and 4:

Dr. Bloom instructed me to use my discretion as the parent who understands and deals with Kim the most often, in making decisions about the frequency of administration of the medication. With extended use of the medication, Kim complains that it makes her sleepy all the time. Because the medication is primarily administered to allow Kim the ability to concentrate on her school work I did not think it was wise to medicate her to spend weekends with her father.

Violation 5 and 6:

I told Ron about Caramel Rose as tutor for Kim and he didn't voice any objection. Because Ron did not object we did not need to seek Harold Beeman's assistance in tutoring the child.

Violation 7:

I have a letter from the Superintendant of Schools, stating that Kim was not eligible for testing because she was in private school.

Violation 8:

Our child does not qualify to be enrolled for services under the Rehabilitation Act, Section 504 or the I.D.E.A. Act within 10 days from the date of the Order. Kim is a good student, well adjusted and has proper medical care and private tutors.

Violation 9:

I told Ron about Kim's meeting with the child's school personnel that took place on October 6, 2000.

Violation 10:

Ron knows Kim sees the tutor twice a week.

Violation 11:

This is the meeting that Ron requested in Violation #7 with the Special Education committee of the school district in which the child resides.

Violation 12:

Ron was invited to attend the meeting by Harold Beeman on October 6, 2000.

Violation 13:

I did forget to notify Ron of Kim's appointment with Dr. Bloom on October 16, 2000.

Violation 14:

The letter mentioned in Violation #1 states that the school director was given Ron's name, address and telephone numbers within seven days of the entry of the Order.

Violation 15 thru 25:

Kim was in class every day as is stated by the school director in the letter mentioned in Violation #1.

Movant prays for general relief.

I think Movant proves that it is not the best interest of the child that is his interest but to harass me. It cannot be in the best interest of any child jail her mother to satisfy the vindictive movant.

Example:

From: Pam Ong Fax: (509) 555-5555
To: Ron Lee Ong Fax: (509) 666-6666

Notification In Compliance with Court Order:

Kim Lee Ong Has an appointment at __________a.m. p.m. On _________ , 2001
With:

Jo Kay Johnson	Tumon Institute
Loretta Chanm	Tutor
Dr. Nick Hudan	University Pediatrics
Harold Beeman	Academic Coordinator
Dr. Bloom	Family Physician
Dr. Golan	Dentist
Susan Smithy	Tester Teaching and Learning Center
Dr. Workman	Teaching and Learning Center
CiCi Julies	Dean of Lower School
Ellen Lynn	3rd Grade Teacher
Marie Seecliff	3rd Grade Teacher

Kindest Regards,

Pam Ong

cc
J.D. Saluter (713) 222-2222
Theo L. Hays, P.C. (713) 333-3333

Speak to Inequity

In this case the primary problem with the original order, was that the parent required to report via fax did not understand that she was in fact required by law to preform the tasks she was agreeing to. She was so disappointed with what her attorney was telling her that she agreed to the demands of the other parent.

When you are faced with frivolous demands and you are not able to escape them entirely, you should demand that the order be reciprocal. Then the other parent would be subject to the same performance standard that you are. An Order Of The Court Is Not A Suggestion. You must comply with any court order. When you are faced with an order, design a method that will allow you to comply. Use a reminder system or a form.

NonCompliance is hazardous to your custody case.

From: Pam Ong Fax: (509) 555-5555
To: Ron Lee Ong Fax: (509) 666-6666

Notification In Compliance with Court Order:
Kim Lee Ong Has a standing appointment from 2:30 to 4:00 p.m. June 4, 7, 11, 14, 18, 21, 25, 28 2001, July 2, 5, 9, 12,16,19, 23, 26, 30, 2001
With: Loretta Chanm her Tutor.
Kindest Regards,
Pam Ong

cc
J.D. Saluter (713) 222-2222
Theo L. Hays, P.C. (713) 333-3333

Visual Impact on the Court

The court's impression of any witness occurs within the first thirty seconds. By the time your witness is observed, the believability quotient has been set by the judge or jury. If the witness made a good impression, the "Halo Effect" kicks in.

From that moment forward all information seen or heard is filtered through the Halo Effect to support opinions already held. Therefore, it is possible for an observer with a "positive" and an observer with a "negative" Halo Effect to "hear" the information given by a witness in two entirely different ways.

On occasion a person will choose to disregard the obvious or proven truth of what they hear if it does not fit what they have decided is so.

This works because, when the information a person is hearing does not correspond with the information that person has decided is so or is seeing, that person will believe what he or she is seeing. Dressing properly for court is very important. Because the court's impression of a witness occurs so quickly and affects how the testimony is heard, choose your witnesses for appearance and demeanor as well as content of testimony.

It does not matter how valuable a witness's testimony is if it will not be believed by the court.

Clothes Make the Witness

If your witnesses must appear in the middle of a work day, ask what you can do to make them more comfortable and look more "court proper" for their testimony. Some may require a subpoena to get time away from work for this appearance. A map of where to park and how to get into the court house will help put your witnesses at ease. The parent and the witness must do their best to down play or avoid the negative impact some visual messages send the court. Avoid strange hair styles, unkempt beards and mustaches on men, the slick salesman look of gold chains and chest hair. Cover skin piercing and tattoos. There is still a considerable prejudice in the legal community against nonconformity. Witnesses should wear a white shirt, a tie and a conservative navy or gray suit for men and dress or ladies suit for women.

If it is necessary for a witness to appear in a work uniform, it is important to have a clean one on in court.

Major Problem Areas

Men --- Strange hair styles and long hair can cost you custody of your children. Even though it may have taken you years to get your hair that long, cut it. Your children's welfare is more important than your hair length, and you can let it grow long again after this case is settled. Beards and mustaches on men, even neatly trimmed, receive much the same negative reaction as long hair. Studies have shown the presence of long hair or facial hair reduces the Believability Factor of a witness by thirty percent or more.

Women --- Avoid coming to court with a shaved, bald head or a short military cut. Strange hair-do's will cause problems with the judge or jury. The legal community has a very set idea about proper parental appearance.

You can use television or magazine advertisements featuring parents with their children as a model of what the court wants to see in you. Unusual hair will offend the court. Avoid see-through blouses, chiffon dresses or glued-on-beads and sparkles. Choose a conservative ladies' suit with skirt in navy, grey, black, brown or pastel colors. Avoid heavy make up.

In the Eye of the Beholder

Skin piercing and tattoos are seen by the conservative mainstream person as immature, defiant and antisocial. Do not wear your skin piercing jewelry. It seems to affect attitude in an, "I know something you don't know," negative way. Tattoos on men or women should be covered at all costs. The opposition may attempt to prejudice a judge by playing up your antisocial behavior, evidenced by tattoos. The opposition's saying you have tattoos is much less effective than the observer seeing you display the "art work." If asked, you would be required to acknowledge the tattoo. Your testifying to the fact that you have a tattoo is still less effective than a person seeing the tattoo.

Your attorney may assist you in preparing a disclaimer to offer about your young age at the time you got the tattoo (if true). Wear concealing clothing, such as long sleeves to cover tattooed arms. A woman should use makeup and several pair of panty hose to hide leg tattoos that show easily. A more permanent option is to have the tattoos removed. Your options include surgical excision (cutting the tattoo out), dermabrasion (scrubbing away the skin layers), salabrasion (using table salt to abrade the tattoo area), and chemical peels (using chemicals to burn away layers of the skin). These methods are expensive, painful and result in scarring. The safest and most effective method is relatively new. It is ruby laser therapy.

A short pulse of laser is absorbed by the tattoo, causing the ink to fragment so your body can carry it away in a matter of four to eight weeks. Large or dark tattoos may require several treatments. Blue or black amateur or "jail house" tattoos are more easily removed because usually they are not as deep as professional art and require only three to five treatments. Professional artwork containing more ink and colors like red and yellow can take six to eight treatments. The object of this exercise is to look as solid, stable, dependable and mainstream as possible.

In Court

You should: Separate the content of your answer from how you deliver the answer. You are on display. Smile politely. Sit in a position that allows your hands to rest in your lap.

Do not whisper anything to your attorney. Judges hate whispering; write a note.

> Prepare a note pad in advance so you can use your pen to point to what you want to say to your attorney. Don't comment on statements about which you know your attorney has the information. Add your own, but these are the most common things you might say:
>
> Yes, its true.
>
> It is a lie.
>
> I have proof. Do you want me to find it?

Do not make noises. Do not tap your pencil, your fingers or your feet.

Eliminate all facial expressions, especially hostile or glaring.

Be prepared to hear the most amazing testimony of your life. Do not laugh, snicker, roll your eyes back, or shake your head at statements made by witnesses. Do not try to intimidate or make friends with anyone. Do not respond to the opposition's assaults. Do not do anything that might limit the opposition's answers. Do not give in to the impulse to make a cheap shot.

Listen carefully to the answers given. Jot down additional questions for your attorney to ask.

The above advice is difficult to follow. However, it will enhance the impression you give the court. If you require professional help to gain and keep your composure, consider a psychologist or therapist.

Witnesses' Demeanor

Your witnesses should:

Separate the content of their answer from how they deliver the answers. They are on display.

Smile politely. Sit in a position that allows hands to rest in one's lap.

Do not make noises. Do not tap a pencil, fingers or feet.

Eliminate all facial expressions, especially hostility or glaring.

Do not respond to the opposition attorney's assaults. Do not do anything that might limit the opposition's question.

The above advice is difficult to follow. However, it will enhance the impression the witness gives the court.

Attitude

The way a witness intends to be seen by the court and the way the court sees the witness is often very different. Often the court can see the witness projecting an attitude of unfiltered belligerence when the witness thinks he or she is being sharp.

What a Witness Cannot Do

1. A witness cannot lie for you.
2. A witness cannot lose a case for you.
3. A witness cannot win a case for you.

Witness Guide for Questions

As a witness appearing for deposition or in court, one's character is very important. The believability factor of the testimony is established by the character of the witness.

It is not a good time for the attorney on your side to learn anything new about one's past or this case. Usually, you are appearing for a friend or associate. If there is some information about you that you realize the attorney should be aware of, but you don't want your friend to know, ask for a few private minutes with the attorney. Give the attorney the information and request that it not be shared with your friend or anyone else. This will allow the attorney to avoid questions that could reveal this information and keep the opposition's attorney from getting into that area by preparing an objection of relevance.

Help fill in the witness outline form. If you have not done so yet, come clean. Tell the attorney everything you have withheld. The attorney will advise you as to subjects that do not apply in this matter and that you should not talk about. There are only two sides in this skirmish - yours and theirs. Do not forget, which side the other attorney represents.

- Listen carefully to the <u>entire</u> question before you begin to think of your answer. When the other attorney asks a question, pause for a moment to allow the attorney to object to the question, if necessary. This gives you a few moments to put your thoughts in order. If your attorney does object, it is probably for the record, and you may, in fact, have to answer the question if instructed to do so by the judge. Be careful and honest.
- Answer only the question for their attorney; do not go into any detail. Avoid long answers to general questions. The opposition's attorney is fishing for information. Example: "Tell me what kind of mother Judy is." Your proper answer to this could be, "The children appear to be well cared for." For your attorney, answer with information the attorney has heard from you before.
- Speak clearly, audibly, using simple free of slang, or bad language.
- If you are asked to supply a list, finish with, "That is all I can think of now."
- Do not make up details based on a spotty or forgotten memory because the attorney pressures you. Example: "Was it between January and March or April and June?" Insist, "I do not remember, and I will not guess."
- Do not attempt to give an answer if the other attorney bases a question on an untrue statement. Example: "Do you still find Gary's children alone at night and have to sleep there until he shows up?" A reasonable response may be, "I stay over and baby-sit, but I have never found the children unattended."
- Answer, "Yes" or "No" to the other attorney as often as possible or, "I do not remember," if that is the case.

Five Days Before Court

Double-check your arrangements for childcare, transportation, leave of absence from work, and any other obligations you have. Make sure any copies of photos or documents you need are ready for court. These are the final days of preparation. Double-check to make sure that your work produces the results your children need.

Prepare for Your Day in Court

Your attorney will know, which information is important to bring before the court. Your attorney is the expert, and as such, will be asking questions in a precise order to create a specific impression. Relax and know that all that could be done has been done. All that remains to be done is in the hands of the person best suited to do it ---your attorney.

Make note of any last-minute information you feel your attorney may need by typing or printing it clearly on white, stick-on address labels that can be easily added to your attorney's notes.

Put some extra blank notes in your pocket or purse.

Place any documents your attorney feels you should take with you in a three-ring binder. Read and re-read any materials for which you are personally responsible, such as letters, interrogatories, or depositions. If there are many papers, or if the documents are long, prepare an index. Refer to the section in this manual on depositions for an example of a workable index.

The Night Before Court

Choose conservative, comfortable clothes. You may be in court all day. Check to see that all the buttons are on, the hems are secure and the zippers work. Press and lay your clothes out the night before.

Put some antacids, cough drops, tissues, aspirin, and the last minute notes for your attorney in your pocket or purse. If you are taking a three-ring binder with documents for court, put it with your purse or wallet. Review your documents one more time.

Make sure your car has enough gas and you have the correct money for parking, or money for the bus or a taxi. If certain things usually make you late, do what you can to avoid those things or get them taken care of beforehand. Perhaps someone else can take care of these responsibilities for you. Stay home the night before and try to rest for your day in court.

Court First Thing in the Morning

If you need a cup of coffee to wake up, have it. After that, avoid beverages with sugar, substitutes, or caffeine. Cool water is recommended by those who have experienced many hours in the courtroom. Water is not as hard on your blood sugar level and will result in fewer trips to the bathroom.

Court Later in the Day

Assemble your clothes and a clean-up kit. This will enable you to put on clean clothes and arrive in court fresh. This can be an important psychological advantage if the opposition arrives less composed. Avoid beverages with sugar and caffeine. Drink cool water; it helps keep up your stamina. If you are aware that your attorney is allergic to perfume or after-shave, do <u>not</u> use it. It is important that nothing you do affects this work negatively.

Dodging Enemy Fire

Words are ammunition in this war. What you and your witnesses testify to in deposition or court can be the most helpful or most damaging evidence to your case. Make sure you and your witnesses understand the process you are about to face and that you have all reviewed any previous sworn statements. The enemy already has a good supply of ammunition. Don't give the opposition any more. This will help you avoid supplying the enemy with any extra. You can win this war with what you do not say. In court, the answer to the question being asked is not necessarily the information being sought.

The information being sought may not surface until several more questions are answered. In real life, we ask a question to get an answer. In court, a attorney must establish the foundation facts in order to ask for the information needed. For example, a attorney may not ask, "Are you still beating the dog?" It must first be established that you had a dog and did beat it at one time. Each attorney will ask questions for which he or she already knows the answers.

The way a question is asked has been carefully calculated in advance to effect the content of the answer. The attorney's questions may also be designed to produce a specific emotional state in the witness. Don't let the attorney manipulate your emotions; remain calm.

The way a question is answered may be more important than the answer itself. Listen very carefully to the entire question before you begin thinking of an answer. Then, think again before you do speak.

Listen carefully to your attorney's questions to see the direction. Likewise, you must listen to the opposition attorney's questions to see the direction. The question being asked may be only a part of the foundation for the real question or point the attorney is trying to make. It is best to answer each question as simply and honestly as possible.

If you are being led, there is not much you can

do about it. Do not worry about where the opposition's attorney is going. Your attorney will take care of that. Your attorney, the opposition's attorney, and the judge can ask you questions.

The processes for asking questions are called direct, cross and redirect.

Their Bullet Your Target

On occasion an attorney is placed in the awkward position of having to rehabilitate a witness he or she has not called to the stand. This can happen with an expert or lay witness. As an example the opposition has called a detective with a poorly written report containing aggravating verbiage. The report is offered to prove that you have a new significant other, therefore, thwarting the other parent's efforts to reconcile the family unit.

Because there is so much value for your case in the report your attorney wants the court to see this detective in the best possible light. Inadvertently the report is offering documentation that, (1) you take excellent care of your children and attend to all their needs yourself, (2) the children are doing better in school since the other parent is out of the home, (3) the children are exhibiting happier behavior, less stress at school and in counseling.

Types of Questions

Open Questions

Open questions allow you to answer as broadly as you wish. This is only the definition of the word "OPEN." Do not answer open-ended questions with broad answers. Keep all answers short and simple. When information on a topic is given in court the opposition's attorney can question you further on the matter. Example of an Open question: "Tell me about the separation."

Leading Questions

Leading questions suggest an expected answer. In other words, the attorney is putting words into the witness' mouth, usually allowing only a yes or no answer. If your attorney cuts you off, SHUT UP. If the opposition's attorney cuts you off, you may turn to the judge and explain that the question asked in this manner seriously distorts the information and you wish to make an explanation.

Leading questions are not permitted, so when it occurs, the other attorney objects on the grounds that the question is leading the witness. If the judge agrees, the question must be rephrased.

Example of a Leading question:

"Isn't it true that because you are on call for your job, it is not unusual for you to leave your children unattended for periods of time?"

1. If the judge does allow you to explain, make it clear and simple. Speak directly to the judge.

2. If the judge does not allow you to explain, do not get upset or feel put out.

Hypothetical Questions

Hypothetical questions allow the attorney to invent a situation and make assumptions. Because this clouds the issue, the judge decides whether the "manufactured" incident is important.

You will be required to answer the questions, but do not agree to any more than necessary. "I do not know," may not be a safe answer. You would have to answer, "No". Example: "If your mother is unavailable to baby-sit in the future and you have to leave the house for an emergency call, would you leave the children alone for half an hour or so?"

Only an expert witness may be asked a hypothetical question. This question may be based upon any theory that can be deduced from the evidence. Attorney may assume any facts within the limits of the evidence and exclude facts not deemed material. It is not proper to ask an expert witness a hypothetical question that assumes facts not in evidence or assumes facts inconsistent with those already in evidence. However, an expert opinion cannot be based on speculation or conjecture. An assumption of facts by an expert contrary to the proof destroys the expert's opinion. A witness testifying in the form of an opinion may state on direct examination the reasons for the opinion unless he or she is precluded by law from using such reasons or matters as a basis for the opinion. It may be as important to learn what facts the expert deemed unimportant as to determine what facts the expert relied upon in forming his or her opinion. This does not empower an expert to testify to legal conclusions in the guise of expert opinion. An expert may not attempt to define a statutory term when its definition is a matter of law.

Types of Questioning

Direct Examination

The direct examination is conducted by the attorney who calls the witness. Try to determine what answers the attorney wants. Your replies should be the result of pretrial planning with your attorney. Don't fall into a trap. Example: "You have, in fact, left your children unattended for as long as an hour on more than one occasion, haven't you?"

Cross Examination

These questions are asked by the attorney who didn't call the witness. Material may not be brought up in cross examination that did not come up in direct examination. Cross examination allows the attorney to challenge answers given to direct questioning.

There are two types of cross-examination: corroborative and destructive. Corroborative cross-examination seeks to have the witness agree with the facts, which support the attorney's position. During this phase, the attorney attempts to get the witness to agree with every good admission previously made about his client. This should include any admissions on positive parenting skills of your client values that are important to your burden of proof, fault grounds and the like. If our adversary starts contradicting his deposition testimony, that is when to use his deposition for impeachment. Destructive cross discredits your adversary and his direct testimony. This type of cross-examination is more difficult to execute. It is on destructive cross that the person pull a knife out and start jabbing the witness. During the cross-examination on fault issues, discuss the adversary's cruel treatment of your client, his illicit affairs, and all the other bad facts, which have been discovered. The witness must be controlled by the examiner at all times. Do not let him waiver from his deposition testimony. Each time the witness attempts to deviate from his prior testimony, impeach.

Corroborative cross must be attempted before destructive cross. At the beginning of a cross-examination, the adversary will be less hostile and more trusting than he will be later in the cross-examination.

There is a two-fold purpose to this method: (1) often times the witness can be "worn down" to the point of answering questions in the manner he believes the attorney wants him to answer because he assumes the deposition testimony is going to be "thrown in his face", and (2) the judge or jury are hearing every contradictory answer and will, hopefully, decide that if the witness cannot tell the truth about unimportant issues, he probably will not tell the truth about issues that will effect his future. A witness may be cross-examined on any matter relevant to any issue in the case, including credibility. The scope of cross-examination is wide open and not limited to the scope of direct examination and credibility. However, the cross-examination of an expert may be limited to the scope of direct examination, credibility, and to areas designated during discovery as being within the scope of the direct examination. The subject matter of the expert's testimony must be disclosed when presented with a proper discovery request at least thirty days prior to the beginning of trial, unless the party affirmatively establishes good cause for the failure to supplement the discovery responses.

There are two primary purposes of cross-examination. One is to overcome, qualify, or explain testimony given on direct examination. The other is to attack the credibility, knowledge, and recollection of the witness by exposing inaccuracies in the direct examination or by exposing the witness' bias or prejudice toward the opposition.

Do not argue with the opposition's attorney. When the opposition's attorney is attempting to make a point, let it happen, even if it's one hundred percent wrong. You will not win the fight, and you may appear belligerent in your effort to right the wrong.

It is your attorney's job to clear up any incorrect impressions the opposing attorney has created. Example: "Didn't you state in your deposition that you had to move to Topeka, near your mother, because you didn't want to leave your children alone anymore?"

Re-Direct

During Re-direct, the attorney who originally called the witness corrects misinformation and attempts damage control. The other attorney will not get another chance to question this witness unless he or she later calls this person as a witness too.

Example: "Referring to your deposition, did you mean, 'I don't want to leave my children alone any more', or, 'I don't want to consider leaving my children alone anymore?'" If the other attorney says something that is not true, say, "No, that is not true." Be polite and stay cool, but do not be afraid to tell an attorney that he or she has said something that is incorrect. It will probably surprise the attorney that you are not intimidated in his or her arena.

Not Sure! Not Sure?

An unsure answer to the opposition attorney is like a red flag to a bull. Do not say, "I think" or "I believe."

Respond with, "I found" or "I saw." If you are unsure say, "I don' know" or "I cannot be sure." Do not be bullied into guessing. Stick to the point of the question. Say what you need to say to answer the question and then stop talking. Use clear, compelling examples to make your point. Preparation with your attorney is the key to making your testimony effective.

Frontal Assault

The opposing attorney will attempt to undermine your testimony and cast doubt on your character. The first target for enemy fire is you as a person. The opposition will try to suggest that you consider your wants and needs to be more important than the children's welfare. The opposition's attorney will question whether your choices in life are sound and reflect proper planning and reliable follow-through.

If he asks, "Did you discuss your testimony with anyone?" He is implying that you were rehearsed or instructed as to what to say. You should be able to reply, "The pretrial meeting let me know what to expect, but I was not instructed as to what to say." Stay calm.

Do not get angry or upset or begin to argue with the attorney.

Do not let this process unnerve you. This is one of the weakest forms of questioning, but it will be the tactic used should the other attorney be unable to find anything real to hang his or her case on. Your attorney will protect you from real badgering. Keep in mind that the practice of law is very demanding emotionally and physically.

The attorney assaulting your efforts to spend time with your children has problems of his or her own with virtually no home life of which to speak. Between taking care of unreasonable, demanding clients like the opposition (you know how ghastly that has to be), the social requirements of the job, ongoing educational requirements and what is left of his or her personal relationships, the attorney will be tired, underpaid and grossly dissatisfied with his or her vocation.

Hey, Were All on the Same Side Here

On the other hand, be wary of "Hey, we are all on the same side here; we all want what is best for the children" attitude. It is not true. If the welfare of the children was all that was important to the opposition, you would not be in court now. Any friendliness on the part of the other attorney, either from the beginning or a change in the way the opposition attorney acts toward you, does not mean he or she can now see that you are the proper parent to have custody of these children. It just means a new tactic is being tested.

It is human nature to want to help someone who is being kind to you. This is especially true in a stressful situation like court. It is amazing how often a witness, who is supposed to be "hostile," will divulge information in the manner the attorney asks for it. "The attorney was nice to me, I didn't want to be a jerk." The opposing attorney is not trying to help you take the best care of your children you can.

The opposing attorney wants you to lose. No matter how nice this person is to you, the opposing attorney is the enemy.

People Who will be Attending the Trial

You will not be able to control the people who may show up in the court room Don't worry about what you can't fix. Enjoy the support of the family and friends who did come with you and ignore the people who came with the opposition. The people essential to the case and who must be there are:

- You
- Your Attorney
- The Opposition
- The Opposition's Attorney
- Guardian ad Litem
- Judge
- Court Reporter
- Bailiff or Clear
- Witnesses

What Will Happen In Court?

This is an indication of how your day in court is supposed to happen. You arrive at the courthouse, meeting your attorney at the prearranged time and place, early enough to be calm and collected. Do not become overly concerned if your attorney is a little late.

They often have one court appearance after another.

1. You enter the court room, where you and your attorney sit at one table. The opposition sits at a table across from you.

2. The bailiff instructs all to rise and the judge enters and sits down. Everyone else then sits down.

3. The bailiff announces the matter at hand and inquires as to whether everyone is there and ready to proceed.

4. Your attorney presents the court and opposition attorney with a Trial Memorandum.

5. The plaintiff's attorney makes a statement. The respondent's attorney makes a statement.

6. The plaintiff's attorney calls witnesses, questions them using direct examination and introduces documentary and physical evidence.

7. The respondent's attorney questions the witnesses using cross-examination. At the end of cross-examination, before the witness leaves the stand, the plaintiff's attorney may question the witness under redirect examination to clear any misconceptions from the cross-examination.

8. The respondent's attorney calls witnesses and questions them, using direct examination, and introduces documentary and physical evidence. The plaintiff's attorney questions the witnesses, using cross-examination, and examines the evidence. The respondent's attorney may call any of the witnesses and question them under redirect examination to clear any misconceptions from the cross-examination. After presentation of the respondent's case, the plaintiff's attorney may introduce impeachment evidence in an effort to compromise the evidence presented by the defense.

9. Each attorney may object to a question asked by the other attorney, using one or more of these reasons:

   Argumentative -Question is designed to make the witness argue.

   Compound -Question requires more than one answer.

   Hearsay -Information requested was not directly experienced by the witness.

   Irrelevant -Testimony cannot be requested that does not have a bearing on the issues raised in the case

   Lack of Foundation -Attorney failed to build a basis for the question asked.

   Leading -The attorney cannot recite the information in a specific order or manner and requests approval or rejection of the statement.

   Presumption - Question based on facts not in evidence -Each question must have roots in previously presented evidence or testimony.

   Repetitive - The question has already been asked in a different way.

   All testimony or evidence is governed by the rules of evidence. Any evidence that violates the rules is inadmissible. When an objection is raised by an attorney, the judge rules on the objection. By objecting to a question, an attorney preserves the rights of the client no matter how the judge ruled on the specific objection. An attorney failing to object is allowing that issue and information to be admitted. Once the judge has ruled on the admissibility of the question or evidence, the witness will be instructed to answer or not. Many times you hear an attorney object and the judge find against the objection.

   The attorney made the objection a matter of record. Without objection on record, that issue cannot be brought up on appeal.

   The plaintiff's attorney makes a summation statement. The respondent's attorney makes a summation statement.

10. The judge will either rule on the spot or advise the attorneys and their clients when and how the ruling will be made.

11. When the decision does arrive, it may de divided into sections;

    Finding of Fact. The history of the case as seen by the judge.

    Conclusions of Law. The precedent that applies to the case.

    Judgment. The judge's actual ruling.

Examples of Judges' Rulings

"I do not feel comfortable making a ruling in this case with the evidence that has been presented. I will appoint a psychologist that the court has worked with on previous occasions, and I will find in accordance with the final report from that professional. Counsel will stop at the Bailiff's desk for name and telephone number of the psychologist so your clients can make their appointments as soon as possible."

"I find that the best interest of the children will be served by approving the shared parenting plan worked out by the parties and their counsel.

If the parties are not back in court for one year, this plan becomes permanent."

"Because of the animosity between these litigants, I feel there is no opportunity for reasonable exchange even when it comes to the children. I find for the petitioner and assign visitation in accordance with long distance guidelines to the respondent."

In addition, the respondent is ordered to pay child support in the amount of $295.00 per month starting in thirty days and is obligated to pay half of any medical and dental expenses not covered by the petitioner's insurance."

It Ain't Over When It's Over

Regardless of the decision, you will want all of this behind you, so you can pick up your life and go on. Nonetheless, you may end up back in court for the following reasons:

- Increase or decrease of child support
- Enforcement of any settlement ordered by the court
- Visitation schedule problems
- Order to pay additional medical or educational costs
- Change of custody. The "loser" may petition for a change of custody one year after original decree.

Reasons original custody decree can be changed are:

- Change in Life-style
- Child Care
- Someone other than the custodial parent has primary responsibility for the child
- Substance abuse or drinks and drives with children in vehicle
- Physical or sexual abuse of children
- Custodial parent desires to relocate
- Children at age of understanding may request a change of residence and guardianship
- Illness or substantial disability requires a change of living arrangements
- Appeal

Whenever you or the opposition initiate action, it will cost you time and money. In many of these matters you can represent yourself, but it is better to save money on gasoline for your car and spend money on an attorney when it comes to your children.

Appeal the Threat

Appeal: The process whereby a higher court reviews the proceedings, resulting in an order or judgment. Appeal is only a review on the record produced in the lower court for errors of law. No new facts or evidence may be considered.

Filing an appeal doesn't disturb the final ruling. If the children have been ordered to move from one home to another, then they must move. If a parent has been ordered to pay child support, the payments must start.

If you don't agree with the decision, you can appeal the decision to the next higher court. The appellate court can change the decision that is binding on the lower court in that state. If the case was decided on a precedent the higher court may change the ruling. The appellate court can decide that the precedent no longer holds or that the case should have been decided on a different point. Each decision creates a precedent.

The appeal process is long and difficult. Even if one wins the appeal (which usually take more than three years) the opposition can challenge that decision in a higher court.

The appeal is primarily a paperwork procedure, and the parties to the action are not in attendance at the appeal. There is a great deal of passion and pain when one loses a custody case. Because the appeal is heard by a different level of the judicial system, the loser feels there is still hope.

It is not unusual for the disappointed parent to immediately fill out the papers to file for an appeal when the decision has not been in one's favor.

Since the initial filing for appeal can be done quickly and with very little money or work, it is often done by the angry, hurt parent. Ninety-eight percent of the request for consideration of appeal are filed within a week of a custody decision and are withdrawn or go "unperfected" before the document deadline of ninety days. An appeal must be filed in a timely manner, usually within thirty days of the initial decision.

If the initial papers are filed and the court has not received anything further within the time limit, the court may automatically extend the time allowed for appeal and notify all the parties. This does not indicate that the appeal has merit; it does indicate that the court is allowing for any unexpected circumstances.

Once the person filing for appeal realizes the complexity of the appeal process, he or she hires an attorney. If the attorney requests additional time too close to the deadline, the attorney on the winning side may ask the court to deny the request.

Attorneys do not pursue appeal in a custody matter "pro bono" (free). The reality of the situation is that appeal is a more expensive and more involved process than the initial action. An advance retainer fee of several thousand dollars is required. Complete transcripts of all court appearances and depositions must be purchased and reviewed.

Many specific documents must be filed within precise time requirements.

If the original attorney does not handle the appeal, a new attorney must be hired. The new attorney must be paid for the many hours required to read and study all of this material to become familiar with the case to determine the merit of an appeal.

In most instances, the new attorney will contact the previous attorney for documents and information. If the client has not pulled the case from the court by this time, the new attorney, after talking to previous council and examining documents, may advise the client to do so.

If an unscrupulous attorney is on a retainer and monthly payment plan, he or she may not care if the case has merit and can delay the process many months to increase the billings.

The Appeal Process

The only grounds for appeal occur when: the court displayed gross bias against one of the parents; the court drew the wrong conclusion from the facts; or a point of law was violated.

To "perfect" an appeal, an appellant's brief must be filed. This document must conform to a rigid format that is bound like a book with a table of contents and an alphabetical list of all the cases to be cited as precedent in the appeal, all the original transcripts and exhibits from the original trial and a brief with the presentation of the facts and the law, with emphasis on why the decision should or should not be upheld.

You must file an answer to the appeal once the brief has been filed, or the side requesting the appeal will win by default. The answer can be to merely oppose the appeal or file a cross-appeal.

The appellate court does not hear testimony since their decision is based on the facts submitted by the attorneys and the questions the court may ask the attorneys. Appeals courts analyze the trial court's decision and judgment for substantive errors in its "conclusions of the law."

In exceptional cases the trial court's "finding of facts" are also reviewed. Most findings of facts are extremely difficult to challenge because appeals courts defer to the trial court's ability to weigh evidence. Unless the trial court's findings of fact cannot possibly be supported by the evidence, such appeals will fail. Judges have Discretion to believe or disbelieve all evidence presented, and appeals courts will not second guess the trial court on its finding of facts. Challenging a trial court's "conclusions of law" is less difficult. States grant domestic relations judges substantial discretion in fashioning judgments.

Appeals are often unsuccessful except for substantial errors of law that significantly and adversely impact a party; otherwise, the mistake is considered "harmless error." Whether your appeal succeeds may depend more on your gender than the merits of your case.

In some states over eighty percent of appeals brought by men were dismissed whereas over eighty percent of appeals brought by women prevailed, although overall fewer appeals are filed by women because of the expense. The decision can take many months. The court can let the original ruling stand and simply state "We affirm."

It can make an entirely different ruling on its own. Or it can send the case back to be retried before the original judge or a new judge.

Once the appellate court decides a case the opinion is published in Case Reporters that are organized by the court and region.

Should You Worry?

Having won the battle, an appeal initiated by the opposition offers very little threat. An appeal:

1. Cannot be raised just because one side does not like the decision of the court.

2. Takes a great deal of time or money or both.

3. Can only be granted on points of law.

4. Does not allow any new issues may be raised in the appeal that were not presented in the original case.

5. Does not allow any new objections if the original attorney did not raise objections to protect points of appeal, any chance for appeal is lost.

This is one of the primary reasons you follow the rules and do not attempt to trick the opposition. If you don't play fair, you can give the opposition grounds for appealing. Once a status quo, also known as "What Is, Shall Remain", is in effect, a judge will resist a change, and the children will remain where the children had been residing after the original decision, unless a problem (such as obvious danger to the children) could be proven to exist. The reasoning behind this attitude is that it is better for children to stay in a less than perfect situation than to inflict radical change on children that the court has no way of knowing will in fact improve the situation for the children. In any case, if the opposition initiates an appeal, it will cost you money. Your attorney must read and draft documents to answer the documents filed by the opposition.

The cost of defending against an appeal is approximately one third of initiating an appeal.

Anger spurs us to action. Loss of patience with the people who have helped us as well as our antagonist and filing for appeal are normal actions. Ninety-eight percent of request for consideration of appeal, filed within a week of a custody decision, are withdrawn before the document deadline of ninety days.

Confidentiality - Court

There is no confidentiality. Every word spoken in court and taken down by the court reporter becomes public record. The exception occurs if the judge seals the records to protect the child. Information in all domestic relations, civil and criminal court cases are accessible to anyone who wishes to look for the documents.

Inexperienced Not Vexatious Litigator

Court Of Appeals of Ohio
Eighth District County of Cuyahoga
No. 74799

Plaintiff-Appellant:	CAROL PISANI, Pro se 30 Common Court Chagrin Falls, OH44022
-vs-	
Defendant-Appellee:	Richard Koblentz, Esq. Koblentz & Koblentz 55 Public Square, #1170 Cleveland, Ohio 44113

Patricia Ann Blackmon, J.:

-2-

Appellant Carol Pisani appeals the trial court's granting her ex-husband's, appellee Glenn Pisani's, motion to declare her a vexatious litigator under R.C. 2323.52. R.C. 2323.52 seeks to prevent abuse of the system by those persons who persistently and habitually file lawsuits without reasonable grounds and/or otherwise engage in frivolous conduct in the trial courts of this state. Central Ohio Transit Authority v. Timson (December 24, 1998), Cuyahoga App. No. 98-AP-509, unreported. Here, the trial court took judicial notice that appellant had, since March 23, 1995, filed in excess of 300 separate pro se filings in her post-divorce custody action.

Additionally, she had failed to first deposit cost before making filings as the court had ordered. The trial court specifically found her conduct involving her January 2, 1996 motion to modify custody most telling.

There, she had not demonstrated her readiness to move forward and prosecute her case. In fact, on December 19, 1997, she voluntarily dismissed the case only to refile the same motion within weeks. Appellant assigns eight errors for our review.1 In one form or another, all the assigned errors address the issue whether the trial court abused its discretion in finding appellant to be a R.C. 2323.52 vexatious litigator. Consequently, we will address the assigned errors together with a focus on the vexatious litigator issue. Having reviewed the record and the legal arguments of the parties, we conclude that the assigned errors that address the vexatious litigator issue have merit and sustain appellant's 1See Appendix.

-3-

arguments; consequently, all other errors are moot except assigned errors seven and eight which are resolved by the law of the case in Pisani v. Pisani (September 24, 1998), Cuyahoga App. No. 74373, unreported. At the outset, we must state that we are mindful that a trial court should be granted deference in matters of this nature and our interference is bridled by the abuse of discretion standard. Clearly, a trial court should be armed with the weapons necessary to control its docket and administer justice. The query is whether Carol Pisani has, at this point, reached the level of vexatiousness by her action to gain visitation with her child. The trial court answered this to the affirmative, but we are not persuaded at this juncture. We agree with the 10th district that R.C. 2323.52(A) is prospective in application and thus we look to appellant's conduct after March 18, 1997. Id. at 8. In reviewing her conduct after March 18, 1997, Carol Pisani is guilty of failing to pay cost and filing numerous motions regarding her request to modify custody. In substance, she has remained persistent in her attempt to obtain visitation with her children, making fifty-six filings since that date. As her daughter has now reached the age of majority, visitation issues no longer pertain to her. However, she was a minor during the majority of the litigation in this case. In January 1997, this court had the opportunity to determine if Carol Pisani's actions constituted frivolous conduct as it related to the number of cases she had appealed. We concluded that she had demonstrated reasonable

-4-

grounds for her appeals, and ruled her conduct not frivolous. Pisani v. Pisani (January 16, 1997), Cuyahoga App. No. 70846, unreported. We here refer to that case because of the analysis used in it regarding two cases from other jurisdictions that had found a pro se litigant's conduct unreasonable. Weltchek v. Weltchek (July 13, 1981), Lucas App. No. C-00-311 and Kondrat v. Byron (1989), 63 Ohio App.3d 495. In both cases, the courts reviewed the number of times the litigant had filed pleadings and held their actions unreasonable and frivolous. In comparing Pisani, we found the difference to be that she had demonstrated reasonable grounds for the matters she had appealed. We concluded that the underlying actions must have been reasonable as well. Consequently, our decision in that case on the reasonableness issue is res judicata as to any conduct prior to March 18, 1997. Thus, we address the issue of whether any of appellant's conduct after March 18, 1997 justified the trial court's finding of vexatiousness. Analyzing whether Ms. Pisani is a vexatious litigator requires an inquiry into whether her filings are warranted under existing law and if they can be supported by a good faith argument for an extension, modification or reversal of existing law. Drummond v. Genoa Banking Co. (1998), Ottawa App. No. OT-97-008, unreported, 3, citing Maines Paper & Food Service- Midwest, Inc. v. Regal Foods, Inc. (1995), 100 Ohio App.3d 454, 460. We must find she was without reasonable grounds, engaged in conduct that, because it is baseless, is not protected under the right-to-remedy/ access-to-courts clause. Timson, supra at 6

. -5-

While Ms. Pisani has been a prolific filer, all of her motions are supportable, and it certainly cannot be said that they are baseless. Examination of the docket and the filings themselves reveals Ms. Pisani's motions primarily revolve around her attempts to have her children seen by a psychologist for evaluation and to regain visitation with them. In fact, many of the filings are efforts to keep the court abreast of problems the children are having and concerns regarding their health. This behavior may be consistent with that of an inexperienced litigant but it is not vexatious. Most recently, the Geauga County Court of Appeals in viewing another action to declare Carol Pisani vexatious held that appellee had failed to specifically reference portions of the docket sheets which indicated vexatious conduct. Catalano v. Pisani (July 23, 1999), Geauga App. No. 98-G-2148, unreported, 4. (Catalano is Carol Pisani's maiden and present last name). The filings and docket sheets referred to in Catalano v. Pisani are the exact filings and docket sheets referred to in this case. Here, as well, the appellee failed at the trial court to point to any specific filings and docket sheets that demonstrate Carol Pisani's vexatiousness. We understand that the trial court specifically pointed to the case she dismissed and later refilled. However, she explained she suffered from poor health during that time. While she could have filed a motion to continue the hearing, she did not. We believe her actions are more in line with an inexperienced litigator as opposed to a vexatious litigator whose goal is to harass and annoy. This record is replete with material showing that the trial court has reached the end of its patience with appellant; however, impatience with a litigant is not the standard. The standard is whether the litigator's conduct is designed to harass and annoy. Here at this time, we are not persuaded that appellant's conduct is vexatious. Judgment reversed. This cause is reversed. It is, therefore, considered that said appellant recover of said appellee her costs herein. It is ordered that a special mandate be sent to said court to carry this judgment into execution. A certified copy of this entry shall constitute the mandate pursuant to Rule 27 of the Rules of Appellate Procedure. TERRENCE O'DONNELL, P.J., and ANN L. KILBANE, J., CONCUR. PATRICIA ANN BLACKMON JUDGE N.B. This entry is an announcement of the court's decision. See App.R. 22(B), 22(D) and 26(A); Loc.App.R. 22. This decision will be journalized and will become the judgment and order of the court pursuant to App.R. 22(E) unless a motion for reconsideration with supporting brief, per App.R. 26(A), is filed within ten (10) days of the announcement of the court's decision. The time period for review by the Supreme Court of Ohio shall begin to run upon the journalization of this court's announcement of decision by the clerk per App.R. 22(E). See, also, S.Ct.Prac.R. II, Section 2(A)(1). APPENDIX ASSIGNMENTS OF ERROR I. The trial court made prejudicial error when it labeled plaintiff as a vexatious litigator violating her constitutional right to due process when it has been the court who has ignored the recommendations of the court-appointed psychologist whom he picked and never ruled on motions which were all of importance to the well being of the children thus prolonging and protracting the litigation. ii. the trial court made prejudicial error when it made a ruling that plaintiff was a vexatious litigator after appellant filed A complaint against the judge at the ohio state bar association and after the judge recused [sic] himself off the case on january 9, 1998, on the record, and never journalizing it. iii. the trial court made a prejudicial error when appellant never received a copy of appellee's motion labeling her a vexatious litigator in which she could not respond to in a brief and opposition violating her due process rights. IV. The trial court made a prejudicial error when appellant never received a hearing on the matter which violates her constitutional rights and also violates her right to due process. v. the trial court made a prejudicial error when appellant never received a copy of the journal entry and only found out about the ruling by a mailing sent to her by the clerk's office which did not say what the ruling was just that something was journalized and appellant found out what it was when it was read to her on the phone at the clerk's office, 443-7960, by ron. vi. the trial court made a prejudicial error when appellant called Frank Pokorney's office and asked for a copy of the journal entry to be sent to her and never received it, only having to go down to the clerk's office and Xerox it herself. VII. The trial court made a prejudicial error when it stated that appellant did not pay a security deposit for filing motions when she is indigent and does file an Affidavit of Indigengy [sic] with her motions and also filed a 60b motion to vacate the judge's journal entry on having to pay for motions when she is indigent and the judge never has ruled on that motion. viii. the trial court made a prejudicial error when it said that appellant withdrew her motion for custody on december 19, 1997 when she was bleeding from female medical problems and violating her federal constitutional right to due process and discriminating against her for being a woman and having female medical .

Civil Appeal Example

Court Of Appeals Of Ohio
Eighth District County Of Cuyahoga
No. 78744

CAROL PISANI : :	:
Plaintiff-Appellant :	: JOURNAL ENTRY
vs. :	: and OPINION

GLENN PISANI : :
Defendant-Appellee :
Date of Decision: March 22, 2001
Character of Proceeding:
Civil appeal from Domestic Relations Division Court of Common Pleas Case No. D-219910
JUDGMENT: AFFIRMED.
APPEARANCES:

For Plaintiff-Appellant: CAROL PISANI, Pro se
30 Common Court
Chagrin Falls, OH44022

For Defendant-Appellee: Richard Koblentz, Esq.
Koblentz & Koblentz
55 Public Square, #1170
Cleveland, Ohio 44113

COLLEEN CONWAY COONEY, J.: Plaintiff-appellant, Carol Pisani, appeals pro se from the trial court's dismissal of her motion requesting access to her son's school records and the trial court's rescheduling of the
-2-
hearing on visitation. We find no merit to the plaintiff's appeal and affirm the lower court's orders. In 1994, the trial court granted a divorce to plaintiff and defendant. The trial court awarded custody of the couple's children to defendant. Although the trial court originally granted plaintiff visitation rights with her children, in a subsequent decision, the trial court completely suspended plaintiff's visitation based on her behavior. On December 12, 1996, defendant filed a motion requesting the trial court to deny plaintiff access to the children's medical and school records based on the plaintiff's alleged harassment of the school officials and doctors. Plaintiff filed a motion in opposition to defendant's request. The trial court granted defendant's motion on January 9, 1998. Plaintiff did not directly appeal this decision. Instead, on January 16, 1998, she filed a motion for relief from judgment pursuant to Civ.R. 60(B)(1), (2) and (3), alleging fraud or mistake on the part of the trial judge due to a pending motion for disqualification against the judge at the time the motion was ruled on. The trial court denied plaintiff's motion without opinion. Plaintiff filed a notice of appeal on January 25, 1999, appealing the trial court's orders denying her access to the children's records and denial of her motion for relief from judgment. This court in Pisani v. Pisani (Apr. 13, 2000), Cuyahoga App. No. 75909, unreported, affirmed the trial court's judgment finding that the appeal of the original action was untimely and
-3-
that plaintiff failed to set forth operative facts entitling her to relief from judgment. On August 7, 2000, plaintiff filed another motion requesting access to her son's school records based on the fact that her son was arrested and charged with vandalizing school property. Defendant filed a motion in opposition to the plaintiff's motion arguing that collateral estoppel prevented the plaintiff from re- arguing this issue and that the matter should therefore be dismissed. On August 17, 2000, plaintiff filed her brief in reply to defendant's motion. After a hearing on the matter, the trial court on October 24, 2000, granted the defendant's motion to dismiss. Plaintiff now timely appeals, asserting five assignments of error. We will address the assignments of error in the order asserted and together where appropriate. I. The trial court committed prejudicial error when it set a full day hearing on october 20, 2000 for visitation and access to school records and then when the court knew that appellant had subpoenaed the school at 1:30 p.m. and that her visitation witnesses were waiting to testify at 9:00 a.m. stated on the record that the court would hear The testimony for access to records at 9:00 a.m. and put off the visitation testimony for another day when it already set a full hearing for the pisani case on that day. Plaintiff argues that the trial court committed error by rescheduling the visitation hearing instead of hearing both the access to school records and visitation matters at the October 20, 2000 hearing.
-4-
Although the trial court's rescheduling the hearing may have inconvenienced the plaintiff and any testifying witnesses, plaintiff fails to show how the trial court's rescheduling the visitation hearing resulted in prejudice. Furthermore, plaintiff conceded during oral argument that the parties have entered an agreement about visitation and this is now a moot issue. Plaintiff's first assignment of error is overruled. II. The trial court committed a prejudicial error in not allowing appellant her right to due process and right to defend herself in why she should not be denied access to her son's records, especially when the court-appointed psychologist diagnosed the children from (sic) suffering from

parental alienation syndrome and a characteristic of the syndrome is to keep everything about the children away from the alienated parent and that report is evidence in this case. IV. The trial court committed a prejudicial error when it was proceeding to start hearing testimony and without notice ruled on appellee's written brief and opposition on the doctrine of collateral estoppel which was already adjudicated when the court set appellant's motion for trial on august 24, 2000. V. The trial court committed a prejudicial error when it applied the doctrine of collateral estoppel on a domestic relations case involving children and according to appellee's argument that the court of appeals already adjudicated the issue when the appeal's opinion dated april 13, 2000 #75909 clearly states that the appeal was filed untimely and the access to records was not looked at by the court of appeals. We will address the above assignments of error together, as they all deal with the trial court's dismissal of the plaintiff's motion based on collateral estoppel.

-5-

We agree with the trial court's conclusion that the doctrine of collateral estoppel precludes the plaintiff from relitigating her right to her son's school records. The general definition of collateral estoppel and its proper application were recently set forth in Teachers Assn. v. SERB (1998), 81 Ohio St.3d 392, 395, as follows: The doctrine of issue preclusion, also known as collateral estoppel, holds that a fact or a point that was actually and directly at issue in a previous action, and was passed upon and determined by a court of competent jurisdiction, may not be drawn into question in a subsequent action between the same parties or their privies, whether the cause of action in the two actions be identical or different. Norwood v. McDonald (1943), 142 Ohio St. 299, 27 Ohio Op. 240, 52 N.E.2d 67, paragraph three of the syllabus; Trautwein v. Sorgenfrei (1979), 58 Ohio St.2d 493, 12 Ohio Op.3d 403, 391 N.E.2d 326, syllabus; Goodson v. McDonough Power Equip. Inc. (1983), 2 Ohio St.3d 193, 2 Ohio B.Rep. 732, 443 N.E.2d 978, paragraph one of the syllabus. While the merger and bar aspects of res judicata has the effect of precluding the relitigation of the same cause of action, the collateral estoppel aspect precludes the relitigation, in a second action, of an issue that has been actually and necessarily litigated and determined in a prior action that was based on a different cause of action. Whitehead v. Gen. Tel. Co. (1969), 20 Ohio St.2d 108, 112, 49 Ohio Op.2d 435, 437-438, 254 N.E.2d 10, 13. In short, under the rule of collateral estoppel, even where the cause of action is different in a subsequent suit, a judgment in a prior suit may nevertheless affect the outcome of the second suit. Id. At 112, 49 Ohio Op.2d at 438, 254 N.E.2d at 13. In the case herein, the trial court in its January 9, 1998 order denied the plaintiff's motion requesting access to her son's records, stating in pertinent part: It is therefore ordered,

-6-

adjudged and decreed that plaintiff shall be denied access to the identities of all care providers to the minor children to wit: Carly and Kyle Pisani, as well as all records of those providers, medical and otherwise. Plaintiff filed a Civ.R. 60(B) motion seeking to have the trial court vacate this order, which was denied. Plaintiff appealed both orders to this court, and we affirmed the trial court's judgments. The matter has therefore been heard and determined by a court of competent jurisdiction and the plaintiff cannot seek to resurrect the issue. Although plaintiff contends that the trial court has failed to previously conduct a hearing on this matter, this is not a defense to collateral estoppel because the failure to conduct a hearing should have been brought to the attention of this court by the bringing of a timely appeal. Furthermore, the trial court has clearly previously considered the issue, albeit without a hearing, based upon the written motions submitted by the parties. We find no authority for plaintiff's contention that the principle of collateral estoppel does not apply to domestic relations cases. In any case, the fact that the plaintiff's son was arrested and suspended from school for vandalizing school property would not be grounds to modify the prior court order denying access to the school records. Her second motion seeking access to the school records cannot be considered a motion to modify a prior court order due to changed circumstances as contemplated in R.C. Chapters 3105 and 3109.

-7-

The plaintiff's second, fourth and fifth assignments of error are overruled. III. The trial court committed a prejudicial error when it ruled on (sic) denied appellant access to school records and according to law without written finding (sic) of fact and opinion as being an insufficient findings according to civ.r. 52 of r.c. 3109.051(f)(1), With no evidence or facts presented to support it which was part of the motion filed by appellant on August 7, 2000. Plaintiff argues the trial court was required to issue findings of fact and conclusions of law pursuant to Civ.R 52 and R.C. 3109.051(F)(1). Civ.R. 52 applies to situations where the trial court hears questions of fact without a jury and requires the court to state in writing findings of fact separately from conclusions of law. Bates v. Sherwin-Williams Co. (1995), 105 Ohio App.3d 529, 534. In the case before us, the trial court made a legal conclusion based on an analysis of law because it dismissed the plaintiff's motion based on the legal principle of collateral estoppel. Therefore, since no factual analysis was necessary, the trial court was not required to issue findings of fact and conclusions of law. Id. Furthermore, the purpose of separately stated findings of fact and conclusions of law is to enable the reviewing court to determine the existence of assigned error. Abney v. W. Rest. Mut. Case. Co. (1991), 76 Ohio App.3d 424, 431. If the court's ruling, together with other parts of the trial court's record, provides an adequate basis upon which a reviewing court can decide the legal issues presented, there is substantial compliance with Civ.R. 52.

-8-

Id. A review of the record in the instant case along with the trial court's ruling provides this court with an adequate basis upon which to decide the assignments of error presented. Although plaintiff argues that pursuant to R.C. 3109.051(F)(1) the trial court was required to issue findings of fact and conclusions of law, we find that a review of this section indicates it pertains only to visitation and companionship issues and not to the right to access of children's records. The plaintiff's third assignment of error is overruled. Judgment is affirmed.

-9-

It is ordered that appellee recover of appellant his costs herein taxed. The court finds there were reasonable grounds for this appeal. It is ordered that a special mandate issue out of this court directing the Domestic Relations Division of the Cuyahoga County Court of Common Pleas to carry this judgment into execution. A certified copy of this entry shall constitute the mandate pursuant to Rule 27 of the Rules of Appellate Procedure. MICHAEL J. CORRIGAN, J. and JAMES D. SWEENEY, P.J., CONCUR JUDGE COLLEEN CONWAY COONEY N.B. This entry is an announcement of the court's decision. See App.R. 22(B), 22(D) and 26(A); Loc.App.R. 22. This decision will be journalized and will become the judgment and order of the court pursuant to App.R. 22(E) unless a motion for reconsideration with supporting brief, per App.R. 26(A), is filed within ten (10) days of the announcement of the court's decision. The time period for review by the Supreme Court of Ohio shall begin to run upon the journalization of this court's announcement of decision by the clerk per App.R. 22(E). See, also, S.Ct.Prac.R. II, Section 2(A)(a). .

Modification

There's an old Army saying that, "no plan survives first contact with the enemy". The decision of the court is a plan ordered by the court. No amount of anger or nasty behavior will change the plan.

If your custody case has gotten as far as a decision by the court you are probably as close to being enemies with the other parent as you will ever be.

Many things can happen from this point on. Generally unless a party files and wins an appeal nothing can be presented to the court for a year. An appeal can be appealed. Once the appeals are decided, nothing can be presented to the court for a year.

During that year the emotional climate can heat or cool. The increase in anger and pain will escalate if both parties participate

If one side decides to cool situations down and make connections easier for the children and themselves, everything will quiet down. If you have decided to make things work and the other parent has decided to make things as difficult as possible, things will still be easier for your child because of you and your child will appreciate your efforts.

Everything in a child custody case can be modified. As a matter of fact everything will be modified with or without your encouragement.

Types of modification:

Temporary
Retroactive
Automatic
Permanent

Things that can be modified are:

Primary Residential Parent
Visitation
Child Support

Ability to Move

Factors that influence modification:

Return to court
Inability to go to court
Destabilized household
Children growing older
School schedule changes
Parent's employment changes
Child's or parent's health change
Temporary modification becomes permanent
Significant change of circumstances (any party)
Custodial interference
Abuse of drink
Abuse of medication or street drugs
Arrest of a parent
Abuse or violence that endangers the child
Death of a parent
Child's Choice of Conservator
Time

Chapter 20: Costs

Family law has become so complicated and therefore expensive that it takes a lot of money to even get beaten. It is neither shallow nor selfish to appreciate and understand the importance of money as it pertains to custody. Disputes over money constitute seventy-five percent of the problems during custody battles. This chapter looks at: (1) legal costs to fight for custody, (2) and a quick look at taxes.

I Don't Understand Why No One Cares

The frustration of this process is aggravated by the fact that no one cares what happens to you or your children. The fact is that until you were became involved in child custody, you were unaware of the problems parents faced. Furthermore, now that you are being eaten alive it is difficult to reach out to others because you need both of your arms just to hang on. Once you have lived through this experience, you will move on to the next of life's challenge. Even the people who love and care about you still have to live their lives. The professionals you hire can't and shouldn't get emotionally involved. It will hamper their efforts on your behalf. They can only gauge your commitment by the support you offer them by doing your part of any process necessary and paying your bill to them on time.

When Your War Chest Is Spent

When you hire most of the professionals you need for your custody case they will require a retainer or down payment against the services you need. The longer a case goes on the more money it costs you. It is hard to believe that you can have an attorney do enough work in six months to use up three thousand dollars, or a detective use up two thousand in seven days, but it happens. Some courts are attempting to speed up the process by having the judges assign dates for the next stage of each case as they make a ruling on the matter at hand. Attorneys do not like having the judges control their cases and you can make it work for you or let it work against you. Get and stay involved in your case. Know and understand what is going on at all times.

There is nothing scientific about this chart. It was compiled from interviews with attorneys and parents who have completed the process. This chart was designed to give you an indication of where in the process your money is spent.

This chart should indicate to you that the earlier you settle this action the better it will be financially.

Legal and Professional Service

When And Where Your Money Is Spent In A Custody Case	
Action	Cost
Initial consultation	none
Second consultation. Acceptance of Documents from you. Organization of Information. Create and file petition of Dissolution and Order to Show Cause for temporary Custody and Support/ or file response to Petition by the opposition.	600.00
Review documents/ prepare for court/ appear at the Order to Show Cause Hearing/ explain what did happen to you after court.	400.00
Confer with other attorneys about the opposition's attorney and/or judge/ discuss results with you.	200.00
Review documents/ confer with you/ prepare for deposition/ depose opposition/ acquire copies of deposition/ review.	600.00
Discuss settlement with Opposition's attorney/ consult with you	200.00
Prepare your disclosure statement/ prepare interrogatories	300.00
Request for production of documents/ including appraisals of businesses and properties. Review when documents arrive	1,200.00
Request/ Review Home Studies and Psychological Evaluations for Custody/discuss results with you	1,400.00
Detectives	5,000.00
Psychological testing or Home Study $600.00 (per person)	1,800.00
Psychologist and/or Expert witnesses	2,500.00
Final attempt to settle with Opposition's attorney	400.00
Review documents/ pretrial conference with you/subpoena witnesses. Court	5,800.00
Total	$20,400.00

Expense Cost Control

You can do a great deal to control costs. But this can only be done if you are willing to manage your case rather than hand over the responsibilities to others. That means you can't wait for other people to call you back. What you are doing is very important to you. To others you are merely one more case to handle, one more file to complete or part of their daily work. You can't let excuses, yours or the excuses of others get in your way. Excuses can slow you down three ways. First, you did not get what you wanted so you can't proceed to the next step. Second, a delay interrupts your momentum and frustrates you causing fatigue, Third, your anger at the obstruction may derail your effort onto unless projects, such as filing complaints.

Once you know what you want, you have to find out what you need and determine exactly what you have to do to get it and then, do it. In most cases it is best to work backward from your goal. When determining your goal, make sure its attainable.
As an example, it would be fruitless if your goal was sole custody in a jurisdiction that will only give joint custody.

Deciding who has the power to give you what you want can mean finding out if a jury trial is an option. Juries tend to be more emotional, but may not hear all of the evidence. If your case will go before a judge, the judge will see all of the evidence. The judge will then determine what evidence will be considered or rejected. Some judges rely on the results of psychological evaluation. That would make it imperative to understand what that psychologist wants to see in a parent. If you find attitudes, behaviors or situations in your life that will keep the professional from seeing what a good parent you are, you must change those things. If the challenges you face are known or discoverable by the opposition, make the corrections quickly and visibly. Problems with anger, decision making, relationships, money and parenting can be addressed with classes through, which you can earn a certificate to show your desire to learn the proper way to do important things.

Keeping proper logs and records will help you demonstrate the life you live. Organizing information so it can be easily accessed is time consuming, tedious as well as expensive if someone must he hired to do it. Obtaining original, or certified copies of documents can save hundreds of dollars.

Establishing and maintaining communication sheets with attorneys and detectives will help you keep the case focused and moving. By recording the questions you asked and the answers you received you will not duplicate your efforts and waste the professional's time and your money. The communication sheets will also make it easy to see if the professionals are doing their job.

Two Ways To Significantly Cut Costs

Negotiation is the fastest and least expensive method of ending the custody battle. There are several options for accomplishing this process. In order to negotiate you must have two willing, concerned parents.

The simplest method is if each parent makes a list of what they want for the children and what they are willing to give to accomplish that goal. Using a form makes the evaluation to the two primary lists much easier than if the lists are done in a free form. Once the number of issues is reduced by the primary list a form should be made for a secondary list. Then if necessary, a third and fourth list. Avoid rehashing 'settled' issues. It may help to have a trained mediator assist with the process.

Fast tracking is the second way to cut the costs of a child custody battle. If the issues in the case are clear, the facts are sharply defined, but hotly in dispute and all that is required is a verdict. Fast tracking can either be agreed upon and requested of the judge or the judge may order it.

In order to successfully accomplish fast tracking a special team of home study, psychologists, accountants and any other professionals that might be necessary assembled. This group of professionals would be required to do their jobs in a matter of days and weeks rather than a matter of months.

Judges may be reluctant to fast track a child custody case. You will have to convince the judge that the professionals you have listed can do a through job on a precise time line rather than drag the process out. The professionals are getting paid to start the file and work on it until it is finished rather than fit the new file into an already crowded calendar of work. Many feel these fast track professionals can do a better job because there is no slippage of information or research. The most important benefit of fast tracking is that a long running initial battle causes more pain for the children and negative economic impact on the parents.

An attorney can present a list of several professionals for each step of the process (so the opposition attorney can choose) to the judge. The judge can assign a completion target date for reports and evaluations from the professionals at thirty days. Professionals expected to fast track their work will charge fifty to seventy-five percent more than for standard service. Set a date for a discovery conference where the attorneys have to meet and exchange the names of potential trial witnesses and documents. Designate thirty days for all depositions, and set a trial date ninety days away. Fast tracking can take the time line of a normal case from eighteen months to six.

Costs Go on Forever

Each job you need done, each bit of information you need will either cost you time or money, sometimes both.

The costs listed in the Legal Service and Professional Service Expense Example are the bare bones expenses. If you add any requests to the original contract, there will be additional costs. An illustration with each service or professional may help.

- **Detective:** You hired a detective and paid a retainer of $6,600.00, which is the hourly rate of $55.00. The assignment is to document a normal five day period in the lives of your children while they are in the care of their custodial mother. The detectives have set up three shifts of operatives so the children, twin girls, six years old will remain under surveillance twenty four hours a day.

During the process the detectives have noted that mom leaves for work at six each morning and does not return until approximately seven in the evening. A man approximately twenty-eight years old takes the twins to school at eight fifteen each day. The twins are dressed well and their hair appears clean and combed. The young man picks the children up from school at three forty-five in the afternoon. They go directly home and do not leave the house again.

Because you have no idea who this man is you are concerned about the situation. After a discussion with the detective agency you decide you want someone to make direct contact with the man. It is arranged to have a young female detective pose as an Avon Lady and make a call on the residence when the children are at school. The additional service will be charged on a per contact, per hour basis at $95.00 per hour with a two hour minimum. The detective was to set up a second meeting if necessary and if possible and all contact would be tape-recorded.

The Avon Lady called on the home at ten thirty in the morning, with free samples and was admitted by the young man.

Zane introduced himself and seemed to accept that the Avon Lady was making rounds in the neighborhood. He was eager to engage in conversation stating that he moved in with his girlfriend and her twin daughters four months ago. He met Sheila because his best friend, who had formerly been her boyfriend, lived there taking care of the children. The Avon Lady was mildly flirtatious and Zane responded. He filled out the top of the order blank and gave the Avon Lady a check for the bottle of after shave and some hair de-tangler for the twins that he ordered. The Avon Lady said she would be back in three days with the order.

After reading the detectives report you request a work-up on Zane. This is billed at $250.00.

The Avon Lady returned with Zane's order. They visited for over an hour. When the Avon Lady asked what he actually did all day she is given a detailed review of his daily chores, responsibilities for the children and his very personal relationship with Sheila. Zane says, the children often sleep with he and Sheila and the girls are not removed from the bed when their mother leaves for work. He is solely responsible for bathing, dressing and feeding the children. Zane considers himself to be a house husband and his personal bills are paid by Sheila. During the visit he offered the Avon Lady; a tour of the house, which she accepted; a Pepsi, which she accepted; and a marijuana cigarette, which she turned down saying her next customer might be able to smell it on her clothes.

It becomes evident that even though the initial $6,600.00 seemed like a great deal, it was only the beginning. The additional costs would be worth it if custody can be reversed because the mother is not the primary caregiver for her children. Additionally, the fact that the children are sleeping with this rogue male and there are drugs in the home are very important.

- **Attorney:** You hired an attorney and paid a $10,000.00 retainer to handle your divorce from Walt, which included some property and custody of your son Danny who is ten years old. The care of Danny had been equally shared between you and your husband. The property division didn't seem to be a problem, but the custody of Danny had become a heated issue because of Walt's parents. The daily living arrangements have not changed and you drop Danny at school just as you do each day. Walt always retrieves Danny at the end of the day, but today they do not come home. You call Walt's cell phone and work phone at his parent's company, Danny's school and Walt's parents. It becomes evident

Walt has taken Danny and no one is giving any information. You know Danny is safe so you are just angry at Walt's behavior. Your attorney gets the court to order Walt to return Danny to the family home pending a final decision. If the child is not returned in three days Walt will be in contempt of court. Two weeks pass and Walt and Danny are in town, but can't be located. The telephone bill comes and your attorney is able to get a record of all the calls made to and from Walt's cell phone.

The cell telephone bill indicates that Walt has called his parents home and office a dozen times each day and that calls have been made from his parents home and office to Walt's cell phone almost as many times each day. In each case the bill indicates that the calls were from three to forty minutes long.

You want you attorney to pursue a civil case against Walt's parents for conspiring with Walt to keep your child from you. Your attorney indicates he could handle this matter, but that it will be a separate lawsuit requiring a new agreement and $10,000.00 retainer.

Eventually you win custody of Danny, in great part because of Walt's actions. Any assurances from his parents that would have normally helped his case were disregarded by their complicity in Danny's abduction.

Because Walt's parents have a great deal of money you will probably be back in court each year to defend your custodial position. Hopefully the judge can be reminded of the cause and result of each action and award you your attorney fees.

- **Home Study:** You have paid $575.00 for a home study and are satisfied that it will show your home to be as good or better than the opposition's home. The opposition has filed a motion to prevent your parents from having the children at their home even during your parenting time because they allege that adults smoke in the presence of the children in that house. You submitted a letter from your father's doctor that he quit smoking eighteen months ago. Because you sometimes have your parent's baby-sit, you have ordered a home study of your parents house at and additional $575.00 to verify that it is a smoke free environment.

Bankruptcy

One of the tactics that will bring a divorce involving a child custody decision for six months to a year is if one party files in filed in the Federal Bankruptcy Court: Federal bankruptcy laws do not vary from state to state. The Bankruptcy Court may grant a specific motion to allow the divorce court to proceed, or until delay the divorce case until the bankruptcy is finally discharged.

Even if the court is ready for the final trial, including the distribution of property and debts. A federal action strips the state court of its jurisdiction to do anything about assets and debts. Child support may be the one exception.

If the other parent has used other dirty tricks to delay the dissolution of the marriage you may need to keep an eye on the 'Legal Notice' section of the newspaper. Any new legal actions will be posted. The sooner you are aware of a problem, the sooner you can fix it.

Rather than let this delay agitate you, use this time to build your case and document any violations of existing orders including, contact or visitation orders.

The (true) story of the PT technique being used against a Mrs. "S", who, after the massive documentation of her persistent access denial, was told by an angry judge "No, Mrs. S, I'm not sending you to jail. Instead, I hereby award temporary custody to Mr. S. See how you like that!"

But what led up to this turnaround? I wouldn't have had a chance to reverse custody for my client, Mr. S, if the trial had occurred on schedule.

Mrs. S had tied Mr. S up in knots. Seemingly hopeless. He hired me only three days before the scheduled final trial, and I was lucky enough to find that the judge had a scheduling conflict. The judge therefore granted me an extra week as the new attorney, to prepare for the final trial.

Mrs. S had a scheme. She planned on getting a "fair division" at trial by assuming all the community debts in exchange for being awarded an equally unbalanced property award of nearly all of the property. Then, in her original plan, she would immediately declare Bankruptcy, getting out of all the debts (and sicking the creditors on the husband, whose divorce decree wouldn't protect him from pre-dissolution contractual debts). And she would still keep all the assets. Nice, huh?

She had the Bankruptcy lawyer all set up to file the day after the divorce trial. He did. But the divorce hadn't gone through yet, because of the trial delay. Mr. S, a banker, read the local Financial Newspaper fine-print-columns, and found his wife's name in it. He called me, and I filed a single-sheet notice to the court that the Bankruptcy court had taken jurisdiction over the parties' property and debts. The trial date was quashed, for the months it would take the Bankruptcy Court to finish.

Acknowledgement of Paternity

Since determining the mother of a child is usually very easy the law focusing on establishing the father. Before the court can order child support, legal paternity must be established for the child.

In many states, the parents were required to sing a AOP and then request the attorney general to receive a legal finding of paternity from the court. New laws require the parents to sign the AOP, which will be furnished by the hospital after the birth of their child. When the AOP is filed with the Bureau of Vital Statistics, the AOP becomes a legal finding of paternity, streamlining the process and eliminating the need for the court to establish paternity. The cost of DNA testing to determine paternity can range from $600.00 to $3,000.00.

Disposable earnings is that part of the payor parent's earnings remaining after deduction of any amounts required by law to be withheld, union dues, nondiscretionary retirement contributions, and medical hospitalization, and disability insurance coverage for the payor parent and the child. Normally, the parent receiving the child support feels the guidelines are too restrictive. Conversely, the parent paying child support feels the guidelines are too generous and does not consider "new" income the custodial parent may receive from a new marriage or the additional obligations the non-custodial parent now has.

2001 DHHS Poverty Guidelines

The Department of Human Health Services poverty guidelines are a simplified version of the Federal Government's statistical poverty thresholds used by the Bureau of the Census to prepare its statistical estimates of the number of persons and families in poverty. The following definitions are derived for the most part from language used in U.S. Bureau of the Census report. They are not binding for administrative purposes to any program. To find out the precise definitions used by a particular program, one must consult the office or organization administering the program in question.

(a) Family. A family is a group of two or more persons related by birth, marriage, or adoption who live together; all such related persons are considered as members of one family.

For instance, if an older married couple, their daughter and her husband and two children, and the older couple's nephew all lived in the same house apartment they would all be considered members of a single family.

(b) Unrelated individual. An unrelated individual is a person 15 years old or over (other than an inmate of an institution) who is not living with any relatives. An unrelated individual may be living in a house or apartment (or in group quarters such as a rooming house) in which one or more person also live who are related to the individual in question by birth, marriage, or adoption. Examples of unrelated individuals residing with others include a lodger, a foster child, a ward, or an employee.

(c) Household. As defined by the Bureau of the Census for statistical purposes, consists of all the persons who occupy a housing unit (house or apartment), whether they are related or not.

(d) Income. Programs, which use the poverty guidelines in determining eligibility may use administrative definitions of "income" or "countable income" which differ from the statistical definition. In many cases, income data for a part of a year may be annualized in order to determine eligibility. For Instance, by multiplying by four the amount of income received during the most recent three months.

Dependent According to the Court

As part of the custody ruling, the judge will make a decision as to who can claim the children as a dependant for purposes of income taxes. Only one parent may claim the children.

Are You Poor Enough?

Poverty Guidelines (Federal Register, Vol. 66, No. 33, February 16, 2001, pp. 10695-10697			
Household Members in Family Unit	**(48) states and D.C.**	**Alaska**	**Hawaii**
One Person	$ 8,590	10,730	9,890
Two People	11,610	14,510	13,360
Three People	14,630	18,290	16,830
Four People	17,650	22,070	20,300
Five People	20,670	25,850	23,770
Six People	23,690	29,630	27,240
Seven People	26,710	33,410	30,710
Eight People	29,730	37,190	34,180
Each additional family member	3,020	3,780	3,470

Dependent According to the IRS

None of the legal or professional expense that you incur while fighting the child custody war is deductible.

As far as taxes are concerned children of divorced or separated parents are subject to special tax rules to determine if the support test is met. The rules also apply to children of parents who lived apart during the last six months of the year, even if they do not have a separation agreement. For these rules, the custodial parent is the parent who had custody of the child for most of the year. A non-custodial parent is the parent who had custody for the shorter period of time or who did not have custody at all.

The general rule is that the custodial parent is treated as having provided over half of the child's total support if both parents together paid over half of the child's support. This means that the custodial parent can claim the child as a dependent if the other dependency tests are also met.

If you are the non-custodial parent, you are treated as having provided over half of the child's support and can claim the child as a dependent if both parents together paid over half of the child's support, the other dependency tests are met, and either one or two below applies.

1. The custodial parent agrees not to claim the child's exemption for 1997 by signing form 8332 or a similar statement. But you must attach this statement to your return. You can attach a copy of certain pages of your divorce decree or separation agreement if it went into effect after 1984.

2. Your divorce decree or written separation agreement went into effect before 1985 and it states that you (the non-custodial parent) can claim the child as a dependent. But you must have given at least six hundred dollars for the child's support in 1997. This rule does not apply if your decree or agreement was changed after 1984 to say that you cannot claim the child as your dependent.

Normally the five tests you must pass in order to claim your children as a dependent on your taxes are:

1. Child must have less than $2,300 gross income for the year.

2. You must have furnished over half of the child's total support for that calendar year.

3. Child must be son or daughter, grandchild, step-child, adopted child, brother or sister, brother or sister by half blood, stepbrother or stepsister, son or daughter of taxpayer's brother or sister, brother or sister of taxpayer's father or mother,

son-in-law, daughter-in-law, and a child who during the taxpayer's entire tax year lives in the taxpayer's home.

4. The child must be a citizen, national, or resident of the United States, Canada or Mexico some time during the calendar year, or an alien child adopted by and living with a US citizen as a member of his household for an entire tax year.

5. The child must not have filed a joint return with his or her spouse.

Dependent Credits

Child and Dependent Care Credit. A Nonrefundable credit is allowed for a portion of qualifying child or dependent care expenses paid for purpose of allowing the taxpayer to be gainfully employed. (Form 2441 or Schedule 2 of 1040A).

Dependent must be under thirteen years old, or physically or mentally incapable of caring for themselves, as well as certain dependent children of divorced parents. Maximum credit $2,400 for one dependent, $4,800 for two or more.

Hidden Assets

Some people attempt to hide assets in order to apply for free or low cost legal assistance. Some of this can be tracked easily and some of it takes a little more work. If you are considering this practice, maybe you rethink the penalties. If you think the other person is hiding assets, the following list of common hiding places should help you devise a search strategy that will locate even the most "deeply" hidden assets. The most common asset protection scheme is to title and transfer all assets to a spouse or business controlled by the subject. Therefore, we suggest you always request an asset search on the subjects spouse and business simultaneously.

1. Under another's name such as spouse, relatives, friends, partners or an alias
2. Pre paid rent or home mortgage paydown
3. Life insurance
4. Savings bonds
5. Postal money orders, travelers or cashiers checks
6. Dissolved corporations
7. Stockbroker accounts
8. Barer bonds
9. Collectibles
10. Safe deposit boxes
11. Offshore foreign accounts
12. Overpayments to IRS
13. Sweetheart lawsuits
14. Overpayments to credit cards
15. Cars, yachts, aircraft
16. Jewelry, collectibles, luxury items
17. Family trusts
18. Offshore corporations, or dead shell corps.

Tax Gifts and Insurance Ownership

Tax gifts can build a secure financial future for your child and give you a tax break at the same time. You can open a Custodian account in your child's name with a parent, guardian, attorney, or mutual fund broker to establish a college fund or for financial maintenance.

There may be tax consequences in connection with the transfer of ownership of policies and collection of insurance proceeds. Find out what they are and plan for them now.

Earned Income Credit

A refundable earned income credit is available to a low-income individual who has a qualifying child, has earned income, and meets adjusted gross income thresholds.

Use a Good Tax Advisor

A good tax specialist will be able to identify the deductions you are allowed and advise you on how best to plan for the future of your children and yourself. The contact log you keep will serve as an important document when you require proof of expenditures for your children.

Adoption of Child and Termination of Rights

The Court will allow relinquishment of rights and responsibilities, if another similar parent is willing and able to take on those responsibilities.

The example used here is that of a father voluntarily relinquishing his rights and responsibilities to another father. The process is the same for a mother who wishes to give up her rights and responsibilities to another mother. Sometimes both parents relinquish their rights to family members such as grandparents who can better provide for the chid.

Voluntary Relinquishment of Parental Rights

[Nonagency]

State of Texas)

County of Harris)

Mark McDavid appeared in person before me today and, in the presence of the undersigned credible witnesses, stated under oath:

My name is Mark McDavid. I am 36 years of age and reside at 1212 Leasing Way, Sites, Idaho. I am the father of the following child:

Sue McDavid, a female child born to me on March 10, 2000.

No person has been appointed or has qualified as guardian of the person or estate of the child.

I am presently obligated by court order to make payments for the support of the child.

A full description, including statement of value, of all property owned or possessed by the child is as follows:

No property of consequence is owned or possessed by the child subject of this suit.

The mother of the child is Marsha Allen, and her address is 35 State St., Houston, TX.

I designate Charles Allen and Marsha Allen, prospective adoptive parents, 35 State St., Houston, TX., as managing conservators of the child. I have been informed that my parental rights, powers, duties and privileges are as follows:

1. the right to have physical possession, to direct the moral and religious training, and to establish the residence of the child;

2. the duty, of care, control, protection, and reasonable discipline of the child;

3. the duty, to support the child, including providing the child with clothing, food, shelter, medical and dental care, and education;

4. the duty, except when a guardian of the estate has been appointed, to manage the estate of the child, including the right as an agent of the child to act in relation to the child's estate if the child's action is required by a state, the United States, or a foreign government;

5. the right to the services and earnings of the child;

6. the right to consent to the child's marriage, enlistment in the armed forces of the United States, medical and dental care, and psychiatric, psychological, and surgical treatment;

7. the right to represent the child in legal action and to make other decisions of substantial legal significance concerning the child;

8. the right receive and give receipt for payments for the support of the child and to hold or disburse funds for the benefit of the child;

9. the right to inherit from and through the child;

10. the right to make decisions concerning the child's education; and

11. any other right or duty existing between a parent and child by virtue of law.

I freely and voluntarily give and relinquish to Charles Allen and Marsha Allen all my parental rights and duties.

Page 1

I fully understand that a lawsuit will be promptly filed in a court of competent jurisdiction to terminate forever the parent-child relationship between me and the child named above. I fully understand that the termination suit may or may not be combined with a suit to adopt my child. I understand that either way, once the Court terminates my parental rights, I have no further say concerning my child, whether or not my child is adopted then or at some later time.

I know that I have the right to appear personally before the Court, with an attorney of my choice, to testify about my desires with respect to my child. However, I do not want to go to court in person and choose not to be represented by a lawyer. I want this Affidavit for Voluntary Relinquishment of Parental Rights presented to the Court.

Because I do not want to testify in person before the Court, I freely and voluntarily waive and give up my right to the issuance, service, and return of citation, notice, and all other process in any suit to terminate my parental rights joined with a suit to adopt. I do not want to be informed further about the lawsuit. I specifically agree that the final hearing in the lawsuit may be held at any time without further notice to me. I waive and give up my right to have the official court reporter make a record of the testimony in the lawsuit. Furthermore, I do not want to be mailed or given a copy of the judgement terminating my parental rights and do not want to be notified of the signing, rendition, or entry of that judgement. I also consent to have any suit affecting the parent-child relationship filed or to b filed with respect to the child named above be decided by an associate judge appointed under section 201.001 of the Texas Family Code.

If I am in the armed services of the United States at this time, the fact in no way has interfered with my freedom to make my decision to execute this affidavit, and, insofar as this matter is concerned, I waive all rights, privileges, and exemptions existing or that may hereafter exist in my favor under the Soldiers' and Sailors' Civil Relief Act of 1940, including the appointment of counsel to represent me in this case.

I FULLY UNDERSTAND THAT I MAY NOT BE FURTHER INFORMED ABOUT THE TERMINATION SUIT OR ABOUT ANY OTHER HEARINGS OR PROCEEDINGS AFFECTING THE CHILD NAMED IN THIS AFFIDAVID.

Termination of the parent-chid relationship is in the best interest of the chid. I understand that I make this termination possible by executing this affidavit.

THIS AFFIDAVIT IS REVOCABLE ONLY IF THE REVOCATION IS MADE BEFORE THE ELEVENTH DAY AFTER THE DATE THE AFFIDAVIT IS EXECUTED..

I understand that, for any revocation to be valid, I must sign a statement before two credible witnesses and a person authorized to take oaths. A copy of the revocation must be delivered to Marsha Allen, 35 State St., Houston, TX..

If I know that a termination suit based on this affidavit has been filed, I must file a copy of the revocation with the clerk of the court.

I have carefully considered alternative plans for my child's future and have obtained the advice of whatever family members, friends, or other persons and professionals I feel were necessary to help me make this decision. This decision is very difficult for me to make, and under other circumstances I might have made a different decision. I know that Charles Allen and Marsha Allen, in accepting my child for adoptive placement and assuming responsibility for my child, is relying on my promise that I will not attempt to reclaim my child. I declare that I fully understand the meaning of this affidavit of relinquishment and the finality of my action in signing it, and I am signing it freely, voluntarily, and with the firm conviction that this decision is the best available alternative for my child.

I am signing this affidavit today because I want to sigh it and not because Charles Allen and Marsha Allen or any other person or persons want me to sign it. I am signing this affidavit in the presence of the two undersigned witnesses. I am also signing this affidavit before a notary public, who has asked me under oath whether or not each and every statement in this affidavit is true and correct.

Page 2

I REALIZE THAT I SHOULD NOT SIGN THIS AFFIDAVIT FOR VOLUNTARY RELINQUISHMENT OF PARENTAL RIGHTS IF THERE IS ANY THOUGHT IN MY MIND THAT I MIGHT SOMEDAY SEEK TO GAIN CUSTODY OF MY CHILD.

AT THE TIME OF THE SIGNING OF THIS AFFIDAVIT FOR VOLUNTARY RELINQUISHMENT OF PARENTAL RIGHTS, I FEEL THAT I AM PHYSICALLY AND EMOTIONALLY PREPARED TO SIGH THIS DOCUMENT. I AM NOT CURRENTLY UNDER THE INFLUENCE OF ANY SUBSTANCE AND/OR MEDICATION THAT WOULD AFFECTMY ABILITY TO EXECUTE THEIS AFFIDAVIT.

I ACKNOWLEGE THAT I AM SIGNING THIS AFFIDAVIT FOR VOLUNTARY RELINQUISHMENT OF PARENTAL RIGHTS MORE THAN FORTY-EIGHT HOURS AFTER THE BIRTH OF THE CHILD NAMED IN THIS DOCUMENT.

Affiant ____Mark McDavid____

Witness at request of affiant. _____Justin A. Tollifson_____________________

Witness _______Ronald Hernandez______________________________

Verification

Mark McDavid appeared in person before me today and stated on his oath that hi is the affiant, that he has read the forgoing Affidavit for Voluntary Relinquishment of Parental Rights, and that the statements contained in it are within his personal knowledge and are true and correct.

This affidavit for voluntary Relinquishment of Parental Rights was signed under oath before me at __5:15___ p.m. on January 8th 2001 by the affiant.

Ruby Ellen Johnson

Notary Public, State of Texas

Page 3

NO. 2001FC-80878

IN THE INTEREST OF	) IN THE COUNTY COUT
Sue McDavid	) a child
	) HARRIS COUNTY, TEXAS

Petition for Termination/Adoption of Stepchild

1. Petitioners.

This suit is brought by Marsha Allen age 34 years and Charles Allen age 35 years, Petitioners, who are husband and wife and who reside at 35 State St., Houston, TX..

Petitioner Marsha Allen is the birth mother of the child.

Charles Allen is the stepfather of the child.

2. Jurisdiction.

This court has acquired and retains continuing, exclusive jurisdiction of this suit and of the child the subject of this suit as a result of prior proceedings.

Because Mark McDavid resides outside Texas, information required by section 152.009 of the Texas Family Code is set forth in the attached affidavit.

3. Interstate Placement Information.

A sworn allegation or statement complying with section 162.002(b) of the Texas Family Code is attached to this petition and incorporated for all purposes.

4. Child.

NAME: Sue McDavid

BIRTHPLACE: Houston, Texas

BIRTH DATE: March 10, 2000

PRESENT RESIDENCE: With Petitioners

5. Persons Entitled to Citation.

The father of the child is Mark McDavid who is 36 years old and who resides at 1212 Leasing Way, Sites, Idaho. No service is necessary at this time.

6. Property.

No property is owned or possessed by the child the subject of this suit.

7. Termination Sought.

Termination of the parent-child relationship between Mark McDavid and the child is in the best interest of the child, and such termination is requested.

8. Ad Litem.

Waiver Requested. Petitioners request the Court to find that the interest of the child will be represented adequately by Petitioners and are not adverse to Petitioners.

9. Inheritance Rights.

It is in the best interest of the child that the Court terminate the right of the child to inherit from and through Mark McDavid, Social Security number is 555-55-5555 and such termination is requested.

Page 1

10. Adoption Sought.

It is in the best interest of the child the subject of this suit to be adopted by Charles Allen and adoption of such child is sought.

11. Residence with Petitioners.

The child will have lived in the home of Petitioners for at lease six months when this cause is heard.

12. Consent of Managing Conservator.

The written consent of the managing conservator is not required, because the managing conservator is one of the Petitioners.

13. Change of Name.

Petitioners request that the name of the child Sue McDavid be changed to Sue Allen.

14. Social Study.

Petitioners request the Court forthwith to appoint an investigator to make and prepare asocial study into the circumstances and condition of the child of the home of Petitioners and to set a date for its filing. Petitioners further request that a copy of the social study be make available to Petitioners prior to a final adoption decree.

15. Sealing of Records.

Petitioners request the Court to order the sealing of the file and the minutes of the Court.

16. Prayer.

Petitioners pray that citation and notice issue as required by law. Petitioners pray that the Court enter its decree in accordance with the allegations of this petition.

Petitioners pray for general relief.

Respectfully submitted, *Gloria Stephens*

Attorney at Law Page 2

NO. 2001FC-80878

IN THE INTEREST OF) IN THE COUNTY COUT

Sue McDavid) a child

) HARRIS COUNTY, TEXAS

Social Study Report of Investigator

This report is filed by the undersigned investigator who was appointed to make the social study in the above-entitled and numbered case.

1. With respect to the background, circumstances, and condition of the child

Sue McDavid was born to Marsha McDavid and Mark McDavid in Houston, Texas on March 10, 2000. Marsha McDavid and Mark McDavid were divorced July 3, 2000. Marsha McDavid married Charles Allen September 1, 2000. Sue McDavid has lived with her mother Marsha Allen since her birth. Mark McDavid reports he has made no effort to maintain regular contact. Sue McDavid is a healthy, happy and verbal fourteen month old. She enjoys constant attention form both Marsha and Charles Allen. They clearly dote on her, and she responds very favorably to them. Dr. Moreland reports that Sue receives regular medical attention and is current on her shots.

2. With respect to the background, circumstances, and condition of Marsha Allen and the Petitioner, Charles Allen.

Marsha (McDavid) Allen has provided Sue's home and primary family since birth. Marsha Allen has been a career homemaker. Marsha and Charles Allen has a marriage that seems strong and secure, and they show excellent parenting skills and experience. They have extended family in the surrounding county, with deep roots in their community. They greatly enjoy being parents and are devoted to Sue and her care.

3. With respect to the background, circumstances, and conditions of the home of the Petitioners, Marsha and Charles Allen, and its suitability to the child;

The Allen family has lived in the area for twenty years. Marsha and Charles live in the home originally purchased by Marsha seven years ago. The three family members share a three bedroom two bathroom home. The home is tidy and neat, with a well-kept fenced yard. The kitchen is fully appointed with modern conveniences, and they enjoy air conditioning.. Their home has all the amenities expected in a typical family home. Sue has her won bedroom which is fully appointed with her bed, chest of drawers, and plenty of nice toys and books appropriate for her age. She enjoys a safe, stimulating and secure living situation. The family owns a pick-up truck and a family sedan. Charles Allen is an insurance agent with a local company and has been employed with them for eleven years.

4. Further I report that:

The Petitioner's household is appropriate for continuing to raise Sue. They are her family, and this adoption formalized the existing relationship dating to the child's infancy. She will have legal recognition of her actual situation. The Allens have proven to be good parents and should continue to fulfill that role.

Accordingly, the undersigned respectfully recommends tat the petition to adopt the child be: APPROVED. SIGNED ON April 4, 2001 Ronald Garcia

NO. 2001FC-80878

IN THE INTEREST OF) IN THE COUNTY COUT

Sue McDavid) a child

) HARRIS COUNTY, TEXAS

Decree Terminating Parental Rights

And Granting Adoption of Stepchild

Appearances.

On June 8, 2001, Marsha Allen and Charles Allen, Petitioners, appeared in person and by attorney and announced ready for trial.

Respondent, Mark McDavid waived issuance and service of citation by waiver duly filed and did not otherwise appear.

Also appearing was Jack Garcia, appointed by the Court to complete a Social Study Report in the interest of Sue McDavid.

Jurisdiction.

The Court, having examined the pleadings and heard the evidence and argument of counsel, finds that it has jurisdiction of this case and of all the parties and that no other court has continuing, exclusive jurisdiction of this cause. All persons entitled to citation were properly cited.

Jury.

Jury was waived, and all questions of fact and of law were submitted to the Court.

Social Study.

The Court finds that the required social study has been made and is on file herein and that a copy of the study has been made available to Petitioners prior to a final decree of adoption.

Health, Social, Educational and Genetic History Report.

The Court finds that making and filing of the health, social, educational, and genetic history report is not required by section 162.005(a-d) of the Texas Family Code.

Interstate Compact.

The Court finds that Petitioners have filed a sworn statement regarding compliance with the Interstate Compact on the Placement of Children as required by section 162.002 (b) of the Texas Family Code.

Consent Of Managing Conservator.

The Court finds that consent of the managing conservator is not required, because the managing conservator is one of the Petitioners.

Adoption Granted.

The court finds that all prerequisites and requirements for adoption have been met and that the adoption in the best interest of the child. IT IS ORDERED AND DECREED that he adoption of the above described child the subject of this suit by Charles Allen is the stepfather of the child.

Page 1

Change of Name.

IT IS FURTHER ORDERED AND DECREED that the child Sue McDavid shall henceforth have the legal name of SUE ALLEN.

Record.

Making of a record of testimony was waived by the parties with the consent of the Court.

Child.

The following child id the subject of this suit;

NAME: Sue McDavid

SEX: Female

BIRTHPLACE: Houston, Texas

BIRTH DATE: March 10, 2000

PRESENT RESIDENCE: With Petitioners

Termination.

The Court finds by clear and convincing evidence that termination of the parent-child relationship between Mark McDavid and the child is in the best interest of the child.

IT IS THEREFORE ORDERED AND DECREED that the parent-child relationship between Mark McDavid and the child the subject of this suit is terminated.

IT IS ORDERED AND DECREED that the right of the child to inherit from

Adoption.

Then, the Court proceeded to consider the application for Charles Allen to adopt the child the subject of this suit.

Residence with Petitioners.

The Court finds that the child has lived in the home of Petitioners for as least six months.

Citizenship.

The Court finds that the child adopted is a citizen by birth of the United States of America.

Costs.

Costs of court are to born by the party by whom such costs were incurred.

Files Transmitted; Records Sealed.

IT IS FURTER ORDERED AND DECREED that the Clerk of this court shall, after entry of final orders in this cause, transmit to the State Department of Human Service at Austin, Texas, certified copies of the petition and judgment in this case; all other papers and records, including the minutes of the Court, in this case are ordered sealed.

Signed on this 12th day of June 2001

Ester Lebowitz

Judge Presiding

Page 2

Chapter 21: Child Support

Family law has become so complicated and therefore expensive that it takes a lot of money to even get beaten. Child support is an issue no matter what your post-custody battle status may be. It is neither shallow nor selfish to appreciate and understand the importance of money as it pertains to custody. Disputes over money constitute 75% of the problems during custody battles. This chapter looks at:

(1) normal daily costs to raise a healthy child
(2) when support starts and ends
(3) how and where support is paid
(4) support collection methods, private and public
(5) child support case law.

Income

Child support guidelines provide that income from full time employment, self-employment, rents, royalties, and benefits allocated to an individual for a business or undertaking in the form of a proprietorship, partnership, joint venture, close corporation, agency, employee or independent contractor, is considered "income" for purposes of child support.

When it comes to looking for income for purposes of child support a certain amount of disclosure is required by law. The parties must disclose income and certain expenses. Some states even require that this information be on a specific form and updated annually, even after the support order is entered.

Shofmaster v. Shofmaster, 138 N.H. 460, 642 A.2d 1361 1994
When financial statement is required by law, parties have ongoing duty to keep statement up to date; Walles v. Walles, 295 N.J. Super. 498, 685 A.2d 508 (App. Div. 1996)

If one party obtains a modification due to a decrease in income, then that party has to provide updated financial data to allow the other party to seek reinstatement of original order if earnings then increase when the financial situation changes.

Verification of Income

Most states also require that the statements made concerning income and expenses be verified and documented, specifically designating the type of verification that is sufficient. The most common forms of verification of income are pay stubs for at least three months, employer statements.

When a parent is self-employed he or she must provide bank statements, receipts for paid expenses, and federal income tax forms.
In the Marriage of Krone, 530 N.W.2d 468 (Iowa Ct. App. 1995) The father's 1992 tax returns and pay stubs verified his income.
Young v. Muthersbaugh, 415 Pa. Super. 591, 609 A.2d 138 (1992) The father's pay stubs and letters from employers were sufficient to substantiate his income.

If you fail to comply with these requirements in a timely manner you may aggravate the judge. The judge could set an arbitrary amount for child support and deny you the opportunity to appeal the decision.
Crefasi v. Crefasi, 628 So. 2d 1274 (La. Ct. App. 1993
Zayed v. Zayed, 100 Ohio App. 3d 410, 654 N.E.2d 163 (1995), In this case the judge prevented the party from appealing his decision.
Hackman v. Hackman, 847 S.W.2d 193 (Mo. Ct. App. 1993) The father was prevented from appealing modification of support where he had not completed the appropriate Form 14
In re Marriage of Bucklin, 70 Wash. App. 837, 855 P.2d 1197 (1993) The father was not entitled to a reduction in support even though his hotel business was destroyed by a hurricane, because he failed to verify his income. In at least one state, the failure to make the required disclosure can result in the presumption that the noncomplying parent's income is the greater of 150% of the most recently available annual average covered wage for all employment as calculated by department of employment or training. Vt. Stat. Ann. tit. 15, § 662.

Each state has it's own method of verifying your income and benefits. The example shown is typical of what each state uses.

Employment / Income Verification Letter

JAMES T. CLARK South Carolina Department of Social Services

State Director Office of Child Support Enforcement

Columbia Region 1Columbia, SC 29202-1150
(803) 253-7566

Kenmor Electric Co., Inc. June 27, 1995

1620 West Hwy. 220, Kenmor, UT 84116

Re: Gregory T. Brian File No.: 02013106

SSN: 613-23-2769
DOB: June 20, 1995

Dear Sir:

We would like to verify employment, income and dependent coverage availability on the above-referenced person. The Office of Child Support Enforcement is exempt from the restrictions of the Privacy Act (P.L. 93-579) due to the fact that the information is needed for legal enforcement of child support. Section 43-5-50(d), Code of Laws of S.C., 1976, as amended, also allows us to obtain the following information.

Please furnish or verify the information requested below:

Please provide social security number.

____

Is referenced person currently employed?
( ) YES ( ) NO

If yes, address where person reports to work.

____

What hours/shifts does person work?

____

Is group health insurance available to this individual? ( ) YES ( ) NO

If so, is dependent coverage carried?
( ) YES ( ) NO

If yes, please list children covered.

____

What is the cost of dependent coverage?

____

If not currently employed, date of termination.

____

Please provide last known home address.

____

If referenced person is not currently employed, do you know where he/she is now employed?

____

____

Any other information, which might help us in locating this employee.______________

____

Current Monthly Salary______________

Your cooperation is appreciated. Thank you.
Sincerely, *Nash Carruthers*

Child Support Specialist Supervisor

Self Employment

The courts have said that payment, in the form of royalties from patents, trademarks, copyrights, and other intellectual property is "income.

- Low v. Low, 79 Colo. 408, 246 P. 266 (1926); Gardry v. Gardry, 481 So.2d 706,708 La. App. 1985
- Hoffa v. Hoffa, 332 N.W.2d 522, 526 (Minn. Ct. App. 1986);
- In re Marriage of Julian, 868 S.w.2d 182 (Mo. Ct. App. 1994)
- Braeman v. Braeman, 192 Neb. 510, 222 N.W.2d 811, 812 (1974)
- Taylor v. Taylor, 333 S.C. 209, 508 S.E.2d 50, 53 (1998)
- Morey v. Morey, No. 01-A-01-9506-CV00243 (Tenn. Ct. App. December 15, 1995)
- Stone v. Gulf American Fire, 554 So. 2d 346 (Ala. 1989)

The illegitimate child of Hank Williams Sr.(a country western singer), acknowledged during his lifetime, was entitled to share in the estate of Williams, including royalty income).

One father argued that the court could not consider his copyright income, for to do so would violate federal law. In Boutz v. Donaldson, 26 Fam. L. Rep. (BNA) 1016 (N.M. Ct. App. September 20, 1999), the father argued that the trial court's consideration of the income he received from his copyrights works was error, specifically basing his argument on a theory of federal preemption. The father argued that The Federal Copyright Act, 17 U.S.C. § 201 (1994) provides that a copyright "vests initially in the author," 17 U.S.C. § 201, and cautions that copyrights "are governed exclusively" by the Act and not by "the common law or statutes of any State," 17 U.S.C. § 301(a) (1994). The father further pointed to language in Section 201(e) of the Act that states may not "seize, expropriate, transfer, or exercise rights of ownership with respect to the copyright." Although the father conceded that his theory of preemption is not explicit in the statute, he relied on these Congressional expressions as an indication of Congressional intent to preempt the field. The court found "Father's argument novel but not persuasive." The court held that copyrights are not federal benefits, but merely contractual benefits that are governed by federal law. This distinction is crucial was crucial to the court. Citing Worth v. Worth, 241 Cal. Rptr. 135, 139 (Cal. Ct. App. 1987), where the court rejected the argument by the author-spouse that income from copyrighted material could not be divided equally under California's community property law for fear of conflicting with the preemptive intent of the Copyright Act, the court concluded:

The trial court only included such income, as it passes unencumbered to Father, for purposes of calculating Father's ability to support his children. In short, the court's actions below are less intrusive on Father's copyright interest than the state judicial actions specifically approved by the California court in Worth. In the absence of any clear federal intent to preempt the effects of generic state law on child support, and relying on the discussion in the Worth opinion, "we are not persuaded that the Copyright Act preempts the court's consideration of Father's income from copyrighted sources."

Lottery Winnings

Lottery winnings are "income" under the child support guidelines, even if the winnings are taken in a one time lump-sum rather than a monthly pay-out.

- County of Contra Costa v. Lemon, 205 Cal. App. 3d 683, 252 Cal. Rptr. 455 (1988)
- In re Marriage of Bohn, 26 Fam. L. Rep. (BNA) 1188 (Colo. Ct. App. 2/3/00); In re Marriage of McCord, 910 P.2d 85 (Colo. Ct. App. 1995)
- In re Marriage of Gudzelak, No. CN90-10675 (Del. Fam. Ct. 10/23/93)
- In re Marriage of Boyden, 164 Ill. App. 3d 385, 517 N.E.2d 1144 (1987)
- Green v. Scott, 687 So. 2d 655 (La. Ct. App. 1997)
- Darden v. Darden, 66 N.C. App. 432, 311 S.E.2d 600 (1984) (father's income was not limited to sporadic income from job, but included income from gambling and numbers running)
- Pratt v. McCullough, 100 Ohio App. 3d 479, 654 N.E.2d 372 (1995)
- Moore v. Youngquist, No. 10A01-9012-CH-00433, 1991 WL 57982 (Tenn. Ct. App. 4/19/91) (holding that lottery winnings paid to the winner over time should be considered income for child support)
- Gerrits v. Gerrits, 167 Wis. 2d 429, 482 N.W.2d 134 (Ct. App. 1992)

Underkofler v. Underkofler, 834 P.2d 1140 (Wyo. 1992).

Knapp v. Levy, 245 A.D.2d 1027, 667 N.Y.S.2d 563 (1997) (one-time prize of automobile is not income).

Hidden Sources of Income

A credit check or insurance policies can find many sources of hidden income. Some hidden sources of income include:

- frequent flyer points
- commissions and bonuses
- points for hotel programs
- country club, golf club, swim clubs, tennis club memberships
- bank accounts, stocks, or bonds
- credit card points
- season tickets to sporting or cultural events
- excessive deductions on pay check
- equity in auto and vacation leases
- transferable government permits such as hunting and grazing leases, individual fishing quotas, taxi medallions
- general powers of appointment
- paper only (fraudulent) loans
- accrued vacation or sick time
- expensive realestate, vehicles, jewelry, or collections
- book royalties

Because the basic income and expense information must be disclosed the support calculation may then be accomplished by means of a calculator, there is no need for further investigation. This isn't true for two reasons. First, the required disclosure only gives you the basics of income and expenses.

Tax law does not cover "income" for purposes of child support.

- In Stepp v. Gray, 58 Ark. App. 229, 947 S.W.2d 798 (1997) the ruling states the, chancellor may not use definitions of income in federal tax code to find true disposable income of child support obligor.
- Beardsley v. Heazlitt, 654 N.E.2d 1178 (Ind. Ct. App. 1995) The tax law is not controlling on definition of income, especially where party is self-employed.
- In re Marriage of McBride, 166 Ill. App. 3d 504, 519 N.E.2d 1095 (1988) The tax law principles did not apply in computing father's net income for purposes of child support..
- Hudson v. Markham, 948 S.W.2d 1 (Tex. Ct. App. 1997) The court is not bound by tax return that could discount business deductions that were really personal in nature.

Second, some people will not tell the truth in the required forms, and further investigation is necessary to check the accuracy of the financial statement.

Your attorney can request additional discovery or you can make investigatory efforts on your own.

Income of the Very Rich

Estevez v. Superior Court, 22 Cal. App. 4th 423, 27 Cal. Rptr. 2d 470 (1994), the court accepted the "millionaire's defense" to discovery, and held that in the case of an extraordinarily high earner who stipulates that he can and will pay any reasonable amount of child support, discovery of the earner's lifestyle and net worth is not warranted. Rather, the only issue before the court is the reasonable needs of the child.

On the other hand, in Miller v. Schou, 616 So. 2d 436 (Fla. 1993), the court rejected this argument. There, the court held that without knowing what the parent's financial status is, it is impossible for the court to determine what the reasonable needs of the child are.

Accord In re Marriage of Shivers, 557 N.W.2d 532 (Iowa App. 1996) (party is entitled to inquire into other party's income, even though total incomes were above the highest amount, because ultimate award is in the court's discretion and the court has the right to be informed)

- Jeffress v. Johnson, No. 279 (Md. Ct. App. slip op. 10/25/96)
- Chambers by Cochran v. Sanderson, 107 Nev. 846, 822 P.2d 657 (1991);
- Shaw v. Cameron, 125 N.C. App. 522, 481 S.E.2d 365 (1997).

But see Woodward v. Berkery, No. 97-0938 (Fla. 4th DCA 12/17/98) (restricting mother's access to complete financial information of father, singer Tom Jones, because of mother's specific statement that she would turn over all information to the press).

Income Not Reflected On Tax Forms

A 1040 form will reflect salary and wages, including tips, commissions, bonuses, profit-sharing, deferred compensation, severance pay, cost of living allowances, over-time pay, pay.
Even second jobs, income from investments. Tax forms will also include payments that are intended to take the place of wages and salary, such as workers' compensation, unemployment insurance, disability insurance, disability pensions.

The following types of "income" that will not necessarily be reflected on a tax form include:

Employer's Contributions to Tax-deferred Savings Plan. Shaver v. Kopp, 545 N.W.2d 170 (N.D. 1996).

Interest and Dividend Income that is reinvested and not received.

- In re Marriage of Tessmer, 903 P.2d 1194 (Colo. Ct. App. 1995)
- Fabiano v. Fabiano, 10 Conn. App. 466, 523 A.2d 937 (1987)
- In re Marriage of Fain, 794 P.2d 1086 (Colo. Ct. App. 1990)
- Tulloch v. Flickinger, 616 A.2d 315 (Del. 1992); Villanueva (Garcia) v. O'Gara, 282 Ill. App. 3d 147, 668 N.E.2d 589 (1996)
- Good v. Armstrong, 218 Mich. App. 1, 554 N.W.2d 14 (1996)
- Mower County Human Services ex rel. Meyer v. Hueman, 543 N.W.2d 682 (Minn. Ct. App. 1996)
- In re Marriage of Durbin, 251 Mont. 51, 823 P.2d 243 (1991)
- Mehne v. Hess, 4 Neb. App. 935, 553 N.W.2d 482 (1996); Cleveland v. Cleveland, 249 N.J. Super. 96, 592 A.2d 20 (App. Div. 1991)
- Erie County Department of Social Services on behalf of Trunfio v. LaBarge, 159 Misc. 2d 806, 606 N.Y.S.2d 520 (Fam. Ct. 1993)
- Geyer v. Geyer, No. 9-92-39 (Ohio Ct. App. 11/25/92)
- Darby v. Darby, Pa. Super., 686 A.2d 1346 (1996)
- Butler v. Butler, 339 Pa. Super. 312, 488 A.2d 1141 (1985)
- Klemetsrud v. Klemetsrud, No. 02A01-9306-CV-00150 (Tenn. Ct. App. 1993).

Social Security Benefits

- In re Marriage of Simon, 856 P.2d 47 (Colo. Ct. App. 1993)
- Forbes v. Forbes, 610 N.E.2d 885 (Ind. Ct. App. 1993)
- In re Marriage of Lee, 486 N.W.2d 302 (Iowa 1991)
- In re Marriage of Benson, 495 N.W.2d 777 (Iowa Ct. App. 1992)
- In re Marriage of Callaghan, 19 Kansas App. 2d 335, 869 P.2d 240 (1994)
- In re Marriage of Durbin, 251 Mont. 51, 823 P.2d 243 (1991)
- In re Marriage of Stringham, 124 Or. App. 626, 863 P.2d 504 (1993)
- Whitaker v. Colbert, 18 Va. App. 202, 442 S.E.2d 429 (1994).

Veterans' Benefits, including military retirement benefits and veterans' disability benefits.

- McCall v. McCall, 596 So. 2d 2 (Ala. Civ. App. 1991)
- Belue v. Belue, 38 Ark. App. 81, 828 S.W.2d 855 (1992)
- Savelle v. Savelle, 650 So. 2d 476 (Miss. 1995)
- Cook v. Cook, 201 Wis. 2d 72, 547 N.W.2d 817 (Ct. App. 1996).

Military Personnel Fringe Benefits, foreign post allotments (FPA), overseas housing allowance (OHA), basic allowance for quarters (BAQ), basic allowance for subsistence or separate rations (BAS/Sep. Rats.), variable housing allowance (VHA).

- Rogers v. Sims, 671 So. 2d 714 (Ala. Civ. App. 1995)
- Berkbigler v. Berkbigler, 921 P.2d 628 (Alaska 1996)
- In re Long, 921 P.2d 67 (Colo. Ct. App. 1996)
- In re Marriage of McGowan, 265 Ill. App. 3d 976, 638 N.E.2d 695 (1994)
- Pegler v. Pegler, 895 S.W.2d 580 (Ky. Ct. App. 1995)
- Peterson v. Peterson, 98 N.M. 744, 652 P.2d 1195 (1982)
- Alexander v. Armstrong, 415 Pa. Super. 263, 609 A.2d 183 (1992)
- Hautala v. Hautala, 417 N.W.2d 879 (S.D. 1988).

Gifts, Prizes, Educational Grants, Lottery

and Gambling Winnings.

- Cummings v. Cummings, 182 Ariz. 383, 897 P.2d 685 (Ct. App. 1994) (gifts)
- Gilbertson v. Graff, 477 N.W.2d 771 (Minn. Ct. App. 1991) (student loan proceeds)
- County of Contra Costa v. Lemon, 205 Cal. App. 3d 683, 252 Cal. Rptr. 455 (1988) (lottery winnings)
- Darden v. Darden, 66 N.C. App. 432, 311 S.E.2d 600 (1984) (father's income was not limited to sporadic income from job, but included income from gambling and numbers running).

The Income of a New Spouse or Paramour to the extent that it reduces living expenses and makes other income available for support.

- Harris v. Superior Court (Smets), 3 Cal. App. 4th 661, 4 Cal. Rptr. 2d 564 (1992)
- Gilpin v. Gilpin, 664 N.E.2d 766 (Ind. Ct. App. 1996)
- Rogers v. Rogers, 923 S.W.2d 381 (Mo. Ct. App. 1996)
- Rodgers v. Rodgers, 110 Nev. 168, 887 P.2d 269 (1994)
- Ribner v. Ribner, 290 N.J. Super. 66, 674 A.2d 650 (1995)
- MacVean v. MacVean, 203 A.D.2d 661, 611 N.Y.S.2d 926 (1994)
- In re Marriage of Hardiman, 133 Or. App. 113, 889 P.2d 1354 (1995);
- McCarty v. Smith, 440 Pa. Super. 280, 655 A.2d 563 (1995)
- In re Paternity of Steven J.S., 183 Wis. 2d 347, 515 N.W.2d 719 (1994).

Expense Reimbursements, such as the company car, employer provided residence (including a church parsonage), monthly or per diem expense allowances, pre-tax flex plan reimbursement for health or day care, transportation expenses, food or beverages provided, relocation expenses, entertainment expenses.

- Gray v. Gray, 242 Mont. 69, 788 P.2d 909 (1990) (housing, utilities, housing fuel, and telephone expenses at farm that lessor provided to husband constituted income).

In-kind Income. Spilovoy v. Spilovoy, 511 N.W.2d 230 (N.D. 1994) (in-kind income contributed by the obligor's spouse included food, shelter, utilities, clothing, health care, and transportation, all of which constituted income).

- Carmon v. Commonwealth, Dept. of Social Services ex rel. Jones, 21 Va. App. 749, 467 S.E.2d 815 (1996) (income includes value of free room at boarding house in exchange for cleaning rooms).

The **Savings Benefit to a Parent as the Result of Being Able to Claim a Child as a Dependent**. Scott v. Scott, 103 Md. App. 500, 653 A.2d 1017 (1995).

The retained earnings of a close corporation, sub-chapter S corporation, or partnership that could be distributed.

- Merrill v. Merrill, 587 N.E.2d 188 (Ind. Ct. App. 1992); Roth v. Roth, 406 N.W.2d 77 (Minn. Ct. App. 1987);In re Marriage of Glueck, 913 S.W.2d 951 (Mo. Ct. App. 1996)
- Boudreau v. Benitz, 827 S.W.2d 732 (Mo. Ct. App. 1992)
- Smith v. Smith, 197 A.D.2d 830, 602 N.Y.S.2d 963 (1993)
- Quamme v. Bellino, 540 N.W.2d 142 (N.D. 1995)
- Williams v. Williams, 74 Ohio App. 3d 838, 600 N.E.2d 739 (1991)
- In re Marriage of Perlenfein, 316 Or. 16, 848 P.2d 604 (1993)
- King v. King, 390 Pa. Super. 226, 568 A.2d 627 (1989)
- Fitzgerald v. Sharum, 857 P.2d 92 (Okla. Ct. App. 1993).

Depreciation On Equipment that was taken for federal taxes may be added back in to income.

- Baker v. Baker, 183 Ariz. 70, 900 P.2d 764 (Ct. App. 1995)
- Pierce v. Pierce, 268 Ark. 864, 596 S.W.2d 364 (Ct. App. 1980)
- Emsley v. Emsley, 467 A.2d 700 (Del. Fam. Ct. 1983)
- Reid v. Reid, 822 P.2d 532 (Idaho 1992)
- Leisure v. Leisure, 589 N.E.2d 1163 (Ind. Ct. App. 1992)
- Cox v. Cox, 580 N.E.2d 344 (Ind. Ct. App. 1991)
- Harloff v. Harloff, 279 So. 2d 91 (Fla. Dist. Ct. App. 1973)

- Miller v. Miller, 610 So. 2d 183 (La. Ct. App. 1992)
- Mireille J. v. Ernst F.J., 220 A.D.2d 503, 632 N.Y.S.2d 162 (1995)
- Eberly v. Eberly, 12 Md. App. 117, 278 A.2d 107 (1971)
- In re Marriage of Pedersen, 261 Mont. 284, 862 P.2d 411 (1993)
- Houmann v. Houmann, 499 N.W.2d 593 (N.D. 1993)
- Kamm v. Kamm, 67 Ohio St. 3d, 616 N.E.2d 900 (1993)
- Sizemore v. Sizemore, 77 Ohio App. 3d 733, 603 N.E.2d 1032 (1991)
- Holland v. Holland, 444 Pa. Super. 251, 663 A.2d 768 (1995)
- Flory v. Flory, 364 Pa. Super. 67, 527 A.2d 155 (1987)
- Hopkins v. Hopkins, 1993 Tenn. App. LEXIS 273 (1993); Powell v. Swanson, 893 S.W.2d 161 (Tex. Ct. App. 1995); Houston v. Smith, 882 P.2d 240 (Wyo. 1994).

Inappropriate Business Expenses for the self-employed obligor may be added back into income.

- In re Marriage of Eaton, 894 P.2d 56 (Colo. Ct. App. 1995)
- McGinley-Ellis v. Ellis, 638 N.E.2d 1249 (Ind. 1994)
- Johnson v. Johnson, 533 N.W.2d 859 (Minn. Ct. App. 1995)
- Roberts v. Wright, 871 P.2d 390 (N.M. Ct. App. 1994)
- Sizemore v. Sizemore, 77 Ohio App. 3d 733, 603 N.E.2d 1032 (1991)
- Minnich v. Minnich, 898 P.2d 747 (Okla. Ct. App. 1995)
- Fettig v. Kailes, 124 Or. App. 455, 863 P.2d 476 (1993).

Voluntary Contributions To Pension, Retirement, Savings Plans, and voluntary debt reduction, although deductible from income for tax purposes, may be added back into income.

- Nelson v. Nelson, 651 So. 2d 1252 (Fla. Dist. Ct. App. 1995) (voluntary contribution to pension plan not deductible)
- State ex rel. Nielsen v. Nielsen, 521 N.W.2d 735 (Iowa 1994) (party cannot claim as deductions to income payments for voluntary savings, indebtedness, current child support, and IRS settlement)
- McCarty v. McCarty, 192 Mich. App. 279, 480 N.W.2d 617 (1991) (voluntary contribution to retirement account is income
- Parzynski v. Parzynski, 85 Ohio App. 3d 423, 620 N.E.2d 93 (1992) (husband's pension contribution was income to him, where he owned 50% of his business and could thus control his contribution).

Financial Child Support Theory

In an effort to remove more children from the welfare system and make non-residential parents financially responsible for their children, during the 1980's each state was required by the federal government to enact child support guidelines or lose federal funding. The guidelines addressed many problems, but ignored other situations entirely. Because the guidelines are the law at this time, that is the information with which we will deal here.

Financial support of the children is the responsibility of both parents. Child support is more important than any other debit or financial obligation either parent may have. Children need support, even if the non-custodial or non-residential parent maintains an additional family that does or does not have children in it.

Child support is a regular payment ordered by the court for the non-custodial parent to send to the custodial parent to help pay for the care and maintenance of the children. The residential or custodial parent is contributing to the support through residential status. The custodial parent can defuse a great deal of resentment or concern the non-custodial parent feels by keeping a log of expenses for the children and making it available to the non-custodial parent.

Guideline Models

Most child support guideline models have name labels that identify the characteristics of the system as an example; Cost Sharing, Income-Shares, Percent-of-Income.

Cost Sharing: The cost-sharing model was developed and established legal principles on making a child support award. Child support is an amount of money paid by the parent who does not have the responsibility of primary care for the child.

This method provided a means of calculating a reimbursement to the custodial parent for expenses in caring for children and to protest the children from the standard of living loss that accompanies the break-up of a two parent home. There was no provision made for a standard of living adjustment. It was never assumed that this method established legally correct result.

Its function was to establish a starting point. Judges were to use Discretion to formulate a final order based on the circumstances of all concerned.

Income-Shares: Often called "mothers' revenge" because it guaranteed the custodial parent a standard of living similar to that she might have if she chose marriage rather than single parenthood and does not have any valid economic basis.

Percent-of-Income: The percent of income model is the simplest of the income redistribution models. Its primary basis comes from highly controlled economies such as that of the Soviet Union. If one imagines that individuals and families have their income controlled according to family size, it is easy to understand how a simple percentage shift from one parent to another can account for the child's entitlement. Use of the percent-of-income formula is a blatant rejection of US Constitutional principles in favor of centrally controlled wealth redistribution as found in the failed communist system.

Child Support Decision Modeling

Relying on principles rather than detailed instructions is one of the major problems with child support decisions. Maurice Franks did a study, which documented statute and case law and attempted to develop mathematics powerful enough to reflect established principles of child support law. The federal government mandated use of child support guidelines as presumptively correct calculators of child support awards. In smith v smith, the Oregon court was asked to require the use of child support calculation formally used only in welfare cases to a non-welfare case. The Oregon Supreme Court decided the Franks' model better fit the principles of statutory law. They rejected use of the welfare model and did not require use of Franks' best-fit model either. Because the Franks' work fit the child support decision modeling, the mathematics fit the description of the cost-sharing model. A judge might start by using Franks' mathematics and them make additions and changes to better fit the full range of circumstances. Then the award level could be adjusted to protect the child's standard of living in a way that reflects the parents' ability to provide.

In the mid 1980's under the pressure of federal reforms, family court Judge Melson created a more complete decision model based on the Delaware state child support statutes that was similar to that used in the county of Sweden. Typical of child support law throughout the United States, Melson's model accounted for the basic and additional needs of children and distributed the obligation of support between the parents. This model accounted for visitation, and provided a standard of living adjustment; all in way that corresponded reasonably to the principles of established Delaware child support law. Though not a replacement for established principles of law. It was an effort to implement established principles. It was also designed to work within the Constitutional system. One could understand the relationship between Melson's mathematical model and the principles of law they were designed to implement. One could also understand the relationship between the mathematics and the details involved in the individual circumstances of each case. If one was not satisfied with the results provided by the mathematical model, because they seemed unjust or inappropriate, one could challenge the results based on established principles of law. The legal principles upon, which child support awards are based must be provided in statute. For example;

1. Child support is for the care and maintenance of children.

2. Both parents have an equal duty to support their children.

3. All relevant circumstantial information may effect the amount of the award.

The child support formula is then designed to conform to the set of principles upon, which a child support award is based. It must be clearly understood how the model fits the legal principles. The logic and data used must also be easily comparable with evidence of actual family circumstances.

Ability to Pay

The court says it uses guidelines that consider the needs of the children as well as the parent's ability to pay that support. Child Support is calculated from the disposable earnings. Earnings means compensation paid or payable to the payor parent for personal services, whether called wages, salary, compensation earned as and independent contractor, overtime pay, severance pay, commission, bonus, or otherwise, and includes periodic payments pursuant to a pension, annuity, workers' compensation, disability and retirement program, and unemployment benefits.

Disposable earnings is that part of the payor parent's earnings remaining after deduction of any amounts required by law to be withheld, union dues, nondiscretionary retirement contributions, and medical hospitalization, and disability insurance coverage for the payor parent and the child. Normally, the parent receiving the child support feels the guidelines are too restrictive.

Conversely, the parent paying child support feels the guidelines are too generous and does not consider "new" income the custodial parent may receive from a new marriage or the additional obligations the non-custodial parent now has.

Ability to Earn

Actual earnings are taken into account, but are not conclusive. When there is evidence that a person could earn more if he or she wished to do so, the court may set the child support based on the higher amount. Often reported income is compared to actual expenditures.

Daily Expenses

Costs can vary significantly depending on which side of the equation you stand and the standard of living to which you have become accustomed. A child with medical problems, a habit of falling out of trees or roller-skating at five miles per hour will have considerably higher expenses. These statistics were compiled using child support data derived from a survey of twenty-five families in a mid-sized metropolitan city in 1994.

Costs to Rear A Child

W.A.,, D.C., April 22, 1999--A family with a child born in 1998 can expect to spend about $156,690 ($240,000 when factoring in inflation) for food, shelter and other necessities to raise that child over the next seventeen years, Agriculture Secretary Dan Glickman announced today in releasing USDA's annual report, "Expenditures on Children by Families."

"While those numbers might seem a bit intimidating to a new parent," Glickman said, "the good news is that with America's strong economy and low inflation, the annual cost of raising a child is up less than $200 from last year." "This report is a very valuable resource for state agencies and courts in determining child support guidelines and foster care payments," said Glickman. "Of primary note to states is the 1998 child-rearing cost estimate for middle income, two-parent families, ranging from $8,240 to $9,340, depending on the age of the child."

The report notes that family income affects child rearing costs, with low-income families projected to spend $115,020, middle-income families $156,690, and upper-income families $228,690 (all in 1998 dollars) over seventeen years. In 1960, a middle-income family could expect to spend $25,229 to raise a child through age seventeen. For the average family, housing was the single largest expenditure on a child, averaging $52,140, or 53 percent of the total costs over seventeen years. Food was the second largest expense, averaging $27,450, or 18 percent of the total.

"As any parent with more than one child knows," said Under Secretary for Food, Nutrition, and Consumer Services Shirley Watkins, "raising a second or third child is less expensive than raising one alone." Watkins noted that families with one child spend approximately 24 percent more on a per-child basis than families with two children, and families with three children spend 23 percent less per child than those with two children.

The report notes geographic variations in the cost of raising a child, with expenses the highest for families living in the urban West, followed by the urban Northeast and urban South. Families living in the urban Midwest and rural areas have the lowest child-rearing expenses.

Copies of the report may be requested by writing to USDA's Center for Nutrition Policy and Promotion, 1120 20th Street, NW, Suite 200 North Lobby, W.A.,, DC 20036-3406.

The report also is also available on the CNPP web site at www.usda.gov/cnpp.

Child Support Expense Survey

Per year, per child	$4,000.00
Per month	$333.00
Per day	$11.11

These were the numbers we arrived at in 1998 from a mail back survey we did. Your standard of living has a great deal to do with how much money you spend. You may not spend as much as you would like to spend on your children because of financial limitations. The cost of everything is higher in San Diego, California than it is in Ellis, Kansas.

Normal expenses include food, clothes, vitamins, medical and dental expenses, braces, eyeglasses, school expenses, toys, Little League uniforms, swimming lessons, dance lessons, musical instrument training, visits to zoos and parks, summer, and other incidents. Money can be depleted at an alarming rate.

Baseball equipment $175.00

Basketball sign-up $75.00

Bible School tithe $114.00 a year

Bicycle $150 +

Computer $1,500.00 +

Gymnastics class $450.00 a year

Gymnastics equipment $100.00

Karate Class $480.00 a year

Karate Equipment 300.00

Montessori or private school $4,000.00 +

Pet $400.00 a year

Scouting equipment $250.00

Soccer Equipment $75.00

Summer Camp and equipment $400.00

Sunday School clothes $200.00 a year

Tennis shoes $25.00 +

College???

Champion Competition or Playoffs $1,000.00+

Child Support Obligation Starts When

The child support obligation starts when a child is born. In an attempt to see that children do not suffer financially during the realignment of the family, either of the parents may request that the court establish Temporary Child Support. The parent who does not have physical responsibility for the children may contact the appropriate agency in the state in which the children reside to determine the proper amount, then tender that amount by check to the parent with physical responsibility for the children. It is best to be consistent with the financial assistance and make the proper notation on the check.

Parents cooperating in this part of the problem (one parent offering proper support and the other parent accepting and using the support for the children) are viewed more favorably by the court. The court will establish Permanent Child Support when the permanent status of the children is decided.

Child Support Ends When

The obligation of child support for natural children and adopted children ends when:

1. The children are emancipated by the court.
2. The court orders the payments stopped.
3. The parent paying child support dies. The inheritance and estate laws in most states don't require that children be provided for when a parent dies.
4. The children go on active military duty.
5. The children reach the age of majority of eighteen or twenty-one years old. Or when a child that is fully enrolled in an accredited secondary school in a program leading to a specific degree or diploma.
6. When the children are adopted by another parent.
7. When the children marry.
8. When the children's disabilities are otherwise removed for general purposes.

April of 2000, the Kansas Supreme Court ruled that even though the parents' divorce agreement said that the father would pay child support until the children "reach the age of 18 years, marry [or] become legally emancipated." The father in the case being decided would still pay child support. The court said that "the act of marriage is merely a factor (as are any of the other factors) for the court to consider in determining whether to modify child support payments.

The marriage of a minor is not a terminating event, which automatically allows a payor parent to stop making child support payments for that child." In this case, the mother "stated that she continued to support her minor son after his marriage, that he was 16 years old at the time, and that she provided food and paid his utilities. The court cited similar rulings from Alabama and Colorado.

Termination of Support

The information listed her is also affected by the emancipation and disability of a child.

Alabama

Child turns 18 or graduates from high school.

Alaska

Child turns 18, or 19 if child enrolled in high school or equivalent and is residing with custodial parent.

Arizona

Child turns 18 or graduates from high school.

Arkansas

Child turns 18 or graduates from high school.

California

Child turns 18, or if child is in high school, then 19 or graduation from high school, whichever happens first.

Colorado

Child turns 19.

Connecticut

Child turns 18.

Delaware

Child turns 18, or if child is in high school, then 19 or graduation from high school whichever happens first.

District of Columbia

Child turns 21.

Florida

Child turns 18, or if child is in high school, then 19 or graduation from high school, whichever is later.

Georgia

Child turns 18, or if child is in high school, then when child turns 20.

Hawaii.

Child turns 18, or court may extend to age 23 if child is enrolled in accredited higher educations institution.

Idaho

Child turns 18, or age 19 by court order if child is enrolled in formal education.

Illinois

Child turns 18.

Indiana

Child turns 21.

Iowa

Child turns18.

Kansas

Child turns 18 or when child graduates high school, whichever is later.

Kentucky

Child turns 18, or if child is in high school, then when child turns 19.

Louisiana

Child turns 18, or if child is in high school, when child turns 19 or graduates, whichever happens first.

Maine

Child turns 18, or if child is in high school, when child turns 19.

Maryland

Child turns 18.

Massachusetts

Child turns 18, or when child turns 21 of child is domiciled with parent, or when child turns 23 if child is enrolled in an educational program.

Michigan

Child turns 18, or when child turns 19½ to allow child to complete high school.

Minnesota

Child turns 18, or when child turns 20 if child attending high school.

Missouri

Child turns 18, or if child is in high school, when child turns 21 or graduates high school, whichever happens first.

Mississippi

Child turns 21.

Montana

Child turns 18 or if child is in high school, when child turns 19.

Nebraska

Child turns 19.

Nevada

Child turns 18, or if child is in high school, when child turns 19

New Hampshire

Child turns 18, or if child is in high school, when child turns 19 or graduates from high school, whichever happens first.

New Jersey

Child turns 18.

New Mexico

Child turns 18.

New York

Child turns 21.

North Carolina

when child turns 18, or if child is in high school, when child turns 20 or graduates from high school, whichever happens first.

North Dakota

Child turns 18, or if child is in high school, when child turns 19 or graduates from high school, whichever happens first.

Ohio

Child turns 18 or when child graduates from high school.

Oklahoma

Child turns 18 or when child graduates from high school.

Oregon

Child turns 18, or if child is in high school half-time or more, when child turns 21.

Pennsylvania

Child turns 18 or completes high school.

Rhode Island

Child turns 18, or if child is in high school, when child turns 19 or 90 days past graduation, whichever happens first.

South Carolina

Child turns 18, or when child graduates from high school.

South Dakota

Child turns 18, of if child is in high school, when child graduates.

Tennessee

Child turns 18, or if child is in high school, when child graduates.

Texas

Child turns 18, or if child is in high school, when child graduates.

Utah

Child turns 18, or if child is in high school, when child graduates.

Vermont

Child turns 18, or if child is in high school, when child graduates.

Virginia

Child turns 18, of if child is in high school, when child turns 19 or graduates, whichever happens first.

Washington

Child turns 18.

West Virginia

Child turns 18, or if child is in high school, when child turns 20 or graduates, whichever happens first.

Wisconsin

Child turns 18, or if child is in high school, when child turns 19 or graduates, whichever happens first.

Wyoming

Child turns 18, or if child is in high school, when child turns 20 or graduates. whichever happens first.

How Much Support is Appropriate?

Each state has its own formula called Child-Support Guidelines. Many factors are considered in computing the amount and frequency of support payments. In most states, child support is a percentage of the combined gross income of both parents. Some of the documents that may be requested by the court from both parents are: income statement, copies of employee check stubs, tax returns, checking and savings account statements, loan and credit card applications, existing support payments and documentation to prove any information the judge requests.

All income from every source must be listed, even if it is exempt, such as child support or social security payments received for other children.

If you feel the opposition will not declare all income, you may, through your attorney, submit correct financial documentation. This is especially important if the opposition is self-employed and can hide a great deal of income. People who remarry can divert assets, including money, to the new spouse. Many courts are making child support an automatic wage assignment, reducing collection problems.

Too Much or Too Little?

Guidelines are just that --- guidelines.

If you are the non-custodial parent paying child support and you feel your children need more than the court has ordered, you can pay more or cover the costs for products or services your children use.

If you are the custodial parent receiving child support and your children require additional support to cover medical, psychological, or educational needs, the judge can increase the amount of money. Child support should be adjusted using the most recent tax return. Make sure you obtain CERTIFIED copies of income tax returns, not just photocopies of returns.

Anyone can photocopy a phony tax return and submit it to court to try and pass it off as legit.

Not sure what the form number is, but there is a form to request a certified copy of any tax return from the past three years directly from the IRS. By doing this, you make sure you get the real deal filed, and not some bogus copy.

If you are the custodial parent receiving child support and you can adequately meet the monetary needs of your children and are aware that the non-custodial parent is having a difficult time financially, you can accept the support payment and send your own check for that amount of money back to the non-custodial parent.

If you are the non-custodial parent and your employment is interrupted or your wages are lowered, you must contact the court and present documentation to prove your change of circumstances right away, requesting a decrease in your child support obligation. If you are out of work, your support obligation goes on and cannot be decreased automatically, so you must petition the court for relief.

In any case, you may check with the state agency that works with child support and request an administrative review of child support. Many states allow you to do this over the telephone. This may allow an adjustment without a formal court appearance. Some of the factors that can influence a modification of child support are these:

Needs of the children.
Medical emergency.
Increase in income.
Financial emergency.
Change in children's living arrangements.
Cost of living adjustment (COLA).
Decrease in income.
Change in the law.
Additional income from remarriage.
Disability.

Support Below the Guidelines

- Custody arrangements that facilitate near-equal sharing of child-rearing duties, such as split or joint custody.
- Costly transportation necessary for non-custodial parent to see the children.
- If the guidelines were applied the high income of payor parent would give the custodial parent funds far beyond the children's reasonable needs.
- Payor's debts if they were incurred during a marriage to the spouse seeking support.
- Large income of current spouse of custodial parent that would insure all of the children's needs would be easily meet.
- Property division award to custodial parent of marital home with no or low mortgage or income-producing property.
- Direct payment by payor of certain expenses that may include mortgage on custodial parent's home, utility payments, vehicle, insurance, private school tuition, summer camp, lessons.
- Payment of spousal support in addition to child support.
- Unfavorable tax consequences to payor.
- Significant earned or unearned income of the children.

Departures from the Guidelines

Although specifics vary from state to state and judge to judge, there are case law and court rules that specify grounds for departing from child support guidelines. Common examples:

- Rules for Child Care expenditures if they are particularly high.
- Special needs of the children including private school, tutoring and speech therapy.
- Extraordinary medical care needs or expenses not covered by insurance that may include physical and psychotherapy.

- Recreational activities, including after-school activities and summer camp.
- Income of new spouse that free funds of parent to pay additional support amount for his or her children.
- Voluntary under-employment or unemployment.
- Assets of parties that may not be reflected in regular income.

Temporary Modification

The court will only consider a permanent change. Requests for temporary modification when a payor is temporarily disabled from an accident or job lay off will not be heard by the court.

Modification

Child support orders are modifiable "at any time as the court deems necessary." Even if the parties have agreed that support may not be modified, child support may be modified at any time to the mandatory statewide child support guidelines.

Typically, the parent seeking a modification must show a "significant change of circumstances" that would support such a modification. These would include:

Child becomes ill or disabledChild's medical needs

Child's emotional or mental needsChild requires more time in school

Child's needs increase with agePayor's income is greatly reduced

Payor looses jobPayor is disabledPayor parent retires

Payor's income increasesPayor gets a new job Change in health of either parent

Substantial change in taxesSubstantial changes in life-style

You will not get an increase in child support if your expenses have increased because you have purchased a new home or car and feel a crunch because of higher payments. Conversely you will not be able to get your payments lowered because you have a new family and are having difficulty supporting the children from that union.

No See - No Pay

It is wrong for the custodial parent to say, "Look, if you will just leave us alone I won't come after you for the child support." It is also wrong for the non-custodial parent to say, "I won't bother you any more if you will drop your demands for child support."

It is also against the law. In 1987, the Nevada Supreme Court and in 1993, the Indiana Supreme Court ruled that a parent does not have the right to sign away or coerce the other parent into signing away the children's right to receive support.

The children have the right to see the non-custodial parent, even when the non-custodial parent cannot or will not pay child support. It is also the right of the children to remain out of the negotiations for the collection of support payments.

In jurisdictions where visitation access is vigorously protected and where custodial parents assist non-custodial parents in maintaining contact with children, the problem of nonpayment of child support is much smaller.

Can't See No-pay

If the children have been removed to purposely deny a non-custodial parent visitation, the child support payments are still due until the order for payment is changed by the court. You must be current on your support payments to ask the court for assistance with visitation problems.

Parent Locate Service is available to individuals who request help in locating the other parent. Parent Locate Service staff seek information from various sources regarding the whereabouts of the person. They then forward their findings to the parent.

The staff does not verify the information before sending it to the requester, so there is no guarantee that the information will enable the parent to locate the other parent. There are no application fees or other charges for this service.

Can't Pay

If you have lost your job or are unable to work, it is important to notify the court with documented evidence of the situation. The court may afford you some temporary relief.

If you have no visual means of income, but

have a place to live, food, and transportation of any kind, the court feels you can find the money to cover your child support payments. If your assets have migrated into another person's name, that person may be subject to questions by the IRS. The parent who is to receive child support payments could file a civil suit against you and your friend, attempting to prove fraud to avoid contributing support to your children.

In any case it is important to send something every month. It indicates a desire to take care of your children and a willingness to comply with the court order even when you are struggling to survive.

The Federal Government has been issued a directive from voters to get children off the public welfare roles and assign the responsibility and burden to the parents of the children. Often the parent required to pay child support may feel that paying child support will put us below the poverty level. Sometimes it does. The poverty guidelines are located in Chapter 20: Costs.

Advised Not to Pay

If you have been advised not to pay court ordered child support there is something you should know. This kind of advice may come from many places including: your attorney, another parent at a support meeting, your parent, a friend, a court official, a book or magazine article. If you don't pay court ordered child support you may be subject to fine and/or imprisonment. Even if you hold, what you think is new law or a letter from your attorney instructing you not to pay, you are still obligated to pay. If you do have a letter from your attorney, you are still obligated to pay according to the court order. Your attorney may be fined or sanctioned for advising you to disregard a court order, but you will still be the one violating the order. Any grounds to remove or change the payment obligation must be submitted to the court by filing proper motions for the court to consider. If ordered you must pay.

Who, When, How, Where to Pay

Pay child support only to whom and in the manner in which the court ordered.

1. Do not pay the money to anyone except to whom the order says to pay. Any other payments can be ruled "not monies for payment for support of child".
2. Regularity of payment will be scrutinized at each hearing, court appearance or proceeding that involve you and your child. Late payments or back child support owed will give you "dirty hands" in the court's eyes.
3. If you are ordered to pay child support directly to the other parent, do so with certified checks or money orders and list your case number with the words "Child support for (put the name of the children) and the month or months the payment covers. Do not pay in cash even with a signed receipt.

No Place to Send Payment

If you have been ordered to pay support, you are obligated to do so regardless of any obstacles you encounter. The most common stumbling block to a parent willing and able to pay support, but unable to do so is when the custodial parent does not wish to be found. This is usually an effort to interfere with visitation or permanently separate the non-custodial parent from the child. Therefore, you must be able to demonstrate to the court that you have in fact fulfilled your obligation to your child despite any handicap. There are several things you can do to protect yourself.

1. By far, the best option is to petition the court to change the order so that your payments are made to the Clerk of The Court, Child Support Section. State the reason for your request in the petition. Primarily this action will lay a solid foundation for a re-evaluation of custody in the future. Secondly, this system will ensure credit for payments made and demonstrate the unfair conditions under, which you must pay, but cannot see your child.
2. Call your attorney and ask if you can have their office keep the monthly payment in their escrow account in trust for your children.
3. Open a savings account for your children with their names on it and make your payments into that account.

No Court Order in Place

If you are the non-custodial parent and there is no court order in place at this time, ask your attorney what you can do to protect yourself from a judge ordering a large amount of back child support some time in the future.

A savings account for your children, that could be turned over to the custodial parent by the court, into which you make monthly payments would greatly lessen the impact of a large judgment against you. It would also be viewed favorably by the court.

Appeal Doesn't Stop Support

Appealing a child custody decision by the court, doesn't stop ordered child support. An appeal will take two years or more and your support obligation is in tact until a judge changes that order.

Best Attitude for Paying Child Support

You always have provided for your children. It is your moral and legal obligation. Your children may get more of your income than you get to keep. Parents have always gotten by on less so their children could have more.

Keep an EXPENSE LOG for money you spend when your children are with you or additional monies sent to the other parent for your children. Do not ever use cash. Always make the instrument of transfer traceable and one that gives you a method of receipt. Bank checks and money orders are best. Let your attorney decide if the presentation of these documents will help or hurt your case. If you are keeping a Contact Log, a separate expense log is not necessary. You can separate the information into an independent document if necessary.

Remove the Sting of Paying

True accountability from the support receiving parent about how the child support money is spent is what most support paying parents would like. In many cases, this is not likely to happen. Therefore, since you cannot change the situation, you must change how you look at the situation and that may allow you to diminish the discomfort the situation causes you.

Use the expense log to estimate what you think to be the costs for the monthly care of your children. You may be able to account for fifty to seventy-five percent of the money you send. The other parent will benefit from what you send for your children. That's not your concern. You can't dictate how the other parent spends the money.

Child Support as a Expense/Debit

Child support you pay out, as far as credit is concerned, is a debit. Any monetary obligation, including child support, may inhibit your ability to qualify for credit cards, auto, boat, plane or home purchase.

FHA (Federal Housing Authority) and VA (Veterans Administration) home financing rules require child support payments be included as a debit in your debit-to-income ratio.

Security for Support Awards

If your financial situation is secure enough so that you could meet the needs of the children now and in the future, security for the child support award may not be a concern. If that is not the case, it could be important to get security for court-ordered payments and obligations. Since a court order could require the non-custodial parent to pay child support and then to provide a four year education for the children, a long-term financial responsibility for the children has been established.

If the non-custodial parent remarries and then dies unexpectedly, the children may lose the security the court order sought to establish. This often happens when the non-custodial parent's will leaves everything to a new spouse. Not only do the employment revenues the children count on stop, but the insurance will also go to the new spouse. Without specific security set up to protect the support protection the court-ordered the children could suffer a dramatic decline in life-style. Even the Social Security benefits for the children end when each reaches age eighteen and no college assistance is provided. With security for the court-ordered child support obligation, there could be continuing support and a college education if the supporting parent dies or becomes disabled.

Some of the options to provide support security would be; disability and life insurance, an annuity or a contract to make a will with support security provided for and defined. Make sure that any obligation is funded with life insurance and disability insurance because once the court has financial information on both parents it may determine, which spouse will be obligated to pay. The court may require this coverage on both parents. If you are the receiving parent, and are financially sound, it may be a wise decision for you to agree to pay the premiums for policies to protect what your children receive. Find out if an existing disability or life policy can be used or whether a new policy is needed. Since governmental and some employee policies have complex rules about beneficiary designations, they should be avoided.

If the other parent is making the premium payment, always make sure that you get regular proof of premium payment and beneficiary designation. If possible, it's always best that you own the policy and pay the premium. This way you don't have to worry about non-performance or going back to court to get information. Find out who will own the cash values of existing policies and how can they be used. If you are going to make the premium payments on an existing policy that builds cash value, you need to make sure that the cash is not taken out of the policy.

It may be wise to ask the court for an annual report on any policies, since only the owner of the policy can change the beneficiary. With this report you would always be able to check into the beneficiaries of all policies to make sure that the appropriate persons are designated. Remember: Only the owner of a policy can change the beneficiary. Beneficiary designations must be considered closely.

Insurance

Health insurance is considered part of child support. The rules that allow for and require medical coverage are federal, but the requirements and regulations for the specific execution vary from state to state. Your attorney may be able to help you through the insurance quagmire.

QMCSO (Qualified Medical Child Support Order) allows the custodial parent to deal directly with the children's health care provider and then be directly reimbursed. If the parent required to provide insurance coverage works for a company that employees more than twenty people, COBRA (the Consolidated Omnibus Budget Reconciliation Act) offers some assistance.

Governmental insurance programs preempt state court orders. If the court order requires a beneficiary designation on a federal insurance program, and it is not accomplished, there is nothing you can do. So consider using separate policies and make sure you get proof of premium payment and beneficiary regularly

If the insurance providing parent is uninsurable, making it impossible for the children to be carried on their policy, check into alternatives, which may be available. Make sure that existing policies are continued for the children's protection.

Insurance and Teens

Parents involved in a custody battle for children under the age of fifteen often forget the small children they are concerned about meeting the needs of now, will soon be teenagers.

At sixteen years of age in many states children are ready to drive, and in some cases, find it necessary. The first thought in the teen's mind is often the availability of a vehicle and how 'cool' the transportation must look. The concern of the parents must be who will provide this expensive vehicle and who will pay for the insurance. A non-custodial parent may be disinclined to provide insurance for a teenager for which that parent does not have control. A custodial parent may not be able to afford insurance on the type of vehicle provided by the non-custodial parent. This issue should be addressed before the need for the transportation and the teenagers' emotions become

Out-Of-Pocket Medical Expenses

Auto Insurance

Walbro Corp. v. Amerisure Cos. U.S. Court of Appeals, 6th Circuit No. 96-2109 Divorced parents' child is covered under both of their auto policies when the parents have joint custody. This is because the child has "two domiciles" for purposes of the no-fault insurance statute in this state (Michigan). The court said that although a person can normally have only one "domicile," it was appropriate to "break with that legal tradition" in this case, so long as "the evidence shows that the child actually resided with both parents." The court relied on public policy, and noted that a child might otherwise be uninsured if only one of the parents was insured or if the child was injured while traveling between the parents' homes. Courts have held similarly in Florida, Illinois, Minnesota, New Jersey, Ohio, Texas and West Virginia.

Child Support and Bankruptcy

Back child support is not discharged and/or current child support payments are not reduced or discharged in Chapter 7, Chapter 11 or Chapter 13 bankruptcy.

Child Support as Income

Child support you receive is, as far as credit is concerned, income. Any monetary inflow you can document with court orders and bank records improves your ability to qualify for credit cards, auto, boat, plane or home purchase. FHA (Federal Housing Authority) and VA (Veterans Administration) home financing rules allow (all or part of) child support payments made to you for your children to be included as income in your debit-to-income ratio.

If you are applying for state or federal financial assistance or food stamps and are completing documentation for evaluation, they will ask if you have been awarded child support. If you have been awarded child support and are not receiving the money, you may have to prove it. The state office responsible for support payments can generate a computer printout of your account. Copies of your bank statements for the last six months are helpful to confirm information you submit.

Best Attitude for Receiving Support

This is not your money. It is to assist you in your efforts to properly care for your children. Disputes can be avoided if you as the custodial parent establish and maintain an Expense Log for your children. If the child support money is being spent on items that do not contribute to the welfare of your children, you may be required to submit monthly accounting to the court.

Is Child Support on the Children?

Knowing the money you send for child support is not being used to take care of your children can be very upsetting. Sometimes the court will let you pay child-related expenses directly to the service provider such as child care or private school expenses. The court will not give any time to consider the matter of children living in comfortable nonthreatening environments. If the custodial parent is not willing to provide an accounting of how child support monies are spent, there is no legal way to make them do it. If the health and welfare of your children are in danger because child support money is not used to meet their needs, you must document those facts. Once you have proven that your children are in crisis and the situation may be remedied by accountability of the custodial parent, payment dispersal for the child's needs directly from you to the child's needs, or a change of custody. The court will always attempt to encourage improvement in the situation in which the child lives now rather than change the custody entirely. It would require a huge amount of documented evidence to prove the children are in danger. Use the Condition of Child Report to document the problems.

Best/Worst States for Collection

The Children's Defense Fund in W.A., D.C. published a list for 1994, rating the state's enforcement of child support collection, using statistics that include establishment of paternity, average collections, number of cases collected on and number of cases filed.

Child Support Hall of:

Fame	**Shame**
Delaware	Arizona
Massachusetts	Washington DC
Michigan	Illinois
Minnesota	Indiana
Montana	Louisiana
Pennsylvania	Mississippi
South Dakota	New Mexico
Utah	Tennessee
Washington	Texas

Child Support Doesn't Come

If you need the support to care for your children, you must go after it. Find evidence that the nonpayer has assets or income and that he or she has been working, and has been intentionally evading support. Document that evidence. Photos of and proof of regular purchases of expensive items such as homes, vehicles, boats and trips. Call the local U. S. Attorney to find out what evidence they would need to investigate the possibility of a charge of criminal non-support under federal law.

Additionally, there may be a state criminal statute regarding non-support that would be prosecuted by the local or state prosecuting attorney under the Deadbeat Parents Act.

Documentation would be critical since criminal charges are and should be reserved for those cases where it is clear that there is a pattern of non-payment, and actions taken by the non-custodial parent specifically to avoid the need to pay. This is done in several ways, such as frequently moving to avoid wage attachment.

Support Accounting in Eleven States

State statutes that allow the court to demand an accounting from the custodial parent of how child support is spent are:

Alabama Authorized an accounting under the specific facts of the case, McDuffie v. Holland, 690 So. 2d 386 (Ala. Civ. App. 1996)

Colorado Rev. Stat. Ann. § 14-10-115(3)(b)(III) (1999)

Delaware Code Ann. tit. 13, § 518 (1994)

Florida Stat. Ann. §61.13(a)(1) (Supp. 2000)

Indiana Code Ann. § 31-16-9-6 (1997)

Kansas Stat. Ann. § 60-1616(f) (1995)

Louisiana Rev. Stat. Ann. § 9:312 (Supp. 1999)

Missouri Rev. Stat. § 452.342 (1997)

Nebraska Rev. Stat. § 42-364(6) (1999)

New York has hinted that such an action.

Oklahoma Stat. tit. 43, § 118(B)(21) (Supp. 1999)

Oregon Rev. Stat. § 107.105(1)(c) (Supp. 1998)

Washington Rev. Code Ann. § 26.23.050(2)(a)(ii) (Supp. 1999)

Where Child Support is Spent

Child Support Expense Log Month___*April*____Year__*2001* ___	**Projected Cost**	**Actual Cost**
Housing (at home)	50.00	50.00
Utilities	10.00	18.00
Food, household supplies	100.00	135.00
Clothing	25.00	70.00
Transportation	10.00	10.00
Day care	0	0
Medical, dental, therapy	25.00	0
School (books, tuition, fees)	264.00	264.00
Insurance	44.50	44.50
Recreation, entertainment, vacation, toys, camp, equipment	25.00	15.00
Allowance and Church tithe	0	20.00
Special events, birthdays, holidays	10.00	0
Lessons (music, dance), Karate Academy	157.50	157.50
Student services fees (college)	0	0
Health services fees (college)	0	0
Housing (college room and board)	0	0
Total	721.00	784.00

Collection Methods

- Employers shall furnish to the Directory of New Hires of the State in which a newly hired employee works, a report that contains the name, address, and social security number of the employee, and the name and address of, and identifying number assigned under section 6109 of the Internal Revenue Code of 1986 to, the employer.

- Wage assignment or payroll deduction order "PDO" (employer is ordered by the court to deduct child support from the employees' earnings each pay period and forward the money to the state ordering the money collected. If the employer does not execute the court order the employer would be responsible for the payments.). This occurs automatically in some states when child support is ordered. Companies are not allowed to fire employees over PDOs. It is a violation of fair employment practices will subject the company to serious fines.
- Government Benefit Diversion includes unemployment benefits. Child support may be deducted from unemployment compensation, worker's compensation and other benefits.
- Obtain financial statements of defaulters.
- Tax refunds may be attached to bring current delinquent support payments or to repay monies funded to a custodial parent through Aid to Dependent Children or the Food Stamp programs. Although second spouse income is normally excused from the contribution for existing or back child support, joint tax refunds are not exempt. The refund from a joint return filed with a new marriage partner can be seized to satisfy back child support.
- States are making it easier to "domesticate" judgments from other states as a foreign judgment entitled to "full faith and credit."
- Lottery winnings are subject to seizure to satisfy back child support.
- Credit Bureaus and credit reporting agency notification from states of debit of back child support effect credit reports negatively.
- Payor parent is required to post a Child Support Bond of up to two years of chid support or deposit money into a security account. Bond or account can be accessed by the Payee parent if the Payor fails to make proper payment,
- The revocation of Professional Licenses and Professional Drivers' Licenses is part of the proposed Federal Child Support act of 1994.
- Suspend motor vehicle, boat, airplane, motorcycle and trailer registration.
- Provide for registration of support orders under the Personal Property Security Act (in Canada)
- The court will take temporary possession of property, freeze assets, garnish wages and throw uncooperative non-payers in jail for contempt.
- Make support orders against third parties who shelter the defaulter's assets (under consideration)
- Seize fifty percent of any funds in a joint bank account with the defaulter's new partner (under consideration)
- Full faith and credit requires that judges recognize and enforce valid decrees and judgments issued by courts in other states. This is not automatic. The person seeking the enforcement must take the legal steps required by the state the person is seeking assistance from.
- The federal government is operating a vast computerized database directory showing every person newly hired by every employer in the country so federal and state investigators can track down parents who owe money to their children.
- States will be able to use the directory to locate parents and dun them, typically by securing court orders to employers to deduct child support from wages and salaries.
- Some states are offering a bounty of over two hundred dollars for anyone reporting a nonpaying parent.
- Deadbeat Parents Punishment Act of 1998, Public Law 105-187

A parent who fails to pay child support for longer than two years or in an amount greater than $10,000 for a child who lives in another state can be fined and imprisoned for up to two years, under a new law that has been signed by President Clinton.

The law applies to any parent who violates the statute as of the effective date of June 24, 1998.

The law amends a statute that already provides that parents who fail to pay child support for longer than one year or in an amount greater than $5,000 can be fined and jailed for up to six months for a first offense, and up to two years for a subsequent offense. (18 U.S.C. Sect. 228)

International Support Enforcement

The United States has no blanket treaty with any other country pertaining to the enforcement of any determinations by U.S. courts.

However, reciprocal arrangements with Australia, Austria, Bermuda, Canada (by province) Czech Republic, Fiji, Finland, France, Germany, Hungary, Ireland, Jamaica, Mexico, New Zealand, Norway, Poland, Slovak Republic, South Africa, Sweden, United Kingdom (England, Scotland, N. Ireland) have produced positive results for parents.

Your first step in the complicated process of obtaining child support enforcement abroad is to contact the office of child support enforcement in your state and exhaust all the possibilities they have to offer. Document who you spoke to, the steps you took and the results of your efforts. Take advantage of the aggressive techniques now available to pursue enforcement, including garnishment of wages and federal income tax refunds, revocation of licenses, direct contact with foreign employers, criminal enforcement proceedings. If the person owing the child support is employed abroad for a U.S.-based company, or for the U.S. government, new provisions in the child support enforcement laws provide a number of steps to obtain enforcement. If the parent from whom you are seeking child support enforcement works for a private U.S.-based employer, ask your local child support enforcement office about procedures for garnishment of wages. In addition, it may be possible to initiate formal enforcement proceedings in accordance with local (foreign) law.

If your state child support officials are unfamiliar with the procedures, they may wish to contact authorities in states, which process these requests on a regular basis, such as California, Texas or Illinois.

These states have developed handbooks and bilingual forms for processing the requests and have regular contacts with their counterparts in the foreign countries. State child support enforcement offices in Texas advise they have found it useful to pursue all possible avenues to attempt to collect child support from the person in the foreign country. They contact the individual's employer, including the president of the company, providing authenticated, translated copies of outstanding court orders, warrants. This is not something you can do on your own. If the other parent lost a job because of your efforts to collect child support you could be subject to law suit. It is critical to have your state follow this path on your behalf.

If no reciprocal arrangement exists, and the aggressive measures are not applicable, it may be necessary for you to initiate a child support enforcement action in the courts in the foreign country. This usually will require retaining the services of an attorney in that country. The Department of State, Office of American Citizens Services may have selected information available concerning general procedures on child support enforcement in particular countries. Some foreign attorneys are willing to proceed on a contingency basis, charging no fee for services until the child support is collected. A list of English speaking attorneys is available from the U.S. State Department Office of American Citizens Services. A general information flyer, “Retaining A Foreign Attorney” or the Martindale-Hubbell Law Directory available in law libraries.

Provide your foreign attorney with copies of any state laws concerning reciprocal enforcement of child support orders with foreign states, including foreign countries (UIFSA, RURESA, URESA). It may be necessary for you to provide foreign authorities or your attorney with authenticated, translated copies of your child support order and any other pertinent documents. Consult your foreign attorney before going to this expense.

Some countries provide legal aid services in child support cases. The legal attache or consular section of the foreign embassy in Washington, D.C. may have specific guidance. Legal aid information may also be available from a local branch of the International Social Service. The ISS' headquarters are in Geneva, Switzerland. Information and assistance is available at 10 W. 40th St., N.Y., N.Y. 10018, (212) 532-6350.

Statute of Limitations

In many states if a parent managed to avoid the efforts to collect child support a statute of limitations would eliminate the obligation. The statute of limitations did not permit the attorney general to pursue unpaid child support claims after the child reached twenty-one years of age. New laws strengthen child support enforcement in eliminating the statute of limitations. This will enable the attorney general to pursue unpaid child support regardless of the age of the child. The law establishes that parents are always responsible for child support and removes the incentive for deadbeats to evade the law until their children reach twenty-one.

Criminal Non-support

In part the new federal criminal non-support law properly titled, Child Support Recovery Act, Deadbeat Parents Act: New Felony Penalties for Egregious Failure to Pay Child Support imposes these tough new penalties creates two new categories of felonies, with penalties of up to two years in prison, for more egregious child support evaders:

- Traveling across state or country lines with the intent to evade child support payments will now be considered a felony if the obligation has remained unpaid for a period longer than one year or is greater than $5,000.
- When the obligation has remained unpaid for a period of longer than two years or is greater than $10,000, willful failure to pay child support to a child residing in another state will be considered a felony.

In Re Marriage of Brent Moss [LLR No. 9609060.CA]. The thirteenth Amendment is cited in reversing jailing of a California father who could not pay the support ordered. Movant in criminal nonsupport proceeding must show that respondent has ability to pay. Forced labor (Pollock v. Williams [1944] and involuntary servitude issues are cited.

Past Due Support Letter

Support Enforcement Division
Central Operations Section (800) 345-9489
Department of Justice
1495 Edgewater NW # 290, Salem, OR

Mr. and/or Ms. Clive Lister
POB 332, Chatsberg, VA

The "Past Due Amount Claimed"
as of: July 31, 2001

Our records show that you owe past due child and/or spousal support of at least the amount shown below. We are referring this past-due amount to the Internal Revenue Service (IRS) for collection. We may collect any federal income tax refund to which you are entitled and apply it to the past-due support you owe.

You have a right to contest our records. You may request an administrative review of the past-due support we show. Please contact us no later than December 31, 2001, at the address or phone number shown above, if you wish to contest our findings. If your support order was issued in another state, we can still conduct the review. If you would prefer, you can request that the state, which issued the order will notify you of the time and place of review.

If you are married and file a joint income tax return, your spouse may be entitled to a portion of the joint refund. To be entitled, your spouse must have no legal obligation for the child and or spousal support debt. Your spouse must also have income and withholding and/or estimated tax payments.

Your spouse may file a Form 8379 "Injured Spouse claim and allocation" to receive a portion of the joint tax return. Form 8379 should be attached to the top of the form 1040 or 1040a when you file, or be filed according to other instructions as indicated on the form 8397.

We may report your past due support amount to the credit reporting agencies. Further, we may also ask your banks, savings and credit associations, investment companies, and other financial institutions, to give us information from your financial records.

SSN & Past Due Amount
555-02-7676 $ 1,580.00
Case Number 446091618150
c:taxnotic (csp) Report # WS64103-A (FED)

Under the Table Employment

One of the most common, but most difficult to prove scams, is putting assets in another's name. Employment in a family business while driving a company vehicle and housing provided by the family offers huge obstacles.

Working "under the table" for cash may also involve tax evasion charges against the other parent and the employer. Documenting the employment situation is important and whether the income is properly reported via a W-4. Bartered or trade off work can be assigned a value and taxed or assigned a child support obligation.

Custodial parents are bringing new types of claims against non-paying parents. A tort claim can add a bargaining advantage and support custody suits. These cases include:

- When a non-payer hides income and assets, fraud, RICO and spoliation of evidence. These cases seek jury trials and punitive damages.

If the non-payor does not have enough money to pay a judgment, third parties can provide a deep pocket Therefore, another advantage to suing in tort is you can bring claims against third parties who may have helped the non-payor hide assets. These third parties could include: accountants, bookkeepers, stockbrokers, lawyers, or family members, and other potential "deep pockets."

- Where one parent is eavesdropping on the children , such as by downloading e-mail files or "chat room" records or intercepting cell-phone or beeper messages, between the other parent and the child, lawyers are suing for invasion of privacy and violations of state and federal wiretapping statutes. Since family law lawyers don't handle domestic torts you will need a different lawyer to sue or defend your case. The family law attorney may call in co-council if the state requires tort claims to be joined during the divorce. You should ask your attorney about any exposure you may have to potential tort and statutory claims or your ability to file such a suit.

The main advantages to suing for fraud rather than reopening the divorce or child support case are getting before a jury and seeking punitive damages. Cheated custodial parents are more sympathetic to juries than to family court judges, who tend to be more jaded.

Family law courts aren't equipped to try these cases. The judges are not interested in hearing "the other parent cheated me." They see and hear it all the time. Their job is to divvy up the assets, assign custody and get on with it.

Additionally, a tort action can be handled on a contingency fee bas whereas in some states a divorce can't.

California, Kansas, Missouri and Pennsylvania have allowed similar suits.

RICO Refer to:

Suing for treble damages and attorney fees under RICO, the federal Racketeer Influenced and Corrupt Organizations Act, 18 U.S.C. Sects. 1961-68.

Woman sued her ex-husband under RICO for using marital assets improperly over a period of several years. (DeMauro v. DeMauro, 712 A.2d 623 (N.H. 1998).)

A suit was filed against a ex-husband, his law firm and accountant for concealing the true amount of his income during the divorce proceeding, by the wife. The court also allowed her state claims for fraud and intentional infliction of emotional distress to be heard with the RICO claim. (Perlberger v. Perlberger, 1998 WL 76310 (E.D. Pa. 1998).)

Assistance with Back Child Support

Example of letter requesting assistance with collecting back child support.

Date:
Honorable [NAME]
U. S. House of Representatives
[ADDRESS]
W.A., D.C. 20515 [Date]
Re: Evasion of Child Support
Dear Representative [LAST NAME]:

I am writing to ask for your assistance or advice in pursuing remedies regarding the collection of child support for my children (names and ages) from my ex-spouse, [SPOUSE NAME]. In 19xx, [SPOUSE NAME] was ordered to pay $xx per month in support.

At the present time, the arrearage is over $xx,xxx! I have sought and received assistance from the child support agency in [COUNTY, STATE]. Little or nothing has come of those efforts, in light of [SPOUSE NAME]'s tactics of evading support by [working "under the table," putting [his/her] assets in [his/her] current spouse's name or [his/her] mother's name, or by quitting any job once a wage attachment is obtained]. In short, traditional civil remedies have not worked. This situation appears to me to be one where the [father/mother] is intentionally evading [his/her] responsibility, and the case should be vigorously pursued under the new federal criminal child support statutes. Any assistance you could offer would be appreciated.

Kindest regards,
Your Name, Address, Phone
Either cc or same letter to:
David Gray Ross, Commissioner,
Office of Child Support Enforcement, 370 L 'Enfant Promenade SW, W.A., D.C. 20447
and
Chief Donald Deering,
Office of Child Support Enforcement
370 L 'Enfant Promenade SW, WA D.C. 20447

Waiting Too Long to Collect

There are consequences for waiting too long to collect back child support. It is not legal for you as the receiver of the child support to punish a non-payor parent. You may not withhold contact or visitation. If you don't legally pursue the child support intended for your children when it is due the amount adds up very quickly. The problem is, that the larger the amount due is, the harder it will be for the non-payor to catch up. If the past due is under three thousand dollars the judge may decide to put the non-payor in jail and require that a cash bond equal to the past due child support is posted in order for the person to be released. When the bond is delivered to the court, you get your child support money. If the past due amount is ten thousand dollars or more the court will order the non-payor to start making the regular payments in a timely manner and add a small payment (most often much less than a regular support payment) to be made against the back child support. When the amounts in back support are between three thousand and ten thousand the court may have other options.

A non-payor who makes the regular support payments and the back support demonstrates to the court that the former non-payor is in fact a responsible parent. A non-payor who unwilling to meet the financial responsibility will be treated more harshly in ongoing court appearances.

Military Service and Child Support

Federal law authorizes the pay of active, reserve, and retired members of the military and the pay of civilian employees of the Federal government to be garnished (or attached) for the payment of child and/or spousal support. The law is found at 42 U.S.C. 659, and the implementing regulations are found at 5 C.F.R. Part 581.

In order to implement a garnishment or wage attachment against any member of the military or any civilian employee of the Department of Defense (DOD), an income withholding order, or similar process, must be served upon DFAS at the following address: Defense Finance and Accounting Service, Cleveland Center, Code L, POB 998002, Cleveland, Ohio 44199-8002, (216) 522-5301 (Customer Service)

The order submitted cannot be the divorce decree or other order that directs the individual (debtor) to make the payment. Rather, the order must direct the government, as the employer, to withhold moneys and remit payments to satisfy the support obligation. The withholding order need not name the specific government office in which the obligor is employed. The order must provide the appropriate information about the person to receive payment.

In order for your withholding order to be processed, it must include the debtor's full legal name and social security number. Other identifying information concerning the debtor, such as a home or work address, would expedite the processing of the order. Also, please be sure to include your return address on any correspondence, not only on the mailing envelope. Questions concerning the child support and alimony processes can be directed to 216-522-5301. Garnishment Operations Facsimile (FAX) Information: Fax Phone Number: Commercial 216-522-6960 or DSN 580-6960.

In updating and improving the processes in the Garnishment Operations we are now using a fax gateway directly into our Electronic Document Management System. To ensure your document is processed in a timely and efficient manner you must include the following information on the fax document and follow the additional guidance provided:

Member/Employee Social Security Number (SSN) - Court Orders/Documents will not be processed if the SSN is not on the document Return Phone Number, Return Fax Number, Ensure original documents are clear and legible. In each fax transmission, include only correspondence for one member or employee (multiple documents can be sent on one fax transmission).

Child Support Court Cases

Religious Objection to Paying Support

Hunt v. Hunt

Vermont a father claimed his religious beliefs and practices kept him from paying a support order. 162 Vt. 423, 648 A.2d 843 (1994), The husband belonged to the Northeast Kingdom Community Church. Members of the Church lead an ascetic, communal existence, eschewing all personal possessions and working for the benefit of the community. The Church forbids no-fault divorce and forbids members to support an estranged spouse

or children who live outside the community.
When the wife left the husband and took the children, the husband, consistent with his religious views, refused to support the wife or their children. The trial court concluded that although these beliefs were sincerely held by the husband, and were not recently acquired but had been practices by the husband throughout the marriage, the law nevertheless demanded that an otherwise able-bodies individual support his or children. "Matter of religious belief, as a matter of law, do not furnish an exemption from that ability to pay." 648 A.2d at 847. The appellate court affirmed. While the support obligation would, indeed, place a burden the husband's religious practices, the state's interest in seeing that children are adequately supported justified that burden.

Pencovic v. Pencovic

45 Cal. 2d 97, 287 P.2d 501 1955, the husband and wife were married in 1937 and divorced in 1944. The husband was ordered to pay child support for the parties two children. From 1945 to 1951, he made no payments of child support. In his defense to the wife's motions for contempt and modification, the husband claimed that after the divorce, he changed his name to Krishna Venta and founded a religious society called the WKFL Foundation (standing for Wisdom, Knowledge, Faith, and Love). The society members live in a commune, and none works outside the commune. Funds are obtained from new members who transfer all their property to the society, and the society provides "gifts" to the members depending on their needs. The trial court concluded, and the appellate court agreed, that a parent cannot evade support obligations by claiming a religious exemption:

By refusing for religious reasons to seek or accept gainful employment defendant may not evade [his child support] obligation. Although the guarantee of religious freedom under the First Amendment of the Constitution of the United States is binding on the states under the due process clause of the Fourteenth Amendment, the states may nevertheless regulate conduct for the protection of society, and insofar as regulations directed towards a proper end and are not discriminatory, they may indirectly affect religious activities without infringing the constitutional guarantee.... Certainly, there are few interests of greater importance to the state that the proper discharge by parents of their duties to their children, and the Constitution does not compel the subordination of the statutory duty of a parent to support his child to a rule of religious conduct prohibiting gainful employment.

McKeever v. McKeever

36 Or. App. 19, 583 P.2d 30 1978. In this case, the father resigned from his job in order to "take on a nonpaying promotional position with a Christian evangelical organization." The father claimed that because he had no income, the court erred in ordering him to pay child support, and that such an order violated his First Amendment rights to free exercise of religion. The court, relying on State v. Sprague, 25 Or. App. 621, 550 P.2d 769 (1976), dismissed this argument out of hand. The court in Sprague had held, "It is of compelling interest to the state that parents of children, when they are able, should be required by law under penalty of criminal sanctions to support their children, and that their actions in such regard should be governed by laws, regardless of their religious beliefs." 25 Or. App. at 628, 550 P.2d at 772.

Dunn v. Dunn

Michigan Court of Appeals 105 Mich. App. 793, 307 N.W.2d 424 1981. During the parties marriage, the husband became an ordained minister in the United Methodist Church. After the divorce, the husband became a member of the Order Ecumenical. As a member of this order, the husband took a vow of poverty and obedience. Members of the Order are given a place to live and a food allowance, and a stipend of the poverty level of the nation to which they are assigned. The Order also provides medical and dental insurance. The trial court found that the husband's actions constituted a willful disregard for the interest of his children, and ordered the husband to pay child support. The husband appealed.

This time, the court held that the trial court erred. "Plaintiff's interest in and association with the Order Ecumenical began long before his divorce from defendant and there is no hint in the record before us that plaintiff became involved in the Order merely to avoid his obligations of child support." 307 N.W.2d at 426. The concurring opinion, per Kallman, J., went further, and said that his case was not a child support case, it was a First Amendment case. A court cannot order a man to get a job and pay child support that will force him to leave his religious order, which he joined during the marriage, and renounce his religious vows.

One might be tempted to conclude that the difference between these cases is that in Pencovic and McKeever, the court imputed income to the support obligor because the decision to become impoverished came after the divorce, whereas in Dunn, the court declined to impute income because decision to become impoverished came before the divorce during the marriage. One would, however, be mistaken, because subsequent cases failed to draw this distinction.

Marriage of Meegan

11 Cal. App. 4th 156, 13 Cal. Rptr. 2d 799 (1992), the parties were divorced in 1988 after 30 years of marriage. At the time of the dissolution, the husband's net income was $56,400 per year. In 1991, the husband left his job, joined an order of the Catholic Church, and entered the Holy Trinity Monastery. The husband then filed a motion to reduce his spousal support, claiming he was impoverished. The trial court reduced his spousal support to zero, and the appellate court affirmed. The court held that since the husband had changed jobs in good faith and without the motive to deny his ex-wife support, he was not guilty of "shirking" and therefore the court would not impute income to him. This case clearly conflicts with Pencovic.

Another case that is difficult, if not impossible, to reconcile with the Pencovic/Dunn rule is Goldberger v. Goldberger, 96 Md. App. 313, 624 A.2d 1328 (1993). In this initial child support case, the father was a lifelong Orthodox Jewish Talmudic scholar who had never held an income-producing job. "It is undisputed that appellant had earned no actual income, as he had never worked at any income-producing vocation. Appellant planned his life to be a permanent Torah/Talmudic scholar. He was a student before he was married and before any of his children were born.... Throughout his life, appellant has been supported by others." 624 A.2d at 1332-33. Nonetheless, even though this man had never held a job, the court imputed income to him. "A parent who chooses a life of poverty before having children and makes a deliberate choice not to alter that status after having children is voluntarily impoverished.... The law requires that parent to alter his or her previously chosen lifestyle if necessary to enable the parent to meet his or her obligations." 624 A.2d at 1335.

After Goldberger, one must draw the conclusion that the voluntary decision to pursue a life of religious poverty, whether before or after marriage, will result in the imputation of income, except in California. More recent decisions support this conclusion.

Bassette v. Bartolucci

38 Mass. App. Ct. 732, 652 N.E.2d 623 (1995), the court also imputed income. In this case, the father claimed a modification of his support obligation because he took early retirement from the U.S. Postal Service to become a religious missionary in Jamaica. The court held that the father's voluntary decision to leave a paying job warranted the imputation of income. "Because his was a voluntary career change, the father retains the ability to pay the ordered amount of child support, based on his potential rather than actual earning capacity." 38 Mass. App. Ct. at 736, 652 N.E.2d at 626.

Elsberry v. Elsberry

967 P.2d 1004 1998, after the father failed to provide tax returns to the court, the court imputed income to him. The father claimed that he could not comply with an order to produce his tax returns because his religious beliefs prevented him from paying federal taxes; hence, he had no tax returns to produce. The appellate court disagreed with the father's contention that the trial court imputed income to him because of his religious beliefs. Rather, the trial court imputed income because he failed to produce any evidence of what his income was. Hence, the father's religious beliefs were inconsequential to his ability to support his children.

In sum, the cases decided since the advent of child support guidelines, which in all states authorize the court to consider not just actual income but potential earning capacity, clearly support the proposition that one cannot avoid a child support obligation on the basis of religious belief.

Child's Adult-Education Not Extend Support

Rowley v. Garvin (Michigan) Support after age 18, which is contingent upon the child being a full-time high school student, is NOT satisfied by the child's being in an adult-education program, therefore there is no post-majority support.

Support Reduced for Time with Child

Holmes v. Holmes (NY, March 6, 1997). The father's support order must be reduced to match the amount of time he spends with the child.

Several states now offer child support credit for time spent with child.

Reduced by Child's Disability Benefits

The Massachusetts Supreme Judicial Court ruled 8/ 12/1998 in Rosenberg v. Merida, No. SJC-07682. A disabled parent's child support payments may be reduced by the amount that the children are receiving from Social Security as a result of the parent's disability.

The courts have ruled that as long as the children are receiving the proper amount of support, the actual source of the payments should be of no concern. Although the benefits are payable directly to the child rather than through the contributing parent, the child's entitlement to payments derives from the parent.

There have been similar decisions from Illinois, Iowa, Michigan, Nebraska and South Dakota.

Decrease in Support Payment

Coons vs. Wilder, 416 N.E. 2d 785 (Ill, 1981). A father whose income decreased while voluntarily attending law school is entitled to a decrease in support payments - law school will increase his income.

Drummond v. State of Maryland. A disabled father can't reduce his child support payments by the amount his child is receiving from Social Security as a result of the father's disability.

Father's Debt Service

County of Lake v. Gerald Anthony Anton. Appeal of case decision where the court properly took into account father's debt service for current liabilities was upheld.

Forced to Provide College Education

Bonita Kline Curtis v. Philip H. Kline 1995. PA.1585. Pennsylvania state law requiring divorced parents to provide college education is held unconstitutional by the Pennsylvania Supreme Court.

Hardship Income Deduction Reversed

In re Marriage of Donald and Lynnette Carlsen [96 C.D.O.S. 7737]. Increase in child support garnered by use of unsupported "DissoMaster" computer printout claiming hardship income deduction for wife is reversed.

Child Support for Kidnapped Child

In Re Marriage of Damico, [CA S033148-OP-5/9/94] [1994.CA.247]. Estoppel defense to support collections where mother kidnaps children, conceals them from father, and later attempts to collect support for the period of concealment.

Case Behind License Revocation

Bell v. Burson, A key case behind license revocation suits.

The License Suspension law, allows custodial parents or their attorneys, certain agencies, and the Office of the Attorney General's Child Support Division to petition for the suspension of a license issued by an agency of the State or political subdivision of the State when past due child support is owed and no attempt is being made to pay it. Professional and occupational licenses as well as personal and commercial driver licenses, and many other licenses, are subject to the statute. This legislation establishes a unique child support enforcement tool that can be used in our most difficult cases: delinquent non-custodial parents who skip from job to job, are self-employed and/or work for cash. It also takes the cost and burden of process administration, notice, and hearing off the various licensing boards and keeps the issues of delinquency and non-compliance in the state child support agency or the family law courts where they belong.

Revocation Requires Due Process

Fitch v. Belshaw [Oregon, 581 F. Supp. 273] Considered minimal procedural due process requirements with respect to revocations.

Revocation for Support Arrears

Thompson, et. al. v. James Ellenbecker, 935 F. Supp. 1037; 1993 U.S. Dist. [S.D. 1995] License revocation for nonsupport (upheld). Revocation for support arrears was only litigated as weak case for procedural process violations over forced signature.

The District Court (in general discussion) unintentionally admits in the ruling that license revocation hinders one's ability to "get around", possibly laying foundation for "heightened scrutiny" litigation over right to travel and work.

Vehicle License Revocation Invalid

Perez v. Campbell, [No. 5175, 1971.SCT.105] Arizona Motor Vehicle license revocation scheme held invalid. Federal bankruptcy codes discharge debt arising from vehicle accidents, preventing state law from denying driver's licenses due to failure to pay the debt.

Federal Government Force States to Comply

The federal government forces states to comply with some laws. Blessing, Director, Arizona Department Of Economic Security v. Freestone et al. [1997, US Sup Ct, 95-1441]. Child Support Enforcement is not a federal right that can be used to force states to substantially comply with Title IV-D.

Law is Partially Unconstitutional

United States of America v. Grigsby March 6, 2000

Deadbeat Parent' Case Could Not Be Dismissed Even Though Law Is Partially Unconstitutional

Judge Ronald R. Lagueux of the U.S. District Court judge has ruled in a case of first impression determining that the unconstitutional statutory presumption will be disregarded at trial because it is severable from the remainder of the statute. Therefore, the indictment against a father under the "deadbeat parents" statute could not be dismissed even though part of the statute unconstitutionally presumes an ability to pay child support. Even though the indictment stands, "In short, [the statute] unconstitutionally forces [the] defendant to rebut the presumption in this case of an element of the criminal offense, which the government must prove and that results in a violation of the [d]ue [p]rocess [c]lause," Lagueux said.

Tougher Proof

Andrew Berg of Providence, who represents the defendant, said "Judge Ronald R. LaGueux's decision is the first in the country to address that the statute, which permitted the presumption that a defendant had the ability to pay simply by virtue of a child support order being issued. This decision will make it more difficult for the government to prove these cases. Instead of just showing up in court with a child support order, it will have to come up with evidence on a defendant's income and expenses, "

Thomas M. Connell, spokesman for the U.S. Attorney's Office, said the government has yet to decide whether to appeal the ruling. "We're carefully considering all the issues in consultation with [U.S.] Department of Justice officials in Washington, D.C. to determine if an appeal is appropriate".

Child Support Payments

On Feb. 7, 1996, the defendant, Mark Grigsby, was ordered by the Rhode Island Family Court to pay child support for his three children, all of whom live in Rhode Island. The defendant, who now resides in California, was later indicted under 18 U.S.C. Sect. 228(a)(3) for "willfully" failing to make the support payments for over two years. The defendant was reimbursed by the federal government for his travel expenses for appearing at his arraignment in Rhode Island, and because he apparently couldn't afford traveling back to California, the government also arranged for his return fare. The defendant filed a motion to dismiss the indictment on the basis that the statute creates an unconstitutional mandatory presumption of his ability to satisfy the child support payments.

Mandatory Presumption

The purpose of the Child Support Recovery Act is to place non-payment of unpaid child support obligations exceeding two years under the federal criminal justice system, Lagueux noted.

To be found guilty under 18 U.S.C. Sect. 228, a defendant must "willfully" fail to pay a child support obligation for a child who resides in a state other than where the defendant lives.

Section 228(b) states that a child support order "creates a rebuttable presumption that the obligor has the ability to pay the support obligation" for the time period set forth in an indictment.

"This section," the judge found, "has the effect of creating a presumption that if a support order is produced by the government, then the jury is to presume that the defendant is able to pay such support order unless the defendant proves otherwise." Since presumptions against criminal defendants are judged according to the due process clause of the 5th Amendment, Lagueux noted, which requires the prosecution to prove every essential element of the crime charged beyond a reasonable doubt.

Rejecting the government's argument that the presumption is not mandatory and that it is rebuttable. Determining that the statute creates a mandatory presumption because it compels the fact finder to determine that the defendant had the ability to pay unless he produces sufficient evidence to rebut that presumption.

"When there is a mandatory presumption the trier of fact is confronted with a command that if fact A is proved, then fact B follows," Lagueux observed. "In effect, the mandatory presumption dictates that the fact finder 'must find the elemental fact upon proof of the basic fact' [such that] the government is relieved of having to produce evidence on an element of the crime at trial." Mandatory presumptions unconstitutionally shift the burden of persuasion to defendants "if the basic fact is not conclusively linked to the presumed, elemental fact in a mandatory presumption," the judge wrote.

Under Section 228, he said, the introduction into evidence of a court order for child support payments compels a jury to find that the defendant has the ability to pay the child support. Because the statute requires that the failure to pay be "willful," a basic element of the crime is that a defendant can pay the child support, but chooses not to do so.

"Therefore, the government is relieved of having to prove that a defendant has the ability to pay so long as there is evidence of an outstanding support obligation," which directly conflicts with the constitutional presumption of innocence, he concluded.

Rebuttable Presumption

Unpersuaded by the fact that the presumption is rebuttable, the Judge noted that Section 228 runs afoul of the constitution because it impermissibly shifts the burden of persuasion to the defendant, Lagueux asserted. "It is readily apparent that the issuance of a support order by a [c]ourt does not establish beyond a reasonable doubt that the parent involved will have the ability to pay that obligation over the next two years," he noted. It is simply unreasonable to conclude that a parent has the means to satisfy court-ordered child support payments solely by virtue of the order itself, which orders are sometimes issued either ex parte or absent evidence on the parent's financial status, the judge determined.

Ruling that the unconstitutional mandatory presumption can be severed from the remainder of the statute allowing it to survive without the presumption. "The unconstitutional mandatory presumption contained in Sect. 228(b) merely established the requirements of proof for the government on the element of [the] defendant's ability to pay the support obligation," The core elements of the offense are stated in a separate provision. "

Canadian Child Support

Many judges appear to be applying the Federal Child Support Guidelines of 1997 to child support matters that were and should be adjudicated under provincial law including non divorce cases, common law cases, paternity cases. The new Standardized Table Approach is now being used to determine the amount of child support to be paid and will be based upon two key factors:

The non-custodial parent's incomeThe number of children to be supported.

Then one looks at standardized tables for one's own province and territory. The income of the non-custodial parent is matched to the number of children; this determines the amount of monthly support. It sounds simple, but it is not. In some cases you may be required to pay more in child support than you earn. Disclosure of income tax returns and company financial statements will be required for financial disclosure to determine child support and may be required before divorce or custody litigation begins. There are four circumstances under which the custodial parent's income could have an effect on the amount of child support to be paid:

1. If the payor's income is over $150,000.00;

2. If any child is over the age of majority (18 in Ontario);

3. If non-custodial parent has the child at least forty percent of the time in a split custody situation;

4. If there are special expenses sought to be added to the base amount;

Or if the payor's income over $150,000.00. Or, if the non-custodial parent's income is over $150,000.00, one consults the standard tables. The base amount is still found on the tables under $150,000.00. The additional amount, as per the standard tables, for one child may be .71% of the income over $150,000.00. Two children is 1.14% of the income over $150,000.00.

Three children is 1.48% of the income over $150,000.00.

Revenue Canada will charge no taxes to the parent who receives child support and no tax deduction will be give to the parent who pays child support. If a separation agreement or a court child support order, it is still valid and the same tax effects will continue, provided neither side does anything.

However, either side will now be able to apply to the court to have the new system apply and there is absolutely nothing that can be done to prevent this. This court application will likely call for a change in the amount of support being paid and the new tax treatment would then apply. Existing separation agreements (such as Ontario's Family Law Act) or even a fairly recent court orders, can be taken back to court to have child support recalculated under the new system.

Provinces: As of May 1, 1997, Quebec has indicated that it intends to implement its own new system. New Brunswick and Saskatchewan are the only provinces that have introduced their own child support guidelines legislation. The other provinces have not yet come on board. It is open to the province to simply adopt the federal scheme or to implement its own system. Therefore, cases heard under provincial law (such as non divorce cases, common law cases, paternity cases) should still, at least in theory, and until a province adopts its own legislation, be subject to the existing law. As developments here may come quickly, it is advisable to ascertain what the up to date law is in one's own province before taking this information as correct.

Chapter 22: End or Beginning

In truth, if custody is solely decided on what is best for the children, there can be no loser.

If the case goes to court, there is a winner and a loser of the court case. The winner will have to take the first steps necessary to heal the wounds of the custody war and make a new beginning possible.

In order to make visitation happy for the children, make visitation as easy as possible for the non-custodial parent. The winner will have to be the fair one, the helpful one, the one willing to make things work for the children, the other parent and oneself. In the end does not matter if you do or do not have custody of your children or if you share custody with the other parent. Because you will miss your children any time they are not with you. In the end you will have to get along with a person you could not or did not want to live with.

Forgiveness

Whether you won or lost custody, the most effective release from the pain of the past is forgiveness of ourselves and of others. If you are holding onto anger, resentment, fear, guilt, hurt, blame, sadness, anger, or even a desire for revenge, you will not be able to enjoy the good things this moment has to offer. Resentment can only be dissolved by forgiveness.

In these busy modern times, it is difficult for us to know what is important to our lives and what we may need from any specific situation as it arises. It is impossible, therefore, for others to begin to figure out what we would want from a particular situation.

If you expect others to consider your needs in a given situation, you will always be disappointed.

Expect all persons you deal with in life to take the best care of themselves that they can. Then you will never be disappointed in their actions.

When You Win Custody

You are the custodial parent, also called most-access. Once you have won custody of your children, everyone will need time for adjustment. Your children, the other parent, even you, as the winner, will need a time of healing. Where custody is concerned there is really no winner and there is no end.

Initially, there is a feeling of relief. After weeks, months and years of being beaten up by the system, the opposition, and your own self-doubts, you may even require professional counseling to handle the emotions.

Is This the Win I Wanted?

My children talk about the non-custodial parent all the time. This makes me feel hurt and less loved.

Every time the children go with the non-custodial parent I am afraid I will never see them again.

The other parent pulls me into court every twelve months. It is very hard on our children's emotions, my finance's and the other parent's mental stability.

The non-custodial parent constantly makes accusations of neglect, abuse and exploitation to any social service or law enforcement agency that will listen. The reports come back in my favor, but it is difficult to live with the constant assault and scrutiny.

When the children visit the non-custodial parent, they are subjected to the parental alienation syndrome and come home angry with me and very confused.

I have the happiness and responsibility of the children's welfare for the next seven years because the court said the children might decide where they want to be when they reach twelve. I feel like I am being blackmailed constantly by the children and the other parent.

The other parent cannot seem to adjust to the loss of this custody case. Our children may be in physical or emotional danger when with the non-custodial parent, and I am not able to do anything.

Mental House Cleaning

Because of the custody battle, your life has been on hold for a long time. Plan your peace as well as you planned your war.

Now is the time to the future for you and your children by establishing some new "family" rituals. Rituals include a pattern of getting into pajamas, brushing teeth and a bedtime story at night, to making homemade ice cream at big family meals on holidays. If the children are with the other parent on the "exact" day, attempt to have your family event the week before or the week after. Plan vacation time (even if you can't afford to go away) and be patient with your children, yourself and the other parent.

The Hard Part

Since custody has been awarded to you, you have obligations to the children with regard to the other parent. Because the children's welfare is more important than your personal desires, the other parent will remain in your life in one way or another.

Make the children's association with the other parent as guilt-free and gratifying for them as possible. The frequency of contact with the non-custodial parent will be greater if that person lives in the same area that you do.

Make visitation happy for your children and less stressful for you. Contact will require careful scheduling, attention to detail and flexibility. If the children must travel out of city or state several times a year, you may have to contend with the pain of separation and concern for their welfare during transport.

Establish a positive attitude and stance to deal with your child's needs as they apply to the other parent. Many valuable books can assist you and the other parent in making your child's life happier, minus many of the permanent emotional scars that can be formed in children when parents live separately.

To Build a Healthy Child

- Establish a positive working partnership with the other parent that is visible to your child. If you are not able to form a happy association, at the very least, build a polite partnership.
- There will be a residue of fear and resentment as a result of the adversarial position imposed by the court proceedings. Assure the other parent that the partnership is for the child's welfare and that you will assist the parent and your child to the best of your ability. This will provide your child with a more secure environment.
- Let your children see and hear your appreciation of all the things the other parent does for them. Compliment the other parent in an honest manner for positive behaviors and things done for the children.

- Do not jump to conclusions if there appears to be a problem. Ask if what you think was said, was, in fact, what was meant by repeating the statement.
- Make it possible for your children to celebrate dates important to the other parent, such as birthdays, anniversaries, and religious holidays. It may be necessary at times to remind the children to acknowledge these occasions, perhaps helping your children to purchase or make cards or gifts.
- Help your children understand and support, in an appropriate manner, the other parent in times of stress or loss.
- Work things out together with the other parent and let your children be part of the process.
- Discard old negative ways of dealing with this person. Extend the respect and patience you would a new acquaintance that shares your love for these children.
- Anticipate questions the other parent will ask, objections the other parent will raise, and concerns the other parent will present. Prepare appropriate responses that will allow the opposition to reach the same goals that you have.
- If there is a matter of disagreement, work out that problem without adding new points to the discussion. Do not insert or allow the opposition to insert any old arguments. Address the matter at hand in a manner that will allow settlement. Offer several acceptable options.
- To avoid misunderstandings during verbal communication, restate the information given to you before you answer or give your information.
- When you are arranging your plans to accommodate the other parent, don't guess. Ask about specific dates and times.
- Do not do anything to the other parent that you would be ashamed for your children to see or know.
- Learn from the times your efforts with the other parent failed. Do not repeat behavior that will initiate a negative response. Do it better each time and without malice. Try to make things work. Do not keep track of the times your efforts failed, only of the times your efforts let everyone win.
- Respond to all situations in the most positive mindset you can. For your children, try yet again.

And the Beat Goes On

As the successful litigant, much of your anxiety and anger will dissipate quickly. Regardless of the age of the children, the judgment of the court may only be for a specific period of time. The court may set a nonspecific date linked to the children's ages to consider the matter of residence at another time.

Therefore, you may be involved in the legal process until the children reach legal age. Your best course of action is to maintain the positive behaviors you have always had and keep exercising the new skills you have developed.

When You Lose Custody

When the fight took years and the battle was constantly uphill, there were many indications that you could not, would not win. You survived the first shock by initiating and sustaining an active period of denial with a strong fight with the best case and attorney you could muster. At some time, the reality of the case became obvious and you anticipated life away from your children. You began to visualize that you would have to cope and make some decisions as to how you would accomplish that task. Then there was a new hope or opportunity that diminished the reality you could not face. Now that the decision has been made, it is hard to believe that there is nothing else you can do. If the fight was short or you had a solid case that moved forward in a reasonable manner and you had every reason to expect to win or have a fair settlement, this is a crushing blow. There was no warning that you could or would lose. You are in an intense state of shock and disbelief.

In any case, you are the non-custodial parent, also called least-access. It is difficult to stop fighting when you have not won. The normal feeling is that, if you can just sustain the battle a little longer, you can win this war. It is equally difficult to get your soldiers to stop fighting. When the decision is rendered, it is the law of the land and that is where your life is now. As the unsuccessful litigant, the anxiety, pain and, anger can consume you. Even if you never felt you had much of a chance to win custody, there is considerable pain in the actual loss.

Emotions and Feelings

Sorting out your emotions will show you that

what you feel is normal and give you an indication as to where you are in the stages that you must live through. Feelings you may experience: grief, denial, lost, daze, shock, fear, mood swings, bitter, let down, depressed, purposeless, crushed, lost, distrust, guilt, unnatural, angry, numb and more. To others you will appear: inconsistent, angry, immature, impulsive, erratic, demanding, unpredictable, blameful, unable to control crying, bitter, aching for a fight. There is a pattern of feelings most people experience. These are shock, anger, denial, guilt, grieving, depression, acceptance and finally adjustment. Each person experiences these emotions in their own time and to varying degrees. Women tend to cry first and men tend to express anger initially.

The process may be delayed or interrupted, but it is necessary to pass through these emotions in order to regain your emotional and physical health. These emotions are legitimate, and you may experience some or all of the emotions several times.

Many Emotions - Most Hurt

Shock immobilizes and disorients us for a time. Emotional shock serves the same purpose for the mind that physical shock does for the body. It removes us from the pain and allows us some time to adjust to what has happened.

Anger spurs us to action. There is a loss of patience with the people who have helped us as well as our antagonists. Hopefully, the targets of displaced anger are able to recognize why they have been assaulted and forgive the person in pain. Filing for appeal of the case is a normal reaction due to angry emotions.

Ninety-eight percent of the request for consideration of appeal are filed within a week of a custody decision, and are withdrawn before the document deadline of ninety days.

Anger will also cause a great deal of blaming and finger pointing for the loss and allow us to vent our feelings.

Denial encourages us to not accept "what is" and allows us to keep functioning under what we choose to believe. Denial also encourages us to blame others and inhibits our ability to move on with more constructive behaviors and thinking.

This stage can last months or years. A conscious effort must be made to grow past denial.

Bargaining gives us a moment of hope, letting us believe that we can give up something else precious and get back that which we cannot bear to lose.

Grief allows us to mourn a loss. The loss is different for each person and all loss is painful. The loss for a parent, grandparent, sibling, psychological parent, and extended family are real and must be recognized and dealt with. Grief is an important stage in our attempt to regain stability.

Guilt comes from our own real or imagined shortcomings. There is a great deal of guilt because we feel we let down our children, ourselves, our parents, the children's grandparents, our families and friends that supported us emotionally and economically.

Shame may be the most insidious of the stages. If this happened to us, what did we do to deserve to be so dishonored? Destroying one's self-esteem and causing humiliation and shame can inhibit our ability to reach out for help.

Depression is the most dangerous of the stages. It inhibits your ability to properly view or deal with our situation. The signs of depression are: crying for no apparent reason, numbness, feelings of helplessness, anger, anxiety, fright, compulsive need to talk, over concern for the people you love, no concern for the people you love, feelings inadequacy, trouble sleeping, thoughts of suicide and deep sadness. Depression is always dangerous and must be addressed.

Acceptance allows us to recognize the existence or meaning of what has happened. We must restore our energy and reaffirm our goals.

Adjustment enables us to make suitable decisions for our children the future and ourselves.

As we work through these feelings, we will feel a need and desire to improve our mental and physical health and then establish new living patterns.

The family members, friends, attorneys, psychologists and others who have supported your efforts share in your loss. Expect to hear and see some of the same pain you feel in them. Remember to thank them for their support.

Don't forget how long they have accompanied you on this trail. It is important to have someone to talk to without having to apologize for your feelings.

Make renewed effort to care for remaining children or family members.
Eliminate discussions about whose fault the loss was. Stay in contact with support groups for guidance and counseling. Members of these organizations can help you cope with the roller coaster of emotions.

If your children are in a good environment, it will be easier to adjust to the idea of not taking care of them yourself. Attempting to portray a good environment as bad in order to change custody will discredit you and harm your children. It will not change the situation you face.

Now is not Forever

Now is not forever and the pain is not forever. Feelings of despair and suicide usually only last a few minutes or hours. Commit to NEVER harming yourself while in this temporary state. Your children will need you in the future. If you're using alcohol or drugs they will increase your despair. They alter your rational state and weaken your resistance. Consider giving them up for a period of time until your crisis passes. Decide to live and heal at least one more day. You probably can't feel much worse than you do now, but you will likely feel at least a little better tomorrow. Make a commitment to one short-term goal or activity.

Make your goal something simple and "do-able." How about visiting a friend, going to a movie, going for a walk or a drive, or cleaning your car? Even when you don't know what to do next, just go on living right now. It will help if you write out every last feeling you have inside. Writing helps you "get out of your head" and transfers the load onto paper. Write as long as needed and each time that you feel upset. Life is all about gaining problem-solving skills. It's normal and even healthy to feel unhappy at times. If you can see your present suffering as transient and normal, it will give you ability to cope with future conflicts. It's true, life can be painful and like a roller coaster, you may have to ride it out. It may not be fun, but it will stop. The best antidote to despair is activity. Lose yourself in something that can fill or replace your void. It might be in accomplishing the goal you set earlier. Life comes one day at a time and needs to be faced one day at a time. Ride it out, take what comes. Already, you're living proof that you've successfully coped with life's challenges for all these years. You can continue to cope. You may need more attention, time, love, and other things. You're building walls right now and shutting people out. Let someone in on your secrets, your private thoughts. Make your needs known. Say it plain "Hey, I need more time with you", or "I need for you to listen to me."

Write an autobiography of your life. Don't just write the bad things. Include the family vacations, Christmas, friends, childhood memories, short moments of joy, funny jokes, and fun times. Conflict is inherent in life. If you are going to have relationships, you are sooner or later going to have some conflict. You may barely remember what is happening now five years from now. If you're skeptical, try to remember exactly what was happening in your life on seven years ago. You probably can't remember. And, several years from now, it's likely that you'll have forgotten what was so upsetting at this particular moment in time. If you are manipulating people to feel sorry for you and to be worried, your tactic may backfire and instead of getting your way, they may avoid you more. Consider building your relationship skills. Talk to a counselor. Read a book. Join support groups -- you can even find some online. You can develop the tools you need to deal with people in difficult times.

It's been said that flexibility is a sign of mental health: The willow tree bends in the wind. It doesn't break. In crisis, we have been given important information to use on our life's journey. We can use this information to make life less painful and more joyful. In the movie, 'Groundhog Day', with actor Bill Murray, Bill's character wakes up to face the same day over and over again. February 2nd, the first day, he steps off a curb and into a puddle. The next day, he stepped off the curb and into the puddle again, so it's February 2nd all over again. But, on the third day, he finally "gets it" and steps around the puddle. That's kind of like life. We step in the same puddles or dilemmas until we understand what we need to do to avoid them the next time around. It's in your power to learn from your crisis and change your life for the better. Of all the dangers in the world, the greatest are the dangers we create for ourselves.

Making the Not-so-good Better

If your children are in a 'Less Than Perfect' environment, there are some things you can do to help the children. Anything you do to help the parent will help your children. Do what it takes to help your children where they are now.

- Help the parent improve his or her self-image.
- Work with dysfunctional parents by taking over or helping with the areas they see they need help in and/or in which they will accept help.
- If the children are abused, the parents should be counseled.
- If the home is dirty and in disrepair, the other parent's needs help to clean and fix what is broken.
- Send books, games and toys for the children to have in their residence.
- Let the school know that you are willing to provide anything the children need.
- Let the rabbi, priest, or minister know of any help they can give the other parent.
- Respond immediately to the children's outstanding needs.
- Supply outdoor toys, swings and secure play areas.
- Make the decision of the court as easy on the children and other parent as possible.

Let Go

Don't let the scars of the battle steal the small joys of today. The past is over and done. It cannot be changed. This is the only moment you can experience. If you relive the painful incidents and angry words of the past, you are wasting this moment and losing the real experience of this life. Allow memories to be just memories. Holding onto the past will only hurt you.

The best reason to forgive is this: It requires energy to maintain anger and bitterness. People who are able to genuinely forgive feel positive physical changes. One of the most painful hurts to forgive is disappointment. Expecting others to know what you need and expecting others to fill your needs causes this emotion. If you find yourself constantly let down, you are a victim, waiting for new disappointments. Take responsibility for your needs and feelings. Meet the needs you can.

Make it clear to others what you need and what, if any, of their needs you are willing to meet. Do what you can and then move on.

Normal Feelings

- I have too much to do and can't work my way through this.
- I have lost control of my entire life.
- As a parent, I am supposed to protect my children. How can I do that when I can't even be with them?
- The world has stopped.
- Everything has changed forever.
- People must feel I am a bad woman since I lost custody of my children.
- My heart is broken and my stomach is raw. There is real physical pain.
- People must feel sure I abandoned my family and am a deadbeat parent.

Usual Challenges

Changes in appetite. No appetite often results in weight loss. Eating ravenously so that you've gained weight.

- Sleep problems. Insomnia or wanting to sleep all the time
- You have no energy and are easily fatigued.
- You're restless and fatigued.
- Feelings of worthlessness, hopelessness or inappropriate guilt.
- Difficult thinking, making decisions or concentrating.
- Chronic aches and pains that don't respond to treatment.
- Excessive crying.
- Challenges that Require Help
- Thoughts of death or suicide or attempts at suicide.
- You feel pessimistic about your life.
- You avoid old friends.
- Crowds bother you.
- You no longer get along with people.
- You have poor memory.
- Your work or school work is not going as well.
- You have unexplained headaches, backaches and stomachaches.
- You have made a will and are thinking about your funeral.

Helpful Applications

Resist victimizing yourself with feelings of guilt. Put your feelings in a diary. It is a sane, healthy way to express and work through your feelings. Custody status does not determine what kind of person you are.
Without the burdened of day-to-day chores that child care requires, many non-custodial parents can still influence the lives of their children in many positive ways.

Avoid imaging vengeance or reprisal against the other parent. These feelings are dangerous for you and negatively impact your children. Get counseling for guilt or anger.

Make every effort to keep bitterness and regret from damaging your relationship with your children.

If you are married or have a significant other, stay as close as possible to this person. The emotional distress you both feel will make communication more difficult. Be patient with each other.

Making out the child support check will be stressful every month. Find the easiest way to handle this obligation. Some options are automatic wage deduction or auto-pay through your bank.

Tell the people who care about you what you are going through and how you feel.

Anticipate pangs of sadness on the children's birthdays, holidays and special family times that they cannot be with you. Make arrangements to celebrate these special days when the children are with you. It is not important that the celebration is not on the "exact" day.

Know that your children are fine and doing all the same activities they always have and that you will see them again.

Recognize personal stress symptoms: fatigue, irritability, isolation, sudden mood swings, and major changes in sleeping, eating and sexual patterns.

Realize there is no right time to feel happy or sad. Your feelings are legitimate.

Allow yourself to feel happiness, joy, success and love. You deserve the feelings.

Weeks may pass where you feel more accepting of your loss of custody, to be replaced by several viciously angry days. These bad days will also pass. The roller coaster of highs and lows can last several years. Take care of yourself even when you don't feel like it.

If you have other children, attend to their nurturing and make appropriate arrangements for them when you are not up to daily parenting. They may feel abandoned, jealous and less loved.

Accept your feelings. They are not right or wrong; they are just how you feel.

Burnout can be avoided by going out and resuming social contacts. This does not mean that you have abandoned your children. It does mean that you are attempting to maintain the balance necessary for a normal life. Maintain whatever contact with your children you have been allowed.

Whatever you think, feel, question, or believe is acceptable. Do not make excessive demands or impose ridged restrictions on yourself or your loved ones. Communicate tolerance, compassion and love. Live through your grief. As you slowly heal, work for balance in yourself in your permanently changed world.

You deserve to be happy regardless of your marital or custodial status.

Write things down to avoid forgetting things.

Safe Answers

I cannot tell you why people say the stupid and insensitive things they do. It is not just a lack of common courtesy. Not everyone is so unthinking. However, even a kind, well-meaning person's question can throw you into sad feelings or depression. Listed are some common questions and statements you will face on a daily basis with suggestions for safe answers. Having safe answers ready is a powerful safety net.

Q. How could you let them take your children?

- *A.* How could you ask such an insensitive question?
- *A.* I did not let them take my children. Your question is very unkind.

Q. I heard you gave your children away. Why?

- *A.* What do you mean by that?
- *A.* Why do you want to know?
- *A.* Our children have two parents, and we are the best qualified to decide what is best for our children.

Q. Why don't your children live with you?

A. Why do you want to know?

A. We all decided the children are where they need to be.

A. I am not the one who gets to decide where the children live and I do not wish to discuss it any further.

A. Are you going to file an appeal for custody of your children?

A. I will do what's best for my children. Thank you for your concern, I will call you if I wish to discuss it further.

A. That, as well as other questions about my children, are not welcome at this time.

Q. What is going on now?

A. Nothing new. How about you?

A. I have been eating, sleeping and living this situation for a long time now. I would appreciate it if you did not ask about it again.

A. I'll let you know if anything interesting happens.

A. Not much. What are your plans for the summer?

Q. Why don't you let me just get rid of them for you?

A. No, their ghosts would just come back to haunt me for the rest of my life.

A. Don't even talk like that; this person is important to my children.

A. I pray that nothing bad happens to them. My children do not need any more stress or pain.

A. Don't be so angry; it doesn't do any of us any good.

A. No thanks. What have you been doing with your time?

Q. What's wrong with you that your children don't live with you?

A. There is nothing wrong with me. Custodial status does not determine what kind of person anyone is.

A. What is wrong with you that you would ask such a rude question?

Q. Are they still giving you problems with the children?

A. Things have been pretty quiet for a long time now.

A. I am sure things will work out the way they are supposed to.

A. We are all working to make this time as easy as possible.

A. Please don't ask about the case every time you see me. I appreciate your concern, but it wears me out.

Q. How can I help you?

A. Just knowing you are there helps.

A. There is nothing anyone can do for now.

A. Please be the one person I get to talk to about other things. That would help me the most.

Concentrate on the Children

Before we are assaulted with a custody battle many things are put off. It is when we are faced with not spending unlimited time with our children that it becomes clear that we must take the time to teach them the important lessons in life. It isn't important if someone else is attempting to teach your children life's lessons. They need to hear what you think and see how you deal with the important issues of life.

Teach your children to be authentic. To be aware of their inner selves and to hear their inner-feeling voices.

Teach your children to transcend their own cultural conditioning, and become world citizens.

Help your children discover their vocation in life, their calling, fate or destiny. This is especially focused upon finding the right career and the right mate.

Teach your children that life is precious, that there is joy to be experienced in life, and if people are open to seeing the good and joyous in all kinds of situations, it makes life worth living.

Accept your children as individuals. Separate from you and the other parent. Help children learn and appreciate their inner nature. From real knowledge of aptitudes and limitations we can know what to build upon. Evaluate the options.

See that your children's basic needs are satisfied. That includes safety, a feeling of belonging and esteem needs.

You should refresh your own consciousness, teaching your children to appreciate beauty and the other good things in nature and in living.

Teach your children that controls are good, and

complete abandon is bad. It takes control to improve the quality of life in all areas.

Teach your children to transcend the trifling problems and grapple with the serious problems in life. When they are mature enough these include the problems of injustice, of pain, suffering and death.

Teach your children to make good choices. They must be given practice in making choices, first between one goody and another. Then more serious decisions.

New Traditions

If the time you will get to spend is infrequent, it is especially important to establish a special ritual that will stick in your child's mind. Not elaborate festivals just small child centered experiences.
make a special kind of cookies
eat with special friends
go to the zoo
plant or harvest
stories at bedtime
feed the pets
act out a story (like 3 Billy Goats Gruff)

Holidays

Even at the best of times, holidays and special events can be difficult. There is no perfect family. Television, movies and advertising can make you feel that Birthdays, Thanksgiving, Christmas, Hanukkah, New Years and other family events, must be done a certain way. Very few people do or have ever had the ideal large, loving family happily sitting around an abundant table. In the background is the lavishly decorated tree surrounded by a mountain of gifts. Laughter and merriment fills the air and everyone obviously loves everyone else.

Unattainable childhood expectations cause us to still want that magical, happy experience. Especially if we never had the ideal experience in our youth, we still somehow want to be part of that experience for our children.

In reality while some of us may have experienced some of that ideal image some of the time, all of us have felt disappointments to some degree or other. As expectations meet the realities of life, we feel the stress, loneliness, depression, hurt or anger that inevitably occurs. During the holidays, the absence of our children intensifies and compounds those feelings at a time when everyone else is striving to be happy and merry.

If you are left out of your children's holidays, it may seem impossible to face the celebrations. The following suggestions are offered to help you through them:

1. A holiday does not go away because you didn't get to celebrate it on the correct day. If your children have to be away on the calendar assigns the holiday to, give it your own day.

2. Be realistic about the holidays. Don't have the expectation they will produce that magical feeling or be a solution to your problems.

3. Accept the reality of your sadness. Allow your feelings to be what they are and feel them without suppression. Cry as much as you need to. Understand that the holidays will seem to intensify your sense of loss.

4. Look for the good in your life. Feel your gratitude for those things you value such as health, family, friends, job, or whatever you value and appreciate. Write them down so you can refer to them whenever you feel there is nothing positive in your life.

5. Take extra good care of yourself. Eat a balanced diet. Minimize sugar, alcohol, tobacco, and caffeine, which can increase depression and lower your immune system. Walk more or exercise regularly. Get plenty of rest and don't overload your limits or your obligations. Take time for yourself to do what nurtures you, alone or with someone of your choosing. Do something special for yourself regularly.

6. Lower your expectations of what you think you "should" or "ought to" do during the holiday season. This might include not sending cards. Instead of giving individual gifts, give a group gift such as a basket of fruit or flowers. Or have a gift for the children only. Have someone help you or do some of it for you.

Consider whether you really need to accept every invitation, or do all the holiday decorations, or bake all the cookies. Keep life simple and low-keyed. Don't try to "make" things happen or force gaiety. It will only create the opposite effect.

7. Choose to be with people that support you. Make special plans for special days in advance.

Decide if you want to be with your family, or leave town, or if you want to volunteer at a homeless shelter. Don't feel you have to do things the traditional way if that doesn't feel right to you. Then meet with your family or friends to let them know about your plans well ahead of time. Tell them what you need to do and what you would like from them. With understanding and agreements in place, there is less likelihood of hurt feelings or resentments later on.

8. Find someone to confide in who can truly understand what you are going through. A grief support or parent's rights group can be invaluable during the holidays (or anytime) to offer support, suggestions, and even companionship. Someone who has "been there" can usually provide the sensitive understanding that even a close and well meaning family member cannot. Ask for help or company when you feel you need it.

9. Maintain and even cultivate your sense of humor. Try not to take the holidays, or any day, too seriously. If you find life becoming too serious or intense, have a good laugh! Watch a funny movie with a good-humored friend. Read a good joke book and share it with someone. Work at it even if it seems difficult. Do something ridiculous. Laughing is a good way to release tension and stress.

10. Rely on your source of spiritual support in your own personal way. Take time to nurture that which sustains your definition of Love or Truth in the highest sense. Take some action to express that in the world. Smile more, praise more, paint a picture, volunteer your time, do something special for someone else. Love given is always returned in some form. Isn't that what these holidays are about after all?

11. Find others, especially those missing someone close. Now is a good time to think about how you want to spend the holidays. What will you or won't you do? Who do you want to be with - and when or where? Nothing, but time can reduce the pain. However, there are ways to help you tolerate it and provide some meaning in the days to come. Rather than trying to control or shove the feelings down, plan to support them instead by remembering in very specific, creative ways during the holiday season. Here are some simple rituals that allow all the feelings to be there and also provide a vehicle for moving through them in a positive, healthful way:

12. Singing - alone or with a group. Sing nostalgic songs that bring up the feelings. Sing the songs especially enjoyed by your children. Sing happy songs in the shower or when driving down the freeway. Sing with family and friends around the dinner table. Organize a group to sing carols at the nearest nursing home.

13. Cook or bake since food like songs, can bring up memories and warm the heart. Nurturing and sustenance can go hand in hand when you make a favorite soup or bake traditional cookies. Sharing food and giving it as gifts to family and friends can be a most healing.

14. Charitable Contributions - To give is to receive! You can donate time, money, talents, resources, clothing, gifts and food. Giving to support or cheer, someone else allows us to feel productive and worthwhile during a time when we might tend to feel despondent and alone.

15. Grow plants and flowers. Flowers and foliage glorify any environment and are perfect ingredients for creating happy memories when your children can be with you. They can be fresh-cut bouquets, potted plants, dried arrangements, or even paper or fabric blossoms if you don't have a green thumb.

16. Collect special photos to make a collage of life's special events, or create a memory card or memory book. Buy or make elegant frames for special gifts. Color-copy selected photos for family and friends. Add a poem or saying to give them special meaning.

17. Sewing Projects - Create a quilt or flag to commemorate significant places or occasions. Cut-up clothing your children have outgrown to be used as quilting squares; or you can incorporate other memorabilia into a creative sewing project such as a cushion cover, wall hanging or lap rug.

18. Stories and Family Histories - Write the family history, or document the special times of the life

of your children. The story can be read aloud at a family gathering or during special times, and copies can be distributed to others as gifts.

19. Decorations - Make creative ornaments, centerpieces, and decorations that mark the holiday. A special ceremony can include the placing of a special decoration on the tree. A significant article can identify each place setting at the holiday table symbolizing something very special about that person. A toast or prayer can be offered before the meal begins.

20. Memory lane - Organize an evening of storytelling with special family members and friends. You can watch family videos, go through photo albums, share stories, play favorite games and prepare favorite foods.

21. There is no right or wrong way to celebrate a holiday. Do whatever feels right for you and include others who can support what you need at that time. Communicate to your close friends and family what you need to do, and what you can and can't do. Do this well ahead of time. It forces you to deal with all the intense feelings that typically arise. Be good to yourself and don't repress the feelings. Instead, promote all those activities that bring up the feelings and turn them all into a way to heal. Honor the feelings and they will lead you to the healing that inevitably will come.

Major Holidays

Before, during or after a custody battle it is important to focus on the children during the holidays.

If you don't live with your child send your holiday cards and gifts to remain close to your children at these important times.

If your children will be at visitation for the holidays send your cards and gifts with the children in their luggage.

Include cards, letters, small amounts of money and kits you can buy or make-up for the child to do easily at the other home.

Valentine's Day

Send a Valentine Day Card. If the children over 8 years old, make a kit of glitter, paste, doilies, and harts so the children can make their own Valentines for the family and friends that live close to them.. Send it out the last week in March. Buy a book appropriate for each child and in the margins on selected pages write a note about a silly, funny or loving thing you remember about the child.

Easter

Buy or make a card to send. If there are unusual or interesting gee coloring kits available in your area that may not be available where the children live buy and send them. You should do that by the first week in April.

Spring

Although not designated as a holiday, it is an opportunity to communicate with your children. If the child has access to and help with a garden send flower or vegetable seeds. If there is on support or opportunity, send wildflowers with instructions on finding a place to spread them.

Earth Day

Make a little book for your children to fill in the pages. Put instructions at the top of the pages. Headings could include: What three wishes would you make for the earth? Make a picture of the ocean. Make a picture of the desert. Make a picture of the woods. Make a picture of your funniest thing you like to do. And on and on...

Passover

Buy and send a card and make a book with some of the Passover stories such as: A Strange Seder, Elijah's Cup, On The Shore Of The Red Sea, Once Upon A Passover Night, Passover in Siberia, The Seder Plate and Midrashic Accounts about the Story of Passover.

Kwanzaa

Make your own book to help your children learn and reaffirm their commitment to themselves, their families, their community, and the black struggle for equality. The seven days of Kwanzaa are from December 26th thru January 1st. Each day focuses on a specific principle: December 26th Unity (Umoja), 27th Self-Determination (Kujichagulia), 28th Collective Work & Responsibility (Ujima), 29th Cooperative

Economics (Ujamaa), 30th Purpose (Nia), 31st Creativity (Kuumba), January 1st Faith (Imani).

Cinco de Mayo

May 5th decorating kit could include rolls of red ,white and green crepe-paper. Make a book with recipes and games such as Loteria and Batalla del Cinco de Mayo for the children to play.

Mothers Day

In addition to what you would expect, cooking is a big deal for this holiday. Send new white t-shirt of the correct size and fabric paint ore markers so the children can decorate it for mom.

Graduation

Dr. Seuss's 'Oh the places You'll Go!' has zoomed to the top of the best

seller list.Gifty advice books and 'Life's Little Instruction' books have done very well.

Father's Day

Books relevant to fatherhood and sports are huge. A package of brownies or cookies that only require water before baking. Send new white t-shirt of the correct size and fabric paint ore markers so the children can decorate it for dad.

Summer

Carry around reading and personal travel.4th of July.suggestion (stuff and instructions to make a red, white, and blue cake or cookies.) If you know the other parent likes to barbecue, send a good bottle of BBQ-sauce.

Back to School

Going back to school is a big deal for most children. Take part in the excitement. Buy or make a book about facing some of the challenges of the new school year. Example, How to do Homework Without Throwing Up. Send an appointment book/ address book to help the children see the whole year as one nice thing after another.

Grandparents Day

Is celebrated every year on the first Sunday after Labor Day. Send paper plates that the children can draw the outline of their hand and paste a photo for the grandparents.

Halloween and Harvest Festivals

Put together and send a kit for pumpkin or harvest decorating. As with any holiday that you can include a single-use camera with the money for photo developing.

Thanksgiving

Make the day better and easier for your children. Send a grocery store gift certificate or money to help pay for the Thanksgiving dinner. Make or buy a card to send.

Christmas

Make your own version of the story of the twelve days of Christmas or the story of the birth of Jesus. If your children can read, make a play out of it that each one can read aloud. Buy or make a card and some gifts to send.

Hanukkah

Make your own version of the story of the eight days of Hanukkah. If your children can read, make a play out of it that each one can read aloud. Buy or make a card to send. Send some gifts or gelt.

After You're Gone

The day-to-day care that you have demonstrated for your children will change, but need not and should not stop with your death. Provide for their financial security by financing their higher education and naming guardians for your children. Naming a guardian for your children does not guarantee where they will end up, but it can influence their lives in a positive way.

Seek Support

You may find the need for support. This is a healthy step and it is important that you know that you are not alone. You may not believe it at times, but there are people who care and are interested in your problem or concern. Many of these people have been through like experiences and are farther down the healing road than you are.

Others need your insight into what they are facing. Look for supportive people and services in your community. Take advantage of every resource.

Start a Support Group

If there are no support groups in your area or you have visited the existing groups and they don't fit your needs, you may consider starting a group. Preparation and knowledge are essential the success of your group. You may wish to become an affiliate to an existing national or regional group that addresses many the topics and concerns you want to cover. They will have a proven, workable model already in place with support and resources at your disposal.

It takes between six and twelve months to really get the group going. Members must understand this and be reasonable in their expectations of the group and themselves. A strong commitment to the group and one another is essential for the group's success. The work of getting a group going is demanding. The stakes are high and the rewards are great. You can start a group, but you can't keep it going alone. Each member shares responsibility for the growth of the group.

Help members to become more than "joiners" by involving them in the group. Members wanting to participate in leadership or organizational type roles should feel encouraged to do so. From the very beginning of the group, think shared leadership. This will help prevent leader and member burnout. It will also promote the life of the group.

You must decide who you want to reach and how you want to make that contact. Who else shares your interest or problem? Think of your group as a circle. Some people will naturally fall within your circle and you will want to include them. Others may not be in your target population, but may wish to be included. As an example you may want to form a Non-Custodial Mothers Group and find that there are several grandmothers that share your interests. Some may want to be included in your circle who are not perfect matches to the group and you will have to decide how if at all they are to be included. You might begin to make a list of other groups or persons who you believe share your interest or problem.

Once you have identified your target population you need to: locate them, decide how to get them involved with your group, and find others who can help you find your target population.

Create a mission statement. It will crystallize your vision of what you want your group to accomplish and where you want your group to go for you and explain your objectives to others. Don't overwhelm yourself or the group by attempting to do too many things. Outline the methods you intend to use to accomplish your objectives and priorities. It is helpful to create a steering committee to be responsible for this process. There are many important issues to consider including meeting format, leadership, officers, funding, for-profit, meeting place, where, when, how often and how long the meetings will be.

Run a few newspaper advertisements. Put flyers up at the churches and the grocery stores to see what kind of response you get. Evaluate your results and go for it.

ANYWAY

People are unreasonable, illogical, self-centered and mean spirited.
Love them anyway.
If you do good, you may be accused of ulterior motives.
Do good anyway.
If you are successful, you win false friends and true enemies.
Succeed anyway.
Others may say you don't measure up.
Love yourself anyway.
What you spend years building may be destroyed overnight.
Build anyway.
People you help may attack you.
Help people anyway.
Honesty, frankness and kindness make you vulnerable.
Be honest, frank and, above all, kind anyway.

- When the court is finished, you still have to deal with the other parent.

Stress Factors

A great number of factors unrelated to the custody issue can cause you stress. Attempt to identify other pressures you may be enduring. Some would include:

death of a loved spouse

change to a different line of work

divorce

increased arguments with your spouse

marital separation

jail term
mortgage you feel is too large
death of a close family member
foreclosure of loan or mortgage
personal injury or illness
change in responsibilities at work
marriage
son or daughter leaving home
fired from employment
trouble with in-laws
marital reconciliation
outstanding personal achievement
retirement
stay home spouse begins or stops work
change in the health of a family member
begin or end school
pregnancy
change in living conditions
gain of a new family member
change in residence or school
business readjustment
change in church or recreation
change in financial state
change in sleeping or social activities
death of a close friend
vacation or Christmas

Once aware of these additional elements, you will have more control. Because you will feel and exhibit more control to the professional, you will present a healthier picture for the evaluation.

Chapter 23: Cases / Decisions

We do not warrant the fitness of cites in this chapter for use in a court of law, and we expresses no legal opinions in providing the educational resources here. You are encouraged to collect relevant cases and give them to your attorney so he has better tools to work with in your case. You are encouraged to utilize this as a starting point in researching your case. Those who go to court with the facts are likely to do better than those who do not.

Since precedent is very important in a custody battle, you should explore your case for similarities to already settled cases. You must know how to find the law whether it is constitutional, statute, regulation, ordinance or case law.

The most efficient research tools are a service known as Shepard's Case Citations. The most efficient method of learning how to use these tools is listed in our Bibliography in category How To as "LEGAL RESEARCH, How To Find and Understand the Law." This method for finding the most recent case that may apply to your case is referred as "Shepardizing" your case.

These are a few of the studies, reports and decisions that came to our attention while writing this book. They are only here to indicate that you can find a decision or study to support any position you take.

It is becoming more common that the principal in a law suit finds decisions of which the attorney was unaware. Your attorney must work on several cases of old and new law at any one time spanning many areas of crises for their clients. You have only one interest. Your passion for the subject, desire for information and ability to compile information is very important. Some of the avenues you may explore are networking with other parents at support groups and parenting organizations. There are usually several very knowledgeable people in each group.

Computer bulletin boards (BBS) for men's, women's, parent's, step-parent's, children's, and grandparent's rights. These groups have huge data bases of case studies and legal opinion as well as thousands of hours of hands on experience. The more proper way to search for recent decisions.

DNA

Negative - Father is Still Father

Nevada Supreme Court February 03, 2000 Justices Bill Maupin, Miriam Shearing and Nancy Becker.

in a 3-0 ruling that a Clark County man cannot deny he is the father of a 9-year-old girl, even though genetic tests showed the child was fathered by another man. The decision ending the parental relationship between Gary William Stenlund and the girl now "would clearly be detrimental to the child's best interests."

"Gary is the only father that the child has ever known, and although Gary contends that he does not now consider the child his biological daughter, he testified that he is bonded to the child as if he was her biological daughter," the court ruled.

Nonetheless, Stenlund sued to end the parental relationship and requested that his former girlfriend, Michele Poliksza, reimburse him for the $250 per month child support he had paid. According to the court, Poliksza contacted Stenlund and told him she was pregnant not long after they broke up in 1990. Stenlund signed affidavits that he was the father and secured joint custody of the child. Then in 1997 he changed employment and was required to provide his health care provider the girl's medical history, including her blood type. When Poliksza refused to enroll the child in his medical plan, Stenlund became suspicious of his paternity. A genetic test in January 1998 concluded he was not the biological father. A family court threw out Stenlund's lawsuit. He then appealed to the Supreme Court. In the order, the Supreme Court said Stenlund failed to take opportunities available to him to determine the parentage of the child shortly after she was born. "Thus, we cannot conclude that Michele's misrepresentations, assuming they were fraudulent, prevented him from contesting paternity in the first instance," the court stated. Stenlund has held the child out as his biological daughter and she has become dependent on that established relationship, according to the court.

Paternity Suits May Never be Settled

In re Paternity of Chad M. G.

Wisconsin Court of Appeals. No.94-3119

The Wisconsin Court of Appeals held that a child can bring his own paternity suit seven years after his mother's suit was dismissed for failure to prosecute. The court joined similar recent rulings from California, Maine, Minnesota, Nevada, Ohio, Wyoming and the appellate courts in Illinois, Michigan and Wisconsin have recently held that paternity settlements violate the federal Equal Protection Clause because child support for legitimate children can be reopened at any time. Taken together, these decisions call into question whether a paternity case can ever be settled. The Wisconsin court acknowledged that its decision resulted in "a potentially serious problem," in that, "A father once acquitted of a paternity charge brought by the mother may be required to face a second paternity claim instituted by a child." To prevent this, the court recommended that whenever a paternity suit is filed, anyone who might have a similar claim should be added as a party. "Taking steps to join the unnamed parties who have an interest in the determination should be neither difficult nor time-consuming, and the benefits of fairness and judicial economy well support whatever additional expense may be required," The child's suit is not barred by res judicata, according to the Wisconsin court, because the interests of the mother and child in establishing paternity "are not sufficiently identical to place them in privity." "While a mother and child will often have a shared interest in pursuing a paternity action against the putative father, there is a significant likelihood that their interest will conflict," the court stated. "There are many instances when a child's interests will be significantly different from those of the mother," such as "the child's need to establish his or her right to support or inheritance, the child's desire to establish the father's right to seek custody or the child's interest in establishing a meaningful relationship with the father."

Can't Sue Wife for Lying About Paternity

Doe v. Doe Maryland Court of Appeals. No. 99 September Term, 1998.

Where a wife told her husband he was the father of their children – but he later discovered that he wasn't – he can't sue her for fraud and emotional distress, says Maryland's highest court in reversing an appellate court. The court said the husband was in effect bringing a "criminal conversation" claim.

That tort has been abolished by a majority of states on public policy grounds. "Regardless of whether [the husband] is suing [his wife] or her paramour, his asserted causes of action are based on the same conduct that formerly gave rise to a criminal conversation action, and he seeks damages for the same injuries recognized in a criminal conversation action. Consequently, the identical public policy considerations, which led to the abolition of criminal conversation, are applicable here." The court cited similar cases from California, Nebraska, New York and Wisconsin.

Non-Biological Father May Get Custody

In re Marriage of Gallagher

Iowa Supreme Court. Ninth State Appellate Court may hold where a husband didn't find out that he wasn't the father of his wife's child until after the couple had filed for divorce, he may get custody anyway, says the Iowa Supreme Court in a 5-4 decision. If a trial court decides if this decision would be in the child's best interests the father will get custody. The court cited similar rulings from Alabama, Kansas, Michigan, New York, Ohio, Oregon, Pennsylvania and Wisconsin. As part of a trend to apply equitable principles in custody cases, this husband can be declared an "equitable parent" if this would be in the child's best interests. The wife didn't reveal that the child was illegitimate until after a divorce had been filed and a "home study" had concluded that the husband should get custody.

"Where both the child and the husband reasonably believe they share a biological relationship, the bonding should and can be expected to develop to such a stage that its rupture might be devastating to both, Devastation to the child is of course the first and paramount concern because the best interest of the child is the dominating consideration in all child custody disputes." The dissenters said it was an "emotional reaction" and added that the court will now have to decide the status of an "equitable" parent in wrongful death cases, loss of consortium claims, inheritance disputes and many other types of cases.

Live-In Boyfriend Doesn't Get Custody

Van v. Zahorik

Michigan Supreme Court No. 111254. 7/799. In a 4-3 decision the court said that, "Even though a man lived with his girlfriend for five years and believed that he was her children's father, he is not entitled to custody as an "equitable parent," The man and his girlfriend lived together for five years and continued to date for several more years, but never got married. He claims his girlfriend told him he was the father of her two children and that he cared for and supported both of them, even after his relationship with her ended. Blood tests later revealed that he was not the biological father. The man argued that he was entitled to custody as an "equitable parent." But the court said that "the equitable parent doctrine applies, upon divorce, with respect to a child born or conceived during the marriage. The rationales for equitable parenthood are consistent with this state's public policy in favor of marriage and legitimacy. These justifications are lacking in the context of a cohabitation relationship." The court also rejected the argument that the girlfriend was "equitably estopped" from denying the man's paternity. The doctrine of equitable estoppel prevents "a husband from denying paternity of a child born during marriage, but of whom he is not the biological father...Application of equitable estoppel in the context of marriage is based in part on the presumption of legitimacy. This fact militates against extension of equitable estoppel outside the context of marriage and demonstrates that such an extension implicates the state's public policy in favor of marriage." The dissent complained that by "placing an artificial restriction on the definition of 'parent,' the majority absolves itself from addressing, as mandated by the legislature in the best interests of the child."

Live-In Girlfriend May Get Custody

North Carolina Court of Appeals. Ellison v. Ramos, No. COA97-1417.

Reversing a trial court, the North Carolina Court of Appeals says, a woman caring for her live-in boyfriend's daughter five days a week for five years, may be awarded custody.

The girlfriend acted in the manner of a parent, taking the diabetic daughter to the doctor and to school, providing in-home medical care, and buying her clothing. When the couple separated, the daughter stayed with the girlfriend. The father later returned and took her to Puerto Rico to live with her grandparents.

The girlfriend then sued for custody, claiming the grandparents couldn't properly care for her diabetes.

The father argued that (1) the girlfriend didn't have standing and (2) the Due Process Clause of the U.S. Constitution required that he get custody of his biological child. But the court said that

(1) "where a third party and a child have an established relationship in the nature of a parent-child relationship, the third party does have standing."

Further, "conduct inconsistent with the parent's constitutionally protected status, which need not rise to the statutory level warranting termination of parental rights, would result in the application of the 'best interests of the child' test...

(2) "The complaint alleges that the father placed his child in the custody of the grandparents who allegedly are not properly caring for the child's diabetes and that he has relinquished custody of his child to others, including the girlfriend, on several occasions.

Conclusion These allegations support a conclusion that the father has acted in a manner inconsistent with his protected status as a parent."

Infliction of Emotional Distress

Sheltra V. Smith, 392 A. 2d 431 (Vt. 1978). In this case, the non-custodial parent brought suit for damages alleging that defendant willfully, maliciously, intentionally, and outrageously inflicted extreme mental suffering and acute mental distress on the plaintiff, by willfully, maliciously, and outrageously rendering it impossible for any personal contact or other communication to take place between the plaintiff and child. Id. at 433. The Superior Court, Caledonia County, dismissed the complaint for failure to state the cause of action on which relief could be granted. The Supreme Court of Vermont, however, found that the plaintiff stated a prima facie case for outrageous conduct causing severe emotional distress.

Wrongful Inclusion in Witness Protection

Ruffalo v. Civiletti, 539 F. Supp. 949 (W.D. Mo. 1982), the court found that although the father had physical custody of the child, the mother had legal custody.

The Judge ruled that the government violated the mother's rights by admitting the child to the witness protection program and preventing the mother from communicating with the child for over four years.

A Study of Families after Divorce

D.A. Luepnitz. Maternal, paternal and joint custody.

Doctoral thesis 1980. State University of New York at Buffalo. UMI No. 80-27618

A Study of Families After Divorce. Luepnitz studied single parent custody and joint custody. Most single parent children were dissatisfied with the amount of visitation they had, whereas the children of joint custody arrangements seemed reasonably happy with their exposure to both their parents. The quality of the parent-child relationship was determined to be better for joint custody. (The NCP-child relationship is described as more like an aunt or uncle - child relationship.)

Joint Custody v. Sole Custody

Effects On Child Development S.A. Nunan. Doctoral thesis 1980. Joint Custody Versus Single Custody. California School of Professional Psychology, Berkley, UMI No. 81-10142

Nunan compared twenty joint custody children (pages 7-11) with twenty age-matched children in sole maternal custody. All families studied were at least two years after separation or divorce.

Joint custody children were found to have higher ego strengths, superego strengths and self-esteem than sole custody children. Joint custody children were also found to be less excitable and less impatient than their sole custody counterparts.

For children under four at the time of separation the differences were very small.

Effects of Custody Arrangements on Children

B Welsh-Osga. Doctoral thesis 1981

Effects Of Custody Arrangements. University of South Dakota. UMI No. 82-6914 Welsh-Osga compared children in intact families with joint custody and single custody families. Ages range four and one-half to ten years old. Children from

joint custody were found to be more satisfied with the time spent with both parents. Parents in joint custody were found to be more involved with their children. (Joint custody parents found to be less overburdened by parenting responsibilities than sole custody parents.)
Children from all four groups (intact families, sole maternal, sole paternal, joint custody) were found to be equally well adjusted by their various standardized measures.

Domestic Violence Report

Domestic Violence Report. NJC-143498 Murder in Families. Available from Department of Justice, Bureau of Justice Statistics, W.A., DC 20531

Good-Enough Parenting

Good-enough Parenting. There is substantial research on adequate or "good-enough" parenting: William F. Hodges, Interventions for Children of Divorce (1968)

Attorney Problems

Hatch (1985) 169 CA3d 1213

It is an abuse of discretion for the trial court to deny a *pendente lite* award of attorney fees or to defer the decision until time of trial without considering need and ability.

Malak (1986) 182 CA3d 1018

Where jurisdiction is declined by reason of petitioner's conduct, upon dismissing the petition, the court may charge the petitioner with attorney fees.

Newport (1984) 154 CA3d 915

A waiver of spousal support does not necessarily include a waiver of attorney fees. Fees and costs can be assessed where the requisite need and ability is established.

Smith v. Smith (1970) 4 CA3d 446

This case deals with an award of attorney fees pending an appeal.

Sullivan (1984) 37 C3d 762

This case deals with an award of attorney fees that may be based upon the actual income of a party or from a determination of their ability to earn.

Work-Product Privilege

Each state has their own rule. This is an example of what you can expect.

Rule 1.280 of the Florida Rules of Civil Procedure codified what is commonly referred to as the "work-product privilege." Generally speaking, documents prepared in anticipation of litigation be discovered by an opposing side "...only upon a showing that the party seeking the discovery has a need for the materials in the preparation of the case and is unable, without undue hardship, to obtain the substantial equivalent of the materials by other means." Rule 1.280(b)(3). Normally any work done in anticipation of litigation, or in furtherance of litigation, is protected unless the party seeking the discovery is able to establish that there is no other reasonable way of obtaining the factual information and that the information is necessary.

If a party seeks to raise the work-product privilege as a basis for not divulging information or turning over documents, the party must specifically identify the documents, which are to be protected and object on the basis of work product. Nationwide Mutual Fire Ins. Co. v. Harmon, 587 So.2d 192 (Fla. 4th DCA 1991). If the specific documents are not identified, and if a specific objection is not raised for each, then the work product privilege is not properly presented and the Court will not be able to rule in favor of the party attempting to protect the work product.

If the discovering party is attempting to establish that there is a need for the documents or materials being sought and that they cannot be duplicated without undue hardship, it would be best for the discovering party to file an affidavit establishing the factual basis as to why the documents or materials are necessary and why it would be undue hardship in attempting to find a substantial equivalent to the materials by other means. North Broward Hospital District v. Button, 592 So.2d 367, 368 (Fla. 4th DCA 1992).

The work-product privilege may encompass witness statements, photographs of relevant scenes or items, sketches, drawings, opinions and theories. The work-product privilege does not protect the party's and opposing party's statement. Rule 1.280(b)(3) specifically allows a party to obtain a copy of a statement concerning the action or a subsequent matter previously made by that party. A witness who has had their statement taken may also request a copy of the statement without having to show need for the documents or undue hardship to obtain the substantial equivalent by other means. Id.

If the documents being sought were not prepared in anticipation of litigation, then the work-product privilege does not apply. Cotton States Mutual Ins. Co. v. Turtle Reef Associates, Inc., 444 So.2d 595 (Fla. 4th DCA 1984).

Even if it appears likely that there will be litigation, the work-product privilege will not attach unless the materials and documents were prepared in anticipation of litigation. Id. Nevertheless, a strong argument may be made in cases where it is obvious that litigation will arise, that any investigation done should be covered under the work-product privilege referred to in Rule 1.280(b)(3) of the Florida Rules of Civil Procedure.

If a party intends on presenting any of the "work-product documents" at trial, then the privilege is non-existent and the documents must be produced to the other side upon request. Once a party intends to use documents as evidence in a case, it becomes discoverable. Florida Power & Light Co. v. Limeburner, 390 So.2d 133 (Fla. 4th DCA 1980).

The landmark case on work product in Florida is Surf Drugs, Inc. v. Vermette, 236 So.2d 108 (Fla. 1970). In that case, the Florida Supreme Court outlines what is protected and what is not. The names and addresses of persons having relevant information concerning a particular case and a request for the general statement about what those persons know is deemed not protected under the work-product privilege. Id.

If the opposing side is attempting to discover work product that includes opinions or attorney's thought processes and theories, then those documents are not discoverable, even if the discovering side shows a need for the documents and undue hardship in seeking the substantial equivalent. Dodson v. Persell, 390 So.2d 704 (Fla. 1980). Rule 1.280(b)(3) specifically states that a court shall "in ordering discovery of the materials when the required showing has been made, the court shall protect against disclosure of the mental impressions, conclusions, opinions or legal theories of an attorney or other representative of a party concerning the litigation." Thus, even if there is a showing by an opposing side of the need for the factual information that would constitute work-product discovery and an inability to find a substantial equivalent without undue hardship, the court will protect those documents containing the mental impressions, conclusions, opinions or legal theories of the attorney. Id. Dodson v. Persell, 390 So.2d at 707. If an attorney inadvertently discloses work-product material, chances are that the work-product privilege has been waived. St.

Paul Fire & Marine Ins. Co. v. Welsh, 501 So.2d 54 (Fla. 4th DCA 1987). Nevertheless, if the work-product privilege is not raised initially, but is raised before the documents are turned over, followed by subsequent raising of the work-product privilege, the failure to raise the work-product privilege initially will not require the disclosure of the information. Truly Nolen Exterminating, Inc. v. Thomasson, 554 So.2d 5 (Fla. 3d DCA 1989). It is extremely important to protect the work-product privilege at the first available opportunity so that there is no question that the documents are not intended to be produced.

Documents Produced by Mistake

Amgen, Inc. v. Hoechst Marion Roussel, Inc.

January 18, 2000 U.S. District Court for the District of Massachusetts,

A law firm reviewed seventy thousand pages of materials for privilege and set aside three thousand eight hundred pages to be withheld. A paralegal mistakenly included those sent to opposing counsel. They asked the opposing firm to return the documents stating that the documents were still protected because it didn't intentionally wave the privilege.

The court said that whether the privilege had been waived depended on several factors, including "the reasonableness of the precautions taken to prevent inadvertent disclosure; the amount of time it took the producing party to recognize tis error and the extent of the inadvertent disclosure.

Although the court recognized that the firm did make some effort to prevent inadvertent disclosure, the court felt easily accomplished additional precautions were obviously needed. For example, particularly because the firm's attorneys out-sourced the copying of the documents a knowledgeable attorney or legal assistant should have quickly reviewed the performance of the vendor to ensure that the proper documents were copied.

In addition, the sheer magnitude of the disclosure far exceeds any inadvertent disclosure the court has encountered in previous cases and it took five days to recognize its error.
Then only after the opposing counsel drew its attention to the privileged documents.

Use and Misuse of Psychological Testing

Use and Misuse of Psychological Testing. In Child Custody Evaluations by David M. Brodzinsky, Copyright 1993 by the American Psychological Association, Inc. Professional Psychological: Research and Practice 1993. Vol. 24, No. 2,213-219

Tender Years Doctrine

This doctrine provides that custody of children of tender years (five and under) had to be awarded to the mother when the parents divorce. This doctrine has been rejected in most states. It is sometimes used as the deciding point when both parents request custody and are fit to have custody.

Anatomical Dolls Don't Meet Frye Test

US v. Gillespie

9th Circuit U.S.C.A.(1993). Anatomical Dolls fail to satisfy Frye Test for scientific reliability.

Override of Right to Travel

City of Spokane v. Julie Anne Por

[716 P.2d 945, 43 Wash. App. 273] [1986.WA.116] The interest of public safety overrides right to travel when license holder operates vehicle in unsafe manner.

Pro Se

Pro Se Not Held Same As Licensed

Attorney

Haines v. Kerner

972.SCT.7 Pro se litigant shall not be held to same standards of expertise as licensed attorney, and has right to offer proof of claim.

Non-Lawyers May Assist

NAACP v. Button

Members of groups who are competent non-lawyers may assist other members of the group achieve the goals of the group in court without being charged with "unauthorized practice of law."

Recording Telephone Conversations

Federal Wiretap Law

Federal Law Permits Recording. The 1986 Electronic Communications Privacy Act makes it illegal to intentionally intercept cellular phone calls, and to possess or divulge the contents of any intercepted conversation. Under federal law it may be permissible for a person to record his/her conversations with others and then use the recording as evidence.

Federal law allows recording when the person making the recording is a party to the conversation, or has consented to the recording (so long as the recording is not for the purpose of committing any criminal or tortuous act). Some states have laws, which differ from the federal approach. For example, in the States of California and Oregon it is a crime to secretly record a conversation (unless all parties to the conversation consent to its recording).

State of Arizona v. Stanley

597 P.2d 998, 123 Ariz.95 (Ariz. App. 1979) Under the Fourth Amendment, there is no invasion of privacy in monitoring, recording, and introduction into evidence a telephone conversation where one party has given prior consent to the interception. Therefore, there is no violation of statute governing unauthorized publication or use of communications or of a statute governing interception of wire or oral communication if one of the parties to the communication has given prior consent .

Absolute Right to Tape Record Trial

Forsythe v. Family Court Commissioner

Dane County [1986.WI.157] [25 Wis. 2d 572, 373 N.W.2d 85 (Ct. App. 1985)].

A pro se litigant has absolute right to tape record trial proceedings.

No Need for Ex Parte Wiretap Order

State of Arizona v. Johnson

592 P. 2d 379, 121 Ariz. 545 (Ariz. App 357, application den. 91.S.Ct 1669,402 U.S.971, 29 L.Ed. 2d 135; cert. den. 91 S.Ct. 2255, 403 U.S. 936, 29 L.Ed.2d 717

It is illegal to wiretap or record another persons phone without a court order. It is not illegal to record your own phone calls. You may only record the phone calls of other persons if one of the other people gives you consent, even if all the other parties to the conversation object.

Calls Between Your Children and the Other Parent

Williams v. Williams 1998

Michigan Court of Appeals. Custodial Parent Tape-Records Child's Phone Call With Non-custodial Parent and is Sued Under Federal Law. A custodial father tape-recorded a phone call between his five-year-old child and his non-custodial mother, the mom sued him under both federal and state wiretapping laws, says the Michigan Court of Appeals in reversing a summary judgment. The Federal wiretapping statutes make it illegal to tape a phone call unless one of the parties consents. The father's argument was that because he was the custodial parent, he could consent on his son's behalf and was a "vicarious participant" in the conversations. The court said that there was no "vicarious consent" exception in either statute, and said,. "We find no indication that the legislature intended to create an exception for a custodial parent of a minor child to consent on the child's behalf to interceptions of conversations between the child and a third party," Even though courts in Alabama, Kentucky, Mississippi and Utah have held to the opposite opinion it is a dangerous practice.

Rule 52 Federal Rules

Findings by the Court; Judgment on Partial Findings (a) Effect pursuant to Rule 58, of the Federal Rules of Civil Procedure and in granting or refusing interlocutory injunctions Requests for findings are not necessary for purposes of review. Findings of fact, whether based on oral or documentary evidence, shall not be set aside unless clearly erroneous.

Due regard shall be given to the opportunity of the trial court to judge of the credibility of the witnesses. The findings of a master, to the extent that the court adopts them, shall be considered as the findings of the court. It will be sufficient if the findings of fact and conclusions of law are stated orally and recorded in open court following the close of the evidence or appear in an opinion or memorandum of decision filed by the court. Findings of fact and conclusions of law are unnecessary on decisions of motions under Rule 12 or 56 or any other motion except as provided in subdivision (c) of this rule. Amendment. Upon motion of a party made not later than 10 days after entry of judgment the court may amend its findings or make additional findings and may amend the judgment accordingly.

The motion may be made with a motion for a new trial pursuant to Rule 59. When findings of fact are made in actions tried by the court without a jury, the question of the sufficiency of the evidence to support the findings may thereafter be raised whether or not the party raising the question has made in the district court an objection to such findings or has made a motion to amend them or a motion for judgment.

Judgment on Partial Findings

If during a trial without a jury a party has been fully heard with respect to an issue and the court finds against the party on that issue, the court may enter judgment as a matter of law against that party on any claim, counterclaim, cross-claim or third-party claim that cannot under the controlling law be maintained or defeated without a favorable finding on that issue, or the court may decline to render any judgment until the close of all the evidence. Such a judgment shall be supported by findings of fact and conclusions of law as required by subdivision (a) of this rule.

Real Advantage Test

Removal (of a minor child) is the legal proceeding, usually brought by complaint or petition, by the custodial parent to remove (move) the minor child(ren) from the state. The recent trend is to allow the custodial parent more flexibility in moving out of state when there are "real advantages" (known as the "real advantage" test) to the custodial parent.

The theory is what's good for the parent is good for the child and is in the child's best interest. Parents' rights groups have lobbied against this trend. Not all states use the "real advantage" test. We have come full circle from Victorian times when children were the personal property of their fathers. Now children are the personal property of the custodial parent.

Many courts are unlikely to allow removal if the child has a close relationship with the non-custodial parent.

Surprise Witness May Not Testify

Binger v. King Pest Control

401So.2d 1310 (Fla. 1981). The Supreme Court of Florida held that a trial court may exclude the testimony of a witness whose name has not been disclosed in accordance with the trial court's pre-trial order requiring disclosure of all witnesses when the opposing party is prejudiced, the opposing party does not have independent knowledge of the existence of the undisclosed witness, testimony by the undisclosed witness may disrupt the orderly and efficient trial of the case, and no diligence has been shown in attempting to find the witness prior to the actual trial of the case. It no longer matters that the undisclosed witnesses are being used simply for impeachment or rebuttal purposes at trial. "All witnesses names should be exchanged before trial, including rebuttal and impeachment witnesses when the pre-trial order so requires.

Appeal Modification Change of Circumstances

Ellis v. Ellis Western District

Missouri Court of Appeals from an order modifying a dissolution decree trans-fearing custody of a minor child, Trinity Ellis, from her mother, appellant Reba Ellis, to her father, respondent Randy Ellis. Appellant alleges that the trial court erred in removing the minor child Trinity Ellis from appellant's custody because: (1) the removal was not in the best interests of the child; (2) substantial evidence established that the father was not a fit custodian; (3) the modified custody decree was a punitive measure taken against appellant; and (4) the court relied on evidence violating § 452.410, RSMO 1986. Appellant also argues that the trial court erred by ordering her to pay the fees of the guardian-ad-litem and court appointed psychologist as this would constitute an unlawful award of child support to a third party. Finally, that the evidence established her inability to pay these fees making it impossible to comply with the order of the court.

Shared Parenting

Leis v. Leis

Court of Appeals of Ohio, Second Appellate District, Case No. 96-CA-20, 06/20/1997 Ohio App. LEXIS 2638, Court of Appeals, Second Appellate District. The court held that "netting out" the child support obligations of the two parents in a shared parenting situation (deducting the child support obligation of the parent with the lower amount on line 24 of the worksheet from the amount of the obligation of the parent with the higher obligation) was required to avoid injustice and to avoid statutory inconsistency. Taken literally, the language of R.C. 3223.215(E) would entail that neither parent in a shared parenting situation could be assessed any child support obligation.

Clearly, that is not the intent of the legislation. Since both parents are residential and custodial parents, either the law must presume that both parents expend these funds directly on the children (and, so, no child support order is required) or that neither does (and, so, both parents are subject to such an order). Since the first is contrary to the intent of the legislature, the second is required. That means that there must either be two orders with child support funds going back and forth or that the lesser amount on line 24(A or B) must be deducted from the greater amount on line 24(A or B) and the person with the larger amount is required to pay the other the difference between these two amounts. Time with the children can then be used (as the Pauly decision says) to adjust this amount if it is unfair and contrary to the interests of the children. This is a

VERY good decision for obligors in shared parenting situations. However, the reasoning can be employed in arguing with CSEA and with courts in other Ohio districts.

Luke v. Luke

Court of Appeals of Ohio, Eleventh Appellate District, Case No. 97-L-044, 02/20/1998 Ohio App. LEXIS 647

This decision, like the Leis decision by the Second District Court of Appeals, concludes that there is no basis for discriminating between the two parents in a shared parenting plan. Since it is unreasonable for the court to conclude that there is never a child support obligation that can be ordered, both parent's obligations must be employed.
Instead of using the language of "netting out", the Luke court calls this an "offset". It clearly distinguishes an offset from an "automatic credit", which the Supreme Court did not allow in Pauly. The outcome is the same as the Leis outcome and the language is very favorable to the idea behind of shared parenting. This is a very recent and extremely important decision for Ohio parents involved in shared parenting situation.

Commonwealth v. Carter

Worcester Jury Session, No. 9566CR002.

In this case, the defendant was under an order not to contact the complainant or any of her children, and to stay at least one hundred yards away from them. The defendant was convicted of violating that order on evidence that he had visited the school that one child attended without permission of the court. The defendant filed a motion for stay of sentencing pending appeal, arguing that the violation of the minimum distance requirement in the order was not within the statutory meaning of contact, which, he argued connotes either the physical act of touching or the state of being in communication. In denying the defendant's motion for a stay, the District Court ruled, following Gordon, that the term contact must include minimum distance requirements as the protective means necessary to shield a victim from contact and potential abuse. In this case, the defendant's conduct in visiting the school threatened the child's zone of safety.

Doubtfire Clause or First Right of Refusal

It is the intention of the courts to facilitate and maintain the contact between children and their biological parents whenever that contact will not be harmful for the children. In many cases, with all other things being equal, the parent that can spend the most time with the children is granted custody. Once custody is granted on this basis it remains a key ingredient to the circumstances in which the children live. If for some reason the custodial parent is unable to care for the children the non-custodial parent should have first right to refuse the available parenting time. The biological parent's rights take president over grandparents, step-parents, siblings and child care professionals. Documentation of a substantial permanent shift in the parenting time from a custodial parent to a non-custodial parent or auxiliary caregiver can constitute a change of circumstances that could give the court reason to consider a change of custody.

Day Care - A Dangerous Experiment?

Wall Street Journal Europe Wednesday 14 January 1998 "Social science confirms that children raised in day-care centers and similar institutions are often emotionally maladjusted and mentally impaired."

Many young families today depend on day care. Single fathers may rely on it even more than single mothers do. But is it good for our children? In this article by Andrew P. Thomas, The Wall Street Journal takes a critical look at the effects of day care on young children. He warns against "the growing practice of abandoning infants to paid strangers."

Even as long as twenty years ago, the early studies of day care were not encouraging: "A 1974 study in the journal Developmental Psychology reported that children who entered day care before their first birthday were 'significantly more aggressive' and more physically and verbally abusive of adults than other children."

Several more recent studies are quoted, which show that children '...who had spent more time in day care suffered proportionately greater ill effects, regardless of the quality of the care' the most extreme case being the kibbutz-raised children of Israel:

"In 1995, the National Institute of Mental Health published a joint US-Israeli study that found children raised in Israeli communes known as kibbutzim, who received 24-hour day care, were at significantly greater risk of developing schizophrenia and other serious mental disorders."

Criticizing American parents for "warehousing infants so that they might accumulate ever-nicer possessions," the article calls on the US Congress to "reject Mr. Clinton's ill-considered plan to subsidize day care."

Move Away

Parent Considered, Joint Custody Move

McGuinness v. McGuiness

NV. 1991 A mother who had joint custody of her son wanted to get primary custody and relocate to another state, the "best interests" of the child can't be determined without considering the mother's interests as well, says the Nevada Supreme Court in reversing a trial court. The mother wanted to move closer to her family after her mother died. She planned to live in her mother's house rent-free while she attended college and got her teaching license. The trial court refused her request, finding that continued joint custody was in the son's best interests. But the Nevada Supreme Court said the lower court should have considered how the move would benefit the mother. "[T]he best interest of the child can never be determined in a vacuum without considering the other members of the family. The circumstances and well-being of the parents are inextricably entwined with the best interest of the child.... "If the parents' needs are not considered, motions to relocate would almost never be granted, because close physical proximity to good parents is almost always in the child's best interest."

Custodial Mother Allowed to Move

A mother with custody of her teenage daughter can relocate to another state if this is in the "best interests of the child," says the North Dakota Supreme Court in allowing the move.

However, the court said the burden of proof was on the custodial parent to show the move should be allowed. This is contrary to the trend in most states, which place the burden of proof on the non-custodial parent. (See 96 LWUSA 889; Search Words for LWUSA Archives: Folks and Wallops.) In the North Dakota case, the father argued that regular contact with him was in his daughter's best interests. But the court said that a "visitation schedule, which provides less frequent, but extended, visitation periods will preserve a non-custodial parent's right to foster and develop a relationship with the child." Further, it held that "the preference of a mature child is particularly significant in determining the child's best interests," noting that the daughter "unconditionally stated her preference is to live with her mother."

Move Away Affects Visitation

Marriage of Burgess (1995) 32 C4th 637
Marriage of Gigliotti (1995) 33C4th 518, 39 Cal. Rptr. 2d 367
Marriage of Selzer (1994) 29 CA4th 637
Marriage of Rosson (1986) 178 CA3d 1094
Marriage of Fingert (1990) 221 CA3d 1575
Marriage of Carlson (1991) 226 CA3d 1330
Marriage of McGinnis (1992) 7 CA4th 473
Marriage of Roe (1993) 18 CA4th 1483
Marriage of Battenburg (1994) 28 CA4th 1338

Parent Left - Not Pay All Costs

Willey v. Willey

21 Fla. L. Weekly (Fla. 4th DCA Dec. 4, 1996). The appellate court found that ordering the father to pay all the travel expenses was "financially onerous." Moreover, the court said, "This one-sided imposition of a significant economic burden on the father may have the practical effect of defeating the limited visitation ordered (abbreviated)" The court reversed for reconsideration of a more liberal visitation schedule and more equitable sharing of transportation costs. A trial court in Palm Beach County abused its discretion when, in approving a custodial mother's request to move away to Chicago, it gave the father less visitation than even the mother offered and made the father bear all the visitation transportation costs.

Burgess v. Burgess

The infamous decision permitted a joint custodial mother to move out of state.

Move Away with Foreign Jurisdiction

In re Stephanie M. (1994) 7 CA4th 295 [see also 7 CA4th 724a]

Zenide v. Superior Court (Ignaccolo) (1994) 22 C4th 1287

Tort - Interference/Relationship

Hall v. Hall-Stradley

Denver (Colorado Dist.Ct.) No. 84-CV-2865, 11/26/86 (was under appeal) A non-custodial father brought suit against the custodial mother, her husband and her attorney for interference with the family relationship and for infliction of distress. The first count of the complaint, interference with the family relationship, was dismissed. The court awarded the non-custodial father damages of three hundred and seventy thousand dollars however, for interference with his right to visit with his children, which resulted from their being removed from the country without his knowledge for approximately two years. Such severe damage awards are indicative of the court's efforts to deter a custodial parent from this type of behavior.

State of Arizona 13-1302

June 1, 1994 Allows for prosecution of those who interfere with visitation. Interference With Visitation. NCP who are denied visitation/access in Arizona are required to present a copy of their custody/visitation order and request that a report be filed, which is forwarded to the city prosecutor for prosecution. State law 13-1302 gives up to five hundred dollars fine and one year in jail.

Custodial Interference Damages

Kajtazi v. Kajtazi

United States District Court, Eastern District New York., 488 F. Supp. 15 [August 29, 1978]. - Federal court awarded damages for custodial interference and kidnapping.

Ruffalo v. United States

590 F. Supp. 706 (W.D. Mo. 1984). Involved a mother who sued the U.S. government for interference with her visitation rights after the U.S. government took her child into the witness protection program along with the father. The mother asserted a claim in excess of one million dollars for federal depravation of her right to custody of her child, denial of due process and interference with her parental role. The court granted the mother damages of only seventeen thousand dollars for loss of communication and visitation with the child, but it should be noted that the amount of the damage award in this case was small because the violation was found not to be of a lasting nature.

Parents Who Smoke

Badeau v. Badeau

LaPlace, LA, 1989 An appeals court upheld a lower court decision reducing a father's visitation rights because his smoking aggravated his child's bronchial problem. {WSJ, 10/18/90}

Wilke v. Wilke

MO1989 Custody awarded to smoke-free mother.

Roofeh v. Roofeh

NY Family Ct., Nassau County, Mineola 1988 Mr. Jahanshah Roofeh's attorney, Stephen W. Schlissel of Mineola, NY's Ruskin, Schlissel, Moscou, Evans & Faltischek, P.C.; Ms. Elizabeth Roofeh represented by Joel R. Brandes of Garden City, NY. Nassau County Judge Ralph Diamond in Mineola issued order forbidding Elizabeth to smoke in front of her husband and three children. Ms. Roofeh was also directed to confine her cigarette smoking to a small television room in the couple's Kings Point mansion. Neal Shayne, dean of the Academy of Law for the Nassau County Bar Association, said he believes the order was legal because it's not Mrs. Roofeh's rights, but the rights of her family that were violated by her smoking.

Reeves v. Reeves, Pricilla Bullock Reeve

TN 1988 Complained about a judge's order restricting her from smoking in confined areas around her four-year-old son. Christopher Reeves is father of the child. Fourth Circuit Court Judge Bill Swann made the ruling on Friday about Bullock's smoking practices and said his decision was based on the child's welfare. Swann granted a request by the ex-husband's lawyer to prohibit her from smoking around the child in a confined environment, such as the home or in an automobile. Bullock plans to pursue legal action to reverse the ruling.

Pizzitola v. Pizzitola

TX 1988 Custody awarded to smokefree father.

Potter v. Potter

MI Ct. of App. 1998 An unpublished Michigan Court of Appeals decision involved a custody battle over a minor child who had respiratory problems. The ex-husband said the mother's smoking was harming the child's health. The circuit judge placed the child with the mother. The appeals panel affirmed the trial court because the father failed to present medical evidence on the smoking issue.

Satalino v. Satalino

NY Sup. Ct., Nassau City., No. 11440-86, Oct. 10, 1999 The New York Supreme Court said that the health risk posed by secondhand smoke in the home was a factor that 'must be considered, as would alcohol consumption for example, when viewing the suitability of a household environment in which a child is to be placed.' Nassau County decision pits Catherine Satalino, a one-pack-a-day smoker, against her husband, Martin, who kicked the habit. Mr. Satalino had argued that giving custody of their six-year-old son to his wife would expose the child to the dangers of secondhand tobacco smoke. Note: NY state Supreme Court Justice John F. O'Shaughnessy of Mineola wrote that smoking is 'one factor among the many that must be considered, as would alcohol consumption for example, when viewing the suitability of a household environment in which a child is to be placed.' Custody awarded to Mrs. Satalino, however, saying that other factors, including Mr. Satalino's prior drug addiction and continuing recovery, outweighed the smoking issue.

Masone v. Tanner

Sacramento, CA, October 13, 1993 A county judge granted a nonsmoking father's request to remove an 8-year-old girl from the custody of her mother, his ex-wife. The child had only 43 percent of her breathing capacity because the mother continued to violate an earlier court order, obtained five years ago, that she not smoke around or near the child. The smoking continued until the child had an asthma attack and a doctor stated that she would end-up in an emergency room if her exposure to tobacco smoke continued. The child was placed in the custody of her grandmother. Attorney Sharon Huddle represented the father.

De Beni Souza v. Kallweit

Sacramento, CA, August 1990 Judge David Stirling ordered a woman (Anna Maria de Beni Souza) not to smoke in front of her five-year-old son; judge issued the ruling at the request of the boy's father, Manfred Kallweit, who had complained of health risks associated with inhaling secondhand smoke. Woman didn't appeal; custody case is pending. Lawyer for father was Charles M. Asbury, Sacramento.

Robert Strathmann v. Linda Foster

Ct. of Common Pleas of Erie County, PA 1991 Judge Stephanie Domitrovich ordered that there will be no smoking in the natural father's home for at least 48 hours before children are to visit. The natural father shall provide a smokefree environment for all of the children while he is exercising his partial custody with them. Natural mother shall also provide a smokefree environment.

Nocera v. Nocera

Cir. Ct. of Kalamazoo, MI, File No. B 89-2922 DM, May 29, 1991 Judge John F. Foley ordered, pending further proceedings, that the Plaintiff, Sharon Nocera, shall not allow the minor children of the parties Nicolas Nocera and Lauren Nocera, to be exposed to cigarette smoke until further Order of this Court.

Brett Lee Bryant/Dept of S.S. v. Wakely

MI Ct. of App., No. 131708, June 13, 1991 The Michigan Court of Appeals upheld the decision of a Civil Court that placement with a grandmother who smoked would not be in a child's best interest. The child had serious respiratory problems and it was highly recommended that he live in close proximity to a hospital in Traverse City (where his grandparents were unable to relocate) and that he should live in a smokefree environment.

Lamacchia v. Lamacchia (O'Brien) (Probate Ct. of Middlesex County, MA Dec. 19, 1991)

Temporary order that neither parent will smoke in front of their three-year-old son who suffers from lung ailments.

Sulva v. Isaacson

IL 1992 Judge William Ward signed an order barring Isaacson from smoking when he visited his son. It was the first time in Illinois history that such an order has been signed. Alex, the son, suffers from bronchitis and it was alleged that his father's smoking might aggravate his condition. The order means that to have a smoke Isaacson will either have to abstain or leave his North Side apartment every other weekend from about 9:30 a.m. Saturday to 6:30 p.m. Sunday, as well as for about a month during the summer when he has Alex for visitation. One smoke in front of his son could lead to a contempt of court finding and a jail sentence of up to 6 months.

Montufar v. Navot

Sup. Ct., Fam. Div., Camden, NJ, Docket No. FM 04-0021-8789, Jul 23, 1993 Judge Orlando granted post-judgment relief to a nonsmoking father whose child, aged ten, was exposed to tobacco smoke by his mother and maternal relatives and suffered adverse effects. The order stated that the custodial mother shall provide the child a complete smokefree environment in the home in which he resides. There must be no smoking by other residents or by visitors. All smoking must be carried on outdoors. The custodial mother is also under obligation to take all reasonable steps in assuring that the child is not unduly exposed to ETS. The custodial mother must remove the child from any situation or location where he is exposed to passive smoke. As far as the grandparents are concerned (they live close to the mother) the order compels the mother to remove the child from the grandparents' presence if they are smoking. There is to be no smoking in any vehicle in which the child is a passenger.

Mitchell v. Mitchell

Ct. of App. of TN, Middle Section Nashville, Appeal No. 01-A-01-9012-CV-00442, April 26, 1991 In this divorce case, the court refused to return custody of an asthmatic child to the mother although the mother had joined a smoking cessation program.

The father had been awarded custody because the child suffered from asthma and, despite the pediatrician's advice, the mother and grandmother had not stopped smoking. The trial judge had found that the failure of the mother and grandmother to stop smoking was strong evidence of lack of proper concern for the welfare of the child. A belated cessation of smoking might evidence desire for the custody of the child rather than concern for the welfare of the child.

Second-Hand Smoke and Children

Second-Hand Smoke Increases Prevalence Of Asthma In Kids BETHESDA, MD -- February 11, 1998

A study sponsored by the National Institutes of Health points to second-hand smoke as an important factor in the increasing prevalence of asthma in children. Peter Gergen and colleagues from the Center for Primary Care, the Agency for Health Care Policy and Research, Rockville, the Klemm Analysis Group, Inc., the National Center for Health Care Statistics, the Centers for Disease Control and Prevention and the National Institute of Child Health and Human Development, report on the study in the Pediatrics Electronic Pages. Researchers evaluated children two months through five years of age from 1988 to 1994. Parents were asked to report on household smoking or maternal smoking during pregnancy and on wheezing, cough, upper respiratory infection, or pneumonia in the previous twelve months and chronic bronchitis or physician-diagnosed asthma at any time. They found that about thirty-eight percent of kids were being exposed to second-hand smoke at home, whereas more than twenty-three percent were exposed by maternal smoking during pregnancy. Kids between two months and two years of age had increased prevalence of chronic bronchitis and wheezing.

When they evaluated the effects of second-hand smoke on kids between two months and five years, they found an increased prevalence of asthma. Although they found no statistically-significant increase in the prevalence of upper respiratory infection, pneumonia or cough and in the severity of asthma in children exposed to second-hand smoke, the researchers found that this group of kids did appear to have an increased prevalence of asthma. "These findings reinforce the need to reduce the exposure of young children to environmental tobacco smoke,"

Second-Hand Smoke Delays Teeth

CHICAGO--Children exposed to tobacco smoke from their parents' cigarettes experience delays in the formation of their permanent teeth, according to dental researchers. In a study published in a recent issue of the Journal of Clinical Pediatric

Dentistry, researchers found that exposing a child to tobacco smoke can delay the development of the child's permanent teeth by an average of four months.

As a result, the normal age for eruption of a child's permanent teeth--between 3 to 6 years--can be delayed. The most significant delays in dental development were observed when both parents smoked, and the least delays occurred when only the mother smoked. Surprisingly, children exposed to smoke only from their fathers showed a high incidence of tooth formation delays.

"This is another study that confirms the damage caused by second hand smoke," says Ingrid Schroetter, DDS, a general dentist who practices in Chicago's Loop. "If parents must smoke cigarettes, they should do so in a well-ventilated, separate area from children. Both parents--especially the mother--should never smoke during pregnancy."

Use of tobacco products by parents sets a bad example for children, says Dr. Schroetter. "Children who smoke are more likely to turn into lifelong smokers," she says. According to the U.S. Centers for Disease Control and Prevention, about 40,000 Americans were diagnosed with oral cancer in 1995, and about 9,000 died from the disease.

"Tobacco products can leave a trail of tell-tale signs in the mouth, including bad breath, gingivitis, tooth loss and cancer," says Dr. Schroetter. "Dentists may be among the first health care professionals to notice that a child or teenager is a smoker or dipper, and can talk to the parent about the oral hazards of tobacco." Dr. Schroetter says she can always tell when she has a patient who smokes or dips. "It's not a pretty picture," she says. "Teeth are stained yellow, the roof of the mouth is white from the heat of cigarette smoke, and gums are inflamed." Dr. Schroetter suggests that all smokers should be considerate of non-smokers, keeping in mind that the second-hand smoke they create can be a detriment to those nearby, including pregnant women and their fetuses.

This information is made available to you by the Chicago Dental Society. For more information contact: Victoria Farster, Director of Communications, (312)836-7330; vfarster@chicagodentalsociety.org.

Parental Alienation Syndrome

Berg v. Perlow

Case No. CD 98-1285-FC, 15th judicial circuit in Palm Beach County Florida dated March 15, 2000, specifically recognizing Parental Alienation Syndrome.

Some quotes include "the wife seeks sole parental responsibility and to eliminate any contact between husband and child based upon the Parental Alienation Syndrome". Husband diagnosed as psychopath, with copious quotes from DSM-IV. Father diagnosed as psychopath and child diagnosed with moderate to severe PAS by mental health professionals including Ellinger, Heller, Gardner and Bush. Court order includes such items as: "The Husband...shall have absolutely no contact with the parties' child (now 8) until the child reaches age 14. No contact with the child forthwith shall include, but not be limited to (the court will specifically reserve jurisdiction as to this issue as the husband will probably find a way to somehow circumvent this order, so that the Court will enter additional orders on behalf of the Wife so as to require strict compliance with this order) the following:

No: telephone contact, e-mail contact, computer contact, videos, visitation, visits at school, No records from school, records from any health care providers, contact indirectly by third parties on behalf of the Husband, whether they are relatives or not."

"The Court finds that the order of the Court in which the Wife should not disparage the Husband to the child is now becoming a detriment to the child. The wife needs to be as truthful to the child as possible taking into consideration the child's youth, but that the wife should advise this child of this Court's specific findings and why this Court has done what it has done, including, but not limited to the husband's extensive background involving his deceitfulness, his lack of remorse, his arrests, his poor behavior control and impulsivity, his lack or empathy, and his total anti-social personality disorder".

Action May Proceed for PAS

Bhama v. Bhama

425 N.W.2d 733 (Mich. App. 1988), the Michigan Court of Appeals allowed a cause of

action to proceed where the custodial parent created a negative relationship between the child and the non-custodial parent through denial of visitation rights.

Children are not Chargeable

Children are not chargeable with the misconduct of their parents and should not be uprooted from their home in order to discipline a recalcitrant parent.

Webb v Kudson

133 NH 665,673 (1990) also Houde v Beckmeyer, 116 NH 719 (1976)

When the alienation of a parent is at it's worst the child no longer defends the target parent, but actively takes part in the alienation. Studies show that only between one percent and five percent of alienation cases become this severe. Even when the alienation is not that severe it may be impossible to encourage or even force a child to be with the target parent. These children demonstrate extremely hostile feelings for the target parent, and will not believe any amount of evidence disproving their reasons for their hatred. In some of these cases, the child would suffer a complete emotional breakdown if custody were awarded to the hated target parent. The child's sense of security and self is totally dependent on the relationship with the alienating parent, and a loss of that relationship would destroy the child. Attempts to change custody would be undermined by the child and involve: running away, reports of physical/sexual abuse and self-destructive behaviors such as drug abuse, suicide attempts, refusal to obey the parent, and refusal to go to school. Therefore, the courts have decided the child must stay with the alienating parent, as it is not proper to use a child to punish a parent for misbehavior. If discontinuance of child support will not harm the child, the courts have suspended a target parent's child support or allowed the target parent to escrow child support so that the target parent does not have to provide financial assistance to the household that hates him so profoundly.

PAS Excluded, Daubert V. Merrell

Parental Alienation Syndrome testimony may be excluded, in light of this case. (PAS) is a theoretical disorder in children that arises almost exclusively in child custody disputes. In most PAS cases one parent causes the children to hate the other parent - often leading to false allegations of physical and sexual abuse. This assigns blame in an area that psychologists and courts recognize as extremely uncertain. It also observes that there is no empirical evidence supporting the theory, nor has PAS been subjected to meaningful peer review or publication. In fact, experts in the field have widely discredited the theory.

Therefore, it is argued that PAS is dangerous because its wide dissemination in the legal community, via the PAS originator's self-published works, lends a questionable aura of reliability to the theory.

DHSS Report on PAS

DHSS report on child abuse issued by HMSO 1983. This report stated that the child says different things to different people. It is well documented that children say to each parent what that parent expects to hear. Therefore, the child says different things to different people. In general they say what they think adults want to hear. After all, they are political animals trying to exist in a crisis: Children fit their responses to the expectations of adults, especially those adults who are in a position of current power. Each parent will take what the child has said at face value and not believe the other parent's claim that he or she has been told the opposite.

Malicious Mother Syndrome

Turkat ID: Child visitation interference in divorce. Clinical Psychology Review 1994; 14:8:737-742

This should actually be called the "Malicious Parent Syndrome." This disorder describes a special class of alienating parents who engage in a relentless and multifaceted campaign of aggression and deception against the ex-spouse, who is being punished for the divorce regardless if they were the parent who ended the relationship or not.

The malicious parent can be male, female, grandparent or other parent figure. Discussing PAS by name, Turkat classified PAS as a moderate form of visitation interference as compared with Divorce Related Malicious Mother Syndrome. The parent with the latter disorder uses an array of tactics including excessive litigation, alienating the child from the target parent, and involving the child and third parties in malicious actions against the ex-spouse. Lying and deception are routinely used. A malicious parent might arrange to have the ex-spouse investigated for use of illegal drugs at work or file a complaint with authorities against the ex-spouse's new partner. Malicious parents are often successful in using the law to punish and harass the ex-spouse, sometimes violating the law themselves but often getting away with it.

Their efforts to interfere with the target parent's visitation are persistent and pervasive, including attempts to block the target parent from having regular, uninterrupted visitation with the child and from having telephone contact, as well as trying to block the target parent from participating in the child's school life and activities.

Kidnapping

Parental Kidnapping Prevention Act

Of 1980 recognizes existing custody orders when a parent flees with a child (interstate or international flight). Provides for the use of a parent locator service for enforcement.

Hague Convention of 1986

The Hague Convention on International Child Abduction of 1986 establishes a legal right and procedures for the return of children kidnapped across national boundaries. The United States adopted the International Child Abduction Remedies Act of 1988 supporting the Hague Convention.

Hague Convention
On The Civil Aspects Of
International Child Abduction

The States signatory to the present Convention, Firmly convinced that the interests of children are of paramount importance in matters relating to their custody, Desiring to protect children internationally from the harmful effects of their wrongful removal or retention and to establish procedures to ensure their prompt return to the State of their habitual residence, as well as to secure protection for rights of access,

Have resolved to conclude a Convention to this effect, and have agreed upon the following provisions.

Chapter I - Scope of the Convention

Article 1

The objects of the present Convention are

a. to secure the prompt return of children wrongfully removed to or retained in any Contracting State; and

b. to ensure that rights of custody and of access under the law of one Contracting State are effectively respected in other Contracting States.

Article 2

Contracting States shall take all appropriate measures to secure within their territories the implementation of the objects of the Convention. For this purpose they shall use the most expeditious procedures available.

Article 3

The removal or the retention of a child is to be considered wrongful where -

a. it is in breach of rights of custody attributed to a person, an institution or any other body, either jointly or alone, under the law of the State in which the child was habitually resident immediately before the removal or retention; and

b. at the time of removal or retention those rights were actually exercised, either jointly or alone, or would have been so exercised, but for the removal or retention.

The rights of custody mentioned in sub-paragraph a above, may arise in particular by operation of law or by reason of a judicial or administrative decision, or by reason of an agreement having legal effect under the law of that State.

Article 4

The Convention shall apply to any child who was habitually resident in a Contracting State immediately before any breach of custody or access rights. The Convention shall cease to apply when the child attains the age of 16 years.

Article 5

For the purposes of this Convention -

a. 'rights of custody' shall include rights relating to the care of the person of the child and, in particular, the right to determine the child's place of residence;

b. 'rights of access' shall include the right to take a child for a limited period of time to a place other than the child's habitual residence.

Chapter II - Central Authorities

Article 6

A Contracting State shall designate a Central Authority to discharge the duties, which are imposed by the Convention upon such authorities. Federal States, States with more than one system of law or States having autonomous territorial organizations shall be free to appoint more than one Central Authority.
And to specify the territorial extent of their powers. Where a State has appointed more than one Central Authority, it shall designate the Central Authority to which applications may be addressed for transmission to the appropriate Central Authority within that State.

Article 7

Central Authorities shall co-operate with each other and promote co-operation amongst the competent authorities in their respective States to secure the prompt return of children and to achieve the other objects of this Convention.

In particular, either directly or through any intermediary, they shall take all appropriate measures

a. to discover the whereabouts of a child who has been wrongfully removed or retained;

b. to prevent further harm to the child or prejudice to interested parties by taking or causing to be taken provisional measures;

c. to secure the voluntary return of the child or to bring about an amicable resolution of the issues;

d. to exchange, where desirable, information relating to the social background of the child;

e. to provide information of a general character as to the law of their State in connection with the application of the Convention;

f. to initiate or facilitate the institution of judicial or administrative proceedings with a view to obtaining the return of the child and, in a proper case, to make arrangements for organizing or securing the effective exercise of rights of access;

g. where the circumstances so require, to provide or facilitate the provision of legal aid and advice, including the participation of legal counsel and advisers;

h. to provide such administrative arrangements as may be necessary and appropriate to secure the safe return of the child;

i. to keep other each other informed with respect to the operation of this Convention and, as far as possible, to eliminate any obstacles to its application.

CHAPTER III - Return Of Children

Article 8

Any person, institution or other body claiming that a child has been removed or retained in breach of custody rights may apply either to the Central Authority of the child's habitual residence or to the Central Authority of any other Contracting State for assistance in securing the return of the child. The application shall contain -

a. information concerning the identity of the applicant, of the child and of the person alleged to have removed or retained the child;

b. where available, the date of birth of the child;

c. the grounds on which the applicant's claim for return of the child is based;

d. all available information relating to the whereabouts of the child and the identity of the person with whom the child is presumed to be.

The application may be accompanied or supplemented by -

e. an authenticated copy of any relevant decision or agreement;

f. a certificate or an affidavit emanating from a Central Authority, or other competent authority of the State of the child's habitual residence, or from a qualified person, concerning the relevant law of that State;

g. any other relevant document.

Article 9

If the Central Authority, which receives an application referred to in Article 8 has reason to believe that the child is in another Contracting State, it shall directly and without delay transmit the application to the Central Authority of that Contracting State and inform the requesting Central Authority, or the applicant, as the case may be.

Article 10

The Central Authority of the State where the child is shall take or cause to be taken all appropriate measures in order to obtain the voluntary return of the child.

Article 11

The judicial or administrative authorities of Contracting States shall act expeditiously in proceedings for the return of children. If the judicial or administrative authority concerned has not reached a decision within six weeks from the date of commencement of the proceedings, the applicant or the Central Authority of the requested State, on its own initiative or if asked by the Central Authority of the requesting State, shall have the right to request the Central Authority of the requested State, that Authority shall transmit the reply to the State, or to the applicant.

Article 12

Where a child has been wrongfully removed or retained in terms of Article 3 and, at the date of the commencement of the proceedings before the judicial or administrative authority of the Contracting State where the child is, a period of less than one year has elapsed from the date of the wrongful removal or retention, the authority concerned shall order the return of the child forthwith. The judicial or administrative authority, even where the proceedings have been commenced after the expiration of the period of one year referred to in the preceding paragraph, shall also order the return of the child, unless it is demonstrated that the child is now settled in its new environment. Where the judicial or administrative authority in the requested State has reason to believe that the child has been taken to another State, it may stay the proceedings or dismiss the application for the return of the child.

Article 13

Notwithstanding the provisions of the preceding Article, the judicial or administrative authority of the requested State is not bound to order the return of the child if the person, institution or other body, which opposes its return establishes that -

a. the person, institution or other body having the care of the person of the child was not actually exercising the custody rights at the time of removal or retention, or had consented to or subsequently acquiesced in the removal of retention; or b. there is a grave risk that his or her return would expose the child to physical or psychological harm or otherwise place the child in an intolerable situation.

The judicial or administrative authority may also refuse to order the return of the child if it finds that the child objects to being returned and has attained an age and degree of maturity at which it is appropriate to take account of its views. In considering the circumstances referred to in this Article, the judicial and administrative authorities shall take into account the information relating to the social background of the child provided by the Central Authority or other competent authority of the child's habitual residence.

Article 14

In ascertaining whether there has been a wrongful removal of retention within the meaning of Article 3, the judicial or administrative authorities of the requested State may take notice directly of the law of, and of judicial or administrative decisions, formally recognized or not in the State of the habitual residence of the child, without recourse to the specific procedures for the proof of that law or for the recognition of foreign decisions, which would otherwise be applicable.

Article 15

The judicial or administrative authorities of a Contracting State may, prior to the making of an order for the return of the child, request that the applicant obtain from the authorities of the State of the habitual residence of the child a decision or other determination that the removal or retention was wrongful within the meaning of Article 3 of the Convention, where such a decision or determination may be obtained in that State. The Central Authorities of the Contracting States shall so far as practicable assist applicants to obtain such a decision or determination.

Article 16

After receiving notice of a wrongful removal or retention of a child in the sense of Article 3, the judicial or administrative authorities of the Contracting State to which the child has been removed or in which it has been retained shall not decide on the merits of rights of custody until it has been determined that the child is not to be returned under this Convention or unless an application under the Convention is not lodged within a reasonable time following receipt of the notice.

Article 17

The sole fact that a decision relating to custody has been given in or is entitled to recognition in the requested State shall not be a ground for refusing to return a child under this Convention, but the judicial or administrative authorities of the requested

State may take account of the reasons for that decision in applying this Convention.

Article 18

The provisions of this Chapter do not limit the power of a judicial or administrative authority to order the return of the child at any time.

Article 19

A decision under this Convention concerning the return of the child shall not be taken to be determination on the merits of any custody issue.

Article 20

The return of the child under the provision of Article 12 may be refused if this would not be permitted by the fundamental principles of the requested State relating to the protection of human rights and fundamental freedoms.

CHAPTER VI - Rights of Access

Article 21

An application to make arrangements for organizing or securing the effective exercise of rights of access may be presented to

the Central Authorities of the Contracting States in the same way as an application for the return of a child. The Central Authorities are bound by the obligations of co-operation, which are set forth in Article 7 to promote the peaceful enjoyment of access rights and the fulfillment of any conditions to which the exercise of such rights may be subject. The central Authorities shall take steps to remove, as far as possible, all obstacles to the exercise of such rights. The Central Authorities, either directly or through intermediaries, may initiate or assist in the institution of proceedings with a view to organizing or protecting these rights and securing respect for the conditions to which the exercise of these rights may be subject.

Article 22

No security, bond or deposit, however described, shall be required to guarantee the payment of costs and expenses in the judicial or administrative proceedings falling within the scope of this Convention.

Article 23

No legalization or similar formality may be required in the context of this Convention.

Article 24

Any application, communication or other document sent to the Central Authority of the requested State shall be in the original language, and shall be accompanied by a translation into the official language or one of the official languages of the requested State or, where that is not feasible, a translation into French or English. However, a Contracting State may, by making a reservation in accordance with Article 42, object to the use of either French or English, but not both, in any application, communication or other document sent to its Central Authority.

Article 25

Nationals of the Contracting States and persons who are habitually resident within those States shall be entitled in matters concerned with the application of this Convention to legal aid and advice in any other Contracting State on the same conditions as if they themselves were nationals of and habitually resident in that State.

Article 26

Each Central Authority shall bear its own costs in applying this Convention.

Central Authorities and other public services of Contracting States shall not impose any charges in relation to applications submitted under this Convention. In particular, they may not require any payment from the applicant towards the costs and expenses of the proceedings or, where applicable, those arising from the participation of legal counsel or advisers. However, they may require the payment of the expenses incurred or to be incurred in implementing the return of the child. However, a Contracting State may, by making a reservation in accordance with Article 42, declare that it shall not be bound to assume any costs referred to in the preceding paragraph resulting from the participation of legal counsel or advisers or from court proceedings, except insofar as those costs may be covered by its system of legal aid and advice. Upon ordering the return of a child or issuing an order concerning rights of access under this Convention, the judicial or administrative authorities may, where appropriate, direct the person who removed or retained the child, or who prevented the exercise of rights of access, to pay necessary expenses incurred by or on behalf of the applicant, including travel expenses, any costs incurred or payments made for locating the child, the costs of legal representation of the applicant, and those of returning the child.

Article 27

When it is manifest that the requirements of this Convention are not fulfilled or that the application is otherwise not well founded, a Central

Authority is not bound to accept the application. In that case, the Central Authority shall forthwith inform the applicant or the Central Authority through, which the application was submitted, as the case may be, of its reasons.

Article 28

A Central Authority may require that the application be accompanied by a written authorization empowering it to act on behalf of the applicant, or to designate a representative so to act.

Article 29

This Convention shall not preclude any person, institution or body who claims that there has been a breach of custody or access rights within the meaning of Article 3 or 21 from applying directly to the judicial or administrative authorities of a Contracting State, whether or not under the provisions of this Convention.

Article 30

Any application submitted to the Central Authorities or directly to the judicial or administrative authorities of a Contracting State in accordance with the terms of this Convention, together with documents and any other information appended thereto or provided by a Central Authority, shall be admissible in the courts or administrative authorities of the Contracting States.

Article 31

In relation to a State, which in matters of custody of children has two or more systems of law applicable in different territorial units -

a. any reference to habitual residence in that State shall be construed as referring to habitual residence in a territorial unit of that State;

b. any reference to the law of the State of habitual residence shall be construed as referring to the law of the territorial unit in that State where the child habitually resides.

Article 32

In relation to a State, which in matters of custody of children has two or more systems of law applicable to different categories of persons, any reference to the law of that State shall be construed as referring to the legal system specified by the law of that State.

Article 33

A State within which different territorial units have their own rules of law in respect of custody of children shall not be bound to apply this Convention where a State with a unified system of law would not be bound to do so.

Article 34

This Convention shall take priority in matters within its scope over the Convention of 5 October 1961 concerning the powers of authorities and the law applicable in respect of the protection of minors, as between Parties to both Conventions. Otherwise the present Convention shall not restrict the application of an international instrument in force between the State of origin and the State addressed or other law of the State addressed for the purposes of obtaining the return of a child who has been wrongfully removed or retained or of organizing access rights.

Article 35

This Convention shall apply as between Contracting States only to wrongful removals or retentions occurring after its entry into force in those States. Where a declaration has been made under Article 39 or 40, the reference in the preceding paragraph to a Contracting State shall be taken to refer to the territorial unit or units in relation to which this Convention applies.

Article 36

Nothing in this Convention shall prevent two or more Contracting State, in order to limit the restrictions to which the return of the child may be subject, from agreeing among themselves to derogate from any provision of this Convention, which may imply such a restriction.

CHAPTER VI - Final Clauses

Article 37

The Convention shall be open for signature by the States, which were Members of the Hague Conference on Private International Law at the time of its Fourteenth Session. It shall be ratified, accepted or approved and the instruments of ratification, acceptance or approval shall be deposited with the Ministry of Foreign Affairs of the Kingdom of the Netherlands.

Article 38

Any other State may accede to the Convention. The instrument of accession shall be deposited with the Ministry of Foreign Affairs of the Kingdom of the Netherlands. The Convention shall enter into force for a State acceding to it on the first day of the third calendar month after the deposit of its instrument of accession. The accession will have effect only as regards the relations between the acceding State and such Contracting States as will have declared their acceptance of the accession. Such a declaration will also have to be made by any Member State ratifying, accepting or approving the Convention after an accession. Such declaration shall be deposited at the Ministry of Foreign Affairs of the Kingdom of the Netherlands; this Ministry shall forward, through diplomatic channels, a certified copy to each of the Contracting States. The Convention will enter into force as between the acceding State and the State that has declared its acceptance of the accession on the first day of the third calendar month after the deposit of the declaration of acceptance.

Article 39

Any State may, at the time of signature, ratification, acceptance, approval or accession, declare that the Convention shall extend to all the territories for the international relations of which it is responsible, or to one or more of them. Such a declaration shall take effect at the time the Convention enters into force for that State. Such declaration, as well as any subsequent extension, shall be notified to the Ministry of Foreign Affairs of the Kingdom of the Netherlands.

Article 40

If a Contracting State has two or more territorial units in which different systems of law are applicable in relation to matters dealt with in this Convention, it may at the time of signature, ratification, acceptance, approval or accession declare that this Convention shall extend to all its territorial units or only to one or more of them and may modify this declaration by submitting another declaration at any time. Any such declaration shall be notified to the Ministry of Foreign Affairs of the Kingdom of the Netherlands and shall state expressly the territorial units to which the Convention applies.

Article 41

Where a Contracting State has a system of government under, which executive, judicial and legislative powers are distributed between central and other authorities within that State, its signature or ratification, acceptance or approval of, or accession to this Convention, or its making of any declaration in terms of Article 40 shall carry no implication as to the internal distribution of powers within that State.

Article 42

Any State may, not later than the time of ratification, acceptance, approval or accession, or at the time of making a declaration in terms of Article 39 or 40, make one or both of the reservations provided for in Article 24 and Article 26, third paragraph. No other reservations shall be permitted. Any State may at any time withdraw a reservation it has made. The withdrawal shall be notified to the Ministry of Foreign Affairs of the Kingdom of the Netherlands. The reservation shall cease to have effect on the first day of the third calendar month after the notification referred to in the preceding paragraph.

Article 43

The Convention shall enter into force on the first day of the third calendar month after the deposit of the third instrument of ratification, acceptance, approval or accession referred to in Articles 37 and 38. Thereafter the Convention shall enter into force -

1. for each State ratifying, accepting, approving or acceding to it subsequently, on the first day of the third calendar month after the deposit of its instrument of ratification, acceptance, approval or accession;

2. for any territory or territorial unit to which the Convention has been extended in conformity with Article 39 or 40, on the first day of the third calendar month after the notification referred to in that Article.

Article 44

The Convention shall remain in force for five years from the date of its entry into force in accordance with the first paragraph of Article 43 even for States, which subsequently have ratified, accepted, approved it or acceded to it. If there has been no denunciation, it shall be renewed tacitly every five years. Any denunciation shall be notified to the Ministry of Foreign Affairs of the Kingdom of the Netherlands at least six months before the expiry of the five year period. It may be limited to certain of the territories or territorial units to which the Convention applies. The denunciation shall have effect only as regards the State, which has notified it. The Convention shall remain in force for the other

Contracting States.

Article 45

The Ministry of Foreign Affairs of the Kingdom of the Netherlands shall notify the States Members of the Conference, and the States, which have acceded in accordance with Article 38, of the following -

1. the signatures and ratifications, acceptances and approvals referred to in Article 37;
2. the accession referred to in Article 38;
3. the date on which the Convention enters into force in accordance with Article 43;
4. the extensions referred to in Article 39;
5. the declarations referred to in Articles 38 and 40;
6. the reservations referred to in Article 24 and Article 26, third paragraph, and the withdrawals referred to in Article 42;
7. the denunciation referred to in Article 44. In witness whereof the undersigned, being duly authorized thereto, have signed this Convention.

Done at The Hague, on the 25th day of October, 1980, in the English and French languages, both texts being equally authentic, in a single copy, which shall be deposited in the archives of the Government of the Kingdom of the Netherlands, and of which a certified copy shall be sent, through diplomatic channels, to each of the States Members of the Hague Conference on Private International Law at the date of its Fourteenth Session. International Adoption & Child Abduction

International Criminal Enforcement

New criminal enforcement procedures. There have been new developments in the use of these procedures in international cases. On May 11, 1997, the state of Massachusetts, working with Interpol, succeeded in having a child support fugitive from its "most wanted" list, who was the subject of an outstanding warrant, deported from the Dominican Republic and arrested on

International Abduction Remedies Act

Of 1988 establishes the legal right and procedures for the return of children kidnapped across national boundaries supporting the Hague Convention of 1986 on International Child Abduction.

Sec. 11601. Findings and declarations.
(a) Findings.
(b) Declarations.
11602. Definitions.
11603. Judicial remedies.
(a) Jurisdiction of courts.
(b) Petitions.
(c) Notice.
(d) Determination of case.
(e) Burdens of proof.
(f) Application of Convention.
(g) Full faith and credit.
(h) Remedies under Convention not exclusive.
11604. Provisional remedies.
(a) Authority of courts.
(b) Limitation on authority.
11605. Admissibility of documents.
11606. United States Central Authority.
(a) Designation.
(b) Functions.
(c) Regulatory authority.
(d) Obtaining information from Parent Locator Service.
11607. Costs and fees.
(a) Administrative costs.
(b) Costs incurred in civil actions.
11608. Collection, maintenance, and dissemination of information.
(a) In general.
(b) Requests for information.
(c) Responsibility of government entities.
(d) Information available from Parent Locator Service.
(e) Record keeping.
11609. Interagency coordinating group.
11610. Authorization of appropriations.
Sec. 11601. Findings and declarations
(a) Findings

The Congress makes the following findings:

(1) The international abduction or wrongful retention of children is harmful to their well-being.

(2) Persons should not be permitted to obtain custody of children by virtue of their wrongful removal or retention.

(3) International abductions and retentions of children are increasing, and only concerted cooperation pursuant to an international agreement can effectively combat this problem.

(4) The Convention on the Civil Aspects of International Child Abduction, done at The Hague on October 25, 1980, establishes legal rights and procedures for the prompt return of children who have been wrongfully removed or retained, as well as for securing the exercise of visitation rights. Children who are wrongfully removed or retained within the meaning of the Convention are to be promptly returned unless one of the narrow exceptions set forth in the Convention applies. The Convention provides a sound treaty framework to help resolve the problem of international abduction and retention of children and will deter such wrongful removals and retentions.

(b) Declarations

The Congress makes the following declarations:

(1) It is the purpose of this chapter to establish procedures for the implementation of the Convention in the United States.

(2) The provisions of this chapter are in addition to and not in lieu of the provisions of the Convention.

(3) In enacting this chapter the Congress recognizes (A) the international character of the Convention; and

(B) the need for uniform international interpretation of the Convention.

(4) The Convention and this chapter empower courts in the United States to determine only rights under the Convention and not the merits of any underlying child custody claims.

References in Text

This chapter, referred to in subsec. (b), was in the original "this Act" meaning Pub. L. 100-300, Apr. 29, 1988, 102 Stat. 437, which is classified principally to this chapter. For complete classification of this Act to the Code, see Short Title note below and Tables.

Short Title

Section 1 of Pub. L. 100-300 provided that: "This Act (enacting this chapter and amending section 663 of this title) may be cited as the 'International Child Abduction Remedies Act'."

Sec. 11602. Definitions

For the purposes of this chapter -

(1) the term "applicant" means any person who, pursuant to the Convention, files an application with the United States Central Authority or a Central Authority of any other party to the Convention for the return of a child alleged to have been wrongfully removed or retained or for arrangements for organizing or securing the effective exercise of rights of access pursuant to the Convention;

(2) the term "Convention" means the Convention on the Civil Aspects of International Child Abduction, done at The Hague on October 25, 1980;

(3) the term "Parent Locator Service" means the service established by the Secretary of Health and Human Services under section 653 of this title;

(4) the term "petitioner" means any person who, in accordance with this chapter, files a petition in court seeking relief under the Convention;

(5) the term "person" includes any individual, institution, or other legal entity or body;

(6) the term "respondent" means any person against whose interests a petition is filed in court, in accordance with this chapter, which seeks relief under the Convention;

(7) the term "rights of access" means visitation rights;

(8) the term "State" means any of the several States, the District of Columbia, and any commonwealth, territory, or possession of the United States; and

(9) the term "United States Central Authority" means the agency of the Federal Government designated by the President under section 11606(a) of this title.

Sec. 11603. Judicial remedies

(a) Jurisdiction of courts

The courts of the States and the United States district courts shall have concurrent original jurisdiction of actions arising under the Convention.

(b) Petitions

Any person seeking to initiate judicial proceedings under the Convention for the return of a child or for arrangements for organizing or securing the effective exercise of rights of access to a child may do so by commencing a civil action by filing a petition for the relief sought in any court, which has jurisdiction of such action and which is authorized to exercise its jurisdiction in the place where the child is located at the time the petition is filed.

(c) Notice

Notice of an action brought under subsection (b) of this section shall be given in accordance with the applicable law governing notice in interstate child custody proceedings.

(d) Determination of case

The court in which an action is brought under subsection (b) of this section shall decide the case in accordance with the Convention.

(e) Burdens of proof

(1) A petitioner in an action brought under subsection (b) of this section shall establish by a preponderance of the evidence -

(A) in the case of an action for the return of a child, that the child has been wrongfully removed or retained within the meaning of the Convention; and

(B) in the case of an action for arrangements for organizing or securing the effective exercise of rights of access, that the petitioner has such rights.

(2) In the case of an action for the return of a child, a respondent who opposes the return of the child has the burden of establishing -

(A) by clear and convincing evidence that one of the exceptions set forth in article 13b or 20 of the Convention applies; and

(B) by a preponderance of the evidence that any other exception set forth in article 12 or 13 of the Convention applies.

(f) Application of Convention

For purposes of any action brought under this chapter -

(1) the term "authorities", as used in article 15 of the Convention to refer to the authorities of the state of the habitual residence of a child, includes courts and appropriate government agencies;

(2) the terms "wrongful removal or retention" and "wrongfully removed or retained", as used in the Convention, include a removal or retention of a child before the entry of a custody order regarding that child; and

(3) the term "commencement of proceedings", as used in article 12 of the Convention, means, with respect to the return of a child located in the United States, the filing of a petition in accordance with subsection (b) of this section.

(g) Full faith and credit

Full faith and credit shall be accorded by the courts of the States and the courts of the United States to the judgment of any other such court ordering or denying the return of a child, pursuant to the Convention, in an action brought under this chapter.

(h) Remedies under Convention not exclusive

The remedies established by the Convention and this chapter shall be in addition to remedies available under other laws or international agreements.

Sec. 11604. Provisional remedies

(a) Authority of courts

In furtherance of the objectives of article 7(b) and other provisions of the Convention, and subject to the provisions of subsection (b) of this section, any court exercising jurisdiction of an action brought under section 11603(b) of this title may take or cause to be taken measures under Federal or State law, as appropriate, to protect the well-being of the child involved or to prevent the child's further removal or concealment before the final disposition of the petition.

(b) Limitation on authority

No court exercising jurisdiction of an action brought under section 11603(b) of this title may, under subsection (a) of this section, order a child removed from a person having physical control of the child unless the applicable requirements of State law are satisfied.

Sec. 11605. Admissibility of documents

With respect to any application to the United States Central Authority, or any petition to a court under section 11603 of this title, which seeks relief under the Convention, or any other documents or information included with such application or petition or provided after such submission, which relates to the application or petition, as the case may be, no authentication of such application, petition, document, or information shall be required in order for the application, petition, document, or information to be admissible in court.

Sec. 11606. United States Central Authority

(a) Designation

The President shall designate a Federal agency to serve as the Central Authority for the United States under the Convention.

(b) Functions

The functions of the United States Central Authority are those ascribed to the Central Authority by the Convention and this chapter.

(c) Regulatory authority

The United States Central Authority is authorized to issue such regulations as may be necessary to carry out its functions under the Convention and this chapter.

(d) Obtaining information from Parent Locator Service

The United States Central Authority may, to the extent authorized by the Social Security Act (42 U.S.C. 301 et seq.), obtain information from the Parent Locator Service.

Sec. 11607. Costs and fees

(a) Administrative costs

No department, agency, or instrumentality of the Federal Government or of any State or local government may impose on an applicant any fee in relation to the administrative processing of applications submitted under the Convention.

(b) Costs incurred in civil actions

(1) Petitioners may be required to bear the costs of legal counsel or advisors, court costs incurred in connection with their petitions, and travel costs for the return of the child involved and any accompanying persons, except as provided in paragraphs (2) and (3).

(2) Subject to paragraph (3), legal fees or court costs incurred in connection with an action brought under section 11603 of this title shall be borne by the petitioner unless they are covered by payments from Federal, State, or local legal assistance or other programs.

(3) Any court ordering the return of a child pursuant to an action brought under section 11603 of this title shall order the respondent to pay necessary expenses incurred by or on behalf of the petitioner, including court costs, legal fees, foster home or other care during the course of proceedings in the action, and transportation costs related to the return of the child, unless the respondent establishes that such order would be clearly inappropriate.

Sec. 11608. Collection, maintenance, and dissemination of information

(a) In general

In performing its functions under the Convention, the United States Central Authority may, under such conditions as the Central Authority prescribes by regulation, but subject to subsection (c) of this section, receive from or transmit to any department, agency, or instrumentality of the Federal Government or of any State or foreign government, and receive from or transmit to any applicant, petitioner, or respondent, information necessary to locate a child or for the purpose of otherwise implementing the Convention with respect to a child, except that the United States

Central Authority -

(1) may receive such information from a Federal or State department, agency, or instrumentality only pursuant to applicable Federal and State statutes; and

(2) may transmit any information received under this subsection notwithstanding any provision of law other than this chapter.

(b) Requests for information

Requests for information under this section shall be submitted in such manner and form as the United States Central Authority may prescribe by regulation and shall be accompanied or supported by such documents as the United States Central Authority may require.

(c) Responsibility of government entities

Whenever any department, agency, or instrumentality of the United States or of any State receives a request from the United States Central Authority for information authorized to be provided to such Central Authority under subsection (a) of this section, the head of such department, agency, or instrumentality shall promptly cause a search to be made of the files and records maintained by such department, agency, or instrumentality in order to determine whether the information requested is contained in any such files or records. If such search discloses the information requested, the head of such department, agency, or instrumentality shall immediately transmit such information to the United States Central

Authority, except that any such information the disclosure of which -

(1) would adversely affect the national security interests of the United States or the law enforcement interests of the United States or of any State; or

(2) would be prohibited by section 9 of title 13; shall not be transmitted to the Central Authority. The head of such department, agency, or instrumentality shall, immediately upon completion of the requested search, notify the Central Authority of the results of the search, and whether an exception set forth in paragraph (1) or (2) applies. In the event that the United States

Central Authority receives information and the appropriate Federal or State department, agency, or instrumentality thereafter notifies the Central Authority that an exception set forth in paragraph (1) or (2) applies to that information, the Central Authority may not disclose that information under subsection (a) of this section.

(d) Information available from Parent Locator Service

To the extent that information, which the United States Central Authority is authorized to obtain under the provisions of subsection (c) of this section can be obtained through the Parent Locator Service, the United States Central Authority shall first seek to obtain such information from the Parent Locator Service, before requesting such information directly under the provisions of subsection (c) of this section.

(e) Record keeping

The United States Central Authority shall maintain appropriate records concerning its activities and the disposition of cases brought to its attention.

Sec. 11609. Interagency coordinating group

The Secretary of State, the Secretary of Health and Human Services, and the Attorney General shall designate Federal employees and may, from time to time, designate private citizens to serve on an interagency coordinating group to monitor the operation of the Convention and to provide advice on its implementation to the United States Central Authority and other Federal agencies. This group shall meet from time to time at the request of the United States Central Authority. The agency in which the United States Central Authority is located is authorized to reimburse such private citizens for travel and other expenses incurred in participating at meetings of the interagency coordinating group at rates not to exceed those authorized under subchapter I of chapter 57 of title 5 for employees of agencies.

Sec. 11610. Authorization of appropriations

There are authorized to be appropriated for each fiscal year such sums as may be necessary to carry out the purposes of the Convention and this chapter.

Uniform Child Custody Jurisdiction Act

The Uniform Child Custody Jurisdiction Act of 1986 resolves child custody disputes by enforcing existing custody orders (presumably made by the court having the most relevant information about the case) across state lines.

Kidnapping Damages Awarded

Pankratz v. Willis,

744 P.2d 1182 [Arizona, 1987], $125,000 damages were awarded to father for intentional infliction of emotional distress resulting from parental kidnapping of children by wife, supported by her parents.

False Allegations

Ross KL, Blush GJ: Sexual abuse validity discriminators in the divorced or divorcing family. Issues in Child Abuse Accusations 1990; 2:1:1-6 Investigation, case management issues, strategies. Issues in Child Abuse Accusations 1990; 2:3:152-160

Wakefield H, Underwager R: Personality characteristics of parents making false accusations of sexual abuse in custody disputes. Issues in Child Abuse Accusations 1990; 2:3:121-136

SAID Syndrome

Blush and Ross have come up with three psychological profiles for mother false accusers and a typical profile of father accusers. Mothers tend to present as "fearful victim," "justified vindicator," or to some degree psychotic. The "fearful victim" presentation involves manipulation of social image around a specific theme to which others respond with sympathy and support, such as child abuse or spousal abuse. The "justified vindicators" initially present as intellectually organized with a knowledgeable, even pseudo-scientific sounding agenda, similar to what Clawar and Rivlin report regarding self-righteousness as an important motivation of some programming parents.

Women in the third group present with a combination of borderline and histrionic features, which interact with the stress of the divorce to impair the mother's reality testing and significantly interfere with her functioning, sometimes to the point of a psychotic or quasi-psychotic presentation. Similar to Wakefield and Underwager's findings, mothers in all three categories tend to be histrionic in presentation, so emotionally convinced of the "facts" that no amount of input, including from neutral professionals, can dissuade them from their perceptions. According to Blush and Ross, the typical profile for father accusers is one of intellectual rigidity and a high need to be "correct," possibly male counterparts of the "justified vindicator" presentation among mothers.

By history, these men were hypercritical of their wives while the marriage was still intact, quick to suspect them of negligence and to accuse their wives of being unfit mothers. Gardner's work is referenced in the second and third SAID syndrome articles by these authors.

Narcissistic

Johnston JR, Campbell LE: Impasses of Divorce: The Dynamics and Resolution of Family Conflict. New York, The Free Press, 1988

Reich W: Character Analysis. New York, WR Farrar, Straus and Giroux/Noonday Press, 1949

Johnston found that to varying degrees, one or both of the parents in high conflict divorce may be narcissistically vulnerable, lacking a well-established self identify and relying on primitive defenses such as externalization, denial and projection. The need of one or both parents to protect and defend themselves against narcissistic injury is at the root of many high conflict divorces. This may be a motivating factor for PAS in some cases, a dynamic described by Wilhelm Reich almost 50 years ago when he foretold how parents of certain character types would seek to defend themselves against narcissistic injury in divorce by fighting for the child, using the technique of defaming the partner in order to alienate the child from that parent.

Medea Syndrome

Jacobs JW: Euripides' Medea: a psycho dynamic model of severe divorce pathology. American Journal of Psychotherapy 1988; XLII:2:308-319

Wallerstein JS, Blakeslee S: Second Chances. New York, Ticknor & Fields, 1989; Wallerstein JS, Kelly JB: Surviving the breakup: how children and parents cope with divorce. New York, Basic Books, 1980

In Greek Mythology Medea murder her sons (and others) out of revenge. The need for revenge is taken to an extreme in Media Syndrome. "Modern Medeas do not want to kill their children, but they do want revenge on their former wives or husbands-and they exact it by destroying the relationship between the other parent and the child. The Medea syndrome has its beginnings in the failing marriage and separation, when parents sometimes lose sight of the fact that their children have separate needs [and] begin to think of the child as being an extension of the self...A child may be used as an agent of revenge against the other parent...or the anger can lead to child stealing". The "embittered- chaotic" parents described earlier by Wallerstein and Kelly may also fall in the revenge category. These parents act out their intense anger in a disorganized, but chronically disruptive way, which bombards the children, rather than protecting them, with the raw bitterness and chaos of the angry parent's feelings about the ex-spouse and the divorce.

Emergency Jurisdiction Ends

Rhode Island Supreme

Emergency Jurisdiction Ends as Emergency Ends

A Rhode Island woman took her children to Connecticut to flee a husband she alleged had been abusing them. Connecticut did assert "emergency" jurisdiction over custody. The mother filed for and was awarded custody in Connecticut. The father appealed to the Rhode Island Supreme court. The Rhode Island Supreme court said that Connecticut must give up jurisdiction as soon as the "emergency" is over. That the state of Rhode Island had jurisdiction and would decide the custody of the children. The mother argued that this order was entitled to full faith and credit in Rhode Island under the Parental Kidnapping Prevention Act, 28 U.S.C. Sect. 1738A. The Rhode Island court said that while

Connecticut could assume "emergency jurisdiction" under the Act, "this jurisdiction continues only for as long as the emergency exists." Once the children were safe, Rhode Island would again assume jurisdiction. The Rhode Island court felt that "To hold otherwise... would provide a license for every unscrupulous would-be custodial parent in the country to take his or her children and make false allegations of emergency situations in states where favorable custody decisions may result." Similar rulings:
New Jersey. Benda v. Benda, 565 A.2d 1121 (1989)
Rhode Island Supreme Court. Nadeau v. Nadeau

Termination of Parental Rights

Joshua M., 274 Cal.Rptr. at 222

Delaware Supreme Court 1998 Case in progress Ten year old girl has won a legal step in her bid to have her mother's parental rights terminated.

Samantha Frazer, with the help of a national child rights' group, asked the state Supreme Court this month to let her challenge a Family Court decision to reunite her with her mother. The high court has approved. Family Court Judge William Walls ruled in March that state family services officials had not done enough to try to reunite Samantha with her mother, Victoria Frazer.

Ms. Frazer was described in court documents as a former crack cocaine and marijuana addict who has been rehabilitated and now lives in South Carolina. Samantha, who was 6 when her mother left, lived in four foster homes, including one where she was abused. She has said she wants to stay in Delaware, where her former therapist wants to adopt her. But a court-appointed child advocate recommended to Walls that Ms. Frazer be allowed to keep her parental rights, and the judge agreed. The Supreme Court justices said that the court-appointed advocate had a conflict of interest and her claim that she acted in Samantha's best interest "is open to significant doubt." The court sent the case back to Family Court to allow the state Division of Family Services and Samantha to seek to reopen the case.

Psychological Parent

In the absence of a statute, under the common law, marriage alone does not obligate a stepparent to support his or her stepchild. Where, however, the stepparent acts in loco parentis to a stepchild, then the stepparent assumes an obligation to support the stepchild. Stated succinctly,

> A step-parent is not under obligation to support the stepchildren, but if he or she takes the children into his or her family or under his or her care in such a way that he or she places himself or herself in loco parentis, he or she assumes an obligation to support them, and acquires a correlative right to their services.

Harris v. Lyon, 16 Ariz. 1, 140 P. 825 (1914). Accord State v. Smith, 485 S.W.2d 461 (Mo. Ct. App. 1972) (position stepparent assumes for himself determines if he stands in loco parentis, and if he voluntarily receives child into family and treats it as a member thereof, he may be said to be standing in place of natural parent); Schneider v. Schneider, 25 N.J. Misc. 180, 52 A.2d 564 (Ch. Div. 1947) (if stepfather voluntarily accepts into his family a child of his wife by a former husband and assumes the obligations of a parent, such obligation continues as long as he permits the child to be in his home). See also In re Teddy's Estate, 214 Cal. App. 2d 113, 29 Cal. Rptr. 402 (1963); Ladd v. Welfare Commissioner, 3 Conn. Cir. 504, 217 A.2d 490 (1965); Kelley v. Iowa Department of Social Services, 197 N.W.2d 192 (Iowa 1972); Duffey v. Duffey, 113 N.C. App. 382, 438 S.E.2d 445 (1994); Palmer v. Harrold, 101 Ohio App. 3d 732, 656 N.E.2d 708 (1995) (stepparent is liable for support of stepchild during marriage to natural parent under doctrine of in loco parentis); Drescher v. Morgan, 251 S.W.2d 173 (Tex. Civ. App. 1952).

As with all other equitable doctrines, the creation of an in loco parentis relationship depends on the facts of the case. Generally, there must be an intent by the stepparent to create the status of in loco parentis. Dodd v. United States, 76 F. Supp. 991 (D. Ark. 1948); Jackson v. Jackson, 278 A.2d 114 (D.C. 1971); Rutkowski v. Wasko, 286 A.D. 327, 143 N.Y.S.2d 1 (1955) (assumption of parental relationship by stepparent is largely question of intention which should not lightly or hastily be inferred); Appeal of Fowler, 130 Vt. 176, 288 A.2d 463 (1972); State ex rel. Gilroy v. Superior Court for King County, 37 Wash. 2d 926, 226 P.2d 882 (1951) (relationship of in loco parentis becomes established only when a person intends to assume toward the child the statue of parent). Most often, stepparents establish de facto in loco parentis relationships with their stepchildren during the course of the marriage of the child's custodial parent by residing in the same household and treating the stepchild as a natural child. Treating a stepchild as one's own includes taking responsibility for the child's care, education, and development, including contributing to the child's support without the expectation of financial compensation. E.g., Deal v. Deal, 545 So. 2d 780 (Ala. Civ. App. 1989); Brummitt v. Commonwealth, 357 S.W.2d 37 (Ky. 1962); Palmer v. Harrold, 101 Ohio App. 3d 732, 656 N.E.2d 708 (1995); In re Custody of H.S.H.-K., 193 Wis. 2d 649, 533 N.W.2d 419 (1995). Quite importantly, the presence or absence of the noncustodial natural parent is not a critical factor in determining whether a stepparent stands in the place of a parent.

For obvious reasons, it may be difficult for a stepparent to prove the intention not to stand in loco parentis to a stepchild when they reside in the same household.
When the stepparent and stepchild share a household, the child naturally benefits from the stepparent's financial contributions to the household, and this benefit creates a presumption that the stepparent intends to assume financial responsibility for the child. Where, however, the stepparent unequivocally expresses a contrary intent, then the presumption may be rebutted. E.g., In re Besondy, 20 N.W. 366 (Minn. 1884) (express agreement between mother and her new husband that child would be supported by government benefits paid to her son, based on the child's father's military service, negated presumption of in loco parentis status).

Because the establishment of an in loco parentis relationship is dependent on the voluntary assumption of responsibility by the stepparent, the relationship is terminable at the will of the stepparent. Ex parte Lipscomb, 660 So. 2d 991 (Ala. 1994); Franklin v. Franklin, 75 Ariz. 151, 253 P.2d 337 (1953); Jackson v. Jackson, 278 A.2d 114 (D.C. 1971); Cavanaugh v. deBaudiniere, 1 Neb. App. 204, 493 N.W.2d 197 (1992); Falzo v. Falzo, 84 N.J. Super. 343, 202 A.2d 192 (App. Div. 1964).

The relationship can also be terminated by the actions of the stepchild. For example, in In re Marriage of Farrell, 67 Wash. App. 361, 835 P.2d 267 (1992), the court held that the in loco parentis relationship between the stepfather and stepdaughter was terminated when the stepdaughter removed herself from her stepfather's home. The court held that the in loco parentis relationship is voluntary and can be terminated at will, the daughter's actions had terminated the relationship.

Quite interestingly, because the law imposes no duty on a stepparent to support a stepchild outside the in loco parentis relationship, if an in loco parentis relationship has not been established during the marriage, a stepparent may argue on divorce that any support actually provided to a stepchild during the marriage constitutes a "drain" on marital resources, and that the stepparent is therefore entitled to a larger share of the equitable distribution award. For example, in Burgess v. Burgess, 710 P.2d 417 (Alaska 1985), the Alaska Supreme Court permitted the stepfather to receive a credit in the property distribution for the contributions he made during the marriage toward the support of his stepchild. See also Cox v. Cox, 882 P.2d 909 (Alaska 1994) (error not to consider husband's support for wife's children by prior marriage as a one relevant factor in dividing marital property). Cf. In re Marriage of Peterson, 211 Mont. 118, 683 P.2d 1304 (1984) (Montana Supreme Court refused to authorize an increase in stepfather's share of assets at divorce to compensate him for the consumption of marital income during the marriage, where in loco parentis relationship was established).

Atkinson v. Atkinson

Michigan 408 N.W. 1987 A spouse who is not the biological or adoptive parent may be assigned custody, visitation or child support under the notation of Equitable Parent. Courts apply this concept when a spouse and a child have a close relationship and consider themselves parent and child and where the biological parent encouraged the relationship.

Flink v. Flink

Arizona District 1. 1993 In "IN LOCO PARENTIS" (Latin for taking the place of a parent) If a child knows you "only as a parent," then the court recognizes that relationship for visitation.

Ellison v. Ramos

North Carolina Court of Appeals. No. COA97-1417. Reversing a trial court, the North Carolina Court of Appeals says, a woman caring for her live-in boyfriend's daughter five days a week for five years, may be awarded custody. The girlfriend acted in the manner of a parent, taking the diabetic daughter to the doctor and to school, providing in-home medical care, and buying her clothing. When the couple separated, the daughter stayed with the girlfriend. The father later returned and took her to Puerto Rico to live with her grandparents. The girlfriend then sued for custody, claiming the grandparents couldn't properly care for her diabetes. The father argued that (1) the girlfriend didn't have standing and (2) the Due Process Clause of the U.S. Constitution required that he get custody of his biological child. But the court said that (1) "where a third party and a child have an established relationship in the nature of a parent-child relationship, the third party does have standing." Further, "conduct inconsistent with the parent's constitutionally protected status, which need not rise to the statutory level warranting termination of parental rights, would result in the application of the 'Best Interests of the Child' Test.

(2) "The complaint alleges that the father placed his child in the custody of the grandparents who allegedly are not properly caring for the child's diabetes and that he has relinquished custody of his child to others, including the girlfriend, on several occasions. Conclusion These allegations support a conclusion that the father has acted in a manner inconsistent with his protected status as a parent."

Child Support

Family Support Act of 1988

This act revises the AFDC (Aid to Families with Dependent Children) program to emphasize work, child support and family benefits to avoid long-term welfare dependence. In divorce cases, that act provides for automatic wage attachments in all new or modified support orders.

Barnes v. Morrow

Arkansas Court of Appeals, April 25, 2001, No. CA00-1089 The wife was awarded child support arrearages, and requested additional arrearages for the time that the child was not in her custody on the basis of equitable estoppel. The court held that the chancellor did not err in failing to award her child-support arrearages through the date husband petitioned for termination of support.

Railing v. Hawkins

Indiana State Court of Appeals, April 23, 2001, No. 72A01-0009-JV-324 The mother successfully argued to the Court of Appeals that the trial court erred in not including in the father's gross income his overtime pay, in accordance with Guideline 3.

MacDougall v. DHS

Maine Supreme Judicial Court, April 24, 2001, 2001 ME 64 Joel MacDougall appealed from a judgment entered in the Superior Court affirming a decision of the Department of Human Services determining the amount of child support he owed. He contended that the DHS hearing officer erred in calculating his gross base pay for purposes of determining the amount of child support due. Because the court concluded that the hearing officer erred in categorically rejecting all of MacDougall's reported business expenses, the court vacated and remanded.

In re Paternity of Cheryl

Massachusetts Supreme Judicial Court, April 24, 2001, No. SJC-08391 The trial court granted relief from a paternity judgment after genetic tests showed that he was not the biological father. The SJC held that he was not entitled to relief more than five years after he voluntarily acknowledged paternity.

White v. Laingor

Massachusetts Supreme Judicial Court, April 27, 2001, No. SJC-08329 Mother appealed enforcement of an agreement in which she agreed to accept a reduced lump-sum payment for child support arrearages in exchange for father's consent to the adoption of children by her new husband even though the adoption did not occur. The court held that agreements between parents to reduce child support obligations in exchange for the surrender of parental rights, without a finding that the proposed agreement is in the best interests of a child, violates public policy.

Ottino v. Ottino

New Mexico Court of Appeals, April 28, 2001, No. 2001-NMCA-012 Wife and daughter appealed an adverse ruling in their action seeking to enforce the husband's obligation to pay half of daughter's education expenses. The court held that Section 40-4-7 did not preclude the court from enforcing a contract between the parents as to the provision of post-minority child support.

Brown v. Birman Managed Care

Tennessee Supreme Court, April 25, 2001, No. M1999-02551-SC-R11-CV The mother, individually and on behalf of her daughter, sued her former husband and his employers for fraud and civil conspiracy to defraud. She alleged that these defendants successfully carried out a plan to reduce the amount of her former husband's child support payments. Part of the plaintiff's conspiracy claim is based on the testimony of her former husband in a child support hearing in which he is alleged to have falsely stated his income. The defendants moved for summary judgment on two grounds: (1) the quality of the plaintiff's evidence and (2) the defense of "testimonial privilege," which grants a witness immunity from subsequent civil liability based on testimony he gave in a judicial proceeding. The trial court granted the defendants' motion.
The Court of Appeals, in an opinion authored by Judge Cantrell, reversed, holding that the defendants were not entitled to summary judgment and that the former husband's testimony comes within the "larger conspiracy" exception to the testimonial privilege. The Supreme Court affirmed the Court of Appeals.

Edwards v. Edwards

West Virginia Supreme Court, April 18, 2001, No. 28213 Ex-wife appealed from a court order regarding dates of commencement of payment of child support and alimony. The court held that the trial court did not have the authority to alter the dates upon which ex-husband was required to begin paying child support and alimony without making any factual findings or conclusions of law.

In re Marriage of Simmons

Wisconsin Court of Appeals, April 25, 2001, No. 00-1428 Husband appealed the modified divorce settlement, arguing that a deviation from the shared-time payer formula was improper. "In this case, the circuit court followed the statutory guidelines for deviating from the shared-time payer formula. The court found that the shared-time payer formula would be unfair to Christine and to the children. Specifically, the court found that the shared-time payer amount would be $51 per month based on Richard's asserted income, $140 per month based on the income the court considered to be reasonable, or $240 based on Richard's income at the time of the divorce. The court found that none of these amounts were sufficient to meet Christine's and the children's needs. The court further explained that the existing child support arrangement created an arrangement where Richard had control over Christine and her resources. The court found that the evidence presented by both parties established that Christine was primarily responsible for the child care costs. Further, by insisting that the children attend private school and by requiring Christine to pay for the private school tuition while paying her only enough money to cover that tuition, Richard was attempting to "control" Christine. The court concluded that this situation was not in Christine's or the children's best interests. The record supports the circuit court's decision to deviate from the shared-time payer formula."

Step-parent and Child Support

The duty of a stepparent to support a stepchild after the marriage to the custodial parent has ceased (including the cohabitant's duty of support to the other cohabitant's child after the period of cohabitation).

A. statutory provision that a stepparent has a duty to support a stepchild, the statute is essentially no more than a codification of the in loco parentis doctrine. No statute or interpretation of the doctrine of in loco parentis imposes a duty of support on a stepparent after divorce where the stepparent and stepchildren are no longer living together as a family and the stepparent is not acting as a parent. For example, the North Dakota statute extends the stepparent's duty of support after divorce, but only so long as the stepchildren remain in the stepparent's family. Thus, the cases have universally held that once the parent and stepparent divorce, there is no duty of a stepparent to support a stepchild, unless an obligation to support a stepchild is established by either estoppel or contract. See U.S. v. Floyd, 81 F. 3d 1517 (10th Cir. 1996) (in loco parentis relationship is by nature temporary, and ends when the person standing in the shoes of the parent ceases to fulfill his or her responsibility of care); Deal v. Deal, 545 So. 2d 780 (Ala. Civ. App. 1989); Fenn v. Fenn, 174 Ariz. 84, 847 P.2d 129 (Ct. App. 1993) (no duty of stepparent to support stepchild after divorce, even though stepparent had begun adoption proceedings); Bryan v. Bryan, 132 Ariz. 353, 645 P.2d 1267 (Ct. App. 1982) (stepparents have no

postdissolution duty to support their stepchildren); In re Krystle D., 30 Cal. App. 4th 1778, 37 Cal. Rptr. 2d 132 (1994) (in loco parentis relationship does not continue after dissolution); Swain v. Swain, 250 Cal. App. 2d 1, 58 Cal. Rptr. 83 (1967); K.A.T. v. C.A.B., 645 A.2d 570 (D.C. 1994); Portuondo v. Portuondo, 570 So. 2d 1338 (Fla. DCA 1990); Burney v. Burney, 233 Ga. 216, 210 S.W.2d 727 (1974); In re Petition of Ash, 507 N.W.2d 400 (Iowa 1993) (there is no duty of support by stepparent); In re Marriage of Bethards, 526 N.W.2d 871 (Iowa Ct. App. 1994) (the duty of support under doctrine of in loco parentis does not continue past dissolution of marriage); Tanielian v. Brooks, 202 Mich. App. 304, 508 N.W.2d 189 (1993) (no duty to support stepchild after divorce); Berisford v. Berisford, 322 N.W.2d 742 (Minn. 1982); Levesque v. Levesque, 773 S.W.2d 220 (Mo. Ct. App. 1989) (obligation of support to stepchild ceases on divorce)
Quintela v. Quintela, 4 Neb. App. 396, 544 N.W.2d 111 (1996) (divorce terminates the in loco parentis relationship); Ruben v. Ruben, 123 N.H. 358, 461 A.2d 733, 735 (1983) (obligation to support stepchildren under statute depends on existence of valid marriage and ceases on entry of divorce); Klipstein v. Zalewski, 230 N.J. Super. 567, 553 A.2d 1384 (1988) (in absence of equitable estoppel, there is no duty of stepparent to support stepchild); Chiarello v. Chiarello, 51 A.D.2d 1089, 381 N.Y.S.2d 156 (1976) (after divorce, relationship as stepparent was terminated, and there was no duty to support former wife's children); Duffey v. Duffey, 113 N.C. App. 382, 438 S.E.2d 445 (1994) (there is no duty of stepparent to support stepchild after divorce); Drawbaugh v. Drawbaugh, 436 Pa. Super. 57, 647 A.2d 240 (1994) (no support obligation after divorce by stepparent to stepchild); Garman v. Garman, 435 Pa. Super. 590, 646 A.2d 1251 (1994); Concerned Parents of Stepchildren v. Mitchell, 645 P.2d 629 (Utah 1982). See generally David B. Sweet, Annotation, Stepparent's Postdivorce Duty to Support Stepchild, 44 A.L.R.4th 520 (1986). But see In re Marriage of Bonnette, 492 N.W.2d 717 (Iowa Ct. App. 1992) (court may order stepparent to support former stepchild after divorce in order to maintain stepchild's standard of living which stepparent established). The principle that a stepparent owes no duty to support a stepchild after divorce that courts have even refused to consider the custodial parent's child support expenses in setting the amount of alimony owed by the former spouse/ stepparent to the custodial parent following divorce, even though the "financial need" of the obligee spouse is almost always a support factor. The courts have reasoned that any reference to the stepchild's future expenses in the award of alimony would, in effect, create an unacceptable postdivorce stepparent support duty. Needel v. Needel, 15 Ariz. App. 471, 489 P.2d 729 (1971); Wood v. Wood, 166 Ga. 519, 143 S.E. 770 (1928); Harrison v. Harrison, 503 So. 2d 116 (La. Ct. App. 1987). But see Commonwealth ex rel. Bulson v. Bulson, 419 A.2d 1327 (1980) (alimony payments to custodial mother should reflect the needs of her child because former husband/stepfather had assumed child support duty).

Garnishment Subject to Federal Cap

Michigan Supreme Court. Genesee County Friend of the Court v. General Motors Corp., No. 115856. May 15, 2001

State's garnishment of awards and bonuses is subject to federal cap. Where GM employees received profit-sharing payments, bonuses, and "recognition awards," these qualify as "earnings" under the federal Consumer Credit Protection Act, 15 U.S.C. Sect. 1673, and therefore the extent to which they can be garnished for child support is capped, says the Michigan Supreme Court.

Under state law, a worker's "income" can be garnished to fulfill support obligations. "Income" is defined as "commissions, earnings, salaries, wages and other income." However, state law incorporates the federal Act, which caps the amount of "earnings" subject to garnishment at between 50 and 60 percent. "Earnings" is defined as "compensation...for personal services, whether denominated as wages, salary, commission, bonus, or otherwise, and includes periodic payments pursuant to a pension or retirement program." (15 U.S.C. Sect. 1673(a).)

The employees in this case received annual profit-sharing payments and a $2,000 "signing bonus" pursuant to a collective bargaining agreement. In addition, some employees received discretionary "recognition awards" in lieu of raises.

The plaintiffs were seeking to enforce support orders against the employees. They argued that the payments the employees received didn't constitute "earnings" and therefore weren't subject to the federal cap because they were lump sum payments of uncertain amounts, rather than consistent amounts of money received at regular intervals.

But the court said that "earnings are 'compensation paid or payable for personal services'...The fact that the amounts of the payments are not known in advance and, in the case of the recognition awards, are subject to the discretion of management, does not change the character of the payments... [They] are unquestionably compensation for personal services."

Both Move – Custodial Parent's State to Modify Support

Groseth v. Groseth

Nebraska Supreme Court, No. S-98-833

In applying the Uniform Interstate Family Support Act, the Nebraska Supreme Court ruled that where a husband and wife each moved to different states after their divorce, the law of the state where the mother is raising the children should be used in determining whether child support should be modified. The couple divorced in Massachusetts. The mother then moved with the children to Nebraska and the father moved to Texas. The mother requested an increase in child support due to a change in circumstances. She argued that Massachusetts' law should apply. But the court said that Nebraska law should control.

"[T]he courts of MA lost continuing, exclusive jurisdiction to modify the child support provisions of the decree under the UIFSA once [the father] moved to Texas and [the mother] moved to Nebraska with the children.

"Under [UIFSA's] choice-of-law provision, the substantive law of the issuing state Massachusetts in the instant case governs the nature, extent, amount, and duration of current payments and other obligations of support. It is implicit by the use of the term 'current' that the substantive law of Massachusetts applies merely to petitions to enforce existing orders and not to subsequent orders resulting from petitions to modify child support orders in a responding state. "We see no persuasive reason why the law of an original issuing state should play a role in deciding the amount of a child support obligation when neither party continues to raise children or earn an income there. It is more sensible to apply the law of the state where at least one party is earning income or raising the children because the substantive law more accurately takes into account the cost of living and factors of raising children in that locale."

Passport Restrictions for Child Support

Sections 370, 652(k) and 654(31) Off the Personal Responsibility and Work Opportunity Reconciliation Act of 1996 (PRWORA) (Pub. L. 104-193), which amends 42 U.S.C. 452, the Secretary of State must deny a passport to a person who is in arrears of child support of more than $5,000 upon certification to that effect by the Secretary of Health and Human Services (HHS). The certification of the Secretary of HHS is based upon the certification by a state agency in accordance with Section 454(31) of the PRWORA. The effective date of Section 370 is October 1, 1997. For further information regarding HHS certification for purposes of passport denial, please contact your local child support enforcement agency or the Department of Health and Human Services, OCSE/ DPO, 370 L'Enfant Plaza, 4th Floor East, W.A., D.C. 20447, phone (202) 401-5367

Missouri Dad Needn't Pay Back Support

Linford v. State of Missouri

Even though a father failed to pay court-ordered child support for his two children for nine years, he doesn't have to pay it back to their mother, the state court of appeals has ruled. The father argued that since the children had lived with his parents and not their mother during the nine year period, she wasn't entitled to support. The court of appeals agreed. "The purpose of child support is to provide for the needs of the children," the court said. "Permitting [the mother] to collect $23,100, plus interest, in child support arrearages would be 'unjust and inequitable enrichment.'" James and Sallie Linford were divorced in Georgia in 1988 after a six-year marriage that produced two children. The divorce decree required the father to pay the mother child support for the two children "so long as the children reside with the mother." The mother then voluntarily allowed the children to live with the father's parents. Neither the mother nor the father paid any support to the grandparents.

16 States Provide Child Support Credit

Alaska, Colorado, W.A., D.C., Maryland, Michigan, Minnesota, Nebraska, New Jersey, North

Carolina, Oregon, Utah, Vermont, Virginia, Wisconsin and Wyoming are giving non-custodial parents child support credit for spending time with their kids. The Family Support Act of 1988, requires states to review their child support guidelines every four years. "Shared-parenting credit" applies if the non-custodial parent provides a separate bedroom for the children in their home and keep their children for (1) two overnights a week, or (2) 28% of the time, not counting holidays and extended visits of five days or more.

All non-custodial parents are eligible for a separate, smaller "visitation" credit to cover expenses such as food and transportation. Fathers' and children's rights groups around the country have mounted extensive lobbying campaigns to persuade the Family Courts to adopt these measures, hoping to distribute spending on children between two households based on the amount of time that the children spend in each household. These measures are meant to encourage non-custodial parents to spend more time with their children and will be fairer to parents who are already spending more time. Some say the guidelines will cause more litigation over whether the credits were really earned, describing the credits as "bribes." Custodial parents say the children will suffer because they will receive less money. Suppose a non-custodial parent is awarded a credit, but spends less time than promised with the child. The custodial parent can't file a claim with the state child support collection bureau, because it has jurisdiction only when support isn't paid. So the custodial parent must return to court and hope the judge will reinstate the full, non-credit award. As with all opportunities for progress some parents may argue for their personal interests rather than what's best for the children. The guidelines will contribute to this game-playing. A non-custodial parent may use this as a new opportunity exercise more time with the children. Custodial parents may feel it is one more opportunity for the non-custodial parent to interfere with the child's normal routine. Or the custodial parent may have to oppose more time with the other parent to ensure a full child support award. The formula for the credits is extremely complicated and varies based on the parents' income, the percentage of time they spend with the children and the expenses they incur. Computers will be necessary to calculate child support awards since the credits are too complicated to figure on paper.

Full Faith and Credit

This term is found in the United States Constitution (Art IV, Sec. 1). It requires each state to honor the legal judgments of other states. Such judgments must comply with the United States Constitution in all other respects. If a court did not have jurisdiction over a party (for instance, the person never set foot in the state), then a judgment affecting that person might violate the "due process" clause of the Constitution.

Payor Reduces Earnings Support Increased

Bassette v. Bartolucci

In 1995 a Massachusetts state Appeals Court has ruled father's child support obligation could be tripled even though a fathers income decreased by a third. The man had retired early to become a missionary, and as a result his income fell.

However, the Appeals Court increased his support obligation because the mother was unable to support the child and the father's earning capacity was much higher than his actual income. "Although there was no evidence that the father made this career change in order to avoid his child support obligations," Judge Kent B. Smith wrote, "because his was a voluntary career change, the father retains the ability to pay the ordered amount of child support, based upon his potential rather than actual earning capacity."

Meagher v. Meagher

1961 190 CA2d 62 Where a payor's earning capacity may be used for support purposes when the payor deliberately or intentionally reduces earning capacity or terminates employment.

Uniform Marriage and Divorce Act

Of 1970 amended in 1971 & 1973: This statute provides uniform standards for governing divorce based upon the concept of no-fault divorce and dividing property in a manner similar to distribution of assets when a business partnership is dissolved. Custody and support provisions emphasize the interests of the children not the wishes of the parents.

Uniform Interstate Family Support Act

Supersedes Acts in 1950, 1952, 1958, and Revised Uniform Reciprocal Enforcement of Support Act (RURESA) of 1968. Support Act of 1992 entitles a state to establish, enforce, and modify child/spousal support and have its existing support orders enforced across state lines.

Actual Earnings Used to Set Support

Philbin v. Philbin

1971) 19CA3d 115 The earning capacity and actual earnings of a party are to be used in setting support, unless there is a deliberate attempt to shirk work or reduce income.

Support Set on Reasonable Work Regimen

In re Marriage of Simpson

1992 4 CA4th 225, 234-235 This case is important as one spouse cannot have income based upon a work regimen that is oppressive or extraordinary, but should have income for support purposes based upon an objectively reasonable work regimen.

Child Support a factor in Life-Style Change

Marriage of Padilla

1995 45 Cal.Rptr.2d 555, 38 Cal.App.4th 1212 This case deals with a parent who may have income imputed if he or she unreasonably fails to take advantage of an employment opportunity. Also, the parent's motivation for reducing available income is irrelevant when ability and opportunity to adequately and reasonably provide for child are present. Child support obligation must be taken into account whenever obligor wishes to pursue different life-style or endeavor.

Lottery Payments Frozen

In 1994 a Denver Colorado judge froze $54,293 in lottery payments to a "deadbeat dad" until a trial can be held to determine whether the money should go to his children in Massachusetts. Denver District Judge Stephen Phillips ordered the money placed in a bank account until he determines whether the money should go to the children or to an Arizona company that loaned Albert Tecci $1.7 million in exchange for part of his winnings. The company is disputing the judge's decision to freeze the money. A former political consultant, Tecci won Colorado's first big Lotto jackpot in 1989. Tecci once was listed on a Massachusetts list of the state's worst deadbeat dads for not sending child support payments to his ex-wife and their two children. They were forced to go on welfare. He was recently released from a Massachusetts prison after serving part of an 18-month sentence for failure to pay child support. Subsequently the state of Colorado sued both Tecci and his current wife, claiming the two established a complicated system of trusts and banking arrangements to make their Lotto winnings "unreachable by his ex-wife" and the states of Massachusetts and Colorado.

Separation of Powers

In Re the Marriage of Chastain

Mo Sup Ct # 78611, October, 1996 Separation of powers requires court approval of all administrative actions in child support. Legislature may not establish a short time period, permitting court approval, should the court not approve an administrative action within that time period.

Parenting Constitutional Right

Santosky v. Kramer

102 S.Ct. 1388, 455 U.S. 745 (1982 "Even when blood relationships are strained, parents retain vital interest in preventing irretrievable destruction of their family life; if anything, persons faced with forced dissolution of their parental rights have more critical need for procedural protections than do those resisting state intervention into ongoing family affairs."

Bell v. City of Milwaukee

746 F.2d 1205, 1242-45 (S.C. Ct. App 7th Circuit 1985 The parent-child relationship is a liberty interest protected by the Due Process Clause in the 14th Amendment.

Franz v. United States

707 F.2d 582, 595-599 (U.S. Ct. App. D.C. Circuit 1983 "A parent's right to the preservation of

his relationship with his child derives from the fact that the parent's achievement of a rich and rewarding life is likely to depend significantly on his ability to participate in the rearing of his children. A child's corresponding right to protection from interference in the relationship derives from the psychic importance to him of being raised by a loving, responsible, reliable adult." (Emphasis added)

Matter of Gentry

369 N.W.2d. 889, Mich. Appellate Div. (1983) A parent's right to the custody of his or her children is an element of "liberty" guaranteed by the Fifth Amendment and Fourteenth Amendment to the Constitution of the United States.

Orr v. Orr

99 S.Ct. 1102, 440 U.S. 268 (1979) Legislative classifications, which distribute benefits and burdens on the basis of gender carry the inherent risk of reinforcing stereotypes about the proper place of women and their need for special protection; thus, even statutes purportedly designed to compensate for and ameliorate the effects of past discrimination against women must be carefully tailored. The state cannot be permitted to classify on the basis of sex.

Doe V. Irwin

441 F. Supp. 1247, U.S. District Court Of Michigan (1977) Their right of parents to the care, custody and to nurture their children is of such character that it cannot be denied without violating those fundamental principles of liberty and justice, which lie at the base of all our civil and political institutions, and such right is a fundamental right protected by amendments 5, 9, and 14.

Langton v. Maloney

]527 F.Supp. 538 (U.S. Dist. Ct. Connecticut - 1981). The liberty interest and the integrity of the family encompass an interest in retaining custody of one's children, and thus a state may not interfere with a parent's custodial right absent due process protections.

Wo v. Hopkins

118 U.S. 356 (1886) Laws and court procedures that are "fair on their faces", but administered "with an evil eye or a heavy hand" were discriminatory and violates the Equal Protection Clause of the Fourteenth Amendment.

Carsen v. Elrod

411 F.Supp. 645, 649 (U.S. District Court Eastern Dist. Virginia 1976) "No bond is more precious and none should be more zealously protected by the law as the bond between parent and child."

In Interest of Cooper

621 P.2d 437, 5 Kansas App. Div. 2d 584 (1980) A parent's interest in custody of her children is a liberty interest, which has received considerable constitutional protection; a parent who is deprived of custody of his or her child, even though temporarily, suffers thereby grievous loss and such loss deserves extensive due process protection.

Mabra v. Schmidt

356 F.Supp. 620 (U.S. District Ct. WI 1973)

"A father enjoys the right to associate with his children, which is guaranteed by this amendment (1st) as incorporated in Amendment Fourteenth, or which is embodied in the concept of 'liberty' as that word is used in the due process clause of Fourteenth Amendment and equal protection clause of Fourteenth."

Kelson v. Springfield

767 F.2d. 651 (U.S. Ct. App. 9th Circuit 1985) That the parent-child relationship is a constitutionally protected liberty interest (see Declaration of Independence - life, liberty and pursuit of happiness and Fourteenth Amendment of U.S. Constitution.- No state can deprive any person of life, liberty -without due process of law nor deny any person the equal protection of the laws).

Mav v. Anderson

345 U.S. 528, 533; 73 S.Ct. 840, 843 (1952) The United States Supreme Court noted that a parent's right to "the companionship, care, custody and management of his or her children" is an interest "far more precious" than any property right.

Stanton v. Stanton

421 U.S. 7. 10; 95 S.Ct. 1373, 1376 (1975) The United States Supreme Court held that the "old notion" that "generally it is the man's primary

responsibility to provide a home and its essentials, "can no longer justify a statute that discriminates on the basis of gender. "No longer is the female destined solely for the home and the rearing of the family, and only the male for the marketplace and the world of ideas."

Commonwealth v. Laskowski

40 Mass. App. Ct. 480 (1996) A defendant claimed that the portion of an order issued under Ch. 209A, which provided that he was not to contact the child he fathered with his ex-girlfriend, violated his constitutional right to familial association. The defendant appealed from his conviction for violating the order, which was based on evidence that he had contacted his ex-girlfriend.
The Appeals Court ruled that the contested part of the order was un-appealable because it was unrelated to his conviction and, further, that even if the order deprived the defendant of due process, his proper avenue for redress was to file a motion for modification, or petition a single justice.

Matter of Delaney

617 P.2d 886, Oklahoma (1980) Parents have a fundamental constitutionally protected interest in continuity of legal bond with their children.

Craig v. Boren

97 S.Ct. 451;429 U.S. 190 (1976) Classifications by gender must serve important governmental objectives and must be substantially related to achievement of those objectives.

Frontiero v. Richardson

93 S.Ct. 1746; 411 U.S. 677 (1973) Classifications based upon sex, like classifications based upon race, lineage or national origin are inherently suspect and must be subjected to strict judicial scrutiny... Any statutory scheme, which draws a sharp line between the sexes, solely for the purpose of achieving administrative convenience, necessarily commands dissimilar treatment for men and women who are similarly situated and therefore involves the very kind of arbitrary legislative choice forbidden by the Constitution.

Johnson v. Robinson

94 S.Ct. 1160, 415 U.S. 361 (1974) A classification must be reasonable, not arbitrary, and must rest upon some ground of differences having a fair and substantial relation to the object of the legislation, so that all persons similarly circumstanced shall be treated alike.

Grayyned v. City of Rockford

92 S.Ct. 2294, 408 U.S. 104 (1972) Vague laws offend several important values; first, vague laws may trap the innocent by not providing fair warning; second, vague law impermissibly delegates basic policy matters to policemen, judges, and juries for resolution on an ad hoc and subjective basis, with attendant dangers of arbitrary and discriminatory application; and third, where a vague statute abuts on sensitive areas of basic First Amendment freedoms, it operates to inhibit the exercise of those freedoms.

Blood v. Margis

322 F.2d 1086 (1971) The pleading of one who pleads pro se for the protection of civil rights should be liberally construed.

Raucci v. Town of Rotterdam

No. 89-7693, U.S. Dist. Ct. --N.Y., April 27, 1990. A parent may bring a suit against a municipality, which failed to provide protection against an ex-spouse, under 42 U.S.C. Section 1983. The parent may recover damages for her son's death and her own injuries, where the police force assured her of protection from a violent ex-spouse.

Bradley v. Fisher

U.S. 13 Wall. 335 (1871)Judges have no immunity from prosecution for their judicial acts." Title 18 U.S.C.A. 241, 242 are the criminal equivalent of Title 42 U.S.C.A. 1983, 1985 et seq.

Pierson v. Ray

386 U.S. 547 at 567 (1967) "When a judge acts intentionally and knowingly to deprive a person of his constitutional rights, he exercises no discretion or individual judgement; he acts no longer as a judge, but as a "minister" of his own prejudice."

Commonwealth v. Butler

40 Mass. App. Ct. 906 (1996), Under the facts, the Appeals Court recently upheld a defendant's conviction for violation of restraining order on

evidence that he arranged to have roses sent to his ex-girlfriend's apartment. Whereas the flowers had arrived with a name on the card, the florist identified the sender as the defendant. Defendant argued on appeal that the prohibition against contacting the victim was unconstitutionally vague. Thereby, rejecting the defendant's claim, the Appeals Court held that the order, which specifically directed the defendant not to contact the victim in person, by telephone, in writing, or otherwise, either directly or through someone else, met the constitutional requirement and that the defendant's action constituted a communication, which elevated to the level of a contact and thereby came within the conduct prohibited by the order.

Gregoire v. Biddle

177 F.2d 579, 581. "We should, of course, not protect a member of the judiciary "who is in fact guilty of using his power to vent his spleen upon others, or for any other personal motive not connected with the public good."

United States v. Scheffer

March 31, 1998 The Supreme Court ruled that criminal defendants have no constitutional right to introduce at trial lie-detector test results that support their claims of innocence. The ruling does not violate his Sixth Amendment right to present a vigorous defense. That there is in fact no constitutional right to present polygraph evidence. Scheffer originally lost his case in a military court and the case was sent to the Supreme Court on appeal.

Military Rule of Evidence 707, prohibits polygraph results from being introduced at trial even though the U.S. government through its Department of Defense conducted more than 400,000 lie-detector tests between 1981 and 1997 to ferret out spies and criminals.

Fair Law - Unfair Enforcement

Yick Wo v. Hopkins, 118 US 356 (May, 1986). A law that is fair on its face, but unfairly enforced is unconstitutional.

Fifth Amendment

On April 5, 1999 A divided Supreme Court ruled that defendants who plead guilty cannot be penalized during sentencing for refusing to detail their crimes. The justices unanimously held that defendants' guilty pleas do not prevent them from later asserting their Fifth Amendment privilege against self-incrimination during the sentencing phase. The court did split 5-4 that a judge cannot hold the defendants' silence against them when handing down a sentence.

Justice Anthony M. Kennedy, writing for the majority, said the government could turn guilty pleas into "a prosecutorial sword" if defendants forfeited their right hot to incriminate themselves simply by admitting to a crime. The Fifth Amendment protects a person from being compelled to take the stand, and also protects the person from adverse inferences drawn from his silence at trial.

In the Matter of U.S. Court of Appeals, 9th Circuit. U.S. v. Oplinger, No. 97-30110. the Fifth Amendment privilege against self-incrimination doesn't extend to out-of-court, pre-arrest statements made to private individuals.

In the Matter of the Welfare of J.G.W. and J.L.W., 433 N.W.2d 885; 1989 (Minn.), A parent's fifth amendment privilege against compelled self-incrimination protects him from being ordered by court to admit sexual abuse as pre-requisite to visiting his children, but the privilege does not protect him from the risk of being denied visitation for any failure in treatment resulting from his failure to admit guilt.

Protective Laws May Not Hide Child

Franz, et. al

707 F2d 582, 1993. Wisconsin protective laws may not be used to hide a child.

U.S. Supreme Court is Fallible

Barsky v. Board of Regents

At the height of the McCarthy era, the license of a New York doctor was taken away because of his political views. A stunning dissent by Justice Douglas is in the footnotes. This case is proof that even the U.S. Supreme Court is fallible in the face of politics.

Judges are not Immune

Peterson v Stanczak

48 F.R.D. 426 "Judges are not absolutely immune from liability to damages under Civil Rights Act. 42 U.S.C.A. Section 1983 & 1985.

Imbler v. Pachtman

424 U.S. 409; 96 S.Ct. 984 (1976) Title 42 USC 1983 is for (federal) civil rights violations. "Judges may be punished criminally for willful deprivation of rights on the strength of Title 18 U.S.A. 241 and 242."

Grandparent

Case #VR921200 Askren

Best Interest of the Child. Billings Montana August 10, 1994

This case found that it was in the best interest of a seven-year-old girl to live with her step father after the death of her mother rather than live with her biological father who has had visitation, or the maternal grandparents.

Ward v. Dibble, Fla. 5th DCA

Dec. 6, 1996. the trial court incorrectly presumed that Florida Statute 752.01 entitled grandparents to visitation rights. The appellate court held grandparents must show why visitation would be in the best interests of the children.

Troxel, Jenifer, v. Granville, Tommie

8094 Order dated: 09/28/99 Docket number: 99-138 Action: The petition for a writ of certiorari is granted. The brief of petitioners is to be filed with the Clerk and served upon opposing counsel on or before 3 p.m., Friday, November 12, 1999. The brief of respondent is to be filed with the Clerk and served upon opposing counsel on or before 3 p.m., Monday, December 13, 1999. A reply brief, if any, is to be filed with the Clerk and served upon opposing counsel on or before 3 p.m., Thursday, December 30, 1999. Rule 29.2 does not apply.

TROXEL, JENIFER, ET VIR v. GRANVILLE, TOMMIE (8094) Order dated: 12/06/99 Docket number: 99-138

Action: The motion of Grandparents United for Children's Rights for leave to file a brief as amicus curiae is granted. 1. Does Revised Code of Washington 26.10.160(3) and the former RCW26.09.240 granting third parties, including grandparents, the right to petition for visitation rights with a minor child if the visitation is "in the best interests of the child" impermissibly interfere with a parent's fundamental interest in the "care custody and companionship of a child" as defined by the liberty and privacy provisions of the United States Constitution? 2. Did the Supreme Court of Washington err in Custody of Smith, 137 Wn.2d 1, 969 P.2d 21 (1998), in holding that RCW 26. 10. 160(3) and the former RCW 26.09.240 are unconstitutional based upon the liberty interest of the Fourteenth Amendment and the fundamental right to privacy inherent in the United States Constitution. When it used the flawed premise that a parent's fundamental right to autonomy in child-rearing decisions is unassailable and that the state's parents patriae power to act in a child's welfare may not be invoked absent a finding of harm to the child or parental unfitness?

Six Months of Grandparents Care

Illinois grandparents who cared for their grandchildren for at least six months must be informed if the children are being offered for adoption, a Florida circuit court has ruled. Ron and Fran Schroeter of Centralia had been trying to gain custody of their granddaughter when they discovered she had been adopted by a Florida couple. The couple argued that notifying the grandparents of the adoption would violate their right to privacy. But the court disagreed. It will now decide who gets custody of the girl.

Utah Grandparent Visitation

In Utah grandparents would be able to obtain court-ordered visitation rights more easily under a bill passed by the state senate. State law currently applies a presumption that it is "reasonable" for parents to deny grandparents visitation rights. Grandparents can ask a court to override that presumption, but they must first prove that they're fit to have contact and it's in the best interest of the child. The bill would limit the presumption's applicability to only "intact families," where both natural or adoptive parents live with the children. State Senator Terry Spender, who sponsored the bill, says he wants to equalize legal rights for grandparents and parents.

Oklahoma Grandparents Get More Protection

Oklahoma grandparents who have raised their grandchildren for over a year would be given more extensive legal protection in custody cases under a bill pending before the state legislature. The proposal gives greater rights to grandparents and other close family relatives who have become surrogate parents in cases where birth parents decide they want their kids back, says Representative Russ Roach. The bill would establish a procedure for giving relatives and the children they raised some protection in informal cases not decided by a court or the state department of human services. Roach says the bill may also help people who have custody of their grandchildren, but haven't established legal guardianship because they can't afford an attorney.

Iowa Grandparent Visitation Unconstitutional

A state law allowing grandparents to petition for visitation of a grandchild raised by married parents is unconstitutional, a Polk County court has ruled. Lois and Joe Santi sought the legal right to visit their granddaughter, Taylor, after their relationship with Taylor's parents deteriorated. They claimed that the loss of contact will be harmful to the three-year-old. But the court said that allowing grandparents to petition for visitation violates the parents' right to raise their children as they see fit. "There has to be finding of substantial risk of serious harm before the court has a right to come in and make a judgment over loving, caring parents," the court said. All states allow grandparents to petition for visitation if the nuclear family is broken up because of divorce or death, but only some states allow petitions when the parents are still together.

FL Grandparent Visitation Unconstitutional

Saul v. Brunetti,

Where a grandparent can obtain visitation whenever this is in the child's "best interests," this is unconstitutional even if the child's parents were never married, says the Florida Supreme Court in affirming the Court of Appeal. The statute violates parents' right to privacy under the state constitution because it interferes with their right to raise their children, the court said. The U.S. Supreme Court has agreed to decide the constitutionality of a similar state statute. In the Florida case, the grandparents, whose unmarried daughter had died, sought visitation with their grandson after his father objected to their visits. The grandparents tried to distinguish a 1998 case that said the statute was unconstitutional as applied to a child whose father was widowed, noting that their grandchild's parents had never been married. Von Eiff v. Azicri But the court said that "if the father of a child born into a marriage has a right of privacy where the biological mother is deceased it follows that the father of an out-of-wedlock child has the same right of privacy... "We recognize that it must hurt deeply for the grandparents to have lost a daughter and then be denied time alone with their [grandson]. We are not insensitive to their plight. However, familial privacy is grounded on the right of parents to rear their children without unwarranted governmental interference."

Troxel v. Granville

Certiorari granted, September 28, 1999. The U.S. Supreme Court will decide whether a state statute permitting grandparents to obtain visitation rights whenever it is in the child's "best interest" is constitutional. The Court will review a Washington Supreme Court decision that said the statute violates parents' right to privacy under the Fourteenth Amendment because it interferes with their right to raise their children as they see fit. The Washington court held that parents have a constitutional right to decide who can visit their children as long as their decisions don't "seriously conflict with the physical or mental health of the child... "Short of preventing harm to the child, the standard of 'best interest of the child' is insufficient to serve as a compelling state interest overruling a parent's fundamental rights. State intervention to better a child's quality of life through third party visitation is not justified where the child's circumstances are otherwise satisfactory. To suggest otherwise would be the logical equivalent of asserting that the state has the authority to break up stable families and redistribute its infant population to provide each child with the 'best family.'" The dissent complained that the decision deprives third parties of "any opportunity to have visitation with a child even where the relationship is significant and in the child's best interest. This is cruel both to the child and to those third parties." A decision from the Supreme Court is expected this term.

Foor v. Foor

In Ohio where children have been adopted by their stepfather, a domestic relations court can't award visitation to their paternal grandparents, a state appeals court has ruled. The grandparents argued that visitation could be awarded to them, pursuant to statutory and case law, upon a finding that it was in the best interest of the children. But the court disagreed. It said that state law was silent on the issue of grandparent visitation in the context of step-parent adoption, and that the state supreme court hadn't ruled on the issue.

"When the supreme court has been presented the opportunity to rule on this issue in the past, it has consistently declined to do so, stating unequivocally that any changes in this area of law must emanate from the general assembly," the court said. "Reluctantly, we find that we are in no position to disagree."

Grandparents Custody Despite Father

Watkins v. Nelson

Grandparents can get custody of their deceased daughter's child when this is in the child's "best interests" – even if the father objects, says the New Jersey Appellate Division. The child had lived with her grandparents since she was born (her mother died 12 days later). The father had regular visitation. The father argued that he was entitled to custody unless the grandparents could show he was "unfit."

But the court said that "where [a] third party is able to show that he or she stands in the shoes of a parent to the child and thus in parity with the natural parent, he or she should be accorded the status of the natural parent in determining the standard to be applied to the quest for custody. In such circumstances the best interest test should apply." The court rejected "an absolute parental preference rule [that] effectively forecloses custody to any other party, even one who has functioned in every way as a parent, unless the biological parent is sufficiently unfit that termination of that parent's parental relationship would be warranted. Such a rule would be a mistake." A dissenting judge complained that "this decision has been infused with concerns over who the child would be 'better' off with. The correct legal standard is parental unfitness."

Religion

Zummo v. Zummo

574 A.2d 1130 (Pa. Super. 1990) A Pennsylvania state court observed that "the vast majority of courts... have concluded that each parent must be free to provide religious exposure and instruction, as that parent sees fit, during any and all periods of legal custody or visitation without restriction, unless the challenged beliefs or conduct of the parent are demonstrated to present a substantial threat of present or future, physical or emotional harm to the child in the absence of the proposed restrictions." The court adopted this view as the law of Pennsylvania.

The court stressed that a "substantial threat of harm" did not include "the speculative possibility of mere disquietude, disorientation, or confusion arising from exposure to contradictory religions." It also concluded that a court could not take into account the "devoutness" of the respective parents in making a decision regarding religious upbringing. choice.

An appeal court overturned a decision that prohibited a father from taking the children to non-Jewish religious services. The court also found the mother had failed to prove tat the father's religious beliefs presented any potential harm to the children and granted the father the right to expose his children to his roman Catholic faith.

Re in the Marriage of Knighton

723 S.W.2d 274 (Tex. App. 1987) Membership in (a certain church) could not be used as a basis for denying a parent custody of a child in a child custody hearing without proof that the parent's religious beliefs were "illegal, immoral, or caused serious mental or bodily injury to the children," concluded a Texas appeals court.

LeDoux v. LeDoux

452 N.W.2d 1 (1990) The Nebraska Supreme Court noted that "courts have a duty to consider whether religious beliefs threaten the health and well-being of a child." If they do, as they did in this case, then a civil court is free to protect a child against such influences.

Zucco v. Garrett

501 N.E.2d 875 (Ill. App. 1986) Religious belief alone cannot be the basis of an award of custody. In The Best Interests Of The Child- The trial court erred in awarding custody of a child to its father on the basis of the father's more active participation in organized religion, ruled an Illinois appeals court. The court concluded that favoring religion in child custody hearings violates the First Amendment's non establishment of religion clause. The court did acknowledge that evidence of a parent's religious faith is admissible in evidence, but cannot be the basis of an award of custody.

Prince v. Massachusetts

3210 U.S. 158, 166 (1944) Moore V. City Of East Cleveland, 431-U.S. 494 (1977)

Recognizing as a fundamental liberty interest the right of parents to raise their children, the Supreme Court has also established that the Constitution's guaranteed fundamental privacy rights also embodies a fundamental right to parental autonomy in child rearing. The Court acknowledged a "private realm of family life, which the state cannot enter."

In re Marriage of Roberts

503 N.E.2d 363 (Ill. App. 1986) The Illinois Court awarded custody of two minor children to their father, but required the children to regularly visit their mother though she was living in adultery. The father, appealed stating that such an arrangement forced him to seemingly condone a lifestyle contrary to his religious beliefs and sought to deny the mother visitation. An appeals court denied the father's request, concluding that there was no evidence that the best interests of the children would be adversely affected by periodic visits to their mother.

Meyer v. Nebraska

262 U.S. 390, 399 (1923) This court did not attempted to define with exactness the liberty thus guaranteed [by the Fourteenth Amendment]... Without doubt, it denotes not merely freedom from bodily restraint, but also the right of the individual to contract, to engage in any of the common occupations of life, to acquire useful knowledge, to marry, establish a home and bring up children, to worship God according to the dictates of his or her own conscience, and generally to enjoy those privileges long recognized at common law as essential to the orderly pursuit of happiness by free men.

Pater v. Pater

588 N.E.2d 794 (Ohio 1992) The discretion, which a court has in custody matters is limited by the federal constitution. A court may violate a parent's constitutional rights if a custody decision is improperly made based on religious bias. Though courts can examine religious practices to determine the best interests of the child, parent may not be denied custody of a child on the basis of the parent's religious practices, unless there is probative evidence that those practices will adversely affect the mental or physical health of the child. A court may not restrict a non-custodial parent's right to expose child to that parent's religious beliefs unless conflict between the parents' religious beliefs is affecting the child's welfare.

Thomas v. Review Board

Stated "religious beliefs need not be acceptable, logical, consistent, or comprehensible to others in order to merit First Amendment protection"

Kendall v. Kendall

SJC-07427 (1997) Divorced parents of different faiths can be prohibited from teaching their religious beliefs to their children if it would harm them, the Massachusetts state Supreme Judicial Court has ruled. The father, Jeffrey P. Kendall, is a member of the fundamentalist Boston Church of Christ. The mother, Barbara Kendall, is an Orthodox Jew. The children, aged 4, 6 and 9, are being raised by the mother as Orthodox Jews and she argued they would be forced to learn teachings that contradict her religion. The high court justices called it a "close question", but said the state and U.S. constitutions permit limitations on individual liberties if there is a compelling interest. "Promoting the best interests of the children is an interest sufficiently compelling to impose a burden on the (father's) right to practice religion and his parental rights to determine the religious upbringing of his children," wrote Justice Neil Lynch. The mother's lawyer, David Cherny, wrote that the children "are experiencing emotional distress because of the exposure to Jeff's religion, which teaches them that in order to be 'saved' they must accept Jesus Christ. "These teachings contradict their Jewish ethnicity, force them to regard their mother as someone doomed to hell and place them in the unenviable position of having to regard choosing between religions as choosing between parents."

Marriage of Mentry 1983

The appeals court found that the father's religious beliefs hadn't harmed the children and that the trial court's order represented an unwarranted intrusion into family privacy.

The appeals court also found that, in order for the court to intervene in a parent's upbringing of their children there needs to be a "clear, affirmative showing of harm or likely harm to the children" as well as "a showing that such harm presents a graver problem than coercive intervention into family privacy."

Yoder v. Wisconsin

The free exercise of religious beliefs includes the right to direct the religious upbringing of one's children. The Supreme Court has clearly established that to constitute a compelling interest, state interference with a parent's right to raise his or her child must be for the purpose of protecting the child's health or welfare.

Carrico v. Blevins

402 S.E.2d 235 (Va. App. 1991). [PCL17] A Virginia appeals court ruled that the original court order requiring a mother to take her son to the church that her ex-husband attended, but which held tenets that she herself found to be "intolerable" was in error when it ordered that: "She is required to attend church with her son or suffer the penalty of losing a portion of her visitation time....Regardless of the trial judge's motivation, the state may not require a citizen to attend any religious worship."

Osteras v. Osteras

859 P.2d 948 (Idaho 1993) A court may not violate the Free Exercise Clause of the First Amendment of the federal constitution by suggesting that parents who choose not to observe a particular (or any) religious faith are subject to having their custodial rights jeopardized because of that choice. Use of religion as a factor in deciding custody disputes would serve to establish a favored religion, over either an unfavored religion or no religion at all, in violation of the Non-Establishment Clause of the First Amendment, since it would have the primary effect of advancing religion. The state, through the courts, cannot prefer one religion over another, or religion over non-religion. To deny a parent custody of children because of a parent's religious beliefs or lack thereof, would deny that parent a civil right because of those religious beliefs. In the absence of a compelling reason, courts cannot favor religion over non-religion or favor one religion over another. In determining custody, a court may, in its discretion, examine the secular ethical traits that the parent will teach children. But this may not serve as a pretext, inadvertent or otherwise, for delving into a parent's religion or degree of devotion.

Parents Can't Choose Modification

Frauenshuh v. Giese

The Minnesota Supreme Court ruled that even though a couple agreed to a different standard for altering custody as part of their divorce agreement, this is invalid and state law still applies, says the Minnesota Supreme Court in reversing the Court of Appeals. The state law, an award of sole physical custody can be modified only if both parents consent or the current arrangement "endangers the child's physical or emotional health." In this case the mother had sole physical custody of the couple's son. As part of their divorce agreement, the parents stipulated that if either of them moved more than 50 miles away, any change in custody would be based on the best interest of the child. But the court said that state law controls. "If the legislature wanted parties to be afforded the opportunity to stipulate to a different modification standard in cases involving sole physical custody, it would have said so with unambiguous language... "We acknowledge the importance of stipulations as a means for resolving marital dissolutions and in no way seek to discourage creative and amicable resolution of these cases within the confines of the law...However, we cannot allow parties to contravene the plain and unambiguous intent of the legislature to provide permanence and closure in child custody matters... "It is one thing to hold for another day issues related to money or property of a party; it is quite another to permit a stipulation, which effectively holds for another day the decision of who has custody of a child."

Mundon v. Mundon

The Indiana Court of Appeals ruled that even though a couple agreed that custody of their child would automatically shift to the father if the mother failed to provide proof of attendance at an alcohol treatment program, the court must still consider the "best interests of the child" before transferring custody. The father argued that the automatic transfer of custody should be enforced.

But the court said that while state law "expressly encourages divorcing spouses to reach...agreements...where provisions are made in the interest of the support and custody of children, as opposed to those that merely set forth rights in property, our legislature and sound public policy dictate that the trial court must play a role... "The trial court may not modify a child custody order unless the modification is in the best interests of the child [and] insofar as the trial court itself could not have circumvented the best interests finding before a custody modification could come into effect...so it cannot in essence 'ratify' an automatic change of custody simply because the divorcing parents agreed to it."

Change of Circumstance

Searcy v. Seedorff

Missouri Court held that even though a mother got a better job and improved her home life after custody of her children was awarded to her husband's parents following her divorce, she could not move to modify custody and get the children back, the state court of appeals has ruled. The mother filed a motion to modify child custody, arguing that a substantial and continuing change in circumstances had occurred because she was gainfully employed and could provide a stable and secure home.

But the court said, "The plain language of [the state custody statute] provides no exception to the requirement that a moving party, any moving party, who seeks to modify a custody order must first establish that a substantial 'change in circumstances of the child or his custodian' had occurred." The decision expressly overrules contrary precedent in this court.

Rich Can't Get Attorney Fees from Richer

Taylor v. Taylor

The North Carolina Supreme Court ruled a wife who is a millionaire can't be awarded attorney fees in a child custody case even though her husband is much wealthier than she is, says the North Carolina Supreme Court in a 4-3 decision. A state statute says that fees can be awarded if a party has "insufficient means to defray the expense of the suit." The court held that the wife had "sufficient means" to pay $100,000 in attorney fees.

The dissenters argued that the statute shouldn't be applied with "literal starkness," and that the wife should get fees because she wasn't rich enough to battle with the husband on an equal financial footing.

Police - Psychologists Sued in Domestic Violence

Third Party Tort is becoming more viable to victims of domestic violence. They are alleging that the police or others such as psychologists should be held accountable for the commission of the crime. The Third, Ninth and Tenth Circuits have upheld the validity of police liability claims based on 42 U.S.C. õ 1983, alleging the victims of domestic violence were not afforded the equal protection of the laws, which would have been afforded to non-domestic violence victims.

The Fifth Circuit also says it upholds the theory, but has not yet rendered a decision in favor of the plaintiffs. A similar equal protection theory is currently pending in the Eighth Circuit. Some state courts are allowing these cases to go forward on the theory of tort liability, whereas previously these actions were dismissed on the grounds of governmental immunity. In the 1990's Illinois and Wisconsin have issued opinions on this subject.

Calloway v. Kinkelaar

Illinois' Court of Appeals held that the issuance of a protective order (or no contact order or Temporary Restraining Order) created a special duty.

Barillari v. City of Milwaukee

In the Wisconsin case, the court held that once

the police promised protection, that promise took the police's duty out of a discretionary function exception. An exception that exists with respect to cases against the government is that you cannot hold the government liable for the doing or the failing to do a discretionary act. The court held that the trial courts' motions for summary judgment granted on the basis of governmental immunity should be reversed.

Ricketts v. City of Columbia, Mo.

The jury came back with a verdict of over a million dollars, but the lower court set it aside.

Does a Police Liability Case Exist?

Some sample questions attorneys should ask domestic violence victims in order to determine whether a police liability suit is an option:
What is the crime?
Where did it occur?
Who is the victim?
Is the victim a person under a protective order?
Is it a person the police have promised protection to?
Where did it occur can be a pertinent question.

For example, A woman was kidnapped by her husband in a parking lot of a mall and dragged 50 feet in broad day light. The mall was ultimately sued, and the case was resolved.

Questions designed to determine whether someone aside from the criminal bears liability for the commission of the crime should include:

Who is the criminal?

Is the criminal a person on parole, probation, under treatment for mental illness or escaped from somewhere?

Once you have determined that the police may be liable, the next step is: Investigation. If it involves a city, you can usually get the information with a Freedom of Information Act request under whatever the local equivalent of the act is. As an example, the police records of the woman's calls.

If the calls were all to the same address, the larger communities usually have a computerized system that you can get the record of all the police calls and reports for that particular address. Each jurisdiction is different. You may have to send someone over to the police station to sit in the basement and look over a year's worth of calls. You need to figure out all of the ways the police department keeps their records to find them all.

In the records you are looking to see whether a liability allegation is feasible. The attorney for the victim, needs to find out at what point something went awry in order to properly draft a petition. It is important to know how much contact has occurred with the third party. For example, sometimes the calls go awry at the dispatcher level. In other words, the dispatcher handles the call by saying, "If he actually hits you, then call me back," or words to that effect. Sometimes a dispatch is made, but nobody ever shows up because of the priority the call is given. It could be in a place where domestic cases are given a low priority and nobody ever shows up.

Sometimes the offender goes away when the officer arrives on the scene and decides that it was the victim's fault. Or, the officer decides that it's just a domestic matter and they should work it out. Other times, the officer takes the assailant out and just walks him around the block.

Any number of things can occur, and the attorney for the victim needs to find out at what point - and sometimes every one of these things has happened over the course of time - the third party's role enables the commission of the crime.

There maybe other parties, other than law enforcement officers, who may be held liable for negligence or violation of equal protection. As an example, a case where the assailant was being treated by a psychiatrist, there may be a third-party liability option. In those cases, its important to file the case first and try to get your records later. Usually you need to sue the assailant directly, and then the court may or may not order the release of the records. In that case, you're looking for a direct threat said by the assailant to the psychiatrist, such as, "I am going to kill my wife."

The keys to holding the police or another third party accountable in a domestic violence case is discovering conduct that is aggravated in nature. Examples of aggravated conduct are repeated police calls with no real response and injury that cannot be denied. We are still a society that looks at domestic violence as a social rather than a criminal problem.

Jurors willing to open their minds to the possibility that domestic violence is certainly a public health problem are critical to the case. It's important to make jurors understand that law-enforcement officials that we count on to protect us from violence committed by strangers have at least as great if not a greater obligation to protect us from family violence.

Skillful drafting is important since these are technically complicated cases. They involve potential negligence claims, such as the state tort claims in Illinois and Wisconsin alleging negligence against municipalities become especially complicated because of governmental immunities. An attorney who doesn't explore police or other third-party liability may be open to a malpractice suit.

The standard of care is not yet established in connection with these matters. Certainly an attorney handling a divorce for a person who has been viciously beaten and bears permanent injuries, better look at third-party liability. There are a lot of reasons not to pursue these lawsuits, not the least of which is the emotional toll on the victim. But the option always ought to be explored, and the victim ought to be the decision-maker. Attorney's clients who are victims of domestic violence should be advised to get mental health assistance. Some attorneys refuse representation of victims of domestic violence who will not go to counseling. This is because attorneys cannot provide counseling while providing legal representation.

These women are traumatized. That is what makes it so hard to persuade them that they need counseling. They trust no one. Their self-esteem is at zero or less. They often believe that whatever happened was in fact their fault - that if they had only cooked better or cleaned better or been a better wife or better mother, then none of this would have occurred. That makes it very difficult to get them to see that what they need in order to heal is counseling. What else is important to know about helping a client who is a victim of domestic abuse? In dealing with domestic abuse victims, if you're lucky enough to have a living victim, the first step is to find out how she can be kept safe. What can the attorney do to ensure that this doesn't end up being a case involving an estate instead of a living person? A lawyer who has a living victim should do everything in his or her power to assure the victim goes on living.

Attorneys need to understand that the most dangerous time for a battered woman is when she decides to break the chains that bind. The lawyer may need to intervene in terms of finding a safe house, a battered women's shelter or even getting her out of the state or community. The attorney also needs to make sure that any children are also safe. All of this is the responsibility of any attorney who undertakes to represent a battered woman. The immediate need of any woman who is a victim of domestic violence is safety.

First take care of the immediate need for safety, and then begin to ask questions. The attorney has to be compassionate and someone who will go the extra mile for the client. The time spent will be very great, and it won't all be legal time. It's unavoidable to not do some counseling.

Expunged Records

NJ 2C:52-17. Use of expunged records by agencies on pending petition for expungement. Expunged records may be used by the agencies that possess same to ascertain whether a person has had prior conviction expunged, or sealed under prior law, when the agency possessing the record is noticed of a pending petition for the expungement of a conviction. Any such agency may supply information to the court wherein the motion is pending and to the other parties who are entitled to notice pursuant to 2C:52-10

Lesbian and Gay Parents

The "Nexus" Approach

The nexus standard requires that there be a clear connection (or "nexus") between a parent's sexual identity and harm to the child before the parent's sexual orientation assumes any relevance in a custody, visitation, or adoption dispute. Under this approach, the sexual orientation of a parent alone can not form the basis of denying parenting rights unless it is demonstrated to cause harm to the child.

As of May 1995, the following states (29) have adopted some variant of a nexus test: Alabama, Alaska, Arizona, California, Connecticut, Delaware, (District of Columbia*), Florida, Illinois, Indiana, Iowa, Kentucky, Maine, Maryland, Massachusetts, Michigan, New Jersey, New Mexico, New York, North Dakota, Ohio, Oregon, South Carolina, Pennsylvania, Utah, Vermont, Washington, West Virginia, Wisconsin, Wyoming.

(*The District of Columbia is currently the only jurisdiction in the country that has an explicit law guaranteeing that sexual orientation by itself cannot be used as a factor in determining custody or visitation.)

Denies Child Custody to Gay Father in Favor of Violent Stepdad

Weigand v. Houghton

730 So. 2d 581 (Miss. 1999)

In The Supreme Court Of Mississippi

NO. 97-CA-01246-SCT

David John Weigand

V.

Machelle "Gil" Weigand Houghton

Date Of Judgment: 07/21/1997

Trial Judge: Hon. Percy Lee Lynchard, Jr.

Court From Which Appealed: Desoto County Chancery Court

Attorneys For Appellant: Robert B. Mcduff

Alison R. Steiner

Elizabeth Jane Hicks

Michael Adams

Jennifer Middleton

Attorney For Appellee: Pro Se

Nature of the Case: Civil - Custody

Disposition: Affirmed In Part; Reversed And Rendered In Part - 02/04/99

Motion For Rehearing Filed:

Mandate Issued:

En Banc.

Roberts, Justice, For The Court:

Statement of the Case

¶1. On May 9, 1997, David Weigand (herinafter "David") filed a petition for modification of the custody and visitation order in effect with regard to his son, Paul Weigand (hereinafter "Paul") in the Chancery Court of Desoto County, Honorable Percy Lee Lynchard, Jr. presiding. Because the original divorce decree was entered by the District Court of Shawnee County, Kansas, David petitioned the chancery court for enrollment of a foreign divorce decree at the same time. The Opinion of the Court, denying the petition for custody modification, was filed on June 17, 1997. In light of new evidence which David found quite important to the case, he filed a Motion for New Trial and Motion to Alter or Amend Judgment, which was heard on August 19, 1997. That motion was denied by the chancellor in an order filed on September 9, 1997. On October 9, 1997, David filed a Notice of Appeal. On December 8, 1997, David filed a Motion For Injunctive Relief Pending Appeal with the chancery court. That motion was denied by the chancery court in an Order filed on December 22, 1997. David asserts four issues on appeal to the Supreme Court:

I. whether this court is required to give deference to the chancellor's finding concerning The Best Interest Of The Child when the chancellor relied on an erroneous view of the law and misapplied the albright factors?

II. Whether the chancellor erred when he found that modification of custody was not in Paul's best interest?

III. Whether the chancellor's sua sponte order that all visitation between David and Paul occur outside the presence of David's life partner is legal error and requires reversal?

IV. Whether the chancery court's ruling requires reversal and an immediate transfer of custody of Paul to his father, David?

Statement Of The Facts

¶2. On November 23, 1987, a divorce was awarded unto David by the District Court of Shawnee County, Kansas, Division 11, in Cause No. 87-D-8111. The District Court awarded the joint legal custody of Paul to both parties with "residential custody" being alternated between the parties until such time as the minor child reached school age. It further provided that at the time the minor child reached school age, the residential custody would be vested with David during the school year and with Machelle during the remaining months. Subsequently, on June 2, 1988, an order modifying that decree was entered by the same court whereby the parties were granted joint custody of the minor child with Machelle having the residential custody of the child. David is presently seeking modification of the prior decrees enrolled in this cause. The requested relief by way of modification includes an award of full care, custody and control of the minor child of the parties subject only to the reasonable and liberal rights of visitation to Machelle, an order terminating his duty of support payments for the benefit of Paul as earlier awarded, an assessment of support on behalf of Machelle to be paid to him for the care, support and maintenance of

the minor child and finally an order directing Machelle to turn over to David all of Paul's personal property. At the trial of this cause, David testified and produced nine witnesses in support of his request for modification of the provisions of child custody. Machelle testified on her own behalf and called no other witnesses. Furthermore, it is important to note that Machelle did not file a brief in response to David's appeal to the Supreme Court; however, her letter is in the nature of a response and is considered accordingly.
Also, David does not dispute the chancellor's finding of facts. After a thorough review of the record, this Court agrees with the chancellor's finding of facts and has adopted them.

¶3. David is a forty-one (41) year old resident of Lake Forest, California. He has resided in the state of California since January of 1994 and is employed as a property manager at this time. He resides in a five bedroom home in an upscale neighborhood and earns a gross annual salary of approximately $40,000.00.

¶4. Following the divorce of the parties in 1987, the minor child resided with David for a period of less than one year. At that time, because he felt that his lifestyle as a single person was not conducive to the rearing of a minor child, he relinquished physical custody of Paul to Machelle. David has throughout the post-divorce period of his life consistently exercised visitation with Paul, having him at his home in California for extended weeks during the summer. David expresses a love and affection for Paul which was unquestioned by the chancellor. He has seen to Paul's needs during the period of time in which Paul has lived with him by furnishing him with not only the necessities of life, but also providing him with certain luxuries including access and use of a home computer which Paul enjoys, availability of an "800" number for the child to contact him at any time he desires, accompanying the child to museums, dinners, shopping and amusement parks as well as other extracurricular activities. He has consistently encouraged Paul to develop his writing skills for which the child shows a talent. David expressed a desire for Paul to receive the highest quality education possible.

¶5. In anticipation of Paul coming to live with David, should David be successful in this modification, David has remodeled and refurbished Paul's room at his home, thoroughly investigated the local school system as well as a local university, and purchased computer and word processing programs for Paul to enhance his writing skills. David also sought information concerning Paul's publication of short stories he has written, which publication would enhance the possibility of Paul's admission to the university program.

¶6. David openly and freely admits to engaging in a homosexual lifestyle for a number of years. He presently resides in a jointly owned home with his life partner of eight years, Wayne Fields. Although prohibited from marrying under California law, David and Wayne have entered into a living trust agreement and domestic partnership agreement, holding themselves out as a couple and describing their relationship as monogamous. According to David, they regularly engage in homosexual activities which include both oral and anal intercourse. However, they described their sexual relations, as well as their open affections between each other, at least in the presence of the child, to be discreet and performed only behind closed and locked doors.

¶7. When Paul was examined in chambers by counsel for both parties as well as the chancellor, he acknowledged that he had been previously embarrassed when he appeared in public with both his father and Wayne "while here in the South." He further indicated that a show of affection between the two might bother him and "definitely would bother me" if any of his friends were present when that affection was shown. While on vacation trips with his father and Wayne, Paul slept in the same hotel room with the two, sleeping in his own bed while David and Wayne slept in the adjacent bed. Paul also indicated that he would be uncomfortable if he believed himself to be a homosexual because of his religious beliefs. He stated that he believed the relationship between his father and Wayne was wrong.

¶8. Paul is an "A" student with no behavioral problems. He presently resides in the custody of his mother and his stepfather, Jeff Houghton, formerly convicted of felony assault and theft in the state of Kansas. He routinely attends the First Baptist Church in Horn Lake, Mississippi. Although of a sufficient age in which he may voice a preference for the parent with whom he would desire to reside, Paul has expressed no clear choice, testifying that he wanted to continue to reside with his mother yet he had a desire to live with his father in California as well. However, Paul did testify that if the recent stress in his home following his stepfather's accident had not occurred, he would not have been interested in moving in with his father, David.

¶9. David seeks a change of custody based upon a material and substantial change in the circumstances of the parties which adversely affects Paul. In support of this he testified that the present custodial situation is exposing Paul to mental and emotional abuse as a consequence of the volatile relationship between Paul's mother and stepfather. As evidence David points to two separate incidents of domestic disturbance involving Machelle and Jeff. On November 4, 1996, Jeff was arrested for disturbance of family and simple assault by the Horn Lake Police Department. This was a result of a domestic disturbance occurring at the home of the parties in which Jeff caused physical injury to Machelle by striking her in the face. As a result of this incident he was subsequently convicted by the municipal court on a charge of simple assault after the entry of a plea of guilty. As a result of this incident, Jeff was sentenced to complete a course in anger management. Subsequently on January 11, 1997, Jeff was again arrested at the family home following an altercation between the parties. As a result of that incident the charge of disturbance of family was remanded and he was convicted of the charges of public drunk and malicious mischief. The use of alcohol by him was also present at this incident.

¶10. Both of the above incidents occurred while Paul was present and apparently greatly disturbed him. The latter incident resulted in Paul himself summoning the police following a 911 emergency call. It is apparent from the testimony of Paul that the relationship between his mother and Jeff is explosive at times, but Paul acknowledges that he has never personally been physically abused by his stepfather.

¶11. Machelle testified in her own behalf. She testified that she had no idea that there was any problem perceived by David in the custody arrangement until she received a letter of March 19, 1997, where David indicated a desire to seek the physical custody of Paul. She further testified that she assisted Paul in school, including extracurricular activities such as the BETA club. She has in recent months begun sending Paul to the First Baptist Church. Both she and Jeff, along with Paul, attend regularly. She is employed at two separate jobs, Wal-Mart and Federal Express, working an average of 50-52 hours per week at both jobs. She admits that the time with the child is limited now because of her two jobs but has intentions of resigning one in August of this year.

¶12. Machelle admits that her relationship and home situation with her current husband has placed a strain on her relationship with Paul. In May of 1996 Jeff was seriously injured in an automobile accident in Memphis, Tennessee and has since been unable to work causing severe financial strain on the family as a result of his absent income and excessive medical bills. Jeff's depression because of his inability to work has caused a strain on the relationship between both him and Machelle as well as he and the child.

¶13. Machelle acknowledged the two incidents as testified by David which involve the arrest of Jeff, but believes them to be isolated incidents which she does not anticipate reoccurring. She is expecting her second child and believes this her third marriage to be stable at this time.

Discussion of the Issues

I. Whether this court is required to give deference to the chancellor's finding concerning the best interest of the child when the chancellor relied on an erroneous view of the law and misapplied the albright factors?

II. Whether the chancellor erred when he found that modification of custody was not in Paul's best interest? ¶14. The standard of review this Court invokes in a child custody case is well-settled. The review is "quite limited in that the chancellor must be manifestly wrong, clearly erroneous, or apply an erroneous legal standard in order for this court to reverse." Wright v. Stanley , 700 So. 2d 274, 280 (Miss.1997) (citing Williams v. Williams , 656 So. 2d 325, 330 (Miss.1995)). This Court will not disturb the findings of a chancellor, "'. . . be they of ultimate fact or of evidentiary fact,'" when supported by substantial evidence in the record. Smith v. Jones , 654 So. 2d 480, 485 (Miss.1995) (quoting Cooper v. Crabb , 587 So. 2d 236, 239 (Miss.1991)).

¶15. This Court has stated that: "[t]he prerequisites to a child custody modification are: (1) proving a material change in circumstances which adversely affects the welfare of the child and (2) finding that the best interest of the child requires the change of custody." Smith v. Jones , 654 So. 2d 480,

486 (Miss.1995).

In order for this Court to say that the chancellor has not abused his discretion in these matters, there must be sufficient evidence to support his conclusions. Id. This Court has also noted that "[t]he 'totality of the circumstances' must be considered." Ash v. Ash , 622 So. 2d 1264, 1266 (Miss.1993) (citing Tucker v. Tucker , 453 So. 2d 1294, 1297 (Miss.1984)).

¶16. "In all child custody cases, the polestar consideration is the best interest of the child." Sellers v. Sellers , 638 So. 2d 481, 485 (Miss.1994). There are a number of factors that should be considered by chancellors in weighing decisions regarding custody:

The age of the child is ... but one factor to be considered. Age should carry no greater weight than other factors to be considered, such as: health, and sex of the child; a determination of the parent that has had the continuity of care prior to the separation; which has the best parenting skills and which has the willingness and capacity to provide primary child care; the employment of the parent and responsibilities of that employment; physical and mental health and age of the parents; emotional ties of parent and child; moral fitness of parents; the home, school and community record of the child; the preference of the child at the age sufficient to express a preference by law; stability of home environment and employment of each parent, and other factors relevant to the parent-child relationship. Id. (quoting Albright v. Albright , 437 So. 2d 1003, 1005 (Miss.1983)).

¶17. The lower court issued a thirty-page opinion in the case sub judice, of which twenty-eight pages were devoted to the issue of Paul's custody. Having found that there had been a substantial and material change in circumstances which adversely affected Paul's welfare, the chancellor addressed and analyzed each of the Albright factors before determining that it was in the best interest of Paul to remain in the custody of his mother, Machelle.

¶18. The chancellor noted that Paul, being almost fourteen (14) years of age, was of such an age that he could by statute express a preference for the parent with whom he wished to live, under certain conditions. As Paul exhibited no specific preference, this factor is of some consequence, as it tends to support maintaining the status quo. There was no testimonial or documentary evidence to suggest that the health of Paul favored either parent. The chancellor noted that Machelle had continuously cared for Paul since 1988 and, thus this factor clearly rested with the mother. The chancellor did not find that one parent had better parenting skills than the other. This factor favored neither parent, but appears to support maintaining the status quo as Paul expressed no opposition thereto.

¶19. The chancellor also noted that the employment responsibilities of Machelle hindered her relationship with Paul. Conversely, he found that the employment responsibilities of David working an average work week were more conducive to a good relationship toward Paul leaving this factor in favor of David. The chancellor found that both parties were in good physical condition.

¶20. The chancellor found that both parents exhibit a great love and affection for Paul which is reciprocal from the child to both parents. However, the factor of the home, school and community record of Paul lies clearly in favor of Machelle because of the continuity of care which she has had with Paul. This is evidenced by Paul's excelling in school, participation in extracurricular activities as well as church attendance.

¶21. Because of the incidents of domestic violence, and the recent eviction of Machelle from her apartment complex as a direct result of that domestic violence, the stability of the home lies more heavily with David.

¶22. The factor of the moral fitness of the parents did cause the greatest concern with the chancellor. David, an admitted homosexual who lives with and engages in sexual activities with another an on a day-to-day basis, obviously has concerns that his homosexual activity and his show of affection between him and his life partner may, at least at this point in Paul's life, have an adverse effect upon Paul. He admits that a heterosexual lifestyle would have no adverse effect, while acknowledging that a homosexual lifestyle or homosexual activity may well have the opposite effect. The chancellor also felt that David placed far too much emphasis on Paul's own decisions without any guidance whatsoever. David further admits that an open sign of affection between homosexual partners is not proper for the child at this age, yet despite refraining from that activity, he merely retreats behind closed and locked door hiding and secreting his own sexuality from Paul. Although the morality of David's lifestyle was one important factor to consider in the eyes of the chancellor, this was not the sole basis for his custody decision.

¶23. Lastly, the chancellor considered the issue of religious training towards the development of a child. He noted that the mother has seen that Paul is taken to church and undergone religious training, along with the entire family. The chancellor determined that Paul's best interest would be served by providing religious training.
The chancellor further stated that the acceptance or rejection of religious beliefs obtained through the church will be the discretion of Paul, but one could hardly argue that his best interest will be served by not presenting that opportunity to him. Because Machelle has seen fit to provide that training for Paul and make that available to him, the chancellor weighed this factor heavily in her favor.

¶24. In weighing a request for modification of child custody, a chancellor's ultimate concern must always be whether such change would be in the child's best interest. Riley v. Doerner, 677 So. 2d 740, 745 (Miss. 1996). After examining all the factors as set forth in Albright, the chancellor found that despite the fact that there has been substantial and material changes in circumstances since the modification of the Kansas decree in 1988, the best interest of the child, would be served by leaving Paul in the actual physical custody of Machelle. On this record, this Court cannot say that the chancellor was manifestly wrong in denying David's petition for modification to change child custody and the chancellor's judgment should be affirmed.

¶25. Based upon this reasoning, Issue IV is moot and will not be addressed.

III. Whether the chancellor's sua sponte order that all visitation between David and Paul occur outside the presence of David's life partner is legal error and requires reversal? ¶26. David next asserts that the chancellor's order banning visitation between David and Paul in the presence of David's life partner, Wayne, burdens and violates the fundamental right of both father and son to an ongoing relationship.

¶27. "The chancellor has broad discretion when determining appropriate visitation and the limitations thereon." Harrington v. Harrington , 648 So. 2d 543, 545 (Miss. 1994) (citing White v. Thompson , 569 So. 2d 1181 (Miss. 1990)). "When the chancellor determines visitation, he must keep the best interest of the child as his paramount concern while always being attentive to the rights of the non-custodial parent, recognizing the need to maintain a healthy, loving relationship between the non-custodial parent and his child." Harrington , 648 So. 2d at 545. This Court will not reverse a chancellor's findings of fact so long as they are supported by substantial evidence in the record. Tedford v. Dempsey , 437 So. 2d 410, 417 (Miss. 1983). However, this Court "will reverse when he is manifestly in error in his finding of fact or has abused his discretion." Hammett v. Woods , 602 So. 2d 825, 828 (Miss. 1992).

¶28. This Court will follow the reasoning set out in Harrington v. Harrington , 648 So. 2d 543 (Miss. 1994), in which this Court reversed a chancellor's decision to restrict visitation by a natural father who cohabitated without the benefit of marriage with a woman. The Court reasoned that there was no evidence that the children were confused by the father's actions in so cohabitating. In the case sub judice, even if Paul is embarrassed, or does not like the living arrangement of his father, this is not the type of harm that rises to the level necessary to place such restrictions on David's visitation with his son. Harrington , 648 So. 2d at 547. Paul's present age of fifteen affords him considerable input as to visitation and it seems obvious that he wishes to continue the same arrangement. Therefore, we reverse and render the chancellor as to this issue and reinstate the visitation as per the chancellor's order but without any restrictions.

Conclusion

¶29. In weighing a request for modification of child custody, a chancellor's ultimate concern must always be whether such change would be in the child's best interest. In this case, the chancellor's decision to deny transfer of Paul's custody from his mother to his father best served Paul's welfare. However, this Court believes that the restriction placed upon David's visitation rights was an abuse of discretion requiring reversal.

¶30. Affirmed in Part; Reversed and Rendered in Part.

Prather, C.J., Pittman, P.J., Smith, Mills and Waller, JJ., Concur. McRAE, J., Dissents with Separate Written Opinion Joined In Part By Sullivan, P.j. Banks, J., Concurs in Part and Dissents in Part With Separate Written Opinion Joined By Sullivan, P.J.

McRAE, Justice, Dissenting: ¶31. The chancellor and majority believe a minor is best served by living in an explosive environment in which the unemployed stepfather is a convicted felon, drinker, drug-taker, adulterer, wife-beater, and child-threatener, and in which the mother has been transitory, works two jobs, and has limited time with the child. The chancellor makes such a decision despite the fact that Paul's father has a good job, a stable home, and does all within his power to care for his son.

The chancellor and majority are blinded by the fact that Paul's father is gay. Such should not be the issue. The issue is that Paul is living in a psychologically and physically dangerous environment from which he should be saved not blindly forced to remain. I dissent.

¶32. From the facts of this case, it is disturbingly clear that the majority, like the chancellor, has based its opinion neither on what is in the best interest of the child nor the law of child custody but on its own moral perceptions of human sexuality. The morality of homosexuality, however, should not be at issue before this Court or the lower court. Rather, the polestar consideration to which we are bound by the law to follow is whether a custody decision is in the best interests of the child.

¶33. Given the explosive environment the chancellor and the majority have found suitable for young Paul Weigand, it is apparent that the decision is more a condemnation of David Weigand's lifestyle than a consideration of his son's best interests. The chancellor even stated that David "expresses a love and affection for the child which is unquestioned by this Court." Yet, the chancellor ordered the child to remain in the custody of his mother and explosive stepfather. Thus, while the child could be living with his father in a safe and stable home with every material and educational opportunity, today's decision affirms the chancellor's finding that he should remain with his mother and her present husband, an adulterer and convicted felon, who has beaten Machelle and threatened Paul's life. No child should be subjected to such a potential for short- and long-term psychological and physical abuse just because the chancellor thinks little of homosexuals. It boggles the mind how the chancellor and this Court thus could deem it in Paul's best interest to remain in his mother's custody.

¶34. The majority dutifully recites the very basic premise of domestic law that the chancellor's ultimate concern in weighing a request for modification of child custody is whether the requested change is in the child's best interest. Riley v. Doerner , 677 So. 2d 740, 745 (Miss. 1996). Yet, the majority holds that "the chancellor's decision to deny transfer of Paul's custody from his mother to his father best served Paul's welfare." How can the majority say that the decision is in Paul's best interest given the facts of the case?

¶35. Indeed, today's decision leaves the youth vulnerable to both psychological and physical harm. Paul's mother, Machelle married and divorced a convicted felon, then married her current husband, Jeff Houghton. Jeff, Paul's stepfather, is a convicted felon who, according to the trial testimony, was in arrearage for past due child support. Paul's stepfather also has been arrested for hitting Paul's mother in the face, swelling her eye, while Paul was in his bedroom. In another incident, in which Paul's stepfather was intoxicated and knocked out the driver's side window of a car driven by Machelle, Paul again was present. Paul screamed and his stepfather told Paul that he (the stepfather) was going to kill Paul. Paul ran to the house and called 911. Another time, Paul's mother and stepfather were arguing when he told them he was going to the library, but he actually went to a gas station, called his father, and told him that he wanted to move to California and live with him.

¶36. Further, the family moved from Kansas; once in Mississippi, the family was evicted from the apartment complex in which they lived because of the stepfather's violent behavior. The Gateway Apartments resident manager, Sue Hosey, testified that Paul was really afraid and stayed in the apartment most of the time. Hosey testified that she feared for Paul's life. Hosey further testified:

> We hate for anyone to move, but I really feared for Machelle's life. This man had beat her so many times, you know, that it was unreal. And I told her, I said, 'Machelle, due to the circumstances', I said, 'if he kills you I don't want this on my conscious [sic] and I think it would be best if you moved.'

37. There is evidence that Paul's stepfather drinks heavily, sometimes unreasonably mixing alcohol with prescription pain medication. He entered a guilty plea in 1997 for possession of marijuana, careless driving, and driving without headlights. Further, Paul is aware that his stepfather has been involved in an adulterous relationship since

his marriage to Machelle. In May, 1996, Jeff was injured in a one-vehicle accident which rendered him unable to work, causing financial strain on the family. Machelle consequently worked two jobs at the time of trial, averaging fifty to fifty-two hours per week, which admittedly limits her time with her son and effectually making the stepfather the primary care-giver.
Indeed, Machelle testified at trial that Jeff-the drunken, wife-beating, convicted felon-takes Paul to and picks him up from school, cooks for Paul, does the housework, and does the cleaning and washing.

¶38. Paul is bright and not sufficiently challenged in the school he now attends; his father has provided Paul a home computer, has set up an "800" number with which he can keep the lines of communication open with his son, actively encourages Paul to develop his writing talent, and has sought the best California and Mississippi-area schools to provide Paul the highest quality education possible in. David has even offered to take out an $8,000.00 loan to send Paul to a private school, the Memphis University School, to provide him a more challenging academic environment while he resides with his mother and stepfather. While Paul chose not to decide with which parent he wishes to live, he has stated that he is attracted by the material benefits of being in California with his father. David owns his own home, has a stable job, and does all a non-custodial parent can do to care for his child. Yet, regarding his stepfather and current living arrangement, Paul stated to the chancellor that "he does have a bad temper . . . ." Further, Paul has recently received disciplinary marks regarding his conduct, despite the majority's comment that he has no behavioral problems. Paul also stated that his mother has tape recorded his conversations with his father, and that she has read his mail.

¶39. The chancellor, nevertheless, states that "it is apparent" that it is in Paul's best interest to remain with Machelle. But, how can it be so clear? Under the chancellor's thirteen-factor totality of the circumstances test articulated in Albright v. Albright , 437 So. 2d 1003 (Miss. 1983), the analysis is basically inconsequential. Hence, we are faced with the critical issue in this case.

¶40. The majority states that "[a]lthough the morality of David's lifestyle was one important factor to consider in the eyes of the chancellor, this was not the sole basis for his custody decision." How can this be? Each party was deemed to have basically the same number of Albright factors in its favor. Given the facts of this case, it is obvious that the key issue in the mind of the chancellor, if not the majority, is that of David's sexual orientation. David is openly gay. Paul even is aware of his father's orientation. The chancellor spent twelve pages analyzing the Albright factors, seven of which are dedicated to the single issue of David's homosexuality. This Court imprudently states that David's sexual orientation was not the sole basis for the chancellor's custody decision. To the contrary, it is obvious that David's homosexuality was the sole basis for the chancellor's decision to decline the father's request and hold that the mother (and stepfather) should retain custody:

(12) Moral fitness of the parents: It is this factor above all others which causes the greatest concern with the Court. The natural father is an admitted homosexual who lives with and engages in sexual activities with another man on a day-to-day basis.. . . .

. . . [T]he fact that the Plaintiff and his "life partner" engage in sexual activity which include both oral or anal intercourse is repugnant to this Court as constituting a felony act under the laws of this state. Section 97-29-59 of the Mississippi Code Annotated (1972 as amended) prohibits unnatural intercourse and provides as follows:

"Every person who shall be convicted of the detestable and abominable crime against nature committed with mankind or with a best, shall be punished by imprisonment in the penitentiary for a term of not more than ten years."

Under Mississippi law, oral intercourse or fellatio violates the statute. (1) Miller vs. State , 636 So. 2d 391 (Miss. 1994). Further, anal intercourse or sodomy falls within the purview of that statute. Miller , supra. The conscious of this Court is shocked by the audacity and brashness of an individual to come into court, openly and freely admit to engaging in felonious conduct on a regular basis (2) and expect the Court to find such conduct acceptable , particularly with regards to the custody of a minor child. The parties are not in Kansas anymore, nor are they in California. Such conduct is only not [sic] condoned by the Mississippi legislature but is prohibited and punishable as a serious crime. Further, other statutes within this state make it clear that the legislative intent for the enforcement of the law prohibiting unnatural intercourse among other reasons, is for the

protection of children. Section 43-15-6 of the Mississippi Cod Annotated (1972 as amended), prescribes that: "No person convicted of a crime affecting children or any other crime as set forth in Section 97-29-59, Mississippi Code of 1972.
This code relating to unnatural intercourse; or any other offense committed in another jurisdiction which, if committed in this state, would be deemed to be such a crime without regard to its designation elsewhere, shall be licenses as a foster parent or a foster home by the Mississippi Department of Public Welfare"

Surely it cannot be argued that conviction for such which would prohibit the Plaintiff from serving as a foster parent should not likewise prohibit him form serving as a custodial parent of a child.

Additionally, Section 37-3-51 of the Mississippi Code Annotated (1972 as amended) requires that: "Upon the conviction of any certificated personnel as defined in Section 37-19-7, employed by a public or private elementary or secondary school, of any felony, or of a sex offense as defined in subsection (2) of this section, the District Attorney or other prosecuting attorney shall identify those defendants for the Circuit Clerk. Each Circuit Clerk shall provide the State Department of Education with notice of the conviction of any such personnel of a felony or a sex offense. Sex offense shall mean any of the following offenses: . . . (h) Section 97-29-59, Mississippi Code of 1972, relating to unnatural intercourse."

Likewise, this Court recognizes the legislature intent of such a statute to be for the protection of children. It is apparent that the legislature, in enacting Section 97-25-59, Section 43-15-6 and Section 37-3-51 of the Mississippi Code did so among other purposes, for the protection of children. This Court refuses to condone, endorse, sanction or tolerate homosexual activity in any fashion, mode or manner. To do so would be to turn a blind judicial eye in the statute promulgated and enacted by the legislature which was obviously passed with the intent to protect children. The element of morality must be resolved against the Plaintiff because of his homosexual activity which, if committed within this state would constitute felonious conduct, same as it would be resolved has he openly admitted and confessed to the ongoing sale or distribution of illegal drugs. This state and particularly this Court is unwilling to accept such conduct at any time. Indeed, the Mississippi Supreme Court in White vs. Thompson , 569 So. 2d 1181 (Miss. 1990), has found that such homosexual activity may well be considered in matters of child custody. (Natural mother's visitation was restricted to times and places where such visitation would occur outside the presence of her lesbian lover.) This Court is unwilling to deviate from that standard. Opinion of the Chancery Court (emphasis added).

¶41. Our unnatural intercourse statute, about which the chancellor is so concerned, applies to both heterosexuals and homosexuals. The chancellor feels that David's sexuality is an issue of morality. David's sexual orientation, however, is an issue both of genetics and personal privacy. If sexual behavior were an issue of morality, why did not the chancellor ask Machelle, who resides in Mississippi, if she engages in heterosexual sodomy or oral intercourse? See Miss. § Code Ann. 97-29-29. No morality argument is relevant. If homosexuality were the accepted perspective, as it was with the Greeks, who most people deem as enlightened, would it then be fair to criticize heterosexuals on the grounds of morality? See Darryl Robin Wishard, Comment, Out of the Closet and Into the Courts: Homosexual Fathers and Child Custody , 93 Dick. L. Rev. 401, 403 (1989). I think not. It appears that the chancellor and majority have created a new Albright factor, that of sexual orientation. Such seems contrived by the majority for the purpose of punishing David for his lifestyle, contrary to the well-established legal principle that child custody decisions are to be made in the best interests of the child and should not be used to punish one parent or the other. Smith v. Jones , 654 So. 2d 480, 487 (Miss. 1995)(quoting Tucker v. Tucker , 453 So. 2d 1294, 1297 (Miss. 1984)); Moak v. Moak, 631 So. 2d 196, 200 (Miss. 1994); Crowson v. Moseley , 480 So. 2d 1150, 1152 (Miss. 1985).

¶42. Given the chancellor's concern about David's sexuality and its affect on Paul, it is unfortunate that David could not bring this case in California, where consensual oral copulation and sodomy behind closed doors are legal. See Cal. Penal Code §§ 286 & 288a. If the case had been so brought, David would have avoided the unfortunate and unnecessary behavior of chancery court. The chancellor cites Mississippi law not applicable to this case. See Miss. Code §§ Ann. 43-15-6 & 37-3-51; see also White vs. Thompson , 569 So. 2d 1181 (Miss. 1990). Even the majority recognizes, and reverses on, the issue that the chancellor erred by

restricting, pursuant to White, David's visitations with Paul to times when David's life partner is not present.
Further, while David's intimacies with his companion may be "illegal" in Mississippi pursuant to § Miss. Code Ann. 97-29-59, they are not illegal in California and are effected in private and behind locked bedroom doors, well outside of Paul's immediate presence.

¶43. One must consider also the scholarly literature which explains that parental homosexuality is not a precursor to the child being homosexual, (3) even in a case such as this where the child is aware of the parent's homosexuality:

"Every study on the subject has revealed that the incidence of same-sex orientation among the children of gays and lesbians occurs as randomly and in the same proportion as it does among children in the general population. . . ." Therefore, despite the concern of many courts about the negative influence on a child, sexual orientation, according to several studies, is developed independently of one's parents and should not be a factor in custody considerations. "Most homosexuals have had parents who are exclusively heterosexual, or primarily so." The concern of judges that a homosexual parent will rear homosexual children is unwarranted by the evidence. Therefore the court's concern about the negative effects of exposure to a same sex relationship is ill-based.. . . .

. . . An irrebuttable presumption really functions to penalize the parent for their sexual orientation rather than rationally evaluating and determining custody upon concrete evidence of the child's current health and stability. At least ten states have rejected presumptions against awarding custody to parents with a same sex orientation. See Courtney R. Baggett, Sexual Orientation: Should It Affect Child Custody Rulings , 16 Law & Psychol. Rev. 189, 191-193 (1992)(citations omitted). The ten states cited by Baggett as rejecting per se rules against same-sex parents are Alaska, California, Indiana, New Jersey, New York, South Carolina, Vermont, Washington, West Virginia, and New Mexico. See S.N.E. v. R.L.B. 699 P. 2d 875, 879 (Alaska 1985); In re Marriage of Birdsall , 243 Cal. Rptr. 287, 289 (Ct. App. 1988); Nadler v. Superior Court , 63 Cal. Rptr. 352, 354 (Ct. App. 1967); D.H. v. J.H. , 418 N.E. 2d 286 293 (Ind. Ct. App. 1983); In re J.S. & C. , 324 A. 2d 90, 92 (N.J. Super. Ct. Ch. Div.1974), aff'd , 362 A.2d 54 (N.J. Super. Ct. App. Div.1976); Guinan v. Guinan , 477 N.Y.S. 2d 830, 831 (App. Div. 1984); Stroman v. Williams , 353 S.E. 2d 704, 705-06 (S.C. Ct. App. 1987); Re: Adoptions of B.L.V.B. and E.L.V.B., 628 A. 2d 1271 (Vt. 1993); In re Marriage of Cabalquinto, 669 P. 2d 886, 888 (Wash. 1983); Rowsey v. Rowsey , 329 S.E. 2d 57, 60-61 (W. Va. 1985); In re Jacinta M. , 764 P. 2d 1327, 1330 (N.M. Ct. App. 1988). Why does Mississippi not become reasonable and follow the lead of these states? Yes, as the majority shows, Mississippi ostensibly follows the lead of the aforementioned states, but I query whether we truly do follow such leads. Do we? Given the chancellor's activities and the majority's decision in this case, I think not.

¶44. Underlying this case is the protection one is guaranteed by the Fourteenth Amendment of the United States Constitution. In a key substantive due process case which considered the right to child-rear, Pierce v. Society of the Sisters , 268 U.S. 510 (1925) , the United States Supreme Court stated that "[t]he child is not the mere creature of the state; those who nurture him and direct his destiny have the right, coupled with the high duty to recognize and prepare him for additional obligations." See Id . ; see also Meyer v. Nebraska , 262 U.S. 390 (1923) ; and see Prince v. Massachusetts , 321 U.S. 158 (1944) . In Bryant v. Brown , 151 Miss. 398, 118 So. 184 (1928), we stated that:

Primarily parents, or those standing in loco parentis to minor children, have the constitutional right, under the Fourteenth Amendment, to the custody and control of such minor children, and may give them such education and training as in their judgment may seem best for the welfare of the child and for the good of society. . . .

As long as parents properly exercise their duty, under their natural rights, to rear, educate, and control their children, their right to do so may not be interfered with solely because some other person or some other institution might be deemed better suited for that purpose. The children of the poor cannot be taken from them, and awarded to the rich or to some rich and powerful institution, merely because such person or such institution might, in the judgment of the court, do a better part by the child than the natural parents. But where the parents fail to perform their natural duty to so rear and educate the child as to make it a useful, intelligent, and moral being. But permit it to go unrestrained and to become vicious in its habits and practices, and a

menace to the rest of society, the state, as parents patriae of all children, may assert its power and apply the curative.
This is to prevent injury to the child and to society by the negligent and wrongful conduct of the parents in failing to exercise the proper control and restraint over the child in its tendencies. See Id. , 151 Miss. at 414-416, 118 So. at 188. Citing Pierce , this Court further has stated that the liberty guaranteed by the Due Process Clause "involves the power to give to children such training and education as in the parents' judgment is best for the children, so long as such training and education do not result in, or tend to develop, tendencies or traits dangerous to society." See Sinquefield v. Valentine , 159 Miss. 144, 151, 132 So. 81, 83 (1931).

¶45. In the instant case, Machelle and Paul's stepfather are breaching the "high duty" required by the Constitution. The chancellor and the majority are forcing Paul to reside in an unhealthy environment from which physical and psychological harm could erupt at any moment, or, at best, from which he is being taught an immoral and abusive lifestyle. Given the facts and the substantive due process requirements that parents have the right and duty to child-rear, it is only reasonable to hold that Machelle has breached her duty and squandered her right. Consider particularly Machelle's choice of "living partners" -her last two marriages have been to convicted felons. David is a stable, loving parent who now wishes to fully utilize his right to child-rear, who are we to take that Constitutional right away from a capable parent? Someone might argue that regardless of the right to child-rear, Bowers v. Hardwick , 478 U.S. 186 (1986) , states that a homosexual has no right to commit sodomy and thus is not fit to be a father. Such an argument is dangerous and unmerited. This is not Bowers -unlike Georgia, in California, where David is intimate with his life partner, consensual sodomy amongst adults is legal. Further, while homosexual behavior may not be a fundamental right, such realization is not even a rational basis for trumping another right-that of child-rearing. Under the equal protection analysis of Romer v. Evans , 571 U.S. 620 (1996) , the chancellor's sexual-orientation based decision burdens the parental right to child-rear. The chancellor's obvious sexual-orientation based action is not rationally related to the legitimate end of considering the best interests of the child in a modification of custody. The rationale is one of homosexuality being a moral block to effective child-rearing. Such a rationale is, as explained above, at least unreasoned and at most unconscionable. As the Supreme Court stated in Romer : "[i]t is a status-based enactment divorced from any factual context from which we could discern a relationship to legitimate state interests; it is a classification of persons undertaken for its own sake, something the Equal Protection Clause does not permit. . . ." See id. at 635 . The Romer Court continued: "[w]e must conclude that Amendment 2 classifies homosexuals not to further a proper legislative end but to make them unequal to everyone else. This Colorado cannot do. A State cannot so deem a class a stranger to its laws." See id. Neither should Mississippi.

¶46. Paul Weigand remains in the custody of a mother who, herself, is trapped in an untenable situation that renders the boy vulnerable to both psychological and physical harm from his stepfather. What is the child being taught in this environment? He is being prepared for a lifestyle of drugs, adulterous relations, wife abuse, and child-threatening. But for the "moral" decision of the chancellor and the majority of this Court, he could be in the custody of his father in California living in a safe and stable home environment and enjoying the educational and material benefits his father desperately seeks to provide him. Accordingly, justice requires that I dissent.

Sullivan, P.J., Joins in Part.

Banks, Justice, Concurring in Part and Dissenting in Part: ¶47. Because of the language used by the chancellor with respect to Don's acknowledgment of a homosexual lifestyle, I cannot help but believe that his findings and ultimate conclusions are impermissibly infected by undue consideration of this factor. Accordingly, I dissent to so much of the majority decision as affirms the custody decision.

¶48. The chancellor's discussion of this issue is set forth in the dissent of Justice McRae, much of which I join. It is my view that a homosexual lifestyle should not ipso facto render one unfit for custody. It is apparent from that the chancellor below had a contrary view. I would reverse his decision with respect to custody and remand this matter for a new trial before a different chancellor.

¶49. Failing complete reversal, I join that portion of the majority decision which reverses the chancellor as to visitation.

Sullivan, P.J., Joins this Opinion.

1. The chancellor fails to recognize that the statute applies to both heterosexuals, whether married or single, and homosexuals.

2. The chancellor directly questioned David. What was he supposed to do, perjure himself?

3. Recent studies have found that more than one-third of all adult males and nearly one-fifth of all adult females have engaged in a homosexual act to the point of orgasm. About one-tenth of all men continue to have homosexual experience after marriage. See J. Thomas Oldham and David S. Caudill, A Reconnaissance of Public Policy Restrictions Upon Enforcement of Contracts Between Cohabitants , 18 Fam. L.Q. 93, 141 n.162 (1984).

Schroeder v. Schroeder

(Illinois) Lambda client Becky Schroeder lost custody of her son and daughter to her former husband several years after the couple's divorce because of her bisexuality and relationship with a woman, and despite a lengthy hearing in which everyone agreed the children were doing very well in her custody. On appeal, the Illinois Appellate Court, sitting in central Illinois, unanimously held that the fact that a parent is gay, is living with her same-sex partner, or may face community disapproval or charges of immorality are not valid reasons to change custody. The court embraced a "sexual-orientation neutral" approach to child custody determinations, allowing gay, lesbian, and bisexual parents in Illinois to breathe a little easier. This is the first Illinois case in which an appellate court has ever awarded custody to a gay parent. (December 1996)

J.A.L. v. E.P.H.

(Pennsylvania) This case, which involved a custody dispute between two lesbian mothers. After the trial court disregarded the parties' intent to create a parental relationship between the non-biological mother and the child, as well as the fact that the child has developed a parental relationship to her non-biological mother, with her biological mother's consent and encouragement, the Superior Court of Pennsylvania held that J.A.L., the non-biological mother, should be allowed to seek visitation and partial custody of the child that she and her former partner had planned for and had during their nine-year relationship. The superior court found that the non-biological mother and child were members of a family and that there is sufficient evidence to establish that J.A.L. has a parental relationship to the child and therefore has standing to seek partial custody. The biological mother did not appeal this ruling from Pennsylvania's second-highest court. (September 1996)

Lesbian Mom Restricted Access

In The Supreme Court of Tennessee At Knoxville

January 3, 2001 Session

Anthony Keith Eldridge

V. Julia Edith Eldridge

Appeal by Permission from the Court of Appeals Chancery Court for Sullivan (Kingsport) County No. 23478(L) Richard E. Ladd, Chancellor No. E1999-02583-SC-R11-CV - Filed May 2, 2001

We granted review of this child visitation case to determine whether the trial court abused its discretion in ordering unrestricted overnight visitation with the mother. The Court of Appeals held that the trial court had abused its discretion and imposed restrictions prohibiting the presence of the mother's lesbian partner during overnight visitation. We hold that the record does not support a finding of an abuse of discretion. Accordingly, we reverse the judgment of the Court of Appeals.

Tenn. R. App. P. 11 Appeal by Permission; Judgment of the Court of Appeals Reversed

Janice M. Holder, J., delivered the opinion of the court, in which E. Riley Anderson, C.J., and Frank F. Drowota, III, Adolpho A. Birch, JR., and William M. Barker, JJ., joined.

Michael May, Kingsport, Tennessee, for defendant-appellant, Julia Edith Eldridge.

Harold Wayne Graves, Johnson City, Tennessee, for plaintiff-appellee, Anthony Keith Eldridge.

Stephen R. Scarborough, Atlanta, Georgia, and William Allen Mynatt, Knoxville, Tennessee, for amicus curiae, Lambda Legal Defense and Education Fund, Inc.

Susan Elizabeth Mackenzie, Memphis, Tennessee, and William Allen Mynatt, Knoxville, Tennessee, for amicus curiae, Memphis National Organization for Women.

Shannon Minter, San Francisco, California, and William Allen Mynatt, Knoxville, Tennessee, for amicus curiae, National Center for Lesbian

Rights.

William Allen Mynatt, Knoxville, Tennessee, for amicus curiae, Tennessee National Organization for Women.

Abby Rose Rubenfeld, Nashville, Tennessee, and Bruce S. Kramer, Memphis, Tennessee, for amicus curiae, The American Civil Liberties Union of Tennessee.

1 No error is alleged as to the trial court's ordered visitation between Andrea and Ms. Eldridge. Accordingly, this Court's comments shall be limited to visitation with Taylor.

-2-OPINION

BACKGROUND

Anthony and Julia Eldridge were divorced in 1992. The couple agreed to joint custody of their minor daughters, Andrea and Taylor, who were ages eight and nine respectively. Two years later, a dispute arose regarding Ms. Eldridge's visitation rights. Ms. Eldridge, who is engaged in a live-in homosexual relationship with Lisa Franklin, moved the court to establish a visitation schedule. In response, Mr. Eldridge moved for sole custody of the children.

In July 1995, the Court awarded sole custody of the children to Mr. Eldridge. The court also appointed a Special Master, Dr. James Granger, Head of the East Tennessee University Division of Child and Adolescent Psychiatry, to counsel the parties and their children and make recommendations to the court regarding visitation. Dr. Granger's written final report and testimony reflected that counseling was unsuccessful. An agreement as to visitation was not reached.

Upon Mr. Eldridge's motion, the trial court appointed a guardian ad litem ("GAL") for both children. The GAL concluded that regular visitation with the mother was essential and recommended regular visitation with standard visitation every other weekend. The first few weekend visitations were recommended to be limited to Saturday morning through Sunday evening and eventually to be extended to Friday through Sunday.

In September 1996, the trial court ordered overnight visitation with Taylor 1 every other Saturday night through Sunday. Eight months later, Ms. Eldridge moved the court to extend Taylor's overnight visitation to include Friday nights, holidays and summer vacation. Ms. Eldridge also moved that another Special Master be appointed. Mr. Eldridge opposed expanding Ms. Eldridge's visitation rights.

In September 1997, the trial court approved an agreement reached by the parties. The agreement provided for a visitation schedule and appointment of Dr. Judy Millington, a counselor at Church Circle Counseling Center, as Special Master. The court's order provided that Dr. Millington's written recommendations were to take effect immediately without further order of the court. Dr. Millington recommended to the court that Ms. Eldridge's overnight visitation be expanded. Various disputes regarding visitation continued.

A hearing was held in October 1998 to resolve the visitation issue. In November 1998, the trial court entered an order adopting Dr. Millington's recommendations and permitting Ms. Eldridge unrestricted overnight visitation with Taylor. The Court of Appeals reversed, finding that the trial -3- court abused its discretion in failing to prohibit Taylor's overnight visitation with Ms. Eldridge while Ms. Franklin was present in the home. One judge dissented. We granted review.

ANALYSIS

The Court of Appeals correctly held that the standard for appellate review of a trial court's child visitation order is controlled by our decision in Suttles v. Suttles, 748 S.W.2d 427, 429 (Tenn. 1988). There, we noted that "'the details of custody and visitation with children are peculiarly within the broad discretion of the trial judge.'" Id. at 429 (quoting Edwards v. Edwards, 501 S.W.2d 283, 291 (Tenn. Ct. App. 1973)). Accordingly, we held that a "trial court's decision [on visitation] will not ordinarily be reversed absent some abuse of that discretion." Id.

In reviewing the trial court's visitation order for an abuse of discretion, the child's welfare is given "paramount consideration," id. (quoting Luke v. Luke, 651 S.W.2d 219, 221 (Tenn. 1983)), and "the right of the noncustodial parent to reasonable visitation is clearly favored." Id. Nevertheless, the noncustodial parent's visitation "may be limited, or eliminated, if there is definite evidence that to permit . . . the right would jeopardize the child, in either a physical or moral sense." Id. (quoting Weaver v. Weaver, 261 S.W.2d 145, 148 (Tenn. Ct. App. 1953)).

Under the abuse of discretion standard, a trial

court's ruling "will be upheld so long as reasonable minds can disagree as to propriety of the decision made." State v. Scott, 33 S.W.3d 746, 752 (Tenn. 2000); State v. Gilliland, 22 S.W.3d 266, 273 (Tenn. 2000). A trial court abuses its discretion only when it "applie[s] an incorrect legal standard, or reache[s] a decision which is against logic or reasoning that cause[s] an injustice to the party complaining." State v. Shirley, 6 S.W.3d 243, 247 (Tenn. 1999). The abuse of discretion standard does not permit the appellate court to substitute its judgment for that of the trial court. Myint v. Allstate Ins. Co., 970 S.W.2d 920, 927 (Tenn. 1998).

Mr. Eldridge challenges the trial court's visitation order on grounds that Ms. Franklin should not be present during Taylor's overnight visitation with Ms. Eldridge. The Court of Appeals held that "the trial court abused its discretion by not prohibiting Ms. Franklin's presence during the court-ordered overnight visitation." To cure this abuse of discretion, it modified the trial court's visitation order by prohibiting Lisa Franklin's presence during Taylor's overnight visitation with her mother.

The Court of Appeals' opinion makes clear that the court did "not rely on the fact that Ms. Eldridge is a lesbian" in modifying the trial court's order. The court fails to state, however, what it did rely upon. The Court of Appeals did not identify any legal or factual error by the trial court that might constitute an abuse of discretion. It also failed to establish how the ordered modification would cure the trial court's supposed error. Cf. Suttles, 748 S.W.2d at 429 (describing multiple facts justifying reversal of visitation as ordered by the trial court). The court offered that "[t]he courts of Tennessee commonly place reasonable restrictions on the visitation rights of heterosexual parents who engage in sexual activity with partners with whom they are not married." Mere observation that -4-restrictions have been imposed in past cases does nothing, however, to reveal why the trial court in this case abused its discretion in permitting unrestricted overnight visitation.

The Court of Appeals cited Dailey v. Dailey, 635 S.W.2d 391 (Tenn. Ct. App. 1982), as having "addressed the issue raised by Mr. Eldridge." In Dailey, the Court of Appeals upheld the trial court's decision to modify a custody order to shift custody from the mother, a homosexual, to the father. The court also, sua sponte, modified the trial court's visitation order to prohibit the visitation in the home where the mother lived with her lesbian partner or from having the child in the presence of any lesbian partner. Id. at 395-96.

The Court of Appeals justified modification of the visitation order in Dailey on grounds that the child should not be "subjected to the type of sexually related behavior that has been carried on in his presence in the past under the proof in this record." Id. at 396. The proof in Dailey showed that the mother flagrantly flaunted her relationship with [her live-in lesbian partner] in the presence of the minor child. They would hug and passionately kiss each other and rub the private parts of their bodies while in the home where the child was. They would go to bed together and during their sexual stimulation of each other make audible expressions of pleasure and satisfaction that could be heard throughout the house and in the area where the child slept. They would have the child in bed with them while they were embracing each other in the nude. The child was five years of age at the time of the trial of this case. He suffers from cerebral palsy and is somewhat handicapped physically and is mentally slow.

Id. at 393.

The record in Dailey established that the noncustodial parent engaged in overt, lascivious, sexual conduct in the presence of her five-year-old, mentally and physically handicapped child. Certainly, this is the type of "definite evidence" that unrestricted visitation "would jeopardize the child, in either a physical or moral sense" that might constitute a finding of an abuse of discretion under Suttles. 748 S.W.2d at 429.The Court of Appeals in this case held that "[t]he facts of this case do not rise to the level of harmful behavior displayed by the mother in Dailey." This statement indicates either: (1) that the court held Dailey to be inapplicable; or (2) that the court found at least some conduct by Ms. Eldridge similar to that in Dailey. The court's recitation of the facts shows no conduct by Ms. Eldridge that might arguably be construed as similar to that of the mother in Dailey, and our independent review of the record reveals none. The only similarity between this case and Dailey is that the mother is homosexual. As the Court of Appeals affirmatively stated that it did not rely on Ms. Eldridge's homosexuality in modifying the trial court's order, we can only infer that the Court of Appeals found Dailey to be completely irrelevant to this case.

We agree. 2 Mr. Eldridge admitted under questioning that he and Chantal cohabited with the children for several months while unwed. That living arrangement, he admitted, also set a b ad example for Taylor. He stated that he would not, however, make that same decision again.

-5-The Court of Appeals' failure to state a basis for its decision leaves us little insight as to what facts in the record show the trial court abused its discretion. Our own review of the record shows that Ms. Eldridge and Ms. Franklin offered substantial testimony regarding their relationship and living arrangement. At the time of the hearing, they had been together for nearly five years. They live in the same home but had slept in separate bedrooms for three months prior to the hearing. Ms. Franklin provides all the financial support for the home. Ms. Eldridge is not a lessor of the home. They have a monogamous relationship but have not been sexually intimate in over a year. Ms. Franklin characterized them as "best friends, roommates." They make no expression of "physical emotion or physical contact" when Taylor is in the home. Taylor has her own bedroom in the home. Ms. Franklin testified that she had a good relationship with Taylor.

Mr. Eldridge and his wife, Chantal Eldridge, testified that unrestricted overnight visitation has a deleterious effect on Taylor. Mr. Eldridge testified that allowing Ms. Franklin to be present during overnight visitation would set a bad example for Taylor. He tries to teach Taylor to live by the Bible and that unmarried persons should not cohabit.2 He also testified that Taylor, based on her own sense of morality, believed that homosexuality and extramarital relationships were wrong. He testified that Taylor does not want Ms. Franklin present during visitation and that Taylor has many questions about Ms. Eldridge's and Ms. Franklin's relationship. Mr. Eldridge did not believe that Taylor would be physically harmed during overnight visitation. He was, however, concerned about her emotional well-being.

Chantal Eldridge testified that Taylor is visibly upset before leaving to spend the night with her mother. She was unsure what produced Taylor's response but opined that Taylor might miss her, Mr. Eldridge, and their children. Ms. Eldridge, however, testified that Taylor refuses to come into her house only until Taylor is certain her father has left. Then, Taylor enters the home and is very comfortable, eating and playing normally. As the time to return to her father approaches, however, Taylor paces, cries, and worries. Taylor makes efforts to hide the fact that she has eaten or enjoyed herself at Ms. Eldridge's home. Larry Davis, Ms. Eldridge's brother-in-law, offered testimony that supported this contention. He stated that during one of his family's visits with Ms. Eldridge, Taylor was playing outside with him and his children and acting normally. In the last hour before Mr. Eldridge came to pick her up, however, Taylor became withdrawn, refused to come outside, and would not associate with anyone in the home.

Dr. Millington testified that Taylor wants to love and please both of her parents. This conflict causes Taylor to lie to her father about having fun while visiting with her mother. Dr. Millington had observed no adverse or detrimental effects on Taylor resulting from overnight visitation with Ms. Eldridge in Ms. Franklin's presence. Dr. Millington stated, however, that Taylor has admitted to being somewhat uncomfortable during overnight visitation in Ms. Franklin's -6-presence. Dr. Millington observed that Taylor's behavior around Ms. Eldridge was very positive and opined that increased visitation would further encourage their relationship.

In her June 30, 1997 report, Dr. Millington suggested that Taylor's overnight visitation every other weekend should be extended from one night to two. Dr. Millington expressed in an addendum to her report that

> [i]nteraction with Lisa appears (from videotapes viewed) to have no deleterious effects on Taylor at present. Does seeing Lisa and Julie together make a difference for the children for the future? . . . Although Taylor most likely will have difficulty with her mother's orientation in the future, I don't know whether it will make a difference having had Lisa there versus not there. Taylor seems comfortable with Lisa now.

In that same document, Dr. Millington opined that "on the continuum the best for Taylor . . . would be to have visitation without Lisa present, because the sexual orientation and modeling behavior issues become less obvious and so less of an issue parent-to-child in the future than it otherwise might be." In her deposition of June 30, 1997, Dr. Millington stated that although overnight visits generally might be stressful for a child, she was not sure that Ms. Franklin was the source of Taylor's stress.

Upon question about what would be the "ideal situation" regarding visitation, she testified that "the very best situation, which would probably be for the girls to see [Ms. Eldridge] just completely by herself, but I don't know how practical that is." At the October 1998 hearing, Dr. Millington ultimately was noncommittal on the issue of overnight visits:

And I think I stated earlier that for [Taylor's] best interest overnight would not be required, but on the other hand that I didn't really think overnight would harm her because I don't think she's going to see anything at [Ms. Eldridge's home]. So I guess I'm kind of leaving that one up to Your Honor as to whether that it ought to be the overnight or not [sic], but that my feeling is that time has to happen and hasn't happened.

The trial court evaluated and resolved this competing testimony and held that overnight visitation without restriction was appropriate. Mr. Eldridge claims on appeal that prohibiting overnight visitation while Ms. Franklin is present is a reasonable way to resolve his concerns and would constitute a minimal inconvenience to Ms. Eldridge. His argument, however, is one to be made in the trial court, not on appeal.

It is not the function of appellate courts to tweak a visitation order in the hopes of achieving a more reasonable result than the trial court. Appellate courts correct errors. When no error in the trial court's ruling is evident from the record, the trial court's ruling must stand. This maxim has special significance in cases reviewed under the abuse of discretion standard. The abuse of 3 See Hansen v. Hansen, 650 So. 2d 9 17 (Ala. C iv. App. 19 94); Gallo v. Gallo, 440 A.2d 782 (Conn. 1981); LeBlanc v. LeBlanc, 490 So. 2d 763 (La. Ct. App. 198 6); Duplantis v. Monteaux, 412 So. 2d 215 (La. Ct. App. 1982); Robison v. Robison, 722 So. 2d 601 (Miss. 19 98); DeVita v. DeVita , 366 A.2d 1350 (N.J. Super. Ct. App. Div. 1976); Dilworth v. Dilworth, 685 N.E.2d 84 7 (Ohio C t. App. 19 96); Somers v. Somers, 474 A.2d 630 (Pa. Super. 198 4); Carrico v. Blevins, 402 S.E .2d 235 (Va. Ct. Ap p. 1991); Palmer v. Palmer, 416 A.2d 143 (Vt. 1980).

-7-discretion standard recognizes that the trial court is in a better position than the appellate court to make certain judgments. The abuse of discretion standard does not require a trial court to render an ideal order, even in matters involving visitation, to withstand reversal. Reversal should not result simply because the appellate court found a "better" resolution. See State v. Franklin, 714 S.W.2d 252, 258 (Tenn. 1986) ("appellate court should not redetermine in retrospect and on a cold record how the case could have been better tried"); cf. State v. Pappas, 754 S.W.2d 620, 625 (Tenn. Crim. App. 1987) (affirming trial court's ruling under abuse of discretion standard while noting that action contrary to action taken by the trial court was the better practice); Bradford v. Bradford, 364 S.W.2d 509, 512-13 (Tenn. Ct. App. 1962) (same). An abuse of discretion can be found only when the trial court's ruling falls outside the spectrum of rulings that might reasonably result from an application of the correct legal standards to the evidence found in the record. See, e.g., State ex. rel Vaughn v. Kaatrude, 21 S.W.3d 244, 248 (Tenn. Ct. App. 2000).

The Court of Appeals cited Edwards v. Edwards, 501 S.W.2d 283 (Tenn. Ct. App. 1973), for the contention that Tennessee courts commonly place reasonable restrictions on the presence of unmarried partners, whether heterosexual or homosexual, during overnight visitation. In Edwards, however, the trial court imposed restrictions on the mother's visitation. On appeal, the Court of Appeals observed that the trial court's restrictions "superficially appear[ed] rather severe." Id. at 291. Still, the appellate court gave appropriate deference to the trial court, found a reasonable basis in the record for the trial court's ostensibly severe ruling, and affirmed the restrictions on visitation. Id. Appellate courts in other jurisdictions have, in a similar fashion, upheld trial court orders prohibiting overnight visitation with a parent in the presence of a non-spouse.3

As a general proposition, we agree that in an appropriate case a trial court may impose restrictions on a child's overnight visitation in the presence of non-spouses. The procedural posture of the case at bar is markedly different. In this case, the appellate court, in spite of the deference to which the trial court is entitled, has displaced the trial court's ruling and imposed a restriction that was considered and rejected by the trial court. Justification for that action must be found in the record and, preferably, be developed in the appellate court's opinion. We find no justification in this record.

There was testimony that Taylor might suffer some deleterious effects from Ms. Franklin's presence during overnight visitation. Still, ample evidence to the contrary was presented orally at the hearing and in writings found in the record.
The trial court was in a far better position than the appellate court to resolve this competing evidence.

See, e.g., Nance v. State Indus., Inc., 33 S.W.3d 222, 229 (Tenn. 2000); Jones v. Hartford Accident & Indem. Co., 811 S.W.2d 516, 521 (Tenn. 1991) ("where the trial judge has seen and heard witnesses, especially where issues of credibility and weight of oral testimony are involved, on review considerable deference must still be accorded to -8-those circumstances"). We cannot find that the trial court's ruling was not among the reasonable alternatives supported by the proof in this case.

We may, however, find an abuse of discretion when the record contains definite evidence that visitation, as ordered, would jeopardize the child in a physical or moral sense. Suttles, 748 S.W.2d at 429. We have carefully scrutinized the entire record for any evidence that Taylor has been, or would be, subject to physical or emotional harm from overnight stays with her mother while Ms. Franklin was present in the home and have found none.

Further, there is no definite evidence in this record that Taylor's moral well-being would be jeopardized if visitation were implemented as ordered by the trial court. There is conclusive evidence in this case of a moral dilemma between the parents. Dr. Millington characterized the parents in this case as "quite polarized in their beliefs, two apparently reasonable people doing the best that they can with their own belief systems." A finding of harm to Taylor's sense of morality, however, does not necessarily follow from her parents' moral dilemma.

Although Dr. Millington opined that overnight visitation in general was not required to promote Taylor's best interests, she never indicated that overnight visitation in Ms. Franklin's presence was contrary to Taylor's best interests. The evidence shows that Ms. Eldridge and Ms. Franklin conduct themselves appropriately in Taylor's presence, as do Mr. Eldridge and Chantal Eldridge. Dr. Millington opined that there was no risk that either parent would engage in sexual conduct in the child's presence. The trial court, in adopting Dr. Millington's recommendations from her report of October 6, 1998, ordered that Ms. Eldridge and Ms. Franklin not share a bedroom during Taylor's overnight visitation. There is no evidence of noncompliance with that order.

The record does not show that Taylor is in moral crisis because of Ms. Franklin's presence during overnight visitation. At most, it appears that Taylor, like many children of divorce, is caught in the crossfire of parental acrimony. It is argued as a general proposition of morality that a parent's unwed love interest should not be present during overnight visitation with the child. A trial court's acceptance of that proposition, taking into account all the facts and circumstances, may give rise to a reasonable conclusion that overnight visitation should be restricted. Nevertheless, that proposition does not in all cases foreclose the possibility of the trial court reaching a reasonable alternative conclusion. In the absence of any evidence of harm beyond the mere unsubstantiated predictions of a vying parent, the trial court's ruling in this case cannot be said to be unreasonable. The evidence adduced in this case supports a reasonable conclusion that unrestricted overnight visitation was in Taylor's best interests. Accordingly, on this record, there was no abuse of discretion by the trial court.

CONCLUSION

We hold that the trial court did not abuse its discretion in ordering unrestricted overnight visitation by Taylor Eldridge with Julia Eldridge. The judgment of the Court of Appeals is reversed. -9-Costs of this appeal are taxed to Appellee, Anthony Eldridge, for which execution may issue if necessary.

Janice M. Holder, Justice

Court Takes Custody of Sons from Gay Father

Pulliam v. Smith

In The Supreme Court of NC No. 499PA96

Filed: 30 July 1998

Carol J. Pulliam

V.

Frederick J. Smith

On discretionary review pursuant to N.C.G.S. § 7A-31 of a decision of the Court of Appeals, 124 N.C. App. 144, 476 S.E.2d 446 (1996), reversing a judgment entered by Burgin, J., on 30 June 1995 in District Court, Henderson County. Heard in the Supreme Court 14 May 1997.

Jackson & Jackson, by Phillip T. Jackson, for plaintiff-appellant.

Lambda Legal Defense and Education Fund, Inc., by Beatrice Dohrn; and N.C. Gay and Lesbian Attorneys, by Ellen W. Gerber and Sharon A.

Thompson, for defendant-appellee.

Stam, Fordham & Danchi, P.A., by Paul Stam, Jr.; and James F. Lovett, Jr., on behalf of North Carolina Family Policy Council, amicus curiae.

Michael P. Adams and Tharrington Smith, by Jaye Meyer, on behalf of American Civil Liberties Union; and Deborah Ross on behalf of ACLU of North Carolina Legal Foundation, amici curiae.

Myrna Ann Miller on behalf of National Association of Social Workers, North Carolina Chapter, and National Association of Social Workers, amici curiae.

MITCHELL, Chief Justice.

The overriding question presented for review is whether there was sufficient evidence to support the trial court's finding of a substantial change of circumstances affecting the welfare of two minor children which would warrant a change of custody. The Court of Appeals held that there was not. Since we conclude that the trial court's judgment modifying a prior order placing custody of the children with their father is supported by adequate findings of fact based on substantial evidence, we also conclude that the trial court's judgment was free of error. We therefore reverse the decision of the Court of Appeals.

As a preliminary matter, we address that portion of the Court of Appeals' decision which concluded that the party seeking modification of custody must show "that the change [in circumstances] has had an adverse effect on the child or will likely or probably have such an effect unless custody is altered." Pulliam v. Smith , 124 N.C. App. 144, 147, 476 S.E.2d 446, 449 (1996) (emphasis added). This Court has never required the party moving for a modification of custody to show that the change in circumstances has had or will have an adverse consequence upon the child's well-being, and we decline to do so now.

The controlling statute provides that, when an order for custody of a minor child has been entered by a court of another state, a court of this state may, upon a showing of changed circumstances, enter a new order for custody. N.C.G.S. § 50-13.7(b) (1995). In Blackley v. Blackley , 285 N.C. 358, 204 S.E.2d 678 (1974), we interpreted N.C.G.S. § 50-13.7(b) which mandates a "showing of changed circumstances." In that decision, we held:

[T]he modification of a custody decree must be supported by findings of fact based on competent evidence that there has been a substantial change of circumstances affecting the welfare of the child, and the party moving for such modification assumes the burden of showing such change of circumstances.

Id. at 362, 204 S.E.2d at 681. In Blackley, we held that the trial court erred in modifying a prior order awarding custody because the evidence was insufficient to show a substantial change of circumstances affecting the welfare of the child; we neither held nor implied that to establish a change of circumstances which would justify a modification of custody, it must always be shown that the change of circumstances adversely affects or will adversely affect the child.

The welfare of the child has always been the polar star which guides the courts in awarding custody. Shepherd v. Shepherd , 273 N.C. 71, 75, 159 S.E.2d 357, 361 (1968). In reviewing a request for modification of custody, courts may not limit the inquiry as to what constitutes the best interests of the child solely to a consideration of those changes in circumstances which it has found to exist and which may adversely affect that child. It is true that we have stated in one case that, "We cannot forecast the future, but if there should be a change of circumstances adversely affecting the welfare of these children, the court is empowered to act . . . ." Thomas v. Thomas, 259 N.C. 461, 467, 130 S.E.2d 871, 876 (1963). However, this statement in the form of obiter dictum should not be read to indicate that a court's consideration of changed circumstances should be limited to those having adverse consequences for the child. The facts in Thomas involved a situation in which the children were affected adversely if at all, and our statement there merely reflected those facts. Further, our statement that a change of circumstances adversely affecting children would empower the court to act is not equal to, and should not be read as, a holding that a court could not change custody where a substantial change of circumstances had occurred which would beneficially affect the child if custody should be modified. Rather, courts must consider and weigh all evidence of changed circumstances which affect or will affect the best interests of the child, both changed circumstances which will have salutary effects upon the child and those which will have adverse effects upon the child.

In appropriate cases, either may support a modification of custody on the ground of a change in circumstances.

In Rothman v. Rothman, 6 N.C. App. 401, 170 S.E.2d 140 (1969), the Court of Appeals wrote, "Professor Lee points out in his treatise on North Carolina Family Law that there must generally be a substantial change of circumstances before an order of custody is changed." Id. at 406, 170 S.E.2d at 144. The Court of Appeals then incorrectly held, "It must be shown that circumstances have so changed that the welfare of the child will be adversely affected unless the custody provision is modified." Id. The Court of Appeals' decision in Rothman, insofar as it mandates that the changed circumstances analysis be limited to a showing of adverse effects on the child, is contrary to N.C.G.S. § 50-13.7(b) and is disapproved. We also disapprove of subsequent Court of Appeals cases to the extent they require a showing of adversity to the child as a result of changed circumstances to justify a change of custody.(1)

We emphasize that an adverse effect upon a child as the result of a change in circumstances is and remains an acceptable factor for the courts to consider and will support a modification of a prior custody order. However, a showing of a change in circumstances that is, or is likely to be, beneficial to the child may also warrant a change in custody. We conclude this analysis by noting that, in either situation, it must always be remembered that

[a] decree of custody is entitled to such stability as would end the vicious litigation so often accompanying such contests, unless it be found that some change of circumstances has occurred affecting the welfare of the child so as to require modification of the order. To hold otherwise would invite constant litigation by a dissatisfied party so as to keep the involved child constantly torn between parents and in a resulting state of turmoil and insecurity. This in itself would destroy the paramount aim of the court, that is, that the welfare of the child be promoted and subserved.

Shepherd, 273 N.C. at 75, 159 S.E.2d at 361. Having resolved the foregoing questions of law, we turn to the evidence presented and the issue raised by the parties in this case.

Uncontroverted evidence before the trial court tended to show that plaintiff Carol J. Pulliam and defendant Frederick J. Smith are the mother and father of two boys, Frederick Joseph Smith, II (Joey) and Kenneth August Smith (Kenny). Plaintiff-mother and defendant-father were married in California in November 1982. They separated in 1990 when plaintiff went to live in Kansas with William Pulliam. Plaintiff and defendant were divorced in November 1991. At that time, Joey was six years old, and Kenny was three years old. The parties entered into a consent decree regarding the custody of the children. Pursuant to the decree, the parties had joint legal custody, and defendant-father had physical custody of the children. Until August 1994, the children lived with defendant and his grandmother in North Carolina. In February 1993, plaintiff married Mr. Pulliam, and they have since resided in Wichita, Kansas. Plaintiff-mother had the boys with her for two months during the summer and at Christmas each year. In August 1994, Tim Tipton moved into defendant's home, and defendant's grandmother moved out a month later. Defendant-father and Mr. Tipton are homosexuals.

The trial court made findings of fact supported by evidence, which included, inter alia, the following:

27. That Tim Tipton first moved into the home located on 9 Roberts Street in Fletcher, North Carolina around March of 1994.

28. That Tim Tipton and the Defendant often kiss on the check [sic] and sometimes on the lips in front of the two minor children. That Tim Tipton and the Defendant would often hold hands in front of the two minor children.

29. Tim Tipton and the Defendant both testified that they engaged in oral sex, in that Tim Tipton would about once a week place his mouth on the penis of the Defendant. The Defendant would also place his mouth on the penis of Tim Tipton. The Court accordingly makes this as a finding of fact.. . .

32. That Tim Tipton and the Defendant engaged in the acts described in paragraph 29 above while the minor children were present in the home. That the minor children share the same bedroom and the said bedroom of the minor children is directly across the hall from the bedroom occupied by the Defendant and Tipton. That the Defendant and Tipton would engage in the acts described in paragraph 29 above while the children were a short distance away.

33. The Defendant and Mr. Tipton on at least one (1) occasion had a party for homosexuals at the

home located at 9 Roberts Road in Fletcher, N.C.. That the occasion was an anniversary party marking the first year since the Defendant and Tim Tipton meet [sic] at a homosexual bar in Asheville, North Carolina.

34. The Defendant and Mr. Tipton on at least three (3) occasions since first meeting have gone to an establishment that caters to homosexuals.

35. Mr. Tipton keeps in the bedroom he shares with the Defendant pictures of "drag queens". These are pictures of men dressed like women. These pictures are not under a lock, and it is possible for the children to gain access to the pictures.

36. Mr. Tipton testified that these materials (photographs of "drag queens") were not something that a child should be subjected to, and the Court finds this as a fact.

37. That the minor child Joey on one or more occasions observed the Defendant and Tipton in bed together.

38. That the two minor children never have friends stay over night while they are residing with the Defendant. . .

43. Uncontroverted evidence was presented that on at least two (2) occasions the Defendant struck the minor child Joey on or about the head, and accordingly the Court makes this as a finding of fact.

44. That on the 27th day of February, 1993, the Plaintiff married William Pulliam.

45. That evidence was presented which indicated that the two minor children have friends in Wichita, Kansas as well as friends in Henderson County, accordingly the Court makes this as a finding of fact.

46. The children spend about two (2) months every summer with the Plaintiff in Wichita, Kansas since the entry of the California Judgment.

47. At the house in Henderson County the children had separate beds in the same bedroom. That the two minor children have separate beds in the same bedroom at the Plaintiff's home in Wichita, Kansas. Furthermore, the Plaintiff's residence in Wichita, Kansas is of ample size for the two minor children.

48. The Plaintiff has in the past during the summer visitations taken more than adequate care of the two minor children.

49. That from the evidence presented the Court would find that the Defendant's conduct is not fit and proper and will expose the (2) minor male children to unfit and improper influences.. . . .

53. The activity of the Defendant will likely create emotional difficulties for the two minor children. That evidence was presented that the minor child Joey cried when he was told by the Defendant that he (Defendant) was homosexual. This evidence leads the Court to find that the minor child Joey may already be experiencing emotional difficulties because of the active homosexuality of the Defendant. Furthermore the Court finds that it is likely that the minor child Kenny will also experience emotional difficulties because of the active homosexuality of the Defendant.

54. That the active homosexuality of the Defendant and his involvement with Tim Tipton by bringing Tim Tipton into the home of the two minor children is detrimental to the best interest and welfare of the two minor children.

55. The Plaintiff is presently in a position to provide an environment more suitable to the two minor children's physical and emotional needs.

Based on such findings of fact, the trial court entered conclusions of law which included, inter alia, the following:

2. That since the entry of the California Judgment the Defendant is exposing the two minor children to conduct which is not fit and proper.

3. That since the California Judgment the Defendant is not providing a fit and proper environment in which to rear the two minor children.

4. That there has been a substantial change of circumstances since the entry of the California Judgment adversely affecting the two minor children or that will likely or probably adversely affect the two minor children.

5. That Plaintiff is a fit and proper person to exercise the exclusive care, custody, and control of the said two minor children. That it is in the minor children's best interest that the Plaintiff have exclusive[] care, custody and control of the minor children, subject to reasonable visitation privileges being awarded to the Defendant as hereinafter set out.

Based upon its findings of fact and conclusions of law, the trial court ordered that plaintiff-mother be awarded the exclusive care, custody and control of the two minor children. Defendant-father was granted one month of visitation during the summers and was directed by the trial court not to allow the boys to live in the same house with Mr. Tipton.

Defendant-father appealed to the Court of Appeals, which held that the findings upon which the trial court based its determination that there had been a change in circumstances adversely affecting the welfare of the children were either speculative or not supported by evidence in the record. The Court of Appeals reversed the trial court. For the reasons stated herein, we reverse the decision of the Court of Appeals.

Since this is a case involving modification of a custody order entered with the consent of both parties by a court in California, the controlling statute is N.C.G.S. § 50-13.7. That statute provides in pertinent part:

[W]hen an order for custody of a minor child has been entered by a court of another state, a court of this State may, upon gaining jurisdiction, and a showing of changed circumstances, enter a new order for custody which modifies or supersedes such order for custody.

N.C.G.S. § 50-13.7(b) (1995).

It is a long-standing rule that the trial court is vested with broad discretion in cases involving child custody. In re Custody of Peal , 305 N.C. 640, 645, 290 S.E.2d 664, 667 (1982). The Court of Appeals correctly explained the rationale for this rule when it stated:

"[The trial court] has the opportunity to see the parties in person and to hear the witnesses, and [its] decision ought not be upset on appeal absent a clear showing of abuse of discretion." Falls v. Falls, 52 N.C. App. 203, 209, 278 S.E.2d 546, 551, [disc. rev.] denied , 304 N.C. 390, 285 S.E.2d 831 (1981). "[The trial court] can detect tenors, tones, and flavors that are lost in the bare printed record read months later by appellate judges." Newsome v. Newsome, 42 N.C. App. 416, 426, 256 S.E.2d 849, 855 (1979).

Surles v. Surles, 113 N.C. App. 32, 36-37, 437 S.E.2d 661, 663 (1993) (first and third alterations in original). As a result, we have held that the trial court's "findings of fact have the force and effect of a verdict by a jury and are conclusive on appeal if there is evidence to support them, even though the evidence might sustain findings to the contrary." Williams v. Pilot Life Ins. Co., 288 N.C. 338, 342, 218 S.E.2d 368, 371 (1975).

The basis for the Court of Appeals' reversal of the trial court's judgment ordering a change of custody was its conclusion that the evidence presented did not support some of the trial court's findings. It is the duty of the reviewing court to examine all of the competent evidence in the record supporting the trial court's findings and to then decide if it is substantial. Thompson v. Wake County Bd. of Educ., 292 N.C. 406, 414, 233 S.E.2d 538, 544 (1977). However, in this case, the Court of Appeals did not afford sufficient weight and deference to the well-established law which severely limits appellate court review of custody orders, especially in the area of fact-finding. The Court of Appeals also failed to note competent, substantial, and critical evidence in the record tending to support the trial court's findings, conclusions, and order.

Where, as here, a case is tried without a jury, the fact-finding responsibility rests with the trial court. Absent a total lack of substantial evidence to support the trial court's findings, such findings will not be disturbed on appeal. The essential ingredient here is "substantial" evidence. The trial court's findings need only be supported by substantial evidence to be binding on appeal. We have defined "substantial evidence" as "'such relevant evidence as a reasonable mind might accept as adequate to support a conclusion.'" State v. Hill, 347 N.C. 275, 301, 493 S.E.2d 264, 279 (1997) (quoting State v. Smith, 300 N.C. 71, 78-79, 265 S.E.2d 164, 169 (1980)); accord Thompson, 292 N.C. at 414, 233 S.E.2d at 544.

Most of the trial court's findings of fact are uncontested. The remaining findings of the trial court are supported by substantial evidence.

With regard to findings of fact 49 and 54, uncontroverted evidence was presented that defendant-father and Mr. Tipton engaged in oral sex approximately once a week in the home with the children present. Defendant-father and Mr. Tipton intended to continue such homosexual activity in the home. Defendant-father saw nothing wrong with such conduct and would not counsel the two minor children that such conduct was improper.

Evidence was also presented tending to show that the children had seen the two men demonstrate physical affection, including kissing each other on the lips. This activity took place in the home in front

of the children as the "provider" of this couple prepared to leave for work.
The minor child Joey had observed his father and Mr. Tipton in bed together.

The evidence further tended to show that the door of the bedroom occupied by defendant-father and Mr. Tipton was directly across the hall and approximately three feet from the door to the children's bedroom. Defendant-father and Mr. Tipton testified that both their bedroom door and the children's bedroom door were open at all times, except when the two men engaged in sexual activity. Further, testimony tended to show that the children went in and out of the two men's bedroom at will, often during the night when the two men were in bed together.

Defendant testified that he had told the children that society was not accepting of such a homosexual relationship. There was also evidence that Mr. Tipton kept photographs of "drag queens" in the home, despite his admission that the children should not be exposed to such material. Further, evidence was presented that Mr. Tipton had, on at least one occasion, taken the children away from the home without defendant's knowledge of their whereabouts.

The foregoing evidence was admitted by the trial court and was not disputed by defendant. This evidence was substantial evidence and clearly supports findings of fact 49 and 54. We conclude that activities such as the regular commission of sexual acts in the home by unmarried people, failing and refusing to counsel the children against such conduct while acknowledging this conduct to them, allowing the children to see unmarried persons known by the children to be sexual partners in bed together, keeping admittedly improper sexual material in the home, and Mr. Tipton's taking the children out of the home without their father's knowledge of their whereabouts support the trial court's findings of "improper influences" which are "detrimental to the best interest and welfare of the two minor children."

We do not agree with the conclusion of Justice Webb's dissent that the only basis upon which the trial court changed custody was that the defendant is a "practicing homosexual." Instead, we conclude that the trial court could and did order a change in custody based in part on proper findings of fact to the effect that defendant-father was regularly engaging in sexual acts with Mr. Tipton in the home while the children were present and upon other improper conduct by these two men. The trial court did not rely on the mere fact that defendant is a homosexual or a "practicing homosexual." Nor does this Court hold that the mere homosexual status of a parent is sufficient, taken alone, to support denying such parent custody of his or her child or children. That question is not presented by the facts of this case. Although the trial court might have worded findings 49 and 54 better or more fully, they are nonetheless supported by substantial uncontroverted evidence. Therefore, they were binding on the Court of Appeals and are binding on this Court.

With regard to finding of fact 53, evidence was presented that when Joey was told that defendant-father was involved in a homosexual relationship, Joey was emotionally distraught, covering his face with his hands and running into the bathroom. Later, Joey cried, grasped onto his mother, and asked his mother to get him out of defendant's home. Evidence was also presented that sometime thereafter, Joey told his stepfather, William Pulliam, that he wanted his mother to come and get him and take him to Wichita where she lived. Further, evidence was presented that Joey expressed confusion over defendant's homosexual relationship with Mr. Tipton by asking Mr. Tipton if he was Joey's stepfather.

The trial court could reasonably find from this substantial evidence, as well as the other evidence discussed above, that "[t]he activity of the Defendant will likely create emotional difficulties for the two minor children." Although the trial court might have worded finding of fact 53 differently, it is nonetheless supported by substantial evidence and is binding on the Court of Appeals and this Court.

Substantial evidence supports all of the above-quoted findings of the trial court. Because these findings are sufficient to support the trial court's conclusions, which in turn justify a change of custody, we conclude that the trial court did not err.

The judgment of the trial court was proper, and the decision of the Court of Appeals to the contrary was in error. The decision of the Court of Appeals must be and is reversed, and this case is remanded to that court for its further remand to the District Court, Henderson County, for reinstatement of the judgment of the trial court.

REVERSED AND REMANDED.

Justice WEBB dissenting.

I dissent. I do not believe the evidence supports a finding that there had been a substantial change in circumstances affecting the welfare of the children so that the custody could be changed.

The majority begins its opinion by saying this Court has never required a party seeking a change in custody to show there has been a change in circumstances adversely affecting the child. The majority then overrules Thomas v. Thomas , 259 N.C. 461, 130 S.E.2d 871 (1963), and eighteen Court of Appeals cases which hold otherwise. We may want to change the law as to the showing necessary to change custody, but if we do so I suggest we do it forthrightly. I note that in this case the majority relies on a change in circumstances which adversely affects the children t o affirm the change in custody.

The majority relies first on findings of fact 49 and 54 to hold that the district court found facts sufficient to justify a change in custody. In these two findings, the district court found only that the defendant is a practicing homosexual and this creates an unfit and improper environment for the children. I do not believe the fact, standing alone, that defendant is a practicing homosexual, is sufficient to support a conclusion that this shows an improper environment which justifies a change in custody.

The majority also relies on finding of fact 53, in which the district court speculated on the possibility that their father's homosexuality will likely create emotional difficulties for the two children. The only evidence that the children actually suffered emotional difficulties was testimony that the older child, when he was told his father was homosexual, cried and asked his mother to remove him from his father's home. This child said at the hearing that he had no preference as to which of the parties was given custody. All the evidence showed the children were well adjusted. They had good attendance records in school and maintained average to above average grades. There was not substantial evidence to support a finding of fact that the defendant's homosexuality will likely create emotional difficulties for the two children.

The difficulty with the majority opinion for me is that it recites actions by the defendant which the majority considers to be distasteful, immoral, or even illegal and says this evidence supports findings of fact which allow a change in custody. There is virtually no showing that these acts by the defendant have adversely affected the two children. The test should be how the action affects the children and not whether we approve of it. I believe the evidence shows only that the defendant is a practicing homosexual without showing any harm has been inflicted on the children by this practice. I do not believe we should allow a change in custody on evidence which shows only that the defendant is a practicing homosexual.

Justice ORR concurring in the result.

N.C.G.S. § 50-13.7(b) provides that "when an order for custody of a minor child has been entered by a court of another state, a court of this State may, upon gaining jurisdiction, and a showing of changed circumstances , enter a new order for custody which modifies or supersedes such order for custody." N.C.G.S. § 50-13.7(b) (1995) (emphasis added). The statutory language does not use the word "substantial" in describing change of circumstances nor does the statute use the phrase "affecting the child's welfare." Both "substantial" and "affecting the child's welfare" have been added by judicial decisions and represent a commonsense interpretation of the legislative intent.

As I read the intent of the legislature in its passage of N.C.G.S. § 50-13.7(b), the trial court would first determine whether a change of circumstances had occurred since the entry of the original custody order and then determine whether the change of circumstances is substantial and has some rational relationship to the polar star issue in all custody determinations, i.e., the welfare of the child.(2)

In other words, the first factor to be considered in evaluating a change of circumstances is whether it is substantial. By this, we mean not inconsequential or minor but instead a change that is significant. Next, the trial court should evaluate whether the change "affects the welfare of the child." By this, we mean that the changes are of the type which normally or usually affect a child's well-being -- not a change that either does not affect the child or only tangentially affects the child's welfare.

It is unnecessary at this stage to determine the quantitative or qualitative degree of effect on a child's welfare. As a practical matter, it may be difficult, if not impossible, to determine how a significant change of circumstances is currently or in the long-term going to affect a child's welfare.

Upon determining that the requirement of N.C.G.S. § 50-13.7(b) has been met, the trial court would then be required to consider modification of custody by applying the best interest of the child test.

Here, there is little, if any, dispute that the father's acknowledgment that he is homosexual and that his companion and admitted lover's moving into the home with the boys constitutes a substantial change of circumstances as envisioned by N.C.G.S. § 50-13.7(b). Obviously, conditions in the home are dramatically different from when the original custody order was entered. Once the trial court reaches the conclusion that there has been a substantial change of circumstances, it is not necessary, as the Court of Appeals believed, for the trial court to make findings as to adverse (or beneficial) effects, but only that the substantial change affects the welfare of the child. Here, there seems little room for argument that the new living arrangement and the father's new lifestyle will have some effect on the boys and their well-being. It was erroneous to require a showing of harm to the children in reaching such a conclusion. Since there was evidence in the record from which the trial court could find that the change of circumstances was substantial and affected the boys' welfare, the trial court then was required to reopen the custody issue and determine what was in the best interest of the boys.

As to the ultimate disposition of this case, there is evidence in the record from which the trial court could find and ultimately conclude that it was in the best interest of the children to change custody. "[T]he trial judge's findings of fact in custody Orders are binding on the appellate courts if supported by competent evidence." Blackley v. Blackley, 285 N.C. 358, 362, 204 S.E.2d 678, 681 (1974).

In determining the best interest of the child, the trial court should consider a number of factors, too numerous to be named here. . . .

Whenever the trial court is determining the best interest of a child, any evidence which is competent and relevant to a showing of the best interest of that child must be heard and considered by the trial court, subject to the discretionary powers of the trial court to exclude cumulative testimony.

In re Shue, 311 N.C. 586, 597, 319 S.E.2d 567, 574 (1984).

However, there is no burden of proof on either party on the "best interest" question. Although the parties have an obligation to provide the court with any pertinent evidence relating to the "best interest" question, the trial court has the ultimate responsibility of requiring production of any evidence that may be competent and relevant on the issue. The "best interest" question is thus more inquisitorial in nature than adversarial.

Ramirez-Barker, 107 N.C. App. at 78, 418 S.E.2d at 679 (citation omitted). In applying the best-interest test, the trial court is vested with broad discretion, and its decision cannot be overturned absent a showing of an abuse of discretion. In re Custody of Peal, 305 N.C. 640, 645-46, 290 S.E.2d 664, 667(1982). Here, despite conclusory aspects of the trial court's order which were unnecessary, I cannot say that the trial court's decision that it was in the best interest of these young boys to now live with their mother and stepfather was an abuse of discretion.

I acknowledge that our case law has emphasized the importance of stability in custody cases and that continual reopening of the issue is harmful to the child. However, I am convinced that the test articulated in this concurring opinion does not substantially create a problem, and, if so, it must be balanced against the Court's ultimate responsibility to do what is in the child's best interest. Shepherd v. Shepherd, 273 N.C. 71, 75, 159 S.E.2d 357, 361 (1968). The party moving for modification of the original custody order must demonstrate that a substantial change in circumstances has occurred that affects the child's welfare. Obviously, this burden is necessary to promote stability in custody orders and discourage frequent petitions for modification of custody decrees. I believe this test will still serve to protect the custodial parent from harassment by repeated litigation and protect the child from being in the midst of ongoing custody battles.

As Justice Ervin said almost fifty years ago: "It may be well to observe, in closing, that the law is realistic and takes cognizance of the ever changing conditions of fortune and society. While a decree making a judicial award of the custody of a child determines the present rights of the parties to the contest, it is not permanent in its nature, and may be modified by the court in the future as subsequent events and the welfare of the child may require." Hardee v. Mitchell, 230 N.C. 40, 42, 51 S.E.2d 884, 885-86 (1949).

ENDNOTES

1. E.g., Wiggs v. Wiggs, ___ N.C. App. ___, 495 S.E.2d 401 (1998); Pulliam v. Smith, 124 N.C. App. 144, 476 S.E.2d 446; MacLagan v. Klein, 123 N.C. App. 557, 473 S.E.2d 778 (1996), disc. rev. denied, 345 N.C. 343, 483 S.E.2d 170 (1997); Speaks v. Fanek, 122 N.C. App. 389, 470 S.E.2d 82 (1996); Garrett v. Garrett, 121 N.C. App. 192, 464 S.E.2d 716 (1995); Benedict v. Coe, 117 N.C. App. 369, 451 S.E.2d 320 (1994); Dobos v. Dobos, 111 N.C. App. 222, 431 S.E.2d 861 (1993); Ramirez-Barker v. Barker, 107 N.C. App. 71, 418 S.E.2d 675 (1992); Perdue v. Perdue, 76 N.C. App. 600, 334 S.E.2d 86 (1985); Wehlau v. Witek, 75 N.C. App. 596, 331 S.E.2d 223 (1985); O'Briant v. O'Briant, 70 N.C. App. 360, 320 S.E.2d 277, disc. rev. denied, 312 N.C. 623, 323 S.E.2d 923 (1984), rev'd in part on other grounds, 313 N.C. 432, 329 S.E.2d 370 (1985); Barnes v. Barnes, 55 N.C. App. 670, 286 S.E.2d 586 (1982); Gordon v. Gordon, 46 N.C. App. 495, 265 S.E.2d 425 (1980); Daniels v. Hatcher, 46 N.C. App. 481, 265 S.E.2d 429, disc. rev. denied, 301 N.C. 87 (1980); Pritchard v. Pritchard, 45 N.C. App. 189, 262 S.E.2d 836 (1980); Dishman v. Dishman, 37 N.C. App. 543, 246 S.E.2d 819 (1978); Searl v. Searl, 34 N.C. App. 583, 239 S.E.2d 305 (1977).

2. I would disavow the test first set forth in Rothman v. Rothman, 6 N.C. App. 401, 406, 170 S.E.2d 140, 144 (1969), and followed in Ramirez-Barker v. Barker , 107 N.C. App. 71, 77, 418 S.E.2d 675, 678-79 (1992), that "[i]n order for a change in circumstances to be substantial, '[i]t must be shown that circumstances have so changed that the welfare of the child will be adversely affected unless the custody provision is modified.'"

Second Parent-adoption

Until recently, in most lesbian and gay families, only one parent was recognized as the legal parent. Distinct from the traditional form of adoption, which extinguishes the parental rights of the biological current legal parent(s), second-parent adoptions leave the parental rights of one legally recognized parent intact and create a second legally recognized parent for the child. While second-parent adoption is currently the only way for gay couples to both become legal parents of their children, it has also become fairly routine among children of non-gay step parents.

As of April 1997, second-parent adoptions by lesbian and gay couples had been approved by courts in the District of Columbia and twenty one (21) states: Alabama, Alaska, California, Illinois, Indiana, Iowa, Maryland, Massachusetts, Michigan, Minnesota, Nevada, New Jersey, New Mexico, New York, Ohio, Oregon, Pennsylvania, Rhode Island, Texas, Vermont, and Washington. (In most of these states, the approvals were from lower level courts.)

* In the Matter of Dana and In the Matter of Jacob (New York) Lambda represented the petitioner in Dana , who sought to adopt her lover's 5 1/2 year old biological child. They had been together for 19 years and raised Dana together since her birth. The Jacob case, in which Lambda submitted an amicus brief, was brought by a man who had lived with the biological mother of the child he sought to adopt since a short time after the boy was born. The Court of Appeals -- the highest court in New York State -- issued a joint opinion in these two cases. The 4-3 ruling established for all of New York State that the adoption code does permit "second parent adoption" (adoption by a person not married to a child's parent). (November 1995)

* In re Petition of D.M. and K.M. to Adopt Olivia M. (Illinois) This second-parent adoption case involves a three-year-old child, known as Olivia M., who was conceived by donor insemination. Olivia's lesbian parents planned for her conception and birth, and have raised and supported Olivia jointly. They filed an adoption petition seeking for Olivia the security of a legally recognized relationship with both her parents. After an initial defeat at the trial court level, the Illinois Appellate Court ruled that Olivia's parents -- and all lesbian, gay and unmarried parents -- have the right to seek to adopt children together. This is the first such appellate ruling in the Midwest. The court-appointed guardian for Olivia, who opposed the petition on legal grounds, joined a post-appeal motion to allow the adoption as he agreed it was in Olivia's best interests. After a lengthy hearing, the trial court granted the adoption petition. (July 1995)

Disallowing a Child to Testify

Posted Date: August 31, 1995

[Majority Opinion]

[Return to IU Law WWW Server]

IN THE INDIANA COURT OF APPEALS

Sandy L. White

-vs.-

Daniel G. White

SULLIVAN, J.

Sandy L. White (Sandy) appeals the trial court's decree dissolving her marriage to Daniel G. White (Daniel) and awarding custody of the couple's two minor children to Daniel.

We affirm.

The sole issue Sandy presents for our review is whether the trial court committed reversible error when it refused to allow her to call the parties' ten-year-old son as a witness at the dissolution hearing.[NOTE 1]

On April 25, 1994, the trial court entered a Decree of Dissolution dissolving Daniel and Sandy's marriage. The decree awarded Daniel custody of the couple's two minor children. The facts most favorable to the trial court's judgment disclose that Daniel and Sandy married in 1982. Two children were born of the marriage, a son, Joshua, and a daughter, Jessica. On April 30, 1993, Sandy filed a dissolution petition. The trial court held a final contested hearing on the dissolution petition on January 13, 1994, at which both Sandy and Daniel sought custody. At the time of the hearing, Joshua was ten years of age, and Jessica was five. Before the submission of evidence at the hearing, Sandy's counsel requested that the trial court conduct an in-camera interview with the couple's two children before it made a custody decision. The trial court took the matter under advisement pending submission of all evidence.

Sandy called Daniel as her first witness, and he testified, among other things, that Sandy had a bad temper. The next witness was Dr. Richard L. Lawlor, a clinical psychologist who conducted a custody evaluation.[NOTE 2] Dr. Lawlor was Daniel's witness, but the parties agreed to allow him to testify out of order during Sandy's case-in-chief. Dr. Lawlor testified at trial that it would be in the best interests of the children for the trial court to award sole custody to Daniel because Sandy was engaging in a pattern of behavior known as parental alienation syndrome, a series of actions and "maneuvers" by which she would attempt to exclude Daniel and to denigrate him in the eyes of the children.[NOTE 3] Dr. Lawlor also stated that Sandy displayed excessive anger and hostility toward Daniel. Daniel's mother, Dorothy White (Dorothy), and his sister-in-law, Elizabeth White (Elizabeth), both testified that Sandy displayed anger and hostility. They also each testified that they saw Sandy kick Joshua.[NOTE 4] Near the end of Daniel's presentation of evidence, the court informed counsel that it would have to resume the hearing at a later date.

On February 11, 1994, four days before the date on which the hearing was set to resume, the trial court denied Sandy's request for an in-camera interview. The hearing continued on February 15, 1994,[NOTE 5] at which time Daniel testified and then rested his case. Sandy presented two rebuttal witnesses, both of whom testified that they had never seen Sandy become physically abusive toward her children, and that she would provide a suitable environment for the children. Next, Sandy's trial counsel attempted to call Joshua as a rebuttal witness. Daniel's counsel objected to "exposing [Joshua] to a Court Room", contending that testifying would have a damaging emotional effect on him. Record at 534. The trial court sustained Daniel's objection and refused to allow Sandy to call Joshua as a witness, stating, in part, as follows:

"It is the position of this Court and has been the position of this Court since day one that children of the parties are not to be called as witnesses. I will allow children of the parties to be called as witnesses if the issue is emancipation for the limited purpose of them testifying as to whether they meet the qualifications of the statute. I will allow children of the parties to be called as witnesses for the limited purpose of them testifying as to advanced educational expenses. . . . I think that it is abundantly clear, based on [I.C. 31-1-11.5-21 (d)] and based on case law, that it is within this Court's discretion to exclude children as witnesses." Record at 542-43.

Sandy then testified as a rebuttal witness and specifically denied allegations that she ever kicked Joshua as Elizabeth and Dorothy White had testified.

On February 25, 1994, the trial court entered findings of fact and an order awarding Daniel custody of the children. The trial court's findings formed the basis for the dissolution decree, which awarded Daniel sole custody subject to Sandy's guideline visitation.[NOTE 6]

At custody hearings, a parent seeking custody bears the burden to demonstrate his or her fitness, and may submit evidence which reflects the other parent's incapacity to serve the child's best interests.

The trial court then exercises its discretion to award custody of the child consistent with the child's best interests. E.g., In re Marriage of Myers (1979) 3d Dist., 180 Ind.App. 284, 387 N.E.2d 1360, 1364. This court generally will not reverse a custody determination absent a manifest abuse of discretion. See Buchanan v. Buchanan (1971) 256 Ind. 119, 267 N.E.2d 155, 158; Myers, supra at 1364; Schwartz v. Schwartz (1976) 1st Dist., 170 Ind.App. 241, 351 N.E.2d 900, 901. A trial judge abuses his or her discretion if he or she renders a decision that is clearly against the logic and effect of the facts and circumstances before the court or the reasonable inferences to be drawn therefrom. Prenatt v. Stevens (1992) 4th Dist. Ind.App., 598 N.E.2d 616, 619; Walker v. Walker (1989) 4th Dist. Ind.App., 539 N.E.2d 509, 510. See also Myers, supra, 387 N.E.2d at 1364; Schwartz, supra at 901; Shaw v. Shaw (1973) 2d Dist., 159 Ind.App. 33, 304 N.E.2d 536, 539.

By refusing to allow Joshua to testify in any manner during the dissolution proceedings, the trial court essentially made two determinations. First, it refused to allow Joshua to rebut Dorothy and Elizabeth White's allegations that Sandy kicked him on a specific occasion or occasions. In addition, the trial court also foreclosed Sandy from eliciting any testimony regarding Joshua's custody preference. We therefore review each of these decisions.

I. Exclusion of Child's Rebuttal Testimony

Sandy contends that the trial court committed reversible error in not allowing Joshua to rebut Dr. Lawlor's allegations that she restricted the children's access to Daniel, as well as the allegations that Sandy kicked him. Daniel responds that the trial court did not err because I.C. 31-1-11.5-21 (d) [NOTE 7] grants a trial judge discretion not to allow a child to testify at dissolution proceedings. Alternatively, Daniel contends that even if the trial court committed error, it was harmless because other evidence in the record addressed the same points that Joshua would have made on the stand. Daniel specifically draws our attention to the fact that Sandy testified on rebuttal and denied the allegations that Dorothy and Elizabeth White had made.

Because Joshua was ten years of age at the time of the hearing, Indiana law does not presume that he was incompetent to testify.[NOTE 8] We mention the issue of Joshua's competency because Sandy devotes a significant portion of her briefs to arguing that the trial judge could not automatically presume Joshua incompetent. We agree. In doing so, however, we note that the trial judge's reluctance to allow Joshua to testify does not appear to arise because of a determination or even a suspicion that Joshua was incapable of understanding the nature and significance of an oath. Rather, it appears that the trial judge was more concerned about the emotional toll on Joshua which testifying in his parents' dissolution proceeding would exact. Nevertheless, while the trial judge's motives were no doubt admirable in trying to shield Joshua from the dissolution and custody proceedings, we must agree that he erred in doing so with regard to certain rebuttal testimony.

The facts here are similar to those presented in Bowman v. Bowman (1948) 118 Ind.App. 137, 77 N.E.2d 900. Bowman involved the proffered testimony of an eleven-year-old child of the parties to a dissolution proceeding whose father offered her as a witness at those proceedings. After the girl gave her age and stated that she was a child of the parties, her mother's attorney objected to any "'further use'" of her testimony due to her age and the "nature of the case." Id. at 901. The trial court sustained the objection and refused to allow the child to testify further. Upon appeal, the Bowman court reversed, first noting that children over ten years of age are competent witnesses. Id. The court then stated that it knew of "no authority vested in the trial court" which would allow the court to exclude the child's testimony in such a situation. Id.

Here, the trial judge determined that I.C. 31-1-11.5-21 (d) as well as case lean-to 9] placed within his discretion whether to exclude children of the parties as witnesses in dissolution proceedings. We disagree with the trial judge's interpretation of I.C. 31-1-11.5-21 (d). I.C. 31-1-11.5-21 addresses child custody orders. Section (a) provides that a trial court "shall determine custody and enter a custody order in accordance with the best interests of the child" and that the court "shall consider all relevant factors" including those which the statute specifies.[NOTE 10] Section (d) provides as follows:

"The court may interview the child in chambers to ascertain the child's wishes. The court may permit counsel to be present at the interview, in which event a record may be made of the interview and the same may be made part of the record for purposes of appeal."

Section (d) is a provision which allows a trial judge to interview minor children in chambers to ascertain their views regarding, for example, a custody preference. The in-camera interview allows the trial judge an alternative vehicle for ascertaining the information which Section (a) delineates without placing the children in the middle of an adversarial, open-court custody battle. See Truden v. Jacquay (1985) 3d Dist. Ind.App., 480 N.E.2d 974, 979.

Contrary to Daniel's assertions, Section (d) merely provides an option for, and governs the conduct of, in-camera interviews. Indeed, a trial judge is vested with rather broad discretion in conducting an interview should the judge decide to hold such an interview pursuant to Section (d). For example, a trial judge may, in his or her discretion, determine whether counsel should be present and whether or not to make a record of the interview. We discern no legislative intent by the creation of such a discretionary in-camera interview process that such discretion carries over into the broader and more general area of testimonial evidence. We conclude, therefore, that Section (d) does not afford a trial judge discretion in determining whether an otherwise competent child may testify in open court during dissolution proceedings.

While it may be good policy to exclude some otherwise competent persons, including children, from the adversarial and confrontational setting, articulation of such policy should be left to the legislature. The present rules of evidence clearly indicate that a party in civil litigation is free to call and to obtain the testimony of competent witnesses. The trial court lacks discretion to accept or reject those witnesses.[NOTE 11]

We next examine the nature of Joshua's proffered testimony. After the trial judge ruled that Joshua could not testify at the hearing, Sandy's counsel made an offer to prove, in which it was stated that Joshua would have, among other things, [NOTE 12] understood the nature of an oath and would have testified that no incidents of kicking as described by Dorothy and Elizabeth White ever occurred. Rebuttal evidence is evidence which tends to explain, contradict, or disprove an adversary's evidence. McCullough v. Archbold Ladder Co. (1993) Ind., 605 N.E.2d 175, 180; Coffman v. Austgen's Electric, Inc. (1982) 3d Dist. Ind.App., 437 N.E.2d 1003, 1005. Thus, any testimony from Joshua indicating that Sandy did not kick him as Dorothy and Elizabeth White earlier testified is proper rebuttal testimony, and the trial judge erred in precluding Joshua from rebutting such allegations.[NOTE 13]

We turn now to Daniel's argument that the error was harmless. If a trial court erroneously excludes evidence, we will reverse only if the error relates to a material matter or is of such character as to affect the "substantial rights of the parties." Ind. Trial Rule 61; see also Manns v. State, Department of Highways, Inc. (1989) Ind., 541 N.E.2d 929, 936; Dynes v. Dynes (1994) 2d Dist. Ind.App., 637 N.E.2d 1321, 1324, trans. denied; Indiana Insurance Co. v. Plummer Power Mower & Tool Rental, Inc. (1992) 4th Dist. Ind.App., 590 N.E.2d 1085, 1088.[NOTE 14] We have likewise recognized that error in the exclusion of evidence is not grounds for reversal unless our refusal to reverse would be "inconsistent with substantial justice." T.R. 61; Indiana & Michigan Electric Co. v. Hurm (1981) 1st Dist. Ind.App., 422 N.E.2d 371, 376, reh'g denied. We are satisfied that the error here does not mandate reversal.

We will deem harmless a trial court's erroneous ruling if the record otherwise indicates that the trial court clearly would have entered the same judgment regardless of the error. See Vollmar by Vollmar v. Rupright (1988) 2d Dist. Ind.App., 517 N.E.2d 1240; Miller v. Faulkner (1987) 3d Dist. Ind.App., 506 N.E.2d 52. Here, even if the trial court had allowed Joshua to rebut the allegations that Sandy had kicked him, such testimony, if examined in conjunction with the other evidence of record, leads unerringly to the conclusion that the trial court did not err in determining that sole custody with Daniel was in the best interests of the children.

In this connection, and as earlier noted, Dr. Lawlor testified that Sandy was engaging in a pattern of behavior he described as parental alienation syndrome. Furthermore, a significant portion of Daniel's evidence revealed that Sandy had a volatile temper and that she displayed socially inappropriate behavior. Testimony also revealed concern over the fact that the five-year-old daughter, Jessica, had yet to be fully potty-trained while under Sandy's primary supervision. Further, we are cognizant of the comparative credence afforded to both the doctor's testimony and that of Dorothy and Elizabeth White, especially in light of the fact that Joshua had been living with Sandy at the time of trial.

Joshua was particularly susceptible to undue pressure, wittingly exerted or not, to favor Sandy in his testimony. Accordingly, we agree that a refusal to reverse here because Joshua was not permitted to rebut Daniel's allegations of abuse is not inconsistent with substantial justice. The error does not mandate reversal.

II. Exclusion of Child's Testimony Regarding Custody Preference

The record reveals that Sandy sought not only to use Joshua's testimony to rebut allegations that she kicked him, but that she also desired to elicit testimony from Joshua regarding which parent with whom he wished or preferred to live.[NOTE 15] She did not, however, seek such testimony until the rebuttal phase of the trial. Sandy closed her case-in-chief before the trial court ruled on her in-camera interview request. By the time the hearing resumed some days later, the trial court, by then, had denied the request. Thus, the rebuttal phase of the proceedings was Sandy's last chance, so to speak, to offer such evidence.

As noted above, rebuttal evidence is evidence that tends to explain, contradict or disprove an adversary's evidence. McCullough, supra, 605 N.E.2d at 180; Coffman, supra, 437 N.E.2d at 1005. Further, trial courts may properly exclude testimony or evidence a proponent offers in rebuttal that he or she should have offered during his or her case-in-chief. Coffman, supra, 437 N.E.2d at 1005; Waugaman v. Gary Methodist Hospital (1972) 2d Dist., 151 Ind.App. 279, 279 N.E.2d 240, 243; see also McCullough, supra at 180; Carter v. AEtna Life Ins. Co. (1940) 217 Ind. 282, 292, 27 N.E.2d 75, 78-79. Whether a trial court may exclude such testimony offered for rebuttal is a decision left to the trial judge's sound discretion. Ind. Trial Rule 43 (C); McCullough, supra at 180; City of Indianapolis, Department of Metropolitan Development v. Heeter (1976) 1st Dist., 171 Ind.App. 119, 355 N.E.2d 429, 438; Waugaman, supra, 279 N.E.2d at 243.[NOTE 16] A trial judge abuses his discretion if he renders a decision that is clearly against the logic and effect of the facts and circumstances before the court or the reasonable, probable and actual deductions to be drawn from those facts and circumstances. See, e.g., Myers v. Myers (1990) Ind., 560 N.E.2d 39.

Here, Joshua's proffered testimony regarding his custody preference was an improper subject for rebuttal. At no time during the hearing does the record reveal that either child had expressed a preference for living with one parent as opposed to the other. Thus, Joshua's testimony cannot be gainsaid to explain, contradict or disprove evidence that Daniel previously elicited.

Furthermore, the trial court made it clear that Sandy's in-camera interview request would be taken under advisement "pending submission of all evidence in this cause." Record at 142 (emphasis supplied). Accordingly, Sandy knew that there would not be a ruling upon her in-camera interview request until after both sides had called all witnesses. Thus, she cannot successfully claim that she did not call Joshua because she assumed that the trial court would have conducted an in-camera interview. In addition, the record reveals that both children were present at the courthouse during the hearing sessions, and nothing appears to have prevented Sandy from calling Joshua as a witness during her case-in-chief in an attempt to elicit testimony addressing his custody preference. Upon appeal we will not substitute our judgments for those of the trial judge. Matters committed to judicial discretion are those requiring an on-the-spot decision made in light of the trial judge's knowledge, sense of fairness and equity, and the facts and circumstances present in the courtroom. See McCullough v. Archbold Ladder Co. (1992) 1st Dist. Ind.App., 587 N.E.2d 158, 162, (Baker, J., dissenting).[NOTE 17] The record simply does not reveal that the trial judge's decision not to allow Joshua to testify as a rebuttal witness regarding his custody preference is clearly against the logic and effect of the facts and circumstances before him or the reasonable, probable and actual deductions he could draw from those facts and circumstances.

CONCLUSION

The error the trial judge committed in precluding Joshua from rebutting allegations that Sandy kicked him does not mandate reversal. The trial judge did not abuse his discretion in disallowing Joshua to testify on rebuttal regarding his custody preference, which was a matter properly for Sandy's case-in-chief. Sandy does not present a frivolous appeal. We therefore deny Daniel's request for appellate attorney's fees.

The judgment is affirmed.

FRIEDLANDER, J. and RILEY, J. CONCUR

Note 1: Daniel presents an additional issue for our consideration: whether we should assess damages against Sandy for initiating a frivolous appeal.

Note 2: Daniel originally requested that Dr. John Ehrmann perform the custody evaluation. Sandy objected to his selection and instead requested that the parties utilize the services of Dr. Lawlor.

Note 3: Daniel reported that Sandy consistently was uncooperative and inflexible with respect to his access to the children. He also said that Sandy consistently acted in an angry and acrimonious manner toward him in the presence of the children. Daniel believed that his relationship with the children was becoming increasingly strained and remote as a result of these activities.

Dr. Lawlor initially made alternative custody recommendations, one recommending sole custody with Daniel and one recommending sole custody with Sandy subject to Daniel's rather liberal visitation. Dr. Lawlor testified that he arrived at alternative recommendations because he initially had believed Daniel was somewhat uncertain about seeking custody. However, Dr. Lawlor testified as he did at trial because Daniel's counsel advised him that Daniel was indeed interested in having full custody of the children.

Note 4: In his brief, Daniel maintains that Dorothy and Elizabeth refer to two separate incidents. It is unclear whether they refer to one incident which they both allegedly witnessed or whether they refer to two distinct incidents.

Note 5: The correct date on which the hearing resumed is not entirely clear. In her brief, Sandy contends that the hearing occurred on February 13, 1994, while Daniel submits that it was held on February 15, 1994. The record only adds to the confusion because the first page of the hearing transcript indicates that the hearing took place on January 13 and February 15, 1994, but the point at which the hearing resumes after concluding on January 13 is dated February 17, 1994. For purposes of this appeal, we assume that the second hearing occurred on February 15, 1994.

Note 6: The decree reads in relevant part as follows:

"Daniel . . . is a fit and proper person to have custody of said children and that it is in the children's best interest that [he] be the person to have care and custody, subject to the right of [Sandy] to visitation as set forth herein below. . . . [Sandy] shall have visitation with the minor children consistent with the Marion County Visitation Guidelines. . . . As a condition of [Sandy's] continued visitation, she shall participate in on-going counselling. . . . Sandy . . . shall pay support for the benefit of the parties' minor children in the sum of $119.00 per week." Record at 125-26.

Note 7: See I.C. 31-1-11.5-21 (d) (Burns Code Ed. Repl. 1994).

Note 8: Rule 601 of the Indiana Rules of Evidence presumes that "[e]very person is competent to be a witness except as otherwise provided in these rules or by act of the Indiana General Assembly." Further, I.C. 34-1-14-4 provides that all persons are competent witnesses in a civil action or proceeding, whether parties to, or interested in, the suit, except as provided by statute. Before its amendment in 1990, I.C. 34-1-14-5 presumed that a child under age ten was incompetent to testify unless the trial court was satisfied that the child understood the nature and the obligation of an oath. In 1990, our legislature amended I.C. 34-1-14-5, deleting the reference to children under age ten. Joshua was ten years of age at the time of the hearing. Therefore, even under Indiana law before 1990, the trial court could not presume him incompetent.

Note 9: The record discloses that the case law to which the trial judge referred is Truden v. Jacquay (1985) 3d Dist. Ind.App., 480 N.E.2d 974, and In re Marriage of Saunders (1986) 1st Dist. Ind.App., 496 N.E.2d 419. After briefly explaining the two cases, the judge concluded as follows:

"I infer from these decisions that it is within this Court's discretion to allow or disallow evidence and testimony from a child of the parties. I think that [I.C. 31-1-11.5-21 (d)] provides for in-camera interview in the Court's discretion as to whether the Court wishes to take evidence as such from the children by interviewing them on an in-camera basis and it is up to the Court to determine whether or not to do that in chambers. . . . The Court exercises its' [sic] discretion against allowing the child to be called as a witness in this cause of action. The Respondent's objection to the calling of this witness is sustained. Joshua White shall not testify in this cause of action." Record at 545-46.

Note 10: The relevant factors the statute enumerates are as follows:

(1) The age and sex of the child;

(2) The wishes of the child's parent or parents;

(3) The wishes of the child. . .;

(4) The interaction and interrelationship of the child with his parent or parents, his siblings, and any other person who may significantly affect the child's best interests;

(5) The child's adjustment to his home, school, and community; and

(6) The mental and physical health of all individuals involved."

Note 11: We note that Rule 403 of the Indiana Rules of Evidence permits the trial court to exclude certain evidence from a competent witness if the probative value of that evidence is outweighed by, for example, prejudice or trauma to the witness. Regardless, exclusion of a witness and exclusion of certain evidence from a witness are two different things.

Note 12: The offer to prove also indicated that Joshua would testify that he preferred to live with his mother and that Daniel punishes Joshua's sister, Jessica, when she says that she misses her mother during visitation. As we will discuss in Part II, infra, such testimony is not proper rebuttal.

Note 13: Sandy argues in her brief that through Joshua's testimony, she might also have "had an opportunity to counter the allegations leveled by Dr. Lawlor that [she] somehow attempted to restrict the children's access to their father." Appellant's Brief at 17. That may well be so, but Sandy's offer of proof reveals that her trial counsel did not seek to elicit such testimony from Joshua. Citing Bowman, supra, 77 N.E.2d 900, and State v. Hamer (1936) 211 Ind. 570, 199 N.E. 589, Sandy maintains that the error is nevertheless preserved because she need not have made an offer of proof in this case. We disagree.

Older Indiana cases have held that when an objection "is to the right of the witness to testify at all, the party introducing that witness need not state what he expects to prove by him, as the question for the court to pass upon in such a case is not as to the competency of his testimony, but as to the competency of the witness himself." Sullivan v. Sullivan (1893) 6 Ind.App. 65, 32 N.E. 1132, 1133; see also Hamer, supra, 199 N.E. at 593-94; Bowman, supra, 77 N.E.2d at 901. Courts have held likewise in cases where the so-called "dead man's statute" has precluded witnesses from testifying at trial. See, e.g., Paullus v. Yarnelle (1994) 4th Dist. Ind.App., 633 N.E.2d 304, 308, trans. denied; Senff v. Estate of Levi (1987) 1st Dist. Ind.App., 515 N.E.2d 556, 559, trans. denied; Satterthwaite v. Satterthwaite's Estate (1981) 4th Dist. Ind.App., 420 N.E.2d 287, 292.

Nevertheless, recent decisions have seemingly required an offer of proof even when the trial court has found a witness incompetent or when it has otherwise prevented a witness from giving any testimony. E.g., Wiseheart v. State (1986) Ind., 491 N.E.2d 985, 991 (witness precluded from offering any testimony because of discovery violation); Tyson v. State (1993) 2d Dist. Ind.App., 619 N.E.2d 276, 281, trans. denied, denial of post conv. relief Aff'd in Part, Rev'd in Part (1993) 2d Dist. Ind.App., 626 N.E.2d 482, U.S. cert. denied (1994) ___ U.S. ___, 114 S.Ct. 1216, 127 L.Ed.2d 562 (witnesses precluded from offering any testimony). Most recently in Donaldson v. Indianapolis Public Transportation Corp. (1994) 4th Dist. Ind.App., 632 N.E.2d 1167, 1170, the trial court excluded the testimony of a purported expert witness after determining that the witness did not qualify as an expert on National Safety Council (NSC) standards and their applicability to the accident at issue. Upon appeal, Donaldson contended that the trial court committed error when it precluded the witness from testifying about the NSC rules. There, the court noted:

"During direct examination, when the trial court rules that a witness may not testify, the proponent of the excluded testimony must make an offer of proof to preserve the ruling for appellate review. [Citations omitted.] 'An offer of proof provides the appellate court with the scope and effect of the area of inquiry and the proposed answers, in order that it may consider whether the trial court's ruling excluding the evidence was proper.' Tyson v. State (1993) Ind.App., 619 N.E.2d 276, 281, trans. denied. Thus, 'the offer of proof must demonstrate the substance, purpose, relevancy, and materiality of the excluded evidence in order to enable the appellate court to determine on appeal whether the exclusion was proper.'Id."

Donaldson involved exclusion of a witness offered for direct examination.
Nevertheless, its rationale is equally if not more appropriate in a situation, such as in the instant case, in which a proponent offers the excluded testimony during the rebuttal phase of the proceeding. When dealing with rebuttal testimony, it is imperative that we, as an appellate tribunal, know what the proponent expects to prove by a particular witness

so that we may be able to discern whether the evidence offered upon rebuttal is proper at that stage of the proceeding. Specifically, we may need to determine whether the proffered testimony is prejudicial or cumulative. That was not at issue in Sullivan, supra, Hamer, supra, and Satterthwaite, supra. In those cases, the only real issue was the competency of the witnesses, not the competency of their proffered testimony. However, when a proponent offers a witness as a rebuttal witness, issues may arise not only with regard to the witness' competency, but often, as is the case here, with regard to the nature of the testimony itself. This is so because, as mentioned above, an appellate court must be able to determine whether such testimony is properly within the scope of rebuttal evidence. See State ex rel. Repp v. Cox (1900) 155 Ind. 593, 596, 58 N.E. 849, 850; see also Robert L. Miller, Indiana Evidence, 12 Indiana Practice § 103.110 (West 1984). Without an offer of proof on record, we are unable to do so. Accordingly, an offer of proof is necessary.

In the case at bar, Sandy's trial counsel did not state that Joshua's proffered testimony would rebut any of Dr. Lawlor's conclusions regarding parental alienation syndrome or any of the facts underlying his custody recommendation, such as whether Sandy restricted Joshua's access to Daniel or whether Daniel may have punished Jessica on occasion. Upon appeal, we will deem waived an issue that was neither presented nor established at trial. See, e.g., Franklin Bank and Trust Co. v. Mithoefer (1990) Ind., 563 N.E.2d 551, 553; Allstate v. United Farm Bureau Mutual Insurance Co. (1993) 4th Dist. Ind.App., 618 N.E.2d 31, 33; Blairex Laboratories, Inc. v. Clobes (1992) 1st Dist. Ind.App., 599 N.E.2d 233, 237, trans. denied; Williams v. City of Indianapolis Department of Public Works (1990) 1st Dist. Ind.App., 558 N.E.2d 884, 887, trans. denied; Kline v. Business Press, Inc. (1987) 4th Dist. Ind.App., 516 N.E.2d 88, 90, trans. denied; Allen v. Scherer (1983) 1st Dist. Ind.App., 452 N.E.2d 1031, 1033; Green v. Green (1983) 4th Dist. Ind.App., 447 N.E.2d 605, 610, trans. denied. In this case, Sandy failed to preserve an argument concerning Joshua's ability to counter Dr. Lawlor's testimony because she did not make such assertions in her offer of proof at trial. Accordingly, when considering what portion of Joshua's proffered testimony was a proper subject for rebuttal, we will not consider the fact that Joshua might have had the opportunity to counter Dr. Lawlor's conclusion or the facts upon which he based that conclusion.

Note 14: See also Posey County v. Chamness (1982) 1st Dist. Ind.App., 438 N.E.2d 1041, 1048; Cornett v. Cornett (1980) 1st Dist. Ind.App., 412 N.E.2d 1232, 1236, reh'g denied; Lovko v. Lovko (1978) 2d Dist., 179 Ind.App. 1, 384 N.E.2d 166, 173, reh'g denied; Dudley Sports Co. v. Schmitt (1972) 2d Dist., 151 Ind.App. 217, 279 N.E.2d 266, 278.

Note 15: When Daniel's counsel objected to Joshua's testimony, the following colloquy occurred:

"[Daniel's Counsel]: I think it's important that the Court know what the wishes of the children are, as clearly the statute requires the Court to take that into account in determining who shall have custody, and to this point, there has been no evidence to indicate what the childrens' [sic] wishes are and if that cannot be acquired by the Court through an in-camera interview, then the only alternative is for me to call Joshua and have him testify. . . ."

THE COURT: . . . How is it proper rebuttal testimony presenting evidence as to the wishes of the child concerning placement?

[Daniel's Counsel]: With respect to rebuttal, it really isn't, your Honor. Well, I take it back.

THE COURT: Well, if it isn't then why are you calling this child as a rebuttal witness if it's not proper rebuttal testimony? . . . [H]ow is this child to testify as to Mrs. White's fitness as a parent? Mr. White's testimony on direct examination in his case in chief was that he had not discussed with the children what their preferences are as to placement. . . .[Daniel's Counsel]: . . . There has been testimony by Mr. White as to the conduct of Mrs. White which would render her a parent who should not have custody and I think Joshua is certainly competent to testify as to some of the allegations that have been made in the testimony of Mr. White and I think that goes to the issues as well as to the wishes of the child.

And without that testimony, the Court has no knowledge as to what the wishes of the children would be and the Court without that information can, it would seem to me, not fulfill it's [sic] statutory duty with respect to taking into consideration those wishes. I would also add to that that I had requested at the outset an in-camera interview. The Court deferred ruling upon that until completion of all the evidence and then the Court did rule upon my written motion for an immediately [sic] ruling.

THE COURT: I denied that.

[Daniel's Counsel]: I realize that, which left me then with no alternative [but to call Joshua as a witness.]" Record at 535-38.

Note 16: See also Stalker v. Breeze (1917) 186 Ind. 221, 114 N.E. 968; Stewart v. Smith (1887) 111 Ind. 526, 13 N.E. 48.

Note 17: The majority opinion was vacated by our Supreme Court upon transfer in McCullough v. Archbold Ladder Co. (1993) Ind., 605 N.E.2d 175.

The Supreme Court
of The State of Alaska

MARLENE M. WEST,	)
	) Supreme Court
Appellant,	) No. S-9666
	) Superior Court No.
v.	) 3KO-99-273 CI
BRIAN S. WEST,	) O P I N I O N
Appellee.	)[No.5394-April27, 2001]

Appeal from the Superior Court of the State of Alaska, Third Judicial District, Kodiak,

Donald D. Hopwood, Judge.
Appearances: Steve W. Cole, Gray, Cole & Razo, P.C., Kodiak, for Appellant. D. Scott Dattan, Law Office of D.
Scott Dattan, Anchorage, for Appellee.

Before: Fabe, Chief Justice, Eastaugh,
Bryner, and Carpeneti, Justices. [Matthews, Justice, not participating.]

BRYNER, Justice.

I. INTRODUCTION

The court presiding over Marlene and Brian West's divorce gave Brian primary custody of the Wests' son Cody; the court based its decision primarily on Brian's anticipated remarriage, which, the court found, would offer Cody the benefit of a "two-parent household." We reverse, holding that custody awards may not be based on the assumption that a divorced parent who remarries can provide a better home than an otherwise equally competent parent who remains single.

II. FACTS AND PROCEEDINGS

Marlene and Brian separated after seven years of marriage. Upon separation Marlene moved to Oregon with two teenage children from a previous marriage, Heather and Gene. At first Marlene and Brian's young son Cody remained with Brian in Kodiak so that Brian could retain his Coast Guard housing. Cody later moved back and forth between his parents' homes every several months. At the time of trial, Cody was enrolled in kindergarten and living in Oregon with Marlene and her sixteen-year-old daughter Heather.

In Oregon Marlene's job required her to leave home early in the morning. Heather was responsible for getting Cody ready and riding the bus with him to school. Marlene was usually back from work by the time Cody returned home in the afternoon. Heather had two years left before graduating from high school; if she moved away from home after her graduation, Marlene planned to leave Cody with his nearby grandparents on school mornings so that they could get him ready for school.

At the time of trial, Brian lived in Coast Guard housing in Kodiak. He was involved in a romantic relationship with Anne Marie Gould, a nurse who lived in Anchorage. Brian and Anne Marie hoped to marry but were reluctant to make definite plans before Brian's divorce became final. Brian expected to remain in Kodiak until July 2001 and then request a transfer to Sacramento. He could not predict his duty locations, other than to say that they would not be outside of the United States.

The evidence at trial included a child custody report describing the family's history and current circumstances and briefly discussing statutorily relevant factors. For the most part, the custody investigator's comments about both parents were equally positive, and she concluded that joint legal custody seemed like a viable option. Under the heading "violence, abuse and neglect," the investigator reported that Marlene expressed "concern [that Brian] may verbally abuse Cody in the future, based on his behavior towards her other children." But the investigator noted that there was no indication that Brian had ever verbally abused Cody and that it "does not seem reasonable to conclude that child abuse is a factor in this case."
The factor that the investigator discussed at greatest length was the amount of time that Cody had lived in

a stable, satisfactory environment and the desirability of maintaining continuity. The investigator commented that Cody could flourish in either home and that, if it were not for the physical distance between Marlene and Brian, she would recommend shared physical custody. She observed that there had been little continuity in Cody's life since his parents' separation. The investigator suggested it would be best for Cody to spend the entire school year in one location. Ultimately, the fact that Heather lived with Marlene and that Marlene's extended family lived near her in Oregon formed the basis for the investigator's recommendation that Cody be placed primarily with Marlene and permitted to visit with Brian as much as possible.

At the close of trial the court commented on the investigator's report, which it generally adopted. The court then made oral findings and concluded that it would be in Cody's best interest for Brian to have primary physical custody after the school year ended. The court began with observations about the quality of parenting that both Marlene and Brian could provide to Cody. It observed that both parents had spent extensive time with Cody. The court addressed Marlene's concerns about Brian's parenting and, like the custody investigator, concluded that abuse was not a significant factor. Aside from the discussion of alleged verbal abuse, the trial court's only mention of Cody's siblings was a remark that Heather would graduate in a couple of years.

The court identified differences in the immediate households as important. The court described the situation as follows: It's likely that Brian will remarry Anne Marie Gould, and she has long-term stability in the nursing field; about 12 years. And that's a situation that, I think, is very positive because of the number of adults it provides in a household for child-rearing. It's likely that's going to happen. I think highly likely in the near future. And that there would be two adults in that household, part of the immediate family, that would be available most of the time. Brian might be subject to deployments as part of his military duties. . . . If it happens, it seems to me that Ms. Gould, who likely would be his wife by then, would be in the household to care for Cody.

The trial court later issued written findings of fact and conclusions of law. The court observed that both Marlene and Brian "provide positive environments and living arrangements" and that one was not necessarily better than the other. However, the court observed:

14. Brian West and Anne Marie Gould plan to get married. Her background as a nurse is a positive factor which adds to the advantages for Cody in a two-parent household when he is with Mr. West.

15. The significant difference between the parties is in what is ahead and the kind of household provided for Cody. Brian's household will be the better one for Cody's future.

The written findings did not mention Heather. The court's conclusions of law stated that it would be in Cody's best interest for primary physical custody to be awarded to Brian once Cody completed the school year. The court went on to establish visitation and child support obligations for Marlene.

III. DISCUSSION

On appeal Marlene argues that the trial court abused its discretion by using improper factors to determine Cody's best interests. In particular, Marlene argues that it was improper to award Brian primary physical custody of Cody based on his anticipated remarriage. Marlene also argues that the trial court improperly failed to take into account three factors -- Cody's bond with Heather, the disruptiveness of Brian's likely continued relocation, and allegations that Brian had verbally abused Marlene's two older children -- which might have supported a determination that it would be in Cody's best interest to live with Marlene. Finally, Marlene asks that we vacate the child support order if we reverse the child custody order.

A. Standard of Review

We will reverse a trial court's custody determination if critical factual findings were clearly erroneous or if there has been an abuse of discretion. [Fn. 1] We will set aside a finding as clearly erroneous if a review of the entire record leaves us firmly convinced that a mistake has been made. [Fn. 2] It is an abuse of discretion to consider improper factors, to fail to consider relevant statutory factors, or to assign disproportionate weight to some factors while ignoring others. [Fn. 3] When a custody determination has been made based on improper factors, we remand for a decision based on proper factors. [Fn. 4]

B. The Award of Primary Physical Custody on the Basis of Anticipated Remarriage Was Improper.
Custody determinations must be based on the best interests of the child as determined using the factors listed in AS 25.24.150(c). [Fn. 5] The trial court must consider each of these factors, but it is only required to discuss relevant factors in explaining its decision. [Fn. 6] Pertinent factors other than the eight specifically listed in the statute can be considered if they are relevant to determining the best interests of the child. [Fn. 7] Here, the trial court determined in its written findings that both Brian and Marlene are excellent parents and that only physical distance and Cody's need to attend one school precluded shared physical custody. The court observed that, although Brian and Marlene differed in their parenting styles, both parents had spent equal time with Cody and both had support networks available to them. The court indicated that there had been no child abuse and that complaints about visitation were not significant. The court also found that both Marlene and Brian "provide[d] positive environments and living arrangements" and that there was no evidence that Cody would be better off with Brian than with Marlene.
Finding all these factors essentially equal, the trial court proceeded to award primary physical custody of Cody to Brian based on the benefits of "a two-parent household": Brian West and Anne Marie Gould plan to get married. Her background as a nurse is a positive factor which adds to the advantages for Cody in a two-parent household when he is with Mr. West.

The significant difference between the parties is in what is ahead and the kind of household provided for Cody. Brian's household will be the better one for Cody's future. In the court's view, then, Brian's plan to marry Anne Marie, who would provide a "two-parent household," gave him the advantage over Marlene, who would continue to work and had no plans to remarry.

Other states have addressed the question of whether a court's ruling on custody in a divorce proceeding may rest on the assumption that a working parent who remarries will be able to provide superior care to the care provided by a single working parent. We agree with the well-reasoned decisions of other courts concluding that the presumed advantages of a two-parent household ordinarily should not determine an award of custody. [Fn. 8] When awarding custody, the superior court is charged with determining the arrangement that will serve the best interest of the child in the specific case at hand. A child custody determination "cannot be based on an assumption, unsupported by scientific evidence, that a working mother cannot provide such care." [Fn. 9] Such an assumption unfairly forces divorcing spouses to choose between parenthood and livelihood; and it is likely to disproportionately deprive women of custody, since statistics indicate that divorced men are more likely to remarry a spouse who does not work outside the home. [Fn. 10] The trial court expressed concern in its oral findings that, once Heather graduated from school and moved away from home, Marlene would need to drop Cody off at his grandparents' home to get ready for school. The court believed that this routine would be disruptive in comparison to the continuity of care that Cody would receive in the two-parent setting of Brian's home once Brian remarried.

But the court's concern rests largely on its unexplained assumption that the added physical convenience of in-home care that Cody might receive from his new second parent -- Anne Marie Gould -- would outweigh the less tangible, but potentially vital emotional benefits he might receive by maintaining his close and already-established ties to Heather and his maternal grandparents.
As other courts have observed, determining which parent can better meet the needs of a child in circumstances like these requires more than "rudimentary hour-counting" or reliance on an assumption that babysitters or extended family are less desirable care givers than stepparents.[Fn. 11]
A presumptive preference for in-home care by a new second parent implicitly treats parenthood as a fungible service, ignores potential stresses associated with stepfamilies, and runs counter to recent scientific evidence. [Fn. 12] A court may certainly give custodial preference to a two-parent household when case-specific evidence points to the conclusion that the second adult custodian would be advantageous under the particular circumstances actually presented. But in our view, a presumptive preference for the two-parent setting is unwarranted. We thus conclude that, absent case-specific evidence indicating that Anne Marie Gould's in-home care would be of superior benefit to Cody than the care he would receive from his grandparents and sister, Cody's custody should not have been

determined by an expressed preference for the advantages of a "two-parent household."

e turn, then, to the evidence presented at trial. Our review of the trial record reveals no case-specific basis for concluding that Cody's care in Brian's proposed two-parent household would be superior to the care that he would receive in the single-parent setting of his home with Marlene.

The record certainly contains substantial evidence indicating that Brian and Anne Marie could provide excellent care. [Fn. 13] But comparable evidence -- accepted by the trial court -- indicated that Cody would also receive excellent care from Marlene, Heather, and his maternal grandparents. What the record lacks, however, is specific evidence establishing which of the two possible home settings -- a single-parent or two-parent household -- would actually be better for Cody. Nor did the trial court appear to see a need for such evidence. As shown in its written findings, the court simply assumed, all other things being equal, that the "two-parent household" should have the advantage, because it offered Cody more time for in-home care.

As we have already indicated above, this is an unfounded assumption. Child custody orders must be based on the best interests of the particular child. Here, we find no sound, case-specific evidentiary basis for concluding that the qualitative benefits of extended-family care that would have been available to Cody with Marlene should be deemed less desirable than the improved physical convenience of the in-home stepparenting that he might experience with Brian. Accordingly, we conclude that it was improper to award primary physical custody of Cody to Brian on the basis of Brian's anticipated marriage to Anne Marie.

C. Other Issues

Marlene separately argues that the trial court abused its discretion by failing to award custody to her based on sibling bonds, the disruptiveness of Brian's likely future relocations, and allegations that Brian abused the older children. But given our decision to remand this case for a redetermination of custody, we need not consider these issues here. [Fn. 14] Marlene will have the opportunity to present these arguments to the trial court on remand. [Fn. 15] We assume that the court will carefully reconsider them, among all other factors relevant to its determination of Cody's current best interests.

IV. CONCLUSION

Because it was error to award primary physical custody of Cody to Brian on the basis of his anticipated marriage to Anne Marie, we VACATE the trial court's custody order and REMAND for a redetermination of custody based on Cody's current best interests.

FOOTNOTES

Footnote 1: See R.I. v. C.C., 9 P.3d 274, 277 (Alaska 2000).

Footnote 2: See City of Hydaburg v. Hydaburg Co-op. Ass'n, 858 P.2d 1131, 1135 (Alaska 1993).

Footnote 3: See Borchgrevink v. Borchgrevink, 941 P.2d 132, 134 (Alaska 1997).

Footnote 4: See Lowdermilk v. Lowdermilk, 825 P.2d 874, 878-79 (Alaska 1992). Cf. Johnson v. Johnson, 564 P.2d 71, 74 (Alaska 1977).

Footnote 5: The statutory factors are:

(1) the physical, emotional, mental, religious, and social needs of the child;

(2) the capability and desire of each parent to meet these needs;

(3) the child's preference if the child is of sufficient age and capacity to form a preference;

(4) the love and affection existing between the child and each parent;

(5) the length of time the child has lived in a stable, satisfactory environment and the desirability of maintaining continuity;

(6) the desire and ability of each parent to allow an open and loving frequent relationship between the child and the other parent;

(7) any evidence of domestic violence, child abuse, or child neglect in the proposed custodial household or a history of violence between the parents;

(8) evidence that substance abuse by either parent or other members of the household directly affects the emotional or physical well-being of the child;

(9) other factors that the court considers pertinent. AS 25.24.150(c).

Footnote 6:
See Park v. Park, 986 P.2d 205, 207 (Alaska 1999).

Footnote 7: See AS 25.24.150(c)(9); see also Evans v. Evans, 869 P.2d 478, 481-82(Alaska 1994)(affirming custody determination made on basis of non-statutory factors when parents were equally qualified to care for child in all other respects).

Footnote 8: See Barchard v. Garay, 724 P.2d 486, 492 (Cal. 1986) ("The essence of the court's decision is simply that care by a mother who, because of work and study, must entrust the child to day-care centers and babysitters, is per se inferior to care by a father who also works, but can leave the child with a stepmother at home. . . . [T]his reasoning is not a suitable basis for a custody order."); Wellman v. Dutch, 604 N.Y.S.2d 381, 383 (N.Y. App. Div. 1993) ("[T]he court's award of custody to petitioner principally because his spouse would be home all day to care for the child has the impermissible effect of depriving respondent, an unmarried working mother, of her equal right to custody."); Brennan v. Brennan, 685 A.2d 1104, 1106 (Vt. 1996).

Footnote 9: Burchard, 724 P.2d at 492.

Footnote 10: See id. at 492 n.10; Linda R. v. Richard E., 561 N.Y.S.2d 29, 33 (N.Y. App. Div. 1990).

Footnote 11: Brennan, 685 A.2d at 1105-06 (reversing a trial court decision awarding custody to father over mother who relied on day care provider); see Wellman, 604 N.Y.S.2d at 383 (reversing an order granting custody to father whose wife would care for child over mother who would take the child to be cared for by an aunt in the mornings); Gerber v. Gerber, 487 A.2d 413, 416 (Pa. Super. 1985) (noting that "a parent's work schedule may not deprive that parent of custody if suitable arrangements are made for the child's care in his or her absence").

Footnote 12: See generally Jennifer E. Horne, Note, The Brady Bunch and Other Fictions: How Courts Decide Child Custody Disputes Involving Remarried Parents, 45 Stan. L. Rev. 2073 (1993) (discussing research indicating that children do not accept stepparents as replacement parents and data about the instability of stepfamilies).

Footnote 13: We note, however, that the record in this case is equivocal in its support of the trial court's findings that Brian would marry Anne Marie and that they would successfully arrange their work schedules to ensure that one of them would usually be at home to care for Cody. Anne Marie -- who by her own estimate had seen Cody on only a dozen occasions -- described her relationship with him as "decent": "I think we have a -- decent relationship. I don't -- I don't inundate Cody. I let him come to me." With respect to marriage, Brian testified that he and Anne Marie would probably get married and start a family of their own. Anne Marie testified that she hoped to marry Brian but that they had not made definite plans. Her testimony concerning her future work schedule was even more tentative. She did say that she hoped to be able to reduce her work hours and to mesh her schedule with Brian's, so that she could "possibly [work] on weekends when Brian would be home." But she said this in describing her hope to "start a family," not in describing her willingness to provide home care for Cody.

Footnote 14: Our decision to remand also moots Marlene's challenge to the superior court's child support order.

Footnote 15: To avoid potentially unnecessary relitigation of a contentious issue, however, we note our conclusion that the superior court was not clearly erroneous in declining to attach significant weight to evidence of verbal abuse by Brian.

Glossary of Terms

The definition of terms given in this glossary may or may not agree with the accepted reference dictionaries. While some of the definitions are not literally proper, they are correct for understanding the whole of this text. This list is not a complete dictionary, rather a quick reference guide.

A

A.A.R.P.: American Association of Retired Persons

Abandon: To knowingly give up without intent to return or re-claim.

Abatement: To reduce, diminish or temporarily suspend.

Abducted Child: The child who has been wrongfully taken, kept, or concealed by the abductor, with or without the child's help or consent. Also called the victim child.

Abduction: Taking and carrying away by force, by means of fraud, persuasion, or open violence.

Abet: As in "to aid and abet." The act of encouraging or inciting another to do a certain thing, such as a crime like concealing a child against a court order. For example, many countries will equally punish a person who aids or abets another to commit a crime.

Abrogate: To annul or cancel. Having been deprived of legal validity, force or authority now brings to an end by formal concerted action.

Abscond: To travel covertly out of the jurisdiction of the courts, or to conceal oneself in order to avoid the process of the court.

Absence of Entry: Refers to evidence that a matter is not included in the reports, records, or data compilations in any form kept in accordance with "records of regularly conducted activity".

Absence of Public Record: Refers to evidence in the form of certification in accordance with testimony that diligent search failed to disclose that a matter is not included in the reports, records, or data compilations in any form made and preserved by a public office or agency.

Abuse: To act in an unjust, corrupt and offensive manner. Verbal, Physical, Emotional or Sexual Abuse against the child, against the people the child cares about or in the child's presence or within the child's knowledge is a crime against the child that will leave permanent scars.

Abuse of Discretion: Unreasonable, arbitrary or unconscionable action taken without proper consideration of the facts and law pertaining to the matter. A standard of review applied by appellate courts in reviewing the exercise of flexible, but sensible course of action taken by trial courts and administrative agencies and persons. Reviewing courts can upset determinations made when such determinations are wholly inconsistent with the facts before the court and the deductions that can reasonably be made from the facts.

Abuse of Process: Malicious use of civil process has to do with the wrongful initiation of such process, such as filing suits to harass another party. The number of cases and the justification of the charges can be used to determine if there is an abuse.

Accessory: One who aids, counsels, procures, or commands the deed perpetrated, or contributes in a secondary way, who may or may not be present at the action, before, during or after a crime. One who receives, comfort or assistance from or gives comfort or assistance to a criminal offender or attempts to hinder or prevent his or her apprehension or punishment.

Accident: An unforeseen, unexpected event; an occurrence by chance and not by design.

Accomplice: Individual or individuals who voluntarily engage with another in the commission or attempted commission of a crime. See Accessory.

Accord and Satisfaction: A compromise agreement between both parties.

Accusation: A charge against a person that may include indictment, presentment and information.

Acknowledged Father: Any biological father of a child born to unwed parents for whom paternity has been established by admission of the father or agreement of the parents.

Acquittal: The not guilty verdict in a criminal trial.

Action: A lawsuit. The formal legal demand on one's rights from another person brought in court.

Actionable: Wrongful conduct, which may form the basis for a civil action.

ADC or AFDC: Abbreviation for Aid to Families with Children.

Addiction: Addiction is chemical dependency that exists against one's own better judgment, and persists in spite of efforts to control or eliminate the use of the substance. The condition of habitually taking a legal or illegal drug or substance with adverse effects on ceasing can have an impact on custody.

Adjourn: To postpone, delay briefly a court proceeding through recess or to another time or place.

Adjudication: The formal pronouncing or recording of a judgement or decree by a court. The court's final order.

Ad Litem: A Guardian Ad Litem is a person appointed by the court to protect the interests of a minor in a lawsuit.

Admissible or Admissibility: Any testimony, document or demonstrative material that is officially considered by the court by allowing it into evidence generally in compliance with the rules of evidence. Any evidence the judge wishes to see. The judge may properly receive only admissible evidence, but need not permit a party to introduce all admissible evidence. Within discretion the judge may exclude otherwise admissible evidence when the court determines that its probative value is outweighed by countervailing factors such as undue consumption of time.

Adoption: The legal process by which the parent/ child relationship is created between persons not related by blood. The act by which a person takes the child of another into his or her own family and makes the child, for all legal purposes, his or her own child.

ADR: Alternative Dispute Resolution is methods other than taking a controversy to court.

Adultery: The voluntary sexual intercourse by a married person with someone other than his or her spouse. Is given very little consideration in most child custody cases.

Adversarial Divorce: A divorce where the divorcing spouses are unable to come to any agreement.

Adversary System: The judicial system where in each of the opposing, or adversary, parties has full opportunity to present and establish its opposing contentions before the court.

Affidavit: A written statement of facts made under oath and signed before a notary public or other person who has been duly authorized so to act. A written statement of fact that is verified by oath or affirmation. Make sure you have personal knowledge of all matters asserted, or else it "can and will be used against you in a court of law." If there is any doubt whatsoever, but you still believe something is true, say "Based on information and belief...."

Affidavit of Preference: A written statement by a child twelve years of age or older, stating desire to reside with one parent over the other or one parenting plan over other options.

Affirmation: A written statement of facts made and executed by a lawyer under penalty of perjury.

Agenda: A conscious or unconscious plan that may or may not be formally contrived to ensure the results desired by an individual.

Agreement: A transcribed or written resolution of the disputed issues when the parties have resolved issues in the case.

Aggravation: or aggravating circumstances are any considerations or factors that may justify an increase in the degree of discipline to be imposed.

Aggressive: Behavior marked by a bold determination and readiness for conflict.

Aid to Families with Dependent Children: A program of public assistance administered by the Family Independence Agency.

Alimony: See spousal support.

Alias: An indication that a person is known by more than one name. Using more than one name is not necessarily criminal. AKA is the abbreviation for "also know as."

Alienation of Affections: A tort suit based upon willful and malicious interference with the marriage relationship by a third party. It includes mental anguish, loss of social position, disgrace, humiliation and embarrassment as well as disruption of the marriage.

Alimony: Payment of support from one party to another; may include property division and attorney fees. Unrelated to child support. Sometimes called "maintenance" and "spousal support." Similarly situated parties are treated dissimilarly when the only difference is gender. Most courts are sympathetic to women, especially in long-term marriages or when the husband has a high income or greater resources. In their enthusiasm to protect women, some courts favor wives despite their economic equality.

Allegation: To bring forward for consideration a claim of one party against the other. A statement of issue, which the contributing party is prepared to prove.

Alternative Dispute Resolution (ADR): Methods other than taking a controversy to court. To resolve disagreements without the direct intervention of the court. See Arbitration, Conciliation, Mediation.

Alternative Lifestyle: Can mean any lifestyle other than a home with a male and a female parent living in the same home with their own biological children. Usually refers to gay or lesbian persons.

Amicus Curiae: Friend of the Court

Anger: An emotion expressed by feeling or showing strong displeasure or bad temper. Anger is also expresses as being: aggravated, enraged, exasperated, incensed, indignant, infuriated, irate, mad, perturbed, put out, stressed, upset, uptight, worked up, wrathful and vexed.

Annulment: The legal ending of an invalid marriage. According to law, neither party was ever married. All children born of the annulled marriage remain legitimate.

Answer: A legal reply; written answer to demands or charges made in the complaint; the pleading filed by the defendant in response to plaintiff's complaint. Denies or admits some and denies others, or admits all and pleads an excuse.

Antenuptial: An event or document, which pre-dates a marriage.

Appeal: The process whereby a higher court reviews the proceedings resulting in an order or judgment. Appeal is only a review on the record produced in the lower court for errors of law. No new facts or evidence may be considered. The Appeal is primarily a paperwork procedure and neither of the parties to the action nor their attorneys are in attendance at the appeal. An appeal requires that an appellant's brief must be filed. This document must conform to a rigged format. The Brief is bound like a book with a table of contents and an alphabetical list of all the cases to be cited as precedent in the appeal, all the original transcripts and exhibits from the original trial and a brief with the presentation of the facts and the law, with emphasis on why the decision should or should not be upheld.

Appellant: The party appealing a decision or judgment to a higher court. The appellant may have been the plaintiff or defendant in the lower court.

Appellee: The party against whom an appeal is taken. The appellee may have been the plaintiff or defendant in the lower court.

Appearance: The manner in which the defendant appears under the jurisdiction of the court. To show up in court. See Compulsory appearance.

Acquittal: To declare not guilty, free and clear of blame of responsibility.

Arbiter: One appointed by the court or chosen by the parties. Responsibilities are to be impartial and decide a controversy according to law or equity. Sometimes called an umpire or referee.

Arbitration: The parties agree to submit their controversies to a person chosen by them for final determination. An arbitration may be binding or non-binding and the award can be made into a court judgment and enforced. Binding Arbitration is not Appealable.

Argument: Is a connected discourse based on a line of reasoning intended to establish a position and to induce belief.

Arraignment: To bring a prisoner to the court to answer criminal charges.

Arrears or Arrearage: Money, which is overdue and unpaid. That, which is unpaid although due to be paid. A person "in arrears" is a person who is behind in payment.

Arrest: To deprive a person of his or her liberty by legal authority. Arrest indicates only that a law enforcement agency believe that probable cause to arrest existed for some offense. The arrest record is not complete, it does not reflect guilt, nor that the person actually committed the offense.

Assault: A verbal or physical attempt or threat with unlawful force to inflict injury. The apparent present ability to cause the harm if not prevented. An assault need not result in physical contact. Therefore, when the changes Assault and Battery are filed it means with assault you don't actually have to "touch" anyone you just put them in fear that they are about to be hit or touched in an offensive way. Battery means there is actual contact and it doesn't have to hurt or leave a injury, it only has to be an unwanted offensive touching.

Assets: Anything owned that has monetary value. Any interest in real or personal property that can be used for payment of debts.

Attachment: Is a lasting psychological connectedness between human beings, which remains one of the most important building blocks for human development. The responses from the child may include crying, smiling, clinging, rooting, and vocalization, and are exhibited a few days after birth. These behaviors are the child's way of making contact and encouraging the caregiver to respond. When a caregiver meets the expressed needs of a child, the child begins to develop trust. This process is often called the Trust Cycle. Without these critical interactions, infants can lose interest in the world, become "insecure" or "anxiously attached" or even die. Attachment is not an "all or nothing" proposition. Attachments run along a continuum between secure and unattached, with the normal child falling somewhere in the middle.

Attachment Disorder: see Attachment. Children with attachment disorder show confusing behaviors, marked by two conflicting drives: approach and avoidance. This child will turn away from the caregiver, refusing to make eye contact, or fight viciously to avoid closeness. Even when distressed the child will not allow comforting. On the other hand, this child will, without fear, ask to be taken home by a stranger. These children are often diagnosed with Attention Deficit Disorder or Separation Anxiety.

Attention Deficit Disorder: A.D.D. is a disability that is neurobiologically based and characterized by attention skills that are not as developed and therefore, are inappropriate, impulsivity, and, in some cases, hyperactivity. Characteristics of children with ADD can include: fidgeting with hands or feet difficult remaining seated difficulty awaiting turns in games difficulty following through on instructions shifting from one uncompleted task to another difficulty playing quietly interrupting conversations appearing to be not listening doing things that are dangerous without thinking about the consequences ADD students have a greater likelihood of grade retention, school drop out, academic under-achievement and social and emotional adjustment difficulties. Making and keeping friends is a difficult task for children with ADD. They may talk too much, dominate activities, intrude in others' games, or quit a game before its done. They may be unable to pay attention to what another child is saying, not respond when someone else tries to initiate an activity, or exhibit inappropriate behavior.

Attest: To swear a statement is true.

Attorney: Also called Lawyer, Counsel. The legal representative of a party at a trial.

Attorney Client Privilege: The indefinite protection of oral, written, actions or gestures of communication between an attorney and client in the course of the professional relationship and cannot be disclosed without the consent of the client.

Attorney Work Product: Material prepared by an attorney, as an attorney, including notes, analysis, and trial strategy is not subject to the process of Discovery.

Audi Alteram Partem: A principle of justice, which prohibits a judicial decision, which impacts upon individual rights without giving all parties in the dispute a right to be heard. Habeas corpus was an early expression of the audi alteram partem principle. In more recent years, it has been extended to include the right to receive notice of a hearing and to be given an opportunity to be represented or heard.

B

Bad Faith: intentionally committing an ethical or legal breech.

Badger: To persist in tormenting or harassing another.

Bail: A financial obligation, which guarantees a person's future appearance in court. Often issued in the form of a document called a Bail Bond. A money bond (usually secured by real estate or valuable personal property) deposited as an assurance for the fulfillment of a condition for an arrested person to be released from arrest as surety that the person will appear at trial and forfeited if the person fails to appear.

Bailiff: A court officer who guards the judge and jurors and keeps order in the court. (Establish a friendship with the bailiff. The bailiff knows how the judge wants things done and sees more cases than any attorney. If your attorney has established a relationship with the bailiff, you have a smart attorney.)

Bar Association: Organizations dedicated to promoting good will between attorneys and their clients. They claim to monitor attorneys and impose sanctions against bad ones.

Barratry: Black's Law Dictionary, 5th Ed., page. 137 defines it as: A common mover, exciter, or maintainer of suits and quarrels either in courts or elsewhere in the country; a disturber of the peace who spreads false rumors and calumnies, whereby discord and disquiet may grow among neighbors. One who frequently excites and stirs up groundless suits and quarrels, either at law or otherwise. State v. Batson, 220 N.C. 411, 17 S.E.2d 511, 512, 513. Since a barretor is a disturber of the peace, in N.J. domestic violence falls under the category of disturbing the peace. The barretor is committing domestic violence through harassment (serious annoyance or serious alarm).

Battered Woman Syndrome (BWS): Is a collection of psychological symptoms, often considered a subcategory of Post Traumatic Stress Disorder, and can be measured by a trained mental health professional. Battered Woman Syndrome can cause a woman to act in ways that confuse those who wish to help her, thus making it extremely difficult for her to cooperate with the legal system, even though she wants the abuse to stop. Symptoms: BWS is a psychological reaction that can be expected to occur in normal people who are exposed to repeated trauma, such as family violence. It includes at least three groups of symptoms that assist the mind and body in preparing to defend against threats. Psychologists call it the “fight or flight” response.

Batterers: People who assault others usually family members such as their spouses and children.

Battery: Physically striking someone without reason.

BBS: Bulletin Board System allows a person with small computer and one or two telephone lines to host groups for you to read and carry on conversations, upload and download files, put (post) messages and announcements usually dealing with a specific subject.

Believability: Is the demeanor or ability to be viewed as right or true. To be able to instill in others a firm conviction in the reality of what you say and are. To have other people who do or do not know you accept, trust and credit what you say. Believability and honesty are not the same thing. It is possible for someone to be believably, but not truthful.

Bench: The court, or more typically the judge or judges who make up the court.

Bench Trial: A hearing before a Judge, but without the presence of a jury.

Bench Warrant: An order issued by the court from the Judge on the Bench in the courtroom) for the arrest of a person, so that (s)he may be brought before the court.

Best Evidence: Primary evidence; the best evidence, which is available; any evidence falling short of this standard is secondary. The original document is "best," a copy is secondary.

Bifurcation: Splitting of a case into separate issues.

Bill of Particulars: The formal title for information attached to a complaint or petition.

Birthfather/Birthmother: The person who's sperm, egg or womb contributed to the life of a child, but who may or may not be involved with the child's emotional, financial or physical support.

Black Letter Statement: In one instance if the law or the court order prohibits a person or the police from doing something, they can't hire or have it done by someone else. In another instance the general rule is that settlement offers and the negotiations concerning them are inadmissible because the law favors the settlement of disputes. J.A. Tobin Construction v. State Hwy. Commission., 697 S.W.2d 183 (Mo. App. 1985); McCammon v. McCammon, supra, 680 S.W.2d at 202. Evidence of (1) furnishing or offering or promising to furnish, or (2) accepting or offering or promising to accept, a valuable consideration in compromising or attempting to compromise a claim, which was disputed as to either validity or amount, is not admissible to prove liability for or invalidity of the claim or its amount. This rule does not require exclusion when the evidence is offered for another purpose, such as proving bias or prejudice of a witness, negativing a contention of undue delay, or proving an effort to obstruct a criminal investigation or prosecution.

Borderline Personality Disorder: Is marked by instability in mood, action and thoughts; however, these different, conflicting ideas, beliefs, and goals are resident within a single personality.

Breaking and Entering: Any act of physical force, however slight, by which obstruction to entrance is removed. Example: The pushing open of a door that is ajar followed by entrance into a building is sufficient to constitute the act of breaking and entering. Abbreviation used by police B&E.

Brief: A written argument concentrating upon legal points and authorities, used to convey the essential facts, a statement of law involved, the law that the lawyer would like applied, and the application desired made of it by the court, in the client's case, and submitted with other paperwork. Often a brief accompanies a motion and is properly bound, footnoted, indexed and with a bibliography to make it easier for the judge to review.

Budding Integrity: Where a child begins to assign his or her role and value identification. A period in a child's life where he or she gradually switches from primary bonding with the parent of the opposite sex to the parent of the same sex.

Bugging: To wire tap a telephone or wire a room for the pick up of sound and/or video by another location.

Burden of Proof: In the law of evidence, the necessity or duty of affirmatively proving a fact or facts in dispute. In civil matters, this burden may be a "preponderance of the evidence" or "clear and convincing evidence."

C

Calendar: The order in which cases are heard during a term of court.

The calendar includes the name of the court, the name of the judge, and the names of the participants and date of the cases.

Calling for the Rule: All witnesses except for the plaintiff and the defendant who may testify for either party will be excluded from the courtroom until they are called to testify. These witnesses are admonished by the judge not to discuss the case or their testimony with other witnesses or persons except the attorneys.

Canon Law: The law of the Christian Church. Has little or no legal effect today. Canon law refers to that body of law, which has been set by the Christian Church and which, in virtually all places, is not binding upon citizens and has virtually no recognition in the judicial system. Some citizens resort to canon law, however, for procedures such as marriage annulments to allow for a Christian church marriage where one of the parties has been previously divorced. Many who attend church and church officers abide by rulings and doctrines of canon law. Also known as "ecclesiastical law."

Case Law: The entire collection of published legal decisions of the courts, which, because of stare decisis, contributes a large part of the legal rules, which apply in modern society. If a rule of law cannot be found in written laws, lawyers will often say that it is a rule to be found in "case law". In other words, the rule is not in the statute books, but can be found as a principle of law established by a judge in some recorded case. The word jurisprudence has become synonymous for case law.

Case in Point: A judicial opinion, which deals with a factual situation similar to the one being researched and substantiates point of law to be asserted.

Caseload: The number of cases a Judge, Court itself, Attorney or Friend of the Court caseworker handles at any given time.

Cash Bond: A payment of a specific amount of money to guarantee future support payments will be made. Certified

Canon Law: The laws that govern churches.

Capacity: A person's mental ability to make rational decisions. Capacity is not necessarily synonymous with sanity.

***Capias Warrant*:** A civil arrest warrant ordering the sheriff or other officer to take a person into custody and deliver that person to court. This procedure is used when a party refuses to appear in court. If one is outstanding and you are stopped by the police, you will be arrested. You will generally also be arrested without an unrelated stop, the cops or sheriff will go and pick you up. If you believe a capias has been entered against you, see a lawyer immediately.

CASA: Court-appointed special advocates (usually volunteers) who serve to ensure that the needs and interests of a child in child protection judicial proceedings are fully protected.

Case Law: Common law. The law of reported appellate judicial opinions as distinguished from statutes or administrative law.

Caseworker Competency: Demonstrated professional behaviors based on the knowledge, skills, personal qualities, and values a person holds.

Cause: A suit, litigation or action - civil or criminal.

Cause of Action: A claim in law and in fact sufficient to bring the case to court; the grounds of an action.

Caveat: Let him or her beware. A warning or emphasis for caution.

Cease and Desist Order: An order of a court prohibiting a person or entity from undertaking or continuing a particular activity or course of action.

Certified Order: A copy of an order signed and certified as a true copy by the Clerk Of The Court with whom the original order was filed.

Chambers: A room near the courtroom where the judge can do private interviews.

Chameleon: An unacceptable person who can appear to be acceptable especially for short periods of time in order to with the observers support.

Change of Venue: A change of the place where the case is to be tried. The removal of a suit begun in one county or district to another for trial, or from one court to another in the same county or district.

Character Witness: A person who testifies as the reputation of a litigant involved in a lawsuit.

Chart: A symbolic depiction of something incapable of direct verbal or pictorial representation. A condensed ordered enumeration of items usually arranged in columns. Charts you create to identify specific information are Demonstrative Evidence. They are admitted in evidence or visual aids that will not be entered in evidence, but are simply used by a witness or by the lawyer to explain matters that are relevant to the trial. Demonstrative evidence includes models, medical devices, diagrams, photographs, sketches, graphs, maps and objects at issue.

Chattel: Any article of personal property. Animate as well as inanimate property, as opposed to real estate or land property.

Chemical Dependence: Reliance on any substance including coffee, sugar, legal medications, drugs or alcohol is an individual choice. All have known health risks and known personal disadvantages including regrettable behavior, social ostracism, relationship problems, child neglect, child abuse, divorce, unemployment, and imprisonment. Regardless of the laws and the best efforts of law enforcement and others who oppose chemical dependence, using alcohol and drugs for pleasure is a choice some make, that cannot realistically be controlled by others.

Child-Snatching Lawsuits: Legal actions the "victim" parent and child may be able to file against the abductor parent and the other people who assisted the abductor.

Child Support: Monies paid by one parent to the other parent to assist with the costs of meeting the child's needs. Child Support Formula: Factors considered by the Friend of the Court and the Prosecuting Attorney when making a recommendation, and by the circuit court when making a determination for an appropriate amount of child support. Both parents' incomes are considered under the formula.

Chronology: A listing of events in sequence of when they happened from beginning to end.

Circumstantial Evidence: Is evidence, which may allow a judge or jury to deduce a certain fact from other facts, which have been proven. In some cases, there can be some evidence that cannot be proven directly, such as with an eye-witness. And yet that evidence may be essential to prove the case. In these cases, the lawyer will provide evidence of the circumstances from, which a juror or judge can logically deduct, or reasonably, directly; it is proven by the evidence of the circumstances. Fingerprints are an example of circumstantial evidence. While there may be no witness to a person's presence in a certain place, or contact with a certain object, the scientific evidence of someone's fingerprints in persuasive proof of a person's presence or contact with an object.

Circuit Courts: Courts whose jurisdiction is over several counties or districts may hold sessions in counties or districts alternately, or a circuit court may hold all its sessions in one county.

Citation: The reference to previous cases (authority) necessary to substantiate the validity of one's argument or position.

Civil Action: A lawsuit that arises from a non-criminal dispute.

Civil Case: A lawsuit is called a civil case when it is between persons in their private capacity or relations. There is no guilt or innocence in a civil trial.

Civil Law: Legal ruling developed from Roman law. The law concerning non-criminal matters in a common law jurisdiction.

Claim: A charge one party makes against the other ascertaining his or her right, as to money or property. The accumulation of facts, which give rise to a right enforceable in court.

Clandestine: Something that is purposely kept from the view or knowledge of others either in violation of the law or to conduct or conceal some illegal purpose.

Class Action: A lawsuit brought by a representative party on behalf of a large group, all of whose members have the same or a similar grievance against the defendant. Used when the group is too large for it to be practical to name every member of the group as a party.

Clean Hands (Doctrine): The concept in equity that people who seek fair relief must be fair.

They must not have themselves have indulged in impropriety in relation to the transaction upon, which relief is sought.

Clear and Convincing Evidence: means the measure or degree of proof that will produce in the mind of the trier of fact a firm belief or conviction as to the truth of the allegations sought to be established.

Code: The laws in force are rewritten and arranged in a classified order, with the addition of material having the force of law taken from judicial decrees. The repealed and temporary acts are eliminated and the revisions are reenacted.

Co-Defendant: Another person defending him or herself against charges in a crime in which another defendant is charged. The guilt or innocence of the codefendant may or may not have impact on the defendant's charges.

Co-Dependent: Behaviors that are positive or negative that one is compelled do, to help another person behave in unacceptable manner, even if the results are to the detriment of both persons.

Codification: The process of collection and arranging systematically, usually by subject, the laws of a state or country. The end product may be called a revised code of statutes.

Cognitive Ability and Memory Loss: The victim begins to have intrusive memories of the abuse or may actually develop psychogenetic amnesia and not always remember important details or events. The victim may have trouble following his or her thoughts in a logical way, being distracted by intrusive memories that may be flashbacks to previous battering incidents. The victim may disassociate himself or herself when faced with painful events, memories, reoccurring nightmares or other associations not readily apparent to the observer. Considered the third major impact of Battered Woman Syndrome is to the cognitive and memory areas.

Cognitive Therapy: The goal of this type of therapy is to reduce immediate behaviors that are either life threatening (suicide threats, self-mutilation) or interfere with quality of life (rages directed toward others).

Cohabitation: The act of living together among unmarried persons of the opposite sex is often proscribed by local laws. Such living conditions will produce an inference of criminal fornication.

Collateral Estoppel: Precludes the relitigation, in a second action, of an issue that has been actually and necessarily litigated and determined in a prior action that was based on a different cause of action.

Collusion: When two or more people plan to act in an unethical manner in unison, such as in giving similar, but incorrect testimony.

Comity: Is other countries recognizing United States custody orders and the United States recognizing theirs.

Commissioner: A person authorized by the court to make judicial decisions.

Commit: To send a person to prison, an asylum, or reformatory by lawful authority.

Common Law: Law discovered in the customs and habits of the people. The strength of the judicial system in which prior decision (case law) is distinguished from statutory law.

Common Law Marriage: The cohabitation of two people living in the same domicile, who consider themselves married.

Community Property: All property owned by husband and wife acquired during a marriage, not including gifts and inheritance.

Complaint: The first papers filed in a lawsuit, stating the facts and allegations and request for relief.

Compulsory Appearance: Where one has been validly served, processed, and so is compelled to appear in court.

Computer: May be used to accurately determine solutions to otherwise complex and tedious equations and arrive at solutions to standard often used equations such as those used for determining velocity, force of impact, or path of trajectory. The data put into the computer and the computers output can be easily verified.

Computer Generated Graphics: Are used to illustrate a proposed sequence of events as testified to by a witness. The evidence is considered demonstrative rather than subsantive.

Computer Modeling: The use of computers to provide visual simulations of car crashes, aircraft crashes and DNA structure of an accused with the perpetrator of a crime. The court will determine the admissibility of computer modeling using the "*Frye* test" or the more liberal standard, as set out in "*Daubert* Test".

Computer Noted Evidence: Printouts from data recorders and other automatic machines including logs and journals, computer generated or created evidence and include two kinds (1) computer models, simulations and forecasts (2) artificial intelligence or fuzzy logic.

Computer Printed Evidence: Is the direct mechanical production of the computer's machine readable contents to a hard copy on paper for example.

Compute Stored Evidence: Is information kept in machine readable form in the computer's hard drive, on a floppy or tape.

Computer Transmitted Evidence: Any computer data transmitted when an automatic system, which logs the incoming message with the date, time, purported identity of sender and dumber of segments received and stores the information on a non-erasable media.

Conciliation: To make a friendly atmosphere for difficult discussions, encouraging the exchange of information and ideas and allowing negotiations.

Conclusion of Fact: Is reached solely through the use of facts and natural reasoning. A conclusion reached without resorting to the rule of law or interferences from evidentiary facts.

Conclusion of Law: Is reached through application of rules of law.

Conclusive Evidence: Is incontrovertible evidence that is not open to question because it is irrefutability proven.

Conflict of Interest: A situation in which regard for one duty leads to disregard for another, or the reasonable expectation that this might happen.

Conflict Resolution: A training of mind and temperament that enables one to work out problems in a positive manner in the face of opposition, hardship, or danger.

Conscience of the Court: Refers to the power of the court to resolve a controversy by applying common standards of decency and fairness of the community rather than the opinion of a particular judge.

Consideration: Usually, refers to money. What one person in a contract offers to induce the other person to cooperate.

Consistent With: During deposition or courtroom questioning when the opposing attorney uses this term it means nothing, but it is a clever devise to convert remote causation to a more likely causal connection. The opposing attorney may try to get you to agree that certain acts are consistent with a particular practice or occurrence. You must be very careful about this. Just because something is consistent with something else, it does not follow that there is necessarily any relationship whatsoever between the two things. This is true even if the opposing attorney identified many factors, which are supposedly "consistent with" the practice or occurrence. Try to avoid agreeing that remote facts are "consistent with" any key fact in the case.

Conspiracy: Two or more persons planning and/or committing a criminal or unlawful act.

Contact Orders: Same as visitation schedule

Contempt of Court: Conduct in court, which interferes or stops a court in the administration of its duties. The willful and intentional failure to comply with a court order, judgment, or decree by a party to the action, which may be punishable in a variety of ways. There are two kinds of contempt: civil and criminal. Criminal is as punishment for disobedience of a court directive, including, but not limited to, failure to pay child support and acting in a naughty manner in open court. Criminal contempt can be detected by its consequence: punishment by incarceration for a definite time period and/or a fine. Then there is civil contempt, incarceration until the person in contempt uses "the keys to the jail house in his hands" i.e., until he obeys the orders of the court.

Contested Custody: Any custody case in which the court must decide one or more issues on which the parties have not agreed.

Contingency Fee: A percentage of the recovery. Contingent fees are generally forbidden in divorce cases but, in some states, are permitted in a proceeding to enforce the judgment.

Contract: A usually legally enforceable arrangement between two or more parties. An attempt to create a "private law" and, except in certain circumstances, courts will give great weight to what the parties have created in that contract.

Controlled Substances: Drugs whose general availability is restricted by law through prescription use or are outlawed. Such drugs include those classified as narcotics, stimulants, depressants, hallucinogens and cannabis.

Conversion: In legal terms the wrongful appropriation to oneself of the personal property of another.

Conviction: Is a societal judgment regarding an individual's actions. Unlike arrest, a conviction record is complete. Guilt and accountability have been finalized.

Copy: A copy of an order signed and certified as an exact true copy by the officer of the court having possession of the original order.

Corporal Punishment: Physical punishment inflicted upon the body. A punishment for some violation of conduct, which involves the infliction of pain on, or harm to the body. A fine or imprisonment is not considered to be corporal punishment (in the latter case, although the body is confined, no punishment is inflicted upon the body). The death penalty is the most drastic form of corporal punishment and is also called capital punishment. Some schools still use a strap to punish students. Some countries still punish habitual thieves by cutting off a hand. These are forms of corporal punishment, as is any form of spanking, whipping or bodily mutilation inflicted as punishment. Although the use of reasonable corporal punishment has been upheld in schools by the courts, many jurisdictions are in constant flux about what constitutes "reasonable." Child psychologists strongly oppose any form of physical assault.

Corpus Delicti: The body or thing the crime was committed against.

Corrigena: Document to make corrections on a deposition. A thing to be corrected.

Corroborating Evidence: Evidence to complement evidence already given and tending to strengthen or confirm the same point.

Costs: An allowance for expenses in prosecuting or defending in a suit.

Counsel: Also called Lawyer, Attorney. The legal representative of a party at a trial.

Counseling, Supportive: This is less intensive than psychoanalytic. The therapist helps the patient with problems that are more current rather than trying to resolve early childhood issues.

Count: Separate and independent claims. Civil and criminal indictments may contain one or more counts.

Counterclaim: Also called Counter-Petition or Cross-Complaint. Constitutes a separate cause of action. A pleading asking for relief filed in response to a Petition or Complaint.

Court: The branch of government, which is responsible for the resolution of disputes arising under the laws of the government. A place or a person entrusted with and assembled for the administration of the law (and sometimes justice).

Court Order: A written document issued by the court, which becomes effective only when signed by a judge. There must be a mechanism for enforcement of a court order for the parties to feel the strength of the court behind the court order.

Court Reporter: An instrument of the court. The court reporter takes down, in shorthand or on a machine, everything that is said in the courtroom, or judges chambers. These notes may be transcribed if necessary.

Court Rules: Refer to court rules by the names given in their title or citation sections, if any. The correct forms are: California Juvenile Court Rules, rule 4-4. California Rules of Appellate Procedure, rule 103.01, subdivision 2.

CP (Custodial Parent): The parent that does have residential responsibility for the children.

Credibility: Whether or not a witness is able to evidence a degree of integrity, knowledge and confidence and the appearance that the witness is being truthful. The primary measure of credibility is whether the testimony is probable or improbable when judged by the common experience of mankind.

Crime: Any act, which the sovereign has deemed contrary to the public good and may be prosecutable.

Criminal Case: A lawsuit to handle crimes when the state is the plaintiff; a person or persons on the opposition are defendant(s) and involves a question of whether the defendant has violated some of the laws defining crimes.

Criminal Law: Criminal law concerns crimes against society.

Cross-examination: Questions asked a witness by the other person's attorney at deposition or trial.

Cross-petition or Cross-complaint: May be filed by the defendant either separately or as part of his answer. It asks for relief or damages on the part of the defendant against the original plaintiff, and perhaps others. When a cross-petition is filed, the plaintiff may then file other motions to the cross-petition, except a motion to quash service of summons.

Culpability: Responsibility for misdeed or delinquency. Blame, fault, guilt or onus found be assigned to one. One could be accountable, answerable, liable, accused, charged, censured, condemned, denounced and reprehended if found to be responsible or involved.

Custodial Parent (CP): Also called Residential Parent. The parent with whom the child lives the majority of the time. This designation may include many other aspects in the court's jurisdiction.

Custody: The legal right and responsibility awarded by the court for the care, possession, and rearing of a child. Usually, refers to the parent's right to (1) have the children live with that parent and (2) make decisions concerning the children. Exact meaning varies greatly from state to state.

Custody Determination: A court order awarding rights of custody and visitation. Also called a custody order or custody decree.

Cyber: Or Cyberspace. Used to describe the whole range of information resources available through computer networks.

D

Damages: Monetary compensation awarded by a court for an injury caused by the act of another. The injured must ask for the compensation for it to be awarded. Damages may be actual or compensatory (equal to the amount of loss), exemplary or punitive (in excess of the actual loss and which is given to punish the person for the malicious conduct, which caused the injury) or nominal (less than the actual loss. Often a trivial amount such as one dollar), which is given because the injury is slight or because the exact amount of injury has not been determined satisfactorily.

***Daubert* Test:** For the admissibility is guided by the liberal premise of Federal Rule of Evidence 402, which states, "[a]ll relevant evidence is admissible. *Daubert v. Merrell Dow Pharmaceuticals, Inc.*, 93 C.D.O.S. 4825,4826 (June 28, 1993)

Debit: The sum of money one person owes another.

Debitor: A person who owes money to a person or company.

Decree: Or Final Decree is the decision of the court. A publicly proclaimed order by the court in the case. An interlocutory decree is a provisional or preliminary decree, which is not final.

Declaration: Written testimony under oath, not necessarily sworn to before a notary.

Declaratory Action: An action taken in a case where litigants need interpretation to understand a law.

Defamation: To make a false statement in public that tends to diminish the reputation so that people think less of that person or company. The two kinds of defamation are slander and libel.

Default: Failure to do something or to do it on time. Order of a court for the plaintiff based on the defendant's failure to answer the filings within the time allowed or make an appearance in the case.

Defendant: Also called a Respondent. In a civil case, the defendant is the person against whom the lawsuit is brought. In a criminal case, the defendant is the person charged with the offense.

Deliberation: The period of time in which a judge or jury determines the facts and declares a verdict.

Dementia: Is a loss of many cognitive functions, usually beginning with memory loss, then leading to confusion and inability to function mentally in normal situations or not be able to recognize normal situations in life. The progress of the decease is not always predictable.

Demonstrative Evidence: Consists of trial exhibits that are admitted in evidence or visual aids that will not be entered in evidence, but are simply used by a witness or by the lawyer to explain matters that are relevant to the trial. Demonstrative evidence includes models, medical devices, diagrams, photographs, sketches, and objects at issue, as well as a variety of other items.

Demur: To file a pleading admitting the truth of the facts in the complaint, or to answer, but contending they are legally insufficient.

Denial: A refusal to satisfy a request. A rejection of the facts in order to create a less painful or more personally acceptable view of reality. A real or contrived inability to accept the truth, often blaming the negative consequences on others.

Dependent: Unable to do without someone or something. As is a child's relationship with it's caregiver.

Dependent-Relationship: There are 3 types: Gross: that existents are established in dependence on causes and conditions. General :that existents are established in dependence on parts and wholes that is the basis. Subtle: that things are established in dependence on imputation by sound(names) & meaning generalities (mental images/concepts). These imply, but are not selflessness/emptiness. Also, these are not to be confused with teachings on the 12 dependent-related links, a synopsis of the mechanism of samsara.

Depersonalization Disorder: Is either a persistent or recurring alteration in one's perception of one's self, such as a feeling of detachment from one's actions or thoughts, or feeling like an observer of one's own actions. Alternatively, one may feel as if one is an automaton, without conscious will of one's actions, or feel as if one is dreaming, rather than actually performing, one's actions. Depersonalization Disorder is caused by severe stress; it is not uncommon to have a single instance of depersonalization (but this is usually not recurrent or persistent) due to stress. It is usually found in younger adults (late adolescence/early adulthood).

Deposition: Testimony of any witness taken out of court under oath, in writing and typed in question and answer form, just as if it were given in court.

Depression: Occurring spontaneously without any obvious reason, possibly from chemical manifestation in the brain affecting a person's mood is intrinsic. Occurring as a result of a depressing life situation or loss it is reactive. Prognosis is good and treatment includes medication and therapy. Sometimes depression can mimic dementia and affects decision related to incapacity.

Developmentally Disabled: Unable to function well mentally these Individuals have been born with some defect, which is lifetime limitation. Some die as children, others may have a normal life expectancy with permanent deficiency. If disability is severe, the person will not be able to function independently and will need outside help.

Diagnostic Statistical Manual III: Also known as the DSM III, lists categories of mental disorders.

Directed Verdict: An instruction by the judge to a jury to return a specific verdict.

Direct Evidence: Proof of facts by witness who saw acts done or heard words spoken, as distinguished from indirect evidence, which is called circumstantial evidence.

Direct Examination: The first questioning of a witness by the party on whose behalf the witness is called. The story being told the way this side wants it told.

Dirty Hands: A person who seeks fair relief from the court in a matter when that person has indulged in impropriety in relation to the matter in which relief is sought.

Disbar: To deprive an attorney the right to practice law; disbarment. A grievance is filed with the State Bar Association where the attorney practices. The State Bar Association has specific procedures they must follow to investigate each grievance. The State Bar Association will either dismiss the charges or exercise any number of sanctions against the attorney. It is very difficult to have an attorney disbarred, and there is no money involved for the party filing against the attorney. Disbarment is a much larger threat than a malpractice suit. If you have a case for disbarment, you may also have a case for malpractice.

Disclosure: Is when the court compels both sides to divulge to the opposition, all of the information either side may have requested from the other in discovery.

Discovery: The processes used to determine the nature, scope, and credibility of the opposition's case before the trial.

Discretionary Transfer: With regards to jurisdiction concerning custody of a minor child,

If the child has resided in another county for less than 6 months, or it would be more convenient for the parties, the court may transfer the motion to modify to the court of another county.

Dismiss: A court ordered end to a lawsuit.

Dismissal Without Prejudice: Permits the complainant to sue again on the same cause of action.

Dismissal With Prejudice: Bars the complainant from filing suit or maintain an action on the same claim or cause.

Disorderly Conduct: Generally means a breach of the peace, disturbing those who hear or see it, or endangers the morals, safety, or health of the community.

Disposable Earnings: is that part of the payor parent's earnings remaining after deduction of any amounts required by law to be withheld, union dues, nondiscretionary retirement contributions, and medical hospitalization, and disability insurance coverage for the payor parent and the child.

Dissolution: The termination of an agreement.

District Attorney: The state's representative in a criminal case. Parents who do not pay their child support are considered criminals in most states.

Divorce: The dissolution of marriage.

DNA: Abbreviation for deoxyribonucleic acid. A chromosome molecule, which carries genetic coding unique to each person with the only exception of identical twins (that is why it is also called "DNA fingerprinting"). Through laboratory process, DNA can be extracted from body tissue such a strand of hair, semen, blood and matched against DNA discovered at a crime scene or on a victim to scientifically implicate an accused. Can also be used to match DNA between parents in a paternity suit.

Docket: A complete list maintained by the county clerk, of cases a court has in its system.

Docket Number: A number, sequentially assigned by the clerk at the outset to a lawsuit brought to a court for adjudication.

Doctrine: A principle accepted as valid and authoritative sometimes a rule of law.

Domestic Violence: Includes beatings, threats, stalking, intimidation, harassment, neglect, and physical, emotional, and sexual abuse. Domestic violence may include any act by one family member that causes harm to another family member.

Domicile: A person's permanent home.

Double Jeopardy: Common-law and constitutional prohibition against more than one prosecution for the same crime, transaction or omission.

Dual Citizenship: Where two different sovereigns within their respective territorial confines may lawfully claim citizenship of the same person and that person of them.

Due Care: The legal duty one owes to another according to the circumstances of a particular case.

Due Diligence: An attorney must be able to demonstrate that all efforts made on behalf of the client were marked by careful attention and persistent application. Some contra-indications would be: not filing proper documents, not answering service on time, not showing up for court.

Due Process: The guarantee that every person has the protection of a fair trial by giving an unbiased hearing to resolve a two-or-more-party dispute.

Duress: Action by a person, which compels another to do what he would not otherwise do. Where a person is prevented from acting (or not acting) according to their free will, by threats or force of another, it is said to be "under duress". Contracts and agreements signed under duress are voidable and, in may places, you cannot be convicted of a crime if you can prove that you were forced or threatened into committing the crime (although this defense may not be available for serious crimes).

D.W.I. (Driving While Intoxicated): Is the offense of operating a motor vehicle while under the influence of alcohol or drugs. This does include only sitting in the vehicle.

E

Earnings: Means compensation paid or payable to the payor parent for personal services, whether called wages, salary, compensation earned as and independent contractor, overtime pay, severance pay, commission, bonus, or otherwise, and includes periodic payments pursuant to a pension, annuity, workers' compensation, disability and retirement program, and unemployment benefits.

EBT, Examination Before Trial: see deposition.

Ecclesiastical Law: The body of church-made law, which binds only those persons, which recognize it, usually only church officers, and based on aged precepts of canon law.

Eighth Amendment: prohibits excessive bail, excessive fines and cruel and unusual punishments.

E-Mail: Electronic main messages sent from one person to another via computer. It will appear something like this divorce@livingston.net

Emancipation: An age, ruling of the court or the activities, behavior and independence that indicates that a child is now an adult. In some states, when the obligation of child support may be terminated.

Enabler: 1. In the recovery group movement, used to describe persons taken advantage of by

addicted people in order to continue

Enforcement: Anyone disobeying an order of the court may be subjected to restriction of contact with children, reversal of custody, forfeit of property, fine or imprisonment.

Entrapment: The inducement, by law enforcement officers or their agents, of another person to commit a crime for the purposes of bringing charges for the commission of that artificially-provoked crime. This technique, because it involves abetting the commission of a crime, which is itself a crime, is severely curtailed under the constitutional law of many states.

Emotional or Verbal Abuse: Would include name-calling, put-downs, and the like. Consistently telling someone that they are worthless is emotional abuse, for example. Telling someone they are not worthy of love is emotional abuse. Withholding of affection is also emotional abuse. Manipulation of someone so that they do precisely what the manipulator wants is emotional abuse. ("If you loved me, you wouldn't want to go to visitation." "If you don't do this, you are worthless.")

Equitable Distribution: A method of fair division of property, which is determined by a fact-finder.

Equitable Parent: A spouse that is not a biological or adoptive parent who has had a parental relationship with the child with the encouragement of the biological parent. The equitable parent may be required to pay child support and have the right to visitation.

Equity: Some circumstances even though they are not fair they are not covered by law or the law is unfair when dealing with them. In the past, there were "courts of equity," but today, most courts have "equity jurisdiction." The court can apply "equitable principles" to cases, including divorce. These are sometimes called "anti-law" courts because they were able to circumvent unfair laws. In most cases judges will not ignore statutes and established common law.

***Et Al*:** Meaning and others.

***Et Ano*:** Meaning and another.

Ethics: Legal, Medical and Professional Ethics. Codes of conduct, also known as the Code of Professional Responsibility, imposed on licensed professionals. Violations may subject the professional to disciplinary proceedings within their profession and malpractice claims.

Evaluation: The act of appraising or valuing the nature, character, quality, status or worth of someone or something.

Evaluation of Family Progress: The stage of the CPS case process where the CPS caseworker measures changes in the family behaviors and conditions (risk factors), monitors risk elimination/ reduction, and determines when the CPS case can be closed.

Evasion. A subtle device to set aside the truth, or escape the punishment of the law; as if a man should tempt another to strike him first, in order that he might have an opportunity of returning the blow with impunity. He is nevertheless punishable, because he becomes himself the aggressor in such a case. Wishard, 1 H. P. C. 81 Hawk. P. C. c. 31,?24, 25; Bac. Ab. Fraud, A.

Evidence: All the means by which any alleged matter of fact, truth of which is submitted to investigation at judicial trail, is established. Evidence includes the testimony of witness, introduction of records, documents, exhibits or any other relevant matter offered. Is the outward evidence of something else. The physical facts including items, documents, objects, and testimony offered to prove or disprove allegations in a case. Evidence is not evidence until the judge accepts it as such. The judge may properly receive only admissible evidence. see Demonstrative Evidence.

Evidence, Computer: Evidence from computers take several forms; computer printed, computer created or generated, computer noted, computer stored, computer printed, computer transmitted.

Exchange Monitoring: Supervision of Transfers is the observation of movement of the child from one parent to the other parent and back at the end of a visitation. The remainder of the parent/child contact may occur unsupervised.

Excited Utterance: Is a statement relating to a startling event or condition made while the declarant was under the stress of excitement caused by the event or condition.

Exhibit: Tangible things presented at trial as evidence such as documents, items produced and identified in court.

***Ex Parte*:** A written or verbal application for court relief without the presence of the other party, or in some states, without formal notice. Hearings and divorces can be *ex parte*. Ex Parte orders have a short life. Anytime during the order you may request and must be granted (14th Amendment) a hearing. If you do not request a hearing or do not appear for a court ordered hearing the temporary order may become permanent.

Expectation of Privacy: A person's reasonable expectation of privacy can be key to whether there was an invasion of privacy or not. A person may not reasonably expect privacy at a televised sporting event, but may reasonable expect privacy in their bedroom.

Expert: Having the knowledge, skill and experience for success in a particular field or endeavor. A person possessing a higher degree of knowledge than would be presumed to be held by the court with regard to the field in which he or she is qualified. This knowledge may be derived entirely from the study of technical works, or specialized education, or practical experience or varying combinations thereof. It is determinative that his or her answers indicate to the court that he or she possesses the knowledge, which will assist the court in making inferences regarding fact issues more effectively than the court could do so unaided.

Expert Witness: An expert is a person with credentials or experience beyond that of the general public and recognized by the court. In divorce cases, most experts are called to testify as to the value of the marital home, pensions, and privately-held businesses. In child related disputes, mental health professionals are often called to testify.

***ex post facto law*:** States are prohibited, under Article 1, Section 10 of the United States Constitution, from making any "ex post facto law." An ex post facto law is a law that applies to crimes, which were committed before the enactment of the law. Thus, a person cannot be prosecuted for violation of a law, which was made after the person committed the crime.

Expunged Records: Information that is eliminated or neutralized with or as if with a stroke of the pen. Normally police do not expunge files on anyone they have ever investigated until many years after their assumed death. Guilt or innocence has nothing to do with their policy. They work on the where there is smoke there is fire principle.

Extended Family: Persons other than the parents and the children, such as grandparents, step-parents, stepchildren, nieces, nephews, aunts and uncles.

Extradition: The surrender by one city, state, county or country to another of an accused or convicted person.

F

Face Fee: Money paid to an attorney that allows you to place the attorney's name on the documents filed while the attorney does not in fact do any of the work in the case.

Fact: An event that has occurred or circumstances that exist, events whose actual occurrence or existence is to be determined by the evidence.

Failure to Appear: Means not showing up for deposition or court when ordered to do so by Subpoena. If only one party shows, and provides evidence, the only thing the judge has to go on is that evidence. If there is no rebuttal to that evidence, that is what the judge uses to make the ruling. If failure is willful, you can be held in contempt of court. Contempt of court is punishable by fine and/or imprisonment. The attorneys may also have a claim against you for out of pocket expenses and their time spent attending the abortive deposition or court appearance. Costs could exceed $400.00 per hour.

Failure to Thrive (FTT): Is defined as a child with whose weight and height are less than the third percentile or whose weight or height have decreased more than two major percentiles growth charts. Fifty percent of FTT is non- organic and fifty percent is due to organic processes. Head size, motor function and IQ may be affected also. There are before birth and after birth types. Before birth FTT may be due to maternal malnutrition, high blood pressure, cigarette smoking, alcohol use, drug use, seizure medicine use (Dilantin) or infections/viruses (rubella, cytomegalic inclusions disease, toxo-plasmosis, syphilis.)

After birth, many factors will affect children's size. Malnutrition, emotional deprivation, digestive problems such as reflux, malabsorption, parasites, milk intolerance and diarrhea will cause significant FTT as will complex heart problems, which are cyanotic. Kidney problems or failure, steroid use, and liver disease can all slow growth. Lung problems such as Cystic Fibrosis, severe stridor, severe recurrent and thyroid hormone deficiency are also causors of FTT. The thyroid child may have normal growth initially and then develop failure to thrive. If a child has FTT, a physician must assess and determine, which of the etiologies exists. Only then can the failure to thrive be corrected.

Fair To Say That: During deposition or courtroom questioning, when this phrase is used, you can be quite sure that the opposing attorney has no intention of being fair to you, but wants to appear fair. Try to avoid agreeing by responses such as, "I don't know if that is fair or not," or "that is not how I would characterize it."

False Accusation: A charge that is not true against a person that may include indictment, presentment and information.

False Claim: An accusation one party lodges against another, knowing it is not true.

False Swearing: Is a 'common law' misdemeanor, which is the same as perjury except that it is not committed in a judicial proceeding.

Family Abduction: The taking, keeping, or concealing of a child by a parent or other family member, or person acting on behalf of the parent or family member, which deprives another individual of his or her rights with or without the child's help or consent.

Family Law: For divorce and custody.

Family Records: Statements of fact concerning personal or family history contained in family Bibles, genealogies, charts, engravings including on jewelry, inscriptions on family portraits, engravings on urns, crypts and tombstones.

Family Violence: Is any form of physical, sexual, or other abuse inflected on any person in a household by a family or household member. Family violence includes abuse of both adults and children.

Fanatics: Persons who manifest extreme and often dangerous ardor, fervor or attachment to a person or a cause. Sometimes referred to as fiends, freaks, maniacs, nuts, extremist or zealots.

FAQ: Abbreviation used on the Internet for frequently asked questions.

Fast-tracking: When the issues in the case are clear, the facts are sharply defined, but hotly in dispute and all that is required is a verdict. Fast tracking can either be agreed upon and requested of the judge or the judge may do it on his own.

Father-absent: Refers to single mother families. Studies indicate that boys raised in this environment have lower self-esteem, are more likely to be rejected by peers and may experience deficits in cognitive functioning.

Fault: Is a term used when a divorce is granted because a spouse was proven to have been guilty of some marital misconduct. Some grounds for a Fault Divorce are abandonment, adultery, drug or alcohol abuse, neglect, criminal activity, some kinds of mental illness, and spousal or child abuse.

Federal Rules of Evidence: The statues and rules that govern evidence. There are state rules of evidence and rules of civil procedure.

Federal Statutes: Most generally deal with issues covered by the U.S. Constitution:

Felony: A generic term employed to distinguish certain high crimes from minor offenses known as misdemeanors. Conviction of a felony crime can result in the imposition of the greatest punishment for violation of law, such as a jail sentence greater than one year and fines exceeding $1,000.

Fifth Amendment: The popular term given to a person's assertion of his or her Fifth Amendment right not to give evidence that will incriminate him or herself. A direct reference to the Fifth Amendment to the Constitution of The United

States. Actually the Fifth Amendment provides several critical protections: prohibition against double jeopardy (you may not be tried more than once for the same offense): prohibition against self-incrimination (you may not be forced to testify against yourself): prohibition against deprivation of life, liberty or property without due process of law.

Fight Response Mode: The body and mind prepare to deal with danger by becoming hyper vigilant to cues of potential violence, resulting in an exaggerated startle response. The automatic nervous system becomes operational and the individual becomes more focused on the single task of self-defense. This impairs concentration and causes physiological responses usually associated with high anxiety. In serious cases, fearfulness and panic disorders are present and phobic disorders may also result. Irritability, rage and crying are typical symptoms of this stage.

Filiation: The court's decision that a man is the father of his child.

Financial Child Abuser: Any person with a moral or legal obligation to monetarily support children, but for any reason does not do so.

Findings of Fact, or Rule 52: In all actions tried upon the facts without a jury or with an advisory jury, the court shall find the facts specially and state separately its conclusions of law thereon, and judgment requires the court to state in writing findings of fact separately from conclusions of law.

Financial Abuse: Is controlling, through whatever means, someone's financial resources, including money for food, clothing, shelter, luxuries, and the like. It is often accompanied by some other form of abuse; for instance, forcing someone to sign their check over to the perpetrator by beating that person.

Financial Statement: A paper required by each party to specify the monthly income and expenses.

First Impression Case: Means that there is no precedent for such a case because it is the first time the subject has ever come before a court.

First Right of Refusal: It is preferable to have the child spend quality time with a parent than with sitters, day-care operators or relatives. Should circumstances require one parent to be away from home, the other parent should be given the "right of primary refusal". The custodial parent is to ask the non-custodial parent to care for the children first before resorting to sitters or relatives. This is sometimes called the "Doubtfire Clause'.

Fixed-Schedule Visitation: High parent conflict cases should have a detailed fixed-schedule visitation order. This schedule will eliminate the fruitless exercise of attempting to get combative parents to negotiate. Dates, times, places and responsibilities must be spelled out precisely.

Flat Fee: A fixed amount of money charged for handling an entire case or a certain part of it.

Flight Response Mode: Alternates with the fight pattern of response when people face danger. When physical escape is actually or perceived as impossible, then mental escape occurs. This is the avoidance or emotional numbing stage where denial, minimization, rationalization and disassociation are subconsciously used as ways to psychologically escape from the threat or presence of violence.

Forensic: An exercise of one's powers of argument.

Fornication: Generally sexual intercourse of two persons not married to each other, which is punished as a misdemeanor by statute in some states.

Fourteenth Amendment: prohibits all the States from enacting or enforcing any law, which violates the privileges and: immunities of the citizens of the United States: prohibits all States from depriving a person of life, liberty or property without due process of: law mandates that all persons are entitled to equal protection of the laws.

Fraud: Intentional deception resulting in an injury or loss to another.

***Frye* Test:** For the admissibility asks if proposed evidence has been "sufficiently established to have gained general acceptance in the particular field in which it belongs. *Frey v. United States*, 54 Appl D.C. 46, 476, 293 F. 1013, 1014 (1923)

Friendly Fire: A combat term that indicates that the bullets or bombs are coming from one's own groups rather than from the enemy. This term is valid for business as well as personal interaction.

Friend of the Court: A person, usually a professional, from which the court has requested information or appearance. The Friend of the Court, submits information on an issue related to, but broader than the case in question, regarding the legal implications of the ruling.

Frivolous: Clearly lacking in substance and clearly insufficient as a matter of law.

Fruits of the Crime: That advantage, which is derived by the criminal who commits a crime.

Fugitive: One who runs away to avoid arrest, prosecution or imprisonment. Many extradition laws also call the suspect a "fugitive" although, in that context, it does not necessarily mean that the suspect was trying to hide in the state or country from which extradition is being sought.

Full Age: The age at which the child becomes an adult on the state in which he/she resides.

Full Faith and Credit: Legal principal requiring judges to recognize and enforce valid decrees and judgments issued by courts in other states. A constitutional requirement for every state to enforce the judgment of another state.

G

Gag Order: To silence by authority of the court to prevent speech about a person or event.

Garnish: The seizing of a person's property, credit or salary, on the basis of a law, which allows it, and for the purposes of paying off a debt. The person who possesses the assets of the debtor and is the subject of the seizure is called a "garnishee". This is frequently used in the enforcement of child support where delinquent debtors will be subjected to salary garnishment. A percentages of their wages is subtracted directly off their pay-check and directed to the person in need of support the employer being the garnishee.

Gett: Is a divorce document required under Jewish law to terminate a marriage. This document is required in addition to the civil divorce. Even if you and you ex are divorced civilly and have been living apart for an extended period, under Jewish law, without the Gett you are still married. In Judaism the giving and accepting of the Gett is a no fault situation. It is the dissolving of the marriage contract, a legal formality only.

Good Faith: Acting with integrity and honesty without intent on cheating.

Grand Jury: Usually, a jury of 16 whose duty is to receive complaints and accusations in criminal cases, hear the evidence and find bills of indictment in cases where they are satisfied that there is probable cause that a crime was committed and that a trial ought to be held. Grand jury proceedings, are private and secret. Prospective defendants are not entitled to be present at the proceedings and no one examines witnesses on the defendant's behalf.

Grievance: A formal complaint filed with a licensing body or regulatory agency against a professional. The process may have strict filing, answering and hearing requirements. Grievances for professionals are a nuisance at best and may endanger their licensing at worst.

Gross Negligence: Any action or an omission in reckless disregard of the consequences to the safety or property of another. Sometimes referred to as "very great negligence" and it is more then just neglect of ordinary care towards others or just inadvertence. Also known as *culpa lata*.

Guardian: An individual who, by legal appointment or by the effect of a written law, is given custody of both the property and the person of one who is unable to manage their own affairs, such as a child or mentally-disabled person.

Guardian Ad Litem (GAL): A person lawfully invested with the power, and charged with the duty, to protect and represent the interests of a minor child in a lawsuit. The status of the guardian ad litem exists only in that specific litigation in which the appointment occurs.

H

Habeas Corpus: May be used to force a parent to produce a child in court. The name given a variety of writs whose object is to bring a person before a court or judge. In most common usage, it is directed to the official or person detaining another, commanding him to produce the body of the prisoner or person detained so the court may determine if such person has been denied his liberty without due process of law. May be used to force a parent to produce a child in court.

Habitability: The condition of residential or other premises being reasonably fit for occupation and does not impair the health, safety, or well-being of the occupants.

Habitual Offender: A person who is convicted and sentenced for crimes over a period of time and even after serving sentences of incarceration, such as demonstrates a propensity towards criminal conduct. Reformation techniques fail to alter the behavior of the habitual offender. Many countries now have special laws that require the long-term incarceration, without parole, of habitual offenders as a means of protecting society in the face of an individual that appears unable to comply with the law.

Hacked: When data on a computer system is accessed and/or amended by persons not authorized to do so.

Halo Effect: Positive Halo Effect; If a good impression on an observer is established, the observed is without further effort deemed worthy of acceptance, believing and trust. After that it becomes much more difficult for anyone to discredit the observed. This works first because once people decide how they feel about someone, they are unwilling to find their judgment was in error. Second, because all information is filtered through to support your opinion. Third, if the information a person is hearing does not correspond with the information that person is seeing, that person will believe what he or she is seeing. "The Negative Halo Effect" is just as pervasive as the Positive is helpful. Once the Negative Halo Effect is in place, it is much more difficult to change than the Positive Halo Effect.

Harassment: Any activity that is unnecessarily oppressive with purposeful actions and conduct motivated by a malicious or discriminatory purpose. Unsolicited words or conduct, which tend to annoy, alarm or abuse another person. An excellent alternate definition can be found in Canadian human rights legislation as: "a course of vexatious comment or conduct that is known or ought reasonably to be known to be unwelcome." Name-calling ("stupid", "retard" or "dummy") is a common form of harassment.

Harmless Error: A mistake that does not merit reversal of judgment by the appellate court. Distinguished from "Prejudicial Error," an error, which warrants the appellate court to reverse the judgment before it.

Hearing: Any proceedings before a court where testimony is given.

Hearsay: Any statement other than that by the person reciting the statement. Evidence not proceeding from the personal knowledge of the witness, such as a rumor.

Heroin: A trademark for certain narcotic. A study released in May 2001 stated that nearly half the heroin addicts tracked in a 33-years study died. Causes of death included murder, suicide, accidents, chronic liver disease and cancer. Many of the survivors, whose average was 57, still were using heroin and other drugs. The study concluded that heroin addiction cannot be cured like an acute disease and suggests treatment be premised on a philosophy of "more harm reduction as opposed to total abstinence which has only led to frustration and to failure."

Hinder: To check, obstruct, hamper, embarrass, debar or shut out. To put obstacles in the way.

Histrionics: Overly dramatic presentation.

Home State: The state in which the child's permanent domicile is located. If the child has a Home State, the suit must be brought in the home state. If the child has no home state, but the child and at least one party has significant connection with a state, and there is substantial evidence concerning the child's care, protection, training, and personal relationship in that state, the suit may be brought in that state.

Home Study: Also known as Social Study may be ordered by the court to evaluate the home environment of people requesting custody of a child.

Honesty: Uprightness as evidenced in character and actions. Also known as: having honor, being moral, possessing virtue, trustworthiness, dependability, and evidencing justness.

Hornbook: A series of textbooks, which review a certain field of law in summary, textural form, as opposed to a case book, which is designed as a teaching tool and includes many reprints of court opinions.

Hostage: A person offered or kept by one party as security for the fulfillment of some promise, agreement, or the like, made by another party.

Hostile Witness: A witness who is subject to cross-examination by the party who called the witness to testify, because of the witness evident antagonism toward that party as exhibited in his direct examination. A lawyer is not allowed to ask leading questions of their own witness. But, if that witness openly shows hostility against the interests (or the person) that the lawyer represents, the lawyer may ask the court to declare the witness "hostile", after, which, as an exception of the examination-in-chief rules, the lawyer may ask their own witness leading questions.

Hostility: Deep-seated dislike or ill will or a manifestation of such feeling, often with bitterness.

Hourly Fee: Cost based on the time not per job. Minimum charges may apply.

Humiliate: To lower the pride, self-respect, status, prestige, or esteem to embarrass, discomfort, humble or mortify.

Husband-Wife Privilege: A special right that married persons have to keep communications between them secret and even inaccessible to a court of law. While this privilege may have been varied in some states, it has always been held to be lifted where one spouse commits a crime on the other. Similar to the client-solicitor privilege. Privilege is compromised if a spouse gives the information to any third party.

Hyperactivity: Commonly refers to behavior in children or adolescents characterized by constant overactivity, distractibility, impulsiveness, inability to concentrate, and aggressiveness. Hyperactivity is often associated with Attention Deficit Disorder (which is then referred to as Attention Deficit Hyperactivity Disorder), but can also be associated with other disorders (for example Fetal Alcohol Syndrome).

Hypothetical Question: A combination of facts and circumstances, assumed or proved, stated in such a forms as to constitute a coherent state of facts upon, which the opinion of an expert can be asked by way of evidence in a trial.

I

Identity Disorder: Is considered a disorder of childhood and adolescence. It is severe and distressing arising from the inability to create an integrated, cohesive and acceptable sense of self. Symptoms include severe stress regarding uncertainty over one's long-term goals, career choice, friendship patterns, sexual orientation, religious identification, morals/values, group loyalties, and other important decisions, accompanied by impairment in one's functioning due to this stress and uncertainty.

Ignorance: Lack of knowledge. Ignorance of the law or a specific law does not justify breaking the law.

Illegal: Against the law.

Illicit: Contrary to or prohibited by law. Unlawful, criminal, illegal, illegitimate, nefarious, improper, intolerable or objectionable.

Immunity: An exemption that a person (individual or corporate) enjoys from the normal operation of the law such as a legal duty or liability, either criminal or civil. An example of an immunity is where a witness agrees to testify only if the testimony cannot be used at some later date during a hearing against the witness. Once you are granted immunity or otherwise won't be prosecuted in a criminal case, you lose your ability to "plead the fifth", since your testimony isn't going to be used against you in a criminal trial. You can be sued after in a civil trial, that may end in your incarceration.

Impeachment of Witness: An Attack on the credibility of a witness by the testimony of other witnesses. Discrediting a witness by proving lies, inconsistencies in stories told, and untrustworthiness. The witness may be impeached during cross-examination or by the direct testimony or evidence of another witness. Prior inconsistent statements made at deposition or in written interrogatories are classic examples of impeachment during cross-examination.

Implied Consent: Actions or facts that imply by inaction or silence that one agrees with the course of conduct transpiring.

Improper Communications: This applies to contact with individuals in the legal process and can cause sanctions to be imposed in cases involving attempts to influence a witness, judge, juror, prospective juror or other official by means prohibited by law.

Imputed Income: Once child support has been set at a level it may not be lowered because the payers income will drop because of retirement or optional educational opportunities. The payor will be held responsible for earning the income the payor is 'capable' of earning. Or it may apply to services received instead of income. Examples might include company paid life insurance, company car, employer provided housing, or stock options. The cost of the premium or vehicle expenses covered by the company is imputed income.

In Camera: Refers to proceedings held in a judge's chambers or where the public is not present.

Inadmissible: That, which, under the established rules of evidence, cannot be admitted or received.

Incriminating Evidence: Items that show involvement of a suspect or an accomplice in a criminal activity. Items could be a weapon bearing blood stains or fingerprints acquired during the crime, e-mail containing references to a crime, a photograph showing some relationship to the crime for a tape recording of accomplices discussing a crime.

Incest: A criminal offense, which involves sexual intercourse between members of a family, among whom marriage would be illegal because of blood relations.

Income Withholding Order: An order of the circuit court. It directs an employer, or source of income, to withhold a fixed amount and send that amount to the Friend of the Court for purposes of support.

Interpreter: An interpreter is a person or machine that can make something comprehendible. Translating information from a medium or language not understood by a witness to a language or medium understood by the witness and then reporting the information given to the court. One form of interpretation is done when a witness communicates in Sign Language and their gestures must be translated for the court. An interpreter may be appointed by the court to facilitate the admission of testimony. An interpreter must take an oath or affirmation to make a true translation.

Interstate Income Withholding Order: An order entered to secure payment of support through an employer in another state.

Indiscreet: Not marked by or according with good sense or sound judgment.

Indictment: An accusation in writing found and presented by a grand jury, charging that a person herein named has done some act, or been guilty of some omission, which, by law, is a crime.

Injunction: A court order, which requires a party to do some act or prohibiting certain actions.

In-Laws: The parents of one's spouse.

***In Loco Parentis*:** A person who has put him or herself in the situation of lawful parent by assuming the obligations incident to the parental relation without going through the formalities necessary to legal adoption.

Incompetence: Lack of sufficient resources or capacity to perform.

Indigent: Lacking money or material possessions. A person who may receive permission to proceed in a lawsuit without paying court fees.

Injunction: A judge's order that a person do or, more commonly, refrain from doing something. It may be preliminary or temporary pending trial of the issue presented, or it may be final if the issue has already been decide in court.

Injury: When dealing with attorney malpractice, is harm to a client, the public, the legal system, or the profession, which results from a lawyer's misconduct. The level of injury can range from "serious" injury to "Little or no" injury; a reference to "injury" alone indicates any level of injury greater than "little or no" injury.

In Pari Delicto: Both parties are equally at fault. Actually, the usual use of this phrase is "in pari delicto, potior est conditio possidentis" which means that where both parties in a dispute are equally at wrong, the person in possession of the contested property will retain it (the law will not intervene).

***In Personam*:** Is the law that deals with the rights of people.

***In Rem*:** Is the law, which deals with property rights

Insanity: Not mentally responsible to some degree.

Insolvent: A person who doesn't have enough money to pay his or her bills.

Instruction: A direction given by the judge to the jury concerning the law of the case.

Intent: A willful act.

Interlocutory Decree: Is a provisional or preliminary decree, which is not final.

Intent: Is the conscious objective or purpose to accomplish a particular result.

Internet: The Internet is best described as a tool to communicate with other people and organizations world wide via computer modem.

Interrogatories: A series of written questions served on the opposition to discover certain facts regarding the disputed issues in the proceeding. The answers to interrogatories must be under oath and served and completed within a prescribed period of time. Typically the answering side is as vague as legally possible.

Interstate: Between two or more states.

Intervention: A parceling in a suit or action by which a third person is permitted by the court to make him or herself a party.

Interview Protocol: A structured format used by all professionals to ensure that all necessary persons are interviewed in a planned strategy to insure that information gathering is thorough.

Invasion of Privacy: The wrongful intrusion into a person's private activities by other individuals or by the government.

***Ipso Facto*:** Latin meaning, "by the fact itself."

Investigation: The act or instance of seeking truth, information, or knowledge about something. A private detective may be hired by one or both parties. The court may assign a social worker or health professional. The process may include interviews with the parents, the children, their teachers, neighbors, doctors, baby-sitters and anyone else the professional feels compelled to talk to. Reports and recommendations may be submitted to the judge.

Irrelevant: Evidence not relating or applicable to the matter in issue.

Islamic Law: The law according to the Muslim faith and as interpreted from the Koran. Islamic law is probably best known for deterrent punishment, which is the basis of the Islamic criminal system and the fact that there is no separation of church and state. Under Islamic law, the religion of Islam and the government are one. Islamic law is controlled, ruled and regulated by the Islamic religion. Islamic law purports to regulate all public and private behavior including personal hygiene, diet, sexual conduct, and child rearing. Islamic law now prevails in countries all over the middle east and elsewhere covering twenty per cent of the world's population.

Issues: The things that are important such as child custody, visitation, child support, alimony and division of property and debits.

Instructions to the Jury: The attorneys for each side submit a number of instructions designed to apply the law to the facts in evidence. The judge will indicate, which instructions he will accept and which he will refuse. The attorneys make objections to such rulings for the purpose of the record in any appeal.

Intrastate: Within the borders of one state.

J

Joinder: This means that you include all the persons and entities and include all the claims, at the time of the original suit, you lose your right to do so. Many states permit a tort claim to be joined during the divorce, but don't require it. Other states, don't allow tort claims to be joined at all. See Mandatory Joiner.

Joint Custody: The parties share the responsibilities and major decisions relative to the child.

Joint Managing Conservator (JMC): Persons who have shared actual care, custody or control of a child for at least six months.

Joint Petition: When both parties want the court to do the same thing, such as "co-custody" due to an existing parenting plan and history, the parties jointly request (by joint petition) the court to grant the shared responsibility arrangement.

Judicial Review: An administrative agency or tribunal, which make decisions or deliver government services of one sort or another, the decisions of which can also be "appealed." In many cases, the "appeal" from administrative agencies is known as "judicial review" which is essentially a process where a court of law is asked to rule on the appropriateness of the administrative agency or tribunal's decision. Judicial review is a fundamental principle of administrative law. A distinctive feature of judicial review is that the "appeal" is not usually limited to errors in law, but may be based on alleged errors on the part of the administrative agency on findings of fact.

Judge: A person appointed or elected who decides the issues of fact and issues of law. The Judge has many duties in connection with a trial. The judge must see that the trial is conducted in an orderly manner according to prescribed rules and laws covering the presentation of evidence and the arguments of the lawyers. The judge must decide the propriety of the questions, rule on objections, and render a verdict. A person who has the authority to make exceptions.

Judgment: Ruling or order of the court.

Judgment Entry: A Judgment Entry is a written document that is signed by a Judge and contains a Judge's order.

Judicial Admission: Evidence of a disputed fact, "a judicial declaration that eliminates the adversary's necessity of providing such element upon, which it relies."

Judicial Immunity: The freedom or charge or obligation, which others are subject from civil liability for any acts performed in the judge's official capacity. The immunity is absolute provided only that the judge is acting within his or her jurisdiction. The scope of the judge's jurisdiction must be constructed broadly to protect the court's independence.

Therefore, the judge will not be deprived of immunity because the action taken was in error, was done maliciously, or was in excess of the judge's authority; rather the judge will be subject to liability only when the action taken was in clear absence of all jurisdiction.

Jurisdiction: The authority given to a court by a Constitution or a legislative body to make legally binding decisions over certain persons or property. Example: A custody suit shall be brought in the county where the child resides, unless another court already has continuing jurisdiction over the child. If the child resides in a jurisdiction other than the one, which has continuing jurisdiction for over six months and there are no actions pending, the jurisdiction may be changed to that in which the child resides. If a child has been improperly brought to or kept in a county, the court may refuse jurisdiction and charge the party who brought the suit with the opposition's travel costs and attorney's fees.

Jurisprudence: (1) The science or philosophy of law; (2) a collective term for case law, as opposed to legislation.

Jury: A group of people summoned and sworn to decide on the facts in issue at a trial. Juries normally consist of six, eight or twelve people. There are usually several alternate Jurors who sit through the entire trial in case one of the regular jurors should require replacement.

Attorneys may photograph potential jurors' homes and autos, search for any litigation they have been involved in, including divorces and bankruptcies, obtain credit and employment histories, including salaries, whether they rent or own their homes and how much the home costs. The attorneys are prohibited from personal contact either directly or through an intermediary.

Justifiable: Capable of being made defensible.

Juvenile: A person less than 18 or 21 years old, depending on the state in which the child resides. Court for these children is referred to as Juvenile Court.

K

Kangaroo Court: A court in which a strong, unlawful bias toward one side is evident.

Ketubah: A Jewish marriage contract.

Key Number: Part of the major indexing system devised for American case law, developed by West Publishing Company. The key number is a permanent number given to a specific point of this case law.

Kidnap: To carry off or hold a person by force or fraud or in violation of a law or of a court order.

Knowledge: Is the conscious awareness of the nature or attendant circumstances of the conduct, but without the conscious objective or purpose to accomplish a particular result.

Knowledge or Awareness: During deposition or courtroom questioning if the other attorney asks questions like "Did you know that. . ." or "Were you aware that. . ." are dangerous because the opposing attorney usually then states a fundamental fact or premise that, if the object of the question had known or been aware of it, the standard would have required him or her to have acted in a particular way, such as doing or not doing a particular act. Also, opposing attorney, having memorized the facts most favorable to his or her client, may be testing your memory of these facts.

L

Lapse: A slip, as of the tongue or pen or behavior. Failure to meet certain requirements.

Larceny: The unlawful taking and carrying away of personal property with intent to deprive the rightful owner of it.

Latent: Present, but not visible.

Law: The rules and boundaries set and enforced by society. A principle governing conduct, action, or procedure. A comprehensive and fundamental rule, doctrine or assumption.

Lawyer: Also called Counsel, Attorney. The legal representative of a party at a trial. A person may give legal advice to another person without risking prosecution for the unauthorized practice of law only if they are licensed to practice law. Lawyers licensed to practice in one state are no more entitled to practice law in another than a lay person. The incompetent and/or unlicensed practice of law does not have to be carried on for profit for it to be subject to civil and/or criminal sanctions. Even licensed lawyers are subject to getting punished for practicing law outside their jurisdiction when they give even free and correct advice on the Internet.

Lawyer Discipline Proceedings: The purpose of lawyer discipline proceedings is to protect the public and the administration of justice from lawyers who have not discharged, will not discharge, or are unlikely to discharge their professional duties to clients, the public, the legal system, and the legal profession properly.

Leading Question: One, which instructs a witness how to answer or puts into a witness' mouth words to be echoed back. One, which suggests to the witness the answer desired. Prohibited in direct examination

Legal: Being in accordance with law.

Legal Separation: A court order or, in some jurisdictions, a written agreement between the parties, arranging the terms under, which the parties will live apart after separating. While signifying the separation of the parties, it does not formally dissolve the marriage or permit the parties to marry other persons legally.

Legitimate: Lawfully begotten. Conforming to recognized principals or standards. No longer applies to the parentage or origination of a child.

LEIN: Law Enforcement Information Network. A computer system containing files on wanted persons.

Leniency: Giving clemency, being indulgent, tolerant or merciful.

Liability: That for which a person is responsible such as money or contract obligations.

Liaison: A bond or an intimacy, especially illicit or sexual meeting between two people.

Libel: To communicate through print, writing, pictures or signs to mark a person's activities or personal or business behavior for the purpose of injuring and without regard for the truth.

Lie: A statement or declaration that is not true.

Lien: A money debit. A claim against property as security for a debit, under, which the property may be seized and sold to satisfy the debit.

Limitation: A certain time allowed by statute in which litigation must be brought. Statute of limitations.

Litigate: To take a question before the court to make a contest by judicial process.

Local Counsel: An attorney whose geographic presence and license for a jurisdiction may assist an out-of-town or out-of-country attorney in the litigation of a case.

Local Venue: Foreclosure of a mortgage on a house is a common action that may be brought only in the county where the subject matter of the litigation is located. Child custody cases are not restricted.

Loco Parentis: A person who stands in the place of a parent such as a step-parent in a common law relationship.

Lurking: A cyber term meaning that a person reads and/or prints out the messages that people post on Internet news groups without making their presence known in any way.

M

Magistrate: Is an experienced attorney who has been hired by the Court to take evidence and decide cases. The magistrate acts as the Judge in assigned cases. He or she will hear the evidence and makes written findings in a magistrate's decision. The magistrate's decision will include recommendations to the Judge as to what the ultimate order in the case should be. The Judge reviews the magistrate's decision and makes the final order in your case. If you disagree with the magistrate's decision, within a time limit, you can file written objections to the decision. An attorney to assist you with filing objections.

Maintaince: Spousal support sometimes called Alimony.

Malfeasance: Evil doing; ill conduct; the commission of some act, which is positively prohibited by law.

Malice: The state of mind that accompanies the intentional doing of a wrongful act without justification or excuse.

Malicious Mother Syndrome:

Malpractice: A legal malpractice suit is only about money. It is a civil remedy for negligence or damages. If you lost your case because your attorney did not show up for court or has not performed adequately on your behalf, you may have a case against the attorney. If you have a case for malpractice, you may also have a case for disbarment.

Managing Conservator (MC): Person who has had actual care, custody or control of a child for at least six months. A person with whom the child and the child's parent or guardian resided for at least 6 months may file such a suit if the child's parent or guardian is dead. A grandparent may bring an original suit to be named MC if the child's present environment presents a serious question concerning the child's physical health or welfare.

Manifestly Unjust: When a decision is so contrary to the overwhelming weight of the evidence as to be clearly wrong and unjust.

Mandamus: The name of a writ, which issues from a court of superior jurisdiction, directed to a lower court, commanding the performance of a particular act.

Mandate: A judicial command or precept proceeding from a court or judicial officer, directing the proper officer to enforce a judgment, sentence, or decree.

Mandatory Joinder: This means that if you don't bring suit against all the persons and entities and include all the claims, at the time of the original suit, you lose your right to do so forever. See Mandatory Joiner.

Mandatory Transfer: On timely motion, a suit must be transferred from the court of original and/or continuing exclusive jurisdiction to the court of another county. This happens if the child has resided in latter county for six months or longer. The time of residency does not have to be continuous and uninterrupted; the court will look to the child's principal residence.

Maneuver: An action planned or taken toward the accomplishment of a purpose.

Marriage: A voluntary union or file or until divorce of a man and a woman.

Maternal Preference Presumption: A presumed preference for the mother, now virtually non-existent legally as courts attempt to move to a gender-free standard, in keeping with equal rights. Still used informally by many courts despite changes in law.

Material Evidence: Such as is relevant and goes to the substantial issues in dispute.

Mediation: A method of settling disputes outside of a court. The imposition of a neutral third party to act as a link between the parties. **Traditional Mediation**, sometimes called a mediated settlement conference, consists of one continuous meeting, attended by the parties and their attorneys, in which all issues are resolved, with general sessions and private caucuses. **Serial Mediation** is when the parties meet with the mediator, usually without counsel present, in a series of short (1 hour) sessions, until all issues are resolved.

Mediator: A mediator is an unbiased third party who can often assist the parties in reaching agreement regarding what is in the best interest of the child.

Medical Support: Means periodic payments or a lump-sum payment made under a court order to cover medical expenses, including health insurance coverage, incurred for the benefit of a child.

Memorandum of Law: A legal document filed along with pleadings or other court papers setting forth your lawyer's legal research in support of a request to the court.

Mental Anguish: Compensable injury embracing all forms of mental pain, as opposed to mere physical pain, including deep grief, distress, anxiety and fright.

Mercenary: The amateurs and professionals who are willing to surrender their time and efforts for assured rewards, usually monetary. They do not have any other real stake in the issue. In this war, the mercenaries are the hired professionals and services who offer legal advice, evaluation and surveillance.

Merit: The substance of a litigant's claim or refutation of a claim. Example: The case has merit or the case does not have merit or is without merit.

Misdemeanor: Offenses less than felonies, generally those punishable by fine or imprisonment otherwise than in penitentiaries. Conviction of a misdemeanor law can result in imposition of punishment greater than that of a petty offense, but not as severe as that of a felony (examples might be a heavier fine, or short jail sentence).

Misfeasance: A misdeed or trespass; the improper performance of some act, which a person may lawfully do.

Mis-joinder: When a person has been named as a party to a law suit when that person should not have been added. When this is asserted, a court will usually accommodate a request to amend the court documents to strike, or substitute for, the name of the mis-joined party.

Mistrial: An erroneous, abortive or invalid trial. A trial, which cannot stand in law because of lack of jurisdiction, wrong drawing of jurors, or disregard of some other fundamental requisite.

Mitigating Circumstance: One, which does not constitute a justification or excuse for an offense, but which may be considered as reducing the degree of moral culpability.

Modify: Almost everything in custody decision is subject to change. In most cases you must show a material change, change of circumstances or show that the best interest of the child(ren) necessitates a change, then the judge will be more inclined to modify your judgment.

Modification: Within one year of the previous order determining possession. May be filed in only three circumstances: 1) the child's present environment may endanger the child's physical health or significantly impair the child's emotional development; 2) the current custodian of the child is seeking or consenting to the proposed modification and the modification is in the best interest of the child; 3) the current custodian has relinquished actual care, control and possession of the child for at least 6 months and the modification is in the best interest of the child.

A court may not modify another state's custody decree unless that state has lost jurisdiction, or has declined to assume jurisdiction to modify the decree, and the new court has jurisdiction. If the child is in the new court because the party seeking modification improperly brought the child to or has improperly kept the child in the new jurisdiction, or violated any other provision of the existing custody decree, the court may refuse jurisdiction, and charge the party seeking modification with the opposition's travel costs and attorney's fees.

Moot: Unsettled or undecided by judicial decision.

Mother-absent: Refers to single father families.

Motion: Is a written or oral request to the Judge by the lawyer of one of the parties. Motions are made to obtain an order, ruling or direction in favor of the applicant. Often motions are accompanied by a brief. Motions are either "contested" or, if the parties stipulate to the matter, "uncontested." Motions are usually heard at a special motion or ex parte "session" of the court. Legal fees for contested motions are expensive and the outcome is rarely certain. Therefore, when possible, you should enter into a written stipulation to be submitted for the court's approval. The stipulation then becomes part of the court's temporary order. Often, motions request temporary orders relating to support, maintenance of health and life insurance, and temporary custody of minor children. Other requests relate to matters such as motions to allow "amendment of pleadings," "more time to answer a complaint," and "continuances." Requests for restraining orders and requests to vacate a shared home are also made by motion.

Motion for Security of Costs: A motion that may be filed by one side if they are in doubt about the opposition's willingness or ability to pay costs if they lose the case and are ordered by the judge to cover filing expenses incurred by both parties.

Motion to Dismiss: Also called Demurer. Asks the court to rule that the plaintiff's complaint does not state a legally sound case of action against the defendant even if, for the purpose of the motion, the defendant admits that all the facts set out by the plaintiff are true.

Motion to Make More Definite and Certain: Asks the court to require the plaintiff to set out the facts of his complaint more specifically, or to describe his injury or damages in greater detail, so that the defendant can answer more precisely.

Motion to Modify: A formal written request to the court to change a prior order regarding custody, child support or any other order that the court may change by law.

Motion to Quash Service of Summons: Questions whether the defendant has been properly served with summons, as provided by law.

Motion to Strike: Asks the court to rule whether the plaintiff's petition contains irrelevant, prejudicial or other improper matter.

Motion to Vacate Premises: A request to the court, on the showing of good cause, ordering one spouse to leave the residence.

Move the Court: Request a decision from the judge on a motion or fact of law.

Multiple Personality Disorder: is defined as the existence within a person of two or more distinct personalities or personality states, in which at least 2 of these personalities "take control" of the functioning of the body at given points. Each personality controls the body separately, and there is a memory loss for at least some personalities when others are in control of the body. Other personalities may have wildly different traits, belief systems, relationships, names, and so forth. Some clinical studies have shown that EEGs differ by personality. Personalities may themselves have other psychological disorders, such as depression; these disorders may be present in only one, some, or all of the personalities. The degree of interaction and/or cooperation of the personalities varies extremely; the degree of co-consciousness (the state of being able to share memories of the various personalties' actions, and being able to cooperate in the control of the body) also varies extremely.

Munchausen Syndrome: A disorder in which people manifest symptoms of factitious disorders by their ability to feign, exaggerate, or actually self-induce illnesses. This makes them a "patient," and in need of attention, nurturance, and lenience that they feel unable to obtain in any other way. Unlike individuals who "malinger," people with factitious disorders are not primarily seeking external gains such as disability payments or narcotic drugs--though they may receive them.

Munchausen Syndrome By Proxy: (MSBP), An individual makes another person sick in order to accrue the same attention, care and concern--but this time vicariously. This is a form of abuse in which children or the elderly are the usual victims.

Murphy's Law: A set of maxims initially assembled by George Nichols in 1949 while working as a project manager for Northrop Corporation in California as a result of a remark made by a colleague, Captain E. Murphy, of the Wright Field-Aircraft Laboratory. The contexts of the early quotations appear to support this explanation. Example; Aviation Mechanics Bulletin May-June 1955 Murphy's Law: If an aircraft part can be installed incorrectly, someone will install it that way.

Mutual Mistake: A mistake made by both sides in a lawsuit.

N

Natural Law: The body of unwritten laws accepted by civilized people everywhere as based on reason. Essential to the well-being of society.

Natural Parent: The biological parent.

NCP (Non-custodial Parent): The parent that does not have residential responsibility for the children.

Negligence: In general, negligence is the failure of a person to exercise the reasonable care of an ordinary person in the same circumstance, and through failure to exercise such reasonable care causing harm to someone or something. People are responsible for the intentional harm they cause, and for their failure to act as a reasonable person would be expected to act in similar circumstances. If the negligence of a child causes injury a liability suit under tort can be filed. Negligence is always assessed having regards to the circumstances and to the standard of care, which would reasonably be expected of a person in similar circumstances. Everybody has a duty to ensure that their actions do not cause harm to others. Between negligence and the intentional act there lies yet another, more serious type of negligence, which is called gross negligence. Gross negligence is any action or an omission in reckless disregard of the consequences to the safety of a person or property of another. When dealing with attorney malpractice; Is the failure of a lawyer to heed a substantial risk that circumstances exist or that a result will follow, which failure is a deviation from the standard care that a reasonable lawyer would exercise in the situation.

Negative Halo Effect: If a bad impression on an observer is established, the observed is without further input deemed unworthy of acceptance, believability and trust. After that, it becomes much more difficult for the observer to respect the observed. This works, first, because once people decide how they feel about someone, they are unwilling to find their judgment was in error. Second, because all information is filtered through to support your opinion. Third, if the information a person is hearing does not correspond with the information that person is seeing, that person will believe what he or she is seeing. "The Positive Halo Effect" is just as helpful as the Negative is pervasive. Once the Negative Halo Effect is in place, it is much more difficult to change than the Positive Halo Effect.

Negotiated: In this book, "negotiate" means to discuss and bargain in good faith to find a solution all can accept.

Next Best Friend: Is a way to file a motion that a person cannot file or is unable to because of disability or death. This is called Petitioning the Court as her "Next Best Friend" and you must state why the person didn't, wouldn't or couldn't file herself.

Nexus: A connection between groups or series.

No-Fault: To end without the necessity to find fault in a person, process or thing. Is a term used when a divorce is granted without the necessity of finding a spouse to have been guilty of some marital misconduct.

***Nolo Contendere*:** A pleading usually used by defendants in criminal cases, which means "I will not contest it."

Noncombatants: People not involved in the conflict. Noncoms rarely exist in a war zone. Family, friends, neighbors, young children, adult children and coworkers are pressed to or voluntarily choose sides.

Non-custodial Parent (NCP): The parent with whom the child does not live the majority of the time. This designation may restrict many areas of influence and behavior in your jurisdiction.

Nonfeasance: Failure to act. Failure to do what ought to be done.

Non-Issue: Not an issue that will assist you in winning your lawsuit.

Non-Support: The failure to provide support that one can provide and that one is legally obliged to provide.

Notice of Hearing: A paper that is served on the opposing lawyer or other parent listing the date and place of a hearing and the motions that will be heard by the court.

O

Oath: A promise not to lie.

Objection: The act of taking exception to some statement or procedure in trial. Used to call the court's attention to improper evidence or procedure.

Obligor and Obligee: The persons entitled to receive and pay child support, respectively. Each parent has the duty to support the child and the right to receive support for the child. However, these rights are subject to a court order.

Of Counsel: Attorney(s) employed to assist in the preparation or management of the case.

This may be for the initial presentation or appeal, but is not the principal attorney of record.

Off-site Supervision: Is contact between the 'visiting parent' and the children, which occurs away from a state, which is under the control of the Provider and Visit Supervisor.

Officer of the Court: Any duly sworn personnel usually bailiffs or attorneys.

Off Calendar: The removal of a case from a judge's calendar.

Off the Record: An attempt to give information or opinion without retaining the responsibility for doing so. There is no such thing. Anything you say to anyone is subject to scrutiny.

On Demand: When requested.

On-site Supervision: Supervision of a visiting parent and children on a site under control of the Provider or Supervisor. This may include a range of closeness of supervision from continuos, close monitoring to periods of time, which the parent and child are intermittently monitored by video or audio.

On the Record: Statement made in public or open court.

Open Court: A court that is formally opened and engaged in the transaction of judicial affairs where all persons who conduct themselves in an orderly manner are admitted.

Opinion: The reason given for a court's judgment, finding, or conclusion, as opposed to the decision, which is the judgment itself.

Opposition: The opposition, the enemy.

Oppositional Defiant Disorder: A pattern of negativistic, hostile, and defiant behavior in children lasting at least six months. If the behavior occurs more frequently than is typically observed in individuals of comparable age and developmental level. The disturbance in behavior causes clinically significant impairment in social, academic, or occupational functioning. The behaviors that are frequently displayed include: loses temper, argues with adults, actively defies or refuses to comply with adults' requests or rules, deliberately annoys people, blames others for his or her mistakes or misbehavior, is touchy or easily annoyed by others, is angry and resentful, is spiteful or vindictive.

Order: The court's ruling in writing and signed by the judge and filed with the court, requiring the parties to do certain things or setting forth their rights and responsibilities.

Order to Show Cause (OSC): Paperwork used to request an action from a judge. An OSC requires the party served to appear before the judge to answer questions.

Order to Vacate: Is an instruction from a court for a person to leave a specific address with or without their personal property.

Out of Court: One who has no legal status in court is said to be "out of court." If by some act of omission or commission, the plaintiff shows the plaintiff is unable to maintain the action initiated, he is frequently said, to have put himself "out of court."

Out-Of-Court Settlement: The resolution of dispute between parties prior to going to court at all or prior to the rendering of a final judgment by the court.

P

Panel: A list of jurors to serve in a particular court or for the trial of a particular action. The list may denote the whole body of persons summoned as jurors for a particular term of court or those selected by the clerk by lot.

Paralegal: A person other than a licensed attorney who is employed to perform a variety of tasks associated with law practice, which can be performed by one not authorized to practice law.

Paranoia: A disorder that causes a person to become very suspicious about people and events. Often a symptom of other diseases, especially schizophrenia. This person may be dangerous if frightened and unwittingly do severe harm to another. Paranoia may be mild or severe and sometimes medical treatment or therapy can help. Often it is difficult to evaluate and deal with because the lack of trust inhibits being susceptible to care of another.

***Parens patrieae*:** The right and responsibility of the state to take charge of the care and custody of minor children or other legal incompetents when their health or safety so requires.

Parental Alienation Syndrome (PAS): Is any function that obstructs contact with or is intentionally denigrating the other parent with the intent of alienating the child. Is a disorder in children that arises almost exclusively in child custody disputes.

Parental Interference: When the parent of a child obstructs access of the other parent to the child. If the parental interference is in violation of a court order, it may precipitate legal action that could result in fines or time in jail or both.

Parental Kidnapping: The taking, keeping, or concealing of a child by a parent or other family member, or person acting on behalf of the parent, which deprives another individual of his or her rights with or without the child's help or consent.

Parental Liability: Statutes that vary widely, but usually make parents responsible for acts of their minor child, and usually limited to a fixed dollar amount.

Parenting Classes: Classes that teach parents effective ways to care for and help their children adjust to life and the divorce of their parents.

Parole: Release of a convicted criminal from state prison with less than full term of incarceration, but with restrictions and conditions. A parolee is usually required to report to a parole officer.

Parties or Party: The persons who are actively concerned in the prosecution or defense of a legal proceeding. In a judicial proceeding, a litigant, plaintiff or defendant, the person directly interested in the subject matter of the case.

Passive Aggression: A style of reaction that is characterized by apparently enduring injury while offering no opposition in a manner, which appears submissive. When in fact provoked or unprovoked attacks or hostile activities are initiated and done by the person with an on-going and insidious agenda of revenge and demoralization. The strategy is never obvious and the toll is only apparent by the cumulative impact on the target person.

Passive Resistance: A style of reaction that appears submissive. Apparently, enduring pressure or injury while offering no opposition. When in fact resistance is offered in a non-violent manner by refusing to cooperate, understand or respond appropriately. Often feigning innocence or ignorance using inadequacy as a tool.

Paternity Lawsuit: An action to establish the fatherhood of a man in order to assign the rights and responsibilities to that parent.

Paternity Testing: Paternity means fatherhood. Paternity is established when a paternity testing laboratory uses genetic testing methods to demonstrate, to a legal standard, that an alleged father is the biological father. Paternity is disproved when these same methods and standards demonstrate that an alleged father is not the biological father.

Peer Review: One of the factors in considering admissibility of a theory or scientific method in court is whether it has been "peer reviewed." A theory or method is released. Other professionals explore the abilities and limitations of the technique. The professionals write articles and hold discussions on it. Generally the steps would be guidelines, developmental validation, internal validation and peer review.

Percipient Witness: One who was there and saw what happened.

Perfected: To "perfect" an appeal requires that an appellant's brief must be filed. This document must conform to a rigid format that is bound like a book with a table of contents and an alphabetical list of all the cases to be cited as precedent in the appeal, all the original transcripts and exhibits from the original trial and a brief with the presentation of the facts and the law, with emphasis on why the decision should or should not be upheld.

Peremptory Challenge: Many states allow the parties to a case to dismiss the judge assigned to the case without having to prove an actual bias. The challenge, which the prosecution or defense may reject a certain number of prospective jurors without giving any explanation or reason.

Perjury: The traditional definition is the criminal offense of making false statements under oath. A willful and corrupt sworn statement made without sincere belief in its truth, and made in a judicial proceeding regarding a material matter. Today, the statutes have been broadened so that in some jurisdictions any false swearing in a legal instrument or legal setting is perjury. Chargeable even if it is not material and even though it is not presented in a judicial proceeding. Some statutes group 'perjury,' 'false swearing,' and 'making false written statements' together as different degrees of the same crime, often called loosely perjury. Perjury can be punishable by imprisonment. See Subornation Of Perjury.

Perpetuating Testimony: The recording of evidence when it is feared that the person with that evidence may soon die or disappear and that this person's evidence, if recorded, could then be used in the future to prevent a possible injustice or to support a future claim.

Permanent Child Support: The final court ordered payments that continue until the child reaches the age of majority.

Per Se: A person representing him or herself in a law suit.

Persuasive Authority:

Petit Jury: The ordinary jury of twelve (or fewer) persons for the trial of a civil or criminal case. So called to distinguish it from the grand jury.

Petition: A formal, written application to a court requesting judicial action on a certain matter.

Petitioner: Also called a Plaintiff. The person who starts a lawsuit; in a criminal case, this would be the State.

Petty Offenses: Petty offense is a sub-group of misdemeanor. Petty offenses typically may be tried before a magistrate in a summary proceeding as the matter typically is handled all on the date of the first appearance by the defendant in court. The defendant may be denied the right to a jury trial without violation of constitutional rights. Offenses such as minor traffic tickets, parking violations, and minor infractions of local ordinances are treated as petty offenses. The typical punishment for violation of a petty offense is the imposition of a fine.

Physical Custody: A child custody decision, which grants the right to organize and administer the day to day residential care of a child. This is usually combined with legal custody.

Physician/Patient Privilege: A "patient" means any person who consults or is seen by a physician to receive medical care. A "physician" means a person licensed to practice medicine in any state or nation, or reasonably believed by the patient so to be. A communication is "confidential" if not intended to be disclosed to third persons other than those present to further the interest of the patient in the consultation, examination, or interview, or persons reasonably necessary for the transmission of the communication, or persons who are participating in the diagnosis and treatment under the direction of the physician, including members of the patient's family.

Pick-Up Order: A court order, usually obtained in the state in which the child is located, which allows the local law enforcement officials in that state to pick up the child.

Plaintiff: Also called a Petitioner. The person who starts a lawsuit; in a criminal case, this would be the State.

Plea Bargaining: The process whereby the accused and the prosecutor in a criminal case work out a mutually satisfactory disposition of the case. It usually involves the defendant's pleading guilty to a lesser offense or to only one of the counts of a multi-count indictment in return for a lighter sentence than possible for the graver charge. In theory this assists the legal system by settling a large volume of cases without costly, protracted litigation.

Pleading: Formal written application (petitions, answer, replies, motions and counterclaims) to the court for relief requiring a written response.

Polling the Jury: A practice initiated by the judge or requested by counsel.

The jurors are asked individually whether they assented, and still assent, to the verdict.

Polygraph: It is an electromechanical instrument that simultaneously measures and records certain physiological changes in the human body, which are believed to be involuntarily caused by the subject's conscious attempts to deceive the questioner.

Positive Halo Effect: If a good impression on an observer is established, the observed is without further effort deemed worthy of acceptance, believing and trust. After that, it becomes much more difficult for anyone to discredit the observed. This works, first, because once people decide how they feel about someone, they are unwilling to find their judgment was in error. Second, because all information is filtered through to support your opinion. Third, if the information a person is hearing does not correspond with the information that person is seeing, that person will believe what he or she is seeing.

Possessory Conservator: A person who is not a blood relative may be granted custody by the court if the person can demonstrate substantial past contact with the child.

Post a Bond: A bond is a special insurance policy large enough to discourage noncompliance with a court order either to perform or appear. A bond may be required in civil or criminal cases for visitation and child support.

Post-Traumatic Stress Disorder (PTSD): Is a debilitating condition that follows a terrifying event. PTSD causes persistent frightening thoughts and memories, and emotional numbness. PTSD, first noticed in war veterans, can result from many traumatic incidents including kidnapping, accidents, violent attacks or child abuse. PTSD symptoms may be mild or severe and seem to be worse if the event that triggered them was initiated by a person--such as a rape, as opposed to a flood. Children often relive the trauma through repetitive play. In young children, distressing dreams of the traumatic event may change into nightmares of monsters, of rescuing others or of threats to self or others. PTSD rarely appears during the trauma itself and often surfaces several months or even years later.

Potential Injury: Is the harm cause to a client, the public, the legal system or the profession that is reasonably foreseeable at the time of the lawyer's misconduct, and which, but for some intervening factor or event, would probably have resulted from the lawyer's misconduct.

Power of Attorney: An instrument authorizing another to act as one's agent or attorney.

Precedent: Stare Decisis. The doctrine of American law, which states when a court has formulated a principle of law as applicable to a given set of fact, it will follow that principle and apply it in future cases where the facts are substantially the same. It connotes the decision of present cases on the basis of past precedent. Is a case or cases that have already been decided whose decision may affect this or following like cases.

Prejudicial Error: An error, which warrants the appellate court to reverse the judgment before it. The same as reversible error. Distinguished from "harmless error," which does not merit reversal.

Prejudice: The inclination to take a stand, with or without just grounds or sufficient information. Also known as bias, one-sidedness or partiality.

Present Sense Impression: Is a statement describing or explaining an event or condition made while the declarant was perceiving the event or condition, or immediately thereafter.

Preliminary Hearing: Same as preliminary examination. The hearing given a person charged with a crime by a magistrate or a judge to determine whether he or she should be held for trial.

Preponderance of Evidence: In a civil case, the plaintiff must prove their case, and the defendant must prove any defense asserted by a preponderance of evidence. This is the greater weight of the credible evidence, which may be less than the proof beyond a reasonable doubt, which would be required in a criminal case. If a criminal case can't be proved, a civil action for theft, called 'conversion' where the burden of proof is : preponderance of the evidence, not beyond reasonable doubt, a lesser standard.

Presumed Father: A man is presumed to be the father of a child in several different ways. Some are: if he welcomes the child into his home and openly acknowledges that he is the father, was married to the mother when the child was conceived or born, or he married the mother after the birth and agreed to have his name on the birth certificate.

Presumption of Fact: An inference as to the truth or falsity of any proposition of fact, drawn by a process of reasoning in the absence of actual certainty of its truth or falsity, or until such certainty can be ascertained.

Presumption of Law: A rule of law that courts and judges shall draw a particular inference from a particular fact, or from particular evidence.

Prima Facie: Something that is self evident. Elements of proof required to prove a basic case.

Privilege: General Rule of Privilege. (1) Confidential communications between a professional such as physician or attorney and a patient or client, relative or in connection with any professional services rendered by a professional to the patient or client, are privileged and may not be disclosed. (2) Records of the identity, diagnosis, evaluation, or treatment of a patient or client by a professional that are created or maintained by the professional. The records are confidential and privileged and may not be disclosed. (3) The privilege of confidentiality may be claimed by the patient or client or by a representative of the patient or client acting on the patient or client's behalf.

The right of a person to make admissions to his/her lawyer, member of the clergy, psychiatrist, or doctor that are not later admissible in evidence.

Privilege Release: Consent for the release of privileged information must be in writing and signed by the patient or client, or a legal guardian or parent if the patient or client is a minor, or a legal guardian if the patient or client has been adjudicated incompetent to manage his or her personal affairs.

Proactive: To react in a positive manner to stimulus.

Probate Case: A legal process to dispense with debits and distribute wealth of a person after the person's death.

Probate Court: The court, which handles wills, estates, and commitment of mentally ill persons. The court also has jurisdiction over matters involving minors, usually through a juvenile division.

Probation: Is a criminal sentence that requires the offender to meet conditions under supervision in the community.

Pro Bono: Refers to an attorney accepting a case with no payment for services rendered on the client's behalf. For the public good or welfare.

Proceedings: A hearing that involves a series of actions, operations, or motions involved in the accomplishment of a purpose before a judge, arbitrator, or government agency.

Procedural Law: That law, which governs the operation of the legal system, including court rules and rules of procedure, as distinguished from substantive law.

Professional Liability: Any dishonest, fraudulent, criminal or intentionally wrongful acts or omissions are illegal. Negligent acts, error or omissions in rendering services as a neutral administrator involving the submission, negotiation, and settlement of disputes involving divorce, marriage, child custody, visitation rights and their family matters. Additionally, professionals are responsible for their staff including secretaries.

Proof: The evidence that tends to establish the existence of a fact. More than just the uncorroborated testimony of an interested party.

Proposed Findings: A document prepared by you or your lawyer and submitted to the court setting forth your best case scenario of how you want the judge to find the facts and make "conclusions of law" to decide the case.

Pro Se: Also Pro Per (In Propria Persona). A litigant who is not represented by a lawyer. Under the U.S. Constitution, anyone may represent himself or herself in court. The act of appearing Pro-se, installs and grants an individual under the constitution of the United States and the constitution of each state in the United States, full authority to act as an officer of the court in all matters both civil and criminal, having the same weight as any attorney for a litigant. A pro se litigant must know: trial procedure, sequence of presentation, evidence, witnesses, experts, scientific evidence, tactics, overcoming the other side's "dirty tricks", pretrial maneuvering, trial memorandum, making a record in case, what to do if you are prevented from presenting your full case, what to do about a bad, inattentive or unprepared judge.

Prosecutor: A person in the criminal justice system who files criminal charges against and prosecutes an abductor who has violated the law. Also called District Attorney, Commonwealth Attorney, State's Attorney, or Solicitor.

Process Server: A person who serves a summons, citation or petition.

Protective Order: The restriction by court order of two parties having contact.

Provider: Is an independent individual or organization providing supervised visitation services.

Psychological Parent: Is someone who cares for a child as a parent would, but has no legal or blood ties to the child.

Psychologist: A person with a degree in Psychology. A professional dealing with the mental and emotional processes of human behavior. A learned person who seriously and systematically explores the mental characteristics of a person. A clinical psychologist deals with the diagnosis and treatment of mental, emotional, and behavior disorders. A forensic psychologist provides psychological services to the courts, to the criminal and civil justice system. Neuropsychology deals with brain behavior relationships. Neuropsychologists diagnose brain injury and brain disease in terms of the dysfunction of the brain or the cognitive processes such as memory, learning, attention, concentration, language, and the higher mental processes.

Psychotherapy: The therapist explores the patient's early childhood and develops a healthy relationship with the patient in an attempt to resolve interpersonal issues.

Public Records and Reports: Reports, records, statements or data compilations in any form made and preserved by a public office or agency.

Punishment: Sanctions imposed on a person because that person has been found to have committed some act.

Q

Qualified Domestic Relations Order: A court decision that assigns a portion of one spouse's pension to the other spouse as part of the equitable distribution of the marital assets.

Quality: The degree of excellence of a thing.

Quantity: A determinable or measurable count of a thing.

Quash: To overthrow; vacate; to annul or void a summons or indictment.

R

Rape: Sex with a woman without her consent. Many states have changed this basic definition to include sex with a minor (with or without consent).

Reactive: To react in an opposite sometimes negative manner to stimulus.

Residence Order: The final decree that identifies where and with whom the child will live.

Reasonable Doubt: In a criminal case, an accused person is entitled to acquittal if, in the minds of the jury, his or her guilt has not been proved beyond a reasonable doubt. The state of mind of the jurors in which they cannot say they feel an abiding conviction as to the truth of the charge.

Reasonable Visitation: Should only be given when parents can work together to set a mutually acceptable and flexible schedule of parenting time for all parties. The alternative is Fixed-Schedule Visitation.

Rebuttal: The introduction of evidence showing that statements of witnesses as to what occurred are not true. The state of a trial at which such evidence may be introduced.

Rebuttable Presumption: Usually, every element of a case must be proven to a judge or a jury. The exception is a "presumption", which means that if certain other facts are proven, then another fact can be taken for granted by the judge (or jury). For example, in some states, an adult caught having intercourse with a minor is presumed as having known that the minor was under-age. Most presumptions are "rebuttable", which means that the person against whom the presumption applies may present evidence to the contrary, which then has the effect of nullifying the presumption. This then deprives the person that tried to use the presumption with the advantage of the "free" evidence and makes him present evidence to support the fact, which might have been proven by the presumption.

Reciprocal Enforcement of Maintenance Orders (REMO): The name of the international system of recognition, registration and enforcement of child and spousal support orders between countries, which have agreed, between themselves, to enforce each other's maintenance orders. Originally created by England, the international REMO system now spreads over many countries. In the USA, the system is known as UIFSA or URESA.

Reconciliation: When all the parties to a domestic relations action are attempting to work out his/her differences and remain as a family unit.

Records of Religious Organizations: Statements of births, marriages, divorces, deaths, legitimacy, ancestry, relationship by blood or marriage of personal or family history, contained in a regularly kept record of a religious organization.

Records of Vital Statistics: Records of data compilations of births, fetal deaths, adult deaths, or marriages if the report was made to a public office within the requirements of the law.

Recusal: When a judge voluntarily removes himself from a case because of bias, conflict of interest, relation to a party, attorney or witness, or for any number of other reasons.

Redirect Examination: Follows cross-examination and is exercised by the party who first examined the witness. Usually, to correct damaged testimony.

Referee: A person to whom a cause pending in a court is referred by the court to take testimony, hear the parties, and report thereon to the court. He is an officer exercising judicial powers and is an arm of the court for a specific purpose.

Relief: Whatever a party to a legal proceeding asks the court to do: award support, enforce a prior court order, enjoin certain behavior, dismiss the complaint of the other party.

Religious Abuse: May not be just ritualistic abuse, but also such things as using religious tenets to excuse physical, sexual, or emotional abuse. Excusing one's physical abuse because the abuse victim is "evil", for instance, would in this author's opinion be religious abuse as well as physical abuse.

Relinquishment: To let go of one's possession and to completely give away control. To abandon.

Remand: To send back to court for further proceedings, as when a higher court sends back to a lower court.

Reply: The pleading filed in answer to the allegations of a claim or counterclaim. Either party may file a reply, which constitutes an answer to any new allegations raised by the other party in prior pleadings.

Reporting Domestic Violence: In some states domestic violence towards children must be reported by day care providers, teachers, doctors, psychotherapists and lawyers to child welfare authorities. A report of child abuse can lead to criminal prosecution and even placing the child in a foster home or public facility.

Reciprocity: To give and receive mutually. If an agreement is reciprocal, both parties must preform in the same manner.

Rescind: To abrogate or cancel a contract or agreement putting the parties in the same position they would have been in had there been no contract or agreement. A contract can be rescinded because of some defect in its formation (such as misrepresentation, duress, or undue influence) or it can be set aside by agreement by the parties, for example if they reach a new agreement.

Residential Parent: The parent with whom the child lives the majority of the time.

Respect: To consider worthy of high regard; to hold in high esteem. Should be offered and earned.

Resolution: A formal expression of the opinion of a rule-making body adopted by the vote of that body.

Respondent: Also called a Defendant. In a civil case, the defendant is the person against whom the lawsuit is brought. In a criminal case the defendant is the person charged with the offense.

Reporter: The person, who's job it is to transcribe testimony and other court related items.

Repression: Is forgetting memories of an unpleasant or unacceptable nature out of psychological need. This may include memories of traumatic events or taboo thoughts and feelings.

Repudiate: To turn away by not accepting, receiving, or considering. To desert a cause or party often in order to expose another.

Response Time: A determination made by the police, or CPS regarding the immediacy of the response and reaction needed for contact with the child and family to begin the initial assessment.

Responsibility: The ability to respond appropriately. Accountability for one's obligations, duties and behavior.

Rest: In legal terms, this means that the lawyer has concluded the evidence the lawyer wants to introduce at that stage of the trial.

Restitution: The act of attempting whole a litigant. Most often restitution is accomplished monetarily.

Restraining Order: An order granted without notice or hearing, demanding the preservation of the status quo or keeping one party from having contact with another party until a hearing can be had to determine the proper decision. A restraining order works both ways. One cannot approach another they have had a restraining order issued against.

Retainer: Money paid by the client to a professional to obtain a commitment to handle a specific assignment. A retainer can be a deposit against charges and may be a non-refundable engagement fee. A retainer that has not been billed against may be entirely or partly refundable regardless of any signed agreement.

Revenge: The act of inflicting or the intent to inflict injury in return for real or imagined injury.

Revised Statutes: A collection of the laws of a state or country systematically arranged usually by subject.

Rights: Something that requires no negotiation, but may require explanation.

Right of Meaningful Access: Is a component of due process, the court said. It cited a 1907 U.S. Supreme Court case for the proposition that "the right of access to the courts is a fundamental right protected by the Constitution." (Chambers v. Baltimore & Ohio Railroad Co., 207 U.S. 142.)

Risk: Is the state of being exposed to injury, pain or loss. To bring into peril as in harm or disaster. The likelihood that there is a danger. Likelihood a child will be maltreated in the future.

Risk Assessment: An assessment and measurement of the likelihood that a child will be maltreated in the future, frequently through the use of checklists, matrices, scales, and/or other methods of measurement.

Risk Factors: Behaviors and conditions present in the child, parent, and/or family that will likely contribute to child maltreatment occurring in the future.

Ritualistic Abuse: Uses false religious reasons to physically, sexually, or emotionally abuse in the context of a religious rite, such as raping someone as part of the ceremony.

Rules of Court: Rules that regulate practice and procedure before the various courts. In most jurisdictions, these rules are issued by the court itself, or by the highest court in that jurisdiction.

Rules of Evidence: The rules that govern the presentation and admissibility of oral and documentary evidence at court hearings or depositions.

S

Sanction: A word with two contradictory meanings. To "sanction" can mean to ratify or to approve, but it can also mean to punish. The "sanction" of a crime refers to the actual punishment, usually expressed as a fine or jail term. Sanctions are punishment for violation of accepted norms of court conduct and may be civil or criminal. Sanctions may be imposed on litigants or attorneys by the judge or they may be requested by one side in an action against the opposition. Failing to obey a scheduling or pretrial order, or if no appearance is made on behalf of a party at a scheduling or pretrial conference, or if a party or party's attorney is substantially unprepared to participate in the conference, or if a party or party's attorney fails to participate in good faith, the judge may upon motion or the judge's on initiative, impose sanctions. The battle over sanctions becomes a separate war in some lawsuits. Sanctions. Courts are reluctant to punish obstructionist lawyers or uncooperative parties.

Sane: The state of sound mental condition. Everyone is presumed sane until the opposite is demonstrated.

Schizophrenia: Sometimes includes fragmented thought and the perception of voices in ones head, as well as a feeling of being controlled by another entity; however, the shift in control does not appear as it does within MPD, and schizophrenic patients generally report their voices as being external in origin.

Sealing of Records: A judge may seal court or investigatory records if the matter deals with a child.

Search Warrant: A special and specific legal order used by police and prosecutors to locate and take private records, evidence, and information from a specific location for criminal investigation.

Secondary Authority: When doing legal research it is sometimes easier to use resources containing secondary rather than Primary Authority in which the actual law is available. Secondary authority is someone else's description, explanation, or analysis of the law. Secondary authority can provide background information as well as references to relevant statutes, regulations and cases. This can be found on the Internet, law review articles, legal forms, legal dictionaries, and full-blown treatises in law books.

Second-Hand Smoke: Also known as passive smoke refers to tobacco smoke in the atmosphere of a room or vehicle, also known as environmental tobacco smoke (E.T.S.). Involuntary smoking is the inhalation of the environmental tobacco smoke from the air. Second-Hand smoke is make up of mainstream smoke the smoker inhales, side-stream smoke that comes from the cigarette between puffs and exhaled smoke, which is the smoke inhaled and then breathed out.

Security of Costs: A motion that may be filed by one side if they are in doubt about the opposition's willingness or ability to pay costs if they lose the case and are ordered by the judge to cover filing expenses incurred by both parties.

Self-authenticated: The ability to attest to its own substantiated truthfulness, genuineness, accuracy or validity. Such as government and public documents, as well as newspapers and periodicals.

Self-Incrimination: When a person tells of a crime that person committed.

Separation Anxiety Disorder: Inappropriate and excessive anxiety concerning separation from home or from those to whom the individual is attached that: lasts at least four weeks, causes significant distress or impairment in personal, social, and academic. Recurrent excessive distress when separation from home or major attachment figures is anticipated or occurs causing persistent and excessive worry. The child worries about losing, or about possible harm such as getting lost or being kidnapped befalling the major attachment figure(s). Reluctance to go to school or sleep without major attachment figure9s0 being near. There may even be repeated nightmares involving the theme of separation repeated complaints of physical symptoms when separation from major attachment figure9(s) occurs or is anticipated.

Service: Also called Service of Process. Delivery of a pleading, notice, or other paper in a lawsuit to the opposite party. Both parties to a lawsuit must receive notice of all court actions. If a person cannot be found or if they deliberately conceal their whereabouts, most states allow alternatives to personal service. Examples: mail service, service to a responsible adult at the primary address, mail (via postal service) and nail (attach to front door of residence) and publication in the newspaper.

Settlement: Agreed resolution of the dispute.

Settlement Depression: Custody battles keep you on an emotional roller coaster for so long that settling is like hitting a brick wall. Since each side must give in so much to reach an agreement it is common to feel a huge let down or even depressed after signing a settlement agreement.

Sexual Abuse: Sexual contact between two relatives is incest and is a form of sexual abuse in some cases, such as a parent and its child. Sexual contact between a caregiver or a teacher and a child is sexual abuse.

Shall: As used in a legal document, it means that the action is mandatory.

Shelters: Many cities have public and private agencies that provide shelters for battered spouses (usually women) and children. Victims of violence fear more violence will result from leaving home, so the locations are kept secret. Most of these facilities provide counseling and legal help when victims cannot afford to pay for such services.

Shepardized: "Shepard's Citations for Cases" is probably the most powerful tool in the law library and was designed predominantly as a tool to update what has happened to a ruling on a case. It is used primarily as a means to checking a case for its precedential or persuasive value to cases you are researching.

Show Cause: Written application to the court for some type of relief, which is made on such notice to the other party as the court directs.

Siblings: Two or more biological or adopted brothers and sisters.

Significant Other: Modern term for husband, wife, betrothed or person you may or may not be living with on an intimate basis.

Sine Die: Adjourned without giving any future date of meeting or hearing. A court that adjourns *sine die* essentially dismisses the case by saying that it never wants to hear the case again! A meeting, which adjourns sine die has simply not set a date for it's next meeting.

Sixth Amendment: provides you with: the right to a speedy and public trial by an impartial jury: the right to be informed of the law and potential punishment faced for violation of the law: the right to confront (examine at trial) witnesses against you: the right to compel witnesses in your favor to appear and testify at trial: the right to have an attorney for your defense.

Slander: Words falsely spoken that tend to damage the reputation of another. Base and defamatory spoken words tending to harm another's reputation, business or means of livelihood. Both libel and slander are forms of defamation.

Sole Custody: One parent is given physical custody of the child and the right to make all the major decisions about the child.

Sole Managing Conservator (SMC): Person who has total care, custody or control of a child's physical health or welfare.

Solicitor: This refers to lawyers in England that restrict their practice to the giving of legal advice and do not normally litigate. That court room. A legal distinction is made between solicitors and barristers, the former with exclusive privileges of giving oral or written legal advice, and the latter with exclusive privileges of preparing and conducting litigation in the courts. In other words, solicitors don't appear in court on a client's behalf and barristers don't give legal advice to clients. Barristers and solicitors work as a team: the solicitor would typically make the first contact with a client and if the issue cannot be resolved and proceeds to trial, the solicitor would transfer the case to a barrister for the duration of the litigation. Lawyers in Canada, sometimes use the title "barrister and solicitor" even though, contrary to England, there is no legal distinction between the advising and litigating roles. Canadian lawyers can litigate or give legal advice. In the USA lawyers are referred to as "attorneys".

Special Master: A court-appointed individual, usually an attorney, who assists the court in moving a case forward. Problems relating to pretrial discovery often are handled by a special master who schedules and coordinates discovery. Such procedure is necessary where one or both parties fail to comply with discovery requests, or when the parties can't agree on a psychologist a special master can make the selection. Note that the special master is not a judge -- his opinions carry weight, but not the final word.

Split Custody: Time with and responsibility for the child are shared, not necessarily on a 50/50 basis.

Stalking: To pursue stealthily or under cover by following, tracking, chasing with a purposeful goal. It is against the law to stalk another person. "Stalking" someone across state lines will be a federal crime punishable by up to five years in prison. "Interstate stalking" is traveling across a state line "with the intent to injure or harass another person" and placing that person "in reasonable fear" of death or injury to themselves or a member of their immediate family. Defendants can be given up to 10 years if they cause a "serious bodily injury" or use a dangerous weapon, and up to 20 years if they cause a "permanent disfigurement" or life-threatening injury.

***Stare Decisis*:** The doctrine of American law, which states when a court has formulated a principle of law, as applicable to a given set of facts, it will follow that principle and apply it in future cases where the facts are substantially the same. It connotes the decision of present cases on the basis of past precedent. The decision is always binding on the parties to the case and it becomes precedent and becomes a Binding Precedent for future cases in lower within its jurisdiction. On all fours a case in which Binding President matches exactly and the judge must decide using. Distinguished the difference.

State Clearinghouse: A state agency that keeps records of missing children and may assist law enforcement agencies in trying to recover missing children.

State's Evidence: Testimony given by an accomplice or participant in a crime, tending to convict others.

State Statutes: Are state laws that cover everything except your Constitutional Rights.

Status Quo: The posture or position, which existed. What is shall remain.

Statute: The written law in contradistinction to the unwritten law.

Statute Law: Law that is made by legislative enactment.

Statute of Limitations: A certain time allowed by statute in which litigation must be brought.

Statutory Rape: The common law definition of rape has not proven adequate to reflect modern values. It is limited to sex without consent and with a woman, and only where the victim is not the wife of the rapist. Many states have enacted laws, which include under the charge of rape, sex with a minor even if done with the minor's consent, sex without consent regardless of whether the victim is male or female, and sex without consent regardless of the matrimonial bond between victim and rapist.

Stay: A stopping of a judicial proceeding by order of the court. A stay can stop an adoption, divorce, execution or release from incarceration.

Step-parent: A parent gained by marriage to one of the child's biological parents. A step-parent is not obligated to support the children of the parent to whom the step-parent is married unless the step-parent legally adopts the children.

Stipulation: Agreement between the parties relating to matters of procedure or certain undisputed facts or issues, which need not be proven during the course of the trail.

Stockholm Syndrome: Is a theory, which describes the children as 'hostages' afraid of the mother, and obeying her as a means of survival.

Substantiated/Founded: A CPS determination that credible evidence exists that child abuse or neglect has occurred.

Subpoena: Is an official document served to notify persons not directly involved in a lawsuit they are to appear for deposition or court at a stated time, date and place. It insures that unwilling witnesses or withheld evidence comes to court.

Subpoena *Duces Tecum*: A process by which the court commands a witness to appear and produce certain documents, records, or other physical things in a trial.

Subornation of Perjury: Is the crime of inducing or paying another to make false oath. Proof of subornation of perjury requires both proof of perjury in fact and that the perjured statement was procured by the accused. There must also be proof that the suborner knew or should have know that such oaths or testimony would be false.

Substantive Law: That law, which establishes rights and obligations as distinguished from procedural law, which is concerned with rules for establishing their judicial enforcement.

Summons: A document served upon the defendant that tells them a suit has been filed against him/her and tells him/her when to file an answer or appear in court.

Surrogate Parent: One who is not a child's parent, but who stands in the place of the parent and is charged with a parent's rights, duties, and responsibilities, either by virtue of voluntary assumption or court appointment. One willing or able to perform some duties of a parent for the benefit of a child while surrendering any rights to the child.

Surveillance or Subrosa: The term "sub-rosa" comes from the old cloak and dagger days and means "beneath the rose." If an agent placed a rose on the table, in meant that they were speaking in secret. Today, the term is commonly used to refer to surveillance work. There are many different types of surveillance including visual, video, telephone, static and rolling.

Suspension: The restraining of a person from doing something for a period of time, generally used as a disciplinary action.

Sustain: When an attorney requests an objection, if the judge wishes to block the testimony or evidence he will support the objection by saying "sustained."

Syllabus: A condensed treatment of a subject. A compendium, diggers abridgment or overview.

Synopsis: A version of a larger work produced by shortening without basic alteration of intent or language.

T

Tainted Evidence: see fruit of the poisonous tree.

Take-Home Pay: The amount of money a person receives after taxes.

Tamper: To interfere improperly or in violation of the law such as to tamper with a document. The term "jury tampering" means to illegally disrupt the independence of a jury member with a view to influencing that juror otherwise than by the production of evidence in open court.

Threat: A declaration of an intention to inflict punishment, loss, or pain on another or to injure another by some wrongful act.

Temporary Custody: Applications to the court for interim relief for custody of a child pending the final decision of the court.

Temporary Injunction: Restraining order.

Temporary Motions: Sometimes called pendente lite motions. Applications to the court for interim relief pending the final decision of the court. Typical temporary motions include child support, attorneys' fees, costs, expert fees, custody, visitation, enforcement or modification of prior temporary orders.

Temporary Restraining Order: An order of the court prohibiting a party from doing something that affects the other party, such as threatening, harassing, or physical abuse on the opposition, or the child.

Tender Years Doctrine: Decisions that weigh the mother's role more heavily than the father's in caring for young children, especially infants. Not as popular as in the past, but still used by individual courts.

Term of Court: A definite time period prescribed by law for a court to administer its duties. Term and session are often used interchangeably, but, technically, term is the statutory time prescribed for judicial business and session is the time a court actually sits to hear cases. In general, terms of court no longer have any special significance, fixed periods of days having replaced the stated terms of court.

Testify: To make statements under oath.

Testimony: Oral evidence given under oath usually in court or deposition in response to questions, as distinguished from evidence derived from writing and other sources.

Therapeutic Supervision: Is the provision of supervision of contacts between the child and parent, as well as intervention and modeling to help improve the parent-child interactions. This service may be offered only by a certified or licensed mental health professional as required by individual states or jurisdictions. Because this service is provided by trained, professionals, evaluations and recommendations for further parent-child contact can be made.

Third-Party: In child custody there are many people with which the child may wish to maintain contact. Often visitation orders will include: grandparents, great-grandparents, stepparents, foster parents, and siblings.

Tooling the Statute of Limitations: A legal extension to the time limit for action.

Tools of the Crime: The devices used in the commission of the illegal act. Tools may include burglary devices, telephone taping equipment, or even a worthless check, a false document, or even a fraudulent advertisement.

Tort: An injury or wrong committed, either with or without force, to the person or property of another. A lawsuit for money to make amends for damages.

Transcript: A typewritten record of testimony taken by a court reporter during court or a deposition. Visual evidence created from audio or video information.

Trespass: An unlawful interference with one's person, property, or rights.

In common law, trespass was a form of action brought to recover damages for an injury to one's person or property or relationship with another.

Trial: A formal court hearing.

Trial Memorandum: A document presented to the court on the eve of the trial or as the case is announced in court. It is an outline of the case an attorney intends to present to the court. The outline includes: a statement of the case, a brief actual summary, names of the witnesses and what they will testify to, evidence and the value of the evidence, the law pertaining to the case, a prayer of what the attorney wants the court to do and a notarized statement as to the truth of the a for mentioned information. If possible a copy was filed and a copy given to the clerk of the court in advance of the proceeding. This is a valuable tool in the event an appeal is necessary.

Truth: Keeping close to fact and avoiding distortion or misrepresentation.

U

UIFSA: The American uniform child and spousal support legislation, the Uniform Interstate Family Support Act already adopted and implemented by most states and expected to be law throughout the USA soon. It is the successor of URESA and is a long-arm statutes as it gives the state, which issues the first support order jurisdiction over the support payor anywhere in the USA for the purposes of varying that order.

Ultra Vires: Without authority. An act, which is beyond the powers or authority of the person or organization, which took it.

Unclean Hands: The principle that a party seeking redress in a court must not have done anything dishonest or unethical or failed to comply in the transaction in which that party seeks fairness.

Unconditional: Absolute, unreserved.

Uncontested Custody: A proceeding in which a person sued for custody does not fight it or may have reached an agreement with the opposition before or during the proceedings.

Under Protest: Making of a payment or the doing of an act under an obligation while reserving the right to object to the obligation at a later date.

Undue Influence: The power exerted over the mind or behavior of another, destroying the requisite of free will. Power that goes beyond a normal or acceptable limit.

Uniform Laws: Are drafts of laws that states may adopt in whole, in part, or not at all. As far as child custody is concerned there are uniform laws that address jurisdiction, kidnapping, abduction remedies, and support.

Ultra Conservative: Used to describe a person, a community or a judge that strongly resists change and often favors a prior condition.

Ultra Liberal: Used to describe a person, a community or a judge that is not bound by traditional forms, tends to depart sharply from the usual. Is tolerant, indulgent and unorthodox, often favoring new approaches to old problems.

Unconstitutional: A specific act, sometimes legal, that is in direct violation of the Constitution of the United States.

Undisputed Fact: A fact in a lawsuit that neither party question.

Undue Influence: Influence of another that destroys the requisite free will of a person nullifying or invalidating the decision making of the person being influenced. The exercise of undue influence is suggested by excessive insistence, superiority of will or mind, the relationship of the parties or pressure on the person by other means to do what he or she is unable, practically to refuse.

Unethical: Not in accordance with the standard followed in a business or profession.

Unfit: Unsuitable, incompetent or not adapted for a particular obligation, use or service.

Unimpeachable Witness: A person with no stake or investment in what they are to see and who may be an observer that can give an account without bias, giving no opportunity for censure.

Unperfected: To fail to file a brief that conforms to a rigid format that is bound like a book with a table of contents and an alphabetical list of all the cases to be cited as precedent in the appeal within the time allotted by law, all the original transcripts and exhibits from the original trial and a brief with the presentation of the facts and the law, with emphasis on why the decision should or should not be upheld.

Unsubstantiated/Unfounded: Being without cause or occasion. A CPS determination that credible evidence does not exist that child abuse or neglect has occurred.

Unwed: Being without a spouse. Having unwed parents does not affect the legal status of a child or the parent's obligation to the child. An unwed parent without custody of the child will be required to pay child support and may have the right to visitation and may seek custody.

Unwritten Law: Law originated in custom, not by enactment.

V

Vacate: To make a place or thing empty. To clear a legal matter by its invalidation.

Venue: The proper county, city or geographical area for the trial.

***Verba fortius accipiuntur contra proferentem*:** Latin: a principle of construction whereby if words of a contract are ambiguous, of two equally possible meanings, they should be interpreted against the author of the words and not against the other party.

Verbatim: Word-for-word.

Verbiage: The way words are assembled to send a message.

Verdict: The formal finding or decision of the court.

Verification: A document signed under penalty of perjury and attached to another document stating the second document is true.

Victim: Is a person injured or destroyed as the result of event or circumstance. It is common for the victim of child abuse in one generation to become the victimizer, inflicting child abuse on the next generation.

Victory: The overcoming of an enemy in battle or of an antagonist in any contest.

Vigilant: To pay close attention with a view to anticipating approaching danger or opportunity.

Vindictive: Actions or words motivated by a desire for malicious damage to another. Thought, action, or appearance of anger to another person.

Visitation: The process facilitating the right of a child to have regular contact with the non-custodial parent, step-parents, grandparents, psychological parents and siblings. Sometimes called Contact Orders.

Visiting Parent: May be a biological parent or other adult, who is authorized to have contact with the children.

Visit Supervisor: Is a Child Access Monitor responsible for observing the contact and seeking to ensure the safety of the children during the visit and transition between parents.

W

Webmaster: The person who designed and/or maintains the website or webpages on the Internet.

Website: A configuration of personal or business information presented as data, graphics, photos and sound on a computer via the Internet.

World Wide Web: Thousands of overlapping information portals that allow users to access sites and send communications via telephone wire and satellite link.

Index

A

Abandonment
- Abandon, definition 564
- Modification for, definition 590
- Neglect 329
- Panic Situation #08 296
- to Grandparents Panic SIT #36 305

Abatement, definition 564
Abduction
- definition 564
- Project Return 264
- Resistant Children 339
- Retrieval Questionnaire 346
- see Kidnapping

Abductor Profile, Parental Kidnapping 344
Abet, definition 564
Abrogate, definition 564
Absence of
- Entry, definition 564
- Public Record, definition 564

Absolute Right to Tape Record Trial, case 488
Abuse 324
- & Kidnapping, Chapter 17, 271, 324
- Abandoned 326
- Arrest for Abuse 333
- Battered Woman Syndrome 568
- Child Prostitution 326
- Children's Reactions to 327
- Cognitive Ability & Memory Loss 572
- Emotional Abuse 326
- Emotional abuse 330
- Emotional Maltreatment 326
- Emotional or Verbal, definition 578
- Excuse 19
- False Accusation, Panic Situation #07 296
- Fight Response Mode 581
- Financial Child Abuser 183
  - definition 581
- Financial, definition 581
- Flight Response Mode 581
- Guidelines for Interviewing Children 273
- Has Your Child Been Abused 334
- Indications of Negligence or 327
- Legal System, Right-to-remedy/access 415
- List in your Contact Log 105
- Munchausen Syndrome by Proxy 334
- Non-Sexual Exploitation 326
- of the system, Vexatious Litigation 414
- Penalty for Reporting Suspected 328
- Physical, Is an Issue 26
- Recognizing Children Exposed to Abuse 326
- Religious, definition 599
- Seeing Abuse is Abuse 271

Serious Physical Injury 325
Sexual Assault 325
Types of
Abandoned 326
Child Prostitution 326
Commercial Sexual Exploitation 325
Emotional Abuse 326
Emotional Maltreatment 326
Molestation of a Child 325
Neglect 325
Physical Abuse 325
Serious Physical Injury 325
Sexual Assault 325
Sexual Conduct 325
Verbal or Mental 26
Violence Lethality Assessment 342
Abuse of Discretion 380
definition 565
Academic Expert 219
Accident
definition 565
Investigation Reconstruction 132
Accomplice, definition 565
Accord and Satisfaction, definition 565
Accusation, definition 565
Acknowledgement of Paternity (AOP) 426
Acquittal, definition 567
Act, How to Behave From Now On 36
Action, definition 565
Actionable, definition 565
Activities
Start a Support Group 479
to Avoid 95
to Cultivate 64
ADC or AFDC, definition 565
Addiction
definition 565
Address Books 353
Administrative Cases 392
Admissible Evidence 101
Not, Fruit of the Poisonous Tree 352
Websites as 101
Admonishment of Attorney 160
Adoption
Adopted Children, Child Support 446
Second Parent-adoption 551
Adultery, Case
In re Marriage of Roberts, Illinois 523
Adversarial Divorce, definition 565
Adversary System, definition 566
Advice
avoid the Rescuer 33
Free on the Internet 14
Not to Comply with Court Order 152
Not to Pay Child Support 451
on the internet, Lawyer 588
Unsolicited Help 32
AFDC 137
Affidavit of Preference 254
definition 566
example 255
Panic Situation # 37 305
Agenda 58, 72
Children's 72
Insidious (Passive Aggression) 594
of others Affecting other Parent 72
other Peoples 58
Rescuer's 33
Aggravation, definition 566
Aggressive 566
Don't Be 359
Passive, definition 594
Aid to Families with Dependent Children 137, 566
Aim to Negotiate, Not to Win 71
Alabama
Child Support Ends 447
Child support for married minor 447
Deal v. Deal, Step-parent 512
Ex parte Murphy, Move away 272
Nexus Gay/Lesbian Parents 527
Non-Bio Father May Get Custody 483
Recorded calls 488
Stone v. Gulf American Fire, Income 439
Support Accounting 455
Alaska
Child Support Ends 447
Elsberry v. Elsberry, Income 463
Indian Child Welfare 387
McQuade v. McQuade, Move away 272
Nexus Gay/Lesbian Parents 527
Poverty Guidelines 427
Provides Child Support Credit 514
Same Sex 536
Spoilation of evidence 104
Alcohol
Home testing kits 131
Treatment, Mundon v. Mundon 525
use or Abuse 27
Alias, definition 566
Alienation
Conscious Messages 268
of Affections, definition 566
Recalcitrant Parent, Children 496
Syndrome, case
Daubert V. Merrell 496
Unconscious Messages 268
Alimony, definition 566
Allegation

Allegation see Abuse
definition 566
False 337
Recognizing Children Exposed 326
False, Request Supervised Visitation 338
Profile Precursor for False Accuser 338
Alternating or Divided Custody 21
Alternative Dispute Resolution, definition 566
Alternative Lifestyle
definition 566
Gay, Lesbian 28
Amendments 5, 9, and 14, Doe v. Irwin 517
Amgen, Inc. v. Hoechst Marion Roussel
Documents Produced by Mistake 486
Amicus Curiae, definition 566
Amphetamines, Home testing kit 131
Analytical, a type of thinking 73
Anatomical Dolls Fail Frye Test, case 487
Anger 320, 414
Against You 273, 398
and Joy 95
Dealing With the Anger in Our Children 321
Dealing With the Anger of Others 321
Dealing With Your 320
definition 566
Legal Papers Cause 294
Medea Syndrome 508
The One I Feed 48
Annulment, definition 566
Anonymity, Security, Privacy on Internet 50
Answer
definition 566
Safe Answers During the Battle 84
Safe, When You Don't Have Custody 473
Answering Machine
Needs no permission to record 132
tapes as evidence 131
tapes at discovery 353
Antenuptial, definition 566
Antisocial Behavior, Appearance of 405
Appeal
Change of Circumstances 491
definition 566
Don't Hire Attorneys That Say Appeal 148
Findings of Fact
Abney v. W. Rest. Mut. Case. Co 419
Harmless Error 583
Prejudicial Error 596
Should You Worry About Oppositions 414
the Process 413
the Threat 412
Appearance, definition 567
Appellant, definition 567
Appellate Court 412
Appellee, definition 567
Appointment Book 99, 353
Arbiter, definition 567
Arbitration 133
definition 567
Argument, definition 567
Arizona
Bryan v. Bryan, Step-Parent 512
Child Support Ends 447
Child Support Hall of Shame 455
Family Support Center 54
Fenn v. Fenn, Step-parent 512
Fink v. Fink, Parent in Fact 16
Kidnapping Damages Awarded 507
Lottery Payments Frozen 516
Must comply with Title IV-D 464
Nexus Gay/Lesbian Parents 527
Perez v. Campbell, License Revocation 464
Prosecution for visitation interference 492
v. Johnson, Illegal wiretap 488
v. Stanley, 4th Amendment 487
Arkansas
Barnes v. Morrow, Support 511
Child Support Ends 447
Spoilation of Evidence 103
Stepp v. Gray, Income 440
Arraignment, definition 567
Arrears, definition 567
Arrest
definition 567
for Abuse 333
Things You Can Get Arrested For 39
When the Police are Called 39
Art Classes 261
Assault, definition 567
Assertive 359
Assets, definition 567
Assumptions for Negotiation 76
Atkinson v. Atkinson, case 510
Attachment 567
Disorder 567
Attention Deficit Disorder (ADD) 567
Case of Kim Lee Ong, A Child 398
Sit #74 Child's Problem Ignored 317
Attest, definition 568
Attitude Adjustment
Abuse Excuse 19
Dead Hand 19
Duck Muck 47
Attorney 133
Admonishment is indicated when 160
Advised Not to Comply with Court Order 152
and Lies 291
Before 10 After 5 148

Breach of Attorney-Client Relationship 159
Breach of Duty 159
calling yours too often 37
Chapter 9, 141
Client Privilege, definition 568
Communicating with the Enemy 152
Communication Notes, example 151, 185
Comparison Form, example 146
Confidentiality 149
Confidentiality of Case File in Question 315
Contingency Fee, defined 573
Damage as a direct result of action 159
definition 568
Disbar, definition 576
Disbarment is indicated when 163
Discharge #1 157, 158
Discharge Letter 157, 158
Don't Hire Attorneys Who 147
Due Diligence, definition 577
Evaluation, example 144
Face Fee, definition 579
Facing the Mad Dog 360
Fails to show a Duty of Care 159
Fees
Cases 485
Comparison 146
for Negotiation 75
Free Internet Advice 14
Help form the Bar Association 159
How to Find One 144
Invoice, example 155
Keep a Good Attorney Happy 146
Local Counsel, definition 588
Malpractice, definition 589
More Work, More Money 424
My Lawyer Really Screwed Me, SIT #47 308
no Statute of limitations to sue 159
of Counsel, definition 592
Opposition's, attorney costing you $$ 305
Panic SIT #34 304
Preparation for Deposition 357
Privilege, General Rules of 596
Privileged Relationship 149
Professional Liability, definition 597
Public Reprimand is indicated when 162
resist close observation by their clients 81
Sanctions Against, definition 600
Sex & Your 153
sue in Small Claims Court 158
Suing Your 158
Suspension is indicated when 161
the Bad Rap Lawyers Get 148
Violations of duties owed to Clients 160
Wants to Quit, Panic SIT #39 306
will not be an Accessory to Crime 156
Work Product, definition 568
Work-Product Privilege 485
Attrition, as a Strategy 57
Audi Alteram Partem, definition 568
Australia, Travel Documents 264
Automatic Transfer of Custody, Mundon 525

B

Bad
But not that bad, Demur 576
Faith, definition 568
Parenting 273
Parenting or PAS? 187
Badger, definition 568
Bail
Child Support Bond 456
definition 568
Visitation Bond 23
Bailiff, definition 568
Bald Heads on Women 404
Banking Records 353
Bankruptcy
Child Support 454
Perez v Campbell 464
will delay trial 425
Bar Association, definition 568
Barratry, definition 568
Barsky v. Board of Regents, case
Politics may inhibit personal rights 519
Battered
Batterers, definition 568
Wife Syndrome
Cognitive Ability & Memory Loss 572
Woman Syndrome (BWS) 568
Battery, definition 568
BBS, definition 569
Beards & Mustaches Effect on Believability 404
Before
10 A.M. After 5 P.M. 148
Next Contact, From Now On 36
Behavior
beware the Rescuer 33
Defensive 58
Requiring Rescue 37
Believability Factor, definition 569
Believe What Is Seen, Not What Is Heard 201, 583
Bell v. Burson, ,License Revocation 464
Bell v. City of Milwaukee, 14th Amendment 516
Bench
defined 569
Trial 569
Warrant, definition 569

Bender Gestalt 240
Benzodiazepines, Home testing kit 131
Best
    /Worst States for Child Support Collection 457
    Attitude for Paying Child Support 452
    Attitude for Receiving Child Support 454
    Evidence, definition 569
    Time to Depose 356
Best Interest 25, 54
    #36 Grandparents' Custody Interrupted 305
    #54 Change of Circumstances 311
    Children Who Want to Choose 254
    Examples of Judges' Rulings 412
    Factors Influencing Decisions 19
    Move Away 271
    of the Child Test 511
    of the Child, non-issue 28
    Psychological Parent 17
    Relationship Inventory 45
    U.S. v. Green (1824) 17
    Uniform Marriage and Divorce Act 28
    Whatever constitutes 51
Better Decisions 55
Bhama v. Bhama, PAS, MI 495
Bifurcation, definition 569
Bill of Particulars, definition 569
Binding or Non-Binding, Arbitration 567
Biological Father v Adoptive Parents, SIT 58 311
Bipolar Disorder, Situation #71 316
Bird Nest Custody 21
Birthfather/Birthmother, definition 569
Black Letter Statement, definition 569
Blameless, for Your Actions, Children 293
Blended Family 26
Blood Type Test for Maternity & Paternity 138
Blood v. Margis, case
    Pro Se protection of civil rights 518
Blush GJ, False Allegations 507
Bond
    Bail Bond, when to arrange for 40
    Bonding with New Traditions 475
    Child Support 456
    of Parent & Child, Carsen v. Elrod 517
    Visitation Bond 23
Bonita Kline Curtis v. Philip H. Kline, College 464
Book of Your Life 201
Borderline Personality Disorder, definition 569
Boyfriend won't get custody 483
Bradley v. Fisher, Judges have no immunity 518
Brazil Travel Documents 264
Breaking and Entering, definition 569
Brent Moss, case 458
Bricklin Perceptual Scales 240
Brief
    definition 569
    for Appeal 413
Buddies & Pals 87
Budding Integrity, definition 569
Bugging, definition 569
Bunker (Your Home) 34
    protect it from Peeping Tom Law 34
Burden of Proof, definition 569
Burgess v. Burgess, case
    Joint custody parent to move out of state 491
Burglar Alarm System 25
Buying the Pain Away 272

C

Calculative a type of Thinking 74
Calendar 129
    As evidence Personal, Kitchen, Business 353
    Court, definition 569
    example 101
California
    Can't Sue Wife 482
    Child Support Ends 447
    Contra Costa v. Lemon, Lottery, Support 439
    CPS can remove Child 332
    Criminal Nonsupport 458
    Estevez v. Superior Court, Income 440
    Has excluded DNA 138
    Husband Can't Sue Wife for Lying 482
    International Support Enforcement 457
    Jordache v. Brobeck, Phlenger & Harrison 158
    Licensed Investigators 166
    Made Move Away Easier 272
    Marriage of Burgess, Move Away 272
    Marriage of Meegan, Religion, Support 462
    Murphy's Law 591
    Nexus Gay/Lesbian Parents 527
    No Limitations on Bar Complaints 159
    Paternity Never Settled 482
    Paternity Suits May Never be Settled 482
    Pencovic v. Pencovic, Religious, Support 461
    Same Sex 536
    Spoilation of Evidence 104
    Swain v. Swain, Step-Parent 513
    Tort action on a contingency 459
    Willfully failing to make support 465
    Wire Tap - Recording 487
    Worth v. Worth, Income 439
Caller Id 129
Calling
    for the Rule, definition 570
    Friends & Attorney Many Times 37
    People Late at Night 37
Camera

35 MM 129
Peeping Tom Law 35
example #2 175
Video 130
Canada's International Project Return 264
Canadian Child Support 466
Canon Law, definition 570
Capacity, definition 570
Capias, definition 570
Caribbean Travel Permission 264
Carsen v. Elrod, case Parent child bond 517
CASA 570
Case
14 Child Support Court Cases 461
Analysis 151
Behind License Revocation 464
Bell v. City of Milwaukee,14th Amend. 516
Blood v. Margis, Pro Se 518
Boosters 59
Bradley v. Fisher, Protection/ Judges 518
Carsen v. Elrod, Bond of Parent & Child 517
Commonwealth v. Butler, RO 518
Commonwealth v. Carter RO 490
Commonwealth v. Laskowski, RO 518
Court may not favor religion over none 524
Craig v. Boren, Gender 518
Doe v. Irwin, Amend. 5, 9, and 14 517
Drummond v. State of Maryland 463
Franz v. United State, Rights 516
Frontiero v. Richardson, Sex, Race, Origin 518
Grayned v. City of Rockford, Vague laws 518
Gregoire v. Biddle, Protection for Judge 519
Imbler v. Pachtman, Title 18 520
in Interest of Cooper, Due Process 517
in Point, definition 570
Intentional Infliction of Distress 484
Johnson v. Robinson, Must Be Reasonable 518
Kelson v. Springfield 14th Amendment 517
Killers 91
Langton v. Maloney Due Process 517
Law, definition 570
Leis v. Leis, Shared parenting 489
Luke v. Luke, Shared Parenting 490
Mabra v. Schmidt 14th Amendment 517
Matter of Delaney, Right to bond 518
Matter of Gentry, 5th Amendment 517
Mav v. Anderson, Parent's right 517
Orr v. Orr, Gender 517
Peterson v Stanczak, Judges not Immune 520
Pierson v. Ray, Judges prejudice 518
Raucci v. Town of Rotterdam, Protect 518
Reporters, appellate decisions 414
Santosky v. Kramer, protections 516
Stanton v. Stanton, Gender 517
Strategy 393
U.S. v. Oplinger 519
Wo v. Hopkins, 14th Amendment 517
Yang v. Government Employees Ins. 103
Case Law, definition 570
Caseload, definition 570
Cases
Administrative 392
Barillari v. City of Milwaukee 525
Black Letter Statement
J.A. Tobin Cons.v. State Hwy. Com. 569
Calloway v. Kinkelaar 525
Case #VR921200 Askren 520
Civil 392
Criminal 392
Dawson v. Emerson, Bio-Father 312
Frauenshuh v. Giese 524
Kendall v. Kendall 523
Law is Partially Unconstitutional 464
Meyer v. Nebraska 523
Mundon v. Mundon 525
Osteras v. Osteras 524
Pater v. Pater 523
Police - Psychologists Sued in D.V. 525
Prince v. Massachusetts 523
Re in the Marriage of Knighton 522
Ricketts v. City of Columbia, Mo. 526
Saul v. Brunetti 521
Thomas v. Review Board 523
Troxel, Jenifer V. Granville, Tommie 520
Types of 392
Watkins v. Nelson 522
Yoder v. Wisconsin 524
Zucco v. Garrett 523
Zummo v. Zummo 522
Caseworker
As an Expert 221
Competency 570
Family Assessment Outline 330
Reporting Suspected Abuse To 328
When CPS Gets A Call 328
When Police Are Called 39
Cash Bond, definition 570
Cause of Action, definition 570
Cause, definition 570
Caveat 570
Cease & Desist Order, definition 570
Cellular Telephone 130
Censorship, Impose it 81
Certified Order, definition 570
Chain of Evidence 103
Chambers, defined 570
Chameleon, definition 570
Change

in Non-Custodial Circumstances, # 54 311, 312, 314, 315
of Venue, definition 570
Strategies 58
Change of Circumstance
Appeal of Custody Modification 489
Doubtfire Clause or First Right of Refusal 490
Lengthy Childcare 26
Searcy v. Seedorff 525
Visitation Denial or Interference 27
Character Witness, definition 570
Chart
Child's Hospital Visit List 209
Computer Generated, definition 572
Computer Modeling, definition 572
definition 570
Identify Concerns #2 Grades/Attendance 235
To Identify Concerns #1 Moving 210
Types of information you can 234
Chattel, definition 571
Check
Expert's Deposition 364
Opposition's Deposition 364
Your Deposition 361
Checking, Savings & Credit Card 25, 353
Chemical Dependence 571
Chickadee 261
Child 26, 455
#38 Won't go to Visitation 306
12 Year Old, may choose Conservator 254
1981 Study, Effects of Custody 484
Abduction
Hague Convention on International 497
Remedies Act, International 503
Resistant 339
American Indian Child Welfare 386
Budding Integrity, definition 569
Condition Report
form Example #1 211
form Example #2 212
Dealing With Your Child's Fears 257
Dependent According to the Court 426
Dependent According to the IRS 427
Disallowing a Child to Testify 551
Endangerment 26
Fear of
Abandonment 258
Failure 257
Fear 258
Monsters 257
Not Being Important 258
Not Doing the Right Thing 258
the Future 257
Time 258
Trying 257
hates going to Visitation 14
I Don't Want to Visit You Anymore 267
in Danger, Panic Situation # 16 299
Information Children Need 270
Make Evaluation Easier for Your 190
Not Charged Misconduct, PAS 496
Phone Calls Upset, Panic Situation #15 299
Pressuring Parent 304
Retraining 36
Should Have Responsibilities 269
Testifying in Court 395
Visitation is a Right of the Child 21, 264
What Can You Do to Help 259
What Do I Tell My 273
Child Abuse 296
Charge, False 296
DHSS report, on PAS 489
Muchausen Syndrome by Proxy 334
Preventing False Allegations of 336
Second-hand Smoke is 324
What is 324
Child Care
#9 During Custody 92
Albright v. Albright, MS 531
Departure from Guidelines 450
Dependent Credits 428
Document Poor Choices 107
in Evaluation 242
Lengthy 26
Letter from Caregiver 204
Parent over Others 490
Strange Situation Test 241
Child Custody
Jurisdiction Act, Uniform 507
when & where Your Money is spent 445
Child Support
Ability to Earn 445
Acknowledged Father 137
Acknowledged Mother 137
Acknowledgement of Paternity (AOP) 426
Adopted Children 446
Advised Not to Pay 152, 451
as an Expense/Debit 453
as Income 454
Bankruptcy 454
Barnes v. Morrow, AR 511
Below the Guidelines 450
Best Attitude for Paying 452
Best Attitude for Receiving 454
Best/Worst States for Collection of 457
Bond 456
Brown v. Birman Managed Care, TN 512
Can't Pay 451

Can't See No-Pay 451
Canada 466
Chambers by Cochran v. Sanderson, Income 440
Chapter 21, 437
Child Reaches Age of Majority 446
Child's Active Military Duty 446
Collection Methods 456
Cost Sharing Guideline 443
Credit from 16 States Provide 514
Custodial Parent's State to Modify 514
Daily Expenses 445
definition 571
Departures from the Guidelines 450
Dependent Credits 428
Doesn't Come 455
Edwards v. Edwards, WV 512
Emancipated Minor 446
Enforcement, Full Faith & Credit 348, 457
Equitable Parent 16
Estevez v. Superior Court, CA, Income 440
Expense Log example 456
Federal Government Force States 464
Financial Support Theory 445
Financial Theory 443
Government Benefit Diversion 456
Guideline Models 443
Hardship Income Deduction Reversed 464
How Much is Appropriate 449
Income of Significant Other 442
Income of Step-parent 442
Income-Shares Guideline 444
Insurance & Teens 454
Insurance Coverage for Child 453
International
  Criminal Enforcement Procedures 503
  Enforcement 457
Is Not Being Spent On My Children 454
Kidnapped Child, Marriage of Damico 464
Law is Partially Unconstitutional 464
Leaving Country, SIT 69 315
Lottery Payments Frozen 516
MacDougall v. DHS 511
Marriage of Shivers, IA 440
Marriage of Simmons, WI 512
Medical 589
Military Service 460
Miller v. Schou, FL 440
Modification 450
No Court Order in Place 426, 452
No Place To Send Payment 452
No See - No Pay 450
Obligation Starts? 449
Obligor & Obligee, definition 592
Ottino v. Ottino, NM 511
Parent Locator Service 134
Passport Issuance Restrictions 514
Past Due Support Letter 458
Paternity of Cheryl 511
Percent-of-Income Guideline 444
Permanent Child Support 446
Presumed Father 137
Railing v. Hawkins 511
Reduced by Child's Disability Benefits 463
Remove the Sting of Paying 452
Security For Support Awards 453
Shaw v. Cameron, NC 440
Suddenly Super Parent 21
Temporary Child Support 446
Temporary Modification 450
The License Suspension law 464
Too Much Or Too Little 449
Under the Table Employment 459
Uniform Interstate Family Support Act 516
Verification of Income 437
What is Considered Income 437
When Does It End? 446
When Does It Start? 449
White v. Laingor, MA 511
Who, When, How, Where 451
Won't have to Pay Back 514
Child's
  Adult-Education Doesn't Extend Support 463
  Affidavit of Preference, definition 566
  Agenda 72
  Fear of Flying 265
  Realities 256
  Testimony, Jersey v. Margaret 397
  Voice 256
Child's Right
  Children Who Cannot Choose 255
  Children Who Want to Choose 254
  to Choose, Situation #72 316
Children
  & the Liar 284
  as hostages, 'Stockholm Syndrome' 603
  As Pawns 19
  Dealing With the Anger in Our 321
  Depend on you for Safety 342
  Guidelines for Interviewing 273
  Open About Their Activities 270
  Revenge 274
  Second-Hand Smoke 494
  When Children Lie 285
  Who Cannot Choose 255
  Who Want to Choose 254
Children's Perspective, Chapter 14, 253
Child-Snatching Lawsuits, definition 571

Choice of Conservator
Child 12 Years or Older 254
Example of Document 255
Choices, Making Poor 56
Chronology, definition 145, 571
Church and State 263
Cigarettes see Second-Hand Smoke
Circuit Court, definition 571
Circumstances
Best for Children 16
Change in Non-Custodial, Sit #54 311
Change in Support 449
Change of, Reason for 2nd Deposition 356
Ellis v. Ellis, MO 489
Extreme 12
Grounds to Continue Investigation 330
Make the Best of and Enjoy Present 254
Of a child's Birth 15
Of Child's Conception 44
Second Best Possible for Children 16
Significant change of, for Modification 450
Therapist Confidentiality is Broken 38
When Attorney Privilege is Broken 149
Circumstantial Evidence, definition 571
Citation, definition 571
City of Spokane v. Julie Anne Port, case
Pro Se litigant may record trial 487
Civil
Action, definition 571
Case 392
Case, definition 571
Federal Rules of Civil Procedure 364
Law, definition 571
Standby 23
Claim, definition 571
Clandestine, definition 571
Class Action, definition 571
Classification by Gender
Craig v. Boren 518
Frontiero v. Richardson 518
Johnson v. Robinson, 518
Orr v. Orr, 517
Stanton v. Stanton 517
Clean Hands (Doctrine), definition 571
Clear and Convincing Evidence 571
Clinical Psychologist 241
Clinical Psychologist see Psychologist 597
Closest Friends 87
Clothes Make the Witness 404
Cocaine
Home testing kit 131
Random Test for 236
Retention Time in Body 237
Code, definition 572
Co-Defendant, definition 572
Co-Dependent
Behavior 37
definition 572
Codes for Log Book, example 105
Codification, definition 572
Cognitive
Ability and Memory Loss 572
Memory's Imperfections 278
Therapy, definition 572
Cohabitation, definition 572
Cold Turkey Truth 286
Collateral
Contact List 211
Estoppel, definition 572
Estoppel, Whitehead v. Gen. Tel. Co. 418
Collection
Past Due Support Letter 458
Collection Methods for Child Support 456
Collusion, definition 572
Colorado
Child Support Credit 514
Child Support Ends 447
Child support for married minor 447
Hall v. Hall, Tort - Interference 492
Has Excluded DNA 138
has made it easier to move away 272
Lottery Payments Frozen 516
Low v. Low, Income 439
Marriage of Bohn, Support, Lottery 439
Marriage of Fain, Income 441
Marriage of Francis, Move Away 272
Marriage of Tessmer, Income 441
Provides Child Support Credit 514
Support Accounting 455
Comity, definition 572
Commissioner, definition 572
Commit, definition 572
Common
Custody Arrangements 19
Law Marriage, definition 572
Law, definition 572
Commonwealth v.
Butler Violation of restraining order 518
Carter Violation of restraining order 490
Laskowski, Violation of restraining order 518
Communication
& Fear 82
Assertive Evaluation 83
Monitor Between Attorneys 81
Privacy on the Internet 50
When Not to Talk 82
with the Enemy 152
With Your Attorney 151

with your Detective 170
Community Property, defined 572
Complaint
definition 572
or Petition in Courts Time Line 382
Compliance
Failure to Comply with Discovery 364
with Court Order 403
with Supervised Visitation 339
Compulsory Appearance, definition 572
Computer 101, 130
Classes 261
Data Retrieval 139
defined 572
Evidence, SIT#60 312
Files 353
Generated Graphics, definition 572
Modeling, definition 572
Noted Evidence, definition 572
Printed Evidence, definition 573
Stored Evidence, definition 573
Transmitted Evidence, definition 573
Websites as Evidence 101
Concerns
About Other Parent 210
Child's Hospital Visit List 209
Second-Hand Smoke 324
Second-Hand Smoke and Children 274, 494
Conciliation
Court 133
definition 573
Services Report Example 191
Services, do I have to go? 14
Conclusion of
Fact, definition 573
Law 412
Law, definition 573
Conclusive Evidence, definition 573
Condition of Child Report
Example #1 211
Example #2 212
Confession of Judgment or Promissory Note 147
Confidentiality
Attorney 149
Court 414
Detective 179
Documentation 105
Documents Produced by Mistake 486
Equipment 132
Evaluator 190
Expert 223
Expert for Opposition 223
How Subpoenas Work 392
Inventories 41
Judge 380
of Case File in Question, SIT 66 315
Paper Shredder 131
Psychologist 239
Services 140
Witnesses 38, 395
Your Children 273
Conflict 73
Assertive Communication Evaluation 83
of Interest, definition 573
of Laws Rules 132
Conflict Resolution
Arbitrate 75
Attorneys 75
Conciliate 75
definition 573
Mediate 75
Mediators 75
Negotiate 75
Poorest Method 382
Conflicting Truths 277
Connecticut
Blake v. Blake, Move Away 272
Child Support Ends 447
Emergency Jurisdiction 508
Fabiano v. Fabiano, Income 441
Langton v. Maloney, custodial right 517
Nexus Gay/Lesbian Parents 527
Conscience of the Court, definition 573
Consequences for the Future 55
Consideration, definition 573
Consistent With, definition 573
Constitutional Right, Parenting 516
Consulting Expert 219
Contact Has Been Denied 267
Contact Log
Admissible Evidence 101
Appointment Book 99
Calendar 101
Chapter 7, 97
Codes for Log Book 105
Computer 101
Crucial Data to Record 104
Dark Side 128
Evaluator 185
Extensive example 106
Fill-In Form 101
Home Study Evaluation 185
Methods of Keeping a 100
Notebook 101
Simplicity & Speed 104
Tape Recorder 101
Value of Specific Entries 106
Contact Orders, definition 573

Contempt
    Filing a Contempt Motion 398
    of Court 398
    of Court, Defending Contempt Charges 402
    of Court, definition 573
Contested Custody, definition 573
Contingency Fee, definition 573
Continuing Jurisdiction 392
Contract, definition 573
Control
    Freak 26
    Take of Your Case 34
    You Voice 81
Controlled Substances, definition 573
Conversion, definition 573
Conviction, definition 574
Coons vs. Wilder, Decrease Support, IL 463
Cooperate
    Development of Cooperation 55
    Why the Opposition will 71
    Why you should 70
Copy, definition 574
Corporal Punishment, definition 574
Corpus Delicti, definition 574
Correcting Mistakes On Your Deposition 361
Corrigena
    Correcting Mistakes 361
    definition 574
    example 361
Corroborating Evidence, definition 574
Cost Sharing, Child Support Guideline 443
Costs
    Chapter 21, 421
    definition 574
    Detective 168
    Fast Tracking to Cut 423
    for Deposition 356
    for Home Study 200
    for Using Experts 219
    making records available 354
    reduce using frequent flyer points 135
Council of Int'l. Investigators 166
Counsel, definition 574
Counseling, Supportive, definition 574
Counselor/Mediator Can Be Both 210
Counterclaim, definition 574
County of Lake v. Gerald Anthony Antoni, case
    Fathers Debit Service 463
Court 574
    All Appearances Equal? 392
    Appellate 384
    Chapter 20, 382
    Circuit Courts, definition 571
    Confidentiality 414
    Contempt of Court 398
    definition 574
    Don't Whisper 405
    Forcing Me Back to Court #73 317
    in Court You Should 405
    Judge or Jury 380
    Last Review for 395
    Military 385
    Non-Issue 394
    of Limited & Special Jurisdiction 384
    of Veterans Appeals 384
    Prepare for Your Day in 406
    Pre-trial Conference 392
    Questions - Dodging Enemy Fire 407
    Refreshed Memory 394
    Reporter, definition 574
    Rules of, definition 600
    Skin Piercing 405
    Superior 384
    Tattoos 405
    the Ultimate Battlefield 383
    Time Line 382
    Tribal 386
    Types of 383
    Video in 130
    Visual Impact on the 404
    What Will Happen in 411
Court Order
    Advised Not to Pay Child Support 152, 451
    and Child's Fear of Flying 265
    As evidence 353
    Attorney, Advised Not to Comply 152
    Child Must Comply, Panic SIT #38 306
    definition 574
    forms for Compliance with 403
    Is Not a Suggestion 403
    Ordered Money, Other Parent Won't Pay 307
    SIT #40 We Comply, They Don't 306
Court Rules, how to refer to 574
Covert Intelligence Division 165
CP Custodial Parent, definition 574
CPA, Penalty, Reporting Abuse 328
CPS
    a Child Protective Service 328
    Aggressively Dealing with False Reports 333
    Child and Family Assessment Outline 330
    Child Protective Services 328
    Child's Hospital Visit List 209
    Court Ordered Cooperation 332
    Gets a call 328
    Getting Your Child Back 333
    Grounds to Continue Investigation 330
    Knocks at Your Door 332
    Parenting Classes 134

Removal of the Children 332
Craig v. Boren, Classification by gender 518
Credibility, definition 574
Credit
16 States Provide Child Support 514
Card Applications, Statements 353
Report, No Permission, SIT 57 311
Credit Report
Yang v. Government Employees 103
Crime, definition 574
Criminal
Case 392
Case, definition 574
Law 574
Records 353
Crises, Real or Manufactured 294
Cross Examination 409
definition 574
Cross-petition or Cross-complaint, definition, 575
Crucial Data to Record 104
Culpability, definition 575
Custodial
Interference, Damages, Kajtazi v. Kajtazi 492
Parent
Move Away, Burgess v. Burgess 491
Travel, Wiley v. Wiley 491
Visitation Bond 23
Parent, CP, definition, 575
Visitation Responsibilities 266
Custody
Arrangements, types of 19
Automatic Shift, Mundon v. Mundon 525
Bird's Nest 21
Boyfriend doesn't get 483
definition 575
Determination, definition 575
Evaluation 246
Girlfriend may get 483
Modification
Change of Circumstances 489
Possessory Conservator 595
Sole Managing Conservator 601
Cyber, definition 575

D

D.W.I. (Driving While Intoxicated) 577
Damages
Awarded for Parental Kidnapping, case 507
for Custodial Interference, case 492
Suing for, definition 575
Danger
Fight Response Mode 581
Flight Response Mode 581
Dark Side 128
Data Sheet
example 88
explanation 88
Data Submitted to Identify Concerns 210
Amber's Homes Since Bobby's Birth 209
Child's Hospital Visit List 209
types of 234
Daubert
Test, defined 575
v. Merrell, Parental Alienation Syndrome 496
Day Care
Doubtfire Clause 490
Letter from Caregiver 204
negative viewpoint 490
Workers 133
Dead Hand 19
Dealing With
Assertive Communication Evaluation 83
Combating Alienation Syndrome 269
Depression & Pain, Duck Muck 47
False Allegations of Child Abuse 336
When CPS Knocks at Your Door 332
Your Child's Fears 257
Decision
Contrary to Evidence, Manifestly Unjust 589
Judge Renders Decision not Justice 376
Laws are designed to give Justice 142
Not Punishment 382
Declaration, definition 575
Declaratory Action, definition 575
Decrease in Support Payments, case 463
Decree
definition 575
Interlocutory, definition 585
Terminating Parental Rights 435
Defamation
definition 575
Sue the Liar 283, 339
Default, definition 575
Defendant, definition 575
Defensive Behaviors 58
Remedies 59
Deficiencies, in Parenting Skills 52
Delaware
Child Support Ends 447
Child Support Hall of Fame 455
Marriage of Gudzelak, Support, Lottery 439
Nexus Gay/Lesbian Parents 527
Support Accounting 455
Delay
During Negotiation 59
New Attorney 158
Tactics, Bankruptcy 425

Delegation 34
Deliberate, Insightful, Rational Enemy 56
Deliberation, definition 575
Dementia, definition 575
Demilitarized Zone 35
Demonstrative Evidence, definition 575
Demur, definition 576
Denial 576
  definition 576
  of Visitation, Incident Report form 154
Dental Neglect 28
Dependence, Chemical 571
Dependent
  According to the Court 426
  According to the IRS 427
  Credits for Child 428
  definition 576
  -Relationship 576
Depersonalization Disorder, definition 576
Deposition
  Attorney Preparation for 357
  Best Time to Depose 356
  Check the Enemy's 364
  Check the Expert's 364
  Check Your 361
  Correcting Mistakes On Your 361
  Corrigenda, definition 574
  Costs for 356
  definition 576
  During Enemy's 363
  During Your 359
  Ending the 361
  Enemy's 363
  Evasive, Incomplete Disclosure, Answer 365
  Failure to Attend Own Deposition 367
  First Thing in the Morning 356
  Four Reasons to Depose 355
  Index, example 365
  Instructions from the Opposition 358
  Later in the Day 356
  Outline Form, example 362
  Prepare for a 356
  Psychological & Emotional Prep. 356
  Rules of 355
  Second 356
  Telephone 205
  the Night Before a 356
  via the Internet 355
  What is a 355
  Who Would You Depose 362
  Your 356
  Your Witnesses' 364
  Your, No New News 357
Depression
  definition 576
  Duck Muck for dealing with 47
Desire VS Reality 52
Detective 133
  A Snake Is A Snake Is A ... 169
  Are You Being Watched? 171
  Assignment #1 Child's Environment 172
  Assignment #2 Children's Environment 174
  Assignment #3 Identify Any Income 176
  Assignment #4 Business Information 177
  Assignment #5 Confirmation of Drug use 178
  Assignment #6 General Investigation 179
  Attorney work-product privilege 177
  Avoid Hot Shots 169
  California Licensed Investigators 166
  Can Do 165
  Communication Note 170
  Council of International Investigators 166
  Covert Intelligence Division 165
  Detectives Chapter 10, 165
  Discovery Bonus In Report 177
  Evaluation Form, example 167, 168
  Finding One 166
  Getting the Evidence 171
  Help Your Detective 169
  More Work, More Money 424
  Opposition Searched My House 314
  Opposition's Detective 171
  Retainer Agreement, example 168
  Sex & Your 180
  Stalking 165
  Understanding the Costs 168
  World Association of Detectives 166
Deterrence 57
Developmentally Disabled, definition 576
Diagnostic Statistical Manual III 576
Diaries or Journals, Business or Personal 353
Direct
  Evidence, definition 576
  Examination 409
    definition 576
Directed or Summary Judgment
  in Courts Time Line 383
Directed Verdict, definition 576
Dirty Hands, definition 576
Dirty Tricks 148
Disallowing a Child to Testify 551
Disbar, definition 576
Disbarment of Attorney 163
Discharge of Attorney #1 157, 158
Discipline 22, 259
  Styles of Parental 260
Disclosure
  definition 576

Evasive or Incomplete Answer 365
Failure to, False or misleading 366
Discover Hidden Agenda 72
Discovery
& Deposition, Chapter 18, 351
Bonus In Detective Report 177
Chambers by Cochran v. Sanderson, Income 440
definition 576
Documents Produced by Mistake 486
Estevez v. Superior, Income 440
Evasive, Incomplete Disclosure, Answer 365
Failure to Comply With 364
Failure to Disclose 177
Good News About You, example #3 178
How Subpoenas Work 392
I Have to Tell Them What? 352
Jeffress v. Johnson, Income 440
Marriage of Shivers, IA 440
Miller v. Schou, Income 440
or Disclosure in Courts Time Line 382
Panic Situation #25 302
Photo Graphs 353
Right of Meaningful Access 600
Shaw v. Cameron, Income 440
Discretion
Abuse of 380
Child Support Issues 444
Judges can disbelieve 413
To Exclude Evidence 101
Vexatious Litigator Issue 415
Discretionary Transfer, definition 576
Dismiss
definition 576
Motion to 590
With Prejudice, definition 577
Without Prejudice, definition 577
Disneyland Parent 261
Disorder
Attachment 567
Attention Deficit 567
Borderline Personality 569
Depersonalization 576
Failure to Thrive (FTT) 580
Hyperactivity 584
Identity 584
Multiple Personality 591
Munchausen Syndrome 591
Oppositional Defiant 593
Paranoia 593
Parental Alienation Syndrome 593
Post-Traumatic Stress 596
Separation Anxiety 601
Situation #71 Biolar 316
Disorderly Conduct, definition 577
Disposable Earnings, defined 577
Dissolution, definition 577
District Attorney
definition 577
to Prosecute Perjury 283
District of Columbia
Child Support Credit 514
Child Support Ends 447
Nexus Gay/Lesbian Parents 527
Support Hall of Shame 455
Division of Church and State 263
Divorce
1980 A Study of Families After, case 484
Act, Uniform Marriage & 515
definition 577
Has Precedent Over Custody, Sit #36 306
Military Divorce & Child Custody 150
Precedent Over Custody, Panic SIT #36 305
Soldiers' and Sailors' Civil Relief Act 385
DNA 482
Court Ordered 137
definition 577
for abandonment or denial of maternity 137
Genetic Testing 137
Home testing kits 131
Negative - Father is Still Father 482
What Is Needed for Testing 138
Docket
definition 577
Number, definition 577
Doctors 133
Doctrine, definition 577
Documentation
Confidentiality 354
Costs for Access and Copies 354
Detective 169
Documents and Records 353
False 362
How Subpoenas Work 392
Methods of 99
Now for Later 267
Origin of Documents 91
Produced by Mistake 486
Production of 353
Reasons for 97
Self-authenticated 601
Doe v. Irwin, 5th ,9th , & 14th Amendments 517
Domestic Violence
definition 577
Forced to Leave 343
Patterns Won't Change 343
Police - Psychologists Sued in Cases 525
Report 485

When the Police are Called 39
Domicile, definition 577
Don't
Think Out Loud 82
Donald & Lynnette Carlsen, case 464
Double Jeopardy, definition 577
Doubtfire Clause 11
or First Right of Refusal 490
Dress for Custody Success 38
Drug
Assignment #5 Confirm Drug Use 178
Controlled Substances, definition 573
Drugs in the Other Home, SIT #42 307
Drugs see Test
Home Testing Kits 131
Home testing kits 131
Prescription Drug Abuse 237
Prescriptions 353
Proper Prescription Drug Use 237
Residue identification wipes 131
Drug Test
Hair Analysis 135, 236
Passive Inhalation 135, 237
Random 236
Will You Take A 136, 238
Dual Citizenship, definition 577
Duck Muck 47
Due Care, definition 577
Due Diligence, definition 577
Due Process
definition 577
Protection in Interest of Cooper 517
Required, License Revocation, case 464, 488
Duress, definition 577
During Opposition's Deposition 363
Dwight D. Eisenhower, quote 51

E

Earned Income Credit 428
Earnings, definition 577
EBT, Examination Before Trial 355
definition 577
Ecclesiastical Law, definition 578
Eighth Amendment 578
Elizabeth Stone, quote i
Ellis v. Ellis, Appeal Custody Modification 489
E-Mail, definition 578
Emancipated Child 446
Emancipation, definition 578
Emergency Jurisdiction Ends with Emergency 508
Emotional
Abuse 326
abuse 330
Distress, Intentional Infliction of, case 484
Emotions When Your Child Gone 346
or Verbal Abuse, definition 578
type of Thinking 73
Employee Expert 219
Employment Records 353
Enabler, definition 578
Ending the Deposition 361
Enemy
Aid to the 33
Deliberate, Insightful, Rational 56
Know Your 88
of My Enemy 86
Enforcement
Advised Not to Pay Child Support 152, 451
definition 578
Fair Law 519
Full Faith & Credit 348
Full Faith and Credit 457
Hearings 392
LEIN, Law Enforcement Info. Network 588
of Court Orders 578
of Maintenance Orders 598
Past Due Support Letter 458
Entrapment, definition 578
Equal Time, Joint Physical & Legal 20
Equipment
and Service Options List 140
Calendar 129
Caller ID 129
Camera, 35 MM 129
Cellular Phones 130
Computer 130
Contact Log 130
Fax Machine 130
Home Testing Kits 131
Internet 131
Pager 131
Paper Shredder 131
Tape Recorder 131
Telephone 130
Telephone Answering Machine 131
Video Camera 130
Equipment & Service
Chapter 8, 129
Confidentiality 132
Spy Shops 134
Equipment & Service Options List 140
Equitable Distribution, defined 578
Equity
definition 578
Doesn't Give Boyfriend Custody 483
No-Biological Father May Get Custody 483
Et Al, definition 578

Et Ano, definition 578
Ethics, definition 578
Evaluation
  Appointment 190
  Bad Results 248
  definition 578
  Easier for Your Child 190
  Eliminate the Trash 216
  Evaluating a Panic Situation 317
  Evaluating the Evaluation 208
  Evaluating the Home Study 216
  If You Gotta Go 190
  of Family Progress 578
  of Your Significant Other 186
  Prescription drugs 237
  Skin Piercing & Tattoos 405
  Social Study Report for Adoption 434
Evaluations, Chapter 11, 181
Evaluator
  & Confidentiality 190
  & Your Significant Other 185
  Best Attitude with the 182
  Contact Log 185
  Looking for? 208
  Other Parent Is A Chameleon 188
  Parental Alienation Syndrome 186
  Recommendation = Decision 186
  Report Example 191, 194, 197, 200
  Sensitive to Case Driven by others 185
  Why are Evaluators Used? 182
Evasion, definition 578
Evasive, Incomplete Disclosure or Response 365
Evidence
  Admissible, definition 565
  Available Information 102
  Best, definition 569
  Chain of Evidence 103
  Chain or Trail of 103
  Circumstantial, definition 571
  Clear and Convincing 571
  Computer Data Retrieval 139
  Computer SIT#60 312
  Computer, definition 579
  Corroborating, definition 574
  definition 578
  Demonstrative, definition 575
  Detective Report Example #1 172
  Direct, definition 576
  Document Court Order Violation 205
  Documents Produced by Mistake 486
  E-mail 103
  Fair Credit Reporting Act 103
  Federal Rules of 580
  Financial Stockpiling #3 176
  Fruit of the Poisonous Tree 352
  How Subpoenas Work 392
  Inadmissible, definition 585
  Lie Detector 136
  Material, definition 589
  News About You, example #3 178
  Peeping Tom Law
    definition 35
    Photos, example #2 175
  Places to Look 349
  Preponderance of, definition 596
  Recorded Conversations 517
  Self-authenticated 601
  Spoliation of 103
  State's, definition 602
  Tainted, definition 603
  Tape Recorded Conversations 354
  The Paper Trail 349
  Under the Table Income 459
  Video 130
  Websites as 101
Ex Parte
  definition 579
  no need for Wiretap Order 488
  see Audi Alteram Partem, definition 568
  SIT #32, Exparte Hearing 304
Ex post facto law 579
Examination
  Before Trial (EBT) 355
  Direct 576
Example
  Attorney Invoice 155
  Chart #1 Frequent Moving 210
  Child Support Expense Log 456
  Codes for Log Book 105
  Condition of Child Report #1 211
  Court Presentation Outline Form 393
  Daily Log Sheets 106
  Data Sheet Form 88
  Deposition Index 365
  Deposition Outline Form 362
  Detective Communication Notes 170
  Detective Evaluation Form, example 167
  Detective Report 172
  Detective Retainer Agreement 168
  Evaluator Contact Log 185
  Evaluator's Report 191, 194, 197, 200
  Home Study, Report #1 211
  Home Study, Report #2 212
  Incident Report for Visitation 154
  Judges' Rulings 379
  Letter from a Friend #1 202
  Letter from Caregiver 204
  Letter from Employee #6 204

Letter from Employer #7 204
Letter from Friend #5 203
Letter from Mother-In-Law #3 203
Letter from Oppositions Co-Worker #4 203
Letter from Son-In-Law #2 202
Letter from Teacher 204
Letter to Document Order Violation 205
Letters of Support 202
Panic Situations 294
Psychological Evaluation #1 241
Psychological Evaluation #2 246
Rulings 412
Transcript of Telephone Deposition 205
When Your Money Is Spent 445
Who Would You Depose 362
Exchange Monitoring 579
Excited Utterance, definition 579
Exercising Visitation 22
Exhibits, definition 579
Ex-Husband Excluded as Guardian, SIT 56 311
Expense Account Records 353
Expert
Academic 219
Consulting 219
Costs Involved 219
definition 579
Employee 219
Experts Chapter 12 218
Fees Reimbursement 220
for the Opposition and Confidentiality 223
New Stricter Standards for 229
Opposition Using An 225
Over or Under Exposed 221
Practical 219
Some are Prostitutes 221
Testifying 219
the Special Thing They Can Do 220
Witness
can be a Loose Cannon 225
definition 579
Deposition Check 364
How to Find an 220
Work-product Privilege 219
Yours and Confidentiality 223
Exploitative or Permanent Retaliation 57
Expunged Records 527
Expunged Records, definition 579
Extended Family
definition 579
In-laws & Outlaws 86
Opposition's Parents 86
Your Friends 87
Extradition, definition 579

F

F. Scott Fitzgerald, quote 94
Face Fee, definition 579
Facing the
Mad Dog Attorney 360
Other Parent 232
Fact, definition 579
Factors that Influence Custody 19
Failure 364
Failure to
Appear, definition 579
Attend at Own Deposition 367
Comply with Discovery 364
Disclose 177
Federal Rules of Civil Procedure 364
Thrive (FTT) 580
Fair Law - Unfair Enforcement, case 519
Fair to Say That, definition 580
False
Claim, definition 580
Documentation 362
or Misleading Disclosure 366
Swearing, definition 580
False Accusations 26
Accusation of Abuse 296
Allegations Examined 337
Allegations of PAS 186
definition 580
In Home Study, Eliminate the Trash 216
of Parental Alienation Syndrome 189
of Sexual Abuse 277
SIT #41 of Sexual Abuse 307
Sue for Making 339
False Accuser, Profile Precursors 338
False Allegations
if you are Arrested 40
In Home Study, Eliminate The Trash 216
of Child Abuse, Dealing with 336
Preventing 336
Studies 507
Family
& Friends, Letters From 201
Abduction, definition 580
Conciliation Services, Don't want to reconcile 14
Eruptions Test 240
Extended, definition 579
Families After Divorce, 1980, study 484
Law definition 580
Records, definition 580
Support Act, case 511
Support Act, Uniform Interstate 516
Tree 348
Violence 580

Fanatics, defined 580
FAQ, definition 580
Far Away Friends 87
Fast Tracking 423
 definition 580
Father 16
 Absent, definition 580
 Acknowledgement of Paternity (AOP) 426
 Against Adoptive Parents, SIT# 58 311
 Can't Sue Wife 482
 DNA Negative - Father is Still Father 482
 Equity No Custody for Live-In Boyfriend 483
 Father 16
 Father's Debt Service, case 463
 Father-absent, definition 580
 Fight for Custody All the Way 16
 Gay Father, Pulliam v. Smith, NC 543
 Paternity No-Bio. Dad May Get Custody 483
 Paternity Suits May Never be Settled 482
 Paternity Testing 594
 Presumed 137
 Second Parent-adoption 551
Fault, defining 580
Fax 130
Fax Machine 130
Fear
 Aggressive or Subdued Child 62
 and Communication 82
 Assertive Communication Helps Control 83
 Causes Sniveling or Whining 37
 Child may fear losing family 335
 Child will gravitate to other parent 256
 Child' Inventory 43
 Child's fear of Abuser 329
 Children Fear Disapproval and Anger 285
 Dealing with 84
 Dealing with Your Child's 257
 Kidnapping Threat 27
 Needs Control of Area 35
 of Flying 265
 Our Fear and Anger Indicate 320
 Panic Situations 293
 Reaction Chart 68
 The One I Feed 48
 What You Can do to Help 259
 Your Parents 86
Federal
 Circuit Court 384
 Government Forces States to Comply 464
 Parent Locator Service 134
 Rules of Civil Procedure 364
  Failure to Comply with Discovery 364
 Rules of Evidence, definition 580
 Statutes, definition 580
Feelings
 Not hateful just incompetent 56
 Other parent is only doing this to hurt me 27
Fees
 #13 Attorney won't take case 145
 (3) Expense and Sanctions 366
 Attorney Problems 485
 Attorney, Billable Hours 152, 155
 Attorney, Promissory Note 147
 Cost for Deposition 356
 Costs Using Experts 220
 Detective Retainer Agreement 168
 Hatch (1985), pendente lite Award 485
 Keep Detective/Attorney Happy 169
 No Pro Se Recovery of Attorney 142
 Sit #23 Other Parent Costing You 301
 Sit #43 Opposition Won't Pay 307
 Suing Under RICO 459
 Violations, Duties as a Professional 160
Felony, definition 580
Fifth Amendment 519, 580
 Matter of Gentry 517
 U.S. v. Oplinger 519
Fight Response Mode 581
Fighting Battles or Playing Games = Strategy 55
Filiation, definition 581
Fill-In Form 101
Financial
 Abuse, definition 581
 Statement 353
 Statement, definition 581
Findings of Facts 412
 Abney v. W. Rest. Mut. Case. Co. 419
 Bates v. Sherwin-Williams Co. 419
 Hard to challenge 413
 or Rule 52, definition 581
 Rule 52 Federal Rules 488
Fined for Following Attorney Advice, SIT 67 315
Fire Drill 35
First
 Impression Case, definition 581
 Right of Refusal or Doubtfire Clause 490
 Strike, Deposition 355
First Amendment
 Osteras v. Osteras 524
 Thomas v. Review Board 523
Fitch v. Belshaw, Due process, OR 464
Fixed 581, 598
fixed 20, 21, 23, 24, 27, 181
Fixed-Schedule Visitation 20, 21, 23, 24, 27, 181, 581, 598
Flat Fee, definition 581
Flawed Process, Home Study 216
Flight Response Mode 581

Flink v. Flink, case, Equitable Parent, AZ 510
Florida
    Berg v. Perlow, PAS 495
    Binger v. King Pest, Surprise Witness 489
    Child Support Ends 447
    Grandparent v. adoptive parents 520
    Grandparent Visitation Unconstitutional 521
    Miller v. Schou, Income 440
    Move Away 272
    Nexus Gay/Lesbian Parents 527
    Out of Pocket Medical Expenses 454
    Portuondo v. Portuondo, Step-parent 513
    Saul v. Brunetti, Grandparent 521
    Spoilation of Evidence 104
    Support Accounting 455
    Ward v. Dibble, Grandparent visitation 520
    Work-Product Privilege 485
Flying, Fear of 265
Forensic
    defined 581
    Psychologist see Psychologist 597
    Testing Services 135
    WAIS-III Intelligence Scales 240
Forms
    Attorney Evaluation, example 144
    Child Support Expense Log, example 455
    Condition of the Child Report 211, 212
    Incident Report for Visitation, example 154
Fornication, definition 581
Forsythe v. Family Court of Dane County, case
    Pro Se may tape record trial 488
Forum Shopping 370
Four Reasons to Depose 355
Fourteen Child Support Court Cases 461
Fourteenth Amendment 581
    Bell v Cith of Milwaukee 516
    Kelson v. Springfield 517
    Wo v. Hopkins 517
Franz
    Laws may not hide child, WI 519
    v. United States, case
        Parent child relationship 516
Fraud, definition 581
Frauenshuh v. Giese 524
Free
    Advice on the Internet 14
    Legal Assistance 142
Freedom of Information Act 526
Frequent Moving 26
Friend
    Next Best 592
    of My Enemy 86
    of the Court 52
        definition 581
    or Enemy, Chapter 5, 80
Friendly Fire 85
    definition 581
Friends
    Buddies & Pals 87
    Closest 87
    Far Away 87
    New 87
    Old 87
    Online 87
    On-The-Job 87
    What They Can Do to Help 201
    Your Extended Family 87
Frivolous, definition 582
From Now On 36
Frontiero v. Richardson, Classification suspect 518
Fruit of the Poisonous Tree 352
Fruits of the Crime, definition 582
Frye Test, definition 581
Fugitive, definition 582
Full
    Age, definition 582
    Faith & Credit 515
        definition 582

G

Gag Order, definition 582
GAL, Guardian Ad Litem 582
Garbage into Gold #3 176
Garnish
    Changes in the future 54
    Collection Methods 457
    definition 582
    in Detective Report 174
    Military Wage Attachment 460
Gay
    Second Parent-adoption 551
    Sons Taken from Gay Father 543
    The "Nexus" Approach 527
Genetic Testing for Maternity or Paternity 137
Georgia
    Burney v. Burney, Step-parent 513
    Child Support Ends 447
Gett, part of a Jewish Divorce 582
Getting
    Your Child Back from CPS 333
Girlfriend May Get Custody 483
Glossary of Terms, for this book 564
Good
    Faith, definition 582
    Faith, Maines Paper & Food Service- Midwest, Inc. v. Regal Foods 415
    Old Lawyer System 146

Gossiping and Anger 95
Government Benefit Diversion 456
Grand
- Jury, definition 582
- Lie, the 277

Grandparent 16
- Case #VR921200 Askren 520
- Change of Circumstance 525
- Custody Interrupted, SIT #36 305
- Fight for Custody of Grandchildren 16
- Florida Visitation Unconstitutional 521
- Foor v. Foor 522
- Get Custody Despite Father 522
- Get More Protection 521
- Husband Interfering with Visitation 314
- Managing Conservatorship 16
- May be Managing Conservator, definition 589
- must justify visitation 520
- Relationship Inventory 44
- Saul v. Brunetti 521
- SIT #36 Custody Interrupted 305
- Six Months of Care 520
- Smoking 494
- Step-Grandparents 17
- Troxel, Jenifer v. Granville, Tommie 520
- Visitation Unconstitutional 521
- Visitation, importance of 22
- Visitation, Situation #27 302
- Visitation, Utah 520

Grayned v. City of Rockford, Vague law 518
Gregoire v. Biddle, case 519
Grievance
- definition 582
- Filing Against Oppositions Attorney 305

Gross Negligence, definition 582
Guarantees, None You Will Win Or Lose 15
Guardian Ad Litem 396
- (GAL), definition 582

Guide for Answering Questions 406
Guidelines
- for Interviewing Children 273
- Income-Shares 444
- Percent-of-Income 444

Gymnastics & Exercise Classes 261

H

Habeas Corpus, definition 582
Habitability, definition 582
Habitual Offender, definition 583
Hacked, definition 583
Hague Convention on Child Abduction, case 497
Haines v. Kerner, case
- Pro Se not same standard as attorney 487

Hair
- Analysis 135, 236
- Analysis, Court Room Samples 236
- drug test, Home testing kit 131
- Men, Long Hair in Court 404
- Women, Strange hair-do's 404

Halo Effect 404
- Negative Halo Effect, definition 583
- Positive Halo Effect, definition 583

Handling
- a Bad Attorney 158
- Interference with Visitation 23
- the Liar 282

Hanoi Hanna 89
Harassment 583
- # 04 Phone Harassment at Work 295
- # 53 Constant Public 310
- # 70 Former Spouse Tips Police 316
- Barriatry 568

Hardship Income Deduction Reversed, case 464
Harmless Error, definition 583
Hashish, Home testing kit 131
Hawaii
- Child Support Ends 447
- Poverty Guidelines 427

Health Issues
- Second-Hand Smoke and Children 274, 494
- Second-Hand Smoke Delays Tooth 494

Hearing, definition 583
Hearsay, definition 583
Help
- avoid the Rescuer 33
- From Hell 205
- Guidelines During a Crisis 49
- Proper Responses 48
- Rescue Mentality. 195
- Rescue, #64 Grandparent 314

Heroin, definition 583
Hidden
- Agendas 72
- Assets 428
- Assets, Detective Report #3 176
- Assets, Under the table employment 459
- Sources of Income 440

Highlights for Children 261
Hinder 583
Histrionics, definition 583
HIV, Home test kit 131
Holidays
- # 14 Denial of Holiday Visitation 298
- Back to School 478
- Christmas 478
- Cinco de Mayo 478
- Earth Day 477

Father's Day 478
Graduation 478
Halloween and Harvest Festivals 478
Kwanzaa 477
Mothers Day 478
Negotiate Schedule 78
Passover 477
Spring 477
Summer 478
Thanksgiving 478
Valentine's Day 477
Holmes v. Holmes, case, Support reduced 463
Home
Bunker 34
Demilitarized Zone 35
State, definition 583
Testing Kits, guidelines for use 131
Videos 353
Home Study
Costs 200
Evaluating the 216
Evaluator Contact Log 185
Example, Report #1 211
Example, Report #2 212
Flaws in the Process 216
for Grandparents Home 425
Items to have Ready 201
Video Inspection 130
What is a 200
Honesty, definition 583
Hornbook, Law in Summary, definition 583
Hostage
Child as, 'Stockholm Syndrome' 603
definition 583
Hostile
Behavior 294
Hostility, definition 584
Witness, definition 583
Hourly Fee, definition 584
How 392
Can My Attorney Question An Expert 219
Do I Handle
Anger, Court Filings SIT #1, 294
Misuse of Insurance Money SIT # 02, 295
Judges Decide 376
Lies Affect Children 284
Much Do People Remember 201
Subpoenas Work 392
to File, Contempt of Court 398
How to
Find an Expert 220
Help Your Detective 169
Make A Chart #1 Frequent Moving 210
Negotiate 77
Repair the Damage 286
Say "Thanks But No Thanks" 33
Human Leucocyte Anitigen (HLA) Test 137
Humiliate, definition 584
Hurt You Worse Than Them 95
Husband
Can't Sue Wife for Lying About Paternity 482
Husband-Wife Privilege, definition 584
No-Biological Father May Get Custody 483
Hyperactivity 584
Hypothetical Question 408
definition 584

I

I
Don't Want to Visit You Anymore 267
Have to Tell Them What? 352
Think I Need A Shrink 38
Ice Skating Classes 261
Idaho 442
Child Support Ends 447
Osteraas v. Osteraas, Move 272
Osteras v. Osteras, 1st Amendment 524
Identify
Concerns About Other Parent 210
The Liar to Others 290
Identity Disorder, definition 584
If You
are Accused of Abuse, Dealing 336
Disregard This Advice 82
Gotta Go 190
Ignorance, definition 584
Illegal
definition 584
Incompetent or Unethical Behavior 158
Illegitimate Children 137
Illicit, definition 584
Illinois
Calloway v. Kinkelaar, Protective Order 525
Child Support Ends 447
Child Support Hall of Shame 455
Grandparent care - adoption 520
International Support Enforcement 457
Marriage of Boyden, Support, Lottery 439
Marriage of McBride, Income 440
Marriage of Roberts, adultery 523
Move Away 271
Nexus Gay/Lesbian Parents 527
Out of Pocket Medical Expense 454
Paternity Never Settled 482
Paternity Suits Never Settled 482
Police - Psychologist, sued 525
Police Liability 527

Sulva v. Isaacson, Smoking 494
Support Reduced by Child's Benefits 463
Zucco v. Garrett, Religion 523
Imbler v. Pachtman, Judges punished 520
Immunity, definition 584
Impeachment of Witness, definition 584
Implied Consent, definition 584
Impose Censorship 81
Improper Communications, definition 584
Imputed Income, definition 584
In
Camera, definition 585
Interest of Cooper, case 517
Loco Parentis, definition 585
Pari Delicto, definition 585
Inadmissible, definition 585
Inappropriate, Behavior 294
Incest, definition 585
Incident Report
for Visitation 154
form example 154
Income
Assignment #4 Confirm Business Losses 177
Child as a Dependent. 442
Depreciation On Equipment 442
Employer's Contributions 441
Employment Verification Letter 438
Expense Reimbursements 442
for Child Support 437
Gifts, Prizes, Grants, Gambling Winnings 441
Hidden Sources of 440
Imputed, definition 584
Inappropriate Business Expenses 443
In-kind Income 442
Interest and Dividend Income 441
Lottery Winnings 439
Military Personnel Fringe Benefits 441
Money 350
of a New Spouse or Paramour 442
of the Very Rich 440
Self Employment 438
Shares, Child Support 444
Social Security Benefits 441
Statements 353
Verification 437
Veterans' Benefits 441
Voluntary
Money contribution 443
Withholding Order, definition 585
Incompetence, definition 585
Incompetent decision makers 56
Incriminating Evidence
definition 585
Documents Produced by Mistake 486
How Subpoenas Work 392
Index Cards for Documentation 101
Indian
Best Interests of Child 390
Child Custody Proceedings 387
Child Welfare 386
Exclusive Jurisdiction 387
Termination of Parental Rights 387
Transfer of Proceedings 387
Tribal Affiliation 390
Tribal Court 386
Indiana
Beardsley v. Heazlitt, Income 440
Can't give away child support 451
Child Support Ends 447
Child Support Hall of Shame 455
Lamb v. Wenning 272
Mundon v. Mundon, Custody Shift 525
Nexus Gay/Lesbian Parents 527
Railing v. Hawkins, Support 511
Same Sex 536
Support Accounting 455
White v. White, Child Can't Testify 551
Indictment, definition 585
Indiscreet, definition 585
Individuality in Court, You or Your Witness 38
Influence, Undue, definition 605
Information
& Mis-Information 89
Documents 91
from the Opposition 90
Gathering Using Their Family Members 348
Gathering, Deposition 355
Gathering, Discovery 353
How Subpoenas Work 392
Opposition's Attorney 90
Outside or questionable source 91
Private Investigator 90
Source of 90
You 91
Your Attorney 90
Your Child 91
Initial Filings 392
Injunction, definition 585
Injury by Legal Counsel 585
In-Laws, definition 585
Insanity, definition 585
Insolvent, definition 585
Inspection, Video 130
Instruction
definition 585
Judge or Jury 380
to the Jury, definition 586
Insurance

Applications & Policies as Evidence 353
Coverage for Child 453
Misappropriation of Money, SIT #02 295
Part of Child Support 453
Security for Child Support Awards 453
Teenage Drivers 454
Intelligence 293
Intended Audience 15
Intent, definition 585
Interference, case
Damages awarded, Kajtazi v. Kajtazi 492
Interim or Temporary Custody 20
Interlocutory Decree, definition 585
International
Child Abduction Remedies Act, case 503
Child Support Enforcement 457
Criminal Enforcement Procedures 503
Internet 131
Anonymity or Security or Privacy 50
definition 585
Deposition via the 355
Free Advice on the 14
Hacked, definition 583
Lawyer advice on the 588
Lurking SIT # 51 310
Online Friends 87
Privacy on the 50
Visitation 131
Interpreter 585
Interrogatories 306
definition 586
Failure to Serve Answers 367
Interrogatory, Objecting in 352
Interstate
definition 586
Family Support Act, Uniform 516
Income Withholding, definition 585
Intervention
definition 586
Interview Protocol 586
Interviewing Children, Guidelines for 273
Intimidation by friends of the other parent 296
Intra-Faith Custody Challenges 263
Intrastate, definition 586
Invasion of Privacy
definition 586
Peeping Tom 35
Inventory
Inventories, Confidentiality 41
Relationship, example #1 44
Relationship, example #2 45
Your, example 45
Invest in Yourself 32
Investigation, definition 586
Iowa
Child Support Ends 447
Child Support Reduced by Child's Pmts. 463
Grandparent Visitation Unconstitutional 521
Marriage of Krone, Income 438
Marriage of Shivers, Income 440
Nexus Standard Gay/Lesbian Parents 527
Non-Biological Father May Get Custody 483
Petition of Ash, Step-parent 513
Second Parent Adoptions 551
Ipso Facto, definition 586
Irrelevant, definition 586
IRS, Dependent According 427
Islamic Law, definition 586
Issue
Alcohol use or Abuse 27
Child Endangerment 26
definition 586
Drug use or Abuse 237
Drug use or Abuse (prescription or street) 27
False Accusations 26
Frequent Moving 26
Kidnapping 27
Lengthy Childcare (10+ hours a day) 26
Lying to Child/ You/ Court 27
Mental Illness 26
Neglect 28
Non Issues 25
Physical Abuse 26
Poor Living Condition 28
Second-Hand Smoke as Abuse 324
Visitation Denial or Interference 27
It Ain't Over When It's Over 412
It's
Your Battle Because 34

J

Jerk Status for lies 292
Johnson v. Robinson, case
Classification 518
Joinder 586
Mandatory 589
Joint
Managing Conservator, definition 586
Petition, definition 586
Physical & Legal Custody 20
Joint Custody
& Shared Responsibility Agreement 52
definition 586
Joint Legal Custody 20
Joint Physical Custody 20
v. Single Custody, study 484
Joshua M., case 509

Judge
a Matter of Perception 379
Abuse of Discretion 380
can Remove Themselves, Recusal 374
Comparison 374
Confidentiality 380
definition 586
Evaluation Form for 373
Filing a Formal Complaint 380
Get Rid of a Bad Judge 375
Guidelines for Unfit Parent, SIT #63 313
How Judges Decide 376
Judges, Chapter 19, 368
Judicial Immunity 380
may be punished, case Imbler v. Pachtman 520
No protection for Bradley v. Fisher 518
No protection for, Gregoire v. Biddl 519
Not Immune Peterson v Stanczak 520
or Jury 380
Prejudice, Pierson v. Ray 518
Should be Removed When 371
Situation # 1 377
Situation # 2 377
Situation # 3 377
Situation # 4 378
Situation # 5 378
Situation # 6 379
What You Cannot Do with the 376
Judgment 412
definition 587
Entry 587
Judicial
Admission, definition 587
Immunity 380
Immunity, definition 587
Review, definition 586
Jurisdiction 369
Automatic Change of, Panic SIT #36 305
definition 587
Discretionary Transfer 576
Ends As Soon As The Emergency Ends 508
Home State 583
Mandatory Transfer 589
Shopping 369
Jurisprudence, definition 587
Jurors see Jury
Jury
definition 587
Grand 582
Instructions to the 586
Judge or 380
Peremptory Challenge 594
Petit, definition 595
Polling the, definition 595
Just Shot Yourself in the Foot 82
Justifiable, definition 587
Justified Vindicator 508
Juvenile Case, definition 587

K

Kajtazi v. Kajtazi, case
Money awarded for custodial interference 492
Kangaroo Court, definition 587
Kansas
Can't Sue Wife 483
Child Support Ends 447
Child Support for Married Minor 446
In Interest of Cooper, Liberty violation 517
Support Accounting 455
Tort- Non-Support 459
Kelson v. Springfield, case, 14th Amendment 517
Kendall v. Kendall 523
Kentucky
Child Support Ends 447
Nexus Gay/Lesbian Parents 527
Williams v. Williams, Phone Calls 488
Ketubah, definition 587
Key Number
definition 587
Specific Point Case Law 587
Kidnapping
$125,000 awarded to father
Pankratz v. Willis, case 507
Abduction by Stranger or Parent 343
Canada's International Project Return 264
Comity, to Another Country 348
definition 587
Emotions When Your Child is Gone 346
Family History Library 349
Family Tree 348
Full Faith & Credit 348
Habeas Corpus, definition 582
Has Your Child Been Kidnapped 345
Jurisdiction, definition 587
Kajtazi v. Kajtazi, Money awarded 492
Money 350
Money awarded for, case 507
Police 328
Prevention 343
Act, Parental 497
Profile of the Abductor 344
Steps to Getting Your Child Back 347
Threat 27
Warning Signals 344
Kill Your Case with These 91
Kinetic Family Drawings Test 239
Know Your Enemy 88

Knowledge or Awareness, definition 587

L

Ladybug, the Magazine for Young Children 261
Langton v. Maloney, case, Due Process 517
Language Interpreter 585
Lapse, definition 588
Larceny, definition 588
Latent, definition 588
Law 588
- Case Law 570
- Civil Law 571
- Common 572
- Criminal Law 574
- definition 588
- Finding the, Shepard's Case Citations 481
- is Partially Unconstitutional 464
- Procedural 597
- Substantive 603
- Where to Find the 143

Laws
- Federal Statutes 580
- Persuasive Authority 595
- State Statutes, definition 602
- Uniform Laws 605

Lawsuit Against Attorneys 158
Lawyer
- Advice on the internet 588
- definition 588
- Discipline Proceedings, definition 588

Leader
- A Strong Confident Leader 37
- A Weak Leader 37

Leading Questions 408, 588
Legal
- Aid 142
  - Clinics 149
- definition 588
- Papers, Panic Situation # 01, 294
- Separation, definition 588
- Services, Corporation 142
- Transcribers 133

Legitimate, definition 588
LEIN, Law Enforcement Info. Network 588
Leniency, definition 588
Lesbian
- Mom Restricted Access, TN 538
- Mom, SIT 55 311
- Second Parent-adoption 551
- The "Nexus" Approach 527

Letters of Support, Examples 202
Liability, definition 588
Liaison, definition 588
Liar
- accuse the children of lying 285
- Document Lying 290
- Forged & Ignored the Court, SIT #44 308
- get others to lie, Subornation of Perjury 603
- Identifying the Liar to Others 290
- Pathological 277
- Personality Disorders, Extensive Pattern 277
- Portrait of the 278
- Seeing the Pattern 280
- their Soldiers see Lies as Truth 281
- they Even Lie to Themselves 280
- Types of 277
- Using Their Lies Against Them 283
- Why Liars Get Caught 280

Libel, definition 588
License revocation, Perez v. Campbell, case 464
Lien, definition 588
Lies
- and Attorneys 291
- and Children, Knowing Truth from Lie 395
- by Familiars 279
- by Strangers 279
- Can't Sue Wife About Paternity 482
- Defense Against 281
- Detector Test 136
  - to Defend Against 282
- False Accusation of Sexual Abuse 277
- False Swearing 580
- Frequency & Scope Indicate Dysfunction 277
- In Home Study, Eliminate the Trash 216
- Memory's Imperfections 278
- No Lie Double Talk 291
- Non-Fatal Flaw 285
- Perjury, definition 594
- Proof or Poof 284
- Reasons not to 277
- Start Repairing the Damage 286
- Sue the Liar 283, 339
- the Grand Lie 277, 282
- the Opposition Tells About You 277
- to Child, You, Court 27
- Types of 276
- Used to Recruit Troops 280
- When Children Lie 285
- When is Someone Lying 279
- Your 286

Lies & Perjury, Chapter 15, 276
Life Insurance Applications & Policies 353
Limitation, definition 588
Limited Presumption in Favor of Move Away 272
Linear type of Thinking 73
List
- Chain of Evidence 103

Child And Family Assessment Outline 330
Dealing with Fear 84
Hospital Visits, evidence 209
of People You Would Depose 362
Quick List of Activities to Avoid 95
Litigation, Litigate, definition 588
Live & Let Live 57
Loan Applications & Payment Records 353
Local Venue, definition 588
Loco Parentis
definition 588
Step-parent and Child Support 512
Step-parent relationship is temporary 512
Look Ahead 57
Loose
Cannon 225
Lips Sink Ships 81
Lottery Payments Frozen 516
Lottery Winnings 439
Louisiana
Child Support Ends 447
Child Support Hall of Shame 455
Crefasi v. Crefasi, Income 438
Gardry v. Gardry, Income 439
Green v. Scott, Support, Lottery 439
Support Accounting 455
Lurking, definition 588
Lying
Can't Sue Wife for Lying About Paternity 482

M

Mabra v. Schmidt, 1st, 14th Amendment 517
Mad Dog Attorney 360
Magistrate, definition 588
Maine
Child Support Ends 447
MacDougall v. DHS, Support 511
Paternity May Never be Settled 482
Paternity Suits Never Settled 482
Rowland v. Kingman, Move Away 272
Maintenance 589
Make
Words Work for You 80
Malfeasance, definition 589
Malice, definition 589
Malicious Mother Syndrome 496
Malpractice
definition 589
Suit Against Attorney 158
Managing Conservator (MC), definition 589
Mandamus, definition 589
Mandate, definition 589
Mandatory
Joinder 589
Transfer, definition 589
Maneuver, definition 589
Manifestly Unjust, defined 589
Marijuana, Home testing kit 131
Marriage 512
& Divorce Act, Uniform 515
definition 589
of Damico, case 464
Marriage of Tessmer, Income, CO 441
Maryland
Can't Sue Wife 482
Cartnail v. State, police stop driver on a tip 316
Child Support Credit 514
Child Support Ends 447
Doe v. Doe, Can't Sue Wife 482
Domingues v. Johnson, Move Away 272
Drummond v. State of MD, Support on SS 463
Jeffress v. Johnson, Income 440
Massachusetts
Amgen v. H.M.R., Documents Mistake 486
Bassette v. Bartolucci, Support 463
Bassette v. Bartoucci, Earnings/Support 515
Child Support Ends 447
Child Support Hall of Fame 455
Groseth v. Groseth, Support Modification 514
International Criminal Enforcement 503
International Support Enforcement 503
Kendall v. Kendall, Religion 523
Lawyer and Lies 291
Lottery Payments Frozen 516
Nexus Gay/Lesbian Parents 527
Paternity of Cheryl, Support 511
Prince v. Massachusetts, Constitution 523
Schiebel Elektronische Geraete v. Polestar 156
Support Reduced by Child's Benefits 463
White v. Laingor, Support 511
Yannas v. Frondistou-Yanna, Move 272
Matahari 89
Material Evidence, definition 589
Maternal Preference Presumption, defined 589
Maternity & Paternity Testing 137
Matter of
Delane, Legal bond with child 518
Gentry, 5th & 14th Amendment 517
Mav v. Anderson, Parent's right 517
McGuinness v. McGuiness 491
Medea Syndrome 508
Mediation
definition 589
Serial, definition 589
Traditional, definition 589
Mediative Type of Thinking 74
Mediator

and Evaluator 183
definition 589
for Negotiation 75
Mediator's Recommendation 186
Professional Liability 597
Medical
Case of Kim Lee Ong, Child 398
Child's Problem Ignored SIT #74 317
Records
Cost of Record Retrieval and Copy 354
People who keep them 354
Records Including Therapists 353
Support 589
Memorandum of Law, definition 589
Memory 572
Cognitive Ability and Memory Loss 572
Criterion Based Content Analysis 273
forgotten 406
in deposition 360
loss, Dementia 575
Memory's Imperfections 278
practice to eliminate hazy answers 394
Reasons for documentation 97
Refreshed, by documents 394
Repressed Memory Disorder 182
When is someone lying 279
Mental
Anguish, definition 590
Illness 26
Illness, Diagnostic Statistical Manual 576
Mercenary, definition 590
Merit, definition 590
Methamphetamines, Home testing kit 131
Methods of Documentation 99
Mexico, Travel Requirements 264
Meyer v. Nebraska, 14th Amendment 523
Michigan
Atkinson v. Atkinson, Equitable Parent 16
Baker v. Oakwood Hospital
Medical Records 355
Bhama v. Bhama, PAS 495
Child Support Credit 514
Child Support Ends 447
Child Support Hall of Fame 455
Dawson v. Emerson, Bio Father 312
Dunn v. Dunn, Religion, Support 462
Horton v. Switzer, Refreshed Memory 395
Nexus Gay/Lesbian Parents 527
Recording Phone Calls 488
Tanielian v. Brooks, Step-parent 513
Walbro Corp. v. Amerisure, Out of Pocket 454
Mickey Mouse Magazine 261
Military
and Child Support 460
Child Custody & Divorce Attorney 150
Child's Active Duty 446
Court 385
Garnishment or Wage Attachment 460
Non Support, SIT #62 313
Service and Child Support 460
Soldiers' and Sailors' Civil Relief Act 385
Minnesota
Berisford v. Berisford, Step-parent 513
Child Support Credit 514
Child Support Ends 447
Child Support Hall of Fame 455
Frauenshuh v. Gies, Parents Can't Modify 524
Hoffa v. Hoffa, Income 439
Multiphasic Personality Inventory 238
Out of Pocket Expenses 454
Paternity Never Settled 482
Paternity Suits Never Settled 482
Silbaugh v. Silbaugh, Move Away 272
Misappropriation of Insurance Money 295
Miscellaneous
Anxiety Inventories 240
Projective Drawings 240
Projective Drawings Test 239
Misdemeanor, definition 590
Misfeasance, definition 590
Mis-Joinder, definition 590
Mississippi
Bell v. Bell, Move Away 272
Child Support Ends 447
Child Support Hall of Shame 455
Hammett v. Woods, Abuse of Discretion 532
Harrington v. Harrington, Cohabited 532
Riley v. Doerner, Best Interest 532
Missouri 447
Child Support Ends 447
Court of Appeals Ellis v. Ellis 489
Dad Needn't Pay Back Support 514
Hackman v. Hackman, Income 438
Levesque v. Levesque, Step-parent 513
Marriage of Julian, Income 439
Searcy v. Seedorff, Circumstance 525
Support Accounting 455
Support Non-payor 459
Mistake
Documents Produced by 486
How Subpoenas Work 392
Mistrial, definition 590
Mitigating Circumstance, definition 590
Modification
After court 419
definition 590
Factors that Influence 420
Modify, definition 590

of Child Support 450
Refusal to Modify Court Order 590
things that can be Modified 419
Types of 419
Money 350
43 Parent Won't Pay Court Ordered 307
Consideration, definition 573
Hidden Assets 428
No Help From Attorney 304
Two Ways to Significantly Cut Costs 423
Under the Table Employment 459
Visitation Bond 23
Montana
Best Interest, Step Father 520
Child Support Ends 447
Child Support Hall of Fame 455
Lorenz v. Lorenz, Move Away 272
Marriage of Peterson, Share of Assets 510
Mood Swings, Index Cards to Track 101
Moot, definition 590
Mother 16
Absent 590
Conservative Sentiment on Your Side 16
Mother-absent 590
Second Parent-adoption 551
With Custody Allowed to Move Away 491
Motion 590
Contempt of Court 398
definition 590
for Security of Costs 590
in Courts Time Line 382
to Dismiss, definition 590
to Make More Definite, definition, 591
to Modify, definition 591
to Quash Service, definition 591
to Strike, definition 591
to Vacate Premises, definition 591
Move Away 271
Affects on Non-Custodial Visitation 491, 508
Best Interest 271
Burgess v. Burgess, joint custodian can 491
Cases with Foreign Nation Jurisdiction 491
Don't Move Out 25
Limited Presumption in Favor 272
Mother with Custody Allowed to 491
No Provision 271
Parents Needs Considered 491
Presumption in Favor of 272
Real Advantage Test 489
Taking Child, SIT #03, 295
Move the Court, definition 591
Multiple Personality Disorder, definition 591
Munchausen Syndrome
by Proxy Indications of 334
By Proxy, definition 591
definition 591
Mundon v. Mundon, Shift in Custody 525
Murphy's Law
About Telling Lies 276
definition 591
Music Classes 261
Mutual Mistake, definition 591

N

NAACP v. Button, Non-Lawyer can assist 487
Napoleon, quote 279
Narcissistic 508
Native American Child Welfare 386
Natural
Law, definition 591
Parent, definition 591
NCP
Non-Custodial Parent
definition 591
Denied Visitation 492
Handling Interference With Visitation 23
Visitation Bond 23
Nebraska
Best Interest, Move Away 271
Braeman v. Braeman, Income 439
Can't Sue Wife 482, 483
Child Support Credit 514
Child Support Ends 447
Groseth v. Groseth, Both Move 514
Harder v. Harder, Move Away 272
LeDoux v. LeDoux 522
Meyer v. Nebraska, 14th Amendment 523
Prescription Abuse 238
Quintela v. Quintela, Step-parent 513
Support Accounting 455
Support Reduced by Child's Benefits 463
Zucco v. Garrett, Religious 523
Negative
Halo Effect, definition 592
Observations 191
Neglect 28, 325, 329
Dental 28
Indications of Negligence or Abuse 327
Negligence, definition 591
Negotiate
Additional Considerations 78
Child's Physical Residence 77
Educational Arrangements 78
Holiday Schedule 78
How to 77
Medical & Dental Arrangements 78
Monetary Arrangements 78

Outline for Discussion, example 77
Professional or Parent Care 77
Right Place & Time 75
Time Limit 79
Using a Professional 75
Negotiation
& Cooperation Techniques 56
Defensive Behaviors 58
definition 592
Delay 59
Going Well? 77
Mediated, Arbitrated Settlement 382
Previous Settlement is Inadmissible 569
Neuropsychology see Psychologist 597
Nevada
Chambers by Cochran v. Sanderson, Income 440
Child Support Ends 448
McGuinness v. McGuines 491
McGuinness v. McGuiness, Move 491
Negative DNA Father Still Father 482
No See - No Pay 451
Paternity Suits Never Settled 482
Prescription Drug Abuse 238
SIT #61 Ex Won't Complete Move 312
Trent v. Trent, Limited Move Away 272
New
Friends 87
Traditions 475
New Hampshire
Child Support Ends 448
DeMauro v. DeMauro, Martial assets 460
Failure to Protect Child 326
Ruben v. Ruben, Step-parent 513
Shofmaster v. Shofmaster, Income 437
New Husband Stops/ Grandparent Visit SIT 64 314
New Jersey
Benda v. Benda, Emergency Jurisdiction 509
Child Support Credit 514
Child Support Ends 448
Holder v. Polanski, Limited Move Away 272
Invasion of Privacy 132
Klipstein v. Zalewski, Step-parent 513
Nexus Gay/Lesbian Parents 527
NJ v. Margaret Kelly, Child's Testimony 397
Out of Pocket Expenses 454
Same Sex 536
Spoilation of Evidence 104
Walles v. Walles, Support Reduction 437
Watkins v. Nelson, Grandparent Custody 522
New Mexico
Boutz v. Donaldson, Income 439
Child Support Ends 448
Child Support Hall of Shame 455
Nexus Gay/Lesbian Parents 527
Ottino v. Ottino, Support 511
Same Sex 536
Spoilation of Evidence 104
New Stricter Standards for Experts 229
New York
Can't Sue Wife 482, 483
Chiarello v. Chiarello, Step-parent 513
Child Support Ends 448
CPS Removal of Child 332
Kajtazi v. Kajtazi, Interference Damages 492
Knapp v. Levy, Support Lottery 440
Nexus Gay/Lesbian Parents 527
Same Sex 536
Satalino v. Satalino, Second Hand Smoke 493
Support Accounting 455
Tropea v. Tropea, Move Away 272
News Flash Junkies 84
Next Best Friend, defined 592
Nexus, definition 592
Night Inspection 35
No
Fault, definition 592
Lie Double Talk 291
Protection for Judge
Bradley v. Fisher 518
Gregoire v. Biddle 519
Sniveling or Whining 37
Nolo Contendere, definition 592
Non Support, Military 313
Noncombatants, definition 592
Non-Custodial
Parent should not pay all travel, case
Wiley v. Wiley 491
Parent's Visitation Emotions 25
Santosky v. Kramer, Protections 516
Visitation Bond 23
Visitation Responsibilities 266
Visitation, Move Away Cases 491
Non-Family
Boyfriend won't get custody 483
Girlfriend may get custody 483
Non-Fatal Flaw 285
Nonfeasance, definition 592
Non-Issue 394
Best Interest of the Child 28
Blended Family 26
definition 592
Domestic Violence 28
EX Won't Complete Move SIT #61 312
False Accusation 26
Kidnapping Threat 27
Lying to Child/ to You/ to the Court 27
New Significant Other or Step-parent 28

Other Parent is a Control Freak 26
Other parent is only doing this to hurt me 27
Poor Living Conditions 28
Non-Lawyer 23
Can Assist, case 487
Getting Started 143
No Recovery of Fees 142
Non–Sexual Exploitation 326
Non-Support, definition 592
North Carolina
Child Support Credit 515
Child Support Ends 448
Darden v. Darden, Support, Lottery 439
Duffey v. Duffey, Step-parent 513
Ellison v. Ramos, Girlfriend Custody 483
Ellison v. Ramos, Step-Mom Custody 312
Pulliam v. Smith, Gay 543
Shaw v. Cameron, Income 440
Taylor v. Taylor, Attorney Fees 525
North Dakota
Child Support Ends 448
Keller v. Keller, Move Away 272
McDonough v. Murphy, Move Away 272
Nexus Gay/Lesbian Parents 527
Shaver v. Kopp, Income 441
Supreme Court Mother's Move 491
Not Admissible Evidence
E-mail 103
Fruit of the Poisonous Tree 352
Notebook 101
Notice of
Exercise of Parenting Time 23
Hearing, definition 592

O

Oath
definition 592
for Interpreter 585
-taking Competency, Child's 395
Objecting in Interrogatory 352
Objection
Argumentative 411
Compound Question 411
definition 592
Hearsay 411
Irrelevant Question 411
Lack of Foundation 411
Leading Question 411
Presumption 411
Repetitive Question 411
to Video in Court 130
Obligor & Obligee, definition 592
Off
Calendar, definition 592
the Record, definition 593
Officer of the Court, definition 592
Off-site Supervision 592
Ohio
Can't Sue Wife 483
Carol Pisani, 300+ Separate Filings 414
Chambers v. Baltimor, Meaningful Access 600
Child Support Ends 448
Foor v. Foor, Grandparent Visitation 522
Leis v. Leis, Shared parenting 489
Luke v. Luke, Shared parenting 490
Nexus Gay/Lesbian Parents 527
Norwood v. McDonald, Question Again 418
Out of Pocket Expenses 454
Pater v. Pater, Constitution 523
Paternity Never Settled 482
Paternity Suits Never Settled 482
Pratt v. McCullough, Support, Lottery 439
Spoilation of Evidence 104
Transit Authority v. Timson, Vexatious 414
Vexatious Litigation
Kondrat v. Byron 415
Weltchek v. Weltchek, ProSe 415
Zayed v. Zayed, Income 438
Oklahoma
Child Support Ends 448
Grandparents Protection 521
Matter of Delaney, Right to Bond 518
Support Accounting 455
Old Friends 87
On 593
Demand, definition 593
the Record, definition 593
Online Friends 87
On-site Supervision 593
On-The-Job Friends 87
Open
Court, definition 593
Questions 408
Opiates, Home testing kit 131
Opinion, definition 593
Opposition
Dealing With the Anger of Others 321
definition 593
Deposition 363
EX Won't Complete Move SIT #61 312
Grinding Me Down, SIT 68 315
Opposition's
Attorney Frontal Assault 410
Attorney to Your Side 154
Deposition During 363
Detective 171
Detective Searched My House, SIT 65 314

Detective, Research 171
Inventory, example 45
Mad Dog Attorney 360
Parents 86
Using An Expert 225
Video Inspection of Home 130
Oppositional 593
Oppositional Defiant Disorder 593
Order
definition 593
for Protection 353
Is Not a Suggestion. 403
to Show Cause (OSC), definition 593
to Vacate, definition 593
Oregon
Child Support Credit 515
Child Support Ends 448
Child Support Modeling 444
Federal Wire Tap Law 487
Fitch v. Belshaw, Due Process 464
McKeever v. McKeever, Religion 462
Nexus Gay/Lesbian Parents 527
Non-bio Father May Get Custody 483
State v. Sprague, Religion, Support 462
Support Accounting 455
Telephone Recorder 132
Orr v. Orr, Classification by Gender 517
Osteras v. Osteras 524
Other
Side Cooperate, Why? 71
Other Parent
Affecting Agenda of the 72
Control Freak and no Responsibility 26
EX Won't Complete Move SIT #61 312
Facing the 232
Hiding Assets in Another's Name 459
Identify Your Concerns About the 210
Implied Threats 296
Is A Chameleon 186
is a Control Freak 26
is only doing this to hurt me 27
Lengthy Childcare 26
Misappropriating Insurance Payment 295
Profile Precursors False Accuser 338
Requesting Supervised Visitation for 341
Retraining 36
Tape-Recording Phone Calls 488
Won't Pay Court Ordered Money 307
Working Under the Table 459
Works Under the Table 459
Out of Court, definition 593
Over or Under Exposed, Expert 221

P

Pager 131
Pain
Dead Hand 19
Dealing with Depression/Pain, Duck Muck 47
of Others, Learning from the 294
Panel, Jury, definition 593
Panic Situations
Chapter 16, 293
Evaluating Your 317
examples 294
Your List 318
Pankratz v. Willis, $125,000 Awarded Father 507
Paralegal
definition 593
Services 134
Paranoia
Are You Being Watched? 171
definition 593
Personal Security 34
Parens Patrieae, definition 593
Parent
busy, uninvolved 260
Effective 260
Expelled from children's lives 267
in Fact 137
Locator Service, Federal 134
-pal 260
Psychological 16
Psychological, 1993 Ruling, case 509
Rights Mav v. Anderson 517
Rights Terminating 435
Soldier Creed 46
to Parent Guidelines for Discussion 76
Unfit SIT#63 313
Who Must Have Perfect Children 260
Parent's
Rights, Wards of the State 392
Visitation Emotions, Non-Custodial 25
Parental
Care Preferred, Doubtfire Clause 11
Caretaker acts/omissions, Abuse 330
Interference
Must still pay support 451
Visitation Bond 23
with Visitation 23
Interference, definition 593
Liability, definition 594
Rights Termination case 509
Voluntary Relinquishment of Rights 429
Parental Alienation Syndrome 186
Combating 269
Daubert V. Merrell, case 496
DHSS on Child Abuse, case 489

DHSS report on 496
Evaluator 186
False Accusations of 189
Legal Action May Proceed for 484
PAS, definition 593
the theory 186
What PAS Is 188
What PAS Is Not 187
Parental Kidnapping
definition 594
Prevention Act, case 497
Profile of the Abductor 344
Parent-Child
Interaction Test 239
Privilege 273
Parenting
Classes 134
Classes, definition 594
Constitutional Right 516
Differences, Panic SIT #29, 303
Good-Enough, 1968 Research, case 485
Parents
Can't Choose Modification 524
Needs Considered Move Away 491
Opposition's 86
rights & child's rights
Franz v. United States 516
Your 86
Parole, definition 594
Parties or Party, definition 594
PAS
Berg v. Perlow, FL 495
Bhama v. Bhama, MI 495
Children are not Chargeable 496
PAS see Parental Alienation Syndrome
Passive
Aggression 594
Inhalation of drugs 135, 237
Resistance, definition 594
Smoke, Second-Hand 324
Passport
Get your Child's 270
Office of the United States
to avoid kidnapping 270
Travel 264
Paternity
DNA Negative - Father is Still Father 482
Equity Doesn't Give Boyfriend Custody 483
Husband Can't Sue Wife for Lying About 482
Lawsuit, definition 594
No-Biological Father May Get Custody 483
Recognition of Parentage 54
Suits May Never be Settled 482
Testing 594
Presumed Father 137
Pathological Liar 277
Patrol Service 134
Payment, Wrongfully Kept by Other Parent 295
PCP- Phencyclidine, Home testing kit 131
Peeping Tom Law 35, 175
Detective Report #2 175
Peer Review 594
Pennsylvania
Baldwin v. Baldwin, Move Away 272
Can't Sue Wife 483
Child Support Ends 448
Child Support Hall of Fame 455
Drawbaugh v. Drawbaugh, Step-parent 513
Forced to Provide College 464
Nexus Gay/Lesbian Parents 527
Parker v. Rodwell, ProSe Fees 142
Perlberger v. Perlberger, Fraud/Distress 460
Wire Tap 459
Young v. Muthersbaugh, Income 438
Zummo v. Zummo, Religion 522
People
Believe What They See 201, 583
Trail 348
Noncombatants 592
Per Se, definition 595
Percent-of-Income Child Support Guideline 444
Percipient Witness, definition 594
Peremptory Challenge 370, 594
definition 594
Perez v. Campbell, case License revocation 464
Perfected, definition 594
Perjury 276
definition 594
Subornation of, definition 603
Sue for 283
Permanent Retaliation 57
Perpetuating Testimony, definition 594
Personality Disorders, Extensive, Lying 277
Persuasive Authority 376
Persuasive Authority, definition 595
Peterson v Stanczak, case 520
Petition
definition 595
Termination and Adoption of Stepchild 432
Petitioner, definition 595
Petty Offenses 595
Phone Calls Between Children and Parent 488
Photos 127, 353
Peeping Tom Law, example #2 172, 175
Take Photos of Everything 127
Physical 26
Abuse 26
Abuse, Munchausen Syndrome by Proxy 334

Custody, definition 595
Physician/Patient Privilege, definition 595
Pick-Up Order, definition 595
Pierson v. Ray, Judges prejudice 518
Pig to Sing, Teaching a 30
Plaintiff, definition 595
Plea Bargaining, definition 595
Pleading, definition 595
Poker Face 89
Police 24
and Restraining Orders 24
Barillari v. City of Milwaukee 525
Child Been Abused 334
Does a Liability Case Exist? 526
If Your are Arrested 40
Kidnapping 343
Restraining Orders 24, 152
Sit #70 Former Spouse Tips 316
Sued in Domestic Violence Cases 525
to get a copy of a Police Report 343
When the Police are Called 39
Pollock v. Williams, case
Forced labor to pay child support 458
Polygraph
definition 595
Machine 136
Poor Choices 56, 273
Rescuer 33
Poor Living Conditions 28
Positive
Halo Effect 583
definition 595
Observations 190
Possessory Conservator, definition 595
Post a Bond, definition 595
Post-Traumatic Stress Disorder (PTSD) 596
Potential Injury, definition 596
Poverty Guidelines 2001 426
Power of Attorney, definition 596
Practical Expert 219
Praise for Win Your Child Custody War iii
Pray for Peace 11
Precedent 376
definition 596
First Impression Case 581
No Longer Holds, Appeal 412
Sense Impression, definition 596
Stare Decisis, definition 602
Prejudice, definition 596
Prejudicial Error, definition 596
Preliminary Hearing 392
Criminal, definition 596
Preparation for Negotiation 76
Prepare for a Deposition 356
Preponderance of Evidence, definition 596
Prescription Drug Use 237
Presumed Father 137
Presumption in Favor of Move Away Provision 272
Presumption of
Fact, definition 596
Law, definition 596
Preventing False Allegation 336
Previous Cases, Civil & Criminal 353
Prima Facie 596
Privacy
Act 295
Peeping Tom Law 35
see Invasion of Privacy
Privilege
Attorney Client 149
General Rule of, definition 596
Husband-Wife 584
Parent-Child 273
Physician/Patient 595
Privileged Relationship 149
Release of, definition 596
Waiver of 149
Work-Product 219, 485
Pro Bono, definition 597
Pro Se
Blood v. Margis 518
definition 597
Has absolute right to tape record trial 488
No Recovery of Attorney Fees 142
Non-lawyers, case, NAACP v. Button 487
Not Held to Same Standards as Attorney 487
Paralegal Service 134
Representing Yourself 142
Proactive, definition 597
Probate Case, definition 597
Probation, definition 597
Procedural Law, definition 597
Proceedings, definition 597
Process Server, definition 597
Production of Documents 353
How Subpoenas Work 392
Professional Liability 597
Profile
of the Abductor 344
Precursors False Accuser 338
Project Return 264
Proof
definition 597
or Poof 284
Proposed Findings, definition 597
ProSe
Kondrat v. Byron, Unreasonable 415
Weltchek v. Weltchek, Frivolous 415

Prosecutor, definition 597
Protection, Failed to provide
Raucci v. Town of Rotterdam 518
Protective
Calloway v. Kinkelaar, IL 525
Laws May Not Hide a Child, case 519
Order of Protection 40
Order, definition 597
Order, Things you can get Arrested for 39
Ricketts v. City of Columbia, Mo. 526
Sit# 01, Legal Papers 294
Provider, Supervised Visitation 597
Psychological
& Emotional Preparation for Deposition 356
Evaluation #1 241
Evaluation #2 246
Parent 16
1993 Ruling, Atkinson v. Atkinson 509
definition 597
Tests, Use & Misuse, case
David M. Brodzinsky 487
Tests, Who can perform them 230
Psychologist
& Tests, Chapter 13, 230
As a Friend of the Court 52
Best Attitude with 231
Check out the 230
Clinical 597
Confidentiality 239
definition 597
Evaluation & Significant Other 233
Filing a Formal Complaint 239
Forensic 597
I Think I Need a Shrink 38
Professional Liability 597
Recommendation = Decision 232
Sex & the 239
Sued in Domestic Violence Cases 525
What Are They Looking For? 233
Psychotherapy, definition 597
Public
Constant Harassment SIT # 51 310
Records & Reports, definition 598
Reprimand, Attorney 162
Safety Overrides Right to Travel, case 487
Punishment, definition 598

Q

Qualified
Domestic Relations Order 598
Medical Child Support Order 453
Quality, definition 598
Quantity, definition 598
Quash
definition 598
Service of Summon 591
Questioning, Types of 409
Questions
Hypothetical 408, 584
Leading 408, 588
Not Sure! Not Sure? 410
Open 408
Safe Answers for Stupid 473
Safe Answers to Hard Questions
During the Battle 84
Types of 408

R

Ralph Waldo Emerson, quote 61
Random 58
Drug Test 236
Rape
definition 598
Statutory, definition 602
Rational Type of Thinking 74
Raucci v. Town of Rotterdam, case
Failure to provide protection 518
Re in the Marriage of Knighton 522
Reactive, definition 598
Real Advantage Test, Removal of child 489
Reality Check 51
Reasonable Doubt, definition 598
Reasonable Visitation 598
Reasons
for Documentation 97
People Think They Have Custody 18
Your Attorney Will Fire You 156
Rebuttable Presumption, definition 598
Rebuttal, definition 598
Recalcitrant
Parent, Houde v Beckmeyer 496
Parent, Webb v. Kundson 496
Receipts for Products & Services 353
Reciprocity
Reciprocal Enforcement, definition 598
Reciprocal Support Arrangements 457
Speak to Inequity 403
Type of negotiation 58
Reciprocity, definition 599
Recognition of Parentage 54
Recording Phone Conversations
Between Children and Other Parent 488
cases 487
Conflict of Laws Rules 132
Federal Wiretap Law 487
No Need for Ex Parte Order 488

Records
- Expunged 527, 579
- Religious Organizations, definition 598
- Vital Statistics, definition 598

Recrimination 186
Recruiting Troops Using Lies 280
Recusal, definition 598
Redirect Examination, definition 598
Reduced Child Support, by Child's Benefits 463
Referee, definition 598
Refreshed Memory, documents 394
Refusal
- to Admit 366
- to go for Visitation, Child 267

Relationship
- Before the Birth 44, 45
- Inventory, example #1 44
- Inventory, example #2 45
- Privileged 149

Release of Privileged Information 596
Relief, definition 599
Religion 263
- As Custody Grounds, SIT 46 308
- Church and State 263
- Court not favor Religion over None, ID 524
- Intra-Faith Custody Challenges 263
- Kendall v. Kendall, MA 523
- LeDoux v. LeDoux, NE 522
- Marriage of Mentry, Privacy 524
- Meyer v. Nebraska, 14th Amendment 523
- Pater v. Pater, OH 523
- Religious Abuse, definition 599
- Thomas v. Review Board, 1st Amendment 523
- Zucco v. Garrett, IL 523
- Zummo v. Zummo 522
- Zummo v. Zummo, PA 522

Relinquishment
- definition 599
- I want to give up 12
- Voluntary 429

Remand, definition 599
Reply, definition 599
Reporter, Court, definition 599
Reporting Domestic Violence, definition 599
Reporting to the Court, Supervised Visitation 340
Repression 599
Repudiate, definition 599
Requiring Opinion from Everyone 37
Rescind, definition 599
Rescuer
- Agenda of the 33
- Lethal help 33

Research
- Opponent's Expert 228
- Opposition's Detective 171
- Your Judge 370

Residence Order, definition 598
Residential Parent, definition 599
Resistance, Passive, definition 594
Resolution, definition 599
Respect, definition 599
Respondent, definition 599
Response
- in Courts Time Line 382
- Time 599

Responsibilities
- I want to give up my rights 12
- Voluntary Relinquishment of 429
- Your Children Have 269

Responsibility
- Accepting 52
- and Rights, Relinquishment of 429
- Custodial Visitation 266
- definition 599
- is Yours 34
- Non-Custodial Visitation 266

Rest
- & Relaxation 33
- definition 599

Restitution, definition 599
Restraining Order 24, 152, 353
- Attorney Advised Not to Comply 152
- Commonwealth v. Butle 518
- Commonwealth v. Carter 490
- Commonwealth v. Laskowski 518
- definition 599
- Situation #32 304

Retainer 150
- definition 599

Retraining 36
Retrieval Questionnaire for Abduction 346
Revenge 12, 274
- definition 599
- Medea Syndrome 508
- The One I Feed 48

Revised Statutes, defining 599
Revocation for Support Arrears, case 464
Rhode Island
- Child Support Ends 448
- Child Support Payments 465
- Emergency ends Jurisdiction 508
- Nadeau v. Nadeau, Emergency 509

Rich Can't Get Attorney Fees from Richer 525
Right
- of Meaningful Access 600
- of Primary Refusal see First Right of Refusal 581
- to be heard see Audi Alteram Parte 568

Rights
definition 599
I want to give up my 12
Visitation is the Child's 21
When the Police are Called 39
Risk 600
Assessment 600
Factors 600
Ritualistic Abuse, definition 600
Rorschach Test 238
Ross KL, False Allegations 507
Rules of
Court, definition 600
Deposition 355
Evidence, definition 600
Evidence, Federal 580
Rulings, Examples of 412

S

S.K.Y. Scream-Kick-Yell 270
Safe Answers
During a Custody Battle 84
When you don't have custody 473
Safety Nets 31
SAID Syndome, Studies 507
Sanctions, definition 600
Sane, definition 600
Santosky v. Kramer, Constitutional Right 516
Saul v. Brunetti, Grandparents, FL 521
Schizophrenia, definition 600
School Records, Children's & Adult's 353
Sealing of Records, definition 600
Search Warrant, definition 600
Second Deposition 356
Secondary Authority 600
Second-Hand Smoke
and Children 274, 494
definition 600
Delays Tooth Eruption 494
Exposure Considered Child Abuse 324
Marijuana 275
Secret Psychologist Help 39
Secret Weapon, Trial Memorandum 604
Secular Humanism Ethics 74
Security
at Your Home 34
Breach 81
Measures 293
of Costs, definition 600
of Costs, Motion for, definition 590
Paper Shredder 131
Personal 34
Seeing Abuse is Abuse 271
Self
Authenticated, definition 601
Deception, Liars Even Lie to Themselves 280
Employment 438
Help Groups, not for you 31
Incrimination, definition 601
pity, Duck Muck 47
Separation Anxiety Disorder 601
Sequester, Calling for the Rule 570
Service
definition 601
Professional Companies 132
You can Hire Options List 140
You Hire out and Confidentiality 140
Settlement
definition 601
Depression 601
Offers in Negotiations are Inadmissible 569
Sex & Your
Attorney 153
Detective 180
Psychologist 239
Sexual
Abuse 325
Abuse, definition 601
Abuse, False Accusation SIT #41 307
Assault 325
Exploitation of a Minor, Commercial 325
Molestation of a Child 325
Shall, definition 601
Shame, Anger 95
Shared parenting
Agreement 53
Leis v. Leis 489
Luke v. Luke 490
Shaver v. Kopp, Income, ND 441
Shelter, definition 601
Shepard's
Case Citations 481
Shepardized, definition 601
Shopping
Forum Shopping 370
Jurisdiction Shopping 369
Venue Shopping 375
Short
and Long Range Planning 55
Time Line 25
Show Cause, definition 601
Shrink-Confidentiality 38
Siblings, definition 601
Sign
Don't Without Attorney 25
Language Interpreter 585
Significant Other

at Evaluation 186
definition 601
Income of 442
Second Parent-adoption 551
Your Role 17
Simplicity & Speed 104
Sine Die, definition 601
SIT #01, Legal Papers 294
SIT #02, Misuse of Money 295
SIT #03, Possible Kidnapping 295
SIT #04, Phone Harassment at Work 295
SIT #05, Physical Abuse of Child 296
SIT #06, Implied Threats 296
SIT #07, False Accusations 296
SIT #08, Abandonment 296
SIT #09, Child Denied Phone Contact 297
SIT #10, Visitation Interference 297
SIT #11, Public Display of Affection 297
SIT #12, Intercepting Child's Mail 298
SIT #13, Dangerous Living Conditions 298
SIT #14, Denial of Holiday Visitation 298
SIT #15, Upsetting Child on Phone 299
SIT #16, Danger to Child 299
SIT #17, Conditions for Pick Up 299
SIT #18, Moving Child Away 299
SIT #19, Restriction of Time With Child 300
SIT #20, Telling Lies to Child 300
SIT #21, Can't Stand Each Other 300
SIT #22, Interference With Contact 301
SIT #23, Attorney Invoice Inflated 301
SIT #24, Alienation of Affections 301
SIT #25, Demand for Information 302
SIT #26, Disneyland Parent 302
SIT #27, Grandparent Visitation Denied 302
SIT #28, Secret Documents 302
SIT #29, Different Parenting Style 303
SIT #30, Conflict During Exchange 303
SIT #31, Misuse of Psychological Evaluation 303
SIT #33, Children Pressuring Parent 304
SIT #34, No Money, No Help 304
SIT #35, Other Attorney Costing You $$ 305
SIT #36, Grandparents Custody Interrupted 305
SIT #37, Child's Affidavit of Preference 305
SIT #38, Child Won't go to Visitation 306
SIT #39, Attorney Wants to Quit 306
SIT #40, We Comply, They Don't 306
SIT #41, Accusation of Sexual Abuse 307
SIT #42, Visitation Home is Dangerous 307
SIT #43, Other Parent Won't Pay 307
SIT #44, Proof They Lied, Forged & Ignored 308
SIT #45, Parent Threatens Suicide 308
SIT #46, Religion as Custody Grounds 308
SIT #47, My Lawyer Really Screwed Me 308
SIT #48, Parent Won't Supply Insurance Card 309
SIT #49, Volunteer Spy 309
SIT #50, Other Parent & Judge Association 309
SIT #51, Internet Lurking 310
SIT #52, Prosecution for Perjury 310
SIT #53, Constant Public Harassment 310
SIT #54, Change in NCP Circumstances 311
SIT #55, Parent in Fact 311
SIT #56, Ex-Husband Excluded as Guardian 311
SIT #57, Credit Report Without Permission 311
SIT #58, Bio - Dad Against Adoptive Parents 311
SIT #59, Step-Mom Wants Custody 312
SIT #60, Computer Evidence 312
SIT #61, EX Won't Complete Move 312
SIT #62, Non Support from Military Parent 313
SIT #63, Unfit Parent 313
SIT #64, Interfering with Grandparent Visits 314
SIT #65, Opposition Searched My House 314
SIT #66, Confidentiality of Case in Question 315
SIT #67, Fined for Attorney Advice 315
SIT #68, Opposition Grinding Me Down 315
SIT #69, Leaving Country Owes Support 315
SIT #70, Tips Police 316
SIT #71, Bipolar Disorder 316, 317
SIT #72, Child's Right to Choose 316
SIT #73, Forcing Me Back to Court 317
SIT #74, Child's Medical Problem 317
Sixteen States Provide Child Support Credit 514
Sixth Amendment 601
Skin Piercing 405
Slander, definition 601
Small Claims Court to sue Attorney 158
Smoking, Grandparents 494
Snivel or Whine 30, 37
Social, Stigma of not having Your Child 267
Soldiers' and Sailors' Civil Relief Act 385
Sole Custody 20
definition 601
I Want 53
Sole Managing Conservator, definition 601
Solicitor, definition 602
Some Experts are Prostitutes 221
South Carolina
Child Support Ends 448
Employment/Income Verification 438
Nexus Gay/Lesbian Parents 527
Same Sex 536
Taylor v. Taylor, Income 439
Termination of Parental Rights 509
South Dakota
Child Support Ends 448
Child Support Hall of Fame 455
Fortin v. Fortin, Move Away 272
Support Reduced by Child's Benefit 463
Special Master, definition 602

Split Custody 20
definition 602
Spoilation
DeLew v. Wagner 104
Goff v. Harold Ives Trucking Co 103
Swekel v. City of River Rouge 104
Sports 261
Spy
Peeping Tom Law 35
Shops 134
Volunteer Spy, SIT # 49 309
Stalking 165
definition 602
Standards
for Experts 229
of Conduct (for Attorneys), case 485
Stanford-Binet Intelligence Testing 240
Stanton v. Stanton, Gender Classification 517
Stare Decisis, Present, definition 602
Start a Support Group 479
State
Clearinghouse, definition 602
Department Travel Requirements 265
has right to take child, Parens Patrieae 593
State's Evidence, definition 602
Statutes, definition 602
Status Quo
definition 602
Or What Is Shall Remain 189, 240, 291
Statute
definition 602
Law, definition 602
of Limitations to sue Attorney 159
of Limitations, definition 602
Statutory Rape, definition 602
Stay, definition 602
Stepfamily
Step Grandparents 17
Step-parent 17
Child Support 512
definition 603
Ellison v. Ramos, Wants Custody 312
Income of 442
Step-Mom Wants Custody, SIT 59 312
Stipulation, definition 603
Stockholm Syndrome 603
Strange Situation Test 241
Stranger
at the Door 35
don't talk to Strangers 81
on the Telephone 35
Strategies 51
& Techniques, Chapter 4, 51
Attrition 57
Changing Your 74
Deterrence 57
Exploitative or Permanent 57
Look Ahead 57
Random 58
Reciprocity 58
Strategic Case Boosters 59
Strategic Interaction 55
Tester 57
Tit for Tat 57
Tranquilizer 57
Strategy, Case 393
Stress
Before a Deposition 356
Causes child to test situation 259
Dealing with Other Parent 65
Don't transfer to children 92
Fear and Communication 82
Last Review reduces 395
of Departure for Children 254
Recognize personal symptoms 473
Secret Psychologist Help 39
Sit#71 Bipolar Disorder 316
Strange Situation Test 241
What's causing it 66
willingness or unwillingness for visit 267
Strike, Motion to 591
Studies & Decisions
Best Interest 28, 520
Chapter 26, 481
Child not Charged with Parent Misconduct 496
Domestic Violence, case 485
Effects of Custody 484
Effects of Custody Arrangements 484
Flink v. Flink 510
Good-Enough Parenting 485
Interference with Visitation 484
Joint v. Sole Custody 484
NCP Denied Visitation 492
Psychological Parent 509
Second-Hand Smoke and Children 494
Second-Hand Smoke Delays Tooth 494
Study of Families After Divorce 484
Termination Parental Rights 509
Use & Misuse of Psych. Testing 487
Visitation Interference 492
Subornation of Perjury, definition 603
Subpoena
definition 603
Duces Tecum, definition 603
How they work 392
Substance Abuse, Home Testing Kits 131
Substantiated/Founded 603
Substantive Law, definition 603

Successful, Visitation 22
Such Behavior Is Bad Parenting 273
Suddenly Super Parent 21
Suffering, Visitation causes Child's 14
Suicide, Parent Threatens, SIT 45 308
Suing
 Attorney for Malpractice, definition 589
 Child-Snatching Lawsuits 571
 Cross-petition or complaint, definition 575
 for Damages, definition 575
 Your Attorney 158
Summons
 definition 603
 Motion to Quash Service of 591
Supervised Visitation 338
 Complying with 339, 341
 Family Violence 580
 for the Other Parent 341
 for Yourself 341
 Off-site Supervision 592
 On-site Supervision 593
 Options 339
 Parent's Responsibilities 266
 Provider 597
 Reason for Referral 340
 Reporting to the Court 340
 Requesting 338
 Therapeutic 604
 Therapeutic Supervision 604
 Types of 340
 Visit Supervisor 606
 visiting Parent 606
Support
 Act, Family 511
 Departures from Guidelines 450
 Group, Start a 31
 Reduced to Match time with Child, case 463
Support Group, start a 479
Supreme Court of the United States 383
Surprise & Ambush 351
Surprise Witness May Not Testify 489
Surrogate
 Parent, definition 603
Surveillance
 definition 603
 in Custody Evaluation 193
 or Subrosa 603
 Right One 166
 the Costs 168
Suspension
 definition 603
 of Attorney 161
Sustain, definition 603
Swimming Classes 261
Syllabus, definition 603
Synopsis, definition 603

T

Tactic, is a Technique, is a Strategy 56
Tainted Evidence, definition 603
Take-Home Pay, definition 603
Tamper, definition 603
Tape Record
 Conversations as Evidence 354
 Conversations, Production of documents 353
 No Need for Court Order, case
  State of AZ v. Johnson 488
 Recorded Conversation 517
 Recorder for Contact Log 101
 Recorder, equipment 131
 Recording Phone Calls
  Between Children and Other Parent 488
 Trial Proceedings, case
  Forsythe v. Family Court 488
Tasks of Emotional Development Test 240
Tattoos 405
 Activities to Avoid 95
 Jail House 405
 on Data Sheet for identification 88
 Removed 405
Tax
 Child Support As A Expense/Debit 453
 Dependent Credits 428
 Earned Income Credit 428
 Gifts 428
 Records 353
Teacher 653
 letter from 204
 Letter of support #9 204
 Testimony from 134
Telephone
 Answering Machine 131
 Caller ID 129
 Cellular 130
 Child is Not Allowed to Call 297
 Deposition 205
 Mobile 132
 Recorder On Phone 132
 Recorder, Spy Shops 134
 Records 353
Telling the Awful Truth 290
Temporary
 Child Support 446
 Child Support Modification 450
 Custody 25
  definition 603
 Injunction, definition 603

Motions, definition 603
or Interim Custody 20
Order Hearings 392
Orders in Courts Time Line 382
Restraining Order, Calloway v. Kinkelaar 525
Restraining Order, definition 604
Restraining Order, vacated 152
Tender Years Doctrine
defined 487, 604
Tennessee
Aaby v. Strange, Move Away 272
Brown v. Birman Managed Care, Support 512
Child Support Ends 448
Child Support Hall of Shame 455
Lesbian Mom Restricted Access 538
Moore v. Youngquist, Support, Lottery 439
Move Away 272
Term of Court 604
Termination of Parental Rights case 509
Tester 57
Testimony
Competence of Child to Testify 395
Content of Child's 397
definition 604
Disallowing a Child to Testify 551
Expert 219
Fear, Bias, Prejudice, Interest 397
Subornation of Perjury 603
Testify, definition 604
Testifying in Court, Children 395
Testimony by
Day Care Workers 133
Detective 133
Doctors 133
Legal Transcribers 133
Patrol Service 134
Spy Shops 134
Teachers 134
Travel Agent 135
Your Child 396
Testing Services 135
Tests
DNA, Genetic Testing 137
DNA, What Is Needed For 138
Drug 135, 236
for Adults
Adult Sentence Completions 239
MMPI 238
Rorschach 238
Sixteen Personality Factor 239
Thematic Apperception 239
WAIS, Intelligence test 240
for Children
Bender Gestalt 240
Bricklin Perceptual Scales 240
Family Eruptions Test 240
Miscellaneous Anxiety Inventories 240
Miscellaneous Projective Drawings 240
Stanford-Binet Intelligence Testing 240
Strange Situation Test 241
Tasks of Emotional Development 240
Thematic or Children's Apperception 240
WAIS, Intelligence test 240
Wide Range Achievement Test 240
WISC, Intelligence test 240
Lie Detector 136
Maternity & Paternity 137
Passive Inhalation 237
Paternity, definition 594
Random Testing 236
Urine 135, 237
Texas 514
Adoption of Stepchild 432
Both Move 514
Child Support Ends 448
Child Support Hall of Shame 455
Decree Terminating Rights 435
Hudson v. Markham, Income 440
International Support Enforcement 457
Marriage of Knighton, Religion 522
Out of Pocket Expenses 454
Relinquishment of Parental Rights 429
Study Report of Investigator 434
Thanks But No Thanks, How to say 33
The
End - Beginning, Chapter 22, 33
One I Feed 48
Their Problem or Ours 25
Thematic Apperception Test 239
Thematic or Children's Apperception Test 240
Theory of PAS 186
Therapeutic Supervision 604
Thinking
Don't Think Out Loud 82
Right 34
Types of, Abstract 73
Types of, Analytical 73
Types of, Calculative 74
Types of, Emotional 73
Types of, Linear 73
Types of, Mediative 74
Types of, Rational 74
Types of, Secular Humanism 74
Third Party Tort 525
Third-Party 604
Thomas v. Review Board, Religious 523
Thompson v. James Ellenbecker, Revocation 464
Threat

Analysis 293
definition 603
Panic Situation #06 296
Risk 600
Violence Lethality Assessment 342
Time Line
Chronology 571
Court 382
If your On A Short 25
Life's 24
of Your Case 145
Timing is Important in all things 284
Tissue Test for Maternity or Paternity 138
Tit for Tat 57
Title 18, Imbler v. Pachtman 520
Tokyo Rose 89
Too Much
Hurt Accidently 272
Tooling the Statute of Limitations, definition 604
Tools of the Crime, definition 604
Tort, definition 604
Trail of Evidence 103
Tranquilizer 57
Transcript, definition 604
Travel 264
Agent 135
Passport Restrictions, Child Support 514
visas, passports 264
Trespass, definition 604
Trial
definition 604
Memorandum, definition 604
Troxel v. Granville, Grandparents 521
Truth
Cold Turkey 286
Conflicting 277
Memory's Imperfections 278
Must start telling the 286
Telling the Awful 290
Their soldiers see lies as 281
Truth, definition 604
Turtle Magazine 261
Type of Law
Case Law 570
Types of
Custody Arrangements 19
Questioning 409
Cross Examination 409
Direct Examination 409
Re-Direct 409
Questions 408
Hypothetical Questions 408
Leading Questions 408
Open Questions 408
Supervised Visitation 340
Types of Law
Civil Law 571
Criminal Law 574
Procedural Law 597
Substantive Law 603
Types of Laws
Federal Statutes 580
Persuasive Authority 595
State Statutes 602
Uniform Laws 605
Types of Visitation
Fixed-Schedule Visitation 20, 21, 23, 24, 27, 181, 581, 598
Grandparent 22
Internet E-mail 131
Internet visitation 131
Reasonable Visitation 598
Requested Supervised Visitation 338
Supervised visitation 340
Telephone Visitation 297
Third-Party 604

U

U.S.
Court of Appeals Armed Forces 384
Court of Federal Claims 383
Supreme Court is Fallible, case 519
v. Gillespie, Dolls fail Frey Test 487
v. Green, 1824 17
UIFSA, definition 604
Ultra
Conservative, definition 605
Liberal, definition 605
Liberal, Judge 370
Vires, definition 604
Ultraconservative, Judge 370
Unclean Hands, definition 605
Unconditional, definition 605
Unconstitutional, definition 605
Uncontested Custody 605
Under
Protest, definition 605
the Table Income 459
Undisputed Fact, definition 605
Undue Influence
definition 605
see Rescind
Visitation, Panic SIT #37 306
Unethical, definition 605
Unfit Parent, SIT#63 313
Unfit, definition 605
Uniform

Child Custody Jurisdiction Act, case 507
Marriage & Divorce Act, case 515
Marriage and Divorce Act 28
Uniform Laws 605
Unimpeachable Witness, definition 605
United States
Court of International Trade 383
Tax Court 384
Unperfected, definition 605
Unsolicited Help, Advice 32
Unsubstantiated/Unfounded 605
Unwed, definition 605
Unwritten Law, definition 605
Urine Analysis 135, 237
Use A Good Tax Advisor 428
Utah
Child Support Credit 515
Child Support Ends 448
Child Support Hall of Fame 455
Concerned Parents of Stepchildren v. Mitchell 513
Grandparent Visitation 520
Nexus Gay/Lesbian Parents 527
Recorded Phone Calls 488

V

Vacate, definition 605
Vague Laws, Grayned v. City of Rockford, 518
Valium, Home testing kit 131
Vehicle License Revocation Held Invalid, case 464
Venue
Local 588
Shopping 375
Verba fortius accipiuntur contra proferentem 605
Verbatim, definition 605
Verbiage, definition 605
Verdict
definition 605
Directed 576
Verification
definition 605
Employment 438
of Income, Support 437
Vermont
Child Support Credit 515
Child Support Ends 449
DNA Excluded 138
Hunt v. Hunt, Religious, Support 461
Infliction of Emotional Distress 484
Lane v. Schenck, Move Away 272
Nexus Gay/Lesbian Parents 527
Same Sex 536
Vexatious Litigation
Kondrat v. Byron, Ohio 415
Not a Vexatious Litigator 414
Pisani, 300+ Separate Filings 414
Sit #73 Forcing Me Back to Court 317
Weltchek v. Weltchek 415
Victim
definition 606
or Victor 49
Victory
definition 606
Is This the Win I Wanted? 468
Video
Camera 130
Evidence 130
Inspection 130
Vigilant, definition 606
Vindictive
definition 606
Parent 267
Violations of
duties
as a professional, Attorney 160
owed to Client, Attorney 160
owed to the Legal System, Attorney 160
Restraining Order
Commonwealth v. Butler 518
Violence
Domestic, report 485
Lethality Assessment 342
Virginia
Carrico v. Blevins, Religious 524
Carsen v. Elrod, Right to Bond 517
Child Support Credit 515
Child Support Ends 449
Visitation 21
Bond 23
Bond, for CP or NCP 23
Child hates going 14
Child Won't Go, Panic Situation #38 306
Complying with Supervised 339, 341
definition 606
Denial or Interference 27
Fear of Flying 265
Flink v. Flink 510
frequent flyer coupons 135
Grandparent 22
Grandparent, Unconstitutional 521
Handling Interference 23
I Don't Want To Visit You Anymore 267
Important Part of Child Support 264
Interference with 23
Internet Visitation 131
is a Right of the Child 21
is Dangerous SIT # 42 307

Notice of Exercise 23
Notice to the Court of Denial of 23
Parental Interference 23
Part of Child Support 21
Reasonable 598
Request Supervised 338
Request Supervised, for You 341
Request Supervised, Other Parent 341
Responsibilities, Non-Custodial 266
Visit Supervisor 606
Your Interference with Your 22
Visiting Parent, definition 606
Visual Impact, Major Problem Areas 404
Voluntary
Decision of religious poverty
Goldberg v. Goldberg, MD 463
Relinquishment of Parental Rights 429
termination of parental rights 389
Termination of, Indian Parental rights 388
Under-employment or Unemployment 450
Volunteer Spy, SIT #49, 309

W

WAIS, Intelligence test, Children & Adults 240
Waive the Privilege
Attorney Client 149
Husband-Wife 584
Walk the Talk 270
War or Peace, Chapter 1, 11
Ward v. Dibble, Grandparents Visitation 520
Wards of the State 392
Warning
Flags About Evaluation 233
Signals for Kidnapping 344
Warrant, Bench, definition 569
Washington
Child Support Credit 514
Child Support Ends 449
Child Support Hall of Fame 455
Custody of Smith, Grandparents 520
Marriage of Bucklin, Income 438
Nexus Gay/Lesbian Parents 527
Same Sex 536
Support Accounting 455
Watkins v. Nelson 522
Webb v Kudson, case 496
Webmaster, definition 606
Website, definition 606
Wechsler Adult Intelligence Scales, for Adults 240
Wedlock, Out of 137
Welfare of J.G.W. and J.L.W., case 519
Well Get Over It 52
West Virginia
Child Support Ends 449
Edwards v. Edwards, Support 512
Nexus Gay/Lesbian Parents 527
Out of Pocket Expenses 454
Same Sex 536
What
a Witness Cannot Do 406
Can Friends do to Help 201
Can You Do to Help Your Child 259
Factors Influence Custody 19
Is Parent Alienation Syndrome 188
Parent Alienation Syndrome Is Not 187
Will Happen During Your Day in Court 411
What is
A Deposition 355
a Home Study 200
a Witness 395
an Allegation 335
an Expert, Should I Use One? 218
an Interrogatory 352
Child Abuse 324
Parent Alienation Syndrome 187, 188
the Evaluator Looking for? 208
What You
Cannot Do with the Judge 376
Consider, A Win 51
When
Children Lie 285
Does Child Support End? 446
Does Child Support Start? 449
Is Your War Chest Spent 421
When Your Child
Testifies in Court 395
Where, Do You Fit? 15
Whining or Sniveling 37
Who
Are Evaluators 182
Should Not Fight for Custody 18
Would You Depose 362
Whose Custody Case is this Anyway 17
Why
Cooperate? 70
Liars Get Caught 280
people make poor choices 56
will the Opposition Cooperate? 71
Wide Range Achievement Test 240
Will You Take a Drug Test 136, 238
Williams v. Williams
Recording Phone Calls 488
Winning
Attitudes 34
Wire-tapping
Between Your Children and Other Parent 488
No Need For Ex Parte Order For 488

Recorded Conversations 517
WISC, Intelligence test 240
Wisconsin
Bohms v. Bohms, Move Away 272
Can't Sue Wife 482
Child Support Credit 515
Child Support Ends 449
Franz, Laws may not hide child 519
Gerrits v. Gerrits, Support, Lottery 439
Marriage of Simmons, Support 512
Nexus Gay/Lesbian Parents 527
Paternity Suits Never Settled 482
Witness
Cannot Do 406
Clothes Make the 404
Confidentiality 38, 395
Demeanor 405
Deposition 364
Guide for Answering Questions 406
Hostile 583
Impeachment of 584
Memory's Imperfections 278
Percipient, definition 594
Surprise Witness May Not Testify 489
the Most Important 37
Unimpeachable 605
What Do I Tell the Other 38
What is a 395
Wo v. Hopkins, case, 14th Amendment 517
Working
Partnership With Other Parent 652
Under the Table 459
Work-Product
Attorney, definition 568
Privilege Florida case 485
Privilege, Expert 219
World Wide Web
Anonymity, Security, Privacy 50
definition 606
Deposition via the 355
Hacked, definition 583
Internet visitation 131
Online Friends 87
Websites as Evidence 101
Worst Reasons to Want Custody 18
Wyoming
Child Support Credit 515
Child Support Ends 449
Love v. Love, Move Away 272
Nexus Gay/Lesbian Parents 527
Paternity Never Settled 482
Underkofler v. Underkofler, Support 439

Y

Yick Wo v. Hopkins, case, 14th Amendment 519
Yoder v. Wisconsin 524
You
Are Arrested 40
are the Package, Chapter 2, 336
Are You Being Watched? 171
Emotions When Your Child is Gone 346
I Have to Tell Them What? 352
Must Focus on Yourself 30
Must Start Telling the Truth 286
Open About Activities With Your Child 270
Stay Alert 169
Walk the Talk 270
You've Been in Court too Long When 95
Your
Battle Because, It's 34
Behavior Requiring Rescue 37
Big Backyard 261
Child, Confidentiality 273
Children 86
Children Testifying in Court 395
Correcting Mistakes on Deposition 361
Dealing With Your Anger 320
Deposition 356
no new news is good news 357
Deposition, check 361
Deposition, During 359
Expectations 377
Expert's Deposition 364
Feelings 37
Friends, Extended Family 87
Interference With Your Visitation 22
Inventory, example 45
Judge, Research 370
Lies 286
Panic Situation List 318
Parents 86
Shrink-Confidentiality 38
Significant Other 186
Significant Other at Testing 233
Witnesses' Deposition 364

Z

Zayed v. Zayed, OH, Income 438
Zucco v. Garrett, NE, Religious 523
Zummo v. Zummo, PA, Religious 522

Witnesses' Guide To Testifying For Deposition Or Court

One of the biggest problems we face as litigants in a lawsuit is figuring out how to tell our side of the story. Just getting people we know to understand what we are saying is difficult, and the thought of a hostile attorney firing trick questions at us in front of others causes terror in the bravest most willing witness.

Our problems are further aggravated if the outcome of our case depends heavily on the testimony of other witnesses. Our strongest supporters can turn into our worst legal nightmare in a matter of minutes under the skilled questioning of the opposition's attorney. A marginal witness with important testimony could destroy your entire case. A negative decision can alter the rest of our lives or cost enormous amounts of money.

Big corporations employ skilled, seasoned professionals who spend many hours and a great deal of money preparing their witnesses for deposition and court in order to minimize potential damage and maximize their witnesses' testimony. Most of us do not have the experience in court or the vast resources of these companies.

The average pre-appearance interview time an attorney spends with a witness before testimony is less than an hour. There is virtually no actual 'witness testimony preparation' time before most appearances. Consequently a witness without proper understanding and expectation is subject to fear and surprise which will prevent the witness from doing a proper job. Even the most dedicated attorney cannot completely prepare you and each of your witnesses for this important experience. Since you have the most to gain or lose, you must make sure you and your witnesses produce the results you need.

Witnesses' Guide To Testifying For Deposition Or Court, is the most comprehensive overview of theory and practical application available offering a realistic introduction to the world of court for the uninitiated. By offering valuable insights and tips, a witness is able to concentrate on the effects and ramification of their behavior before and during testimony. It gives a comprehension to a process that would leave the uninformed wondering what happened even after they have been through it, illuminating the strategies, tactics and techniques used by opposing counsel. How one's answers fit into the complicated puzzle of a court case prepares a witness to be powerful and persuasive.

This book explains why and how to prepare as well as many valuable tips, allowing a witness to concentrate on the effects of his or her behavior and testimony before and during his or her appearance. Understanding of how one's answers fit into the complicated puzzle of a court case prepares a witness to be powerful and persuasive. This book gives the witness an insight into a process that would otherwise leave many wondering what happened even after they have been through the process. Illuminating the strategies, tactics and techniques used by opposing counsel will help the witness avoid being an easy target.

This book applies a great deal of information from the Win Your Child Custody War manual and expands on it as it pertains to the witness by addressing each situation from the witnesses point of interest and need-to-know.

Professionals report this inexpensive book is the most comprehensive overview of theory and practical application available offering a realistic easy-to-understand introduction to the world of court for the uninitiated.

Custody Case Killers & Boosters

Attitude Adjustment for Custody Case Litigants

Ever since we were forced into the custody case arena in 1991, we have looked for "The Answer." We wanted to know what the mediators, evaluators, and judges wanted to hear. We were willing to paint ourselves yellow if that's what they wanted. (I don't even look good in yellow.)

After years of working with thousands of other parents in parents' rights groups, child protective service agencies in nine major cities, attending seminars with counselors, attorneys and psychologists and interviewing attorneys, judges, mediators and guardian ad litems; reading many books on custody and writing several of our own, we have found out here is no "answer."

Our cases, lives, children, communities and the laws that affect us vary to such a huge degree that there are too many answers. This book deals with what others do to us, what we do to ourselves: our love, pain, and fear in the past, present, and future, and our perception and perspective. There is no The Answer. This is not a book of legal advice or pat answers just a book of suggestions and options. Use what you can and ignore the rest. The listings in the book are in numerical order. Here is a sample of the more than 1,400 listed.

1. Each day of our lives we make deposits in the memory banks of our children. Charles R. Swindoll
2. Court is not designed to give you justice; it gives you a conclusion.
3. The greatest test of courage on earth is to bear defeat without losing heart. Robert Green Ingersoll
4. 90% of good parenting is just being there. Be there whenever the courts let you. Let the other parent be there whenever the other parent can. Children need as much good parenting as they can get.
5. Sometimes it is more important to discover what one cannot do than what one can do. Lin Yutang
6. When you find a solution to a problem, it is usually a comfortable solution. Find several other solutions. Then pick the best not the most comfortable.
7. Everyone has dreams for their children and for themselves. What is rare is the courage to take action and follow through.
8. Two parents living apart will not see their children as much as two parents living together.
9. Courage is like a muscle, it is strengthened by use.
10. Only by taking the risk of going too far can we determine how far we can go.
11. For the truly faithful, no miracle is necessary. For those who doubt, no miracle is sufficient. Nancy Gibbs
12. To have a crisis and act upon it is one thing. To live in perpetual crisis is another.
13. Establish a positive working partnership with the other parent that is visible to your child. If you are not able to form a happy association, at the very least, build a polite partnership.
14. What one has to do usually can be done. Eleanor Roosevelt
15. Help your children understand and support, in an appropriate manner, the other parent in times of stress or loss.

16. Almost everything comes from almost nothing. Frederic Amiel

17. There will be a residue of fear and resentment as a result of the adversarial position imposed by the court proceedings. Assure the other parent that the partnership is for the child's welfare and that you will assist the parent and your child to the best of your ability. This will provide your child with a more secure environment.

18. Don't look for ways to change others, look for opportunities to become a better parent yourself.

19. Good clear ice two inches thick will bear the weight of a grown person; four inches thick will bear a horse and rider; six inches thick will bear the weight of a compact car. But your skin never gets thick enough to bear an unkind word about your child.

20. No person is your enemy. No person is your friend. Every person is your teacher.

"I bought Killers & Boosters because I was buying everything you had. The other books are more serious but this turned out to be the one that lifts my spirits so I can put the bull behind me and go on with the real work. Thanks." Mike Barbs Killeen, TX

"You must have listened to me cry alone at night to know what to put in this book. You hit all the hurt places and made them better. These short mind-benders took me out of the short sighted hole I was in so I could get a clearer cleaner perspective on each situation. I understand where I am and where my is and it's easier now." Stevie McCoy Little Rock, AK

"I had never purchased anything from the internet. I am glad "Killers & Boosters" was my first experience. It has been a wonderful catalyst to find healthier and stronger ways to think about the challenges I have been facing." Carmen Modesto Safety Harbor, FL

Dear Judge,

Children's Letters to the Judge. These letters deal with Fear, Anger, Confusion, Love, Grief an Hope

It is difficult for parents to know what children think. Often children feel helpless and only give the answers they think the grown-ups want. These letters are straight from the hearts and minds of children to the person they think can fix everything.

This book was created in an entirely different manner than any of our other books. I was sitting in a continuing education class for attorneys. During a break the gentleman next to me and I introduced ourselves to each other. I showed him a copy of the Win Your Child Custody War manual. He asked if he could keep it for a day or two. I made arrangements to pick up the manual at his office later in the week.

When I arrived at his office, his clerk informed me that the judge was out but that he had left my manual and an envelope for me. I thanked her and left.

In addition to several very good suggestions and two important case cites. Finally, there was a stack of letters with a hand written note that said,

"I have been on the bench in family court for twenty-two years. I have always worked to protect children and secure a safe happy future for them. Often I have had to work with laws with which I disagreed, attorneys I didn't like and parents I couldn't get to see past their won pain and anger. I have lost more sleep about decisions I had to make than anyone would believe.

I don't know why but I have saved these letters, since I got one the first month I was on the bench. Because they are ex parte communications and from children there was nothing I could really do with them. I hope you will use them to help parents to understand what their children are going through. Children trusted me with their true feelings and I am trusting them to you. I would appreciate it if you would find a way to get these letters to the public."

I hope these letters mean as much to you as parents as they did to the judge and to me. At your service, Charlotte Hardwick

Help and Where to Find It

There are many organizations offering a great diversity of assistance. Some are very selective as to whom they will help, and others welcome anyone with problems. A listing in this book is not necessarily an endorsement of the group or its ideas by Pale Horse Publishing. It is up to you as a responsible adult to exercise caution when dealing with any group.

Many groups are small and have been started by a person who has gone through, or is going through, the same trials you are and can offer advice and direction. Others are international in scope and ability.

This list will give you an indication of where to look in your community. Call the numbers listed here and ask if they can help you. If not ask for a recommendation for a group in your area. If the telephone number listed here is not valid, look in your local telephone book for a facility near your home.

Just as with people, socially conscious groups have a limited life-span. Some of these organizations will have disbanded, and some will not be available in your area. As you locate one group, ask if they are aware of any other resources you may contact. Groups that do not have a chapter in your area may be interested in helping you start one.

This book is 5 1/2" X 8". Updated July 1999 Finding competent support, help and advice is difficult for child custody litigants. If you live in a small community, often there are no services offered. This book identifies what other communities have and how you can contact them for long distance help or information on how to start an affiliated group in your area. If you live in a very large community you may not know where to start looking. This book contains listing of More than 1,000 Groups, Organizations and Professionals

Name of group or organization

Telephone and Fax number

E-mail address

World Wide Web site address

Description of what they do or have to offer

Putting Kids First:

Walking Away From A Marriage Without Walking Over The Kids is a positive guide for parents to assist in dealing with issues of custody and visitation of children. Midwest Book Review

At last: a guide which advises parents on how to walk away from a marriage with the least effects on the children. New attitudes about children and divorce's effects are needed: Oddenino provides these insights, juxtaposing case history examples of parent interactions and experiences with the legal system with keys to therapies which help heal the entire family.

Healing Hearts

Helping Children and Adults Recover from Divorce

This book is dedicated to the children of divorce who shared their pain, so we could discover the pathways to healing hearts. Illustrated with B&W drawings throughout. Non-Fiction, Divorce, Counseling, Mediation, Children, Families. 215 pages. This is an outstanding book to use on an individual basis or as a parenting class.

CHILDREN: The Experts on Divorce

CHILDREN KNOW BEST HOW DIVORCE AFFECTS THEM!!!

Without any prompting or coaching the children in this video speak from their own experience of going through their parents' divorce. Their experiences represent the bulk of the research findings related to what children need from their parent in a divorce. The children didn't read the research. They know from living it. If we listen closely to what these children have to say we can prevent much of the long term harm that too many children feel from being caught in their parent's divorce. This video was created for parents who want to learn what children really think about divorce and what children need from parents during and after separation.

I Love You More Than . . .

This book will help build happy memories for your child. Wonderful memories that will last a life time.

Boys and girls will delight in this wonderful dream adventure. Sure to be a classic bedtime story!" Valerie Hale, Ph.D. Child Psychologist

A charming book, good for everyone who ever wanted to tell someone just how much they love them. Kind and loving, it's a sentiment that everyone should want to share with a loved one- child, sibling, parent, friend or whatever. There is no way you'll feel bad after reading this book..

Elizabeth Hickey's new book, I Love You More Than . . ., offers a beautiful way to deliver this message of love and caring. The story is a conversation between a little girl and her father, part real and part imagined. The photographs, illustrations and text combine to create a moving and powerful message of love between a parent and child.

I Love You More Than . . . is cleverly constructed to be universally applicable since the family structure of the characters is ambiguous. While father speaks of his love for his daughter, the message is acknowledged "from Mommy, too." The story does not state whether the parents are together, separated, unmarried, married or divorced. It was heart-warming to share this book with my eleven year old son, Mark. Here are Mark's comments:

The story I Love You More Than . . . walks you through a little girl's dream about how much her father loves her. The beautiful illustrations contribute to the story greatly by giving the reader a picture of the child's wonderful dream. I thought that the photographs were adorable. They reminded me of when I was a toddler and my parents read stories to me. I think that all children and adults will find this story inspiring and touching to the heart.

Unlike fairy tales, this story makes the child whose parents read them this book feel that their parents really love them. I am sure that all kids would enjoy having this book read to them as much as I did. This book is sure to be a classic bedtime favorite.

Mark's responses reflect those of other children and adults who have encountered this book. I Love

You More Than . . . conjures warm memories of the best parts of the reader's relationship with his or her parents. These combine in such a positive and gentle way to melt the heart of all parents and help them share the warm glow of their parental love with their children. This book is a treasure. The world is a better place because it is available.

Will establish a wonderful love link between parent and child. This is a magical book that will take both parent and child on a lovely journey reminding them both of the love they have for each other. The illustrations are done in wonderful detail and will provide lots of opportunity for conversation and expectation during subsequent readings. It is sure to become a favorite with many, especially the Daddy/Daughter combination. I have sent copies to each of my young grandchildren and they all love it!

This Hardcover - 32 page book is a charming and refreshingly different story about a little girl and her teddy bear as they go on a dream adventure and learn all the ways she is loved by her parents. Illustrated with colored photographs and a brightly colored dream sequence, this keepsake book affirms the love a parent has for their child as well as the love one person may have for another,. Hearing 'I love you" makes us all feel good and this book fills that need in the child in all of us.

The Authors by Elizabeth Hickey, James Cohen, Lynda Smart Brown (Illustrator)

The Reading level for this book is Children's Ages 4-8

These materials are used in the United States and Canada. Elizabeth Hickey, previously co-authored a book titled “Healing Hearts” and produced two national award winning videos on family issues. She learned first-hand the importance of children hearing the works “I love you”. This book fills that need every child has and enriches a parent's reading time with their child.

The co-author James Cohen is an aspiring writer and film maker living in New York whose talents of continuity and humor are well displayed in this wonderful book.

Pale Horse Publishing Order Form

P.O.Box 1447 Livingston, TX 77351-1447

Phone (936) 327-1104 (800) 646-5590 Fax (967) 936-0950

Web Pages http://www.custodywar.com E-Mail booksale@samlink.com

Name: ____

Address: ____

City, State, Zip: _____________________________________

Type of Credit Card: ________ Credit Card #:_______________Xp Date:____/____

SIGNATURE ____

Description	U.S. $	S&H
Buy 6 Litigation Books (1) Win Your Child Custody War (2) Witness (3) Killers (4) Dear Judge (5) Case Forms (6) Help (savings of $15.00)	169.90	15.00
Win Your Child Custody War (Child Custody Help SourceBook)	79.95	7.95
Witness Guide To Testifying For Deposition Or Court All types of cases. More than 200 pages of easy to read valuable information.	15.00	4.95
Killers & Boosters Custody Case (Attitude Adjustment for Custody Case Litigants) 1,400+ tips, traps, quotes and advice for parents	15.00	4.95
Dear Judge, Children's Letters to the judge. More than 90 letters children have written to judges.	15.00	4.95
Help & Where to Find it for Custody Cases	15.00	4.94
Custody Case Management Forms More than 240 Blank Forms & Examples, to Copy, Adapt And Use) No Legal Advice Included	29.95	7.95
Building A Bridge: Long Distance Loving for Divorced Parents	19.95	4.95
Children the Experts on Divorce, Award Winning Tape	25.00	4.95
Healing Hearts, Outstanding manual for Helping Children and Adults Recover.	19.95	4.95
I Love You More Than... Wonderful bedtime story for building happy memories.	19.95	4.95
Putting Kids First, Walking away from a marriage without walking over the kids.	16.95	4.95
Total Purchase		$

Pale Horse Publishing Order Form

P.O.Box 1447 Livingston, TX 77351-1447

Phone (936) 327-1104 (800) 646-5590 Fax (936) 967-8962

Web Pages http://www.custodywar.com E-Mail booksale@samlink.com

Name: ______________________________

Address: ______________________________

City, State, Zip: ______________________________

Type of Credit Card: _________ Credit Card #:_______________Xp Date:____/_____

SIGNATURE ______________________________

Description	U.S. $	S&H
Buy 6 Litigation Books (1) Win Your Child Custody War (2) Witness (3) Killers (4) Dear Judge (5) Case Forms (6) Help (savings of $15.00)	169.90	15.00
Win Your Child Custody War (Child Custody Help SourceBook)	79.95	7.95
Witness Guide To Testifying For Deposition Or Court All types of cases. More than 200 pages of easy to read valuable information.	15.00	4.95
Killers & Boosters Custody Case (Attitude Adjustment for Custody Case Litigants) 1,400+ tips, traps, quotes and advice for parents	15.00	4.95
Dear Judge, Children's Letters to the judge. More than 90 letters children have written to judges.	15.00	4.95
Help & Where to Find it for Custody Cases	15.00	4.94
Custody Case Management Forms More than 240 Blank Forms & Examples, to Copy, Adapt And Use) No Legal Advice Included	29.95	7.95
Building A Bridge: Long Distance Loving for Divorced Parents	19.95	4.95
Children the Experts on Divorce, Award Winning Tape	25.00	4.95
Healing Hearts, Outstanding manual for Helping Children and Adults Recover.	19.95	4.95
I Love You More Than... Wonderful bedtime story for building happy memories.	19.95	4.95
Putting Kids First, Walking away from a marriage without walking over the kids.	16.95	4.95
Total Purchase		$